Contents

MARKETING

HANDBOOK
of
MARKETING

Edited by
BARTON WEITZ
and ROBIN WENSLEY

SAGE Publications
London • Thousand Oaks • New Delhi

First published 2002
Paperback edition published 2006

SAGE Publications Ltd
1 Oliver's Yard
55 City Road
London EC1Y 1SP

SAGE Publications Inc.
2455 Teller Road
Thousand Oaks, California 91320

SAGE Publications India Pvt Ltd
B-42, Panchsheel Enclave
Post Box 4109
New Delhi 110 017

British Library Cataloguing in Publication data

A catalogue record for this book is available from the British Library

ISBN-10 1 4129 2120 1 (pbk)
ISBN-13 978 1 4129 2120 6 (pbk)

Library of Congress Control Number: 2005935813

Typeset by C&M Digitals (P) Ltd., Chennai, India
Printed in Great Britain by The Cromwell Press Ltd, Trowbridge, Wiltshire
Printed on paper from sustainable resources

The Editors

Barton Weitz is the J.C. Penney Eminent Scholar Chair and Executive Director of the Miller Center for Retailing Education and Research in the Warrington College of Business Administration at the University of Florida. He earned a B.S.E.E. at MIT and an M.B.A. and Ph.D. at Stanford. In 1998, he was honored as the Educator of the Year by the American Marketing Association for his contributions to the marketing discipline. Professor Weitz's current research interests focus on the development of long-term relationships between firms in a channel of distribution (retailers and vendors), firms and their employees, and salespeople and their customers. He has co-authored three textbooks – *Retailing Management*; *Selling: Building Partnerships*; and *Strategic Marketing: Making and Implementing Decisions*. He was editor of the *Journal of Marketing Research* and is presently the co-editor of *Marketing Letters* and editor of *Marketing Management Abstract* journal, part of the Social Science Research Network.

Robin Wensley is Professor of Policy and Marketing at Warwick Business School and was Chair of the School from 1989 to 1994, Chair of Faculty of Social Studies from 1997 to 1999, and Deputy Dean from 2000 to 2004. He is Director of the ESRC/EPSRC Advanced Institute of Management Research as well as convenor of the new Public Management and Policy subject group within the Warwick Institute of Governance and Public Management, and was co-editor of the *Journal of Management Studies* from 1998 to 2002. His research interests include marketing strategy and evolutionary processes in competitive markets, investment decision making, the assessment of competitive advantage and the nature of choice processes and user engagement in public services. He has published a number of articles in *Harvard Business Review*, *Journal of Marketing*, and *Strategic Management Journal* and has twice won the annual Alpha Kappa Psi Award for the most influential article in the US *Journal of Marketing* as well as the Millennium Prize for the best article in the UK *Journal of Marketing Management*. He has worked closely with other academics and practitioners both in Europe and the USA. His books include (with G.S. Day and B.A. Weitz), *Interface of Marketing and Strategy* (JAI Press, 1990) and (with D. Brownlie, M. Saren and R. Whittington), *Rethinking Marketing: Towards Critical Marketing Accountings* (Sage, 1999).

The Contributors

Sönke Albers has been Professor of Innovation, New Media and Marketing at the Christian-Albrechts University at Kiel (Germany) since 1990. Prior to Kiel, he served on the faculties of WHU-Koblenz and the University of Lüneburg. He was also a Visiting Professor at Stanford University, INSEAD (Fontainebleau) and the Australian Graduate School of Management (Sydney).

He has published and edited 12 books and over 150 articles that appeared in international journals such as *Marketing Science*, *Journal of Marketing Research*, *International Journal of Research in Marketing*, *European Journal of Operational Research*, and the leading German journals. His research areas are marketing planning and controlling, sales force management, innovation research, and electronic commerce. He is co-editor of the 'Zeitschrift fuer betriebswirtschaftliche Forschung/Schmalenbach Business Research'. He is also consulting editor of the *International Journal of Research in Marketing*. He was a dean in Koblenz and the president of the German Association of Marketing Professors. Currently, he serves as an associate dean of the faculty in Kiel where he was recently appointed as the chairman of a research unit on electronic business, with 13 doctoral students, funded by the German National Research Foundation.

Erin Anderson is the John H. Loudon Professor of International Management and Professor of Marketing at INSEAD, holding her Ph.D. in Management from the University of California, Los Angeles. She specializes in the management, organization, and performance of sales forces and distribution channels. Among other topics, she also studies vertical integration (make-or-buy decisions), managing independent agents, and designing effective commissioned sales forces. She approaches these topics through the viewpoint of New Institutional Economics.

The author of numerous articles on sales force management and distribution channels, Erin Anderson is co-author (with Anne T. Coughlan, Louis W. Stern, and Adel I. El Ansary) of *Marketing Channels,* currently in its 6th edition with Prentice Hall. She serves on the editorial boards of the *Journal of Marketing*, *Journal of Marketing Research*, and *International Journal of Research in Marketing*, and she has received several awards for her contributions to the fields of marketing and international management.

Patrick Barwise is Professor of Management and Marketing at London Business School and co-author (with Seán Meehan, IMD, Lausanne) of *Simply Better* (HBS Press, 2004: www.simply-better.biz), winner of the 2005 Berry-AMA Prize for the best recent book in marketing. He joined London Business School in 1976, having spent his early career with IBM. His previous publications include *Television and its Audience*, *Accounting for Brands*, *Strategic Decisions*, *Predictions: Media*, and *Advertising in a Recession*, as well as numerous papers and articles on brands, consumer and audience behavior, marketing expenditure trends (www.london.edu/marketing/met), and new media. In 2004, he led an independent review for the UK government of the BBC's digital television services. He is also a Fellow of the Sunningdale Institute, a government think-tank and virtual academy on public service management.

Kurt A. Carlson is Assistant Professor of Marketing at the Fuqua School of Business, Duke University. He received his Ph.D. in management from Cornell University, with specializations in marketing and decision making. He also holds an M.S. (1990) and B.S. (1993) in Agricultural and Applied Economics, both from the University of Wisconsin.

His research explores consumer decision making, with a special focus on the role of goals. With colleagues, he has developed methods for tracking the evolution of pre-choice preferences and the activation of consumers' goals during the choice process. Dr Carlson has published articles in the *Journal of Consumer Research*, *Journal of Experimental Psychology: Applied*, *Management Science*, *Organization Behavior and Human Decision Processes*, and *Psychological Science.*

Anne T. Coughlan is on the Marketing Faculty at the Kellogg School of Management at Northwestern University. Her research interests lie in the areas of distribution channel management and design, pricing, competitive strategy, and the international applications of these areas. She is the lead author of *Marketing Channels* (6th edition), and has also published scholarly research articles in journals such as *Marketing Science*, *Management Science*, *International Journal of Research in Marketing*, *Journal of Business*, and *Journal of Marketing*.

She is currently an associate editor at the *Journal of Economics and Management Strategy* and serves on the editorial boards of *Marketing Science*, *Journal of Retailing*, and *Journal of Marketing*. She is a co-editor of the Quantitative Marketing Network of the Social Sciences Research Network. Professor Coughlan was elected Secretary-Treasurer (1988–89) and President (1992–93) of the College on Marketing of the Institute for Management Sciences.

Ely Dahan is Assistant Professor of Marketing at the Anderson School of Business at UCLA, where he was awarded the Dean George Robbins Teaching Award. His research focuses on internet-based market research methods, securities trading of concepts, mass customization, models of new product prototyping, and the economics of cost reduction. His work has been recognized by the John D.C. Little Best Paper Award by INFORMS, the Thomas Hustad Award for Best Paper in the *Journal of Product Innovation Management*, the Frank Bass Outstanding Dissertation Award, and the American Marketing Association's Explor Award. Dr Dahan holds a Ph.D. from Stanford Business School's Operations, Information and Technology program, an M.B.A. from the Harvard Business School, and a Bachelor's degree in Civil Engineering from MIT. He worked as a national product manager for W.R. Grace and NEC until 1984, when he founded a computer networking company in Maryland, serving as CEO until the firm was acquired in 1993.

George S. Day is the Geoffrey T. Boisi Professor, Professor of Marketing, co-Director of the Mack Center for Technological Innovation at the Wharton School of the University of Pennsylvania and Visiting Professor at the London Business School. He previously taught at Stanford University, IMD (International Management Development Institute) in Lausanne, Switzerland, and the University of Toronto, and has held visiting appointments at MIT and Harvard Business School. Prior to joining the Wharton School, he was Executive Director of the Marketing Science Institute, an industry-supported research consortium.

He is a member of the board of directors and Chairman of the Audit Committee of Footstar Corporation and a Fellow of Diamond Cluster International. His primary areas of activity are marketing, the management of new product development, strategic planning, organizational change and competitive strategies in global markets.

Dr Day obtained his doctorate from Columbia University in 1968. He presently serves on five editorial boards and has authored 14 books in the areas of marketing and strategic management. His most recent books are *Wharton on Dynamic Competitive Strategy* (with David Reibstein), published in 1997, *Wharton on Managing Emerging Technologies* (with Paul Schoemaker), published in 2000, and *The Market Driven Organization*, published in 1999. He is the co-editor (with David Montgomery) of the 1999 special issue of the *Journal of Marketing, Harvard Business Review, California Management Review, Strategic Management Journal, Planning Review, Journal of Marketing Research*, and *Sloan Management Review.*

Dr Day has received various awards, including two Alpha Kappa Psi Foundation Awards and two Harold H. Maynard Awards for the best articles published in the *Journal of Marketing.* In 1994, he received the Charles Coolidge Parlin Award, which each year honors an outstanding leader in the field of marketing, and in 1996 he received the Paul D. Converse Award for outstanding contributions to the development of the science of marketing. He was selected as the outstanding marketing educator for 1999 by the Academy of Marketing Science, and in 2001 he received the Mahajan Award from the American Marketing Association for career contributions to marketing strategy.

Eric M. Eisenstein is an Assistant Professor of Business at the S.C. Johnson School of Management at Cornell University. His areas of research include managerial decision making, the psychology of expertise, and intuitive statistics. Dr Eisenstein earned his Ph.D. in Managerial Science and Applied Economics and an M.A. in Statistics at the Wharton School, University of Pennsylvania.

Prior to entering the Ph.D. program at Wharton, Dr Eisenstein worked for four years at Mercer Management Consulting, where he primarily focused on management of technology and consumer research in the financial services and telecommunications industries. Dr Eisenstein has maintained his relationship with the business community through participation in executive education and consulting.

Dr Eisenstein graduated from the Management and Technology Dual Degree program at the University of Pennsylvania, where he earned a B.S. in Economics from the Wharton School and a B.S. in Computer-Systems Engineering from the School of Engineering and Applied Science.

Anita Elberse is an Assistant Professor of Business Administration in the marketing unit at Harvard Business School. She received a Ph.D. from London Business School, an M.A. in Communication from the Annenberg School for Communication, University of Southern California, and an M.A. in Communication Science from the University of Amsterdam. In her research, she primarily aims to understand what drives the success of products in 'creative industries', such as entertainment, advertising, sports and fashion, and how firms can develop effective marketing strategies for such products. More generally, she is interested in the diffusion of innovations, the impact of new technologies on marketing practice, and the application of econometric modeling techniques to marketing problems.

Her work has been published in a number of journals, including the *Harvard Business Review* and *Marketing Science*. She has also completed case studies on several firms in the entertainment and media sector.

Hubert Gatignon is the Claude Janssen Chaired Professor of Business Administration and Dean of the Ph.D. Program at INSEAD. He is also the Research Director of the INSEAD-Wharton Alliance, and the Director of the INSEAD-Wharton Alliance Center for Global R&D. He joined INSEAD in 1994 from the Wharton School of the University of Pennsylvania, where he was Professor of Marketing. He holds a Ph.D. in Marketing from the University of California, Los Angeles. His research interests involve modeling the factors influencing the adoption and diffusion of innovations, and explaining and econometrically measuring how the effects of marketing mix variables change over conditions and over time. His most recent research concerns strategies for entering a market and for defending a brand's position, as well as international marketing strategy.

Håkan Håkansson is Professor in International Management at the Norwegian School of Management, BI in Oslo. Earlier, he was at the University of Uppsala. He is one of the founding members of the IMP-Group and has published articles and books regarding purchasing, industrial marketing, and technological development, especially in an international context. His latest book is *Rethinking Marketing: Developing a New Understanding of Markets*, published in 2004 by Wiley (co-edited with Alexandra Waluszewski, University of Uppsala and Debbie Harrison, Norwegian School of Management, BI).

Kathy Hammond is a Managing Director at Duke Corporate Education, where her role includes designing and developing customized corporate education programs for a variety of European corporations, and client relationship management. Her design and teaching interests center on consumer behavior, particularly patterns of consumer purchasing, brand loyalty, and customer-to-customer recommendation – and their implications for customer relationship management. Before joining Duke Corporate Education, Kathy was an Assistant Professor of Marketing at London Business School, and also co-founder and Director of London Business School's Future Media Research Program from 1998 to 2004. This program provided a focus for research on new media products, trends, and consumer behavior. Kathy

Preface

In writing this preface we were conscious of the inevitable question as to how, in the last three years, the domain of marketing has shifted? A good place to look for an answer to this question is both in terms of what research and scholarship has been undertaken and also the ways in which our stakeholder communities are defining the current priorities. A cursory glance at both the last three years' prize-winning papers in the *Journal of Marketing* and the current Marketing Science Institute priorities would suggest that many of the key topics, such as brand equity, growth and the role of marketing itself, remain the same.

However, one debate examined in the book has become more dominant than we suggested: the issue of relationship versus transactional marketing. This is really part of the wide and ongoing debate about the relationship between firms and customers, or between marketing management and customer behaviour. Many of the underlying research and theoretical questions however have not changed much. It remains true that a so-called relationship perspective has a much longer pedigree in many business-to-business marketing contexts and that issues of a relationship perspective raise equal questions of expectations, choice and power in many business-to-consumer marketing contexts. A relationship perspective often needs to give as much emphasis to the active role of the consumer in generating value as to the fact of repeated transactions let alone the possible role as a 'trusted' intermediary.

Chapters 9 and 20 continue to provide a good introduction to the issues involved in developing long-term relationships in business-to-business markets. From a broader perspective, critical issues related to customer relationship management (CRM), fostering relationships in business-to-consumer markets, are reviewed in Chapter 7 on branding and Chapter 14 on customer service. However, the trend among product and service retailers to identify their 'best' customers, tailor attractive offerings toward these customers, and increase 'share of wallet' is a developing research area.

Another trend of growing importance is the increasing role of retailers in the consumer products distribution channel. Most marketing research has taken the perspective of the manufacturer and treated retailers as a manufacturer's marketing decision variable. As power is shifting from manufacturers to retailers, more attention is being directed towards retail issues, such as the effect of assortments on buying behaviour, category management, pricing over time for assortments and supply chain management.

There are two other key areas in which debate has developed significantly where the handbook contributions continue to provide an excellent starting point and the passage of time has had little effect on the specific nature of the research commentary in the handbook. The nature of the Internet and its twin effects in both the behaviour of consumers and also the business models of providers has remained an important and evolving domain for research. For example, the Internet facilitates the use of auctions as a pricing mechanism in consumer and business markets which raises concerns about an emphasis on price affecting long-term relationships and service quality. In addition, the Internet facilitates the tailoring of offerings to smaller groups of customers and even individuals but raises privacy concerns. However we believe that Chapter 21 remains an excellent starting point.

Chapter 1 addresses the vexed question of the wider impact of consumption and marketing on the nature of society. To tackle this question adequately we need to take a long historical perspective. From such a perspective it is clear that issues of consumption and attendant questions of luxury goods and conspicuous consumption predate by a considerable margin the formalization of any marketing activities. The question is more whether the adoption of marketing and what might be termed the attendant technology has exacerbated trend beyond the effect of increased economic activity. In this area, as in a number of marketing areas, there is more research to be done.

Barton Weitz and Robin Wensley
December 2005

Introduction

BARTON WEITZ and ROBIN WENSLEY

A wide variety of research activities contribute to the development of knowledge about marketing issues and problems. Marketers use a panoply of methods and draw on and extend theories developed in the social sciences to examine issues ranging from the consumption of high-risk sports such as sky diving, to the development and use of sophisticated econometric modeling on POS scanner data to estimate the consumer response to price promotions.

Scope of the Handbook of Marketing

Research Domains

Brinberg and McGrath (1985) offer a scheme for classifying a social science research that can be used to delineate the research reviewed in this book. They suggest that academic research involves three interrelated but distinct domains – substantive, conceptual, and methodological. Research in each of the domains has unique objectives, and thus addresses unique sets of issues.

Research focusing on the *substantive domain* examines relationships between problems, phenomena, and processes that arise in the real world such as the relationship between sales compensation and salesperson performance, or the relationship between the use of cross-functional teams to develop products and the success of the products in the marketplace. The objective of research in the substantive domain is to improve the performance of the agents and organizations and the system in which they interact. In the previously stated marketing illustrations, the objective would be to improve the performance of salespeople and new product development teams.

Research focusing on the *conceptual or theoretical domain* considers relationships between abstract constructs and concepts such as the impact of incentives on salesperson motivation, or the effect of team cohesiveness on the level of conflict between the members of a new product development team. The objective of research focusing on the conceptual domain is to develop a parsimonious but deeper understanding of the broad range of the relationships observed in the real world.

Finally, research in the *methodological domain* develops techniques for measuring the properties of phenomena, agents, and organizations and assessing the degree to which properties are related to each other. The objective of methodological research is to develop precise, robust measures and assessments.

What Is in the *Handbook of Marketing?*

Most academic marketing research involves all of these domains. Research typically (1) examines some problem or issue facing a marketer or customer, (2) proposes some abstract constructs and concepts that may offer greater understanding of the issue and generalization of the results, and (3) uses some method for studying the problem and measuring the concepts and relationships. However, the focal contribution of a specific research article or book tends to be in one of the three domains.

The chapters in the *Handbook of Marketing* summarize research in the substantive domain of marketing. Each of the chapters:

1. provides an overview of academic research addressing a particular substantive area of marketing. The overviews are designed to help scholars and sophisticated marketers understand issues involved in the area and the knowledge that has been developed to address those issues. While the authors are experts in substantive areas, they review all of the important research streams on the topic rather than just summarizing their individual research contributions
2. offers a bibliography of important research in the topic area
3. identifies productive areas for future research in the substantive area.

The *Handbook of Marketing* is problem-focused and thus methodological and conceptual issues are not explored in depth. When the understanding of a methodological issue or conceptual debate is needed to appreciate and/or interpret results of substantive research, the authors identify the methodological or conceptual issues, explain their specific impact on the substantive conclusions, and provide references for examining these issues in more detail.

In addition, the *Handbook of Marketing* focuses on just a subset of substantive marketing issues. Marketing is the study of relationships between buyers and sellers, between firms and their markets, marketing managers and their customers. Clearly effective marketing is based on a thorough understanding of the needs and buying behaviors of customers, both consumers and organizational buyers, and both as collectivities and as individuals. However, the chapters in this book focus primarily on the substantive issues facing marketing managers and, to some extent, market regulators and policy makers, not their customers.

We elected to focus on the managerial and policy issues for two reason. First, the body of research on consumer behavior is so extensive that it merits its own handbook (see Robertson & Kassarjian, 1990). Second, the objective of much consumer behavior research is no longer to directly improve the practice of marketing, not even sometimes to develop a better understanding of consumer behavior in substantive terms, but solely for its own sake. To paraphrase Lutz (1991), it is of little interest to anyone else except the researcher. Thus we have not included reviews on the extensive research solely examining consumer behavior or organizational buying. However, behavioral research with managerial implications in specific substantive areas is included in the chapter reviews.

Who Should Read the *Handbook of Marketing?*

The primary audience for the Handbook is students in any introductory doctoral seminar on marketing management issues and problems. The chapters in the Handbook provide the necessary background for reading, understanding, and discussing specific empirical and/or theoretical articles in a substantive area. In addition, the chapters can be used by academics, both within marketing and from other fields, who want to become familiar with research issues in a substantive area outside their primary area of expertise. Finally, analytically oriented practitioners might be interested in reading chapters to learn about research that has been conducted in a problem area they confront.

Overview of Chapters

The twenty-one chapters in the book are divided into five sections, together with some concluding thoughts. The sections are: (1) Introduction; (2) Marketing Strategy; (3) Marketing Activities; (4) Marketing Management; and (5) Special Topics. The chapters in the first section review research examining the context in which marketing issues and problems arise. The following two sections then review research examining the strategic and more tactical decisions confronting marketing managers. The fourth section examines research on how managers process information and make decisions and the use of decision aids to improve their decision-making. The final section examines research on some specific contextual environments – global, services, and business-to-business markets – in which marketing management issues arise, and the evolving implications of the Internet for marketing management.

Introduction

The Introductory section consists of three chapters and provides reviews of research about the role of marketing in society and in the firm, and the history of marketing thought. These chapters provide the background for examining the specific substantive areas of marketing research outlined in the subsequent chapters.

In Chapter 1, 'Marketing's Relationship to Society,' Professors William Wilkie and Elizabeth Moore examine the research on how society affects marketing and how marketing affects society. The chapter begins with an overview of the aggregate marketing system, the activities performed by the system, the properties of the system, and an approach for assessing the scope of the system. Then marketing's contributions to the larger system, economic development, and to individual buyers are reviewed. Research critiquing marketing from a societal perspective is discussed, concluding with a discussion on how marketing can be used to increase the level of societal benefits.

Chapter 2, 'History of Marketing Thought' by Professors Brian Jones and Eric Shaw, reviews the history of marketing thought. Rather than reviewing the history of marketing practice, they examined the evolution of research about marketing as discipline over the last 100 years. The review is organized chronologically, beginning with studies of the marketing ideas of ancient scholars and the writings of economists on marketing issues during the late nineteenth century, followed by the emergence of the marketing discipline between 1900 and 1957, and concluding with the more recent era that has seen a proliferation of schools of thought (e.g., marketing management, consumer behavior, macromarketing).

In the final chapter in the section, 'The Role of Marketing and the Firm,' Professor Frederick Webster traces the evolution of marketing's role in the firm from its identification as a distinct management function in the 1920s, through the expansion of its activities beyond selling and sales management, to the developing perspective that marketing should be a pervasive business philosophy. He concludes by suggesting that, paradoxically, the role of marketing is becoming even more important while the importance of the traditional marketing activities might be diminishing.

Marketing Strategy

The second section of the Handbook reviews the research involving the identification of target markets of customers, the analysis of competitive actions and reactions, and the marketing strategies directed toward realizing a sustainable competitive advantage.

Professors George Day and Robin Wensley, in Chapter 4, 'Market Strategies and Theories of the Firm,' relate research on marketing strategies to three theories of the firm: (1) the resource-based perspective, focusing on the firm as a portfolio of resources; (2) the positioning perspective, based on industry structure and spatial competition; and (3) the configuration, or forms of organization perspective, which incorporates sociological considerations. Then research on marketing strategy issues associated with each perspective is reviewed.

The objective of a marketing strategy is to develop a sustainable competitive advantage – an advantage that cannot be easily duplicated by competitors. To develop a marketing strategy, marketers need to understand the structure of the market in which they are participating – who are their customers and who are their competitors? In Chapter 5, 'Determining the Structure of Product Markets: Practices, Issues and Suggestions,' Professor Allan Shocker reviews the research approaches used to analyze market structures, with emphasis on the relationships between assumptions regarding the definition and structure of competitive relationships (e.g., measuring the degree of competition) and various methods for operationalizing and representing that structure. The chapter focuses on understanding the structure of competitive markets, not on the algorithms used to analyze market structures.

This section concludes with Chapter 6, 'Competitive Response and Market Evolution,' by Professors Hubert Gatignon and David Soberman. This chapter provides a framework for understanding the research that has been conducted on two inextricably linked topics – competitive response and market evolution. The authors first identify the key dimensions of competitive response and market evolution. Then, they review the research addressing the impact of competitive responses on market evolution, and how the evolution of a market can impact and constrain the competitive responses. The chapter also considers the impact that environmental (exogenous) factors can have on both competitive response and market evolution.

Marketing Activities

The eight chapters in this third section of the Handbook review research related to the traditional marketing decision variables – the 4Ps of product, price, promotion, and place (distribution). Due to the extensive amount of research on promotion, there are separate chapters for marketing communications (primarily advertising), personal selling and sales management, and sales promotions. Two additional chapters on branding and brand management, and customer service are included because of their strategic importance. Both the development of strong brands and the provision of excellent service result in customer loyalty, a sustainable competitive advantage.

In Chapter 7, 'Branding and Brand Equity,' Professor Kevin Lane Keller begins by reviewing the conceptual foundations of branding including the research on brand personality, experiences, relationships, and communities, as well as corporate images. This research examines how the brand provides meaning beyond the attributes and benefits of the product or service. He then presents the research on some brand management implementation issues, such as factors affecting the choice and design of brand elements such as brand names and logos, legal issues, involving branding, factors affecting the success of brand extensions, and means by which brands leverage their brand equity through brand alliances.

Professors Ely Dahan and John Hauser review the research on developing new products in a highly competitive, dynamic environment in Chapter 8, 'Product Development – Managing a Dispersed Process.' The chapter begins with an overview of the integrated end-to-end product development process. The remainder of the chapter addresses specific research challenges relating to the new product development process organized around the development stages. Specifically the authors review research on the front end of customer opportunity identification and idea generation, the process of concept selection and detailed design and engineering of products and processes, the testing phase where concepts and products are prototyped and tested, and the enterprise and organizational strategy necessary for success.

Chapter 9, 'Channel Management – Structure, Governance and Relationship Management' by

Professors Erin Anderson and Anne Coughlan, reviews research on a subset of managerial decisions that are crucial to the functioning of a marketing channel. The three issues examined are: (1) channel structure – the number of separate firms and levels that constitute the distribution channel; (2) channel governance – the frameworks used to coordinate and control the activities of the channel members so that the channel operates efficiently and the channel members realize their goals; and (3) relationship management – the management of the daily activities undertaken by channel members. Managerial decisions regarding these three issues determine how firms in the channel coordinate their activities to successfully compete against other sets of channel members promoting different solutions to a market's needs.

Professor Sönke Albers in Chapter 10, 'Salesforce Management – Compensation, Motivation, Selection and Training,' provides an overview of the research examining the management of salespeople – the most costly and effective element in a firm's communication mix. The chapter begins with a discussion of the problems encountered in measuring the performance of salespeople, and then examines the research directed toward improving salesperson performance through selection and hiring, training, motivation and compensation, and the dismissal of poor performers.

Chapter 11, 'Pricing – Economic and Behavioral Models,' by Professors Chezy Ofir and Russell Winer, reviews the research on the pricing element in the marketing mix. The review is organized into the following five sections:

1. the measurement of the customer response to price changes emphasizing the importance of price threshold
2. research on how customers actively process price information and use this information to evaluate alternatives and make choices
3. approaches for incorporating price and price promotions into brand choice models
4. theoretical models considering competitive activity in making pricing decisions
5. the potential impact on pricing by the lowering of search costs and dynamic pricing opportunities arising with the sales of products and services over the Internet.

Professors David Stewart and Michael Kamins in Chapter 12, 'Marketing Communications,' review the extensive research on marketing communication focusing on impersonal communication through mass media. The chapter examines research investigating the effects of marketing communications on primary and secondary demand, the mediating role of awareness and attitudes, the impact of these communications over time, and the factors moderating these effects such as the stage in the advertised product's life cycle, the competitive position of the advertised product and the intensity of competitive activity within the market, customer familiarity with the product, the customer's level of involvement in the purchase decision, and the nature and execution of the communication message.

Sales promotions include price discounts, feature advertising, special displays, trade deals, reward programs, coupons, rebates, contests, and sweepstakes have become the dominant expense in the communication program of many firms. In Chapter 13, 'Sales Promotion,' Professor Scott Neslin organizes his review of the research on sales promotion into three sections: (1) the behavioral and economic bases for the existence of sales promotion; (2) the various customer behaviors or responses that are influenced by sales promotion; and (3) the impact of different forms of promotion on customer behavior.

In the final chapter in the section, 'Understanding and Improving Service Quality: A Literature Review and Research Agenda,' Professors Parsu Parasuraman and Valarie Zeithaml review research on customer service. The chapter begins with a review of the literature on the conceptualization and definition of the service quality construct, including how it relates to the concept of product quality. Following the review, the chapter examines research relating service quality to profitability and customer loyalty, and then describes studies that offer conceptual frameworks and approaches for improving service quality. The chapter then discusses research on the quantitative assessment of customer perceptions of service quality. Finally, the chapter provides a synthesis of recent work on the role, meaning and measurement of service quality in the context of market offerings delivered through technology.

Marketing Management

The 11 chapters following the introductory section review research examining the factors that influence the effectiveness of strategic and tactical marketing activities. The three chapters in this section review research related to how managers make decisions, the relative importance of different types of decisions, and the use of decision support systems in making these decisions.

In Chapter 15, 'Individual Decision Making,' Professors Jay Russo and Kurt Carlson summarize the research on how individuals make decisions – how they identify and commit to a course of action. While the primary focus of the chapter is on managers and decisions that confront them, the theories and empirical findings reviewed typically extend to consumers and other individual decision-makers.

The phases of decision-making are used to organize the chapter. The discussion on each phase is divided into sections. The first section deals with decisions, called errors of untutored performance, that can be corrected or improved. The second section deals with challenges to effective decision-making that make decisions difficult even for skilled decision-makers. These two decision categories, errors and challenges, correspond roughly to the controllable (or internal) and uncontrollable (or external) obstacles to a satisfactory decision. Novice decision-makers must deal with both errors and challenges. Skilled decision-makers, no matter how great their expertise, must still confront the uncontrollable obstacles to a successful decision.

Dr. Murali Mantrala in Chapter 16, 'Allocating Marketing Resources,' reviews the research concerning a specific type of decision – that of the allocation of scarce marketing resources such as salesperson time, advertising expenditures, and retail shelfspace across products, customers, and markets. While these allocation decisions are complicated, managers often rely on fairly arbitrary and simplifying heuristics and decision rules. The chapter provides a survey of normative-theoretical decision models and provides insights for allocating marketing resources. Then the research on the implications of using decision rules versus normative models is presented. Specific areas covered in the chapter are the budgeting and allocation of resources related to advertising, salesforce, manufacturer promotions, retailing and the marketing mix as a whole.

Corporations spend billions of dollars each year on decision support systems designed to improve the decision-making of their managers. In the final chapter in this section, Chapter 17, 'Are Marketing Decision Support and Intelligent Systems "Worth It"? Precisely Worthwhile or Vaguely Worthless,' Professors Eric Eisenstein and Leonard Lodish review research that examines approaches for improving marketing decision-making using decision support systems. The chapter provides a taxonomy of decision support systems, offers an integrative framework showing the factors affecting implementation of these decision systems, and reviews the research on the effectiveness of decision support systems.

Special Topics

The four chapters in the last section of the Handbook examine the unique considerations affecting global marketing, the marketing of services, marketing in business-to-business environments, and the impact of the Internet on marketing activities.

Global marketing involves the coordination of marketing activities across national boundaries and thus is affected by potential institutional and cultural difference between nations. In Chapter 18, 'Global Marketing: Research on Foreign Entry, Local Marketing, Global Management,' Professor Johny Johansson reviews the research on the set of issues facing firms involved in global markets including foreign entry (research on mode of entry issues, the internationalization process, and exporting); local marketing (cultural factors, country-of-origin effects, and environmental issues which facilitate or impede foreign market acceptance); and global management (product standardization, global branding, global marketing communications, and global services).

A unique property of services is that they cannot be inventoried. Thus management of capacity and the matching of supply and demand are crucial issues in services marketing. Professor Steven Shugan, in Chapter 19, 'Services Marketing and Management: Capacity as a Strategic Marketing Variable,' begins his review with the classic discussion of whether service marketing is different from the marketing of manufactured and extractive products. Next he demonstrates that the key problem facing service providers is the coordination of marketing and operations. He then reviews the literature on capacity constrained strategies when demand is predictable and unpredictable, and examines specific strategies for coordinating supply and demand in these situations such as demand shifting through peak pricing strategies and rationing.

The dominant characteristic of business markets is that the exchange relationships exist between organizations rather than individuals. In Chapter 20, 'Marketing in Business Markets,' Professors Håkan Håkansson and Ivan Snehota organize their review of the research on business marketing into five sections: (1) the distinctive characteristics of business markets, including the continuous interaction and interdependency of firms; (2) the different theoretical perspectives for examining buyer – seller relationships; (3) the variety of business relationships found in business markets; (4) the task of marketing management in business markets; and (5) strategy development in business markets.

The Internet will potentially impact the topic of every chapter in this book, especially marketing strategy, channel management, pricing, marketing communications, customer service, decision support systems, global marketing and business marketing. The final chapter, Chapter 21, 'Marketing and the Internet,' by Professor Patrick Barwise and Drs Anita Elberse and Kathy Hammond, explores the emerging research on how the Internet is or can be used by both firms and consumers to support the marketing process. The review concentrates on research in consumer behavior, advertising, pricing, channels, and marketing strategy, because empirical research is most advanced in these areas.

References

Brinberg, David & McGrath, Joseph E. (1985) *Validity and the Research Process*. Beverly Hills, CA: Sage.

Lutz, R. (1991) Editorial, *Journal of Consumer Research*, 17 (March), 1–3.

Robertson, Thomas S. & Kassarian, Harold H. (eds) (1990) *Handbook of Consumer Behavior*. Englewood Cliff, NJ: Prentice-Hall.

PART ONE

Introduction

1

*Marketing's Relationship to Society**

WILLIAM L. WILKIE and ELIZABETH S. MOORE

SECTION I: 'MARKETING'S CONTRIBUTIONS TO SOCIETY'

Introduction

We originally chose to study the field of marketing because we found it to be one of the most stimulating, complex, and intellectually challenging of academic areas in a university setting. In curious contrast to its general reputation as a 'soft' area, we found that this field welcomes insights from many disciplines, including economics, psychology, history, mathematics, sociology, law, political science, communications, anthropology, and the creative arts. Its scholarship combines elements of objectivity and subjectivity, demands both quantitative and qualitative insights, requires persistence yet rewards creative leaps, and allows freedom of imagination and nuance yet grounds its efforts in real actions with measured consequences. Further, marketing can be studied from a number of intriguing perspectives.

As the academic field of marketing nears its 100th birthday, its focus is squarely on firms, markets, and household consumers. Relatively few persons, even in the mainstream of the field, have recently been able to examine marketing's contributions to society. However, this subject is worthy of consideration from the broad college of thinkers in the field. It is worthy of exposure to thoughtful practitioners, to students in MBA and undergraduate programs, and to emerging scholars in doctoral programs (and probably why the Marketing Science Institute named it a key topic for the special Millennium Issue of the *Journal of Marketing*). Thus our purpose here is to provide a *different* look at marketing, one that engages thoughtful deliberation on the larger system and its contributions. *Taken together, the issues in this domain help us to better see both the nature of marketing and the remarkable potentials of our field.*

Background: A Century of Progress

It may be merely trite to point out that the world is changing and that marketing is an active participant in this process. It is not trite, however, to inquire into the nature of such change – to delve more deeply into the history, substance and controversies concerning marketing's roles in society. It is stimulating, moreover, to pursue the implications for all of this for our present and our future. For example, let us briefly consider that the formal academic field of marketing began just about 100 years ago, at the turn of the last century, with the first offerings of courses on 'market distribution' (Bartels, 1988). Substantively, these courses reflected the realities of their time and place (e.g., courses in the Midwest tended to stress the distribution system for agricultural and other products; those on the East Coast covered distribution and merchandising). Theoretically, interest was on

---

**Note to readers:* In a recent survey, two-thirds of Marketing Ph.D. students reported that they had a personal interest in marketing and society, but fewer than one in ten had ever had a course in it, and they did not feel proficient. This chapter should go a long way to remedying this situation. In Section I we present an abridged version of "Marketing's Contributions to Society" (Wilkie and Moore, 1999), to provide you with a new perspective on our field. Then, in Section II, we discuss the research in this area and present guides for learning more.

pursuing benefits flowing from distributive activities that had been missed by economic thinkers concentrating on land, labor and capital. However, it is clear in the literature of that time that issues of marketing's performance on behalf of society were a serious concern for this fledgling field.

Of course, the 'society' at hand was much less developed, and consumer lifestyles were very different. For example, the typical US housewife carried 9,000 gallons of water into the house each year, and she then had to boil the water before using it because only 25% of homes had running water (and only 3% had electricity). Cooking, baking and food preservation required some 42 hours per week. Central heating would not arrive until the 1920s, so many households heated only the kitchen for the winter, using fuel hauled in daily by family members. On the health front, infant mortality was common – about one in every ten births – life expectancy was only 47 years.[1] Now let us contrast this with today's US society: life expectancy is nearing 80 years, gross domestic product is some 400 times greater, and time spent gathering and preparing food has dropped to less than 10 hours per week. Typical homes are filled with comforts and conveniences based on electricity and water, and autos, airplanes, television and the Internet have stretched our personal borders far beyond the distance we could reach within a day's walk or ride on horseback.

This recognition of historical changes serves to make the academic challenge in the study of marketing and society a bit more daunting than we might at first imagine. We know beyond doubt that US *society* has changed greatly, and that the aggregate *marketing system* also has changed; but what about the relationship between the two? What about 'marketing's relationship to society?' Has that also changed, or is it in some larger sense immutable? Either answer will, of course, be interesting. If 'immutable' is correct, merely clarifying this answer will itself be an heroic achievement. And if 'has changed' is our answer, what exactly are our present and future goals for the relationship of marketing to society, and who (or what) is taking us toward meeting them? Altogether, this poses a worthy challenge for marketing academics!

The Importance of Perspective

To understand a topic well it is helpful to walk around it mentally, adopting different perspectives on it. Viewing a topic from a single perspective highlights certain characteristics, but can hide other aspects that may also be important. For example, four perceptual barriers related to this topic involve *time, system limits, culture,* and *personal experience.* The brief lifestyle comparison noted above raised the issue of the slow diffusion of marketing's contributions over time by contrasting extremes across the twentieth century. When viewed in this way, contributions that the aggregate marketing system has delivered to society are apparent: it is clear that Americans today are living very differently – and mostly in better ways – than did their ancestors a century ago. With respect to system limits, not only is the marketing system vast, but its operations converge and coordinate with the operations of other aggregate systems within a society's larger economic system. (In a Venn diagram, then, we might conceive of aggregate systems in marketing, finance, technology, production, etc. as partially overlapping large circles, reflecting areas where activities are in common and those where activities lie only in that field.)

With respect to culture, marketing is a social institution that is highly adaptive to its cultural and political context. Thus we can easily go around the world to locate societies with very different marketing systems. In some global locations we will find rudimentary marketing systems offering none of the conveniences we currently enjoy. Elsewhere, as in parts of Brazil, we would find people just discovering installment credit, and using it to obtain the first home conveniences they have ever enjoyed. In parts of China we would find incredible levels of investment – one out of every five construction cranes in the world are reportedly at work just in Shanghai – to bring modern elevators, air conditioners, and other conveniences to the citizenry. *Thus our coverage of aggregate marketing systems is culture-bound: we need to take care to distinguish which lessons are generalizable and which are not.* Finally, in regard to personal experience, many marketing contributions are 'behind the scenes,' unseen by those of us not directly involved. It is thus important that we remain mentally open to the discovery of new possibilities about marketing and its relationship to society.

The Aggregate Marketing System

Studies have shown that the less familiar one is with our field, the more likely a person is to equate marketing with advertising or selling: as one learns more, the view broadens, and one begins to appreciate the richness of the field of marketing (Kasper, 1993). We now turn to a concept we will term the 'aggregate marketing system.' We begin with an illustration of one small part of the system, to see what it does. If marketing thinkers are to appreciate the range of contributions our field makes, it is good to remind ourselves about the scope and details of the work that it takes on.

The System at Work

Our illustration begins with an American household at breakfast. Here the outputs of a small number of marketing channels are brought together for the purpose of consumption.

'Breakfast at Tiffany's' [Note: The idea for this illustration is based on Vaile, Grether and Cox's

(1952) classic textbook on marketing, though our description is different and updated. We here join Tiffany Jones and her family in New York, as Tiffany reaches for her breakfast pastry and blows softly across her cup of coffee...]

A Cup of Coffee Although a commonplace-enough event, a breakfast represents an interesting confluence of forces from the aggregate marketing system. Let us first consider Tiffany's coffee, and how it got to this morning's meal. Tiffany has chosen a leading brand that delivers a consistent color, scent, and taste that is favored by its many customers. How exactly does this brand's marketing system achieve this? The coffee Tiffany has prepared is, in fact, a combination of beans grown in different countries, then brought to the US and blended into a specified mixture to deliver this brand's unique qualities. Due to different growing seasons and bean characteristics, the source nations for the coffee change as the year progresses: coffee is grown in some fifty nations around the world.

As shown in Figure 1.1, Panel A, we assume that some beans in this cup came from a Colombian hillside, hand-picked (to ensure ripeness) in the grower's field. The process was highly structured: from basket, to tractor, to truck, the beans were transported to the coffee grower's de-pulping mill, where the inner beans were separated from their cherries. Still wet and protected by a parchment-like cellulose shell, the beans were spread on a sun-filled patio to dry for several days. They were then milled (removing the parchment sheath to produce a green bean), then graded against set national coffee standards. Samples of the beans were sent to buyers and the government coffee board to check the grading process. The beans were then put into 60 kilo (132 pound) burlap or polyester bags bearing the grower's name and quality level, and warehoused at the grower's facility. Brokers and large buyers were contacted by the grower to arrange for sale and delivery. In the case of Tiffany's brand, this process continued a long-term business relationship with this grower, based on trust in the quality of the beans, his capability to deliver needed quantities at agreed-upon times, and willingness to stand behind agreements. This seller has similar views about buyers, and will only deal with certain buyers. Thus the actual agreement on these beans was sealed with a handshake.

Continuing with Panel A, the beans were loaded on trucks and driven from the mountains to the port city (ocean humidity levels could damage the beans had they been warehoused there). Here they were loaded directly into 20-ton 'piggyback' containers designed to transport seamlessly amongst ships, trains and trucks. After four or five days at sea, the beans arrived at the port of New Orleans, were again tested for quality, and given over to a warehouse service. This service handled customs' clearance, then unloaded the bags into trucks driven to the coffee firm's 'silo' facility. Here loads of different beans are stored, then blended together into 20-ton hopper trucks and sent to the firm's New Orleans roasting plant (alternatively, they might have been sent to the firm's Midwest or Southwest roasting plants in 80-ton hopper cars). Here the final coffee is carefully prepared, tested for quality, and packaged into the familiar red cans or bricks. As indicated in Panel A, from this point the route depends on the purchaser: it may be shipped in large volume to one of the firm's seven regional distribution centers, thence to be sold to wholesalers, then to retail outlets, or – in the case of very large national accounts – trucked directly from the plant in 40,000-pound loads. As Tiffany had bought her coffee from the neighborhood IGA store, it had taken the longer route. Even so, the vacuum-pack containers had kept it quite fresh, and lent pleasure to her cup this morning. Thus we see how one marketing system has operated to provide a branded cup of coffee to an American family on a typical morning.

A Breakfast Pastry While coffee provides us with useful insights, it is a relatively simple product. We can move to a further level of complexity with another item in Tiffany's meal: a new breakfast pastry produced by a major food marketer to compete in the fast-growing 'premium' breakfast segment. Its marketing system is shown in Panel B of Figure 1.1 (for ease of communication we have shown only portions of this system to complement points of the coffee channel: neither system is portrayed in its true complexity). Note at the left that the pre-production marketing system here is much more involved than the linear system for coffee, as there are 15 ingredients in each unit of this pastry. Though not shown in the panel, each ingredient has its own system, similar to coffee's, for collection and transport to its processors. The pastry brand is similar to the coffee brand in requiring a very high level of uniformity in the brand units sold to consumers. Thus we find exacting product specifications for each ingredient at the left side of Panel B.

The next set of activities focus on product management decisions. Excited by consumer research showing unmet demand for bakery quality pastry that can be stored at home, and concerned by the success of competitors' new entries, this firm began a major new product development project. Experts in food science and nutritional technologies were challenged to translate this benefit concept into an actual food product. A long process ensued, as numerous attributes – size, icing, taste, consistency, flavoring, shelf-life, preparation, packaging, reasonable costs for pricing, production feasibility, and so forth – had to be brought to acceptable levels. The process included consumer research on reactions to prototypes, in-home use tests, and BehaviorScan controlled-store tests of pricing and promotions (including studies of purchase substitution patterns). The firm's Board of Directors now had to decide to launch the product or not. Key factors included internal rate of return over a six-year period, capital needs (new plant vs. conversion), options for co-packing or outsourcing

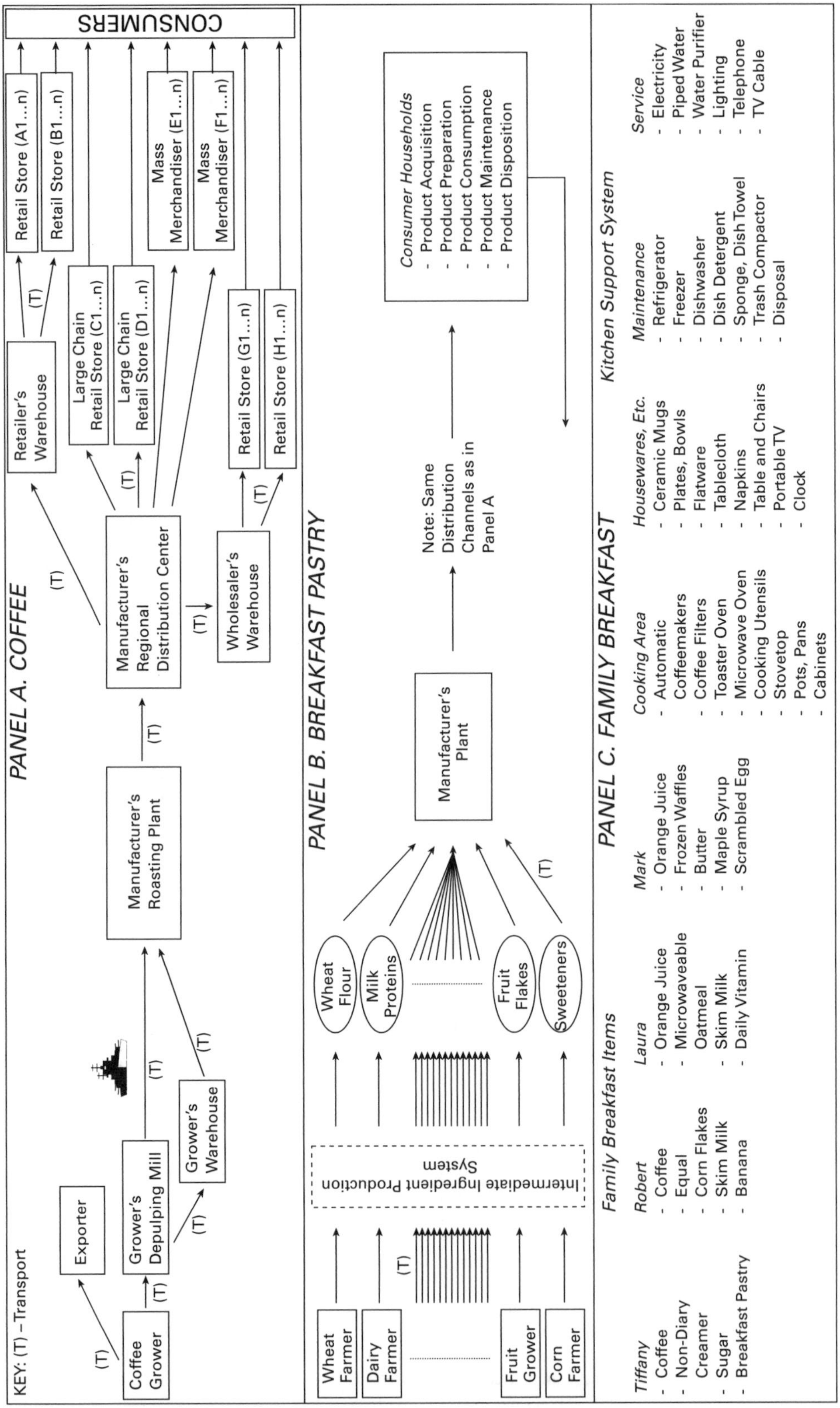
PANEL A. COFFEE
KEY: (T) – Transport
Coffee Grower
Exporter
Grower's Depulping Mill
Grower's Warehouse
Manufacturer's Roasting Plant
Manufacturer's Regional Distribution Center
Wholesaler's Warehouse
Retailer's Warehouse
Large Chain Retail Store (C1...n)
Large Chain Retail Store (D1...n)
Retail Store (A1...n)
Retail Store (B1...n)
Mass Merchandiser (E1...n)
Mass Merchandiser (F1...n)
Retail Store (G1...n)
Retail Store (H1...n)
CONSUMERS
PANEL B. BREAKFAST PASTRY
Wheat Farmer
Dairy Farmer
Fruit Grower
Corn Farmer
Intermediate Ingredient Production System
Wheat Flour
Milk Proteins
Fruit Flakes
Sweeteners
Manufacturer's Plant
Note: Same Distribution Channels as in Panel A
Consumer Households
- Product Acquisition
- Product Preparation
- Product Consumption
- Product Maintenance
- Product Disposition
PANEL C. FAMILY BREAKFAST
Family Breakfast Items
Tiffany
- Coffee
- Non-Diary Creamer
- Sugar
- Breakfast Pastry
Robert
- Coffee
- Equal
- Corn Flakes
- Skim Milk
- Banana
Laura
- Orange Juice
- Microwaveable Oatmeal
- Skim Milk
- Daily Vitamin
Mark
- Orange Juice
- Frozen Waffles
- Butter
- Maple Syrup
- Scrambled Egg
Kitchen Support System
Cooking Area
- Automatic Coffeemakers
- Coffee Filters
- Toaster Oven
- Microwave Oven
- Cooking Utensils
- Stovetop
- Pots, Pans
- Cabinets
Housewares, Etc.
- Ceramic Mugs
- Plates, Bowls
- Flatware
- Tablecloth
- Napkins
- Table and Chairs
- Portable TV
- Clock
Maintenance
- Refrigerator
- Freezer
- Dishwasher
- Dish Detergent
- Sponge, Dish Towel
- Trash Compactor
- Disposal
Service
- Electricity
- Piped Water
- Water Purifier
- Lighting
- Telephone
- TV Cable

PANEL D. SELECTED MARKETING SYSTEM ACTIVITIES (present in the coffee and breakfast pastry examples)

Sales and Delivery

The Classic Function of Distribution

- Transportation (2)
- Storage (2)
- Financing (2)
- Risk-bearing (2)
- Assembly (1)
- Selling (1)
- Standardization (2)
- Market Information (1)

N.B., Detailed Levels of Activities Exist: (e.g., Transport Activities)

- Truck to Depulping Mill
- Beans to Drying Area

....

- Ship to New Orleans
- Hopper Truck to Roasting Plant

....

- Truck to Retail Store

... additional steps in text

Purchasing and Use

Organizations:

- Sourcing Raw Material Supply (2)
- Quality Specifications (2)
- Purchase of Capital Equipment (3)
- Outsourcing: Specialist/ Expert Services (2)
- Purchase for Resale (1)
- Assortment Building (1)
- Bulk Breaking (2)
- Order Processing (2)
- Negotiation: Terms of Sale (1)
- Transfer of Ownership (2)

Consumers:

- Product Acquisition (2)
- Product Preparation (3)
- Product Consumption (3)
- Product Maintenance/Repair (2)
- Product Disposition (2)

Knowledge Development/Intelligence

Organizations:

- Market Analysis (1)
- Market Demand Assessment (1)
- Analysis of Competitive Strategies (1)
- Market Segmentation (1)
- Market Forecasts (1)
- Performance Monitoring (1)
- Program Evaluation (1)

Consumers:

- Consumer Education (2)
- Information Search (2)
- Word of Mouth (3)
- Store Visits (2)
- Post-Purchase Analysis (3)

Marketing Plans and Programs/Government Actions

Organizations:

- Financial Projections (2)
- Board of Directors Approval (2)
- Product Design (2)
- Product Line Decisions (1)
- Budget Setting (2)
- Distribution Planning (1)
- Brand Name Selection (1)
- Packaging (1)
- Market Testing (1)
- Positioning Strategy (1)
- Pricing Decisions (1)
- National Advertising (1)
- Direct Marketing (1)
- Consumer Promotion (1)
- Trade Promotion (1)
- Trade Advertising (1)
- Communication to Sales Force (1)
- Point of Purchase Materials (1)
- Publicity (2)
- Warranty Terms (2)
- Customer Service (2)
- Retailer Assortment (1)
- Merchandising (1)
- Retail Advertising (1)
- Inventory Management (2)

Government Agencies:

- Standard Setting (2)
- Export/Import Controls (2)
- Trademark Protection (2)
- Financing Arrangements (2)
- Nutritional Labeling (2)
- Inspections (3)
- Regulartory Rules and Guidelines (2)

Numerical Key:

(1) = Largely or entirely controlled by marketing managers
(2) = Largely controlled by others, but influenced by or coordinated with marketing managers
(3) = Little or no influence by marketing managers
(n) = Activity does not involve market

Centers of Little or No Marketing Involvement

Organizations:

- Internal Management of Work Force (n)
- Management of Plant & Equipment (n)
- Financial Mgmt., Accounting & Control (n)
- Basic Research, etc. (n)

Government:

- All non-commerce/non-consumer sectors (n)

Consumers:

- All non-consumer aspects of daily life (n)

PANEL E. DEPICTING THE ENTIRE AGGREGATE MARKETING SYSTEM

Brand Coffee System (Panel A) →	***All system activities given for the cup of coffee,*** beginning with harvest of beans on left, Ending with consumer use and disposition on right. (2) (2) (2) (2) (1) (1)..... (note: not all activities controlled by marketers, see key in panel D) ..... (2) (3) (3) (2) (2)		
(Multiplicative Increase) →	***Add <u>all</u> coffee systems***	→	**(Similar sets of activities, participants and forms of value creation)**
Brand Pastry System (Panel B) →	***All system activities*** *given for pastry* beginning with creation, storage and transport of 15 pastry ingredients and ending with consumer use and disposition.	→	"
(Large Geometric Increase) →	***Add <u>all</u> breakfast systems, on-premise restaurants and home kitchen systems***	→	"
(Larger Geometric Increase) →	***Add <u>all</u> other food and beverage systems***	→	"
(Huge Geometric Increase) →	***Add <u>all</u> product systems and <u>all</u> service systems***	→	"
(Huge Geometric Increase) →	***Add <u>all</u> not-for-profit marketing activities***	→	"
(Huge Geometric Increase) →	***Add <u>all</u> government and <u>all</u> consumer marketing system activities***	→	"

Figure 1.1 *The System at Work*

production, and effects on the firm's current product line. As this would be a 'bakery quality' item, the Board was very concerned about the system at the left of Panel B – that the ingredients be regularly available, cost-controlled, and geared to precise recipe quality. The Board did give the green light to the project, and the entire marketing mix was finalized and implemented. The distribution system (the right side of Panel B) was quite similar to that for coffee, as was the consumer's purchase and use system (which concludes with a disposition service purchase for trash removal). In terms of the system's dynamics, each consumer purchase feeds back into stocking and production plans: through feedback derived from both internal accounting and formal market research projects this firm will monitor and adapt its management of this product. Over time, therefore, consumers' actual use satisfactions and repurchases will determine its success or failure.

Further Considerations Although the illustration is getting long, we are only a little way toward capturing the true scope of the aggregate marketing system (however, we'll now dispense with details and simply point to key issues). We have only covered two breakfast items: as shown in Panel C, the four family members have different preferences, which the aggregate marketing system is easily able to accommodate. Also, the breakfast depends on more than food, and an entire kitchen support system is available to assist this consumption episode. In terms of our broader topic it is important to recognize that *all* aspects of Panel C have been brought to the Jones household through the aggregate marketing system, some many years ago (e.g., the plumbing and the furniture), and others more recently (e.g., the new dishwasher bought last week, and the coffee, pastry and fresh fruit bought yesterday). Also, each element listed in Panel C had its own complex marketing system that brought it to this point. Global sourcing was involved in some systems: the coffeemaker from Germany, artwork from the Far East, microwave from Korea, and so forth. In every case, a complete system was planned, created, and run in order to deliver these products to households like Tiffany's, and in most cases had to compete and win out over others' systems to gain Tiffany's purchase. If we were to analyze each system, many pages would be used: the total number of system interactions needed to create this meal is truly impressive. When we further recognize that the aggregate marketing system routinely provides breakfast for 100 million US households every morning – and that breakfast is only a trivial element of its total activity – we are ready to appreciate its immensity and significance.

The Scope and Size of the System

The foregoing illustration is a useful basis for summarizing system scope: Panel D of Figure 1.1 provides a partial listing of system activities that allowed this breakfast to occur. Several points emerge:

1. There are a surprisingly large number of entries: *the aggregate marketing system undertakes a wide range of activities* in order to provide for a simple breakfast meal.
2. *There are participants besides marketers in the aggregate marketing system.* Organizational customers and ultimate consumers are key players (buying is crucial at every stage), and governments provide services intended to facilitate system operations (shown at the right, these cross all stages).
3. As indicated by the keyed entries in Panel D, *marketing managers control (#1) only some of the activities of the aggregate marketing system. Other necessary activities are carried out by persons who do not consider themselves to be marketers. In most of these cases, marketing managers do serve as influences within organizations (#2) on these actions*, while in some cases (#3) necessary system activities may be carried out with little or no direct influence from marketers (note that this is particularly apparent in the consumer realm). *This property of the system calls for a perspective on marketing that reaches beyond a sole focus on a manager's controllable decisions.* (Note: numbers assigned to each activity are generalized: readers may wish to consider whether they would agree.)
4. *The three classes of participants all engage in activities apart from the aggregate marketing system: the system is very broad, but not entirely dense.* Some parts of virtually every organization work on tasks only indirectly related to the marketing activities listed, and carry these out independently (shown as 'n' in the bottom right of Panel D). We would not define these as marketing system activities. Nor would we include activities of government agencies or consumers that are directed entirely toward other sectors of society and life. Thus our visual conception of the aggregate marketing system resembles a cross-section of fine swiss cheese or steel mesh – similar to Panels A and B, with numerous linkages between organizations as we move across to the consumer sector, but with holes inside each organization to represent parts where the work is arguably outside of the marketing system.
5. *Finally, Panel D significantly understates system activity:* most listings have many detailed steps (e.g., advertising, promotion, merchandising, etc.), or transportation steps, as in bottom left column.

Panel E of Figure 1.1 next depicts an approach to assessing the scope of the US aggregate marketing system. *Horizontally,* note that it extends from extraction of raw materials/crops at the left, through many levels of value creation, to end consumption and disposition in far-off locales at the right (again, the earlier Venn diagram analogy should clarify our conception that some of these activities are properly seen as also belonging to other intersecting aggregate systems). *Vertically,* we first add all competing coffee and pastry systems, then add all other food systems, then add all other goods and services. In concept, this process will include all organizations that engage in marketing system activities of the types shown in Panel D, all levels of government activities that impact on this system, and all forms of consumer participation by all societal members. Our next illustration provides estimates of the magnitudes involved.

'From Here to Eternity' The aggregate marketing system is huge and growing rapidly.[2] As we move past the year 2000, in the US alone we find some *275 million final consumers* arrayed in *100 million households,* all on the consumption side of the system. They *spend 5 trillion dollars* each year, or two-thirds of the nation's Gross Domestic Product. To place this spending in perspective, if we were to try to count it at the rate of one dollar per second, it would take us over 150,000 years, or much longer than the history of civilization. While the aggregate marketing system in the US may not stretch quite to 'eternity,' it certainly does stretch a very long way.

Further, we should recall that yearly data are merely compiled for convenience, and can easily understate true impacts. For example, as in Tiffany's kitchen, households accumulate many consumer durables that continue to provide benefits to them for years. As opposed to annual sales, then, consider that some *200 million motor vehicles* are currently registered for road use in the US: all of these have been provided through the marketing system (and many are used to carry out its functions on a daily basis). In terms of the work of marketing, *a significant portion of Americans are employed entirely or in part assisting the system to perform its functions.* While exact figures are elusive due to categorization problems, it appears that over 30 million Americans work directly within the aggregate marketing system, with salespersons accounting for the largest portion. There are almost 20 million businesses acting as buyers: 3 million of these are retailers that resell to consumers, with another one-half million wholesaling firms (interestingly, because of multiple steps in the wholesale channel, total sales of wholesalers are larger than those of retailers). Advertising spending is huge and growing, now some $200 billion per year: other areas of recent growth include services (now over half of all consumer spending) and direct marketing, which has doubled in recent years.

Even though these numbers are huge, still we have understated the true scope of the aggregate marketing system in our society. Professional practices (attorneys, accountants, architects) were not included in these counts, but must engage in accepted forms of marketing to build and maintain their clientele. Numerous persons in not-for-profit organizations, also not included in our formal numbers, employ marketing actions both in garnering resources and carrying out their missions. Government workers at local, state and federal levels regularly negotiate contracts, buy goods and services, and monitor marketing performance. Further, because marketing is an intrinsic function in those 20 million business firms noted above, a portion of the responsibilities of many positions – from Chief Executive Officer to quality inspectors to shipping and fulfillment clerks – are involved with carrying out the firm's marketing activities. Finally, the US aggregate marketing system in no way stands alone in the world: by not including other nations' numbers we have understated by many times the actual impact of marketing around the globe (as an aside, this analysis also helps us to appreciate the enormity of the challenges faced by command systems, which cannot hope to replicate the millions of allocation decisions being made within a market system each day).

Characteristics of the Aggregate Marketing System

Figure 1.2 completes our background on the system with a summary of its key properties. Propositions I, III, and IV have been discussed at length, but the others deserve brief comment. Proposition II gives a system perspective that we have long viewed to be powerful: *the concept of continuous flows in various modalities,* including physical, persuasive, informational and monetary. Flows occur in both directions (e.g., money flows backwards in the system in payment for goods; information and influence flow forward from advertising and sales efforts, but also backward with marketing research). Some are simultaneous, but many are not: the investment flow forward (in plant, labor, production, and promotion in advance of sales) represents levels of risk-taking and confidence in marketing activity.[3] Meanwhile, Proposition V reflects that in a market-based system, consumers' response to marketers' offerings will drive supply allocations and prices. Depending on a society's decisions on public vs. private ownership, the aggregate marketing system plays a greater or lesser role in allocating national resources.[4] The US has given substantial freedoms to its aggregate marketing system; apart from certain restrictions, a person may choose to produce almost any good or service he or she desires, in any form and name, offer it for sale at places, prices and terms of his or her choosing, and may advertise it or not, using virtually any appeal seen to be effective. While restrictions do exist in each of these areas, these are primarily to protect the rights of competing marketers or consumers.

The Aggregate Marketing System:

I. ***Incorporates numerous activities,*** including the classic distribution functions, marketers' plans and programs, and actions by consumers and government.

II. ***Is comprised of planned and continuous flows*** among participants, including flows of goods and materials, service deliveries, dollar payments, and flows of information and influence.

III. ***Is extensive, in several respects,***

A. Extending all the way from the collection of raw materials, through multiple intermediate processes, to use and disposition at each individual household.

B. Combining materials/goods from around the globe into market offerings.

C. With multiple sets of marketers, acting as competitors, performing activities in parallel.

D. In its geometric exchange activity, with multiple producers selling to multiple purchasers, and multiple buyers purchasing from multiple sellers.

IV. ***Is structurally sophisticated,*** relying upon a massive physical and communications infrastructure that regularly and routinely creates and delivers goods and services across the society.

V. ***Is a key basis for resource allocation in a market economy,*** as consumer responses to market offerings determine which goods and services are and are not created in the future.

VI. ***Is governed by forces for efficiency,*** most notably self-interest, competition, and characteristics of market demand.

VII. ***Is constrained by social forces,*** including laws, government regulations, cultural norms, and ethical codes of business and consumer conduct.

VIII. ***Relies upon coordinated processes,*** with producers and resellers seeking interdependent purchases to fit pre-specified standards, with the later expectation of purchasing by consumers.

IX. ***Operates through human interactions, experience and trust,*** as participants develop and maintain marketplace relationships as a basis for conducting their system activities.

X. ***Is an open system, geared toward growth and innovation,*** as participants seek to solve problems and pursue opportunities, investing with faith in the future operations of the market.

Figure 1.2 *Propositions on the Aggregate Marketing System*

Proposition VI reflects that our aggregate marketing system does more than physically deliver goods and services: it also works to bring a *dynamism* to society that encourages continual growth and progress (Vaile, Grether & Cox, 1952). Marketers know that observed demand is not really fixed: consumers can be highly responsive to different marketing programs. *Thus competition is the main driving force*, leading marketers to search for areas of comparative advantage that will lead to greater financial success.[5] New competitors are attracted to areas of opportunity. Over time prices can be adjusted downward through competition and/or production efficiencies. New buyers join in buying the favored offerings, and some markets grow while others wither away. Not all marketing system programs are successful: the effort to support dynamism can lead to excesses, failures, and sometimes unforeseen consequences. Proposition VII reflects this underlying tension by reflecting the *need for controls*. A market system needs a legal infrastructure for property rights, performance of contracts, freedom of choice, and so forth. The role of government as society's representative is thus central, though this can be contravened if politicians allow cynical self-seeking interests to circumvent either competition or desirable restraints. Thus government achieving a proper balance to best serve a society's goals becomes a key issue for aggregate marketing systems.[6]

Propositions VIII and IX, meanwhile, refer back to the bonding forces that constitute the heart of the marketing effort. The existing infrastructure requires coordination in space, time, and 'fit,' as offerings require the intermarriage of components within a context of high efficiency. We indeed have been impressed by the serious concerns given to process quality control within this system. Further, we have been reminded that at its roots this is a human institution in which both experience and trust play major roles, a point that has also recently emerged in relationship marketing thought. Even economists have recognized the role of trust within the system, as Kenneth Arrow, Nobel Laureate in Economics explained, '*...virtually every commercial transaction*

A. TEN CONTRIBUTIONS TO THE LARGER ECONOMIC SYSTEM

- *Employment and Personal Incomes*
- *Freedom of Choice in Consumption*
- *Delivery of a Standard of Living*
- *Assistance in Infrastructure Development*
  (e.g., Transportation, Communications, Financial Sector)
- *Tax Payments for Public Purposes*
- *Mass Market Efficiencies*
- *Diffusion of Innovations*
- *Enhanced Balance of Trade Accounts*
- *International Development*
- *Integral to Economic Growth and Prosperity*

B. INSIGHTS ON MARKETING AND ECONOMIC DEVELOPMENT

- *Marketing Employment/GDP Relationship*
- *Roles Depend on Stage of Development:*
  - *Traditional Subsistence: Assure Prices*
  - *Transitional: Infrastructure*
  - *Market-oriented: Financing, Credit*
- *Roles Depend on Government Policies*
- *Roles Depend on Consumers and Culture*
- *Marketing Expertise and Systems are Key*
- *Marketing's Development Functions:*
  - *Organization of Networks*
  - *Speculation in Time*
  - *Equalization*
  - *Spatial Connectivity*
  - *Capital Accumulation*
  - *Entrepreneurial Entry*

Figure 1.3 *Marketing's Contributions to Economic Well-being*

has within itself an element of trust ... much of the economic backwardness in the world can be explained by the lack of mutual confidence' (Arrow, 1972). In asking why all societies do not become equally wealthy and successful, recent work by Hunt (1997) and others (e.g., Etzioni, 1988) points to differences in societal institutions that promote trust and personal moral codes as a key differentiator. Finally, Proposition X notes this 'open system' stresses achievement, growth, and progress. These are the elements of the US aggregate marketing system that helped to bring the century of progress noted at the start of our discussion.[7]

We now turn to the system's contributions. Our discussion here is presented in three sections: (1) benefits to economic well-being, (2) benefits to buyers, and (3) several broader perspectives on benefits.[8] While most entries are not new to marketing thinkers, we are hopeful that in combination they will prove useful in stimulating further thought about our field and its value to society.

Marketing's Contributions to Economic Well-being

Contributions to the Larger Economic System

Whatever the political choices, an aggregate marketing system is integral to a society's economic system. Figure 1. 3A lists ten areas in which marketing contributes here in the US. First, it offers *employment and incomes* for the millions of persons engaged in this field, allowing them to be productive and earn money needed for consumption. As noted, consumers' exercising *freedom of choice* means that the preferences of society's members are largely reflected in the system's goods and services; this should mean that aggregate satisfaction is enhanced in this sector of life. As Adam Smith pointed out in his classic *The Wealth of Nations* (1776), 'Consumption is the sole end and purpose of all production...' In this regard, the aggregate marketing system is directly involved in *delivering the standard of living* enjoyed by society's members. Further, private investments for the marketing system have been important in *assisting national infrastructure development* in such areas as distribution facilities, transportation, communication, medical care, and the financial sector. Related to this, monies gathered by governments (sales and excise taxes) are actually gathered by operations of the marketing system. Together with income taxes paid by firms and individuals engaged in marketing, these represent substantial sources of the tax payments to fund public programs.

With respect to consumption, the system's *mass market efficiencies* have led to lower costs, lower prices, and increased total consumption for citizens. The system's dynamic character also fosters *diffusion of innovations,* bringing new benefits to daily life. Internationally, the aggregate marketing system is a crucial contributor to the nation's *balance of trade* and, in seeking new areas of opportunity, is a *force for international development.* Overall, then, in a number of significant and positive ways, the aggregate marketing system has played an integral role in the economic growth and prosperity of the US.

While obvious in the abstract, marketing's contributions to economic well-being have not actually been recognized by many businesspersons nor, indeed, by many economists. This is probably because they are not factors in the classic macroeconomic equations (Kinnear, 1994). Here, aggregate supply is seen to depend on the stock of capital, labor, raw materials, and technology. Kinnear asserts that marketing's importance would be more clear if efficiencies and skills in wholesaling, retailing and logistics were included in this equation. Similarly, aggregate demand is a function of expenditures for consumption, investment, government, and net foreign trade. However, we all know that marketing impacts on aggregate demand: if economists' equations were to identify effects of marketing programs (on autonomous consumption and marginal propensity to consume, on prospects for success of an investment in a new product, and on the volume of exports and imports), the value of marketing efforts in our economic system would be more starkly obvious. Further, this would stimulate interest in calibrating the magnitudes of these contributions.

Marketing and Economic Development

The societal benefits that flow from the aggregate marketing system are nowhere more apparent than in the area of economic development. Peter Drucker, the noted business thinker, raised this issue years ago in a stirring speech, reprinted by the *Journal of Marketing* as 'Marketing and Economic Development' (Drucker, 1958). His view of marketing as an entrepreneurial 'multiplier' and organizer of resources casts a quite different light on our field. Later work has done much to explore and refine this view. The points in Figure 1.3B illustrate several key insights about marketing's roles and contributions.[9]

First, the role for marketing in economic development is real. Nations with higher proportions of their populations in marketing also have higher gross domestic products: the development of the marketing system is necessary for this to occur (e.g., Preston, 1968; Wood and Vitell, 1986). However, the specific roles for the marketing system differ by stage of economic development. In a subsistence economy, production is barely sufficient for self-needs, and is not separated in time or distance from consumption. The immediate priority is incentives to increase production, with price assurance being most significant. In economies just becoming urbanized, the priority is to develop distribution infrastructure (i.e., transport, storage, and selling networks). In market-oriented systems, all marketing functions are important, with investment financing and consumer credit as primary tools for market growth (US Department of Agriculture, 1972).

As noted in Figure 1.3B, a host government's policies help determine opportunities for marketing's contributions to the society (e.g., Thorelli, 1996). However, governments typically pursue five possibly contradictory goals: growth, fuller employment, income distribution, price control (inflation), and balance of payments – and may do so with too few tools to handle the task (Slater, 1978). Treatment of the aggregate marketing system is thus part of a complex political context. As a social institution, the marketing system must be embedded in the society's culture. For the US in the international sphere, this can be problematic in some societies, as aspects of the culture are not welcoming of some features of the US marketing system (Ger, 1997). Where a US-style system is desired, moreover, certain consumer behaviors (e.g., handling of finances, planned saving and choice processes, defenses to persuasion) have to be learned for the system to work well. As to linkages among efficiency, consumer behavior, and culture in developing marketing systems, Slater identified literacy, achievement desires, cooperation, fatalism, mass media and innovativeness as key dimensions (cf. Nason & White, 1981). Today's marketing experts working in the 'transitional economies' (i.e., those moving from centralized planning to market-based systems) of Eastern Europe, the former Soviet Union, and China are noting that entrepreneurial risk-taking, marketing management expertise, and the use of strong business planning and control systems are crucial in determining success (e.g., Batra, 1997). They differ as to the ease of the transfer of such knowledge, but the large number of international students educated in business schools in recent years does give cause for optimism.

Finally, Figure 1.3B's 'Marketing's Development Functions' reflects marketing's roles in more basic settings (modified from Moyer, 1965). First, marketing encourages increased production by *conceiving, organizing, and operating networks* for communication and exchange. *Speculation across time* is needed to bring future production and consumption, using entrepreneurial risk of capital and effort. *Equalization of supply and demand* occurs across distance (transport), time (storage), and quantity (price), while *spacial connectivity* joins diverse locales into a larger marketplace to offer efficiencies of scale and lower prices to consumers. Over time, these can grow into a center for *capital accumulation* (investment), and serve as a springboard for *marketing entrepreneurs' entry* to become industrialists. For example, some years after its independence, nearly half of the leading industrialists of Pakistan were found to have come from the marketing sector (Papenek, 1962). Here they had learned, in Adam Smith's words, 'the habits ... of order, economy, and attention' that characterize success in market distribution (Smith, 1776).

Contributions to Buyers from Specific Marketing Activities

We now focus on marketers' actions that benefit buyers. As there are millions of competing firms in our aggregate marketing system, at any time a huge number of these benefits are being offered in parallel. Across time, these benefits accumulate, through billions of purchase occasions, to be truly formidable. Our framework in Figure 1.4 will be quite familiar to marketing thinkers, but persons outside the field are likely to be surprised at the scope of contributions offered. We begin with the economic concept of utility.

Marketing's Bundle of Utilities

Economists traditionally employ *utility* to represent value. As a prominent economist observed nearly 80 years ago, '*... marketing and advertising are interested primarily in the creation of value*' (Moriarty, 1923). Identification of marketing's special utilities, shown in Figure 1.4A, proved helpful to economists who argued that distributive services did add value beyond that derived from production.[10] Of the five utilities listed, note that only *elemental utility,* which refers to cultivation or extraction of crops and raw materials, is arguably beyond marketing's purview. The second, *form utility,* comes primarily from operations, but marketing activities do contribute here by (1) physically supplying essential inputs to the production process, and (2) providing insights from the marketplace (e.g., market research) that help decide specific attributes for goods and services. *Place utility* is clearly in marketing's province, representing the value added by providing goods where buyers need them. Marketing adds *time utility* through preplanning, inventory, and promotion activities to ensure customers can obtain goods when they are needed. Finally, *possession utility* is offered through marketing transactions, and allows customers to use goods for desired purposes.

The Eight 'Classic Functions' of Market Distribution

Our appreciation of marketing's contributions is enhanced by the 'functional approach,' which arose early in the twentieth century in reaction to mainstream economists' lack of attention to the value of distribution. It became a basic approach for the study of marketing for over five decades, describing marketers' activities and their reasons for them. With the rise of the managerial approach, however, this descriptive view of marketing has now all but disappeared (Hunt and Goolsby, 1988).

Among many frameworks, the eight functions listed in Figure 1.4B are widely accepted (Maynard, Weidler & Beckman, 1927). Given the emphasis at that time on agriculture and manufacturing, functional frameworks stressed physical supply services, beginning with *(1) transportation.* Closely allied, *(2) storage* helps to nullify timing discrepancies in supply and demand, smooths production schedules to reduce costs, and allows the mixing of ingredients or stock (as in our coffee bean example). Innovations in these areas (consider refrigeration and freezing) have brought major improvements to our society over the past century. The next one of marketing's classic functions, *(3) financing,* receives little attention by marketing scholars today, but is still a key topic in economic development settings. A firm must finance the time-gap between the start of the productive process (when machines, material, labor, marketing, etc. must be paid for) and the later receipt of money from sales. Such investment financing may be undertaken directly by marketers or, when stakes are high, by financial institutions. Within our overall system, financing has fostered entry by many small businesses, while consumer credit has allowed purchases of millions of homes, autos, etc., and thus has been a key factor in society's prosperity. Number *(4), assumption of risk,* reflects transactions, and arises out of uncertainty. In marketing channels, for example, risk comes with ownership of goods for which future demand may be less than expected (e.g., negative price changes, demand shortfalls, improved designs, deterioration in quality, or credit problems with repayments). Risk is substantial throughout the aggregate marketing system – a fact apparent to those who forecast demand.

(5) Assembly refers to the broader buying process – seeking out sources of supply and deciding on goods and services to be purchased. Buying is pervasive across the aggregate marketing system, leading to successive changes in ownership that end in final consumer purchases. The other side of a purchase is

Traditional Views	Managerial Sectors		System Outcomes

A. Five Types of Utility:
– *Elemental Utility*
(marketing not a contributor)
– *Form Utility*
(marketing a partial contributor)
– *Place Utility*
(marketing a major contributor)
– *Time Utility*
(marketing a major contributor)
– *Possession Utility*
(marketing a major contributor)
 	
B. The Eight Classic Functions of Market Distribution:
– *Transportation*
– *Storage*
– *Financing*
– *Risk-bearing*
– *Assembly*
– *Selling*
– *Standardization*
– *Market Information*
	C. Marketing Mix Elements:
	Products and Service Offerings
	– Two-Way Exchange
	– Benefits From Each Use Occasion
	– Benefit Bundles (Multiattribute)
	– Frequent New Offerings
	– Continued Improvements
	– Considerable Product Variation
	– Stress on Quality Control
	– Guarantees and Redress
	
	Benefits of Branding/Trademarks
	– Indentification of Specific Offerings
	– Efficiency in Future Search
	– Consumer Confidence/Meaning
	– Possible Symbolic Benefits
	
	Market Distribution
	– Most Marketing Functions (at left)
	– Eases Access to Products/ Services
	– Reduces Information Search Costs
	– Enables Inter-brand Comparisons
	– Lowers Prices via Competition
	– Increases Quantity of Information
	– Facilitates Transaction Processes
	– Offers Credit Opportunities
	– Post-Purchase Support Structure
	  – Delivery and Set-up
	  – Liberal Return Policies
	  – Maintenance and Repair
	– Provides Entry for New Competitors
		Salespersons and Representatives
		– Consultation on Problem Solutions
		– Crystallization of Needs
		– Education About Alternatives
		– Introduction of New Offerings
		– Customization of Offerings
		– Facilitation of Transactions
		– Access to Technical Support
		– Customer Satisfaction
		– Feedback From Field
		
		Advertising and Promotion
		– Provides Information
		  – Product Knowledge/Use
		  – New Products and Services
		  – Prices and Specials
		– Decision Making Enhancements
		  – Shopping Patronage
		  – Lowers Search Costs
		– Enlarges Market Demand
		  – Reduces Distribution Costs
		  – Lowers Prices
		  – Entry of New Competitors
		  – Acceptance of Innovations
		– Subsidizes Media and Events
		  – News and Editorial
		  – Entertainment and Sports
		– Provides Entertainment
			D. Summary: The Marketing System's Resultant Benefits
			I. Promotes the Production of Desired Products and Services
			II. Delivers Products and Services
			III. Provides for Market Learning
			IV. Stimulates Market Demand
			V. Offers Wide Scope for Choice
			VI. Close/Customized Fits With Needs
			VII. Facilitates Purchases (Acquisitions)
			VIII. Saves Time/Promotes Efficiency
			IX. Provides for Postpurchase Support
			X. Brings New Entries to Market
			XI. Fosters Innovations/ Improvements
			XII. Enables Larger Total Consumption
			XIII. Seeks Customer Satisfaction for Repeat Purchase Relationships
			XIV. Provides a Pleasant 'Approach' Environment for Buyer Behavior

Figure 1.4 *Contributions to Buyers from Specific Marketing Activities*

another's sale. Though much maligned, *(6) selling* harnesses the forces of competition to improve the value of offerings, and brings about the exchanges that allow the system to operate. *(7) Standard setting* is often unseen and quite underestimated. Once set by a society, standards serve as buying guides in a vast range of business and consumer categories: in essence they provide assurance for critical 'credence' attributes such as safety, strength, or other elements of an offering that may be difficult to determine via inspection, and they aid in price and value comparisons as well. Marketers are important users of standards in our society, and also participate in their creation (in contrast to general perceptions, the vast majority of standardization is a voluntary activity in the US, rather than being imposed by government). Finally, the gathering and use of *(8) market information* is quite familiar. Inputs can come from sources – experts, government, customers, the sales force, library – beyond formal market research projects. As a key activity in marketing today, this function increasingly stimulates improvements in the benefits we will now discuss.

Benefits From Product and Service Offerings

A marketing exchange relies on *both* transacting parties expecting to be better off. *As sellers benefit from payments for purchases, it is not surprising to see marketers' focus on purchase processes. However, it is important to recall that benefits received by customers accrue from use or consumption.* As indicated in Figure 1.4C, this has an interesting implication; *each single use occasion creates an opportunity for another benefit delivery from the system.* Further, as products and services are 'benefit bundles,' users are deriving multiple benefits (Green, Wind, & Jain, 1972). For example, toothpaste attributes such as decay prevention, whitening, tartar control, and good taste can be combined to create multiple sources of value in a single use occasion. Extensive product variation further allows closer fits with users' preferences. In our system, frequent new offerings and improvements to current offerings are also pursued. Further, we should recognize that *much of the care taken by marketers in design, creation, and delivery of offerings remains unseen* (and is thus underappreciated by the general public). This care aids a brand's competitive success by providing an intended, identical service or use experience expected by loyal customers. Last, our marketing system generally stands behind its offerings, with buyers often protected by guarantees.

To check our impression of this system stress on quality, we checked ratings in some 200 product and service classes. Ratings were given in 1996–97 in *Consumer Reports,* published by Consumers Union, an independent testing organization that accepts no advertising or other funds from the marketing community. Our tabulation of scores showed that, of 3028 ratings, only 51 items (1.7%) were rated as 'Poor' in quality. Including 'Fair' as a passing grade, 98% of marketers' offerings received satisfactory ratings: 88% received ratings of good, very good, or excellent.[11] Clearly the system is delivering quality offerings to its public.

Benefits of Branding/Trademarks

Unique identification is not only significant to marketers (Aaker, 1991), but also benefits buyers in four ways.[12] As shown in Figure 1.4C, unique source names assist:

(1) organizing future behaviors (if problems are encountered, the source can be re-contacted: if satisfied, favorable attitudes can direct future decisions);
(2) efficiency in locating favored sellers (while appearing innocuous, summed across products, time, and competing demands, this efficiency is actually quite significant in total);
(3) rapid, confident choices in self-service settings (the average time for a single choice in a US supermarket aisle is only a few seconds); and
(4) deriving symbolic benefits from purchase, ownership, or use. Symbolic benefits can be public (driving a high-status car) or private (enjoying a finely crafted product). While at times a target for criticism, symbolic benefits' mechanisms are varied and subtle, involving sustaining personal identity as well as communicating about oneself (Belk, 1988, 1989; Cohen, 1989; Levy, 1959).

Benefits From Market Distribution

As noted in the first entry of this section of Figure 1.4C, the key benefits in this area were captured in our discussion of marketing's eight classic functions. As it is performed largely out of the sight of non-participants, however, the performance of distribution can be underappreciated. It is useful to recall that the marketing system performs these functions repetitively and routinely, millions of times daily, each time offering benefits to receivers. Beyond this, wholesale and retail activities offer the additional benefits noted in the remaining listings of Figure 1.4C. The first five of these are well-recognized and need no amplification. The final four entries, however, do deserve separate discussion.

One powerful aspect of the US marketing system is *facilitating the transaction process,* thus saving consumers' time and effort while maximizing purchase opportunities. Consider, for example, the benefits of extended store hours, convenient locations, free parking, stocked shelves, posted prices, displays, fast and smooth checkouts, advertising price specials, salespersons' pleasant and efficient completion of transactions, and so forth (consumers from some other cultures express surprise, and delight, upon discovering this of the US retailing system). Further, processes for *extending consumer credit* allow some expensive purchases to occur that otherwise would be delayed, while bank credit cards have greatly eased transaction processes for buyers and sellers alike (the fact that stores will pay significant fees, about 3%, for bank card charges is a good indicator of how much the system desires to facilitate purchase transactions). When a durable good purchase is made, moreover, consumers enter a use phase that can last for many years. During this time the marketing system offers a *postpurchase support structure* with benefits such as delivery, installation, repair services, and liberal return policies. Our final entry is quite different, but has done much to improve the lives of everyone in our society, in that our channels of distribution *serve as the entry point (gatekeeper) for new products and services.* Receptivity by wholesalers and retailers to offerings providing better value or new benefits has made this dynamic work for society's gain (similarly, government actions to reduce competitive barriers to entry allow innovations and price competition to work to the benefit of society's consumers and competitors).

Benefits From Salespersons and Representatives

Sales representatives facilitate flows within the aggregate marketing system. *While advertising receives more public attention, marketers frequently rate personal selling as more important for business success.* In one study, executives rated selling as five times more important than advertising for industrial goods, and almost twice as important for consumer durable goods; for consumer nondurables, the two were rated about equally important (Udell, 1972). An estimated 20 million sales representatives are at work daily in the system – 9 million in business-to-business selling, and 11 million others dealing directly with consumers. Roles vary widely, as do levels of performance. Figure 1.4C lists some contributions offered in business-to-business sales, where the salesperson is a professional representative dealing with generally well-informed buyers, as well as with current users who may need to have problems resolved. To start, salespersons may be called on to consult on large programs (e.g., plant construction, advertising campaigns), often as part of account teams that include specialists. During this process a representative may help crystallize the client's needs, educate the client about alternatives, introduce new entries, and customize the offering when feasible. He or she then works to facilitate the entire transaction, payment, and product delivery or project completion. During this process, which can extend for years, the sales representative provides access to technical support and offers personal service to ensure customer satisfaction and a continuing relationship. Our final entry – feedback from the field – reflects salespersons reports back to the firm on opportunities to enhance its offerings.

Benefits From Advertising and Promotion

Each year an incredible amount of money is spent on advertising and sales promotion: advertising is a major industry in its own right, accounting for about 3% of US Gross Domestic Product. Due to its high visibility, advertising is probably the most criticized facet of the aggregate marketing system, though it in fact provides important benefits. In their classic study, *Advertising in America*, Bauer and Greyser (1968; see also Pollay & Mittal, 1993) asked consumers about this institution. Their findings fit four of the five entries in Figure 1.4C. First, appreciation for the *information* advertising provides on products and prices was expressed by a majority of consumers.[13] Few consumers noted our second benefit: clearly, however, advertising can *enhance consumer decisions* through lower search costs (product proliferation, however, does raise search costs). The consumers did mention *enlarging market demand,* noting special appreciation for advertising's contribution to lowering prices. Less obvious are three related benefits here: reducing distribution costs, aiding entry by new competitors, and fostering acceptance of new innovations by a society. The consumer sample also recognized the final entries in Figure 1.4C, applauding advertising's role in *subsidizing media,* as well as expressing pleasure with advertising's own *creative offerings.*

Summary: Marketing's Key Benefits to Buyers

As our detailed listings risk 'losing sight of the forest for the trees,' Figure 1.4D abstracts what we see as 14 of the key benefits consumers derive from marketing activities. First is marketing's role in *driving the production of offerings most desired in the marketplace.* In many organizations marketers act as internal advocates representing the customer in decisions on what to produce, then other elements of the aggregate marketing system advance the creation of those offerings by carrying out their functions (e.g., assembly, transport) at all intermediate stages leading to final production. The marketing system then manages the *delivery of products and services* to consumers. It also expends funds to *provide for market learning* via sales representatives, advertising, brochures, specialized brokers, etc. The persuasive aspect of these vehicles serves to *stimulate market demand:* this creates sales, and may lead to lowered costs and prices. Through competition, the system offers a *wide array of choices.* This allows consumers to judge how best to satisfy their needs to obtain desired quality (in this regard, it is interesting to realize that *every* available good and service is being purchased by some fellow consumers). The system's variety allows some marketers *to offer close- or even customized-fits* with a user's needs. The system is also *designed to facilitate purchases*, easing acquisitions of benefits for buyers. Numerous elements of *time-saving* are

A. Contributions from Improvements in Marketing System Activities

Transportation
- e.g., Real-time Monitoring

Materials Handling
- e.g., Containerization

Distribution
- e.g., Order Processing

Assembly
- e.g., Global Sourcing

Retailing
- e.g., Checkout Scanners

Product Design
- e.g., Match or Better

Promotion Programs
- e.g., Loyalty Clubs

Product Management
- e.g., Brand Equity

Market Segmentation
- e.g., Mass Customization

Database Marketing
- e.g., Personalized Offerings

Marketing Research
- e.g., Expert Systems

Packaging Innovations
- e.g., Environmental Impacts

Pricing Programs
- e.g., Value/Bonus Packs

Services Marketing
- e.g., Consumer Satisfaction

B. Contributions to Quality of Life

I. Illustrative Social/Psychological Benefits to Marketing Participants (Opportunities for):

- Achievement
- Success
- Growth
- Action
- Discovery
- Creativity
- Humor
- Invention
- Influence
- Service
- Beauty
- Morality
- Interpersonal Relationships
- Understanding
- Trust

II. Illustrative Social/Psychological Benefits Created by Consumers Engaged with the System:

- Accomplishment
- Beauty
- Safety
- Health
- Nurturance
- Joy
- Gift-giving
- Bonding
- Belonging
- Excitement
- Prestige
- Pleasure
- Self-enhancement
- Escape
- Socializing
- Learning
- Authority
- Control
- Status
- Play
- Leisure

Figure 1.5 *Some Broader Views of Benefits*

offered in both products and purchasing: these increase societal members' efficiency, leaving time for other activity. Also, the marketing system offers a *postpurchase support structure* to enable continuing benefits over time.

Our marketing system continually *brings new entries* for customers to consider, and actively works on behalf of *product innovations and improvements,* some of which will enhance a society's quality of life over the long run. Further, it enables buyers to *engage in larger total consumption* than they would otherwise be able, through credit, price specials, discount versions of goods, and/or bundled attributes. Most sellers seek long-term repeat purchases from patrons, so *customer satisfaction is a real goal of the system.* Last, but not least, our marketing system often offers *pleasant environments within which consumers can act,* a distinct benefit in itself (as those experienced with some monopolists or government agencies can attest).

Two Broader Views of Benefits

Contributions From Improvements in Marketing Processes

In our analyses to this point it has become clear that the system's current level of performance is based on its emphasis on a continual search for improvement. Thus our interest is not only in *kinds* of benefits, but also increased *levels* of benefits emanating daily, as indicated in the following:

'Back to the Future' The constant press for improvements characterizes the world of marketing. Many efforts don't work out; some yield minor advances; and a few lead to norms of the future. Figure 1.5A displays a few illustrative cases of recent breakthroughs. For example, trucking firms now combine on-board computers and satellite tracking systems for *real-time monitoring* of their cargo. One firm uses this system to coordinate routes and communicate with all 10,000 trucks in its fleet, adapting instantly to weather or traffic delays. The result is better delivery service with lower costs for the firm. Similarly, *containerization* has added efficiency in shipping and handling: our coffee beans, for example, shifted easily from ocean to ground transport and were less susceptible to damage, spoilage, and theft. As distribution channels have embraced relationship marketing, *order processing systems* have saved time and costs. For example, two firms may use electronic data interchange, in which inventories (e.g., a drugstore's entire stock in a line) are automatically replenished as sales movement data are transmitted to the wholesaler: humans are limited to oversight of the system. Also, improvements in communications, transport, and technology have allowed marketers increasingly to move worldwide to obtain materials at much lower costs. While *global sourcing* has generated legitimate criticisms, it has also provided consumers with quality goods at lower prices, and has added to the aggregate marketing systems of other societies as well. In retailing, *checkout scanners* have brought about a revolution: computerized pricing allowed stores to lower labor costs, better manage inventory, and promote goods more effectively through information on what works best with each store's customers. For food manufacturers, this technology speeds adjustments to developments in the marketplace, allowing increased responsiveness to consumers.

In product development, '*match or better*' means a search for value parity on most key attributes, and advantage on the others. For example, in the early 1980s Ford Motor Company had just lost $3 billion when it created 'Team Taurus,' a group of marketers, designers, engineers, and plant personnel charged with developing a new car to rescue the firm. The team relied on consumer research, choosing 700 features for the new car from this source. In addition, the team bought models of popular competing cars, and then tore them apart to analyze their best features (over 400 were 'borrowed' in this process). The net result of Team Taurus's efforts? One of the most popular cars ever produced, and a turnaround for Ford, whose market share rose from 16% to 29% (Wilkie, 1994). The general lesson? Marketers know that demand is highly responsive to advantages consumers perceive a product to have (or lack), and can be quite responsive to price as well (Day & Wansink, 1994). At this point we need not detail the remaining items in Figure 1.5A, as marketing readers can easily appreciate the potentials of each. As noted above, pressures for improvements in the system are relentless: the positive benefits of this force should be clearly appreciated.

Contributions to Quality of Life

In this final section on contributions we'll shift away from the economic calculus that reports on the system as if it were a relentless machine spewing out streams of utiles. Instead we examine – briefly – the aggregate marketing system as a *human* institution, composed of people living their lives on a variety of fronts. Our effort here is illustrative, intended to raise this topic as worthy of further attention by marketing scholars. We first examine benefits in the work of marketing (where aggregate effects could be very large).

Social/Psychological Benefits to System Participants In the first set of entries in Figure 1.5B we have listed several social and psychological benefits we believe are offered to persons who work in marketing. For example, drawing on the system's stress on competition, *achievement* is highly rewarded in this field. This is one reason for steep increases in marketing incomes in the early years of one's career (in contrast to accounting or engineering, where salaries begin at higher levels, but increase much more slowly). Because of the marketing system's openness to change, opportunities abound for feelings of personal growth and individual autonomy. Whether pursuing clearer understanding of the consumer marketplace, creating a new ad campaign, managing a retail store, closing an important sale, or planning a new product launch, marketing offers challenges to creativity and ingenuity, as well as opportunities to influence others. Marketers in many areas can offer service to others, and those in the arts can foster aesthetic values within society. Many marketing positions require teamwork toward a common goal, which can provide valued group affiliations. It is common for sellers to develop friendly relationships with their clients as a consequence of ongoing exchange activities. In our breakfast illustration, for example, the large transaction between the coffee buyer and major grower was sealed with a handshake. To marketing scholars, many of whom who have come to this field from other disciplines, these attributes are well-understood. Further, with the globalization of markets these opportunities are expanding.

Social/Psychological Benefits to Individual Consumers Since the study of consumer behavior entered marketing's mainstream during the 1950s and 1960s, consumers' goals and motivations have been much studied. Most research has been instrumental (e.g., what can we learn about consumers so that we can sell more effectively to them?), but some reveals interest in deeper human issues. Examples include two older books by well-known marketing consultants – Daniel Yankelovich (1981), who revealed concerns about society's direction at the time, and Arnold Mitchell (1983), who designed the VALS system by using Maslow's humanistic need theory. More recently, the interpretivist orientation (e.g., Sherry, 1991) has honed our appreciation of goods' meanings in consumers' lives. A carefully cultivated lawn and flower garden can give a homeowner a sense of accomplishment, while a parent may derive special satisfaction from selecting food, clothing, or furniture for a safe, healthy home. Gift-giving can involve significant emotional and symbolic dimensions. Movies, sporting events, or theatrical productions can lead to feelings of belonging, prestige, escape, or excitement. Consumer activities allow learning, socializing and self-enhancement: the benefits are emotional, subjective and experiential (Holbrook & Hirschman, 1982). Spending money can bring feelings of achievement, status, control, and even play. Shopping is an enjoyable activity for many. Although intangible and difficult to express, treatment of the marketing system's contributions to consumers would be incomplete without these meaningful consequences.

As a final point in this section, and as will be amplified in our closing section's coverage of current research on marketing and society, *we need to stress that the aggregate marketing system is comprised of more participants than only business marketers.* Private marketing *is* the mainstay of the system in the US, but government, the entire consumer sector, and many individuals in the not-for-profit sector are also participants. The system's issues extend to societal concerns and, in turn, are influenced by them as well.

Criticisms and Problems of the Aggregate Marketing System

Our focus in this article has been on accomplishments, but balance calls on us to also acknowledge that the aggregate marketing system has long been controversial in some respects. Figure 1.6 summarizes many of the most prominent criticisms, controversies and problems that have been raised. Space limitations preclude an extended analysis: this is available elsewhere (Moore & Wilkie, 2002). We begin with *critiques of system values*. These are usually made by persons speaking from vantage points outside the system, raising philosophical points about its nature. These criticisms tend to say little directly about the practice of marketing, the focus is on broader issues such as the 'consumer culture' and our economic system that sustains it. Political theory is the root of some of these critiques, but not all of them. These are not simplistic arguments, and we do not wish to do them an injustice in such a brief summary. Readers will find writings by Galbraith (1958) of interest, as well as the Pollay (1986,1987)/Holbrook (1987) advertising debate and recent collections by Goodwin, Ackerman and Kiron (1997) and Schor and Holt (2000).

Classic social and economic debates are next in Figure 1.6. These have a long history, though they have evolved over time. For example, the distribution cost debate of the early 1900s had farmers questioning why they received only a low percentage of the consumer's food dollar: today buyers (and farmers) ask why cereal brands are priced so high relative to ingredient costs. Much attention has also been directed to advertising, as reflected in four out of eight debates. These debates likely persist because:

(1) strong proponents on each side won't concede;
(2) generalizations are at times based on particular episodes;
(3) decisive empirical evidence has not been available, due to severe measurement difficulties; and
(4) the underlying issues actually *are* complex.

The second column reflects *views of the consumer movement.* These tend *not* to be antagonistic to the aggregate marketing system itself (recall the high ratings *Consumer Reports* gives system offerings), but are aimed at having the system serve consumers' interests rather than only those of marketers. Thus President John F. Kennedy's 1962 proclamation of the 'Consumer Bill of Rights' was seen as crucial in placing the power of government squarely on the side of consumers in the four basic ways listed (that is, it affirmed that US society would pass laws, restricting marketers if necessary, to ensure consumers received their rights). During the past century there were three eras (Mayer, 1989) of high public receptivity to consumer movement issues. Consumer issues have shifted over time, as earlier concerns have been largely attained (e.g., food processing safety). *A root belief sustaining the consumer movement, however, is that major economic imperfections persist within the system – especially reflecting pricing and value received per dollar:* these are listed in the next entries of this section (Maynes, 1997). Some debates continue, in part, because consumers themselves disagree. Again, our treatment here cannot do justice to the arguments' sophistication: excellent books are available, including Aaker & Day (1982), Mayer (1989), Maynes et al. (1988), and Brobeck (1997).

The third column of Figure 1.6 highlights difficult issues that arise naturally in marketing and which must be addressed.[14] Handling of these issues by *some* marketers may spark legitimate criticisms, while others may merit commendation for their efforts to be responsible. Problems may also arise

Broad Social and Economic Concerns	Views of the Consumer Movement	Continuing Challenges for Marketing Practice	Problem Episodes Through Deliberate Behaviors
Critiques of System Values **Promotes Materialism** – Stresses Conformity – Social Competitiveness, Envy – Exacerbates Pain of Poverty **Negatively Impacts Cultural Values** – Creates Insidious Cycle of Work and Spend – Discourages Participation in Noneconomic Activities (e.g., Arts, Community, Leisure) – Undermines Families, Alters Socialization **Is Fundamentally Persuasive/ Manipulative in Character** – Creates Artificial Wants and Needs – Invokes Imbalance Between Marketer and Consumer **Cultural Imperialism** – Cultural Impacts – Natural Resource Depletion – Global Warming **Purposes Limitless, Unsustainable Aggregate Consumption Levels** **Capitalist System Promotes Inequality in Benefit Distribution (Fairness vs. Allocative Efficiency)**	***The Consumer Bill of Rights*** – The Right of Safety – The Right to Be Informed – The Right to Choose – The Right to Be Heard ***Consumerism's Three Major Eras: Key Issues*** **I. Turn of the Century** – Food and Drug Safety – Regulation of Competition **II. 1920s and 1930s** – Objective Information – Consumer Representation **III. 1960s and 1970s** – Product Safety – Advertising's Social Impact – Avenues for Redress ***Economic Imperfections: The Asymmetric Power of Marketing*** – Difficult Product Quality Assessment – Incomplete or Biased Information – Too Few Sellers in Some Local Markets – Uncaring Civil Servants – Too Little Time for Considered Decisions – Under-representation of Consumer Interest	***Limits to Information and Persuasion*** **Advertising Content** – Limits to Persuasion – Themes, Executions and Copy – Intrusiveness: Environmental Clutter – Ad Approval Processes **Sales, Pricing and After Sales Practices** – Limits to Persuasion – Control of Sales Abuses – Warranties and Guarantees – Retailer and Distributor Pricing Practices **Information Disclosure** – Limits to Disclosure – Effective Warning Labels – Use of Disclaimers ***The Broader Environment*** **Environmental Concerns** – Natural Resource Depletion – Threats to Ecology – Re-usability and Disposition **Product Safety** – Hazardous Products – Regulatory Approval Processes – Product Failure and Liability	***Marketing Sector*** – Deceptive Advertising – High-pressure Sales Techniques – Misrepresentations of Sales Intent – Inferior Products and Services – Bait and Switch – Price Fairness: High–Low Pricing – Price Fixing – Predatory Pricing – Franchise Abuses – International: Bribery – Gray Market Goods – Counterfeit Goods – Internet Fraud ***Consumer Sector*** – Uninformed Decisions – Consumer Fraud (e.g., Shoplifting, Credit Abuse) – Bankruptcy – Product Liability: Frivolous Lawsuits – Compulsive Consumption ***Government Sector*** – Errors of Omission – Errors of Commission

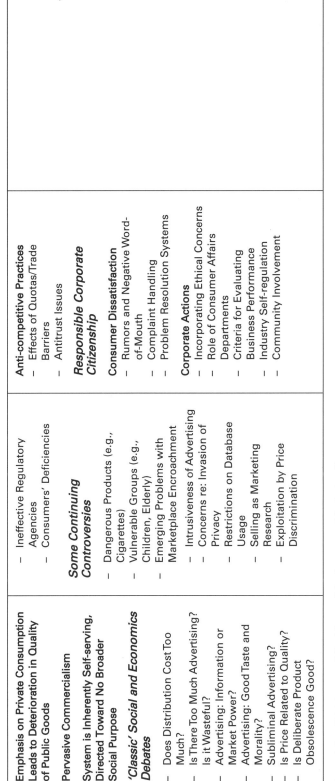

Emphasis on Private Consumption Leads to Deterioration in Quality of Public Goods

Pervasive Commercialism

System is Inherently Self-serving, Directed Toward No Broader Social Purpose

'Classic' Social and Economics Debates

- Does Distribution Cost Too Much?
- Is There Too Much Advertising? Is it Wasteful?
- Advertising: Information or Market Power?
- Advertising: Good Taste and Morality?
- Subliminal Advertising?
- Is Price Related to Quality?
- Is Deliberate Product Obsolescence Good?

- Ineffective Regulatory Agencies
- Consumers' Deficiencies

Some Continuing Controversies

- Dangerous Products (e.g., Cigarettes)
- Vulnerable Groups (e.g., Children, Elderly)
- Emerging Problems with Marketplace Encroachment
  - Intrusiveness of Advertising
  - Concerns re: Invasion of Privacy
  - Restrictions on Database Usage
  - Selling as Marketing Research
  - Exploitation by Price Discrimination

Anti-competitive Practices

- Effects of Quotas/Trade Barriers
- Antitrust Issues

Responsible Corporate Citizenship

Consumer Dissatisfaction

- Rumors and Negative Word-of-Mouth
- Complaint Handling
- Problem Resolution Systems

Corporate Actions

- Incorporating Ethical Concerns
- Role of Consumer Affairs Departments
- Criteria for Evaluating Business Performance
- Industry Self-regulation
- Community Involvement

Figure 1.6 *Criticisms and Problems of the Aggregate Marketing System*

when trying to balance the goals of different stakeholders. Illustrative issues are organized in three topics. First, limits for persuasive influence arise in both advertising and selling: a firm must focus on both policy and daily control levels to address these. Second, specific problems arise from certain products, or from markets that pose societal externalities if only short-term sales and profits are pursued: we expect increasing conflict here if societies' controls of marketer actions are challenged by further globalization. The third topic raises the need for consistently responsible actions by all members of an organization. Efforts here include design of systems to assist customers with problems, and formalizing the presence of influential 'voices' for all stakeholders, including employees, consumers, and the broader society. The right-hand column of Figure 1.6 then shifts to deliberate problem behavior, as in our final illustration:

'Ruthless People' On rare occasions a participant in the aggregate marketing system *chooses* to act in ways that injure others. This occurs in all system sectors, as indicated in the following reports (Wilkie 1994):

Marketing Sector 'Creating a consumer want' has cynical meaning among a certain stratum of marketers, who first alter a consumer's product, and then point out the problem to gain a sale. Gas stations on interstate highways, for example, have been caught plunging ice picks into tires and placing chemicals into batteries to cause adverse reactions. 'Termite inspectors' have been caught placing the bugs in houses, and then informing frightened residents of an imminent home collapse unless repaired immediately. Some traveling 'tree surgeons' thrive by pointing out imagined diseases in large trees over a house, and then removing the trees at high prices. The classic case of this fear selling, however, was used by the Holland Furnace Company, which employed 5000 persons in its 500 US offices. Its sellers were to introduce themselves as 'safety inspectors,' go down to the furnace and dismantle it, and then condemn it as 'so hazardous that I must refuse to put it back together – I can't let myself be an accessory to murder!' One senator called the selling 'merciless.' One elderly woman was sold *nine new* Holland furnaces in six years, costing over $18,000 at the time.

Consumer Sector We have pointed out that one hallmark of the marketing system is its emphasis on providing satisfaction after the sale, including liberal return policies. Some consumers abuse this service, as this quote shows:

> Mark is a soccer player who needs new shoes frequently. He has developed a system to get them from a local store that takes back defective shoes. Once or twice a year, Mark removes the sole, slices off a cleat, or places a rip in the tongue, each in a way that is hard to detect. He then brings the shoes to the store to exchange … at last count he'd received eight new pairs this way. Mark is sure to go to a different clerk on each visit, and … probably won't get caught.'

Government Sector Government abuses are harder to identify because of few legal cases and difficulty in observation. Errors of omission (failure to act when warranted) may be more common than errors of commission, given the incentive structure of a bureaucratic system. For example, New York City's health department discovered that a dispute between two laboratory managers had *led to delays of up to one year in reading cancer test results* for women using city clinics. Of 3000 delayed Pap smear readings, 500 abnormalities called for immediate follow-up, 93 more appeared malignant, and 11 were clearly malignant. On discovery, the commissioner denounced his department for 'betrayal of the public trust,' as he demoted four people; evidently none could be fired.

Several points remain. This is a complex area involving the law: it may not be clear that an act was deliberate or that a certain party was responsible. Also, criticisms are usually aimed at marketers, but *all* system participants have responsibilities, including public policymakers and consumers, and negative acts do occur in each sector regularly. Third, some acts *deserve* to be criticized by all participants. Our system is designed for dealings to be open, honest, and well-informed. Deceptive and irresponsible behaviors injure honest competitors and consumers. Thus it is disingenuous to simply defend the actions of fellow marketers or fellow consumers because system roles are shared: it is not clear why we would want disreputable persons' actions to define either the standards or image for the system overall.

Implications

Our goal has been to stop at this unique point in time, consider the larger picture of our field, then fairly portray its structure, activities, and benefits to society. Our system is huge and dynamic. Its imperfections stand as challenges for improvement; it is appropriate for participants to work to rectify them. Beyond this, the aggregate marketing system offers much that is impressive.

Interesting Insights From the Project

This project has been illuminating, and six 'lessons learned' stand out for us (depending on background and interests, other readers may have had different observations):

1. *Tremendous potentials exist for marketing contributions to economic development, which can literally change the world for citizens of developing nations.* Each aggregate marketing system is specific to its own society and its own time. While a society's choices will constrain

options, development also does proceed in identifiable stages. Thus there is a potential to transfer knowledge, products, and methods found useful in prior stages of advanced systems. Aggregate marketing systems are in flux daily across the globe. Will the 'transitional'-nations trying to move from command economies to free market systems be successful? Strong linkages between marketing, public policy, and aggregate marketing system performance are starkly clear in these cases.

2. *The central role for innovation in improving a society's quality of life has been underscored.* The contributions from innovations and improvements were striking. Conceptually, this underscores the value of *dynamism* in an aggregate marketing system, as well as the key role of *competition* in providing the system's impetus. In turn, the societal importance of a government's policies to foster and protect both innovation and competition – antitrust, patents, trademarks, etc. – became clearly apparent (but global differences may impede future progress). We also found the system's twin reliance on competition as a driver and trust as a bonding agent to be impactful, yet somehow paradoxical. Finally, it is clear that success in discovering, developing and managing new products is a central issue for our field (which calls for closer ties with other areas, as in more joint programs for science and marketing).
3. *The size, power, and practiced performance of the aggregate marketing system has emerged in this project.* Several points accompany this realization: (a) there is a real need to conceptually appreciate the magnitudes in this system; (b) many 'hidden aspects of marketing' may be being excluded from thinking about the field; and (c) those marketing elements the public experiences directly, such as advertising and retail selling, are likely receiving disproportionate weight in people's view of our field.
4. *Not all lessons are entirely positive: future developments will likely place marketers at the center of further controversies.* 'Society,' as referenced in the chapter's title may be losing cohesion, and global marketers can be seen as assisting in this process (though this may not be intentional). Consider challenges to ethical systems (e.g., bribery), religious beliefs and customs (e.g., interest rates), government protections for home industries and workers (trade barriers), and the growing need for adaptations in national antitrust policies (Federal Trade Commission (FTC) 1996). Meanwhile, the Internet not only seamlessly crosses societal boundaries, but the incredible efficiency of its reach offers huge potentials for marketing fraud. In one recent FTC (1997) case, an Internet pyramid scam promised investors $60,000 per year for an initial investment of $250: 15,000 consumers had bought in before it was stopped. Overall, concerns are increasing about marketer intrusions in areas like privacy of records, security of financial resources, and selling to children.
5. *This chapter has concentrated on benefits and system potentials. However, at this point in time it is reasonable for every marketing person to ask whether our current aggregate marketing system actually does represent 'the best of all worlds.'* Our emphasis here is not critical, but philosophical. The system is very powerful, and we are at work to help it achieve its ends. The fact that our society has granted marketers substantial freedoms, and that these serve to allocate much of the nation's resources, is in fact a key statement about a societal purpose of the aggregate marketing system. However, to what extent do marketing managers view themselves, or we marketing academics view ourselves, as personally holding reponsibility for improving the public interest, or acting as stewards of a society's resources? What implications, if any, do these views have for our field as presently constituted?
6. *Implications for marketing scholarship are bright, if differing perspectives are pursued. Adopting the perspective of the aggregate marketing system helps one to 'see' the field of marketing in its true expanse and complexity.* One wonderful aspect of the academic life is its freedom to speculate. This project has more generally highlighted for us the potentials of higher *'levels of analysis'* aggregated beyond a single firm, market, or household. Much current research in marketing can be quite useful for understanding the aggregate marketing system if we invoke only a slightly different frame of reference: of particular note, the 'Value of Marketing' offers special potentials as an organizing framework for new contributions to marketing thought. A multi-university project with this title was begun by Yoram Wind at Wharton in the early 1990s, and led to some of the insights cited in this chapter. Assessing the value of marketing activities is congenial to much current research in marketing management (e.g., new product development), marketing science (e.g., long-term value of promotion versus advertising), and consumer research (e.g., consumer information). Further, 'value' can be assessed at either a firm level, across firms, or for society generally.

Into the Future

Having begun this article by looking back over a long time, we now know not to look forward very far! As just one example, new information technologies will clearly change our world in the future, though exact impacts are unknown. Some firms will gain new efficiencies, others will develop new offerings, and all will have to adapt to new competitive realities.

In closing, we reiterate that we feel privileged to have had this opportunity to step back, explore, and recognize the achievements of the aggregate marketing system. Through this process we have gained a better understanding of the nature of our field, the challenges that it faces, and the contributions it makes to societal welfare.

Section II: Overview of Research

Conceptual Frameworks for Marketing and Society Research

Now that we have an understanding of the larger system of marketing and its relationships to society, what about research in this area? As we'll discuss shortly, there exists a vibrant academic infrastructure and some excellent sources available for interested scholars to begin, to learn more, and contribute over time. At this point, however, it is useful to develop a clearer understanding of research issues that are most likely to be examined, as the vast expanse of the aggregate marketing system gives rise to a huge number of potential topics. We briefly examine three interesting and distinctly different conceptual frameworks, each of which identifies research possibilities.

Bloom and Gundlach's 'Handbook' Framework

Paul Bloom and Gregory Gundlach have recently edited the extremely useful *Handbook of Marketing and Society* (2001), which presents 22 chapters summarizing recent research in this area. Figure 1.7 depicts the framework they developed to represent current knowledge in this field and to identify topics in need of further investigation. It is important to note that this framework is proactive in its intention to advance work in the area. It explicitly points to areas for knowledge development, in addition to reflecting existing research activity. Several notable elements in this framework include its emphasis on 'marketing knowledge' as a positive causal factor on the left, and the enhancement of 'consumer welfare' (as representative of societal welfare) as the system goal at the right. Note also that the framework is organized around the three institutional actors noted in our study of the Aggregate Marketing System – marketers (here divided into 'corporate' for-profit and 'social' not-for-profit), consumers, and public policymakers (as representative of society's interests).

The division of the 22 chapter-contents along the framework's linkages then provides us with a reasonable reflection of the issues marketing academics have focused on in the Marketing and Society area. We begin by observing that four links (numbers 1, 6, 9, and 11) account for over half of the Handbook chapters.

How Knowledge About Marketing Improves Public Policy Decisions (Link 1) There are three chapters reflecting this link. They assess how marketing knowledge can, and has, improved public policy regulatory decisions on *consumer protection* (especially at the Federal Trade Commission (FTC) and the Food and Drug Administration (FDA)), on *antitrust policies* (at FTC and the US Justice Department), and with regard to *deceptive advertising and selling techniques* (FTC and the court system).

Impacts of Corporate Marketing Decisions on Competition (Link 6) These chapters focus on mainstream marketing management research topics, but here exploring their implications for potential legality and effects on competition as well as consumer decisions. The three topics explored here are *advertising's effects on price and competition, socioeconomic consequences of franchising distribution, and positive and negative aspects of pricing strategies.*

Impacts of Public Policy Decisions (Links 9 and 11) Relevant chapters return attention to public policy decisions and their impact on both competition and consumers. Two of the topics here reflect attention to technical aspects of product and service offerings: *how public policymakers and marketers can best regulate product safety* as well as *emerging issues and challenges in the arena of consumer privacy.* Four other chapters reflect the clear interest on behalf of consumer researchers in some of these topics, here represented by *consumer response to warnings, the effectiveness of nutritional labels on foods, the effectiveness of environmental product claims, and the effects of deceptive advertising regulation.*

Social Marketing Initiatives (Links 3, 5, 12, and 13) The bottom of the framework reflects efforts to work on improving society through *Social Marketing.* Here we find (Link 3) marketing tools increasingly being adopted by not-for-profit, agencies whether governmental or private, involved with education, health, poverty, religion, crime prevention, and myriad other social programs. Formally, social marketing differs from traditional marketing in aiming to directly benefit the target audience (e.g., AIDS awareness or childhood immunization) or society as a whole (e.g., recycling programs, blood donations) rather than the firm sponsoring the program (Andreasen, 1994). Again, there is not a large base of research within the mainstream of marketing on this topic, but interesting issues are available to be studied, and additional chapters are devoted to

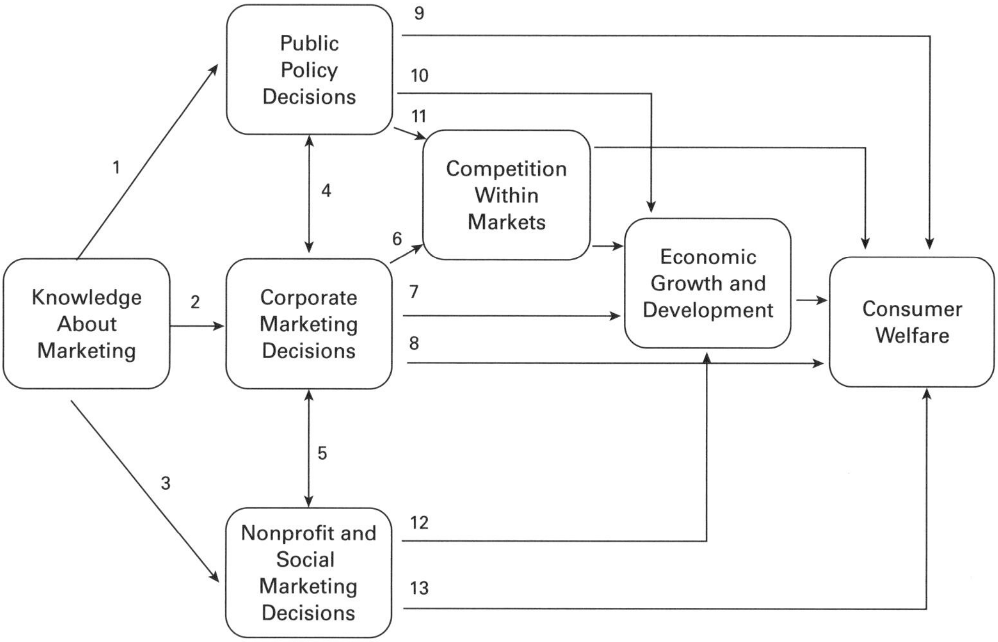

Figure 1.7 Bloom and Gundlach's Framework for the Handbook of Marketing and Society
Source: Bloom, Paul N. and Gundlach, Gregory T. (2001) Handbook of Marketing and Society, Thousand Oaks, CA: Sage.

'*corporate societal marketing,' involving alliances with social causes* (Link 5), *social marketing and development* (Link 12), and *social marketing theories* (Link 13).

Remaining Linkages The remaining links to public policymakers and marketers have actually seen little research undertaken within the academic marketing community, though interesting issues are present, as explained in the Handbook. Chapters here include issues of corporate response to alterations in the legal environment (e.g., *how grocery manufacturers changed their marketing mixes in response to the nutritional labeling law, and how companies react to antitrust enforcement)* and to issues with public relations or reputational overtones (e.g., *corporate responses to boycotts).* Chapters are also devoted to *intellectual property laws* (trademarks, patents, copyrights), *marketing and economic development,* and *marketing's long-term impacts on consumer welfare.* As was indicated in Section I, these topics have not been much studied within marketing, but are of potentially great impact in the global environment.

The 'Consumer Bill of Rights' as a Research Framework

While Bloom & Gundlach were attempting to conceptualize all of the Marketing and Society area, a much simpler framework has also proven useful in organizing the portion that is of special interest to the consumer research community. As was described in Section I, in 1962 President John F. Kennedy sent the US Congress a now famous message enunciating a *Consumer Bill of Rights* for our society. These Rights are:

1. *The Right to Safety* Consumers have the right to be protected against products and services that are hazardous to health and life.
2. *The Right to Be Informed* Consumers have the right to be protected against fraudulent, deceitful, or misleading advertising or other practices, and to be given the facts they need to make an informed choice.
3. *The Right to Choose* Consumers have the right to be assured, whenever possible, access to a variety of products and services at competitive prices. In those industries where competition is not workable, government regulation is substituted to assure satisfactory quality and service at fair prices.
4. *The Right to Be Heard* Consumers have the right to be assured that consumer interests will receive full and sympathetic consideration in the formulation of government policy, and fair and expeditious treatment in its administrative tribunals.

This statement by the President had the effect of creating a framework of criteria by which a 'marketing/consumer environment' could be examined in our market-based society. Our general goal is that such a marketplace be both 'fair' and 'efficient' for marketers, competitors and consumers alike. The statement has generally been welcomed by marketers: only the fourth element has been controversial, and this due only to no clear limitations on the extent of the government's potential intrusion into the free market. Meanwhile, the statement was popular with the public and was heavily applauded by representatives of consumer interests, since it awards consumers an equal standing within our system, promising that their interests will be represented fully in public policy deliberations. It has since been used as an organizing framework for research in this area, in a major research compendium authored by consumer advocates (Maynes et al., 1988), and in an excellent overview prepared for consumer researchers (Andreasen, 1991).

Wilkie and Gundlach's Research Framework for Marketing and Public Policy

In an ambitious effort to capture all of the public policy-related research published in major journals between 1970 and the early 1990s, William Wilkie and Gregory Gundlach developed the framework of research topics depicted in Figure 1.8 (Gundlach & Wilkie, 1990). We should take care to note that, in contrast to the frameworks above, this framework was designed to proceed from the research literature itself. Through an iterative process, research articles were examined, and then assigned to primary, secondary, and tertiary framework categories, with the creation of new categories and reassignments when necessary.

Figure 1.8 depicts a slightly adapted version of this framework, which contains over 100 categories. Every category has been the topic of some research by marketing academics, but the number of gradations is a reasonable reflection of areas of greater or lesser stress. Here we see a strong emphasis on 'Marketing Mix' issues in general. Promotion issues receive the most attention, but authors have actually pursued each of the 4Ps to a considerable extent. It is also apparent that 'Consumer Protection' has been heavily stressed, reflecting both the prominence of consumer research among many marketing academics, and also the fact that the FTC, FDA, and the courts have called upon marketing academics to provide expertise in operating some of the programs in this area. In contrast, antitrust attorneys and economists have only very recently begun to discern that marketing academia might be a source of useful expertise. Using this framework and the article counts within it, Gundlach & Wilkie (1990, 2001) have been able to provide detailed evidence about research progression across time (e.g., the total amount of work rose throughout the 1970s, fell off during the 1980s, then rose again during the 1990s). They were also able to document the rise and fall of research interest in specific topics that occurred during this period. Here, however, our primary concern is to communicate the wide array of research opportunities that exist. In scanning the listings of Figure 1.8, moreover, notice how interesting many of the topics are, and why they may be of significance both to marketers and to the public.

Where to Go Now

A Diverse Academic Infrastructure Exists

One of the true prerequisites of a vibrant research field is the presence of an 'academic infrastructure' that assists in learning about important developments, provides vehicles for the publication of quality research, and generally facilitates communication and interchange among researchers with common interests. Commonly this consists of an association that offers an annual conference, a newsletter, and a journal. Over the past 20 years the Marketing and Society research area has created a strong infrastructure, with opportunities to achieve all of these ends. However, rather than a single unified presence, there are at least *six subgroups* hard at work on research dealing with Marketing and Society issues, some with their own journals, and all with conferences and means to share communications:

1. **Public Policy and Marketing** This group has its own annual conference and the specialized *Journal of Public Policy & Marketing,* published by the American Marketing Association. Its focus is on government's regulatory policies with regard to marketing, and it enjoys strong ties to the Marketing Science Institute, and to professional staffers at the FTC and FDA. Its membership is open to government and industry persons as well as academics from any discipline, but the dominant membership group is from marketing academia.
2. **International Consumer Policy** Distance and cultures still do present some barriers. These persons are at work in other nations, with only sporadic interactions with the US groups. They publish two journals that focus on different aspects of this topic: the *Journal of Consumer Policy* and the *Journal of Economic Psychology.*
3. **Macromarketing** This group has its own annual conference and the specialized *Journal of Macromarketing,* published by Sage. It represents the closest ties to an overall marketing system view as represented at the start of this chapter. It also has formalized small subgroups focused on economic development, quality of life studies, and marketing history.

4. **Consumer Economics** The American Council on Consumer Interests (ACCI) is an organization consisting primarily of consumer economists who study marketing issues from the perspective of advancing the consumer interest. This group also holds its own annual conference and publishes the *Journal of Consumer Affairs*. Some consumer-oriented marketing academics are members and publish in this journal.
5. **Social Marketing** This has been a loosely affiliated group of researchers who are interested in assisting not-for-profit and government agencies in designing effective interventions. It does not publish a journal, but does have ties to the more practice-oriented *Social Marketing Quarterly* and an annual conference, 'Innovations in Social Marketing.' Opportunities for volunteer projects are also available through the Social Marketing Institute, now based at Georgetown University.
6. **Marketing Ethics** The Society for Business Ethics draws its membership from various business disciplines, but does not publish its own journal. *Business Ethics Quarterly* is the major outlet in this area. Within marketing, this is more a community than a formal group. It has been quite active in creating special sessions at the major marketing conferences. Given difficult issues in crossing cultures, the International Society of Business, Economics and Ethics (ISBEE) is also worthy of note.

Thus the current area of Marketing and Society research is itself fragmented. Moreover, prospects for future integration are hindered by significant differences in levels of analysis, methods, and substantive focus. At the risk of over-simplifying, it is yet instructive to note that among these groups we today find persons who wish to focus on social change and help those managing these efforts to be more effective (*social marketing*), to focus on corporate marketing managers and help them to make more ethical decisions (*marketing ethics*), to focus on the aggregate marketing system and its effects on economic development, quality of life, or other issues (*macromarketing*), or focus on helping government decision makers and marketing managers to devise more efficient and effective regulatory policies (*public policy and marketing*). Further, some persons are approaching problems within different cultural and political contexts (*international consumer policy*), and some with different aims and methods (consumer interest economists). During the 1990s efforts were made to integrate these groups into a larger area of focus, and over 200 marketing academics joined the Marketing and Society Special Interest Group (SIG) of the American Marketing Association. However, each of the specialized conferences and journals continued to exist on their own as well.

For publication purposes, these specialized journals have been receptive to a variety of topics and approaches. In addition, the mainstream marketing journals, especially the *Journal of Marketing*, are quite willing to publish work on marketing and society (note: as with any topic, there is a need for the article to 'fit' the other criteria characterizing each journal). So there really is no shortage of infrastructure available for someone wishing to pursue work in this area.

Some Good Places to Start

This chapter's introduction to Marketing and Society research may have raised your interest in learning more about it in the coming years. This is not only possible, but is rather easy to accomplish, as the academic infrastructure is quite accessible and excellent sources are available to offer further research overviews. Several of the best places to start have already been mentioned. A trip to the library will allow perusal of past and current issues of the journals listed above, and will provide a better appreciation for both the topics discussed and the approaches taken in this research area. Of particular note, the Spring 1997 issue of the *Journal of Public Policy and Marketing* contains a section of six useful retrospective commentaries by leading researchers on the development of this field during the period dating from about 1970.[15]

Also as noted earlier, *The Handbook of Marketing and Society*, edited by Paul Bloom and Gregory Gundlach (2001), offers useful research overviews in 22 areas, together with citations for in-depth follow-up. For those interested in the Federal Trade Commission, *Marketing and Advertising Regulation*, edited by Patrick Murphy and William Wilkie (1990) provides background and commentaries by a number of experts. Also, the websites for the Federal Trade Commission (www.ftc.gov) and the Food & Drug Administration (www.fda.gov) are user-friendly, and full of interesting information about the operations of these agencies that regulate the marketing community. For those wanting to learn about how consumer advocates view these issues, volumes edited by E. Scott Maynes (1988) and Robert Mayer (1989) provide excellent and interesting background, as does the *Encyclopedia of the Consumer Movement* (1997), edited by Stephen Brobeck, head of the Consumer Federation of America. Finally, it is helpful to attend conferences, listen to talks, and meet the people working in areas of interest to you. You will find, just as with any of the other research areas covered in this Handbook, that people will be pleased to see you there.

Authors' Closing Note: Please be aware that the authors of this chapter, together with Gregory Gundlach, are presently developing a 'Center for the Study of Marketing and Society.' Plans are to

General Topics	Marketing Management Topics		Consumer Protection Topics
International Issues – Marketing and Economic Development – Protectionism – Corrupt Practices – General International ***Public Policy Participants*** – US Supreme Court – Administrative Agencies – State and Local Government ***General Antitrust*** – Antitrust Regulation ***Other Governmental Regulation*** – Commercial Speech – General Governmental Regulation	***Product Issues*** – Protection of Trade Secrets – Patents – Copyright – Trademarks – Certification Marks – Warranty – Product Liability – Safety – Package and Labeling – Nutrition Information – Services – Product Standards – General Product ***Place Issues*** – Exclusive Dealing – Tying Contracts – Territorial and Customer Restrictions – Resale Price Maintenance – Reciprocity – Refusals to Deal – Functional Discounts	***Pricing Issues*** – Price Fixing – Exchanging Price Information – Parallel Pricing – Predatory Pricing – Discriminatory Pricing – Credit Practices – Robinson-Patman Act – Unit Pricing – Reference Price – Item Price Removal – General Price ***Promotion Issues*** – Deceptive Advertising – Unfairness in Advertising – Advertising to Children – Advertising Substantiation – Affirmative Disclosure – Corrective Advertising – Multiple Product Remedy – Comparative Advertising	***Consumerism and Consumer Protection Issues*** – Consumerism – Socially Conscious Consumers – Quality of Life – Legal Aspects – Comparative Marketing – Marketing of Governmental Programs – Competition – General Macro Issues – Marketer Behavior – Management of Consumer Protection – Consumer Information – Consumer Education – Consumer Complaining – Vulnerable Segments – Ethnic Targeting – Consumer Practices – Environmental Issues – Energy Conservation – Minority Owned Businesses – Consumer Affairs

Self Regulation – Advertising Self-regulation – Local Business Bureaus ***Information Technology Issues*** – Internet Marketing – Consumer Welfare Impacts of the 'Digital Divide' – Impacts on Marketing Productivity – Consumer Privacy ***Market Research Issues*** – Using Marketing Research – Market Research Problems	– Vertical Integration – Gray Markets – Mergers – Franchising – Slotting Allowances – General Place	– Endorsements – Price Promotions – Warranty Promotions – Credit Promotions – Sweepstakes and Contests – Personal Selling Practices – Mail Order Selling – Referral Selling – Brokerage Allowances – Promotional Allowances – Promotion of Prof. Services – Cigarette Advertising – Political Advertising – Sex Roles in Advertising – General Promotion	– Ethnics – Consumer Satisfaction/Dissatisfaction – Consumer Information Search – Medical Programs – Objective Price/Quality – Social Marketing – General Consumer Protection

Figure 1.8 *Wilkie and Gundlach's Framework of Topics in Marketing and Public Policy Research*

initially base the center at Notre Dame, and to aim its efforts toward fostering future research in this area. We would like to compile an e-mail list of persons interested in this topic so that we can alert them to future developments and research opportunities. We are especially interested in doctoral students who may not undertake work in the near-term, but who do have longer-term interests. If this describes you, please send us an e-mail at wilkie.1@nd.edu, letting us know of your possible interest. Thanks!

Notes

1. Comparative numbers are from a variety of sources, especially Lebergott (1993) and US News and World Report (1995).

2. For a classic effort to assess magnitudes of the US distribution system alone, see Cox, Goodman and Fichandler (1965). The figures reported in the following illustration are from the *Statistical Abstract of the United States (1996)*, tables 12, 66, 685, 691, 1003, 1252, 1253, 1255, 1272, 1274, 1278, 1279, and 1280. Calculated comparisons are by the authors. The advertising spending estimate is from *Advertising Age* (1997).

3. We are unsure where the concept of marketing flows originated, but have seen it in both Vaile, Grether and Cox (1952) and Kotler (1976) (McInnes (1964), in his discussion of marketing systems, also discusses flows, as well as some other elements present in our propositions). This analysis also highlights marketing's contributions at the firm level by showing marketing to be the function that reaches out from a firm to the outside world (marketplace), with flows of products, information, and promotion activity, and further shows marketing as using its learning about that world (through an inward flow of research) to influence decisions within the firm. Finally, the fact that marketing generates an inward flow of dollars to sustain the firm's continued existence earns marketing the title of 'lifeblood of the business.'

4. As societal boundaries become more permeable, especially through immigration and trade, the linkage of production, employment of human resources, and end consumption become more complex.

5. This has been the subject of significant recent theoretical developments within marketing, challenging the tradition of equilibrium economic theory (e.g., Dickson, 1992, 1996, 1999; Hunt & Morgan 1995, 1996).

6. Unfortunately, extensive discussion of government's role is beyond the purview of this chapter. Readers may wish to access the excellent volume by Stern and Eovaldi (1984) for discussions pointed to marketing.

7. Of course, any aggregate system will bring serious issues as well. Here, for example, probing questions can be posed about destruction of natural resources, social inequality in life chances, the nature of growth in affluence, and others. We shall see these in our later section on controversies and criticisms.

8. While the aggregate system includes marketers, customers, and public policy makers, given the purpose of this article, we here concentrate on contributions emanating from the marketing sector of the system.

9. Much of our discussion to follow is based on overviews provided by Batra (1997), Moyer (1965), Nason & White (1981), Thorelli (1996), & Wood & Vitell (1986).

10. The recent emphasis on supply chain management incorporates a systems approach to the provision of these utilities, aimed at enhancing efficiencies. Although this may alter marketing's identification within a firm, these clearly remain as activities within the aggregate marketing system.

11. Every quality test rating using the five-point 'Excellent–Poor' scale given by the organization was used. Ratings by members were not included, nor were relative scales in which distributions were forced.

12. This term is being used in a broad sense, as price and value are relevant issues as well. Health insurance firms, for example, are pushing for 'debranding' (generic drugs) to obtain lower prices.

13. A number of leading marketing thinkers believe that firms would benefit from increased attention to providing consumer information/education programs that would assist consumers to make better decisions, as opposed to the simple emphasis on persuasion/entertainment in advertising.

14. The essential point here – that social issues shape aspects of marketing practice – is based upon Day's (1994) framework, which we have modified to reflect our purposes in this section.

15. If your library doesn't carry the *Journal of Public Policy and Marketing*, it should. It can be ordered through the American Marketing Association's website, www.ama.org.

References

Aaker, David A. (1991) *Managing Brand Equity*. New York: Free Press.

——— & Day, George S. (1982) *Consumerism: Search for the Public Interest*, 4th edn. NewYork: Free Press.

Advertising Age (1997) Immune to crash. October 20, p. 22.

Andreasen, Alan R. (1991) Consumer behavior research and social policy. In *Handbook of Consumer Behavior*, edited by Thomas S. Robertson & Harold H. Kassarjian. Englewood Cliffs, NJ: Prentice Hall, pp. 459–506.

——— (1994) Social marketing: its definition and domain. *Journal of Public Policy and Marketing*, 13 (1), 108–14.

Arrow, Kenneth (1972) Gifts and exchanges. *Philosophy and Public Affairs*, 343–61 (cited in Hunt 1997, 335).

Bartels, Robert (1988) *The History of Marketing Thought*, 3rd edn. Columbus, OH: Publishing Horizons.

Batra, Rajeev (1997) Executive insights: marketing issues and challenges in transitional economies. *Journal of International Marketing*, 5 (4), 95–114.

Bauer, Raymond A. & Greyser, Stephen A. (1968) *Advertising in America: The Consumer View.* Boston, MA: Research Division, Harvard Business School.

Belk, Russell W. (1988) Possessions and the extended self. *Journal of Consumer Research*, 15 (September), 139–68.

Belk, Russell W. (1989) Extended self and extending paradigmatic perspective. *Journal of Consumer Research*, 16 (June), 129–32.

Bloom, Paul N. & Gundlach, Gregory T. (eds) (2001) *Handbook of Marketing and Society*. Thousand Oaks, CA: Sage.

Brobeck, Stephen (ed.) (1997) *Encyclopedia of the Consumer Movement*. Santa Barbara, CA: ABC-Clio.

Cohen, Joel B. (1989) An over-extended self? *Journal of Consumer Research*, 16 (June), 125–8.

Cox, Reavis, Goodman, Charles S. & Fichandler, Thomas C. (1965) *Distribution in a High-Level Economy*. Englewood Cliffs, NJ: Prentice Hall.

Day, George S. (1994) Social issues shaping marketing practice. Presentation at the American Marketing Association Summer Educators' Conference, San Francisco, CA, August.

——— & Wansink, Brian (1994) Marketing and the stimulation of market growth. Paper presented to the Conference on the Value of Marketing, Stanford University, August.

Dickson, Peter R. (1992) Toward a general theory of competitive rationality. *Journal of Marketing*, 56 (January), 69–83.

——— (1996) The static and dynamic mechanics of competition: a comment on Hunt and Morgan's Comparative Advantage Theory. *Journal of Marketing*, 60 (October), 102–6.

——— (1999) A general theory of competitive rationality and economic evolution, working paper. Madison, WI: College of Business Administration, University of Wisconsin.

Drucker, Peter F. (1958) Marketing and economic development. *Journal of Marketing*, 23 (January), 252–9.

Etzioni, Amatai (1988) *The Moral Dimension: Toward a New Economics*. New York: Free Press.

Federal Trade Commission (1996) *Anticipating the 21st Century: Competition Policy in the New High-Tech, Global Marketplace*. Washington, D.C., May.

——— (1997) *Anticipating the 21st Century*. Washington, D.C., Spring.

Galbraith, John K. (1958) *The Affluent Society*. Boston, MA: Houghton Mifflin.

Ger, Guiliz (1997) Human development and humane consumption: well-being beyond the good life. *Journal of Public Policy and Marketing*, 16 (Spring), 110–25.

Goodwin, Neva R., Ackerman, Frank & Kiron, David (eds) (1997) *The Consumer Society*. Washington, D.C.: Island Press.

Green, Paul E., Wind, Yoram & Jain, Arun K. (1972) Benefit bundle analysis. *Journal of Advertising Research*, 12 (April), 31–6.

Gundlach, Gregory T. & Wilkie, William L. (1990) The marketing literature in public policy: 1970–1988. In *Marketing and Advertising Regulation – The Federal Trade Commission in the 1990s*, edited by Patrick E. Murphy & William L. Wilkie. Notre Dame, IN: University of Notre Dame Press, pp. 329–44.

——— (2001) Updated framework, unpublished, private correspondence.

Holbrook, Morris B. (1987) Mirror, mirror, on the wall, What's unfair in the reflections on advertising? *Journal of Marketing*, 51 (July), 95–103.

——— & Hirschman, Elizabeth C. (1982) The experiential aspects of consumption: consumer fantasies, feelings and fun. *Journal of Consumer Research*, 9 (September), 132–40.

Hunt, Shelby D. (1997) Resource-advantage theory and the wealth of nations: developing the socio-economic research tradition. *Journal of Socio-Economics*, 26 (4), 335–57.

——— & Goolsby, Jerry (1988) The rise and fall of the functional approach to marketing: a paradigm displacement perspective. In *Historical Perspectives in Marketing–Essays in Honor of Stanley C. Hollander* edited by Terence Nevett and Ronald A. Fullerton. Lexington, MA: D.C. Heath, pp. 35–51.

——— & Morgan, Robert M. (1995) The comparative-advantage theory of competition. *Journal of Marketing*, 59 (April), 1–15.

——— & Morgan, Robert M. (1996) The resource-advantage theory of competition: dynamics, path dependencies, and evolutionary dimensions. *Journal of Marketing*, 60 (October), 107–14.

Kasper, Hans (1993) The images of marketing: facts, speculations, and implications, working paper 93–015. Maastricht, Netherlands: University of Limburg.

Kinnear, Thomas C. (1994) Marketing and macroeconomic welfare. Presentation at the Value of Marketing Conference, Stanford University, August.

Kotler, Philip (1976) *Marketing Management: Analysis, Planning, and Control*, 3rd edn. Englewood Cliffs, NJ: Prentice Hall.

Lebergott, Stanley (1993) *Pursuing Happiness*. Princeton, NJ: Princeton University Press.

Levy, Sidney J. (1959) Symbols for sale. *Harvard Business Review*, 37 (July/August), 117–24.

Mayer, Robert N. (1989) *The Consumer Movement: Guardians of the Marketplace*. Boston, MA: Twayne.

Maynard, Harold, Weidler, W.C. & Beckman, Theodore (1927) *Principles of Marketing*. NewYork: The Ronald Press Co.

Maynes, E. Scott, and the ACCI Research Committee (eds) (1988) *The Frontier of Research in the Consumer Interest*. Columbia, MO: American Council on Consumer Interests.

——— (1997) Consumer problems in market economies. In *Encyclopedia of the Consumer Movement*, edited by Stephen Brobeck. Santa Barbara, CA: ABC-Clio. pp. 158–64.

McInnes, William (1964) A conceptual approach to marketing. In *Theory in Marketing*, edited by Reavis Cox, Wroe Alderson and Stanley J. Shapiro. Homewood, IL: Irwin, pp. 51–67.

Mitchell, Arnold (1983) *The Nine American Lifestyles*. New York: Macmillan.

Moore, Elizabeth S. & Wilkie, William L. (2002) Why is marketing controversial? Working paper, Notre Dame, IN: Graduate School of Business, University of Notre Dame.

Moriarty, W.D. (1923) *The Economics of Marketing and Advertising*. New York: Harper & Brothers.

Moyer, Reed (1965) Marketing in economic development. Working paper, East Lansing, MI: Graduate School of Business, Michigan State University.

Murphy, Patrick E. & William L. Wilkie (eds) (1990) *Marketing and Advertising Regulation – The Federal Trade Commission in the 1990s*. Notre Dame, IN: University of Notre Dame Press.

Nason, Robert W. & White, Phillip D. (1981) The visions of Charles C. Slater: Social consequences of marketing. *Journal of Macromarketing*, 1 (Fall), 4–18.

Papenek, Gustav F. (1962) The development of entrepreneurship. *American Economic Review*, 52 (2), 46–58.

Pollay, Richard W. (1986) The Distorted Mirror: reflections on the unintended consequences of advertising. *Journal of Marketing*, 50 (April), 18–36.

——— (1987) On the value of reflections on the values in The Distorted Mirror. *Journal of Marketing*, 51 (July), 104–10.

——— & Mittal, Banwari (1993) Here's the beef: factors, determinants, and segments in consumer criticism of advertising. *Journal of Marketing*, 57 (July), 99–114.

Preston, Lee E. (1968) Market development and market control. In *Changing Marketing Systems: Consumer, Corporate and Government Interfaces*, edited by Reed Moyer. Washington, D.C. American Marketing Association, pp. 223–27.

Schor, Juliet B. & Holt, Douglas B. (eds) (2000) *The Consumer Society Reader*. New York: The New Press.

Sherry, John F. Jr. (1991) Postmodern alternatives: the interpretive turn in consumer research. In *Handbook of Consumer Behavior*, edited by Thomas S. Robertson & Harold H. Kassarjian. Englewood Cliffs, NJ: Prentice Hall, pp. 548–91.

Slater, Charles C. (1978) Toward an operational theory of market processes. In *Macro-Marketing: Distributive Processes From a Societal Perspective, An Elaboration of Issues,* edited by Phillip White and Charles Slater. Boulder, CO: University of Colorado Press, pp. 115–29.

Smith, Adam (1776) *The Wealth of Nations*, 1937 Modern Library Edition. New York: Random House.

Statistical Abstract of the United States (1996) Washington, D.C.: US Government Printing Office.

Stern, Louis W. & Eovaldi, Thomas (1984) *Legal Aspects of Marketing Strategy*, Englewood Cliffs, NJ: Prentice Hall.

Thorelli, Hans B. (1996) Marketing, open markets and political democracy: the experience of the PACRIM countries. *Advances in International Marketing*, 7, 33–46.

Udell, John G. (1972) *Successful Marketing Strategies in American Industry*. Madison, WI: Mimir.

US Department of Agriculture (1972) *Improving Marketing Systems in Developing Countries*. Washington, D.C.: US Department of Agriculture.

US News and World Report (1995) By the numbers. August 28, p. 83.

Vaile, Roland S., Grether, E.T. & Cox, Reavis (1952) *Marketing in the American Economy*. New York: The Ronald Press Co.

Wilkie, William L. (1994) , *Consumer Behavior,* 3rd edn. New York: John Wiley & Sons.

——— (1997) Developing research on public policy and marketing. *Journal of Public Policy & Marketing*, 16 (Spring), 132–6.

——— & Moore, Elizabeth S. (1997) Consortium survey on marketing and society issues: summary and results. *Journal of Macromarketing*, 17 (2), 89–95.

——— & Moore, Elizabeth S. (1999) Marketing's contributions to society. *Journal of Marketing*, 63 (Special Millennium Issue), 198–218.

Wood, Van P. & Vitell Scott (1986) 'Marketing and economic development: review, synthesis and evaluation', *Journal of Macromarketing*, 6 (1), 28–48.

Yankelovich, Daniel (1981) *New Rules: Searching for Fulfillment in a World Turned Upside Down*. New York: Random House.

2

A History of Marketing Thought

D.G. BRIAN JONES and ERIC H. SHAW

INTRODUCTION

This section considers the nature of historical research in marketing, why this research should matter to marketing scholars, the various approaches to studying the history of marketing thought, and the organization of this chapter.

Historical Research in Marketing

Marketing historians have generally followed the tradition long held by economists, which is to separate the history of practice from the history of thought and to focus their studies on one or the other. Thus, historical research in marketing divides roughly into marketing history and the history of marketing thought. It is the latter we are reviewing in this chapter. Of course, as Stanley Hollander once observed, 'practice is not entirely thoughtless and thought is often practice-driven' (1989, p. xx). Some of the research reviewed herein examines marketing history together with marketing thought and, as we point out at the end of the chapter, more of this would be desirable. We have also restricted our review primarily to historical research by marketing scholars publishing in the literature intended for a marketing audience. We do not directly review literature dealing with historiography, but for the interested reader there is a growing body of work describing the methods of historical scholarship in marketing (e.g., Brown et al., 2001; Golder, 2000; Jones, 1993; Nevett, 1991; Savitt, 1980; Smith and Lux, 1993; Stern, 1990; Witkowski, 1993).

The practice of marketing is quite ancient and as long as thoughtful individuals have reflected on marketing behavior, there has been marketing thought. For example, early sections of this chapter examine the ideas about markets, marketing and marketers of Greek philosophers such as Plato and Aristotle. However, the formal study of marketing is of much more recent origin. As a subject taught in universities, studied and written about in a systematic, scholarly way, the marketing discipline has existed for only about 100 years. Interestingly, when such scholarship emerged during the early twentieth century, history was a prominent part of what marketing professors studied and taught – a quality we have since lost.

Why History Matters to Marketing

The classic justification for history is that those who don't know their past are doomed to repeat its mistakes. Ideas or concepts that have not worked or have not proven useful should be discarded. This appears self-evident. However, knowledge of history can also help us to avoid repeating its successes! This is the re-inventing-the-wheel phenomenon. One example well known to marketing historians is the reincarnation of the marketing concept, first as relationship marketing, and then as customer relationship management (CRM). Even if it is only a marginal change in the broader concept, with each new generation of terminology there seems to be no recognition that the basic idea has remained the same. As Mark Twain has been credited with observing, history may not repeat itself, but it often rhymes. When it does, variations on a theme should be recognized for what they are.

That brings us to a second value in studying history. It establishes a baseline for recognizing changes in theory. How can we advance our knowledge of marketing if we have no prior knowledge?

In a sense, this is the purpose served by a literature review. The problem is that far too many literature reviews only go back as far as the researcher can personally remember because, as many faculty tongue-in-cheek state, 'if it occurred before my Ph.D. it's ancient history,' or as one presenter at a recent marketing history conference suggested, 'if it happened during my lifetime it isn't history!'

Closely related to its value in serving as a baseline for recognizing change, history also helps us to frame the right questions to ask in teaching and research. A review of previous research on an idea or issue allows us to identify what has been previously studied and how extensively, which are the unanswered questions, and which are the unquestioned answers.

Perhaps the most practical value of history for students of marketing comes from its unique ability to provide a framework for building and integrating knowledge. Nowhere is this more apparent than in the work of Robert Bartels. His seminal study of the development of marketing thought, published in three editions (1962, 1976, 1988), provides us with one of the most comprehensive overviews of the development of marketing as a discipline during the past 100 years. At the same time, it gives us an introspective look at our discipline.

In addition to its practical value, history can be a thing of beauty. It is valuable for its own sake. It is a story worth telling. It adds perspective, richness, and context to marketing ideas. And, it gives us an intellectual heritage and sense of origin. It is difficult to understand how any serious student of marketing can possibly not be curious about what has changed and what has remained constant over the century of our discipline's existence.

Approaches to the History of Marketing Thought

There have been several different approaches used, separately or together, to study the history of marketing thought. Perhaps the most obvious and relevant approach is the study of ideas or concepts. The simplest version of this is a literature review where an author traces previous work on the topic or idea in question. This chapter might be considered as an example. Strictly speaking, however, few historians would consider such reviews as history. A better example is provided by the historical studies done by Hollander (1986) and Fullerton (1988) of the marketing concept, or by Shaw (1994) of the four utilities concept.

A second approach, one that might be considered a natural extension of the study of ideas or concepts, is to study schools of marketing thought. Now called the traditional approaches to marketing thought, by 1930 three such schools had emerged: functional, commodity, and institutional, and a good deal of historical research has involved those schools of thought. More recently, Sheth et al. (1988) have identified and examined the evolution through the twentieth century of 12 schools of marketing thought, including the three traditional ones.

Perhaps the earliest approach to studying the history of marketing thought, one that continues to have relevance and popularity, is a marketing discipline approach. Disciplinary studies refer to the history of the associations, organizations, and journals, identified with the marketing discipline. For example, as journals in marketing have reached milestones in their history, historical accounts of their development have been written (e.g., Berkman, 1992; Grether, 1976; Kerin, 1996; Muncy, 1991).

As an approach to the history of marketing thought, biography has been used to trace the contributions of pioneer scholars in the marketing discipline. This approach began during the 1950s and continues today. Between 1956 and 1962, the *Journal of Marketing* published a series of 23 biographical sketches that seemed to establish a tradition continued by Converse (1959), Bartels (1962, 1988), Hollander (1995), Jones (1994), and others. Often, biography is applied in combination with other approaches, as it was by Bartels (1988).

Organization of the Chapter

Naturally enough, this review of historical research on marketing thought proceeds chronologically, beginning with studies of the marketing ideas of ancient scholars through medieval times to the industrial revolution. Those earlier ideas about marketing began to crystallize in the writings of economists during the late nineteenth century. Most historical research has focused on developments during the twentieth century, which we have divided into two broad eras. The first, from 1900 to 1957, deals with the emergence of the marketing discipline. This was a time during which the first university courses were offered, the first textbooks were written, the traditional schools of thought emerged, and so on. With the publication of Wroe Alderson's (1957) *Marketing Behavior and Executive Action*, the modern era of marketing began. This more recent era has seen a proliferation of schools of thought (e.g., marketing management, consumer behavior, macromarketing), and with it a dramatic increase in historical study. In the final section of the chapter we reflect on the current status of historical research on marketing thought and make some suggestions about what research needs to be done.

Ancient and Medieval Marketing Thought

The birth of trade has disappeared in the mist of time, but the archeological evidence for trading goes back more than 10,000 years (Dixon et al., 1968). Trading continued for many millennia in a rudimentary form of barter known as the silent trade, first noted by Herodotus ([fifth century BCE] de Selincourt, 1972: 336), the Father of History. Barter in any form is relatively primitive and, as necessity is often the mother of invention, with the growth of civilization a more sophisticated trading mechanism emerged – marketing.

The earliest historical statement about the origin of marketing activity was made by Herodotus (de Selincourt, 1972: 80): 'The Lydians were the first people we know of to use a gold and silver coinage and to introduce the retail trade.' Marketing, in the sense of selling and buying, originated in the seventh century BCE, in Asia Minor (now modern Turkey). Because marketing was so much more efficient than barter, it quickly spread to neighboring Greek cities along the Mediterranean, and then rapidly diffused throughout the civilized world.

Marketing represented a strange new form of behavior. Emphasizing individual gain and competition, marketing activity appeared detrimental to maintaining the social bonds uniting the members of societies traditionally based on altruism and cooperation. During a famine, the socially acceptable thing to do was share the plight of one's neighbors, but marketers were more likely to raise prices. Deep thinkers of the time, such as the Socratic philosophers (fourth century BCE), were concerned with how this newly emerging, rapidly growing, form of human behavior would affect the social order. Their discussions represented the earliest thinking about marketing from the social perspective, what is now termed macromarketing thought. After the fall of Rome, marketing thought was developed largely by the medieval scholars, from St. Augustine of Hippo (fifth century CE) to St. Thomas Aquinas (thirteenth century), then by a variety of Enlightenment philosophers and scholars, leading to the early economists.

Some of the earliest writers discussing the history of ancient and medieval thought in the marketing literature include Cassels (1936), Kelley (1956), Steiner (1978) and Dixon (1979a). Cassels (1936), an economist by training, was probably invited to introduce the origins of marketing thought to the marketing discipline in the newly published *Journal of Marketing*. Laying the groundwork, Cassels noted that the central reason for studying the historical development of marketing thought was to shed light on a current question:

> the amount of systematic study given to [marketing] problems has increased tremendously since the beginning of the present century; but *the great central problem of marketing, the problem of carrying on efficiently from the social point of view* this final stage in the general production process, has remained essentially the same since it was so intelligently discussed by Plato twenty-three hundred years ago. (1936: 129, italics added)

Unfortunately, Cassels did not methodically discuss Plato's explanation of the efficiency of the marketing system. Yet Plato provided a systematic framework for discussing macromarketing thought that has been followed (knowingly or unknowingly) by almost every thinker since. Although the terms are modern, the concepts are Plato's, stated simply and succinctly:

> In summary, Plato has shown that because people are not self-sufficient societies evolve to satisfy human needs. Since individuals have different skills, their comparative advantages lead to a division of labor, which results in increased efficiency in production. The division of labor, however, also results in a separation of producers and consumers. To bridge this gap, market exchange – selling and buying – is necessary. The exchange process requires work, work takes time, and time has an opportunity cost. Hence, marketing intermediaries emerge because of their increased efficiency in market exchange. (Shaw, 1995: 10)

Attempting to provide a relatively balanced treatment of the views of the Socratic philosophers, Cassels noted 'the views of Aristotle on marketing are strikingly at variance with those of Plato.' However, their differences in viewpoint are due less to their actual arguments than to Cassels selectively choosing comments attributed to each. For example, Cassels (1936: 130) greatly exaggerated 'the views of Aristotle [toward marketers] as useless profiteering parasites.'

On the other hand, Cassels astutely attributed Plato's view of middlemen as 'unsuited to more strenuous occupations' to his recognition of the importance of comparative advantage in the division of labor, with a contrary view proposed by Adam Smith:

> Plato … recognized the existence of innate differences between individuals and attached much importance to the advantage of fitting people into the occupations for which their 'natural gifts' best suited them, whereas Smith, writing in an era of revolutionary democracy and liberalism, accepted the general view that men were born equal and was obliged, therefore, to develop an explanation of division of labor in which 'natural gifts' play no part at all. (Cassels, 1936: 130)

Cassels' observation is particularly noteworthy, because subsequent writers (e.g., Kelley, 1956;

Steiner, 1978) regarded Plato's views as no less hostile than those of Aristotle. For example, both Kelley and Steiner mistakenly attributed Plato's concern with comparative advantage to hostility, even prejudice, against middlemen.

Tracing the favorable and unfavorable views of trade in the early and medieval Christian church Cassels compared viewpoints ranging from the simple, e.g., Cassiodorus, who preached that 'he who in trading sells a thing for more than he paid for it must have paid for it less than it was worth or must be selling it for more than it is worth' Cassels, 1936: 130 to the perceptive, e.g., St. Thomas Aquinas, who argued that a trader may sell for a higher price 'either because the price has changed with a change of place or time, or because of the risk he takes in transporting the thing from one place to another' (p. 131), anticipating place (and possibly time and possession) utility in what is now termed the four utilities concept.

Cassels also commented on a few early British philosophers who held favorable opinions of marketing, including Thomas Mun and David Hume, as well as a couple of French Physiocrats, whom he said did not, including A.R.J. Turgot and Richard Cantillion. The problem with Cassels' work is that, lacking a framework to organize marketing thought, only a few favorable and unfavorable comments by historically noteworthy writers are offered. They are interesting as historical facts, but they do not advance our knowledge of marketing thought very far. Based on his observation that 'it is widely recognized' that 'pure competition' is lacking in marketing, 'even where the number of middlemen in the market is large and the rivalry between them … keen, their policies may nevertheless be non-aggressive,' Cassels concluded 'the system as a whole may be wastefully inefficient from a social point of view' (1936: 133). Thus, Cassels subjected himself to the same type of criticism Kelley and Steiner make about other historical figures who 'denigrate' marketing.

In contrast to Cassels, who at least sought to provide a balanced perspective, Kelley's (1956) study focused exclusively on unfavorable views of marketing to support the position 'when we go back into early history we find that the trader was not well regarded by society' (p. 62). Similarly, Steiner (1978: 2) took the same position: 'The prejudice against marketing and marketers is of ancient origin.' As evidence for this notion of bias, both Kelley and Steiner started with Plato's comment about marketing being delegated to those people 'weakest in bodily strength,' leading both to conclude: 'The marketer … was considered a rather immoral person by nature and his status was low indeed' (Kelley, 1956: 62). This was not bias, however; it was a logically thought-out position. The weak were more suited to sitting in the marketplace, exchanging goods for money, which does not require heavy lifting, rather than toiling in the fields or performing hard labor. As Cassels noted above, Plato placed great significance on a division of labor based on comparative advantage.

Kelley (1956) based his arguments for bias on the eighteenth-century Physiocratic philosophers' position 'that all value was thought to come from the land' (1956: 62); consequently, agriculture ranked higher (provided greater value) than manufacture, and manufacturing ranked higher than trade. Steiner (1978: 5) also linked this notion to the now discredited Marxian theory of value, 'Already in the minute when the commodity is finished, before it leaves the hands of its first vendor, it must be worth as much as the final purchaser, i.e., the consumer, pays for it in the end.' Steiner's main argument for prejudice rested on the four utilities concept that was developed by nineteenth-century American Institutional economists and refined by marketing academics of the twentieth century (Shaw, 1994). According to Steiner: 'By the prejudice against marketing we mean an attitude that denigrates the economic role of the three marketing utilities [time, place and possession] and magnifies the importance of form utility' (1976: 2). This was an argument often invoked by twentieth-century marketing pioneers to justify the idea that marketing, like agriculture and manufacturing, provides value.

There is one point on which these two writers diverge, when the bias against marketing ended. Kelley (1956: 67) believed that 'by the early part of the twentieth century, most of the community accepted [marketing] as useful and necessary,' although early marketing academics up to almost the mid-twentieth century found themselves defending marketing against the popular criticism of 'high costs, wastes, and inefficiency' (Bartels, 1988). Alternatively, Steiner (1978: 2) suggested that 'the prejudice against marketing … is a presence very much to be reckoned with today.' Although with the advent of non-profit marketing, social, political, religious and charitable causes seem quite comfortable embracing modern marketing techniques.

The most comprehensive and exhaustive treatment of the history of marketing thought prior to the twentieth-century is found in the works of Dixon (1978, 1979a, 1979b, 1980, 1981, 1982, 1991). One article in particular (1979a) refuted the bias issue raised by Kelley and Steiner. Using Ambrose's definition of prejudice as 'a vagrant opinion without visible means of support' (1979a: 39), Dixon argued that the Greek philosophers, medieval schoolmen and many subsequent scholars ignored in the literature, offered well-reasoned arguments for their opinions of marketing. To present his case Dixon used a cost–benefit framework. On the social benefits side, he pointed out classical Greek philosophers argued that marketing was not only useful to society, but it was essential.

According to Plato, 'The natural purpose for which all retail trading comes into existence is not a loss, but precisely the opposite for how can any man be anything but a benefactor if he renders even and symmetrical the distribution of goods' (1979a: 37). According to Aristotle, 'One of the essential activities of states is the buying and selling of goods to meet their varying needs' (p. 38). Consequently, Dixon concluded that the ancient Greek philosophers clearly recognized the importance of marketing and 'The specialists who ... do the work of marketing have an important place in the system, and perform socially beneficial work' (1979: 38).

This classical analysis carried over to the church fathers of the early medieval period, seeking to understand under what conditions profit making was morally justifiable. Early churchmen struggled with the notion of profit making or the value added by marketing, and Dixon (1979a) discussed the thinking of several. For example, St. Jerome (fifth century) believed marketing a zero-sum game, so 'the seller's gain must be the buyer's loss.' Pope Leo argued marketing was not sinful unless the profit was unreasonable: 'The nature of the gain either convicts or excuses a man doing business, for there is a gain which is honest another which is disgraceful' (1979a: 38). But a conceptual breakthrough was made by St. Augustine, who distinguished between marketing as an activity and the people who perform marketing. By separating the two, he could focus on the nature of marketing itself, rather than confound the issue with honest or sinful marketers. St. Augustine, giving words to an imaginary merchant, makes the argument 'I bring merchandise from afar' to those places in need. This is socially useful work, not without risk; consequently, 'I ask a wage for my labor, so that I buy more cheaply than I sell.' Profit is the wage, because 'the laborer is worthy of his hire' (p. 38).

Thus, contrary to Steiner's (1978: 3) assertion, 'By the fall of the Roman Empire, the major foundations of the anti-marketing bias had been sunk deep into intellectual soil,' Dixon reached a diametrically opposite conclusion. According to Dixon (1979a: 38), 'Hence, by the fall of the Western Roman Empire (*c.* 476), the best known of the early church writers not only had demonstrated the marketer made a social contribution by creating "place utility" but he had also shown that the profit earned represents nothing more than a wage paid for the labor expended.'

Later medieval church fathers also recognized the beneficial nature of marketing. Dixon cited several examples:

> Alexander of Hales (13th C.) remarks that trading is in harmony with the law of nature. St. Thomas (13th C.) says that 'Buying and selling seem to be established for the common advantage of both parties.' ... Duns Scotus (14th C.) says that 'Trade is necessary and useful for the well being of society.' Martin Luther (1524) remarks that 'It cannot be denied that buying and selling are necessary. They cannot be dispensed with. (Dixon, 1979a: 39)

Along with social benefits, there were also social costs. Dixon contended that discussions of costs should not be confused with hostility or prejudice but with the logic of the cost–benefit analysis. For example, he cited Plato, 'Let us see wherein trade is reputed to be ... not respectable ... in order that we may remedy by law parts of it' to show that Plato wished to fix the illegal and immoral aspects of retailing so that it 'will benefit everyone, and do the least possible injury to those in the state who practice it' (1979a: 39–40).

Marketing had other social costs. It reduced a state's self-reliance and preparedness for war, as well as encouraging foreign merchants with strange customs. Dixon quoted St. Thomas Aquinas:

> The State, which needs a number of merchants to maintain its subsistence, is liable to be injured in war through a shortage of foods ... Moreover, the influx of strangers corrupts the morals of many of the citizens ... whereas, if the citizens themselves devote themselves to commerce, a door is open to many vices ... the pursuit of a merchant is as contrary as possible to military exertion. For merchants abstain from labors and while they enjoy the good things of life, they become soft in mind and their bodies are rendered weak and unsuitable for military exercises. (1979a: 40)

Steiner (1978: 2) stated, 'An inevitable corollary of the hostility toward marketing institutions and practices is the "rub-off" to individuals engaged in them. Marketers thus get portrayed as less worthwhile persons than the honest farmer.' Dixon argued the contrary, however: the directionality of the causal arrow should be reversed; sinful marketers were corrupting the activity of marketing.

Dixon noted a variety of Greek and Roman writers (e.g., Herodotus, Dionysius) who disapproved of manual labor in general, not marketing in particular; citing Cicero (first century BCE), as just one example, 'vulgar are the means of livelihood of all hired workmen whom we pay for mere manual labor ... Vulgar we must consider those also who buy from wholesale merchants to retail immediately ... and all mechanics [artisans and manufacturers] are engaged in vulgar trades' (1979a: 40). Cicero also differentiated among types of marketing based on the scale of operations: 'Trade, if it is a small scale [such as retail] is to be considered vulgar; but if it is wholesale and on a large scale ... is not to be greatly disparaged' (p. 40). There was no bias against trade *per se*, but these writers were mostly aristocrats, and having the leisure to think and write they disdained all forms of manual labor.

The medieval churchmen, concerned with morality, condemned a variety of marketing practices as sinful. Dixon (1979a: 41) cited several marketing 'stratagems' including 'selling a different article for more than was first bargained, hiding the fault of a thing, as horse dealers do, and making a thing look better than it is, as do cloth sellers who choose dim places to sell their cloth.' Many all-to-common trade practices, such as using false weights, hiding defects in merchandise, and adulterating food, however, were condemned in the earliest codified laws, back to the Code of Hammurabi (eighteenth century BCE), and such practices are also illegal today.

It was, however, clearly recognized that the fault lay in the man, not the activity. As one of many writers in the early literature, Dixon (1979a: 41) cited Gower (fourteenth century): 'There is a difference between the merchant whose thoughts are set on deceit, and he whose day is spent in honest work, both labor alike for gain, but one cannot be compared with the other.' Thus it is apparent that marketing activity was not looked down upon because of prejudice. The problem lay mostly with dishonest marketers. As Plato stated: 'The class of men is small ... who when assailed by wants and desires, are able to hold out and observe moderation, and when they might make a great deal of money are sober in their wishes and prefer a moderate to a large gain, but the mass of men are the very opposite' (Kelley, 1956: 62). It was the concern with excessive profits that was the issue. Marketers were violating the 'golden mean' – everything in moderation, nothing in excess. They were confusing the means (making money) with the ends (the good life). Thus, Plato concluded, 'If the best men were to follow the retail trade, the latter would be an honored occupation' (pp. 62–3). St. Augustine says much the same, 'I do not approve of a covetous trader ... but these failings are in the man and not in his trade, which can be carried out honestly' (Dixon, 1979a: 42). Because it dealt with money, there were few who could avoid such temptation, and Plato recommended limiting the number engaged in marketing and assigning the work to those whose corruption would cause society the least harm, namely resident aliens. Again, this was not evidence of prejudice, but the logic of his analysis. Medieval writers were concerned with the same problem. Dixon (1979a: 42) cited St. Cyprian's criticism of churchmen, who after 'deserting the people ... sought the market places for gainful business ... they wished to possess money in abundance.'

Thus, from the earliest discussions of marketing to the close of the medieval period, it is clear that many scholars were seeking to understand the impact of marketing on society. Their discussions have contributed significantly to our knowledge. The Socratic philosophers produced the earliest framework that integrated marketing into society. It was expanded and deepened by subsequent scholars. During the medieval period church writers were concerned with the morality of profit making, because it caused marketers to fall into temptation. Consequently, classical philosophers suggested laws to moderate the excesses, and medieval churchmen preached against greed. Throughout history thinking about marketing has evolved through a distinguished lineage of scholars who have enriched our heritage of marketing thought.

Economics and Marketing Thought During the Late Nineteenth Century

Marketing historians agree that the discipline emerged as a branch of applied economics at the turn of the twentieth century (Bartels, 1988). There is some variance of evidence and opinion, however, about which economic ideas and schools of thought were most influential. The late nineteenth century was a time of division and debate among different economic schools, especially in North America, and it was from such diverse streams of economic thinking that the study of marketing emerged in the academy.

One of the first detailed studies of this era was Coolsen's (1960) examination of the collected works of four 'selected empirical liberal economists,' Edward Atkinson, David Wells, Arthur Farquhar, and Henry Farquhar, writing in the US between 1870 and 1900. Coolsen considered this a time during which marketing emerged as an important problem of modern capitalism, but just prior to the emergence of marketing as a field of inquiry in its own right. When marketing problems and issues were considered, it was as part of the study of economics. As was common at that time, these four economists used the phrase 'distribution of products' instead of the term 'marketing.' Coolsen made it clear that they did not intend, nor did they, develop an organized body of marketing knowledge (1958: 210). They did, however, provide a fairly comprehensive view of the scope and importance of marketing at that time. Their primary interest was in promoting laissez-faire – a belief in free trade and economic liberalism. They conducted studies of the effects of changes in transportation on market size and product availability, of credit and consumption, of the relationship between the marketing of commodities and income distribution, and of the effects of buying and selling on aggregate consumption. In this way, their work had an unmistakable macromarketing focus, but it also highlighted the relatively sophisticated marketing techniques of that time period. Coolsen concluded that these four economists did not have as much impact on the early development of the 'science' of marketing as they might otherwise have, because their discussions of marketing were imprecise and somewhat vague, and because they were neither academically trained nor academically employed (1958: 215). As a result, their influence on early students of marketing is uncertain.

Shortly after Coolsen's work, Bartels published his seminal book titled *The Development of Marketing Thought* (1962), in which he included an early chapter surveying some of the various economic theories, ideologies, and philosophies on which the emerging marketing discipline might have been founded. He pointed out that the 'traditionally trained marketing economist around 1900' would have studied the writings and ideas of classical economists, including Adam Smith, David Ricardo, John Stuart Mill; the neoclassical school, particularly Alfred Marshall; and the marginal economists, such as Menger and Bohm-Bawerk; concerning market, value, government and business, the consumer, and the state of the economy. Bartels was equivocal, however, about the precise nature and extent of various influences noting, for example on the issue of laissez-faire, that there was much disagreement among economists (and presumably, therefore, among early students of marketing). He added, 'By 1900, the body of economic thought consisted of many theories that had been developed in England, France, Austria, Germany, the United States, and other places. Their suitability to our own [American] problems at that time was strongly debated' (1962: 12).

Jones and Monieson (1990) used Bartels' work as a point of departure (inasmuch as it had identified the original universities and teachers associated with the academic study of marketing at the turn of the century) and traced back a generation the late nineteenth-century economists who were the teachers of those earliest students of marketing. Their research was among the first to make extensive use of primary, archival data such as personal correspondence, diaries, and unpublished manuscripts and records belonging to many pioneer marketing scholars, as well as to their teachers. Using that evidence, they examined the ideas and teachings of economists at Harvard University and the University of Wisconsin to identify the methodological, philosophical, ideological, and pedagogical assumptions that may have influenced early marketing scholars. They discovered that the German Historical school of economics and its American offspring, the Institutional school, played a profound role in determining which marketing issues were studied and why, how those issues were studied, and why pedagogies such as the case method were used. At the University of Wisconsin, under the well-known Institutional economists Richard T. Ely and John Commons, early marketing students such as Edward Jones, Henry Taylor, Benjamin Hibbard, and James Hagerty used historical, statistical, descriptive studies of marketing problems such as efficiency in the marketing process, distributive justice, and the basic functions of marketing – believing, as their teachers did, that their inductive approach would eventually result in the development of theory. They also held a critical view of the effectiveness and efficiency of the marketing process.

At Harvard, German-trained economists such as Edwin Gay and Frank Taussig were the teachers of early marketing students such as Arch Shaw and Paul Cherington, who later became pioneers in the marketing discipline. There, the same philosophical ideas of the German Historical school were influential in creating an intellectual environment receptive to the ideas of Scientific Management, which, when applied to marketing problems, resulted in Shaw's work on the basic functions of marketing (Jones, 1997; Jones & Monieson, 1990). An argument is also made that the German Historical school's pedagogy may have some claim to laying the foundations of the case method that was developed and popularized by the Harvard Business School. This is relevant because, as odd as it may seem today, the case method was later considered one of the most important 'concepts' in the early development of the marketing discipline (Converse, 1945).

Generally, however, the philosophy of German Historical economics led to the collection of marketing facts rather than the development of marketing theory. That began to change during the 1950s with the work of Wroe Alderson, who is now widely recognized as the most important marketing theorist of the twentieth century. Many of Alderson's concepts and theories can be traced to earlier ideas developed by economists from a wide range of eras and schools of thought.

For example, the role of marketing in creating utility or satisfaction was better understood by Alderson (1957), who relied on a 'value-in-use' reasoning, than by most marketing writers of recent generations who never read Alderson's work. Dixon (1990) traced Alderson's value-in-use concept of marketing back through the ideas of Aristotle, Thomas Aquinas, Nicholas Barbon (the seventeenth-century English economist), Ferdinando Galiani (an eighteenth-century Italian economist), Etienne de Condillac (a French philosopher of the eighteenth century), J.B. Say (a nineteenth-century French economist), and Karl Menger (an Austrian economist of the same period). At the same time, Dixon traced Theodore Beckman's (1957) value-in-exchange concept of marketing through Classical economists such as Adam Smith, James Mill, and John Stuart Mill, the neoclassical economist Alfred Marshall and his American disciple Frank Taussig, as well as late nineteenth-century American economists including the Institutionalist, Richard T. Ely. Both streams of economic thought provided justification for Alderson's rejection of the notion that different aspects of utility should be attributed to production and marketing, but Alderson failed to recognize any of those earlier economic arguments. Dixon concluded that by the turn of the twentieth century economists had developed a clear concept of marketing as a productive process – something early marketing theorists seemed to understand, but whose arguments have since been forgotten.

Shaw's (1994) study of the four utilities concept followed historical lines similar to Dixon's work, but focused on the efforts by American Institutional economists during the late nineteenth century to separate the concept of value, or utility, into four component parts. In particular, Shaw noted the work of John Bates Clark (1886) and Richard T. Ely (1889), who used the four utilities concept to distinguish between different types of labor (originally: elemental – linked with farming; form – related to manufacturing; time; and place – associated with marketing), thereby crediting anyone who produced utility of some type for creating economic value. Early students of marketing, especially those trained under Institutional economists, seized on this concept because it served to distinguish marketing from production, and at the same time demonstrated that marketing activities created value. Economists eventually dismissed the four utilities concept, but marketing scholars made it a cornerstone of their discipline.

Where Shaw's work departs significantly from Dixon's is in tracing the evolution of the utility concept in marketing from the earliest principles of marketing texts to marketing management texts of today, and in describing efforts by marketing scholars throughout the twentieth century to relate the four utilities concept, first to the marketing functions, next to the nature and scope of marketing, and later to the four Ps of marketing management. Shaw concluded, as the neoclassical economists had a century earlier, that the four utilities concept offers little that isn't better explained by the value-added concept. As Alderson had done a half century earlier, Shaw observed that what is needed is a marketing interpretation of the whole process of creating utility.

Alderson was also concerned with the role of marketing in system-environment interactions, but apparently overlooked earlier writings by economists on that same issue (Dixon, 1999). Dixon examined work done during the late nineteenth century by Alfred Marshall and by Austrian economists such as Carl Menger, Eugene von Bohm-Bawerk, and Fredrich von Wieser, describing late nineteenth- century theories of the consumer, production and exchange, marketing effort (especially pricing), system structure (firm size), and interactions between the system and its environment. Dixon then compared them with Alderson's mid-twentieth-century treatment of the same concepts in his attempts to develop a general theory of marketing. Many similarities were identified between Alderson's theories and those of Marshall and the Austrians, but the main difference was in their respective recognition of the interactions between marketing and its environments. Here, Alderson's focus was decidedly more micro-analytic because he was concerned with developing a theory of the firm usable by marketing executives. Because of that difference, Dixon suggested that the contributions of those late nineteenth-century economists have not been recognized, leading him also to wonder whether the focus of marketing theory on the behavior of the firm was a cause or result of the failure to appreciate this intellectual heritage.

System interrelationships were also at the root of an issue that dogged marketing scholars through much of the twentieth century, even though it had been largely solved by economists a century earlier – the cost of distribution. A debate about whether or not distribution cost too much culminated in well-known studies designed to estimate those costs, first by Stewart and Dewhurst (1939), and later by Cox et al. (1965). According to Dixon (1991), both studies were flawed because they did not fully appreciate concepts and approaches to measurement of the structure of economic systems developed by economists between the eighteenth and late nineteenth centuries. As a result, those early estimates of the cost of distribution by marketing scholars were overestimated and then repeated for half a century. It is only in the last 20 years that a better application of input-output models to understanding marketing system structure and its relationship with the environment has been made.

Another of Shaw's studies (1990) complemented Dixon's work by distinguishing between marketing costs and marketing productivity. Shaw reviewed five cost studies for a single year, and seven productivity studies carried out between 1869 and 1968. In response to the often-asked question, 'Does distribution cost too much?' he concluded the question of costs cannot be answered without considering the benefits provided. On the other hand, input costs and output benefits are considered in the productivity ratio and Shaw discovered a rising secular trend, concluding that over the past century marketing has become more productive.

It is ironic that while the marketing discipline was founded by scholars trained in economics, so much of that economic thinking, some of it very relevant today, has either been misunderstood or forgotten. Fortunately, the relationship between the history of economic thought and history of marketing thought remains a topic of considerable interest to marketing historians, and so may ultimately be rediscovered.

EMERGENCE OF THE MARKETING DISCIPLINE: 1900–1957

Most of the research on the history of marketing thought has dealt with the era when marketing was first taught in universities and a clearly recognizable body of literature began forming. No historian has been more dedicated to the genesis of marketing in the academy than Robert Bartels.

Robert Bartels and The Development of Marketing Thought

No other scholar has become so identified with the history of marketing thought as has Robert Bartels. He is credited with 'almost single-handedly [keeping] interest in the history of marketing thought alive through his book on the subject and his doctoral seminars' (Hollander, Nevett & Fullerton, 1990: 267). Bartels' books on the *History of Marketing Thought* (1962, 1976, 1988) contain discussions of the meaning of marketing, early theories of marketing, and the beginnings of marketing thought, as well as a number of special areas of marketing thought, such as advertising, sales management, retailing, and marketing research, among others. Although the period prior to 1960 dominates Bartels' *History*, marketing management and several other areas of thought since the 1960s, such as marketing systems, channels, and international marketing are included in later editions of the book. In all this, Bartels regards the general literature as most important, because it represents 'A distillation and integration of thought ... in the specialized areas ... [And in it] are found the best measures of marketing thought: its scientific character, its historical evolution, its social orientation, its philosophic, economic, and cultural characteristics' (1988: 141). To describe the marketing thought literature Bartels divided the period from 1900 to the 1970s into eleven-year decades:

1900–1910 – The Period of Discovery
1910–1920 – The Period of Conceptualization
1920–1930 – The Period of Integration
1930–1940 – The Period of Development
1940–1950 – The Period of Reappraisal
1950–1960 – The Period of Reconceptualization
1960–1970 – The Period of Differentiation
from 1970 – The Period of Socialization

It is not clear why Bartels overlaped the beginning and ending year of each decade, but it presents an immediate source of confusion. He regarded 1910 as the year the term 'marketing' was first used to identify the discipline. Consequently, given the overlap in decades, Bartels was forced to include the origin of the term marketing both at the end of the Period of Discovery as well as the beginning of the Period of Conceptualization – one of several sources of confusion that would not otherwise arise if his eleven-year decades followed the standard dating convention of ten years per decade!

Before tracing the evolution of marketing thought from 1900, there is the question of those who influenced the early academics who first started thinking about marketing. This is discussed in a chapter on 'The Beginnings of Marketing Thought' based on Bartels' (1951) article 'Influences on the Development of Marketing Thought, 1900–1923.' Tracing the lineage of marketing influence provides a particularly useful reference source for understanding the history of marketing thought. In a genealogical chart, Bartels (1988: 28) primarily credited the Institutional economists at Wisconsin, such as Richard T. Ely and John Commons, and economists at Harvard, such as Frank Taussig and Edwin Gay, for training several early marketing pioneers.

In the Period of Discovery, 1900–1910, Bartels noted the first American college marketing courses were taught in 1902 and identified the early teachers and universities, including Edward Jones at Michigan, Simon Litman at California-Berkeley, and George M. Fisk at Illinois. He regarded the *Report of the Industrial Commission on the Distribution of Farm Products* (1901), dealing with the costs of distributing agricultural goods, as the first book on general marketing. Most early scholars focused on understanding this distribution system because of concerns with the large price spread in agricultural products between producers and consumers, and popular criticisms of high costs, waste and inefficiencies in marketing.

Bartels believed he found the origins of marketing thought, placing it in America 'between 1906–1911' (1988: 3), with his best approximation 'about 1910' (1988: 143). His argument was based on when the term 'marketing' was first used as a noun and where academic thought about marketing began. There is disagreement on both counts – time and place. In regard to time, Bartels apparently erred on the year marketing entered the language as a noun, signifying marketing thought, rather than its use as a verb, indicating marketing practice. One writer traced the 'academic use of the term marketing' back to 1897 (Bussiere, 2000: 142), and even before marketing emerged as an academic discipline, another author discovered marketing as a noun in 1856, implying it might be even earlier (Lazer, 1979: 654); still another writer tracked the term back to 1561 (Shaw, 1995). Bartels also believed that marketing thought originated in university courses in the US. However, there is contrary evidence that marketing courses were offered in Germany before those offered at American institutions (Fullerton, 1988; Jones and Monieson, 1990).

Bartels named the first epoch in the history of marketing thought the Period of Conceptualization, 1910–1920, because the 'commodity, institutional, and functional approaches … were conceived' (1988: 143). Now known as the traditional approaches to (or schools of) marketing thought, they dominated academic thinking about marketing until the mid 1950s. The functional approach was concerned with the activities of the marketing process (e.g., buying and selling, transporting and storing, advertising, research, credit, standardizing and grading). The institutional approach focused on the types of organizations known as marketing institutions (e.g., merchant wholesalers, agents, brokers, rack jobbers, catalog, general, specialty and department store retailers) that performed marketing activities on various products. And the commodity approach centered on the products (e.g., farming, forestry, fisheries, mining, manufacturing, and occasionally services) that were processed by marketing institutions.

Bartels described the Period of Integration, 1920–1930, as the 'Golden Decade,' because *Principles* texts were integrating knowledge in marketing and many sub-disciplines such as advertising, credit, sales management and salesmanship. Bartels credited Ivey (1921) with the first use of the title *Principles of Marketing*, as well as one of marketing's best known principles: 'the middleman himself can be eliminated, but his functions cannot' (Bartels, 1988: 148). Other early marketing textbook writers during this period include Cherington (1920), Converse (1921), Clark (1922), Brown (1925), and Maynard, Weidler and Beckman (1927).

The years 1930–1940 are called the Period of Development. The most notable comment about the decade is that 'The "principles" texts were kept up to date.' Revisions of Converse and Hugey's *Elements of Marketing* (1930, 1935, 1940), Clark's *Principles of Marketing* (1932), and Maynard and Beckman's *Principles of Marketing* (1932, 1939) dominated sales of entry-level college textbooks. Consequently, only one new principles text by Phillips (1938) was able to break into the market. Some newly published books focused on the commodity approach for non-agricultural products (and occasionally services) such as Breyer's *Commodity Marketing* (1931) and Comish's *Marketing Manufactured Goods* (1935). However, the most important new book of the decade was largely overlooked – then and now. Described as 'unorthodox,' Breyer's *The Marketing Institution* (1934) provided the most systematic and theoretical approach in marketing thought to that date. Bartels regarded Breyer's work as rising 'above the mechanistic concept of marketing … portrayed as separate functions … in conventional works … to present a *theory* of a compound operation; [however,] his effort failed to make much impression on the market for ideas at the time' (1988: 155, italics in original).

One of the most significant developments affecting marketing thought during this decade, and indeed the entire century, is noticeably absent in Bartels' treatment of the history of marketing thought. Only mentioned in a single sentence, in one section of chapter dealing with Associations, the *American Marketing Journal* was first published in 1934, became the *National Marketing Review* in 1935, and then the *Journal of Marketing* in 1936 (Bartels, 1988: 29). Of all the publications in marketing, the '*JM*' undoubtedly represents one of the most dominant influences on the development of marketing thought.

The Period of Reappraisal, 1940–1950, saw the incipient development of two new conceptual approaches to marketing – management and systems. The seeds of marketing management were planted in the 1940 text *Marketing* by Alexander, Surface, Elder and Alderson. This book focused on planning and controlling marketing activities within a business firm. Following Breyer's 1934 work, another systemic treatment of marketing was that of Duddy and Revzan (1947), who viewed 'the marketing structure as an organic whole made up of interrelated parts, subject to growth and change' (Bartels, 1988: 156). For unexplained reasons, the 1952 work of Vaile, Grether and Cox is also included in this decade, rather than the next. Their book, *Marketing in the American Economy,* is yet another early systematic approach to marketing.

The developing conceptual approaches of the prior decade reached maturity, according to Bartels, in the 1950–1960 Period of Reconception. The distinction between this and the previous decade 'was thin,' according to Bartels, but rested on the 'degree of concern with a theoretical statement of marketing knowledge' and 'the replacement of the "functional-institutional-commodity"' schools of marketing thought. One of the earliest theoretical works, Cox and Alderson's *Theory in Marketing* (1950), offered a collection of essays that included a diverse array of marketing topics with a theoretical bent. In addition to the usual economic theorizing, essays included theories related to consumer psychology, demographics and organizational behavior, among others.

The early developments in marketing management and systems thinking of the previous decades, were both more fully developed in Wroe Alderson's seminal work *Marketing Behavior and Executive Action* (1957). Bartels regarded this work as 'unquestionably the most fully developed theoretical exposition of marketing up to that time' (1988: 238). This book represents a landmark in distinguishing 'modern marketing thought' from the 'traditional marketing thought' that had gone before. Alderson combined management and systems into a single unified approach, focusing on firms (and households) as 'organized behavior systems' processing inputs into outputs. Most subsequent writers, however, focused on either the 'micro' firm perspective of marketing management, or the more 'macro' view of marketing systems (which often included firms as a sub-system) as alternative perspectives to marketing thought.

With the growth of these two new conceptual schools, the traditional functions-institutions-commodities approaches to marketing thought followed the life cycle of ideas into decline. Most writers of the time (e.g., Howard, 1957; Kelley and Lazer, 1958; McCarthy, 1960) pursued the growing interest in marketing management, which since the 1970s developed into the dominant paradigm of marketing thought, replacing 'principles' as the entry-level course in the marketing curriculum. Marketing systems, and several other approaches to marketing thought awaited developments in the next and subsequent decades.

During the Period of Differentiation, 1960–1970, a few principles texts remained but they were laggards and the traditional approaches to marketing thought were almost entirely replaced by an increasing array of specialty areas of marketing thought, including marketing management, marketing systems, quantitative analysis in marketing, international marketing, and consumer behavior. Although given impetus in earlier decades, marketing systems analysis was greatly enhanced and significantly expanded by Alderson's (1965) *Dynamic Marketing Behavior*, another seminal work in marketing thought during the last half century. Despite its popularity across a wide variety of disciplines among the physical, biological and social sciences, the systems approach attracted only a few adherents in marketing, fewer books, and a brief flurry of journal articles. These were mostly written by Alderson's students, such as Fisk's (1967) *Marketing Systems*, Fisk and Dixon's (1967) *Theories for Marketing Systems Analysis*, Dixon's (1968) 'Social Systems,' and Narver and Savitt's (1971) *The Marketing Economy*. The area of marketing systems has been relatively quiescent during the past few decades. This is surprising, because the systems approach offers the only possibility of providing a unity to all the other sub-areas of marketing thought in the general theory that was an underlying concern of Bartels' work (e.g., 1988: 241, 287).

Marketing models and quantitative methods also became popular during the 1960s (e.g., Bass et al., 1968; Buzzell, 1964; Day, 1964; Frank & Green, 1967; King, 1967; Kotler, 1971 Langhoff, 1965). Also popularizing this specialty, the *Journal of Marketing Research* increasingly moved from qualitative articles to those more quantitatively oriented. There was also an array of *International Marketing* books (e.g., Fayerweather, 1965; Hess & Cateora, 1966; Kramer, 1964; Leighton, 1966) and more recently several journals published in the international marketing arena. Unexpectedly, Bartels ignored consumer behavior in his decade-by-decade coverage – the specialty attracting the greatest number of adherents after marketing management. He did include it, however, in his chapter on 'Influences on the Development of Marketing Thought, 1950–1987.' For the most part the area started its rapid growth with the development of extended and complex consumer/buyer behavior models. The two most notable books were Engel, Kollat and Blackwell's (1968) *Consumer Behavior* and Howard and Sheth's (1969) *Theory of Buyer Behavior*. Spurring its rapid growth, several dedicated journals were published in the 1970s, including the *Journal for Consumer Research*.

The Period of Socialization, beginning in 1970, only discussed work until the mid-1970s, because the 1988 *History of Marketing Thought* is largely a reprint of the previous 1976 edition, with one new chapter bringing the book up to date. Bartels' discussion of this half decade is more tentative than other periods, as he noted 'the 1970s are distinguished by a larger social element in marketing thought.' He specifically cited in that connection Kotler's (1975) work on *Marketing for Non-Profit Organizations,* which translated marketing terminology and technology to social causes. Social marketing is a result of more fundamental concepts that Bartels glossed over. They pose a critical problem for marketing thought, however, because they define marketing's nature and scope. The latter is based on Kotler and Levy's (1969) 'broadening concept' of marketing, and the former on Kotler's (1971) 'generic concept' of marketing. Both are very briefly described in Bartels' *History* but neither is critically examined. This is surprising, because in other publications (1974, 1983, 1986) Bartels regards these views as limiting and diverting marketing thought.

'Broadening' is the notion that all organizations, including government agencies, political parties, and charities deal with stakeholders, of one type or another, and could therefore benefit from using marketing concepts and techniques, such as target marketing, focus groups, survey research, and persuasive communication ranging from advertising to personal selling. The 'generic' concept expresses the idea that market transactions can be generalized to any social or economic form of exchange. The problem this poses for marketing thought is whether marketing is determined by subject matter or by techniques (Bartels, 1974: 74–5).

It is a weakness of his history books that Bartels seldom integrated new material into old chapters, but simply added newer chapters onto his older editions. Consequently, the later books have more of a layered, than integrated, quality about them. For example, in addition to the decade-by-decade approach in the 1962 book, Bartels added a chapter on the 'Maturing of Marketing Thought' in the 1976 book, which includes subheadings of 'The Development of Thought – 1900 to 1960,' and 'The Development of Thought Since 1960.' These two periods in the revised book clearly overlap his decade-by-decade coverage in the original 1962 book. Similarly, in the 1988 book, one new chapter is added: 'Influences on the Development of

Marketing Thought 1950–1987.' However, this chapter starts with a discussion of the early influences of turn-of-the-century marketing pioneers, and overlaps both the 1962 decade-by-decade history and the 1976 'Maturing of Marketing Thought' chapter.

As a reference source for the historian of marketing thought, Bartels' appendices are invaluable. A notable achievement of the books is Bartels' biographical sketches of 18 leaders of marketing thought from the first half of the twentieth century, and 20 more thought leaders since 1950. Another notable historical accomplishment is Bartels' chronological listing of marketing books, organized by topic area, from the turn of the century up to the 1970s. Taken as a whole, despite the criticisms, this work is a monumental contribution to the literature of marketing. No other work in the discipline offers such a sweeping, detailed perspective of marketing thinking in twentieth-century America as Bartels'.

Emergence of a Marketing Literature

Bartels wasn't the only marketing historian who considered the general literature a starting point for studying the academic history of marketing thought; he wasn't even the first. With all the usual caveats that go with that claim, this review suggests that the first publication by a marketing academician to look at the history of marketing thought was an article titled 'The First Decade of Marketing Literature' by Paul D. Converse, published in 1933 in the *NATMA Bulletin* (National Association of Teachers of Marketing and Advertising). Converse identified several books published between 1915 and 1924 as the first to be written about marketing. The earliest was Arch Shaw's (1915) *Some Problems in Market Distribution*, which, Converse also pointed out, initiated the functional approach to marketing. Converse considered Butler's (1917) *Marketing Methods and Policies* to be the first 'teachable' book. Interestingly, the editor of the *NATMA Bulletin* was critical of Converse for omitting several books believed worthy of inclusion, some of which were published prior to 1915.

There is also clear historical evidence of an even earlier periodic literature dealing with marketing, and not surprisingly it was found in economics. Bussiere (2000) studied the early publications of the American Economic Association and identified articles dealing with marketing topics as early as 1894. The first use of the term 'marketing' there, in a manner consistent with modern use, was by Hammond in 1897. Prior to the formation of the NATMA, most marketing professors belonged to the American Economic Association and its periodic publications, especially the *American Economic Review* (AER), were probably the most popular publishing outlets for marketing academics. According to Bussiere, the number of marketing articles published in the AER increased until 1925, when marketing academics began to organize their own associations, culminating in the American Marketing Association.

The history of the American Marketing Association (AMA) actually goes beyond the NATMA and was chronicled by Agnew in 1941. In 1915 the National Association of Teachers of Advertising was formed under the leadership of Walter Dill Scott. There were 13 original members, including Agnew. In 1926 its name was changed to the National Association of Teachers of Marketing and Advertising in order to recognize the broadening membership that included marketing professionals and teachers. NATMA published the *NATMA-Graphs*, which later became the *NATMA Bulletin*. In 1933 the name of the association was changed again, this time to the National Association of Teachers of Marketing, as it became increasingly recognized that advertising was part of the broader field of marketing. NATM first published the *American Marketing Journal* in 1934, which became the *National Marketing Review* in 1935, and began publication of the *Journal of Marketing* in 1936. Finally, in 1937 the NATM and the American Marketing Society merged, to form the American Marketing Association (AMA).

In 1947 the first of several retrospectives (others appeared in 1952, 1976 and 1996) was written about the *Journal of Marketing's* development and contribution to the marketing literature. Applebaum (1947) described the various sections of the Journal and provided copious statistics about the publishing activities over its first 10 years including, for example, the number of articles by subject (by far the most popular were marketing research and government regulation of marketing) and by type of author/occupation (practitioners, university teachers, and government employees). Surprisingly, business practitioners wrote approximately half of the 435 regular articles published between 1936 and 1947. Because the history of the Journal was so intimately tied to that of the AMA, Applebaum also included several facts about the history of that association. For example, the total membership of 584 at inception in 1937 had quadrupled to 2300 members by 1947. Five years later, Applebaum (1952) published a post-war update to his statistical summary of the Journal's activities. Among the changes reported, government regulation as a subject in the journal had retreated significantly in importance. Marketing research was still the most common subject, followed by wholesaling, then teaching of marketing. Practitioners still dominated as authors.

It is disappointing that the subject categories used in those first two retrospectives did not include 'marketing history,' because we know that history was a relatively common theme during that period. Many of the articles dealing with the teaching of marketing (the third most common category in

1952) were retrospectives on early experiences of marketing teachers.

The notion that a marketing 'literature' first appeared after the turn of the twentieth century was challenged by Lazer (1979), who pointed out that early writers did not use the term 'marketing,' but rather, terms like 'commerce' and 'distribution,' which were synonymous with 'marketing.' If marketing historians redirected their research based on that broader interpretation of terminology, they would find new insights into the development of marketing thought. Viewed from this perspective, Lazer traced the development of marketing thought to a pre-1800 stage that focused on the role of middlemen, ideas of mercantilism, the acceptance of capitalist thought, and the development of national markets. That was followed by a period from 1800 to 1900 when marketing was seen as part of economics and the marketing literature was characterized by books such as *The Retailer's Manual,* published in 1869 (Hoagland and Lazer, 1960).

Similarly, an advertising literature developed earlier than, and separately from, the general marketing literature and some of that development was chronicled by Coolsen (1947). Using *The American Catalogue, 1876–1905*, and *The United States Catalogue, 1912*, as publication records, Coolsen identified 10 books on the technique of advertising which pre-dated 1895, four more published between 1895 and 1900, and another 75 volumes published between 1900 and 1910. Coolsen grouped the contributors to this literature into three categories: advertising practitioners (especially copywriters and agents), academic psychologists, and correspondence textbook writers. The earliest book, according to Coolsen, was Edwin T. Freedley's (1852) *Practical Treatise on Business*.

Goodman (1996) also noted that there was a periodic literature before the *Journal of Marketing* and its contributors were often not marketing academics. Goodman reviewed the *Annals of the American Academy of Political and Social Science*, which began publication in 1890, as an outlet for marketing ideas and discovered articles by economists, practitioners, and government officials as far back as 1903. Between 1903 and 1940 various issues of the *Annals* dealt with marketing-related topics such as intermediary sorting, retailing practices, price controls and inflation, pricing legislation and controls, channels of distribution, government regulation of marketing, and a wide variety of agricultural marketing and food marketing topics. The latter was by far the most common general marketing subject covered in the *Annals* during the time period reviewed by Goodman. Its contributors 'viewed marketing phenomena largely as seen by outside, often critical, observers whose goal was to improve the system' (Goodman, 1996: 142). A 1940 special issue, titled 'Marketing in Our American Economy,' dealing with marketing costs and efficiency, for the first time included a significant number of marketing scholars as contributors, such as Wroe Alderson, Theodore N. Beckman, Paul D. Converse, and N. H. Engle. The timing was noteworthy because in 1939 Stewart and Dewhurst had published their critical book *Does Distribution Cost Too Much?*

There is little doubt that a literature focusing on marketing education existed outside the US. However, there is almost no published discussion of this in the American marketing literature. The few exceptions mentioned here deal with translations of American work. Fullerton (1994) translated and analyzed a book published by H.F.J. Kropff (1939) in Germany. The misleading title, *The Totality of Promotion*, obscured the fact that it included a chapter reviewing and evaluating marketing practices and education in the US. The book dealt with market and advertising research, applied psychology, and the state of marketing education. Similarly, Usui (2000) cited examples of Japanese publications as early as 1929 that looked at American marketing practices. The American pioneer scholar who most captured the attention of the Japanese was Arch Shaw, whose work has been the subject of no fewer than 27 historical studies.

Collegiate Education in Marketing

A development paralleling the marketing literature was higher education; indeed, those two are, perhaps, the most tangible residue of the origins of a marketing discipline. Once marketing in the academy was recognizable, its professors began to reflect on the first courses, programs, and people involved. A stream of biographical and autobiographical research during the 1950s and 1960s contributed in a tangential way to the history of university teaching, but several earlier publications focused specifically on identifying the origins of higher education in marketing.

The very first volume of the *Journal of Marketing* featured an essay by one of the discipline's first professors, James Hagerty, who began a tradition of pioneer teachers reflecting on their experiences. Hagerty (1936) identified several of the earliest American universities to offer marketing courses, including the University of Illinois (1902), New York University (1902), the Ohio State University (1905), the University of Pittsburgh (1909) and the Harvard Business School (1908), although he focused on early curriculum development at the Ohio State University, where he was a faculty member and later dean. Hagerty also pointed out the difficulty that had characterized efforts to identify early books about marketing; that marketing was originally thought about under names other than 'marketing.' For example, until 1916 the marketing course at OSU went by several different names including 'Mercantile Institutions.' Since there was little or no literature on the subject, teachers of that era relied on local businessmen and students' interviews of them. Hagerty added, however, that *The Distribution of Farm Products*, volume six, published by the US Industrial Commission in 1901, was one of the earliest studies used as a marketing textbook.

L.D.H. Weld, who began his teaching career at the University of Minnesota in 1912, was another pioneer teacher to publish his reminiscences in the *Journal of Marketing*. Weld (1941) credited the University of Michigan as the first to offer a course in marketing in 1902, followed by the Wharton School at the University of Pennsylvania (1904) and Ohio State (1905). According to Weld, the course at Wharton was the first to use the word 'marketing' in its title, but he questions whether or not the subject matter of some of those early courses bore much resemblance to marketing at that time.

In that same issue of the *Journal of Marketing*, Harold Maynard (1941a) wrote about marketing courses prior to 1910, with the specific objective of determining once and for all which university course was the 'first' to teach marketing. All the institutions cited above were also mentioned in Maynard's article. He dealt with the issue of course title by arguing that actual subject matter, rather than title, should establish when marketing was first taught in universities. Based on that position and his extensive research, Maynard determined that the first university marketing course was offered in 1902 at the University of Michigan and taught by Professor Edward David Jones. Maynard included as evidence the university calendar course description, and followed up by describing other marketing courses offered by Jones at Michigan in subsequent years. Interestingly, Maynard published an update later that year (1941b) in response to comments he received from other pioneer teachers. They led Maynard to acknowledge courses offered by George M. Fisk at the University of Illinois in 1902, one semester following Jones' course at Michigan, as well as previously ignored contributions (albeit in 1910) by Ralph Starr Butler at the University of Wisconsin. However, the status of being first remained with Jones and Michigan.

The University of Illinois' distinction, mentioned above, motivated one of its pioneering teachers, Simon Litman, to write about his early teaching experiences (1950). Litman actually began his career at the University of California and believed that west coast institutions had been overlooked in the efforts to identify original course offerings. He had taught a marketing course in 1902 at the University of California, although because it was offered in the second semester that year, could only claim a second place tie with the University of Illinois' offering that same year. Litman described in detail the content of his first marketing courses, including the lack of an established literature, his attempts to use local businessmen in class, and the topics about which students wrote in their papers.

Another study of origins warranting mention is Schultze's (1982), which examined the early development of university education in advertising. Schultze documented the role played by advertising clubs and the ad industry, a perspective largely ignored in retrospectives on higher education in the general field of marketing.

Most of the writings summarized above were echoed in an article by Bartels (1951) that anticipated his seminal book on the development of marketing thought in 1962. By that time, the debate about the origins of collegiate education in marketing appeared settled, at least as far as such development in the US was concerned. The history in other countries has largely been ignored. A study by Jones (1992) looked at Canadian university courses in marketing and credits Queen's University, the University of Western Ontario, and the University of Toronto as the pioneer institutions in that country with the earliest courses offered in 1919 at Queen's.

In a follow-up study, Cunningham and Jones (1997) examined the early development of collegiate education in international marketing at Queen's University in Canada and compared it with similar developments at the University of Illinois and the Harvard Business School. In addition to dating courses and writings on international marketing much earlier than previously believed, Cunningham and Jones discussed some of the differences between Canadian and American marketing education at that time – those differences being driven by Canada's relatively heavier reliance on international trade.

As previously mentioned, Bartels' research relied quite heavily on interviews with pioneer scholars still living at the time of his dissertation research and many of those interviews formed the basis of short biographical sketches included as an appendix to the various volumes of his book (1962, 1976, 1988). Numerous other biographical sketches and longer, biographical articles have since contributed to our understanding of the *thinkers* of marketing ideas over the last century. Converse (1959) wrote a collection of 25 short biographical sketches of early marketing scholars including the four nineteenth-century economists studied by Coolsen, discussed on p. 44 above. Each of the 25 sketches is only a page or two in length, but highlights the major contributions of its subject. Between 1956 and 1962 the *Journal of Marketing* featured 23 biographical sketches of 'Pioneers in Marketing' as the series was known. Several of those were later revised with additional information and two others added in a compilation by Wright and Dimsdale (1974). More recently, a series of article-length biographies has been published by Jones (1993a, 1993b, 1994, 1995, 1999) about pioneer marketing scholars, including H.C. Taylor, E.D. Jones, T.N. Beckman, G.B. Hotchkiss, and W.R. Davidson, some of whom were included in the shorter *JM* pieces. Hollander, whose career began in the pioneer era and continues to flourish, has published an autobiography (1995) that stands on its own as a contribution to the history of marketing thought. And finally, Shaw and Tamilia (2001) have written a biography/historiography on 'Robert Bartels and the History of Marketing Thought.' Taken together, this body of biographical research has contributed many insights into the influences, motivations, approaches, and ideas of the scholars who built the marketing discipline.

From the teachers, courses, and schools, we move to the larger picture of collegiate education. Following World War II, there was an explosion of attendance at universities in western countries that led to phenomenal growth in the number of institutions offering business programs, and the number and variety of marketing courses. Statistics on such growth in the US between 1930 and 1950 were included in Hardy's (1954) study of collegiate marketing education. This period was later described by Lazer and Shaw (1988) as one of 'expansion and diversification' when the academic quality of marketing education was open to question, course specialization was rampant, and many practitioners taught in universities on a part-time basis due to a lack of sufficient faculty members. That period was followed by one of 'reassessment and reorganization' with growth in graduate programs, increased emphasis on quantitative methods, social and behavioral sciences, and the addition of doctorally qualified faculty members (Lazer and Shaw, 1988). The period from 1960 to the late 1980s was described as one of 'differentiation and legitimization,' marked by the recommendations of the Ford and Carnegie Foundation reports of 1959. Of particular interest is the commentary by Lazer and Shaw on the negative reactions in universities to the founding of business schools at the turn of the century. This explains in part the characterization of the latter period as one of legitimization.

The period of expansion and diversification referred to above included some positive developments in the marketing discipline. As it grew, the ideas and concepts appearing in its articles, books, and university course offerings had matured into schools of thought.

Traditional Schools of Marketing Thought

By the 1920s, the study of marketing was becoming organized into three approaches. The functional approach focused on marketing activities – the basic work done in marketing. The commodity approach focused on goods (originally agricultural goods, hence the name 'commodity') classified according to common product characteristics. The institutional approach was concerned primarily with the various organizations that did the work of marketing. While they came to be known individually as schools of thought, it would have been rare as well as difficult for any comprehensive discussion of marketing at that time, say, in a principles text, to rely on just one of those basic approaches because of their interrelationships. Organizations (institutions) performed activities (functions) with goods (commodities). Hollander (1980) pointed out this problem in his attempt to describe early examples of the institutional approach. Nevertheless, historians have studied the origins and development of these three schools individually and collectively.

As part of a broader study of 12 schools of marketing thought, Sheth et al. (1988) examined the three traditional schools in some detail. While their attempts to categorize and meta-theoretically evaluate the schools detracted somewhat from the historical description, the latter provided sufficient material to understand the origin, essence, and major contributors to each school. In fact, their criteria for status as a school included association with a 'pioneer thinker' and with a 'significant number of scholars who have contributed toward the thought process' (Sheth et al., 1988: 19). Accordingly, the functional school was said to have originated with Arch Shaw's (1912) article titled 'Some Problems in Market Distribution' (lengthened and published as a book under the same title in 1915). This claim was reinforced by Converse, among others, whose 1945 survey of early twentieth-century marketing scholars also pointed to the functional approach as the 'most valuable concept' in marketing at that time. Other notable contributors included Weld, Vanderblue, Ryan, and numerous other scholars who alternately elaborated or condensed the list of basic marketing functions over the years, until the work of McGarry (1950) which served to bridge our thinking from the functional school to the four Ps of marketing management.

Jones (1997) recently examined Shaw's (1912) use of machine metaphors in the latter's seminal work on marketing functions, and offered some insights into Shaw's thinking about those functions. Shaw believed that marketing involved the application of motion to material. He felt that scientific study of marketing should focus on identifying the motions operating in the marketing system. Shaw identified five such motions, but insisted that the analysis was incomplete. Once it was completed, he suggested, the ultimate goal of the marketing system should be to identify and eliminate all nonessential motions in order to make the marketing machine operate more efficiently. Shaw's motions became known as the basic functions of marketing.

Usui's (2000) detailed history of Japanese scholarship in marketing focuses on the profound and lasting influence that Arch Shaw has had in that country, especially through his pioneering work on marketing functions. Both Jones (1997) and Usui also pointed to the influence of Scientific Management on Shaw's work in this area.

Hunt and Goolsby (1988) used a life-cycle metaphor to study the history of the functional approach, suggesting that it survived a contest with the commodity and institutional schools, growing and outnumbering the latter in applications between 1920 and 1940, then reaching maturity with McGarry's analysis in 1950. Its decline began with McCarthy's four Ps and the managerial approach that followed the Gordon and Howell report in 1959. Their conclusion was that the functional approach is dead, swept away in the dustbin of history.

Sheth et al. (1988) dated the origin of the commodity school to a classification by C.C. Parlin in 1912, although most historians would probably cite Copeland's (1923) article in the *Harvard Business Review*, which proposed the now familiar convenience-shopping-specialty goods classification. Copeland himself credited Parlin for the convenience and shopping goods categories. Just as the functional school had generated numerous lists of different functions, the commodity school generated a number of variations of the original three classes and a plethora of methods for assigning goods to the various classes. Long after the functional school faded away, discussions of good classifications continued to the present day. Nevertheless, Zinn and Johnson (1990) wondered whether the commodity approach was 'obsolete,' citing numerous papers during the 1970s that had proclaimed it dead. They carried out a content analysis of the *Journal of Marketing* (1936–1989) and AMA Proceedings (1957–1989), and determined that the commodity approach had exhibited a cyclical adoption rate, that with each cycle different commodities were studied, and that more recent articles have attempted to develop the theoretical side of commodity classification systems.

According to Sheth et al., the institutional school focused on organizations in marketing channels and how they performed functions to achieve channel efficiency. It originated with L.D.H. Weld's book *The Marketing of Farm Products* (1916), followed by important contributions from Butler (1923), Breyer (1934), Converse and Huegy (1940), and Duddy and Revzan (1947). As with most marketing thought during the first half of the twentieth century, institutionalists relied on ideas from economics to develop their thinking. During the 1970s an influx of behavioral science ideas helped change institutionalism into what Sheth et al. (1988) called the organizational dynamics school of thought, which is examined later in this section.

Hollander's 1980 study of early institutional work was cited previously in connection with the problems historians have had in differentiating between functional, commodity, and institutional approaches. Hollander also pointed out that the traditional approaches were not mutually exclusive. The differences between them were not as obvious or substantial as, say, the differences between economic schools of thought. It is relatively easy to find applications of different traditional approaches in a single scholar's work and Hollander cited Weld, credited by Sheth et al. (1988) with originating the institutional approach, in that connection. It is also not uncommon to find one pioneer's work categorized as one approach by some historians, and a different approach by others. With the institutional approach, the root of the problem is multiple definitions. Institutionalism is almost always said to deal with channel intermediaries, although some believe the discussion must involve the struggle by various intermediaries to survive. Some scholars even define marketing institutionalism in terms of economic institutionalism, which is based on philosophy and methodology as much as on subject matter. Economic institutionalism typically held a critical view of the economic system, which was not always the case for marketing institutionalists. Ultimately, Hollander advocated a definition of institutionalism based on the writings of the nineteenth-century economist Amassa Walker, summarized as the 'description and prescription of methods for organizing marketing agencies and practices' (Hollander, 1980: 46).

Although not generally considered one of the traditional schools in marketing, another body of ideas emerged during the 1930s with a focus on the geographic or spatial gaps between buyers and sellers. This approach is associated with what Sheth et al. (1988) labeled the regional school. Its founders are E.T. Grether and William Reilly, whose 1931 book *Law of Retail Gravitation* was most responsible for the initial interest in the regional approach. Brown stated that Reilly's book 'ranks among the classics of marketing thought' (Brown, 1994: 117). Babin et al. (1994) noted that the earliest contributions to the regional school coincided with great technological improvements in the transportation infrastructure in North America. They went on to trace the connections between Reilly's seminal work and that of Converse in the 1940s and Huff in the 1960s, concluding that those early writings were conceptually simple, yet provided a scientifically rigorous framework for studying the attraction of trade centers through space and time. But it was Grether, who used geographic concepts to develop a fairly broad perspective of interregional trade, who is most identified with the approach (Sheth et al., 1988).

Other Ideas and Concepts

There are several topics relevant to the first half of the twentieth century that do not fall neatly into the major themes used in this section. Included is research that examined influences from Scientific Management on marketing ideas, changing definitions of the term marketing, and early developments in consumer/buyer behavior theory.

In connection with previously cited work by Jones and Monieson (1990) and Usui (2000), mention was made of the influence of the pioneers of Scientific Management, such as Taylor (1911) and Gilbreth (1911), on Arch Shaw's (1912) ideas about marketing functions. It is surprising there hasn't been more historical study of the influence of Scientific Management. One such history by LaLonde and Morrison (1967), focused on the period from World War I to 1930 and described applications of Scientific Management to sales force management by such writers as Lyon (1926) and Hoyt (1912), and applications to marketing more generally by Shaw (1912) and White (1927). An interesting point made by LaLonde and Morrison was that in 1924 the *Bulletin of the Taylor Society* cited the J. Walter Thompson Company as the first to apply the concept of market segmentation. While the historical claim is debatable, it is interesting that efficiency experts regarded segmentation as an application of Scientific Management.

While many marketing historians have commented on the problems associated with early terminology and meaning, one study has traced the definition of marketing as presented in principles textbooks from 1900 to 1980. Lichtenthal and Beik (1984) identified five distinct periods associated with changes in that definition over 80 years. Early periods saw marketing defined informally, as part of economic production, or in terms of functions as marketing developed into a discipline separate from economics. Not surprisingly, they found that definitions shifted towards a marketing management orientation beginning with Alderson's 1957 book, *Marketing Behavior and Executive Action.*

A subdiscipline of marketing with a curious history is consumer behavior. Neoclassical consumer theory never seemed very useful to marketing practitioners and, therefore, marketing academics pretty much ignored it. But neither did they develop many ideas of their own during the early twentieth century. In fact, Sheth and Gross (1988) listed no concepts before 1930 in their study of the parallel developments of the marketing discipline and consumer behavior. During the 1930s, the most interesting and potentially relevant consumer theory was developed by home economists, most of whom were women, and it is in that area that we find a lone historical voice for the contributions of women to marketing thought (Zuckerman and Carsky, 1990). In particular, Zuckerman and Carsky have documented the contributions of Hazel Kyrk (1929), Elizabeth Hoyt (1928), and Christine Frederick (1923) as pioneers in educating consumers and in providing some understanding of consumers to marketers.

Despite some important works on consumer theory by home economists during the 1930s, as marketing grew apart from economics, buyer behavior received less and less attention from both groups with a resulting lack of much focus on consumer behavior until the formation of the Association for Consumer Research in the early 1970s. The events of that period, especially those between 1930 and 1950, were described by Mason (1994), who focused on the causes of tension between marketing practitioners, marketing academics, and economic theorists during that period.

Chronologically as well as substantively, those developments constituted a bridge with the modern marketing management era that was marked by the publication of Wroe Alderson's *Marketing Behavior and Executive Action* in 1957. Among the many other fields of knowledge from which Alderson borrowed, the behavioral sciences were the most important.

MARKETING MANAGEMENT ERA: POST 1957

This section begins by examining historical analyses of the work of Wroe Alderson who pioneered the development of marketing management. Alderson's work focused on developing a theory of the firm that would enable marketing executives to make better decisions. Thus Alderson moved the discipline from a macro functions-institutions-commodities framework to a micro marketing management paradigm. Before Alderson, marketing academics were primarily concerned with description and classification. Alderson developed marketing theory in his own writings, but he also played a major role in stimulating others to do theoretical work by organizing his renowned Marketing Theory Seminars.

Alderson's 'school' of functionalism signaled the beginning of a multidisciplinary movement in marketing that led to several new schools of thought. In this section we also review historical studies of those developments. Part of that history includes the formation of new associations and journals as well as milestones celebrated by some of the original institutions in the marketing discipline. Those have also received historical attention and are discussed in this section. Finally, this section ends with an examination of research into the history of the marketing concept.

Wroe Alderson and Functionalism

In his comments about Wroe Alderson's *Marketing Behavior and Executive Action*, Bartels observed 'with one sweeping stroke [Alderson] created a new pattern for considering marketing management' (1988: 178). Together with *Dynamic Marketing Behavior* in 1965, these two books represent the fullest exposition of what Alderson called his 'functionalist theory' of marketing. Sheth et al. (1988)

admitted that, while they included functionalism as one of their *schools* of marketing thought, it was largely the result of a single scholar's work. Similarly, Barksdale (1980) noted that, while Alderson had many followers, he did not establish a tradition or school of scholars to continue his work. As we discuss below, Alderson was widely recognized as the leading marketing thinker of his time. Yet curiously, other writers pursued few of Alderson's ideas after his death in 1965. The general consensus seems to be that Alderson's work was unfinished, and only he could have finished it.

As Sheth et al. (1988) pointed out, functionalism is not easy to summarize. It should not be confused with the functional approach mentioned several times earlier in this chapter. The latter was simply concerned with identifying and classifying the basic activities or work performed in marketing. *Functionalism* was based on a systems approach to the study of marketing and developed around three core concepts: organized behavior systems, heterogeneous markets, and a unique concept Alderson termed 'transvections' (1965). A transvection is a set of sequential transactions from the original seller of raw materials, through intermediate purchases and sales, to the final buyer of a finished product. The transvection concept parallels a channel of distribution. Whereas a channel represents structure and is analogous to the banks of a river, a transvection represents process and is analogous to the flowing water.

Alderson was much more concerned with developing theory than had been scholars working in the traditional schools of thought. *Dynamic Marketing Behavior* included 150 hypotheses in one appendix, titled 'Research Agenda for Functionalism.' Unfortunately, few of those hypotheses have been tested and little was ever done to further develop Alderson's theory subsequent to his untimely death in 1965. The most common reason for that given by those who have studied Alderson's work is that his writings were difficult to comprehend. While he was widely recognized as a brilliant and creative thinker, his writing has been criticized for its confusing terminology (Sheth et al., 1988), a lack of close reasoning, and poor development of concepts (Barksdale, 1980). In fact, many of the historical reflections on Alderson's work have consisted of attempts to interpret various aspects of his theory.

Barksdale, for example, presented a detailed summary of Alderson's core concepts, mentioned above, although he focused on the narrower concept of 'sorting functions' rather than 'transvections.' He singled out the hypotheses proposed in *Dynamic Marketing Behavior* as a goldmine for Ph.D. students searching for dissertation topics, and lamented the lack of empirical work on them since their initial publication in 1965. Monieson and Shapiro (1980) focused on biological and evolutionary dimensions of Alderson's writing in order to clarify ideas he had borrowed from the life sciences and sociological thought. In the latter they singled out writings by Talcott Parsons in social systems theory and C. West Churchman in general systems theory, and then speculated about how Alderson might have used them to develop his general theory of marketing. Monieson and Shapiro concluded that, 'given Alderson's prodigious and eclectic reading habits, contemporary life science thought and research findings would almost certainly have been incorporated into a re-fashioned Alderson theory of marketing behavior' (1980: 7). Similarly, Rethans (1979) examined more recent work in general systems theory and used it to update Alderson's theory of functionalism.

Dawson and Wales (1979) looked at Alderson's writings in *Cost and Profit Outlook,* which was the bulletin published from 1947 until 1958 by Alderson's consulting firm. Their focus was on Alderson's ideas about consumer motivation, carefully documenting examples from 22 different issues of the bulletin. Like other historians of marketing thought, they concluded that little of Alderson's work is now recognized and that almost none of his concepts appear in leading principles texts. Lusch (1980) also examined issues of *Cost and Profit Outlook* to develop a profile of how Alderson and his partner, Robert Sessions, viewed the role of theory in marketing practice. A brief history of the Alderson & Sessions consulting firm was given, followed by an analysis of the bulletin's editorial content. It was clear Alderson believed that theory should be communicated to managers, that while marketing consultants and marketing scientists had different purposes it was in the best interests of consultants to foster the development of theory, and, more generally, the idea that theory and practice go together hand in hand (Lusch, 1980).

Much has been made of Alderson's efforts to organize and stimulate other scholars to develop marketing theory. Barksdale (1980) suggested that Alderson's efforts in this connection might have been more important than his own theoretical contributions. Dawson and Wales (1979: 222) agreed, writing 'one of the greatest contributions made by Wroe Alderson to the field of marketing theory was his organization of and leadership in the Marketing Theory Seminars.' These unusual and exclusive conferences were held from 1951 until 1963, first at the University of Colorado and later alternating between Colorado and the University of Vermont. As Sheth et al. described them,

> These 'invitation only' seminars were used by Alderson to both encourage those present to think of marketing in conceptual ways and develop marketing theory, and also to develop and explain the functionalist approach to marketing. By his own powerful intellect and his dominating personality, he was clearly 'in charge' of these seminars and put his stamp on the introduction of a formal theory approach to marketing science. (1988: 86)

Despite their reputation, or perhaps because of it, the theory seminars suffered the same posthumous fate as Alderson's unfinished theoretical work. It wasn't until 1979 that the profile of marketing theory was renewed in the Marketing Theory Conferences, now named the AMA Winter Educators' Conference.

Clearly, historians believe that marketing scholars have ignored Alderson and his functionalist ideas, and we have paid a considerable intellectual price for this ignorance. However, there is ongoing interest in Alderson's work by marketing historians, and that pursuit may yet rekindle a broader interest in some of those ideas.

Functionalism is one the post-traditional 'schools,' but is treated separately here because of the relatively greater interest in it by marketing historians. Along with the institutionalism of Breyer (1934), Duddy and Revson (1947), and Vaile, Grether and Cox (1952), Alderson's (1957, 1965) functionalism has evolved into the marketing systems school of thought. For example, Savitt (1990) elaborated on the 'systemic' ideas found in textbooks by Fred Clark (1922, 1932), Ralph Breyer (1934), Duddy and Revzan (1947), and Vaile, Grether and Cox (1952). These ideas clearly influenced Alderson's thinking about marketing systems. Savitt traced several propositions, which he considered to be antecedents to both modern macromarketing thought and systems analysis through the books listed above. All of them addressed such questions as: why society requires a marketing system? how the system operates? environmental and institutional factors affecting marketing, and the boundaries between marketing and other social institutions – harkening back to similar discussions by ancient and medieval scholars. These ideas were transmitted from Alderson to several of his students, such as Fisk (1967) and Dixon (1967).

The remainder of this section relies heavily on Sheth et al. (1988). In addition to the previously discussed schools of thought, Sheth et al. identified several others that emerged during or following Alderson's work. Along with marketing systems, two other schools were linked directly to Alderson's functionalism: marketing management, and social exchange.

Modern Schools of Marketing Thought

The *managerial school* emerged during the late 1950s and was represented in books such as Alderson's *Marketing Behavior and Executive Action* (1957), Howard's *Marketing Management* (1957), Kelley and Lazer's *Managerial Marketing: Perspectives and Viewpoints* (1958), and McCarthy's *Basic Marketing: A Managerial Approach.* (1960) Ideas such as the marketing concept, marketing myopia, marketing mix, and market segmentation, were popularized in a series of influential articles by scholars such as Borden (1964), Keith (1960), Levitt (1960), and McKitterick (1957), and continue to be popular in textbooks today. One idea, the marketing concept, has more recently been the subject of intense, critical analysis by marketing historians, and that research is reviewed in a separate section below. Sheth et al. (1988) described the managerial school as the most comprehensive and influential in the discipline, a status that continues today. It has had a tremendous influence, not only in the classroom, but in the profession as well.

Next to the managerial school, the greatest impact on the discipline has been by the *consumer/buyer behavior school.* If economic thinking and approaches dominated the first half of the twentieth century, then the last half was dominated by ideas from the behavioral sciences. In contrast to functionalism, the buyer behavior school is not associated with any one dominant scholar, such as Alderson, and has benefited from ideas developed by numerous scholars in many different disciplines outside of marketing. Sheth et al. (1988) identified three areas of research that emerged during the 1950s which laid the foundation for the buyer behavior school: motivation research, social determinants of consumer behavior, and household decision-making. During the 1960s there was growing interest in brand loyalty behavior and a new research tradition based on laboratory experiments and experimental design. Comprehensive theories (Engel, Kollat & Blackwell, 1968; Howard & Sheth, 1969) of consumer/buyer behavior also gained popularity during this period. Research and interest in consumer/buyer behavior experienced phenomenal growth during the 1970s. This was stimulated by two important developments: the formation in 1970 of the Association for Consumer Research, and the publication of the *Journal of Consumer Research* beginning in 1974. Many of these developments were also described by Mittelstaedt (1990), who ascribed the status of 'subdiscipline' to consumer behavior.

While critics of the marketing process have long written about the imbalance of power between buyers and sellers and about marketing malpractices, Sheth et al. (1988) suggest it is only since the 1960s that marketing scholars have participated in that discussion. They label this the *activist school* of marketing thought. Similar concerns about the role of business in society gave rise to the *macromarketing school,* which has focused on the role and impact of marketing activities on society and *vice versa.* Of course, a macro focus on marketing existed, certainly in the traditional schools and even in the marketing ideas of earlier economists. Instititionalists were interested in how channels could be structured more efficiently for the ultimate benefit of consumers. During the 1970s a critical mass of research began to look at channels of distribution again, this time with a focus on the goals and needs of channel members. This *organizational dynamics school* added social psychological concepts such as 'power,' 'conflict,' and 'cooperation' to the discussion.

According to Sheth et al. (1988), books written by Holloway and Hancock (1964) and by Fisk (1967) signaled a new level of interest in macromarketing, and were accompanied by conferences beginning in the 1970s under the leadership of Charles Slater, and the publication of the *Journal of Macromarketing,* starting in 1981.

One last school of thought, according to Sheth et al., is also associated with Alderson, based on his 1965 Law of Exchange. The so-called *social exchange school* focuses on exchange as the fundamental concept of marketing. Some contributors to this line of research included Kotler and Bagozzi during the 1970s and Hunt during the 1980s (Sheth et al., 1988), along with critics of social exchange, such as Shaw and Dixon (1980).

Continuing Development of the Marketing Literature

In the previous section we mentioned the formation of the Association for Consumer Research and the founding of new journals, such as the *Journal of Consumer Research* and *Journal of Macromarketing,* connected with some of the modern schools of thought. Other scholarly organizations have formed in the past few decades, such as the Academy of Marketing Science, and there are too many new journals to list here. Indeed, the marketing literature has grown so much in size and complexity, including health care marketing, sports marketing, and non-profit marketing, that the sort of sweeping review conducted by Bartels in the 1960s may no longer be possible. The 1988 edition of Bartels' *History of Marketing Thought* did not even attempt to update the vast number of new textbooks published since the previous edition of 1976.

Published since 1936, the *Journal of Marketing (JM)* is the oldest surviving academic periodical published about general marketing (in fact, the *Journal of Retailing* precedes *JM* by some 20 years). In 1976 the *JM* published a 40-year retrospective on its content by analyzing the number of articles over time in 12 subject categories (Grether, 1976). The 'highest continuing interest' was in marketing research, marketing mix variables, and marketing management. This reflected the dominant influence of the managerial school. Areas of 'medium and relatively stable interest' included consumer behavior, the role of government, marketing institutions, marketing theory, international marketing, and the role of marketing in society. In this grouping we see the rising interest that soon became associated with schools of thought such as consumer behavior and macromarketing. (Remember as well that Grether's retrospective was published on the 40th anniversary of *JM*, just two years after the *Journal of Consumer Research* and four years before the *Journal of Macromarketing* began publication.) Areas of 'lowest relative interest' in 1976 were marketing education, industry studies, and marketing history. One of these, marketing education, now claims its own specialized journal and another, marketing history, has become a regular section in the *Journal of Macromarketing,* as well as the subject of a new online journal that began publication in 2001. It is noteworthy that marketing history was included among the 12 categories in Grether's 1976 review. Although the subject had disappeared from *JM*'s pages by 1976, marketing history had been a theme for a substantial number of articles published during the first two decades of the Journal's history.

Grether also commented about surveys of *JM*'s readers carried out during the 1950s and 1970s. The first survey in 1956 left the impression that the *JM* was a 'stodgy, long-hair booklet written by impractical scholars, in terminology not understood by laymen, containing boring articles arranged in a way which makes them hard to find' (1976: 68). This was an image that became hard to shake. A subsequent survey in the 1970s reinforced the image as too academic, even for the academic readers!

In 1996 *JM* celebrated its 60th anniversary with a history of its editorial orientation and literary content (Kerin, 1996). This retrospective included insights into the tensions between the predecessors of the AMA and the *JM.* It also elaborated on the ideals and goals of the Journal, as well as the lack of direction *JM* seemed to experience during the 1950s. Further shifts in editorial policy occurred to make the *JM* more scholarly after 1979 and to narrow its scope so that articles dealing with methods and models were directed to its sister periodical, the *Journal of Marketing Research.* During this period, the *JM* transformed itself into a scholarly professional journal, and various measures of impact suggest that its influence and quality were growing.

In his analysis of the literary history of the *JM,* Kerin developed themes for each of its six decades, which added insights to the frequency counts of earlier retrospectives. The changing themes again reflected the shift during the 1960s to managerial concerns, and during the 1970s to buyer behavior. Subsequent to those influences, Kerin described the period 1976–1985 as one which viewed marketing as a decision science. Not surprisingly, practitioner authorship had fallen to less than 1% by 1982, from the 42% reported in Applebaum's original analysis in 1947. Finally, for the period 1986–1995, Kerin described the content of the *JM* as reflecting marketing as an integrative science. Average article length had grown considerably; the number of references per article had increased by 600% over those of the 1970s. These changes reflected attempts to integrate a larger literature. In addition, a quarter of the articles published in this last period featured integrative conceptual frameworks and an interdisciplinary approach. In his concluding comments, Kerin observed that more than 3000 articles were published during the *JM*'s 60-year history, making it an indispensable archive for those wishing to track developments and changes in marketing thought over time.

The Standard Chronology: Production–Sales–Marketing Concept Eras

One historical hypothesis has come to be cynically known by marketing historians as the 'standard chronology.' The standard chronology hypothesizes that marketing went through a sequence of three eras, from a production orientation to a sales orientation to the marketing orientation/concept. In 1960, Keith proposed that American business was undergoing a revolution in the way it treated customers. He called it the 'marketing oriented era' and its core characteristics have been immortalized in the 'marketing concept.' According to Keith, this marketing oriented era had been preceded, first, by a production era between 1870 and 1930 when businesses supposedly had to focus on production because of excessive demand for most consumer products. This was followed by a sales era, beginning around 1930, when a collapse in consumer demand forced businesses to emphasize selling in order to 'dispose of all the products we make at a favorable price' (Keith, 1960: 36). This inherently historical hypothesis of production–sales–marketing eras was based on evidence from a single company (Pillsbury) for which its author was then Executive Vice-President. Even the case for Pillsbury was based solely on Keith's personal recollections and ignored the fact that it was a conservative company that was engaged primarily in a commodity business. It also ignored the tremendous amount of consumer marketing that its leading (and much more successful) competitor, Washburn-Crosby (later General Mills), had practiced for 30 or 40 years. Surprisingly, Keith's chronology has become accepted wisdom in almost every principles textbook today. That status persists in spite of thorough and convincing historical scholarship that contradicts it.

One of those critics, Hollander (1986), began by carefully explaining the implications of the ordering and timing of the three eras for assumptions about the levels and types of consumer demand that would have necessarily accompanied each era. He also listed the sorts of marketing activities that would not have existed prior to the marketing era if businesses had not embraced the marketing concept prior to that period in time. Hollander presented economic statistics that clearly demonstrated that the US market absorbed a substantial and increasing amount of discretionary purchases between 1900 and 1941, including many new products and product modifications. He recounted well-known facts about developments in marketing education and the profession to demonstrate the sheer number and magnitude of marketing activities and institutions there must have been well before 1950 when the marketing era supposedly began. Examples of marketing activities, such as product planning to meet customer preferences, integration of promotional efforts, customer service, merchandising functions, and employment of a profit criterion, were detailed for firms such as Eastman Kodak, John Deere, General Electric, Washburn-Crosby (General Mills), and Proctor & Gamble, all of which suggested a marketing orientation. Statistics on the number of traveling salesmen in the US during the 1880s indicated the way in which firms reached out to their customers and competed for business. Examples of market research as early as 1911 were reported, and many large companies were doing an extensive amount of such research by the 1930s. Hollander identified 14 companies that carried out large-scale consumer surveys at that time. Evidence of internal coordination of marketing activities was given for DuPont and General Electric as well as in the reports of the Taylor Society. The simplification movement initiated by the Hoover government during World War I was used as evidence of the product diversification and market segmentation which simplification was designed to 'correct.' Product diversification and market segmentation, however, are hallmarks of the marketing concept. Hollander then drew on accounting history to demonstrate clearly a profit orientation that existed at least as early as 1940, and cited the views of department store magnate, E.A. Filene, on profit-based pricing practices used in 1927. Hollander's historical analysis leaves no doubt that sales era tactics and marketing era activities have been practiced and thought about at least as long as those associated with the production era.

Fullerton's 1988 study came to similar conclusions by focusing on the case for, and against, a production era. His research uncovered evidence for Britain, Germany, and the US that confirmed that serious and sophisticated marketing is not a recent phenomenon, as suggested by the 'myth of the production era,' nor was it exclusive to America. Fullerton cited numerous examples of producers' involvement with marketing mix strategies for the period 1870 to 1930 as well as examples of marketing education that developed in Germany and the US during the 1890s. His conclusion was that there was no production era, and the development of modern marketing was well under way by the time the Great Depression was supposed to have ushered in the sales era.

At the beginning of this chapter we suggested that the most obvious justification for history is that people who don't know theirs are doomed to repeat past mistakes. There is no better example of this than the persistence of this infamous, misleading doctrine. Hollander included in his study a convenience sample of 25 general marketing textbooks from the mid-1980s that adhered to the 'standard chronology.' Surprisingly, and disappointingly, that situation has changed little since the publication of the two historical studies described above.

Looking Back to See Ahead: Future Research on the Past

It has been said that every generation re-writes history. That being the case, future marketing historians will continue to document and argue ideas about marketing behavior back to antiquity. They will continue to explore the connections between early scholarship in marketing, its parent discipline of economics, and its sister discipline of management. They will continue to trace their intellectual genealogy and interpret the achievements of their teachers and grand-teachers. And a discipline that has grown more tolerant during the past 20 years of its history being written will hopefully continue to welcome this work.

Since the early 1980s there has been a new level of interest in historical research in marketing. It has helped create what Hollander and Rassuli (1993) call the 'New' marketing history (p. xv). Beginning in 1983, under the leadership of Stanley Hollander and with the support of Michigan State University, a marketing history conference has been held biennially in North America with a steadily increasing level of participation from scholars around the globe. Proceedings have been published for all 10 conferences to date including a total of 313 papers.* An Association for Historical Research in Marketing has been formed as a support structure for CHARM (Conference on Historical Analysis & Research in Marketing), and to promote interest and research in marketing history and the history of marketing thought. Other marketing history conferences have been organized and two were held at the University of Reading in the UK in 1991 and 1993. Both the Academy of Marketing Science and American Marketing Association held conferences in 1988 where marketing history was a major theme. And the Association for Consumer Research hosted a conference in 1985 on historical perspectives in consumer research. The *Journal of the Academy of Marketing Science, Journal of Retailing,* and *Journal of Public Relations* have all published special issues focusing on marketing history. Since 1994, the *Journal of Macromarketing,* which has always been hospitable to historical research, has featured a regular section on historical research and, as of the summer of 2001, had published 64 marketing history articles, commentaries, and reviews. And, an online journal titled the *Journal of Marketing History* has recently been established. The 'new' marketing history has sought to build on the tradition of history developed during the early decades of marketing scholarship, but it has primarily focused on marketing history and only secondarily on the history of marketing thought.

The opening section of this chapter started with Hollander's observation about the symbiotic relationship between marketing thought and marketing practice. Hollander has gone even further.

> The long-standing distinction between economic history and the history of economic thought provides a model for a similar dichotomy in marketing. Perhaps the two types of histories in economics is not a perfect model for us … I have come to really wonder why we want to teach our doctoral students the history of marketing thought without teaching them the history of marketing. (1980: 45–6)

Hollander's (1986) own historical analysis of the standard chronology, discussed in the previous section, serves as a model for integrating the two. He weaves together evidence of both the ideas and practice of modern marketing. We will write better history of marketing thought if we consider the work of both marketing scholars and marketing practitioners.

Hollander also raises the issue of doctoral seminars on the history of marketing thought. Once a fairly common requirement in Ph.D. programs in North America, that is no longer the case. There are only a few universities that regularly offer its doctoral students a full course in the subject. Some include a session or two, but it is embarrassing how little exposure doctoral students receive to what should be an indispensable aspect of graduate education in any discipline. More needs to be done about this.

Very little research has been written about the role of women in the development of marketing thought. The sad truth is that most business teachers during the early twentieth century were male, but there have been exceptions. Zuckerman and Carsky (1990) looked in an unconventional place – home economics – to find their women pioneer marketing scholars. Perhaps we need to look for more such sources.

Very few historical studies have been made of marketing thought outside the US. We now know some of that history for Canada, Japan, and Germany. Hollander (1998) recently cited a rich collection of interesting marketing books published in England during the 1920s, 1930s, and 1940s. The first university business program in the British Empire was started at the University of Birmingham in 1901 when there still were only a handful in the US. But

* This is a thorough, but not exhaustive, review. All but a handful of conference proceedings papers are omitted.

we know little more about the development of marketing thought in England. More historical research should be done on marketing thought outside the US.

As discussed in an earlier section, even in his last, (1988), edition Bartels virtually ignored the burgeoning literature in the field of consumer behavior. One reviewer of Sheth et al.'s 1988 book lamented the lack of detail and scope in the discussion about the consumer behavior school (Johnson, 1990). The same could be said of their discussion of the managerial school of marketing thought. Other historians have examined the development of particular ideas or concepts, but no one has attempted a careful and comprehensive historical analysis. These two bodies of research, marketing management and consumer behavior, have dominated the literature for the past 30 or 40 years, yet there has been little historical study of that development.

There should be more use of primary source materials in our historical research, and they are becoming available in surprising quantities. Most university archives collect, as a matter of policy, the papers of important faculty members. As a consequence there are often considerable collections of personal papers that have been donated to universities by their retired or deceased marketing professors, providing important source materials for biographical research. The contents of these collections range from curriculum vitae to unpublished autobiographies, diaries, lecture notes, unpublished papers, and correspondence. Typically, such collections are held closed for a certain period of time, a waiting period to provide some measure of security and privacy, before opening them to researchers. Many such collections are now open to researchers and the list of available collections reads like a who's who of pioneer marketing scholars. Jones (1998) recently summarized the contents of several such collections.

Ultimately, for almost any marketing idea in which the reader is interested, there is a history. Whatever your subject of interest, we heartily encourage you to investigate its history. History provides insights not found in other forms of analysis. It will help you appreciate the subject's complexity. It will teach you to recognize changes and consistencies in its meaning over time. It will add a new dimension to your understanding of the issues. And we suspect you will find the task interesting and enjoyable. All research should be such fun!

References

Agnew, Hugh E. (1941) The History of the American Marketing Association. *Journal of Marketing*, 5 (4), 374–9.

Alderson, W. (1965) *Dynamic Marketing Behavior.* Homewood, Ill.: Richard D. Irwin.

Alderson, W. (1965) (1957) *Marketing Behavior and Executive Action.* Homewood, Ill.: Richard D. Irwin, Inc.

Applebaum, W. (1947) The *Journal of Marketing:* the first ten years. *Journal of Marketing*, 11 (4), 355–63.

——— (1952) The *Journal of Marketing:* postwar. *Journal of Marketing,* 16 (January), 294–300.

Babin, Barry J., Boles, James S. & Babin, Laurie (1994) The development of spatial theory in retailing and its contribution to marketing thought and marketing science. In *Research in Marketing: Explorations in the History of Marketing*, edited by Ronald A. Fullerton. Greenwich: JAI Press, pp. 103–16.

Barksdale, H.C. (1980) Wroe Alderson's contributions to marketing theory. In *Theoretical Developments in Marketing*, edited by Charles W. Lamb & Patrick M. Dunne, Chicago: AMA, pp. 1–3.

Bartels, Robert (1951) Influences on the development of marketing thought, 1900–1923. *Journal of Marketing*, 16 (July), 1–17.

——— (1962) *The Development of Marketing Thought.* Homewood Ill.: Richard D. Irwin.

——— (1974) The identity crisis in marketing. *Journal of Marketing*, 38 (October), 73–6.

——— (1976) *The History of Marketing Thought*, 2nd edn. Columbus: Grid.

——— (1983) Is marketing defaulting its responsibilities. *Journal of Marketing*, 47 (Fall), 32–5.

——— (1986) Marketing: management technology or social process at the twenty-first century? In *Marketing Management Technology as a Social Process,* edited by George Fisk. New York: Praeger, pp. 30–42.

——— (1988) *The History of Marketing Thought*, 3rd edn. Columbus: Publishing Horizons.

Bass, F.M., King, C.W. & Pessemier, E.A. (1968) *Application of the Sciences in Marketing Management.* New York: John Wiley and Sons.

Berkman, Harold W. (1992) Twenty years of the journal. *Journal of the Academy of Marketing Science*, 20 (4), 299–300.

Borden, Neil H. (1964) The concept of the marketing mix. *Journal of Advertising Research*, 4 (June), 2–7.

Breyer, R.F. (1931) *Commodity Marketing.* New York: McGraw-Hill Book Co.

——— (1934) *The Marketing Institution.* New York: McGraw-Hill Book Co.

Brown, E., Jr. (1925) *Marketing.* New York: Harper & Row.

Brown, Stephen (1994) Reilly's Law of Retail Gravitation: what goes round, comes around. In *Research in Marketing: Explorations in the History of Marketing*, edited by Ronald A. Fullerton, Greenwich: JAI Press, pp. 117–47.

Brown, Stephen, Hirschman, Elizabeth & Maclaren, Pauline (2001) Always historicize! Researching marketing history in a post-historical epoch. *Marketing Theory,* 1 (1), 49–90.

Bussiere, David (2000) Evidence of a marketing periodic literature within the American Economic Association: 1895–1936. *Journal of Macromarketing*, 20 (December), 137–43.

Butler, Ralph Starr (1923) *Marketing and Merchandising.* New York: Alexander Hamilton Institute.

Buzzell, R.D. (1964) *Marketing: An Introductory Analysis.* New York: McGraw-Hill Co.

Cassels, J.M. (1936) The significance of early economic thought on marketing. *Journal of Marketing*, 1 (October), 129–33.

Cherington, Paul T. (1920) *The Elements of Marketing.* New York: Macmillan Co.

Clark, Fred (1922) *Principles of Marketing.* New York: Macmillan Co., 2nd edn 1932, 3rd edn 1942 with Carrie P. Clark; rev. edn 1962 by R.D. Tousley, Eugene Clark & F.E. Clark.

Comish, N.H. (1935) *Marketing Manufactured Goods.* Boston, MA: Stratford Co.

Converse, Paul D. (1921) *Marketing: Methods and Policies.* New York: Prentice-Hall.

——— (1930) *Elements of Marketing.* New York: Prentice-Hall, Inc. Rev. edn 1935 with H.W.Huegy; 2nd edn 1940.

——— (1933) The first decade of marketing literature. *NATMA Bulletin Supplement,* (November), 1–4.

——— (1945) The development of the science of marketing – an exploratory survey. *Journal of Marketing*, 10 (July) 14–23.

——— (1959) *The Beginnings of Marketing Thought in the United States.* Texas: Bureau of Business Research, University of Texas.

Coolsen, Frank (1947) Pioneers in the development of advertising. *Journal of Marketing*, 12 (July), 80–6.

——— (1958) Marketing ideas of selected empirical liberal economists 1870 – 1900. Doctoral Dissertation, Urbana: University of Illinois.

——— (1960) *Marketing Thought in the United States in the Late Nineteenth Century.* Texas: Texas Technical Press.

Cox, Reavis & Wroe Alderson (eds) (1950) *Theory in Marketing.* Chicago: Richard D. Irwin.

Cox, Reavis, Goodman, Charles S. & Fichandler, Thomas C. (1965) *Distribution in a High-Level Economy.* Englewood Cliffs, NJ: Prentice-Hall.

Cunningham, Peggy & Jones, D.G. Brian (1997) Early development of collegiate education in international marketing. *Journal of International Marketing*, 5, 87–102.

Dawson, Lyndon & Wales, Hugh G. (1979) Consumer motivation theory in historical perspective: an Aldersonian view. In *Conceptual and Theoretical Developments in Marketing*, edited by O.C. Ferrell, Stephen W. Brown & Charles W. Lamb, Chicago: AMA, pp. 210–22.

Day, R.L. (ed.) (1964) *Marketing Models – Quantitative and Behavioral.* Scranton, PA: International Textbooks.

Dixon, Donald F. (1967) A social systems approach to marketing. *Social Science Quarterly,* (September), 164–73.

——— (1978) The origins of macro-marketing thought. In *Macromarketing: New Steps on the Learning Curve,* edited by George Fisk & Robert W. Nason. Boulder: University of Colorado, Business Research Division, pp. 9–28.

——— (1979a) Prejudice v. marketing? An examination of some historical sources. *Akron Business and Economic Review*, (Fall), 37–42.

——— (1979b) The origins of macromarketing thought. In *Macromarketing*, edited by Charles C. Slater. Boulder: University of Colorado, pp. 9–18.

——— (1980) Medieval macromarketing thought. In *Macromarketing,* edited by George Fisk & Phillip White. Boulder: University of Colorado, pp. 59–69.

——— (1981) The role of marketing in early theories of economic development. *Journal of Macromarketing*, 1 (Fall) 19–27.

——— (1982) The ethical component of marketing: an eighteenth century view. *Journal of Macromarketing*, 2 (Spring) 38–46.

——— (1990) Marketing as production: the development of a concept. *Journal of the Academy of Marketing Science*, 18 (Fall), 337–44.

——— (1991) Marketing structure and the theory of economic interdependence: early analytical developments. *Journal of Macromarketing*, 11 (Fall), 5–18.

——— (1999) Some late nineteenth-century antecedents of marketing theory. *Journal of Macromarketing*, 19 (December), 115–25.

Dixon, J.F., Cann, J.R. & Renfew, Colin (1968) Obsidian and the origins of trade. *Scientific American*, (March), 38–46.

Duddy, E.A. & Revzan, D.A. (1947) *Marketing: An Institutional Approach.* New York: McGraw-Hill; 2nd edn 1953.

Engel, James F., Kollat, David T. & Blackwell, Roger D. (1968) *Consumer Behavior.* New York: Holt, Rinehart, and Winston.

Fayerweather, J. (1965) *International Marketing.* Englewood Cliffs, NJ: Prentice-Hall.

Fisk, G. (1967) *Marketing Systems.* New York: Harper & Row.

Fisk, G. & Dixon, Donald F. (eds) (1967) *Theories for Marketing Systems Analysis.* New York: Harper & Row.

Frank, R.E. & Green, P.E. (1967) *Quantitative Methods in Marketing.* Englewood Cliffs, NJ: Prentice-Hall.

Frederick, Christine (1923) *Household Engineering: Scientific Management in the Home.* Chicago: American School of Home Economics.

Fullerton, Ronald A. (1988) How modern is modern marketing? Marketing's evolution and the myth of the production era. *Journal of Marketing*, 52 (January), 108–25.

——— (1994) 'And How Does It Look in America?': H.F.J. Kropffs historic report on US marketing. *Journal of Macromarketing,* 14 (Spring), 54–61.

Golder, Peter (2000) Historical method in marketing research with new evidence on long-term market share stability. *Journal of Marketing Research*, 37 (May), 156–72.

Goodman, Charles, (1996) The Annals of the American Academy of Political and Social Science as a pre-1940 source of marketing thought. *Journal of Macromarketing*, 16 (Fall), 141–4.

Government Printing Office (1901) *Report of the Industrial Commission on the Distribution of Farm Products, (VI).* Washington, DC: Government Printing Office.

Grether, E.T. (1976), The first forty years. *Journal of Marketing*, 40 (July), 63–9.

Hagerty, J.E. (1936) Experiences of an early marketing teacher. *Journal of Marketing*, 1, 20–7.

Hardy, Harold (1954) Collegiate marketing education since 1930. *Journal of Marketing*, 19 (2), 325–30.

Hess, J.M. & Cateora, P.R. (1966) *International Marketing*. Homewood, Ill: Richard D. Irwin.

Hoagland, William & Lazer, William (1960) *The Retailer's Manual* of 1869. *Journal of Marketing*, 24 (January), 59–60.

Hollander, Stanley C. (1980) Some notes on the difficulty of identifying the marketing thought contributions of the early institutionalists. In *Theoretical Developments in Marketing*, edited by Charles W. Lamb & Patrick M. Dunne. Chicago: American Marketing Association, pp. 45–6.

——— (1986) The marketing concept: a deja-vu. In *Marketing Management Technology as a Social Process*, edited by George Fisk. New York: Praeger, pp. 3–28.

——— (1989) Introduction. In *Marketing History: The Emerging Discipline*, edited by Terence Nevett, Kathleen Whitney, & Stanley C. Hollander. Lansing: Michigan State University, pp. xix–xx.

——— (1995) My life on Mt. Olympus. *Journal of Macromarketing*, 15 (Spring), 86–106.

——— (1998) Lost in the library. *Journal of Marketing*, 62 (January), 114–23.

Hollander, Stanley C. & Rassuli, Kathleen (1993) Introduction. In *Marketing*, Volume I, edited by Stanley C. Hollander & Kathleen Rassuli. Bookfield: Edward Elgar Publishing, pp. xv–xxxiii.

Hollander, Stanley C., Nevett, Terence & Fullerton, Ronald (eds) (1990) The history of marketing thought: editors' introduction. *Journal of the Academy of Marketing Science*, 18 (4), 267–8.

Holloway, Robert J. & Hancock, Robert S. (eds) (1964) *The Environment of Marketing Behavior: Selections from the Literature*, New York: John Wiley and Sons Inc.

Howard, J.R. (1957) *Marketing Management: Analysis and Decision*. Homewood, Ill.: Richard D. Irwin; rev. edn 1963: 3d edn 1973.

Howard, J.R. & Sheth, J.N. (1969) *The Theory of Buyer Behavior*. New York: John Wiley and Sons.

Hoyt, Charles W. (1912) *Scientific Sales Management*. New Haven, CT: George Woolsen and Co.

Hoyt, Elizabeth E. (1928) *The Consumption of Wealth*. New York: The Macmillan Co.

Hunt, Shelby D. & Goolsby, Jerry (1988) The rise and fall of the functional approach to marketing: a paradigm displacement perspective. In *Historical Perspectives in Marketing: Essays in Honor of Stanley C. Hollander*, edited by Terence Nevett & Ronald A. Fullerton. Lexington: Lexington Books, pp. 35–52.

Johnson, Jean L. (1990) Marketing theory: evolution and evaluation, review. *Journal of Macromarketing*, 10, 38–40

Jones, D.G. Brian (1992) Early development of marketing thought in Canada. *Canadian Journal of Administrative Science*, 9 (2), 126–33.

Jones, D.G. Brian (1993a) Historiographic paradigms in marketing. In *Marketing*, Volume I, edited by Stanley Hollander & Kathleen Rassuli. Brookfield: Edward Elgar Publishing, pp. 136–45.

——— (1993b) Theodore N. Beckman: portrait of a scholar. In *Contemporary Marketing History*, edited by Jeffrey B. Schmidt, Stanley C. Hollander, Terence Nevett & Jagdish N. Sheth. Lansing: MSU, pp. 473–84.

——— (1994), Biography and the history of marketing thought: Henry Charles Taylor and Edward David Jones. In *Research in Marketing: Explorations in the History of Marketing*, edited by Ronald A. Fullerton. Greenwich: JAI Press, pp. 67–85.

——— (1995) George Burton Hotchkiss: a voice that carried well. In *Marketing History: Marketings Greatest Empirical Experiment*, edited by Stanley C. Hollander. Lansing: MSU, pp. 83–94.

——— (1997) The machine metaphor in Arch W. Shaw's (1912) 'Some Problems in Market Distribution'. *Journal of Macromarketing*, 17 (1), 151–8.

——— (1998) Biography as a methodology for studying the history of marketing ideas. *Psychology & Marketing*, 15 (2), 161–74.

——— (1999) William Davidson: a life in retailing management. In *Marketing History: The Total Package,* edited by Peggy Cunningham & David Bussiere. Lansing: MSU, pp. 51–60.

Jones, D.G. Brian & Monieson, David D. (1990) Early development of the philosophy of marketing thought. *Journal of Marketing*, 54 (1), 102–13.

Keith, Robert J. (1960) The Marketing Revolution. *Journal of Marketing*, 24 (January), 35–8.

Kelley, E.J. & Lazer, W. (eds) (1958) *Managerial Marketing: Perspectives and Viewpoints*. Homewood, Ill.: Richard D. Irwin; rev. edn 1962, 3rd edn 1967.

Kelley, William T. (1956) The development of early thought in marketing and promotion. *Journal of Marketing*, 21 (July), 62–76.

Kerin, Roger (1996) In pursuit of an ideal: the editorial and literary history of the *Journal of Marketing*. *Journal of Marketing*, 60 (January), 1–13.

King, W.R. (1967) *Quantitative Analysis for Marketing Management*. New York: McGraw-Hill.

Kotler, Philip (1971) *Marketing Decision Making: A Model Building Approach*. New York: Holt, Rinehart and Winston.

——— (1975) *Marketing for Nonprofit Organizations*, Englewood Cliffs, NJ: Prentice-Hall Inc.

Kotler, Philip & Levy, Sidney J. (1969) Broadening the concept of marketing. *Journal of Marketing*, 33 (January), 10.

Kramer, R.L. (1964) *International Marketing*. Burlingame, CA: South-Western.

Kyrk, Hazel (1929) *Economic Problems of the Family*. New York: Harper Bros.

Langhoff, P. (1965) *Models, Measurement and Marketing*. Englewood Cliffs, NJ: Prentice-Hall.

LaLonde, Bernard J. & Morrison, Edward J. (1967) Marketing management concepts, yesterday and today. *Journal of Marketing*, 31(January), 9–13.

Lazer, William (1979) Some observations on the development marketing thought. In *Conceptual and Theoretical Developments in Marketing*, edited by O.C. Ferrell, Stephen Brown & Charles W. Lamb Jr. Chicago: American Marketing Association, pp. 652–64.

Lazer, William & Shaw, Eric (1988) The development of collegiate business and marketing education in America: historical perspectives. In *Marketing: A Return to the Broader Dimensions,* Proceedings of the Winter Educators Conference, edited by Stanley Shapiro and A.H. Walle. Chicago: American Marketing Association, pp. 147–52.

Leighton, D.S.R. (1966) *International Marketing: Text and Cases.* New York: McGraw-Hill.

Levitt, Theodore (1960) Marketing myopia. *Harvard Business Review*, 38 (July–August), 45–56.

Lichtenthal, J. David & Beik, Leland L. (1984) A history of the definition of marketing. In *Research in Marketing*, Volume 7, Greenwich: JAI Press, pp. 133–63.

Litman, Simon (1950) The beginnings of teaching marketing in American Universities. *Journal of Marketing*, 15 (October), 220–3.

Lusch, Robert (1980) Alderson, Sessions, and the 1950s manager. In *Theoretical Developments in Marketing*, edited by Charles W. Lamb & Patrick M. Dunne, Chicago: AMA, pp. 4–6.

Lyon, Leverett (1926) *Salesmen in Marketing Strategy.* New York: Macmillan Co.

Mason, Roger (1998), Breakfast in Detroit: economics, marketing, and consumer theory, 1930 to 1950. *Journal of Macromarketing*, 18 (Fall), 145–52.

Maynard, H.H. (1941a) Marketing courses prior to 1910. *Journal of Marketing*, 5 (April), 382–4.

——— (1941b) Notes and communications – early teachers of marketing. *Journal of Marketing*, 7 (October), 158–9.

Maynard, H.H. Weidler, W.C. & Beckman, T.N. (1927) *Principles of Marketing.* New York: Ronald Press.

McCarthy, E.J. (1960) *Basic Marketing: A Managerial Approach.* Homewood, Ill: Richard D. Irwin, Inc.; rev.edn 1964, 3rd edn 1968, 4th edn 1971.

McGarry, E.D. (1950) Some functions in marketing reconsidered. In *Theory in Marketing*, edited by Reavis Cox & Wroe Alderson. Chicago: Irwin, pp. 263–79.

——— (1953), Some new viewpoints in marketing. *Journal of Marketing*, 18 (1), 33–40.

McKitterick, John B. (1957) What is the marketing management concept? In *The Frontiers of Marketing Thought and Action*, edited by Frank Bass. Chicago: AMA, pp. 71–82.

Mittelstaedt, Robert (1990) Economics, psychology, and the literature of the subdiscipline of consumer behavior. *Journal of the Academy of Marketing Science*, 18 (Fall), 303–12.

Monieson, David D. & Shapiro, Stanley (1980) Biological and evolutionary dimensions of Aldersonian thought: what he borrowed then and what he might have borrowed now. In *Theoretical Developments in Marketing*, edited by Charles W. Lamb & Patrick M. Dunne. Chicago: AMA, pp. 7–12.

Muncy, James A. (1991) The *Journal of Advertising:* a twenty year appraisal. *Journal of Advertising*, 20 (December), 1–12.

Narver, J.C. & Savitt, R. (1971) *The Marketing Economy: An Analytical Approach.* New York: Holt, Rinehart and Winston.

Nevett, Terence (1991) Historical investigation and the practice of marketing. *Journal of Marketing*, 55 (3), 13–23.

Phillips, C.F. (1938) *Marketing.* New York: Houghton Mifflin Co.

Rethans, Arno J. (1979) The Aldersonian paradigm: a perspective for theory development and synthesis. In *Conceptual and Theoretical Developments in Marketing*, edited by O.C. Ferrell, Stephen W. Brown & Charles W. Lamb. Chicago: AMA, pp. 197–209.

Savitt, Ronald (1980) Historical research in marketing. *Journal of Marketing,* 44 (4), 52–8.

——— (1990) Pre-Aldersonian antecedents to macromarketing: insights from the textual literature. *Journal of the Academy of Marketing Science*, 18 (Fall), 293–302.

Schultze, Quentin J. (1982) An honourable place: the quest for professional advertising education 1900–1917. *Business History Review*, 56 (1), 16–32.

Shaw, Eric (1990) A review of empirical studies of aggregate marketing costs and productivity in the United States. *Journal of the Academy of Marketing Science*, 18 (Fall), 285–92.

——— (1994) The utility of the four utilities concept. In *Research in Marketing: Explorations in the History of Marketing*, edited by Ronald A. Fullerton. Greenwich: JAI Press, pp. 47–66.

——— (1995) The first dialogue on macromarketing. *Journal of Macromarketing*, 15 (Spring), 7–20.

Shaw, Eric & Dixon, Donald (1980) Exchange conceptualization. In *Theoretical Developments in Marketing*, edited by C.W. Lamb & P.M. Dunne. Chicago: AMA, pp. 150–3.

Shaw, Eric & Tamilia, Robert (2001) Robert Bartels and the history of marketing thought. *Journal of Macromarketing*, 21 (December) 156–63.

Sheth, Jagdish N. & Gross, Barbara L. (1988) Parallel development of marketing and consumer behaviour: a historical perspective. In *Historical Perspectives in Marketing: Essays in Honor of Stanley C. Hollander*, edited by Terence Nevett & Ronald A. Fullerton. Lexington: Lexington Books, pp. 9–34.

Sheth, Jagdish N., Gardner, D.M. & Garrett, D. (1988) *Marketing Theory: Evolution and Evaluation.* New York: John Wiley & Sons.

Smith, Ruth Ann & Lux, David S. (1993) Historical method in consumer research: developing causal explanations of change. *Journal of Consumer Research*, 19, 595–610.

Steiner, Robert L. (1978) The prejudice against marketing. *Journal of Marketing*, 40 (July), 2–9.

Stern, Barbara B. (1990) Literary criticism and the history of marketing thought: a new perspective on reading marketing theory. *Journal of the Academy of Marketing Science*, 18 (Fall), 329–36.

Stewart, Paul W. & Dewhurst, J. Frederic (1939) *Does Distribution Cost Too Much?* New York: The Twentieth Century Fund.

Usui, Kazuo (2000) The interpretation of Arch Wilkinson Shaw's thought by Japanese scholars. *Journal of Macromarketing*, 20 (December), 128–36.

Vaile, Roland S., Grether, E.T. & Cox, Reavis (1952) *Marketing in the American Economy*, New York: Ronald Press.

Weld, L.D.H. (1941) Early experience in teaching courses in marketing. *Journal of Marketing,* 5 (April), 380–1.

White, Percival (1927) *Scientific Marketing Management: Its Principles and Methods.* New York: Harper Bros.

Witkowski, Terrence (1993) A writer's guide to historical research in marketing. In *Marketing*, Volume I, edited by Stanley C. Hollander & Kathleen Rassuli. Brookfield: Edward Elgar Publishing, pp. 146–55.

Wright, John S. & Dimsdale, Parks B. (1974) *Pioneers in Marketing.* Atlanta: Georgia State University.

Zinn, Walter & Johnson, Scott D. (1990), The commodity approach in marketing research: is it really obsolete? *Journal of the Academy of Marketing Science*, 18 (Fall), 345–54.

Zuckerman, Mary-Ellen & Carsky, Mary (1990) Contribution of women to U.S. marketing thought: the consumers perspective, 1900–1940. *Journal of the Academy of Marketing Science*, 18, (Fall), 313–18.

3

The Role of Marketing and the Firm

FREDERICK E. WEBSTER, JR.

The role of marketing and the firm has been evolving for almost a century, ever since marketing was first recognized as a distinct activity. Putting marketing within the context of the firm is a fairly recent development from an historical perspective. Prior to that, it was regarded as a socioeconomic process taking place within markets, not firms. It was identified as a distinct management function in the 1920s, and since then has experienced continued elaboration as both management practice and academic discipline. Most recently, the idea of marketing as a separate management function is being challenged and modified dramatically by a new conceptualization of marketing as a set of organizational processes that pervades the whole firm, and is not the sole responsibility of marketing managers. Our field is very much a field in intellectual and practical transition, as evidenced by the changing role of marketing in the firm (Day & Montgomery, 1999).

Marketing was recognized as a set of human activities long before it was identified with the firm. Obviously, people had been doing many of the things we call 'marketing' long before it was given a name. Even before the earliest commercial traders, who might be considered to be the first marketing firms (most of the great voyages of discovery were launched in search for goods to be traded), people were undoubtedly exchanging things such as one type of food, tool, or clothing for another. For most of history, marketing was thought of as a societal, economic process through which goods and services were exchanged between buyers and sellers, activities that even preceded the existence of money and a market economy.

Competing Views of the Role of Marketing

There have been many conceptualizations of marketing. These different viewpoints prove to be useful in understanding the evolution of marketing as a management and business activity within the firm and as a relationship between buying and selling firms.

There has been a kind of 'border war' among competing interests in both the academic and business worlds about the proper boundaries for the field. In both practice and theory there has been an on-going struggle to define marketing as an academic intellectual domain on the one hand, and as a management function with prescribed scope of organizational responsibility and authority on the other. On the academic side, marketing as a discipline, which arguably has its roots in economics, overlaps with many other fields including psychology, sociology, anthropology, political science, organization theory, strategic management, and quality management (as part of operations).

For a time in the 1960s and 1970s, there was a trend in academia to define marketing in terms of its analytical tools and techniques, especially mathematical and statistical modeling and behavioral theory. Today, it appears that the debate has been resolved in favor of those who argue, following the logic of philosopher of science Karl Popper (1963), that marketing is defined by the problems it studies and attempts to resolve rather than its techniques or its subject matter (Bagozzi, 1975; Day & Montgomery, 1999). The subject matter of marketing is markets, but that doesn't define it as a field of study. Marketing is not alone among the behavioral disciplines in using markets as its subject matter. The problems that are studied in marketing must be unique for it to be a distinct scientific discipline. Defining what those problems are is central to the challenge of defining marketing as both discipline and practice, and to understanding its role in the firm.

Conflict with Sales and Other Functions

Within the firm, marketing managers have found themselves in turf battles with other management functions including sales, research and development, engineering, strategic (long-range) planning, purchasing, logistics, and operations. The problem of demarcating marketing from sales has perhaps been the most persistent and remains largely unresolved. On the one hand, marketing in the firm developed essentially within the sales function, to provide market analysis and communications support for the sales force. On the other hand, the development of the marketing concept (Drucker, 1954) was based on the fundamental premise that marketing is much more than selling. According to the integrated view of marketing, selling (and more generally promotion) is just one of several marketing functions.

If marketing is more than selling, it is also less than all of the management functions taken together. Several authors have asserted that 'marketing is the whole firm seen from the customer's point of view' (Drucker, 1954). McKenna (1991) asserted that 'marketing is everything.' Webster (1992) agreed with several business executives who had argued that 'marketing is too important to be left to the marketing people.' Haeckel (1999) says that marketing isn't *a* function of business; it is *the* function of business.

While all of these authors are striving to assert, correctly, the fundamental importance of customer orientation to the success of the firm, they do not help to clarify the issue of marketing's intellectual domain and practical scope. In fact, if it can be agreed that the fundamental purpose of the firm is to create satisfied customers, as proposed by the marketing concept as a management philosophy (Borch, 1959; Drucker, 1954; Levitt, 1960; McKitterick, 1957), then it follows logically that marketing as a management function cannot be uniquely and solely responsible to and for the customer. Customer orientation does not, by itself, define the role of marketing within the firm.

Marketing exists both within the firm and outside it. It is both a set of organizational management activities and a set of institutional actors and functions within the marketplace, external to the firm, in which the firm participates. Marketing channels, or vertical market structures, consist of multiple organizational entities, each firm engaged in marketing management activities, interacting with one another in a set of market-based processes. Complex interorganizational networks, such as strategic alliances, are increasingly responsible for marketing activities. The role of marketing and the firm is very complex, a fact reflected in the many rather distinct definitions of marketing. We will now review some of these definitions as they relate to the role of marketing and the firm.

Marketing as Exchange

Exchange as a human activity is as basic as any social process and it is certainly not surprising that marketing scholars are attracted to a definition of their field as exchange. It is fundamental to assert that 'exchange forms the core phenomenon for study in marketing' and that marketing is 'a general function of universal applicability. It is the discipline of exchange behavior, and it deals with problems related to this behavior' (Bagozzi, 1975: 32, 39). This definition is more than tautological, as exchange involves many specific problems related to processes for negotiation, determining value, managing transactions, etc. This definitional point of view was implicit in the attempts of several scholars in the 1970s to broaden the concept of marketing beyond the firm to include *all* exchanges of value between social actors of all kinds (Kotler & Levy, 1969; Kotler, 1972).

The so-called 'resource-based' or 'constituency-based' theory of the firm looks at the firm as a set of negotiated exchanges with multiple constituencies including employees, suppliers, financiers, customers, the community in which it operates, and the public-at-large (Anderson, 1982; Grant, 1991; Pfeffer & Salancik, 1978). The theory recognizes that the firm depends upon resources such as cash, labor, materials, supplies, and community support, each controlled by a different set of people and institutions. The relative influence of each upon the firm is a function of the power that constituency has as a result of its control of these resources. (The marketing concept argues that customers should have the most power. It is normative, not descriptive.) Since each member of each of these constituencies is involved in some exchange of value with the firm, it can be argued that each of these exchanges is within the intellectual domain of the field of marketing.

Most scholars would agree that this goes too far (Arndt, 1978; Luck, 1969, 1974). A traditional point of view would argue that only exchanges with *customers* fall within the domain of marketing. Some would use the broadened concept of marketing as exchange to argue that each management function and organizational sub-unit has its own 'internal' customers within firm who use its services. Once again, traditionalists would counter that the only true customer is one who pays the firm for the goods and services that it produces for exchange in the open marketplace. (A dictionary definition of a customer is 'a patron, shopper, or buyer.') Simply put, a reasonable conclusion is that marketing exchanges must take place within markets. Not all exchanges are marketing exchanges because not all exchange partners are customers. Customers are the essence of marketing.

Marketing as Demand Stimulation

A competing and widely held alternative definition of marketing is that it is the stimulation of demand for the firm's output or, more generally, its 'productive resources' (Davis, 1961). This viewpoint gained broad support as the practice of modern marketing developed in the late nineteenth and early twentieth centuries in Britain, the US, and Germany. The important context for this development was the rapid increase in mass production and the concomitant appearance of intense competition and excess manufacturing capacity (Fullerton, 1988; Tedlow, 1990). Aggressive personal selling and advertising were in full bloom by the early 1900s as firms faced the need to create new customers for their products, especially innovations such as the mechanical harvester, the typewriter, the automobile, and a plethora of health and beauty aids, packaged foods, and household cleansers (Rowsome, 1959).

Firms began to differentiate their products, hoping to do a better job than their competitors of responding to and satisfying customers' needs (Shaw, 1916). The practice of, if not the term, market segmentation was well known at the turn of the twentieth century (Shaw, 1916: 106; Fullerton, 1988: 113). While Henry Ford is celebrated for his vision for mass production and design of a standard product for the working class (the Model T), he also purchased the Lincoln Motor Company in order to offer a luxury car. He used advertising and publicity of all kinds, including racing, to stimulate demand for Ford products (Ford, 1922; Fullerton, 1988: 118).

Clearly, firm managers a century ago understood the importance of marketing as demand stimulation, although they did not often call it marketing. Selling, advertising, and other forms of promotion (the terms that were used) were essentially synonymous with 'marketing' in the common understanding. Business people were focused on the problem of stimulating demand and creating preference for their products, and on pricing and distribution as part of the demand stimulation process. Marketing presented the company and its products to the customer. Communications were one-way, from producer to consumer. Within the firm, marketing was synonymous with selling.

Marketing as Creating and Managing Markets

While business people were focused on the problems they faced, academic theorists were trying to define marketing as a field of study and a distinct academic discipline. The first marketing management case book to be used as a text was published in 1920 (Copeland, 1920), but it did not offer an analytical framework for decision making.

Early academic definitions of marketing grew out of an attempt to understand how markets actually worked in moving the products of farm, forest, sea, mine, and factory from the producer to the consumer. Thus, many early scholars attempted to understand the differences among commodities in terms of their unique market structures and processes (Breyer, 1931). There was a heavy emphasis on the functions (McGarry, 1950; Weld, 1917) and institutions (Breyer, 1934; Duddy & Revzan, 1947) involved in the marketing process as marketing scholars attempted to discern the fundamental principles of marketing (Ivey, 1921; Maynard et al., 1927). On the other hand, there was relatively little attention paid to the management of those institutions (Shaw, 1916; Copeland, 1920). [Chapter 2 has provided a much more complete review of the history of marketing thought.]

Nonetheless, the *functional* approach to marketing in particular contained the intellectual root stock for the development of marketing management as a distinct approach to the discipline, and for defining the role of marketing within the firm. Obviously, marketing functions had to be managed. In 1948, after due study and consideration, the Definitions Committee of the American Marketing Association (AMA) offered the first 'official' definition of marketing: 'The performance of business activities directed toward, and incident to, the flow of goods and services from producer to consumer or user' (American Marketing Association, 1948: 210). A stronger interest in marketing theory also developed at this time (Alderson & Cox, 1948).

While the AMA statement is not a clear definition of the role of marketing within the firm, it blends the functional and institutional approaches. It defines marketing as a business activity rather than an economic function performed by markets and anonymous institutions. The recognition that these activities (functions and institutions) must be managed within the firm opened the door to consideration of the specific problems that marketing managers must deal with and that require analysis, planning, implementation, and control as basic management processes.

Marketing as Tactics: 'The Four P's'

It did not take long for an explicitly managerial approach to the study of marketing and its role within the firm to develop. Several textbooks incorporating a managerial approach appeared in the 1950s and 1960s (Alderson, 1957; Davis, 1961; Howard, 1957; Kotler, 1967; McCarthy, 1960). The subtitles of these texts demonstrate clearly where the field was going: 'Marketing Behavior and Executive Action' (Alderson); 'Analysis and Planning' (Howard); 'Analysis, Planning, and Control' (Kotler), and 'A Managerial Approach' (McCarthy).

Analysis of these texts shows quite clearly that the authors were still in the demand stimulation business, with a focus on the problem-solving required in each of four specific areas in order to develop an optimum offering of products, prices, promotion, and place (distribution), immortalized as 'the four P's' by Professor McCarthy's treatment.

The early approaches to marketing management as a distinct discipline were based on the fundamental microeconomic theory of the firm (also called 'price theory') and the assumed focus on profit maximization as the ultimate objective of all firm decision making (Anderson, 1982). When two famous studies of management education were published in 1959 (Gordon & Howell; Pierson) calling for a more rigorous analytical approach on the part of business schools, marketing scholars eagerly turned their attention to the application of quantitative techniques and behavioral science theory to the study of marketing problems (Webster, 1992). The new emphasis on rigorous, quantitative analysis was totally consistent with the fundamental optimization approach of microeconomic theory. Interestingly, from a constituency-based theory point of view, it implicitly gives primacy to the interests of the owner-shareholders because it emphasizes profitability as the sole decision criterion.

The marketing management approach is still the dominant paradigm underlying academic research in the field. Marketing management is treated as an optimization problem in which the dependent variables (sales revenue, market share, gross margin, return on investment, etc.) are a function of product quality, price, promotion (advertising, selling effort, price discounts, etc.), and distribution. The assumed functional form of the relationship, with few exceptions, is the classic S-shaped curve where initially increasing returns give way to decreasing returns to scale as expenditures (more generally, efforts) increase. The relationship is usually characterized by time lags, interactions among the 'independent' variables, and other complicating factors, making it difficult to estimate the i in any particular variable. Ho optimizing condition of 'marg marginal revenue' persists as the obj analysis and managerial action. [See Chapter a thorough discussion of the optimum allocation o marketing resources.]

This is the fundamental microeconomic, price theory model. The primary focus of this approach is short-term and tactical, not long-term and strategic. The time horizon in most analyses is a week, month, or quarter, seldom beyond a year (Hayes & Abernathy, 1980). In contrast to the customer orientation called for by the marketing concept, this tactical view remains product- and marketer-oriented.

Organizing the Marketing Function

Within this view of marketing function as the 'four P's' of marketing tactics, there were a number of different, often competing, views as to how the marketing function should be organized within the firm. Before we return to a consideration of marketing as customer orientation and organizational culture, we will first look at marketing from the point of view of marketing organization structure. Different organizational forms imply basically different views of the role of marketing in the firm.

There has been surprisingly little solid research on the organization of the marketing function, probably reflecting the complexity of the issue, the general lack of training in the organizational theory area by academic marketing specialists, and the absence of meaningful databases across a reasonable sample of firms. Furthermore, gathering data about marketing organization is a time-consuming process, not readily amenable to traditional survey methodologies. A set of common questions in a questionnaire or interview guide are difficult to create because of the inherent complexity and ambiguity of organizational issues. Defining simple terms like 'product manager' or 'applications engineer' in words with similar meanings across a sample of respondents is very, very difficult.

The small amount of research that has been reported on the organization of the marketing function has often relied upon clinical analysis and observational data of the case study variety. For example, Workman (1993) spent many months observing and interviewing managers in a well-known computer manufacturing organization and concluded that marketing was able to play only a limited role in the new product development process. Workman has worked with others and used the insights from his field research experience to offer an integrative framework for issues of marketing organization (Workman et al., 1998). Dougherty (1992) studied interactions between marketing and research and development managers in the new product development process with special attention to their differing perceptions. She concluded that effective coordination requires developing specific organizational arrangements and routines.

Corey and Star (1971) analyzed program management in 13 companies in 11 industries to develop generalizable answers to three sets of questions:

1. How do corporate managements delineate the overall enterprise by businesses?
2. How are individual businesses organized? What design principles are at work?
3. What coordinating mechanisms are most effective in managing resource allocations across programs?

Their analysis identified four ways in which companies segment markets, leading to four different forms of marketing organization: by product, by end-use technology, by buyer behavior, and by geography for both industrial and consumer markets (Corey & Star, 1971: 23). They found that decentralized marketing organizations were more common, not surprisingly, when markets varied greatly by geography, buyer behavior, and local or regional government regulations. They also found that the program management structures could be either 'unilateral,' with single managers responsible for both products and markets, or 'bilateral' with both a product manager and a market manager for each program, where diverse markets are served by technically related product lines, and where marketing strategy as well as applications technology varies considerably across markets (Corey & Star, 1971: 25).

It is common for authors to define alternative marketing organization forms along these lines. Product, market, and geographic forms, and combinations of them, represent broadly the options available (Weitz & Anderson, 1981). In the background lurks the never-resolved issue of the appropriate relationship between sales and marketing. Should marketing and sales be separate organizational functions? Is marketing part of sales? Is sales part of marketing?

It is not uncommon to find in one corporate structure almost all combinations of marketing organization forms. For example, a chemical firm might have a product-centered organization with managers for each distinct group of products; a market-centered organization with separate managers for several distinct end-use markets; and a geographically organized sales force. Within the product organization, there might be market specialists and within the market organization there might be product specialists. Within the sales organization, there might very well be both market and product specialists located at regional offices reflecting the industry concentration in that area. These specialists might have a dual reporting relationship to the regional sales manager and to the relevant product or market manager. When organizations become this complex, there are almost certainly major issues of efficiency, coordination, and control and noticeable difficulties in responding to changes in the competitive marketplace and in customer needs and wants. Issues of coordination and control and the resolution of organizational conflict are likely to take a significant portion of management time.

Brand management (sometimes called product management) structures, pioneered by the Procter and Gamble Company, are common in consumer packaged-goods firms and similar companies (Low & Fullerton, 1994). In recent years, however, brand management systems have undergone significant re-evaluation (Shocker et al., 1994). One of the major problems that must be addressed is the lack of coordination between brand marketing strategy and its implementation through the field sales organization. Whereas the brand manager may be focused on the nuances of product positioning and brand equity, the field sales manager may be more concerned with attaining volume objectives and using short-term price incentives for the trade to achieve those short-term results (Webster, 2000). [Brand management systems are reviewed in more detail in Chapter 7.]

The wide variety of marketing organization forms found in practice reflects the basic fact that structure generally derives from strategy (Chandler, 1962) and that strategy reflects the unique circumstances of each firm in terms of market and product characteristics. Clearly, there can be no single answer to the questions 'What is the optimal form of marketing organization?' and 'How should the marketing function be organized?'

Marketing as Organizational Culture

The articulation of the so-called 'marketing concept' in the 1950s was a seminal event in the development of the marketing field and brought the field of marketing into the center of discussions about management in general (Borch, 1959; Drucker, 1954; Levitt, 1960; McKitterick, 1957). We referred to the marketing concept earlier in order to make the point that marketing can be defined as 'the whole business seen…from the customer's point of view' (Drucker, 1954: 39). The essence of Drucker's argument can be summarized with five assertions paraphrasing his words:

1. The only valid definition of business purpose is to create a customer.

2. What the business thinks it is producing is not as important as what the customers think they are buying; what they consider to be 'value' is decisive.
3. Any business has only two basic functions: marketing and innovation.
4. It is not enough to entrust marketing to the sales department.
5. Marketing is the whole business seen from the point of view of its final result, that is, from the customer's point of view.

It is especially relevant to note that Drucker was talking about *customer-defined value* almost 50 years ago – a concept which has only reappeared in the marketing and strategy literature in the last 10 years or so. This early articulation of customer orientation as a guiding principle has once again become a central focus of the marketing field (Lehmann & Jocz, 1997). By the late 1960s some authors were using this concept to redefine the totality of marketing as a management function. *Customer* orientation was enlarged as a concept to become *marketing* orientation, and the terms were used interchangeably. For example, John Keith, the CEO of Pillsbury, wrote a famous article in which he argued that the marketing focus was the ultimate stage in corporate development from manufacturing- to sales- to marketing-orientation (Keith, 1960). He also argued that marketing, in the sense of customer focus, was the best way to insure management responsibility in a corporation grown too large to be controlled by its owners. Likewise, McKitterick (1957) stressed the ethical content of the marketing concept when he noted that it represented a basic change in management philosophy from seeing the customer as a means to the end of profit, toward the view that the customer's welfare must be an end in itself. McKitterick's view is founded on Kant's 'categorical imperative' that no person should be viewed as a means to an end and, more generally, that one's actions should always be capable of serving as the basis for universal law that one would be willing to have applied to oneself.

The fundamental mandate of the marketing concept was simple: To put the customer's interests first, always. It is interesting to note that the moral philosopher Adam Smith, in his famous *The Wealth of Nations* (1776) wrote that: 'Consumption is the sole end and purpose of production; and the interest of the producer ought to be attended to only so far as it may be necessary for promoting that of the consumer.' (Vol. II, Book IV, Ch. 8.) Today, Smith's 'invisible hand' of the marketplace is usually invoked as the mechanism by which producers' pursuit of self-interest (profits) is justified because it maximizes social welfare. However, Smith clearly gave primacy to the consumer's self-interest as he approached the question of how to create the greatest good for the greatest number. Consumer orientation for the firm is a very old idea. However, the articulation of the marketing concept in the 1950s brought it into the management literature.

There followed a period when researchers (e.g., Felton, 1995, Hise, 1965; Houston, 1986; McNamara, 1972; Webster, 1981) examined whether firms had actually adopted the marketing concept. Results were mixed. McNamara found that the marketing concept had been more readily adopted by consumer (vs. industrial) products companies, and by larger (vs. small and medium-sized) companies. He also concluded that Keith's total 'marketing control' had yet to be found. In general, the conclusion was that the marketing concept was easy to articulate but hard to implement in practice. Among the barriers to implementation were the traditional turf battles among management's functional silos (Anderson, 1982); the dominance of a product, engineering, and manufacturing orientation; powerful retailers and distributors; a focus on short-term profitability (or return-on-investment – Hayes & Abernathy, 1980); under-investment in marketing activities; and imperfect and incomplete information about customers' needs and wants (Webster, 1981, 1994: 14–28).

For the first 15 or 20 years of its existence, the marketing concept remained essentially a question of corporate culture, a basic set of values and beliefs about putting the customers' interests in a position of primacy relative to all other claimants. It competed directly with other value systems including those which emphasized technology (R&D), manufacturing excellence, product performance, and financial control, any of which could easily dominate the customer-oriented culture. There was a seemingly endless stream of articles in the management literature (not, it should be noted, in the more academic, scientific marketing literature), emphasizing both the importance of customer orientation and the lack of it in most organizations (Bell and Emory, 1971; Kotler, 1977; Lavidge, 1965; Shapiro, 1988; Webster, 1981, 1988). There was also considerable semantic confusion over the meaning of the terms 'customer orientation,' 'market orientation,' and 'marketing orientation.'

As we will investigate in the next section, the emphasis on marketing as customer orientation and organizational culture left a large gap between concept and implementation, a gap that was filled by authors and scholars in a new field that came to be known as strategic management (Ansoff, 1965). By the mid-1970s, a strategic emphasis in marketing had pushed aside the focus on customer orientation in favor of a competitor-focused approach to planning (Anderson, 1982; Buzzell et al., 1975; Day & Wensley, 1988; Schoeffler et al., 1974). The pendulum began to swing back to customer orientation and organization culture in the late 1980s.

Deshpandé and Webster (1989) surveyed the literature and adopted the scheme of Smircich (1983) that identified five different paradigms of organizational culture: comparative management, contingency management, organizational cognition, organizational symbolism, and the structural/psycho-dynamic perspective. The first two were said to regard culture as a variable (grounded in a sociological framework), whereas the latter three saw it as a metaphor (grounded in anthropology) for the organization itself. In this latter view, culture is not something the organization 'has' but what it 'is.' Deshpandé and Webster defined organizational culture as 'the pattern of shared values and beliefs that help individuals understand organizational functioning and thus provide them norms for behavior in the organization' (1989: 4). They proposed that the organizational cognition perspective offered the richest research opportunities in marketing, especially for understanding the customer focus called for by the marketing concept, because it views organizational culture as a metaphor for organizational knowledge systems with shared cognitions (1989: 11).

Kohli and Jaworski were among the first researchers to revisit the concept of market orientation in a more analytical framework (Kohli & Jaworski, 1990; Jaworski & Kohli, 1993). They were concerned about both the lack of a clear definition of the construct and the gap between concept and implementation. Their approach was not grounded in the culture paradigm but instead relied upon a 'discovery-based' approach to theory construction using empirical data. Their interviews with managers from multiple functions and levels within a cross-section of companies included questions about what marketing meant to these managers and its consequences for action and results.

Analyzing the responses, they found widespread agreement that customer focus was the central element of market orientation. However, they noted that marketing was seen as much more than simple customer research or a vague sense of customer commitment. Kohli and Jaworski proposed a definition of market orientation as 'the organization-wide *generation* of market intelligence pertaining to current and future customer needs, *dissemination* of the intelligence across departments, and organizationwide *responsiveness* to it' (Kohli & Jaworski, 1990: 6, italics in original). They developed a series of testable propositions relating market orientation to antecedent organizational factors (senior management, interdepartmental, and systems) and consequences (customer and employee responses and business performance measures), mediated by such external factors as market and technological turbulence, competitive intensity, and general economic conditions. They agreed with Shapiro (1988) that the phrase market*ing* orientation was too restrictive, limiting the concept to the marketing department rather than seeing it as a firm-wide construct.

At the same time, Narver and Slater (1990) were conducting an intensive study of one company's 140 business units (incorporating both commodity and differentiated products), relating unit profitability to a carefully developed and validated measure of market orientation. Their definition of market orientation was broader than that of Kohli and Jaworski and incorporated customer orientation, competitor orientation, and interfunctional coordination, giving each set of factors equal importance. Market orientation proved to have a positive and linear impact on the profitability of non-commodity businesses, whereas the impact for commodity businesses was positive but non-linear. The most profitable commodity businesses had either high or low market orientation, whereas those with medium market orientation scores were least profitable. This was an important first step in establishing the relationship between market orientation and profitability, an unproved assumption of the marketing concept.

Deshpandé and Webster, following their work on organizational culture and marketing, teamed up with Farley (Deshpandé et al., 1993) to examine the relationships among corporate culture, customer orientation, innovation, and company performance. They used a model of organizational culture types adapted from Cameron and Freeman (1991) and Quinn (1988) that characterized firms as having either an internal or external focus, and either flexible and spontaneous or mechanistic and controlled management processes. The four culture types that result from this two-by-two scheme were labeled Clan (internal/flexible); Adhocracy (external/flexible); Market (external/controlled); and Hierarchy (internal/controlled). Each organization demonstrates some of the characteristics of each type of culture; the measurement scales are used to characterize firms in terms of their dominant cultural orientation. Previously developed measures of organizational climate, innovativeness, and business performance were also used, along with a new scale for customer orientation. Performance was measured as a combination of profitability, size of firm, market share, and sales growth relative to the firm's largest competitor – measures adopted from the PIMS (Profit Impact of Market Strategy) studies (Buzzell & Gale, 1987).

Their first published results (Deshpandé et al., 1993) concerned only Japanese firms, based upon interviews with two managers in each of 50 marketing firms and two managers in a randomly chosen customer organization for each marketer, resulting in four observations for each firm, called a 'quadrad' design. Thus, the Japanese sample was a total of 200 interviews. Subsequently, smaller samples of managers in both marketer and customer firms were interviewed in France, Germany, the UK, and the US. The total sample in all five countries represented 640 managers from 320 organizations, including 160 marketers. The results shed light on the basic question of the relationship of customer orientation and organizational culture to business performance.

Customer orientation, whether measured from the perspective of the marketer or the customer, had no significant impact upon business performance. Simply stated, customer orientation by itself, as part of the organization's values and beliefs, just doesn't count for very much. It has to be transformed into action. This finding lends strong support to the Narver and Slater definition of *market* orientation as a combination of customer-, competitor-, and profit-orientation, not just customer focus.

Combining data from all five countries in the sample, organizational culture did have an effect on performance (Deshpandé et al., 1997). Market-type culture had a positive and significant effect on performance. Adhocracy-type culture had a positive but not statistically significant impact. Hierarchy had no significant impact and Clan had a significant negative impact. (The Market-type firm is distinguished by its focus on competitors more than customers and should not be confused with 'customer orientation.') In other words, firms that are externally oriented outperform those with an internal focus. The Market-type firms are both externally focused and flexible in their responsiveness to changes in the marketplace. In contrast, the Clan-type firms, both internally focused and flexible in their organizational response, are least effective. Hierarchical organizations, internally focused and tightly controlled, do not show any significant influence of culture, positive or negative, on business performance.

As would be expected, there were differences in dominant cultural types across countries. However, consistent with the analysis of the pooled data, there were only minor effects of cultural type on performance in the individual country results. Similarly, at the individual country level customer orientation had no effect on performance.

Innovativeness had the strongest impact on performance. This result was found in individual countries and in the pooled data and was strongly significant in every instance. Likewise, an organizational climate characterized as 'friendly' had a significant incremental effect on performance when the effects of innovativeness and culture were present. Innovativeness was by far the most important variable in impact on performance, followed by culture (either Market – positive or Clan – negative) and climate. Customer orientation, as measured in this study, had no impact on firm performance. Thus, by separating customer orientation from the more general corporate culture, this study shows that it does not have a direct effect. Furthermore, customer orientation does not have any relationship with type of culture; no particular type of culture is more or less conducive to customer orientation.

Continuing their research programs, the several authors just reviewed have developed additional data and analyses that tend to strengthen their conclusions about the importance of customer and market orientation to successful business performance (Slater and Narver, 1994, 1995). They have also developed better scales for measuring market orientation with improved validity and reliability (Deshpandé and Farley, 1998).

To conclude this discussion of marketing as culture and the marketing concept with its emphasis on customer orientation and innovation, we can see that recent research linking these concepts to business performance has considerably extended our understanding. Customer orientation by itself cannot translate into profitability as asserted by the original marketing concept. However, when customer orientation is folded into a broader definition of *market* orientation, incorporating competitor focus and an emphasis on profitability, and combined with innovation, there is a positive impact on the firm's performance.

Limitations of the Marketing Concept

Frustration with the speed of implementation of the marketing concept reflected a number of limitations of the concept itself. These can be summarized as follows:

1. It is an incomplete idea. It says nothing about *how* a company should go about satisfying customer needs. It ignores the question of company capabilities and limitations.
2. It does not specify *which* customers a firm should focus its attention on.
3. It *assumes* a causative relationship between customer orientation and profitability without an underlying argument or proof.
4. It *assumes* that customers can articulate their needs and wants and does not consider how to *anticipate* consumer needs, especially in the case of rapidly developing technology.
5. It has weak *strategic* content. It does not define a good strategy or how to develop one.

In other words, as stated earlier, the marketing concept is only a statement of corporate culture, values, and beliefs with an emphasis on customer orientation. It has little strategic content in its simple form. As we have just seen, more recent research confirms both these limitations and the positive impact of a market-oriented culture when combined with a stronger strategic focus.

The limitations of the marketing concept were, understandably, a cause of the slowness in its implementation. Marketing as culture and marketing as tactics were both incomplete views of the role of marketing in the firm. Recognizing that there was a need to integrate a strategic focus with the concept of customer orientation, companies such as General Electric developed *strategic planning* as a separate corporate level activity, motivated, in part, by a desire to make customer orientation operational.

Marketing and Business Strategy

An important stimulus to the adoption of formal strategic planning systems in many large corporations was the work of Professor H. Igor Ansoff (1965). He noted that customer orientation and market opportunities needed to be matched with the firm's capabilities and resources; no firm could be all things to all potential customers. He was specifically critical of the marketing concept, arguing that it was unreasonable to define a business around customer needs. Strategy formulation required finding market niches where the firm could gain competitive advantage by using and developing its unique competitive strengths.

Ansoff defined three types of decisions. *Operating* decisions set levels of input variables. *Administrative* decisions determine the shape and structure of the firm. *Strategic* decisions define markets to be served and products to be offered in those markets. It was somewhat confusing that Ansoff defined 'marketing strategy' (his words) as operating decisions, not strategic. Using our earlier terminology, this is equivalent to saying that marketing is tactics, not strategy.

Strategic planning concentrated on matching the firm's strengths and weaknesses with market opportunities where the firm could achieve a competitive advantage. This came to be called SWOT analysis: Strengths, Weaknesses, Opportunities, and Threats. The focus in the planning process shifted subtly from customers to competitors, defining markets as collections of competitors vying for advantage. Strategic planning thus undermined customer orientation, instead of supplementing and implementing the concept.

The path to sustained growth, in Ansoff's view, depended upon the firm's unique capabilities and the definition of market segments which valued them. The most attractive markets were those that were growing the fastest and where the firm could achieve a dominant market share. The PIMS studies, mentioned earlier (see page 72), supported this viewpoint by reporting that regression analysis using 37 variables describing a firm's marketing strategy, showed that market share (relative to that of the largest competitor) had the strongest influence on its profitability, measured as return-on-investment (Buzzell et al., 1975; Schoeffler et al., 1974). Later work (Aaker & Jacobson, 1985; Prescott et al., 1986) called into question these results, suggesting that the correlation could be spurious or that the causal relationship could actually go the other way. Profitability may lead to market share by permitting higher levels of spending for product development and other marketing activities (Webster, 1994: 54–8). Even the original authors of the PIMS studies now conclude that product quality relative to competition, not market share, has the strongest influence on long-term return on investment (Buzzell and Gale, 1987: 7). [See Chapter 6 for an extended discussion of the PIMS project.]

Ansoff's pioneering work in strategic planning, along with others who followed (e.g., Glueck, 1970; Hofer & Schendel, 1978) gave rise to an entire new field that today is identified as *strategic management* (Ansoff, 1972; Schendel & Hofer, 1979). Strategic planning had its heyday in the 1970s and early 1980s. Product portfolio models were a common tool for strategic planners (Abell & Hammond, 1979; Day, 1977; Haspeslagh, 1982). These models incorporated a cashflow paradigm that viewed the objective of planning as the allocation of financial resources to alternative growth opportunities. Financial management criteria came to dominate business strategy, and they can compete directly with customer focus (Hayes & Abernathy, 1980; Webster, 1988).

Critics of strategic planning were concerned with its narrow focus on return-on-investment and other short-term measures of business performance, as well as its lack of customer focus. The emphasis on market share led many business managers to increasingly narrow definitions of their 'served markets' so as to assure that they could tell their corporate bosses that they were 'Number One or Number Two' in their markets (Kiechel, 1981).

By the late 1970s, the infatuation with strategic planning had begun to fizzle out (Kiechel, 1982). American firms in industries as diverse as automobiles, chemicals, tires, construction equipment, consumer electronics, and photography had lost substantial market share to global competitors that were doing a better job of responding to customer needs. Formal strategic planning approaches were identified as part of the problem of slow response to a changing marketplace (Hayes & Abernathy, 1980). The large, bureaucratic strategic planning staffs that were created in many corporations became a major burden in terms of costs and, more importantly, response time to changing market conditions. 'Paralysis by analysis' was a serious problem for the large, hierarchical organization that had developed large strategic planning operations.

The focus shifted from formal strategic planning to strategy implementation and strategic management (Gluck et al., 1980; Porter, 1980; Schendel & Hofer, 1979). The shift from strategy formulation, and its emphasis on competitor actions, to strategy implementation and the need to understand customers and how they will respond to the firm's product offering, brought marketing competence back into the strategic management process. Now, customer value is at the center of most strategic management frameworks (Day, 1990, 1999; Webster, 1994). However, the line between marketing management and strategic management has blurred.

There is cause for concern about where this leaves the marketing field as an academic discipline. Many of the issues once considered to be the intellectual domain of marketing such as customer orientation, market segmentation, competitor analysis, product management, and pricing, are now central to the field of strategic management.

Meanwhile, the preponderance of marketing scholarship appears to be concentrated still in the traditional areas of marketing tactics, not strategy, centered around the micro-economic paradigm. This is perhaps seen most clearly in the substantial number of journal articles, doctoral dissertations, and research conferences devoted to the area of sales promotion and other short-term price incentives, a primary concern of firms selling consumer products and services, especially frequently purchased packaged goods. Using impressive analytical models and statistical tools, these scholars are attracted to the sales promotion area by the availability of large-scale databases, most easily available on retail transactions of frequently purchased products, even though the quality of the data is often less than desired. In contrast, the scholarly work in the area of the role of marketing and the firm, which, by definition, is concentrated on issues of strategy and organization, can often be criticized for its reliance on anecdotal and observational data and the use of much less rigorous forms of analysis.

Summary: Marketing as Culture, Strategy, and Tactics

The debate about the role of marketing in the firm and the definition of its intellectual domain is far from over. Marketing's role in the firm simultaneously encompasses culture, strategy, and tactics. A huge research challenge remains to understand each of these subsystems and to integrate them into a comprehensive model of the role of marketing in the firm. The challenge is further complicated by the fact that many firms, perhaps even a majority of them, are evolving from traditional hierarchical, bureaucratic organizations into new organizational forms characterized by extensive relationships with other firms in strategic relationships, partnerships, and alliances in which each firm concentrates on that small part of the total value chain where it has distinctive, world-class competence.

The distinction between the firm and its market environment is breaking down (Achrol & Kotler, 1999; Badaracco, 1991). The network 'captain' or 'hub' of the networked organization is the firm that has the ultimate relationship with the end-user customer. Firms are increasingly defined by their customer relationships as their major strategic asset, not their offices and factories, and not even their products and technology. The customer is the only part of the value chain that cannot be 'outsourced'.

One attempt to conceptualize the role of marketing in this new and still evolving environment is organized around a more flexible view of the traditional corporate hierarchy paradigm, looking at the role of marketing at the corporate (culture), business unit (strategy), and functional (tactics) levels (Webster, 1992).

At the corporate level, the role of marketing is to determine what business the company is in, as defined by the customer needs it wishes to serve, and to determine the mission, scope, shape, and structure of the firm. This requires considering customer needs, the firm's distinctive competence vs. competitors (Prahalad & Hamel, 1990) and its position in the value or supply chain. At the corporate level, decisions are required about where to form strategic alliances and with what types of partners, to form new strategic business units such as joint ventures. These decisions in every instance should be determined primarily by customer needs and the definition of the combinations of distinctive competencies (e.g., converging technologies, some possessed by the firm and some outsourced) that will be required to satisfy them.

At the corporate level, top management has the important marketing responsibility of creating a culture of customer orientation and advocating for the customer's welfare in all decisions. The focus on the customer's definition of value must pervade the organization in every management function from accounting to manufacturing to research-and-development to human resources. In some firms, for example, customers participate in the hiring of key managers. In others, customer visit programs are a regular part of the new product development process. Many firms require that their top executives, including the C.E.O., spend at least one day each month visiting customers.

The role of marketing at the corporate level is therefore three-fold:

1. to promote a culture of customer orientation and to be an advocate for the customer in the deliberations of top management strategy formulators;
2. to assess market attractiveness by analyzing customer needs and wants and competitive offerings; and
3. to develop the firm's overall value proposition, the vision and articulation of how it proposes to deliver superior value to customers.

At the corporate level, the definition of the firm's distinctive competence must be robust enough to have strategic value across multiple markets and business opportunities as the marketplace evolves and customers' definition of value changes.

At the level of the individual strategic business unit (SBU), the role of marketing is somewhat more traditional and the focus is upon how the firm will compete in the businesses it has chosen to be in. Here the focus shifts to individual customers and competitors as the firm develops its competitive strategies for specific market segments. The definition of those segments, selection of market targets, and the development of positioning strategies for each of them is a major marketing management responsibility at the SBU level. At the SBU level, marketing and strategic planning are virtually synonymous.

At the SBU level, marketing management should be actively involved in strategic decisions about the procurement of materials, components, subassemblies, systems, and services that will become part of the firm's product offering, as the firm forms its strategic partnerships with vendors. Beyond that, marketing management must consider strategic partnerships with other marketing partners at multiple points in the value chain including market research providers, marketing strategy consultants, independent sales representation, communications media, distributors and other types of resellers, packaging designers and suppliers, transportation companies, customer credit facilitators, etc. Each of these decisions requires make vs. buy analysis – the definition of the service specification in terms of the firm's value proposition, and the identification and selection of suppliers.

At the third level, tactical and operating decisions, there is the ground most familiar to marketing managers of defining the marketing mix and managing customer relationships. Marketing specialists are responsible for market research and market segment analysis; product management, including new product development, pricing and sales promotion; communications; distribution; and related functions. Although sales force management may be a separate function (either within or across strategic business units), the strategic guidance of sales force activities is a marketing management responsibility built around market segmentation, targeting, and positioning (Rackham & DeVincentis, 1999). In practice, however, marketing strategy implementation often breaks down at the sales force management level, usually due to defects in the sales compensation system and in sales force training and supervision.

The analytical tools of segmentation and optimum allocation of marketing expenditures and other financial, human, and technological resources, apply primarily at the tactical level. In addition to the individual decision variables, however, the marketing management team must manage the interrelationships and synergies of the marketing mix and create an integrated, short-term marketing strategy to achieve business unit performance goals most efficiently.

However, this integrated view of marketing as culture, strategy, and tactics does not go far enough. It leaves unanswered some important questions about the role of marketing in the firm. If, as has been argued at different points in this chapter, marketing is not a separate management function: if it is the whole firm seen from the customer's point of view; if it is not merely creating demand for the firm's productive resources; if everybody in the firm has responsibility for customer value delivery, and marketing is 'too important to be left to the marketing people,' then we have yet to define what it *is* in terms of organizational tasks, structure, skills, roles, and technology. Current thinking about these questions has moved strongly in the direction of re-conceptualizing marketing as a set of organizational processes as distinct from a separate management function.

Marketing as Organizational Processes

Marketing as Value Delivery

Understanding of the role of marketing and the firm has evolved to a point where the focus on customer orientation that was the hallmark of the marketing concept has broadened from a statement of organizational culture to its implementation in strategy and tactics. Customer value is the intellectual linking mechanism bringing together views of marketing as culture, strategy, and tactics (Webster, 1997, 52–4). Marketing is undergoing re-conceptualization as the link between commitment to, and understanding of, customers' needs and wants and various processes for defining, developing, and delivering solutions to customer problems. Marketing inputs become the guiding force in matching customer needs, company capabilities, and financial results. The only way to increase the value of the firm for its owners is to deliver superior value to customers, and to have a business model that allows the firm to retain a fair share of the value created for the customer (Slywotsky, 1996; Slywotsky & Morrison, 1997).

Customers define the business in the sense that they make demands on the firm, which the firm responds to by collecting, organizing, and deploying resources to respond to customer demands. Understanding those demands and responding to them with a keen sense of the firm's strengths and limitations defines the essential role of marketing within the firm. Marketing is fundamentally an informational process. Marketing is not something the firm does to the customer, which can be said to be the old persuasion or selling view of marketing. Marketing is how the customer is able to influence the firm. This is the essence of Haeckel's (1999) paradigm of 'sense and respond' as opposed to 'make and sell.' Or, to go all the way back to Drucker (1954), marketing is the whole firm seen from the customer's point of view.

Earlier we reviewed research that connected innovativeness, organizational culture, and organizational climate with firm performance. Further evidence of the positive impact of marketing competence on firm performance has been provided by Moorman and Rust (1999). In their model, marketing links customers to product development, service delivery, and financial accountability. They surveyed a sample of managers from multiple functional areas. Their research found that the marketing function contributes to firm performance beyond the shared values of market orientation, by linking customers to new product development, service delivery, and financial accountability. Strong customer relationships and information about customer needs and wants can simultaneously contribute to successful new product development and, ultimately, higher levels of financial performance in both product and service firms. They suggest that marketing's role can be strengthened by placing more emphasis on the link between customers and financial performance.

This broad view of marketing as defining, developing, and delivering value calls forth a view of marketing not as a separate management function distinct from other management specialties within the firm, but rather as a set of processes for guiding firm activities toward the creation of satisfied customers who are willing to pay the firm for the productive resources it has committed to solving their problems. Some important definitional issues must again be resolved.

What is a Marketing Process?

Defining what we mean by a marketing process once again raises the question of the borders on the intellectual domain of marketing. What is it and what is it not? There is no need to review the arguments developed earlier in this chapter, but we must recognize that marketing involves markets which are aggregations of customers and competitors, and that the role of marketing in the firm is to guide the firm in managing its linkages with the market. Our understanding of marketing as value delivery, combined with the recognition that the firm itself can only occupy a limited space in the value chain, means that it must also involve linkages with suppliers who must be guided by the firm's value proposition and its commitment to a given customer set. In this aspect, marketing includes processes for managing linkages with suppliers (marketers) as well as customers (buyers).

Recognizing that this definition pushes the limits of marketing as an intellectual domain, we can define a *marketing process* as any activity which generates or uses information about customers to organize and deploy resources for providing solutions to customer problems. Marketing is any business process that gathers and disseminates information about customers, guides value creation and delivery with information about customers, or produces information evaluated and used by customers. A culture that values customer orientation provides the necessary organizational predisposition to use market-back information in all value-creation and value-delivery processes. Marketing is the design and management of all of the business processes necessary to define, develop, and deliver value to customers. Marketing cannot operate alone in these processes but must provide the customer focus that guides and directs all activities. As we will argue, marketing can therefore be most effective not as a separate function, but as part of a team of managers where marketing provides the guidance and leadership for the customer-oriented enterprise.

Types of Marketing Processes

Marketing processes are defined by customer information, but many of these processes are not solely the responsibility of marketing managers. Product development, for example, is a marketing process but it is not exclusively owned by marketing. Certain other processes, such as financial accounting, are probably minimally affected by marketing inputs. Many processes which we would consider to be marketing processes have traditionally been the province of other management functions, especially operations management, purchasing, engineering, and research-and-development. This new view of marketing asserts that these processes that used to be managed primarily from a cost-control perspective need to be repositioned, and be managed from a customer-value perspective. This is a fundamental shift in point of view.

Marketing processes have been defined in several different (but not conflicting) ways. One framework is organized around a definition of marketing as defining, developing, and delivering value (Webster, 1997: 53–4). Examples include:

Value-defining processes:

- Market research – studies of customer needs, preferences, expectations, buying behavior, product use, etc.
- Analysis of the firm's core competencies

- Strategic positioning of the firm in the value chain
- Economic analysis of customer use systems

Value-developing processes:

- New product development
- Design of distribution channels
- Development of sourcing strategy
- Vendor selection
- Strategic partnering with service providers (e.g., customer credit, database management, product service and disposal)
- Developing pricing strategy
- Developing the value proposition
- Sales force and dealer training

Value-delivering processes:

- Managing distribution and logistics
- Deployment of the sales force
- Order-entry, credit, and post-sales service
- Advertising and sales promotion
- Applications engineering
- Product upgrades and recalls
- Customer training

Other classifications of marketing processes identify the linkages between the firm and its continuencies. For example, Srivastava et al. (1999) define an 'organizationally embedded' view of marketing in terms of three core business processes that generate value for customers: product development, supply chain management, and customer relationship management. A.T. Kearney, management consultants, have identified four key marketing processes of a very macro nature (Bluestein, 1994), with an emphasis on strategy – except for the fourth, which is tactical:

1. Establishing competitive position
2. Defining target markets and designing products/services to serve those markets
3. Delivering products/services to those target markets
4. Creating and managing demand

This classification is easily mapped onto the Webster categories. Establishing competitive position and defining target markets are part of the value-definition process. Designing products and services are value-development processes. Delivering products/services and creating and managing demand are primarily value-delivery activities.

Beddow (1995) has described how 3M Company defines marketing 'competencies,' which encompass both processes and marketing capabilities:

Core Marketing Competencies:

- Planning – defining the business and its customers
- Product development – strategy for business unit growth
- Value-pricing – understanding the utility the customer places on the company's products and services
- Channel management – developing and managing the institutions through which the company goes to market
- Customer analysis – analyzing individuals, organizations, and institutions in terms of needs, desires, and ability to buy
- Research – gathering and interpreting market information for marketing decision making
- Brand management – developing and managing strong global brands and corporate assets

Advanced Marketing Competencies:

- International – marketing products and services across national borders
- Financial analysis – identifying profitable strategies that increase the lifetime value of the customer
- Strategic planning – developing strategic fit between organizational goals and capabilities and changing market opportunities
- Quality function deployment – translating customer inputs into design requirements
- Process management – interrelating critical organizational functions in product development, manufacturing, selling, and distribution
- Value-added – continually improving customer value
- Customer – focused selling – demonstrating a consistent ability to meet and exceed customer expectations

Complementary Marketing Competencies:

- Teamwork – ability to function as a member of a cross-functional team
- Interpersonal skills – ability to listen and understand the needs of others, to manage conflict, and to convey information
- Marketing communications – exchange of product information between buyers and sellers
- Computer literacy – ability to use data retrieval systems, develop databases, apply computer-based models, etc.

Perhaps the leading marketing theorist involved in redefining marketing as organizational process rather than separate function, is Professor George S. Day. Central to his definition of the market-driven organization (Day, 1999) are capabilities for market sensing (creating a shared base of market knowledge throughout the organization) and market relating (strategic thinking). He sees these marketing capabilities combining with an externally oriented culture to create a flexible, adaptable organizational configuration, with integrated organization structure, and systems focused on superior customer value. The result is a superior ability to understand markets and sense emerging opportunities and competitors' moves, and superior ability to attract and retain customers by leveraging market investments and delivering superior customer value. The firm is more closely aligned with its changing market environment. The bottom-line benefits are increased revenues, cost efficiency, enhanced employee satisfaction, and price premiums that result in stronger profit margins and the preemption of rivals.

Future Research on the Role of Marketing and the Firm

Paradoxically, as the traditional marketing function becomes less important, the role of marketing in the firm becomes ever-more critical. As traditional hierarchical organization forms give way to hybrid forms for aligning the firm with its rapidly changing marketing environment, our understanding of the role of marketing and the firm is challenged and must be renewed. The movement from an economy consisting primarily of firms engaged in manufacturing, to one emphasizing services, and now toward one in which the predominant value-delivery activities involve information technology in one form or another, unquestionably calls for paradigm shifts in our thinking about organization strategy and structure (Achrol & Kotler, 1999; Haeckel, 1999). Marketing is an essential part of that transformation. As noted by Srivastava et al., 'traditional marketing perspectives almost certainly contain within them the seeds of marketplace failure' (1999: 178).

Under the very broad rubric of the role of marketing and the firm, it is hard to draw lines around directions for important future research. At the broadest level, we need to know more about the way marketing activities are conducted within the firm, and how these are changing. We need to compare and contrast alternative organization forms, to identify the benefits and drawbacks of each, and evaluate them in terms of efficiency and performance. Increasingly, marketing activities will take place across firm boundaries, in various forms of network organizations. Inter-organizational issues will become much more important in marketing research.

Research on the role of marketing and the firm must be by definition interdisciplinary, incorporating the theories and methodologies of diverse intellectual fields from anthropology to organization science, political science, psychology, sociology, and strategic management. Given the very traditional structures of most universities, the scholar who wishes to breach the boundaries of his or her chosen discipline will face a challenge that must, nonetheless, be met in order to move the marketing field forward.

A research workshop of the Marketing Science Institute, in December 1996, addressed the question of the future scope of the marketing discipline and the shape of the marketing organization (Lehmann & Jocz, 1997). In their review of these proceedings, Montgomery and Webster (1997) identified several important research directions. Among these were the need to understand 'value migration' (Slywotsky, 1996), the process by which delivering superior value to customers results in a shift in the market valuation of firms that compete for the customers' patronage. The fundamental notion of market orientation needs further study and elaboration, as does the process of creating and sustaining customer orientation as part of organizational culture. The assumptions of the traditional paradigms guiding research in marketing and management practice need to be made explicit and evaluated. Interfunctional conflict within marketing itself and between marketing and other business functions can be usefully examined for both positive and negative consequences on firm performance.

Montgomery and Webster proposed a three-dimensional grid with a total of 120 cells for thinking about research opportunities for examining marketing's interfunctional interfaces: Three dimensions of marketing (culture, strategy, and tactics) across five other management functions (operations, human resources, research-and-development, finance, and purchasing) with eight sets of marketing activities (customer orientation, market segmentation, targeting and positioning, product development, pricing, promotion, relationship management, and channel strategy). Each cell in the matrix identifies specific issues relating to the role of marketing and its inherently interfunctional dimensions.

In summary the future role of marketing and the firm requires understanding, if not total resolution, of conflicts on several dimensions. First, there is a need to continue to work on the integration of three traditionally competing viewpoints of marketing as culture, strategy, and tactics. Second, we need to develop an up-to-date understanding of when transactional marketing activities should dominate the marketing mix, versus when relationship management processes are more strategically valuable and financially rewarding. Third, the trade-offs between bureaucratic control of asset and resource allocation and organizational flexibility with team-based structure and hybrid organization forms need to be studied. Fourth, the inherent conflict between marketing's broad, strategic, long-term orientation and the sales function's more immediate, tactical requirements must be understood and managed carefully. Fifth, better measures of marketing performance incorporating a process and customer-value oriented view must be integrated with traditional, short-term, financially oriented performance measures such as sales volume, profit margins, and return-on-investment. However, the traditional concerns of cost and economic efficiency must not become victims to the new concern for superior customer value.

In summary, our understanding of the role of marketing and the firm has changed from an emphasis on revenue to profit, from price to customer value, from products to customer needs and preferences, from traditional bureaucratic, functional structures to networked organizations, from function to process, and from 'make and sell' to 'sense and respond.'

References

Aaker, David A. & Jacobson, Robert (1985) Is market share all it's cracked up to be. *Journal of Marketing*, 49 (Fall), 11–22.

Abell, Derek & Hammond, John S. (1979) *Strategic Market Planning: Problems and Analytical Approaches.* Englewood Cliffs, NJ: Prentice-Hall.

Achrol, Ravi S. & Kotler, Philip (1999) Marketing in the network economy. *Journal of Marketing*, 63 (Special Issue), 146–63.

Alderson, Wroe (1957) *Marketing Behavior and Executive Action.* Homewood, IL: Richard D. Irwin, Inc.

——— & Cox, Reavis (1948) Towards a theory of marketing. *Journal of Marketing*, 13 (October), 137–52.

American Marketing Association (1948) Report of the Definitions Committee, R. S. Alexander, Chairman. *Journal of Marketing,* 13 (October), 202–10.

Anderson, Paul F. (1982) Marketing, strategic planning, and the theory of the firm. *Journal of Marketing*, 46 (April), 7–23.

Ansoff, H. Igor (1965) *Corporate Strategy: An Analytical Approach to Business Policy for Growth and Expansion.* New York: McGraw-Hill Book Company.

——— (1972) The concept of strategic management. *Journal of Business Policy*, 2 (Summer), 2–7.

Arndt, Johan (1978) How broad should the marketing concept be? *Journal of Marketing*, 42 (January), 101–3.

Badaracco, Joseph L. (1991) *The Knowledge Link: Compete through Strategic Alliances.* Boston, MA: Harvard Business School Press.

Bagozzi, Richard P. (1975) Marketing as exchange. *Journal of Marketing*, 39 (October), 22–39.

Beddow, Thomas F. (1995) Panel discussion on Developing Future Market Leaders. Marketing Science Institute Board of Trustees Meeting, Dana Point, CA. November 9–10.

Bell, M.L. & Emory, C.W. (1971) The faltering marketing concept. *Journal of Marketing*, 35 (October), 37–42.

Bluestein, Abraham I. (1994) Leadership practices in marketing. *Planning Review*, 22 (September–October), 35–36.

Borch, Fred J. (1959) The marketing philosophy as a way of business life. In *The Marketing Concept: Its Meaning to Management.* New York: American Management Association, pp. 1–6.

Breyer, Ralph F. (1931) *Commodity Marketing.* New York and London: McGraw-Hill Book Company.

——— (1934) *The Marketing Institution.* New York: McGraw-Hill Book Company.

Buzzell, Robert D. & Gale, Bradley T. (1987) *The PIMS Principles: Linking Strategy to Performance.* New York: The Free Press.

Buzzell, Robert D., Gale, Bradley T. & Sultan, Ralph G.M. (1975) Market share – key to profitability. *Harvard Business Review*, 53 (January–February), 97–106.

Cameron, Kim S. & Freeman, Sarah J. (1991) Cultural congruence, strength and type: relationships to effectiveness. In *Research in Organizational Change and Development*, 5, edited by R.W. Woodman & W.A. Passamore. Greenwich, CT: JAI Press.

Chandler, Alfred D. (1962) *Strategy and Structure: Chapters in the History of the Industrial Enterprise.* Cambridge, MA: MIT Press.

Copeland, Melvin T. (1920) *Marketing Problems.* Cambridge, MA: Harvard University Press.

Corey, E. Raymond & Star, Steven H. (1971) *Organization Strategy: A Marketing Approach.* Boston, MA: Division of Research, Graduate School of Business Administration, Harvard University.

Davis, Kenneth R. (1961) *Marketing Management.* New York: The Ronald Press Company.

Day, George S. (1977) Diagnosing the product portfolio. *Journal of Marketing*, 41 (April), 29–38.

——— (1990) *Market Driven Strategy.* New York: Free Press.

——— (1994) The capabilities of market-driven organizations. *Journal of Marketing*, 58 (October), 37–52.

——— (1999) *The Market Driven Organization.* New York: Free Press.

Day, George S. & Montgomery, David B. (1999) Charting new directions for marketing. *Journal of Marketing,* 63 (Special Issue), 3–13.

Day, George S. & Wensley, Robin (1988) Marketing theory with a strategic orientation. *Journal of Marketing*, 47 (October), 79–89.

Deshpandé, Rohit & Farley, John U. (1998) Measuring market orientation: generalization and synthesis. *Journal of Marketing*, 62 (July), 213–32.

Deshpandé, Rohit & Webster, Frederick E., Jr. (1989) Organizational culture and marketing: defining the research agenda. *Journal of Marketing*, 53 (January), 3–15.

Deshpandé, Rohit & Farley, John U. & Webster Frederick E., Jr. (1993) Corporate culture, customer orientation, and innovativeness in Japanese firms: a quadrad analysis. *Journal of Marketing*, 57 (January), 23–37.

——— (1997) *Factors Affecting Organizational Performance: A Five-Country Comparison*, Report No. 97–108. Cambridge, MA: Marketing Science Institute (May).

Dougherty, Deborah (1992) Interpretive barriers to successful product innovation. *Organization Science*, 3 (May), 179–202.

Drucker, Peter F. (1954) *The Practice of Management.* New York: Harper & Row Publishers, Inc.

Duddy, Edward A. & Revzan, David A. (1947) *Marketing: An Institutional Approach.* New York: McGraw-Hill Book Company.

Felton, A.P. (1959) Making the marketing concept work. *Harvard Business Review*, 37 (July–August), 55–65.

Ford, Henry (1922) *My Life and Work.* New York: Doubleday, Page & Company. (Reprinted by Ayer Company, Publishers, Salem, NH, 1987).

Fullerton, Ronald A. (1988) How modern is modern marketing? Marketing's evolution and the myth of the 'Production Era'. *Journal of Marketing*, 52 (January), 108–25.

Gluck, Frederick W., Kaufman, Stephen P. & Walleck, A. Steven (1980) Strategic management for competitive advantage. *Harvard Business Review*, 58 (July–August), 154–63.

Glueck, William (1970) *Policy, Strategy Formation, and Management Action.* New York: McGraw-Hill Book Company.

Gordon, R.A. & Howell, J.E. (1959) *Higher Education for Business.* New York: Columbia University Press, a study sponsored by The Ford Foundation.

Grant, Robert M. (1991) The resource-based theory of competitive advantage: implications for strategy formulation. *California Management Review*, 33 (Spring), 114–35.

Haeckel, Stephan H. (1999) *Adaptive Enterprise: Creating and Leading Sense-and-Respond Organizations.* Boston, MA: Harvard Business School Press.

Haspeslagh, Philippe (1982) Portfolio planning: uses and limits. *Harvard Business Review*, 60 (January–February), 58–73.

Hayes, Robert H. & Abernathy William, J. (1980) Managing our way to economic decline. *Harvard Business Review*, 58 (July–August), 67–77.

Hise, Richard T. (1965) Have manufacturing firms adopted the marketing concept? *Journal of Marketing*, 29 (July), 9–12.

Hofer, Charles W. & Schendel, Dan (1978) *Strategy Formulation: Analytical Concepts.* St. Paul, MN: West Publishing Company.

Houston, Franklin S. (1986) The marketing concept: what it is and what it is not. *Journal of Marketing*, 50 (April), 80–7.

Howard, John A. (1957) *Marketing Management: Analysis and Planning.* Homewood, IL: Richard D. Irwin, Inc.

Ivey, Paul (1921) *Principles of Marketing.* New York: The Ronald Press Company.

Jaworski, Bernard J. & Kohli, Ajay K. (1993) Market orientation: antecedents and consequences. *Journal of Marketing*, 57 (July), 53–71.

Keith, Robert J. (1960) The marketing revolution. *Journal of Marketing*, 24 (January), 35–8.

Kiechel, Walter III (1981) The decline of the experience curve. *Fortune*, October 5, 139–46.

——— (1982) Corporate strategists under fire. *Fortune*, December 27, 34–9.

Kohli, Ajay K. & Jaworski, Bernard J. (1990) Market orientation: the construct, research propositions, and managerial implications. *Journal of Marketing*, 54 (April), 1–18.

Kotler, Philip (1967) *Marketing Management: Analysis Planning and Control.* Englewood Cliffs, NJ: Prentice-Hall, Inc.

——— (1972) A generic concept of marketing. *Journal of Marketing*, 36 (April), 46–64.

——— (1977) From sales obsession to marketing effectiveness. *Harvard Business Review*, 55 (November–December), 67–75.

Kotler, Philip & Levy, Sidney J. (1969) Broadening the concept of marketing. *Journal of Marketing*, 33 (January), 10–15.

Lavidge, Robert J. (1965) Marketing concept often gets only lip service. *Advertising Age*, 37 (October), 52.

Lehmann, Donald R. & Jocz, Katherine E. (eds) (1997) *Reflections on the Futures of Marketing.* Cambridge, MA: Marketing Science Institute.

Levitt, Theodore (1960) Marketing myopia. *Harvard Business Review*, 38 (July–August), 45–56.

Low, George S. & Fullerton, Ronald A. (1994) Brands, brand management, and the brand manager system. *Journal of Marketing Research*, 31 (May), 173–90.

Luck, David J. (1969) Broadening the concept of marketing – too far. *Journal of Marketing*, 33 (January), 10–15.

——— (1974) Social marketing: confusion compounded. *Journal of Marketing*, 38 (October), 70–2.

Maynard, Harold, Weidler, W.C. & Beckman, Theodore (1927) *Principles of Marketing.* New York: The Ronald Press Company.

McCarthy, E. Jerome (1960) *Basic Marketing: A Managerial Approach*, Homewood, IL: Richard D. Irwin, Inc.

McGarry, Edmund D. (1950) Some functions of marketing reconsidered. In *Theory in Marketing*, edited by Reavis Cox & Wroe Alderson. Homewood, IL: Richard D. Irwin, Inc.

McKenna, Regis (1991) Marketing is everything. *Harvard Business Review*, 69 (January–February), 65–79.

McKitterick, John B. (1957) What is the marketing management concept? In *The Frontiers of Marketing Thought and Science,* edited by Frank Bass. Chicago: American Marketing Association. Proceedings of the December 1957 Educators' Conference of the AMA, Philadelphia, pp. 71–82.

McNamara, Carlton P. (1972) The present status of the marketing concept. *Journal of Marketing*, 36 (January), 50–7.

Montgomery, David B. & Webster, Jr. Frederick E. (1997) Marketing's interfunctional interfaces: the MSI workshop on Management of Corporate Fault Zones. *Journal of Market Focused Management*, 2 (1) (September), 7–26.

Moorman, Christine & Rust, Roland T. (1999) The role of marketing. *Journal of Marketing*, 63 (Special Issue), 180–97.

Narver, John C. & Slater, Stanley F. (1990) The effect of a market orientation on profitability. *Journal of Marketing*, 54 (October), 20–35.

Pfeffer, Jeffrey & Salancik, Gerald R. (1978) *The External Control of Organizations.* New York: Harper & Row.

Pierson, F.C. (1959) *The Education of American Businessmen.* New York: McGraw-Hill Book Company, a study sponsored by The Carnegie Foundation.

Popper, Karl R. (1963) *Conjectures and Refutations.* New York: Harper & Row Publishers, Inc.

Porter, Michael E. (1980) *Competitive Strategy.* New York: The Free Press.

Prahalad, C.K. & Hamel, Gary (1990) The core competence of the corporation. *Harvard Business Review*, 68 (May–June), 79–91.

Prescott, John E., Kohli, Ajay K. & Venkatraman, N. (1986) The market share – profitability relationship: an empirical assessment of major assertions and contradictions. *Strategic Management Journal*, 7, 377–94.

Quinn, Robert E. (1988) *Beyond Rational Management.* San Francisco: Josey-Bass.

Rackham, Neil & DeVincentis, John (1999) *Rethinking the Sales Force: Redefining Selling to Capture Customer Value.* New York: McGraw-Hill.

Rowsome, Frank Jr. (1959) *They Laughed When I Sat Down.* New York: McGraw-Hill Book Company.

Schendel, Dan & Hofer, Charles W. (1979) *Strategic Management: A New View of Business Policy and Planning.* Boston, MA: Little, Brown & Company.

Schoeffler, Sidney, Buzzell, Robert D. & Heany, Donald F. (1974) Impact of strategic planning on profit performance. *Harvard Business Review*, 52 (March–April), 137–45.

Shapiro, Benson P. (1988) What the hell is 'market oriented'? *Harvard Business Review*, 66 (November–December), 119–25.

Shaw, Arch W. (1916) *An Approach to Business Problems.* Cambridge, MA: Harvard University Press.

Shocker, Allan D., Srivastava, Rajendra K. & Rueckert, Robert W. (1994) Challenges and opportunities facing brand management: an introduction to the special issue. *Journal of Marketing Research*, 31 (May), 149–58.

Slater, Stanley F. & Narver, John C. (1994) Does the competitive environment moderate the market orientation–performance relationship? *Journal of Marketing*, 58 (January), 46–55.

——— (1995) Market orientation and the learning organization. *Journal of Marketing*, 59 (July), 63–74.

Slywotsky, Adrian (1996) *Value Migration: How to Think Several Moves Ahead of the Competition.* Boston, MA: Harvard Business School Press.

Slywotsky, Adrian & Morrison, David J. (1997) *The Profit Zone.* New York: Times Books.

Smircich, Linda (1983) Concepts of culture and organizational analysis. *Administrative Science Quarterly*, 28 (3), 339–58.

Smith, Adam (1776) *The Wealth of Nations.* London: W. Strahan and T. Cadell.

Srivastava, Rajendra K., Shervani, Tasadduq A. & Fahey, Liam (1999) Marketing, business processes, and shareholder value: an organizationally embedded view of marketing activities and the discipline of marketing. *Journal of Marketing*, 63 (Special Issue), 168–79.

Tedlow, Richard (1990) *New and Improved: The Story of Mass Marketing in America.* New York: Basic Books.

Webster, Frederick E., Jr. (1981) Top management concerns about the marketing function: issues for the 1980s. *Journal of Marketing*, (Summer), 9–16.

——— (1988) The rediscovery of the marketing concept. *Business Horizons*, 31 (May–June), 29–39.

——— (1992) The changing role of marketing in the corporation. *Journal of Marketing*, 56 (October), 1–17.

——— (1994) *Market-Driven Management: Using the New Marketing Concept to Create a Customer-Oriented Company.* New York: John Wiley & Sons, Inc.

——— (1997) The future role of marketing in the organization. In *Reflections on the Futures of Marketing*, edited by Donald R. Lehmann & Katherine Jocz. Cambridge, MA: Marketing Science Institute, 39–66.

——— (2000) Understanding the relationships among brands, consumers, and resellers. *Journal of the Academy of Marketing Science*, 28 (Winter), 17–28.

Weitz, Barton & Anderson, Erin (1981) Organizing the marketing function. In *Review of Marketing*, edited by B. Enis and Kenneth Roering. Chicago: American Marketing Association, 134–42.

Weld, L.D.H. (1917) Marketing functions and mercantile organization. *American Economic Review*, (June), 306–18.

Workman, John P., Jr. (1993) Marketing's limited role in new product development in one computer systems firm. *Journal of Marketing Research*, 30 (November), 405–21.

Workman, John P., Jr., Homburg, Christian & Gruner, Kjell (1998) Marketing organization: an integrative framework of dimensions and determinants. *Journal of Marketing*, 62 (July), 21–41.

PART TWO

Marketing Strategy

4

Market Strategies and Theories of the Firm

GEORGE S. DAY and ROBIN WENSLEY

Many different theories of the firm have been advanced to address such fundamental questions as why firms exist, and what determines their scale and scope. Three of these theories, emphasizing in turn the resources, the positioning and the configuration of the firm, are especially useful for advancing our understanding of the nature of market strategies, and the process of market-based competition over time.

Each of these theories of the firm takes a different perspective on the evolution of market strategies because of differences in (1) *the unit of analysis* – whether it is the firm, the business unit or the intra-organizational network; (2) their *theoretical premises* – the emphasis on opportunism versus asymmetries in knowledge between firms, for example; and (3) the *role of time* – are they a snapshot or a movie? Taken together these three theories provide a reasonably coherent and complete picture of the dynamics of strategy in competitive markets.

Our approach is in the spirit of Henry Mintzberg's 'strategy safari' (Mintzberg et al., 1998), which dissected 10 perspectives on strategy, represented as 10 different schools of thought. Although the focus was more eclectic, and emphasized the process of strategy formation, we share the same intent to show that no single perspective can stand on its own.[1] Each of the three theories is part of a more balanced and integrative understanding.

We begin with the 'Resource-based' view of the firm as a bundle of resources that may be superior or inferior to rivals' in enabling it to offer products and services to the market. Here the unit of analysis may be the firm, but is more likely to be the individual business unit serving a distinct market. This is predominantly an inside-out perspective, which starts with the capabilities and assets of the firm before considering the competitive context.

The second theory of the firm adopts an outside-in perspective, which views the strategy of the firm as finding an advantageous positioning in a multidimensional space in which other competitive offerings are located. These positions are shaped and changed by the push and pull of the forces of competitive rivalry, the exercise of bargaining power by customers and suppliers, and the evolution of market expectations and requirements.

The final theory, of the configuration of the firm, is more ambidextrous by looking from the outside-in and inside-out at the co-evolution of the firm or business within a continually changing market context. This configurational perspective sees the evolution of markets as a consequence of iterative interactions between firms, suppliers, and customers – each with shifting boundaries. The resulting webs of connections and networks inevitably require a perspective that is wider than any particular market, because a product- or service-analysis may be less wide than the total portfolio of the business activities of the firm.

The Resource-based Perspective. The resource-based perspective has been developed from Penrose (1959) by, particularly, Wernerfelt (1984) and Barney (1991) to consider the firm as heterogeneous bundles of assets and capabilities. This approach has also directed attention to the nature of resources that are difficult to imitate and competitively superior.

Hunt (2000a), however, has argued that it is also important to consider much more directly the issue of heterogeneous demand, which is especially pertinent in a marketing strategy context. This approach also highlights questions relating to the more dynamic aspects of market-based competition. Indeed others, such as Dickson (1996) have gone further to argue that such an approach should mean that learning processes are indeed the only basic competence likely to result in sustained competitive advantage.

The Positioning Perspective. In the broad sense the positioning perspective focuses attention on the nature of the territory over which the competitive process evolves and the impact and effect of different positioning strategies of individual firms within this context. The most obvious approach is that of spatial competition originally developed in the Hotelling (1929) model. Spatial competition provides a useful means of understanding the basics of a positioning perspective, which can then be contrasted with other positional approaches, particularly ones derived from Michael Porter's work in Industrial Organization economics. More complex models of spatial competition lead us to notions of fitness landscapes and the evolution of competitive strategies, as well as ways of formulating some basic issues in game theory modelling.

The Configuration Perspective. Firms are, of course, particular forms of organization and a key question relates not only to the boundaries of firms and their wider links but also to the nature of their internal organization. In this chapter we will focus more on issues of the wider network of interrelationships within which any firm is located. We will also consider approaches in this area that help us to understand the extent to which configurational choices appear to facilitate certain types of strategic change for the firm itself.

Strategic issues include questions such as why are we losing market share? How can we regain our competitive edge? Should we enter a related market? These questions can clearly be answered in various ways. From a marketing perspective, we might focus on the ability or inability of the business to understand its customers, create relationships with trade partners, develop new products or fulfil orders compared to rivals. This set of answers reflects a broadly resource-based view of the firm and leads us into questions of key capabilities that determine the success of the firm. On the other hand, we could look for answers in terms of how we might position the products or services from our understanding of the nature of both customer demand and the way in which our competitors position their offerings. This brings us into the domain of positioning and, in the broad sense, 'spatial' competition. Finally we could go further and look at the ways in which the whole supply chain in our markets is changing and the areas in which we want to maintain direct control over activities, those where we wish to 'contract out' activities, either within or outside the firm itself, and finally those where we will rely on traditional intermediate market mechanisms. This leads us directly to issues of organizational design and what we have labelled as configurational choices.

The Resource-based Perspective

The basic argument of the resource-based view (RBV) is that the resources controlled by the firm are the basis for a sustainable competitive advantage, when they are competitively superior and valuable in the market (Wernerfelt, 1984), difficult to imitate, durable, and unlikely to be trumped by a different resource (Barney, 1991; Collis & Montgomery, 1995)

This view of a business as a tightly integrated bundle of productive resources is not new. An emphasis on resources can be found in Penrose (1959), and distinctive capabilities or competencies were introduced by Selznick (1957) and featured in the strengths and weaknesses component of the early business policy frameworks (Learned et al.,1969). Although these early frameworks provide useful insights, the lack of a thorough theoretical understanding of capabilities meant that in practice firms did little more than compile lengthy and indiscriminate lists of strengths and weaknesses. A common flaw in these evaluations was that the resource was not compared to the competitors', but instead was based on an internal assessment of which activity, of all of its activities, the business performed best.

Types of Resources

The further development of the resource-based view has been impeded by a plethora of terms, such as resources, assets, capabilities, and core competencies, being used loosely and interchangeably. Thus, it is obligatory in any exposition of the RBV to define and distinguish the terms carefully. We follow a convention that adopts elements of Day (1994), Teece et al. (1997), and Amit and Schoemaker (1993)[2] to make the following distinctions among the different types of resources.

Assets. This includes all the factors of production that are readily available in factor markets, and easily valued and traded, and privileged or firm-specific assets that are hard to obtain or replicate. Among the most valuable of the privileged assets are the investments in the scale, scope and efficiency of facilities and systems, intellectual property including patents and trade secrets, the scale and efficiency of a distribution network, the equity in a brand name, and detailed customer information that can be used to adjust or customize the product offering. These privileged assets are difficult to transfer among firms because of transaction and transfer costs, and embedded tacit knowledge.

Capabilities provide the glue that brings these assets together and enables them to be deployed advantageously. They are complex bundles of skills and accumulated knowledge, exercised through organizational processes, that enable firms to coordinate activities and carry on learning how to perform these activities better. Capabilities are manifested in such typical business processes as order fulfillment, new product development and service delivery.

Capabilities and business processes are closely entwined, because it is the collective skills, and accumulated learning that determines how well the linked activities in a process are carried out. Each business will have as many processes as necessary to carry out the natural business activities, defined by the stage of the firm in the supply chain and the key success factors in the market.[3] The processes needed by a life insurance company that sells direct will be very different from the process found in a microprocessor fabricator. Each process has a beginning and end state that facilitates identification and implies all the work that gets done in between. Thus, new product development proceeds from concept screening to market launch, and the order fulfillment process extends from the receipt of the order to payment.

Distinctive capabilities and core rigidities. Some capabilities will be done adequately,[4] others poorly, but a few must be clearly superior if the business is to consistently out-perform the competition. These are the distinctive capabilities that support a market position that is valuable and difficult to match. The most defensible test of distinctiveness is whether the capability makes a disproportionate contribution to the provision of superior customer value, or permits the business to deliver value in an appreciably more cost-effective way. Another test is whether the capability can be readily matched by rivals. Because distinctive capabilities are difficult to develop, they often resist imitation.

The flip side of distinctive capabilities are core rigidities (Leonard-Barton, 1992). These are inappropriate processes, where the values, skills, and accumulated knowledge that may have served the firm in the past get in the way of effectively managing the current process. The consequences are poor implementation and high costs that disadvantage the firm.

Dynamic capabilities. Some authors (notably Teece et al., 1997) separate distinctive front-line execution capabilities, which enable superior performance with the current business model, from growth enabling or dynamic capabilities. These are dynamic because they reflect the firm's ability to reconfigure its resources to address rapidly changing environments and achieve new and innovative forms of advantage. Among these dynamic capabilities are insight/foresight capabilities that enable business to anticipate or discern patterns which present first-mover advantages, or enable rapid responses to competitive moves (Coyne et al., 1997). Value ultimately is derived from the insight itself. Other growth-enabling capabilities include acquisition or partnering abilities, financing and risk management skills, or capital management skills.

For the remainder of this section, the emphasis will be on the capabilities component of the resource base of a business unit, since this is where advantages will be gained or lost. Because our focus is primarily on the business unit and the market or markets in which it operates, we will not talk about 'core competencies' that are the capabilities of a corporation which span and support multiple lines of business (Prahalad & Hamel, 1990). Each of the separate business units draws on these corporate-wide resources to develop or enhance some or all of its distinctive capabilities.

Identifying Capabilities

Because capabilities are deeply embedded within the fabric of the organization they can be hard to identify. One way to overcome this problem is to create detailed maps of the sets of process activities in which the capabilities are employed (Hammer, 1996). These maps usually show that capabilities and their defining processes span several functions and organizational levels, and involve extensive communication.

Capabilities are further obscured because much of their knowledge component is tacit and dispersed. This knowledge is dispersed along several dimensions (Leonard-Barton, 1992):

- Accumulated *employee knowledge and skills* that come from technical knowledge, training, emulation of proficient people, and long experience with the process.
- Knowledge embedded in *technical systems*, comprising the information in linked databases, the formal procedures and established 'routines' for dealing with given problems or transactions (Nelson & Winter, 1982), and the computer systems themselves.
- *Managerial systems*, which guide and monitor the accumulation of knowledge, and comprise the training processes, rewards, incentives, and controls.
- *Values and norms* that dictate what information is to be collected, what types are most important, who gets access to the information, and how it is to be used, which are a part of the overall culture.

The contribution of knowledge to the functioning of a capability also exposes a persistent tension in the identification of distinctive capabilities. On the one hand it is important to be precise in specifying the capability by disaggregating the scope down to a level where the skills and execution of the capability are competitively superior. Broad generalizations like consumer marketing skills are misleading, when the distinctive capability may be only in demand stimulation through image-based advertising, while other ingredients such as pricing or channel linking may be merely average.

While disaggregation is useful, it may also be misleading if it doesn't consider the relationships with other capabilities, the institutional context[5] in which the capability is embedded, and the central themes and methods that prioritize, orchestrate and direct the resources toward the delivery of superior customer value. Sometimes the valuable resource is an adroit combination of capabilities, none of which is superior by itself, but when combined, makes a better package. Then competitive superiority is due either to (1) the weighted average effect – the business does not rank first on any asset or capability but is better on average than any of the rivals, or (2) the firm's system-integration capability, so the capabilities, are mutually reinforcing, or (3) the superior clarity and focus of the strategic thrust that mobilizes the resources.

Bundling capabilities. One concept of aggregation is that all capabilities are nested within a complex network with many direct and indirect links to other resources (Black & Boal, 1994). Thus, Day (1999) embeds the distinctive market-sensing, market-relating and strategic-thinking capabilities of a market-driven organization within an externally oriented culture and a configuration with an adaptive-organization design. Competitive success comes when all these elements are aligned with a compelling value proposition.

An alternative view is that there is a hierarchy progressing from culture at the top, through strategy formulation, with capabilities at a tactical or operational level (Hooley et al., 1999). This highlights the role of culture as a distinct resource by separating it from the capabilities, and gives the marketing strategy choices of segments to target and competitive positions to adopt, the dominant influence on the strategic thrust of the business. In reality, of course, the choice of thrust will also be constrained and shaped by the distinctive, hard-to-imitate capabilities the organization had developed, since the likelihood of success with a new strategy increases directly with the ability to exploit these capabilities. A further argument against a hierarchical ordering of culture-strategy-capabilities is that some capabilities are dynamic (Teece et al., 1997), and enable the business to anticipate the need for strategic shifts.

Appraising the Guiding Premises

The resource-based perspective has enjoyed great popularity during the past decade. Managers find it a useful lens for understanding their sources of competitive advantage and addressing strategic issues. Academics have probed and extended the concept with a stream of conceptual analyses. While this has been persuasive, it is also troubling that much of the support has been based on inductive reasoning using ex-post case studies. There is a lurking concern that in the absence of rigorous empirical work the identification process could be tautological: 'Show me a success story and I will uncover a core competence (Williamson, 1999: 1093). There are also legitimate concerns about the practical problems of identification – given that the few distinctive capabilities are usually embedded in a rich network of other resources – and of action implications.

At this stage in the development of the resource-based perspective the question is whether it will be able to live up to its promise as a fundamentally different way of thinking about strategy, and the basis for an alternative theory of the firm.[6] This will depend on whether the underlying premises are found to be valid or not, and expansive in applicability or narrowly restrictive to specific environments. For this purpose we will examine the four premises that define the logic of this theory.[7] This analysis will expose a number of limitations to the applicability of this theory, and will help place it in a broader context.

Performance premise. A firm's positional advantage and performance relative to its competitors is a function of the strength, expert exploitation and leveraging of its assets and distinctive capabilities. When these resources are valuable and durable they are the basis for a sustainable competitive advantage.[8]

There are two corollaries to this premise. The first is that distinctive capabilities are robust and can be used in different ways to speed the firm's adaptation to environmental changes and facilitate entry into new markets. The second is that these capabilities are more fundamental to the prospects for the firm than any particular product or service in which they are used. Therefore, strategies should be designed to 'compete on capabilities' (Stalk et al., 1992) rather than by seeking a position in an attractive market that can be defended against rivals. This premise is a direct challenge to the competitive forces approach (Porter, 1991), and the related entry-deterrence approach that held sway as the dominant perspectives on strategy selection during the 1980s and early 1990s. However, the shift in emphasis towards capabilities and assets doesn't mean that strategy position and market attractiveness are any less important. On the contrary, the choice of which capabilities to nurture and which investment commitments to make must be guided by a shared understanding of the industry structure, the needs of the target customer segments, the positional advantages being sought, and the trends in the environment.

Priem (2001) develops further the Williamson critique we mentioned earlier – the issue of measurement and definition of superior resources – and indeed the extent to which the whole RBV approach is tautological when it comes to empirical falsification. In a robust defense of RBV empirical research, Barney (2001) points out that a number of previously useful theoretical frameworks, such as those of Michael Porter (1985, 1991) are in a strict sense tautological, but at the same time they provide useful guidance for both empirical research and, indeed, the development of a better understanding of competitive processes and impacts. Much of this argument reflects the continued problem of researching individual firm performance in a competitive market context (Powell, 2001).

Development premise. This premise holds that resource and capability development is a selective and path-dependent process. The need for focus and selectivity requires an organization to concentrate attention on a few capabilities that correspond to key success factors in the target market. Indeed this logic leads to outsourcing any activities that are judged to be non-core because they don't contribute to gaining a competitive advantage that can be protected, or they can be done better by others.

There is a path dependency in the choice of capabilities to develop in the sense that we build on what we know (Liebowitz & Margoles, 1994). Behind the immediate choices are a history of prior choices that sensitize one to certain issues and possibilities, create a knowledge platform on which one can keep building, and constrain or 'lock in' a firm to a particular path. This premise has face validity, in view of the considerable inertia behind most strategies and the demonstrable inability of incumbent organizations to respond to challenges from disruptive technological or social change.

An interesting corollary of the path dependency of strategic choices is the notion of time compression diseconomies. Because some resources can only be developed painstakingly over long periods of time, a rival that tries rapidly to achieve the same result through a crash program is likely to find it has incurred much higher costs than if it had made the same expenditures over a longer period.

Sustainability premise. If key resources and capabilities are to keep their value they must be protected from imitation, or substitution. Barriers to imitation are created by causal ambiguity and barriers to duplication.

There is causal ambiguity when it is unclear to competitors how the source of advantage works, so the causal connection between the actions of a firm and the observed results cannot be uncovered. The greater the uncertainty over how successful firms realize their results, the more likely it is that potential entrants will be deterred. Causal ambiguity deepens when the distinctive capability requires a complex pattern of coordination among diverse types of resources. This means that few people have a complete grasp of the entire system and no single element can be singled out for examination. There will be further ambiguity when the resources are specifically committed to the activities in the process and cannot be used elsewhere. These create interdependencies that are hard to disentangle and even harder to emulate.

Once a potential rival comprehends the sources of advantage, however imperfectly, imitation requires that it acquires or develops the resources necessary to mount a competitive challenge. Sustainability of the advantage against these attacks depends on the barriers to duplication, i.e.,

- the immobility or scarcity of the resources
- the accuracy of the information about the value of the resource. The established firm will usually have better insights into the productivity of the individual assets, whereas the rivals face an imperfect market with poor information about how much to pay
- even if the resources can be acquired, there is a risk that the value may not be realized because of a degradation in their productivity after the transfer.

The problem with the sustainability premise is that a position of advantage derived from a distinctive capability may not be sustained even if the capability is inimitable (Collis, 1994). First, if there is profound causal ambiguity with a high level of tacit knowledge, the capability will not be well understood by those inside or outside the firm. This could potentially impede the ability of the firm to adapt to new circumstances. Second, even if each of the distinctive capabilities is inimitable, there will be rivals trying to invalidate these sources of advantage by developing substitute capabilities or new business models that utilize different capabilities. Indeed, capabilities may be especially vulnerable to this threat because there are so many possible variants derived from different combinations of each of the linked activities in a business process. If the new capability becomes a competitive threat because it delivers superior value, the defender may be handicapped in adapting if its deeply embedded and imperfectly understood distinctive capability becomes a core rigidity or disability.

A counter-argument is that firms that have sustained their advantages and maintained superior performance have higher order capabilities for developing new capabilities[9]. These 'meta-capabilities' might include the flexibility to shift between capabilities more efficiently or faster than rivals, or the ability to carry through major change initiatives, or speedily acquire and act on insights into emerging opportunities.

Equilibrium premise. The emphasis on sustaining the advantage presumes an evolutionary equilibrium context. This may be a 'punctuated' equilibrium, with long periods of continuous but incremental change that may be disrupted by a discontinuity which is followed by new equilibrium conditions (Lengnick-Hall & Wolff, 1999). This does not preclude a firm applying 'strategic foresight' to find an opportunity to disrupt the status quo that they can exploit with their capabilities. The intent is to create a new equilibrium state where their advantage can be protected from imitation and be sustained.

This premise is at odds with an emerging hypercompetitive/high velocity logic of strategy (D'Aveni, 1994) that presumes an equilibrium will never be reached, that change is continuous and unpredictable, and that competitive advantages are fleeting in fluid, competitive arenas. The hallmark of success strategies is the ability to take preemptive action that challenges existing strategies, and adaptive organizations and capabilities that can respond quickly to unpredictable requirements and challenges. Strategies based on this disruptive logic deliberately aim to foment disequilibrium.

These conditions certainly are found in embryonic markets for high technologies, and especially in the intensely contested markets with low barriers to entry found in Internet commerce. The unpredictability and uncertainty of these markets demands organizational flexibility that is incompatible with the equilibrium-seeking emphasis of the resource-based perspective. However, life-cycle patterns suggest that once these markets have passed through their early high growth, turbulence period, on their way to maturity, that a capability logic would be more relevant (at least until another transformative technology of equal power came along to rewrite the rules of competition in a similar way).

An important part of the art of applying either a disruptive, guerilla logic or an equilibrium-seeking, capability logic is knowing when they are appropriate. Of course the transition from one strategic logic to another could be traumatic, because most prevailing premises and practices will need to be overhauled. The question is whether adroit practitioners of a guerrilla logic can adapt to the discipline and efficiency orientation of a capability logic, or whether the incumbents who have mastered the capability logic and have abundant assets, will eventually prevail.

The RBV and Market Strategies

In the context of this chapter we now return to our central question: in what ways does the RBV approach enable us to understand and interpret market strategies themselves, i.e., the behaviour over time of individual firms or business units. Perhaps inevitably, because the RBV approach starts from the nature of resources at the firm or unit level, it has rather more to say about the nature of supply than demand.

Indeed Priem (2001), in the critique of the RBV approach which we have already mentioned, notes the extent to which demand value is seen as exogenous. As they recognize, Shelby Hunt has also emphasized this limitation in a number of key contributions (Hunt & Morgan, 1996; Hunt, 2000a), and pointed out that whilst the resource-based view clearly recognizes firm heterogeneity in terms of assets, it places no equivalent emphasis on customer heterogeneity, which is, of course, central to any notion of the value of, say, market segmentation. Barney (2001) also recognizes that the RBV approach has relatively little to contribute to a direct understanding of market value. Indeed Hunt (2000a) goes as far as to argue that a more comprehensive theoretical approach, which he labels 'Resource Advantage' is required.

There are some concerns, however, as to whether Hunt's framework actually provides the most effective way of incorporating heterogeneity of demand (Wensley, 2002a), particularly in the context of the evolution of market structure. For instance, one of the most established issues in the nature of a market structure is what Wroe Alderson referred to as the sequential processes of 'sorting' between supplier offerings in order to 'match' specific portfolios to customer demands. As Hunt himself observes in addressing the issue of how this might be incorporated within his framework:

> My reply to Savitt's [2000] complaint that [I] did not develop a completely new lexicon and new theory that incorporated Alderson's 'sorting' and the competitive behaviors of consumers is simple: I do not know how to develop the lexicon and the theory he proposes. Nonetheless, [it] does include (in Figure 6.1) the behaviors of consumers as an important factor that influences the process of competition among firms. I see no reason why the competitive behaviors of consumers, as well as the 'sorting' aspects of Alderson, could not be incorporated in a systematic manner into the theory's lexicon and overall framework. I encourage him and others to work at doing so. (Hunt, 2000b)

At best, therefore, it remains an open question how far the RBV, even with the developments proposed by Hunt, will help us to understand not only a static view of market demand but even more a dynamic and evolving one, although it does provide a very useful perspective on the nature of strategic choices for the individual firm or business unit.

The Positioning Perspective

As Mintzberg et al., describe it:

> The positioning school … argued that only a few key strategies – as positions in the economic marketplace – are desirable in any given industry, ones that can be defended against existing and future competitors. Ease of defense means that firms which occupy these

> positions enjoy higher profits than other firms in the industry. And that, in turn, provides a reservoir of resources with which to expand and so to enlarge as well as consolidate position.
>
> Cumulating that logic across industries, the positioning school ended up with a limited number of basic strategies overall, or at least categories of strategies – for example, product differentiation, and focussed market scope. These were called generic.
>
> By thereby dispensing with one key premise of the design school that strategies have to be unique, tailor-made for each organization, the positioning school was able to create and hone a set of analytical tools dedicated to matching the right strategy to the conditions in hand (themselves also viewed as generic, such as maturity or fragmentation in an industry). (Mintzberg et al., 1988: 83)

From a market strategy perspective, however, we need to deconstruct some of the essential elements in this description: positions in the 'economic marketplace', the nature of differentiation, the concept of generic strategies and, finally, the equivalent notion of generic market conditions.

Our analysis will show that just as with some of the aspects of the resource-based perspective, where it proves rather difficult to link specific resources to actual market-based capabilities, so each of these essential elements only maps in a rather problematic manner onto our more detailed understanding of markets and market behaviour.

3-4-5 Analytical Framework

The most obvious codification of market strategies within the positioning perspective can be best described in terms of the three generic strategies, the four boxes (or perhaps more appropriately strategic contexts), and the five forces.

These particular frameworks also represent the substantial debt that marketing strategy owes to economic analysis; the three strategies and the five forces are directly taken from Michael Porter's (1985, 1990) influential work, which derived from his earlier work in Industrial Organization Economics. The four contexts was initially popularized by the Boston Consulting Group under Bruce Henderson (see Morrison & Wensley, 1991), and again strongly influenced by micro-economic analysis. Whilst each of these approaches remains a significant component in much marketing strategy teaching, we also need to recognize some of the key considerations and assumptions which need to be taken into account in any critical application.

The Three Strategies

It could reasonably be argued that Porter (1985) really reintroduced the standard economic notion of scale to the distinction between cost and differentiation to arrive at the three generic strategies of focus, cost and differentiation. Indeed, in his later formulation of the three strategies they really became four in that he suggested, rightly, that the choice between an emphasis on competition via cost or differentiation can be made at various scales of operation.

With further consideration it is clear that both of these dimensions are themselves not only continuous but also likely to be the aggregate of a number of relatively independent elements or dimensions. Hence scale is in many contexts not just a single measure of volume of finished output but also of relative volumes of sub-assemblies and activities which may well be shared. Even more so in the case of 'differentiation', where we can expect that there are various different ways in which any supplier attempts to differentiate their offerings. On top of this, a number of other commentators, most particularly John Kay (1993), have noted that not only may the cost–differentiation scale be continuous rather than dichotomous, but it also might not be seen as a real dimension at all. At some point this could become a semantic squabble, but there clearly is an important point that many successful strategies are built around a notion of good value for money, rather than a pure emphasis on cost or differentiation at any price. Michael Porter (1980) might describe this as a 'middle' strategy but, rather crucially, he has consistently claimed that there is a severe danger of getting 'caught in the middle'. In fact it might be reasonable to assume that in many cases being in the middle is the best place to be: after all, Porter has never presented significant systematic evidence to support his own assertion (cf. Wensley, 1994).

The Four Contexts

The four boxes (contexts) relates to the market share/market growth matrix originally developed by the Boston Consulting Group (BCG) under Bruce Henderson. Although there have inevitably been a whole range of different matrix frameworks that have emerged since the early days, the BCG one remains an outstanding exemplar not only because of its widespread popularity and impact, but because there was an underlying basic economic logic in its development. Many other similar frameworks just adopted the rather tautologous proposition that one should invest in domains which were both attractive and where one had comparative advantage!

The market growth/market share matrix, however, still involved a set of key assumptions which was certainly contestable. In particular, alongside the relatively uncontroversial assumption th
general the growth rate in markets tends t
there were the assumptions that it was

sense both easier to gain market share in higher growth-rate markets, and also that the returns to such gains were likely to be of longer duration. This issue, which can be seen as assumptions about first the cost and then the benefit of investment in market share, and has been discussed and debated widely in marketing over the last 20 years (see Jacobson & Aaker, 1985; Jacobson, 1994). The general conclusion would appear to be that:

1. Market share as an investment is not on average under-priced, and may well be over-priced.
2. The cost of gaining market share is less related to the market growth rate and much more to the relationship between actual growth rates and competitors' expectations.
3. Much of the benefit attributed to market share is probably better interpreted as the result of competitive advantages generated by more specific resources and choices in marketing or other corporate areas.[10]

On this basis, it would seem that the bias implied in the BCG matrix towards investment in market share at the early stages of market growth is not really justified, particularly when one takes into account that at this stage in market development many investments are likely to be somewhat more risky as well. If, however, a focus on market share position does encourage companies to place greater emphasis on the marketing fundamentals for a particular business then it could well be justified – but as very much a means to an end, rather than the solution itself.

More generally, as an analytical device, the matrix suffers from some of the problems which we illustrated for the three strategies approach: an analysis that is essentially based on extreme points when, in practice, many of the portfolio choices are actually around the centre of the diagram. This implies that any discrimination between business units needs to be on the basis of much more specific analysis rather than broad general characteristics.

Five Forces

The five forces analysis was originally introduced by Michael Porter (1985) to emphasize the extent to which the overall basis of competition was much wider than just the rivalries between established competitors in a particular market. Whilst not exactly novel as an insight, particularly to suggest that firms also face competition from new entrants and substitutes, it was presented in a very effective manner and served to emphasize not only the specific and increasing importance of competition as we discussed, but also the extent to which competition should be seen as a much wider activity within the value chain as Porter termed it, although it might now be more likely to be seen as the supply chain.[11] Actually, of course, the situation is a little more complex than this. Porter used the term 'value chain' when in essence he was concentrating more on the chain of actual costs. Whilst *ex post* from an economic point of view there is no difference between value and cost, it is indeed the process of both competition and collaboration between various firms and intermediaries that finally results in the attribution of value throughout the relevant network. In this sense, as others have recognized, a supply chain is an intermediate organization form, where there is a higher degree of cooperation between firms within the chain and a greater degree of competition between firms within different chains.

In this context Porter's analysis has tended to focus much more clearly on the issue of competition rather than cooperation. Indeed, at least in its representational form, it has tended to go further than this and focus attention on the nature of the competitive pressures on the firm itself rather than interaction between the firm and other organizations in the marketplace.

Each of these positioning approaches were still, however, driven by rather simplistic models of the nature of the marketplace itself, and in relating them to market strategies we need to consider this issue more critically. Marketing is not about the idealized world of some economic models, where competition takes place between a multitude of homogeneous small firms in an environment in which a market clearing price is set instantaneously in each time period. Of course, much of economics has evolved in various ways, some systematic, some rather *ad hoc,* to develop different and more complex theories and models about the nature of firm competition, and indeed many of the tools and techniques owe much of their development to particular economists. We will return to some of these developments shortly but need first to consider in more detail the central notion of differentiation, and hence the allied issue of positioning.

What makes a real market interesting is that (1) the market demand is heterogeneous, (2) the suppliers are differentiated, and (3) there are processes of feedback and change through time. Clearly these three elements interact significantly, yet in most cases we find that to reduce the complexity in our analysis and understanding we treat each item relatively independently. For instance, in most current textbook treatments of these issues in marketing we would use some form of *market segmentation* schema to map heterogeneous demand, some notion of the *resource-based view* of the firm, which we have reviewed already, to reflect the differentiation amongst suppliers, and some model of market evolution such as the *product life cycle* to reflect the nature of the time dynamic.

Spatial Competition

In the broad sense the positioning perspective focuses attention on the nature of the territory over which the competitive process evolves and the impact and effect of different positioning strategies of individual firms within this. We therefore need to consider means of representation which accommodate more complex ways of reflecting the nature of the territory or the market space. The most obvious initial approach is that of spatial competition, originally developed in the Hotelling (1929) model.

In formal terms, Hotelling considers two identical firms that supply a single homogeneous product with a constant production cost in a bounded linear market over which consumers with inelastic demand are uniformly distributed. The firms compete in location and price and consumers purchase the product from the cheapest source and pay a transport cost which is assumed linear with respect to the distance between the locations of the consumer and the supplying firm. Hotelling (1929) was, however, interested not in the strategies that the firms would adopt but the equilibrium outcome, which, at least given the simple form of the problem, can turn out to be independent of both starting conditions and intermediate actions.

Hence, the problem about this basic representation of firms locating in the 'strategy space' is that it does not recognize the likely dynamics of such a process. The most obvious way of modelling this is via some form of inertia–incentive representation, which recognizes that there will be some level of organizational inertia to any movement but also some form of incentive, which if substantial enough will overcome this inertia. In principle this incentive can be either because of the unacceptable nature of the existing position or the attractive nature of the new position. This is the basic logic behind the SIOP (Stress, Inertia, Opportunity) model of strategic change developed by Huff et al. (1992). In a later paper, Huff & Huff (1995) test this model against data on strategic change within the pharmaceuticals industry, with some success.

Broadly, Huff et al. set down three components which make up 'stress':

1. firm underperformance compared with the mean in terms of annual return on sales or annual sales growth in the base year
2. the extent to which the firm exhibits abnormal (in either direction) performance in terms of return on sales and/or sales growth
3. the extent to which the firm is, as Huff & Huff put it, 'stretching the strategic envelope' in committing a high level of resources within a narrow product line.

They also suggest that 'highly attractive opportunities constitute a source of stress and may well trigger second order changes in strategy' and 'inertia', which is represented by the period of persistence of the current strategy, is itself affected by:

1. the level of resources available to actually undertake a major strategic change
2. the future potential of the current strategy: they argue this can be measured by the relative concentration of the firm's products in high growth therapeutic classes.

Finally Huff et al. characterize opportunity in terms of the performance surface revealed by competitor performance. More specifically Huff & Huff consider the partial differentials with respect to sales growth along the three strategic dimensions in the analysis (R&D spend, advertising spend and scope of pharmaceutical categories covered by their product line) for the firm's near neighbours.

Whilst we might wish to question some of the specific operationalization(s) of their variables, which as usual in this sort of empirical work have to be proxied against what data are or can be available, it is important to recognize that Huff & Huff manage to test their model against some useful empirical data. Their results are supportive of their model, particularly in terms of the general incidence of strategic changes themselves, and also direction – the latter particularly in the case of advertising expenditure and product portfolio scope.

Game Theory

Varadarajan and Jayachandran (1999) assert, 'game theory has emerged as a dominant conceptual framework in marketing to analyze the behavior of competing (interdependent) firms in oligopolistic markets' (1999: 126), and Moorthy (1985) provides a broad list of possible applications.

In an analytical sense, game theory has indeed provided a very effective framework within which to investigate a whole series of contexts where the outcomes are a result of the interactions between the intermediate choices of various actors. It has ensured that we systematically model the impact of various decision rules for the actors themselves and do not assume, without defining them carefully, distortions such as information asymmetries between the actors. It has provided us with a better understanding of robust competitive strategies in many situations of direct competition (such as the so-called 'tit-for-tat' approach), as well as the impact of changes in rules and regulations. When we come, however, to the complex, and to some extent contested, context in which market strategies actually operate, the benefits are perhaps a little less clear. There are three reasons for this. First, the pay-off matrix is itself uncertain; second, there is a more complex continuum of competitive or cooperative behaviour than can easily be represented in a game theory model; and third, it often turns out in practice that trying too hard to think about the situation 'from a competitor viewpoint' can itself prove rather dysfunctional (Waterman, 1988).

Equally, game theory-type thinking may be usefully applied at some stages when it is necessary to interpret the relationship between competitive behaviours and market response. Leeflang & Wittick (1993) argued that there was evidence of what might be termed 'over-competition', and were particularly interested in the notion that forms of conjoint analysis could be used to determine the underlying customer trade-off matrix, which is, of course, only partly revealed in the empirical customer elasticities (because individual customers can only respond to the actual offerings that are available), and is 'assumed' (with some degree of bias and error) by individual competitors in determining their competitive actions and reactions. More recently, they have argued that much of the managerial behaviour they observed could be explained by the imbalance in incentive structures in that management will rarely get criticized for reacting to competitive moves, whilst Clark & Montgomery (1995) have argued that such 'paranoia' can actually help improve firm performance!

The Nature of Market Space: Differentiation and Positioning

We have so far considered various ways in which, implicitly or explicitly, the market space is represented by making various simplifying assumptions. Such approaches have two major limitations which may act to remove any benefit from the undoubted reduction of analytical complexity. First, they assume implicitly that this decomposition is reasonably first-order correct: that the impact of the individual elements is more important than their interaction terms. To examine this assumption critically we need some alternative form of analysis and representation such as modelling the phenomenon of interest as the co-evolution of firms and customers in a dynamic phase space, which allows for the fact that time and space interact. A particular difficulty in this representation would appear to be how we introduce what might be termed learning behaviour into the system.

Second, they assume that the ways of representing the individual elements that we use, in particular market segmentation and product life-cycle concepts, are in fact robust representations of the underlying phenomena. In terms of the adequacy of each element in its own terms, we need to look more closely at the ways in which individual improvements may be achieved, and we might wish to consider whether it would be better to model partial interactions, say, between two elements only rather than the complete system.

The Various Ways of Modelling the Market Space: Imperfect Competition, Product Markets and Networks

When we come to the question of the modelling and representation of the market space, we again face a range of forms from simple to complex. In economic terms, perhaps the simplest form lies in the developments we discussed above, heralded by both Chamberlain and Robinson when they originally and independently developed the notion of imperfect or monopolistic competition. It was, with hindsight, not a dramatic move but it remains a crucial insight that there is no reason why the demand curve should be horizontal except the particular logic of perfect competition. To make the demand curve downward sloping would be to recognize the possibility of some form of price differentiation between suppliers in the market.

How then do we characterize the nature of the market space? To move beyond the traditional notion of each firm facing a separate downward sloping but non-interacting demand curve, we need to develop a way to characterize the nature of the space in which the firms compete. For convenience we will call this the market space and we will focus on the issue of what might be called the dimensionality of competition. This is a crucial construct in understanding the likely development of firm strategies in a competitive market: broadly speaking the dimensionality is the basis upon which different strategies can be viable because of relative independence of the positions in a sustainable multi-dimensional space. In the limits the traditional imperfect competition model assumes N firms compete in N dimensional space, that is that they do not interact, whereas direct competition of the traditional economic model implies competition in $N = 1$ dimension only.

Differentiation in space: issues of market segmentation The analysis of spatial competition has of course a long history, back at least, as we have already mentioned, to the classical and very simple Hotelling (1929) model of linear competition such as that faced by the two ice-cream sellers on the sea-front. Despite its evident simplicity, the basic Hotelling model captured the two critical issues in spatial competition: the notion of a space dimension which separated the various competitive suppliers as well as the fact that these suppliers themselves would have some degree of mobility. As we have already discussed, in traditional economic terms Hotelling was interested in establishing the equilibrium solution under these two considerations, whereas in marketing we are often more concerned with the impact and likelihood of particular spatial moves although some notion of the stable long-term equilibrium, if it exists, is obviously important. The Hotelling model provides us with the basic structure of spatial competition: a definition of the space domain, some model of the relationship between the positioning of the relevant suppliers within this space, and their relative demands.

In marketing, the competitive space is generally characterized in terms of market segmentation. Market segmentation has, of course, received considerable attention in both marketing research and practice, and this is summarized in Chapter 5 on The Structure of Product-Markets in this Handbook. In the terminology used by Shocker in Chapter 5, we are most obviously concerned with spatial models.

It is also worth noting the particular caveats that Shocker emphasizes when it comes to market structure analysis (MSA), particularly of a factor-based spatial type which we may wish to use to investigate the strategic issue of positioning further. He emphasizes that the aggregation issue can mean that we fail to reflect on different use situations, but also points out that under certain circumstances spatial models can be used to interpret the more dynamic aspects of market evolution.

There is undoubtedly a case that both the longevity of popular brands and the stability of individual purchase patterns (see early work by Ehrenberg (1972) and more recently Ehrenberg & Uncles (1995)) might suggest that any positional changes in competitive space are not only difficult to predict but also likely to be infrequent.

Therefore how far do spatial forms of MSA provide us with an appropriate definition of the space within which competition evolves? In this sense the key questions are about the dimensionality of the space concerned, the stability of the demand function, and the degree of mobility for individual firms (or more correctly individual offerings) in terms of repositioning.

In principle we can describe the nature of spatial competition in a market either in demand terms or in supply terms. Market segmentation represents the demand perspective on structure, whilst competitive positioning represents the supply perspective.

Market segmentation takes as its starting point assumptions about the differing requirements that individual customers have with respect to bundles of benefits in particular use situations. Most obviously in this context, it is an 'ideal' approach in that it is effectively assumed that each customer can/does specify their own ideal benefit bundle and their purchase choice in the relevant use situation is based on proximity to this ideal point. In consumer psychology this is equivalent to an assumption that individuals have strong and stable preferences.

The competitive positioning approach uses consumer judgements, normally on an aggregate basis, on the similarities and differences between specific competitive offerings. In principle this provides an analytical output roughly equivalent to the spatial distribution in the Hotelling model. Such an analysis can also be used to provide an estimate of the dimensionality of the discriminant space, but in many situations the results are given in a constrained two-dimensional format for ease of presentation. Equally, benefit segmentation studies can be used, as we have discussed above, along with techniques such as factor analysis to try and arrive at an estimate of the dimensionality of the demand side.

We can be reasonably certain that the attitude space for customers in any particular market is generally, say, $N > 3$: factor analytical studies might suggest at least four or five dimensions on average, and that of competitive offerings is of at least a similar order. Indeed in the latter case if we considered the resource-based view of the firm very seriously we might go for a dimensionality as high as the number of competitors.

Of more interest from a strategy point of view is a relatively parsimonious view as to how we represent what happens in terms of actual purchase behaviour through time. Although there is relatively little high quality empirical and indeed theoretical work in this area so far, there are intriguing results to suggest that the dimensionality of this space can be effectively much reduced, although we may still then have problems with some second-order effects in terms of market evolution. There have been a number of attempts to apply segmentation analysis to behavioural data with much less information as to attitudes or intention. In one of the more detailed of such studies, Chintagunta (1994) suggested that the dimensionality of the revealed competitive space was two-dimensional, but even this might be an over-estimate.[12] In his own interpretation of the results Chintagunta focuses on the degree to which the data analysis reveals interesting differences in terms of brand position highlighted by individual purchase patterns through time.

In terms of second-order anomalies, we can also consider some of the issues raised by the so-called 'compromise effect' in choice situations, where the choice between two alternatives depends on other, less attractive, alternatives. In an intriguing paper Wernerfelt (1995) argues that this effect can be systematically explained by the notion that consumers draw inferences about their own personal valuations from the portfolio of offerings. However it may be that a compromise effect can also be seen as the result of mapping an $N > 1$ attribute and preference space onto an $N = 1$ set of purchase decisions.[13]

A simple model of spatial competition might therefore be one in which a considerable amount of competition can be seen along a single dimension, in circumstances in which multiple offerings are possible, and where there is no reason to believe *a priori* that individual offerings will be grouped either by common brand or specification, with a fixed entry cost for each item and a distribution of demand which is multi-modal. To this extent it may actually be true that the very simplifications that many criticize in the Porter 'three generic strategies' approach may be reasonably appropriate in building a first-order model of competitive market evolution (see Campbell-Hunt, 2000). In the short-term, following the notion of 'clout' and 'vulnerability' (Cooper & Nakanishi, 1988), we might also expect changes in position in this competitive dimension could be a function of a whole range of what might often be seen as tactical as well as strategic marketing actions.

Cooper in his more recent work (see Cooper & Inoue, 1996) has extended his own approach to understanding market structures and developed an approach which marries two different data types – switching probabilities and attribute ratings. Despite the fact that the models developed appear to perform well against the appropriate statistical test, there remain basic issues with the approach adopted which link to the issue of the time-dynamic evolution of the market or demand space. When the model is applied to the well-established data set on car purchase switching behaviour (Harshman et al., 1982) it is clear that it provides an interesting and informative analysis of the ways in which various customer 'segments' have evolved over time, both in terms of their size and attribute preferences. However, given the nature of the data and the form of analysis, the dynamic process whereby customer desires change in response both to new competitive offerings and other endogenous and exogenous factors can only be seen in terms of changes in attributes and specific switching decisions. We must now consider, however, in the context of understanding the time-based nature of market strategies, how we might incorporate in more detail a longer-term time dimension with a stronger customer focus.

Differentiation in time: beyond the Product Life Cycle. Characterizing the nature of competitive market evolution

> Few management concepts have been so widely accepted or thoroughly criticised as the product life cycle. (Lambkin & Day, 1989: 4)

The product life cycle remains an oft-used model to represent the nature of time effects in product markets. It has the advantage that it does represent the most simple form of path development for any product (introduction, growth, maturity, decline) but, as has been widely recognized, this remains a highly stylized representation of the product sales pattern for most products during their lifetime. Whilst it is reasonably clear that it is difficult if not impossible to propose a better single generic time pattern, any such pattern is subject to considerable distortion as a result of interactions with changes in technology as well as customer and competitor behaviour.

It would seem that this is an area in which we lack some important research evidence. It is currently not only difficult to provide any advice on the reduced set of likely patterns (given that we know that the single pattern is relatively infrequent) but also to provide any advice on the most significant contingencies and interactions. Anecdotal evidence might suggest that the most important positive moderating effects (those which shift the sales level upwards) are to be found in new uses amongst customers encouraged by supplier behaviour, whilst the most common causes of downward moderation are to be found in competitive reaction. However a cynic might suspect this was another case of attribution bias and that we need more systematic and rigorous research.

Lambkin & Day (1989) suggested that an understanding of the process of product–market evolution required a more explicit distinction between issues of the demand system, the supply system, and the resource environment. However, they chose to emphasize the nature of the demand evolution primarily in terms of diffusion processes, an approach which is covered in detail elsewhere in this Handbook. This approach tends to underestimate the extent to which demand side evolution is as much about the way(s) in which the structure of the demand space is changing as the more aggregate issue of the total demand itself. Lambkin & Day, themselves, treat these two issues at different levels of analysis, with 'segmentation' as an issue in market evolution, which is defined as the resource environment within which the process of the product life cycle takes place.

Beyond this, more recent research on the process of market evolution, partly building on some the ideas developed by Lambkin & Day (1989), has attempted to incorporate some insights from, amongst other areas, evolutionary ecology. In particular, work on the extensive Disk-drive database, which gives quarterly data on all disk-drive manufacturers, has allowed Christiansen (1997) and Freeman (1997) to look at the ways in which the existence of competitive offerings at the early stages in the market development seems to encourage market growth, whereas of course at later stages the likelihood of firm exit increases with firm density. Other computer-related industries have also provided the opportunity for empirical work on some of the issues relating to both the impact of standardization, modularization, and the nature of generation effects (Sanchez, 1995), although in the latter case it must be admitted that the effects themselves can sometimes be seen as marketing actions in their own right.

Much of the market shift towards standardization as it evolves can be seen as analogous to more recent work on the mathematics of chaos and particular questions of the nature of boundaries between domains of chaos and those of order: often labelled the phenomena of complexity (Cohen & Stewart, 1995). Whether we can use such models to provide a better understanding of the nature of market evolution beyond the basic analogy remains an important question for empirical research.

More recent attempts to apply spatial competition models that demonstrate some level of chaotic or complexity characteristics, either to competitive behaviour in a retailing context (Krider & Weinberg, 1997) or multi-brand category competition (Rungie, 1998) and competition between audit service providers (Chan et al., 1999), show that such models may be able to give us significant new insights as to the nature of competitive market evolution.

The Configurational Perspective

Firms are, of course, particular forms of organization and a key question relates not only to the boundaries of firms and their wider links but also to the nature of their internal organization. In this section we will focus more on issues of the boundary of the firm, following Coase (1937) and Williamson (1975), with insights from Chandler (1962) and Stinchcombe (1965) too, and on the issues of the wider network of interrelationships within which any firm is located. We will also consider approaches in this area that help us to understand the extent to which configurational choices appear to facilitate certain types of strategic change for the firm itself.

The Boundaries of the Firm

The classical economics treatment for the boundaries of the firm is that of Coase (1937) and Williamson (1975) around the issue of transaction costs – the administrative costs of any internal relationship between activities compared with the costs inherent in opportunism and uncertainty which are a result of incomplete contingent contracts in a market-based transaction. Clear though this distinction is in conceptual terms, there have been major problems about how it applies in practice, both to issues of internal organization of firms themselves (particularly those that adopt what might be termed pseudo-market relationships between various units, represented as an ideal type in the M-Form described by Chandler (1962) and others), and the complex network of relationships and relative stable series of transactions between firms (most clearly enunciated by Hakansson (1987) and others in terms of resources, activities and actors) that we observe in almost all industrial configurations.

The Transaction Cost Approach

Williamson & Winter (1991) provide a good review of how the transaction cost approach is applied to questions relating to the nature of the firm, whilst Perrow (1986) provides a critique of the approach in the context of complex organizations. From a marketing perspective, whilst the debate about the extent to which the internal organization of the firm can be understood, primarily framed in terms of economic efficiency as compared with totally different perspectives around the nature of firms as sociological entities, or indeed as a wider class of organizations that provide their incumbents with various defences against anxiety (cf. Menzies-Lyth, 1988), remains an interesting one, our key concern is the relationship between the internal organization and the nature of the market or markets for the firm's products or services. Hence as others have observed (Peng et al., 2000), we are in fact more interested in the choice between a Schumpeterian dynamic view of the nature of entrepreneurial activity in the context of a continually evolving marketplace compared with a more static perspective, which Williamson (1991) describes as 'economising', represented by the transaction cost approach. The other key issue in the transaction cost approach is the extent to which, in practice, we observe a wide range of what might be termed intermediate governance arrangements between, at the one end of the spectrum, the 'pure' market and, at the other, the administered hierarchy.

In a marketing context, we most commonly apply a transaction cost approach in considering the traditional 'make or buy' decisions which relate to the marketing function, such as in the use of advertising agents and, more particularly, sales intermediaries (Anderson, 1996; Anderson & Weitz, 1986). The more general issue of supply chains and the relationships between buyers and sellers, however, has proved to be one where a number of different perspectives are evident (Faria & Wensley, 2002). In general, what might be termed the supply chain management perspective, strongly influenced by work in operations management, has emphasized what was formerly termed in marketing the channel 'captain' perspective, with a key organization assumed to have power and control over the other members of the chain whilst the industrial networks perspective, which forms the basis of another chapter in this Handbook (Håkansson & Snehota, Chapter 20), has tended to emphasize the embedded nature of every firm (Grabher, 1993; Hakansson & Johanson, 1993) and hence the mutual dependencies within which they all act.

The Firm as a Bundle of Contracts

John Kay, in his analysis of the foundations of corporate success, developed the notion of the architecture of the firm, which he defined as:

> … the first of the three primary sources of distinctive capability. It is a network of relational contracts within, or around, the firm. Firms may establish these relationships with and among their employees (internal architecture), with their suppliers or customers (external architecture) or amongst a group of firms engaged in related activities (networks).
>
> The value of architecture rests in the capacity of organisations which establish it to create organisational knowledge and routines, to respond flexibly to changing circumstances, and to achieve easy and open exchanges of information. (Kay, 1993: 66)

This view of the firm is clearly linked to that developed by Jensen & Meckling (1976) in their earlier analysis of the firm as a bundle of contracts and the particular issues of agency between the owners and the managers. More recently, Blois (2002) has looked at the Macneil (1981) approach to relational contracting, and in comparing it to Menger's (1871) writing on exchange suggests that the distinction between discrete and relational contracting, which is often used to argue that a transaction-based cost approach is inadequate, is itself potentially misleading. As Blois puts it:

> Thus an exchange is [the] sum of a number of attributes passing between the two organizations and because of the nature of these attributes and the involvement of many different people the norms that are applicable may vary. Indeed there can be elements of exchange that are discrete – even within an exchange which is overall perceived to be relational. Alternatively, within an exchange that is seen overall as being discrete, there may be elements that are subject to relational norms. (Blois, 2002: 1545)

Strategy, Structure and Evolution

As we have suggested above, a configuration perspective suggests that a combination of the internal and external forms of organization of the firm has a significant impact on the enacted strategy of the firm and the way it evolves. Two central and early contributors to this understanding were Alfred Chandler & Arthur Stinchcombe.[14]

Chandler, of course, enunciated the key principle of the relationship between structure and strategy. Of course, as often with key ideas which are widely developed and disseminated, it is also clear that the richer picture that he described in his analysis got rather lost in its widespread development and adoption:

> In the Harvard studies, the focus is exclusively on firms, their strategies and organizational structure. The relationship between firms and their environment is largely simplified. The same can also be said about the relationship between the firm and its past. While Chandler had clearly examined the socio-economic interaction between firms and the external environment, at Harvard the only relation considered is a competitive one, which is supposed to vary across industries. This is done by examining the effect of industries on performance. (It has to be noted that in the initial studies no environmental variable was considered at all. Only in 1982 Rumelt published a paper where he introduced a variable analysing the effect of industry on performance.) Having separated the firms from their environment, firms are separated from their past. In the account of how firms had changed their strategies in the post-war period and how they had increasingly diversified their strategies and changed their structure, there is no process. It seemed that the changes firms were making in their strategies and structures were all logical, straightforward and necessary measures to improve their performance. Nothing of Chandler's narrative of the process of change in firms' strategies and structure appears in the Harvard research.
>
> The simplification process and the separation between the firm and its environment enable research to use linear equation techniques to measure the effect of firms' strategies and their organisational structures on performance, and the formulation of clear cause-effect relationships (Curto & Wensley, 1997)

Such developments meant that the work related to Chandler became focused almost exclusively on the internal organization (or configurational) questions.

Alfred Stinchcombe's influence has been somewhat less marked. He started by taking a much wider (but not, as we have discussed, so much wider when compared with Chandler's original one) approach to the issue of organizational form and, particularly, new organizational form. His analysis concluded:

> Organizations which are founded at a particular time must construct their social systems with the social resources available. Particularly, they have to build their elites so that they can recruit necessary resources from the society and to build the structure of the organization so that in the historically given labor market they can recruit skills and achieve motivation of workers. Once such going concerns are set up in a particular area, they may preserve their structures for long enough to yield the correlations we observe by any one of three processes: (a) they may still be the most efficient form of organization for a given purpose; (b) traditionalizing forces, the vesting interests, and the working out of ideologies may tend to preserve the structure; (c) the organization may not be in a competitive structure in which it has to be better than alternative forms of organization in order to survive. (1965: 169)

Broadly speaking, we can link these issues to work which has developed in two areas of sociology to try and understand the process of firm evolution.[15] One has been in population ecology (Aldrich & Pfeffer, 1976; Hannan & Freeman, 1977), where the emphasis has been on the process of organizational selection and the twin notions of structural inertia and a changing fitness landscape that relates to some of the work we discussed in the previous section on the nature of the market space. The other approach has been labelled 'institutional theory' and has been concerned with the degree to which populations of firms share similar characteristics (DiMaggio & Powell, 1983). Again we can recognize twin notions, in this case isomorphism and resource partitioning. 'Isomorphism' is a limiting process that makes companies in a market resemble other companies that confront the same set of commercial conditions. 'Resource partitioning' explains how competition among mass-producing firms generates the exploration of peripheral niches within the resource space available to specialist organizations (Carroll & Swaminathan, 1992). Carroll & Swaminathan's framework is developed on the differences between a fundamental niche (the resource space on which a population can thrive) and a realized niche (the actual sub space of the niche utilized by the population).

We can also find strong echoes of Stinchcombe's approach in more recent work looking at the issues of organizational evolution (Aldrich, 1999) or the co-evolutionary process in particular industries and markets (Lewin et al., 1999). Aldrich shows how the traditional neo-Darwinian model of variation-selection-retention model can be applied to the study of organizational transformation:

Variation. In Aldrich's evolutionary model of transformation, the greater the frequency of variations the greater the opportunities for transformation. The level of variation may be reduced by endogenous selection norms favouring inertia. Otherwise, it may be helped along by institutional experimentation, incentives to innovate, authorization of unfocused variation, and creative acting out of organizational practices.

Selection. Changes in selection criteria open avenues for new practices. Internal selection criteria, which are not linked to environmental fitness, may be realigned. External discontinuities may trigger changes in selection pressures, such as changes in competitive conditions, government regulations, or technological breakthroughs.

Retention. Transformations are completed when the knowledge required for reproducing the new form is embodied in a community of practice. Retention is operated by individuals and groups, structures, policies and programmes, or networks.

Aldrich looks at the above model as the basic dynamic within organizations that brings about change and transformation. He defines transformation as a major change in an organization involving a break with existing routines and a shift to new kinds of competencies that challenge organizational knowledge. He views this as happening along three dimensions of the organization: goals, boundaries and activities.

Goals. Organizations that are driven by goals engage in collective action towards a target. Transformation would occur when major changes in the goals are effected. Ginsberg & Bucchholtz (1990) look at the example of the conversion of Health Maintenance Organizations (HMOs) from non-profit to profit status. Haverman (1992) looks at the changes in the breadth of the goals of Savings and Loan organizations when they entered the market for direct investment in real estate.

Boundaries. Organizations experience expansion or contraction of their boundaries. Expansion occurs through acquisition, mergers, or going into new market segments. Contraction occurs through downsizing, divestitures, or a reduction in the market base being targeted. Contraction and expansion can be exogenous or endogenous to the organization. Aldrich (1999) sees ITT is a prime example of the transformation of boundaries. ITT had spent billions acquiring more than 150 companies during the 1960s in order, according to the firm's president, to escape the status of a 'one product company'. Its acquisition policy sent the firm to 10th on the *Fortune 500* list. A decade after its acquisition spree, ITT was mired in poor performance and bureaucratic inertia. Its stock, which formerly traded in the $70 range, sunk to the $30 range. In response to this judgement of the financial markets, ITT embarked on a bold departure in 're-engineering' itself. It divested some 100 subsidiary businesses during the 1980s. In 1995, when the number of formerly acquired operations divested by the firm exceeded 200, ITT divided itself into three independent trading firms.

Activities. According to Aldrich (1999) activity systems in organizations are the means by which members accomplish work, which can include processing raw materials, information or people. Transformation occurs when changes in the activities have a major effect on organizational knowledge. The University of Michigan set up the M-Pathways Project in 1995 to focus on how the University did its administrative work in order to improve processes, simplify policies, and eliminate policies and procedures that did not add value.

In Aldrich's terms, it is the issue of 'boundaries' that most concerns us, when we try to understand the configurational choices that are made either individually or collectively by firms, particularly in respect to assumptions about the nature of the organization of demand. Here, however, we face a problem in terms of detailed empirical data, as Lewin and Volberda note:

> However, studies of simultaneous evolution or co-evolution of organizations and their environments are still rare. We define co-evolution as the joint outcome of managerial intentionality, environment, and institutional effects. Co-evolution assumes that change may occur in all interacting populations of organizations. Change can be driven by direct interactions and feedback from the rest of the system. In other words, change can be recursive and need not be an outcome of either managerial adaptation or environmental selection but rather the joint out-come of managerial intentionality and environmental effects. (Lewin & Volberda, 1999: 526)

As an exception they note the Galunic & Eisenhardt (1996) study on selection and adaptation at the intra-corporate level of analysis, which used charter changes to align and realign the competencies of various divisions with co-evolving markets and opportunities. Whilst this approach provides not only an interesting way of researching intra-organizational restructuring over time, but also a direct link to Chandler's original interest in the M-form organization, it is worth noting that even in this case, the model adopted for the process of market evolution was a simple three-stage life cycle one: start-up, growth, and maturity. They found that, broadly speaking, the process of charter changes, which equate with the agreed domain of any division's activity, could be seen as one which was based on selecting the successes from a portfolio of start-ups, the reinforcing focus, and finally required disposals as the particular market opportunity went through the three stages.

Lewin & Volberta (1999) also note the much more historical analysis in which Kieser (1989) describes how medieval guilds were replaced by mercantilist factories as markets and institutions co-evolved, where he shows how co-evolutionary processes resulted in an increase of functional specialization of institutions, a de-monopolization of social monopolies, and a decoupling of individual motives and organizational goals.

From a market strategy perspective, however, it is noteworthy that even those few studies which attempt to model the nature of market evolution specifically, rather than treat it more as a backcloth upon which other sociological and economic processes take place, tend to represent the actual process in very limited ways. Only in the resource partitioning approach do we perhaps see the direct opportunities for a more complex model of market development which represents both its continuity, in the sense that one can reasonably expect cycles of competitive imitation followed by the emergence of new forms and market positions for competition, and its indeterminacy, in that various new 'realized niches' could emerge. Even here, however, the implicit emphasis is on the individual firms as the motivating force rather than the collective choice of customers in the various markets. Much as Levins & Leowontin (1985) intended to emphasize a more dialectic and interactive approach between any species and its 'environment' by, amongst other things, titling their book *The Dialectical Biologist*, so we need to develop a more interactive approach to the modelling of firm and market co-evolution.

The Research Challenge: Linking Market and Firm Evolution

Our understanding of the development and evolution of markets and business strategies has made steady progress in the past decade – but the result is still modest when compared with the complexity of the issues. The challenge still remains to integrate the three major perspectives on these issues, epitomized by the resource-based view, the positioning, and configuration approaches to the theory of the firm. Each of these perspectives gives valuable insights into the role played by heterogeneous demand and supply, and the processes of market feedback and change. But none gives a full perspective. Continuing progress on the convergence of these theories will require the simultaneous consideration of the impact of time and space along the following three levels of evolution.

The evolution of a market space (and the shape of the product life cycle in particular), is shaped by the interaction of buyers and sellers over time and can clearly be seen as an evolutionary or, more correctly, co-evolutionary process. This has been recognized by marketing scholars from Wroe Alderson onwards, but seems to be stalled by, amongst other things, the lack of a viable taxonomy. Whilst on the supply side Day & Lambkin initially applied the general notion of specialist and generalist organizations with some success,[16] we still lack any reasonably agreed aggregate framework on the demand or customer side beyond the product life cycle and adopter groups based on the original Rodgers (1962) analysis of the diffusion of innovation.[17] Among the complexities to incorporate are feedback effects of the collective choices of strategy; such as the self-fulfilling prophecy whereby the established competitors in a mature market simultaneously decide to reduce their marketing and R&D investments to a sustaining level. Under what conditions is there a resulting slowdown in category sales that confirms and reinforces the initial decision?

We also need to develop new ways of understanding the ways in which the market space evolves. For instance, Rosa et al. (1999) and Rosa & Porac (2002) have argued that we need to adopt a much more socio-cognitive perspective to appreciate the dynamic nature of the market space as 'an outcome of the interaction between producers and consumers around ever-developing product concepts: product concepts are consensually understood categories that define for producers and consumers what counts as an instance of a product' (Rosa & Porac, 2002).

Richer and more useful models of market evolution may benefit by narrowing the scope of theory development, while using a mix of theories. Such an approach could be used, for example, to address the question of whether markets become more complex as they evolve. Is there an increase in the number of viable competitive positions in the market space? Does that market space have more dimensions? Both complexity theory (Kaufmann, 2001) and thermodynamic theory (Chaisson, 2001) have dealt with similar questions, and advances in agent-based modelling promise new ways of simulating more complex interactive processes of spatial competition (Ishibuchi, et al., 2001; Tesfatsion, 2001).

The positioning of each firm within a market space (relative to rivals) over time, is a second level of evolutionary process. Individual firms make constrained positioning choices, and these choices develop over time to become what we may label individual market strategies. We need to understand more specifically the ways in which choices are made, the nature of the assumptions about the market space or fitness landscape that informs these choices, and the nature of subsequent learning processes with respect to both other firms and revealed market response. As we have indicated above, at the individual level there is some tentative evidence that firm-level strategies tend to result in convergent positioning through a process of imitation which itself provides the opportunity for new competition to position itself on the boundaries of the resource space, thus supporting a continuing cycle of innovation and imitation between firms (cf. Metcalf et al., 2000). In understanding the evolution of individual firm level market strategies, we need to develop both better models of 'appropriate' decision choices against which to benchmark actual empirical evidence (see for instance Marks et al., 1998) and to incorporate the central strategic issue of managerial intent in any strategic choice process (Lewin & Volberda, 1999; Wensley, 2002b)

The co-evolution of the resources of each firm with the market. Many organizational capabilities emerge, are refined, or decay as a result of product market activity. As a consequence the particular sub-markets a firm chooses to serve will engender a distinctive set of resources. The choices of activities to be performed within the firm, and the external relationships that are formed, provide managerial discretion over the evolutionary path that the resource set takes.

Heterogeneity in the population of firms in a market space can in theory be amplified by feedback effects (Cohen & Levinthal, 1994). For example, the concept of absorptive capacity (Cohen & Levinthal, 1990) suggests that a firm with greater expertise in a particular technology domain than its rivals will more readily acquire further knowledge in the same domain.[18] In the same way a positional advantage may be self-reinforcing. For example, research in brand equity consistently shows that a strong brand name enhances the ability of a firm to extend its product line into related products. But if there is a discontinuous change in the competitive space, due to a technological disruption or a change in customer requirements, these same self-reinforcing mechanisms may weaken a position by reducing the ability of a firm to adapt successfully. This is because the returns from exploiting existing resources may appear to be more certain and immediate to established firms than returns from the exploration of new resources and market opportunities. Again the issue becomes more complex when we also introduce the phenomenon of demand heterogeneity (Adner & Levinthal, 2001).

In short, there are numerous sustaining and inhibiting forces to be accounted for in any dynamic analysis of the strategic positions of rivals in the market space. These issues are surely at the frontier of our understanding of market strategies. By integrating on-going progress in the relevant theories of the firm and the research discussed elsewhere in this Handbook, this knowledge frontier will continue to advance.

Notes

1. In fact our general approach is actually closer to that used by Allison (1969) in his seminal study of the Cuban missile crisis. He used three distinct levels of analysis – nation state, bureaucratic entities, and individuals – to interpret the nature of the choices made and actions undertaken.

2. Our use of assets is more restrictive than Amit & Schoemaker (1993), who refer to strategic assets as the subset of all resources and capabilities that form the basis of the firm's competitive advantage.

3. Srivastava et al. (1999) adopt a process perspective, and argue that the crucial or core processes are product development, supply chain management, and customer relationship management.

4. Leonard-Barton (1995) distinguishes 'core' or distinctive capabilities from 'supplemental' capabilities that add value to the core capability, but could be imitated, and from 'enabling' capabilities that are necessary but not sufficient to distinguish competitively a firm.

5. Some authors (e.g., Oliver, 1997) define this context broadly to encompass the firm's culture and broader influences such as traditions, network ties, and regulatory pressures.

6. Our focus will be on the issue of the ability of the RBV to explain firm heterogeneity, rather than the more fundamental concerns of many theories of the firm to

explain the existence of firms and why they are needed. These latter questions have become very controversial. See for example, Connor & Prahalad, 1996; Foss, 1996; Kogut & Zander, 1996; Williamson, 1999.

7. These premises are adapted from Lengnick-Hall & Wolff (1999).

8. As Mintzberg et al. (1998) put it, 'SWOT is alive and well in strategic management; it is just that the SWs (strengths and weaknesses) have taken over from the OTs (opportunities and threats)'.

9. Indeed this perspective has led some commentators in the marketing field such as Dickson (1996) to argue that organizational learning is the key major capability, or what might be termed meta-competence, in contradistinction to Hunt & Morgan's (1996) and others' emphasis on market orientation. This however leads us into further difficulties since, on the one hand, as Dickson recognizes, following Sinkula (1994), such higher order learning is a complex construct, whilst on the other, the market orientation construct is also to be seen as a mixture primarily of a so-called 'cultural' construct derived from Narver & Slater's (1990) empirical work, along with a more 'behavioural' one linked to the original work by Kohli & Jaworski (1990). Of course, since this original work there have been various attempts to produce and empirically test an integrated construct, for a partial review see, for instance, Stoelhorst & Raaij (2002).

10. For a specific meta-analysis which considers findings from 48 studies, see Szymanski et al. (1993).

11. More recent commentators such as McGee (2002) maintain a distinction between the *value chain*, which represents those activities undertaken by a firm, and the *supply chain*, of which the value chain is a subset, which refers to all the activities leading up to the final product for the consumer.

12. In fact, on closer inspection it is clear that we can achieve a high level of discrimination with the one-dimensional map where there are two distinct groupings, and one intermediate brand and one 'outlier' brand. It is significant that these groupings are not either brand or pack-sized based but a mixture. In fact the only result in moving from the one-dimensional to the two-dimensional analysis, is that one brand has become less discriminated (see Wensley, 1996). Hence it would appear that we can rather surprisingly reduce the effective competitive space to a single dimension with the possibility of only some second-order anomalies.

13. The classical Victorian monograph 'Flatland' (Abbott, 1884; 1992) provided an early illustration of many perceptual problems of moving between space of different dimensions.

14. For a more detailed analysis of the contribution of these two see Curto & Wensley, 1997.

15. For a more detailed recent review of the literature in this area see Sammut-Bonnici & Wensley, 2002.

16. Even in this case, we might heed McKelvey's (1982) concern that developing an appropriate taxonomy for this purpose is a challenging task which also raises key questions as to the appropriate unit of analysis.

17. Of course many of the more complex models for the cross-sectional analysis of market structure, based on consumer-level data, model heterogeneity in various ways (see the discussion, for instance, in Cooper & Inoue, 1996), but it is important to remember that in general they use statistical artifacts, such as product moments, as a parsimonious way of representing continuous distributions. In terms of interpretation we are often in danger of treating these artifacts as if they were genuine groupings or clusters.

18. However, we should also recognize that in a recent review Zahra & George (2001) argued that despite the growing use of the absorptive capacity construct in the study of organizations, problems remained with definitions, components, antecedents and outcomes.

References

Abbot, E.A. (1992) *Flatland: A Romance of Many Dimensions.* Mineola, NY: Dover Publications (first published by Seeley and Co Ltd., London, 1884).

Adner, R. & Levinthal, D. (2001) Demand heterogeneity and technology evolution: implications for product and process innovation. *Management Science*, 47, 5, May, 611–28.

Aldrich, H. (1999) *Organizations Evolving.* Thousand Oaks, CA: Sage.

Aldrich, H.E. & Pfeffer, J. (1976) Environments of organizations. *Annual Review of Sociology*, 2, 121–40.

Allison, G.T. (1969) Conceptual models and the Cuban Missile Crisis. *American Political Science Review*, 63 (3), 689–718.

Amit, Raffi & Schoemaker, Paul J.H. (1993) Strategic assets and organizational rent. *Strategic Management Journal*, 14, 33–46.

Anderson, Erin (1996) Transaction cost analysis and marketing. In *Transaction Cost Economics and Beyond*, edited by John Groewegen. London: Kluwer Publishing, pp. 65–84.

Anderson, Erin & Weitz, Barton A. (1986) Make or buy decisions: vertical integration and marketing productivity. *Sloan Management Review*, 27 (Spring), 3–20.

Barney, Jay (1991) Firm resources and sustained competitive advantage. *Journal of Management*, 16, 99–120.

——— (2001) Is the resource-base 'view' a useful perspective for strategic management research? Yes. *Academy of Management Review*, 26 (1), January, 41–56.

Black, Janice A. & Boal, Kimberly B. (1994) Strategic resources, traits, configurations and paths to sustainable competitive advantage, *Strategic Management Journal*, 15, 131–48.

Blois, K. (2002) Business to business exchanges: a rich descriptive apparatus derived from Menger's and Macneil's analyses. *Journal of Management Studies*, 39 (4) (June), 523–52.

Campbell-Hunt, Colin (2000) What have we learned about generic competitive strategy? A meta-analysis. *Strategic Management Journal*, 21, 2, 127–54.

Carroll, Glenn R. & Swaminathan, Anand (1992) The organizational ecology of strategic groups in the American brewing industry from 1975 to 1990. *Industrial and Corporate Change*, 1, 65–97.

Chaisson, E.J. (ed.) (2001) *Cosmic Evolution: The Rise of Complexity in Nature.* Cambridge, MA: Harvard University Press.

Chamberlin, E. (1933) *The Theory of Monopolistic Competition.* Cambridge, MA: Harvard University Press.

Chan Derek K., Feltham, Gerald A. & Simunic, Dan A. (1999) A Spatial Analysis of Competition in the Market for Audit Services, August (available at http://www.ecom.unimelb.edu.au/accwww/seminars/Papers 99/paper30.pdf).

Chandler, Alfred D., Jr. (1962) *Strategy and Structure: Chapters in the History of the Industrial Enterprise.* Boston, MA: The MIT Press.

Chintagunta, P. (1994) Heterogeneous logit model implications for brand positioning. *Journal of Marketing Research*, 31, May, 304–11.

Christensen, Clayton M. (1997) *The Innovator's Dilemma.* Boston, MA: Harvard Business School Press.

Clark, B.H. & Montgomery, D.B. (1995) Perceiving competitive reactions: the value of accuracy (and paranoia). Stanford GSB Research Paper, 1335R.

Coase, R.H. (1937) The nature of the firm. *Economica,* 4, 386–405.

Cohen, Jack & Stewart, I. (1995) *The Collapse of Chaos.* New York: Penguin Books.

Cohen, W.M. & Levinthal, D.A. (1990) Absorptive capacity: a new perspective on learning and innovation. *Administrative Science Quarterly*, 35, 128–52.

——— (1994) Fortune favors the prepared firm. *Management Science*, 40, 227–51.

Collis, David J. (1994) Research note: how valuable are organizational capabilities? *Strategic Management Journal*, 15 (Winter), 143–52.

Collis, David J. & Montgomery, Cynthia A. (1995) Competing on resources: strategy in the 1990s. *Harvard Business Review*, 73 (July–August), 118–28.

Connor, K.R. & Prahalad, C.K. (1996) A resource-based theory of the firm: knowledge versus opportunism. *Organizational Science*, 7, 477–501.

Cooper, L. & Nakanishi, M. (1988) *Market Share Analysis: Evaluating Competitive Marketing Effectiveness.* Boston, MA: Kluwer Academic Press.

Cooper, L.G. & Inoue, A. (1996) Building market structures from consumer preferences. *Journal of Marketing Research*, 33, August, 293–306.

Coyne, Kevin P., Hall, Stephen J.D. & Clifford, Patricia Gorman (1997) Is your core competency a mirage? *The McKinsey Quarterly*, 1, 40–54.

Curto, F. & Wensley, R. (1997) New organisational forms in old writings: revisiting the contributions of Arthur Stinchcombe & Alfred Chandler Jr. Modes of Organizing: Power, Knowledge Shifts Conference, April, University of Warwick.

D'Aveni, Richard A. (1994) *Hypercompetition: Managing the Dynamics of Strategic Maneuvering.* New York: Free Press.

Day, George S. (1994) The capabilities of market-driven organizations. *Journal of Marketing*, 58 (October), 37–52.

——— (1999) *The Market-Driven Organization.* New York: Free Press.

Dickson, P. (1996) The static and dynamic mechanics of competition: a comment on Hunt & Morgan's comparative advantage theory, *Journal of Marketing*, 60, October, 102–6.

DiMaggio, P. & Powell, W.W. (1983) The iron cage revisited: institutional isomorphism and collective rationality in organisational fields. *American Sociological Review*, 48: 147–60.

Ehrenberg, A.S.C. (1972) *Repeat Buying: Theory and Applications*, London: North-Holland.

Ehrenberg, A.S.C. & Uncles, M. (1995) Dirichlet-type markets: a review. Working Paper, November, London Business School.

Faria, A. & Wensley, R. (2002) In search of 'inter-firm management' in supply chains: recognising contradictions of language and power by listening. *Journal of Business Research*, 55 (7) (July), 603–10.

Foss, N.J. (1996) Knowledge-based approaches to the theory of the firm: some critical comments. *Organizational Science*, 7, 470–6.

Freeman, Jonathan (1997) Dynamics of market evolution. *European Marketing Academy. Proceedings of the 26th. Annual Conference*, May.

Galunic, D.C. & Eisenhardt, K.M. (1996) The evolution of intracorporate domains: divisional charter losses in high-technology, multidivisional corporations. *Organizational Science*, 7(3) 255–82.

Ginsberg, Ari & Buchholtz, Anne (1990) Converting to for-profit status: corporate responsiveness to radical change. *Academy of Management Journal*, 33 (3), September, 447–77.

Grabher, G. (1993) Rediscovering the social in the economics of interfirm relations. In *The Embedded Firm: On the Socioeconomics of Industrial Networks*, edited by G. Grabher. London: Routledge, pp. 1–32.

Håkansson, H. (ed.) (1987) *Industrial Technological Development: A Network Approach.* London: Croom Helm.

Håkansson, H. & Johanson, J. (1993) The network as a governance structure: interfirm cooperation beyond markets and hierarchies. In Grabher, G. (ed), *The Embedded Firm: On the Socioeconomics of Industrial Networks*, edited by G. Grabher. London: Routledge, pp. 35–51.

Hammer, Michael, (1996) *Beyond Reengineering: How the Process-Centered Organization is Changing Our Work and Our Work Lives*, New York: Harper Business.

Hannan, M.T. & Freeman, J.H. (1977) The population ecology of organizations. *American Journal of Sociology*, 82 (5), 929–63.

Harshman, R.A., Green, P.E., Wind, Y. & Lundy, M.E. (1982) A model for the analysis of asymmetric data in marketing research. *Marketing Science*, 1, Spring, 205–42.

Haverman, Heather A. (1992) Between a rock and a hard place: organizational change and performance under conditions of fundamental environmental transformation. *Administrative Science Quarterly*, 38, 1, March, 20–50.

Hooley, Graham, Fahy, John, Cox, Tony, Beracs, Jozsel, Fonfara, Brzysztof & Snoj, Boris (1999) Marketing capabilities and firm performance: a hierarchical model. *Journal of Market Focused Management*, 4, 259–78.

Hotelling, H. (1929) Stability in competition. *Economic Journal*, 39 (March), 41–57.

Hunt, Shelby D. (2000a) *A General Theory of Competition: Resources, Competences, Productivity and Economic Growth.* Thousand Oaks, CA: Sage.

Hunt, Shelby D. (2000b) A general theory of competition: too eclectic or not eclectic enough? Too incremental or not incremental enough? Too neoclassical or not neoclassical enough? *Journal of Macromarketing*, 20 (1), June, 77–81.

Hunt, S.D. & Morgan, R.M. (1996) The resource advantage theory of competition: dynamics, path dependencies and evolutionary dimension. *Journal of Marketing*, 60, October, 107–14.

Huff, A.S., Huff, J.O. & Thomas, H. (1992) Strategic renewal and the interaction of cumulative stress and inertia. *Strategic Management Journal*, 13, 55–75.

Huff, James, O. & Huff, Anne S. (1995) Stress, inertia, opportunity and competitive position: a SIOP model of strategic change in the pharmaceuticals industry. *Academy of Management Journal*, special issue: best paper proceedings, 22–6.

Ishibuchi, Hisao, Sakamoto, Ryoji & Nakashima, Tomoharu (2001) Evolution of unplanned coordination in a market selection game, *IEEE Transactions on Evolutionary Computation*, 5 (5), 524–34.

Jacobson, R. (1994) The cost of the market share quest. Working Paper. Seattle: University of Washington.

Jacobson, R. & Aaker, D. (1985) Is market share all that it's cracked up to be? *Journal of Marketing*, 49 (4), Fall, 11–22.

Jensen, M.C. & Meckling, W.H. (1976) Theory of the firm: managerial behaviour, agency costs and ownership structure. *Journal of Financial Economics*, 3, 305–60.

Kauffman, S. (2001) *Investigations*. London: Oxford University Press.

Kay, J. (1993) *Foundations of Corporate Success*. London: Oxford University Press.

Kieser, A. (1989) Organizational, institutional, and societal evolution: medieval craft guilds and the genesis of formal organizations. *Administrative Science Quarterly*, 34 (4), 540–64.

Kogut, B. & Zander, U. (1996) What firms do? Coordination, identity, and learning. *Organizational Science*, 7, 502–18.

Kohli, A. & Jaworski, B. (1990) Market orientation: the construct, research propositions and managerial implications. *Journal of Marketing*, 54, (April), 1–18.

Krider, R.E. & Weinberg, C.B. (1997) Spatial competition and bounded rationality: retailing at the edge of chaos. *Geographical Analysis*, 29, 1 (January), 17–34.

Lambkin, M. & Day, G.S. (1989) Evolutionary processes in competitive markets: beyond the product life cycle. *Journal of Marketing*, 53, July, 4–20.

Learned, Edmund, Christensen, Chris, Andrews, Ken & Goth, William (1969) *Business Policy: Text and Cases.* Homewood, IL: Richard D. Irwin, Inc.

Leeflang, P.S.H. & Wittick, D. (1993) Diagnosing competition: developments and findings, In *Research Traditions in Marketing*, edited by G. Laurent, G.L. Lillian, & B. Pras. Norwell, MA: Kluwer Academic, pp. 133–56.

Lengnick-Hall, Cynthia A. & Wolff, James A. (1999) Similarities and contradictions in the core logic of three strategy research streams. *Strategic Management Journal*, 20 (December), 1109–32.

Leonard-Barton, Dorothy (1992) Core capabilities and core rigidities: a paradox in managing new product development. *Strategic Management Journal*, 13, 111–25.

——— (1995) *Wellsprings of Knowledge*, Boston, MA: Harvard Business School Press.

Levins, R. & Leowontin, R. (1985) *The Dialectical Biologist.* Cambridge, MA: Harvard University Press.

Lewin, Arie Y. & Volberda, Henk W. (1999) Prolegomena on coevolution: a framework for research on strategy and new organizational forms. *Organizational Science*, 10 (5), Sept–Oct, 519–34.

Lewin, Arie Y., Long, Chris P. & Carroll, Timothy N. (1999) The coevolution of new organizational forms. *Organization Science*, 10 (5), 535–50.

Liebowitz, S.J. & Margoles, Stephen E. (1994) Path dependence, lock-in and history. *The Journal of Law, Economics and Organization*, 10, 205–26.

Macneil, I.R. (1981) Economic analysis of contractural relations: its shortfalls and the need for a 'rich' classificatory apparatus. *Northwestern University Law Review*, 75, 6, 1018–63.

Marks, R.E., Midgley, D.F., Cooper, L. G. & Shiraz, G.M. (1998) The complexity of competitive marketing strategies. *Complexity International*, vol. 6.

McGee, J. (2002) Strategy as Knowledge. In *Images of Strategy*, edited by S. Cummings & D. Wilson. Oxford: Blackwells.

McKelvey, B. (1982) *Organizational Systematics: Taxonomy, Evolution, Classification.* Berkeley, CA: University of California Press.

Menger, C. (1871) *Principles of Economics,* trans. J. Dingwall & B.F. Hoselitz, 1976. New York: State University of New York Press.

Menzies-Lyth, I. (1988) *Containing Anxiety in Institutions: Volume 1.* London: Free Association Books.

Metcalfe, J.S., Fonseca, D. & Ramlogan, R. (2000) Innovation, growth and competition: evolving complexity or complex evolution? Complexity and Complex Systems in Industry Conference 2000, University of Warwick.

Mintzberg, Henry, Ahlstrand, Bruce & Lampel, Joseph (1998) *Strategy Safari: A Guided Tour Through the Wilds of Strategic Management.* New York: Free Press.

Moorthy, J.S. (1985) Using game theory to model competition. *Journal of Marketing Research*, 22 (August), 262–82.

Morrison, A. & Wensley, R. (1991) A short history of the growth/share matrix: boxed up or boxed in? *Journal of Marketing Management*, 7 (2), April, 105–29.

Narver, J. & Slater, S. (1990) The effect of market orientation on business profitability. *Journal of Marketing*, 54 (October), 20–35.

Nelson, R.R. & Winter, S.J. (1982) *An Evolutionary Theory of Economic Change*. Cambridge, MA: Belknap Press of Harvard University Press.

Oliver, Christine (1997) Sustainable competitive advantage: combining institutional and resource-based views. *Strategic Management Journal*, 18, 697–713.

Peng, M.W., Hill, C.W.L. & Wang, D.Y.L. (2000) Schumpeterian dynamics versus Williamsonian considerations: a test of export intermediary performance. *Journal of Management Studies*, 37 (2), March, 167–84.

Penrose, Edith T. (1959) *The Theory of the Growth of the Firm*. London: Basil Blackwell.

Perrow, C. (1986) *Complex Organizations: A Critical Essay*. Glenview, IL: Scott Foresman.

Porter, Michael E. (1980) *Competitive Strategy*. New York: Free Press.

——— (1985) *Competitive Advantage*. New York: Free Press.

——— (1991) Towards a dynamic theory of strategy. *Strategic Management Journal*, 12 (Winter), 95–118.

Powell, T.C. (2001) Competitive advantage: logical & philosophical consideration. *Strategic Management Journal*, 22, 875–88.

Prahalad, C.K. & Hamel, Gary (1990) The core competence of the corporation. *Harvard Business Review*, 68 (May–June), 79–91.

Priem, Richard L. (2001) Is the resource-based view a useful perspective for strategic management research? *Academy of Management Review*, 26 (1) (Jan.), 22–41.

Robinson, J. (1933) *The Economics of Imperfect Competition*. London: MacMillan.

Rodgers, E.M. (1962) *Diffusion of Innovations*. New York: Free Press.

Rosa, J.A. & Porac, J.F. (2002) Category dynamics in mature consumer markets through a socio-cognitive lens. *Journal of Management Studies* (forthcoming).

Rosa, J.A., Porac, J.F., Runser-Spanjol, J. & Saxon, M.S. (1999) Sociocognitive dynamics in a product market. *Journal of Marketing*, 63 (special issue), 64–77.

Rungie, C. (1998) Measuring the impact of horizontal differentiation on market share. Working Paper. Marketing Science Centre, University of South Australia, November.

Sammut-Bonnici T. & Wensley, R. (2002) Darwinism, probability and complexity: market-based organizational transformation and change explained through the theories of evolution. Working Paper. Warwick Business School.

Sanchez, R. (1995) Strategic flexibility in product competition. *Strategic Management Journal*, 16 (special issue), 135–59.

Saunders, John, Forrester, Ros, Stern, Philip & Wensley, Robin (2000) In search of the lemmus lemmus: an investigation into convergent competition. *British Journal of Management*, 11, September (Special Issue), S81–S95.

Savitt, Ronald (2000) A philosophical essay about a general theory of competition: resources, competences, productivity, economic growth. *Journal of Macromarketing*, 20 (1), June, 73–6.

Selznick, Philip (1957) *Leadership in Administration*. New York: Harper & Row.

Sinkula, J.M. (1994) Market information processing and organizational learning. *Journal of Marketing*, 58 (1), 34–45.

Srivastava, Rajendra, Shervani, Tassaddua A. & Fahey, Liam (1999) Marketing, business processes, and shareholder value: an organizationally embedded view of marketing activities and the discipline of marketing. *Journal of Marketing*, 63 (special issue), 168–79.

Stalk, George, Evans, Philip & Shulman, Lawrence (1992) Competing on capabilities: the new rules of corporate strategy. *Harvard Business Review*, 70 (March/April), 57–69.

Stinchcombe, A.L. (1965) Social structure and organizations. In *Handbook of Organizations*, edited by J.G. March. Chicago: Rand McNally, pp. 142–93.

Stoelhorst, J.W. & van Raaij, E.M. (2002) On explaining performance differentials: marketing and the managerial theory of the firm. *Journal of Business Research*, (forthcoming).

Szymanski, D., Bharadwaj, S.G. & Varadarajan, D. (1993) An analysis of the market share–profitability relationship. *Journal of Marketing*, 57 (July), 1–18.

Teece, David J., Pisano, Gary & Shuen, Amy (1997) Dynamic capabilities and strategic management. *Strategic Management Journal*, 18, 509–33.

Tesfatsion, L. (2001) Guest editorial: agent-based modelling of evolutionary economic systems. *IEEE Transactions on Evolutionary Computation*, 5, 5.

Varadarajan, P.R. & Jayachandran, S. (1999) Marketing strategy: an assessment of the state of the field and outlook. *Journal of the Academy of Marketing Science*, 27 (2) (Spring), 120–43.

Waterman, R.H. (1988) *The Renewal Factor*. London: Bantam Books.

Wensley, R. (1994) Strategic marketing: a review. In *The Marketing Book*, edited by M. Basker. London: Heinemann Butterworth, pp. 33–53.

——— (1996) Forms of segmentation: definitions and empirical evidence. MEG Conference Proceedings (CD version), Session G, Track 8. Department of Marketing, University of Strathclyde, July 9–12, 1996, pp. 1–11.

——— (2002a) Marketing for the new century: issues of practice and consumption. *Journal of Marketing Management*, 18 (1–2) (Feb), 229–38.

——— (2002b) Strategy as intention and anticipation. In *Images of Strategy*, edited by S. Cummings & D. Wilson. Oxford: Blackwells.

Wernerfelt, Birger (1984) A resource-based view of the firm. *Strategic Management Journal*, 5 (2) (September–October), 171–80.

——— (1995) A rational reconstruction of the compromise effect. *Journal of Consumer Research*, 21 (March), 627–33.

Williamson, Oliver E. (1975) *Markets and Hierarchies: Analysis and Anti-trust Implications*. New York: Free Press.

——— (1991) Strategizing, economizing, and economic organization. *Strategic Management Journal*, 12, Special Issue, Winter, 75–94 .

——— (1999) Strategy research: governance and competence perspectives. *Strategic Management Journal*, 20 (December), 1087–108.

Williamson, O. & Winter, N. (1991) *The Nature of the Firm*. London: Oxford University Press.

Zahra, S.A. & George, G. (2001) Absorptive capacity: a review and reconceptualisation. Working Paper. School of Management, Syracuse University NY (shorter version published in the Best Paper Proceedings, Academy of Management Meeting 2000, Toronto, Canada).

5

*Determining the Structure of Product-Markets: Practices, Issues, and Suggestions**

ALLAN D. SHOCKER

Among the more important advances in marketing over the past three decades is the development of tools and techniques for analyzing ways in which consumers perceive product offerings and make choices from among alternatives. These tools, which are concerned with the analysis of competitive relationships, take many forms and have numerous names – market structure analysis (MSA), customer perceptual mapping, choice modeling, image analysis, and quality function deployment (QFD), to name a few. Whatever their names and characteristics, all are concerned with aiding management in understanding customer perceptions of the marketplace, e.g., how many and what products/brands are in competition in a product-market of interest, how substitutable are they, what factors determine competitiveness, and how are these factors used when customers choose from among a set of alternatives? These perceptions are likely to be different from managers' own perceptions of competitive relationships for the reason that managers are better informed about direct competitors and may not recognize less direct ones, and may understand competitive products more in terms of their physical features and characteristics than their benefits and costs.

These analytical tools have been widely employed in industry, although until very recently they tended to be used largely by marketing managers. But increasingly they are being employed by managers in R&D, and by design engineers, operations specialists, and even senior management. Manufacturers of consumer packaged goods, consumer and business services, consumer durables, and many industrial products routinely employ such tools. Such activity serves to encourage these managers to become more familiar with MSA so as to be able to make better use of these methods. For both management and representative customers must become active participants in the design and interpretation of relevant research for the MSA exercise to assure meaningful and actionable results. These tools are in active use by marketing researchers – both in industry and academia – and frequently appear in published work (see the references for this chapter).

The purpose of this paper is to provide a primer for academic researchers (and managers) seeking to advance their understanding of these approaches and improve their ability to use them well. We will examine basic approaches to the analysis of market structure, with emphasis on the relationships between assumptions regarding the definition

*This chapter is an edited and updated version of Shocker, Stewart and Zahorik (1990a). Time and space did not permit the complete integration of newer material, as the purpose of this chapter was not to review literature. Supplemental references to more recent literature are included to aid the reader and support the conclusion that Market Structure Analysis (MSA) remains an active area for research and application. Unfortunately, many of our concerns expressed more than a decade ago still remain relevant.

and structure of competitive relationships (e.g., measuring the magnitude of competition) and various methods for operationalizing and representing that structure. There exist important interactions between the purposes of competitive analysis and the methods used to implement them. Our focus will *not* be on specific algorithms, except when key assumptions of algorithms are related to particular conceptualizations of structure and competitive dynamics. Several papers reviewing the characteristics of various algorithms and the issues related to their use already exist (see, for example, Arabie et al., 1981; Cooper, 1983; Dillon et al., 1985; Punj & Stewart, 1983b; Stewart, 1981; Zahorik, 1994). Missing from these prior works is explicit discussion of the assumptions that various methods and techniques imply about the phenomenon being represented, i.e., market structure. Options, conceptual issues, and problems that exist in dealing with MSA will be emphasized.

The paper is organized into four broad sections. Part one is concerned with various conceptualizations of competition and methods for measurement. Of necessity, this leads to a discussion of market definition. Part two focuses on two classes of method for representing structure: spatial and non-spatial models. Part three elaborates several problems that exist in representing the structure of a market. Finally, part four offers guidance for the use and interpretation of MSA.

Operationalizing Competition

Numerous ways to represent market structures exist, ranging from a) spatial models, in which products and customers are located in a characteristics space which helps 'explain' their positioning, with distances between products providing an indicant of how competitive they are, and distances between products and customers a measure of attractiveness to those customers; to b) hierarchical structures, where broadly competing products are partitioned into increasingly competitive subsets, usually on the basis of physical attribute differences; to c) non-hierarchical overlapping clusters, where products are represented spatially by locations, but are also grouped together into submarkets in a way which permits each product to be a competitor in possibly more than one submarket. Each mode of representation offers certain advantages and contributes to an understanding of competition. Yet, different methods can also provide different perspectives. These competing perspectives arise from differences in the measures and data used to derive structure and, importantly, the assumptions of each method, which can sometimes *impose* a particular result whether it is there or not (e.g., by fitting an erroneous model).

It is only when MSA leads to managerial action that one learns whether the underlying analyses have validity. There is no other standard of truth; no 'true' market structure with which the results of particular analytic approaches may be compared. Statistical fit is at best a fit to data under the assumption that the estimating model is accurate and not a measure of fit to the true structure. Market structure is an idea, like a demand curve or an attitude, that cannot be observed; it can only be inferred. It represents the aggregation of individual customer choices within some specified product domain over a given time period. Yet, in this fact there lies danger. Much as the average of many diverse measures can provide no insight to any single one, a representation of market structure can result in something which provides little insight, or even faulty guidance. Particular methods do, however, almost always provide *results*; it is only whether they be sense or nonsense that is sometimes unclear.

One reason different methods provide different results is the continuous nature of the concept of competition or substitutability. At one extreme, all purchasable goods compete because they are claimants for a consumer's limited resources. A telephone call is a plausible substitute for an e-mail, as are a postal letter or a fax transmission. Near the other extreme, two brands of toothpaste compete because they can be substituted for virtually all the same purposes. Competition is a matter of degree rather than a simple dichotomy and attempts to partition the world into competitors and non-competitors is often arbitrary. Even within what appears to be a nominal product category, competitors may differ in their imagery and degree of typicality (Ratneshwar & Shocker, 1991), so that sometimes brands in a given product class will compete more effectively with members of a seemingly different product category than with other brands in their own (e.g., Quaker's Kudos are chocolate-covered granola bars, but are often sold as candies). The first stage in examining competitive relationships is to produce an operational definition of a competitive set that reflects customer perspectives. Although it is arbitrary, it is a necessary step and is referred to as 'product-market definition.'

Product-market Definition

Product-market definition seeks to identify the set of 'product' alternatives or competitors which are sufficiently consequential to a firm that they need monitoring. For many applications a product-market can be thought of as the totality of product alternatives that could be actively considered for purchase or use by at least some minimal percentage of people for whom such purchase or use is relevant. (Since all directly competing goods are not available everywhere, or even actively considered by every customer at any given time, the 'potential' nature of such a definition is appropriate.) Product-market definition thus requires simultaneous determination of the people, products, and conditions of purchase/use (Ratneshwar et al., 1999). At successively lower levels of substitutability, product variants or types compete for a more broadly defined set of purposes. Hence, different levels of analysis could yield different definitions of product-markets. Thus the setting of some boundaries (market definition) is an important pragmatic task.

Market definition becomes a critical determinant of the structural representation of a market because various measures of substitutability or competitive intensity (e.g., market shares) are dependent on the particular set of products for which those measures are obtained (e.g., a brand of potato chips has a larger share of the 'potato chip' market than of the 'salty snack' market, even though it may be competitive in both). It should be remembered that competitiveness is relative, rather than absolute. In real markets the degree of competitiveness of products does not appear to be independent of customer purpose; the same product or brands often compete more intensely for some purposes or in some usage situations or contexts than others. For example, two products, possibly from different product categories, may compete more intensely as gifts than they do for regular or personal use. Two food brands may be more competitive when they are to be used as ingredients than when they are consumed as a main dish, or alone rather than in a social setting. Because product-market definition is affected by user, user purpose, or context (situation), separate MSA may be desirable.

For many researchers, however, market definition has been ignored. They apply their method for determining structure to any convenient set of competitors (usually only ones for which they have data, thereby presuming the research data supplier has already performed adequate product-market definition). If pressed, they might claim that the set of competing products was 'obvious.' Aren't competing products those which are called by similar names, bear some physical resemblance, perform similar functions, are sold through similar channels, or are made by similar manufacturing processes or firms in the same nominal 'industry?' While such rules of thumb may prove sufficient in many instances (and indeed can be those many customers actually use to decide from which products to choose), they have several disadvantages as criteria for defining 'the' competitive set. For one, they are not 'necessary' criteria; e.g., certain wines (inexpensive ones) may compete more strongly with beers and wine coolers than they do with other, pricier varietal wines. Certain automobile makes may be more competitive with the used versions of some makes than with their new automobiles. Alternatives such as these might be excluded from analysis by blind application of the criteria above. Moreover, they tend to restrict consideration of competition to commercial product alternatives and exclude the effect of the customer's own ability to produce their own options in certain instances. Particularly in industrial marketing, customer-created products are quite common in 'make versus buy' decisions (Von Hippel, 1986).

Further complicating the problem of market definition are changes in customer tastes and preferences. Whatever their cause, they can alter competitive relationships and necessitate another MSA. Recognition, for example, that caffeine or sodium is harmful may make products containing those ingredients less competitive than previously with others. Marketer-controlled activities such as the introduction of new product entries (possibly to fill gaps in the array of competitive offerings) can change both the nature of competitive relationships and possibly the boundaries of existing categories (Hauser & Shugan, 1983). Distribution decisions affect the availability of competing alternatives and thus the effectiveness of their competition. Pricing and promotion decisions are particularly critical, for these can change the nature of the offering and have the effect of creating a new competitor in a previous array (Oren et al., 1984). For example, the prices set, say for a line of fashion clothing, may determine with which other garments they compete. The possibility of purchasing an item 'on sale' when other item prices are unchanged may temporarily also change those products with which it competes. Product positioning and imagery suggested by promotional activity can lead to broader (or narrower) acceptance of the brand. Market definition under such dynamic conditions is but a temporary state.

Measuring Inter-product Competition

The traditional concept of competition is rooted in the notion of 'marketing impact,' as typified by the economic concept of *cross-elasticity*. Products whose market performance (i.e., sales) can be 'substantially affected' by the marketing actions (e.g., price, promotion) of other products compete with such products. Discontinuities in such effects become the basis for sorting potential competitors into categories, or otherwise establishing the boundaries of what is termed a 'product-market definition.' They also permit identification of complementary as well as substitute products since they are also affected by competitive marketing action.

The '*marketing impact*' criterion, based as it is upon marketing behaviors, cannot easily permit the consideration of potential, or even recently introduced, alternatives in determining a market definition, since they have either not been marketed or are too new to have attracted sufficient patronage. 'What if' and equilibrium issues are thus more difficult to address with such measures. Products less familiar to potential customers, or which have limited distribution may not be initially affected by a given product's pricing actions, and thus not be determined as part of its competitive array.

A second criterion, termed '*substitutability-in-use*,' (or simply, substitutability) has found increasing use in studies of market definition and structure because it affords a rationale for the existence of competition rather than merely noting its outcome. It holds that products are competitive if customers regard them as interchangeable for some relevant purpose(s). Having usages in common is one reason a product can substitute for another. 'Substitutability' overcomes certain of the problems mentioned earlier. It can be used to assess competition posed by products not yet or only recently marketed. It can be used in the context of hypothetical situations and with product descriptions, as well as real products. And it may be particularly useful in suggesting which products might compete (i.e., market definition) as a prelude to obtaining 'marketing impact' measures. 'Substitutability' has yet another important implication: customer purpose becomes the organizing 'theme' for considering competition. It dictates not only what products are competitive, but also the people for whom such purposes are relevant (i.e., the 'market' or market segments). Moreover, since customer purposes probably change less than do the products competing for a given market, purpose-defined product-markets tend to be relatively stable, even though the specific products in the product-market may change in their competitiveness.

While the creation of a classification system permits the potentially large number of *ad hoc* usages to be reduced to a more manageable set, this can create problems in aggregation of individual-level results into market-level measures. If one desires a measure of overall substitutability between two products, one needs a measure, say, of submarket importance to define weightings appropriate for such aggregation. Measures of frequency of occurrence of each category of usage could suffice, but these may not be reliably obtainable. The problem arises because respondents may not be able to relate as well to a whole category of usages as distinct from specific examples of that category. And an aggregate measure of 'substitutability' may fail to provide a specific measure of the impact of one product's marketing efforts on another.

'Substitutability' is not without its own problems as a criterion for competition. Measures of association of products with customer purposes can only be obtained judgmentally or through costly experiment or observation. Multiple purposes may be relevant and these can be difficult to operationalize (Srivastava et al.,1981). Common usage as the purpose of substitution, for example, may be defined broadly or narrowly (e.g., to clean objects, to clean clothes, to clean delicate fabrics). There can be idiosyncratic usages to which products may be put, which can make inter-customer comparisons difficult and preclude some customers from even identifying with a specific usage. Belk (1975, 1979), and Srivastava et al. (1981), among others, have emphasized the importance of creating a specific classification of product-market usages as a way to manage this problem. Idiosyncratic usages would presumably be grouped together if they elicited similar product-usage associations. The characteristics such usages have in common (i.e., the bases for their classification) could then be inferred as a way of further understanding choice behavior. These authors have also demonstrated generalizable processes for creating such taxonomies.

A third criterion, *brand switching*, should be briefly mentioned since it occasionally appears in the literature (e.g., Colombo & Morrison, 1989; Kumar & Sashi, 1989; Novak, 1993). Brand switching is measured by the frequency with which the same customer purchases brands sequentially (i.e., a switch occurs if a different brand is purchased on a subsequent occasion and no switching occurs in the case of a repeat purchase of the same brand on the subsequent occasion). Brand switching measures presume that a valid market definition is already available (i.e., the products amongst which a customer switches must have been previously confirmed as substitutes and brand switching measures the degree or magnitude of such competition. Cross-elasticity and substitution can first be used to establish such a definition). Brand-switching measures are easily calculated from longitudinal packaged goods scanner panel data. But such data exist largely at the 'household' level, and thus what appears to be a switch may merely be demand from a different household member. Nonetheless, the ready availability of such data for grocery and drugstore products has encourage the use of brand- switching measures in MSA.

The two primary criteria – marketing impact and substitutability – although clearly related (i.e., products useable for similar purposes should be sensitive to each others marketing actions), are not themselves perfect substitutes. For example, if customers who purchased Cadillac and Lincoln automobiles were each extremely brand loyal (say because product differences were insufficient to induce variety-seeking, and because pricing and sales promotion activities were equivalent), then the potential for substitutability could not be revealed by 'marketing impact' measures. Whenever price variability is small, actual substitution may not take place. We would suggest that the more descriptive, behaviorally relevant 'marketing impact' is more useful for evaluating tactical decisions; whereas the more prescriptive, judgmental 'substitutability' criterion is more relevant for 'what if' departures from past behavior and for contemplating strategic moves. Measures of competition which have been proposed by various approaches to determining market structure are based upon one or other of these two criteria. Before discussing specific measures, however, let us consider a few additional concerns for the determination of market structure.

Determination of Market Structure

Once the relevant product-market has been defined, a second stage of analysis, which (despite potential for confusion) we also term 'market structure analysis,' seeks to measure the nature and strength of competitive relationships among those product alternatives included in the definition. One can conceptualize a market structure for each customer in the market, with overall structure determined by aggregating individual structures. Individual structures are likely, however, to be based upon different market definitions and differ in the degree of substitutability among the products included. An aggregate structure can thus not guarantee to be 'representative' of any segment or individual. Approaches to the aggregation problem fall into one of two classes. The first of these analyzes individual-level data to derive a structure, with the structures themselves aggregated. The second aggregates individual-level measures of behavior or judgment and derives a single market structure based upon this aggregation. These approaches need not, and frequently do not, result in the same structure. The advantage of the former is that more insight into customer dynamics and segmentation may be possible than by the latter approach. Existing research does not make clear which is the more valid, however. We discuss aggregation again later.

MSA requires a measure of inter-product competition. There is no shortage of such measures in the literature, though none appear fully satisfactory for all purposes. These measures fall into two broad classes: judgmental and behavioral (Day et al., 1979). This distinction is somewhat different from that previously made between 'marketing impact' and 'substitutability' since either criterion can, in principle, be measured behaviorally or judgmentally. However, in practice 'marketing impact' is more likely to be measured using behavioral data, whereas 'substitutability' is more likely to be measured judgmentally.

Behavioral measures (e.g., brand switching, cross-elasticity) are more traditional and, hence, familiar (although some, such as variety-seeking measures and similarity of inter-purchase times, are not). They tend to be based upon secondary data collected for other purposes, so that either their incremental cost can be small, or much larger sample sizes are possible, or both. Many prefer behavioral measures because they reflect customers' actual behaviors rather than intentions (notwithstanding that they are obtained under historical market conditions rather than those which might prevail in the future).

Judgmental measures (e.g., perceived similarity, substitution for an unavailable preferred product, substitution-in-use) require primary data collection often with higher costs and/or smaller samples. Because of their flexibility, judgmental measures are useful in addressing a variety of 'what if' questions (whereas behavioral measures must, by definition, be based upon 'what was'). The researcher has greater control of stimuli (e.g., by including hypothetical new products or deleting existing ones) when developing judgmental measures and thus can induce greater variability in competitive conditions, consumers, attributes (e.g., new features) and attribute levels to which consumers are asked to respond (i.e., higher/lower levels than those represented by existing products or in existing markets, possibly leading to more reliable measurement). When individual-level market structures need to be constructed, behavioral data requirements (e.g., based upon brand-switching measures) tend to be very extensive (i.e., very long series of individual purchases would be required for reliable estimates of switching rates between all possible brands). Consequently, judgmental measures may be required to make individual-level analysis feasible.

Behavioral measures of competition tend to be highly dependent upon the adequacy of prior market definition, even though they sometimes can be used to confirm that definition (e.g., cross-elasticity measures the degree of substitution or complementarity among products, but may prove expensive to implement without prior understanding of what brands to calculate cross-elasticities among). Some can be constructed for virtually any set of products and therefore could provide misleading guidance if the products were not actually in competition (e.g., a measure of 'brand switching' in principle can be calculated between almost any two products). Some behavioral measures are also dependent upon the validity of relevant 'theories' of market behavior (e.g., similarity of inter-purchase times; variety-seeking). One is then caught in circular logic: only if one assumes the 'theory' correct does the measure become useful; whereas one must assume the measure useful in order to test the 'theory' (Day et al., 1979).

Judgmental measures are particularly useful for determining market definition and for dealing with strategic questions which are more likely to involve 'what if' questions, whereas behavioral measures are more useful for tactical or descriptive concerns. This suggests the two types of measure might usefully serve complementary roles. The impact of the selection of a measure of competition on the representation of market structure is well illustrated by research on the soft-drink market. Representations of market structure based on preference data tend to be different from those produced when similarity (i.e., perceptual) data are employed. Studies of the soft-drink market carried out with similarity data (Bass et al., 1972; Best, 1976; Cooper, 1973) identified cola–non-cola and diet–non-diet dimensions as being of almost equal importance in defining distances among products. Studies of the same market using preference data (Cooper, 1973; Lehmann, 1972), however, found the diet–non-diet dimension the major determinant of product position, although a cola–non-cola dimension was also identified.[1]

The literature on market definition and structure is rich and varied. The large number of publications authored by a diverse set of researchers provides evidence of substantial and continuing research interest. Space does not permit discussion of the numerous procedures that have been proposed, but the Appendix provides a good sampling of references to this literature. These procedures differ in terms of whether a) their primary concern is with market definition or market structure; b) they use behavioral or judgmental measures (and what general type of measure); and c) whether they lead to a specific structure or suggest 'theory' which can be used to test structures which have been hypothesized *a priori*. They also differ in the types of data called for, the concept of competition employed, the way they represent structure (i.e., spatial versus hierarchical – see below), the level of analysis (i.e., individual versus aggregate and single versus multiple usage), and the degree to which physical product attributes or features, or other product characteristics (e.g., benefits) are used for constructing and/or interpreting the obtained structure.

The existence of so many procedures and methods suggests that no single approach has emerged as dominant. It is also useful to note that various measures of competition and methods for representing structure are confounded in that authors typically describe only one combination, making it difficult, if not impossible, to evaluate measurement issues separately from issues of method. Various approaches to the representation of structure could possibly incorporate a variety of measures. This interaction of data and method for representing structure remains a relatively unexplored area of research. The questions of the validation of methods have hardly been addressed by published literature. There exists little documentation regarding the outcome of management actions based upon the insights gained from particular methods. Market structure is, of course, more than the mere measurement of competitive relationships among product alternatives within a given market definition. Relationships must also be displayed in a manner that effectively communicates their managerial content. Representation will be discussed next.

THE REPRESENTATION OF MARKET STRUCTURE

Just as there are many methods for *determining* market structure, there are also many for *representing* it. Most of these representations can be categorized into two broad classes, which we will call 'spatial' and 'non-spatial.' Spatial methods represent products as points in a space whose axes are defined by relevant product attributes, as in the hypothetical perceptual map in Figure 5.1. The 'position' of a product, as defined by the attribute axes, indicates the amounts of those attributes the product possesses (or is perceived to possess by the customers on whom the map is based). Relative distances between product points in such a map are usually interpreted as measures of competitiveness of the products, and products can conceivably be moved to new positions in the space by changing features or altering levels of the attributes they are perceived to possess.

Non-spatial techniques encompass a wide variety of forms (DeSarbo et al.,1993), but the hierarchical tree diagram shown in Figure 5.2 is typical. Here, products are classified on the basis of the various attributes they possess, but these are considered in a particular order. The attribute classifications are typically discrete, as indicated by the presence or absence of certain features. 'Slight

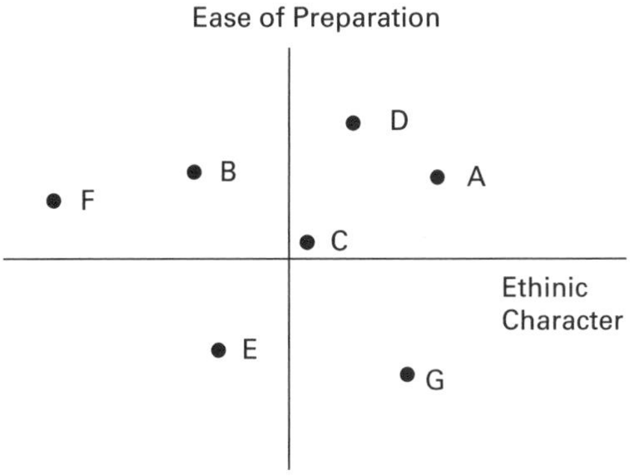

Figure 5.1 *A Hypothetical Map for Prepared Foods*

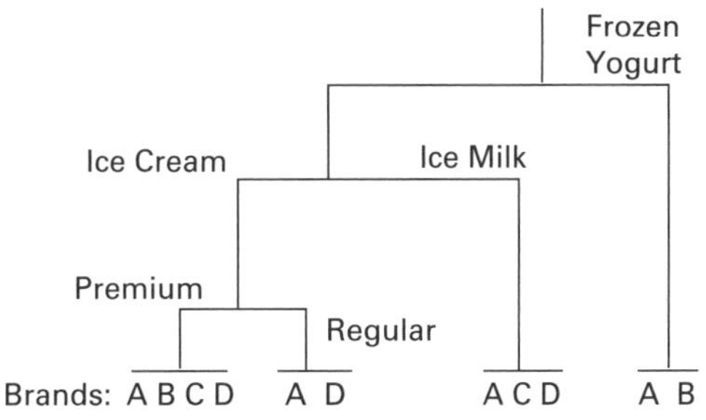

Figure 5.2 *A Hypothetical Tree Structure for Frozen Dairy Products*

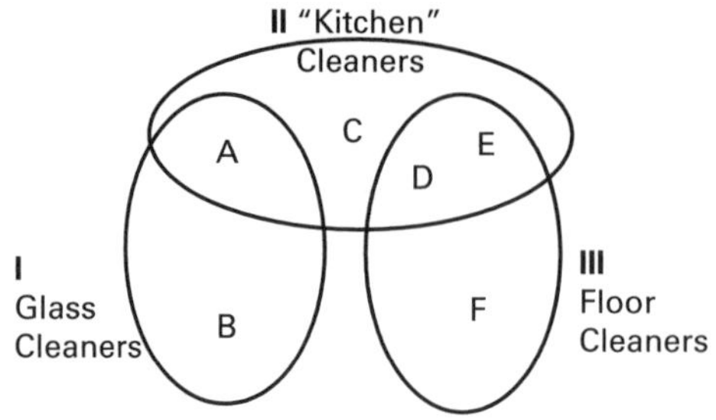

Shares of Sales in Submarkets	I	II	III
A	.60	.25	.00
B	.40	.00	.00
C	.00	.15	.00
D	.00	.35	.15
E	.00	.25	.25
F	.00	.00	.60

Figure 5.3 *A Hypothetical Market with Overlapping Clusters*

repositionings' of products and the positioning of products that could fall into more than one existing category (e.g., chocolate-covered granola bars might be categorized as either candy, or cookie, or a new form of cereal), are difficult to operationalize in this framework.

An emerging class of techniques describes competitive markets in terms of overlapping clustering procedures and is something of a hybrid. (We discuss them below along with non-spatial techniques.) An illustration is shown in Figure 5.3. The graph is informative, although these representations are better described in terms of tables of numbers, such as that shown, which indicate the extent to which the various products belong in one or more of the identified clusters. Finally, some work exists which produces genuine hybrids of spatial and non-spatial structures (Corter & Tversky, 1986).[2]

Within each of these broad classes there are numerous and very different procedures for generating representations. Each may, in turn, be applied to a variety of data types, yielding a still larger number of combination possibilities. Historically, users of spatial methods have employed judgmental data, while those using non-spatial techniques have more often employed behavioral data, although exceptions are easy to find. This is a reflection of a fundamental difference between spatial and non-spatial methods. Because they assume a continuous dimensional structure, spatial methods are consistent with many judgmental tasks, such as estimating inter-product similarity or competitiveness. Non-spatial methods need not make such continuity assumptions and are more suitable for discrete data, such as choice behavior (i.e., a product is either purchased or not). This distinction is by no means rigid, and several methods (e.g., GENFOLD2 (DeSarbo & Rao, 1986), correspondence analysis (Hoffman & Franke, 1986), and CHOICEMAP (Elrod, 1988)) offer spatial representations even when behavioral choice data are used.

Some types of product categories seem better described by only one method. Shepard (1974) and Sattath and Tversky (1977) made observations which suggest the assumption that a set of objects, such as a product-market, can always be represented as a continuous space with well-defined dimensions, is not reasonable for all situations. Some categories may be viewed by customers as inherently more discrete, categorical, and bi-polar, and these qualities may influence their market decisions. For example, pain relievers contain aspirin or they do not, personal computers have wireless capability or they do not; automobiles either have automatic or standard transmissions. In fact, few product features (even price) are available in such a wide range of gradations so as to be considered truly continuous – though if the number of product models and steps of variation are sufficient, it may be desirable to treat such attributes as if they were. Benefits are often continuous and sometimes it is possible to transform features into levels of an overriding benefit (e.g., discrete prices may represent different levels of 'economy,' pain relievers may be characterized in terms of their levels of 'effectiveness' or 'safety' instead of aspirin content).

The appropriateness of various methods for representing structure, given particular types of data, might be left to academic debate were it not for the fact that rather different pictures of competitive structure, often with very different managerial implications, can be derived when different methods of representation are applied to the same set of data. Sattath and Tversky (1977), in their investigation of spatial and tree models as rival means for representing structure, have shown that very simple configurations in one model may be incompatible with the other. For example, tree-structure methods tend to produce mostly large distances between stimuli and few small distances, whereas spatial models tend to result in the opposite. Therefore two different interpretations of market structure could emerge from these two methods (Srivastava et al., 1984), in that products distant from one another in a tree structure may appear quite similar in a dimensional one. Or, to the extent that distance between products is indicative of their similarity, dimensional maps will tend to produce sets of products which appear, on average, more 'similar' to each other than would be found were a tree structure employed, and *vice versa*. This has implications for the traditional interpretation of 'distance' as a measure of substitutability or competitive intensity.

A caveat should also be offered about what consumers may mean by the term 'similar.' One needs to distinguish between similarity of preference and similarity of perception. In a perceptual representation, two products which are perceived similarly (i.e., as having similar attributes) should be positioned proximate to each other; but in a representation based upon preferences, products which are similarly *liked* should be proximate. This interpretation of inter-product 'distance' in a preference space may also depend upon the *criteria* used by customers to make their choices among products (Cooper & Inoue, 1996). While not always clear under what circumstances particular spatial or non-spatial structures might be the better choice, or how the results produced by the two classes of methods might be reconciled, it does appear that there are situations in which one model form may be more appropriate, or at least more consistent with consumer choice processes, than the other (see further discussion below).

Spatial Models

Spatial models or product maps, appear to be more appropriate for situations in which consumers perceive products as 'similar,' in that they vary on common, continuous dimensions, and where consumers choose among products using a compensatory decision rule requiring trade-offs (e.g., between fuel economy and riding comfort in the choice of an automobile). Thus, when inter-product competition is modeled in terms of different degrees of benefits, perceptual dimensions, or physical characteristics, a spatial representation is likely to prove useful.

Spatial representations can be created in different ways and from many types of data, and the managerial implications of these resulting maps can be quite different. Four common approaches are:

1. *Non-metric multidimensional scaling* (MDS), which produces a map which 'best reflects' consumers' judgments about product similarities or preferences (Green et al., 1989). Relevant attributes underlying competition in the market must be inferred from the position of products in the map or correlation with pre-specified known descriptors.
2. *Direct scaling* of products on attributes, in which the researcher predetermines the relevant attribute axes and merely asks respondents to state where each product of interest lies in that space (Shocker & Srinivasan, 1974).
3. *Factor analysis* (or principal components analysis), a statistical procedure which analyzes customer ratings of products on many attributes to find how products rate on the few important underlying dimensions (or factors) on which the original attributes appear to be based (Howard & Sheth, 1969; Urban, 1975).
4. *Multiple discriminant analysis*, another statistical technique for determining the underlying attributes that consumers use to distinguish between the different products (Johnson, 1971; Pessemier, 1982).

Additional methods are the subject of recent academic research (e.g., Bockenholt & Dillon, 1997; Elrod, 1991; Holbrook & Moore, 1982; Jain & Rao, 1994). Each method has its adherents and possesses strengths and weaknesses, some of which have been extensively documented elsewhere (e.g., see Bourgeois et al., 1982; Myers & Tauber, 1977). Very little work has been done to understand the contrasting implications of maps obtained by each of these methods. However, in one study done at the level of individual consumers, Hauser and Koppelman (1979) found that factor analysis outperformed all other methods in terms of ease of use, interpretability, and the ability to predict preferences. Huber and Holbook (1979) compared the conceptual differences between factor analysis and multiple discriminant analysis and found that factor analysis, by putting more weight on the attributes about which people disagree in their product ratings, is more sensitive to the meaning of attributes, making it particularly useful when the purpose of analysis is the formulation of a new product.

Non-Spatial Representations

Non-spatial representations appear more appropriate for situations satisfying the following two conditions:

1. Consumers use sequential, non-compensatory decision processes for choice, i.e., they evaluate products first on the attribute they consider most important, eliminating from further consideration any which do not meet their standard for their attribute, and then so on through attributes of decreasing importance until a selection is made.

2. Products are best described by features or by nominally scaled (i.e., categorical) attributes, particularly those in which different products are described by different, rather than common features (Johnson, 1984).

These conditions may be especially applicable to broadly defined categories (soft drinks), as opposed to sets of brands in 'direct competition' (diet colas). Indeed, this conjecture is consistent with theories of consumer decision-making that suggest that consumers use a non-compensatory decision process to limit their consideration set to a reasonable few, followed by a compensatory weighting of the remaining alternatives to arrive at a final choice (Bettman, 1979; Punj & Stewart, 1983a; Wright & Barbour, 1977). Even when product attributes can be described along continuous scales, tree structures may be appropriate when consumers only respond to changes of certain minimal size, rather than arbitrarily small changes in attribute levels.

Use of non-spatial models to represent structure has a shorter history than is true for spatial models, and much research continues (DeSarbo et al., 1988; DeSarbo et al., 1993). Reasons for this are several. First, as noted earlier, non-spatial models are a natural way to organize items that can be classified in terms of discrete variables or features. Second, research on individual decision making has shown that in many circumstances consumer choice processes can be effectively modeled as a sequence of choices through nodes of some hierarchical structure (Bettman, 1979; Moore et al., 1986). Hence, these models may offer a means for representing consumers' cognitive structures and decision processes, as well as competitive market structure. Third, these models are particularly well suited for analyses of scanner panel data – behavioral data readily available to many packaged goods firms.

A wide range of non-spatial techniques for representing market structure exist. Typical of the methods which produce hierarchical diagrams of market structure, such as that shown in Figure 5.2, are Rao and Sabavala (1981), the procedures of the Hendry Corporation (see Kalwani & Morrison, 1977), and Novak (1993). The Rao and Sabavala method is simplest, using a standard hierarchical clustering program in which objects are successively grouped together on the basis of a 'similarity' measure. (In their model, two brands are considered more similar the greater the degree of consumer switching between them.) A tree diagram such as that in Figure 5.2 can be used to indicate the order and distance at which groups of objects were clustered together. Hierarchical clustering algorithms are generally inexpensive to implement, and the resulting diagram is plausibly interpreted as a description of some aggregate customer's hierarchical choice process. But as noted before, an aggregate customer is a fiction and the process of aggregation need not lead to the decision process that any actual customers or segments use. Moreover, as there are many 'similarity' measures and many clustering algorithms available, each may produce a structure with different managerial implications, implying the strong need to confirm any inferences drawn by further research evidence.

A potentially serious limitation of (non-spatial) hierarchical representations is that each product is limited to a single branch of the competitive tree, whereas in reality products may compete simultaneously on a number of different bases, and have different substitutability for each. For example, a brand of glass cleaner may be highly competitive with other window cleaners but less competitive with specialized products for cleaning woodwork and countertops. While these specialized products might not be among its effective competitors in window-cleaning applications, the fact that there is some competition suggests the need for overlapping partitions in some product categories where multipurpose products may compete (in varying degrees) in several special-purpose markets. Fraser and Bradford (1983), Zahorik (1994), and Grover and Srinivasan (1987) have developed models which describe product markets in terms of overlapping clusters, based on scanner panel data. Overlapping clusters are also useful when different segments of consumers give different priorities to the relative importance of product attributes. For an example of an aggregate market consisting of such segments see Zahorik (1994).

Non-spatial techniques also suffer from another important limitation. It is generally not possible to consider the position of a new product concept without actually collecting data about that concept. In an attribute space it is possible to examine the probable position of a new concept, because its attributes are presumed known, and so it can be mapped into the space without collecting additional data. With non-spatial methods, the probability of group membership will in general not be known without additional primary data. Thus, non-spatial techniques are not likely to be methods of choice where the purpose of MSA is to aid generation of new product concepts.

All spatial, and most non-spatial techniques assume a symmetrical measure of competition between products, i.e, product A is as competitive with product B as B is with A. However, competitive relationships need not be symmetric (Cooper, 1988). For example, a minor brand may view a market leader as its chief rival, but the reverse is rarely true. Secondly, in markets in transition, consumer loyalties may be shifting, so that the flow of brand switches from A to B may be much greater than in the opposite direction. Only certain non-spatial techniques, such as DEDICOM (Harshman et al., 1982), an algorithm which derives a market structure of overlapping clusters, can accommodate such asymmetries.

Conclusions

Two broad classes of procedures, spatial and non-spatial, are as much complements as substitutes for the overall task of representing structure. Spatial techniques appear more useful for representing structures based on perceptual or preference data and in situations where compensatory decision rules are likely to be employed by customers (e.g., a final choice rather than consideration). Such representations provide opportunities for considering the positioning of new product concepts without the necessity of collecting primary data for them. Non-spatial methods appear more useful for representing behavioral rather than judgmental data and for capturing structures arising from non-compensatory decision strategies (e.g., deciding what items are 'acceptable'). Spatial and non-spatial methods rest on very different assumptions about the perceptual and decision-making processes that give rise to particular patterns of competitive relationships. Unfortunately, it may not always be clear which sets of assumptions apply in a given circumstance. Further, different assumptions may hold at different levels of analysis – for example, selection between product forms (e.g., type of fast food restaurant, chicken versus hamburgers) versus brand within form (e.g., McDonald's versus Burger King), and for different groups of consumers. Hybrid models (Urban & Hauser, 1993: 108), where trees are used for broad market partitions and maps are used to represent competition within each product type, exemplify an intelligent use of both methods. This suggests the wisdom of undertaking analyses of customer decision-making prior to selecting a particular approach to represent the structure of one's market. Carroll and Arabie (1980: 638) observe:

> we find increased realization that no particular model, in general, gives 'the true representation'. Most analyses choose a model that at best captures part of the structure inherent in the data; the part not fitted often awaits another analysis with a different model and perhaps a complementary interpretation as well.

It has become common to generate structures of markets based on both judgmental and behavioral data as a means for cross-validation. If the structure of a market based on behavioral data is not consistent with that expected on the basis of perceptual or preference data, this should prompt an examination of distribution, pricing, or other non-product characteristics not adequately captured by the perceptual structure.

Issues in Using Market Structure Analysis

There are certain issues associated with MSA that transcend individual methods. Four are *aggregation, validation, changes over time,* and *actionability* of findings. This section will briefly discuss these issues. Shocker et al. (1990b) provide a much fuller discussion and note promising research paths suggested by the literature.

The Aggregation Problem

An ideal judgmental approach to the analysis of market structure would, perhaps, model the perceptions and decisions of each individual consumer. Indeed, individual approaches are increasingly being employed by industrial marketers and manufacturers of consumer durables with the aid of personal computer-based choice modeling software (see Mancuso & Shaw, 1988 for a collection of representative software packages for the elicitation of perceptions, personal knowledge, and decision rules). The advantage of such individual-level modeling is that it eliminates many of the problems associated with the analysis of aggregate data that were noted above.

We alluded to the aggregation problem earlier, in suggesting that market structures could usefully be constructed independently for different usage categories or applications. The simplicity of a single representation of market structure (along with a desire to restrict the result to 2–3 dimensions to enhance interpretability and communication) may be comforting to many managers, but can be seriously misleading. Even where individual-level analysis is not feasible or economically justified, as is frequently the case for markets for consumer packaged goods, separate analyses of submarket structures are possible and provide insights into differing segmentation, product positioning, new product idea generation, assessment of competitor strengths and weaknesses, and other managerial issues. Classification tools, such as cluster analysis, make it possible to identify relatively homogeneous groups of consumers with respect to perceptions and decision rules used. These homogeneous groups can become foci for the determination of market structure.

Differing objectives for purchase or usage are among factors that influence perception and decision-making and thereby provide a basis for segmentation (Ratneshwar et al., 1999). In addition, differing cultural or geographic settings, time periods, or the like could also produce different perceptual structures and decision rules. Individuals also have different product alternatives available and differing familiarity with those alternatives as the consequence of factors such as time of entry into the product-market, store choices, shopping behavior, media habits, social network support, etc.[3] When one considers that customers may also have differing experiences with the conditions under which products are to be used, different responses to marketing activity – particularly price and promotion – potentially different goals to achieve from their purchase and consumption, and possibly different means and capabilities for arriving at their market choices, etc., one should be most respectful of the enormous diversity that must be summarized by a single market structure. It is for this reason that individual-level analyses are most useful as a starting point for MSA, and why at minimum, some search for segments that are homogeneous with respect to perceptions and decision-making is a critical first step. This is not to suggest that a single, uniform structure for the entire market might not emerge, but it seems better to begin the MSA task by first looking for segments than it is to start by deriving an aggregate structure without investigating whether it is representative of any consumers in the marketplace.

Virtually all market structures, regardless of the method used to derive them, are *interpretable* in terms of customer decision processes. Some methods for deriving structure even impose a customer decision model as an integral part of their approach (e.g., Cooper & Inoue, 1996; Elrod, 1988; Moore & Winer, 1987; Shugan, 1987). Despite disclaimers by some researchers that their perceptual models or hierarchical structures are based on aggregate brand switching data and thus do not necessarily represent underlying choice processes, it is rare that some reference is not made to customer decision-making when attempting to make results actionable. Notwithstanding such tradition, problems arise when a particular structure is interpreted in terms of a stylized choice process. Incomplete *judgmental* rating-data based, for example, upon abstract product attribute descriptions without pricing information or brand identifiers, may reveal the relative importance of the product attributes actually included in the product descriptions, but not all important dimensions of choice in the marketplace. Ratings based simply on product or brand names leave too many options for respondents in construing the rating task, and any rating so obtained can be a function of the respondent's familiarity with a broader set of characteristics of the product (e.g., in various usage contexts).

Analyses of market structure based on *behavior*, say, using scanner panel data, can likewise fail to provide an adequate picture, interpretable as a decision-making process. Market structure is, after all, the *outcome* of customer decisions, not the decisions themselves. Products which are similar and different as judged by relative position in a perceptual product space or tree structure are there for reasons, reasons which might be inferred from the structure. But it would be naive to assume that all individuals in a market make decisions the same way, so that an aggregate map need not capture any single process or even the dominant process. It is at best an 'average.' While customers are similar with respect to the product actually purchased, they may be quite different regarding the decision processes that led them to the purchase, or even the important benefits sought from the products. Creation of market structure only to a level justified by aggregation of homogeneous units, affords some protection against drawing misleading inferences from analysis.

Validation of the Structure

The fact that a 'correct market structure' or standard does not exist makes it difficult to determine the usefulness of any proposed approach to MSA (notwithstanding some attempts to compare competing structures, e.g., Allenby, 1989; Novak & Stangor, 1987). Methods are proliferating at a rapid rate, thereby making the question of validity the more important. Several researchers have developed 'theory' to dictate conditions that a 'correct' market structure should satisfy (e.g., Kalwani & Morrison, 1977 have argued that for a market in equilibrium, 'switching within a partition [of the market] should be proportional to market share within that partition'). The difficulty with this approach is that the 'theory' may not be demonstrated as valid except through its implications, thus resulting in a circularity of logic wherein to test the market structure: we must assume the theory correct and to test the theory we must assume the market structure to be correct. An alternative approach is by considering the usefulness of the guidance to managers that a specific approach provides. Do the firm's marketing actions have differential effects on competitors that mirrors the magnitude of their MSA-measured competitiveness? If changes are introduced to the marketplace either by the firm or competing firms, does MSA prove insightful in estimating their impact? Since MSA is a planning tool, however, and consequences (outcomes) are based both upon the quality of the resulting action plan *and its implementation*, it will not always be easy to judge unambiguously the worth of any specific approach to MSA. But reliable prediction can certainly be suggestive of validity.

Unfortunately, the preceding approach to validation requires a method be accepted and its analyses implemented before determining the value of such implications. The risks associated with this 'test pilot' approach can be reduced by a simpler first test. A test of validity for any approach is its ability to provide not only a plausible (face valid) structure for a set of 'known' competitors, but also to distinguish those products which the analyst feels are strongly competitive from those which are believed less so. We noted earlier the relation between market definition and structure. Thus, a proposed MSA approach might first be tested by using it to define broad market groups as well as the structure within each group. If it cannot produce a plausible structure for this broader market, then the method might be questioned. Bass et al. (1969), for example, once proposed a method to examine substitutability and complementarity among a diverse set of products. While their approach often produced reasonable results, it also produced several that were counter-intuitive: e.g., beer and bleach were classified as complements; butter and water softeners as substitutes; and waxed paper and other food wraps as unrelated. In this case the lack of intuition for certain results appears clear and thus the method should become suspect. All too often methods have been demonstrated on sets of products believed *a priori* to be close substitutes (e.g., nationally distributed brands of coffee). Intuition alone (face validity) is fallible here in the sense that almost any partition of such a market, even a random one, could have plausibility (Shocker et al., 1984).

Static Representation of a Dynamic World

A structural representation of a market is at best a snapshot at a moment in time. While a snapshot is certainly helpful and suggestive, its usefulness may be limited, particularly for strategic planning. Markets are dynamic. Changes in marketing plans, actions by competitors, and general changes in the economic, political, or socio-cultural environments can serve to make any market structure obsolete over time. Consumers learn and adapt to such factors (Ratneshwar et al., 1999). When an environment radically changes, structures generated prior to that change may prove of limited value. New dimensions of competition (e.g., different attributes) may come into prominence while previously important dimensions may become latent.[4] A product-market definition may be broadened by new alternatives offering higher levels of existing attributes (e.g., higher clock speeds in PCs). 'Hybrid products' may forge linkages between previously distinct product-markets (e.g., wine coolers link fruit juice and inexpensive wines; 'Twix' and chocolate-covered 'Oreos' may blur the candy–cookie distinction). Shocker et al. (2002) discuss product-market dynamics extensively in their discussion of the effects of other product categories upon competition in a given product-market.

It is sometimes plausible (depending upon how aggregation issues can be dealt with) to view spatial models for MSA as *measuring* product position or image. Such quantification allows these measures to be systematically related to change in the marketing mixes of the firm and its competitors and to changes in environmental variables. The effect of such analyses could be to enable the firm to acquire a better understanding of market response to its own and others' actions, and of its ability to influence market structure by changing the structural positioning of its own or, possibly, competitors' products.

Actionability

As noted above, the utility of an MSA ultimately rests on the degree to which it provides a basis for managerial action (i.e., actionability) (Shocker & Srinivasan, 1974). Regardless of method, market structure is often represented in terms of product attributes or features. Some MSA methods directly map attributes into the market structure, while others force the analyst to infer attributes from product membership in particular partitions of the market. Knowledge of relevant attributes provides diagnostic benefits that help in deciding what actions to take based upon the analysis. However, issues involved in a valid specification of attributes together with their action implications are not trivial.

Perceptual attributes can, in principle, include any that are meaningful to customers and which affect their preferences or market choices. These may correspond to psychological or emotion-evoking characteristics rather than being unambiguously rooted in tangible or physical product features. 'Good taste' in a food product may be affected not only by the mixture of ingredients in the product recipe, but also by suggestions (of others) or cues provided by the firm's advertising. High price or high value may be conveyed by a product's nominal price, but also by product-styling features, by the distribution outlets chosen, and by the objects with which a product is compared in promotion or display. Unfortunately, customers and managers often think in different terms and use different language (Griffin & Hauser, 1993). Consequently, the very attempts to make procedures managerially useful often impose a structure or nomenclature on modeling efforts that can interfere with the effort to capture customer reality.

An example of this is the effort to define a 'product' in managerial terms. A manager's view of a product is typically narrower than that of customers. Managers may see two distinct products (e.g., cameras and film, workstation and software), whereas consumers may view them as 'systems' for accomplishing some task (e.g., capturing memories, developing a materials requirements planning system). Certain 'products' may be seen by managers as substitutes, e.g., Grand Marnier, B&B, and Kahlua, whereas customers may view them as part of a portfolio of cordials designed to offer selection to guests. Analyses of market definition or structure often ignore customer-created product alternatives (e.g., homemade pies and cakes, Canon cameras with Vivitar lenses) or products typically purchased through different channels (e.g., whole coffee beans through specialty stores rather than ground coffee purchased in supermarkets). It is plausible that inclusion of such alternatives in market structure methodologies would affect the revealed structure and the analyst's understanding of why it is as it is. In B2B marketing, customer ability to create or manufacture alternatives to marketed products has been explicitly recognized (Von Hippel, 1986). These factors complicate analyses of market structure; although their effect might be less with greater sensitivity on the part of researchers and more 'qualitative' research up front (reaffirming the importance of market definition before MSA).

The issue of actionability is comparatively mute when MSA is used to evaluate well-specified products or positioning alternatives. New products can be 'positioned' in a structural configuration, along with existing products, by customers providing the original data.[5] But when new concepts are inserted into a previously constructed spatial model without additional data collection, or when unfamiliar concepts are evaluated by customers, the issue of actionability (i.e., knowing what different locations in perceptual space 'mean') becomes relevant for the new product to be positioned as intended. Often this can better be done by noting to which of the already located products the new one is more similar and positioning it nearby. With spatial models developed via reduced space methods (e.g., factor analysis, discriminant analysis), the products rather than the space itself have the greater substantive meaning.

The problems of actionability are most severe when trying to decipher what a specific 'optimal location' or 'gap' in market structure means. This occurs in searches of a spatial representation for 'optimal' new product locations or in observing what appear to be potentially attractive new positioning opportunities (Sudharshan et al., 1987). The problem is not only one of relating perceptions to preferences but also of determining the relationship of product attributes to perceptions. Thus, at least three data sets (i.e., people, product attribute perceptions, and preferences) must be simultaneously considered. While spatial representation models such as GENFOLD2 consider such data simultaneously (DeSarbo & Rao, 1986), and may provide insight into characteristics of the current market, it remains to be shown that they can be generalized to products and concepts different from those used in estimating the original spatial structure (i.e., to 'really new' products). In any event, MSA represents products only in terms of attributes important to a purchase/choice among existing competitors, and not the full set of characteristics needed to *define* the product.

In fact, so called 'image' attributes – the 'sportiness' of a car, the 'nutrition' of a food product, or the 'innovativeness' of a new computer product – are particularly difficult to act upon. While it may be certain that consumers make distinctions among products on the basis of such attributes, it is not at all clear how a product design engineer should act on the basis of such information (Griffin & Hauser, 1993; Hauser & Clausing, 1988). Perceptions of such image attributes generally emerge from other more fundamental and objective product attributes, as well as the marketing mix strategy employed by the firm. Thus, knowledge that a particular group of consumers desires a 'sportier' automobile may be informative and provide 'direction,' but still leave numerous options for product design which may ultimately vary considerably in their appeal to consumers. In cases where image attributes are important, management action may need to proceed in two stages. MSA may be used to provide direction and to narrow options in an initial opportunity identification stage. This initial stage should then be followed by research in which consumers are asked to evaluate specific design options.

A related problem, that also influences the actionability of any given MSA, is attribute interaction. Attributes may interact in one of two ways. Preference for one attribute (or level) may be dependent upon the presence or level of another. For example, a consumer may prefer more power in an automobile, but only if the level of safety remains the same. A second type of interaction is related to technical feasibility. A particular level of one attribute may not be achievable without sacrificing performance on some other, e.g., it may not be technologically feasible to obtain both high gas mileage and high speed and power. Interactions do not make interpretation of market structure impossible, but analysts need to be aware of their potential for ambiguity, and be prepared to qualify their interpretation of a structural representation accordingly. Good qualitative research up front may help in sensitizing the researcher/analyst. MSA is without doubt a highly useful set of methodologies, but it is not able to answer all managerial concerns about competitive relationships. The problems and issues raised in this paper may stimulate new research in improving MSA methods and their interpretability.

Summary and Conclusions Regarding Implementation of MSA

Only a few years ago accessibility of computer routines for MSA was quite limited. Algorithms were not 'user friendly.' Further, the computational power required for analyses necessitated use of powerful mainframe computers and often required that the size of a problem (i.e., number of products, attributes, and consumers) be restricted. One of the reasons that procedures for aggregate analyses have been so widely available is that such analyses were often the only ones feasible. The ready availability of scanner data for packaged goods (meaning that data for analysis did not have to be collected by academic researchers) also contributed. Advances in computer power have removed many of these limitations and algorithms have become more accessible and user friendly. This greater accessibility only eliminates the need for expensive hardware and substantial programming expertise. The conceptual issues, data availability, and problems associated with MSA remain.

In this paper we have attempted to highlight many of the options, conceptual issues, and problems that exist in dealing with MSA. There are a large and growing number of approaches. One reason for so many could be that they serve different purposes or provide different insights. Further research is needed to determine the extent to which this rationale is correct and to provide validation for and a classification of methods in terms of their conditions for use. With the diversity that exists, it is easy to see how even a seasoned researcher could be confused and frustrated by the many approaches and options. There do not exist overriding criteria for deciding whether any given structure is 'correct.' It is a topic for research to demonstrate that different approaches may not reveal radically different solutions, provided there actually exists structure in a product-market; i.e., that the market is defined in the same way, that the same relevant product attributes are included in all analyses, and that the level of analysis is at the level of homogeneous segments.

Thus, we conclude by offering guidance for the use and interpretation of analyses of market structure:

1. *Define the purposes of MSA*
This will help in determining the appropriate market definition, measure(s) of competitive intensity or substitutability, and data type. In general, the use of MSA for new product generation or for contemplating potential re-positioning for an established brand will likely require the use of perceptual or preference data and a spatial representation. Such analyses should almost always be considered directional, and be followed by research designed to have consumers evaluate specific product alternatives. On the other hand, determination of whether a particular positioning is producing the desired result is better realized through the use of behavioral data, if available, and either a spatial or non-spatial representation. In this latter type of analysis, the purpose of MSA is less the identification of opportunities and more an evaluation of the outcome of specific marketing actions.

2. *Explicitly define the product-market before analysis of market structure*
MSA intends to provide a customer-based perspective on competitive relationships. Explicit research should be undertaken to identify relevant customers and products (desirably including customer-produced solutions, if any). It may take the form of customer visits, focus groups, or in-depth individual interviews. The critical question is how consumers define the set of alternatives for achieving some purpose. In addition, many methods that have been proposed for MSA have been designed for the purpose of analyzing certain types of data (e.g., multiple classification analysis) without raising the question of whether such data have inherent advantages for the examination of structure. Determining market structure on the basis of data or methods which are merely convenient could prove shortsighted. Even though analysis to establish defensible product-market definitions can be expensive and time consuming, this paper may sensitize a reader to the factors that complicate product-market definition so that low cost researcher judgment may be of value. Procedures such as those used by Srivastava et al., (1981) were inexpensive and, through added academic research, might be refined further.

3. *Non-spatial models, based upon discrete data, seem better able to capture non-compensatory customer decision-making; spatial models seem better able to capture compensatory decision-making*
Where aggregation is defensible, we would expect non-spatial models to be more useful in representing submarkets within a broad market definition (i.e., the competition between product forms and types) and spatial models to be more useful in representing competition within a form or type (i.e., between specific brands). If products are represented by features as distinct from continuous attributes (or in cases where customers assign acceptable threshold values to attributes, thus rendering continuous attributes discrete and dichotomous), the issue becomes more muddled. Non-spatial models may be more useful for representing competition in such cases because they are more compatible with a features representation. In fact, in many cases, a two-stage approach to MSA will be most appropriate. The first stage would examine screening strategies consumers use for reducing the set of alternatives to a smaller number; the second stage would examine the way choices are made among the remaining alternatives. The first stage would almost certainly involve non-compensatory decision rules and would be best represented by a hierarchical structure. The second stage might involve compensatory or possibly different non-compensatory decision rules, and either a spatial or tree structure would be appropriate, depending on the rules used by customers. The possibility that the same object (i.e., product type, form, or brand) could appear in more than one partition of the market should also be explored.

4. *Analysis of aggregate data is most appropriate when there is strong reason to believe that customers*

are relatively homogeneous with respect to product perceptions and decision-making
This is an empirical issue, but it is most likely to be the case for very mature product categories in which there has been little product innovation or change and widescale distribution. When homogeneity is not a reasonable assumption, analysis should *begin* at the individual level in order to determine an appropriate basis for segmentation and subsequent aggregation. It may also be necessary to work with multiple submarket structures.

5. *Market structure is often dependent upon usage occasion or application of product*
The purpose(s) for which consumers buy products should be discovered prior to the initiation of MSA, for they can provide an important anchor to use in defining the competitive array (Ratneshwar et al., 1999; Shocker et al., 2002). Purposes should not be confounded within an analysis of market structure. Rather, purpose should provide a basis for defining the product-market. Since measures of substitutability, competitiveness, and similarity can vary with definition of the product-market, this stage can be of critical importance.

6. *Different methods for representing structure are better for some purposes than others and are based on different assumptions about the structure of the market*
The choice of method, if it is not made wisely, can impose a particular structure on the market (Srivastava et al., 1984). After all, most methods for determining structure rely upon statistical fit to a specific model or form. The procedure merely tries to find the best fit to that form. The selection of an approach to MSA should be based upon the researcher's prior intuition or other qualitative evidence. Qualitative research, including direct discussion with representative customers before and after the MSA exercise, should become an indispensable component of market structure studies. If strategic issues are of interest, judgmental data and methods that are based upon such data should prove more useful because buyers can be asked to respond to hypothetical changes in product alternatives. Such analyses should not be viewed as tests of specific product alternatives, however. Rather, they should be viewed as means for identifying opportunities and for establishing general directions in R&D and marketing planning. Responses to specific marketing stimuli (e.g., specific product designs, price points, and advertising messages) are more likely to be illuminated by behavioral data-based approaches.

7. *Structural representations of markets will be actionable only to the extent that they can be interpreted*
In most cases this will require that the researcher obtain product attribute data from customers.

8. *In most cases, more than one method for representing structure could be appropriate*
While they can be more complementary than substitute, the nature of many approaches for the representation of structure provides an opportunity for the analyst to cross-validate findings using a multimethod approach and to discover aspects of competitive structure that are uniquely revealed by a particular method. Multiple methods should be applied to the same data whenever feasible. Much additional research remains to be carried out to examine the distinctiveness of solutions revealed by different methods and, indeed, the intrinsic worth of different methods or data. Until this is completed, the full nature of the benefit provided by complementarity will not be knowable. It is important to note that the differing results obtained with different approaches may be more a function of differences in the market definition employed by the procedure and the type of data used than of the algorithm *per se*. Thus, conceptual foundations of a given MSA exercise are particularly critical. These are the responsibility of the manager as well as the research analyst. Since non-critical use of virtually any statistical approach to MSA will yield a plausible result, it is vital that the product management team and representative customers be active participants in the design and interpretation of an MSA exercise.

9. *MSA also provides a means for* testing *a priori notions about competitive relationships*
Competition between items within a defined market should be more intense than competition (substitutability) between items in different markets. Since determining an appropriate market definition is a critical first step in the analysis of market structure, tests of assumptions regarding market definition and competitive relationships should precede further analyses of structural relationships. Such tests may only support intuition, but they must be conducted in a manner that permits disconfirmation. Methods and criteria have been proposed to carry out such testing, but if the 'correct' structure is not included in those tested, even such methods cannot confirm its superiority.

We conclude by noting what by now might be all too obvious:

10. *For all its elegant technique and mathematical sophistication, MSA remains inherently an art form*
Structural representations of markets are the outcome of data, algorithms, and judgment. All are important and if any are missing, the consequences could be severe. Decisions about the analysis and the interpretation of the results should not be left exclusively to the analyst. Managers need to be active participants in MSA to assure meaningful and actionable results.

Notes

1. Best (1978), Moore, Pessemier and Little (1979), and Moore and Holbrook (1982) provide evidence that maps based on preference data provide superior predictions of choice but at the cost of obscuring the perceptual attribute structure. On the other hand, use of similarities data preserves the perceptual attribute structure but at the cost of some predictive power. The resolution of this dilemma appears to lie with the purposes for which the market structure analysis is undertaken. If the purpose is prediction of choice among existing products, the use of preference data is probably more desirable. If it is an improved understanding of the competitive dimensions of the market, including dimensions that may not currently be important for choice, then similarities data may be more suggestive. DeSarbo and Rao (1986) have offered a procedure, GENFOLD2, that provides the opportunity to examine attributes and preferences simultaneously. The procedure allows the analyst to manipulate the derived multidimensional representation to incorporate any of a variety of product attributes for which data are available, and determine the impact of such manipulations on consumer preferences.

2. Tabular (e.g., matrix) representations are also plausible. These have been infrequently used and often do not communicate well to managers. They will not be discussed further.

3. Srinivasan (1979) investigated what he termed 'brand specific effects' which, for certain brands, grow out of their long-term presence in the market. He found that in some categories these effects can be quite pronounced, e.g., 25% of the variance in preference for soft drinks could be attributed to such effects. Elrod (pers. comm.) has reported that in some product categories rote brand choice decisions (as opposed to decisions based upon competing product attributes) account for more than half the purchases in the category. The presence of such habitual decision-making has implications for the marketing of new products and creates ambiguity in considering the position and acceptance of brand extensions which seek to capitalize on the reputation of an established brand.

4. New products can succeed because they introduce a new attribute dimension. This new dimension may not have been important for the choice among existing products, but its introduction differentiates the new product from existing ones. (It can sometimes also cause a new product to define a new category or submarket by being too different. This phenomenon is not well understood.) It should be noted, however, that even when a data collection task is such that fictitious products containing the new attribute are presented to respondents, the effect of the change may not be captured fully. Promotion to highlight the change and its implications, or to make the subject aware of the existence of a support system (e.g., the comments and actions of significant others) will be absent and the respondent may therefore not realize the full significance of the change at the time of data collection. Thus an attribute that had the power to eventually redefine the structure of a market (e.g., fluoride in toothpaste; artificial sweeteners in soft drinks) could remain latent or be inconsequential in this initial analysis of market structure.

An additional factor affecting the ability of MSA to predict well is the variation of products along an existing dimension – which could influence the relative importance of that dimension (Wittink et al., 1982). When all existing products are similar on some dimension, it is unlikely to manifest an effect upon choice (e.g., safety among airlines). Yet, a new product that varies from the norm of the existing product class on that dimension could be perceived as very desirable (or undesirable) because of this.

5. The fact that the 'new' are often still concepts, while the existing products are 'real' can create problems, of course, and requires that the analyst ensure concept descriptions are 'complete' in the sense that they convey the information customers would learn from exposure to the real alternatives (Nelson, 1974) and that customers comprehend this information accurately.

References

Allenby, Greg M. (1989) A unified approach to identifying, estimating, and testing demand structures with aggregate scanner data. *Marketing Science*, 8 (Summer): 265–80.

Arabie, Phipps, Carroll, J. Douglas, DeSarbo, Wayne & Wind, Yoram (1981) Overlapping clustering: a new methodology for product positioning. *Journal of Marketing Research*, 18 (August): 310–17.

Bass, Frank M., Pessemier, Edgar A. & Lehmann, Donald R. (1972) An experimental study of relationships between attitudes, brand preferences, and choice. *Journal of Marketing Research*, 17 (November): 532–41.

Bass, Frank M., Pessemier, Edgar A. & Tigert, Douglas J. (1969) Complementary and substitute patterns of purchasing and use. *Journal of Advertising Research*, 9 (June): 19–27.

Belk, Russell W. (1975) Situational variables and consumer behavior. *Journal of Consumer Research*, 2 (December): 157–64.

——— (1979) A free-response approach to developing product-specific consumption situation taxonomies. In *Analytic Approaches to Product and Marketing Planning, Report No. 79–104*, edited by. Allan D. Shocker. Cambridge, MA: Marketing Science Institute, pp. 177–96.

Best, Roger J. (1976) The predictive aspect of a joint-space theory of stochastic choice. *Journal of Marketing Research*, 13 (May): 198–204.

Bettman, James R. (1979). *An Information Processing Theory of Consumer Choice.* Reading, MA: Addison-Wesley.

Bockenholt, Ulf & Dillon, William R. (1997) Some new methods for an old problem: modeling preference changes and competitive market structures in pretest market data. *Journal of Marketing Research*, 34 (February): 130–42.

Bourgeois, Jacques C., Haines, George H., Jr. & Sommers, Montrose S. (1980) Defining an industry. In *Market Measurement and Analysis*, edited by David B. Montgomery & Dick R. Wittink. Cambridge, MA: Marketing Science Institute, pp. 120–33.

——— (1982) Product/Market structure: problems and issues. In *Analytic Approaches to Product and Marketing Planning: The Second Conference, Report No. 82–109*, edited by Rajendra. K. Srivastava & Allan D. Shocker. Cambridge, MA: Marketing Science Institute, pp. 79–116.

Carroll, Douglas J. & Arabie, Phipps (1980) Multidimensional scaling. *Annual Review of Psychology*, 31: 607–49.

Colombo, Richard A. & Morrison, Donald G. (1989) A brand switching model with implications for marketing strategies. *Marketing Science*, 8 (Winter): 89–99.

Cooper, Lee G. (1973) A multivariate investigation of preferences. *Multivariate Behavioral Research*, 8: 253–72.

——— (1983) A review of multidimensional scaling in marketing research. *Applied Psychological Measurement*, 7 (Fall): 427–50.

——— (1988) Competitive maps: the structure underlying asymmetric cross-elasticities. *Management Science*, 34 (June): 707–23.

Cooper, Lee G. & Inoue, Akihiro (1996) Building market structures from consumer preferences. *Journal of Marketing Research*, 33 (August): 293–306.

Corter, James E. & Tversky, Amos. (1986) Extended similarity trees. *Psychometrika*, 51 (September): 429–51.

Day, George S., Shocker, Allan D. & Srivastava, Rajendra K. (1979) Consumer-oriented approaches to identifying product-markets. *Journal of Marketing*, 43 (Fall): 8–19.

DeSarbo, Wayne S., & Rao, Vithala R. (1986) A constrained unfolding methodology for product positioning. *Marketing Science*, 5 (Winter): 1–19.

DeSarbo, Wayne S., Manrai, Ajay K. & Manrai, Lalita A. (1993) non-spatial tree models for the assessment of competitive market structure: an integrated review of the marketing and psychometric literatures. In *Handbooks of Operations Research and Management Science: Marketing*, Vol. 5, edited by Joshua Eliashberg & Gary L. Lilien. Amsterdam: North-Holland Publishing CO., pp. 193–257.

DeSarbo, Wayne S., De Soete, Geert, Carroll, J. Douglas, & Ramaswamy, Venkatram (1988) A new stochastic ultrametric tree unfolding methodology for assessing competitive market structure and deriving market segments. *Applied Stochastic Models and Data Analysis*, 4 (3): 185–204.

Dillon, William R., Frederick, Donald G. & Tangpanichdee, Vanchai (1985) Decision issues in building perceptual product spaces with multi-attribute rating data. *Journal of Consumer Research*, 12 (June): 47–63.

Elrod, Terry (1988) Choice map: inferring a product-market map from panel data. *Marketing Science*, 7 (Winter): 21–40.

——— (1991) Internal analysis of market structure: recent developments and future prospects. *Marketing Letters*, 2 (August): 253–66.

Fraser, Cynthia, & Bradford, John (1983) Competitive market structure analysis: principal partitioning of revealed substitutability. *Journal of Consumer Research*, 10 (June): 15–30.

Green, Paul E., Carmone, Frank J. Jr. & Smith, Scott M. (1989) *Multidimensional Scaling: Concepts and Applications*. Boston, MA: Allyn and Bacon.

Griffin, Abbie & Hauser, John R. (1993) The voice of the customer. *Marketing Science*, 12 (1): 1–27.

Grover, Rajiv & Srinivasan, V. (1987) A simultaneous approach to market segmentation and market structuring. *Journal of Marketing Research*, 24 (May): 139–53.

Harshman, Richard, Green, Paul E., Wind, Yoram & Lundy, M.E. (1982) A model for the analysis of asymmetric data in marketing research. *Marketing Science*, 1 (Spring): 205–42.

Hauser, John R. & Clausing, Donald (1988) The House of Quality. *Harvard Business Review*, 66 (May–June): 63–73.

Hauser, John R. & Koppelman, Frank S. (1979) Alternative perceptual mapping techniques: relative accuracy and usefulness. *Journal of Marketing Research*, 16 (November): 495–506.

Hauser, John R. & Shugan, Steven M. (1983) Defensive marketing strategies. *Marketing Science*, 2 (Fall): 319–60.

Hoffman, Donna L. & Franke, George R. (1986) Correspondence analysis: graphical representation of categorical data in marketing research. *Journal of Marketing Research*, 23 (August): 213–27.

Holbrook, Morris B. & Moore, William L. (1982) Using canonical correlation to construct product spaces for objects with Known feature structure. *Journal of Marketing Research*, 19 (February): 87–98.

Howard, John & Sheth, Jagdish N. (1969) *The Theory of Buyer Behavior*. New York: John Wiley and Sons, Inc.

Huber, Joel & Holbrook, Morris B. (1979) Using attribute ratings for product positioning: some distinctions among compositional approaches. *Journal of Marketing Research*, 16 (November): 507–16.

Jain, Dipak & Rao, Ram C. (1994) Latent class models to infer market structure: a comparative analysis. *European Journal of Operational Research*, 76 (2): 331–43.

Johnson, Michael (1984) Consumer choice strategies for comparing non-comparable alternatives. *Journal of Consumer Research*, 11 (December): 741–53.

Johnson, Richard M. (1971) Market segmentation: a strategic management tool. *Journal of Marketing Research*, 8 (February):13–18.

Kalwani, Manohar U. & Morrison, Donald G. (1977) A parsimonious description of the Hendry System. *Management Science*, 23 (January): 467–77.

Kumar, Ajith & Sashi, C.M. (1989) Confirmatory analysis of aggregate hierarchical market structures: inferences from brand switching behavior. *Journal of Marketing Research*, 26 (November): 444–53.

Lehmann, Donald R. (1972) Judged similarity and brand switching data as similarity measures. *Journal of Marketing Research*, 9 (August): 331–4.

Mancuso, James C. & Shaw, Mildred L.G. (1988) *Cognition and Personal Structure: Computer Access and Analysis*. New York: Praeger Press.

Moore, William L. & Holbrook, Morris B. (1982) On the predictive validity of joint-space models in consumer evaluations of new concepts. *Journal of Consumer Research*, 9 (September): 206–10.

Moore, William L. & Winer, Russell S. (1987) A panel-data based method for merging joint space and market response function estimation. *Marketing Science*, 6 (Winter): 25–42.

Moore, William L., Pessemier, Edgar A. & Lehmann, Donald R. (1986) Hierarchical representations of market structures and choice processes through preference trees. *Journal of Business Research*, 14 (5): 371–86.

Moore, William L., Pessemier, Edgar A. & Little, Taylor E. (1979) Predicting brand purchase behavior: marketing application of the Schonemann and Wang Unfolding Model. *Journal of Marketing Research*, 16 (May): 203–10.

Myers, James J. & Tauber, Edward (1977) *Market Structure Analysis*. Chicago: American Marketing Association.

Nelson, Philip E. (1974) Advertising as information. *Journal of Political Economy*, 81 (July–August): 729–45.

Novak, Thomas P. (1993) Log-linear trees: models of market structure in brand switching data. *Journal of Marketing Research*, 30 (August): 267–87.

Novak, Thomas P. & Stangor, Charles (1987) Testing competitive market structures: an application of weighted least squares methodology to brand switching data. *Marketing Science*, 6 (Winter): 82–97.

Oren, Schmuel, Smith, Stephen & Wilson, Robert (1984) Pricing a product line. *Journal of Business*, 57 (January), 73–99.

Pessemier, Edgar A. (1982) *Product Management: Strategy and Organization*. New York: John Wiley and Sons Inc.

Punj, Girish N. & Stewart, David W. (1983a) An interaction approach to consumer decision making. *Journal of Consumer Research*, 11 (September): 181–96.

——— (1983b) Cluster analysis in marketing research: review and suggestions for application. *Journal of Marketing Research*, 20 (May): 134–48.

Ratneshwar, S. & Shocker, Allan D. (1991) Substitution in use and the cognitive structure of product categories. *Journal of Marketing Research*, 28 (August): 281–95.

Ratneshwar, S., Shocker, Allan D, Cotte, June & Srivastava, Rajendra (1999) Product, person, and purpose: putting the consumer back into theories of dynamic market behavior. *Journal of Strategic Marketing*, 7 (September): 191–208.

Sattath, Schmuel & Tversky, Amos (1977) Additive similarity trees. *Psychometrika*, 42 (September): 319–46.

Shepard, Roger (1974) Representation of structure in similarity data: problems and prospects. *Psychometrika*, 39 (December): 373–421.

Shocker, Allan D. & Srinivasan, V. (1974) A consumer based methodology for the identification of new product ideas. *Management Science*, 20 (February): 921–37.

Shocker, Allan D., Bayus, Barry L. & Kim, Namwoon (2002) Product complements and substitutes in a dynamic world: the relevance of 'other products.' Working Paper. College of Business, San Francisco State University.

Shocker, Allan D., Stewart, David W. & Zahorik, Anthony J. (1990a) Determining the competitive structure of product-markets: practices, issues, and suggestions. *Journal of Managerial Issues*, 11, 2 (Summer): 127–159. Reprinted as a Marketing Science Institute Special Report 90–115 (1990).

——— (1990b) Modeling competitive market structures: practices, problems, promise. In *The Interfaces of Marketing and Strategy*, edited by George Day, Barton Weitz & Robin Wensley. Greenwich, CT: JAI Press, pp. 9–56.

Shocker, Allan D., Zahorik, Anthony J. & Stewart, David W. (1984) Competitive market structure analysis: a comment on problems. *Journal of Consumer Research*, 11 (December): 836–41.

Shugan, Steven M. (1987) Estimating brand positioning maps using supermarket scanning data. *Journal of Marketing Research*, 24 (February): 1–18.

Srinivasan, V. (1979) Network models for estimating brand-specific effects in multi-attribute marketing models. *Management Science*, 25 (January): 11–21.

Srivastava, Rajendra K., Alpert, Mark I. & Shocker, Allan D. (1984) A customer-oriented approach for determining market structures. *Journal of Marketing*, 48 (Spring): 32–45.

Srivastava, Rajendra K., Leone, Robert P. & Shocker, Allan D. (1981) Market structure analysis: hierarchical clustering of products based on substitution-in-use. *Journal of Marketing*, 45 (Summer): 38–48.

Stewart, David W. (1981) Application and misapplication of factor analysis in marketing research. *Journal of Marketing Research*, 18 (February): 51–62.

Sudharshan, D., May, Jerrold & Shocker, Allan D. (1987) A simulation comparison of methods for new product location. *Marketing Science*, 6 (Spring): 182–201.

Urban, Glen L. (1975) PERCEPTOR: a model for product positioning. *Management Science*, 21 (April): 858–71.

Urban, Glen L. & Hauser, John R. (1993) *Design and Marketing of New Products* 2nd edn. Englewood Cliffs, NJ: Prentice-Hall.

Urban, Glen L., Johnson, Philip L. & Hauser, John R. (1984) Testing competitive market structures. *Marketing Science*, 3 (Spring): 83–112.

Von Hippel, Eric (1986) Lead users: a source of novel product concepts. *Management Science*, 32 (July): 791–805.

Wittink, Dick R., Krishnamurthi, Lakshman & Nutter, Julia B. (1982) Comparing derived importance weights across attributes. *Journal of Consumer Research*, 8 (March): 471–3.

Wright, Peter L. & Barbour, Frederick (1977) Phased decision strategies: sequels to an initial screening. In *Multiple Criteria Decision Making: TIMS Studies in the Management Sciences, Volume* 6, edited by Martin K. Starr & M. Zeleny. Amsterdam: North-Holland Publishing Co., pp. 91–109.

Zahorik, Anthony J. (1994) A non-herarchical brand switching model for inferring market structure. *European Journal of Operational Research*, 76 (2): 344–58.

Appendix: Supplemental References (relevant research not cited in the chapter)

Andrews, Rick L. & Srinivasan, T.C. (1995) Studying consideration effects in empirical choice models using scanner panel data. *Journal of Marketing Research*, 32 (February): 30–41.

Bayus, Barry L, Shocker, Allan D. & Kim, Namwoon (2000) 'Growth models for multi-product interactions: current status and new directions. In *New Product Diffusion Models*, edited by Vijay Mahajan, Eitan Muller & Jerry Wind. Boston, MA: Kluwer Academic Publishers, pp. 141–64.

Blattberg, Robert C. & Wisniewski, Kenneth J. (1989) Price-induced patterns of competition. *Marketing Science*, 8 (Fall): 291–309.

Bridges, Eileen, Yim, Chi Kin (Bennett) & Briesch, Richard A. (1995) A high-tech product market share model with customer expectations. *Marketing Science*, 14 (Winter): 61–81.

Bronnenberg, Bart J., Mahajan, Vijay & Vanhonacker, Wilfried R. (2000) The emergence of market structure in new repeat-purchase categories: the interplay of market share and retailer distribution. *Journal of Marketing Research*, 37 (February): 16–31.

Bucklin, Randolph E. & Srinivasan, V. (1991) Determining interbrand substitutability through survey measurement of consumer preference structures. *Journal of Marketing Research*, 28 (February): 58–71.

Carpenter, Gregory & Lehmann, Donald (1985) A model of marketing mix, brand switching, and competition. *Journal of Marketing Research*, 22 (August): 318–29.

Chaturvedi, Anil & Carroll, J. Douglas (1998) A perceptual mapping procedure for analysis of proximity data to determine common and unique product-market structures. *European Journal of Operational Research*, 111 (2): 268–84.

DeSarbo, Wayne S. & Manrai, Ajay K. (1992) A new multidimensional scaling methodology for the analysis of asymmetric proximity data in marketing research. *Marketing Science*, 11 (Winter): 1–20.

Deshpande, Rohit & Gatignon, Hubert (1994) Competitive analysis. *Marketing Letters*, 5 (July): 271–88.

Elrod, Terry & Keane, Michael P. (1995) 'A factor-analytic probit model for representing the market structure in panel data. *Journal of Marketing Research*, 32 (February): 1–16.

Ghose, Sanjoy (1998) Distance representations of consumer perceptions: evaluating appropriateness by using diagnostics. *Journal of Marketing Research*, 35 (May): 137–53.

Glazer, Rashi & Nakamoto, Kent (1991) Cognitive geometry: an analysis of structure underlying representations of similarity. *Marketing Science*, 10 (Summer): 205–28.

Grover, Rajiv & Dillon, William R. (1985) A probabilistic model for testing hypothesized hierarchical market structures. *Marketing Science*, 4 (Fall): 312–35.

Grover, Rajiv & Rao, Vithala R. (1988) Inferring competitive market structure based on a model of interpurchase intervals. *International Journal of Research in Marketing*, 5 (1): 55–72.

Hauser, John R. & Wernerfelt, Birger (1990) An evaluation cost model of evoked sets. *Journal of Consumer Research*, 16 (March): 393–408.

Holbrook, Morris B. & Moore, William L. (1982) Using canonical correlation to construct product spaces for objects with known feature structure. *Journal of Marketing Research*, 19 (February): 87–98.

Hruska, H. (1986) Market definition and segmentation using fuzzy clustering methods. *International Journal of Research in Marketing*, 3 (2): 117–34.

Jain, Dipak, Bass, Frank M. & Chen, Yu-Min (1990) Estimation of latent class models with heterogeneous choice probabilities: an application to market structuring. *Journal of Marketing Research*, 27 (February): 94–101.

Johnson, Michael D. & Fornell, Claes (1987) The nature and methodological implications of the cognitive representations of products. *Journal of Consumer Research*, 14 (September): 214–28.

Kamakura, Wagner A. & Russell, Gary J. (1989) A probabilistic choice model for market segmentation and elasticity structure. *Journal of Marketing Research*, 26 (November): 379–90.

Kannan, P.K. & Sanchez, Susan M. (1994) Competitive market structures: a subset selection analysis. *Management Science*, 40, 11 (November): 1484–99.

Kannan, P.K. & and Wright, Gordon P. (1991) Modeling and testing structured markets: a nested logit approach. *Marketing Science*, 10 (Winter): 58–82.

Kim, Namwoon, Chang, Dae Ryun & Shocker, Allan D. (2000) Modeling inter-category and generational dynamics for a growing information technology industry. *Management Science*, 46 (April): 496–512.

Lattin, James M. & McAlister, Leigh (1985) Using a variety-seeking model to identify substitute and complementary relationships among competing products. *Journal of Marketing Research*, 22 (August): 330–9.

Lehmann, Donald R. & Pan, Yigang (1994) Context effects, new brand entry, and consideration sets. *Journal of Marketing Research*, 31 (August): 364–74.

Mackay, David B. & Droge, Cornelia (1990) Extensions of probabilistic perceptual maps with implications for competitive positioning and choice. *International Journal of Research in Marketing*, 7: 265–82.

Mackay, David B., Easley, Robert F. & Zinnes, Joseph L. (1995) A single ideal point model for market structure analysis. *Journal of Marketing Research*, 32 (November): 433–43.

Ramaswamy, Venkatram & DeSarbo, Wayne S. (1990) SCULPTRE: a new methodology for deriving and analyzing hierarchical product-market structure from panel data. *Journal of Marketing Research*, 27 (November): 418–27.

Rao, Vithala R. & Sabavala, Darius (1981) Inference of hierarchical choice processes from panel data. *Journal of Consumer Research*, 8 (June): 85–96.

Rao, Vithala R., Sabavala, Darius & Zahorik, Anthony J. (1982) Market structure analysis using brand switching data: a comparison of clustering techniques. In *Analytic Approaches to Product and Marketing Planning: The Second Conference*, edited by Rajendra K. Srivastava & Allan D. Shocker. Cambridge, MA: Marketing Science Institute.

Ratneshwar, S., Pechmann, Cornelia & Shocker, Allan D. (1996) Goal-derived categories and the antecedents of across-category consideration. *Journal of Consumer Research*, 23 (December): 240–50.

Redmond, William H. (1989) Effects of new product pricing on the evolution of market structure. *Journal of Product Innovation Management*, 6: 99–108.

Roberts, John H. & Lattin, James M. (1991) Development and testing of a model of consideration set composition. *Journal of Marketing Research*, 28 (November): 429–40.

——— (1997) Consideration: review of research and prospects for future insights. *Journal of Marketing Research*, 34 (August): 406–10.

Russell, Gary J. (1992) A model of latent symmetry in cross-price elasticities. *Marketing Letters*, 3 (2): 157–169.

Russell, Gary J. & Bolton, Ruth N. (1988) Implications of market structure for elasticity structure. *Journal of Marketing Research*, 25 (August): 229–41.

Russell, Gary J. & Kamakura, Wagner A. (1994) Understanding brand competition using micro and macro scanner data. *Journal of Marketing Research*, 31 (May): 289–303.

Russell, Gary J. & Ratneshwar S, Shocker, Allan D., et al. (1999) Multi-category decision-making: review and synthesis. *Marketing Letters*, 10 (August): 319–32.

Shocker, Allan D. & V. Srinivasan, (1979) Multiattribute approaches to product concept evaluation and generation: a critical review. *Journal of Marketing Research*, 16 (May): 159–80.

Shocker, Allan D., Ben-Akiva, Moshe, Boccara, Bruno & Nedungadi, Prakash (1991) Consideration set influences on consumer decision-making and choice: issues, models, and suggestions. *Marketing Letters*, 2, 3 (August): 181–97.

Stefflre, Volney (1968) Market structure studies: new products for old markets and new markets (foreign) for old products. In *Applications of the Sciences in Marketing Management*, edited by Frank M. Bass, Charles W. King & Edgar A. Pessemier. New York: John Wiley and Sons.

Tversky, Amos & Sattath, Shmuel, (1979) Preference trees. *Psychological Review*, 86 (November): 542–73.

Wind, Yoram J. (1977) The perception of a firm's competitive position. In *Behavioral Models for Market Analysis*, edited by Franco M. Nicosia & Yoram Wind. Hinsdale, IL: Dryden Press.

Zenor, Michael J. & Srivastava, Rajendra K. (1993) Inferring market structure with aggregate data: a latent segment logit approach. *Journal of Marketing Research*, 30 (August): 369–79.

6

Competitive Response and Market Evolution

HUBERT GATIGNON and DAVID SOBERMAN

Introduction

Our objective is to review the major areas of research that relate to the dimensions of 'competitive response' and 'market evolution.' We develop a conceptual framework that considers the interactions between these two key constructs of 'competitive response' and 'market evolution.' We, therefore, first identify what the key dimensions of competitive response and market evolution are. Then, we review the literature that addresses the impact that competitive responses (to a variety of market initiatives) can have on the evolution of a market. We then examine the research that considers how the evolution of a market can constrain and influence the responses of firms within an industry. Our framework also considers the impact that environmental (or exogenous) factors can have on both dimensions of 'competitive response' and 'market evolution.' Such factors may assist to distinguish between the cause and effects of some of the interactions between competitive response and market evolution. In each section, we identify several areas where we believe that further research is both necessary and can yield fruitful advances.

More specifically, we can represent the area of investigation using the framework shown in Figure 6.1. This framework can be useful for organizing and structuring our review of this literature. The focus of this chapter is about the links between the competitive dynamics dimensions (bottom left box in Figure 6.1) and the dimensions of market evolution (bottom right box in Figure 6.1).

In the second section of this paper, we characterize the dimensions along which competitive responses can be described, and we then define the characteristics of market evolution. Within each box in Figure 6.1, the list of dimensions that are discussed in this chapter is shown for both competitive dynamics and market evolution. In the third section, we review the literature and propose new directions for research concerning how competitive responses affect market evolution and *vice versa* (how market evolution impacts competitive responses). While each aspect has received individual attention in past research, the interaction between the two remains under-researched. Lambkin and Day (1989) made this observation over a decade ago, yet their call for research in that direction has remained for the most part unanswered. We propose a stream of research that goes beyond the population ecology concepts that they suggest. In this section, we include an analysis of the role of external forces in explaining changes in these dimensions.

Dimensions of Competitive Responses and Characterization of Market Evolution

The Primary Dimensions of Competitive Dynamics

Two streams of research concerned with competitive dynamics have received considerable attention in the marketing literature. The first of these streams concerns the entry and exit of competitors. This is the focus of population ecology, which provides a source of explanations for the evolution of markets from a supply-side point of view. Lambkin and Day

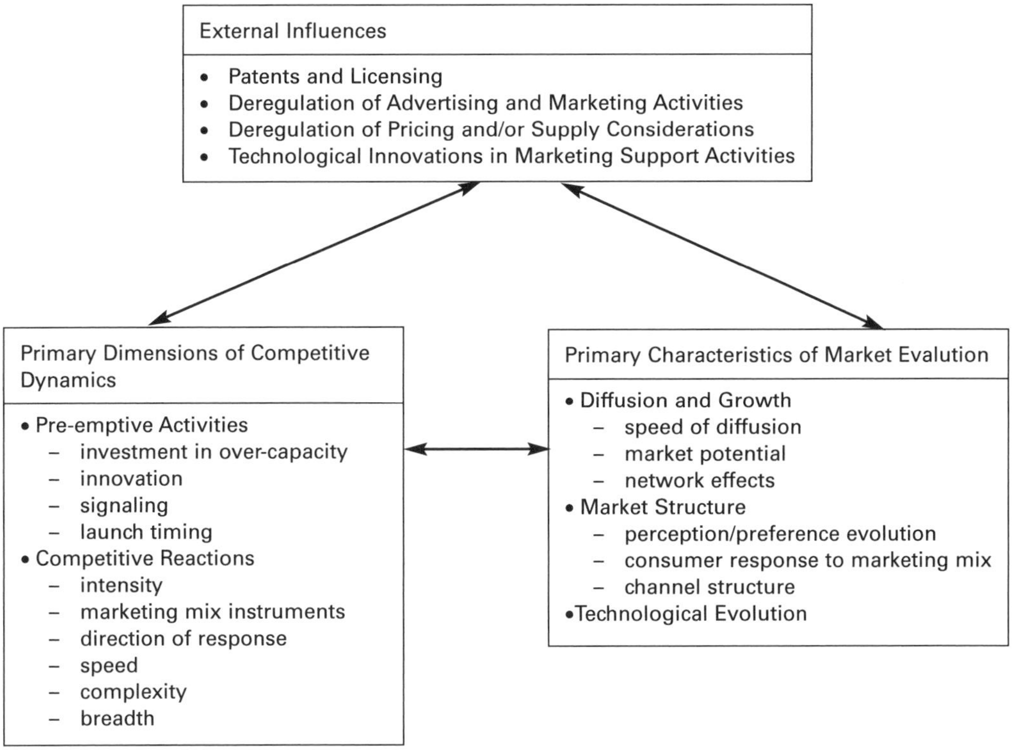

Figure 6.1 *A Framework for Understanding Interactions Between Market Evolution and Competition Dynamics*

(1989) clearly establish the importance of that perspective and explain the role of key population ecology concepts (e.g., structural inertia, r-strategists versus k-strategists, specialists versus generalists). The essence of the theory consists in the impact of strategic choices concerning the firm (e.g., technological or organizational) at the time of entry as a function of the stage of the product life cycle. Beyond the questions of whether multiple types of organizations can coexist at the same stage, and of the ability to develop a valid harmony of firms, Carroll's (1985) argument of resource partitioning combines the dynamics between generalists and specialists. Aldrich (1999) summarizes this approach and especially the notion that generalists can stratify the market, which stimulates the entry of specialists. However, the theory remains at the level of competition between these firm types and does not consider the specific action or strategies used by the firms to compete, and does not develop implications on evolution of demand. We devote our discussion to actions of the firms that may occur at any time when entry is likely or when entry has already happened. Consequently, even though we do recognize the existence of structural inertia (Hannan & Freeman, 1977), we focus our analysis on *pre-emptive activities* of incumbents, i.e., the decisions firms make that stifle or encourage competition, with emphasis on the impact of firm entries and exits over time.

The second broad stream of research concerns the dynamics of competition between firms and brands competing in a single or multiple markets. In this section, we focus our discussion on the characterization of these *competitive reaction patterns*. The goal will not be to review all the issues surrounding competitive reactions, but only the literature as it relates to describing the types and forms of reactions that can be used to categorize competitive reaction strategies. In the second part of this paper, we then relate these reaction strategies to the evolution of markets.

Pre-emptive Activities

Pre-emptive activities are strategies to control the speed with which new products or firms enter a market. Naturally, this determines the extent to which products proliferate over time and, ultimately, the competitive density in the market.

With the threat of entry or the threat of additional competition in a market, incumbents devote considerable time and energy to pre-emptive activities. The objective of these activities is to limit competition by a) making the market less attractive to new competitors in order to reduce their likelihood of entering the market; or b) signaling information to the new entrants about the market (or the incumbents) that affects the marketing decisions of new competitors. For example, an incumbent could develop new technology that makes the market less attractive to an entrant who does not have access to the technology. Alternatively, an incumbent may make irreversible and observable investments in plant, distribution or service capabilities that reduce the cost of responding aggressively to a new competitor. In this section, we discuss the important literature on various pre-emptive actions that are undertaken by incumbents: investment in over-capacity, innovations, signaling and launch timing.

Investment in Over-capacity In the industrial organization literature, there exists a long tradition of examining barriers to entry that are created as the result of competition between oligopolistic firms (see Bain, 1956; Scherer & Ross, 1990). This literature examines how branding, advertising and distribution channels of existing firms can constitute significant barriers to new entrants. In general, however, these barriers form naturally and do not obtain from the specific intent of incumbents to 'deter' or alter the decisions of potential incumbents. More recently however, a number of researchers have examined how incumbents can take decisions that have the express intent of changing the decisions of potential entrants (Demsetz, 1982; Dixit, 1979; Spence, 1977b). This literature focuses on the decision of an incumbent to invest in excess capacity in order to reduce the cost of responding to an entrant that does enter. The authors focus their discussion on manufacturing capacity; however, the logic advanced by this work is as applicable to investments relating to distribution and after-sales service. In the following section, we consider a more complex response by incumbents – that of investing in R&D.

Innovation Amongst the strongest deterrents to a potential entrant are technological disadvantages either in the production of a good or service or in the performance of the good or service (from the perspective of an end-user). As a result, incumbents devote considerable time, effort, and resources to the identification and creation of technological advantages. This literature has its roots in the 'Diffusion of Innovation' literature (Arrow, 1962). While it is possible for any agent in an economy to engage in R&D, it is generally accepted that incumbents are in a better position to engage in innovative activity within a sector due to their knowledge, their expertise, and their ownership of plants and laboratories suitable for the testing of new products and processes (Adams & Encaoua, 1994; Gilbert & Newbery, 1982).

Types of Innovations

Generally, the literature looks at innovations that either improve the quality of existing products or reduce the cost of producing them (Abernathy & Utterback, 1978; Athey & Schmultzer, 1995). *Improvements in quality* are observed to generate upward shifts in demand or in the prices people are willing to pay for a good or service. In contrast, process innovations provide a *reduction in the unit cost* of production, but do not affect end-users' willingness to pay for the product. Some innovations provide a combination of performance and production cost benefits, but in most cases an R&D project can be categorized based on whether its primary thrust is to affect the benefits that consumers obtain from the product or to provide benefits to the firm in terms of producing the product.

This distinction is useful, but recent work demonstrates, however, that product innovation is a richer concept than simply an improvement in quality. The use of differentiation as a pre-emptive action by incumbents has received considerable attention (Bain, 1949, 1956). This view of pre-emptive product differentiation has been analyzed in the context of spatial models (Judd, 1985; Lane, 1980) with focus on an incumbent's 'crowding' the product space by launching additional products. Incumbents are assumed to have cost advantages in launching line extensions. An interesting extension to this idea relates to R&D that focuses on *innovations that add benefits to a product* beyond the products available in a market place (Eswaran & Gallini, 1996). An example of this would be the child seat recently developed for Polaris personal watercraft (aka Wave Runners). Such innovations broaden the appeal of a product to other end users (families with a small child) without materially affecting the benefit obtained by other users.

Therefore, we identify three different types of innovation that are observed to have different effects on market evolution: 1) quality improvement; 2) added benefits to reach new segments of consumers; and 3) cost reduction for producers.

Innovation Strategy

The quintessential problem for an incumbent is how to retain the ownership of an innovation (and the incremental profits it generates) once it has been discovered. It is not easy for an innovator to establish full property rights over an innovation because of spillover, or the degree to which an innovator discloses the 'secret' of the innovation to other firms by simply making the product available in the marketplace (Schumpeter, 1943). Clearly, this problem is most severe with product-related innovations such as the above-mentioned child seat for Wave Runners. In the same way as end-consumers can, competitors can purchase the new product and, through reverse engineering, attain the capability to produce the product themselves.

The problem of spillover with innovations leads to the need for a system of patents to allow firms to recoup R&D costs through 'temporary monopolies' (Arrow, 1962; Schumpeter, 1943). When an incumbent is able to obtain patent protection for an innovation, the pre-emptive effect is high, and there are many categories such as pharmaceuticals and high technology where incumbents devote significant energy to R&D leading to 'patentable' innovations.

However, obtaining and enforcing patents requires considerable capital and expertise and some incumbents do not have this option. Moreover, there are processes and products where obtaining patents is extremely difficult. Until recently, many business processes were ineligible for patent protection. A US Supreme Court decision in January of 1999, *State Street Bank & Trust Co. vs. Signature Financial Group Inc.*, suggests that new processes, as well as products, can be patented.[1] Nonetheless, the ultimate impact of this decision and the definition of what constitutes a *business process* remain to be seen.

Without patent protection, process innovations (i.e. that provide reductions in unit cost) are easier to protect since they are implemented within the manu-facturing or delivery system of the innovating firm (and, by definition, the physical product is unchanged). In theory, a competitor needs to observe the production or delivery process of the innovator for spillover to be significant. Often the innovator can prevent this. Nonetheless, there are situations where process innovations are subject to spillover (d'Aspremont & Jacquemin, 1988; Choi, 1989; Kamien et al., 1992; Vonotras, 1989).

The idea that incumbents create advantage by obtaining access to innovations that are not available to entrants is simple, but this idea leads to three types of actions that incumbents can take:

1. Invest in R&D that has high probability of producing an attractive innovation
2. Form alliances with other incumbents to develop innovations
3. License existing technological advantages to other incumbents.

We now discuss each of these actions in detail.

1. *Invest in R&D that has high probability of producing an attractive innovation*
Much of the R&D literature focuses on the impact of R&D investment on consumer welfare.[2] Nonetheless, significant research is devoted to managerial decisions that need to be faced in the context of R&D policy. Because R&D is a strategic investment, much of the literature follows the spirit of work mentioned earlier by Spence (1977b) and Dixit (1979, 1980), where strategic decisions allow an incumbent to improve the ex-post profitability of a market threatened with entry by a new firm. Adams and Encaoua (1994) examine the activity of a monopolist faced with a potential entrant and they find that a monopolist might invest in technologies that are *socially undesirable* in order to prevent the entry of a new competitor.

2. *Form alliances with other incumbents to develop innovations*
The formation of associations in industry has received considerable attention and the objectives of these associations invariably involve the sharing of costs, information, facilities or the adoption of common standards. Bloch (1995) notes that these associations are considered to be major factors in the profitability and technological innovation of many industries. There are a number of papers that examine the challenges of managing cooperative R&D including Katz and Shapiro (1986), d'Aspremont and Jacquemin (1988), Suzumura (1992), Bhattacharya et al. (1992) and Gandal and Scotchmer (1993). Without delving into the detailed findings of this work, suffice to say that alliances can be an effective framework for facilitating innovation and this can serve to make the market less attractive to entrants. Others, such as Leahy and Neary (1997) and Brod and Shivakumar (1997), consider the public policy implications of cooperative R&D and the potential need for government intervention.

3. *License existing technological advantages to other incumbents*
Gallini (1984) shows how an incumbent firm might license its technology to an entrant in order to reduce the entrant's incentive to invest in R&D. Eswaran (1994) extends this idea to the strategy of deterring an entrant by licensing to other, weaker incumbents. The literature also highlights the potential shortcomings of licensing as a strategy to deter entrants. For example, Yi (1999) shows how entrants can form R&D joint ventures among themselves to counter strategic licensing by an incumbent.

The purpose of reviewing these various innovation strategies is to highlight the different approaches that firms can use to create advantages within a market. A key observation is that the differential impact of these alternate innovation strategies on 'market evolution' has been largely ignored by academics and will prove to be a fruitful area for future research.

Signaling Signaling is a competitive response that can be undertaken by an incumbent or an entrant in order to provide information to a party that lacks the information in question. As noted by Bergen et al. (1992), when a key party to a transaction lacks quality information (which is also known as a problem of 'Hidden Information'), it can create problems in many marketing situations. Rothschild and Stiglitz (1976) analyze one of the most famous examples: the insurance market in which the principal (the insurance company) cannot distinguish between high and low risk customers. With many durable products, the same problem is evident when products cannot be evaluated prior to purchase.[3] The literature generally focuses on the equilibrium outcomes that result when a market is characterized by a spectrum of quality levels and buyers cannot determine quality prior to purchase.

Spence (1974) introduced the logic of signaling to economics, i.e., that a high quality seller may engage in costly activity to identify himself as higher quality than his competitors. This is possible when sellers of high quality have cost advantages over sellers of low quality in making signals. Kreps (1990) provides further insight into the manner by which signaling can facilitate the exchange of higher quality in the context of products and workers. The economics and marketing literature identifies a number of potential signals including advertising (Klein & Leffler, 1981; Milgrom & Roberts, 1986; Schmalensee, 1978), price (Bagwell & Riordan, 1991; Balachander & Srinivasan, 1994; Chu, 1992; Srinivasan, 1991) and the strategic use of signage in retail settings (Anderson & Simester, 1998; Mishra et al., 1998). Given the alternative signals available to a manufacturer or retailer, a number of questions remain unanswered. These include issues such as how a marketer chooses between signals, and why certain signals that seem to be as costly for a high quality seller as for a low quality seller, nevertheless, seem to function. Reconciling the single shot signaling models (Spence, 1974) with those that rely on repeated transactions (Klein & Leffler, 1981) appears to be an important area for further investigation. Another application of signaling is proposed in the context of distribution strategy where a retailer's reputation can be used to signal quality about a manufacturer's product (Chu & Chu, 1994). From a perspective of channel research, this raises a number of interesting issues such as how a retailer might use a manufacturer to signal quality or taking, this idea one step further, how consumers might use different channels to signal information to retailers or manufacturers. Because a fundamental dimension of quality is performance (higher quality products either fail less, cost less to fix, or perform better), the use of performance warranties as signals has also received considerable attention (Gal-Or, 1989; Grossman, 1981; Lutz, 1989; Spence, 1977a). With performance as a primary dimension of quality, it costs a seller less to 'guarantee' performance for a high quality product (independent of whether the guarantee is provided as insurance or as a commitment to repair or replace the product). Thus, an incumbent with higher quality can use a longer warranty to 'signal' higher quality. A further extension of this idea is the use of a money-back guarantee to signal higher quality (Moorthy & Srinivasan, 1995).

Of course, entrants sometimes develop products that exceed the quality of incumbents' products and in this case, they will face a similar challenge (i.e. that of credibly communicating to consumers that their products are better). In order to charge a premium for their product, they may be forced to engage in costly signaling behavior (such as offering non-standard warranty protection). In the following section, we consider a form of communication by a firm that, in contrast to signaling, is of negligible cost.

Pre-Announcements

An endemic characteristic of signaling situations is that consumers have strict preferences for high quality over low quality and there is generally one primary attribute of interest 'quality.' In such situations, costless signals (or *cheap talk*) will never function effectively since it is 'costless' for a low quality seller to do whatever a high quality seller does. Thus, it is not possible for a high quality seller to separate himself from the norm. However, there are clearly a number of situations in which the preferences of buyers are not strict, i.e., *ceteris paribus*, some consumers prefer a focal firm's product and other consumers prefer the competitor's products. In these situations, simple low cost announcements by firms about their attributes may suffice to improve the matching of buyers with sellers. As noted by Calantone and Schatzel (2000), pre-announcements are inexpensive options to inform customers, employees, competitors, channel members, and other related parties of a firm's intentions. The attractiveness of pre-announcements needs to be balanced against their costs. For example, pre-announcements may imply legal obligations on the part of the firm making the announcement. An interesting area for future research is to examine the 'tying one's hands' effect that pre-announcements can have in markets with uncertainty. When a firm's reputation is powerful, a further challenge with pre-announcements is that the cost of making an unfulfilled pre-announcement can be high.[4]

Nevertheless, the marketing literature highlights the use of pre-announcements. Eliashberg and Robertson (1988) conceive pre-announcements as a form of signaling where, because of their impact, costs can ultimately be incurred. First, pre-announcements can provide valuable advance information to competitors (who can then use it to the detriment of the focal firm), and second, pre-announcements can result in a significant loss of reputation for a focal firm if it is unable to deliver on the pre-announcement.[5] This suggests that an interesting area for future research would be to analyze the perceived costs and the use of pre-announcements by firms with a range of reputations. Eliashberg and Robertson consider both consumer and competitive rationales for pre-announcing, and these ideas are further developed in Robertson et al. (1995). Here the use of pre-announcements to influence competitor behavior is highlighted (to pre-empt competitors and provide them with a basis for not pursuing a product in the same market). The use of pre-announcements for pricing is also considered by Heil and Langevardt (1994) and, not surprisingly, a primary focus of this research regards anti-trust issues (it is evident that communication between competitors focused on price can facilitate price collusion).[6] The marketing literature focuses primarily on the use of pre-announcements, their impact and their antecedents, yet advances little in the way of theoretical justification for their effectiveness.

An important question is why costless announcements work as 'conveyors of information' when it is equally easy for a seller to convey false information (recall that the greater expense incurred by a low quality seller to send a high quality signal is the theoretical basis for the effectiveness of signaling). As noted earlier, when pre-announcements involve legal obligations (making a given pre-announcement irreversible), or when a firm's reputation is at stake, the question is less difficult. However, even in the absence of these conditions, pre-announcements may be a useful mechanism for an entrant or an incumbent. As long as there is a degree of alignment in the preferences of the sender and the receiver, Crawford and Sobel (1982) show that costless talk or pre-announcements can reduce information asymmetry and allow a market to function more effectively (even when a direct penalty is not incurred by a sender for sending a false message). By allowing groups of consumers to find or interact with sellers of specific types, this form of communication can facilitate greater alignment (or matching in the marketplace) in the needs of both buyers and sellers (Gibbons, 1992). Practical applications of these ideas are found in the marketing literature on pre-announcements. In fact, Moore (1992) provides an example of 'cheap talk' in the context of a simulated market where participants take action to avoid destructive price wars. Similar to a real market, participants communicate with each other by sending coded signals of retaliation in order to reduce the likelihood of price cuts by the competitor. The benefits of sending costless messages in this environment follow from the long-term alignment of firms' incentives (i.e., it is better to avoid price wars).

When neither signaling nor pre-announcements are viable or feasible for firms to communicate information to their competitors or consumers, they may be forced to resort to alternative strategies. Nevertheless, with the advent of the Internet and the low cost it implies for sending messages, conventional wisdom suggests that firms may find it easier to resolve detrimental information asymmetries through the use of pre-announcements. As the reach and importance of the Internet as a marketing channel increases, the importance of pre-announcements is likely to increase. However, there will always be situations in which high quality sellers cannot provide credible information about quality. Here, the only alternative may be to engage in significant trial activity with users who are unfamiliar with their products.

Trial Programs

Trial activity is tantamount to a disclosure of quality, and high quality firms have an incentive to disclose that they are, in fact, high quality or they will not be recognized by consumers (Grossman, 1981; Stiglitz, 1987). However the cost of trial is frequently a barrier to such disclosure (i.e. the cost of trial programs). For high-ticket items, which include many durable goods, the cost of trial is clearly very expensive. However, even for products with low per-unit costs, the cost of an extensive trial program can be prohibitive. For example, an extensive trial for a new beer in the US can cost upwards of $12 million (Sellers & Welsh, 1994). A further issue concerns the multi-dimensional nature of many products. As noted by Lancaster (1990), the most difficult challenge for a marketer with a multi-attribute product is perhaps the matching of attributes to customer needs. Here, trial can play the role of both disclosing experience attributes and matching attributes with customer preferences. An application of this idea is found in Gerstner et al. (1995) where money-back guarantees can be used to provide free trial opportunities to consumers. Nevertheless, the cost of the trial, even in situations where the firm can repossess the product (as with a money-back guarantee) can be prohibitive.

Certification Procedures

Where an external certification organization exists within a market, this may be the optimal approach for an incumbent or entrant to demonstrate the relative qualities of their products (Stiglitz, 1989). Frequently, the existence of external certification depends on the involvement of the government to protect the public interest (Carlton & Perloff, 1994). When available, certification can provide a useful vehicle for a firm with high or unique quality to communicate its characteristics to new consumers.

Launch Timing Perhaps the single most effective response to a potential entrant who is 'threatening' to enter, because, she is known to offer advantages to consumers over the existing products, is to pre-empt her by launching a comparable product. The benefits of pioneering advantage are well-documented in the empirical literature by Robinson and Fornell (1985), Urban et al., (1986) or Bowman and Gatignon (1996). In addition, explanations for the advantage based on individual consumers are proposed by Carpenter and Nakomoto (1989) and Kardes and Kalyanaram (1992). These advantages are argued to come from the 'setting' of consumer expectations, or because consumers find it easier to remember products that were available first. Frequently these advantages can lead to situations where inferior existing products can retain leadership in the face of superior new entrants.

Disadvantages of going first are that the first entrant may not choose the optimal levels for the attributes and it may be easier for a second entrant (without the baggage of an existing consumer franchise), to adopt preferred levels of certain attributes. Carpenter and Nakomoto (1989) also note that later entrants tend to perform better when they offer levels on certain attributes that are significantly different than those offered by the pioneer. In a sense, the pioneer plays the role of 'test marketing' for the later entrants. If the pioneer launches a product that is close to the revealed preferences of consumers, then the pioneering advantage can be enormous. It follows that Carpenter and Nakomoto (1989) find that 'me-too' products fare poorly even when they provide similar attributes at a somewhat lower price.[7] However, if the pioneer's offering is a) significantly different on certain attributes from the preferences of consumers, and b) difficult to modify because of either supply or demand-side considerations, the later entrants have the advantage of learning from the pioneer's mistakes. Note that this situation, which is not uncommon, contributes to the higher risk that is often associated with 'going first.'

A further consideration appears to be the role that pioneers play in creating awareness for 'the category,' as opposed to building awareness and brand equity for themselves. Late entrants have the advantage of free-riding on the market-making investments of the pioneer. Support for the importance of the pioneer's creation of category awareness for the benefit of later entrants is found in the work by Zhang and Markman (1998). They assume that a number of defining category characteristics are those that are possessed by the pioneer. When a late entrant bases its positioning on those characteristics (alignable differences) and is perceived to be superior on those attributes, it can be preferred over the pioneer. In contrast, when a late entrant bases its positioning on differences that are not characteristic of the pioneer, consumers find it more difficult to remember and process the late entrant's message. In a sense, the pioneer not only plays the role of test marketing for the late entrant, but also provides a framework (product attributes) that a late entrant can use to communicate effectively with consumers.

In summary, 'moving first' is certainly a common and frequently successful response to pre-empt an initiative by a new entrant. Nevertheless, it is a strategy that can also lead to a number of disadvantages when the category is new and consumers need to learn in order to become regular consumers in the category.

Competitive Reactions

An important dimension of marketing strategy concerns the understanding and the predictability of how a competitor responds to a move made by another competitor. This includes the marketing interaction behavior among existing competitors or brands, as well as the reactions of incumbent firms to new entrants in the market. Research on this topic generally follows a normative approach, an analytical approach (especially game theoretic), a behavioral approach or an empirical approach (i.e., data driven). As a result, this topic has provided the marketing field with a rich array of research (Gatignon & Bansal, 1990; Kuester et al., 1999; Robertson & Gatignon, 1991).

Early work focused on investigations of the *intensity* of competitive rivalry among competitors and made significant progress to better understand the conditions that engender intense rivalry. A next step was to understand more specifically, which *marketing mix instruments* are being used, when, and under what circumstances. While the attention has been primarily directed to understanding pricing and advertising reactions, some recent work considers the innovativeness of the new product or entry and the innovativeness of the product response (Kuester et al.,1999; Shankar et al., 1999).

Product modification due to competitive entry is an important aspect of normative models such as Defender (Hauser, 1988; Hauser & Shugan, 1983). For example, Defender prescribes that an incumbent firm should modify its product in the direction of the attribute of strength. Reactions may also entail decisions about how many brands a firm should have in its product line. Villas-Boas (1998) models the number of brands as a decision by the manufacturer. He shows that the number of brands depends on how many of the market segments are actually offered an acceptable product and whether the manufacturer coordinates his decision with the retailer. Schmalensee (1978) also considers the product proliferation issue, but as a pre-emptive move to prevent entry in the industry.

Reactions involving product modifications or the introduction of new products require understanding of the dimensions of the products on which to innovate and the technological aspects of such changes. The variables that have been considered to characterize innovations offer opportunities for new research directions. These characteristics are typically derived from the consumer's perspective in terms of both the adoption decision-process and in terms of the sociological aspects of that process. The technological viewpoint offers perspectives that have not been considered in marketing, although the extant literature in technology management and strategy addresses some of them.

Gatignon et al. (2000) develop a structural approach to assessing innovation. They suggest that an innovation can be comprehensively described by distinguishing between the locus of innovation in a product's hierarchy (core/peripheral), between different types of innovation (generational/architectural), and between the characteristics of an innovation (incremental/radical, competence enhancing/competence destroying). The results show that competence-based innovations have the most powerful and consistent effects, while innovation types have the weakest and most inconsistent effects on innovation performance and organizational change. The characteristics of the innovation in terms of radicalness and competences appear to be important dimensions for understanding how innovation affects competitive behavior dynamics.

While most reactions are assumed to be retaliatory, the Defender model underlines that the best reaction is sometimes to cut expenditures or increase price. Consequently, a third stream of research analyzes the *direction of the response*, i.e., retaliation, accommodation, complete withdrawal, or the competitor's move is ignored (not reacted to). Iyer and Soberman (2000) provide insight about optimal reactions in terms of product modifications that firms can implement to neutralize or accommodate offensive or defensive product modifications by a competitor. The literature also recognizes the multi-market nature of competition and the importance of including the domain of the reaction for fully understanding the way firms respond to each other (Shankar, 1999). A dimension of reactions that has not been the object of attention until recently concerns the timing of these reactions (Heil & Robertson, 1991), that is the *speed* with which firms react to a competitor's move. While speed had been typically assimilated to the aggressiveness of the reaction, and consequently to the reaction intensity, Bowman and Gatignon (1995) show that speed needs a different set of explanatory mechanisms, mostly based on organizational variables. The timing of reactions has also been shown to have a significant impact on performance (Smith et al., 1989; Gatignon, Robertson & Fein, 1997). Recent research has moved away from looking at each of these characteristics one by one and considers the *complexity* of the reaction patterns. The reaction can involve a single marketing mix variable or multiple ones. The reaction can use the same marketing mix like a price match or a different mix variable (Leeflang & Wittink, 1996). Therefore, the reactions can be simple or complex and involve a single variable or multiple variables. Ramaswamy et al. (1994) analyze these patterns with the PIMS data. More specifically, Gatignon, Robertson and Fein (1997) consider the *breadth* of the reactions as a key factor explaining the success of a defense strategy, finding that the most successful defense concentrates on few mix variables rather than spreading resources on too many. Nevertheless, the role of the breadth of reactions has not been fully explored. In particular, the difference in the nature of the effects of breadth versus the intensity of a reaction with a single mix variable needs further study.

The Primary Characteristics of Market Evolution

Most of the literature concerned with market evolution, whether normative or descriptive, considers the evolution of the market as predetermined mostly by demand. In fact, demand cannot evolve if the manufacturers do not produce and market the product appropriately. While this idea has been advanced, it is still a relatively recent concept that has received little attention. We will, therefore, take the perspective that the evolution of a market depends on the strategic decisions of the firms that manufacture and market the products in addition to evolution of demand (i.e., changes in the needs of customers). In order to structure our analysis of the impact of competitive dynamics on market evolution, we first define the key dimensions of market evolution. These can be structured as: 1) diffusion and growth; 2) market structure; and 3) technological evolution.

Diffusion and Growth

The diffusion of an innovation can be described in terms of the time of the first adoption and in terms of the speed and pattern with which the innovation reaches its maximum potential level. This can be expressed, as Rogers (1983) does, at the individual unit of adoption, where adoption necessitates the acquisition of the innovation and then its use by the adopter. It can also be described in terms of breadth of use and depth of use. A parallel is made by Dekimpe et al. (2000) where the diffusion in a country is described by the time between an innovation's availability and its eventual adoption within a specific country. Once an innovation is adopted, it then diffuses throughout the country in question. Diffusion modeling in recent years has contributed explicitly to recognize the key elements of the process. First, in terms of describing the phenomenon, the characterization of the diffusion is explicit in terms of 1) the patterns of diffusion; 2) the potential penetration level; and 3) the speed of the diffusion within the population. Second, the phenomenon's units of analysis include the total market or product category and the market segments or the brands within a market. Third, the explanation of the diffusion process has emphasized the presence of network externalities, as well as the critical role played by marketing decision variables. Most of the research to date has considered the speed of diffusion at the product category level with a network effect due to the existing set of adopters. Recently, Kuester et al., (2000) have considered the role of key marketing strategy decisions on the speed of the diffusion. We do not intend to repeat these points here. Instead, we will focus on the factors that relate more directly to competitive dynamics.

Speed of Diffusion The seminal approach of Bass (1969), suggests that the diffusion process can be understood as the result of an innovation effect (which is exogenous) and an imitation effect (which is proportional to the number of adopters at any point in time). The key parameters of the Bass model are thus, a coefficient of external influence (driving the innovative behavior), a coefficient of internal influence (during this imitative behavior), and the ultimate number of adopters (when the diffusion process is complete). While much of the focus of diffusion research, especially with a strategic orientation, has been about the speed with which an innovation diffuses, the explanation for differences in the speed of diffusion across markets remains limited. Following the theory of Rogers (1983), a number of researchers have conducted empirical tests of how relative advantage, compatibility, trial-ability, observability, complexity and perceived risk affect the speed of diffusion (Ostlund, 1974). Srivastava et al. (1985) model and estimate directly the influence of these variables on the parameters of the Bass diffusion models that relate to the speed of diffusion. In the context of multinational marketing, explanations about differences in the diffusion of the same innovation across countries have been analyzed. These explanations concern differences in the social system characteristics. For example, Gatignon, Eliashberg and Robertson (1989) study the role of mobility and Dekimpe et al. (2000) consider the heterogeneity of the social system, as measured by the number of ethnic groups in the country. Still much remains to be done to understand the determinants of diffusion speed.

Network Effects Network externalities have gained considerable popularity in many fields, including in the study of new product diffusion in Marketing. Three different kinds of network externalities should be considered. The first one concerns the utility derived by the users of the innovation that increases as a function of the number of users of that innovation. This corresponds to the standard imitation or coefficient of internal influence in the Bass model. The second kind relates to the increased utility derived from the use of other related products or technologies co-evolving with the innovation. This could include the co-evolution of computer hardware and software. The third aspect concerns the influence of the installed bases of older related technologies (Dekimpe et al., 2000). The existence and the importance of these three different kinds of network effects may be critical to understanding market evolution and competitive dynamics.

Market Structure

While the diffusion of innovations is typically studied at the aggregate level, the process implies the interactions of multiple segments purchasing among several competing brands with some level of differentiation made available through diverse distribution channels. These typically evolve over time. It is, therefore, critical to analyze the structural changes that occur in the market over the product life cycle. Three basic changes occur: 1) perceptions and preferences of consumers change over time; 2) their responses to the marketing mix variables change over the product life cycle; and 3) the structure of the distribution of the product changes over time.

Evolution of Perceptions and Preference Evolution Preferences are not anterior to the introduction of the innovation in the consumer's mind. Instead, the perceptions and the preferences of consumers are to a great extent formed by the first products available on the market. Carpenter and Nakamoto (1989) provide a theory of the first mover's advantage based on this explanation. Rosa et al. (1999) define markets as 'knowledge structures' that are unstable. Over time, these knowledge structures become more stable (Rosa et al., 1999). Buzzell (1999) mentions how useful it would be to better understand the changes in perceptions that occur during the early periods of a new market.

Consumer Response to Marketing Mix Variables A significant literature now exists on how the marketing mix elasticities change over the product life cycle. Based on early normative theories (Mickwitz, 1959), the patterns across product categories tend to share similarities but also show significant departures from a unique pattern. For background on price elasticity, see Wildt (1976), Simon (1979), Liu and Hanssens (1981), Lilien and Yoon (1988), Parker (1992), Parker and Neelamegham (1997) or Parker and Gatignon (1996). For background on advertising elasticity, see Parsons (1975), Arora (1979), Winer (1979) and Parker and Gatignon (1996). Changes in a marketing elasticities (such as advertising), which may be in part due to the actions of marketers (such as the introduction of new brands and/or new versions of products that fulfill the same needs), force firms to adapt their marketing strategies. Their ability to adapt to these changes can also influence market evolution.

Channel Structure It is difficult to dissociate a market from its distribution channel. In fact, distribution is a key variable that may condition the diffusion of an innovation. The role of the channels of distribution has been shown to influence the selection of which products to market. In addition, early studies of the power of supermarkets provide evidence that big retailing chains actually have power over the manufacturers. Therefore, while in theory the manufacturer decides through which channels to distribute its new products, this choice is often restricted and the success of a new product may depend on the distribution in some key channels. In that respect, because of their mere size or because of the leading role they play as scouts of the market, some channels have a different influence on the diffusion process than others. This is complicated by the fact that the channels monitor the early performance of new products and may decide to carry them or not as a function of their early market performance (Bronenberg et al., 2000).

Technological evolution

One area which may show the greatest promise for new research concerns the role of technology in today's markets. As pointed out by Buzzell (1999), technology is important even in relatively mature consumer product categories like diapers. Naturally, it plays a critical role in technology intensive markets (John et al., 1999). However, our understanding of how technology evolves, how it perturbs markets and creates opportunities for others, how it affects firm performance and the organization are questions begging for answers. Anderson and Tushman (1990, 1991) theorize about the evolution of markets in terms of technological discontinuities. They argue especially for periods of turmoil that exist before a dominant design emerges (Tushman & Murmann, 1998). The concepts of competence-destroying and competence-enhancing innovations provide a possible explanation for the changes in a market, especially changes in competitive dynamics due to the enhancement or obsolescence of the competences of the firms in the market (Tripsas, 1997). Competence-destroying and competence-enhancing innovations may also provide a basis to understand market dynamics from the resource-based perspective of firm strategies.

Interactions Between Competitive Responses and Market Evolution

We now examine the interrelationships between competitive responses and market evolution. First, we discuss how some of the competitive actions described above can explain the evolution of markets. Then, we evaluate how these competitive responses depend on the market evolution itself. We also review the literature that considers how environmental or exogenous factors can affect competitive responses and market evolution. These include the characteristics of the regulatory environment (patents, licensing, and competition laws), ownership of resources, and appropriability factors.

The Effects of Competitive Responses on Market Evolution

A number of studies have analyzed the relationship between competitive response and demand in the marketplace. These are related to a few of the possible links between the primary dimensions of competitive dynamics on the left hand side of Figure 6.1 (page 127) and the characteristics of the market shown in the right hand side of Figure 6.1. Therefore, this leaves significant areas for future research by filling the gap of possible links not yet covered across the items in these two boxes.

There are clearly many possible combinations among the dimensions of competitive responses and the characteristics of market evolution. We discussed, for example, innovation strategies and whether to form alliances for R&D development. This immediately raises the research question of the role that an 'innovation' alliance strategy may have on a) the speed of market development, and b) the level of competitive rivalry that is obtained in such markets. A key objective might be to compare the level of competitive rivalry in markets where new product development is done internally to markets where R&D is frequently a cooperative activity.

Kuester et al. (2000) review how strategic firm decisions can influence the speed of diffusion of an innovation. These decisions concern technological strategic choices and entry strategy choices. By restricting attention to the firm introducing an innovation only, a number of the issues relevant to this chapter are considered in their work. The R&D strategy, in terms of competence-enhancing and competence-destroying innovation, is shown to affect the speed of diffusion of the innovation. Part of their discussion is suggestive of new research as well. For example, many innovation-strategy variables are also essential elements of the competitive behavior of a market. In fact, the authors devote a section of the paper to a discussion of how the timing of product launches is an important dimension of competitive dynamics. In a thorough study of pharmaceutical products, Shankar et al. (1999) show that an innovative late entrant outperforms the pioneer by realizing higher sales growth and obtaining higher repeat buying rates. In addition, they demonstrate that that entrant has a significant negative impact on the pioneer, both in slowing the diffusion of its brand but also in reducing the effectiveness of its marketing mix instruments. Their study also illustrates the impact of innovativeness on the market potential of the brands. Innovativeness appears to dominate any effects which might have been due to order and timing of entry, because an innovative entrant's potential surpasses non-innovative late entrants and is at least as high as the pioneer's. This brand-level analysis of the evolution of demand is also supported at the aggregate level by Mahajan et al. (1993) who develop a model with cross-brand effects and use it to estimate the impact of entry on aggregate demand. They show that in the case of Kodak's entry into the instant camera market, Polaroid benefited from the expansion of demand due to the Kodak introduction, even though Kodak drew a significant portion of its sales from Polaroid's potential market.

The marketing mix plays a critical role in developing markets, both in terms of making consumers aware of the product and communicating its features, i.e., developing a market potential and in terms of speeding the diffusion. More specifically, Jain and Rao (1990) conclude their modeling of the impact of price on the demand for consumer durables by suggesting that price influences the consumer's decision to buy or not buy, but the timing of *when* to buy is governed by the diffusion process.

It is also important to recognize the role that declining price has on market expansion. There are clearly two effects that drive the diffusion or growth of markets. The first is the growth in potential users of a product or service as they become aware of it either through media channels or myriad social processes. The second is the natural expansion of a market that occurs due to declining prices. As noted by Tellis (1988), as categories mature, product-level elasticities increase because the number of potential substitutes increases and consumers become better informed of alternative brands (see also Liu & Hanssens, 1981). Following the inverse elasticity rule, in these conditions, the optimal response for firms is to reduce price (Tirole, 1988). The reduction in price of course leads to an increase in volume. This is effectively a simple descent down a demand curve and may have little to do with consumer acceptance of a new innovation. Frequently in empirical studies, the second effect is ignored and the growth rates are attributed entirely to the speed by which a population accepts and ultimately embraces a new product or service. In building a model of the diffusion process, it would appear important to both discriminate between and recognize these two effects.

The role of marketing mix variables differ at different stages of the product life cycle and are themselves subject to a diffusion process of their own. Jones and Ritz (1991) modeled this directly for the distribution mix. However, as pointed out by Robertson and Gatignon (1991), the effects of the marketing mix variables are not instantaneous, but follow a process themselves over time. Not surprisingly, this determines in part the diffusion of the product (Franses, 1994). Bronnenberg et al. (2000) show that the marketing mix variables have not only strong effects on market share but also that, through a feedback mechanism, market share impacts (with some lag) the levels of marketing mix, especially distribution. This effect is most intense early after introduction of the product category but decreases over time.

Marketing mix activities are, however, partly conditioned by competitive activities, which could explain in part the varying nature of marketing mix elasticities over the product life cycle. For example, Gatignon (1984) shows that competitive reactions influence the effect of advertising on price elasticities. Consequently, competitive markets where firms react strongly to each others' moves may develop the total demand for the product category directly by making the product category more salient in the consumer's mind and indirectly by making consumers more responsive to other marketing mix elements. The sheer higher density of competition may also impact the consumers' response to marketing mix variables (Bowman & Gatignon, 2000)

It should also be noted that the technological evolution in a market has not, to our knowledge, been treated as a dependent variable resulting from the competitive nature of markets. A resource-based view of strategy would consider that the technological evolution of a market follows from strategic choices of firms based on their competitive competences. Therefore, perhaps the technological evolution of a market is an endogenous outcome rather than an exogenous factor, as typically considered. Accordingly, this view also offers new avenues of investigation.

The Impact of Market Evolution on Competitive Responses

Much of the research about explaining competitive reactions has been done in the context of incumbent reactions to new product entry. Although firm specific factors have been analyzed to explain firm differences in responses (Gatignon, Anderson and Helsen, 1989), market evolution explanations correspond directly to the research stream demonstrating the importance of the structural factors of the industry (Biggadike, 1979; Robinson, 1988).

Several characteristics of market evolution have been studied in terms of their impact on competitive responses. We group these variables by the explanation of the reasons why they impact competitive responses. Three types of explanations can be found in the literature: 1) the strategic attractiveness of the market inherent to its evolution; 2) the changing competitive market structure with the entry of new competitors and exit of others; and 3) the evolution of consumer response.

Strategic Attractiveness of the Market

Market Growth The growth rate of a market is a major indicator of the attractiveness of a market in market/portfolio analysis. High growth suggests higher market potential in the future and leads to investments by firms in these markets. Also, share gains in growing markets are worth more than in mature markets because the returns will grow as the market grows (Day, 1986). Several empirical studies indicate that firms defend their investments strongly in high growth markets. This has been observed within established industrial markets (Ramaswamy et al., 1994) as well as in the context of reactions to new entries (Robinson, 1988). High growth markets have also been observed to exhibit faster competitive reactions (Bowman & Gatignon, 1995).

Interestingly, however, there is both empirical support and argument for the opposite. Cubbin and Domberger (1988) find that advertising reactions to an entry are more likely in static than in growing markets, and the portfolio literature argues that gaining share is easier in high growth markets (Aaker & Day, 1986). An underlying explanation is that competitive reactions are low if sales increase at an acceptable rate. However, Day (1986) and Wensley (1981) have questioned this view. They argue that expectations about sales and deviations from these expectations are critical in determining the nature of competitive reactions. Day (1986) contends that expectations are very high in high growth markets and disappointments explain strong reactions.

There are further arguments for why competitive reactions may be lower in high growth markets. First, as sales increase in a high growth market, there may simultaneously be increases in the complexity of market structure, i.e., different firms may be generating growth by focusing their marketing activity on distinctive groups of customers. As a consequence, sales' cross-elasticities might be smaller than if primary demand were relatively flat. Given that competitive reactions are stronger when cross-elasticities are high, this might result in less reaction.

Second, it may also be that market growth has different effects on different marketing mix variables. Advertising clearly has long-term effects. Thus, managers might avoid making immediate changes to advertising when there are sudden changes in the competitive environment. This tendency would be stronger when the market is growing and advertising is already planned as a long-term investment.

Finally, it is also possible that high growth markets are more uncertain and firms might wait and see before reacting. This would follow the findings of Biggadike (1979) and Robinson (1988), who find that start-up businesses react less because of higher uncertainty associated with the impact of their actions.

In spite of these arguments, the majority of evidence supports the idea that market growth is positively correlated with stronger reactions. This is consistent with Bowman and Gatignon (1995) who find that firms react *more quickly* in high growth markets.

Capacity Utilization Another explanation for lower competitive responses in high growth markets would be that firms in such markets might be at full capacity. This variable does not itself fully explain competitive reactions, but it certainly affects them. If an industry is currently at full capacity, the urgency to react is less critical because a successful reaction could lead to increased demand that the firm might not be able to supply. Consequently, this variable acts as a moderator of the growth factor. The impact of market growth on competitive response should increase as capacity utilization decreases.

Product Standardization As markets evolve, so do the products offered in the industry. At least from the technological perspective, standards tend to develop, even if segmentation leads to some differentiation. This standardization reduces the ability of firms to distinguish their products and as a result, markets become more price sensitive. Consequently, as a market evolves toward standardization, price becomes a typical instrument of reaction. Thus, we should expect the commoditization of markets to lead to strong price competition and lower prices. Interestingly, in a study of retail markets, Campbell and Hopenhayn (1999) find that larger markets are associated with lower margins and more customers per establishment. However, Fershtman and Pakes (2000) demonstrate that there may be forces that counteract the tendency to standardize as a market evolves. In an evolutionary dynamic model, these authors show that a collusive environment (which is more likely as the number of firms in an industry decreases) can lead to greater variety in the products offered to consumers. Given these countervailing effects, it is perhaps unsurprising that Ramaswamy et al. (1994) obtained inconclusive results in their analysis of how the degree of price competition changes as a function of the age of the market. The study is based on PIMS data and it is also possible that PIMS data may be too aggregate (in terms of the unit of analysis) to measure the strength and speed of price responses in new markets. Longitudinal data may be more appropriate to observe these effects.

Environmental Stability Environmental instability refers to environments/markets in which many changes occur and/or where the timing of these changes is difficult to predict. A critical source of instability is the rate of technological change (Mansfield, 1961). For example, in some industries firms typically renew all or part of their product line frequently. The technological standard may also change often in some industries, while others conserve the same technology throughout the entire history of the industry. Organizations born in periods of technological change may be better adapted to new changes in technology than others. This would follow from population ecology research and is supported by Bowman and Gatignon's (1995) finding that firms respond faster to new product entry if they face a high rate of technological change.

Market Entry and Exit

The competitive structure of a market evolves throughout the product life cycle with new entrants but also with exits. A newcomer causes a disruption in the market (Schumpeter, 1943) and a new brand poses a threat to existing brands that typically monitor the behavior of their competitors to the extent that they can. Therefore, incumbents who are focused on maintaining their position in a market are typically the firms that respond most aggressively to new entries. Monitoring of competitors is a typical characteristic of markets with a limited number of competitors. As markets contain many players, it may become harder to monitor each competitor. Although several studies have failed to identify market concentration as a significant factor explaining the extent or the speed of responses, Kuester et al., (1999) found a strong but negative impact on several aspects of the reactions: retaliation with changes in the product mix are less likely in concentrated markets, reactions tend to be slower and more concentrated with fewer marketing mix variables (low breadth). These cross-sectional results are consistent with economic theory which argues that concentrated markets are less competitive. Therefore, if these results were to apply within an industry over time, one could hypothesize that, if a market evolves with new competitors, concentration typically decreases and incumbent reactions increase in intensity, speed and breadth. Conversely, in an industry with strong network effects, where markets typically become more concentrated over time, we might expect incumbent reaction to decrease in intensity, speed, and breadth.

In addition to this direct impact of entry on the competitive nature of markets, a market entry may change the elasticities of the competitors' marketing mix variables. Using this idea, Shankar (1997) explains why some firms retaliate while others may not. It also explains changes in marketing mix allocation. There is little research to provide insight as to what factors would allow a prediction of how the marketing mix elasticities would change across firms and for different entrants. Research on changes in marketing mix elasticities over time focus on how environmental factors affect competitors (Bowman & Gatignon, 1996; Parker, 1992).

One possible moderator is the impact of the entry itself on primary demand. Most studies of competitive reactions ignore the primary demand effects. If an entry increases primary demand, the incumbents do not necessarily feel the effect of the entry on sales or profitability. The threat should be expected to be stronger if the primary demand for the industry is not anticipated to improve due to the entry. This factor could be added to the framework presented by Shankar (1999) to understand the entrant's expectations of the incumbent's reactions. Jayachandran et al. (1999) discuss multi-market competition as a function of the product line strategies of the competitors. Competitors that develop products positioned differently and/or targeted at different segments of consumers in order to take advantage of the varying nature of customer needs, lead to market expansion and deter potential new entrants, thus reducing the competitiveness of the market.

A further issue is to consider how the creation of barriers to entry (for example through experience, fixed assets, or advertising) as an industry matures affects the nature of competitive response. On the one hand, the creation of barriers to entry may remove the need for the incumbent firms to innovate since the likelihood of an aggressive new competitor is reduced by the entry barriers. On the other hand, increased barriers to entry may create an incentive for incumbent firms to increase their efforts to innovate, since the barriers to entry can provide an opportunity for the incumbents to price a new innovation aggressively and thereby recoup the costs of development. An interesting area for future research is to measure the nature and gravity of competitive response as the degree of concentration changes.

Evolving Consumer Response

Regardless of the market structure, as markets gain maturity, consumer expectations and behaviors change. While dynamics of customer expectation and behaviors may be more easily tractable in B2B markets, generalization and theorizing with respect to demand evolution has been sparse. For consumer markets, research has focused on the changes in marketing mix sensitivity resulting from changes in consumer expectations and behaviors. No general pattern appears consistently across the many empirical studies studying the evolution of marketing mix elasticities over the product life cycle. One potential explanation for this is that customer characteristics themselves change as markets move from early growth to late growth and, eventually, to maturity. For example, Bergemann and Välimäki (1996) analyze the impact on competing firms of 'customer learning through experimentation.' In this model (where a key aspect of the product is not observable), the firms choose introductory prices below marginal cost to sustain experimentation. Prices rise thereafter, as the relative merits of competing products become better known. In general, however, as markets mature and growth slows, customers typically become more price sensitive and less responsive to advertising. Beyond the explanation due to increased competitiveness of the markets, these relationships follow the changes in the buyers' profiles (innovators versus imitators or leaders versus followers) and theories of consumer learning. These changes in market-demand characteristics affect competitive responses. Gatignon, Anderson and Helsen (1989), followed by Shankar (1997, 1999), and Kuester et al. (1999) use marketing elasticities to predict competitive responses. The higher the elasticity relative to the competitors, the stronger are the reactions.

External Influences and their Impact on the Relationship between Market Evolution and Competitive Interactions

Having considered the relationships between competitive dynamics and market evolution that may exist without the influence of external mechanisms, we now analyze four external factors that appear to have played a significant role recently in changing competitive dynamics and market evolution (Figure 6.1). These are

1. the use of patents and licensing
2. the deregulation of advertising and marketing activities,
3. the deregulation of pricing and/or supply considerations
4. technological innovations in marketing support activities.

Patents and Licensing

As noted by Tirole (1988), patents provide the patent holder with a temporary monopoly in order to provide incentives *ex ante* for companies to invest in R&D. In most countries, a patent holder also has the option of licensing her innovation. Thus, without loss of generality, we assume that patent protection and the potential to license are both external factors that increase the attractiveness of investing in speculative R&D. It is important to note that the degree of patent protection across industries and across countries is highly variable. In the pharmaceutical industry and computer industry, patents have been primary drivers behind the success of major firms (see *The Economist*, 'Patent Wars,' April 8, 2000 and 'Pfizers prize,' February 12, 2000). Yet in many sectors, patent protection is weak (Scherer & Ross, 1990) and a current focus of government attention in recent months has been to strengthen patent protection.

For example, the Canadian government increased patent protection for pharmaceuticals in 1992 (http://cbc.ca/consumers/market/files/health/drugpric.htmlhas) and this led to important structural changes in the competitive marketplace, i.e., R&D spending as a percent of sales has doubled since the regulatory change.

Thus, it seems apparent that the direct impact of increased patent protection is to increase the amount that firms invest in R&D. Our interest is in the secondary effects that such regulatory changes might create. One possibility is that pre-announcements will tend to have greater weight in industries where patent protection is strong (it will be more difficult for competitors to generate a viable response to a pre-announcing competitor). Therefore, when firms have the ability to pre-announce, increases in patent protection should lead to greater pre-announcing, thereby amplifying the impact of technology (and creating greater disparity in firm size and higher industry concentration). A further possibility is that the *ex post* incentive for an incumbent to invest in technology may be lowered since replacing the inferior technology will cannibalize existing sales (Ghemewat, 1991).

While the primary effect of increasing patent protection is ultimately to increase the elasticity of R&D spending, there are two further potential effects that such changes may generate:

1. Given R&D's strategic character, an analogy can be made with the findings of Shaked and Sutton (1982) and Iyer (1998) with respect to quality or service investments. This analogy suggests that firms are likely to become asymmetric competitors, where one firm becomes the technology leader and others continue to supply the existing technology to the market but at much lower prices.
2. Given that firms are spending large sums to develop technology that may ultimately be nullified by the patent of a competitor, such changes also increase the motivation for firms to merge. Consistent with this observation, Scherer and Ross (1990) find high concentration indices in industries where patent protection is strong and R&D spending is high.

Deregulation of Advertising and Marketing Activities

A number of well-known markets such as pharmaceuticals and tobacco, and service markets such as lawyers and doctors face significant barriers to marketing activity. In most Western countries, downstream advertising of prescription drugs is banned and most tobacco companies face significant regulation with respect to the form of communication that they can utilize.

Due to advances in technology, certain industries are becoming better understood in terms of their negative externalities and these industries may well face more (not less) regulation. In the tobacco, alcohol, and over-the-counter drugs industries, the net effect of regulation is to create artificial distortions in the spending budgets of firms. For example, tobacco firms in North America diverted significant funds from advertising to event sponsorships (car racing, cultural events, skiing) with the restrictive regulations that were implemented in the 1970s. On the one hand, this may have limited the growth and popularity of tobacco, and its consumption has declined steadily since the 1970s. On the other hand, these regulations tend to limit the degree to which tobacco firms compete with each other and may have contributed to higher profits.[8]

Nevertheless, a significant factor that affects economic development in many Western economies is the freeing up of many facets of business that in the past have been heavily regulated (notably telecoms, utilities, transportation, and the media). Interestingly, an effect of deregulation for certain marketing activities is to make reaching and communicating with consumers less costly. With profit maximizing behavior, this means that a number of customers that were previously 'too expensive' to reach may become attractive with deregulation. We need only think of the degree of marketing activity that one now observes in many of the previously regulated industries. Thus, an obvious first order effect is to increase the spending that firms allocate to marketing.

A second order effect in mature categories where the differences between brands are not major may be an overall reduction in industry profitability (Tirole, 1988). As noted above, a first order effect of advertising deregulation is for firms to spend more on advertising (the *de facto* impact of advertising deregulation is to reduce the cost of sending messages to potential consumers). When overall category demand is inelastic, the main objective of a company's advertising is to attract consumers who would otherwise have purchased from a competitor. In these conditions, it follows that higher advertising increases competition between firms and, ultimately, this can lead to lower profits (Soberman, 2000). As a result, many firms have responded to the deregulation of marketing activity by trying to increase the level of perceived differentiation of their products. For example, with the deregulation of long-distance telephone service, a significant factor has been the efforts of competitors to differentiate themselves through numerous call plan options and special services.

Deregulation of Pricing and or Supply Considerations

A second level of deregulation concerns the regulation of pricing and supply. Regulation has been used by many governments to protect certain industries and ensure profitability for firms that might otherwise have been unable to finance large up-front fixed costs. In addition, regulation has been a preferred form of ensuring reasonable levels of investment in industries which are natural monopolies (industries with declining marginal costs).[9] The best examples of natural monopolies are industries with significant network effects (telecommunications, railroads, utilities). A number of papers highlight the challenge of network access pricing for firms that wish to compete after deregulation (Armstrong & Vickers, 1996, 1998; Spulber & Sidak, 1997). For example, how much should Sprint (a long-distance telecommunications provider) have to pay in order to access lines that are owned by Southwestern Bell (a local service provider that also competes with Sprint in providing long-distance service)? A key observation is that even with deregulation, there continues to be a need for government involvement, especially when there is an absence of a competitive network.

Deregulation is also an important factor in many industries where until recently there was heavy government involvement for military or strategic reasons. The usual impact of deregulation is to increase demand (in the case of price deregulation) or to increase supply (in the case of supply deregulation).[10] In general, the impact of deregulation is increased sales volume and greater economic efficiency in the short term. The ability of firms to limit the profit erosion created by pricing deregulation is affected positively by the degree to which there is cross-ownership and multi-market contact between operating firms (Parker & Roller, 1997). Nevertheless, the main effect of pricing deregulation is the lowering of prices, which generally leads to reduced profits for firms in the industry. When significant R&D expenditures or fixed costs are essential to compete in this market, deregulation may even lead to a reduction in the quality of service. This is especially true when these investments are sunk and prices charged for products are unrelated to these expenditures. In this case, strategic investments have a money-burning character (Iyer & Soberman, 1999) and pricing deregulation has the potential to make firms strictly worse off.

A second order effect of such deregulation when it leads to reduced profits for industry players may be the appearance of intermediaries who take on the role of coordinating the market (Bernheim & Whinston, 1986). Iyer and Soberman (1999) also show how an intermediary can be used to better coordinate strategic decisions even when active firms continue to compete on the basis of price. An interesting area for future research is to analyze the activity and growth of intermediaries in markets where deregulation has occurred recently.

Another point, which affects companies that have been deregulated, is that the lowering of prices tends to push all firms to the 'lowest common denominator.' That is, firms feel pressure on their profit margins and, as a result, they reduce the level of service that they provide. In these conditions there are strong incentives for firms to distinguish themselves by offering a variety of price/service combinations. Firms can avoid the dilemma of 'lowest common denominator' competition by providing different service for different customers.[11] Hence, over the past 20 years, the deregulation of the airline industry has led to the creation of a new level of service: 'business class' (in addition to economy class and first class). In addition, frequent flyer programs provide further opportunities for firms to distinguish the level of service they provide to different customers.

In sum, deregulation of supply and prices generally has positive economic effects because it increases the level of competition between participating firms. On the other hand, the reduction in profits generally associated with deregulation can also lead to strategies by competing firms such as delegation or increased differentiation through a broadening of the product-line, for example.

Technological Innovations in Marketing Support Activities

The main technological innovation that has impacted marketing support activities is the arrival of the Internet (Balasubramanian et al., 1997). This has led to a number of behaviors that are likely to impact the evolution of a market. First, the greater ease of contacting customers and transacting with them may lead to greater competition. As noted in Balasubramanian (1998), the direct marketer effectively enters into competition with all 'bricks and mortar' retailers, because location is not relevant for a retailer whose presence is Internet-based. This paper highlights the complexity of competition that exists when the Internet marketer competes with traditional retailers and manipulates the coverage of the direct channel. Nevertheless, a key observation from this research is the degree to which the direct channel can bring prices down in traditional markets. In fact, Sheridan (1999) suggests that websites may lead to a commoditization of banking.[12]

However, we must also balance this observation with the potential of less competition. When not all firms are able to make the switch to electronic-based services and communication (for financial or resource-based reasons), industries may evolve to have one or two dominant firms. For example, a number of large PC manufacturers such as Wang, Packard Bell, IBM and Compaq have all suffered due to the tremendous growth of Dell and Gateway, which specialize in Internet-based distribution.[13]

Second, the increased importance of Internet business and shopping is likely to lead to greater price competition and comparison-shopping by consumers (Lal & Sarvary, 1999). This is especially true for products that are primarily search goods (Nelson, 1974).[14] As noted by Balasubramanian et al., (1997), firms may be quite strategic in letting their consumers use the Internet to obtain information easily. Nevertheless, the advent of search engines and shopping agents is likely to have an important impact on the level of competition for products that are highly substitutable. These institutions have the role of assisting consumers to process and use the enormous amount of information that is available on the Internet (Iyer & Pazgal, 1999). Iyer and Pazgal show that in some cases these institutions may actually reduce the intensity of price competition in the market.

Other institutions have also formed as a result of the ease by which the Internet can bring diverse sellers and buyers together. As noted by Klein and Quelch (1997), these include on-line auctions, exchanges, and post-and-buy websites. The impact of these institutions on markets is difficult to predict, however, auctions sites such as Freemarkets Online are observed to provide significant benefits to their clients.[15] The impact is to make it more difficult for a supplier to charge a price that is non-competitive to a downstream firm. Ultimately, this has the potential to accelerate consolidation or exit by firms that cannot charge competitive prices.

Finally, a key concern raised by the growth of the Internet concerns the way that information is generated and collected on the Internet. In fact, consumers' concern about an invasion of privacy is an important barrier to the growth of Internet-based business (Wang et al., 1998). Because users of the Internet leave traces with every keystroke, there are a number of key issues including the access, collection, monitoring, analysis, transfer, and storage of personal information. While the direct effect of privacy concerns will be to slow growth, the Internet may have the side effect of sensitizing consumers to the collection of information in all arenas. Over time, this might make it more expensive to collect and use customer-specific information.

Conclusion

The objective of this chapter has been to provide an integrative framework for better understanding how two key research areas in marketing, Competitive Response and Market Evolution, are inextricably linked. In the past, researchers have studied competitive response primarily through analyzing how firms react to initiative actions (product, price, or marketing mix) made by competitors. For the most part, this research is focused in well-established markets primarily due to the lack of reliable time-series data in new markets and virgin categories.

In contrast, the study of market evolution has focused primarily on the diffusion and growth approach or on the analysis of market structure (which has its origins in the early industrial organization literature). In general, the literature does not address how the manner in which competitors respond to each other affects the development of markets, and *vice versa*.

Yet we have significant intuition that the interaction of competitors has a strong and important effect on the development of markets. We need only look at the difference between markets that have been highly regulated in some countries (and competitive response is effectively eliminated) and deregulated in others to highlight the difference in the evolution of markets.

For example, the landscape and the evolution of the broadcast/cable TV market in the USA (largely deregulated) is significantly different than that of Europe (highly regulated) and these differences can be largely attributed to the efforts of US broadcasters to respond to each other while at the same time meeting the needs of a rapidly growing market.

Thus, we have attempted to provide a basis for better understanding the links between these two areas by highlighting the areas where much work remains to be done. We do this by first, providing a comprehensive review of the primary dimensions of competitive response. It proves useful to divide the dimensions of competitive response into those that are pre-emptive and those that are responses to existing competitors. We then review the important literature on market evolution that follows from these two approaches. The most important parts of the chapter are the sections that discuss the impact of competitive response on market evolution and *vice versa*. There is already some research that is useful to understand these impacts in the context of our framework. Yet these sections highlight a number of links where our understanding remains limited or conjectural at best. Our discussion of external influences is intended to provide a richer basis for considering these links in the future. With the rapid changes in technology and communication that appear to be impacting all markets of significance, we believe it is necessary to consider external factors in order to better understand the relationship between market evolution and competitive response. It is our hope that the framework we present here will assist in that regard.

Notes

1. Heckman (1999) discusses the implication of this US Supreme Court decision to marketers.

2. See, for example, Eswaran and Gallini (1996) where the authors study the ultimate impact of patent policy on consumer welfare.

3. Nelson (1974) refers to these products as 'experience goods.' Akerlof (1970) underlines how 'hidden information' can interfere with the operation of markets.

4. Kreps (1990) and Milgrom et al. (1990) model the reputation effect as a Repeated Prisoners' Dilemma game and show how reputation can be an effective vehicle for promoting honest trade. Similarly, Landes and Posner (1987) show how branding provides a form of insurance or guarantee to the buyer about a product so branded.

5. Eddy and Saunders (1980), Chaney et al. (1991) and Lane and Jacobsen (1995) discuss the role of announcements of new product introductions and brand extensions as a basis for stock market evaluations.

6. An interesting application of these issues can be found in the HBS case 'American Airline and Value Pricing' (5/11/94).

7. The most likely situation for the launch of me-too products is clearly when the pioneer has launched a product without any weaknesses.

8. In spite of creating supra-normal profits for firms in these industries, the regulations may be well justified. Our discussion does not include the negative externalities of products such as tobacco and alcohol (i.e., the societal cost of tobacco or alcohol-related health problems), which is beyond the scope of this paper.

9. A thorough discussion of natural monopolies can be found in Varian (1992) and Tirole (1988).

10. Quotas are the most direct form of supply control; however, restrictive licensing can also be used to achieve the same objective.

11. Pruzan (1996) underlines the 'vast marketing opportunities' that result from deregulation where firms can now 'target' many customers through a variety of media and 'special business customer services.'

12. Sheridan (1999) underlines that banks feel compelled to invest heavily in Internet services without having a clear strategy of how they intend to compete (at the very least, the natural outcome of such behavior is likely to be reduced profits).

13. Wysocki, B. (1999) Corporate Caveat: Dell or Be Delled. *Wall Street Journal Europe*, May 10, 1999.

14. These attributes have also been called experiential and non-experiential attributes (Smith & Kempf, 1998), or non-digital and digital attributes (Lal & Sarvary, 1999).

15. See HBS Case *Freemarkets Online* 1999 for further information.

References

Aaker, David A. & Day, George S. (1986) The perils of high growth markets. *Strategic Management Journal*, 7, 409–21.

Abernathy, W. & Utterback J.M. (1978) Patterns of industrial innovation. *Technology Review*, 80, 41–7.

Adams, William & Encaoua, David (1994) Distorting the direction of technological change. *European Economic Review*, 38, 663–73.

Akerlof, George A. (1970) The market for 'lemons': quality uncertainty and the market mechanism. *Quarterly Journal of Economics*, 84 (August), 488–500.

Aldrich, Howard E. (1999) *Organizations Evolving*. London: Sage Publications.

Anderson, Eric T. & Simester, Duncan I. (1998) The role of sale signs. *Marketing Science*, 17, 2, 139–55.

Anderson, Philip & Tushman, Michael L. (1990) Technological discontinuities and dominant designs: a cyclical model of technological change. *Administrative Science Quarterly*, 35, 604–33.

——— (1991) Managing through cycles of technological change. *Research and Technology Management*, 34, 3, 26–31.

Armstrong, Mark & Vickers, John (1996) The access Pricing problem with deregulation: a synthesis. *Journal of Industrial Economics*, 44, 113–50.

Armstrong, Mark & Vickers, John (1998) The access pricing problem with deregulation: a note. *Journal of Industrial Economics*, 46, 1, 115–21.

Arora, Rejinder (1979) How promotion elasticities change. *Journal of Advertising Research*, 19, 3, 57–62.

Arrow, Kenneth J. (1962) Economic welfare and the allocation of resources for invention. In *The Rate and Direction of Inventive Activity*, edited by R. Nelson. Princeton, NJ: Princeton University Press, pp. 609–26.

Athey, S. & Schmultzer, A. (1995) Product and process flexibility in an innovative environment. *Rand Journal of Economics*, 26, 557–74.

Bagwell, K. & Riordan, M.H. (1991) High and declining prices signal product quality. *American Economic Review*, 81, 224–39.

Bain, Joseph (1949) A note on pricing in monopoly and oligopoly. *American Economic Review*, 39, 448–64.

——— (1956) *Barriers to Competition*. Cambridge, MA: Harvard University Press.

Balachander, Subramanian & Srinivasan, Kannan (1994) Selection of product line qualities and prices to signal competitive advantage. *Management Science*, 40, 7 (July), 824–41.

Balasubramanian, Sridar (1998) Mail versus mall: a strategic analysis of competition between direct marketers and conventional retailers. *Marketing Science*, 17, 3, 181–95.

Balasubramanian, Sridhar, Peterson, Robert A. & Bronnenberg, Bart J. (1997) Exploring the implications of the Internet for consumer marketing. *Journal of the Academy of Marketing Science*, 25, 4, 329–46.

Bass, Frank M. (1969) A new product growth for model consumer durables. *Management Science*, 15, 5 (January), 215–27.

Bergemann, Dirk & Välimäki, Juuso (1996) Learning and strategic pricing. *Econometrica*, 64, 5 (September), 1125–49.

Bergen, Mark E., Dutta, Shantanu & Walker, Orville C. Jr. (1992) Agency relationships in marketing: a review of the implications and applications of agency and related theories. *Journal of Marketing*, 56 (July), 1–24.

Bernheim, Douglas B. & Whinston, Michael D. (1986) Common agency. *Econometrica*, 54 (July), 923–42.

Bhattacharya, S., Glazer, J. & Sappington, D.E.M. (1992) Licensing and the sharing of knowledge in research joint ventures. *Journal of Economic Theory*, 56, 43–69.

Biggadike, R.E. (1979) *Corporate Diversification: Entry, strategy and performance*. Harvard University Press, Cambridge, Mass.

Bloch, Francis (1995) Endogenous structures of association in oligopolies. *Rand Journal of Economics*, 26, 3 (Autumn), 537–56.

Bowman, Douglas & Gatignon, Hubert (1995) Determinants of competitor response time to a new product introduction. *Journal of Marketing Research*, 32, 1 (February), 42–53.

——— (1996) Order of entry as a moderator of the effect of the marketing mix on market share. *Marketing Science*, 15, 3, 222–42.

Bowman, Douglas & Gatignon, Hubert (2000) The impact of competitive context on the allocation of marketing mix resources. Working Paper, INSEAD.

Brod, Andrew & Shivakumar, Ram (1997) R&D cooperation and the joint exploitation of R&D. *Canadian Journal of Economics*, 30, 3, 673–84.

Bronnenberg, Bart J., Mahajan, Vijay & Vanhonacker, Wilfried R. (2000) The emergence of market structure in new repeat-purchase categories: the interplay of market-share and retailer distribution. *Journal of Marketing Research*, 37, 1 (February), 16–31.

Buzzell, Robert D. (1999) Market functions and market evolution. *Journal of Marketing*, 63 (special issue), 61–3.

Calantone, Roger J. & Schatzel, Kim E. (2000) Strategic foretelling: communication-based antecedents of a firm's propensity to preannounce. *Journal of Marketing*, 64, 1, 17–30.

Campbell, Jeffrey R. & Hopenhayn, Hugo A. (1999) Market size matters. Working Paper, University of Chicago, Chicago, IL.

Carlton, Dennis W. & Perloff, Jeffrey M. (1994) *Modern Industrial Organization*, New York: HarperCollins Publishers.

Carpenter, Gregory S. & Nakamoto, Kent (1989) Consumer preference formation and pioneering advantage. *Journal of Marketing Research*, 26, 3 (August), 285–98.

Carroll, Glenn R. (1985) Concentration and specialization: dynamics of niche width in populations of organizations. *American Journal of Sociology*, 90, 6 (May), 1262–83.

Chaney, P.K., Devinney, T.M. & Winer, R. (1991) The impact of new product introductions on the market value of firms. *Journal of Business*, 64, 573–610.

Choi, Jay Pil (1989) An analysis of cooperative R&D. Working Paper, Department of Economics, Harvard University, Cambridge, MA.

Chu, Wujin (1992) Demand signaling and screening in channels of distribution. *Marketing Science*, 11, 4, 327–47.

Chu, Wujin & Chu, Woosik (1994) Signaling quality by selling through a reputable retailer: an example of renting the reputation of another agent. *Marketing Science*, 13, 2, 177–89.

Crawford, V. & Sobel, J. (1982) Strategic information transmission. *Econometrica*, 50, 1431–51.

Cubbin, J. & Domberger, S. (1988) Advertising and post-entry oligopoly behaviour. *Journal of Industrial Economics*, 37, 2, 123–40.

d'Aspremont, Claude & Jacquemin, Alexis (1988) Cooperative and noncooperative R&D in duopoly with spillovers. *American Economic Review*, 78, December, 1133–7.

Day, George S. (1986) *Analysis for Strategic Marketing Decisions*. St. Paul, MN: West Publishing Co.

Dekimpe, Marnik G., Parker, Philip M. & Sarvary, Miklos (2000) Global diffusion of technological innovations: a coupled-hazard approach. *Journal of Marketing Research*, 37 (February), 47–59.

Demsetz, Harold (1982) Barriers to entry. *American Economic Review*, 72, 1 (March), 47–57.

Dixit, A. (1979) A model of duopoly suggesting a theory of entry barriers. *Bell Journal of Economics*, 10, 20–32.

——— (1980) The role of investment in entry deterrence. *Economic Journal*, 90, 95–106.

Eddy, Albert R. & Saunders, George B. (1980) New product announcements and stock prices. *Decision Sciences*, Atlanta, 11, 1 (January), 90.

Eliashberg, Jehoshua & Robertson, Thomas S. (1988) New product preannouncing Behavior: a market signaling study. *Journal of Marketing Research*, 25 (August), 282–92.

Eswaran, Mukesh (1994) Licensees as entry barriers. *Canadian Journal of Economics*, 27, 3 (August), 673–88.

Eswaran, Mukesh & Gallini, Nancy (1996) Patent policy and the direction of technological change. *Rand Journal of Economics*, 27, 4, 722–46.

Fershtman, Chaim & Pakes, Ariel (2000) A dynamic oligopoly with collusion and price wars. *Rand Journal of Economics*, 31, 2 (Summer), 207–36.

Franses, P.H. (1994) Modeling new product sales: an application of cointegration analysis. *International Journal of Research in Marketing*, 11, Nov–Dec, 491–502.

Gal-Or, Esther (1989) Warranties as a signal of quality. *Canadian Journal of Economics*, 22, 1, February, 50–61.

Gallini, Nancy T. (1984) Deterrence by market sharing: a strategic incentive for licensing. *American Economic Review*, 74, 5, 931–41.

Gandal, Neil & Scotchmer, Suzanne (1993) Coordinating research through research joint ventures. *Journal of Public Economics*, 51, 173–93.

Gatignon, Hubert (1984) Competition as a moderator of the effect of advertising on sales. *Journal of Marketing Research*, 21, 4 (November), 387–98.

Gatignon, Hubert, Weitz, Barton A. & Bansal, Pradeep (1990) Brand introduction strategies and competitive environments. *Journal of Marketing Research*, 27, 4 (November), 390–401.

Gatignon, Hubert, Anderson, Erin & Helsen, Kristiaan (1989) Competitive reactions to market entry: explaining interfirm differences. *Journal of Marketing Research*, 26, 1 (February), 44–55.

Gatignon, Hubert, Eliashberg, Jehoshua & Robertson, Thomas S. (1989) Modeling multinational diffusion patterns: an efficient methodology. *Marketing Science*, 8, 3, 231–47.

Gatignon, Hubert, Robertson, Thomas S. & Fein, Adam (1997) Incumbent defense strategies against innovative entry. *International Journal of Research in Marketing*, 14, 2, 163–76.

Gatignon, Hubert, Tushman, Michael L., Anderson, Philip & Smith, Wendy (2000) A structural approach to assessing innovation: construct development of innovation types and characteristics and their organizational effects. Working Paper, INSEAD.

Gerstner, Eitan, Davis, Scott & Hagerty, Michael (1995) Money back guarantees in retailing: matching products to consumer tastes. *Journal of Retailing*, 71, 1 (Spring), 7–22.

Ghemewat, Pankaj (1991) Market incumbency and technological inertia. *Marketing Science*, 10 (Spring), 161–71.

Gibbons, Robert (1992) *Game Theory for Applied Economists*. Princeton, NJ: Princeton University Press.

Gilbert, Richard & Newbery, David (1982) Preemptive patenting and the persistence of monopoly. *American Economic Review*, 72, June, 514–26.

Grossman, Sanford J. (1981) The informational role of warranties and private disclosure about product quality. *Journal of Law & Economics*, 24, 3 (December), 461–83.

Hannan, Michael T. & Freeman, John (1977) The population ecology of organizations. *American Journal of Sociology*, 82, 5, 929–64.

Hauser, John R. (1988) Competitive price and positioning strategies. *Marketing Science*, 7, 1 (Winter), 76–91.

Hauser, John R. & Shugan, Steven M. (1983) Defensive marketing strategies. *Marketing Science*, 2, 4 (Fall), 319–60.

Heckman, James (1999) Marketers can say 'Mine'. *Marketing News*, 33, 4 (February 15), 1–2.

Heil, Oliver P. & Langvardt, Arlen W. (1994) The interface between competitive market signaling and antitrust law. *Journal of Marketing*, 58 (July), 81–96.

Heil, Oliver & Robertson, Thomas S. (1991) Toward a theory of competitive market signaling: a research agenda. *Strategic Management Journal*, 12, 403–18.

Iyer, Ganesh (1998) Coordinating channels under price and nonprice competition. *Marketing Science*, 17, 4, 338–55.

Iyer, G. & Pazgal, A. (1999) Internet shopping agents: virtual collocation and competition. Working Paper, Olin School of Business, Washington University, St Louis.

Iyer, G.K. & Soberman, D.A. (1999) 'Hands Off' or 'Hands On': the marketing of service innovations. Working Paper #99/77/MKT, INSEAD.

——— (2000) Markets for product modification information. *Marketing Science*, 19, 3, 203–25.

Jain, Dipak C. & Rao, Ram C. (1990) Effect of price on the demand for durables: modeling, estimation, and findings. *Journal of Business and Economic Statistics*, 8 (April), 163–70.

Jayachandran, Satish, Gimeno, Javier & Varadarajan, P. Rajan (1999) The theory of multimarket competition: a synthesis and implications for marketing strategy. *Journal of Marketing*, 63, July, pp. 49–66.

John, George, Weiss, Allen M. & Dutta, Shantanu (1999) Marketing in technology-intensive markets: toward a conceptual framework. *Journal of Marketing*, 63 (special issue), 78–91.

Jones, Morgan J. & Ritz, C.J. (1991) Incorporating distribution into new product diffusion models. *International Journal of Research in Marketing*, 8, 91–112.

Judd, K. (1985) Credible spatial pre-emption. *Rand Journal of Economics*, 16, 153–65.

Kamien, Morton I., Muller, E. & Zang, I. (1992) Research joint ventures and R&D cartels. *American Economic Review*, 82, 1293–1306.

Kardes, Frank R. & Kalyanaram, Gurumurthy (1992) Order-of-entry effects on consumer memory and judgment: an information integration perspective. *Journal of Marketing Research*, 29, 3 (August), 343–57.

Katz, M.L. & Shapiro, C. (1986) How to license intangible property. *Quarterly Journal of Economics*, 16, 153–66.

Klein, Benjamin & Leffler, Keith B. (1981) The role of market forces in assuring contractual performance. *Journal of Political Economy*, 89, 4, 615–41.

Klein, Lisa R. & Quelch, John A. (1997). Business-to-business marketing on the internet. *International Marketing Review*, 14, 5, 345–61.

Kreps, David (1990) *A Course in Microeconomic Theory*, Princeton, NJ: Princeton University Press.

Kuester, Sabine, Gatignon, Hubert & Robertson, Thomas S. (2000) Firm strategy and speed of diffusion. In Vijay Mahajan, Eitan Muller and Yoram Wind, *New-Product Diffusion Models*. Boston, MA: Kluwer Academic Publishers.

Kuester, Sabine, Homburg, Christian & Robertson, Thomas S. (1999) Retaliatory behavior to new product entry. *Journal of Marketing*, 63, 4 (October), 90–106.

Lal, Rajiv & Sarvary, Miklos (1999) When and how is the internet likely to decrease price competition? *Marketing Science*, 18, 4, 485–503.

Lambkin, Mary & Day, George S. (1989) Evolutionary processes in competitive markets: beyond the product life cycle. *Journal of Marketing*, 53, 3, 4–20.

Lancaster, Kelvin (1990) The economics of product variety: survey. *Marketing Science*, 9, 3 (Summer), 189–206.

Landes, William & Posner, Richard (1987) Trademark law: an economic perspective. *Journal of Law & Economics*, 30, 265–309.

Lane, Vicki & Jacobsen, Robert (1995) Stock market reactions to brand extension announcements: the effects of brand attitude and familiarity. *Journal of Marketing*, 59, 1 (January), 63–77.

Lane, W.J. (1980) Product differentiation in market with sequential entry. *Bell Journal of Economics*, 11, 237–59.

Leahy, Dermot & Neary, J. Peter (1997) Public policy towards R&D in oligopolistic industries. *American Economic Review*, 87, 4, 642–62.

Leeflang, Peter S.H. & Wittink, D.R. (1996) Competitive reaction versus competitive response: do managers overreact? *International Journal of Research in Marketing*, 13, 2, 103–19.

Lilien, Gary L. & Yoon, Eusang (1988) An exploratory analysis of the dynamics behaviour of price elasticity over the product life cycle: an empirical analysis of industrial chemical products. In *Issues in Pricing: Theory and Research,* edited by T.M. Devinney. Lexington, MA: Lexington Books, Chapter 12.

Liu, L. & Hanssens, Dominique (1981) A Bayesian approach to time-varying cross sectional regression models. *Journal of Econometrics*, 15 (April), 341–56.

Lutz, Nancy A. (1989) Warranties as signals under consumer moral hazard. *The Rand Journal of Economics*, 20, 2 (Summer), 239–55.

Mahajan, Vijay, Sharma, Subhash & Buzzell, Robert D. (1993) Assessing the impact of competitive entry on market expansion and incumbent sales. *Journal of Marketing*, 57 (July), 39–52.

Mansfield, Edwin (1961) Technical change and the rate of imitation. *Econometrica*, 29, 4 (October), 741–65.

Mickwitz, G. (1959) *Marketing and Competition*. Societas Scientarium Fennica, Helsingfors, Finland (available from University Microfilms, Ann Arbor, MI).

Milgrom, Paul R. & Roberts, John (1986) Price and advertising signals of product quality. *Journal of Political Economy*, 94, 4, 796–821.

Milgrom, Paul, North, Douglass & Weingast, Barry (1990) The role of institutions in the revival of trade. *Economics and Politics*, 2, 1–24.

Mishra, Debi Prasad, Heide, Jan B. & Cort, Stanton G. (1998) Information asymmetry and levels of agency relationships. *Journal of Marketing Research*, 35, 3 (August), 277–95.

Moore, M. (1992) Signals and choices in competitive interactions: the role of moves and messages. *Management Science*, 38, 4, 483–500.

Moorthy, Sridhar & Srinivasan, Kannan (1995) Signaling quality with a money-back guarantee: the role of transaction costs. *Marketing Science*, 14, 4, 442–66.

Nelson, P. (1974) Advertising as information. *Journal of Political Economy*. 82, 4 (July–August), 729–54.

Ostlund, Lyman E. (1974) Perceived innovations attributes as predictors of innovativeness. *Journal of Consumer Records*, (June), 23–9.

Parker, Philip M. (1992) Price elasticity dynamics over the adoption life cycle. *Journal of Marketing Research*, 29, 3 (August), 358–67.

Parker, Philip M. & Gatignon, Hubert (1996) Order of entry, trial diffusion, and elasticity dynamics: an empirical case. *Marketing Letters*, 7, 1, 95–109.

Parker Philip M. & Neelamegham, Ramya (1997) Price elasticity dynamics over the product life cycle: a study of consumer durables. *Marketing Letters*, 8, 2, 205–16.

Parker, Philip M. & Roller, Lars-Hendrik (1997) Collusive conduct in duopolies: multimarket contact and cross-ownership in the mobile telephone industry. *Rand Journal of Economics*, 28, 2 (Summer), 304–22.

Parsons, Leonard M. (1975) The product life cycle and time varying advertising elasticities. *Journal of Marketing Research*, 12, 32 (August), 476–80.

Pruzan, Todd (1996) Phone companies ready explosion of marketing. *Business Marketing*, 81, 1 (February), 11–13.

Ramaswamy, Venkatram, Gatignon, Hubert & Reibstein, David J. (1994) Competitive marketing behavior in industrial markets. *Journal of Marketing*, 58 (April), 45–55.

Robertson, Thomas S. & Gatignon, Hubert (1991) How innovators thwart new entrants into their markets. *Planning Review*, 19 (5), 4–11.

——— (1998) Technology development mode: a transaction cost conceptualization. *Strategic Management Journal*, 19 (6), 515–31.

Robertson, T.S., Eliashberg, J. & Rymon, T. (1995) New product announcement signals and incumbent reactions. *Journal of Marketing*, 59, 1, 1–15.

Robinson, William T. (1988) Marketing mix reactions to entry. *Marketing Science*, 7, 4 (Fall), 368–92.

Robinson, William T. & Fornell, Claes (1985) Sources of market pioneer advantages in consumer goods industries. *Journal of Marketing Research*, 22, 3 (August), 305–17.

Rogers, E.M. (1983) *Diffusion of Innovations*, 3rd edition. New York: The Free Press.

Rosa, José Antonio, Porac, Joseph F., Runser-Spanjol, Jelena, & Saxon, Michael S. (1999) Sociocognitive dynamics in a product market. *Journal of Marketing*, 63 (special issue), 64–77.

Rothschild, Michael & Stiglitz, Joseph (1976) Equilibrium in competitive insurance markets: an essay on the economics of imperfect information. *Quarterly Journal of Economics*, 90, 629–50.

Scherer F. & Ross, David (1990), *Industrial Market Structure and Economic Performance*, 3rd edition. Dallas, TX: Houghton Mifflin.

Schmalensee, Richard (1978) A model of advertising and product quality. *Journal of Political Economy*, 86, 3, 485–503.

Schumpeter, J. (1943) *Capitalism, Socialism and Democracy*, 2nd edition. London: Allen & Unwin University Books.

Sellers, Patricia & Welsh, Tricia (1994) Competition: a whole new ball game in beer. *Fortune*, September 9, 79.

Shaked, A. & Sutton, J. (1982) Relaxing price competition through product differentiation. *Review of Economic Studies*, 49 (155) (January), 3–13.

Shankar, Venkatesh (1997) Pioneers' marketing mix reactions to entry in different competitive game structures: theoretical analysis and empirical illustration. *Marketing Science*, 16, 3, 271–93.

——— (1999) New product introduction and incumbent response strategies: their interrelationship and the role of multimarket contact. *Journal of Marketing Research*, 36, 3 (August), 327–44.

Shankar, Venkatesh, Carpenter, Gregory S. & Krishnamurthi, Lakshman (1999) Late mover advantage: how innovative late entrants outsell pioneers. *Journal of Marketing Research*, 35, 1 (February), 54–70.

Sheridan, Kevin (1999) All revved up with no place to go. *Bank Marketing*, 31, 4 (March), 33–8.

Simon, Hermann (1979) Dynamics of price elasticity and brand life cycles: an empirical study. *Journal of Marketing Research*, 16, 4 (November), 439–54.

Smith, Ken G., Grimm, Curtis M., Chen, Ming-Jer & Gannon, Martin J. (1989) Predictors of response time to competitive strategic actions: preliminary theory and evidence. *Journal of Business Research*, 18, 245–58.

Smith, Robert E. & Kempf, DeAnna S. (1998) Consumer processing of product trial and the influence of prior advertising: structural modeling approach. *Journal of Marketing Research*, 35, 3 (August), 325–38.

Soberman, D.A. (2000) Informative advertising: an alternate viewpoint and implications. Working Paper 2000/05/MKT, INSEAD.

Spence, Michael (1974) *Market Signaling*, Cambridge, MA: Harvard University Press.

——— (1977a) Entry, capacity, investment and oligopolistic pricing. *Bell Journal of Economics*, 8, 534–44.

Spence, Michael (1977b) Consumer misperceptions, product failure and producer liability. *Review of Economic Studies*, 44, 561–72.

Spulber, Daniel F. & Sidak, J. Gregory (1997) Network access pricing and deregulation. *Industrial and Corporate Change*, 6, 4 (December), 757–82.

Srinivasan, K. (1991) Multiple market entry, cost signalling and entry deterrence. *Management Science*, 37, 1539–55.

Srivastava, Rajendra K., Mahajan, Vijay, Ramaswami, Sridhar N. & Cherian, Joseph (1985) A multi-attribute diffusion model for forecasting the adoption of investment alternatives for consumers. *Technological Forecasting and Social Change*, 28 (December), 325–33.

Stiglitz, Joseph E. (1987) The causes and consequences of the dependence of quality on price. *Journal of Economic Literature*, 25, 1 (March), 1–48.

——— (1989) *Information and Economic Analysis*, New York: Oxford University Press.

Suzumura, Kotaro (1992) Cooperative and noncooperative R&D in an oligopoly with spillovers. *American Economic Review*, 82, 5, 1309–20.

Tellis, Gerard J. (1988) The price elasticity of selective demand: a meta analysis of econometric models of sales. *Journal of Marketing Research*, 25 (November), 331–41.

Tirole, Jean (1988) *Modern Industrial Organization*, Cambridge, MA: MIT Press.

Tripsas, M. (1997) Unraveling the process of creative destruction: complementary assets and incumbent survival in the typesetter industry. *Strategic Management Journal*, 18, 119–42.

Tushman, M.L. & Murmann, J.P. (1998) Dominant designs, technology cycles, and organisational outcomes. In *Research in organisational behavior*, edited by L.L. Cummings & B.M. Staw. Greenwich: JAI Press, pp. 231–66.

Urban, Glen L., Carter, Theresa, Gaskin, Steven & Mucha, Zofia (1986) Market share rewards to pioneering brands: an empirical analysis and strategic implications. *Marketing Science*, 32, 6 (June), 645–59.

Varian, Hal R. (1992) *Microeconomic Analysis*, 3rd edition. New York: W.W. Norton & Co.

Villas-Boas, J. Miguel (1998) Product line design for a distribution channel. *Marketing Science*, 17, 2, 156–69.

Vonotras, Nicholas S. (1989) Inter-firm cooperation in imperfectly appropriable research: industry performance and welfare implications. Working Paper, Department of Economics, New York University, New York.

Wang, Huaiqing, Lee, Mathew & Wang, Chen (1998) Consumer privacy concerns about Internet marketing. *Communications of the ACM*, 41, 3, 63–70.

Wensley, Robin (1981) Strategic marketing: betas, boxes, or basics. *Journal of Marketing*, 45 (Summer), 173–82.

Wildt, Albert R. (1976) The empirical investigation of time dependent parameter variation in marketing models. In *Educators' Proceedings*, Chicago: American Marketing Association, pp. 466–72.

Winer, Russell S. (1979) An analysis of the time varying effects of advertising: the case of Lydia Pinkham. *Journal of Business*, 52 (October), 563–76.

Wysocki, Bernard (1999) Corporate caveat: Dell or be Delled. *Wall Street Journal Europe*, May 10.

Yi, Sang-Seung (1999) Entry, licensing and research joint ventures. *International Journal of Industrial Organization*, 17, 1–24.

Zhang, Shi & Markman, Arthur B. (1998) Overcoming the early entrant advantage: the role of alignable and non-alignable differences. *Journal of Marketing Research*, 35, 4 (November), 413–26.

PART THREE

Marketing Activities

7

Branding and Brand Equity

KEVIN LANE KELLER

Introduction

Although brand management has been an important activity for some companies for decades, branding has only emerged as a top management priority for a broad cross-section of organizations in the last decade or so. A number of factors have contributed to this trend, but perhaps the most important is the growing realization that one of the most valuable assets that firms have is the intangible asset that is their brands. As will be outlined below, creating strong brands can have a number of bottom-line and other benefits to a firm. As a consequence, branding principles have been applied in virtually every setting where consumer choice of some kind is involved, e.g., with physical goods, services, retail stores, people, organizations, places, or ideas. Driven in part by this intense industry interest, academic researchers and marketing commentators have explored a number of different brand-related topics in recent years, generating literally hundreds of papers, articles, research reports, and books on branding.[1]

The purpose of this chapter is to review and provide some context and interpretation to this explosion of research. The goal is to highlight what has been learned, from an academic perspective, in the study of branding and brand equity, as well as what gaps still exist. Although emphasis is placed on research published since 1990 or so, earlier 'classics' or noteworthy studies are highlighted where appropriate.[2] We concentrate on those important issues in building, measuring, and managing brand equity that have received some academic attention. Consequently, we do not cover all brand management issues and challenges, e.g., important managerial branding issues such as brand recovery, revitalization of classic or heritage brands, brand architecture design, and brand stewardship are not addressed in detail. Note, however, that many of these topics have been discussed in the large number of trade books in the area.

We begin by reviewing the fundamentals of branding in terms of some conceptual foundations and brand equity measurement issues. Next, we turn to a consideration of brand intangibles – the means by which a brand transcends a product – and review research concerning brand personality, experiences, relationships, and communities as well as corporate images. Third, we discuss factors affecting the choice and design of brand elements such as brand names and logos, as well as some related legal issues with respect to branding. Fourth, we review a number of issues with respect to brand extensions – the most widely studied area of branding – examining moderating and mediating factors and managerial issues in detail. Fifth, we examine brand strategies and brand alliances and the means by which brands leverage their brand equity, as well as borrow brand equity from others. Finally, the chapter concludes by offering some summary observations and identifying research priorities in the study of branding and brand management.

Branding Fundamentals

Before considering how brand equity has been conceptualized and measured, it is useful first to define what a brand is. According to the American Marketing Association, a brand is 'a name, term, sign, symbol, or combination of them that is designed to identify the goods or services of one seller or group of sellers and to differentiate them from those of competitors.' Technically speaking then, whenever a marketer creates a new name, logo, symbol, etc. for a new product, he or she has created a brand. It should be recognized that many practicing managers, however, refer to a brand as more than that – defining a brand in terms of having actually created a certain amount of awareness, reputation and prominence in the marketplace. In some sense, a distinction can thus be made between the AMA definition of a 'small "b" brand' versus the sometimes industry practice of a 'big "b" brand' – i.e., a 'brand' versus a 'Brand.' It is important to recognize this distinction as disagreements about branding principles or guidelines can often revolve around the definition of what is being meant by a 'brand' as much as anything. With this caveat in mind, we turn to the topics of conceptualizing branding effects and measuring brand equity.

Conceptual Foundations

Brand functions

A number of studies have, one way or the other, explored the various effects of brands on consumer behavior and the effectiveness of marketing programs (see Hoeffler and Keller (2001) for a comprehensive review, as well as Yoo et al. (2000) for some empirical tests). In these studies, 'brand type' or some such variable has been included directly in the research design as an independent variable, or indirectly in the design as a moderator variable interacting with one or more other independent variables. Regardless of how incorporated, this research has revealed numerous positive effects and advantages from having created a 'strong' brand, where brand strength may reflect macro brand considerations such as market leadership or market share position, as well as more micro brand considerations such as consumer familiarity, knowledge, preferences, or loyalty. Some of the findings from these studies include the following.

Product-related Effects Brand name has been shown to be positively associated with consumer product evaluations, perceptions of quality and purchase rates (Brown & Dacin, 1997; Day & Deutscher, 1982; Dodds et al., 1991; Leclerc, et al., 1994; Rao & Monroe, 1989). This tendency may be especially apparent with difficult-to-assess 'experience' goods (Wernerfelt, 1988) and as the uniqueness of brand associations increases (Feinberg et al., 1992). In addition, familiarity with a brand has been shown to increase consumer confidence, attitude toward the brand, and purchase intention (Feinberg et al., 1992; Laroche et al., 1996) and mitigate the potential negative impact of a negative trial experience (Smith, 1993). Chaudhri & Holbrook (2001) show that brand trust and brand effect combine to determine purchase loyalty and attitudinal loyalty, and, in turn, that purchase loyalty leads to greater market share and attitudinal loyalty leads to higher relative price for the brand. Although these various factors have contributed to long-term category leadership for some brands, as an important caveat, Golder (2000) found that, based on an unbiased sample of 100 categories, many leading brands have lost their leadership over a 76-year period. A number of factors and changes in the marketing environment helped to contribute to such changes in brands' fortunes.

Price-related Effects Several studies have demonstrated that brand leaders can command larger prices differences (Agrawal, 1996; Park & Srinivasan, 1994; Sethuraman, 1996; Simon, 1979) and are more immune to price increases (Bucklin et al., 1995; Sivakumar & Raj, 1997). In a competitive sense, brand leaders draw a disproportionate amount of share from smaller share competitors (Allenby & Rossi, 1991; Grover & Srinivasan, 1992; Russell & Kamakura, 1994). At the same time, prior research has demonstrated that market leaders are relatively immune to price competition from these small share brands (Bemmaor & Mouchoux, 1991; Blattberg & Wisniewski, 1989; Bucklin et al., 1995; Sivakumar & Raj, 1997). In addition, lower levels of price sensitivity have been found for households that are more loyal (Krishnamurthi & Raj, 1991). Advertising may play a role in the decreases in price sensitivity (Kanetkar et al., 1992). Boulding et al. (1994) claim that unique advertising messages (e.g., product differentiation for high quality products and low price messages for low price leaders) led to a reduction in the susceptibility to future price competition.

Communication-related Effects A number of communication effects have been attributed to well-known and liked brands (Sawyer, 1981). Brown & Stayman (1992) maintain that 'halo effects' related to the positive feelings toward a brand can positively bias the evaluation of advertising of the brand. Humor in ads seems to be more effective for familiar or already favorably evaluated brands than for unfamiliar or less-favorably evaluated brands (Chattopadhyay & Basu, 1990; Stewart & Furse, 1986; Weinburger & Gulas, 1992). Similarly, consumers appear to have a more negative reaction with ad tactics such as comparative ads (Belch, 1981), depending on the nature of the brand involved (see also Kamins & Marks, 1991). Consumers are more likely to have a negative reaction to ad repetition with unknown as opposed to strong brands (Calder & Sternthal, 1980; Campbell & Keller, 2000). Familiar brands appear to withstand competitive ad interference better (Kent & Allen, 1994). Van Osselaer & Alba (2000) showed that when the relationship between brand name and product quality was learned prior to the relationship between product attributes and quality, inhibition of the latter could occur.

In addition, panel diary members who were highly loyal to a brand increased purchases when advertising for the brand increased (Raj, 1982). Other advantages associated with more advertising include increased likelihood of being the focus of attention (Dhar & Simonson, 1992; Simonson et al., 1988) and increased 'brand interest' (Machleit et al., 1993). Ahluwalia et al. (2000) demonstrated that consumers who have a high level of commitment to a brand are more likely to counter-argue with negative information (see also Laczniak et al., 2001). This may be the reason why strong brands were shown to be better able to weather a product-harm crisis (Dawar & Pillutla, 2000).

Channel-related Effects Finally, Montgomery (1975) found that products that were from the top firms in an industry had a much higher chance of being accepted in the channel and gaining shelf space in supermarkets. Also, research suggests that stores are more likely to feature well-known brands if they are trying to convey a high quality image (Lal & Narasimhan, 1996).

In short, across a wide range of marketing activity, there have been demonstrable advantages from creating a strong brand.

Theoretical Approaches

As with advertising and other marketing phenomena, a number of different theoretical mechanisms and perspectives have been brought to bear in the study of branding. Although there are a number of industry perspectives that highlight important concepts and relationships with respect to branding and brand management, three main streams of academic research that have formally defined or conceptualized brand equity, based on either consumer psychology, economics, or biology and sociology, are briefly summarized here.

Psychology-based Approaches Researchers studying branding effects from a cognitive psychology perspective frequently have adopted associative network memory models to develop theories and hypotheses, in part because of the comprehensiveness and diagnostic value they offer (see Krishnan (1996) and Henderson et al. (1998) for empirical demonstrations, as well as Lassar et al. (1995)). The brand is seen as a node in the memory with a variety of different types of associations, varying in strength, linked to it. Relatedly, prior research has also often adopted a categorization perspective to memory representations of branding (Boush & Loken, 1991). This approach assumes that consumers see brands as categories that, over time, have come to be associated with a number of specific attributes, based in part on the attributes associated with the different products that represent individual members of the brand category (Loken & Roedder John, 1993).

Researchers have also relied on numerous concepts and principles from social psychology and social cognition in developing models of consumer brand-related decisions, e.g., such as affect referral mechanisms, attributional processes, accessibility–diagnosticity considerations, expectancy value formulations, and so on. Researchers have also used models of consumer inference-making fairly extensively. Teas & Grapentine (1996) construct a framework of the role of brand names in consumer purchase decision-making processes from a marketing research perspective that highlight some of these considerations.

Two well-established models of brand equity that rely in various ways on consumer psychology principles in their development are highlighted here (see also Farquhar, 1989). In three books and numerous papers, Aaker (1991, 1996; Aaker & Joachimsthaler, 2000) has approached brand equity largely from a managerial and corporate strategy perspective but with a consumer behavior underpinning. He defines brand equity as a set of four categories of brand assets (or liabilities) linked to a brand's name or symbol that add to (or subtract from) the value provided by a product or service to a firm and/or to that firm's customers:

1. brand awareness
2. perceived quality
3. brand associations
4. brand loyalty.

In his writing, he has developed a number of distinct and useful concepts related to brand identity, brand architecture, and brand marketing programs, and has addressed a number of managerial branding challenges (Aaker, 1994; Aaker & Joachimsthaler, 1999; Joachimsthaler & Aaker, 1997).

Keller (1993, 1998) has approached brand equity from somewhat more of a consumer behavior perspective. He defines 'customer-based brand equity' as the differential effect that brand knowledge has on the consumer or customer response to the marketing of that brand. According to this model, a brand is said to have positive customer-based brand equity when customers react more favorably to a product and the way it is marketed when the brand is identified, as compared to when it is not (e.g., when it is attributed to a fictitiously named or unnamed version of the product). Customer-based brand equity occurs when the consumer has a high level of awareness and familiarity with the brand and holds some strong, favorable, and unique brand associations in memory. Keller views brand building in terms of a series of logical steps: establishing the proper brand identity, creating the appropriate brand meaning, eliciting the right brand responses, and forging appropriate brand relationships with customers (Keller, 2001). Achieving these four steps, according to his model, involves establishing six core brand values – brand salience, brand performance, brand imagery, brand judgments, brand feelings, and brand resonance. He also develops a number of different concepts and considers a number of different managerial applications (Keller 1999a, 1999b, 2000).

Despite their somewhat different foundations, the Aaker & Keller models share much in common with each other, as well as with other psychologically based approaches to brand equity. Most importantly, both acknowledge that brand equity represents the 'added value' endowed to a product as a result, in part, of past investments in the marketing for the brand. It should be noted that the Aaker & Keller models rely to some extent on spreading activation processes from an associative network model of memory. Janiszewski & van Osselaer (2000) offer some evidence to suggest that a connectionist model of brand-quality association may provide a more robust explanation of consumer reactions to various branding strategies than a spreading activation account, under certain conditions (see also van Osselaer & Janiszewski, 2001). With this model, consumers are assumed to be adaptive learners who are 'learning to value,' as opposed to the spreading activation perspective, which they argue is more relevant for consumers who are 'learning to recall.' Note too that Meyers-Levy (1989) showed that a large number of associations were not necessarily advantageous and could produce interference effects and lower memory performance.

Economics-based Approaches Although behavioral models have been perhaps the dominant basis to studying branding effects and brand equity, as noted above, other valuable viewpoints have also emerged. For example, Erdem (1998a, 1998b) takes an information economics perspective on the value (or equity) ascribed to brands by consumers (see also Montgomery & Wernerfelt, 1992; Sappington & Wernerfelt, 1985; Wernerfelt, 1988). Based in part on a premise of the imperfect and asymmetrical information structure of markets, Erdem's approach centers on the role of credibility as the primary determinant of what she dubs 'consumer-based brand equity.' When consumers are uncertain about product attributes, according to Erdem, firms may use brands to inform consumers about product positions and to signal that their product claims are credible. By reducing consumer uncertainty, brands are seen as lowering information costs and the risk perceived by consumers. She provides empirical support for these signaling mechanisms in an umbrella branding application to the oral hygiene market.

Similarly, Rao et al. (1999) have argued that a brand name can credibly convey unobservable quality when it is the case that false claims would result in intolerable economic losses, due to either losses of reputation, sunk investments, or losses of future profits. In a brand alliance application with hypothetical television brands, they showed that consumers' evaluations of the quality of a product with an important unobservable attribute were enhanced when the brand was allied with a second brand that was perceived to be vulnerable to consumer sanctions.

Sociology- and Biology-based Approaches Some researchers have studied branding from more of a sociological, anthropological, or biological perspective. For example McCracken (1986, 1993) considered the broader cultural meaning of brands and products (see also Richins, 1994). As outlined in subsequent sections, other researchers have explored topics such as brand communities (Muniz & O'Guinn, 2001; Schouten & McAlexander, 1995; Solomon & Englis, 1992) and brand relationships (Fournier, 1998). (See Ratneshwar et al. (2000) for some recent commentary.)

Other researchers have adopted more of a perceptual or even subconscious approach to branding. For example, as described in more detail below, Schmitt (1999a, 1999b) views branding in a more experiential way in terms of the effects on all five senses. Zaltman (Zaltman & Higie, 1995; Zaltman & Coulter, 1995) use metaphors as a guiding theme and qualitative research techniques to uncover the mental models driving consumer behavior with respect to brands.

Summary All three of these theoretical approaches to branding have their roots in basic disciplines and thus, to some extent, share the corresponding strengths and weaknesses of those disciplines. Like other areas of marketing, however, adopting or at least recognizing the advantages of multiple perspectives can potentially offer deeper and richer understanding of branding and brand equity.

Finally, it should be recognized that the concept of brand equity is not without its critics (see Feldwick, 1996 for some insightful commentary). For example, the principle of 'double jeopardy' (DJ) is based on the robust observation that large share brands have more buyers who buy more often and who exhibit unusually high behavioral loyalty (Ehrenberg et al., 1990; Ehrenberg, et al., 1997). In downplaying the importance of brand equity, Ehernberg (1997) interprets this pattern to mean '... there are large brands and small ones rather than any evidence of strong brands and weak ones...'

Critics, however, have countered this charge. Dyson et al. (1997) point out that the DJ model describes 'aspects of buyer behavior in steady markets with readily substitutable brands' but notes that the task of marketing is often to change the setting or situation to the benefit of the brand. In other words, the role of marketing often may be to create a violation of the DJ assumptions. Similarly, Baldinger & Rubinson (1997) maintain that loyalty cannot be assumed and that 'in order to become a large brand and stay a large brand, consumers must not only buy it, but like buying it.' Finally, Fader & Schmittlein (1993) note that part of the explanation for the DJ effect is the existence of an extremely brand-loyal segment for high share brands, and their increased availability at retail locations (smaller stores that carry fewer brands are likely to carry the high share brand) – both indicators of brand equity. (See Chaudhuri (1999) for some additional discussion.)

Resolving the debate depends in part on assumptions and beliefs about market stability and the power of marketing actions to influence consumers. DJ proponents find short-term marketing actions relatively impotent, whereas brand equity proponents believe marketing activities can be disruptive and influence consumer behavior.

Measuring Brand Equity

The manner by which brand equity is conceptualized has obvious implications for how it is measured. Keller & Lehmann (2001) provide a broad, integrative perspective on measuring brand equity (see also Srivastava et al. (1998), Ambler (2000), and Epstein & Westbrook (2001)). They define the 'Brand Value Chain' in terms of a series of three steps in the creation of a value of a brand. According to this model, the first step in value creation is when an investment in marketing activity affects the consumer/customer mind set or brand knowledge (e.g., in terms of brand awareness, associations, attitudes, attachment, and activity). The second step is when brand knowledge, in turn, affects market performance (e.g., in terms of price premiums and elasticities, cost savings, market share, profitability, and expansion success). Finally, the third step is when market performance affects shareholder value (e.g., in terms of stock price and market capitalization).

Keller & Lehman identify key measures associated with each stage of this value creation process, as well as a set of 'filters' or moderator variables that impact the transfer or flow of value between stages of the model. Although a review of all the possible marketing research methods, techniques, and measures associated with each of the three different stages of brand-value creation is beyond the scope of this chapter, it is useful to highlight some notable recent research advances for each stage.

Consumer/Customer Brand Knowledge

In terms of measuring brand awareness, Hutchinson et al. (1994) developed a general Markov model of brand name recall and explored the implications of three special cases of the model as applied to the soft drinks and beverages categories. Their model analysis addressed a number of managerial issues and showed that 1) market structure played an important role in determining brand name recall, and, as a result, brands in certain situations could therefore be completely ignored; and 2) usage rates, advertising expenditures, market penetration and various product attributes were found to be significant predictors of recall latency. In an entirely different approach, Duke (1995) showed how indirect memory measures of awareness – the Ebbinghaus Savings Test and word fragment completion – could supplement more traditional measures of free recall.

In terms of measuring brand image, the Zaltman Metaphor Elicitation Technique (ZMET) uses qualitative methods to tap into consumers' visual and other sensory images (Zaltman & Coulter, 1995a, 1995b). Specifically, based on a belief of the importance of nonverbal channels of communication, as part of the research process ZMET attempts to: 1) reveal the 'mental models' that drive consumer thinking and behavior; and 2) characterize these models in actionable ways using consumers' metaphors. In part, ZMET requires study participants to take photographs and/or collect pictures from magazines, books, newspapers or other sources, and use these visual images to indicate what the brand means to them in various ways.

Product/Market Performance

Several researchers have applied conjoint analysis to measure aspects of brand equity. For example, Rangaswamy et al. (1993) used conjoint analysis to explore how brand names interact with physical product features to affect the extendability of brand names to new product categories. Swait et al. (1993) proposed a related approach to measuring brand equity, which designs choice experiments that account for brand name, product attributes, brand image, and differences in consumer sociodemographic characteristics and brand usage. They defined the *equalization price* – a proxy for brand equity – as the price that equated the utility of a brand to the utilities that could be attributed to a brand in the category where no brand differentiation occurred. They illustrated their approach with an application to the deodorant, athletic shoe, and jeans market, and described its managerial implications.

Using similar techniques, Bello & Holbrook (1995) found comparatively little evidence of price premiums across a number of categories (see also Holbrook, 1992), but suggested that this absence may be due in part to the preponderance of 'search' goods as opposed to 'experience' goods in their sample. Finally, Mahajan et al. (1994) described a methodology to assess the importance of brand equity in acquisition decisions. Their approach involves defining relative attributes for acquisition such as financial performance, product market characteristics, and marketing strategy-related variables, and having key executives provide ratings of real and hypothetical firms based on that information. They illustrate their approach in the all-suites segment of the hotel industry.

Several researchers have employed 'residual approaches' to estimate brand equity. According to these (e.g., Bong et al., 1999; Srinivasan, 1979), brand equity is what remains of consumer preferences and choices after subtracting out objective characteristics of the physical product (although some researchers, e.g., Barwise et al. (1989), have challenged the separability assumption implicit in these approaches). Kamakura & Russell (1993) employed a single-source, scanner panel-based measure of brand equity that modeled consumer choices as a function of two factors: 1) brand value (perceived quality, the value assigned by consumers to the brand, after discounting for current price and recent advertising exposures); and 2) brand intangible value (the component of brand value not directly attributed to the physical product and thus related to brand name associations and 'perceptual distortions'). In an application to the laundry detergent market, they show that brand equity was closely related to order of entry of brands and their cumulative advertising expenditures.

Park & Srinivasan (1994) also have proposed a residual methodology that estimates the relative sizes of different bases of brand equity by dividing it into two components: 1) the attribute-based component of brand equity, defined as the difference between subjectively perceived attribute values and objectively measured attribute values (e.g., collected from independent testing services such as Consumer Reports or acknowledged experts in the field), and 2) the non-attribute-based component of brand equity, defined as the difference between subjectively perceived attribute values and overall preference. They proposed a survey procedure to collect information to estimate these different perception and preference measures, and illustrate their approach in the toothpaste and mouthwash categories.

Dillon et al. (2001) present a model for breaking down ratings of a brand on an attribute into two components: 1) brand-specific associations (i.e., features, attributes or benefits that consumers link to a brand), and 2) general brand impressions (i.e., overall impressions based on a more holistic view of a brand). They empirically demonstrate their model properties in three product categories: cars, toothpaste, and paper towels. Finally, using established notions of health found in the epidemiology literature, Bhattacharya & Lodish (2000) defined 'brand health' in terms of 'current well-being' and 'resistance.' They provided an empirical application of these constructs using store scanner data, demonstrating that their proposed resistance indicator was able to predict the share loss that was suffered by the existing brands in a category in the event of a new product introduction.

Shareholder Value

Several researchers have studied how the stock market accounts for and reacts to the brand equity for companies and products. Simon & Sullivan (1993) developed a technique for estimating a firm's brand equity derived from financial market estimates of brand-related profits. Under the assumption that the market value of the firm's securities provides an unbiased estimate of the future cash flows that are attributable to all of the firm's assets, their estimation technique attempted to extract the value of brand equity from the value of the firm's other assets. They illustrated their approach in part by tracing the brand equity of Coca-Cola and Pepsi over three major events in the soft drink industry from 1982–1986.

Aaker & Jacobson (1994) examined the association between yearly stock return and yearly brand equity changes (as measured by EquiTrend's perceived quality rating as a proxy for brand equity) for 34 companies during the years of 1989 to 1992. They also compared the accompanying changes in current-term return on investment (ROI). They found that, as expected, stock market return was positively related to changes in ROI, but that there was also a strong positive relationship between brand equity and stock return. They concluded that investors can and do learn about changes in brand equity – although presumably indirectly through learning about a company's plans and programs.

Using data for firms in the computer industry in the 1990s, Aaker & Jacobson (2001) found that changes in brand attitude were associated contemporaneously with stock return and led accounting financial performance. They also found five factors (new products, product problems, competitor actions, changes in top management, and legal actions) that were associated with significant changes in brand attitudes. Similarly, using *Financial World* estimates of brand equity, Barth et al. (1998) found that brand equity was positively related to stock return and that this effect was incremental to other accounting variables such as the firm's net income.

Adopting an event study methodology, Lane & Jacobson (1995) showed that a stock market participant's response to brand extension announcements, consistent with the trade-offs inherent in brand leveraging, depended interactively and non-monotonically on brand attitude and familiarity. Specifically, with their sample the stock market appeared to respond most favorably to extensions of high esteem, high familiarity brands and to low esteem, low familiarity brands (in the latter case, presumably because there was little to risk and much to gain with extensions). The stock market reaction appeared to be less favorable (and sometimes even negative) for extensions of brands where consumer familiarity was disproportionately high compared to consumer regard, and to extensions of brands where consumer regard was disproportionately high compared to familiarity.

Brand Elements

At the heart of branding and brand management is the brand itself, which can be thought of as composed of various brand elements. Brand elements can be defined as those trademarkable devices that serve to identify and differentiate the brand (e.g., brand names, logos, symbols, characters, slogans, jingles, and packages). A number of broad criteria have been identified as to how to choose and design brand elements to build brand equity (Keller, 1998):

1. memorability
2. meaningfulness
3. aesthetic appeal
4. transferability both within and across product categories as well as across geographical and cultural boundaries and market segments
5. adaptability and flexibility over time
6. legal and competitive protectability and defensibility.

Although a robust industry exists to help firms design and implement these various elements (see Kohli & LaBahan, 1997 for a descriptive account of the brand name selection process), comparatively little academic attention, even in recent years, has been devoted to this topic. Nevertheless, several research studies and programs have emerged around designing and legally protecting brand elements, as follows.

Brand Names

Sensory or Phonetic Considerations

Research on choice criteria for brand names extends back for years (see Robertson, 1989 for an overview). A number of studies have considered sensory or phonetic aspects of brand names. For example, in a study of computer-generated brand names containing random combinations of syllables, Peterson & Ross (1972) found that consumers were able to extract at least some product meaning out of these essentially arbitrary names when instructed to do so. Specifically, 'whumies' and 'quax' were found to be remindful of a breakfast cereal, and 'dehax' was remindful of a laundry detergent.

Researchers studying phonetic symbolism have considered how the sounds of even individual letters can contain meaning that may be useful in developing a new brand name (see Klink (2000) and Yorkston & Menon (2001) for a review of the conceptual mechanisms involved and some managerial applications). For example, some words begin with phonemic elements called 'plosives' (i.e., the letters b, c, d, g, k, p, and t), whereas others use 'sibilants' (i.e., sounds like s and a soft c). Because plosives escape from the mouth more quickly than sibilants and are hasher and more direct, they are thought to make names more specific and less abstract, and be more easily recognized and recalled (Vanden Bergh et al., 1984). A survey of the top 200 brands in the *Marketing and Media Decision's* lists for the years 1971 to 1985 found a preponderance of brand names using plosives (Vanden Bergh et al., 1987). On the other hand, because sibilants have a softer sound, they tend to conjure up romantic, serene images and are often found with products such as perfumes (e.g., Cie, Chanel, & Cerissa) (Doeden, 1981). Heath et al. (1990) found a relationship between certain characteristics of the letters of brand names and product features: as consonant hardness and vowel pitch increased in hypothetical brand names for toilet paper and household cleansers, consumer perception of the harshness of the product also increased.

Cultural Aspects

Similarly researchers have examined some cultural and linguistic aspects of branding. Leclerc et al. (1994) showed that certain hypothetical products that had brand names acceptable in both English and French (e.g., Vaner, Randal, & Massin) were perceived as more 'hedonic' (i.e., providing much pleasure) and better liked when pronounced in French than in English, although these effects did not completely generalize in a follow-up replication study (Thakor & Pacheco, 1997). Schmitt et al. (1994) showed that Chinese speakers were more likely to recall stimuli presented as brand names in visual rather than spoken recall, whereas English speakers were more likely to recall the names in spoken rather than visual recall. They interpreted these findings in terms of the fact that mental representations of verbal information in Chinese are coded primarily in a visual manner, whereas verbal information in English is coded primarily in a phonological manner.

Extending that research, Pan & Schmitt (1996) found that a match between peripheral features of a brand name (i.e., 'script' aspects such as the type of font employed, or 'sounds' aspects as to how the name is pronounced) and the associations or meaning of the brand resulted in more positive brand attitudes than a mismatch: Chinese native speakers were affected primarily by script matching; English native speakers' attitudes were primarily affected by sound matching. Pan & Schmitt also interpreted these results in terms of structural differences between logographic systems (e.g., Chinese, where characters stand for concepts and not sounds) and alphabetic systems (e.g., English, where the writing of a word is a close cue of its pronunciation), and their resulting visual and phonological representations in memory.

Finally, Zhang & Schmitt (2001) present a conceptual framework for managing brand name creation in an international, multilingual market, e.g., China. Their empirical results indicated that the choice of a translation should be guided by considerations of contextual factors: which brand name (the English or Chinese name) will be emphasized, and which translation approach (phonetic, which preserves the sound of the original name, versus phonosemantic, which preserves the sound of the original name and creates product category and brand associations) for similar products are considered the standard in the marketplace.

Semantic Meaning

In terms of more direct semantic meaning, applying basic associative memory theory, Keller et al. (1998) showed that a brand name explicitly conveying a product benefit (e.g., PicturePerfect televisions) led to higher recall of an advertised benefit claim consistent in meaning with the brand name (e.g., picture quality), compared with a non-suggestive brand name (e.g., Emporium televisions). On the other hand, a suggestive brand name led to lower recall of a subsequently advertised benefit claim unrelated in product meaning (e.g., superior sound), compared with a non-suggestive brand name.

Sen (1999) explored how a brand name's semantic suggestiveness interacted with the type of decision task involved in an initial encounter with a brand to influence the brand information encoded and recalled during a subsequent encounter with a proposed extension. He found that when information about an efficient set of new brands was learned through a choice task, brand names that suggested general superiority appeared to benefit subsequent brand extensions more than names that were suggestive of category-specific, attribute-based superiority. After a judgment task, however, the category-specific names appeared to benefit brand extensions more than the general superiority names.

Finally, in an exploratory study of alpha-numeric brand names (i.e., containing one or more numbers in either digit form (e.g., 5) or in written form (e.g., 'five'), Paiva & Costa (1993) found that alpha-numeric brand names were more favorably evaluated when designating technology-related products. This effect was moderated by a number of factors, including the visual or aural aspects of the name, the actual numbers that were used in the name, and the words or letters, along with the number(s), that comprised the brand name.

Logos

Little academic research has explored the consumer behavior effects of logo design or other visual aspects of branding (see Schmitt & Simonson (1997) for some background discussion). Henderson & Cote (1998) conducted a comprehensive empirical analysis of 195 logos that were calibrated on 13 different design characteristics in terms of their ability to achieve different communication objectives. They interpreted their findings as suggesting that: 1) logos with a high recognition goal should be very natural, very harmonious and moderately elaborate; 2) low investment logos intended to create a false sense of knowing and positive affect should be less natural and very harmonious; and 3) high image logos intended to create strong positive affect without regards to recognition should be moderately elaborate and natural but with high harmony. Overall, the results suggest that logos should generally be natural and fairly elaborative, but not overly so.

Janiszewski & Meyvis (2001) suggest that a dual-process model is most applicable in describing consumer responses to repeated exposure to static brand names, logos, and packages. The dual process model assumes a passive processing system by consumers, and posits that their response to a stimulus is a function of sensitization and habituation. They provide experimental evidence to that effect.

Legal Considerations

Several academics have considered legal issues involved with branding. Cohen (1986, 1991) has argued that trademark strategy involves proper trademark planning, implementation, and control, reviewing issues in each of those areas. Zaichovsky (1995) provides a comprehensive treatment of brand confusion (see also Foxman et al., 1992). Simonson (1994) provides an in-depth discussion of these issues and methods to assess the likelihood of confusion and 'genericness' of a trademark. He stresses the importance of recognizing that consumers may vary in their level or degree of confusion, and that as a result it is difficult to identify a precise threshold level above which confusion 'occurs.' He also notes how survey research methods to assess confusion must accurately reflect the consumers' state of mind when engaged in marketplace activities.

Simonson has provided behavioral perspectives to consider a number of issues related to appropriation, dilution, etc. (e.g., Simonson, 1995). Harvey et al. (1998) considered the legal and strategic implications of the look-a-like 'trade dress' practice of major food chains that adopt the visual cues (e.g., shape, size, color and the like) of national brands in branding their own, private labels (see also Kapferer, 1995; Loken et al., 1986). Oakenfull & Gelb (1996) have described how to avoid 'genercide' – i.e., when consumers employ the brand name as the product category label – through research and advertising. Finally, Sullivan (2001) considered the optimal number of registered trademarks to protect a brand.

Brand Intangibles

An important and relatively unique aspect of branding research is the focus on brand intangibles – aspects of the brand image that do not involve physical, tangible, or concrete attributes or benefits. For a review of some seminal work in this area, see Levy (1999). Brand intangibles are often a means by which marketers differentiate their brands with consumers (Park et al., 1986) and transcend physical products (Kotler, 2000).

Product Brand Level

Brand Personality

Brand personality has been defined as the human characteristics or traits that can be attributed to a brand. Aaker (1997) examined 114 possible personality traits and 37 well-known brands in various product categories to create a brand personality scale composed of five factors:

1. Sincerity (e.g., down-to-earth, honest, wholesome, and cheerful)
2. Excitement (e.g., daring, spirited, imaginative, and up-to-date)
3. Competence (e.g., reliable, intelligent, and successful)
4. Sophistication (e.g., upper class and charming)
5. Ruggedness (e.g., outdoorsy and tough).

In a cross-cultural study exploring the generalizability of this scale outside the United States, Aaker, Benet-Martinez & Berrocal (2001) found that three of the five factors applied in Japan and Spain, but that a 'peacefulness' dimension replaced 'ruggedness' in both countries, and a 'passion' dimension emerged in Spain instead of 'competency.'

Aaker (1999) also explored how different brand personality dimensions affected different types of people in different types of consumption settings. She found that self-congruity (i.e., brands which were chosen whose personality matched those of subjects) was enhanced for low versus high self-monitoring individuals, whereas situation congruity (i.e., brands which were chosen whose personality matched those of the situation involved) was enhanced for high versus low self-monitoring individuals. She interpreted these results in terms of a 'malleable self,' which is composed of self-conceptions that are chronically accessible or made accessible by a social situation.

Relatedly, Graef (1996) found that increased self-monitoring was associated with a greater effect of image congruence on consumers' evaluations of publicly consumed brands, but not privately consumed brands. Moreover, consumers' evaluations of publicly consumed brands were also more affected by the congruence between brand image and ideal self-image, than actual self-image. In the case of privately consumed brands, however, these effects were equal. Graef (1997) also found that when considering a specific consumption situation, the congruence between brand image and a dynamic measure of consumers' situational ideal self-image was more strongly correlated with consumers' brand evaluations than was the congruence between brand image and static measures of either their actual or ideal self-image.

Brand Experiences

Arguing that marketers and brand managers have largely ignored sensory, affective, and creative experiences, Schmitt (1997) outlines the SOOP ('superficial – out of profundity') model of the branding of customer experiences. He distinguishes between three type of experiential brands – 'sense,' 'feel,' and 'think' brands – based on the primary type of appeal that they present and the type of experience they target. Schmitt argues that common to all types of brands is the idea of providing value to consumers by enhancing relations between the brand and the consumer through rewarding, sensory stimulation, emotional binds, or creative rewards. He also defines five types of sensory experiences (which he calls 'SEMs,' Strategic Experiential Modules): 'Sense' experiences involving sensory perception, 'Feel' experiences involving affect and emotions, 'Think' experiences, which are creative and cognitive, 'Act' experiences, involving the physical and possibly incorporating individual actions and lifestyles, and 'Relate' experiences that result from connecting with a reference group or culture. (See also Schmitt (1999a, 1999b).)

Brand Relationships

Fournier (1998) extended the metaphor of interpersonal relationships into the brand domain to conceptualize the relationships that consumers form with brands (see also Fournier & Yao (1997) and Fournier et al. (1998)). Fournier views brand relationship quality as multi-faceted and consisting of six dimensions beyond loyalty/commitment along which consumer-brand relationships vary: 1) self-concept connection; 2) commitment or nostalgic attachment; 3) behavioral interdependence; 4) love/passion; 5) intimacy; and 6) brand partner quality. Based on lengthy, in-depth consumer interviews, Fournier defined 15 possible consumer-brand relationship forms: 1) arranged marriages, 2) casual friends/buddies; 3) marriages of convenience; 4) committed partnerships; 5) best friendships; 6) compartmentalized friendships; 7) kinships; 8) rebounds/avoidance-driven relationships; 9) childhood friendships; 10) courtships; 11) dependencies; 12) flings; 13) enmities; 14) secret affairs; and 15) enslavements. Additionally, Fournier (2000) developed the Brand Relationship Quality (BRQ) scale to empirically capture these theoretical notions.

Aaker, Fournier & Brasel (2001) conducted a two-month longitudinal investigation of the development and evolution of relationships between consumers and brands. They found that two factors – experience of a transgression and personality of the brand – had a significant influence on developmental form and dynamics. Specifically, brands associated with Sincerity traits (e.g., sincere, wholesome, sentimental) relative to those with Exciting traits (e.g., exciting, young, trendy) demonstrated increasing levels of relationship strength over time, but those results held only when relationship development proceeded without the experience of a transgression. In cases where a transgression occurred, relationship strength dramatically suffered for sincere brands, whereas some aspects of relationship strength eventually rebounded for exciting brands.

Brand Communities

Muniz and O'Guinn (2000) have defined 'brand communities' as a specialized, non-geographically bound community, based on a structured set of social relationships among users of a brand. They note that, like other communities, a brand community is marked by 1) a shared consciousness, 2) rituals and traditions, and 3) a sense of moral responsibility. They demonstrated these characteristics in both face-to-face and computer-mediated environments for the Apple Macintosh, Ford Bronco, and Saab brands.

Somewhat relatedly, Schouten & McAlexander (1995) have defined a 'subculture of consumption' as a distinctive subgroup of society that self-selects on a basis of a shared commitment to a particular product class, brand, or consumption activity. They note that characteristics of a subculture of consumption include an identifiable, hierarchical social structure; a unique ethos, or set of shared beliefs and values; and unique jargons, rituals, and modes of symbolic expression. As an illustration, they presented results of a three-year ethnographic field study with Harley-Davidson motorcycle owners. They later expanded their investigation to include the Jeep brand and explore various relationships that consumers could hold with the product/possession, brand, firm, and/or other customers as a measure of loyalty (McAlexander & Schouten, 2001).

Corporate Brand Level

Corporate Image

Much research has considered corporate image in terms of its conceptualization, antecedents, and consequences (e.g., see reviews by Barich & Kotler, 1991; Biehal & Shenin, 1998; Dowling, 1994; Schumann et al., 1991). A corporate image can be thought of as the associations that consumers have in their memory to the company or corporation making the product or providing the service as a whole. Corporate image is a particularly relevant concern when the corporate or company brand plays a prominent role in the branding strategy adopted. In establishing a corporate image, a corporate brand may evoke associations wholly different from an individual brand, which is only identified with a certain product or limited set of products (Brown, 1998).

For example, a corporate brand name may be more likely to evoke associations of common products and their shared attributes or benefits; people and relationships; and programs and values. Brown & Dacin (1997) distinguish between corporate associations related to corporate ability (i.e., expertise in producing and delivering product and/or service offering) and corporate social responsibility (i.e., character of the company with regard to important societal issues). In terms of the latter consideration, much research has explored the implications of cause-related marketing (e.g., Drumwright, 1996; Sen & Bhattacharya, 2001; Varadarajan & Menon, 1988) and green marketing (e.g., Journal of Advertising, 1995; Menon & Menon, 1997) strategies.

Keller & Aaker (1992, 1998) defined corporate credibility as the extent to which consumers believe that a company is willing and able to deliver products and services that satisfy customer needs and wants. Based on past consumer behavior research (e.g., Sternthal & Craig, 1984), they identified three possible dimensions to corporate credibility:

1. Corporate expertise – the extent to which a company is seen as being able to competently make and sell their products or conduct their services
2. Corporate trustworthiness – the extent to which the company is seen as motivated to be honest, dependable, and sensitive to consumer needs
3. Corporate likability – the extent to which the company is seen as likable, prestigious, interesting, etc.

Experimentally, Keller & Aaker (1992) showed that successfully introduced brand extensions can lead to enhanced perceptions of corporate credibility and improved evaluations of even more dissimilar brand extensions. Keller & Aaker (1998) showed that different types of corporate marketing activity, by impacting different dimensions of corporate credibility, as well as perceptions of extension fit and attribute beliefs, differentially affected consumer evaluations of a corporate brand extension. Specifically, corporate marketing activity related to product innovation produced more favorable evaluations for a corporate brand extension than corporate marketing activity related to either the environment or, especially, the community. Their findings also revealed that corporate marketing activity influenced evaluations even in the presence of advertising for the extension (see also Brown & Dacin, 1997).

Brand Extensions

The area of branding research that has seen by far the most attention in recent years has been on how firms should leverage brand equity, especially in terms of brand extensions. To develop managerial guidelines, research has addressed a number of factors affecting extension success.

Basic Processes

Modeling Consumer Evaluations of Brand Extensions

Much research has adopted a categorization perspective in modeling consumer evaluations of brand extension (e.g., Boush & Loken, 1991; Hartman et al., 1990; Loken & Roedder John, 1993). According to this perspective, if a brand were to introduce an extension that was seen as closely related or similar in 'fit' to the brand category, then consumers could easily transfer their existing attitude about the parent brand to the extension. On the other hand, if consumers were not as sure about extension similarity, then they might be expected to evaluate the extension in a more detailed, piece-meal fashion. In this case, the favorability of any specific associations that would be inferred about the extension would be the primary determinant of extension evaluations.

Fit has thus been identified as a key moderator as to how consumers evaluate brand extensions (Boush et al., 1987). Consistent with these notions, Aaker & Keller (1990) found that a perception of fit between the original and extension product categories, as well as a perception of high quality for the parent brand, led to more favorable extension evaluations. A number of subsequent studies have explored the generalizibility of these findings to markets outside the US. Based on a comprehensive analysis of 131 brand extensions from seven such replication studies around the world, Bottomly & Holden (2000) concluded that this basic model clearly generalized, although cross-cultural differences influenced the relative importance attached to the model components. In attempting to understand why some brands have been able to extend into 'perceptually distinct' domains, however, Klink & Smith (2001) show that effects of fit can disappear when attribute information is added to extension stimuli and are applicable only for later product adopters, and that perceived fit increases with greater exposure to an extension.

On the other hand, applying Mandler's congruity theory, Meyers-Levy et al. (1994) showed that suggested products associated with moderately incongruent brand names could be preferred over ones that were associated with either congruent or extremely incongruent brand names (see also Zinkhan & Martin, 1987). They interpreted this finding in terms of the ability of moderately incongruent brand extensions to elicit more processing from consumers that could be satisfactorily resolved (assuming consumers could identify a meaningful relationship between the brand name and the product).

Bases of Extension Fit

Prior research has examined a number of different factors concerning fit perceptions. In general, this research has reinforced the importance of taking a broad and contextual view of fit. Adopting a demand-side and supply-side perspective of consumer perceptions, Aaker & Keller (1990) showed that perceived fit between a parent brand and extension product could be related to the economic notions of perceived substitutability and complementarity in product use (from a demand-side perspective), as well as the perceived ability of the firm to have the skills and assets necessary to make the extension product (from a supply-side perspective).

Subsequent research has shown that virtually any association about a parent brand held in memory by consumers may serve as a potential basis of fit. Park et al. (1991) distinguished between fit based on 'product-feature-similarity' and 'brand-concept-consistency' (i.e., how well the brand concept accommodates the extension product). They also distinguished between function-oriented brands, whose dominant associations relate to product performance (e.g., Timex watches), and prestige-oriented brands, whose dominant associations relate to consumers' expression of self-concepts or images (e.g., Rolex watches). Experimentally, Park et al. showed that the Rolex brand could more easily extend into categories such as grandfather clocks, bracelets, and rings than the Timex brand; but, on the other hand, that Timex could more easily extend into categories such as stopwatches, batteries, and calculators than Rolex. They interpreted these results to suggest that, in the former case, there was high brand-concept-consistency for Rolex that overcame a lack of product-feature-similarity; in the latter case there was enough product-feature-similarity to favor a function-oriented brand such as Timex.

Broniarczyk & Alba (1994) showed that a brand that may not even be as favorably evaluated as a competing brand in its category – depending on the particular parent brand associations involved – may be more successfully extended into certain categories. For example, in their study, although Close-Up toothpaste was not as well liked as Crest toothpaste, a proposed Close-Up breath mint extension was evaluated more favorably than one from Crest. Alternatively, a proposed Crest toothbrush extension was evaluated more favorably than one from Close-Up.

Broniarczyk & Alba (1994) also showed that a perceived lack of fit between the parent brand's product category and the proposed extension category could be overcome if key parent-brand associations were deemed valuable in the extension category. For example, Froot Loops cereal – which has strong brand associations to 'sweet,' 'flavor,' and 'kids' – was better able to extend to dissimilar product categories such as lollipops and popsicles than to even similar product categories such as waffles and hot cereal because of the relevance of their brand associations in the dissimilar extension category. The reverse was true for Cheerios cereal, however, which had a 'healthy grain' association that was only relevant in similar extension product categories.

Thus, extension fit is more than just the number of common and distinctive brand associations between the parent brand and the extension product category (e.g., see Bijmolt et al., 1998). Along these lines, Bridges et al. (2000) refer to 'category coherence' of extensions. Coherent categories are those categories whose members 'hang together' and 'make sense.' According to this view, to understand the rationale for a grouping of products in a brand line, a consumer needs 'explanatory links' that tie the products together and summarize their relationship. For example, the physically dissimilar toy, bath care, and car seat products in the Fisher-Price product line can be united by the link, 'products for children.'

Similarly, Schmitt & Dube (1992) proposed that brand extensions should be viewed as conceptual combinations. A conceptual combination (e.g., 'apartment dog') consists of a modifying concept or 'modifier' (e.g., apartment) and a modified concept or 'header' (e.g., dog). Thus, according to this view, a proposed brand extension such as McDonald's Theme Park would be interpreted as the original brand or company name (e.g., McDonald's) acting on the 'head concept' of the extension category (e.g., theme parks) as a 'modifier.' Bristol (1996) adopted a similar view and suggested that consumers often seem to construct on-line 'conjunctive inferences' about extensions without exclusively using knowledge about the retrieved brand, product class, product-type category or subcategory, or exemplar.

Finally, researchers have explored other, more specific aspects of fit. Boush (1997) provides experimental data as to the context sensitivity of fit judgments. Similarity judgments between pairs of product categories were found to be asymmetrical, and brand name associations could reverse the direction of asymmetry. For example, more subjects agreed with the statement 'Time magazine is like Time books' as compared to the statement that 'Time books are like Time magazine,' but without the brand names, the preferences were reversed. Smith & Andrews (1995) surveyed industrial goods marketers and found that the relationship between fit and new product evaluations was not direct, but was mediated by customers' sense of certainty that a firm could provide a proposed new product. Finally, Martin & Stewart (2001) explore the multidimensional nature of product similarity ratings and the moderating effects of goal congruency.

Extension Feedback Effects

Much research has considered the reciprocal effects on the parent brand from having introduced an extension. Keller & Aaker (1992) and Romeo (1991) found that unsuccessful extensions in dissimilar product categories did not affect evaluations of the parent brand. The Keller & Aaker study also showed that unsuccessful extensions did not necessarily prevent a company from 'retrenching' and later introducing a more similar extension. Sullivan (1990) found that the 'sudden acceleration' problems associated with the Audi 5000 automobile had greater spillover to the Audi 4000 model than to the Audi Quattro model, which she interpreted as a result of the fact that the latter was branded and marketed differently.

Loken & Roedder John (1993) found that dilution effects were evident, but only under certain conditions (e.g., when extensions were perceived to be moderately typical and when extension typicality was not made salient to consumers), and for certain types of beliefs (e.g., gentleness beliefs rather than quality beliefs). In their study, however, dilution effects were largely unrelated to the similarity of the brand extension. Roedder John et al., (1998) found that dilution effects were less likely to be present with 'flagship' products and occurred with line extensions, but were not always evident for more dissimilar category extensions.

Gürhan-Canli & Durairaj (1998) extended the results of these studies by considering the moderating effect of consumer motivation and extension typicality. In high motivation conditions, they found that incongruent extensions were scrutinized in detail and led to the modification of family brand evaluations, regardless of the typicality of the extensions. In low motivation conditions, however, brand evaluations were more extreme in the context of high (versus low) typicality. As the less typical extension was considered an exception, its impact was reduced. In a similar vein, Ahluwalia & Gürhan-Canli (2000) adopted an accessibility-diagnosticity perspective to explain the effects of brand extensions on the family brand name and observed comparable experimental results. Finally, Milberg et al. (1997) found that negative feedback effects were present when 1) extensions were perceived as belonging to a product category dissimilar from those associated with the family brand, and 2) extension attribute information was inconsistent with image beliefs associated with the family brand.

In terms of individual differences, Lane & Jacobson (1997) found some evidence of a negative reciprocal impact from brand extensions, especially for high need-for-cognition subjects, but did not explore extension similarity differences. Kirmani et al. (1999) found dilution effects with owners of prestige-image automobiles when low-priced extensions were introduced, but not with owners of non-prestige automobiles or with non-owners of either type of automobile. Using national household scanner data, Swaminathan et al. (2001) found positive reciprocal effects of extension trial on parent brand choice, particularly among non-loyal users and prior non-users of the parent brand, and consequently on market share. Category similarity, however, appeared to moderate the existence and magnitude of these effects. Evidence was also found for potential negative effects of unsuccessful extensions among prior users of the parent brand, but not among prior non-users. Additionally, experience with the parent brand was found to have significant impact on extension trial, but not on extension repeat.

Morrin (1999) examined the impact of brand extensions on the strength of parent brand associations in memory. Two computer-based studies revealed that exposing consumers to brand extension information strengthened rather than weakened parent brand associations in memory, particularly for parent brands that were dominant in their original product category. Higher fit also resulted in greater facilitation, but only for non-dominant parent brands. Moreover, improvements in parent brand memory due to the advertised introduction of an extension was not as great as when the same level of advertising directly promoted the parent brand.

In reviewing this literature, Keller & Sood (2001a) put forth a conceptual model that posits that changes in consumer evaluations of a parent brand as a result of the introduction of a brand extension, is a function of three factors: 1) strength and clarity of extension evidence; 2) diagnosticity or relevance of extension evidence; and 3) evaluative consistency of extension evidence with parent brand associations. One implication of their conceptual model is that existing parent brand knowledge structures, in general, will be fairly resistant to change. In order for parent brand associations to change, consumers must be confronted with compelling evidence that is seen as relevant to existing parent brand associations, and they must be convinced that the evidence is inconsistent enough to warrant a change (Roedder John et al., 1997).

Thus, an unsuccessful brand extension can potentially damage the parent brand only when there is a high degree of similarity or 'fit' involved, e.g., in the case of a failed line extension in the same category. When the brand extension is farther removed, consumers can 'compartmentalize' the brand's products and disregard its performance in what is seen as an unrelated product category. Keller & Sood provided experimental evidence consistent with all of these conjectures.

Number and Types of Extensions

Line Extensions

Prior research (Farquhar 1989; Keller 1998) has distinguished between line extensions (i.e., when the parent brand is used to brand a new product that targets a new market segment within a product category currently served by the parent brand) and category extensions (i.e., when the parent brand is used to enter a different product category from that currently served by the parent brand). Several studies have examined the market performance of real brands to determine the success characteristics of line extensions (see Quelch & Kenney (1994) for some useful managerial insights and guidelines, and Hardie et al. (1994) for some commentary).

Using data on 75 line extensions of 34 cigarette brands over a 20-year period, Reddy et al. (1994) found that:

1. Line extensions of strong brands were more successful than line extensions of weak brands
2. Line extensions of symbolic brands enjoyed greater market success than those of less symbolic brands
3. Line extensions that received strong advertising and promotional support were more successful than line extensions that received meager support
4. Line extensions entering earlier into a product subcategory were more successful than line extensions entering later, but only if they were line extensions from strong brands
5. Firm size and marketing competencies also played a part in a line extension's success
6. Earlier line extensions helped in the market expansion of the parent brand
7. Incremental sales generated by line extensions could more than compensate for the loss in sales due to cannibalization.

Based on data collected from 166 product managers in packaged goods firms, Andrews & Low (1998) found that meaningful product line extensions had been launched in companies that: 1) had longer planning and reward horizons; 2) encouraged risk taking; 3) rotated brand assignments regularly; 4) had a product-focused management structure; 5) required comparatively more evidence to justify new stock keeping units and 6) utilized smaller new product development teams.

In an empirical study of the determinants in product line decisions in the personal computer industry from 1981–1992, Putsis and Bayus (2001) found that firms in the industry expanded their product lines when there were low industry barriers (e.g., few market-wide introductions, low industry concentration) or perceived market opportunities (e.g., due to high market share, recent market entry). High market share firms were found to expand aggressively their product lines, as did firms with relatively high prices or short existing product lines. They also found important substantive differences between the factors affecting the direction of a product line change (i.e., expansion or contraction of its current line) and the magnitude of any line change (i.e., how many products were introduced or withdrawn).

In the context of fast moving packaged goods, Cohen et al. (1997) developed a decision support system to evaluate the financial prospects of potential new line extensions. The model incorporated historical knowledge about the productivity of the firm's new product development process, as well as R&D resource factors that affect productivity, to provide shipment forecasts at various stages, allow for a product line perspective, and facilitate organizational learning.

Vertical Extensions

For market reasons or competitive considerations, firms often consider introducing lower priced versions of their established brand name products. Additionally, some marketers have attempted to migrate their brand up-market through brand extensions. Many strategic recommendations have been offered as to the topic of 'vertical extensions' (e.g., Aaker, 1994). For example, Farquhar et al. (1992) describe how to use 'sub-branding' strategies as a means to distinguish lower-priced entries, and 'super-branding' strategies to signal a noticeable, although presumably not dramatic, quality improvement (Ultra Dry Pampers or Extra Strength Tylenol). Comparatively little empirical academic research, however, has been conducted on this topic.

In an empirical study of the US mountain bicycle industry, Randall et al. (1998) found that brand price premium was significantly positively correlated with the quality of the lowest-quality model in the product line for the lower quality segments of the market; and that for the upper quality segments of the market, brand price premium was also significantly positively correlated with the quality of the highest quality model in the product line. They concluded that these results suggest that managers only wishing to maximize the equity of their brands would offer only high-quality products and avoid offering low-quality products, although overall profit maximization could dictate a different strategy.

Kirmani et al. (1999) examined the 'ownership effect' – by which owners have more favorable responses than non-owners to brand extensions – in the context of brand line stretches. They found that the ownership effect occurred for upward and downward stretches of non-prestige brands (e.g., Acura) and for upward stretches of prestige brands (e.g., Calvin Klein and BMW). For downward stretches of prestige brands, however, the ownership effect did not occur, because of the owners' desire to maintain brand exclusivity. In this situation, a sub-branding strategy protected owners' parent brand attitudes from dilution.

Multiple Brand Extensions

Keller & Aaker (1992) showed that when consumers did not already have strongly held attitudes, the successful introduction of a brand extension improved evaluations of a parent brand that was originally perceived only to be of average quality. By changing the image and meaning of the brand, the successfully introduced extension also could make *subsequent* brand extensions, that otherwise may not have seemed appropriate to consumers, make more sense and be seen as a better fit. Experimentally, they showed that by taking 'little steps,' i.e., by introducing a series of closely related but increasingly distant extensions, it was possible for a brand ultimately to enter product categories that would have been much more difficult, or perhaps even impossible, to have entered directly.

Similarly, Dawar & Anderson (1994) showed that undertaking extension introductions in a particular order could allow distant extensions to be perceived as coherent, and that following a consistent direction in extension strategy allowed for greater coherence and purchase likelihood for a target extension (see also Jap, 1993).

Boush & Loken (1991) found that far extensions from a 'broad' brand were evaluated more favorably than from a 'narrow' brand. similarly, Dacin & Smith (1994) showed that if the perceived quality levels of different members of a brand portfolio were more uniform, then consumers tended to make higher, more confident evaluations of a proposed new extension. They also showed that a firm that had demonstrated little variance in quality across a diverse set of product categories was better able to overcome perceptions of lack of extension fit (i.e., as consumers would think, 'whatever they do, they tend to do well').

Dawar (1996) showed that for brands with a single product association, brand knowledge and context interacted to influence evaluations of fit for extensions to products that were only weakly associated with the brand. Specifically, retrieval inhibition effects appeared to reduce the activation of 'less relevant' product associations, lowering the perceived fit of extensions closer to such products, especially for individuals more knowledgeable about the brand. For brands strongly associated with more than one product, only context – by selectively eliciting retrieval of brand associations – influenced the evaluations of the fit of the extensions.

In an empirical study of 95 brands in 11 nondurable consumer goods categories, Sullivan (1992) found that, in terms of stages of the product category life cycle, early-entering brand extensions did not perform as well, on average, as either early-entering new-name products or late-entering brand extensions. DeGraba & Sullivan (1995) provided an economic analysis to help interpret this observation. They posited that the major source of uncertainty in introducing a new product is the inability to know if it will be received by customers in a way that will allow it to be a commercial success. They further argued that this source of uncertainty could be mitigated by spending more time on the development process. Under such assumptions, they showed that the large spillover effects triggered by introducing a poorly received brand extension caused introducers of brand extensions to spend more time on the development process than did introducers of new-name products. Finally, Sullivan (1990) found that when Jaguar launched its first new model in 17 years, the older models of Jaguar experienced an increase in demand as a result of advertising used to promote the new 1988 model.

Moderating Factors

Characteristics of Consumers

Perceptions of fit and extension evaluations may depend on how much consumers know about the product categories involved. Muthukrishnan & Weitz (1990) showed that knowledgeable, 'expert' consumers were more likely to use technical or manufacturing commonalties to judge fit, considering similarity in terms of technology, design and fabrication, and the materials and components used in the manufacturing process. Less knowledgeable 'novice' consumers, on the other hand, were more likely to use superficial, perceptual considerations such as common package, shape, color, size, usage, etc. Relatedly, Broniarczyk & Alba (1994) also showed that perceptions of fit on the basis of brand-specific associations were contingent on consumers having the necessary knowledge about the parent brand. Without such knowledge, consumers tended again to rely on more superficial considerations, such as their level of awareness for the brand or overall regard for the parent brand, in forming extension evaluations. Finally, Zhang & Sood (2001) showed that 11–12-year-old consumers, relative to adults, evaluated brand extensions by relying less on category similarity between the parent brand and the extension category and more on the inherent characteristics of the name itself used to brand the extension (see also Achenreiner & Roedder John, 2001; Nguyen & Roedder John, 2001).

In a cross-cultural study, Han & Schmitt (1997) found that for US consumers, perceived fit was more important than company size in extension evaluations, but that for Hong Kong consumers, company size mattered for low fit extensions. They suggest that the value of collectivism may explain the relative higher importance of corporate identity as a quality cue for East Asian consumers.

Characteristics of the Parent Brand

Perceptions of fit and extension evaluations may also depend on aspects of the parent brand involved. Prior research has shown that one important benefit of building a strong brand is that it can be extended more easily into more diverse categories (e.g., Rangaswamy et al., 1993). High quality brands are often seen as more credible, expert, and trustworthy at what they do (Keller & Aaker 1992). As a result, even though consumers may still believe a relatively distant extension does not really fit with the brand, they may be more willing to give a high quality brand the 'benefit of the doubt.' When a brand is seen as more average in quality, however, such favorable source attributions may be less forthcoming, and consumers may be more likely to question the ability or motives of the company involved.

As a caveat to the previous conclusion, prior research (e.g., Farquhar & Herr, 1992) has shown that if a brand is seen as representing or exemplifying a category too much, it may be difficult for consumers to think of the brand in any other way. Farquhar et al. (1992) define a master brand as an established brand so dominant in customers' minds that it 'owns' a particular association – the mention of a product attribute or category, a usage situation, or a customer benefit instantly brings a master brand to mind. Recognizing that the exceptionally strong associations of a master brand often make it difficult to extend it directly to other product categories, they have proposed various branding strategies to extend master brands *indirectly* by leveraging alternative master brand associations that come from different parts of their brand hierarchies (e.g., via sub-branding, super-branding, brand-bundling, and brand-bridging).

The limits to extension boundaries potentially faced by master brands may be exacerbated by the fact that, in many cases, brands that are market leaders have strong concrete product attribute associations (Farquhar et al. 1992). In general, concrete attribute associations may not transfer as broadly to extension categories as more abstract attribute associations. For example, Aaker & Keller (1990) showed that consumers dismissed a hypothetical Heineken popcorn extension as potentially tasting bad or like beer; a hypothetical Vidal Sassoon perfume extension as having an undesirably strong shampoo scent; and a hypothetical Crest chewing gum extension as tasting like toothpaste or, more generally, tasting unappealing. In each case, consumers inferred a concrete attribute association with an extension that was technically feasible even though common sense might have suggested that a manufacturer logically would not be expected to introduce a product with such an attribute.

Because of their intangible nature, on the other hand, more abstract associations may be seen as more relevant across a wide set of categories (Rangaswamy et al., 1993). For example, the Aaker & Keller study also showed that the Vuarnet brand had a remarkable ability to be exported to a disparate set of product categories, e.g., sportswear, watches, wallets, and even skis. In these cases, complementarity may have led to an inference that the extension would have the 'stylish' attribute associated with the Vuarnet name, and such an association was valued in the different extension contexts.

Two caveats should be noted, however, concerning the relative extendibility of concrete and abstract associations. First, concrete attributes can be transferred to some product categories (Herr et al., 1996). Farquhar et al. (1992) have argued that if the parent brand has a concrete attribute association that is highly valued in the extension category because it creates a distinctive taste, ingredient, or component, an extension on that basis can often be successful. Second, abstract associations may not always transfer easily. Bridges et al. (2000) examined the relative transferability of product-related brand information when it was either represented as an abstract brand association (e.g., 'durable') or when it was represented as a concrete brand association. Surprisingly, the two types of brand images extended equally well into a dissimilar product category, in part because subjects did not seem to believe that the abstract benefit would have the same meaning in the extension category (e.g., durability does not necessarily 'transfer' because durability for a watch is not the same as durability for a handbag).

Finally, Joiner & Loken (1998), in a demonstration of the inclusion effect in a brand extension setting, showed that consumers often generalized possession of an attribute from a specific category (e.g., Sony televisions) to a more general category (e.g., all Sony products) more readily than they generalized to another specific category (e.g., Sony bicycles). This inclusion effect was attenuated when the specific extension category increased its typicality to the general category (e.g., Sony cameras vs. Sony bicycles).

Characteristics of the Extension Category

Prior research has shown that some seemingly appropriate extensions may be dismissed because of the nature of the extension product involved. If the product is seen as comparatively easy-to-make, such that brand differences are hard to come by, then a high quality brand may be seen as incongruous or, alternatively, consumers may feel that the brand extension will attempt to command an unreasonable price premium and be too expensive. For example, Aaker & Keller (1990) showed that hypothetical extensions such as Heineken popcorn, Vidal Sassoon perfume, Crest shaving cream, and Häagen-Dazs cottage cheese received relatively poor marks from experimental subjects, in part because *all* brands in the extension category were seen as being about the same in quality, suggesting that the proposed brand extension was unlikely to be superior to existing products. When the extension category is seen as difficult to make, on the other hand, such that brands potentially vary a great deal in quality, there is a greater opportunity for a brand extension to differentiate itself, although consumers may also be less sure as to what exactly will be the quality level of the extension (Kardes & Allen, 1990).

Other researchers have looked at the choice context faced by the extension in the new category. For example, McCarthy et al. (2001) found that brand extension advantages over suggestive new brand names were confined to situations of limited information processing and better fit. When consumers processed information more deeply, however, new brands could perform as well as or better than brand extensions. The researchers also found differences in their experimental study between consumer attitudes and their choices, suggesting an important caveat to generalizations from lab studies (see also Hem & Iverson, 2001).

Characteristics of the Extension Marketing Program

Prior research suggests that introductory marketing programs for extensions can be more effective than if the new product was launched with a new name (Kerin et al., 1996; Smith, 1992; Smith & Park, 1992). Moreover, a number of studies have shown that the information provided about brand extensions through its supporting marketing programs, by triggering selective retrieval from memory, may 'frame' the consumer decision process and affect extension evaluations (e.g., see Boush, 1993).

For example, Aaker & Keller (1990) found that cueing or reminding consumers about the quality of a parent brand did not improve evaluations for poorly-rated extensions. Because the brands they studied were well-known and well-liked, such reminders may have been unnecessary. Elaborating briefly on specific extension attributes about which consumers were uncertain or concerned, however, by clarifying the nature of an important attribute of the new product, appeared to be effective in inhibiting negative inferences and in reducing the salience of consumers' concerns about the firm's credibility in the extension context, leading to more favorable evaluations.

Bridges et al. (2000) found that providing information could improve perceptions of fit in two cases when consumers perceived low fit between a parent brand and an extension. When the parent brand and the extension shared physical attributes but the parent brand image was non-product-related and based on abstract user characteristics, consumers tended to overlook an obvious explanatory link between the parent brand and extension. Information that raised the salience of the physical relationship relative to distracting non-product-related associations – a 'relational' communication strategy – improved extension evaluations. When the parent brand and the extension only shared non-product associations and the parent brand image was product-related, consumers often made negative inferences on the basis of existing associations. In this case, providing information that established an explanatory link on an entirely new, 'reassuring' association – an 'elaborational' communication strategy – improved extension evaluations. They concluded that the most effective communication strategy for extensions appeared to be one which recognized the type of information that was already salient for the brand in the minds of consumers when they first considered the proposed extension, and highlighted additional information that would otherwise be overlooked or misinterpreted (see also Chakravarti et al., 1990).

Lane (2000) found that repetition of an ad that evoked primarily benefit brand associations could overcome negative perceptions of a highly incongruent brand extension. Moreover, for moderately incongruent brand extensions, even ads that evoked peripheral brand associations (e.g., brand packaging or character) could improve negative extension perceptions with sufficient repetition. Process measures revealed that, as a result of multiple exposures to ads for incongruent extensions, positive extension thoughts and thoughts of extension consistency eventually overcame the initial negative thoughts of inconsistency. In a somewhat similar vein, Barone et al. (2000) experimentally demonstrated that positive mood primarily enhanced evaluations of extensions viewed as moderately similar (as opposed to very similar or dissimilar) to a favorably evaluated core brand. These effects of mood were found to be mediated by perceptions of the similarity between the core brand and the extension, as well as the perceived competency of the marketer in producing the extension.

Finally, research has explored several other aspects of extension marketing programs. Keller & Sood (2001a) found that 'branding effects,' in terms of inferences based on parent brand knowledge, operated both in the absence and presence of product experience with an extension, although they were less pronounced or, in the case of an unambiguous negative experience, even disappeared. In considering the effects of retailer displays, Buchanan et al. (1999) found that evaluations of a 'high equity' brand could be diminished by a unfamiliar competitive brand when: 1) a mixed display structure led consumers to believe that the competitive brand was diagnostic for judging the high equity brand; 2) the precedence given to one brand over another in the display made expectations about brand differences or similarities accessible; and 3) the unfamiliar competitive brand disconfirmed these expectations.

BRANDING STRATEGIES AND ALLIANCES

Branding Strategies

Brand strategies concern how brand elements such as the brand name are employed across the products of a firm. LaForet & Saunders (1994) conducted a content analysis of the branding strategies adopted by 20 key brands sold by each of 20 of the biggest suppliers of grocery products to Tesco and Sainsbury, Britain's two leading grocery chains, and found that a variety of different branding approaches had been adopted. Essentially, these different approaches involved using common and/or distinct brands in various ways across the products sold by the firms (see also LaForet & Saunders, 1999).

One frequently employed branding strategy, a sub-brand strategy – whereby an existing name is combined with a new name to brand new products – has received some research attention. Prior research has shown that a sub-branding strategy can enhance extension evaluations, especially if the extension is more removed from the product category and less similar in fit (Keller & Sood, 2001a; Milberg et al., 1997; Shenin, 1998). Moreover, it has also been shown that a sub-brand can also protect the parent brand from any unwanted negative feedback (Janiszewski & van Osselaer, 2000; Kirmani et al., 1999; Milberg et al., 1997), but only if the sub-brand consists of a meaningful individual brand that precedes the family brand (Keller & Sood, 2001b). Thus, it appears that the relative prominence of the brand elements determines which element(s) becomes the primary one(s) and which element(s) becomes the secondary one(s) (see also Park et al., 1996).

Wänke et al., (1998) showed how a sub-branding strategy could help to set consumer expectations. Experimentally, a new compact car manufactured by a sports car company that had existing sports cars branded Winston Silverhawk, Winston Silverpride, and Winston Silverstar, received a more sports-car typical evaluation when its name reflected the continuation (Winston Silverray) rather than the discontinuation of previous models (Winston Miranda). The contrast effect created by the name discontinuation strategy was more pronounced for non-experts than experts.

In an econometric study of 'twin automobiles' (i.e., made in the same plant with essentially the same physical attributes but different names, such as Ford Motor Company's Ford Thunderbird and Mercury Cougar), Sullivan (1998) found that twins were not perceived as perfect substitutes – their relative prices differed. Most importantly, parent brand quality reputation affected the relative prices of the twin pairs. Specifically, the average quality of the parent line increased the demand for used cars sold under the parent brand name.

Finally, Bergen et al. (1996) studied branded variants – the various models that manufacturers offer different retailers (see also Shugan, 1989). They argued that as branded variants increased, consumers' cost of shopping for a branded product across stores increased, leading to less such behavior. Because reduced shopping implies reduced competition, they reasoned that retailers presumably should be more inclined to carry the branded product and provide greater retail service support. An empirical examination with data from three retailers across 14 product categories supported these notions.

Brand Alliances

Brand alliances, where two brands are combined in some way as part of a product or some other aspect of the marketing program, come in all forms (Rao, 1997; Rao et al., 1999; Shocker et al., 1994). Prior research has explored the effects of co-branding, ingredient branding strategies, and advertising alliances.

Co-branding

Park et al., (1996) compared co-brands to the notion of 'conceptual combinations' in psychology. Experimentally, they explored the different ways that Godiva (associated with expensive, high-calorie boxed chocolates) and Slim-Fast (associated with inexpensive, low-calorie diet food) could introduce a chocolate cake mix separately or together through a co-brand. The findings indicated that a co-branded brand extension that combined two brands with complementary attribute levels appeared to have a better attribute profile in the minds of consumers than either a direct extension of the dominant brand, or an extension that consisted of two highly favorable, but not complementary, brands.

Consistent with the conceptual combination literature, they also found that consumers' impressions of the co-branded concept were driven more by the header brand (e.g., Slim-Fast chocolate cake mix by Godiva was seen as lower calorie than if the product was called Godiva chocolate cake mix by Slim-Fast; the reverse was true for associations of richness and luxury). They also found that consumers' impressions of Slim-Fast after exposure to the co-branded concept were more likely to change when it was the header brand than when it was the modifier brand. Their findings show how carefully selected brands can be combined to overcome potential problems of negatively correlated attributes (e.g., rich taste and low calories).

Simonin & Ruth (1998) found that consumers' attitudes toward a brand alliance could influence subsequent impressions of each partner's brands (i.e., such that spillover effects existed), but these effects also depended on other factors such as product 'fit' or compatibility, and brand 'fit' or image congruity. Brands less familiar than their partners contributed less to an alliance but experienced stronger spillover effects than their more familiar partners. Similarly Voss & Tanshuhaj (1999) found that consumer evaluations of an unknown brand from another country were more positive when a well-known domestic brand was used in an alliance.

Finally, Levin & Levin (2000) explored the effects of dual branding, which they defined as a marketing strategy in which two brands (usually restaurants) share the same facilities while providing consumers with the opportunity to use either one or both brands. They found that when two brands were linked through a dual-branding arrangement and both brands were described by the same set of attributes, then the effect of dual branding was to reduce or eliminate the contrast effects. When two brands were linked through a dual branding arrangement and the target brand was less well-specified than the context brand, then the effect of dual branding was to increase assimilation effects.

Ingredient Branding

A special case of co-branding is ingredient branding, which involves creating brand equity for materials, components, parts, etc. that are necessarily contained within other branded products (McCarthy & Norris, 1999; Norris, 1992). Carpenter et al. (1994) found that the inclusion of a branded attribute (e.g., 'Alpine Class' fill for a down jacket) significantly impacted consumer choices even when consumers were explicitly told that the attribute was not relevant to their choice; subjects evidently inferred certain quality characteristics as a result of the branded ingredient. Brown & Carpenter (2000) offer a reasons-based account for the trivial attributes effect and show that the effect will depend on the choice context involved. Finally, Broniarszk & Gershoff (2001) show that the effect of trivial differentiation is more pronounced with strong brands.

Desai & Keller (2001) conducted a laboratory experiment to consider how ingredient branding affected consumer acceptance of an initial line extension, as well as the ability of the brand to introduce future category extensions. Two particular types of line extensions, defined as brand expansions, were studied: 1) slot filler expansions, where the level of one existing product attribute changed (e.g., a new type of scent in Tide detergent); and 2) new attribute expansions, where an entirely new attribute or characteristic was added to the product (e.g., cough relief liquid added to Life Savers candy). Two types of ingredient branding strategies were examined by branding the target attribute ingredient for the brand expansion with either a new name as a self-branded ingredient (e.g., Tide with its own EverFresh scented bath soap) or an established, well-respected name as a co-branded ingredient (e.g., Tide with Irish Spring scented bath soap). The results indicated that with slot filler expansions, although a co-branded ingredient facilitated initial expansion acceptance, a self-branded ingredient led to more favorable subsequent extension evaluations (see also Janiszewski & van Osselaer, 2000). With more dissimilar new attribute expansions, however, a co-branded ingredient led to more favorable evaluations of both the initial expansion and the subsequent extension.

Finally, Venkatesh & Mahajan (1997) derived an analytical model based on bundling and reservation price notions to help formulate optimal pricing and partner selection decisions for branded components. In an experimental application in the context of a university computer store selling '486 class' laptop computers, they showed that at the bundle level, an all-brand Compaq PC with Intel 486 commanded a clear price premium over other alternatives. The relative brand 'strength' of the Intel brand, however, was shown to be stronger in some sense than that of the Compaq brand.

Advertising Alliances

Samu et al., (1999) showed that the effectiveness of advertising alliances for new product introductions depended on the interactive effects of three factors: the degree of complementarity between the featured products, the type of differentiation strategy (common versus unique advertised attributes with respect to the product category), and the type of ad processing (top-down or bottom-up) that an ad evoked (e.g., explicitness of ad headline).

Conclusions and Future Prospects

Branding and brand management has clearly become an important management priority in the past decade or so. The academic research that was reviewed has covered a number of different topics and incorporated a number of different studies that have collectively advanced our understanding of brands. Before considering future research opportunities, it is worth taking stock of the progress that has been made and the kinds of generalization that might be suggested by the research reviewed.

Summary Observations

Prior research has convincingly demonstrated the power of brands. Branding effects are pervasive, and the effects of virtually any marketing activity seem to be conditioned or qualified by the nature of the brands involved. In particular, consumer response to a product and its prices, advertising, promotions, and other aspects of the marketing program have been shown to depend on the specific brands in question. In understanding how these effects are manifested, essentially all the theoretical approaches one way or another interpret these branding effects in terms of consumer knowledge about the brand and how that knowledge affects consumer behavior. The particular dimensions or aspects of brand knowledge that drive these differences vary, however, by theoretical account and by the particular problem being investigated.

Similarly, the exact mechanism involved also varies according to the brand setting under study.

Because of the primary explanatory role that brand knowledge plays as an antecedent, however, branding effects are highly dependent on the context involved. Highlighting brand-related information can activate certain brand associations and not others in a manner to produce different outcomes. This differential accessibility may be a result of the cues in the marketing environment from the marketing program, or through other means. Branding effects can thus be surprisingly complex. Moreover, there is inherent complexity with brands themselves as brand names, logos, symbols, slogans, etc. all have multiple dimensions, which each can produce differential effects on consumer behavior.

As a result, brand management challenges can be especially thorny. There are a number of input variables that come into play and a number of outcome variables that may be of interest. Only by understanding the totality of the possible antecedents and consequences of brand marketing activity and the possible mechanisms involved can proper analysis be conducted and decisions executed.

Future Research

Although much progress has been made, especially in the last decade or so, a number of important research priorities exist that suggests that branding will be a fertile area for research for years to come (see Shocker et al. (1994) for an historical overview of branding progress and research agenda, as well as Berthon et al. (1999)). The review of the different areas highlights a number of specific research directions in those various research programs. The summary observations above help to suggest a broad research agenda for branding and brand management research. Six potential lines of such research are highlighted here.

Deeper, More Integrated Branding Research

In a general sense, progress in our understanding of branding and brand management will depend critically on three key areas: 1) the development of new conceptual models of brand equity; 2) the calibration of new brand equity measures and metrics; and 3) increased attention to the effects of integrated marketing programs and activities. The reality is that marketing has become increasingly complex as more and more ways to communicate with consumers, distribute products, etc. are being adopted by leading-edge firms. As a consequence, to provide greater managerial insight and guidance, there also need to be more sophisticated conceptual approaches to branding, as well as correspondingly more varied and detailed measures of branding effects. Specifically, research imperatives in these three areas and their rationale are as follows:

1. *Develop richer, more comprehensive, and actionable models of brand equity*. There is still a need to develop more fully articulated models of brand equity that provide greater expository detail and which are useful in aiding managers across a broad range of decision settings. At the same time, there also need to be more parsimonious representations of these models to facilitate their applicability and use. Because of their central role, models that provide a more complete articulation of brand knowledge are especially needed. Along those lines, more work needs to be done to better conceptualize 'brand intangibles' in terms of structure and processes. In all these pursuits, much opportunity exists for multi-disciplinary work that relies on complementary theoretical approaches and perspectives.
2. *Design better 'brand metrics' and more insightful measures of brand equity*. As in virtually any area of marketing, there is a need to develop more insightful, diagnostic measures of branding phenomena. As is often the case, this will clearly involve multiple methods and measures. As suggested above, different decision makers have different interests and therefore will require different types of information. To practicing managers, it is especially important to develop better measures that are able to directly relate marketing activity to actual brand performance. To senior management, it is especially important to develop highly reliable brand valuation techniques and means of assessing returns on brand investments. Of critical importance in that regard is achieving a better understanding of the value and contribution of brands in various joint branding contexts and arrangements, be it with another brand, a person, an event, or whatever.
3. *Understand the effects of the increasingly diverse array of marketing activities and how to optimally integrate these various activities to maximize their collective contribution*. As new, alternative marketing approaches supplement more traditional strategies and tactics – especially in terms of communication and distribution – it will be important to fully understand their effects on consumers and how they should best be designed and implemented. At the same time, there is a critical need to understand how these different marketing activities should best be assembled as part of the marketing program. The advantages and disadvantages of different marketing activities and their potential interactions must be understood so that they can be properly 'mixed and matched' and integrated so that the 'whole can be greater than the sum of the parts.'

Broader Branding Research

It will be especially important for branding research to take a broad perspective and account for all the different forces involved. In particular, it will be important to take a strong internal branding point of view and consider the role of employees and other individuals inside the company in building and managing brand equity. At the same time, it has become harder and harder for companies to 'go it alone' with their brands in the marketplace. As a result, it will also be important to take a strong external point of view and consider how brands can 'borrow' equity in various ways. These realizations suggest the fourth and fifth lines of research.

4. *Consider organizational, 'internal' branding issues.* A relatively neglected area of branding is prescriptive analysis of how different types of firms should best be organized for brand management. Additionally, there needs to be more insight into how to align brand management within the organization and those efforts directed to existing or prospective customers outside the organization.
5. *Obtain greater understanding of how meaning 'transfers' to and from brands.* As brands are often linked with other entities – people, places, companies, brands, events, etc. – it is important to understand how the knowledge about these other entities impacts brand knowledge. In what ways do the images of country-of-origin or country-of-brand, celebrity spokespeople, retail store, etc. change or supplement the image of a brand? At the same time, it is important to understand how the meaning of a brand transfers to other brands, products, etc.

More Relevant Branding Research

Finally, as branding is applied in more and more different settings, brand theory and best practice guidelines need to be refined to reflect the unique realities of those settings, as suggested by the following.

6. *Develop more refined models for specific application areas of branding.* Finally, greater attention must be applied to understanding similarity and differences in branding for different types of application areas. Obviously, one priority area of study is 'virtual' branding and how brands should be built on the Internet. In a general sense, how broadly applicable are the guidelines that emerge from academic research? Which principles are valid and which ones need to be modified or supplemented in some way?

One challenge in pursuing research in this area, as well as the other five areas, will be to achieve the necessary rigor to satisfy the highest academic standards, while also achieving the necessary relevance to satisfy the most demanding industry practitioners.

Notes

1. A number of books, conferences (e.g., see summaries from the Marketing Science Institute and the Advertising Research Foundation), journals (*Journal of Brand Management*), and special issues of journals (*Journal of Marketing,* May 1994) have been devoted to the topic of branding in recent years.

2. Some early, seminal research of special note includes Allison & Uhl (1964); Dichter (1964); Gardner & Levy (1955); Haire (1950); and Levy (1959).

References

Aaker, D.A. (1991) *Managing Brand Equity.* New York: Free Press.

——— (1994) Should you take your brand to where the action is?. *Harvard Business Review*, September/October, 135–43.

——— (1996) *Building Strong Brands.* New York: Free Press.

Aaker, D.A. & Jacobson, R. (1994) The financial information content of perceived quality. *Journal of Marketing Research*, 31 (May), 191–201.

——— (2001) The value relevance of brand attitude in high-technology markets. *Journal of Marketing Research*, 38 (November), 485–93.

Aaker, D.A. & Joachimsthaler, E. (1999) The lure of global branding. *Harvard Business Review*, November/December, 137–44.

——— (2000) *Brand Leadership.* New York: Free Press.

Aaker, D.A. & Keller, K.L. (1990) Consumer evaluations of brand extensions. *Journal of Marketing*, 54 (1), 27–41.

Aaker, J.L. (1997) Dimensions of brand personality. *Journal of Marketing Research*, 34 (August), 347–56.

——— The malleable self: the role of self-expression in persuasion. *Journal of Marketing Research*, 36 (2), 45–57.

Aaker, J.L., Benet-Martinez, V. & Berrocal, J.G. (2001) Consumption symbols as carriers of culture: a study of Japanese and Spanish brand personality constructs. *Journal of Personality and Psychology*, 81 (3), 492–508.

Aaker, J.L., Fournier, S. & Brasel, S.A. (2001) Charting the development of consumer-brand relationships. Working Paper, Stanford Business School.

Achenreiner, G.B. & Rodder John, D. (2001). The meaning of brand names to children: a developmental investigation. *Journal of Consumer Psychology*, forthcoming.

Agrawal, D. (1996) Effects of brand loyalty on advertising and trade promotions: a game theoretic analysis with empirical evidence. *Marketing Science*, 15 (1), 86–108.

Ahluwalia, R. & Gurhan-Canli, Z. (2000) The effects of extension on the family brand name: an accessibility-diagnosticity perspective. *Journal of Consumer Research*, 27 (December), 371–81.

Ahluwalia, R., Burnkrant, R.E. & Unnava, H.R. (2000) Consumer response to negative publicity: the moderating role of commitment. *Journal of Marketing Research*, 37 (May), 203–14.

Allenby, G.M. & Rossi, P.E. (1991) Quality perceptions and asymmetric switching between brands. *Marketing Science*, 10 (3), 185–204.

Allison, R.I. & Uhl, K.P. (1964) Brand identification and perception. *Journal of Marketing Research*, 1 (August), 80–5.

Ambler, T. (2000) *Marketing and the Bottom Line*. London: Pearson Education.

Andrews, J. & Low, G.S. (1998) New but not improved: factors that affect the development of meaningful line extensions. Working Paper Report No. 98–124, November. Cambridge, MA: Marketing Science Institute.

Baldinger, A.L. & Rubinson, J. (1997) In search of the Holy Grail: a rejoinder. *Journal of Advertising Research*, 37 (1), 18–20.

Barich, H. & Kotler, P. (1991) A framework for marketing image management. *Sloan Management Review*, 32 (2), 94–104.

Barone, M.J., Miniard, P.W. & Romeo, J.B. (2000) The influence of positive mood on brand extension Evaluations. *Journal of Consumer Research*, 26 (3), 386–400.

Barth, M.E., Clement, M., Foster, G. & Kasznik, R. (1998) Brand values and capital market valuation. *Review of Accounting Studies*, 3, 41–68.

Barwise, P., Higson, C., Likierman, A. & Marsh, P. (1989) *Accounting for Brands*, London: London Business School.

Belch, George E. (1991) An examination of comparative and noncomparative television commercials: the effects of claim variation and repetition on cognitive responses and message acceptance. *Journal of Marketing Research*, 18, 333–49.

Bello, D.C. & Holbrook, M.B. (1996) Does an absence of brand equity generalize across product classes? *Journal of Business Research*, 34, 125–31.

Bemmaor, A.C. & Mouchoux, D. (1991) Measuring the short-term effect of in-store promotion and retail advertising on brand sales: a factorial experiment. *Journal of Marketing Research*, 28 (May), 202–14.

Bergen, M., Dutta, S. & Shugan, S.M. (1996) Branded variants: a retail perspective. *Journal of Marketing Research*, 33 (February), 9–21.

Berthon, P., Hulbert, J.M. & Pitt, L.F. (1999) Brand management prognostications. *Sloan Management Review*, Winter, 53–65.

Bhattacharya, C.B. & Lodish, L.M. (2000) Towards a system for monitoring brand health from store scanner data. MSI Working Paper, Report No. 00-111.

Biehal, G.J. & Sheinin, D.A. (1998) Managing the brand in a corporate advertising environment: a decision-making framework for brand managers. *Journal of Advertising*, 27 (2), 99–110.

Bijmolt, T.H.A., Wedel, M., Pieters, R.G.M. & DeSarbo, W.S. (1998) Judgments of brand similarity. *International Journal of Research in Marketing*, 15, 249–68.

Blattberg, R.C. & Wisniewski, K.J. (1989) Price-induced patterns of competition. *Marketing Science*, 8 (4), 291–309.

Bong, N.W., Marshall, R. & Keller, K.L. (1999) Measuring brand power: validating a model for optimizing brand equity. *Journal of Product and Brand Management*, 8 (3), 170–84.

Bottomly, P.A. & Holden, S. (2000) The formation of attitudes towards brand extensions: empirical generalizations based on secondary analysis of eight studies. *Journal of Marketing Research*, 38 (November), 494–500 .

Boulding, W., Lee, E. & Staelin, R. (1994) Mastering the marketing mix: do advertising, promotion, and sales force activities lead to differentiation? *Journal of Marketing Research*, 31 (May), 159–72.

Boush, D.M. (1993) How advertising slogans can prime evaluations of brand extensions. *Psychology & Marketing*, 10 (1), 67–78.

——— (1997) Brand name effects on interproduct similarity judgments. *Marketing Letters*, 8 (4), 419–27.

Boush, D.M. & Loken, B. (1991) a process tracing study of brand extension evaluations. *Journal of Marketing Research*, 28 (2), 16–28.

Boush, D., Shipp, S., Loken, B., Gencturk, E., Crockett, S., Kennedy, E., Minshall, B., Misurell, D., Rochford L. & Strobel, J. (1987) Affect generalization to similar and dissimilar brand extensions. *Psychology & Marketing*, 4 (3), 225–37.

Bridges, S., Keller, K.L. & Sood, S. (2000) Explanatory links and the perceived fit of brand extensions: the role of dominant parent brand associations and communication strategies. *Journal of Advertising*, 29 (4), 1–11.

Bristol, T. (1996) Consumers' beliefs resulting from conceptual combinations: conjunctive inferences about brand extensions. *Psychology & Marketing*, 13 (6), 571–89.

Broniarcysyk, S.M. & Alba, J.W. (1994) The importance of the brand in brand extension. *Journal of Marketing Research*, 31 (5), 214–28.

Broniarcysyk, S.M. & Gershoff, A.D. (2001) The reciprocal effects of brand equity and trivial differentiation. Working Paper, Univeristy of Texas at Austin.

Brown, C.L. & Carpenter, G.S. (2000) Why is the trivial important? A reasons based account for the effects of trivial attributes on choice. *Journal of Consumer Research*, 26 (March), 372–85.

Brown, S.P. & Stayman, D.M. (1992) Antecedents and consequences of attitude toward the ad: a meta-analysis. *Journal of Consumer Research*, 19 (June), 34–51.

Brown, T.J. (1998) Corporate associations in marketing: antecedents and consequences. *Corporate Reputation Review*, 1 (3), 215–33.

Brown, T.J. & Dacin, P. (1997) The company and the product: corporate associations and consumer product responses. *Journal of Marketing*, 61 (January), 68–84.

Buchanan, L., Simmons, C.J. & Bickart, B.A. (1999) Brand equity dilution: retailer display and context brand effects. *Journal of Marketing Research*, 36 (8), 345–55.

Bucklin, R.E., Gupta, S. & Han, S. (1995) Brand's eye view of response segmentation in consumer choice behavior. *Journal of Marketing Research*, 32 (February), 66–74.

Calder, B.J. & Sternthal, B. (1980) Television commercial wearout: an information processing view. *Journal of Marketing Research*, 27 (May), 173–86.

Campbell, M. & Keller, K. (2000) The moderating effect of brand knowledge on ad repetition effects. Working Paper, University of Colorado at Boulder.

Carpenter, G.S., Glazer, R. & Nakamoto, K. (1994) Meaningful brands from meaningless differentiation: the dependence on irrelevant attributes. *Journal of Marketing Research*, 31(August), 339–50.

Chakravarti, D., MacInnis, D. & Nakamoto, K. (1990) Product category perceptions, elaborative processing and brand name extension strategies. In *Advances in Consumer Research*, Vol. 17, edited by Marvin Goldberg, Gerald Gorn & Richard Pollay. Provo, UT: Association for Consumer Research, pp. 910–16.

Chattopadyay, A. & Basu, K. (1990) Humor in advertising: the moderating role of prior brand evaluation. *Journal of Marketing Research*, 27 (November), 466–76.

Chaudhuri, A. (1999) Does brand loyalty mediate brand equity outcomes? *Journal of Marketing Theory and Practice*, Spring, 136–46.

Chaudhuri, A. & Holbrook, M.B. (2001) The chain of effects from brand trust and brand affect to brand performance. *Journal of Marketing*, 65 (April), 81–93.

Cohen, D. (1986) Trademark strategy. *Journal of Marketing*, 50 (January), 61–74.

——— (1991) Trademark strategy revisited. *Journal of Marketing*, 55 (July), 46–59.

Cohen, M.A., Eliashberg, J. & Ho, T.H. (1997) An anatomy of a decision-support system for developing and launching line extensions. *Journal of Marketing Research*, 34 (2), 117–29.

Dacin, P. & Smith, D.C. (1994) The effect of brand portfolio characteristics on consumer evaluations of brand extensions. *Journal of Marketing Research*, 31 (5), 229–42.

Dawar, N. (1996) Extensions of broad brands: the role of retrieval in evaluations of fit. *Journal of Consumer Psychology*, 5 (2), 189–207.

Dawar, N. & Anderson, P.F. (1994) The effects of order and direction on multiple brand extensions. *Journal of Business Research*, 30, 119–29.

Dawar, N. & Pillutla, M. (2000) Impact of product-harm crises on brand equity: the moderating role of consumer expectations. *Journal of Marketing Research*, 37 (May), 215–26.

Day, G.S. & Deutscher, T. (1982) Attitudinal predictions of choices of major appliance brands. *Journal of Marketing Research*, 19 (May), 192–8.

DeGraba, P. & Sullivan, M.W. (1995) Spillover effects, cost savings, R&D and the use of brand extensions. *International Journal of Industrial Organization*, 13, 229–48.

Desai, K.K. & Keller, K.L. (2002) The effects of brand expansions and ingredient branding strategies on host brand extendibility. *Journal of Marketing*, 66 (January), 73–93.

Dhar, R. & Simonson, I. (1992) The effect of the focus of comparison on consumer preferences. *Journal of Marketing Research*, 29 (November), 430–40.

Dichter, E. (1964) *Handbook of Consumer Motivations*. New York: McGraw-Hill.

Dillon, W.R., Madden, T.J., Kirmani, A. & Mukherjee (2001) Understanding what's in a brand rating: a model for assessing brand and attribute effects and their relationship to brand equity. *Journal Of Marketing Research*, 38 (November), 415–29.

Dodds, W.B., Monroe, K.B. & Grewal, D. (1991) Effects of price, brand, and store information on buyers' product evaluations. *Journal of Marketing Research*, 28 (August), 307–19.

Doeden, D.L. (1981) How to select a brand name. *Marketing Communications*, November, 58–61.

Dowling, G.R. (1994) *Corporate Reputations*. London: Kogan-Page.

Drumwright, M. (1996) Company advertising with a social dimension: the role of noneconomic criteria. *Journal of Marketing*, 60 (October), 71–87.

Duke, C.R. (1995) Exploratory comparisons of alternative memory measures for brand name. *Psychology & Marketing*, 12 (1), 19–36.

Dyson, P., Farr, A. & Hollis, N. (1997) What does the marketing team need, description or prescription? *Journal of Advertising Research*, 37 (1), 13–17.

Ehrenberg, A.S.C. (1997) In search of Holy Grails: two comments. *Journal of Advertising Research*, 37 (1), 9–12.

Ehrenberg, A.S.C., Barnard, N. & Scriven, J. (1997) Differentiation or salience. *Journal of Advertising Research*, 37 (6), 82–91.

Ehrenberg, A.S.C., Goodhardt, J. & Barwise, T.P. (1990) Double jeopardy revisited. *Journal of Marketing*, 54 (3), 82–91.

Epstein, M.J. & Westbrook, R.A. (2001) Linking actions to profits in strategic decision making. *MIT Sloan Management Review*, Spring, 39–49.

Erdem, T. (1998a) An empirical analysis of umbrella branding. *Journal of Marketing Research*, 35 (8), 339–51.

——— (1998b) Brand equity as a signaling phenomenon. *Journal of Consumer Psychology*, 7 (2), 131–57.

Fader, P.S. & Schmittlein, D.C. (1993) Excess behavioral loyalty for high-share brands: deviations from the Dirichlet Model for repeat purchasing. *Journal of Marketing Research*, 30 (11), 478–93.

Farquhar, P.H. (1989) Managing brand equity. *Marketing Research*, 1 (September), 24–33.

Farquhar, P.H. & Herr, P.M. (1992) The dual structure of brand associations. In *Brand Equity and Advertising: Advertising's Role in Building Strong Brands*, edited by David A. Aaker & Alexander L. Biel. Hillsdale, NJ: Lawrence Erlbaum Associates, pp. 263–77.

Farquhar, P.H., Han, J.Y., Herr, P.M. & Ijiri, Y. (1992) Strategies for leveraging master brands. *Marketing Research*, 4 (September), 32–43.

Feinberg, F.M., Kahn, B.E. & McAllister, L. (1992) Market share response when consumers seek variety. *Journal of Marketing Research*, 29 (May), 227–37.

Feldwick, P. (1996) Do we really need 'Brand Equity'? *The Journal of Brand Management*, 4 (1), 9–28.

Fournier, S.M. (1998) Consumers and their brands: developing relationship theory in consumer research. *Journal of Consumer Research*, 24 (3), 343–73.

——— (2000) Dimensioning brand relationships using brand relationship quality. Presentation at the Association for Consumer Research annual conference.

Fournier, S.M. & Yao, J.L. (1997) Reviving brand loyalty: a reconceptualization within the framework of consumer – brand relationships. *International Journal of Research in Marketing*, 14, 451–72.

Fournier, S.M., Dobscha, S. & Mick, S. (1998) Preventing the premature death of relationship marketing. *Harvard Business Review*, January–February, 42–51.

Foxman, E.R., Berger, P.W. & Cote, J.A. (1992) Consumer brand confusion: a conceptual framework. *Psychology & Marketing*, 9 (2), 123–41.

Gardner, B.B. & Levy, S.J. (1955) The product and the brand. *Harvard Business Review*, March–April, 33–9.

Golder, P.N. (2000) Historical method in marketing research with new evidence on long-term stability. *Journal of Marketing Research*, 37 (May), 156–72.

Graeff, T.R. (1996) Image congruence effects on product evaluations: the role of self-monitoring and public/private consumption. *Psychology & Marketing*, 13 (5), 481–99.

——— (1997) Consumption situations and the effects of brand image on consumers' brand evaluations. *Psychology & Marketing*, 14 (1), 49–70.

Grover, R. & Srinivasan, V. (1992) Evaluating the multiple effects of retail promotions on brand loyal and brand switching segments. *Journal of Marketing Research*, 29 (February), 76–89.

Gürhan-Canli, Z. & Durairaj, M. (1998) 'The effects of extensions on brand name dilution and enhancement. *Journal of Marketing Research*, 35 (11), 464–73.

Haire, Mason (1950) Projective techniques in marketing research. *Journal of Marketing*, April, 649–56.

Han, J.K. & Schmitt, B.H. (1997) Product category dynamics and corporate identity in brand extensions: a comparison of Hong Kong and US consumers. *Journal of International Marketing*, 5 (1), 77–92.

Hardie, B.G.S., Lodish, L.M., Kilmer J.V., Beatty, D.R., Farris, P.W., Biel, A.L., Wicke, L.S., Balson, J.B. & Aaker, D.A. (1994). The logic of product line decisions. *Harvard Business Review*, November–December, 53–62.

Hartman, C.L., Price, L.L. & Duncan, C.P. (1990) Consumer evaluation of franchise extension products: a categorization processing perspective. *Advances in Consumer Research*, 17, 120–6.

Harvey, M., Rothe, J.T. & Lucas, L.A. (1998) The 'trade dress' controversy: a case of strategic cross-brand cannibalization. *Journal of Marketing Theory and Practice*, Spring, 1–15.

Heath, T.B., Chatterjee, S. & Russo, K. (1990) Using the phonemes of brand names to symbolize brand attributes. In *The AMA Educator's Proceedings: Enhancing Knowledge Development in Marketing*, edited by William Bearden & A. Parasuraman. Chicago: American Marketing Association.

Hem, L.E. & Iverson, N.M. (2001) Context effects in brand extensions: implications for evaluations. Working Paper, Norwegian School of Economics and Business Administration.

Henderson, G.R., Iacobucci, D. & Calder, B.J. (1998) Brand diagnostics: mapping branding effects using consumer associative networks. *European Journal of Operational Research*, 111, 306–27.

Henderson, P.W. & Cote, J.A. (1998) Guidelines for selecting or modifying logos. *Journal of Marketing*, 62 (2), 14–30.

Herr, P.M., Farquhar, P.H. & Fazio, R.H. (1996) Impact of dominance and relatedness on brand extensions. *Journal of Consumer Psychology*, 5 (2), 135–59.

Hoeffler, S. & Keller, K.L. (2001) The marketing advantages of strong brands. Working Paper, University of North Carolina at Chapel Hill.

Holbrook, Morris B. (1992) Product quality, attributes, and brand name as determinants of price: the case of consumer electronics. *marketing Letters*, 3 (1), 71–83.

Hutchinson, J.W., Raman, K. & Mantrala, M.K. (1994) Finding choice alternatives in memory: probability models of brand name recall. *Journal of Marketing Research*, 31 (1), 441–61.

Janiszewski, Chris & Meyvis, Tom (2001) Effects of brand logo complexity, repetition, and spacing on processing fluency and judgement. *Journal of Consumer Research*, 28 (June), 18–32.

Janiszewski, C. & van Osselaer, S.M.J. (2000) A connectionist model of brand-quality associations. *Journal of Marketing Research*, 37 (August), 331–50.

Jap, S.D. (1993) An examination of the effects of multiple brand extensions on the brand concept. *Advances in Consumer Research*, 20, 607-–11.

Joachimsthaler, E. & Aaker, D.A. (1997) Building brands without mass media. *Harvard Business Review*, September–October, 135–43.

Joiner, C. & Loken, B. (1998) The inclusion effect and category-based induction: theory and application to brand categories. *Journal of Consumer Psychology*, 7 (2), 101–29.

Journal of Advertising (1995) Special issue on green advertising.

Kamakura, W.A. & Russell, G.J. (1993) Measuring brand value with scanner data. *International Journal of Research in Marketing*, 10, 9–22.

Kamins, M.A. & Marks, L.J. (1991) The perception of kosher as a third party certification claim in advertising for familiar and unknown brands. *Journal of Academy of Marketing Science*, 19, 3 (Summer), 177–85.

Kanetkar, V., Weinberg, C.B. & Weiss, D.L. (1992) Price sensitivity and television advertising exposures: some empirical findings. *Marketing Science*, 11 (Fall), 359–71.

Kapferer, J. (1994) *Strategic Brand Management*, New York: Free Press.

Kapferer, J. (1995) Stealing brand equity: measuring perceptual confusion between national brands and 'copycat' own-label products. *Marketing and Research Today*, May, 96–103.

Kardes, F. & Allen, C. (1990) Perceived variability and inferences about brand extension. In *Advances in Consumer Research*, edited by Rebecca H. Holman & Michael R. Solomon. Provo, UT: Association for Consumer Research, pp. 392–8.

Keller, K.L. (1993) Conceptualizing, measuring, and managing customer-based brand equity. *Journal of Marketing*, 57 (January), 1–22.

——— (1998) *Strategic Brand Management*. Upper Saddle River, NJ: Prentice-Hall.

——— (1999a) Effective long-run brand management: brand reinforcement and revitalization strategies. *California Management Review*, 41 (3), 102–24.

——— (1999b) Designing and implementing branding strategies. *Journal of Brand Management*, 6 (5), 315–31.

——— (2000) The brand report card. *Harvard Business Review*, January–February, 147–57.

——— (2001) Building customer-based brand equity: a blueprint for creating strong brands. *Marketing Management*, July–August, 15–19.

Keller, K.L. & Aaker, D.A. (1992) The effects of sequential introduction of brand extensions. *Journal of Marketing Research*, 29 (2), 35–50.

——— (1998) Corporate-level marketing: the impact of credibility on a company's brand extensions. *Corporate Reputation Review*, 1 (August), 356–78.

Keller, K.L. & Lehmann, D.R. (2001) The brand value chain: optimizing strategic and financial brand performance. Working Paper, Dartmouth College.

Keller, K.L. & Sood, S. (2001a) The effects of product experience and branding strategies on brand evaluations. Working Paper, University of California at Los Angles.

——— (2001b) The effects of alternative sub-branding strategies on consumer brand evaluations. Working Paper, University of California at Los Angles.

Keller, K.L., Heckler, S. & Houston, M.J. (1998) The effects of brand name suggestiveness on advertising recall. *Journal of Marketing*, 62 (January), 48–57.

Kent, R.J. & Allen, C.T. (1994) Competitive interference effects in consumer memory for advertising: the role of brand familiarity. *Journal of Marketing*, 58 (July), 97–105.

Kerin, R.A., Kalyanaram, G. & Howard, D.J. (1996) Product hierarchy and brand strategy influences on the order of entry effect for consumer packaged goods. *Journal of Product Innovation Management*, 13, 21–34.

Kirmani, A., Sood, S. & Bridges, S. (1999) The ownership effect in consumer responses to brand line stretches. *Journal of Marketing*, 63 (1), 88–101.

Klink, R.R. (2000) Creating brand names with meaning: the use of sound symbolism. *Marketing Letters*, 11,1, 5–20.

Klink, R.R. & Smith D.C. (2001) Threats to the external validity of brand extension research. *Journal of Marketing*, 38 (August), 326–35.

Kohli, C. & LaBahn, D.W. (1997) Creating effective brand names: a study of the naming process. *Journal of Advertising Research*, January/February, 67–75.

Kotler, P. (2000) *Marketing Management*. Upper Saddle River, NJ: Prentice-Hall.

Krishnamurthi, L. & Raj, S.P. (1991) An empirical analysis of the relationship between brand loyalty and consumer price elasticity. *Marketing Science*, 10 (2), 172–83.

Krishnan, H.S. (1996) Characteristics of memory associations: a consumer-based brand equity perspective. *International Journal of Research in Marketing*, 13, 389–405.

Laczniak, R.N., DeCarlo, T.E. & Ramaswami, S.N. (2001) Consumers' responses to negative word-of-mouth communication: an attribution theory perspective. *Journal of Consumer Psychology*, 11 (1), 57–73.

——— (1999) Managing brand portfolios: why leaders do what they do. *Journal of Advertising Research*, January/February, 51–65.

LaForet, S. & Saunders, J. (1994) Managing brand portfolios: how the leaders do it. *Journal of Advertising Research*, September/October, 64–76.

Lal, R. & Narasimhan, C. (1996) The inverse relationship between manufacturer and retailer margins: a theory. *Marketing Science*, (15) 2, 132–51.

Lane, V.R. (2000) The impact of ad repetition and ad content on consumer perceptions of incongruent extensions. *Journal of Marketing*, 64 (4), 80–91.

Lane, V.R. & Jacobson, R. (1995) stock market reactions to brand extension announcements: the effects of brand attitude and familiarity. *Journal of Marketing*, 59 (1), 63–77.

——— (1997) The reciprocal impact of brand leveraging: feedback effects from brand extension evaluation to brand evaluation. *Marketing Letters*, 8 (3), 261–71.

Laroche, M., Kim, C. & Zhou, L. (1996) Brand familiarity and confidence as determinants of purchase intention: an empirical test in a multiple brand context. *Journal of Business Research*, 37, 115–20.

Lassar, W., Mittal, B. & Sharma, A. (1995) Measuring customer-based brand equity. *Journal of Consumer Marketing*, 12 (4), 11–19.

Leclerc, F., Schmitt, B.H. & Dube, L. (1994) Foreign branding and its effects on product perceptions and attitudes. *Journal of Marketing Research*, 31 (5), 263–70.

Lee, M., Lee, J. & Kamakura, W.A. (1996) Consumer evaluations of line extensions: a conjoint approach. *Advances in Consumer Research*, 23, 289–95.

Levin, I.P. & Levin, A.M. (2000) Modeling the role of brand alliances in the assimilation of product evaluations. *Journal of Consumer Psychology*, 9 (1), 43–52.

Levy, S.J. (1959) Symbols for sale. *Harvard Business Review*, 37 (March–April), 117–24.

——— (1999) *Brands, Consumers, Symbols, and Research: Sydney J. Levy on Marketing*. Thousand Oaks, CA: Sage Publications.

Loken, B. & Roedder John, D. (1993) Diluting brand beliefs. When do brand extensions have a negative impact? *Journal of Marketing*, 57 (7), 71–84.

Loken B., Ross, I. & Hinkle, R. (1986) Consumer confusion of 'origin' and brand similarity perceptions. *Journal of Public Policy and Marketing*,

Machleit, K.A., Allen, C.T. & Madden, T.J. (1993) The mature brand and brand interest: an alternative consequence of ad-evoked affect. *Journal of Marketing*, 57 (October), 72–82.

Mahajan, V., Rao, V. & Srivastava, R.K. (1994) An approach to assess the importance of brand equity in acquisition decisions. *Journal of Product Innovation Management*, 11, 221–35.

Martin, I.M. & Stewart, D.W. (2001) The differential impact of goal congruency on attitudes, intentions, and the transfer of brand equity. *Journal of Marketing Research*, 38 (November), 471–84.

McAlexander, James H., Schouten, John W. & Koenig, Harold F. (2002) Building brand community. *Journal of Marketing*, 66 (January), 38–54.

McCarthy, M.S. & Norris, D.G. (1999) Improving competitive position using branded ingredients. *Journal of Product & Brand Management*, 8 (4), 267–85.

McCarthy, M.S., Heath, T.B. & Milberg, M.J. (2001) New brands versus brand extensions, attitudes versus choice: experimental evidence for theory & practice. *Marketing Letters*, 12 (February), 75–90.

McCracken, G. (1986) Culture and consumption: a theoretical account of the structure and movement of the cultural meaning of consumer goods. *Journal of Consumer Research*, 13, 71–83.

——— (1993) The value of the brand: an anthropological perspective. In *Brand Equity and Advertising: Advertising's Role on Building Strong Brands*, edited by D. Aaker & A. Biel. Hillsdale, NJ: Lawrence Erlbaum Assocs., pp. 125–39.

Menon, A. & Menon, A. (1997) Enviropreneurial marketing strategy: the emergence of corporate environmentalism as market strategy. *Journal of Marketing*, 61 (January), 51–67.

Meyers-Levy, J. (1989) The Influence of a brand name's association set size and word frequency on brand memory. *Journal of Consumer Research*, 16 (September); 197–207.

Meyers-Levy, J., Louie, T.A. & Curren, M.T. (1994) How does the congruity of brand names affect evaluations of brand name extensions? *Journal of Applied Psychology*, 79 (1), 46–53.

Milberg, S.J., Park, C.W. & McCarthy, M.S. (1997) Managing negative feedback effects associated with brand extensions: the impact of alternative branding strategies. *Journal of Consumer Psychology*, 6 (2), 119–40.

Montgomery, C.A. & Wernerfelt, B. (1992) Risk reduction and umbrella advertising. *Journal of Business*, 65 (1), 31–50.

Montgomery, D.B. (1975) New product distribution: an analysis of supermarket buyer decisions. *Journal of Marketing Research*, 12 (August), 255–64.

Morrin, M. (1999) The impact of brand extensions on parent brand memory structures and retrieval processes. *Journal of Marketing Research*, 36 (4), 517–25.

Muniz, A.M. Jr. & O'Guinn, T.C. (2000) Brand community. *Journal of Consumer Research*, 27 (March), 412–32.

Muthukrishnan, A.V. & Weitz, B.A. (1990) Role of product knowledge in brand extensions. In *Advances in Consumer Research*, edited by Rebecca H. Holman & Michael R. Solomon. Provo, UT: Association for Consumer Research, pp. 407–13.

Nguyen, L.T. & Roedder John, D. (2001) 'Abercrombie & Fitch – That's Me': brand names in children's self concepts. Working Paper, University of Minnesota.

Norris, D.G. (1992) Ingredient branding: a strategy option with multiple beneficiaries. *Journal of Consumer Marketing*, 9 (Summer), 19–31.

Oakenfull, Gillian & Gelb, Betsy (1996) Research-based advertising to preserve brand equity but avoid 'Genericide'. *Journal of Advertising Research*, September/October, 65–72.

Paiva, T.M. & Costa, J.A. (1993) The winning number: consumer perceptions of alpha-numeric brand names. *Journal of Marketing*, 57 (7), 85–98.

Pan, Y. & Schmitt, B. (1996) Language and brand attitudes: impact of script and sound matching in Chinese and English. *Journal of Consumer Psychology*, 5 (3), 263–77.

Park, C.S. & Srinivasan, V. (1994) A survey-based method for measuring and understanding brand equity and its extendibility. *Journal of Marketing Research*, 31 (5), 271–88.

Park, C.W., Jaworski, B.J. & MacInnis, D.J. (1986) Strategic brand concept-image management. *Journal of Marketing*, 50 (10), 135–45.

Park, C.W., Jun, S.Y. & Shocker, A.D. (1996) Composite branding alliances: an investigation of extension and feedback effects. *Journal of Marketing Research*, 33 (11), 453–66.

Park, C.W., Milberg, S. & Lawson, R. (1991) Evaluation of brand extensions: the role of product feature similarity and brand concept consistency. *Journal of Consumer Research*, 18 (9), 185–93.

Peterson, R.A. & Ross, I. (1972) How to name new brands. *Journal of Advertising Research*, 12 (6), 29–34.

Putsis, W.P. Jr. & Bayus, B.L. (2001) An empirical analysis of firms' product line decisions. *Journal of Marketing Research*, 38 (February), 110–18.

Quelch, J.A. & Kenny, D. (1994) Extend profits, not product lines. *Harvard Business Review*, September–October, 153–60.

Raj, S.P. (1982) The effects of advertising on high and low loyalty consumer segments. *Journal of Consumer Research*, 9 (June), 77–89.

Randall, T., Ulrich, K. & Reibstein, D. (1998) Brand equity and vertical product line extent. *Marketing Science*, 17 (4), 356–79.

Rangaswamy, A., Burke, R.R. & Oliva, T.A. (1993) Brand equity and the extendibility of Brand Names. *International Journal of Research in Marketing*, 10 (3), 61–75.

Rao, Akshay R. (1997) Strategic brand alliances. *The Journal of Brand Management*, 5 (2), 111–19.

Rao, Akshay R. & Monroe, K.B. (1989) The effects of price, brand name, and store name on buyers' perceptions of product quality: an integrative review. *Journal of Marketing Research*, 26 (August), 351–7.

Rao, A.R., Qu, L. & Ruekert, R.W. (1999) Signaling unobservable product quality through a brand ally. *Journal of Marketing Research*, May, 258–68.

Ratneshwar, S., Mick, D.G. & Huffman, C. (eds.) (2000) *The Why of Consumption: Contemporary Perspectives on Consumer Motives, Goals and Desires*. London: Routledge.

Reddy, S.K., Holak, S.L. & Bhat, S. (1994) To extend or not to extend: success determinants of line extensions. *Journal of Marketing Research*, 31 (5), 243–62.

Richins, M.L. (1994) Valuing things: the public and private meanings of possessions. *Journal of Consumer Research*, 21 (December), 504–21.

Robertson, K.R. (1989) Strategically desirable brand name characteristics. *Journal of Consumer Marketing*, 6 (4), 61–71.

Roedder John, D., Loken, B. & Joiner, C. (1998) The negative impact of extensions: can flagship products be diluted? *Journal of Marketing*, 62 (January), 19–32.

Romeo, J.B. (1991) The effect of negative information on the evaluations of brand extensions and the family brand. *Advances in Consumer Research*, 18, 399–406.

Russell, G.J., & Kamakura, W.J. (1994) Understanding brand competition using micro and macro scanner data. *Journal of Marketing Research*, 31 (May), 289–303.

Samu, S., Krishnan, H.S. & Smith R.E. (1999) Using advertising alliances for new product introduction: interactions between product complementarity and promotional strategies. *Journal of Marketing*, 63 (1), 57–74.

Sappington, D.E.M. & Wernerfelt, B. (1985) To brand or not to brand? a theoretical and empirical question. *Journal of Business*, 58 (3), 279–93.

Sawyer, A.G. (1981) Repetition, cognitive response, and persuasion. In *Cognitive Responses to Persuasion*, edited by R. Petty, T. Ostrum & T. Brock, Hillsdale, NS: Erlbaum, pp. 237–62.

Schmitt, B.H. (1997) 'Superficial out of profundity': the branding of customer experiences. *Journal of Brand Management*, 5 (2), 92–8.

——— (1999a) Experiential marketing. *Journal of Marketing Management*, 15, 53–67.

——— (1999b) *Experiential Marketing. How to Get Customers to Sense, Feel, Think, Act and Relate to Your Company and Brands*. New York: Free Press.

Schmitt, B.H. & Dubé, L. (1992) Contextualized representations of brand extensions: are feature lists or frames the basic components of consumer cognition? *Marketing Letters*, 3 (2), 115–26.

Schmitt, B.H. & Simonson, A. (1997) *Marketing Aesthetics: The Strategic Management of Brands, Identity and Image*. New York: Free Press.

Schmitt, B.H., Pan, Y. & Tavassoli, N.T. (1994) Language and consumer memory: the impact of linguistic differences between Chinese and English. *Journal of Consumer Research*, 21 (12), 419–31.

Schumann, D.W., Hathcote, J.M. & West, S. (1991) Corporate advertising in America: a review of published studies on use, measurement, and effectiveness. *Journal of Advertising*, 20 (September), 36–56.

Schouten, J.W. & McAlexander, J.H. (1995) Subcultures of consumption: an ethnography of the new bikers. *Journal of Consumer Research*, 22 (6), 43–61.

Sen, S. (1999) The effects of brand name suggestiveness and decision goal on the development of brand knowledge. *Journal of Consumer Psychology*, 8 (4), 431–55.

Sen, S. & Bhattacharya, C.B. (2001) Does doing good always lead to doing better? consumer reactions to corporate social responsibility. *Journal of Marketing Research*, 38 (May), 225–43.

Sethuraman, R. (1996) A model of how discounting high-priced brands affects the sales of low-priced brands. *Journal of Marketing Research*, 33 (November), 399–409.

Sheinin, D.A. (1998) Sub-brand evaluation and use versus brand extension. *The Journal of Brand Management*, 6 (2), 113–22.

Shocker, A.D., Srivastava, R.K. & Ruekert, R.W. (1994) Challenges and opportunities facing brand management: an introduction to the Special Issue. *Journal of Marketing Research*, 31 (5), 149–58.

Shugan, Steven M. (1989) Branded variants. In *1989 AMA Educators Proceedings*, edited by Bloom et al. pp. 33–8.

Simon, Carol J. & Sullivan, Mary W. (1993) Measurement and determinants of brand equity: a financial approach. *Marketing Science*, 12 (1), 28–52.

Simon, H. (1979) Dynamics of price elasticity and brand life cycles: an empirical study. *Journal of Marketing Research*, 16 (November), 439–52.

Simonin, B.L. & Ruth, J.A. (1998) Is a company known by the company it keeps? Assessing the spillover effects of brand alliances on consumer brand attitudes. *Journal of Marketing Research*, 35 (2), 30–42.

Simonson, A.F. (1995) How and when do trademarks dilute: a behavioral framework to judge 'likelihood' of dilution. *The Trademark Reporter*, 83, 149–74.

Simonson, I. (1994) Trademark infringement from the buyer perspective, conceptual analysis and measurement implications. *Journal of Public Policy and Marketing*, 13 (2), 181–99.

Simonson, I., Huber, J. & Payne, J. (1988) The relationship between prior brand knowledge and information acquisition order. *Journal of Consumer Research*, 14 (March), 566–78.

Sivakumar K. & Raj, S.P. (1997) Quality tier competition: how price change influences brand choice and category choice. *Journal of Marketing*, 61 (July), 71–84.

Smith, D.C. (1992) Brand extensions and advertising efficiency: what can and cannot be expected. *Journal of Advertising Research*, November–December, 11–20.

Smith, D.C. & Andrews, Jonlee (1995) Rethinking the effect of perceived fit on customers' evaluations of new products. *Journal of the Academy of Marketing Science*, 23 (1), 4–14.

Smith, D.C. & Park, C.W. (1992) The effects of brand extensions on market share and advertising efficiency. *Journal of Marketing Research*, 29 (August), 296–313.

Smith, R.E. (1993) Integrating information from advertising and trial. *Journal of Marketing Research*, 30 (May), 204–19.
Solomon, M.R. & Englis, B.G. (1992) Consumption constellations: implications for integrated marketing communications. In *Integrated Marketing Communications*, edited by Jeri Moore & Esther Thorson. Hillsdale, NJ: Erlbaum, pp, 65–86.
Srinivasan, V. (1979) Network models for estimating brand-specific effects in multi-attribute marketing models. *Management Science*, 25 (1), 11–21.
Srivastava, R.K., Shervani, T.A. & Fahey, L. (1998) Market-based assets and shareholder value. *Journal of Marketing*, 62 (1), 2–18.
Sternthal, Brain & Craig, C.S. (1984) *Consumer Behavior: An Information Processing Perspective*. Englewood Cliffs, NJ: Prentice-Hall.
Stewart, D.W. & Furse, David H. (1986) *Effective Television Advertising: A Study of 1000 Commercials*. Lexington, MA: D.C. Heath and Co.
Sullivan, M.W. (1990) Measuring image spillovers in umbrella-branded products. *The Journal of Business*, 63 (3), 309–29.
——— (1992) Brand extensions: when to use them. *Management Science*, 38 (6), 793–806.
——— (1998) How brand names affect the demand for twin automobiles. *Journal of Marketing Research*, 35 (5), 154–65.
——— (2001) How many trademarks does it take to protect a brand? The optimal number of trademarks, branding strategy, and brand performance. Working Paper, US Department of Justice.
Swait, J., Erdem, T., Louviere, J. & Dubelar, C. (1993) The equalization price: a measure of consumer-perceived brand equity. *International Journal of Research in Marketing*, 10, 23–45.
Swaminathan, V., Fox, R.J. & Reddy, S.K. (2001) The impact of brand extension introduction on choice. *Journal of Marketing*, 65 (October), 1–15.
Teas, R. Kenneth & Grapentine, Terry H. (1996) Demystifying brand equity. *Marketing Research*, 8 (2), 25–29.
Thakor, M.V. & Pacheco, B.G. (1997) Foreign branding and its effect on product perceptions and attitudes: a replication and extension in a multicultural setting. *Journal of Marketing Theory and Practice*, Winter, 15–30.
van Osselaer, S.M.J. & Alba, J.W. Consumer Learning and Brand Equity. *Journal of Consumer Research*, 27 (June), 1–16.
van Osselaer, S.M.J. & Janiszewski, C. (2001) Two ways of learning brand associations. *Journal of Consumer Research*, 28 (September), 202–23.
Vanden Bergh, B.G., Adler, K. & Oliver, L. (1987) Linguistic distinction among top brand names. *Journal of Advertising Research*, August/September, 39–44.
Vanden Bergh, B.G., Collins, J., Schultz, M. & Adler, K. (1984) Sound advice on brand names. *Journalism Quarterly*, 61 (4), 835–40.
Varadarajan, P.R. & Menon, M. (1988) Cause-related marketing: a coalignment of marketing strategy and corporate philanthropy. *Journal of Marketing*, 52 (July), 58–74.
Venkatesh, R. & Mahajan, V. (1997) Products with branded components: an approach for premium pricing and partner selection. *Marketing Science*, 16 (2), 146–65.
Voss, K.E. & Tansuhaj, P. (1999) A consumer perspective on foreign market entry: building brands through brand alliances. *Journal of International Consumer Marketing*, 11 (2), 39–58.
Wänke, M., Bless, H. & Schwarz, N. (1998) Context effects in product line extensions: context is not destiny. *Journal of Consumer Psychology*, 7 (4), 299–322.
Weinburger, M.G. & Gulas, C. (1992) The impact of humor in advertising: a review. *Journal of Advertising*, 21 (4), 35–60.
Wernerfelt, B. (1988) Umbrella branding as a signal of new product quality: an example of signaling by posting a bond. *Rand Journal of Economics*, 19(3), 458–66.
Yoo, B., Donthu, N. & Lee, S. (2000) An examination of selected marketing mix elements and brand equity. *Journal of the Academy of Marketing Science*, 28 (2), 195–211.
Yorkston, E.A. (2000) Construction through deconstruction: a compositional approach to the development of brand names. Ph.D. dissertation, New York University.
Yorkston, E.A. & Menon, G. (2001) A sound idea: phonetic effects of brand names on consumer judgments. Working Paper, Marshall School of Business, University of Southern California.
Zaichowsky, J. (1995) *Defending Your Brand Against Imitation.* Westpoint, CO: Quorom Books.
Zaltman, G. & Coulter, R.H. (1995a) Seeing the voice of the customer: metaphor-based advertising research. *Journal of Advertising Research*, 35 (4), 35–51.
——— (1995b) Seeing the voice of the customer: the Zaltman Metaphor Elicitation Technique. *Marketing Science Institute Report Number 93–114.*
Zhang, S. & Schmitt, B.H. (2001) Creating local brands in multilingual international markets. *Journal of Marketing Research*, 38 (August), 313–25.
Zhang, S. & Sood, S. (2001) 'Deep' and 'surface' cues: brand extension evaluations by children and adults. *Journal of Consumer Research*, 29 (June), 129–41.
Zinkhan, G.M. & Martin, C.R. Jr. (1987) New brand names and inferential beliefs: some insights on naming new products. *Journal of Business Research*, 15, 157–72.

8

Product Development – Managing a Dispersed Process

ELY DAHAN and JOHN R. HAUSER

The Challenge of a Dispersed Product Development Process

New product development has a long history in marketing, including research on customer preferences (Green & Wind, 1975; Green & Srinivasan, 1990; Srinivasan & Shocker, 1973), product positioning and segmentation (Currim, 1981, Green & Krieger, 1989a, 1989b; Green & Rao, 1972; Hauser & Koppelman, 1979), product forecasting (Bass, 1969; Jamieson & Bass, 1989; Kalwani & Silk, 1982; Mahajan & Wind, 1986, 1988; McFadden, 1974; Morrison, 1979), and test marketing (Urban, 1970; Urban et al., 1990). The applications have been many and varied and have led to a deeper understanding of how to gather and use information about the customer in the design, testing, launch, and management of new products. Many integrative texts on product development have been published to review the issues, the methods, and the applications from a marketing perspective (Dolan, 1993; Lehmann & Winer, 1994; Moore & Pessemier, 1993; Urban & Hauser, 1993; Wind, 1982).

Marketing, with its focus on the customer, has had great success. Tools such as conjoint analysis, voice-of-the-customer analysis, perceptual mapping, intention scaling, portfolio optimization, and lifecycle forecasting are now in common use. Firms that continuously and efficiently generate new products that are in tune with their end customers' needs and wants are more likely to thrive (Griffin & Page, 1996). Direct communication with customers allows firms to learn from customers and tailor products to their requirements.

In parallel with the development of prescriptive tools, researchers have studied the correlates of new product success, identifying communication between marketing and engineering as one of the most important factors in success (Cooper, 1984a, 1984b; Cooper & Kleinschmidt, 1987; Dougherty, 1989; Griffin & Hauser, 1996; Souder, 1987, 1988). As a result, organizational process tools such as cross-functional teams (Kuczmarski, 1992; Souder, 1980), quality function deployment (Hauser & Clausing, 1988), and co-location (Allen, 1986) were developed to promote the sharing of ideas and the close integration of engineering decisions with customer needs. Process-oriented textbooks now routinely consider marketing issues and the need to integrate engineering with the marketing function (McGrath, 1996; Ulrich & Eppinger, 2000). Clearly, the ultimate effectiveness of the tools discussed in this chapter is moderated by the incentives, behavior and effectiveness of the people implementing those tools in the organization.

As we move into the twenty-first century, new challenges and opportunities are arising driven by global markets, global competition, the global dispersion of engineering talent, and the advent of new information and communication technologies such as electronic mail, the world-wide web, and increased electronic bandwidth. The new vision of product development is that of a highly disaggregated process, with people and organizations spread throughout the world (Holmes, 1999). At the same time products are becoming increasing complex with typical electro-mechanical products requiring close to a million engineering decisions to bring them to market (Eppinger, 1998; Eppinger et al., 1994). Even software products such as Microsoft Word or Netscape require disaggregated, but coordinated processes involving hundreds of developers (Cusumano & Selby, 1995; Cusumano & Yoffie, 1998). Competitive pressures mean that time-to-market has been proposed as key to new product success as has marketing's orientation toward customer needs and customer satisfaction (Smith & Reinertsen, 1998). Because products are marketed throughout the world, firms face the tradeoff between standardization for cost reduction and variety for satisfying a broad set of customers. This has expanded the need for marketing to look beyond the single product to focus on the product platform (Moore et al., 1999).

In this chapter we look at the state of the art in research that addresses these new challenges for the marketing community. We begin with an overview of the integrated end-to-end product development process, indicating marketing's role in addressing the challenges of developing profitable products (and platforms). The remainder of the chapter addresses specific research challenges relating to the end-to-end process. We organize the remaining sections around the various stages of development, recognizing that in practice, these stages are often iterative and/or integrated. Specifically we address, in order, the strategic end-to-end product development process, the fuzzy front end of customer opportunity identification and idea generation, the process of concept selection and detailed design and engineering of products and processes, the testing phase where concepts and products are prototyped and tested, and the enterprise and organizational strategy necessary for success. We close with a vision of the future of research on product development.

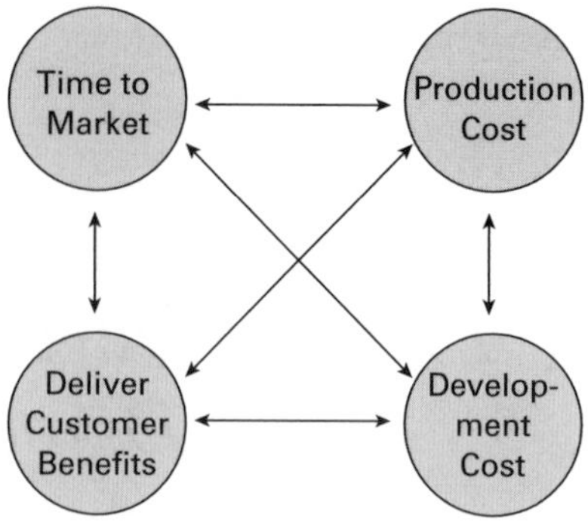

Figure 8.1 *Tradeoffs in New Product Development (Based on Smith & Reinertsen, 1998)*

Product Development – End-to-End

In the late 1980s and early 1990s a marketing focus on product development stressed customer satisfaction. Researchers in marketing believed that the key to success was a better understanding of the voice of the customer and a better ability to link that voice to the engineering decisions that are made in launching a product. For example, Menezes (1994) documents a case where Xerox moved from a focus on ROA and market share to a focus on customer satisfaction. Important research during that period included new ways to understand the voice of the customer (Griffin & Hauser, 1993), new ways to develop optimal product profiles in the context of competition (Green & Krieger, 1989a, 1991), more efficient preference measurements (Srinivasan, 1988), and the ability to handle larger, more complex customer information (Wind et al., 1989). At the same time the quality movement focused product development engineering on improved reliability through continuous improvement, such as Kaizen methods (Imai, 1986), statistical quality control (Deming, 1986), modified experimental design (Taguchi, 1987), and design for manufacturing (Boothroyd & Dewhurst, 1994). There were many successes including a turnaround of the major US automobile manufacturers. Many engineers came to believe that the key to success was a better quality product.

Also during that time both marketing and engineering realized that time-to-market was critical. Marketing saw the phenomenon as that of rewards to early entrants (Golder & Tellis, 1993; Urban et al., 1986) while engineering saw, among other things, the lost profits due to rework and delays (Smith & Reinertsen, 1998). Both customer satisfaction and time-to-market became panaceas that would guarantee success and profitability, if only the firm could achieve them.

An Integrated Process

Today, both industry and academia view successful product development as an integrated process that must overcome many tradeoffs, as depicted in Figure 8.1. Customer satisfaction, time-to-market, and cost reduction through total quality management are all important, but none is viewed as a guarantee of success.

All else being equal, a product will be more profitable if it delivers customer benefits better, is faster to market, costs less to produce, and costs less to develop. Figure 8.1 puts research on product-development tools and methods into perspective. Research should be directed to assure that: (1) the firm is operating on the efficient frontier with respect to each of these strategic goals; and (2) the firm is making the best tradeoffs among these goals.

Research must recognize that there are tradeoffs along the efficient frontier. For example, if we focus on just two of the many goals of product development, then the efficient frontier in Figure 8.2 suggests that there are tradeoffs between customer satisfaction and platform reuse. A firm can become too committed to either. For example, the significant reuse of components in platforms, software, and designs may get the product to the market faster

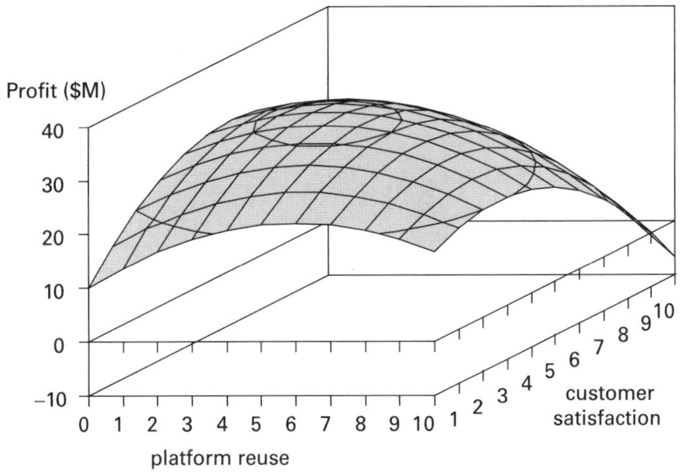

Figure 8.2 *Quantifying the Tradeoffs in Product Development*

and reduce development costs (e.g., Witter et al., 1994), but the firm may sacrifice the ability to satisfy customer needs and may miss out on ways to reduce product costs. Similarly, quality function deployment (QFD) may be an effective means to deliver customer benefits by improving communication and coordinating the efforts of multiple players in the NPD process, but some applications are too cumbersome, reducing time-to-market and increasing development cost.

In response, product development teams have modified QFD to deliver the right benefits at the right costs. Such modifications include just-in-time QFD (Tessler & Klein, 1993), turbo QFD (Smith & Reinertsen, 1998), and simplified QFD (McGrath, 1996). Platform reuse and QFD are just examples. As we review various product-development tools and methods, the reader should keep in mind that the tools work together to enable the firm to make the appropriate tradeoffs among the four strategic goals in Figure 8.1.

Product Development as an End-to-End Process

In order to make these tradeoffs effectively, most firms now view product development (PD) as an end-to-end process that draws on marketing, engineering, manufacturing, and organizational development. Figure 8.3, a representation of such an end-to-end process, is modified from a process used at Xerox and advocated by the Center for Innovation in Product Development (Seering, 1998). It summarizes many of the forces affecting product development and highlights opportunities for research.

From our perspective, the five forces on the outer square of Figure 8.3 present the external challenges to the PD team. All actions are contingent on these forces. For example, speed to market might be more critical in the highly competitive world of Internet software. Rather than three-year planning cycles, such firms might adopt three-year horizons with adaptive implementation strategies that are reviewed monthly or even weekly (Cusumano & Yoffie, 1998). The descriptions in the seven rectangles indicate actions that must be taken. For example, the firm must have a strategy for dealing with technology ('Technology Strategy') and employ methods to understand the benefits provided to customers by competitive product offerings, identify gaps where benefits are demanded but not supplied, and understand how competition will respond ('Competitive Positioning'), while 'Supply Chain Management' helps the firm (and extended enterprise) include suppliers in developing products to meet customer needs. In this chapter we review those actions that are of greatest interest to a marketing audience, namely those in the four darker rectangles. In-bound marketing ('Voice of the Customer, Conjoint Analysis, etc.') provides the window on the customer. The myriad perspectives from marketing, engineering, design, and manufacturing that must be integrated for successful PD manifest themselves in the form of a 'Core Cross-Functional Team,' supporting an 'Effective Organization.' 'Human Resources' are important, including the need to understand the context and culture of the organization and the need to develop human capabilities through training, information technology, and communities of practice (Wenger, 1998). 'Marketing, Engineering, and Process Tools' enable the end-to-end PD process to be both more efficient and more effective.

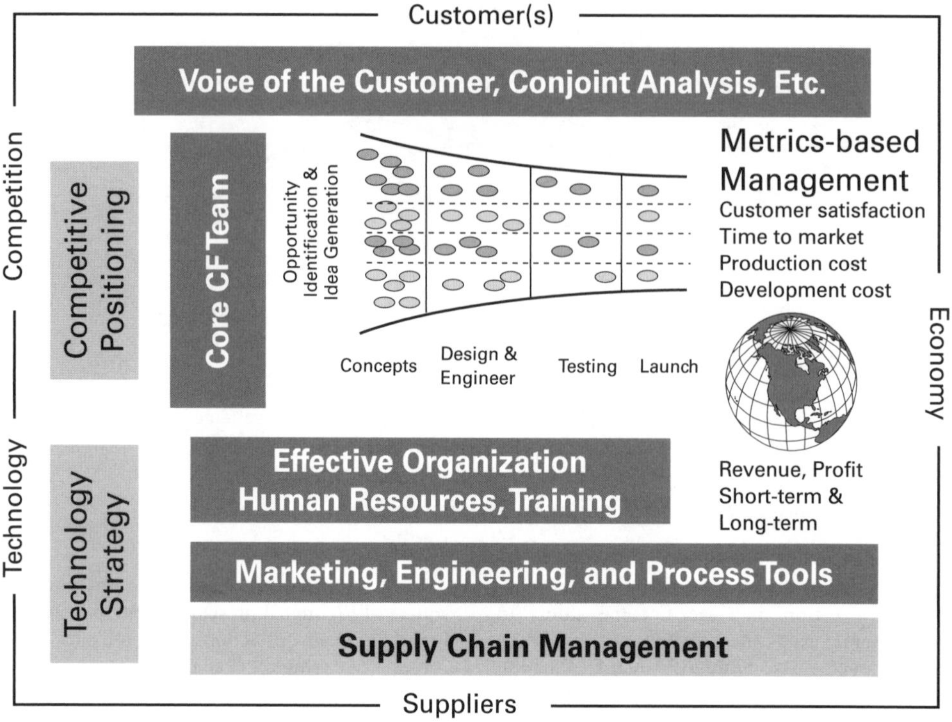

Figure 8.3 *Product Development – End-to-End*

The Product Development Funnel, Stage-gate, and Platforms

The PD funnel is at the center of Figure 8.3. The funnel represents the traditional view that PD proceeds in stages as many ideas are winnowed and developed into a few high-potential products that are ultimately launched. We have adopted here the stages of opportunity identification (and idea generation), concept development and selection, detailed design and engineering, testing, and launch used by Urban and Hauser (1993). Each text and each firm has slightly different names for the stages, but the description of PD as a staged process is fairly universal. The key management ideas are (1) that it is much less expensive to screen products in the early stages than in the later stages, and (2) that each stage can improve the product and its positioning so that the likelihood of success increases. Simple calculations in Urban and Hauser demonstrate that such a staged process is likely to reduce development costs significantly. This staged process is best summarized by Cooper (1990), who labels the process stage-gate. Figure 8.4 summarizes a typical stage-gate process adapted to the structure of this chapter. Stage-gate processes provide discipline through a series of gates in which members of the PD team are asked to justify the decision to move to the next stage – later stages dramatically increase the funds and efforts invested in getting a product to market successfully.

The funnel in Figure 8.3 also attempts to illustrate the concept of pipeline management by having multiple, parallel sets of projects moving through the funnel. Often the best strategy for a firm is to have sufficiently many parallel projects so that it can launch products to the market at the most profitable pace. Research challenges include questions of how many parallel projects are necessary, the tradeoffs between more parallel projects and faster time for each project, and the number of concepts that are needed in each stage of a parallel project to produce the right pace of product introduction. Figure 8.3 does not explicitly capture the important characteristic of real PD processes: that stages often overlap. For example, with new methods of user design and rapid prototyping, it is possible to test concepts earlier in the design and engineering stage or to screen ideas more effectively in the concept stage. Figure 8.3 also does not explicitly capture the iterative nature of the entire process (although we have tried to illustrate that with the feedback arrows in Figure 8.4). For example, if a product does not

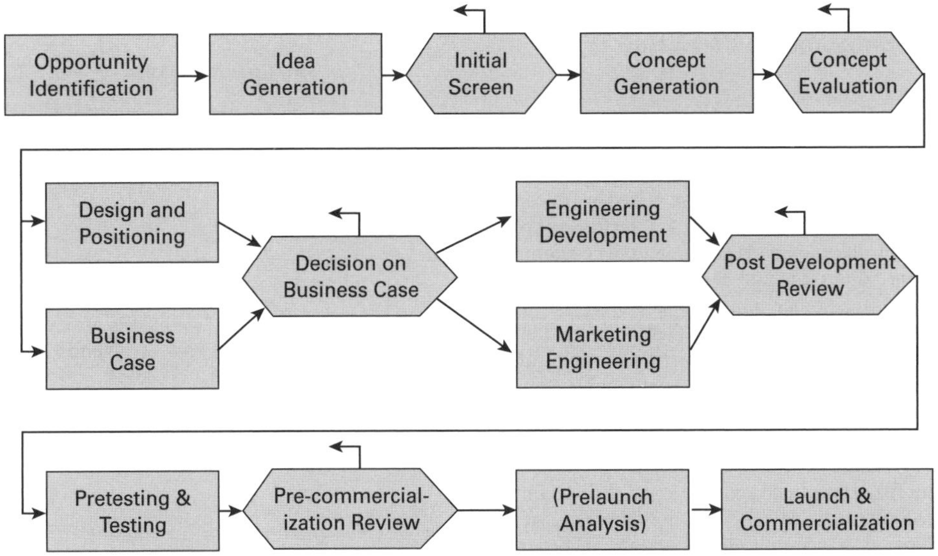

Figure 8.4 *Cooper's Stage-gate Process (Adapted to the Structure of this Chapter)*

test well, it might be cycled back for further development and retested. In fact, many firms now talk about a 'spiral process' in which products or concepts move through a series of tighter and tighter stages (e.g., Cusumano & Selby, 1995). The key difference between a funnel process and a spiral process is that, in the latter, there is a greater expectation of iterative feedback loops as successive journeys through the funnel lead to improvements. One interesting research challenge is to formalize the organizational implications of spiral vs. funnel processes, and to determine the circumstances where one is favored over the other.

The small ovals in the end-to-end PD process (Figure 8.3) are either individual products or product platforms. In many industries, including complex electro-mechanical products, software, and pharmaceuticals, firms have found that it is more profitable to develop product platforms. A platform is a set of common elements shared across products in the platform family. For example, Hewlett Packard's entire line of ink-jet printers is based on relatively few printer-cartridge platforms. By sharing elements, products can be developed more quickly, and at lower cost. Platforms might also lower production costs and inventory carrying costs, and provide a basis for flexible manufacturing. On the customer side, platforms enable a firm to customize features in a process that has become known as mass customization (Baldwin & Clark, 2000; Cattani et al., 2002; Gilmore & Pine, 1997; Gonzalez-Zugasti et al., 1998; Meyer & Lehnerd, 1997; Sanderson & Uzumeri, 1996; Ulrich & Eppinger, 2000).

Finally, the right side of the end-to-end process in Figure 8.3 illustrates the growing trends toward metrics-based management of PD. As the process becomes more dispersed among various functions, various teams, various suppliers, and throughout the world, and as products become more complex, there is a greater need to balance top-management control with the empowerment of self-managed, cross-functional teams. To achieve this balance, firms are turning to a metrics-based approach, in which teams are measured on strategic indicators such as customer satisfaction, time-to-market, production cost, and development cost. If the weights on these metrics are set properly, then the teams, acting in their own best interests, will take the actions and make the decisions that lead to the greatest short- and long-term profit (Baker et al., 1999a, 1999b; Gibbons, 1997).

This completes our marketing overview of the end-to-end product development process. The important lesson that we hope to illustrate throughout the remainder of this chapter, is that the process depends upon all of its elements. Although the detailed implementation of each element varies depending upon technology, competition, customers, and suppliers, a firm is more effective if it understands all of these elements and can manage them effectively.

We now examine research opportunities within each stage of the PD process, beginning with the fuzzy front end of opportunity identification and idea generation.

The Fuzzy Front End: Opportunity Identification and Idea Generation

Perhaps the highest leverage point in product development is the front end, which defines what the product will be – represented by the (leftmost) opening of the funnel in Figure 8.3. This decision balances the firm's core strengths versus competition with the demands of potential customers. Relevant topics include technology strategy and readiness, customer input, and newer, virtual-customer methods. Because this is a marketing handbook, we focus this section on obtaining information to satisfy customer needs and on idea generation. We recommend that readers interested in technology readiness review Roussel, Saad, & Erickson (1991) or McGrath (1996).

The fuzzy front end may be viewed through the lens of *uncertain search*. That is, the design team must consider a multitude of designs in order to find an ideal solution at the intersection of customer preferences and firm capabilities. Once the firm has determined the strategic value of developing a new product within a particular category, but before it can specify the detailed requirements and features of the design, it must select the more promising designs to develop and test so as to meet development cost, production cost, customer satisfaction, and time-to-market targets. Promising designs are those that are technically desirable, i.e. feasible designs that exploit the firm's competitive advantages, and are attractive to potential customers. Marketing's role at the fuzzy front end of PD is to reduce uncertainty during the design team's search for winning product concepts by accurately capturing customers' points-of-view and communicating customer preferences to the design team. In some cases, the process is more direct, with engineers/designers observing and communicating directly with potential customers, possibly facilitated by marketing personnel. The ease of communication and interaction over the Internet has the potential to increase the frequency and effectiveness of such unfiltered observations. The process of listening to customers in order to optimize a new product is iterative, as depicted in Figure 8.5, consistent with the feedback loops in the funnel processes and with the basic intent of the spiral processes.

Recognizing the iterative nature of Figure 8.5, we begin this section by reviewing techniques for gathering raw data on customer needs. These methods include direct survey methods with which marketing researchers are familiar, but include as well Kano's model of delighting customers, the concept of disruptive technologies, methods to get at underlying meanings and values, methods for the 'mind of the market,' and benefit chains. We then review methods for characterizing and refining customer needs based on apparent patterns and themes, and

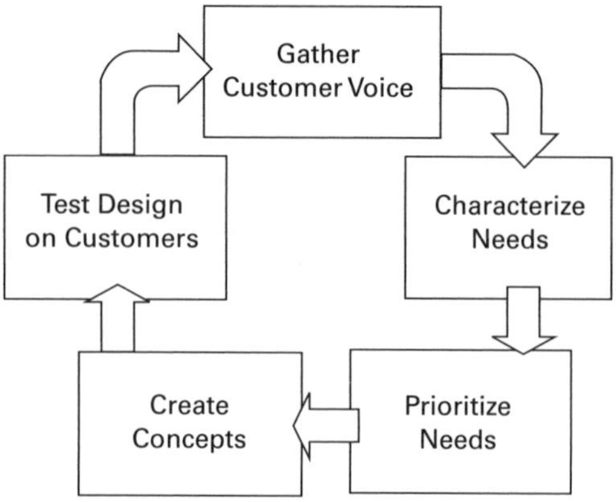

Figure 8.5 *Listening to Customers*

we review methods for organizing needs and identifying market segments. Needs must be prioritized and many marketing methods are quite effective. In the fuzzy front end we use the simpler and less costly methods, recognizing that any information will be refined in the design and prototype phases. Thus, we save a review of these 'high-fidelity' methods until the next section of this chapter. However, in this section we do review some of the more common methods of ideation. We close this section by examining how the Internet is changing the way we view the process of identifying and measuring customer needs.

Surveys and Interviews

There are many challenges when attempting to capture the voice of the customer, measure preference, and predict new product purchase behavior. During the fuzzy front end the methods must recognize that: (1) customers may still be forming their preferences and may change their opinions by the time actual products ship; (2) it may be difficult for customers to express their true preferences (e.g. degree of price sensitivity) due to social norms; (3) the questioning process itself can be intrusive, so it is best to use multiple, convergent methods; and (4) information gatherers may 'filter' the voice of the customer through their own biases (see Bickart, 1993; Feldman & Lynch, 1988; Nowlis & Simonson, 1997; Simmons et al., 1993; Tourangeau et al., 2000). Researchers have developed and validated multiple methods in attempts to address these issues.

Mahajan and Wind (1992) surveyed firms about techniques they used to identify customer needs. They found that 68% of firms used focus groups, and 42% used limited product roll-outs. In addition, many firms used formal concept tests, conjoint

Table 8.1 *Customer Selection Matrix for Coffee Makers*

Market Segment	Current Customers	Competitors' Customers	Lead Users	Untapped Customers	Lost Customers
Countertop 12-cup Drip Users					
Specialty (e.g., Espresso) Users					
High-Volume (24-cup) Users					

analysis, and Quality Function Deployment (QFD). The study also suggested the following improvements for customer research:

- More quantitative approaches
- More efficient in-depth probing
- Greater accuracy and validity
- Simpler and better customer feedback
- Greater customer involvement
- More effective use of lead users and field salespeople
- Methods that address a long-term, functionally-integrated strategy

The new methods we review attempt to address many of these concerns. However, research is still underway. Each method has its limitations and the value of the information depends on the quality of execution of the research.

Experiential Interviews

For evolutionary designs targeted at an existing or familiar customer base, focus groups (Calder, 1977; Fern, 1982), provide valuable information. However, focus groups are subject to social norms within the group and often focus on inter-subject interactions and thus miss many of the customer needs that are hard to articulate or which the customer cannot express effectively in a group setting. Thus, many firms are turning to experiential interviews in which the needs and desires of customers are explored in one-on-one interviews, in which the customer describes his or her experience with the product class. The interviewer probes deeply into the underlying, more stable, and long-term problems that the customer is trying to solve. Research by Griffin and Hauser (1993) indicates that 10 to 20 experiential interviews per market segment elicit the vast majority of customer needs. Qualitatively rich interviews at the customer's location are most effective, but are expensive to conduct. One challenge is to limit the session length, usually to an hour or less, that engages, but does not inconvenience, the participant. In selecting interview candidates, a selection matrix that segments the market according to type-of-use and customer source, like the one in Table 1, ensures that a diversity of customers is contacted (Burchill & Hepner-Brodie, 1997; Hepner-Brodie, 2000). The key concept is a representative rather than a random sample, in which the PD team gathers information from all the relevant segments and from customers with varying perspectives on current and future needs. In addition, if there are multiple decision makers, say doctors, lab technicians, and patients for a medical instrument, then each type of decision maker needs to be consulted. See examples in Hauser (1993).

Multiple members of the PD team should review the transcripts. For example, Griffin and Hauser (1993) suggest that each team member recognizes approximately half of the needs in a transcript, and that multiple team members are very effective at identifying more than 95% of the needs. Because non-verbal communication is critical, many firms now videotape interviews in addition to transcribing them. Such interviews, often distributed on CDs to team members, have become known as the 'Face of the Customer (FOC).' For example, hearing a customer say 'I use Windows on my notebook and need an accurate, built-in pointing device that doesn't require me to move my hands from the keyboard' carries more information than a filtered summary of 'Good pointing device is important.' Seeing the user struggle with existing pointing devices is even more persuasive. In the past, FOC methods have been expensive to implement and are used only by those firms with larger budgets. Fortunately, new developments in the use of digital video photography are making this process less expensive and easier to implement.

Many firms now include the actual design-engineers in the interviewing process when the process is cost-effective (cf. Leonard-Barton et al., 1993). However, in complex products where the PD team often consists of over 400 engineers and other professionals, key members observe the interviews and use methods, such as the videotapes or the CD-based FOC, to carry this information to the PD team in a form that can be used effectively.

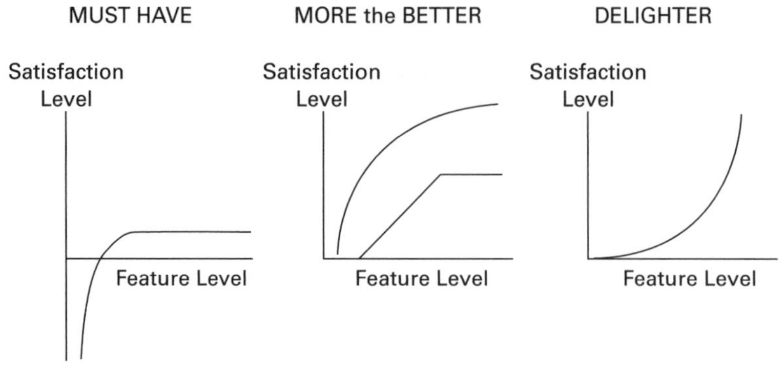

Figure 8.6 *Kano Taxonomy of Customer Needs*

Table 8.2 *Examples of Kano Feature Types (circa 2000)*

	Must Have	More the Better	Delighter
Car	(4) Reliable Tires	Gas Mileage	GPS-based map
Notebook	AC Adapter	Hard Drive Capacity	Built-in wireless
Software	Compatibility	Processing Speed	Auto-fill-in

The Kano Model: Delighting Customers

'Customer needs' are often verbal statements of benefits that customers gain from the product or service. For example, a customer might want a safer car, a computer monitor that takes up less space on the desk, or a portable computer that makes six hours in an airplane cabin more pleasant. However, in order to design a product, the PD team must map these needs into product features. One widely used conceptual method is the Kano model.

The conceptual Kano model characterizes product features according to their relationship to customer expectations (Clausing, 1994), as in Figure 8.6. In particular, features are characterized, roughly, according to the shape of the feature-to-satisfaction function. Although this taxonomy is an approximation to a more continuous categorization, it is nonetheless useful as a conceptual aid to understand how features affect satisfaction.

Some features address 'must have' needs. Such needs are usually met by current technology and any new product must satisfy these needs. However, it is difficult to differentiate a product by increasing the satisfaction of these needs because they are already satisfied well by the competitive set of existing products. In other words, the competitive equilibrium has dictated that all viable products address these needs. If the PD team does not meet the needs then the product will elicit customer dissatisfaction and lose sales. For example, an automobile must have four properly inflated tires that perform robustly under all driving conditions. Recent problems with tire tread separation reveal the powerful negative impact of not meeting 'must have' needs. However, there are opportunities to save costs if new creative technology can address these needs as well or better with lower cost. For example, Hauser (1993) gives an example where a basic need for medical instruments – printing patient records – was met with a new technology (parallel port to connect to the physician's office printer) that was significantly less expensive than existing technology (built-in thermal printers), yet met the need better.

Other needs are 'more the better.' When new technology or improved ideas increase the amount by which these needs are satisfied, customer satisfaction increases, but usually with diminishing returns. Such needs are usually relevant when technology is advancing rapidly, such as with computer processor clock speed. In order to stay on top of the market, a computer manufacturer must always be developing more powerful and easier to use computers.

Finally, a special class of needs are those which customers have difficulty articulating or rarely expect to have fulfilled. When features are included in a product to satisfy such customer needs, often unexpectedly, customers experience 'delight!' Sources of customer delight can become strong motivators for initial purchase and for customer satisfaction after the sale. Examples include complimentary fruit baskets in hotel rooms, software that anticipates your next move, automobiles that rarely need a service, and others such as those in Table 8.2. Conceptually, once a product has such a 'delighter' feature that passes a threshold of functionality, customers become extremely satisfied and seek out the product for that feature.

It is important to remember that the Kano model is dynamic. Today's 'delighter' features become tomorrows 'must have' features. For example, a graphical user interface (GUI) and multi-processing were once 'delighter' features, but today they are 'must have' features for any desktop computer operating system. However, the basic underlying customer needs of an effective and easy to use operating system remain. Antilock braking systems and premium sound systems were once delighter features for high-end cars, but today are 'must have' features for any brand competing in the high-end segment. New 'delighter' features include automatic mapping and location systems, satellite-based emergency road service, side-view mirrors that dim automatically, night-vision warning systems, and Internet access. However, the basic underlying needs of safety and comfortable transportation remain. Really successful products are frequently due to newly identified 'delighter' features that address those basic customer needs in innovative ways. The dynamic nature of Kano's model suggests a need for ongoing measurement of customer expectations over a product's life cycle.

The Innovator's Dilemma and Disruptive Technologies

The Kano model cautions us that as new technology develops, today's excitement needs can become tomorrow's must-have needs. However, the size and nature of the customer base also evolve as technology evolves. For example, as more computer users purchase laptop computers rather than desktop computers, their needs for improved levels of previously unimportant features, such as reduced disk drive size and weight, increase dramatically. If a disk-drive manufacturer is focused only on its current desktop computers, it may miss opportunities when customers move to laptop computers or new customers enter the market.

Bower and Christensen (1995) and Christensen (1998) formalize this concept and point out that listening to one's *current* customers, while consistent with the firm's financial goals, may enable entrants with new technologies to eventually displace incumbents. This may happen even though the new technologies are not initially as effective as the incumbent technologies on 'more-the-better' features. For example, the initial small hard drives for portables were not as fast nor could they store as much information as the larger disk drives used in desktop computers. But an emerging class of portable users demanded them because they were smaller and lighter in weight. Eventually, the technology of smaller drives caught up to the technology of the larger drives on the 'more-the-better' features (storage, speed). However, they dominated on the 'delighter' features (size and weight). Because these delighter features were relatively more important to this new market (portable computers) than the old market (desktop computers), the new drives became the dominant technology for the new market.

Firms fall into disruptive-technology traps because current customers may not appreciate the new benefits of a new technology because it does not perform as well on the traditional features they value. However, new users, not well known to the firm, may value the new features more highly and forgive the below-average performance on traditional features. In addition, new entrants may be willing to settle for lower sales and profits than incumbents in order to gain a foothold in the market. Eventually, as the new technology achieves higher performance on traditional features, the incumbent's old customers begin switching and the firm loses its leadership position. To avoid the disruptive-technology trap and to stay on top of the needs of *all* customers, Christensen proposes that incumbent firms partner with (or develop) independent, 'entrepreneurial' entities to explore disruptive technologies. Christensen proposes that the entrepreneurial entities be held to less stringent short-term financial and performance objectives, so that they might focus on long-term performance by satisfying the 'delighter' needs of the new and growing markets.

While we agree with Christensen's description of the dynamics of the disruptive phenomenon, we are less pessimistic about the ability of incumbent firms to be innovative. His prescriptions do not take into account the evolving nature of customer needs nor the ability of marketing research to identify excitement needs, changes in customer preferences, and new customers. When there is an organizational will to use these proven methods, incumbent firms can innovate on such disruptive technologies.

The dynamic nature of technology and the possibility of disruptive innovation suggest that marketers carefully monitor the preferences of both customers and non-customers over time, and develop a deep understanding of the needs of both customers and non-customers. Marketers should pay careful attention to evolving, difficult-to-articulate customer needs, and to potentially new tradeoffs among customers who contemplate a different use of the technology. Tools to facilitate such ongoing monitoring, such as web-based conjoint analysis, are discussed later in this chapter.

Empathic Design and User Observation

Many firms realize that no matter how refined the research methodology and no matter how much data is collected, some insights can only be gained by observing customers in their natural habitat (Leonard-Barton et al., 1993). This is particularly true when customer needs are difficult to verbalize or are not obvious. The technique of empathic design requires that members of the design team immerse themselves in the customer environment for a period long enough to absorb the problems and feelings experienced by users. If a product is inconvenient, inefficient, or inadequate, the designer gains first-hand experience with the problem. Empathic methods are particularly effective at determining the ergonomic aspects of a product. The empathic methods can be carried out by members of the PD team (after receiving the appropriate training) or by marketing professionals, but in either case, rich media should be used to capture the users' experience so that it can be shared with the entire PD team.

Intuit, makers of Quicken®, the leading personal financial software package on the market, pioneered the 'Follow-Me-Home' program in which Intuit employees observe purchasers in their homes from the moment they open the box to the time they have Quicken functioning properly (Case, 1991). Using empathic design and user observation, Intuit has steadily improved Quicken's ease-of-use with features such as auto fill-in of accounts and payees, on-screen checks and registers that look like their paper counterparts, and push buttons to automate common tasks. More importantly, Intuit took responsibility for the entire process of producing checks, including working to improve printers and printer drivers even though these were made by third parties. Empathic design highlighted problems that explained why customers were not buying Intuit's products. Even though the problem was not Intuit's technical responsibility in the value chain, Intuit took responsibility and solved the customers' perceived problems. Specifically, Intuit recognized that it could lose its share of the software market if it did not solve the printer manufacturers' software and hardware problems. Intuit's focus on customer needs has kept the company on top of a highly competitive, ever-changing marketplace.

Holtzblatt and Beyer (1993) developed a technique known as contextual inquiry, in which a member of the design team conducts an extensive interview with a customer at his or her site while the customer performs real tasks. The interviewer can interrupt at any time to ask questions about the why's and how's of the customer's actions. The results of these contextual inquiries are shared with other design-team members and synthesized using affinity diagrams (described below) and workflow charts.

Underlying Meanings and Values

In addition to exploring customers' stated needs, PD teams often seek to understand customers' underlying meanings and values. One method to get at underlying meanings and values is through in-depth experiential interviews that seek to get customers to express such needs. (In other words, underlying meanings and values are really just difficult-to-articulate needs.) In addition, some firms have explored anthropological methods.

Cultural anthropology (cf. Levin, 1992) is the study of hidden meanings underlying products, or meanings which are sought, but left unmet. The approach is broader than psychology-based motivational research in that it accounts for customers' social values, not just emotional needs. Issues such as a company's environmental impact and minority hiring record gain significance.

How does cultural anthropology affect product design? The key is consistency with the social significance of the product. For example, if customers buy zero emission electric vehicles because of their concern about the environment, they may object to a design with batteries which produce toxic waste.

Zaltman's (1997) Metaphor Elicitation Technique (ZMET) suggests that the underlying values and meanings that drive customers toward specific product-choice decisions, may be uncovered through a process of visual self-expression. ZMET requires participants to provide pictures and images that capture what they seek in the product category. Because ZMET allows the research stimuli to be controlled by the respondents, they can express their feelings, product meanings, and attitudes.

Kansei Analysis and the Mind of the Market

A select group of products, especially 'high-touch' consumer durables such as automobiles and personal information appliances, are purchased as much for the emotional responses they evoke as for the function they provide. For such products, measuring customers' true feelings toward potential designs, especially their look and feel, may prove invaluable.

Kansei analysis may be described as the 'Lie Detector' of customer research methodologies. Most techniques of listening to the customer assume that respondents provide answers that accurately reflect their preferences and perceptions. But for various reasons such as social pressure, vanity, or even inaccurate self-perception, further probing is necessary. Kansei analysis seeks these true preferences by measuring non-verbal responses to product stimuli, in much the same way that galvanic skin response, voice stress, and breathing rate are

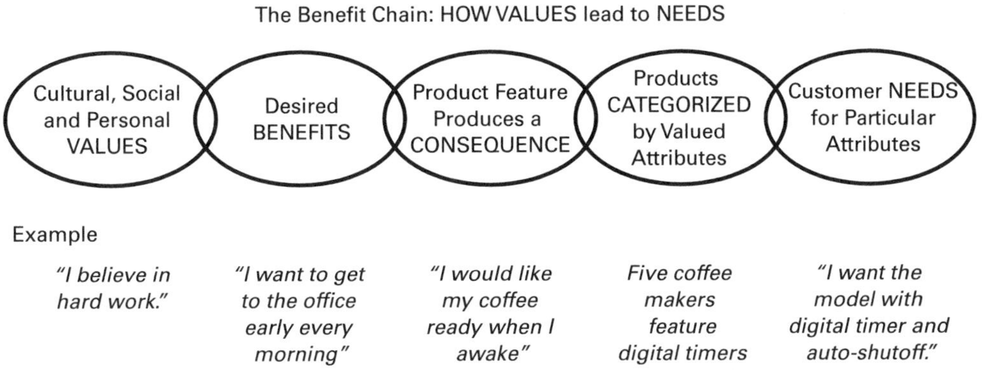

Figure 8.7 *Benefit Chain Structure for a Coffee Maker*

recorded in lie-detector testing. Examples of other non-verbal responses that can be measured are facial muscle contractions and eye movement and dilation. By measuring these subtle physiological responses while a customer views or interacts with a new product, the PD team gauges the customer's feelings and attitudes. A grimace during sharp steering might indicate poor response in a car, while visual focus on a particular coffee maker prototype might reveal a preference for the outward appearance of that design. By correlating the non-verbal reactions of customers with the specific stimuli that produced those reactions, customer preferences for a product's 'look and feel' can be determined. Similarly, by observing detailed click stream data, software and web-site designers can optimize the user interface for maximum customer satisfaction.

Kosslyn et al., (1999) describe a method that delves even deeper into the physiological aspects of customer response mechanisms, a method they term 'The Mind of the Market.' This work utilizes brain imaging of respondents viewing marketing stimuli, in this case automobile dealership scenarios, to assess negative and positive reactions. By comparing their results to those of another research team utilizing more conventional market research methods, they suggest that their method has promise.

Benefit Chains

Benefit chains focus on *why* customers have a particular need that is not yet addressed by existing products. For example, while a focus group or Kano analysis might determine that customers want smaller, lighter-weight notebook computers that perform faster, the underlying values driving those needs may not be so obvious. Are customers so ambitious that they want to accomplish twice the amount of work (notebook performance) and work everywhere they go (lightweight)? Or could it be that customers seek more leisure time (i.e., less time working), and prefer to do their work outside of the office? The underlying values driving those needs might differ dramatically and the difference in underlying values might imply different product development solutions. The workaholic notebook-computer user might need more features and battery life, while the leisure-seeker might need ease-of-learning and low-price. Figure 8.7 illustrates a benefit chain for coffee makers. Here, the user's work ethic leads to a desire for either a digital timer with auto-shutoff (or another solution such as Internet control) that helps the user satisfy his or her cultural work-ethic values.

Related methods include a *Means-End Chain* model of customer choice behavior (Gutman, 1982) and a *Value-Systems* model (Rokeach, 1973). These authors view customer needs as a chain reaction beginning with the cultural, social, and personal values held by the individual. The underlying values held by customers then guide their choices toward products that produce desired benefits. Since there are numerous choices for a given product, people categorize them into sets or classes, thereby simplifying the decision. The categories created by each customer are influenced by his or her values. While the leisure seeker may categorize notebook computers based on price, the workaholic may consider machines grouped according to performance.

Gutman and Reynolds' (1979) technique for measuring such benefit chains begins with Kelly's (1955) repertory grid technique. After respondents have drawn distinctions within a set of three products (by determining similarities between two products and differences with a third), they are asked which attribute they prefer. They are then asked why they prefer that attribute at higher and higher levels of abstraction until some core values are

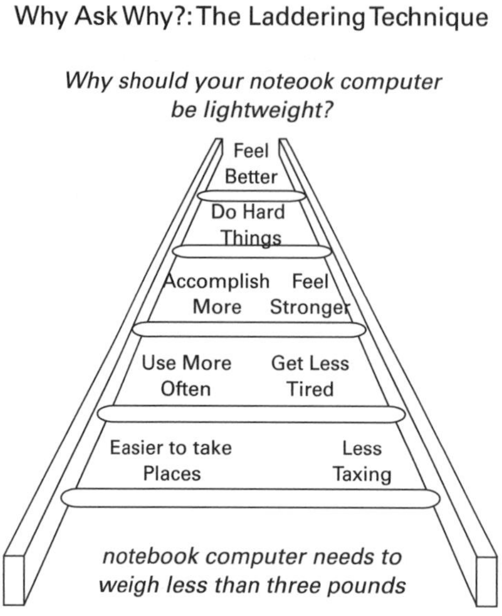

Figure 8.8 *Laddering Example for a Notebook Computer*

reached. This technique is sometimes referred to as laddering. It is illustrated in Figure 8.8.

Focusing the Design Team by Identifying Strategic Customer Needs

Traditional surveys and interviews, experiential interviews, Kano analysis, disruptive-technology analysis, empathic design, the study of meanings, Kansei analysis, benefit chains, and laddering all identify customer needs and desires which, if fulfilled, lead to successful new products. However, these methods are sometimes too effective, producing not just a few needs, but rather hundreds of customer needs. Even for a simple product such as a coffee maker, it is not uncommon to generate a list of 100–200 customer needs. For complex products such as copiers and automobiles, such lengthy lists might be generated for subsystems (interior, exterior, drive train, electronics, climate control). But the needs are not all independent.

To proceed further in idea generation, the PD team needs focus. This focus is provided by recognizing that the needs can be grouped into strategic, tactical, and detailed needs. If we call the raw output of the various needs-generation methods 'detailed needs,' then we often find that the 100–200 detailed needs can be arranged into groups of 20–30 tactical needs. For example, detailed statements by customers of a software package about the on-line help systems, 'wizards,' on-line manuals, documentation, telephone support, and Internet support might all be grouped together as a need by the customer 'to get help easily and effectively when I need it.' The detailed needs help the PD team create technology and other solutions to address the tactical need. However, the tactical need is sufficiently general so that the PD team might develop totally new ways of meeting that need, such as communities of practice within large customers. The tactical needs might also be grouped into 5–10 strategic needs such as 'easy to use,' 'does the job well,' 'easy to learn,' etc. The strategic needs help the team develop concepts that stretch the product space and open up new positioning strategies.

Later in the PD process (see Figure 8.3, page 182) the PD team needs to decide on which strategic need to focus or which features best fulfill a strategic need. In later sections we review methods to prioritize these needs (and features). However, in the fuzzy front end it is more important that we get the grouping right, that is, it is more important that the right strategic and tactical groups be identified. This is because, at this stage of the process, the PD team wants to generate a larger number of potential product concepts, each of which might stretch one or a few strategic needs. The PD team also wants to explore new ideas to address these strategic needs by solving the relevant tactical needs in new and creative ways. In this chapter we review the two most common methods of grouping needs.

Team-based Needs-grouping Methods: Affinity Diagrams and K-J analysis

The Japanese anthropologist Jiro Kawakita (denoted K-J by the Japanese custom of last name first) developed a method of synthesizing large amounts of data, including voice-of-the-customer data, into manageable chunks based on themes that emerged from the data themselves (Mizuno, 1988). The K-J method uses a team approach to develop *affinity diagrams*, in which each voice-of-the-customer statement is grouped with other similar statements. The K-J technique requires an open mind from each participant, encourages creativity, and avoids criticism of 'strange' ideas. The K-J method claims to be based on stimulating the right-brain creative and emotional centers of thought rather than relying on pure cause-and-effect logic.

Typically, each data element, preferably in the original language of the customer, is recorded onto a card or Post-it® note. The cards are well shuffled to eliminate any pre-existing order bias and are then grouped based on feelings rather than logic. The impression or image given by each customer statement suggests the group to which that card has the greatest affinity rather than any pre-conceived category. When a few cards are grouped, they are labeled with a description that captures the essence of their meaning. Card groups are then assembled into a larger diagram with relationships between the groups of cards indicated. The end result is a diagram showing the top five to ten customer needs, relationships between needs, and detailed customer voice data expressing those needs.

Customer-based Needs-grouping Methods: the Voice of the Customer

While affinity diagrams and K-J analysis methods have proven to be powerful in many applications, they can also suffer when the team is too embedded in its corporate culture. For example, Griffin and Hauser (1993) compare affinity diagrams developed by PD teams with those developed by actual customers. While PD team members group customer needs based on how the firm *builds* the product, customers instead group needs by the way they *use* the product. Griffin and Hauser also apply hierarchical clustering (Green et al., 1969; Rao & Katz, 1971) to needs gathered from a larger sample of customers. Here each customer performs a relatively simple sort of needs into a small number of piles. The hierarchy of strategic, tactical, and detailed needs comes from the statistical analysis. This method, called both the Voice of the Customer and Vocalyst®, has proven effective in literally hundreds of applications. Although we know of no head-to-head comparison between customer affinity diagrams and voice-of-the-customer methods, customer-based methods seem to provide more useful structures than do PD team-based methods, and lead to more creative solutions as a result.

New Web-based Methods for the Fuzzy Front End

Information pump

The methods reviewed above provide a breadth of means to identify customer needs, whether they are articulated or unarticulated, individual-specific or bound in the culture, verbal or non-verbal, etc. Recently, the Internet has made it possible for groups of customers to communicate directly and iteratively with one another and, together, produce a set of needs that might not have been identified any other way. The 'Information Pump' is a novel method of objectively evaluating the quality and consistency of respondents' comments, in which 'virtual focus group' participants opine on a common stimulus such as a new product concept (Prelec, 2001). The method transforms the market research task into a 'parlor' game in which respondents create true/false questions about the product concept. Other respondents in the game guess the answers and state their confidence in their answers. Those who answer the questions are rewarded on the accuracy of their answers, while those who create the questions are trying to create questions that informed customers (those who see the concept) can answer better than uninformed customers (those that do not see the concept). The incentives in the game are based on 'honest reward theory' and are fine-tuned to encourage both truth-telling and creativity. Early tests suggest that the Information Pump uncovers statements that independent judges view as more creative than traditional approaches with the same look and feel.

'Listening in' to Customers on the Internet

The Internet also provides the means to identify customer needs by passively observing interactive customer behavior on a web site. By organizing the web site by agendas based on features or customer needs, a virtual engineer can listen in and observe how customers process attributes and, in particular, when they search for attributes, features, or needs that cannot be satisfied by any extant product. Urban (2000) demonstrates this indirect method of capturing unmet customer needs by observing customer interactions with an Internet-based sales recommendation system for trucks. While the virtual agent attempts to identify the ideal, current-model truck for each respondent, a virtual design engineer notes which product attributes leave the customer the most unsatisfied. The virtual engineer then 'interviews' the customer to better understand the unmet needs and how to best resolve the inherent tradeoffs that prevent those needs from being met.

Ideation Based on Customer Needs (and Other Inputs)

Once the PD team has identified and grouped customer needs it must generate ideas on how to address those needs (Goldenberg et al., 1999). In the next section (on designing and engineering concepts) we discuss formal methods, such as QFD, by which the PD team can systematically generate effective concepts. But not all concepts can be generated systematically. Sometimes the PD team needs crazy and bizarre solutions which, when refined, solve the customers' needs in new and creative ways. A wide variety of ideation methods have been proposed including brainstorming (Arnold, 1962), morphological analysis (Ayres, 1969), group sessions (Prince, 1970), forced relationships (Osborn, 1963), systems approaches (Campbell, 1985), varied perspectives (De Bono, 1995), archival analysis (Altschuler, 1985, 1996), and inventive templates (Goldenberg et al., 1999a, 1999b). In this chapter we review the three most

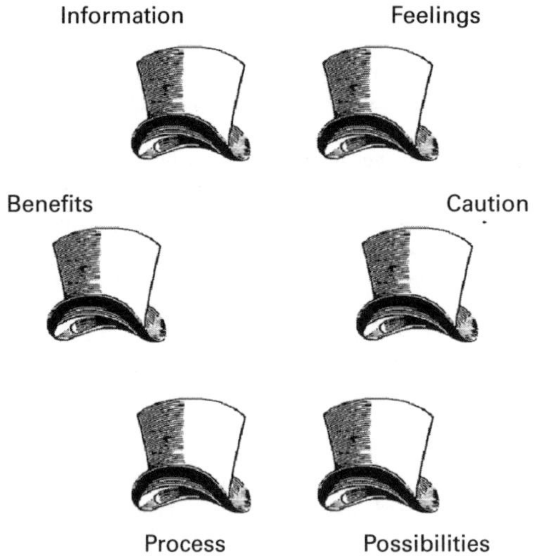

Figure 8.9 *De Bono's Six Hats Method*

recent proposals and refer the reader to the references for the more traditional ideation methods.

Overcoming Mental Blocks

Adams (1986) and De Bono (1995) propose methods for overcoming the mental blocks most of us have that derive from our particular approaches to problem solving. Figure 8.9 depicts De Bono's six hats, representing the diverse perspectives of potential members of a product design team. Typically, each participant in a new product debate feels most comfortable wearing one or two of the hats, frequently leading to conflict. The 'six hats' exercise require team members to 'wear the other guy's hats' so as to improve communications and foster creative exchange. For example, one might ask members of the design team to react to a novel situation such as, 'A pill is invented that makes people dislike the taste of fatty foods,' from the perspective of each of the six hats. By identifying the types of thinking in which each team member engages, participants gain insight into their own problem-solving approaches as well as those of others.

TRIZ (Theory of Inventive Problem Solving)

Altschuler (1985, 1996) developed a technique for generating creative solutions to technical problems by harnessing archival knowledge, an early version of knowledge management. Specifically, Altschuler reviewed tens of thousands of patents and noticed that their genius was in applying inventive principles to resolve tradeoffs between a limited set of 'competing' physical properties (approximately 40 in number). These solutions typically resulted in no tradeoff being made at all, for example the way aluminum cans are both lightweight and strong by virtue of their cylindrical design. Altschuler organized the patents according to the fundamental tradeoffs they resolved, and created tables so that future designers could apply the inventive principles to similar problems. More recently, others have advanced Altschuler's work into other domains of science and technology. Marketing's role in applying a method such as TRIZ is to represent the customer's voice in comparing the multiple technical alternatives generated.

Inventive Templates

Goldenberg, Mazursky, and Solomon (1999a, 1999b, 1999c) extend Altschuler's methods to propose that ideation is more effective when the PD team focuses on five templates – well-defined schemes that are derived from an historical analysis of new products. The authors define a template as a systematic change between an existing solution and a new solution and provide a method by which the PD team can make these changes in a series of smaller steps called 'operators:' exclusion, inclusion, unlinking, linking, splitting, and joining. For example, the 'attribute dependency' template operates on existing solutions by first applying the inclusion and then the linking operators. The authors give an example of how a new car concept was developed by creating a dependency between color and the location of a car's parts. Specifically, Volkswagen's 'Polo Harlequin' features differently colored parts and has become quite popular in Europe, even though it was initially intended as an April Fools' joke. Other templates include component control (inclusion and linking), replacement (splitting, excluding, including, and joining), displacement (splitting, excluding, and unlinking), and division (splitting and linking).

Summary of Methods for the Fuzzy Front End

The fuzzy front end of the PD process is the least well defined, but, perhaps, the most important phase of the process. Without good customer input and creative ideas, the process is doomed from the start. Customers do not buy products that do not satisfy their needs. Success is elusive unless the PD team generates ideas that satisfy those needs in novel ways. Thus, it is not surprising that there has been significant research to propose and test many different ways to identify customer needs and generate creative ideas in response to those needs. In this section we have reviewed the most common methods that we believe are relevant to a marketing audience. They are rich and varied; each has its own strengths and none should be used alone. For example, if a PD team uses only the Kano model it could become overly focused on the product's technological features and miss underlying psychological or social needs. On the other hand, a pure focus on the mind of the customer could cause the team to miss the obvious solutions that will ultimately dominate the market. Good practice suggests that the PD team consider a variety of approaches to customer-need identification and use them in parallel. If the final output is subjected to a rigorous needs-grouping method such as customer-based affinity diagrams or customer sorts, then the PD team will be able to assure that the ideas it creates solve one or more strategic customer needs.

Once the PD team knows the strategic needs, it needs ideas. Once again there are a variety of methods. Our own experience suggests that different teams will be comfortable with different approaches. Some teams prefer the formal systems approaches, others need the wilder approaches that 'take a vacation from the problem,' and still others prefer just to work alone. The organization's culture (see 'Enterprise Strategy' later in this chapter) must be conducive to these myriad approaches. While creativity is lauded by most PD teams, the organizational challenges and frustrations of dealing with truly creative people frequently preempt the benefits (Staw, 1995). However, if idea generation is successful, the teams will suggest large numbers of initial ideas that can later be systematically engineered into effective concepts, prototypes, and products. We now turn to systematic methods by which these winning concepts are selected and developed and ultimately shaped into products.

Selecting Concepts, and Designing and Engineering Products

Returning to the PD funnel at the center of the PD process in Figure 8.3 (page 182), we see that the many ideas created in opportunity identification are funneled to a smaller set of concepts that are winnowed still further to a viable set of products or platforms. In this section we address concept selection and the design and engineering processes that develop concepts into viable products. We begin with methods such as lead-user analysis, Kaizen and Teian analysis, set-based design, and Pugh concept selection. Each of these methods builds on the customer-needs identification and ideation that took place during the fuzzy front end of product development.

Lead Users

Sometimes the best ideas come from outside the firm and, in particular, from end-users themselves. In some categories the average customer can recognize and appreciate new solutions to their basic needs, and in other categories it is more difficult. More importantly, PD teams are often embedded in their corporate culture and view PD through the lens of their current products.

Von Hippel (1986) suggests that some of the best sources of insight into user needs and potential product prototypes are 'lead users,' customers whose strong product needs in the present foreshadow the needs of the general marketplace in the future. These users often have such a compelling need to solve their problems that they develop their own solutions. In some cases these users represent a very specialized market, but in many cases they anticipate the needs of the larger market. For example, automobile manufacturers follow NASCAR racing carefully because the racing teams face new challenges and often invent new solutions that can later be applied to a more general market. Computer projection systems manufacturers monitor early adopters, such as NASA investing in display equipment for its flight simulators, because as technology advances and costs drop, the problems faced by simulator users will suggest solutions for broader markets such as video gamers.

Von Hippel describes how to identify lead users, and then how to incorporate their insights into the product-design process in a five-step process:

1. Identify a new market trend or product opportunity (e.g., greater computer portability, zero emission vehicles, etc.).
2. Define measures of potential benefit as they relate to customer needs.
3. Select 'lead users' who are 'ahead of their time' and who will benefit the most from a good solution (e.g., power users).
4. Extract information from the 'lead users' about their needs and potential solutions and generate product concepts that embed these solutions.
5. Test the concepts with the broader market to forecast the implications of lead-user needs as they apply to the market in general.

Urban and von Hippel (1988) applied this technique to computer-aided design (CAD) systems. Although the conventional wisdom of the CAD developers was that the systems were much too complex for users to modify, Urban and von Hippel found that lead users who faced difficult problems had not only modified their systems, but had generated significant improvements. For example, designers of complex, integrated circuits developed 3-dimensional CAD systems that could deal with curved surfaces, multiple layers, and non-surface-mounted components. When 3-D CAD software packages were developed based on these lead users' solutions, they were highly rated by the more general market.

Employee Feedback: *Kaizen* and *Teian*

Another source of insight into ways in which to address customer needs better is the company's own workforce. In his writings on *Kaizen*, the Japanese concept of continuous improvement, Masaaki Imai (1986) explains that each employee is responsible for both maintaining the status quo and destroying it. This refers to the notion that employees must follow certain standards, but also eliminate waste and contribute to innovation. One way in which employees can contribute is by making frequent suggestions on product and process improvements through a system the Japanese call *Teian*. See *Kaizen Teian 1* by the Japan Human Relations Association (1992). Of course, the scope of such an employee suggestion system covers more than just customer needs, but the essence of continuous improvement is meeting customer needs more effectively.

Set-based Design and Modularity

In addition to getting ideas from lead users and from the production employees, the PD team can pursue systematic methods such as set-based design. This method generates multiple design options by breaking a product into smaller subsystems, standardizing the interfaces between those subsystems, and generating one or more design options for each key subsystem. Given interchangeability between the subsystems, multiple design solutions become available to the firm, limited only by the number of combinations of subsystems that are feasible.

Ward and co-workers describe a set-based design process in which the freezing of the final choice of subsystems is delayed until the product is closer to launch (see Liker et al., 1996; Sobek et al., 1999; Ward et al., 1996). The firm can then check the pulse of a dynamic market in order to optimize the final choice of modular designs, thereby exploiting the flexibility inherent in the set-based approach. Baldwin and Clark (2000) further characterize flexibility due to product and process modularity as forms of real options, and demonstrate the potentially high value of holding such options.

Pugh Concept Selection

When mass customization is not prevalent in an industry, the firm must narrow options from a broad array of possible design solutions to a few critical solutions (sometimes just one). Pugh (1996) developed a method of winnowing multiple new product concepts, which he terms 'controlled convergence.' In essence, Pugh suggests that each member of the design team independently generate conceptual solutions to the design problem. The competing ideas are then compared to a standard datum, selected for its typicality in the product category, and are evaluated as being better than, equal to, or inferior to the datum on the key dimensions that will contribute to product success. The group proceeds to eliminate weaker ideas, but also attempts to cull the advantages of each concept and incorporate it into the remaining ones before discarding it. In this way, the 'winning' concept incorporates many of the best ideas of all of the other concepts. Of course, some ideas are highly integral to a specific concept, making such 'cherry-picking' particularly difficult, which is why consensus-building and tradeoffs amongst the members of the cross-functional team are crucial elements of the Pugh process. Marketing's role in this process is to identify the key customer criteria on which concepts will be based and to ensure that each concept is evaluated with customer needs and preferences in mind.

Using inputs from the ideation processes, lead-user analysis, set-based design, and Pugh concept selection, the PD team outputs a smaller set of high-potential product concepts. Following the PD funnel, the PD team then focuses on these concepts and develops each to their greatest potential. This means linking engineering solutions to customer needs and *vice versa*.

Value Engineering

From a customer's point-of-view, a product consists of a bundle of features and benefits resulting from its use, while from the firm's perspective, the product consists of a bundle of parts and the processes that result in its manufacture. When making cost and feasibility tradeoffs, it is important for the design team to connect the customer and firm perspectives. Ulrich and Eppinger (2000) describe one method of doing so, known as value engineering, which relates the importance customers place on each function performed by a product to the cost of the parts contributing to that function. A key principle underlying value engineering is that the marginal cost of each part of a product should be less than its marginal contribution to customer value. To implement value engineering the team must know (1) the value placed by customers on each function, and (2) the cost of the parts and manufacturing to provide that function. We address (1) below as it is most relevant to the marketing

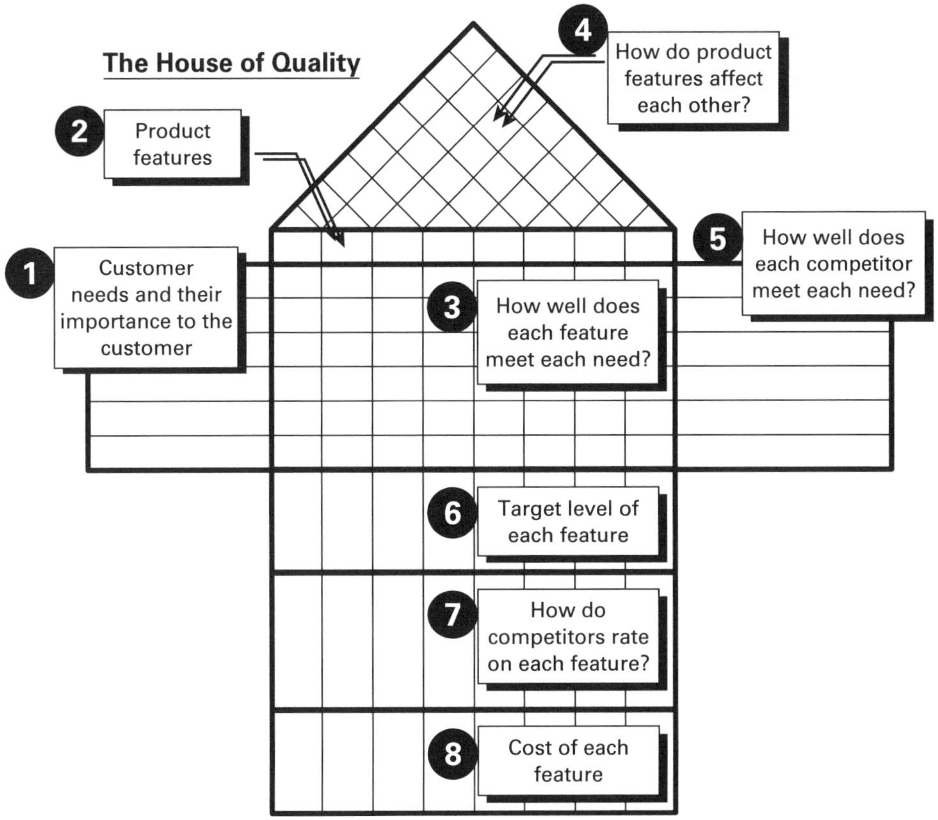

Figure 8.10 *The House of Quality*

audience. For greater detail on (2) see Ulrich and Eppinger (2000). As with Pugh Concept Selection, PD teams must be extremely careful of highly integrated features and look for synergies in both value creation and cost reduction.

Quality Function Deployment and the House of Quality

Value engineering requires that we link customer needs to product solutions so that the PD team can make intelligent tradeoffs and, perhaps, find creative solutions that do not require tradeoffs. Quality Function Deployment (QFD) and its more-recent progeny (McGrath, 1996; Smith & Reinertsen, 1998; Tessler et al., 1993) provide the means to make this linkage. QFD itself is a set of processes that link customer needs all the way through to production requirements. Although the full QFD process is sometimes used, most notably in Japan, it is the first matrix of QFD, called the House of Quality (HOQ), that is used most often (Fig. 8.10). The driving force behind the HOQ is the short, accurate, relevant list of key customer needs identified in the fuzzy front end and structured into strategic, tactical, and detailed needs. In the HOQ, these needs are related to product features, which are then evaluated as to how well they meet customer needs. Product features are 'benchmarked' against competitors' features in their ability to meet customer needs, and the HOQ is used to compare the benchmarking on features to benchmarking on customer needs. Finally the total product is evaluated by the ability of its features to meet customer needs more effectively and at lower costs than competitive products.

The HOQ provides and organizes the information that the PD team needs to refine each concept. It has proven effective in a variety of applications, including consumer frequently purchased goods, consumer durables, consumer services, business-to-business products, and business-to-business services (cf. Hauser, 1993). See Griffin's (1992) review of HOQ applications for an in-depth discussion of when it works well and when it does not. A further advantage of the HOQ and related techniques is that it enhances communication among PD team members (see quasi-experiment in Griffin & Hauser, 1992). This is becoming even more important as PD teams become more dispersed and global. The downside of QFD is that strict adherence to the method can lead to overly complex charts and become extremely time-consuming, especially for products with many customer needs and engineering 'key characteristics.' Clearly, firms must adapt the House of Quality to produce benefits commensurate with these implementation costs. Ironically, complex projects that make QFD difficult to implement may be the very ones that benefit most from improved communication and coordination within the firm.

Marketing's primary input to the HOQ includes identifying customer needs (fuzzy front end), measuring how products fulfill those needs (e.g., Churchill, 1998; Green Tull, & Albaum, 1988; Moore & Pessemier, 1993; Urban & Hauser, 1993), and understanding the tradeoffs among customer needs and among potential product features. Ultimately, the HOQ method translates customer priorities, as captured by a prioritized list of needs, into engineering/design priorities by identifying those product features that contribute the most to satisfying customers better than competitive offerings.

Tradeoffs Among Needs and Features: Conjoint Analysis

After customer needs are identified and grouped, after critical features are identified and linked to customer needs, and after high potential concepts are developed, the PD team's next step is to focus on those features and concepts that are most likely to improve customer satisfaction and lead to profitable products. Developing methods to measure such tradeoffs among customer needs and/or features is, arguably, one of the most studied problems in marketing research. We have been able to identify over 150 articles published in the top marketing journals on conjoint analysis in the last 20 years. In this section we review some of the basic ideas. See also reviews by Green (1984), and Green and Srinivasan (1978, 1990). Also, because they continue to be used by PD teams, we include self-explicated methods such as those reviewed in Wilkie and Pessemier (1973).

Suppose that the PD team is developing a new laundry product and has identified the strategic needs of 'cleans effectively,' 'safe for delicate clothes,' 'easy to use in all situations,' 'good for the environment,' and 'inexpensive.' The team now wants to evaluate a series of product concepts, each of which stretches one of the five strategic customer needs. Conjoint analysis, applied to customer needs, is the general method to measure the customers' tradeoffs among those needs. By identifying and quantifying the tradeoffs, perhaps by customer segment, conjoint analysis helps to focus the PD team on those concepts that have the highest potential. Conjoint analysis can also be applied to product features; for example, the maker of an camera might want to know how highly customers value such features as one-step vs. two-step picture taking, styling covers, automatic vs. manual focusing, and automatic vs. controllable lighting. Conjoint analysis can tell the PD team which of the features is most highly valued by which segment and can associate a willingness to pay for those features.

Camera Example

We begin by illustrating conjoint analysis with the most common type of application – providing preferences with respect to products (or product concepts) in which the experimenter has varied the features (or other aspects) of the products systematically. We then review other types of conjoint analysis and suggest new forms that are now feasible with state-of-the-art information and communication technology.

Suppose that we have identified a set of features for a new camera from a combination of sources including experiential interviews, empathic design, Kansei analysis, and the Information Pump. In general, this feature list will be quite extensive, but for the purpose of this chapter we will illustrate the feature list with a reduced set of five features.[1] We might conclude that customers have needs that can be addressed through various levels of the five product features in Figure 8.11.

For example, one product permutation would cost $25, weigh 16oz., have automatic light control, produce 3-inch square pictures, and require the user to focus manually. In all there are $4 \times 4 \times 2 \times 3 \times 2 = 192$ permutations, each of which might be a viable product. In principle, we could ask a sample of customers to evaluate each of the 192 potential products, but this would be an extremely unwieldy task. As the number of potential products increases the task becomes quite burdensome (Green, Carroll, and Goldberg, 1981; Green, Goldberg, and Montemayor, 1981; Malhotra, 1986) and the quality of the data degrades (Bateson et al., 1987; Huber et al., 1993; Moore & Semenik, 1988). We must also be concerned with biases that can result when the number of levels varies across features (Wittink, 1989), potentially drawing more attention and importance to those features with more levels.

Factorial Designs It would be even more cumbersome if we asked customers to evaluate products that varied on the 22 camera features in Note 1 – if these were a mix of two-level and three-level

Product Feature	Alternative Levels			
Price(P)	$15	$20	$25	$30
Weight (W)	16 oz.	20 oz.	32 oz.	64 oz.
Light control (L)	Auto	1-step		
Size of picture (S)	Postage stamp	3 inch square	Standard	
Focusing (F)	Auto	Manual		

Figure 8.11 *Simplified Conjoint Features and Levels*

features this would yield almost 400 million potential products. Instead we would like to capture the information that customers would provide about tradeoffs among features by asking each customer to evaluate a much smaller number of products. For example, for the five features in Figure 8.11 we may not need to ask each customer to evaluate all 192 feature combinations. Instead, we could use a more efficient experimental design known as a fractional factorial design. If we assume that all of the features are independent we can simplify the number of combinations still further by using a special fractional factorial design known as an orthogonal array. For example, we might use one orthogonal design called a 'hyper-greco-latin-square' design, and ask each customer to evaluate just 16 carefully chosen products. (A similar experimental approach, known as Taguchi methods (Taguchi, 1987), is used in describing reliability testing and statistical sampling.) The actual details of a particular fractional factorial design, that is, the specific levels of price, weight, light control, picture size, and focusing for the 16 potential products, can be determined using listings compiled by Addelman (1962) and Hahn and Shapiro (1966), or by using computer programs produced by SAS, Systat, Sawtooth Software, Bretton-Clark Software, and others. The key research area here is in determining the best designs for a given number of combinations. For example, a common criterion is called D-efficiency – a measure based on the determinant of the information matrix (Kuhfeld, 1999; Kuhfeld et al., 1994).

Respondents' tasks The task by which customers express their evaluations of products varies. See Cattin and Wittink (1989) for a survey of industry practice. By far the most common task is to simply ask the respondents to rank order the product profiles in terms of preference. For example, each respondent might order a set of cards according to his or her preferences for (or likelihood of buying) the products depicted. Each card, known as a full-profile, describes a product consisting of differing levels of the key features. Other tasks include asking the respondent to evaluate pairs of profiles (Bateson et al., 1987; Srinivasan & Shocker, 1973) or tradeoffs among features displayed two at a time (Johnson, 1974; Segal, 1982). The respondent might be simply asked to rank-order the profiles (Green & Wind, 1975) or the customer can provide a scaled evaluation (Carmone et al., 1978; Currim et al., 1981; Hauser & Shugan, 1980; Leigh, et al., 1984; Srinivasan & Park, 1997). Another common data collection procedure simply presents the customer with sets of alternative products' profiles chosen from an experimental design, and asks the customer to select the product he or she prefers from each set of product profiles. This method, known as choice-based conjoint analysis, uses a quantal choice model such as a logit or probit model to estimate the part worths from the choice data (Arora & Huber, 2001; Carroll & Green, 1995; Elrod et al., 1992; Haaijer et al., 1998; Huber & Zwerina, 1996; Louviere et al., 2000; Oppewal et al., 1994; Orme, 1999). All forms of data collection appear to be reliable (Bateson et al., 1987; Green & Srinivasan, 1990; Louviere et al., 2000); none seem to dominate either practice or the academic literature.

Part worth functions Once we have the ratings (or rankings or choices) for each profile in the experimental design, we represent this information by a utility function, that is, a real-valued function of the feature levels chosen such that differences in utility represent differences (or rank orders) in preference among the products. If the features are independent, as is assumed in an orthogonal array, then the utility of a product is simply the sum of the uni-attributed utilities of each of the features (Keeney & Raiffa, 1976). If the features are specified by discrete levels, as in Figure 8.11, then the utility of each of the levels of each of the features is called a part worth. That is, the utility of a camera that costs $25, weighs 16 oz., has automatic light control, produces 3-inch square pictures, and requires the user to focus manually would be equal to the part worth of $25, plus the part worth of 16 oz., plus the part worth of automatic light control, plus the part worth of 3-inch square pictures, plus the part worth of manual focus. (We can also represent utility as the

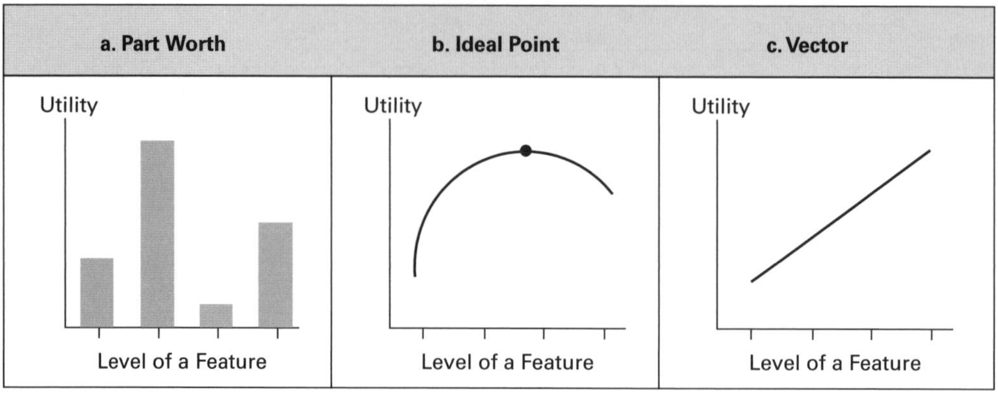

Figure 8.12 *Conjoint Utility Functional Forms*

product of the part worths – it is only separability that is implied by independence.) Part worths are illustrated in Figure 8.12a. However, if the features are continuous we might also represent the utility by a more continuous function. An ideal point model for features where more is not always better (e.g., picture size, Figure 8.12b) is one such continuous function, and a vector model, where more *is* better (e.g., quality of picture, Figure 8.12c), is another such continuous function. Decreasing functions (e.g., price), concave functions (e.g., clarity of sound), and anti-ideal point (e.g., the temperature of tea) models are also possible. See the discussion in Pekelman and Sen (1979).

In some cases the features might not be independent. For example, the desire of the customer for manual focusing might depend upon the quality of image that can be produced with the camera's lens and film. In this case, conjoint analyses use more complex experimental designs that allow interactions and estimate utility functions that cannot be represented simply as the sum (or product) of the part worths. See Green and Devita (1975), Akaah and Korgaonkar (1983), and Johnson et al., (1989).

Estimation In order to estimate the utility or part worth functions we must *decompose* the overall preference rating (or ranking) into the utilities of the features (with or without interactions). Early applications assumed that only the rank-order information was relevant and used monotonic analysis of variance (monanova) to estimate the part worths (Green & Srinivasan, 1978). Alternatively, linear programming provides accurate estimates based on a criterion of mean absolute or directional errors (Jain et al., 1979; Malhotra, 1982; Srinivasan & Shocker, 1973). However, many researchers have discovered that customers can provide valid preference data that have strong metric properties (Currim et al., 1981; Hauser & Shugan, 1980; Huber, 1975), while other researchers have found that treating rank data as if it were metric provides accurate estimates (Carmone et al., 1978). Thus, many applications use OLS regression or other metric methods. If risk is important in the design decision, then von Neumann–Morgenstern utility estimation can be used by asking respondents to evaluate product profiles in which one or more of the features is uncertain (Eliashberg & Hauser, 1985; Farquhar, 1977; Hauser & Urban, 1979; Kahn & Meyer, 1991).

Compositional Methods Conjoint analysis is usually thought of as a decompositional technique in which part worths are estimated by asking respondents to evaluate potential products (or reduced sets of features of those products). However, there is also a long tradition in marketing of compositional methods, in which the customer is asked to specify directly the importance or part worth of a need or feature. These methods, also known as expectancy-value or self-explicated methods, were reviewed by Wilkie and Pessemier in 1973. In these methods, the customer rates each product on each need (rates) and evaluates the importance of each need (weights). The utility of a product is then the sum of the weights times the rates, summed over customer needs. More recently, Srinivasan (1988), Srinivasan & Wyner (1988), and Bucklin & Srinivasan (1991) used a method called Casemap in which they modified self-explicated methods for part worth estimation. After an initial conjunctive phase (described below), Casemap asks customers to specify the importance of each feature or need and the relative value of each level of each feature or need (relative to a base level of that feature or need). The part worth is then the product of these two values. Such self-explicated methods have the advantage of being relatively easy for the respondent; Casemap can be completed over the telephone and does not require that a sample of customers come to a central location. Casemap and other self-explicated methods have proven to be accurate and reliable (Akaah & Korgaonkar, 1983; Bateson et al., 1987; Green & Helsen, 1989; Hoepfl & Huber, 1970; Huber et al., 1993; Leigh et al., 1984).

Conjunctive Processes Standard conjoint analysis asks respondents to evaluate products that vary on all levels of all of the features or needs. But many researchers have hypothesized that not all levels of all features or needs are acceptable to respondents. For example, a customer who wants a camera for a wedding might not accept a postage-stamp size picture; no levels of the other features will compensate the customer enough to make him or her buy a wedding camera that produces such small pictures. When features have such minimum acceptable levels (at least a 3-inch square picture) the customer is said to follow a *conjunctive* process (Einhorn, 1971; Grether & Wilde, 1984). This is similar to the 'must haves' identified by the Kano hierarchy of needs outlined earlier. Casemap and other methods (Sawtooth, 1996) have modified conjoint analysis to account for such conjunctive processes by first asking the respondent to specify those levels of the features that are unacceptable. Prior specification of unacceptable levels improves prediction if done carefully. However, Green Krieger & Bansal (1988) and Klein (1986) caution that if the questions are not pre-tested and implemented carefully, the respondent will falsely reject feature levels that he or she would have later accepted.

Reducing Respondent Burden While the basic concept of conjoint analysis is both powerful and simple, a key implementation barrier has been the respondents' task. Although we can reduce the number of profiles based on the five features in Figure 8.11 to an orthogonal array of 16 profiles, such a reduction is not always possible if the number of features and levels is large. For example, Wind et al., (1989) report a successful application of conjoint analysis to the design of Marriott's Courtyard Hotels, in which there were 50 factors at a total of 167 levels. Clearly, we cannot ask respondents to evaluate even a reduced experimental design for such problems. As a result, researchers and practitioners have focused on means to reduce the burden on respondents. We have already reviewed tradeoff analysis (e.g., Johnson, 1974), in which respondents compare two features at a time, choice-based conjoint analysis, in which respondents choose among sets of profiles (e.g., Carroll & Green, 1995), and the elimination of unacceptable feature levels (e.g., Srinivasan, 1988; Malhotra, 1986, also proposes a method that screens unacceptable profiles.) There has also been much effort allocated to very efficient experimental designs (e.g., Kuhfeld et al., 1994). We review here three other methods for reducing respondent burden: (1) methods that mix individual and market-level data (hybrid conjoint); (2) methods that employ multi-stage data collection, in which the first task is simplified (hierarchical integration and customized designs); and (3) methods that adapt the questions to the respondent's early answers (adaptive conjoint analysis).

Hybrid conjoint analysis (cf. Green, 1984) combines self-explicated methods at the level of the individual respondent with decompositional methods which split the experimental design across respondents to reduce the complexity of the data collection task. For example, respondents might explicitly rate the part worths of each feature on a 1–10 scale and then rank order a subset of full-profile cards. The estimated utilities are based on both types of data. Although, at the level of the individual respondent, hybrid conjoint analysis may not provide the detailed accuracy of full-profile methods, hybrid methods have proven quite accurate at the segment or market level (Akaah & Korgaonkar, 1983; Green, Goldberg & Montemayor, 1981). Recently, Lenk et al. (1996) proposed a hybrid method in which they used hierarchical Bayes (HB) methods to estimate individual utility functions with reduced numbers of questions per respondent. The HB methods improve accuracy by the use of heavy computation, and will become more common as the cost of computation decreases dramatically with the advent of inexpensive but powerful computers. With HB methods caution should be exercised, as the number of parameters to be estimated grows in relation to the number of data points obtained from the respondents' conjoint tasks.

In *hierarchical integration*, respondents evaluate products on higher-level features, facets, or needs. They then evaluate the relative impact of features that affect those higher-level constructs. Methods for the more-detailed evaluations include traditional conjoint analysis (Hauser & Simmie, 1981), hybrid conjoint analysis (Wind et al., 1989), choice-based conjoint analysis (Oppewal et al., 1994), and self-explicated methods (Hauser & Griffin, 1993). In a related method, Srinivasan & Park (1997) used *customized conjoint analysis* – a modified method in which respondents use self-explicated methods to evaluate all features and then evaluate a subset of the most important features with full-profile conjoint analysis. The subset chosen for the drill-down is customized to each respondent.

The third stream of research directed at reducing respondent burden employs adaptive methods. The most common is Sawtooth Software's *adaptive conjoint analysis* (ACA: Sawtooth, 1996). In ACA respondents are first asked a series of self-explicated questions. They are then asked to evaluate pairs of profiles in which a subset of the features vary. The method is adaptive because each question after the first is chosen with an heuristic that attempts to gather the most information per question. Final questions then establish the relative scales of the self-explicated and adaptive components. ACA has proven accurate under the right circumstances, and has proven to add incremental information relative to the self-explicated portion of the interview (Huber et al., 1993; Johnson, 1987; Orme, 1999). However, Green et al., (1991) caution that ACA might not be as accurate as the full profile method when the latter is feasible. Johnson (1999) proposes that one can post-analyze ACA data with hierarchical Bayes analysis to improve its accuracy.

Recently, Toubia et al. (2002) proposed an improved algorithm based on the new interior-point algorithms in mathematical programming. They ask an initial question, but then choose subsequent paired-comparison questions such that the answers maximally reduce the feasible set of utility parameters. Simulations suggest that (1) the interior-point algorithms can gather as much information as traditional ACA, but with fewer questions, and (2) for many situations the initial self-explicated questions can be skipped for a further reduction in the respondents' burden. The new 'polyhedral' methods appear to do well relative to traditional ACA approaches when the researcher is seeking to obtain part-worth estimates with relatively few questions, when respondent wear out is a concern, and when the responses to self-explicated questions are noisy. Dahan et al. (2002) further test the polyhedral methods in an empirical application to laptop computer bags. In their study, they allocate respondents to questions chosen by either (1) the polyhedral methods, (2) traditional ACA, or (3) efficient fixed designs. After completing the conjoint task, respondents are allowed to select and keep a laptop computer bag (plus any change in cash) worth approximately $100. The new methods appear to improve predictions relative to the extant methods and appear to provide valid and reliable part worths with relatively few questions. These polyhedral methods have been extended to produce an adaptive choice-based conjoint method that does well in simulation, but there have not yet been any empirical tests of the polyhedral choice-based method. In general, the polyhedral methods show interesting potential, but need further testing.

Dahan and Orlin (2002) propose a different adaptive approach to conjoint analysis, in which full-profile, web-based conjoint cards from a fractional factorial design are ranked by respondents. By limiting respondents to sort orders that are perfectly consistent, that is, sort orders for which the estimated utility function exactly reproduces the sort order when applied to the conjoint cards, the Conjoint Adaptive Ranking Database System (Cards) approach significantly reduces questioning burden and internal inconsistency. Of course, the method weighs the ranking of more desirable cards higher than low-ranking cards, necessitating careful priming for respondents' early choices. In order to speed web-based response times between clicks, all feasible sort orders are calculated in advance and stored in a high-speed database. This new approach has yet to be tested empirically.

Summary of Conjoint Analysis

Conjoint analysis is a powerful tool for understanding the tradeoffs customers make between various features of a product. Conjoint analysis uses the list of key customer needs or product features determined by the techniques discussed in the fuzzy front end. It prioritizes those features based on the amount of extra benefit customers derive from a feature or from another way of satisfying a customer need. The results can be used to improve designs, optimize them for value, and predict market share and product success.

New Web-based Methods for Designing and Engineering Product Concepts

The advent of new information and rapid-communication technologies such as extremely powerful desktop computers, the Internet, and the worldwide web are leading to new and exciting methods of concept evaluation. We review some of these methods here. Demos, open source software, and working papers describing the methods in this section (and the polyhedral methods of the previous section) are available at mitsloan.mit.edu/vc.

Web-based Conjoint Analysis

McArdle (2000) reports on the application of conjoint analysis to the design of a new camera. The advantages of such web-based applications are that rich, contextual, yet virtual media can be used to illustrate products. For example, in Figure 8.13a the respondent is shown how he or she can use the camera – with a single click the respondent can view animations of the camera or pictures in use. Similar screens enable the respondent to better understand the features that are being varied. Then the respondent is presented with a conjoint analysis task, in this case paired comparisons (Figure 8.13b). The task is made easier for the respondent by animating the scale and by making detailed feature descriptions or product demonstrations available with a single click.

The advantage of web-based conjoint analysis is that the respondents can complete the task remotely. For example, McArdle (2000) compared samples of respondents who answered the questions in the comfort of their homes to respondents who completed the questions on a more traditional,

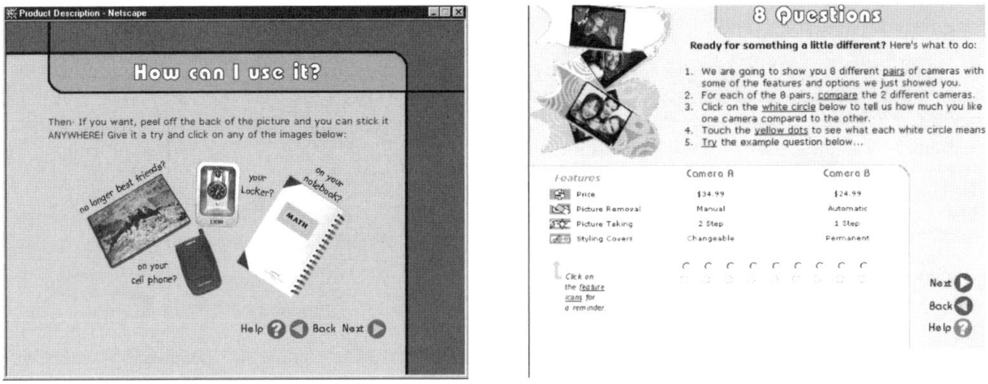

Figure 8.13 *Web-based Product Demonstration and Pairwise Tradeoffs for a Camera*

dedicated computer in a mall-intercept environment. The qualitative results were quite similar, although there was some slight variation due to sample selection. Certainly with further development the methods can be made to converge. Although McArdle used a fixed, orthogonal design, both Sawtooth and Toubia et al. (2002) provide web-based adaptive methods.

With further testing and development, web-based conjoint analysis has the potential to grow dramatically. For example, many companies are forming panels of web-enabled respondents who can complete conjoint tasks. NFO Worldwide, Inc. has a balanced panel of over 500,000 web-enabled respondents; DMS, Inc., a subsidiary of AOL, uses 'Opinion Place' to recruit respondents dynamically, and claims to be interviewing over 1 million respondents per year; Knowledge Networks has recruited 100,000 respondents with random digit dialing methods and provides them with web access if they do not already have it; Greenfield Online, Inc. has an online panel of 3 million respondents, and Harris Interactive, Inc. has an online panel of 6.5 million respondents (Buckman, 2000). Prototypes of automated web-based systems have demonstrated that it is technically feasible to enable an inexperienced user to conduct a web-based study, complete with analysis, in under a week (Faura, 2000).

User design with DnD

The interactivity of the web, coupled with rapidly advancing computer power, makes it possible to explore creative methods to gather information on customers' preferences. For example, Dahan and Hauser (2002) describe a method of feature-based user design on the web in which respondents drag and drop (DnD) their preferred features onto a design palette that illustrates the fully configured product, as seen in Figure 8.14.

As these choices are made, tradeoffs such as price and performance are instantly visible and updated, so the respondent can interactively learn his or her preferences and reconfigure the design until an 'ideal' configuration is identified. The method includes full configuration logic, so that only feasible designs can be generated, i.e., choices on one feature can preclude or interact with choices on other features. User design provides an engaging, interactive method of collecting data on customer tradeoffs. This data can be used to narrow the set of features. The reduced set of features can then form the basis of a more extensive conjoint analysis. McArdle (2000) reports that the conjoint analysis of the camera features in Figure 8.13 predicted well those features that customers selected with DnD (Figure 8.14). See explicit comparisons for this and other applications in Dahan and Hauser (2002). See also Leichty et al. (2001).

The DnD interface employed in user design market research may presage that which will be used to sell mass-customized goods over the web. For example, as shown in Figure 8.15, customers may appreciate a highly visual interface in which product features are literally dragged and dropped into place. Park et al. (1999) demonstrate that customers arrive at different 'ideal configurations' depending on whether they are asked to add options to a base model or subtract options from a fully loaded model, suggesting that the initial configuration of a user design web site may have high impact on the data collected (in the case of market research), or sales effectiveness (in the case of mass-customized e-commerce).

Securities Trading of Concepts (STOC)

One criticism of concept testing methods that rely on direct feedback from potential customers is that customers may not have the incentive to be completely truthful. Further, in most real purchase

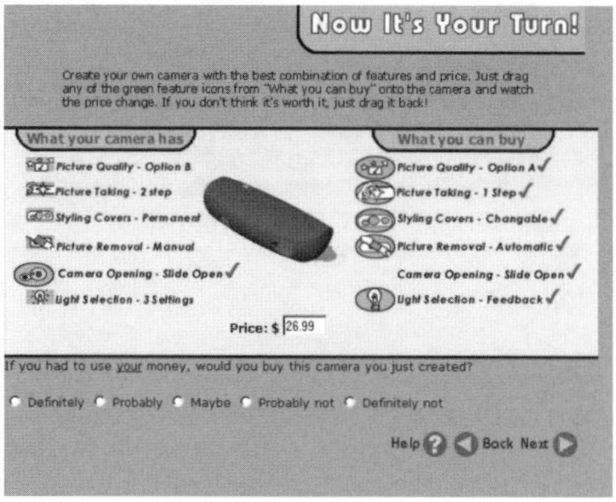

Figure 8.14 *User Design of an Instant Camera*

Figure 8.15 *User Design of a Printer/Copier*

situations, customers may be influenced by others' opinions and choices – a network externality not easily accounted for with traditional concept testing methods. Chan et al. (2000) offer a potential solution to these concerns in the form of a proposed market research methodology – Securities Trading of Concepts (STOC) – depicted in Figure 8.16.

Utilizing the communications and conceptualization technologies of the Internet, participants compete in a simulated trading game in which the securities traded are new product concepts. The prices and trading volumes of these securities provide information as to the underlying preferences of the individual traders and of the group as a whole. The idea that the price mechanism conveys information efficiently is well understood in financial contexts. Early applications of the STOC method suggest that it can identify those concepts that have the highest customer-demand potential, but further application and validation are necessary.

Summary of Methods for Designing and Engineering Concepts and Products

Marketing plays a major role in the design and engineering of product concepts and in the selection of product features. Lead-user analysis, *Kaizen* and *Teian* methods, set-based design, and Pugh concept selection provide means by which PD teams can selectively winnow product concepts down to focus on those that are most likely to succeed. However, a key criterion in any winnowing process is customer acceptance and customer willingness to pay for product features that solve their needs. Thus, QFD and the HOQ provide the means by which product focus and customer focus converge.

Perhaps the most important marketing input to the design and engineering process is the analysis of the tradeoffs that customers make with respect to needs and product features. These methods, generally called conjoint analysis, include both decompositional methods, in which customers evaluate bundles of needs or features, and compositional methods, in which customers directly evaluate the needs or features. Both methods work well and provide valuable input to the HOQ and other concept selection and refinement methods. Finally, new methods are being developed to take advantage of new computing and communications technologies such as the world wide web. Web-based conjoint analysis, new adaptive methods, user design methods, and Securities Trading of Concepts all have the potential to increase the effectiveness and reduce the cost of the marketing input to concept selection and refinement. In some cases, we expect the costs to drop dramatically and the time-to-completion of the market input to drop from six weeks to a few days. These improvements are most likely for consumer products for which web-based panels are available. For business-to-business products, where it is harder to recruit the appropriate respondents, cost reductions may be more difficult to realize, but the time reductions should be achieved. Once fully developed and tested, web-based developments should enhance the ability of the PD team to design and engineer concepts.

Prototyping and Testing Concepts and Products

Returning to the PD funnel in the end-to-end process in Figure 8.3 (page 182), we see that after the product concepts have been generated, winnowed and refined, they need to be tested before they can be launched. The goal in this phase of the PD process is to evaluate the concepts (and engineer the final product) so that any launch is highly likely to

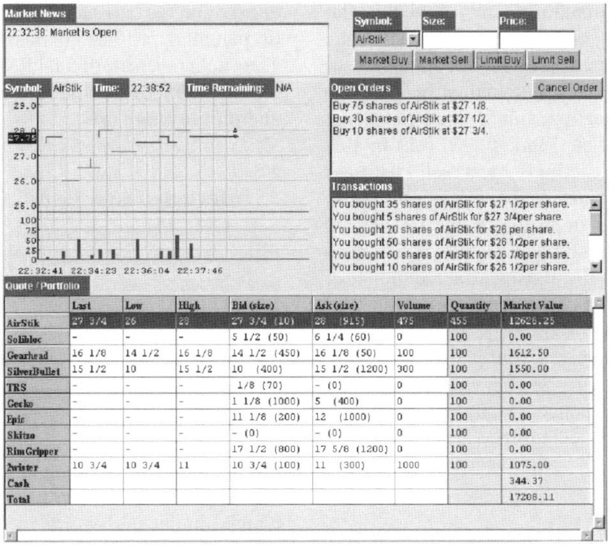

Figure 8.16 *Securities Trading of Concepts (STOC)*

succeed. The team must make tradeoffs among the cost of testing, the advantage of further development, and any delays in product launch. A testing method should be accurate and cost effective.

Recently, there has been significant new work done to understand the role of testing and the optimization in the PD process. The PD process is examined as a unified entity such that reductions in cost and uncertainty at one stage affect cost and uncertainty at subsequent stages. Thus, the tradeoffs between time-to-market, development expense, production cost, and quality can be viewed as an optimal search for the best product design. Testing thus becomes a search process under uncertainty and can be optimized. This section will review this new work, as well as cover many of the testing methods in the literature.

Target Costing: Design for Manufacturing and Assembly (DFMA)

Dahan and Srinivasan (2002) highlight the potential importance of unit production cost in the marketing success of a new product. Specifically, they suggest that investments to reduce unit manufacturing costs increase profitability through six mechanisms: (1) market share improvements due to lower prices; (2) primary market growth due to lower prices; (3) reduced channel costs due to greater volume; (4) 'virtuous cycles' of learning due to higher cumulative volumes; (5) quality improvements due to simplified designs; and (6) strategic benefits due to competitive disincentives. In short, they suggest that marketers work with their operations counterparts at the early phases of new product design to ensure that low costs are locked in early.

Boothroyd et al., (1994) describe methods of dramatically reducing unit manufacturing costs for a broad array of products, primarily through part-count reduction and simplification of the assembly process. Because cost reductions may require changes in the appearance or performance of the product itself if taken to extremes, marketing input, to the extent that it captures cost-benefit tradeoffs as customers would make them, is invaluable to making these decisions.

Ulrich and Pearson (1998) demonstrate empirically, using a method they term 'product archaeology,' that unit manufacturing costs for products competing in the same category (coffee makers) vary greatly, holding quality constant and standardizing for feature variation. They argue that while some of these cost differences may be the result of local manufacturing economics or variations in plant efficiency, a significant portion of the cost differences result directly from design decisions made early in the product development process. Once these design decisions are frozen, reducing the excess costs that may result from them is nearly impossible.

Rapid Prototyping Methods

Thomke (1998a, 1998b), together with von Hippel, and Franke (Thomke et al., 1998) discuss the increasing importance of new technologies such as rapid prototyping, simulation and combinatorial methods in exploring multiple technical solutions during the early phases of product development. In essence, these techniques automatically generate and test variations on a product concept theme using parametric design. Marketing's role in this context is to provide methods by which customer response can be estimated for different feature combinations, combinations that make up part of the objective function used to evaluate those potential designs that pass the technical screening test. For example, while a certain percentage of potential automobile body designs might pass a computer-simulated crash test, only a subset of those body designs might meet other customer requirements for aesthetics and performance. Methods of testing multiple designs with customers are needed, as described next.

Parallel Concept Testing of Multiple Designs

Gross (1967) suggested that multiple advertising campaigns be developed and pretested so as to improve the expected effectiveness of the 'best' campaign. Srinivasan, Lovejoy, and Beach (1997) apply similar thinking to PD and suggest the need for more parallel concept testing prior to 'freezing' the design of a new product. They base their analysis on experience with PD classes taught at Stanford University, in which teams of students design competing products within the same product category. Over years of teaching the course, they note the difficulty of accurately predicting which student designs would fare best in simulated market competitions based on actual respondent preferences. They suggest carrying forward multiple concepts until a later stage of development, testing these with potential customers, and then selecting from among the winning concepts. Once the winning concepts are selected, they can be tested further (funnel PD process), or the team can iterate to opportunity identification and ideation (spiral PD process).

Dahan and Mendelson (2001) quantify this argument and determine the optimal number of concepts to test given the cost per test and the nature of upside profit uncertainty. Their analysis suggests that the statistical theory of extreme values is relevant to concept testing, and that the optimal number of tests is related to the ratio of profit uncertainty (e.g. standard deviation of the profit distribution) to the cost-per-concept test. Further, they show that the nature of upside profit uncertainty, whether fat-tailed, exponential-tailed, or bounded, significantly impacts the degree of optimal parallel testing. Specifically, they show that the effect of declining unit testing costs, as might result from moving to web-based testing, on total concept test spending, depends on the tail-shape parameter of the distribution of potential profits, not just on the cost per test. They note reversals of total R&D spending depending on the interaction between this tail-shape parameter and unit testing cost.

Internet-based Rapid Concept Testing

Dahan and Srinivasan (2000) developed and tested a web-based method of parallel concept testing using visual depictions and animations, in this case bicycle pumps. Respondents viewed eleven new product concepts, and expressed their preferences by 'buying' their most preferred concepts at varying prices. These choices were converted into individual part worths for each concept, using price and product as the only features in a conjoint analysis. These results were compared to a control cell in which similar part-worth measurements were conducted using working physical prototypes of the bike pump concepts. The results showed that both the verbal and web-based visual methods identified the top three concepts from the control group, and that the web-based methods measured these preferences with greater accuracy. As in the fuzzy front end and in the design and engineering phase, we expect that these web-based methods will grow in power and applicability as more researchers address the challenges of implementing these methods. With further development and testing, these virtual concept testing methods have the potential to reduce the cost and time devoted to concept testing.

Automated, Distributed PD Service Exchange Systems

As new methods are developed to model and test customer response to new products more rapidly and inexpensively, it is becoming more important that PD teams can design and cost out these concepts rapidly and inexpensively. However, as product development becomes more dispersed, firms are outsourcing more and more services. Even within a firm, members of the PD team who are experts in gathering the voice of the customer might be in California (say near lead users for automobiles), while experts in the physical design of the car door might be in Detroit, experts in developing the wiring harness (for the door) might be in Mishima, Japan, and experts in wind tunnel simulation might be in Seattle. Furthermore, each sub-team might represent their expertise in a computer model that is not compatible with the other experts. One model might employ a spreadsheet (e.g., Excel), another might utilize a statistical package (e.g., SPSS), another a CAD system, and the last a mathematical modeling system (e.g., MatLab). But all must work

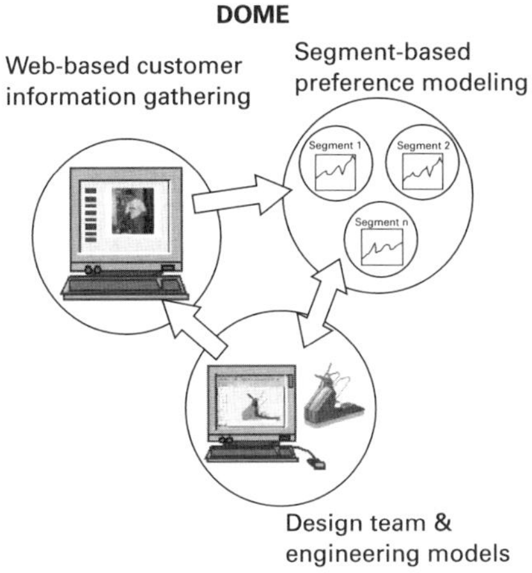

Figure 8.17 *Distributed Object Modeling Environment (DOME)*

together if they are to design a car door for the new Ford Thunderbird.

While in the past, these teams would spend considerable time communicating and developing compatible analytical systems, new automated and distributed service exchange systems such as DOME, depicted in Figure 8.17, make it possible to reduce dramatically the communications costs and speed the product to market (Senin et al., 2001; Wallace et al., 2000). The key idea behind DOME is service (and data) exchange rather than just data exchange. For example, the voice-of-the-customer team might invest in a conjoint analysis of the features of a car door – sound insulation, ease of opening and closing windows, styling, etc – and build a choice simulator that predicts sales as a function of these features. The physical modeler might build a CAD system in which physical dimensions (height, width, length, curvature, wiring requirements, etc.) are input and in which shape is output. The wind tunnel expert might build a simulator in which shape and insulation are input and in which noise level and drag are output. The wiring harness designer might want all of these inputs and can output information such as the power delivered to the electric windows and automatic door locks. Each of these teams, and many others, require and generate information that is connected through a virtual web: the voice-of-the-customer expert cannot run the conjoint simulator without the noise level, the wind tunnel expert cannot estimate noise level without a physical model; and the physical modeler cannot produce a CAD drawing without interfacing with the wiring harness expert.

Systems such as DOME address these communication problems by setting up a 'services' exchange on a common computer platform. Each expert team need only access a software envelope for its program (Excel, SPSS, MatLab, etc.) and post its input requirements and output services. Then either a central administrator, such as the core PD team, can build an integrated system or each expert can trade information in a services marketplace. In the latter case the services exchange provides the means for the market to function and information is exchanged in a free market of services. To date, DOME has been implemented with Ford Motor Company and the US Navy, however, testing continues. The challenge to marketing researchers is to develop systems that are compatible with such service-exchange platforms so that customer information is as fully integrated as engineering-design and production-cost information.

Information Acceleration

Web-based rapid concept testing provides the means to gather customer input about virtual concepts, and service exchanges provide the means to design quickly these virtual concepts. However, in order to make the demand vs. cost tradeoffs, the PD team needs to simulate product acceptance in a marketplace where sales are affected by marketing variables such as advertising, word-of-mouth, and sales force presentations.

Furthermore, really new products often stretch technology and customer comprehension of the benefits of technology. For example, prior to the development of the personal computer, word processing was done by professionals rather than by virtually everyone, spreadsheet analysis was limited to a few financial professionals, and personal finance was done with the checkbook rather than programs like Quicken. There was little demand for web browsers before the Internet became widely available, and little demand for home networking before broadband capabilities were ubiquitous. Thus, in testing really new products and concepts, it is often necessary to place potential customers in new information states with new perspectives on the world. Some of the early attempts at simulating future environments for the customer were called information acceleration (IA). They relied heavily on central location interviewing with multimedia computers that, at the time, were high end. Today, with the rapid advancement of the web, and with streaming video and other multimedia capabilities, we expect that IA methods will become more widespread.

We illustrate IA with Figure 8.18 from Urban et al. (1996). Figure 8.18 is a prototype electric vehicle. Customers could view this vehicle on the computer, walk around it virtually, and even (virtually) open the hood, truck, and doors. In addition, customers could 'talk' to other consumers like them, interact with a virtual salesperson, view advertising

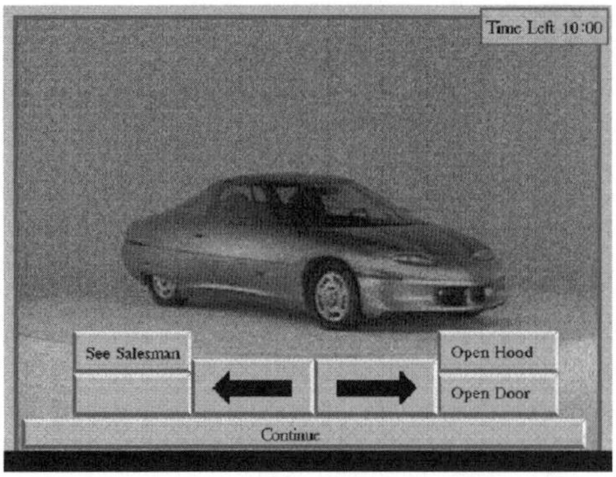

Figure 8.18 *Example of Information Acceleration*

mock-ups of consumer magazines, and other stimuli they were likely to see when shopping for a new vehicle. Furthermore, they were accelerated into the future with accounts of alternative future environments that were either favorable, neutral, or unfavorable towards electric vehicles. IA has been tested and validated in a number of other environments, including medical equipment and durable consumer products (Urban et al., 1997).

Pretest-market and Prelaunch Forecasting

Web-based concept testing, service exchanges, and IA deal with product concepts or virtual prototypes. However, once the virtual prototype is developed and the actual product is engineered, the PD team still seeks to reduce the risk of a full-scale launch. Thus, once a firm has refined its product concepts, developed prototypes, and can produce its products in limited quantities, it needs to test the full-benefit proposition that includes the physical product, service, distribution, and marketing actions such as advertising, detailing, sales force presentations, word-of-mouth, and publicity. We call such testing either pretest-market or prelaunch forecasting.

In a typical pretest-market analysis, potential customers are shown products in a setting that is chosen to simulate the purchase experience. For consumer products they might be shown television advertising, magazine articles, tapes of other consumers talking about the product, sales force presentations, consumer magazine reports or whatever media are appropriate to the product category. For consumer packaged goods, they might be recruited at a mall, brought to a room to see advertising, then brought to another room that simulates a grocery store. They would be asked questions about perceptions, preferences, and purchase intentions and allowed to make an actual purchase in the simulated store.

The methods of analysis include trial/repeat analysis (Eskin & Malec, 1976), recursive analysis (Pringle et al., 1982), norms (Blackburn & Clancy, 1980), econometrics (Blattberg & Golanty, 1978), logit analysis (Silk & Urban, 1978), and preference distribution modeling (Hauser & Gaskin, 1984; Hauser & Shugan, 1983). Indeed, most of these models combine multiple methods. For example, Silk & Urban (1978) explicitly use two parallel models and examine the convergent validity between the two before making forecasts. In general, the models predict well and have proven robust across many applications (Urban & Katz, 1983). In recent years the set of product categories has broadened tremendously. For example, the Assessor group at MARC, Inc. reports applications from frequently purchased products (candy, soda, deodorants) to consumer durables (personal computers). See critical reviews in Narasimhan and Sen (1983), Shocker and Hall (1986), and Ozer (1999).

In some situations, such as automobiles, the PD team wants to test the market before launch, but after the production facilities have been built. Although volume is less of an issue, the team needs to know what it will take to sell the product. That is, it needs an estimate of the required investment in advertising, dealer incentives, and promotion. To the extent that production is flexible, it also wants to know how many items it will likely produce with each set of features, such as global-positioning and mapping systems, premium sound systems, or even metallic paint. In this case, pre-launch methods are used (e.g., Urban et al., 1990). In a typical prelaunch application, consumers are shown advertising, magazine articles, and word-of-mouth simulations. This is similar in nature to pretest-market analyses. However, customers are also allowed to experience the product through test drives (for automobiles) or home use. 'What-if' models are built to forecast the impact of market variables and diffusion models are used to forecast the timing of sales (Bass, 1969; Mahajan & Wind, 1986, 1988; Mahajan et al., 1990).

Mass Customization and Postponement

In some cases, the best strategy might be expeditionary marketing, in which many products are placed on the market simultaneously – allowing the market to decide which are fit to survive (Hamel & Prahalad, 1991). However, expeditionary marketing only makes sense if the firm can easily ramp up production on the successful products and if the cost of failure is low (both directly and in loss of goodwill). The combination of efficient retailing (including e-commerce), product and process modularity, and flexible manufacturing systems are now making these conditions common in a variety of product categories. In particular, we are seeing an explosion in the sale of custom-configured goods that are only assembled after demand is observed. Perhaps the prototypical application of this system has been the build-to-order system used by Dell Computer to dominate the market for personal computers (Rangan & Bell, 1998). The direct sales approach makes particular sense when obsolescence costs are high and 'middleman' markups are significant, as in the PC business. Cattani et al. (2001) model these tradeoffs and show that in many cases a hybrid approach including make-to-order and make-to-stock is optimal. Gilmore and Pine (1997) characterize four approaches to 'mass customization' and suggest that the optimal approach depends heavily on the nature of the product and the markets it serves. These concepts represent a radical shift not only in manufacturing strategy, but also in the marketing thinking underlying product development. Specifically, once a firm adopts a mass-customization approach, the design problem shifts from searching for optimal bundles of features and optimal product lines to defining optimal common platforms, features, and level options, component-by-component pricing and custom-configuration user interfaces. Feitzinger and Lee (1997) provide extensive examples of products that benefit from modularity and postponement of at least some aspects of production until after demand is observed. For example, by pre-sewing 'white' sweaters in various sizes and delaying the dyeing of sweater yarns until after early demand has been observed, Benetton mitigates against the risks of overproducing unpopular colors or under-producing the season's 'hottest' colors, while still being able to respond to demand quickly. Similarly, Hewlett Packard reduces its inventory risk by postponing differentiation of its printers based on geography (affecting power supplies and the language of the manuals) until very late in the distribution process. The manuals and power supplies are treated as separate modules to be inserted into the pre-manufactured, generic printer box.

However, it is still vitally important that the PD team use the methods described earlier to winnow the concepts and features that are made available to the customer. Customers are limited in their ability to search among features – without some focus, even the best mass-customization process might fail.

Summary of Prototyping and Testing Concepts and Products

In most cases the launch of a new product is very costly in terms of commitments to production, distribution, and marketing. It is good management strategy to invest early to refine the product and its marketing and to reduce the risk of failure. This includes methods to reduce cost and risk (DFMA), methods to develop and test prototypes rapidly, and parallel development to manage the pipeline. As the product nears market, PD teams have used effectively pretest and prelaunch forecasting experiments to get early readings on how well the market will accept the product or product line. These methods have been in use for almost thirty years and have proven accurate in a wide variety of circumstances.

With the advent of new information and communications technologies, improved prototyping and testing methods are becoming available. Web-based rapid concept testing, information acceleration, and automated and distributed service exchange systems are enabling PD teams to work together and develop products faster and more profitably. The true advantage of these methods is that they can be used with virtual prototypes, thus enabling the PD team to forecast market response in parallel (or prior to) the development of the physical product. We expect these trends to continue, especially as the Internet and the worldwide web transform the final development and testing of concepts and products. For researchers in marketing, there are exciting opportunities to explore web-based methods for prototyping and testing products and concepts and there are exciting opportunities for seamless integration with engineering, operations management, and production through methods such as services exchanges.

Enterprise Strategy

Previous sections addressed the concept of an end-to-end product development process with stages of opportunity identification and idea generation (the fuzzy front end), the design and engineering of concepts and products, and the prototyping and testing of concepts and products. In each stage there are many tools and methods available to understand the customer and to make use of that information to develop profitable products. However, product development is not done in a vacuum. Rather, its success or failure depends heavily on the organization in which it is embedded. (Review Figure 8.3.) To be successful, the firm must align its culture, incentives, and processes to ensure that the people involved in the process can do their jobs effectively. While tools and methods might work well in theory or in demonstration programs, to make a difference they must improve the effectiveness of the entire organization. And this is not trivial.

The Challenge of Developing an Effective Product Development Organization

Despite many new tools and methods in the design of an end-to-end product development process, and despite the new web-based tools, many organizations are struggling with the execution of those processes. For example, Wheelwright and Clark (1995) document that despite the fact that their suggestions in earlier work have produced isolated successes, many organizations are facing difficulties in using these methods on an ongoing basis. Repenning (2001) and Repenning and Sterman (2000b) document this phenomenon further, suggesting that while new processes might be excellent, it is difficult to implement them in real organizations facing the challenge of actually getting products out the door. Of course this in not limited to product development. Many previous management practices have had trouble with implementation including customer satisfaction programs, quality circles, total quality management, business process re-engineering, and some information technology (Anderson et al., 1994; Howe et al., 1995; Klein & Sorra, 1996; Lawler & Mohrman, 1987; Orlikowski, 1992).

One reason for failure has been communication and suspicion – a new tool or method challenges those team members who have enjoyed the rewards of being an expert in the use of the old tool. New methods and priorities shift the importance of people and functions. Another reason for failure is that too much is expected too soon. New tools and methods take time to learn and they divert energies from the task of getting a project out the door. If the benefits of the new tool are obvious right from the beginning it will be adopted quickly. But if the benefits of the new tool are spread over future projects while the cost is incurred on the current project, then team members may not have the incentives to invest. See the examples in Griffin (1992). Indeed, if the investment in the new tool is so great that it detracts from current performance, then the process can enter a death spiral of self-confirming attribution errors. That is, team members see that the current project takes longer or is more difficult and they attribute this to the new tool or method (Repenning, 1999, 2001). Managers attribute the delays or costs to the team members, which leads managers to suggest the use of more tools (beyond optimal allocations), which just reinforces the delays and costs (Repenning & Sterman, 2000a, 2000b).

To overcome some of the problems of implementation, researchers have proposed boundary objects, communities of practice, relational contracts, and balanced incentives. We review each in turn.

Boundary Objects

Carlile (1999) suggests that tools and methods are more likely to be used in a real organization if differences and dependencies across boundaries in the firm are represented and understood by product development team members. He suggests that certain objects, called boundary objects, effect communication by allowing team members to learn different thought worlds, propose alternatives, test tradeoffs, transform knowledge, and create new solutions. The key ideas here are that these boundary objects must be accessed by two or more team members, that the team members often have disparate skills or thought-worlds, and that, in order to work together on the boundary object, the team members must evolve a means to communicate. In some cases, the technical value of the boundary objects pale in comparison to their implicit ability to enhance communication among team members.

For example, CAD/CAE tools, by generating frequent virtual prototypes during the development process, help assure that components are integrated and that development proceeds in a closely coordinated manner. Similarly, Cusumano and Selby (1995) describe a process at Microsoft where disparate programmers provide code to the common program (say Microsoft Office). Frequently and periodically, the entire program is 'built' in order to synchronize and stabilize the entire package of code. Each component of code must, in this process, work with the entire package. Finally, Carlile and Lucas (1999) argue that

> technical work in cross-functional settings will be more effective when it: (1) establishes a common model and language, (2) uses that logical structure and language as a shared team process to explore constraints and risks, and (3) keeps the interactive process alive by continuing to carry forward alternatives and some degree of design flexibility.

Communities of Practice

Organizational studies suggest that process knowledge is often deeply embedded in social groups within the organization (Brown & Duguid, 1991; Lave & Wenger, 1991; Wenger, 1998). There are new challenges to tap such implicit and tacit knowledge about processes so that human capabilities in product development tools and methods diffuse within organizations. This includes encouraging such communities of practice through mechanisms by which they can share knowledge. In the coming years we expect that interest in this area will grow as the Internet and information technology makes possible internal markets (and external markets) through which such implicit process knowledge is shared.

Relational Contracts

Recent research in agency theory suggests that formal incentive mechanisms are not sufficient to 'induce the agent to do the right thing at the right time' (Gibbons, 1997). Thus formal mechanisms are often supplemented or replaced with long-term implicit relationships in which decisions are delegated informally to self-managed PD teams through self-enforcing relational contracts. By viewing the relationship as a repeated game, Baker et al. (1999a, 1999b) suggest that the greater information inherent in the informal relationships enables these relational contracts to succeed.

Balanced Incentives

Cockburn et al. (1999) suggest that those best practices that diffuse are practices that are complementary to one another – they must be adopted as bundles rather than individually. For example, they suggest that science-based drug discovery in the pharmaceutical industry required that organizations adopt more high-powered incentives within the research organization. Their research suggests that PD tools and methods cannot be viewed in isolation, but as part of a more comprehensive end-to-end process. The tools and methods that the organization accepts will be those that work well in the context of the overall process.

Dynamic Planning

Repenning and Sterman (2000a, 2000b) suggest that firms wishing to adopt new tools and methods adopt a dynamic rather than a static mental model. That is, firms should view the diffusion of new tools and methods as an investment that is amortized over multiple projects rather than requiring immediate return on a single project. They suggest, further, that the firm study the dynamic interrelationships between the expectations of managers and the self-allocation of effort among product development teams. Repenning (2001) further develops these analysis tools by coupling ethnographic inquiry with formal dynamic modeling. The ethnographic inquiry provides the basic hints; the formal modeling generalizes these hints and highlights the key feedback loops that are driving the dynamic behavior of the systems.

Deployment of Capabilities with Web-based Tools

The adoption of new tools and methods does not just happen. New capabilities and knowledge are required on the part of the product development team. For example, Ford Motor Company has a technical staff of 25,000 professionals that are expected to undertake 40 hours of training each year – a total of 500 person-years of effort to learn new processes. This is indeed a substantial commitment. On the other hand, industry estimates that approximately 75% of the training materials in *Fortune 100* companies are redundant, with some of these costing $300,000 each to create and $50,000 to translate into each additional language (Learnshare, 2000). While traditional methods of apprenticeship are still important (Lave, 1991), new opportunities are available with web-based training in which materials are less expensive to reproduce, can be shared across firms (subject to competitive issues), and can be updated easily. For example, Ford expects web courses to take on average one-third less time for the equivalent learning gain (e.g., a three-day instructor-led course takes two days on average with the web-enhanced version).

Process Studies of the Antecedents of Product Development Success

Complementing the study of the organizational culture under which product development teams operate, there is an extensive literature on the antecedents and consequences of product development success. The goal of this literature is to identify variables and constructs that are correlated with success across firms. For example, earlier in this chapter we reviewed some of this literature to suggest that communication between the marketing function and the technical development function is a strong correlate of product development success.

This literature relies primarily on questionnaires sent to product development professionals. These professionals report their perceptions of various constructs and their perceptions of the success of the product development project. Griffin and Page (1993, 1996) provide a comprehensive review of this literature (referencing 77 articles). To date, the strength of this research stream has been exploratory in nature – identifying potential constructs that affect success. Table 8.3 summarizes, in alphabetical order, 82 of the constructs that have been found to affect product development success, either directly, indirectly, or in interactions with other constructs.[2]

Although each of these constructs is correlated with success to some degree, few studies have included a broad set of constructs and few have used regression analysis or path analysis to identify the relative impact of these constructs (Montoya-Weiss & Calantone, 1994). Furthermore, researchers are only now beginning to model the full implications of endogenous decisions by firms. For example, a high-potential market is likely to

Table 8.3 *Antecedents of Product Development Success*

address clear needs	information acquisition	product definition
adequate resources	innovativeness	product differentiation
adequate team	instrumental market information	product-firm compatibility
clear strategy	interdepartmental collaboration	product-market fit
company resources	internal commitment	product organization
competitive intelligence	management accountability	proficiency of formal PD activities
conceptual market information	management commitment	quality of launch execution
concurrent engineering	management support	quality of service
costs	market competitiveness	R&D, marketing integration
cross-functional integration	market growth	relational norms
cultural antecedents	market intelligence	resource availability
customer needs and benefits	market orientation	rigorous tools
customer satisfaction	market potential	service expertise
customer service	market size	standards
decentralization	marketing orientation	strategy
degree of product newness	marketing skills and resources	superior product
empowerment	marketing synergy	supplier involvement
entrepreneurial climate	newness to firm	synergy
environmental uncertainty	newness to market	technical complexity
evaluation and reward procedures	novelty	technical innovativeness
execution of marketing	organizational memory	technical skills and resources
execution of technical	organizational memory dispersion	technical synergy
experience with market	pioneering advantage	templates of change
focus	platform reuse	time-to-market
formal cross-functional integration	pre-development proficiency	uniqueness
formal processes	product advantage	value to the customer
formalization of user inventions	product champion involvement	
high quality teams	product complexity	

attract competitors, thus the net impact of 'market potential' and 'market attractiveness' might be to neither heighten nor diminish observed success (Cooper, 1984b).

Perhaps the best summary of this literature to date is the meta-analysis of 47 scientific studies by Montoya-Weiss and Calantone (1994). These researchers identified the 18 constructs that were reported most. For ease of comparison they grouped these constructs into four categories: strategic factors, development process, market environment, and organization. According to the authors, all 18 constructs had a significant impact on success (Fisher combined test) and all but three had medium to large correlations (0.2 to 0.3) with some measure of success. The remaining constructs were included in only one study (speed-to-market) or no studies (costs, market competitiveness). Because this literature is still developing, not all of the studies reported correlations, thus the authors also report the number of times a construct was found to affect a measure of success. Table 8.4 summarizes the average correlations and number of studies.

This literature has the potential to enlighten and focus future research on the antecedents of product development success. The greatest research need is for studies that combine a comprehensive set of constructs, deal with endogeneity in a sophisticated manner, and develop measures with greater internal and external validity.[3]

Adjusting Priorities to Maximize Profit

Although process studies provide valuable insight with respect to the constructs which correlate with success across firms, they do not provide a tool that managers can use to adjust the emphasis they place on these constructs within their firms. This is particularly challenging because the impact of these constructs is contingent upon the capabilities of the firm and the context in which it operates. Furthermore, because the impact of these constructs is likely to be non-linear, the process studies do not indicate the optimal level for a particular firm. Furthermore, there are tradeoffs among foci (say customer satisfaction vs. platform reuse – review Figure 8.2) and it is possible to overshoot if too much emphasis is placed on one construct, say customer satisfaction, at the expense of another construct, say cost reduction through platform reuse. For example, too large an emphasis on customer satisfaction might prove too costly and reduce profit even as it increases long-term revenue.

Table 8.4 *Meta-analysis of Academic Literature (from Montoya-Weiss and Calantone, 1994: 408, 410)*

Construct	Quantitative Comparisons: Number of Studies	Quantitative Comparisons: Average Correlation	Qualitative Comparisons: Number of Studies	Qualitative Comparisons: Percent of Studies
Strategic factors				
Technological synergy	6	0.27	18	67%
Product advantage	5	0.36	16	59%
Marketing synergy	5	0.30	14	52%
Company resources	3	0.30	9	33%
Strategy	1	0.32	8	30%
Development process				
Protocol	7	0.34	19	70%
Proficiency of technical activities	7	0.28	18	67%
Proficiency of marketing activities	5	0.33	18	67%
Proficiency of pre-development	5	0.29	11	41%
Top management support/skill	2	0.26	9	33%
Financial/business analysis	1	0.27	8	30%
Speed-to-market	1	0.18	8	30%
Costs	0	–	4	15%
Market environment				
Market potential	4	0.24	23	85%
Environment	2	0.29	15	56%
Market competitiveness	0	–	2	7%
Organization				
Internal/external relations	3	0.31	13	48%
Organizational factors	3	0.30	12	44%

To address the issue of selecting priorities *within a firm*, we turn to adaptive control (Hauser, 2001; Little, 1966, 1977). The concept is quite simple. Suppose that we are operating within a division of a firm. It is likely that the implicit culture and relational contracts are relatively homogeneous within this division. The product development teams understand the culture and operate accordingly. Thus, they understand the implicit priorities that are placed on constructs such as customer satisfaction and platform reuse. The net result of the firm's culture, its competitive environment, its capabilities, and its human capital produces a response surface such as that illustrated in Figure 8.2 (page 181). Such a response surface summarizes how achievement with respect to metrics, such as customer satisfaction, affects profits. However, response surfaces are rarely static. New challenges for the firm, both internal and external, are likely to shift the response surface in Figure 8.2. As the response surface shifts, the firm must adjust its priorities.

To understand and adjust its priorities through adaptive control, we must first understand, conceptually, the relationship between metrics, such as customer satisfaction, and the firm's profits. In Figure 8.19, we reproduce the response surface from Figure 8.2 and examine its 'local' properties. At any given time we are likely to observe the firm operating on some portion of this curve, as indicated in Figure 8.19 by the dark circle. Moreover, because the implicit culture is relatively homogeneous, most of the observations of customer satisfaction, platform reuse, and profit for launched products will be in the neighborhood of the operating point, as indicated by the tangent hyperplane in Figure 8.19. Thus, a regression of profit on customer satisfaction and platform reuse *within the hyperplane* will suggest to the firm how to adjust their emphasis on customer satisfaction and platform reuse in order to increase the profitability of their product development projects.[4] While this example is based on two constructs, customer satisfaction and platform reuse, it is readily extended to a larger number of constructs. For example, adaptive control can be applied to top-level constructs such as customer satisfaction, platform reuse, and time-to-market and, simultaneously, to a larger number of lower-level constructs that enable the firm to achieve those strategic priorities.

These methods have been applied to a major product development firm (three strategic constructs, ten enabling constructs, and seven covariates). Based on data from almost all of the development projects over a five-year period for a

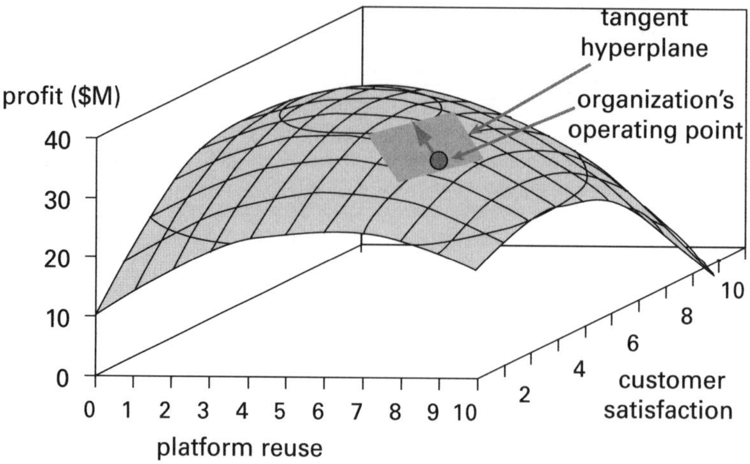

Figure 8.19 *The Metrics Thermostat*

key division of the firm, the 'metrics thermostat' was able to identify that the firm (or at least that division) was placing too little emphasis on customer satisfaction and too much emphasis on platform reuse. Because the results had high face validity, the firm reacted with three initiatives: (1) the firm created the role of a 'marketing engineer' who was responsible for assuring that the voice of the customer was incorporated into the design process and that the product was designed to be marketed; (2) the firm adjusted its channels to reach the customer better and to match customers with the appropriate products; and (3) the firm undertook a major study of platform reuse to optimize their portfolio with respect to upstream/downstream technological development, a balance of product variants and major redesigns, and enterprise coherence in software development.

The metrics thermostat has been applied at a major office equipment firm, a major automotive firm, the US Navy (acquisition reform), and the US Air Force (sustainment of the fleet). In each case, basic insights were obtained and suggestions were developed for improving profit (or capability for the military applications). Nonetheless, the metrics thermostat needs further testing, especially for marketing applications. The basic theory is remarkably robust – for example, directional improvements can still be identified even if the hyperplane approximation includes projects further from the operating point, even if the response surface is changing over time, and even if there is some heterogeneity – as long as none of these violations is 'too severe.' However, the weakness of the metrics thermostat is that the data upon which it is based are often difficult to obtain. Despite directives to manage by metrics, firms often do not collect metrics systematically, or maintain them in a central database. Furthermore, the number of data points for any of the within-firm metrics regressions are quite small, requiring statistics to be supplemented with judgment.[5]

A Vision of the Future of Product Development

Throughout the 1980s and 1990s the focus of research on product development by marketing academics has been on bringing customer information into the product development process and on using that information. Significant strides were made in conjoint analysis, voice-of-the-customer methods, product optimization, demand forecasting, and market testing. Toward the end of the 1990s the challenges of product development began to change as markets and competition became more global, as engineering and design talent became more dispersed, as internal product development efforts migrated into the extended enterprise, and as information and communication technologies changed the way people worked. The new challenges call for a product development process that is integrated, information intensive, almost instantaneous, and makes strong use of new technologies such as the Internet. We call this new vision i4PD: integrated, information, instantaneous, and Internet.

Integrated

The research challenges of the next decade are those that address product development as an integrated, end-to-end process that requires a detailed understanding and coordination of customers, competition, and internal capabilities. Research points to core teams that are either cross-functional or have the ability to make use of cross-functional knowledge embedded in the firm. Furthermore, design now means the design of the product, the assembly and manufacturing process, the service delivery process, the entire value chain, and the marketing materials – all integrated to provide high value to the customer. For example, research on voice-of-the-customer methods in the next decade must consider not just data collection, but how the PD team will use that data.

Information

Ultimately, it is people who design products, but as the process becomes more integrated the demands for information have grown. For example, cutting-edge PD teams must integrate information from the customer, the assembly process, the manufacturing process, the channel-delivery process, and the marketing process. In some cases, this means new roles – some firms now use 'marketing engineers' who help design a product so that it is easy to market. However, integration demands information – the right information to the right people at the right time so that they can make the right decisions. Thus, many of the research challenges in the next decade will involve methods to assure this information transfer. Methods such as services exchanges are just the beginning of integrated information systems that could lead to greater product development competitiveness.

Instantaneous

Speed-to-market has been proposed as a competitive advantage, at least if it can be obtained without sacrificing cost or customer satisfaction. New methods such as virtual prototypes, web-based voice-of-the-customer methods, web-based conjoint analysis, the Information Pump, listening in, Securities Trading of Concepts, and user design all have the potential to provide information to the PD team almost instantaneously. We call this entire set of methods the virtual customer. For example, traditional conjoint analysis studies take a minimum of six to eight weeks. New web-based methods have the potential to reduce that to two days, opening up the potential for the PD team to have its customer-preference questions answered almost instantaneously. In fact, it might soon be possible to get statistical information about customer wants and needs almost as fast as it used to take to debate them. Virtual prototypes mean that products can be 'created' in days, and Internet connectivity means that these prototypes can be tested with customers in hours. Service integration methods mean that many engineering design decisions can be reduced from months to days. Interestingly, in the future we might be in a situation where the decision on how fast to introduce products might be more of a strategic decision on product positioning rather than constrained by the firm's ability to design and test products.

Internet

By Internet we really mean information and communications technologies. It is these technologies that are enabling the process to be integrated, information intensive, and instantaneous.

The i4PD paradigm is one perspective on the future of product development; a perspective that describes how the process will look. But we must not forget the human side of product development. One of most important insights of the late 1990s was the need to study the use of PD tools and methods *within the organization*. By understanding corporate culture and incentives, the new end-to-end processes should be robust, knowledge-based, people-based, and market-based. By robust we mean a process that can adapt to changes in the environment, market conditions, and organization. By knowledge-based we recognize that the firms that will be most competitive will be those that can train their PD teams to design and build products most effectively. We cannot study the process in isolation of the people we are asking to implement the process. The process will not succeed if we do not assure that the team members have the capabilities to exploit it. This means not only training, but also communities of practice, boundary objects, and dynamic thinking. By people-based, we mean that the process respects the teams' needs *and* that the metrics and incentives (explicit and implicit) are designed so that team members, acting in their own best interests, make decisions and take actions aligned with the best interests of the firm. Finally, by market-based we mean two things: first that the process will be responsive to customers and competitors, and second, that it empowers teams to make their own choices in the context of their own specific expertise and knowledge.

In the end, we believe that research on product development in the twenty-first century will concentrate on understanding an end-to-end process *that really works in real organizations*. We do not expect a fad of the month, but rather research to understand the science of organizations, marketing, and product development so that methods and tools are embedded in a self-learning and self-evaluation process that is right for the firm and its markets.

Notes

1. Some features might include price, picture quality, picture delivery, opening of the camera, removable cover or not, picture taking process (1 vs. 2 steps), light selection (3 settings vs. feedback), disposable camera, camera with cartoon characters, metallic vs. plastic camera, battery type: AA vs. AAA, picture size, color vs. black & white, chemical vs. digital picture vs. both at the same time, zoom lens vs. regular, holster for the camera, picture has a sticky backing, the film is decorated, the film contains some advertising to reduce cost, panoramic pictures, waterproof camera, manual control over the picture, picture cutter included in the camera, etc.

2. See, for example, Atuahene-Gima (1995), Ayers et al. (1997), Bonner et al. (1998), Calantone & di Benedetto (1988), Cooper & de Brentani (1991), Cooper & Kleinschmidt (1993, 1994, 1995), Datar et al. (1997), Goldenberg et al. (1999), Griffin (1997), Griffin & Hauser (1994), Ittner & Larcher (1997), Kahn (1996), Lambert & Slater (1999), Lee & Na (1994), Mishra et al. (1996), Moorman (1995), Moorman & Miner (1997), Olson et al. (1995), Rosen et al. (1988), Sharda et al. (1999), Song & Parry (1997a, 1997b), Song et al. (1999), and Song et al. (1997).

3. Montoya-Weiss and Calantone (1994) provide an excellent discussion of the threats to internal and external validity including issues that only significant correlations are reported even when a large number of constructs are included in the study, issues that respondents often are allowed to self-select successes and failures, and issues that much of the literature relies on respondents perceptions rather than objective measures.

4. Figure 8.19 indicates the suggested change in customer satisfaction and platform reuse. To achieve this, the firm must adjust its *priorities* with respect to these measures, thus we need a mapping from measures to priorities on measures. This relies on agency theory and is beyond the scope of this chapter. For more details see Hauser (2001). For more details on agency theory see Gibbons (1997).

5. Fortunately, the metrics thermostat is robust with respect to a small number of data points. It 'does no harm' in the sense of not recommending changes when the results are not statistically significant.

References

Adams, James L. (1986) *Conceptual Blockbusting: A Guide to Better Ideas*, 1st edn. Reading, MA: Addison-Wesley Publishing Company, Inc.

Addelman, S. (1962) Orthogonal main effect plans for asymmetrical factorial experiments. *Technometrics*, 4, 21–46.

Akaah, Ishmael P. & Korgaonkar, Pradeep K. (1983) An empirical comparison of the predictive validity of self-explicated, Huber-hybrid, traditional conjoint, and hybrid conjoint models. *Journal of Marketing Research*, 20, (May), 187–97.

Allen, Thomas J. (1986) *Managing the Flow of Technology*. Cambridge, MA: MIT Press.

Altschuler, Genrich (1985) *Creativity as an Exact Science*. New York: Gordon and Breach.

——— (1996) *And Suddenly the Inventor Appeared*. Worcester, MA: Technical Innovation Center, Inc.

Anderson, Eugene W., Fornell, Claes & Lehmann, Donald R. (1994) Customer satisfaction, market share, and profitability: findings from Sweden. *Journal of Marketing*, 58, (July), 53–66.

Anthony, Michael T. & McKay, Jonathon (1992) Balancing the product development process: achieving product and cycle time excellence in high-technology industries. *Journal of Product Innovation Management*, 9, 140–7.

Arora, Neeraj & Huber, Joel (2001) Improving parameter estimates and model prediction by aggregate customization in choice experiments. *Journal of Marketing Research*, 28, (September), 273–83.

Arnold, J.E. (1962) Useful creative techniques. In *Source Book for Creative Thinking*, edited by S.J. Parnes & H.F. Harding. New York: Charles Scribner & Sons.

Atuahene-Gima, Kwaku (1995) An exploratory analysis of the impact of market orientation on new product performance: a contingency approach. *Journal of Product Innovation Management*, 12, 275–93.

Ayers, Doug, Dahlstrom, Robert & Skinner, Steven J. (1997) An exploratory investigation of organizational antecedents to new product success. *Journal of Marketing Research*, 34, 1, (February), 107–16.

Ayers, R.U. (1969) *Technology Forecasting and Long Range Planning*. New York: McGraw-Hill Book Company.

Baker, George, Gibbons, Robert & Murphy, Kevin J. (1999a) Informal authority in organizations. *Journal of Law, Economics, and Organization*, 15, 56–73.

——— (1999b) Relational contracts and the theory of the firm. Working Paper, Sloan School of Management, MIT, Cambridge, MA 02142. Forthcoming, *Quarterly Journal of Economics*.

Baldwin, Carliss Y. & Clark, Kim B. (2000) *Design Rules: The Power of Modularity*. Cambridge, MA: MIT Press.

Bass, Frank M. (1969) A new product growth model for consumer durables. *Management Science*, 15, 5, (January), 215–27.

Bateson, John E.G., Reibstein, David & Boulding, William (1987) Conjoint analysis reliability and validity: a framework for future research. *Review of Marketing*, edited by Michael Houston. New York: AMA, pp. 451–81.

Bickart, Barbara A. (1993) Carryover and backfire effects in marketing research. *Journal of Marketing Research*, 30, 1, (February), 52–62.

Blackburn, J.D. & Clancy, Kevin J. (1980) Litmus: a new product planning model. In *Proceedings: Market Measurement and Analysis,* edited by Robert P. Leone. Providence, RI: The Institute of Management Sciences, pp. 182–93.

Blattberg, Robert & Golanty, John (1978) Tracker: an early test market forecasting and diagnostic model for new product planning. *Journal of Marketing Research*, 15, 2, (May), 192–202.

Bonner, Joseph, Ruekert, Robert & Walker, Orville (1998) Management control of product development projects. Working Paper 98–120, Cambridge, MA: Marketing Science Institute.

Boothroyd, Geoffrey, Dewhurst, Peter & Knight, Winston (1994) *Product Design for Manufacturability and Assembly*. New York: Marcel Dekker.

Bower, Joseph L & Christensen, Clayton M. (1995) Disruptive technologies: catching the wave. *Harvard Business Review*, (January–February), 43–53.

Brown, J.S. & Duguid, P. (1991) Organizational learning and communities-of-practice. *Organization Science*, 1 (1), 40–57.

Bucklin, Randolph E. & Srinivasan, V. (1991) Determining interbrand substitutability through survey measurement of consumer preference structures. *Journal of Marketing Research*, 28, (February), 58–71.

Buckman, Rebecca (2000) Knowledge networks' Internet polls will expand to track web surfers. *Wall Street Journal*, September 7.

Burchill, Gary W. (1992) *Concept Engineering: The Key to Operationally Defining Your Customers' Requirements*. Cambridge, MA: Center for Quality Management, pp. 155.

Burchill, Gary W. & Hepner-Brodie, Christina (1997) *Voices into Choices*. Cambridge, MA: Center for Quality Management, pp. 113–36.

Calantone, Roger J. & di Benedetto, C. Anthony (1988) An integrative model of the new product development process: an empirical validation. *Journal of Product Innovation Management*, 5, 201–15.

Calder, B.J. (1977) Focus groups and the nature of qualitative marketing research. *Journal of Marketing Research*, 14, 353–64.

Campbell, Robert (1985) *Fisherman's Guide: A Systems Approach to Creativity and Organization*. Boston, MA: New Science Library.

Carlile, Paul (1999) *Crossing Knowledge Boundaries in New Product Development*. Cambridge, MA: Center for Innovation in Product Development, MIT.

Carlile, Paul & Lucas, William (1999) *Cross-Boundary Work and The Effectiveness of Technology Development Teams*. Cambridge, MA: Center for Innovation in Product Development, MIT.

Carmone, Frank J., Green, Paul E. & Jain, Arun K. (1978) Robustness of conjoint analysis: some Monte Carlo results. *Journal of Marketing Research*, 15, (May), 300–3.

Carroll, J. Douglas & Green, Paul E. (1995) Psychometric methods in marketing research: Part I, conjoint analysis. *Journal of Marketing Research*, 32, (November), 385–91.

Case, John (1991) Customer service: the last word. *Inc. Magazine,* (April), 88–92.

Cattani, Kyle, Dahan, Ely & Schmidt, Glen M. (2002) Textured and spackled: dual strategies of make-to-stock and make-to-order that integrate marketing and operations perspectives. Working Paper, Cambridge, MA: MIT.

Cattin, Philippe & Wittink, Dick R. (1982) Commercial use of conjoint analysis: a survey. *Journal of Marketing*, 46, (Summer), 44–53.

Chan, Nicholas, Dahan, Ely, Lo, Andrew & Poggio, Tomaso (2000) *Securities Trading Of Concepts (STOC)*. Cambridge, MA: Center for eBusiness, MIT Sloan School.

Christensen, Clayton (1998) *The Innovator's Dilemma: When New Technologies Cause Great Firms to Fail*. Boston, MA: Harvard Business School Press.

Churchill, Jr., Gilbert A. (1998) *Marketing Research: Methodological Foundations,* 7th edn. New York: The Dryden Press.

Clausing, Don (1994) *Total Quality Development*. New York: ASME Press.

Cockburn, Iain, Henderson, Rebecca & Stern, Scott (1999) *Balancing Incentives: The Tension between Basic and Applied Research*. Cambridge, MA: Center for Innovation in Product Development, MIT.

Cooper, Robert G. (1984a) New product strategies: what distinguishes the top performers? *Journal of Product Innovation Management*, 2, 151–64.

——— (1984b) How new product strategies impact on performance. *Journal of Product Innovation Management*, 2, 5–18.

——— (1987) New product strategies: what distinguishes the Top Performers? *Journal of Product Innovation Management*, 2, 3, 151–64.

——— (1990) Stage-gate systems: a new tool for managing new products. *Business Horizons*, May–June, 44–54.

——— (1994) Third-generation new product processes. *Journal of Product Innovation Management*, 11, 3–14.

Cooper, Robert G. & de Brentani, Ulricke (1991) New industrial financial services: what distinguishes the winners. *Journal of Product Innovation Management*, 8, 75–90.

Cooper, Robert G. & Kleinschmidt, Elko (1987) New products: what separates winners from losers? *Journal of Product Innovation Management*, 4, 169–84.

——— (1993) Major new products: what distinguishes the winners in the chemical industry? *Journal of Product Innovation Management*, 10, 90–111.

——— (1994) Determinants of timeliness in product development. *Journal of Product Innovation Management*, 11, 381–96.

——— (1995) Benchmarking the firm's critical success factors in new product development. *Journal of Product Innovation Management*, 12, 374–91.

Crawford, C. Merle (1991) *New Products Management,* 3rd edn. Homewood, IL: Richard D. Irwin, Inc.

Currim, Imran S. (1981) Using segmentation approaches for better prediction and understanding from consumer mode choice models. *Journal of Marketing Research,* 18, (August), 301–9.

Currim, Imran S., Weinberg, Charles B. & Wittink, Dick R. (1981) Design of subscription programs for a performing arts series. *Journal of Consumer Research*, 8, (June), 67–75.

Cusumano, Michael A. & Selby, Richard W. (1995) *Microsoft Secrets*. New York: The Free Press.

Cusumano, Michael A. & Yoffie, David B. (1998) *Competing on Internet Time*. New York: The Free Press.

Dahan, Ely & Hauser, John R. (2002) The virtual customer. *Journal of Product Innovation Management*, 19 (September).

Dahan, Ely & Mendelson, Haim (2001) An extreme value model of concept testing. *Management Science* (Special Issue on New Product Development), 47, 1, (January), 102–16.

Dahan, Ely & Orlin, James (2002) Conjoint Adaptive Ranking Database System (Cards). Working Paper. Cambridge, MA: MIT.

Dahan, Ely & Srinivasan, V. (2000) The predictive power of internet-based product concept testing using visual depiction and animation. *Journal of Product Innovation Management*, 17, (March), 99–109.

——— (2002) The profit saddle: do unit cost reductions yield increasing or decreasing returns? Working Paper. Cambridge, MA: MIT Center for Innovation in Product Development, MIT.

Dahan, Ely, Hauser, John R., Simester, Duncan & Toubia, Olivier (2002) Application and predictive test of fast polyhedral adaptive conjoint estimation. Working Paper, (October). Cambridge, MA: MIT Center for Innovation in Product Development.

Datar, Srikant, Jordan, C., Clark, Kekre, Sunder, Rajiv, Surendra & Srinivasan, Kannan (1997) Advantages of time-based new product development in a fast-cycle industry. *Journal of Marketing Research*, 34, 1, (February), 36–49.

De Bono, Edward (1995) *Mind Power*. New York: Dorling Kindersley.

Deming, W. Edwards (1986) *Out of Crisis*. Cambridge, MA: MIT Press.

Dolan, Robert J. (1993) *Managing the New Product Development Process*. Reading, MA: Addison-Wesley Publishing Co.

Dougherty, Deborah (1989) Interpretive barriers to successful product innovation in large firms. *Organization Science*, 3, 2, (May), 179–202.

Einhorn, Hillel J. (1971) Use of nonlinear, noncompensatory models as a function of task and amount of information. *Organizational Behavior and Human Performance*, 6, 1–27.

Eisenstein, Paul (1994) Your true color. *Family Circle*, November 1, 40.

Eliashberg, Jehoshua & Hauser, John R. (1985) A measurement error approach for modeling consumer risk preference. *Management Science*, 31, 1, (January), 1–25.

Elrod, Terry, Louviere, Jordan & Davey, Krishnakumar S. (1992) An empirical comparison of ratings-based and choice-based conjoint models. *Journal of Marketing Research* 29, 3, (August), 368–77.

Eppinger, Steven D. (1998) Information-based product development. Presentation to the Research Advisory Committee of the Center for Innovation in Product Development, MIT, Cambridge, MA (January 12).

Eppinger, Steven D., Whitney, Daniel E., Smith, Robert P. & Gebala, David A. (1994) A model-based method for organizing tasks in product development. *Research in Engineering Design*. 6, 1, 1–13.

Eskin, Gerry J. & John Malec (1976) A model for estimating sales potential prior to test marketing. *Proceedings of the American Marketing Association Fall Educators' Conference*. Chicago: AMA, pp. 230–3.

Farquhar, Peter H. (1977) A survey of multiattribute utility theory and applications. *Studies in Management Sciences*, 6, 59–89.

Faura, Julio (2000) Contribution to web-based conjoint analysis for market research. Management of Technology S.M. Thesis, Cambridge, MA: MIT (June).

Feitzinger, Edward & Lee, Hau L. (1997) Mass customization at Hewlett-Packard: the power of postponement. *Harvard Business Review*, January–February, 116–21.

Feldman, Jack M. & Lynch, John G. Jr. (1988) Self-generated validity: effects of measurement on belief, attitude, intention, and behavior. *Journal of Applied Psychology*, 73, (August), 421–35.

Fern, E.F. (1982) The use of focus groups for idea generation: the effects of group size, acquaintanceship, and moderator on response quantity and quality. *Journal of Marketing Research*, 9, 1–13.

Gibbons, Robert (1997) Incentives and careers in organizations. In *Advances in Economic Theory and Econometrics*, edited by D. Kreps & K. Wallis. Cambridge: Cambridge University Press, pp. 1–37.

Gilmore, James H. & Pine, Joseph II (1997) The four faces of mass customization. *Harvard Business Review*, January–February, 91–101.

Goldenberg, Jacob, Lehmann, Donald R. & Mazursky, David (1999) The primacy of the idea itself as a predictor of new product success. Marketing Science Institute Working Paper, 99–110, forthcoming *Management Science*.

Goldenberg, Jacob, Mazursky, David & Solomon, Sorin (1999a) Toward identifying the inventive templates of new products: a channeled ideation approach. *Journal of Marketing Research*, 36, (May), 200–10.

——— (1999b) Templates of original innovation: projecting original incremental innovations from intrinsic information. *Technology Forecasting and Social Change*, 61, 1–12.

——— (1999c) Creative Sparks. *Science*, 285, (September 3), 1495–6.

Golder, Peter & Tellis, Gerald (1993) Pioneering advantage: marketing logic or marketing legend. *Journal of Marketing Research*, 30 (May), 158–70.

Gonzalez-Zugasti, Javier, Otto, Kevin. & Baker, J. (1998) A method for architecting product platforms with an application to interplanetary mission design. *Proceedings of the 1998 ASME Design Automation Conference*, Atlanta, GA.

Green, Paul E. (1984) Hybrid models for conjoint analysis: an expository review. *Journal of Marketing Research*, 155–69.

Green, Paul E. & Devita, M.T. (1975) An interaction model of consumer utility. *Journal of Consumer Research*, 2, (September), 146–53.

Green, Paul E. & Helsen, Kristiaan (1989) Cross-validation assessment of alternatives to individual-level conjoint analysis: a case study. *Journal of Marketing Research*, 26, 346–50.

Green, Paul E. & Krieger, Abba (1989a) Recent contributions to optimal product positioning and buyer segmentation. *European Journal of Operational Research*, 41, 2, (July), 127–41.

——— (1989b) A componential segmentation model with optimal product design features. *Decision Science*, 20, 221–38.

——— (1991) Product design strategies for target-market positioning. *Journal of Product Innovation Management*, 8, 3, (September) 189–202.

Green, Paul E. & Rao, Vithala R. (1971) Conjoint measurement for quantifying judgmental data. *Journal of Marketing Research*, 8, (August), 355–63.

——— (1972) *Applied Multidimensional Scaling*. New York: Holt, Rinehart and Winston, Inc.

Green, Paul E. & Srinivasan, V. (1978) Conjoint analysis in consumer research: issues and outlook. *Journal of Consumer Research*, 5, 2, (September), 103–23.

——— (1990) Conjoint analysis in marketing: new developments with implications for research and practice. *Journal of Marketing*, 54, 3–19.

Green, Paul E. & Wind, Jerry (1975) New way to measure consumers' judgments. *Harvard Business Review*, July–August, 107–17.

Green, Paul E., Carmone, Frank J. & Fox, Leo B. (1969) Television programme similarities: an application of subjective clustering. *Journal of the Market Research Society*, 11, 1, 70–90.

Green, Paul E., Carroll, J. Douglas & Goldberg, Stephen M. (1981) A general approach to product design optimization via conjoint analysis. *Journal of Marketing*, 45, (Summer), 17–37.

Green, Paul E., Goldberg, Stephen M. & Montemayor, Mila (1981) A hybrid utility estimation model for conjoint analysis. *Journal of Marketing*, 45, 33–41.

Green, Paul E., Krieger, Abba & Agarwal, Manoj K. (1991) Adaptive conjoint analysis: some caveats and suggestions. *Journal of Marketing Research*, 28, 215–22.

Green, Paul E., Krieger, Abba & Bansal, Pradeep (1988) Completely unacceptable levels in conjoint analysis: a cautionary note. *Journal of Marketing Research*, 25, (August), 293–300.

Green, Paul E., Tull, Donald S. & Albaum, Gerald (1988) *Research for Marketing Decisions*. Englewood Cliffs, NJ: Prentice-Hall, Inc.

Grether, David & Wilde, Louis (1984) An analysis of conjunctive choice theory and experiments. *Journal of Consumer Research*, 10, (March), 373–85.

Griffin, Abbie J. (1992) Evaluating QFD's use in US firms as a process for developing products. *Journal of Product Innovation Management*, 9, 3.

——— (1997) The effect of project and process characteristics on product development cycle time. *Journal of Product Innovation Management*, 34, 24–35.

Griffin, Abbie J. & Hauser, John R. (1992) Patterns of communication among marketing, engineering, and manufacturing – a comparison between two new product teams. *Management Science*, 38, 3, (March), 360–73.

——— (1993) The voice of the customer. *Marketing Science*, Winter, 1–27.

——— (1996) Integrating mechanisms for marketing and R&D. *Journal of Product Innovation Management*, 13, 3, (May), 191–215.

Griffin, Abbie J. & Page, Albert L. (1996) PDMA success measurement project: recommended measures for product development success and failure. *Journal of Product Innovation Management*, 13, 478–96.

Gross, Irwin (1967) An analytical approach to the creative aspects of advertising operations. Cleveland: Case Institute of Technology, Unpublished Ph.D. thesis.

Gutman, Jonathan (1982) A Means-end chain model based on customer categorization processes. *Journal of Marketing*, 46, (Spring), 60–72.

Gutman, Jonathan & Reynolds, T.J. (1979) A pilot test of a logic model for investigating attitude structure. In *Attitude Research Under the Sun*, edited by J. Eighmey. Chicago, IL: American Marketing Association pp. 128–50.

Haaijer, Rinus, Wedel, Michel, Vriens, Marco & Wansbeek, Tom (1998) Utility covariances and context effects in conjoint MNP models. *Marketing Science*, 17, 3, 236–52.

Hahn, G.J. & Shapiro, S.S. (1966) *A Catalog and Computer Program for the Design and Analysis of Orthogonal Symmetric and Asymmetric Fractional Factorial Experiments*, 66-C-165. Schenectady, NY: General Electric Research and Development Center, May.

Hamel, Gary & Prahalad, C.K. (1991) Corporate imagination and expeditionary marketing. *Harvard Business Review*, July–August, 81–92.

Hauser, John R. (1988) Competitive price and positioning strategies. *Marketing Science*, 7, 1 (Winter), 76–91.

——— (1993) How Puritan Bennett used the House of Quality. *Sloan Management Review*, 34, 3 (Spring), 61–70.

——— (2001) Metrics thermostat. *Journal of Product Innovation Management*, 18, 3, (May), 134–53.

Hauser, John R. & Clausing, Don (1988) The House of Quality. *Harvard Business Review*, 3, (May–June), 63–73.

Hauser, John R. & Gaskin, Steven P. (1984) Application of the 'DEFENDER' consumer model. *Marketing Science*, 3, 4, (Fall), 327–51.

Hauser, John R. & Koppelman, Frank S. (1979) Alternative perceptual mapping techniques: relative accuracy and usefulness. *Journal of Marketing Research*, 16, 4, (November), 495–506.

Hauser, John R. & Shugan, Steven M. (1980) Intensity measures of consumer preference. *Operation Research*, 28, 2, (March–April), 278–320.

——— (1983) Defensive marketing strategy. *Marketing Science*, 2, 4, (Fall), 319–60.

Hauser, John R. & Simmie, Patricia (1981) Profit maximizing perceptual positions: an integrated theory for the selection of product features and price. *Management Science*, 27, 2, (January), 33–56.

Hauser, John R. & Urban, Glen L. (1979) Assessment of attribute importances and consumer utility functions: von Neumann–Morgenstern Theory applied to consumer behavior. *Journal of Consumer Research*, 5, (March), 251–62.

Hauser, John R., Simester, Duncan & Wernerfelt, Birger (1994) Customer satisfaction incentives. *Marketing Science*, 13, 4, (Fall), 327–50.

Hepner-Brodie, Christina (2000) Invigorating strategy with the voices of the customer. *PRTM's Insight*, (Summer), 31–5.

Hoepfl, Robert T. & Huber, George P. (1970) A study of self-explicated utility models. *Behavioral Science*, 15, 408–14.

Holmes, Maurice (1999) Product development in the new millennium – a CIPD vision. *Proceedings of the Product Development Management Association Conference*, Marco Island (October).

Holmstrom, Bengt (1979) Moral hazard and observability. *Bell Journal of Economics*, 10, 74–91.

Holmstrom, Bengt & Milgrom, Paul (1987) Aggregation and linearity in the provision of intertemporal incentives. *Econometrica*, 55 (March), 303–28.

Holtzblatt, Karen & Beyer, Hugh (1993) Making customer-centered design work for teams. *Communications of the ACM*, October, 93–103.

Howe, Roger J., Gaeddert, Dee & Howe, Maynard A. (1995) *Quality on Trial: Bringing Bottom-Line Accountability to the Quality Effort*. New York: McGraw-Hill.

Huber, Joel (1975) Predicting preferences on experimental bundles of attributes: a comparison of models. *Journal of Marketing Research*, 12 (August), 290–7.

Huber, Joel & Zwerina, Klaus (1996) The importance of utility balance in efficient choice designs. *Journal of Marketing Research*, 33 (August), 307–17.

Huber, Joel, Wittink, Dick R., Fiedler, John A. & Miller, Richard (1993) The effectiveness of alternative preference elicitation procedures in predicting choice. *Journal of Marketing Research*, 30, 105–14.

Imai, Masaaki (1986) *Kaizen: The Key to Japan's Competitive Success*. New York: Random House.

Ittner, Christopher D. & Larcher, David F. (1997) Product development cycle time and organizational performance. *Journal of Marketing Research*, 34, 1 (February), 13–23.

Jain, Arun K., Acito, Franklin, Malhotra, Naresh K. & Mahajan, Vijay (1979) A comparison of the internal validity of alternative parameter estimation methods in decompositional multiattribute preference models. *Journal of Marketing Research*, 16 (August), 313–22.

Jamieson, Linda F. & Bass, Frank M. (1989) Adjusting stated intention measures to predict trial purchase of new products: a comparison of models and methods. *Journal of Marketing Research*, 26 (August), 336–45.

Japan Human Relations Association (1992) *Kaizen Teian 1: Developing Systems for Continuous Improvement Through Employee Suggestions*. Cambridge, MA: Productivity Press.

Johnson, Eric J., Meyer, Robert J. & Ghose, Sanjoy (1989) When choice models fail: compensatory models in negatively correlated environments. *Journal of Marketing Research*, 26, 255–70.

Johnson, Richard (1974) Tradeoff analysis of consumer values. *Journal of Marketing Research*, May, 121–7.

——— (1987) Accuracy of utility estimation in ACA. Working Paper, Sawtooth Software, Sequim, WA (April).

——— (1999) The joys and sorrows of implementing HB methods for conjoint analysis. Working Paper, Sawtooth Software, Sequim, WA (November).

Kahn, Barbara & Meyer, Robert J. (1991) Consumer multiattribute judgments under attribute-weight uncertainty. *Journal of Consumer Research*, 17 (March), 508–22.

Kahn, Kenneth B. (1996) Interdepartmental integration: a definition with implications for product development performance. *Journal of Product Innovation Management*, 13, 137–51.

Kalwani, Manohar U. & Silk, Alvin J. (1982) On the reliability and predictive validity of purchase intention measures. *Marketing Science*, 1, 3 (Summer), 243–86.

Keeney, Ralph & Raiffa, Howard (1976) *Decisions with Multiple Consequences: Preferences and Value Tradeoffs*. New York: John Wiley & Sons.

Kelly, George A. (1955) *The Psychology of Personal Constructs*, Vol. 1. New York: W.W. Norton.

Klein, K. & J. Sorra (1996) The challenge of innovation implementation. *Academy of Management Review*, 21, 4, 1055–80.

Klein, Noreen M. (1986) Assessing unacceptable attribute levels in conjoint analysis. *Advances in Consumer Research*, XIV, 154–8.

Kosslyn, Stephen M., Zaltman, Gerald, Thompson, William, Hurvitz, David & Braun, Kathryn (1999) *Reading the mind of the market*. Boston, MA: Harvard Business School, January.

Kuczmarski, Thomas D. (1992) *Managing New Products*. (Englewood Cliffs, NJ: Prentice-Hall, Inc.

Kuhfeld, Warren F. (1999) Efficient experimental designs using computerized searches. Working Paper, SAS Institute, Inc.

Kuhfeld, Warren F., Tobias, Randall D. & Garratt, Mark (1994) Efficient experimental design with marketing research applications. *Journal of Marketing Research*. November, 545–57.

Lambert, Denis & Slater, Stanley F. (1999) Perspective: first, fast, and on time: the path to success. Or is it? *Journal of Product Innovation Management*, 16, 427–38.

Lave, J. & Wenger, S. (1990) *Situated Learning*. Cambridge: Cambridge University Press.

Lawler, E. & Mohrman, S. (1987) Quality circles: after the honeymoon. *Organizational Dynamics*, Spring, 42–54.

Learnshare (2000) http://www.learnshare.com/brochure/brochure1.htm

Lee, Mushin & Na, Dohyeong (1994) Determinants of technical success in product development when innovative radicalness is considered. *Journal of Product Innovation Management*, 11, 62–8.

Lehmann, Donald R. & Winer, Russell S. (1994) *Product Management*. Boston, MA: Richard D. Irwin, Inc.

Leigh, Thomas W., MacKay, David B. & Summers, John O. (1984) Reliability and validity of conjoint analysis and self-explicated weights: a comparison. *Journal of Marketing Research*, 21, 456–62.

Lenk, Peter J., DeSarbo, Wayne S., Green, Paul E. & Young, Martin R. (1996) Hierarchical Bayes conjoint analysis: recovery of partworth heterogeneity from reduced experimental designs. *Marketing Science*, 15, 2, 173–91.

Leonard-Barton, Dorothy E., Wilson, Edith & Doyle, J. (1993) Commercializing technology: imaginative understanding of user needs. Sloan Foundation Conference on the Future of Research and Development, Harvard University, Boston, MA, February.

Levin, Gary (1992) Anthropologists in Adland. *Advertising Age* (February 2), 3, 49.

Liechty, John, Ramaswamy, Venkatram & Cohen, Steven (2000) Choice-menus for mass customization: an experimental approach for analyzing customer demand with an application to a web-based information service. *Journal of Marketing Research*, 38, 2, (May), 183–96.

Liker, Jeffrey K., Sobek, Durward K. II, Ward, Allen C. & Cristiano, John J. (1996) Involving suppliers in product development in the United States and Japan: evidence for set-based concurrent engineering. *IEEE Transactions on Engineering Management*, 43, 2, (May), 165–78.

Little, John D.C. (1966) A Model of adaptive control of promotional spending. *Operations Research*, 14, 6 (November–December), 1075–98.

——— (1977) Optimal adaptive control: a multivariate model for marketing applications. *IEEE Transactions on Automatic Control*, AC-22, 2, (April), 187–95.

Louviere, Jordan J., Hensher, David A. & Swait, Joffre D. (2000) *Stated Choice Methods: Analysis and Application*. New York: Cambridge University Press.

Mahajan, Vijay & Wind, Jerry (1986) *Innovation Diffusion Models of New Product Acceptance*. Cambridge, MA: Ballinger Publishing Company.

——— (1988) New product forecasting models, directions for research and implementation. *International Journal of Forecasting*, 4, 341–58.

Mahajan, Vijay, Muller, Eitan & Bass, Frank M. (1990) New product diffusion models in marketing: a review and directions for research. *Journal of Marketing*, 54, 1 (January), 1–26.

Malhotra, Naresh (1982) Structural reliability and stability of nonmetric conjoint analysis. *Journal of Marketing Research*, 19, (May) 199–207.

——— (1986) An approach to the measurement of consumer preferences using limited information. *Journal of Marketing Research*, 23 (February), 33–40.

McArdle, Meghan (2000) Internet-based rapid customer feedback for design feature tradeoff analysis. LFM Thesis, Cambridge, MA: Massachusetts Institute of Technology (June).

McFadden, Daniel L. (1974) Conditional logit analysis of qualitative choice behavior. In *Frontiers of Econometrics*, edited by P. Zarembla. New York: Academic Press, pp. 105–42.

McGrath, Michael E. (1996) *Setting the Pace in Product Development: A Guide to Product and Cycle-Time Excellence*. Boston, MA: Butterworth-Heinemann.

Menezes, Melvyn A.J. (1994) Xerox Corporation: The Customer Satisfaction Program (A). Harvard Business School Case 9-594-109, Boston, MA: Publishing Division, Harvard Business School.

Meyer, Mark & Lehnerd, Alvin (1997) *The Power of Product Platforms*. New York: The Free Press.

Mishra, Sanjay, Kim, Dongwook & Lee, Dae Hoon (1996) Factors affecting new product success: cross-country comparisons. *Journal of Product Innovation Management*, 13, 530–50.

Mizuno, S. (1988) *Management for Quality Improvement*. Cambridge, MA: Productivity Press.

Montoya-Weiss, Mitzi & Calantone, Roger (1994) Determinants of new product performance: a review and meta-analysis. *Journal of Product Innovation Management*, 11, 397–417.

Moore, William L. & Pessemier, Edgar A. (1993) *Product Planning and Management: Designing and Delivering Value*. New York: McGraw-Hill, Inc.

Moore, William L. & Semenik, Richard J. (1988) Measuring preferences with hybrid conjoint analysis: the impact of a different number of attributes in the master design. *Journal of Business Research*, 16, 261–74.

Moore, William L., Louviere, Jordan J. & Verma, Rohit (1999) Using conjoint analysis to help design product platforms. *Journal of Product Innovation Management*, 16, 1 (January), 27–39.

Moorman, Christine (1995) Organizational market information processes: cultural antecedents and new product outcomes. *Journal of Marketing Research*, 32 (August), 318–35.

Moorman, Christine & Miner, Anne S. (1997) The impact of organizational memory on new product performance and creativity. *Journal of Marketing Research*, 34, 1 (February), 91–106.

Morrison, Donald G. (1979) Purchase intentions and purchase behavior. *Journal of Marketing*, 43, 2 (Spring), 65–74.

Narasimhan, Chakravarthi & Sen, Subrata K. (1983) New product models for test market data. *Journal of Marketing*, 47, 1 (Winter), 11–24.

Nowlis, Stephen M. & Simonson, Itamar (1997) Attribute-task compatibility as a determinant of consumer preference reversals. *Journal of Marketing Research*, 36 (May), 205–18.

Olson, Eric M., Walker, Orville C. Jr., & Ruekert, Robert (1995) Organizing for effective new product development: the moderating role of product innovativeness. *Journal of Marketing*, 59 (January), 48–62.

Oppewal, Harmen, Louviere, Jordan J. & Timmermans, Harry J.P. (1994) Modeling hierarchical conjoint processes with integrated choice experiments, *Journal of Marketing Research*, 31 (February), 92–105.

Orlikowski, Wanda J. (1992) The duality of technology: rethinking the concept of technology in organizations. *Organization Science*, 3, 3, 398–427.

Orme, Bryan (1999) ACA, CBC, or both? Effective strategies for conjoint research. Working Paper, Sawtooth Software, Sequim, WA.

Osborn, A.J. (1963) *Applied Imagination*. New York: Charles Scribner's Sons.

Ozer, Muanmmer (1999) A survey of new product evaluation models. *Journal of Product Innovation Management*, 16, 1 (January), 77–94.

Park, C. Whan, Jun, Sung Youl & MacInnis, Deborah J. (1999) Choosing what I want versus rejecting what I don't want: an application of decision framing to product option choice decisions. Cambridge, MA: Marketing Science Institute.

Pekelman, Dov & Sen Subrata K. (1979) Improving prediction in conjoint analysis. *Journal of Marketing Research*,16 (May), 211–20.

Prelec, Drazen (2001) A two-person scoring rule for subjective reports. Working Paper, Center for Innovation in Product Development, Cambridge, MA: Massachusetts Institute of Technology, February.

Prince, George M. (1970) *The Practice of Creativity*. New York: Harper & Row Publishers.

Pringle, Lewis, Wilson, R.D. and Brody, E.I. (1982) News: a decision-oriented model for new product analysis and forecasting. *Marketing Science*, 1 (Winter), 1–30.

Pugh, Stuart (1996) *Creating Innovative Products Using Total Design: The Living Legacy of Stuart Pugh*, edited by Don Clausing & Ron Andrade. Reading, MA: Addison-Wesley, Inc.

Rao, Vithala & Katz, Ralph (1971) Alternative multidimensional scaling methods for large stimulus sets. *Journal of Marketing Research*, 8 (November), 488–94.

Rangan, Kasturi & Bell, Marie (1998) Dell Online. Harvard Business School Case 9-598-116.

Repenning, Nelson (1999) A dynamic model of resource allocation in multi-project research and development systems, *The System Dynamics Review*, 16 (3), 173–221.

——— (2001) Understanding fire fighting in new product development. *Journal of Product Innovation Management*, 18, 5 (September), 285–300.

Repenning, Nelson & Sterman, John (2000a) Getting quality the old-fashioned way: self-confirming attributions in the dynamics of process improvement. In *The Quality Movement and Organization Theory*, edited by R. Cole & W.R. Scott. Thousand Oaks, CA: Sage Publications, pp. 237–70.

——— (2000b). *From Exploitation to Degradation: Self-Confirming Attribution Errors in the Dynamics of Process Improvement*. Cambridge, MA: Center for Innovation in Product Development, MIT.

Rokeach, M.J. (1973) *Beliefs, Attitudes, and Values*. New York: The Free Press.

Rosen, Barry Nathan, Schnaars, Steven P. & Shani, David (1988) A comparison of approaches for setting standards for technological products. *Journal of Product Innovation Management*, 5, 2 (June), 129–39.

Roussel, Philip A., Saad, Kamal N. & Erickson, Tamara J. (1991) *Third Generation R&D*. Boston, MA: Harvard Business School Press.

Sanderson, Susan & Uzumeri, Mustafa (1996) *Managing Product Families*. Homewood, IL: Irwin.

Sawtooth Software, Inc. (1996), ACA system: Adaptive Conjoint Analysis. *ACA Manual*. Sequim, WA: Sawtooth Software, Inc.

Seering, Warren (1998), Annual Report – Second Year. Center for Innovation in Product Development, MIT, Cambridge, MA (October).

Segal, Madhav N. (1982) Reliability of conjoint analysis: contrasting data collection procedures. *Journal of Marketing Research*, 19, 139–43.

Senin, Nicola, Wallace, David R. & Borland, Nicholas (2001) Object-based simulation in a service marketplace forthcoming, *ASME Journal of Mechanical Design*.

Sharda, Ramesh, Frankwick, Gary L., Deosthali, Atul & Delahoussaye, Ron (1999) Information support for new product development teams. Working Paper, 99–108, Cambridge, MA: Marketing Science Institute.

Shocker, Allan D. & Hall, William G. (1986) Pretest market models: a critical evaluation. *Journal of Product Innovation Management*, 3, 3 (June), 86–108.

Shocker, Allan D. & Srinivasan, V. (1979) Multiattribute approaches to product concept evaluation and generation: a critical review. *Journal of Marketing Research*, 16 (May), 159–80.

Silk, Alvin J. & Urban, Glen L. (1978) Pre-test-market evaluation of new packaged goods: a model and measurement methodology. *Journal of Marketing Research*, 15 (May), 171–91.

Simmons, Carolyn J., Bickart, Barbara A. & Lynch, John G. Jr. (1993), Capturing and creating public opinion in survey research, *Journal of Consumer Research*, 30 (September), 316–29.

Smith, Preston G. & Reinertsen, Donald G. (1998) *Developing Products in Half the Time*, 2nd edn. New York: John Wiley & Sons, Inc.

Sobek, Durward K. II, Liker, Jeffrey K. & Ward, Allen C. (1998) Another look at how Toyota integrates product development. *Harvard Business Review*, 76, 4 (July/August), 36–49.

Sobek, Durward K. II, Ward, Allen C. & Liker, Jeffrey K. (1999) Toyota's principles of set-based concurrent engineering. *Sloan Management Review*, 40, 2 (Winter), 67–83.

Song, X. Michael & Parry, Mark E. (1997a) The determinants of Japanese new product successes. *Journal of Marketing Research*, 34, 1 (February), 64–76.

——— (1997b) A cross-national comparative study of new product development processes. Japan and the United States. *Journal of Marketing*, 61 (April), 1–18.

Song, X. Michael, di Benedetto, C. Anthony & Zhao, Yuzhen Lisa (1999) Does pioneering advantage exist? a cross-national comparative study. Working Paper, 99-111. Cambridge, MA: Marketing Science Institute.

Song, X. Michael, Montoya-Weiss, Mitzi M. & Schmidt, Jeffrey B. (1997) Antecedents and consequences of cross-functional cooperation: a comparison of R&D, manufacturing, and marketing perspectives. *Journal of Product Innovation Management*, 14, 35–47.

Souder, William E. (1980) Promoting an effective R&D/marketing interface. *Research Management*, 23, 4 (July), 10–15.

——— (1987) *Managing New Product Innovations*. Lexington, MA: Lexington Books.

——— (1988) Managing relations between R&D and marketing in new product development products. *Journal of Product Innovation Management*, 5, 6–19.

Srinivasan, V. (1988) A conjunctive-compensatory approach to the self-explication of multiattributed preferences. *Decision Sciences*, 19, 295–305.

Srinivasan, V. & Park, Chan Su (1997) Surprising robustness of the self-explicated approach to customer preference structure measurement. *Journal of Marketing Research*, 34 (May), 286–91.

Srinivasan, V. & Shocker, Allen D. (1973) Estimating the weights for multiple attributes in a composite criterion using pairwise judgments. *Psychometrika*, 38, 4 (December), 473–93.

Srinivasan, V. & Wyner. Gordon A. (1989) CASEMAP: Computer-Assisted Self-Explication of Multiattributed Preferences: In *New-Product Development and esting*, edited by Walter Henry, Michael Menasco & Hirokazu Takada. Lexington, MA: Lexington Books, pp. 91–112.

Srinivasan, V., Lovejoy, William S. & Beach, David (1997) Integrated product design for marketability and manufacturing. *Journal of Marketing Research*, 34, February, 154–63.

Staw, Barry M. (1995) Why no one really wants creativity. In *Creative Action in Organizations*, edited by Cameron M. Ford & Dennis A. Gioia. Thousand Oaks, CA: Sage Publications, pp. 161–6.

Taguchi, Genichi (1987) *Introduction to Quality Engineering: Designing Quality into Products and Processes*. White Plains, NY: Kraus International Publications.

Tessler, Amy, Wada, Norm & Klein, Robert L. (1993) QFD at PG&E, Transactions from The Fifth Symposium on Quality Function Deployment (June).

Thomke, Stefan H. (1998a) Managing experimentation in the design of new products. *Management Science*, 44, 6 (June), 743–62.

——— (1998b) Simulation, learning and R&D performance: evidence from automotive development. *Research Policy*, 27, 55–74.

Thomke, Stefan H., von Hippel, Eric A. & Franke, Roland R. (1998) Modes of experimentation: an innovation process – and competitive – variable. *Research Policy*, 27, 315–32.

Toubia, Olivier, Simester, Duncan & Hauser, John R. (2002) Fast polyhedral adaptive conjoint estimation, Working Paper, Cambridge, MA: Center for Innovation in Product Development, MIT.

Tourangeau, Roger, Rips, Lance J. & Rasinski, Kenneth A. (2000) *The Psychology of Survey Response*. New York: Cambridge University Press.

Ulrich, Karl T. & Eppinger, Steven D. (2000) *Product Design and Development*. New York: McGraw-Hill, Inc.

Ulrich, Karl T. & Pearson, Scott (1998) Assessing the importance of design through product archaeology. *Management Science*, 44, 3 (March), 352–69.

Urban, Glen L. (1970) Sprinter Mod III: a model for the analysis of new frequently purchased consumer products. *Operations Research*, 18, 5 (September–October), 805–53.

——— (2000) Listening in to customer dialogues on the web. Working Paper, Cambridge, MA: Center for Innovation in Product Development, MIT.

Urban, Glen L. & Hauser, John R. *Design and Marketing of New Products,* 2nd edn. Englewood Cliffs, NJ: Prentice-Hall, Inc.

Urban, Glen L. & Katz, Gerald M. (1983) Pre-test market models: validation and managerial implications, *Journal of Marketing Research*, 20 (August), 221–34.

Urban, Glen L. & von Hippel, Eric (1988) Lead user analysis for the development of new industrial products. *Management Science*, 34, 5 (May), 569–82.

Urban, Glen L., Weinberg, Bruce & Hauser, John R. (1996) Premarket forecasting of really-new products. *Journal of Marketing*, 60, 1 (January), 47–60.

Urban, Glen L., Hauser, John R. & Roberts, John. H. (1990) Prelaunch forecasting of new automobiles: models and implementation. *Management Science*, 36, 4 (April), 401–21.

Urban, Glen L., Carter, Theresa, Gaskin, Steven & Mucha, Zofia (1986) Market share rewards to pioneering brands: an empirical analysis and strategic implications, *Management Science*, 32, 6 (June) 645–59.

Urban, Glen L., Hauser, John R., Qualls, William J., Weinberg, Bruce D., Bohlmann, Jonathan D. & Chicos, Roberta A. (1997) Validation and lessons from the field: applications of information acceleration, *Journal of Marketing Research*, 34, 1 (February), 143–53.

von Hippel, Eric (1986) Lead users: a source of novel product concepts. *Management Science*, 32, 791–805.

——— (1988) *The Sources of Innovation*. New York: Oxford University Press.

Wallace, David, Abrahamson, Shaun, Senin, Nicola & Sferro, Peter (2000) Integrated design in a service marketplace, *Computer-aided Design*, 32, 2, 97–107.

Ward, Allen C., Liker, Jeffrey K., Cristiano, John J. & Sobek, Durward K. II (1995) The second Toyota paradox: how delaying decisions can make better cars faster. *Sloan Management Review*, 36, 3 (Spring), 43–61.

Wenger, Etienne (1998) *Communities of Practice: Learning, Meaning, and Identity*. New York: Cambridge University Press.

Wheelwright, Steven C. & Clark, Kim B. (1992) *Revolutionizing Product Development*. New York: The Free Press.

Wilkie, William L. & Pessemier, Edgar A. (1973) Issues in marketing's use of multi-attribute attitude models. *Journal of Marketing Research*, 10 (November), 428–41.

Wind, Jerry (1982) *Product Policy*. Reading, MA: Addison-Wesley, Inc.

Wind, Jerry, Green, Paul E., Shifflet, Douglas & Scarbrough, Marsha (1989) Courtyard by Marriott: designing a hotel facility with consumer-based marketing models. *Interfaces*, 19, 1 (January-February), 25–47.

Witter, Jerome, Clausing, Don, Laufenberg, Ludger & Soares de Andrade, Ronaldo (1994) Reusability – the key to corporate agility. Proceedings of the Conference on New Approaches to Development and Engineering, Gothenburg, Sweden (May).

Wittink, Dick R. (1989) The effect of differences in the number of attribute levels in conjoint results. *Marketing Letters*, 1, 113–23.

Wittink, Dick R. & Cattin, Philippe (1981) Alternative estimation methods for conjoint analysis: a Monte Carlo study. *Journal of Marketing Research*, 18 (February), 101–6.

Zaltman, Gerald (1997) Rethinking market research: putting people back in. *Journal of Marketing* Research, 23 (November), 424–37.

Zentner, Rene D. & Gelb, Betsy D. (1991) Scenarios: a planning tool for health care organizations. *Hospital & Health Services Administration*, Summer, 211–22.

9

Channel Management: Structure, Governance, and Relationship Management

ERIN ANDERSON and ANNE T. COUGHLAN

INTRODUCTION

To go to market, producers of services and products create at least one channel of distribution, or path, through which they access a potential buyer, convert the prospect into a customer, and fulfill the orders the customer places. The importance of distribution channels can be seen in many industries in the US, where channel members collectively earn margins that account for 30 to 50% of the ultimate selling price. In contrast, advertising typically accounts for less than 5 to 7% of the final price (Stern & Weitz, 1997). The importance of the distribution function is not due solely to the accounting costs of the channel's activities. Marketing channels represent a substantial opportunity cost as well. Finding the *potential* buyer and converting mere potential into profitable orders from paying customers is a major part of the channel's role. The marketing channel does a great deal not only to serve the market, but also to *make* the market.

In short, the management of channel activities has great potential for developing competitive advantage, either by lowering costs or by differentiating the final product to a market developed by channel members. And the advantage accrued from good channel management is strategic, because it is often durable, difficult to put into place, and difficult to imitate (Stern & Weitz, 1997).

Much of the early work in channels, circa the 1950s and 1960s, focuses on identifying the somewhat mysterious functions of channels, and explaining when and why these functions have utility (e.g., Alderson, 1965; Bucklin, 1969, 1972). Pioneering institutional work in channels established in fact that marketing channels exist without anyone's knowledge (Cox & Goodman (1956) noted that in the 1950s, even General Electric did not know how a humble lightbulb got from the factory to a kitchen socket). In general, we now recognize that channels perform eight major functions as they interface between suppliers and markets: taking title (ownership); taking physical possession (stewardship); promotion; negotiation; financing; risk taking; ordering; and payment. Along the way, channels achieve competitive advantage by providing support services after the sale and by composing appealing assortments (assortments of products and services to offer to buyers, assortments of potential buyers to offer to suppliers). In short, channels make markets and execute transactions by bringing together potential suppliers and demanders.

Considering the range of functions involved in accessing a market, it is not surprising that the management of marketing channels is no small matter. Going to market at all is not easy. Going to the *right* market, and doing so *quickly*, in the *manner* the customer desires, with few *errors*, and at low *cost* is ... a fairly rare achievement.

This chapter focuses on a subset of managerial decisions that are crucial to the functioning of a marketing channel. These decisions concern *structure* (essentially, strategic choices that can be represented graphically, such as how many separate firms constitute a channel), *governance* (the frameworks that are meant to insure orderly pursuit of goals and resolution of conflict), and *relationship management* (the myriad actions that frame the daily environment of a marketing channel). There are many other issues in channel management, such as the physical movement of goods, logistics and number of levels in the channel, the number of intermediaries at each level, transfer prices, and so on. See Frazier (1999) for an excellent discussion of these and other issues, and Coughlan et al. (2001) for a discussion of institutional arrangements and types of intermediaries.

Channels are typically composed of multiple organizations (either separate firms or separate divisions of one firm), all of them interdependent in that their results derive from the channel's ability to create transactions. But multiple organizations performing a myriad of functions often work at cross purposes. The mediocrity of the resulting channel performance will hurt at least some of its members, leading to recrimination and conflict. To avoid this scenario, channel members attempt to influence each other to operate in a coordinated fashion, one that recognizes that their interdependence creates common interests. Structure, governance, and relationship management shape how firms actually garner and then exert influence over each other, in order to be successful against competing systems (other sets of channel members promoting different solutions to a market's needs).

Roughly, seven governance structure issues concerned with achieving coordination are prominent in the channels literature (Jap & Weitz, 1995). This classification is somewhat arbitrary, as a given research work often covers several categories. This review is organized around these issues, as follows:

1. Vertical integration or not (whether to *own* the channel)
2. Managing conventional channel relationships
   a) Selection of channel members
   b) Design of contracts (both explicit and implicit) governing the relationship
      - Terms of the contract
      - The use of incentives
      - The use of monitoring
   c) Use of relational norms
   d) Accumulation and use of power.

The ordering of this list is carefully chosen. The first decision for the organization is whether or not to vertically integrate, that is, whether to *own* the channel (as opposed to outsourcing, or distributing through independent parties). *The decision making organization can be any player in the channel.* While it may be the manufacturer (considering integrating forward), it may also be a downstream channel member (e.g., a retailer, a logistics services provider, a distributor, or an agent) considering integrating backward into production and/or forward toward the final point of sale. If the organization chooses to vertically integrate from production down to the level of the final buyer (e.g., through direct selling), exerting influence to coordinate channel activities is relatively easy, and hence not the most interesting research problem. But this typically is not the most cost-effective or demand-enhancing solution.

When complete channel integration is unattractive, the organization must then engage in the *recruitment of channel members*. Channel members are generally selected and courted both for their superior abilities to perform specific channel functions, and for their potential interest in cooperative, coordinative behavior. The greater is this interest, the more amenable the member is to working together with the organization to achieve coordination as a channel system. Several other governance issues then come to the forefront.[1] The channel members must establish their *contract* defining at least minimal rights and responsibilities, even if they do not express their agreement as a document. Apart from the *terms* of the contract, a key understanding concerns how *incentives* can be used to directly influence action. To the extent that incentives are not effective, the organization can directly *monitor* channel members to verify their performance levels.

The contract does not fully define the parties' expectations. Norms of behavior can be cultivated, as the relational governance approach would suggest. Further, *channel power* can be brought to bear to affect behavior. Together, contracts, norms, and power drive the behavior of the channel as a system. This influences the channel's success in competing against other channel systems for delivering value to buyers. Figure 9.1 depicts these major issues involved in governing a channel system. We use this schematic as a device to organize the literature surveyed in this chapter.

As a research area, marketing channels is in a pre-paradigmatic state (Kuhn, 1969): there is little agreement about how to frame issues and what is the appropriate mode of inquiry. In pursuit of generalizability, causality, and managerial implications, channels researchers have been eclectic in theory and in method. In addition to carrying out purely descriptive field research (to find patterns of practice and performance outcomes), channels scholars have borrowed from a number of frameworks to generate new patterns and explain existing ones. A partial list of frameworks used in the field includes:

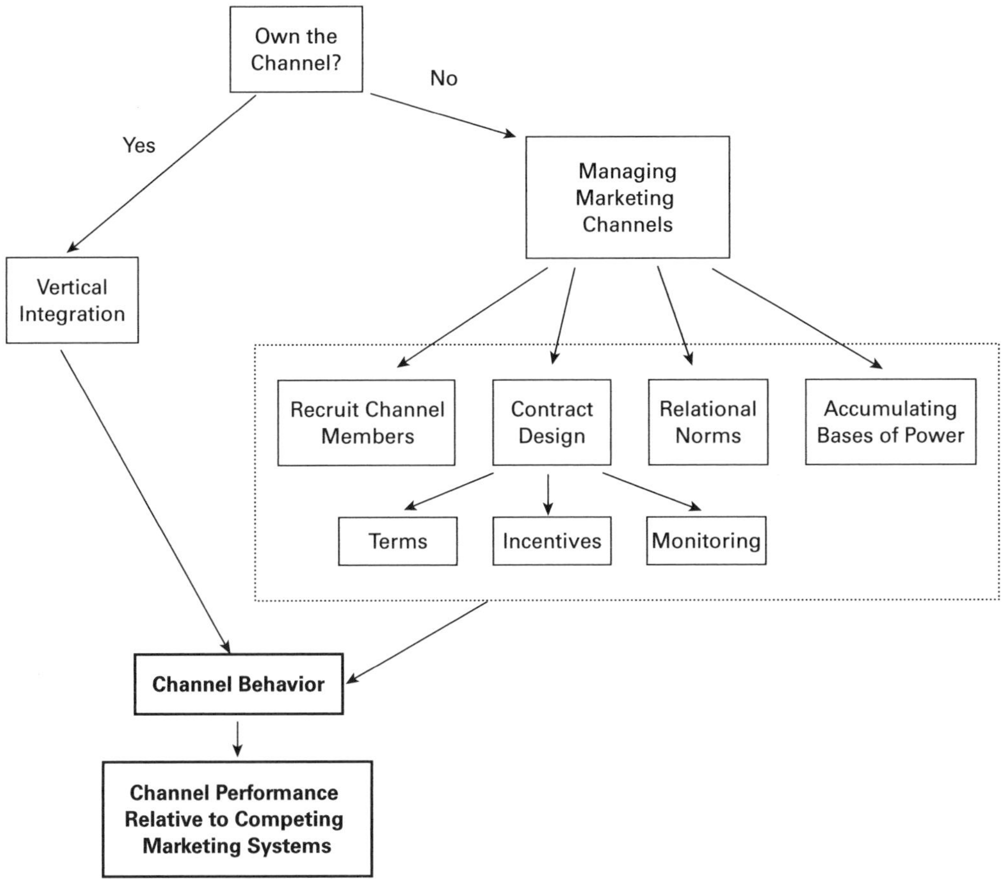

Figure 9.1 *Governance Issues in Channels of Distribution*

1. From economics: transaction cost analysis, agency theory, game theory, analytical models of competition and market response, evolutionary economics
2. From sociology: theories of dependence and group processes, institutional theories of legitimacy
3. From psychology: theories of social influence, interpersonal relationships, and conflict
4. From marketing theory and strategic management: trust, competitive advantage, path dependence
5. From eclectic approaches: political economy, life-cycle theories

As if channels research needed more variety, there are many points of difference about the appropriate methodology to develop and test proposed generalizations. Must there be a field test? If so, should the data be correlational (versus quasi-experimental), dyadic (versus one side – or versus the whole network), longitudinal (versus cross-sectional), archival (versus perceptual), primary (versus secondary), single informant (versus multiple), and so forth? Given the data, how should it be modeled? Do experiments have a role? Are qualitative approaches appropriate? What is the value of inductive or exploratory (versus hypothesis testing) approaches?

The good news is that channels researchers have considerable freedom in how to proceed. The bad news is that it is difficult to achieve consensus, and thus to accumulate findings into robust generalizations. Further, many approaches compete, and their competition focuses on their differences (particularly in the causal mechanism employed, as well as in the research approach taken).

The position of this review is that results from these multiple approaches are converging, almost surprisingly so. Beneath semantic and methodological differences, there is considerable agreement in findings and in explanations for them. Further, there is an emerging consensus about what are the issues that merit further inquiry.

This review gives center stage to the substantive conclusions that are emerging from this large and vital area of inquiry. The issues of how research gets done (i.e., differences in framework and method) will be treated, but given a low priority here.

The Channel Ownership Choice

Perhaps the first question in channel design and management is how many organizations should be involved in a channel: should one entity perform not only production but all channel activities (Lilien, 1979)? A vertically integrated channel is the shortest, simplest structure. But is it the most efficient, or the most effective?

Transaction Cost Analysis and Game Theory in the Channel Ownership Decision

Two useful theoretical approaches have been particularly influential in the literature on channel ownership: transaction cost economics (TCE; see, for example, Rindfleisch & Heide, 1997; Williamson, 1996) and game theory (Moorthy, 1993). Both approaches originated in the economics literature and have been adapted to the channels context by researchers in marketing. TCE's maintained hypothesis is the fundamental superiority of the market mechanism, leading to what economists call 'decentralization' (that is, composing a channel of third parties) as the default channel choice, except in cases of 'market failure.' TCE therefore informs the channel ownership choice by identifying factors leading to market failure and hence to vertical integration of the channel. The game theoretic approach, by contrast, views interaction within a channel as the choice of strategic actions by each channel 'player' that jointly affect channel profitability, and hence ultimate channel-ownership choice. Some of the key strategic factors on which the game theoretic approach focuses are wholesale and retail pricing, service decisions, the intensity of distribution, and nonprice actions such as returns policies and warranty policies. In some sense, the game theoretic approach takes as given the deviation of decentralized channel relationships from the perfectly competitive benchmark, and seeks to identify the conditions (or proactive actions of the channel captain) that nevertheless make outsourcing an optimal channel decision. Thus, TCE starts from the premise that outsourcing (the 'market') should be the default unless certain conditions hold; game theory starts from the premise that outsourcing has inherent deficiencies relative to vertical integration. As we will see, the two approaches are much more complementary than contradictory.

Transaction Cost Economics (TCE) and Channel Ownership

In the TCE approach, the issue is whether to perform a given function (e.g., selling) or set of functions (e.g., taking title, then reselling) via the buy option (outsource, or 'decentralize') or via its polar opposite, make (vertically integrate). Outsourcing is, *a priori*, considered preferable to vertical integration on grounds of long-term efficiency. This is because the outsider, a specialist (such as a distributor or a sales agent), pools the demands of many producers for given distribution services. Thus, the outsider can achieve economies of scope and scale, which are all-important advantages in the competitive world of distribution channels.

The advantage of economies of scope, in particular, is often featured in the channels literature, where it is known as the benefit of assortment, or one-stop shopping (Coughlan et al., 2001). Channel members create economies of scope by judiciously creating a bundle of brands and products/services that appeal to a market they know well. The economies of scale phenomenon has been demonstrated in the channels literature in Coughlan (1985) and Anderson and Coughlan (1987), who show that channel choice for an incremental product in a firm's line tends to follow the pre-existing channel (whether vertically integrated or decentralized), in order to spread fixed costs of distribution across a broader volume base.

The cost advantage created by pooling the products and services of many suppliers is important; so is the discipline of the market itself. Under the assumption that a true market for the services performed by the channel member exists (that is, that other competitors offer similar services and that other buyers value these services), the independent channel intermediary with whom a manufacturer partners has every incentive to perform well. First, the manufacturer can credibly threaten termination, since alternative partners exist. Second, the existence of other potential buyers for the intermediary's services means that poor performance with this manufacturer could threaten the intermediary's future earning opportunities; other manufacturers will stay away from a channel member without a proven success record.

This assumption of the superiority of outsourcing is consistent with the broad usage of outsourcing in channels of distribution. It suggests, for example, that manufacturers' ability to sell direct over the Internet will not result in mass disintermediation, because the Internet merely narrows, but does not eliminate, the upstream-downstream gap in distribution efficiency. Indeed, to the extent that using Internet technologies for channel management (order taking and fulfillment, warehouse management, complaint management, and many others) requires specialized skills, the spread of online commerce could be expected to perpetuate, rather than lessen, the attractiveness of decentralization in channels (Alba et al., 1997).

In TCE logic, a vertically integrated firm cannot generally match the scope or scale of an outsider's specialized skills (Anderson, 1988). An important linchpin of the arguments above about the superiority of outsourcing is the assumption of a true market for the channel member's skills. The violation of this assumption is one example of what TCE calls a 'market failure.' For example, for some transactions, the organization cannot credibly threaten to terminate the channel member because there are no other viable organizations to replace this one (the so-called 'small-numbers bargaining' problem). This could be true from the start (for example, in a small economy or market, there may be few players). But even when there are many potential channel members to choose from at the time of inception of the channel, investment by either or both parties in assets specific to this channel can turn what was a large-numbers situation into a small-numbers one after the channel is established. This arises when the channel builds what are known as *transaction-specific assets* – assets that are difficult to redeploy to another relationship without loss of substantial productive value. In either case (small numbers before or after a channel begins to operate), a barrier to exit from this channel relationship is created, thereby destroying the market mechanism and precipitating a market failure.

How does this happen? Opportunism is self-interest seeking *in a deceitful manner,* as opposed to the normal economic motive of self-interest seeking, but without misrepresenting one's intentions, distorting information, or reneging on one's obligations. Transaction cost economics maintains that, given the chance, some players will practice opportunism: since it is difficult to know which players will do so, it is prudent to structure transactions so as to discourage opportunism. In normal circumstances, third parties can be discouraged by the threat of retaliation or termination. But small-numbers bargaining reduces the credibility of the threat. The 'unique' channel member can practice 'opportunistic behavior' against other channel members, with little fear of negative consequences. Thus, the motivation to contribute to the good of the whole channel diminishes or disappears. When the likelihood of opportunistic behaviors is predicted to be high, the firm is well advised to bypass the market mechanism and, instead, vertically integrate the channel. Vertical integration (e.g., by using an employee sales force instead of an independent sales representative firm as a channel member) increases the agent's (here, salesperson's) dependence on the manufacturer (by removing all its other business), permits the exercise of an employer's legitimate authority to investigate and discipline employees, and creates an atmosphere that motivates employees to perform out of loyalty (Williamson, 1996).

In general (Rindfleisch & Heide, 1997), the transaction-cost predictions about integrating the channel under asset specificity hold up well in the field. The principal transaction-specific assets identified as having a high impact on channels are intangible, human assets that revolve around the type of product/service and the manner in which it is sold. Most of the physical assets employed in distribution can be put to another good use fairly readily: they are general purpose, rather than transaction specific. But the intangibles are considerable. Brand- and partner-specific learning, and personal relationships head the list. Where they are likely to arise and to play a major role in distribution, the firm is more likely to perform a function itself. This is particularly the case for products that are new to the world and/or technically complex. These products tend to be idiosyncratic to their producers. This requires people performing the distribution function to invest in idiosyncratic learning and to interface heavily between prospective customers and the factory. The nature of the job demands investing in personal relations and idiosyncratic (brand-specific) learning (Anderson, 1985). Both transaction cost theory and empirical evidence (Anderson & Coughlan, 1987; Rindfleisch & Heide, 1997) suggest that firms tend to 'take distribution in house' (assume ownership of the channel) for products and services of this nature.

TCE posits that another motive to vertically integrate is to gain information when it is very difficult to judge how well the agent is doing its job using only the information available when contracting with the agent. For example, the selling function is taken in house when observable measures (such as recorded sales) are not good indicators of sales performance (Anderson, 1985): this is a condition of performance ambiguity, or internal uncertainty. By integrating, the firm gains access to more and better information. This information advantage may also explain why some firms use *both* their own and an outside sales force: in situations where performance is hard to judge, each side provides information against which to benchmark the other (Dutta et al., 1995).

Taken together, extant research in the TCE tradition suggests that if cost differences between vertically integrated and decentralized channels are not too great, vertical integration in channels will occur when performance ambiguity is rife and when what is being sold demands investment in brand-specific products and relationships (Rindfleisch & Heide,

1997). These are not the most common scenarios (nor is vertical integration always a lower cost channel alternative than decentralization!); thus, TCE suggests that outsourcing in channels should be common – which indeed it is.

The Game Theoretic Approach to Channel Ownership

The game theoretic approach to channel ownership decisions, similarly to TCE, recognizes the inherent tendency of an independent *agent* (a third party, agreeing contractually to provide services) to behave in its own self-interest, rather than in the interest of the firm hiring it, the *principal*. The game theoretic approach assumes that this is the default behavior of independent members with whom the firm might partner. Although any party could be viewed as the principal, in a channels context, the agent is generally viewed as an intermediary, and the manufacturer is the principal; we will follow this convention in what follows here. Under the game-theoretic view of channel member behavior, the use of an intermediary (or, in the language of game theory, 'decentralization') may or may not bestow cost efficiencies on the channel (that is, the intermediary's ability to perform channel functions and flows at lower cost than could the manufacturer may or may not be strong). However, the independent intermediary induces a different sort of inefficiency in the channel that diminishes the attractiveness of outsourcing: an inefficiency in setting downstream prices to the market. This key transfer pricing problem in the channel is the *double marginalization* problem, written about in the economics literature by Spengler (1950) and Machlup and Taber (1960), and a key focus of Jeuland and Shugan's (1983) paper on channel coordination. When title to the product being sold changes hands as it passes through the channel, each channel member sets a new transfer price to the next downstream channel member (for example, a manufacturer sets a wholesale price to its distributor, who sets a transfer price to the retailers to whom it sells; the retailer sets the final retail price paid by the consumer). Since these transfer prices are not set at the perfectly competitive, no-rents level, but rather are set to generate an economic profit to each channel member (remember the small-numbers bargaining problem raised in TCE!), the result is a retail price that is demonstrably higher than the retail price that would prevail were the channel vertically integrated. In the absence of any other compensating factor (such as significantly lower costs to perform channel functions in the decentralized channel), the double marginalization problem suggests that vertical integration is preferable to a decentralized channel.[2]

Starting from this insight, analytic research in the channels area has focused on identifying conditions where, despite the double marginalization problem, and even under no cost advantage for the decentralized channel, decentralization can nevertheless be the profit-maximizing channel structure. Clearly, this is a strict test: if there are additional significant cost declines available from using specialized intermediaries, the benefit of decentralization would of course increase. The profit level achievable in a vertically integrated channel (holding the efficiency with which channel flows are performed constant) is termed the *coordinated* level of profits. The literature we review here assumes that no efficiency changes accrue to changes in the channel structure; it instead focuses on the strategic role played by vertically interacting channel members and by horizontally competing channel members and entire channels.

Jeuland and Shugan (1983) model a simple dyadic channel to highlight the double marginalization problem in channel transfer pricing. They show that double marginalization causes channel profits to be lower under decentralization (the use of the intermediary) than under vertical integration when a simple single-part transfer price is charged, holding efficiency of performance of channel flows constant. They provide an elegant solution to the problem: a jointly negotiated quantity discount schedule that causes the retailer to price so as to maximize *channel* profits, not just its own retail profits. Moorthy (1987) applies the economic literature on two-part tariffs[3] (see, e.g., Oi, 1971) to show that a wide variety of multi-part pricing options can also coordinate the dyadic channel. These articles together have insights for the *contracting* issue (to be discussed in a later section), but also suggest that ownership of the channel is not necessary for achievement of a vertical-integration pricing and profit benchmark and a reduction of the inefficiencies of double marginalization.

McGuire and Staelin (1983) and Coughlan (1985) examine the channel ownership problem from a different point of view. They restrict their attention to single-part transfer pricing (i.e., a constant wholesale price), but investigate the effect of *competition* on the channel structure, profitability, and coordination problem. Coughlan's model generalizes the linear demand system of McGuire and Staelin to allow for nonlinearities in demand. They model a channel consisting of two competing manufacturers, each of whom can choose to sell through a vertically integrated retail channel or through an exclusive decentralized retailer. The overall market can therefore be completely vertically integrated; completely decentralized (with exclusive retailers); or mixed, with one manufacturer vertically integrating and one decentralizing. They show that the degree of substitutability between the products being sold is a determining factor in optimal ownership choices of the manufacturers. A market with little product substitutability is optimally served through vertically integrated channels, while sufficiently high product substitutability generates two equilibria: complete decentralization, and complete vertical integration. The result is attributed to the fact that in very competitive markets, decentralizing permits the manufacturers to commit to less intense price competition. In effect, the double marginalization 'problem' becomes a benefit in very competitive markets. Coughlan (1985) adds an empirical test to show support for the model's findings in the context of the international semiconductor industry.

Coughlan and Wernerfelt (1989) tie together the threads of the double-marginalization approach of Jeuland and Shugan (1983) with those in the competition-between-channels approach of McGuire and Staelin (1983) and Coughlan (1985), to examine the implications for optimal channel structure in a competitive channel whose manufacturers are not restricted to one-part pricing. When two-part pricing is possible, manufacturers can replicate the vertically integrated level of channel coordination, despite the actual decentralization of the channel. Thus, decentralization becomes optimal because of the benefits of being able to commit (in the sense of Stackelberg leadership) to a coordinated price.[4] However, if these contracts within the channel are not observable and credible to members of the competing channel, and cannot be truly committed to, there is an incentive to 'cheat' on the coordinated pricing level for individual gain. When this is possible, the rational expectation of cheating causes the system to devolve back to more competitive, less profitable levels. This approach thus highlights the importance of contract observability and the ability to commit to contracts as a mechanism for preserving the profitability of the decentralized channel.

Later papers in this vein of the literature expand on these concepts. Coughlan (1987) models the channel-choice problem in a market with complementary goods; Coughlan and Lal (1992) consider how long the channel can and should be as a function of product substitutability in the market; Choi (1991) considers a different channel structure where two manufacturers sell through a common retailer; and Ingene and Parry (1995a, 1995b) model a manufacturer selling through two non-identical retailers. All of these compare the non-integrated channel structure's profitability to a vertically integrated benchmark, under the assumption that the channel intermediary is equally efficient at performing channel functions as would be the vertically integrated manufacturer. The underlying theme is that, in general, a decentralized channel structure can be less attractive than a vertically integrated channel, both because of the double marginalization problem and because of the intermediary's divergent goals from those of the manufacturer. For example, in Choi's channel structure, the retailer seeks to maximize profit across the two competing product lines, which is not the incentive of the individual manufacturer. Further inefficiencies within the channel system are induced when intermediaries are not identical (as in Ingene and Parry); then the antitrust requirement of equal treatment of intermediaries prevents the manufacturer from using effective price discrimination with each of them to coordinate the channel. The underlying thread in this literature is that despite these inefficiencies, there are certainly situations where the manufacturer does not have the choice to vertically integrate, or the fixed cost of doing so is simply prohibitive; thus, the manufacturer needs to appropriately structure the decentralized channel to maximize its profitability.

The game-theoretic approach to the channel ownership problem thus focuses on factors such as transfer pricing inefficiencies; sophisticated transfer pricing mechanisms to get rid of inefficiencies; the impact of competition at various levels of the channel; channel length; and the nature and observability of channel contracts, to see their effects on the value of ownership versus decentralization. The common theme in these results is that decentralization induces strategic inefficiencies in the channel, and that the channel manager's (typically, the manufacturer's) problem is therefore to structure contracts and incentives to do the best job of restoring a coordinated outcome to the channel.

Future Research Directions

This discussion suggests some interesting and provocative avenues for future research in the channel-ownership area. Currently, research on vertical integration in the TCE vein is turning to examining the causal effect of opportunism on channel choice. This mechanism is controversial, and distinguishes TCE from competing approaches. Wathne and Heide (2000) offers an excellent review that traces the second-order effects (such as providing a signal to customers) that can accompany efforts to forestall opportunism. On these lines, Ghosh and John (1999) offer an interesting marriage of TCE and marketing strategy.

Two research issues are particularly promising. First, TCE makes no allowance for the logic of simultaneously making and buying the same function (dual distribution), nor for the possibility of making some channel functions and buying others (hybrid channels). (TCE concerns making or buying a given set of functions, but is silent about how to bundle the functions in the first place.) Both of these non-pure options are increasingly common in channels (some analytic approaches to the dual distribution problem are discussed below in the section on selection of channel members). In particular, the Internet opens new routes to market, both vertically integrated and decentralized, as well as offering the possibility of allocating some (but not necessarily all) specific functions to the online channel presence. This is obviously an issue deserving of considerable research attention.

A second issue concerns the role of external uncertainty, or the inability to forecast frequent environmental changes (volatility) on the choice to vertically integrate or decentralize. TCE theorists differ in their interpretation of what impact volatility should have, and the empirical findings are contradictory and inconclusive (Rindfleisch & Heide, 1997). A new conceptualization is needed, perhaps from another framework such as real-options theory (Kogut & Kulatilaka, 1994).

The Recruitment of Channel Members

If the decision has been made to abandon vertical integration in favor of a decentralized channel, it is necessary to choose what type of channel intermediaries to recruit, and which particular ones to (attempt to) partner with.[5] The marketing literature has looked at the first issue through investigations of the choice of one versus another *form* of channel intermediary. The second question – which specific retailer to recruit, for example, given the choice to sell via retailers at all – has been attacked through *signaling* and *screening* models, which were first used in the economics literature.

Choice of the Form of Intermediary

The question of which type of intermediary to recruit has been approached in several different substantive channels contexts. One is the automobile market channel. A set of three articles looks at different aspects of this problem. Purohit and Staelin (1994) and Purohit (1997) examine the tradeoffs among rentals, sales, and buybacks in the automotive channel, finding that the manufacturer's sales increase with the use of a rental channel that sells off old cars originally sold to rental fleets. However, dealer profitability varies under the different regimes, as these rental agency sales compete with the dealer's used car lots. This is consistent with recent moves by automobile manufacturers to switch from an overlapping system to a buyback system, in which the automakers buy back their used cars from the rental agencies and resell them to dealers. The use of rentals and buybacks changes the dynamics of working with the standard dealer channel. Desai and Purohit (1999) extend this analysis to consider the more general choice between leasing and selling as modes of revenue generation in the channel. They show that the optimal proportion of leasing in the lease/sell mix falls as manufacturers' products become more competitive with each other. This is because products leased today are returned to the manufacturer in the future and then sold on the used car market, competing with future new cars in the market. This extra competition from used leased cars is more problematic, the greater is the degree of competition between the manufacturers.

In the retailing context, the question of which type of intermediary to use has been investigated by Balasubramanian (1998) in a paper examining the nature of competition between direct marketers (such as catalog houses) and conventional retailers. While this paper does not model the whole channel interface between manufacturer and retailer, it does show that the competitive incursion of a direct marketer fundamentally changes the nature of competition in the retail marketplace. The direct marketer has the advantage of 'location-less' competition, but the disadvantage of an inability to let consumers 'touch and feel' products before buying. The tension between these factors makes some consumers prefer bricks-and-mortar stores to direct buying, while others are comfortable with the direct channel. Balasubramanian also considers the importance of *information* about the direct seller's offering: catalog retailers, for example, do not send catalogs to every household, and therefore competition between the cataloguer and the conventional retailer is incomplete. He shows that the optimal coverage level for the direct marketer, interestingly, may not be complete. This suggests the need for a manufacturer seeking to sell through retail channels to take into account the coverage choices of its retailers.

Another treatment of the retailing choice is given in Coughlan and Soberman (2000). Here, the question is whether competing manufacturers of branded retail goods, such as apparel, should open their own vertically integrated outlet stores in addition to selling through their standard primary retail outlets. The authors show that the answer depends on the nature of segmentation in the market. The more different consumers are in their price sensitivity (holding service sensitivity differences constant), the more likely selling through outlet stores as well as primary retailers is to be profitable. Conversely, the more different consumers are in their service sensitivity (holding price sensitivity differences constant), the more likely manufacturers are to choose *not* to sell through outlet stores. Standard segmentation and price discrimination arguments suggest the former insight, but the latter insight is counterintuitive and explained by the usefulness of price-sensitive consumers in limiting the amount of costly service competition by the primary retail channel. Thus, here the choice of what types of retail formats to use depends not just on the fact of segmentation, but how consumers are segmented.

Therefore, the issue of what type of channel intermediaries to partner with is shown to depend variously on demand and segmentation issues; the nature and degree of competition; and the similarity or differences between competitive products in the marketplace.

An ambitious effort in this area is Rangan et al. (1992). This work offers a comprehensive decision-support approach to the selection of a channel structure for new products.

Which Specific Channel Member to Recruit?

The second question, of which *specific* channel members to work with, corresponds to the institutional issue of channel member selection criteria. New approaches to this problem are using the logic of screening and signaling to examine which players will do business with each other to form a channel. The term *screening* refers to the process by which a manufacturer (for example) takes actions designed to uncover the nature or type of intermediary a potential candidate really is. The term *signaling* refers to an action taken by the candidate itself to reveal its quality or type to the manufacturer considering partnering with it.

An excellent example is Mishra et al. (1998), which examines a double channel problem: 1) how can a channel member credibly promise consumers that it provides high quality in cases where quality is hard to verify; and 2) how can that channel member then induce its employees to live up to the quality promise? This paper shows that premium pricing and investing in décor serve as a signal to help to solve the first problem, while screening employees on skills, building a service culture, paying well, and tying pay to customer satisfaction help to solve the second problem.

Other uses of the signaling and screening concept in the channels literature include:

- The use of *signaling* by a *manufacturer* to convince the channel (and consumers) of its new product's high quality, versus the *retailer's* use of *screening* new products via demanding slotting allowances from suppliers. Manufacturers are shown to prefer signaling, while retailers prefer screening; in general, screening through slotting allowances yields higher total channel profit and social welfare (Chu, 1992).
- The manufacturer's choice of a retailer to reinforce its reputation and *signal* its product quality. Manufacturers of higher-quality products choose to distribute through more reputable retailers, while manufacturers of lower-quality products distribute through retailers with no reputation (e.g., discounters) (Chu & Chu, 1994).

The Design of Contracts with Channel Members

The channel relationship is extremely complex, and therefore lends itself to formal contract design (clauses and their wording), or informal contracting (relational governance), over many aspects. In this section we touch on both formal and informal contracting applied to

(a) the form of transfer pricing used;
(b) non-price aspects of the channel relationship;
(c) non-formal, bureaucratic structuring of the channel relationship;
(d) the form of strategic leadership in the channel;
(e) vertical restraints and channel exclusivity;
(f) franchising; and
(g) gray marketing.

The Form of Transfer Pricing in the Channel

The manufacturer is typically the agent choosing the form of transfer pricing applicable to the channel intermediary. As discussed above in the section on channel ownership, the form of transfer price used significantly affects the profitability of the channel. In the simplest channel relationship, like that modeled by Jeuland and Shugan (1983), the manufacturer using a single-part price – a constant wholesale price per unit – is really trying to accomplish two tasks with just one decision variable. The manufacturer seeks both to create an incentive for appropriate retail pricing, and to appropriately split the total channel profit pie, through its choice of wholesale price. Just as in the problem of insufficient degrees of freedom in statistics, here too, the double-marginalization problem really arises because of the manufacturer's inability to manage these two tasks with just one instrument – the wholesale price. This is why Jeuland and Shugan's (1983) solution, as well as the insights of Moorthy (1987) and Coughlan and Wernerfelt (1989), involve a multi-part transfer pricing scheme.

Ingene and Parry (1995a, 1995b, 1998) investigate closely the effects of transfer pricing form on a manufacturer's profits in a channel. They focus on a channel structure where the manufacturer sells through multiple retailers, who may or may not compete directly with one another. One of their contributions is to point out the divergence between transfer pricing contracts that *coordinate the channel* (that is, maximize *total channel profit*) and those that *maximize manufacturer profit* alone. They show that even if the manufacturer's retailers do not compete with each other, the channel-coordinating two-part tariff contract generally does not maximize manufacturer profits (1995b). When the retailers are heterogeneous, they show that there does not exist a single two-part tariff of the sort devised by Jeuland and Shugan (1983) that replicates the channel coordination outcome, but an appropriately devised quantity discount schedule will do so. However, under many conditions, the manufacturer would actually make more profit by offering a two-part tariff than by offering the channel-coordinating quantity discount scheme (1995a). Further, although there does exist a menu of two-part tariffs that mimics the coordinated channel, proper separation of the retailers does not always occur (that is, each retailer does not always choose the 'right' tariff for it). There are therefore many situations where a second-best two-part tariff generates manufacturer profits superior to those available under a channel-profit-maximizing menu of tariffs. Finally, they show the importance of truly jointly choosing both the fixed fee and the per-unit fee in the optimal two-part tariff, and that both of these are a function of the divergence in fixed-cost positions of the two retailers used (1998). In short, these articles show that (a) channel coordination, which has been held up as a goal for pricing models in the channels literature, is not likely to be chosen by a profit-maximizing manufacturer under various circumstances, and (b) while a multi-part pricing scheme dominates the simple single-part pricing structures assumed in many articles, often the manufacturer prefers a second-best version of such a contract to the supposed first-best, channel-coordinating solution.

Non-Price Aspects of the Channel Relationship

Manufacturers and their intermediaries must decide not only how the product is priced, but how it is marketed in non-price ways as well. Several non-price aspects of the channel relationship have been investigated, including manufacturers' returns policies, and product information or after-sales service. While a complete inventory of non-price channel contracting mechanisms is impossible to provide here, this subset serves to illustrate the principles involved.

In some product markets, product returns are routinely accepted by manufacturers. The book market is a good example. A returns policy may be viewed by the retailer as an insurance against unsold inventory; manufacturers may view it as a costly inducement to retailers to carry their products. Padmanabhan and Png (1997) provide another, more strategic rationale for offering a returns policy in the channel contract. By offering returns, competitive manufacturers transform retail competition from *quantity-based competition*, or so-called Cournot competition, to *price-based competition*, or so-called Bertrand competition. In effect, by allowing unlimited product returns, the manufacturers induce the retailers to order *at least* as many units (e.g., books) as they think they will sell; price competition between the retailers then clears the market. In contrast, without a returns policy, retailers will seek to order *no more than* the number of units they think they will sell, and in this situation, the quantity ordered is often sufficiently low to make quantities the market-clearing mechanism. It has been long-known that price-based competition results in lower retail prices and higher quantities sold than quantity-based competition. Thus, by inducing price-based competition in the channel, the manufacturers cause the retailers to compete more fiercely on retail prices and drive down retail margins – effectively reducing the double-marginalization problem mentioned earlier. Of course, the viability of using a returns policy can be limited by its costliness, but if it is not too costly, the strategic competitive benefits outweigh the costs of running such a program.

A general approach to channel contracting in the presence of non-price sales-enhancing activities is given by Iyer (1998). He considers how the channel contract should be structured when consumers are segmented into relatively more service-sensitive and less service-sensitive groups, and shows how the channel contract can be explicitly designed to induce retail differentiation, even if the retailers are, *ex ante*, identical to each other. Such retail differentiation is optimal when retailers' locational differentiation is small enough relative to differences among consumers in willingness to pay for products. Iyer finds that a menu of contracts from which the retailers can choose can be structured to induce the correct level of retail differentiation in service provision and pricing.

These examples show that, in general, the channel-contracting mechanism should be chosen carefully to induce channel intermediaries to do the tasks that need to be done, as well as to effectively manage intra- and inter-channel competition. A good example of the complex ways in which the contract structure influences channel member behavior is Dwyer and Oh (1988).

Bureaucratic Structuring of the Channel

A literature on bureaucratic structuring examines the way that suppliers deal with downstream channel members. The means by which they do so are often (though not always) embedded in contract clauses. Bureaucratization (see Paswan et al., 1998 for a review) in channels comprises multiple constructs, of which two dominate this literature: formalization (decision-making via explicit rules and procedures), and centralization (decision-making by a handful of people, typically at the supplier level).[6] In general, centralization is negatively related to relational norms, meaning that positive norms are less likely to arise without the broad involvement of many people. One reason is that centralization is tied to making threats, in accord with the idea that the possession of power encourages its use (Geyskens et al., 1999).

The effects of formalization are mixed. It is widely considered a negative in interfirm relationships – a heavy-handed imposition of one-sided bureaucracy that discourages initiative, erodes trust, and encourages the target of influence to behave opportunistically (John, 1984). However, recent evidence suggests that in some situations, formalization may function, as a way to achieve role clarity. By reducing confusion over who does what, formalization may actually decrease opportunism and increase inter-firm cooperation – at least in one-sided relationships, such as franchising, where it is understood from the beginning that one party is dominant (Dahlstrom & Nygaard, 1999). Further, formalization is connected to using noncoercive influence strategies, which boosts channel member satisfaction (Geyskens et al., 1999).

A different approach comes from Celly and Frazier (1996), which examine how suppliers apportion their efforts to influence downstream channel members. Suppliers have only so much influence: do they focus it primarily on the channel member's outputs (results, without regard for how they are obtained), primarily on their inputs (competences and activities, regardless of results), or a combination? This has implications for the way a contract is written; some of these tradeoffs are consented to in a contract.

The Form of Strategic Leadership in the Channel

On a completely different level, some recent work on the economics-based modeling side of the channels literature has considered the benefits and costs of 'channel leadership.' In institutional parlance, a 'channel leader' is a channel member who plays a key role in bringing channel members together and has a strong voice in managing channel activities and behaviors. The channel leader's will is usually expected to prevail. This description begs how such leadership is in fact exercised. One way it is dealt with in the game-theoretic literature is by describing the 'leader' (generally known as the Stackelberg leader) as that member who can pre-commit to an action in the channel, which must be taken as given by the other channel member(s) as they take their actions. The classic example is the manufacturer, acting as a Stackelberg leader, who pre-commits to a wholesale pricing rule, which is therefore taken as given by the retailer (who in this case is known as the Stackelberg follower). Those who are interested in the nuts and bolts of Stackelberg game models are referred to sources such as Fudenberg and Tirole (1993).

It has been generally believed that Stackelberg leadership confers benefits, and this has in fact been shown in many models (see, for example, Coughlan & Wernerfelt, 1989). Choi (1991) explicitly addresses this problem in his analysis of a channel with two manufacturers and one retailer. He examines both a linear demand system and a Cobb-Douglas nonlinear demand system, and finds the standard result for linear demand: the manufacturer makes the most profit when manufacturers are Stackelberg leaders in the channel, while the retailer makes the most profit when it is the Stackelberg leader in the channel. However, curiously, the results change under the Cobb-Douglas demand function: here, each manufacturer's profit is largest when the *retailer* is the Stackelberg leader, while the retailer's profit is largest if the *manufacturers* are the Stackelberg leaders in the channel. Apparently the form of the demand function affects whether the manufacturer would rather be the leader or the follower in the channel!

Lee and Staelin (1997) extensively analyze this phenomenon and show that indeed, the nature of demand in a competitive market – in particular, the way consumers view the substitutability of the products in the market – determines the optimal form of channel leadership. They extend the concept of strategic substitutes and strategic complements from economics (Bulow et al., 1985) to the channels context by defining *vertical strategic interaction*. Vertical strategic interaction is defined by the slope of the best-response functions of channel members: that is, the optimal action of an agent in the channel in response to the action of another agent in the channel. Where *rm* denotes the retailer's gross profit margin, and *mm* denotes the manufacturer's gross profit margin, Lee and Staelin define vertical strategic complementarity (VSC) as holding when one channel member's actions move in the same direction as those of the other channel member, that is,

$$\partial rm^*/\partial mm > 0 \text{ and } \partial mm^*/\partial rm > 0.$$

Vertical strategic substitutability (VSS) holds when one channel member's actions move in the opposite direction as those of the other channel member, that is,

$$\partial rm^*/\partial mm < 0 \text{ and } \partial mm^*/\partial rm < 0.$$

And *vertical strategic independence* (VSI) holds when it is optimal not to respond to a move by the channel member, that is,

$$\partial rm^*/\partial mm = \partial mm^*/\partial rm = 0$$

Given this taxonomy, Choi's linear demand model is shown to be an example of VSS (but not the only possible example of it), while his Cobb-Douglas demand function exhibits VSC (but again, not the only possible example of VSC). Lee and Staelin show that under VSS, the manufacturer's profit is highest when the manufacturer is a Stackelberg leader, but the retailer's profit is highest when the retailer is Stackelberg leader. Conversely, under VSC, manufacturer profit is highest when the retailer is the Stackelberg leader, but retail profit is highest when the manufacturer is the Stackelberg leader. Thus, the nature of demand, and in particular the way in which consumers' propensity to buy one brand depends on the price of the other brand, strongly affects the contractual and leadership structure each channel member would prefer.

Nothing in this research speaks explicitly to the issue of how to contractually agree on who will be the Stackelberg leader and who the Stackelberg follower in the channel. The *bargaining* literature in economics, which has been recently applied in a few instances in the literature in marketing, speaks to issues such as these, but not specifically to bargaining over the identity of the Stackelberg leader. The general insight one can draw, however, is that when *total channel profits* are higher under one outcome than another (e.g., if they were higher when the manufacturer(s) play the role of Stackelberg leader), the channel members have an incentive to strike a contract that creates that channel structure. The game theory literature in economics speaks to issues such as the ability to commit to such contracts, but is beyond the scope of this review (the interested reader can refer to Fudenberg & Tirole, 1993, or to Osborne & Rubinstein, 1994).

Vertical Restraints and Channel Exclusivity

The phenomenon of exclusive representation, or category exclusivity, is seldom examined. An exception is Fein and Anderson (1997), which shows that higher degrees of category selectivity (at the limit, exclusivity) are offered by retailers in return for concessions from suppliers. The principal concession is that the supplier, in turn, restricts its coverage of the channel member's market. This means selective (at the limit, exclusive) distribution. More generally, upstream channel members appear to demand (and get) the concession of selective category representation to offset (any of) their vulnerabilities, while downstream channel members appear to demand (and get) the concession of selective coverage to offset (any of) their vulnerabilities. In short, restricting one's options (market coverage for the upstream, brand representation for the downstream) is a negotiating strategy to balance dependence in a channel.

Restricting coverage in a market is a major decision for a supplier, and a significant public policy issue. Surprisingly little empirical research on this topic exists. An exception is Frazier and Lassar (1996), which shows that limiting coverage is a key way to build effective distribution for niche brands and for brands pursuing a high-end positioning strategy. The reason is that, in return for their concession of coverage, suppliers can demand unusual cooperation. (An intriguing way to simulate selective distribution is a strategy of branded variants (Bergen et al., 1996), which merits systematic inquiry.)

Intensity of coverage (of a market, of brands in a product category) is part of a more general issue: vertical restraints. These are brute-force ways of influencing channels (e.g., restrictions on resale price, and on distribution practices in general). Such issues deserve far more study from scholars, who have been too inclined to cede the area to economists and legal scholars (Dutta et al., 1999; see also Tirole, 1994). Some research in the economics literature of interest to marketing scholars concerns resale price maintenance (O'Brien & Shaffer, 1992; Shaffer, 1991a, 1991b) and limited and/or exclusive dealing (O'Brien & Shaffer, 1993; Shaffer, 1995). One of the points made in these articles is that slotting allowances, which until recently endured no antitrust scrutiny at all, can achieve channel outcomes very similar to those under resale price maintenance, which endures significant antitrust scrutiny. Insights such as these suggest that a more comprehensive and formal analysis of all of the non-price contracting mechanisms available to coordinate the channel could help policy makers better manage their oversight of these practices.

Franchising

Perhaps the best institutional example of relational governance (to be discussed) is franchising. Yet, here, much of the relationalism actually comes from explicit, detailed contracts, which is why we cover it under contract design. Franchising should be a prime object of inquiry for channels research, and there has been a resurgence of interest. This is a large area. Notable recent contributions include:

- exploration of the purposes of contract clauses (Dnes, 1993; Klein, 1995)
- a careful examination of the subtle cost/benefit tradeoffs to a franchisor (Kaufman & Lafontaine, 1994)
- insights into the relative importance of royalties and monitoring in the franchisor/franchisee relationship (Lal, 1990)
- a review indicating that there are good economic reasons why franchisors often buy out franchisees, and that buyout is not merely cynical exploitation of those who built a franchisee's reputation (Dant et al., 1996)
- examinations of why and how franchisees relinquish autonomy to franchisors, whether or not their contracts oblige it (Anand & Stern, 1985; Dant & Schul, 1992)

- demonstration of synergies when a franchisor judiciously combines vertical integration and franchising in the same operation (Bradach, 1997)
- a demonstration of the importance to franchisors of gaining legitimacy early (Shane & Foo, 1999).

This body of work, reviewed in Coughlan et al., (2001), points to the conclusion that franchising is a prototypical form of relational governance that appears to be highly political, but that has a greater economic rationale than meets the eye.

Gray Marketing

A focus on contractual issues in channels need not be merely on the presence or absence of contractual clauses, but can also focus on the degree to which the parties actually enforce them. Gray marketing is a classic example of this issue. Gray-marketed products are authentic, branded goods, sold through unauthorized channels of distribution. They are argued to have both negative and positive effects. On the negative side, unauthorized distributors or retailers disrupt a selective or exclusive channel of distribution and take away both authorized retailers' profits and their incentive to invest in customer service (Bucklin, 1993). On the positive side, gray marketing can provide an informal way of segmenting the offerings a company provides to the market: the authorized resellers provide higher-priced, high-service alternatives, while the gray market provides lower-priced, lower-service options (Cespedes et al., 1988; Coughlan & Soberman, 1998). The gray market may also expand total sales, by inducing new consumers to buy the firm's product who are unwilling to buy it through the authorized, higher-priced channel (Ahmadi & Yang, 2000). The classic concern with separation of highly service-sensitive (and less price-sensitive) consumers from less service-sensitive (and more price-sensitive) ones prevails here; authorized resellers may lose core customers to the gray market, and may not be able to easily perceive whether their *profits* rise or fall as a result (they instead focus on the immediately observable decline in *sales*).

Gray markets are a common international channel problem. In a typical situation, a multinational company sets a different transfer price in one market than in another; for example, it may charge a lower price in an emerging market than in a developed country. Alternatively, it may use all-units quantity discounts in some or all of its markets. In either case, there is an arbitrage incentive for the low-price buyer to over-buy and resell the extra units in the high-priced market. It could therefore be argued that it is the manufacturer's own contractual decisions, in areas such as pricing, that in fact spur the gray market (Ahmadi & Yang, 2000). Indeed, segmentation arguments suggest that policing the gray market may not always be in the manufacturer's best interest. Coughlan and Soberman (1998) even show that allowing the gray market to exist can be in the authorized retailer's best interest, if it helps the authorized retailer focus more tightly on those consumers willing to pay a high price for high service levels.

Bergen, Heide, and Dutta (1998) show that suppliers often overlook a downstream channel member's gray marketing activities, even when prohibited by their own contracts. Suppliers take a pragmatic perspective, weighing the costs and benefits of enforcement. A curious factor is the channel member's willingness to offer exclusive representation (that is, carry no competing brands in the product category). Such resellers are unusually valuable, as few will agree to such a contract. Typically, they are high performers for their sole brand. Hence, suppliers hesitate to disrupt their relationship by enforcing anti-gray-market clauses: to a point, they look the other way.

Should gray marketing be banned? Some might argue this is a reasonable response to a channel-management problem that is very difficult for manufacturers to control contractually. The current legal atmosphere is mixed in different countries, but does not uniformly prohibit gray markets (Duhan & Sheffet, 1988). Bucklin's (1993) analysis suggests that banning gray marketing would be unwise. He shows that gray market competition does not deny profits to the manufacturer (who holds the international trademark for the product) in general, and that gray marketing can be mitigated by lessening the price spread between different world markets. Currency fluctuations can harm authorized resellers, but Bucklin argues that this is insufficient to merit a public policy action against gray marketers. Further, prohibiting the gray market harms consumers, and therefore Bucklin advocates active management of the channel pricing strategy, rather than a governmental solution to the problem.

Incentives for Partner Performance

Having chosen a decentralized channel, the manufacturer (or other channel captain) has given up the right to control directly the activities of its channel members. Yet the need to coordinate the activities of the channel remains. The use of incentives to motivate channel member behavior thus becomes an important tool (monitoring, an alternative to incentives, is discussed in the next section).

The need for and design of appropriate incentive systems is a core focus of the *agency theory* literature. Agency theory arose first in economics (see, e.g., Grossman & Hart, 1983; Harris & Raviv,

1979; Holmstrom, 1979; Mirrlees, 1976; Ross, 1973). In the classic agency relationship, a *principal* (e.g., a manufacturer) contracts with or hires an *agent* (e.g., a distributor or retailer) to act on its behalf. There are three aspects of the relationship that cause problems. First, the agent and the principal typically have divergent goals and objectives (for example, the manufacturer seeks to maximize its profit over its own product line, while the multiline distributor seeks to maximize its profit over *all* its product lines, only one of which belongs to the manufacturer). Second, the principal typically cannot perfectly observe the agent's effort. And third, the principal cannot *infer* the agent's effort level from market outcomes (e.g., sales) because of a stochastic relationship between the agent's effort and the market outcome. This concatenation of conditions gives the agent both the incentive and the opportunity to *shirk* on the provision of effort on behalf of the principal. Agency theory seeks to uncover incentive systems that do the best job of inducing effort from the agent consistent with the principal's goals. In essence, appropriate incentive design causes the agent's behavior to mimic what it would do if it in fact had the same objectives as the principal.

In the marketing and channels literature, agency theory has been applied to many problems (for an excellent review, see Bergen et al., 1992). Attention has focused on both *outcome-based contracts* and *behavior-based contracts*. Outcome-based contracts provide incentives tied to observable outcomes in the market, such as sales, market share, or profits. Behavior-based contracts reward the inputs to the production of sales, such as sales calls. Discussion of behavior-based management in channels has often been tied to the use of monitoring (discussed in the next section), the logic being that inputs must be measured and monitored to implement behavior-based management. But this does not deny the possibility that behavior-based contracts provide incentives just as do outcome-based contracts. One example of such an incentive, already discussed above, is manufacturers' payment of slotting allowances to retailers in return for access to key shelf space in the store. This payment rewards the provision of an input (shelf space) rather than an output (e.g. a bonus for selling more than a target amount).

The franchising literature (see above) focuses on the use of incentives such as royalty payments as motivators for franchisee behavior. The franchise channel is a classic agency relationship, where the franchisor recruits franchisees to execute on the marketing concept designed by the franchisor. The franchisee is a residual claimant to the profits of the franchised outlet; this makes the franchisee want to maximize the profits of the outlet. This behavior is consistent with franchisor profit maximization for at least two key reasons: first, because well-run franchised outlets help in the recruitment of more franchisees; and second, because the typical franchise contract provides for royalty payments from the franchisee to the franchisor, typically quoted as a percentage of sales in the franchisee's outlet. One of the arguments in favor of franchising over running owned outlets with employee managers is precisely that the franchisee acts in a profit-maximizing way, while an employee, paid a salary, has no incentive to improve the profitability of a retail outlet beyond the satisficing level.

The other primary application of agency-theoretic insights into incentive design is in the sales compensation literature (see, for example, Basu et al., 1985). Although this is generally perceived to be an area distinct from channel management, there is no doubt that any real-world channel manager views part of his or her job as the motivation and compensation of the sales people making sales in the channel. Two reviews of the sales force compensation literature (Coughlan, 1993; Coughlan & Sen, 1989) summarize the agency-theoretic approach and the insights it derives into optimal use of salary versus incentive pay (e.g., commissions and bonuses) (see, for example, Table 13.7 in Coughlan (1993) for a summary of the factors affecting the optimal salary, commission rate, and ratio of salary in the total pay package). An empirical test of the agency-theoretic approach (Coughlan & Narasimhan, 1992) shows support for the agency-theoretic prescriptions for compensation.

The study of incentives in channel management is so widespread that it would be impossible to summarize every example. To give a flavor of the ubiquity of this focus, consider the following:

- Jeuland and Shugan's (1983) solution to the double-marginalization problem, discussed above, involves the use of a two-part pricing scheme. The per-unit sharing arrangement is an example of an incentive for the retailer to set retail price so as to maximize total channel profits rather than its own retail profits alone.
- Chu and Desai (1995) look at the problem of coordinating the channel for maximum customer satisfaction. In this context, they consider the use of a bonus linked to customer satisfaction index ratings.
- Gerstner and Hess (1995) examine the effect of pull promotions (promotions by manufacturers directly to final consumers) and their effect on channel coordination. The use of pull promotions creates an indirect incentive for the retailer to stock the manufacturer's product, because it enhances demand at the consumer level.
- In a more general context, Anderson et al. (1987) show that the overall economic attractiveness of one option versus another is the single largest influence on actual resource allocation by downstream channel members in

developed economies. But the impact of elements of economic attractiveness, one by one, may be cancelled out by competing considerations, suggesting that the effect of single incentives on channel member behavior can be difficult to disentangle.

These and many of the other examples we have already cited in other sections of this review show the prevalent use of incentives to alter channel members' behavior to better mimic a coordinated, vertically integrated channel.

Monitoring of Channel Members

The monitoring of channel members is not a highly-researched area in the channels literature. There is much more interest in the use of incentives and rewards to motivate appropriate behavior. In one area, franchising, there is a clear interest in monitoring, since the explicit monitoring of franchisees is common and there is a tradeoff between using indirect incentives (e.g. making the franchisee a residual risk-bearer of the business) and monitoring, given the possibility for free-riding in the franchise channel (see Bergen et al., 1992 for a discussion of this tradeoff). Lal (1990) explicitly considers the tradeoff between the use of royalties and monitoring in controlling franchisee behavior, and shows that both may be necessary when demand-enhancing investments are made both by franchisees (in service in the retail outlets) and the franchisor (in brand-building in the franchise business). Monitoring is also shown to be valuable in limiting the free-riding of one franchisee on the service efforts of other franchisees in the system.

Another context in which monitoring of channel members makes sense is that of bootlegging: the sale of product by one dealer in another dealer's territory. This phenomenon bears a great resemblance to the gray marketing problem discussed earlier. Dutta, Bergen and John (1994) use a TCE approach to argue that monitoring and complete prevention of bootlegging is generally not optimal. Some bootlegging should be tolerated because of the lack of full enforceability of contracts between channel members. Bootlegging is less likely to be tolerated rather than controlled when reseller services are very important, when margins are seriously eroded through bootlegging, and when the manufacturer is very committed to the channel relationship. Monitoring and controlling negative channel member behavior is thus not always the optimal channel management policy, but is valuable under particular market and intra-channel conditions.

As one of the more under-researched areas of channel management, monitoring offers opportunities for future research. Sales force and franchising applications are clearly appropriate for research, but in any channel relationship where channel members are responsible for costly and valued channel functions and where the possibility of shirking or free-riding exists, the potential for monitoring as an alternative to incentives can be studied. An example of such work is Murray and Heide (1998), which compares the effectiveness of incentives versus monitoring as tools for manufacturers to induce retailers to participate in a supplier's promotional campaign. This work suggests that in sectors where monitoring (by such means as mystery shoppers and surprise inspections) is uncommon, channel members actively resist it, which renders incentives a much more effective means of persuasion.

Relational Governance

Vertical integration and outsourcing may be viewed as end points on a continuum: control, responsibility, and residual profits are assigned entirely to the principal (vertical integration) or entirely to the agent (using the market, or outsourcing). Between these polar opposites lies relational governance, in which control, responsibility, and profits are *shared* according to the (often unspoken) rules of an *enduring* relationship between upstream and downstream channel members.

The roots of relational governance lie in contracting law (Kaufman & Stern, 1988; Macneil, 1980). The premise is that no contract can or does spell out the myriad understandings, processes, expectations, and norms that grow up during a channel relationship. Yet, this 'implicit contract' or 'relational contract' is what truly drives the channel (by implication, courts should – and do – examine the implicit contract and sometimes even enforce it). Channels research has focused on indexing the degree to which a channel holds 'norms,' that is, expectations of reciprocal behavior. The norms most studied are 1) flexibility (ready adaptation); 2) information exchange (free, open communication); and 3) solidarity (working for mutual benefit).

Typically, positive norms are highly correlated, leading to a research strategy of combining them into a single higher-order factor or relationalism. However measured, relationalism is associated with lower conflict and opportunism, and greater trust, satisfaction, and continued communication (Heide, 1994; Heide & John, 1992; Morgan & Hunt, 1994). However, the causal order of these outcomes has been imposed on correlational data, rather than established, and the manner in which norms come about is not well understood.

This issue – how norms arise – is critical, and several theories address it. One viewpoint is that relationships organically build norms through progressive interaction and risk taking, so that relationships have recognizable stages of development (Dwyer et al., 1987). Increasingly candid and complete communication among an expanding number of organizational actors is a critical feature of this process (Mohr & Nevin, 1990). Others hold that that process is unpredictable, impossible to chart, and based on incidents that the players may fail to recollect (Anderson, 1995). Still others suggest that norms are constructed, but do not specify how. In general, channels research has focused on demonstrating that norms accompany positive affect (sentiment) and channel performance, but has not devoted longitudinal or experimental investigation to norm creation.

A complementary approach focuses on commitment, which is the channel member's desire for a relationship to continue indefinitely, combined with willingness to sacrifice in order to grow and maintain the relationship. This can be interpreted as the ultimate in relationalism, with the exception that commitment is conceptually one-sided, while norms are conceived as mutual states. In transaction cost economics (TCE), commitment is viewed as a hybrid governance structure, a compromise between vertical integration and outsourcing (decentralization). In this vein, commitment can be built in a semi-calculated way by altering each party's incentive structure. The logic is a somewhat curious notion of a self-enforcing contract, or of a balance of dependence (Williamson, 1996). In this view, a relationship can be secured by binding oneself to it – on condition that the channel counterpart take reciprocal action. The relationship becomes one of mutual dependence. This mutuality discourages opportunism, as each side loses if the relationship ends.

Anderson and Weitz (1992) show this logic at work in manufacturer-distributor relations. When one party makes idiosyncratic investments in the other (such as dedicated personnel and the acquisition of relationship-specific knowledge), those investments ('pledges') serve three purposes. First, they serve to bind the maker to the relationship (thereby raising the maker's commitment to the counterpart). Second, they signal to the counterpart that the maker *is* committed – which generates reciprocity. Third, they increase the maker's value to the counterpart – which again generates reciprocal commitment. Reciprocity of commitment (or lack thereof) is common in channels. However, asymmetric commitment does exist, for structural reasons, and has deleterious effects on relationship outcomes (Ross et al., 1997).

Much of the commitment research focuses on idiosyncratic investments as a way to forestall opportunism. However, these investments also serve a function that may be more important: they make channel members more effective in differentiating a brand and making a market for it (Wathne & Heide, 2000). One of the few field research studies that takes a longitudinal perspective shows that when channel members make investments in each other that are difficult to redeploy, they also make more effort to coordinate. As a result, they enjoy higher channel performance *one year later* (Jap, 1999). Further, each party derives benefits from their shared value creation.

A key feature of work on relationship norms is the notion that the channel has a future, and that the players will sub-optimize now to achieve a better outcome later. This 'shadow of the future,' the key element of the theory of repeated games, is critical to achieving competitive advantage (Anderson & Weitz, 1989; Heide & Miner, 1992). The underlying notion in this literature is that channels will not stay together long enough to achieve exceptional performance unless a channel member is dependent. But one-sided dependence is exploitable: dependent parties are vulnerable, and perceive themselves to be so (Jap & Ganesan, 2000). How can the weaker party guard against this risk?

The solution is to create two-sided, or mutual, dependence, to oblige the parties to respect each other and their engagements. The dependent party enjoys 'countervailing power' when the channel counterpart is also dependent. For example, a sales agent becomes dependent on a supplier when it makes supplier-specific investments, such as brand-specific learning. To balance that dependence, some agents work to achieve leverage over suppliers by cultivating strong ties with the principal's customers, seeking ways to bind these customers to the *agent* (rather than to the principal). Agents that engage in such dependence balancing forestall the principal's opportunism – and generate better financial performance (Heide & John, 1988).

This notion – either eschew dependence, or craft ways to make it mutual – underlies much recent channels research on influence. This thinking is reflected in the design of incentives and structure, the subjects of earlier sections.

Much of the current research on relational governance focuses on trust, which is generally operationalized as a belief that a channel member is honest (i.e., reliable, stands by its word, sincere, fulfills obligations) and/or benevolent (concerned about the other party's welfare). A meta-analysis by Geyskens, Steenkamp, and Kumar (1998) concludes that trust, no matter how it is measured, shows a variety of relationships with variables that may be antecedent or may be consequent. On the whole, trust is most strongly tied with positive sentiments (e.g., perceived fairness, satisfaction), and with action variables such as communication and cooperation. This suggests that trust is not difficult to infer, even though it is difficult to observe.

Channel Power

Prior to the late 1960s, channels research comprised four main branches of inquiry (Gattorna, 1978). The institutional approach focused on describing the current state of affairs by categorizing the types of organizations comprising a channel. The functional perspective sought to identify what work was performed, by whom, under what circumstances, and for what purpose. These two approaches were primarily inductive and descriptive. In contrast, a micro-analytic economic stream focused on deducing normative generalizations about how channels should look and function. The fourth approach was essentially an application of industrial organization theory to channels, as though channels were an industry.

Beginning in the late 1960s, channels research was galvanized by the development of the power-and-conflict approach. The seminal idea here is that channels can be characterized as inter-organizational systems in which power is unevenly distributed. How power is gained and then used in these systems is the central question (El-Ansary & Stern, 1972). This 'behavioral' approach to channels, in which institutions are actors with complex, unarticulated motives (more than profit maximization), is now commonplace. Initially, however, the framework was attacked from all sides: it was too deductive for the institutional and functional schools, and too behavioral for the industrial organization and microeconomic schools.

Operationalizing and Measuring the Concept of Power

Channel power is defined as the ability to alter channel members' behavior so that they take actions they would not have taken otherwise. (Influence is a related concept but somewhat broader: to influence a channel member is to change anything in its fields of perception or goals, as well as its field of action.) While intuitively appealing, the concept of power is in itself difficult to apply. Abilities, if unused, are unobservable, and it is difficult to know what channel members would have done in the normal course of events.

The utility of power theory is to predict outcomes. Thus, the pitfall of power theory is that the presence of power may be merely inferred whenever an outcome is observed. This issue arises when channel members are asked to report how much power they have over other channel members: it is plausible that they don't know, but if they see the results they want, they infer they must have power. This begs the questions of whether 1) they have an ability they have not exercised (thereby underestimating their power), or 2) they would have gotten the desired results anyway (thereby overestimating their power). We shall return to this issue shortly.

One way to circumvent this problem is to search for observable proxy indicators of power that are independent of any outcomes that might be attributable to the presence of power. Hence, a popular approach to measuring power is to back up one step in the causal chain by measuring not perceptions of power but the *sources* of power. Borrowing from psychology, a large research stream was sparked by making an analogy between two channel members in a commercial arrangement and two people in an interpersonal relationship. French and Raven's (1959) five bases (sources) of power is a taxonomy in which person A has more power over person B the more

1. A can offer *rewards* (positive utility) to B
2. A can *coerce* (inflict damage on) B
3. A can offer *expertise* that B can use
4. A can appeal to a *legitimate* authority (e.g., law, contract, morality, religion, social obligation) to make B feel obliged to comply
5. B views A as a positive *referent*, such that B identifies with A and wishes to be associated with A.

The translation of reward, coercive, expertise, and legitimate bases of power to channel members is straightforward. Referent power is more perplexing in a commercial setting: it is generally viewed as B's desire to share A's favorable image (e.g., to benefit by associating with a brand name or a recognized market position).

According to French and Raven, these five bases largely exhaust the ways power can be attained, and are conceptually and operationally separable. In particular, an important distinction is between reward and coercion (which are fairly demonstrable to all parties) and the other three bases. Expertise, referent, and legitimate bases are more subjective: B can more readily choose whether to acknowledge or deny their presence, so that A does not directly mediate these sources of power. For example, a franchisee may or may not acknowledge a franchisor's legitimate power to exert direction. This is why many franchisors screen prospective franchisees for a predisposition to accord legitimacy to the franchisor's intervention (some would say a compliant attitude toward authority) (Dant & Gundlach, 1998).

Field research in channels suggests it is difficult to retain this taxonomy intact, as the data often do not support it (Gaski, 1986; Hunt & Nevin, 1974). One common pairing that emerges from data reduction methods is coercion versus all-other-combined (roughly, stick versus carrots) (e.g., Lusch & Brown, 1982). There is some indication that channel members overestimate their own autonomy when their counterparts possess considerable non-coercive power: carrots are less obtrusive than sticks.

Conceptually, the five bases could be combined into a formative indicator of the overall degree of power sources, in the same way that diverse variables (e.g. education, occupational status) are combined to index socioeconomic status. But channels research often keeps the bases separate because they are thought to create different outcomes (to be addressed in a later section).

A competitor to the five-bases approach (which comes from psychology) is the dependence approach, borrowed from sociology (Emerson, 1962). The simple premise here is that A's power over B increases with B's dependence on A. Dependence, in turn, rises with two terms: the utility that A can offer B (*benefits*), and the *scarcity* of A as a source of that utility. Party A is powerful (i.e., B is dependent) the more A is irreplaceable to B (ultimately, a monopolist) *and* the more A offers utility to B. Conversely, when A offers little utility, *or* B can find (and switch over to) many alternative suppliers, then B's dependence is low and A's power is therefore low.

A key element of dependence theory is its focus on the alternative channel members that B could realistically employ. This is absent in the five-bases approach. Dependence theory holds that benefits *per se* are irrelevant: if others could supply those benefits, party A has no leverage over B. (Conversely, scarcity is irrelevant if A doesn't provide much utility to B, since a monopoly over mediocre valuation affords little leverage.)

Dependence may be indexed directly by asking a respondent for an overall estimate of how much it needs the other party. Of course, this direct approach can be questioned: do respondents really know their level of dependence (or their channel counterpart's dependence on them), and if so, will they report it truthfully? To get around this, much channels research composes an overall dependence measure by indexing, then combining, utility and scarcity. Operationally, this means that a measure of dependence should *multiply* an index of benefits (often, these are measured as sales, profits, or an overall perceptual estimate of utility provided) by an index of scarcity (often measured as the reverse of the perceived ease of switching to a comparable channel member, or the number of comparable channel members in existence). But in practice, multiplication is seldom used. Apart from its psychometric complications, multiplication often proves unnecessary. Data reduction techniques frequently reveal that high utility and high scarcity are positively correlated, and therefore may simply be combined additively as reflective indicators of dependence (e.g., Anderson et al., 1987).

If one eschews direct elicitation, it is cumbersome to measure either the five bases or dependence. Some alternative conceptualizations of power are really proxies. In particular, *role performance* has been suggested as a useful approximation of dependence (Frazier, 1983). The premise is that competence and motivation are in limited supply. Thus, a channel member that performs its role in the channel well is distinctive. The better the channel member performs its role in an existing relationship, the more distinctive (and therefore scarce) it is. And since performing a role is useful, higher role performance makes a channel member distinctively valuable to its trading partner. Therefore, a channel member depends more on another party the higher that party's role performance in their relationship. This reasoning would explain why separate measures of utility and scarcity are often correlated, making it unnecessary to multiply utility and scarcity to create an index of dependence.

What is the best way to measure power? Which ways, if any, are invalid? This debate has generated considerable, occasionally acrimonious controversy. A comprehensive paper by Brown, Johnson, and Koenig (1995) suggests the controversy is overblown. These measurement approaches converge: all the indicators point in the right direction. Indeed, the best way to measure power appears to be the simplest way: directly ask the target of influence how much power the source possesses. Power appears to be like love: you recognize it when you see it.

The most recent branch of the power literature is the influence strategies approach. This stream treats power as manifest in the way that boundary spanners between two organizations communicate with each other. Six styles of attempting to exert influence via communication are common in channels (Frazier & Summers, 1984). Although these have been identified inductively through field observation, they map neatly onto a variation of the five bases of power. Research in this vein notes that the way influence strategies are perceived is culture-bound. In particular, influence strategies that seem heavy-handed and provoke channel resistance in Western markets may be acceptable in some cultures (e.g., Frazier et al., 1989).

Consequences of Power: Conflict

The centerpiece of power research has been the prediction that power generates conflict, in which channel members view each other as opponents. This matters because conflict is thought to damage the performance of the channel and hasten its dissolution, as well as reduce the satisfaction of channel members.

At high levels, conflict is experienced as negative emotion. Therefore, measuring conflict in a manner separable from dissatisfaction (also a negative emotional state) is challenging. A comprehensive article by Brown and Day (1981) establishes that the level of channel conflict is best captured as:

$$\text{Conflict} = \sum_{i=1}^{N} \text{Importance}_i \times \text{Frequency}_i \times \text{Intensity}_i$$

where N is the number of issues (i) a channel dyad confronts. By multiplying, this formulation eliminates the influence of any issue that is minor, or that rarely comes up, or that does not involve large differences in the firms' positions on the issue. On the other hand, a major issue that comes up frequently, over which the parties are far apart, will contribute to conflict. A large number of issues also increases conflict, which is why complex relationships with ample role definitions are prone to conflict.

The conceptual research on conflict is somewhat at odds with the empirical research. In principle, the channels literature acknowledges that some conflict can actually benefit the channel, by spurring the parties to work actively to resolve their differences and improve their performance. This functional conflict spurs the channel to new heights and improves the relationship. However, functional conflict is somewhat difficult to find in the field. Overwhelmingly, data suggest that higher conflict accompanies declining satisfaction by channel members (Geyskens et al., 1999).

Perhaps that by the time conflict has increased enough to be reported by channel members, it has passed functional levels. Or perhaps relationships that could use the spur of conflict are so minor that they seldom become objects of study. Alternatively, the jostling that functional conflict creates may be viewed as normal behavior by respondents, and is therefore not encoded as being in opposition. In any event, conflict and dissatisfaction are strongly related.

Does power generate conflict? Results that center around the five-bases approach point to the conclusion that coercion generates conflict, but that all other power sources actually dampen it; results that center around the dependence approach suggest that dependence and conflict are not strongly related, if at all (Geyskens et al., 1999).

Does conflict decrease the channel's performance? Curiously, this issue has seldom been examined. Most of the research in the power tradition appears to assume that if satisfaction declines, performance declines as well. Therefore, satisfaction alone is the object of study. Satisfaction, in turn, can be subdivided into economic satisfaction (appraisal of overall financial outcomes, direct and indirect) and non-economic satisfaction (appraisal of the psychosocial aspects of the relationship). Conflict is negatively associated with both. In terms of causality, current thinking holds that economic dissatisfaction, because it goes to the *raison d'être* of channels, *causes* conflict, which *then* builds non-economic dissatisfaction (Geyskens et al., 1999). Fundamentally, the economics of the situation influence opponent-centered behavior, which influences how smoothly the relationships operate in interpersonal terms.

But is satisfaction a good proxy for performance? A host of factors suggest that it is not. Performance is what the channel (or a channel member) achieves. Satisfaction is the channel member's *evaluation* of that performance. And the evaluation is made against some unspoken baseline, which is itself difficult to assess. It could be the channel member's expectations. Or the baseline could be the channel member's sense of the rewards available from the next best use of resources (Anderson & Narus, 1984). Research using equity theory as a basis suggests that the baseline is even more complicated: it is the channel member's sense of the distributive and procedural justice of the relationship (Kumar et al., 1995).

In short, satisfaction is a complex judgment influenced by many factors, of which the absolute level of performance is only one. Therefore, satisfaction may be a poor proxy for performance. Does satisfaction, then, matter in and of itself? Yes, in that satisfaction (in both its economic and psychosocial forms) is a driver of longer-term channel behavior, such as trust and commitment (Geyskens et al., 1998, 1999). These long-term behaviors translate into extraordinary influence.

The channels literature must develop multiple ways of conceptualizing and measuring performance. This is a difficult task: performance has many facets (Kumar et al., 1992), there are complex tradeoffs among these facets, and performance exists at different levels. Each member of a dyad, the entire channel, and the end buyer all have different (and to some extent conflicting) definitions of performance.

Further, performance is difficult to assess in the absolute. It is necessary to compare an entity's realized performance to some baseline representing a reasonable expectation, given the circumstances. (This is the unspoken rationale behind satisfaction research: it is assumed that the assessor has an appropriate baseline in mind when calibrating satisfaction.) This performance expectation could be established by comparing one firm's outcomes to the results generated by similar firms. An alternative research strategy is to model raw outcomes but include covariates tapping the circumstances that have substantial impact on outcomes (e.g., intensity of competition, size of potential market).

One approach to cracking the performance measurement problem is to develop a very comprehensive index, such as Kumar, Stern, and Achrol (1992). While laudable for its ambition, this approach suffers from obvious challenges to execution. Comprehensive approaches such as this should be employed. However, in the spirit of developing middle range theory, channel researchers should also study a single facet, or a small set of facets, at a time. For example, Anderson (1988) models the performance of a sales agent as the cost-to-sales ratio the agent realizes for the principal.

The power-and-conflict research tradition has expanded to embrace other concepts, many of them more economic and less sociological in nature. Now known as the 'political economy' approach (Stern & Reve, 1980), the behavioral stream has left an enduring mark. Power theory *per se* receives relatively little attention: so many viewpoints have proliferated that they are very difficult to separate and test (see Kumar et al., 1998 for a review). Similarly, conflict *per se* is seldom studied, although it is often invoked in one form or another as an unobserved explanatory mechanism. The channels literature has moved on to other ways to frame the problem of achieving and exercising influence. These are reviewed below: the reader will notice that many of the issues central to discussions of power also feature in these approaches to gaining influence.

A novel approach, which merits more usage, is historical analysis. Messinger and Narasimhan (1995) provide an example by reconstituting the history of the supermarket in the US. They demonstrate that power has shifted in the grocery channel, first to manufacturers, then to retailers, and finally to consumers (who have benefited substantially as a consequence of supplier/grocer rivalry).

Conclusion

This review has noted robust generalizations section by section. At this point, a good deal is known about how to attempt to coordinate a distribution channel, and the costs and benefits of various approaches. Going forward, it is clear that channels research needs more explanation of how to create relationships with positive relationship norms. Further demonstrations that positive affects correlate at one point in time will not add to our knowledge base. Research needs to drive to relationship antecedents that managers can observe, suggesting relationship-building strategies they can adopt, and tracing the costs, as well as the benefits, of these strategies. Research should also focus on incentives, without presuming an alliance (partnership) strategy is envisioned by either side. And, ultimately, channels research needs more contingency thinking and more precise causal reasoning to point to what works, when, and why.

Channels research has developed to the point that competing causal mechanisms are observed to lead to the same predictions. This suggests that a contribution to channels research would be to devise tests to tease out causality. This includes 1) pursuing a theory's implications to find and test unique predictions (implications that do not follow from other theories); 2) longitudinal tests, to rule out reverse causality; and 3) experiments.

This latter is of critical importance. For reasons of implementation, quasi-experimental field designs are non-existent in channels. However, they occur in other fields, such as advertising. Why not channels? In the same vein, naturally occurring field experiments are common in channels (they often occur without management's awareness, given the chaotic nature of channels initiatives in many firms). They merit more research attention.

But the field is not the only place to test a causal mechanism. Historically, channels research has made little use of laboratory experiments, perhaps due to an informal consensus that the lack of external validity outweighs the value of internal validity. But once a phenomenon is known to occur in the field, this concern becomes minimal. Channels research needs to enlarge the currently very small place given to laboratory experiments. This may be particularly productive when seeking to test analytic models, which by force must abstract away from many factors in order to concentrate on the one of interest. Such models are difficult to test in the field environment, but in a laboratory context, the relevant factors can be isolated and tested.

A point of contention in the channels literature is the normative versus positive tradeoff. Early channels work was freely positive, describing channel actions without concern for whether they made normative sense. There has been an about-face in the literature, driven in part by the exigencies of the review process. Later and current channels research now emphasizes finding a normative rationale for prevailing practice. Some research does this by beginning with a normative theory (such as TCE or agency theory), then fitting it (sometimes forcibly) to descriptive data about actual practice. Misfits are either ignored or explained away, sometimes by a convoluted efficiency rationale. Other research begins by searching for any patterns of practice, but ends with (occasionally tortuous) efforts to justify the findings in normative terms. Both approaches (force fitting or retrofitting) pose difficulties.

A third way is suggested by Roberts and Greenwood (1997), which proposes a 'constrained-efficiency' framework, in which actors try to be rational but are limited by preconscious pressures (inability to imagine a better channel), and post-conscious pressures (inability to implement a better channel, for reasons of losing legitimacy or institutional support). A related approach is that of economic sociology (Smelser & Swedberg, 1994). This sort of balanced approach is needed in channels research, because channel actors *are* motivated to make the best normative choice, but are also limited in their ability to do so. Such an approach re-opens the door to descriptive research by removing the review-process penalty for finding a channel practice that no one can justify – yet.

While the field has moved beyond pure documentation of phenomena, channels research still needs description. This is particularly the case for an enormous area in which channels research has barely scratched the surface: channels operations outside of North America. The logic, methods, and institutional environments of channels in the rest of the world merit investigation; such research has a high likelihood of sparking exciting new insights and debates.

More generally, channels research (and its attendant review process) should acknowledge that, while the field has progressed considerably, it is still in a pre-paradigmatic state. This is healthy: the phenomenon is too large and important to be bounded easily. Research on influence has demonstrated that multiple competing approaches *do* make headway: it is not necessary (and is probably harmful) to force a paradigm in the name of progress. In general, channels research should be more eclectic, not less. Indeed, one paradigm can fruitfully inform another on richer ways to consider any particular channels problem.

This is not a call for an anything-goes approach. Over the decades, channels research has greatly increased in rigor, and this is to the good. In particular, there is a greater emphasis on good measurement. This is manifested in greater attention to the wording of questions, to the definition of constructs, and to the correspondence between construct and measures in empirical channels research. On the analytic side, the sophistication of channels models has increased significantly as well. There is also greater attention to the source of data. At one time, channels researchers focused on finding multiple informants to craft a single observation. It is now widely recognized that the benefits of multiple informants are offset by costs. More informants per observation (channel) can be had, but usually by asking fewer questions of each informant, and by discarding many observations where multiple informants fail to respond. Current channels research tends to qualify one best-informed source, rather than aggregate several inferior-but-available ones. It is unusual to see a channels article today that does not justify the choice of informant. This is a major advance in the standards of channels research.

At the same time, channels research risks falling into the trap of trading off validity to gain higher reliability (Kopalle & Lehmann, 1997). This is manifested in excessive deletion of variables that have face validity, and in the exercise of boosting reported reliability by failing to vary the format and nature of the information sought. This, in turn, feeds an historical weakness of much field research in channels, which is to rely solely on the very subjective perceptions and impressionistic judgments of one person. This reliance makes it easy for the informant to retrofit 'reports' of constructs to fit his/her personal theory of how channels work. The result is a possibly spurious, albeit entirely sensible, model, with artificially high fit to the data.

One antidote is to use multiple data sources (e.g., archives, reports of other channel members, industry observers). This is particularly useful to separate the dependent variable from the independent variables. Another antidote is to oblige the informant to report more concrete observables (which are harder to distort), and then to anchor the informant's more subjective judgments in these observables. It is one thing to ask a manager how difficult it is for a new salesperson to learn a job (judgment). It is quite another to combine this estimate with the informant's report of how much the company invests in training salespeople (observable) and how long a new salesperson takes to recapture the performance of his/her predecessor in the same job (somewhat observable). Putting all this information together into one scale reduces reported reliability, because these variables tap different domains of a construct and are in different formats. But combining these variables increases validity, which is essential. In this vein, channels research relies excessively on the reflective indicators approach, built around the idea that a narrow, unitary phenomenon manifests itself in reflections that, taken together, are highly reliable. The complexity of channel phenomena suggests that formative indicators are also appropriate in many cases.

On the analytic side, the increased complexity of channels models – now commonly including multiple channel levels, horizontal competition at the manufacturing as well as downstream levels, and price as well as non-price inputs to the demand function – creates a need for numerical analysis to gain substantive insights. Earlier work, building on simpler model structures, could derive insights in a purely analytic setting, but these insights came at the price of complexity and sophistication of the models themselves. To move forward on the analytic side, the field needs to not only allow, but also encourage, numerical analysis of these increasingly realistic models.

Although the channels area has been extensively researched, using many academic paradigms and investigating a myriad of different channel institutions, there is ample room for future contribution to the field. In an ever-changing real-world marketplace, the challenges of efficient channel design for effective satisfaction of end-users' demands remain. Businesspeople have come to realize the critical importance of an effective channel effort, and this bodes well for access to fascinating problems and data, no matter what basic toolkit the channels researcher brings to the area.

Notes

1. Of course, a contracting system may be designed concurrently with the recruitment of channel members or even in advance of channel member selection. However, the

literature frequently considers optimal contract design, taking as given the identities of members of the channel, suggesting our ordering of the process.

2. Note that this is a manufacturer's view of the issue. The channels literature tends to take the manufacturer's perspective, even though any channel member's perspective (e.g., the retailer's) is equally valid. Frazier (1999) and Stern and Weitz (1997) call for research to balance this excessive emphasis on the channel as viewed from upstream.

3. A two-part tariff involves charging a fixed fee and a per-unit price for the purchase of multiple units of a product. For example, the classic franchising contract requires the franchisee to pay a fixed franchise fee at the beginning of the franchise contract, as well as an ongoing percentage royalty based on sales.

4. The Stackelberg leader chooses its action in the knowledge of the other party's reaction function (rule). For example, a manufacturer (Stackelberg leader) would set its wholesale price in the knowledge of the way in which the retailer (Stackelberg follower) will factor that wholesale price into its retail pricing decision.

5. The literature employs terms such as 'choose,' 'use,' or 'select' channel members. This implies that the supplier need only take a decision. We prefer the term 'recruit' because prospective channel members must be persuaded to join a given supplier's channel – and they frequently choose *not* to be 'selected.'

6. Note that 'centralization' in this literature is unrelated to 'decentralization,' the term economists use to denote vertical integration.

References

Ahmadi, Reza & Yang, B. Rachel (2000) Parallel imports: challenges from unauthorized distribution channels. *Marketing Science*, 19, 3 (Summer), 279–94.

Alba, Joseph, Lynch, John, Weitz, Barton, Janiszewski, Chris, Lutz, Richard, Sawyer, Alan & Wood, Stacy (1997) Interactive home shopping: consumer, retailer, and manufacturer incentives to participate in electronic marketplaces. *Journal of Marketing*, 61 (July), 38–53.

Alderson, Wroe (1965) *Marketing Behavior and Executive Action*. Homewood, IL: Richard D. Irwin Inc.

Anand, Punam & Stern, Louis W. (1985) A sociopsychological explanation for why marketing channel members relinquish control. *Journal of Marketing Research*, 22 (November), 365–76.

Anderson, Erin (1985) The salesperson as outside agent or employee: a transaction-cost analysis. *Marketing Science*, 4 (Summer), 234–54.

——— (1988) Selling efficiency and choice of integrated or independent sales forces: a test of Darwinian economics. *Management Science*, 34 (May), 599–618.

Anderson, Erin & Coughlan, Anne T. (1987) International market entry and expansion via independent or integrated channels of distribution. *Journal of Marketing*, 51,1 (January), 71–82.

Anderson, Erin & Weitz, Barton (1989) Determinants of continuity in conventional channel dyads. *Marketing Science*, 8 (Fall), 310–23.

Anderson, Erin & Weitz, Barton (1992) The use of pledges to build and sustain commitment in distribution channels. *Journal of Marketing Research*, 24 (February), 18–34.

Anderson, Erin, Lodish, Leonard M. & Weitz, Barton (1987) Resource allocation behavior in conventional channels. *Journal of Marketing Research*, 24 (February), 85–97.

Anderson, James C. (1995) Relationships in business markets: exchange episodes, value creation, and their empirical assessment. *Journal of the Academy of Marketing Science*, 23 (4), 346–50.

Anderson, James C. & Narus, James A. (1984) A model of the distributor's perspective of distributor-manufacturer working relationships. *Journal of Marketing*, 48 (Fall), 62–74.

Balasubramanian, Sridhar (1998) Mail versus mall: a strategic analysis of competition between direct marketers and conventional retailers. *Marketing Science*, 17 (3), 181–95.

Basu, Amiya K., Lal, Rajiv, Srinivasan, V. & Staelin, Richard (1985) Salesforce compensation plans: an agency theoretic perspective. *Marketing Science*, 4 (Fall), 267–91.

Bergen, Mark, Dutta, Shantanu & Shugan, Steven M. (1996) Branded variants: a retail perspective. *Journal of Marketing Research*, 33 (February), 9–19.

Bergen, Mark, Dutta, Shantanu & Walker, Orville C. Jr (1992) Agency relationships in marketing : a review of the implications and applications of agency and related theories. *Journal of Marketing*, 56 (3), 1–24.

Bergen, Mark, Heide, Jan B. & Dutta, Shantanu (1998) Managing gray markets through tolerance of violations: a transaction cost perspective. *Managerial and Decision Economics*, 19 (1), 157–65.

Bradach, Jeffrey L. (1997) Using the plural form in the managment of restaurant chains. *Administrative Science Quarterly*, 42 (June), 276–303.

Brown, James R. & Day, Ralph L. (1981) Measures of manifest conflict in distribution channels. *Journal of Marketing Research*, 18 (August), 263–74.

Brown, James R., Johnson, Jean L. & Koenig, Harold F. (1995) Measuring the sources of marketing channel power: a comparison of alternative approaches. *International Journal of Research in Marketing*, 12 (2), 333–54.

Bucklin, Louis P. (1969) *A Theory of Distribution Channel Structure*. Berkeley, CA: IBER Special Publications.

——— (1972) *Competition & Evolution in the Distributive Trades*. Englewood Cliffs, NJ: Prentice-Hall.

——— (1993) Modeling the international gray market for public policy decisions. *International Journal of Research in Marketing*, 10, 387–405.

Bulow, Jeremy, Geanakoplos, John & Klemperer, Paul (1985) Multimarket oligopoly: strategic substitutes and strategic complements. *Journal of Political Economy*, 93 (3), 488–511.

Celly, Kirti Sawhney & Frazier, Gary L. (1996) Outcome-based and behavior-based coordination efforts in channel relationships. *Journal of Marketing Research*, 33 (May), 200–10.

Cespedes, Frank, Corey, Raymond & Rangan, V. Kasturi (1988) Gray markets: causes and cures. *Harvard Business Review*, 88 (July–August), 75–82.

Choi, S. Chan (1991) Price competition in a channel structure with a common retailer. *Marketing Science*, 10, 4 (Fall), 271–96.

Chu, Wujin (1992) Demand signaling and screening in channels of distribution. *Marketing Science*, 11 (Fall), 327–47.

Chu, Wujin & Chu, Woosik (1994) Signaling quality by selling through a reputable retailer: an example of renting the reputation of another agent. *Marketing Science*, 13, 2 (Spring), 177–89.

Chu, Wujin & Desai, Preyas S. (1995) Channel coordination mechanisms for customer satisfaction. *Marketing Science*, 14 (4), 343–59.

Coughlan, Anne T. (1985) Competition and cooperation in marketing channel choice: Theory and Application. *Marketing Science*, 4, 2 (Spring), 110–29.

——— (1987) Distribution channel choice in a market with complementary goods. *International Journal of Research in Marketing*, 4, 85–97.

——— (1993) Salesforce compensation: a review of MS/OR advances. In *Handbooks in Operations Research and Management Science: Marketing*, Vol. 5, edited by Gary L. Lilien & Jehoshua Eliashberg. Amsterdam: North-Holland, pp. 611–51.

Coughlan, Anne T. & Lal, Rajiv (1992) Retail pricing: does channel length matter? *Managerial and Decision Economics*, 13, 201–14.

Coughlan, Anne T. & Narasimhan, Chakravarthi (1992) An empirical analysis of salesforce compensation plans. *Journal of Business*, 65, 1 (January), 93–122.

Coughlan, Anne T. & Sen, Subrata K. (1989) Salesforce compensation: theory and managerial implications. *Marketing Science*, 8, 4 (Fall), 324–42.

Coughlan, Anne T. & Soberman, David A. (1998) When is the best ship a leaky one? Segmentation, competition and gray markets. INSEAD Working Paper, April.

——— (2000) Good marketing to 'bad consumers': outlet malls, gray markets, and warehouse sales. INSEAD Working Paper, October.

Coughlan, Anne T. & Wernerfelt, Birger (1989) On credible delegation by oligopolists: a discussion of distribution channel management. *Management Science*, 35 (February), 226–39.

Coughlan, Anne T., Anderson, Erin, Stern, Louis W. & El-Ansary, Adel I. (2001) *Marketing Channels*, 6th edn. Englewood Cliffs, NJ: Prentice-Hall.

Cox, Ronald & Goodman, Charles S. (1956) Marketing of housebuilding materials. *Journal of Marketing*, 21 (July), 36–61.

Dahlstrom, Robert & Nygaard, Arne (1999) An empirical investigation of ex post transaction costs in franchised distribution channels. *Journal of Marketing Research*, 36 (May), 160–70.

Dant, Rajiv P. & Gundlach, Gregory T. (1998) The challenge of autonomy and dependence in franchised channels of distribution. *Journal of Business Venturing*, 14 (1), 35–67.

Dant, Rajiv P. & Schul, Patrick L. (1992) Conflict resolution processes in contractual channels of distribution. *Journal of Marketing*, 56 (January), 38–54.

Dant, Rajiv P., Paswan, Audehesh K. & Kaufman, Patrick J. (1996) What we know about ownership redirection in franchising: a meta-analysis. *Journal of Retailing*, 72 (4), 429–44.

Desai, Preyas S. & Purohit, Devavrat (1999) Competition in durable goods markets: the strategic consequences of leasing and selling. *Marketing Science*, 18 (1), 42–58.

Dnes, Anthony W. (1993) A case-study analsyis of franchise contracts. *Journal of Legal Studies*, 22 (June), 367–93.

Duhan, D.F. & Sheffet, M.J. (1988) Gray markets and the legal status of parallel importation. *Journal of Marketing*, 52 (3), 75–83.

Dutta, Shantanu, Bergen, Mark & John, George (1994) The governance of exclusive territories when dealers can bootleg. *Marketing Science*, 13, 1 (Winter), 83–99.

Dutta, Shantanu, Heide, Jan B. & Bergen, Mark (1999) Vertical territorial restrictions and public policy: theories and industry evidence. *Journal of Marketing*, 63 (October), 121–34.

Dutta, Shantanu, Bergen, Mark, Heide, Jan B. & John, George (1995) Understanding dual distribution: the case of reps and house accounts. *Journal of Law, Economics, and Organization*, 11 (1), 189–204.

Dwyer, F. Robert & Oh, Sejo (1988) A transaction cost perspective on vertical contractual structure and interchannel competitive strategies. *Journal of Marketing*, 52, 2 (April), 21–34.

Dwyer, F. Robert, Schurr, Paul H. & Oh, Sejo (1987) Developing buyer-seller relationships. *Journal of Marketing*, 51 (April), 11–27.

El-Ansary, Adel & Stern, Louis W. (1972) Power measurement in the distribution channel. *Journal of Marketing Research*, 9 (February), 47–52.

Emerson, Richard M. (1962) Power-dependence relations. *American Sociological Review*, 27 (February), 31–41.

Fein, Adam J. & Anderson, Erin (1997) Patterns of credible commitments: territory and category selectivity in industrial distribution channels. *Journal of Marketing*, 61 (April), 19–34.

Frazier, Gary L. (1983) On the measurement of interfirm power in channels of distribution. *Journal of Marketing Research*, 20 (May), 158–66.

——— (1999) Organizing and managing channels of distribution. *Journal of the Academy of Marketing Sciences*, 27 (2), 226–40.

Frazier, Gary L. & Lassar, Walfried M. (1996) Determinants of distribution intensity. *Journal of Marketing*, 60 (October), 39–51.

Frazier, Gary L. & Summers, John O. (1984) Interfirm influence strategies and their application within distribution channels. *Journal of Marketing*, 48 (Summer), 43–55.

Frazier, Gary L., Gill, James D. & Kale, Sudhir H. (1989) Dealer dependence levels and reciprocal actions in a

channel of distribution in a developing country. *Journal of Marketing*, 53 (January), 50–69.
French, John R. Jr. & Raven, Bertram (1959) The bases of social power. In *Studies in Social Power*, edited by Dorwin Cartwright. Ann Arbor, MI: University of Michigan Press, pp. 150–67.
Fudenberg, Drew & Tirole, Jean (1993) *Game Theory*. Cambridge, MA: The MIT Press.
Gaski, John F. (1986) Interrelations among a channel entity's power sources: impact of the exercise of reward and coercion on expert, referent, and legitimate power sources. *Journal of Marketing Research*, 23 (February), 62–77.
Gattorna, John (1978) Channels of distribution. *European Journal of Marketing*, 12 (7), 471–512.
Gerstner, Eitan & Hess, James D. (1995) Pull promotions and channel coordination. *Marketing Science*, 14 (1), 43–60.
Geyskens, Inge, Steenkamp, Jan-Benedict E.M. & Kumar, Nirmalya (1998) Generalizations about trust in marketing channel relationships using meta analysis. *International Journal of Research in Marketing*, 15 (1), 223–48.
——— (1999) A meta-analysis of satisfaction in marketing channel relationships. *Journal of Marketing Research*, 36 (May), 223–38.
Ghosh, Mrinal & John, George (1999) Governance value analysis and marketing strategy. *Journal of Marketing*, 63 (Special), 131–45.
Grossman, Sanford & Hart, Oliver (1983) An analysis of the principal-agent problem. *Econometrica*, 51 (January), 7–45.
Harris, Milton and Raviv, Artur (1979) Optimal incentive contracts with imperfect information. *Journal of Economic Theory*, 20 (April), 231–59.
Heide, Jan B. (1994) Interorganizational governance in marketing channels. *Journal of Marketing*, 58 (April), 71–85.
Heide, Jan B. & John, George (1988) The role of dependence balancing in safeguarding transaction-specific assets in conventional channels. *Journal of Marketing*, 52 (January), 20–35.
——— (1992) Do norms matter in marketing relationships? *Journal of Marketing*, 56 (April), 32–44.
Heide, Jan B. & Miner, Anne S. (1992) The shadow of the future: effects of anticipated interaction and frequency of contact on buyer-seller cooperation. *Academy of Management Journal*, 35 (2), 265–91.
Holmstrom, Bengt (1979) Moral hazard and observability. *Bell Journal of Economics*, 10 (Spring), 74–91.
Hunt, Shelby D. & Nevin, John R. (1974) Power in a channel of distribution: sources and consequences. *Journal of Marketing Research*, 11 (May), 186–93.
Ingene, Charles A. & Parry, Mark E. (1995a) Channel coordination when retailers compete. *Marketing Science*, 14 (4), 360–77.
——— (1995b) Coordination and manufacturer profit maximization: the multiple retailer channel. *Journal of Retailing*, 71 (Summer), 129–51.
——— (1998) Manufacturer-optimal wholesale pricing when retailers compete. *Marketing Letters*, 9 (1), 65–77.
Iyer, Ganesh (1998) Coordinating channels under price and nonprice competition. *Marketing Science*, 17 (4), 338–55.
Jap, Sandy D. (1999) 'Pie-expansion' efforts: collaboration processes in buyer-supplier relationships. *Journal of Marketing Research*, 36 (November), 461–75.
Jap, Sandy & Ganesan, Shankar (2000) Control mechanisms and the relationship lifecycle: implications for safeguarding specific investments and developing commitment. *Journal of Marketing Research*, 37, 2 (May), 227–45.
Jap, Sandy D. & Weitz, Barton A. (1995) Relationship marketing and distribution channels. *Journal of the Academy of Marketing Sciences*, 23 (Fall), 305–20.
Jeuland, Abel P. & Shugan, Steven M. (1983) Managing channel profits. *Marketing Science*, 2 (Summer), 239–72.
John, George (1984) An empirical investigation of some antecedents of opportunism in a marketing channel. *Journal of Marketing Research*, 21 (August), 278–89.
Kaufman, Patrick J. & Lafontaine, Francine (1994) Costs of control: the source of economic rents for McDonald's franchisees. *Journal of Law and Economics*, 36 (October), 417–53.
Kaufman, Patrick J. & Stern, Louis W. (1988) Relational exchange norms, perceptions of unfairness, and retained hostility in commercial litigation. *Journal of Conflict Resolution*, 32 (September), 534–52.
Klein, Benjamin (1995) The economics of franchise contracts. *Journal of Corporate Finance*, 2 (1), 9–37.
Kogut, Bruce & Kulatilaka, Nalin (1994) Options thinking and platform investments: investing in opportunity. *California Management Review*, 36 (June), 52–71.
Kopalle, Praveen K. & Lehmann, Donald R. (1997) Alpha inflation? The impact of eliminating scale items on Cronbach's Alpha. *Organizational Behavior and Human Decision Processes*, 70 (June), 189–97.
Kuhn, Thomas S. (1969) *The Structure of Scientific Revolutions*, 2nd edn. Chicago: The University of Chicago Press.
Kumar, Nirmalya, Scheer, Lisa K. & Steenkamp, Jan-Benedict E.M. (1995) The effects of supplier fairness on vulnerable resellers. *Journal of Marketing Research*, 32 (February), 54–65.
——— (1998) Interdependence, punitive capability, and the reciprocation of punitive actions in channel relationships. *Journal of Marketing Research*, 35 (May), 225–35.
Kumar, Nirmalya, Stern, Louis W. & Achrol, Ravi S. (1992) Assessing reseller performance from the perspective of the supplier. *Journal of Marketing Research*, 29, 2 (May), 238–53.
Lal, Rajiv (1990) Improving channel coordination through franchising. *Marketing Science*, 9 (4), 299–318.
Lee, Eunkyu & Staelin, Richard (1997) Vertical strategic interaction: implications for channel pricing strategy. *Marketing Science*, 16 (3), 185–207.
Lilien, Gary L. (1979) ADVISOR 2: modeling the marketing mix decision for industrial products. *Management Science*, 25 (February), 191–204.

Lusch, Robert F. & Brown, James R. (1982) A modified model of power in the marketing channel. *Journal of Marketing Research*, 19 (August), 312–23.

McGuire, Timothy W. & Staelin, Richard (1983) An industry equilibrium analysis of downstream vertical integration. *Marketing Science*, 2 (Spring), 161–92.

Machlup, F. & Taber, M. (1960) Bilateral monopoly, successive monopoly, and vertical integration. *Economica*, 27 (May), 101–19.

Macneil, Ian R. (1980) *The New Social Contract: An Inquiry into Modern Contractual Relations*. New Haven, CT: Yale University Press.

Messinger, Paul R. & Narasimhan, Chakravarthi (1995) Has power shifted in the grocery channel? *Marketing Science*, 14, 2 (Spring), 189–223.

Mirrlees, James (1976) The optimal structure of authority and incentives within an organization. *Bell Journal of Economics*, 7 (Spring), 105–31.

Mishra, Debi Prasad, Heide, Jan B. & Cort, Stanton G. (1998) Information asymmetry and levels of agency relationships. *Journal of Marketing Research*, 35 (August), 277–95.

Mohr, Jakki & Nevin, John R. (1990) Communication strategies in marketing channels: a theoretical perspective. *Journal of Marketing* (October), 36–51.

Moorthy, K. Sridhar (1987) Managing channel profits: comment. *Marketing Science*, 6, 375–9.

——— (1993) Theoretical modeling in marketing. *Journal of Marketing*, 57 (April), 92–106.

Morgan, Robert M. & Hunt, Shelby D. (1994) The commitment-trust theory of relationship marketing. *Journal of Marketing*, 58 (July), 20–38.

Murray, John P. & Heide, Jan B. (1998) Managing promotion program participation within manufacturer-retailer relationships. *Journal of Marketing*, 62 (January), 58–68.

O'Brien, Daniel P. & Shaffer, Greg (1992) Vertical control with bilateral contracts. *Rand Journal of Economics*, 23, 3 (Autumn), 299–308.

——— (1993) On the dampening-of-competition effect of exclusive dealing. *Journal of Industrial Economics*, 41, 2 (June), 215–21.

Oi, Walter (1971) A disneyland dilemma: two-part tariffs for a mickey mouse monopoly. *Quarterly Journal of Economics*, 85, 77–96.

Osborne, Martin J. & Rubinstein, Ariel (1994) *A Course in Game Theory*. Cambridge, MA: The MIT Press.

Padmanabhan, V. & Png, I.P.L. (1997) Manufacturer's returns policies and retail competition. *Marketing Science*, 16 (1), 81–94.

Paswan, Audhesh K., Dant, Rajiv P. & Lumpkin, James R. (1998) An empirical investigation of the linkages among relationalism, environmental uncertainty, and bureaucratization. *Journal of Business Research*, 43 (4), 125–40.

Purohit, Devavrat (1997) Dual distribution channels: the competition between rental agencies and dealers. *Marketing Science*, 16 (3), 228–45.

Purohit, Devavrat & Staelin, Richard (1994) Rentals, sales and buybacks: managing secondary distribution channels. *Journal of Marketing Research*, 31, 325–38.

Rangan, V. Kasturi, Menezes, Melvyn A.J. & Maier, E.P. (1992) Channel selection for new industrial products: a framework, method, and application. *Journal of Marketing*, 56 (July), 69–82.

Rindfleisch, Aric & Heide, Jan B. (1997) Transaction cost analysis: present, past, and future. *Journal of Marketing*, 41 (October), 30–54.

Roberts, Peter W. & Greenwood, Royston (1997) Integrating transaction cost and institutional theories: toward a constrained-efficiency framework for understanding organizational design adaptation. *Academy of Management Review*, 22 (2), 346–73.

Ross, Steven (1973) The economic theory of agency: the principal's problem. *American Economic Review*, 63 (2), 134–9.

Ross, William T., Anderson, Erin & Weitz, Barton (1997) Performance in principal-agent dyads: the causes and consequences of perceived asymmetry of commitment to the relationship. *Management Science*, 43 (May), 680–704.

Shaffer, Greg (1991a) Slotting allowances and resale price maintenance: a comparison of facilitating practices. *Rand Journal of Economics*, 22, 1 (Spring), 120–35.

——— (1991b) Capturing strategic rent: full-line forcing, brand discounts, aggregate rebates, and maximum resale price maintenance. *Journal of Industrial Economics*, 39, 5 (September), 557–75.

——— (1995) On vertical restrictions and the number of franchises: comment. *Southern Economic Journal*, 62, 1 (July), 264–8.

Shane, Scott & Foo, Maw-Der (1999) New firm survival: institutional explanations for new franchisor mortality. *Management Science*, 45 (February), 142–59.

Smelser, Neil J. & Swedberg, Richard (1994) The sociological perspective on the economy. In *Handbook of Economic Sociology* edited by Neil J. Smelser & Richard Swedberg. Princeton, NJ: Princeton University Press, pp. 3–26.

Spengler, J. (1950) Vertical integration and anti-trust policy. *Journal of Political Economy*, 58, 347–52.

Stern, Louis W. & Reve, Torger (1980) Distribution channels as political economies: a framework for comparative analysis. *Journal of Marketing*, 44 (Summer), 52–64.

Stern, Louis W. & Weitz, Barton A. (1997) The revolution in distribution: challenges and opportunities. *Long Range Planning*, 30 (6), 823–9.

Tirole, Jean (1994) *The Theory of Industrial Organization*. Cambridge, MA: The MIT Press.

Wathne, Kenneth H. & Heide, Jan B. (2000) Opportunism in interfirm relationships: forms, outcomes, and solutions. *Journal of Marketing*, 64 (October), 36–51.

Williamson, Oliver E. (1996) *The Mechanisms of Governance*. New York: Oxford University Press.

10

Salesforce Management – Compensation, Motivation, Selection and Training

SÖNKE ALBERS

1 Introduction

Selling products or services is critical to the success of any business and salespeople often play a critical role in generating sales by communicating the advantages and purchase conditions of offers. Even though personal selling is of utmost importance for free market economies, salesforce management issues are an under-researched area within marketing. Perhaps the reason for this neglect is that the task of selling has had a negative image in society (Mason, 1965) and continues to have this image as people equate all salespeople with the aggressive used-car and door-to-door salespeople they have personally encountered. Despite this poor image, selling is a serious profession that involves many complex management problems.

A salesforce is one of the elements in the communication mix used by companies to communicate with their customers. Personal selling is the most expensive and most effective element in a communication mix that includes advertising, promotions, and publicity. Rather than sending the same messages to anonymous recipients via mass media, salespeople communicate individualized messages about the advantages of the products offered by their firms typically in face-to-face encounters. Due to the very high costs of a sales call, salesforces are typically used for products of considerable value with attributes that need to be explained, such as industrial products, pharmaceutical products, and financial services (leasing, building societies), as well as for selling to wholesalers or big retailing chains.

Employing human beings as a communication channel involves management problems that are generally discussed in the research literature on organizational and human behavior. However, many unique problems arise in managing salesforces because salespeople work in the field without close supervision, their outputs are readily observable, and compensation is often closely tied to sales outputs. Managerial advice is available in textbooks (cf. Churchill et al., 1997; Ingram et al., 2000), and there are excellent reviews of academic research addressing specific topics such as factors affecting salesperson performance (Churchill et al., 1985), methods for the selection of salespeople (Randall & Randall, 1990), the effects of sales compensation (Coughlan, 1993; Coughlan & Sen, 1989), and the implementation of compensation schemes (Albers, 1996). The focus of this review is on systematizing the many problems facing sales management and discussing research that could provide help for management. Therefore, this review is problem-oriented with a critical review of what research has been done to solve managerial problems. The review also focuses on economic problems with direct financial impact, while the typical psychological problems in managing people are neglected.

Managing a salesforce involves hiring of promising salespeople; training, motivating, and compensating them; and dismissing low-performers. These salesforce management activities must be based on an evaluation of the performance of salespeople. Thus, the review begins with a discussion of performance measurement problems. Based on an understanding of what high-performance is and what characteristics of salespeople are correlated with performance, Section 3 examines issues related to hiring promising salespeople. Since training improves performance and leads to salespeople acting in the best interest of the company, Section 4 discusses how to identify the training needs and how to choose the right training method. If a company determines it has not recruited the right people in the first place, it has to decide on the dismissal of salespeople, which is discussed in Section 5. Supervision not only involves training of selling skills but also motivation to work as hard as possible. How this motivation can be achieved, and which problems are associated with it, are discussed in Section 6. Salespeople have to be compensated for their work, but financial incentives can also be used to motivate salespeople. The design of compensation plans is covered in detail in Section 7. The chapter closes with a summary and conclusions in Section 8.

2 Performance Measurement

The evaluation of salesperson performance is a necessary ingredient in the control of a salesforce. However, evaluating performance can be challenging because one needs to control for external factors such as the nature of the sales territory and the state of the economy. By controlling for these factors, the assessment of performance is fair, equitable, and comparable across all members of a salesforce. While a wide variety of performance measures has been suggested, there probably is no one single measure that satisfies this criterion.

Researchers have conducted empirical studies inventorying measures applied in practice (Jackson et al., 1983, 1995). These studies show, for example, that more than 50% of the responding companies use output measures such as sales volume in terms of absolute dollars or relative to previous year's sales or to a quota, market share achieved, and net profit dollars. With respect to input measures, companies use the number of customers and selling expenses in terms of absolute dollars or relative to sales or budget.

Clearly, firms hire salespeople with the expectation that sales and profits will increase. However, this does not imply that using an output measure, such as the gross margin of sales recorded, is always appropriate. Albers (2000) points out that it is not appropriate if sales are affected by external factors in addition to the effort and ability of the salespeople. It may be appropriate if the territories are equal with respect to external factors, such as the number of customers, the economic value of individual customers, the geographical dispersion of customers, and the strength of competition. However, this is rarely the case. In fact, if companies follow a profit-contribution maximizing territory design, then potentials will differ across the resulting territories (Skiera & Albers, 1998), and the company will need to correct for external influences or use input measures. Data on environmental factors such as the number of customers, the number of inhabitants, and square miles of an area can be obtained from easily accessible public databases, but measures of competitive activities are generally not available.

The time horizon also needs to be considered when selecting performance measures. Short-run measures can neglect future profitability. For example, sales may rise in the short-term but customer satisfaction decreases, which leads to a lower probability of repurchasing. To assess long-term profitability, a company therefore needs to consider the impact of salespeople on customer loyalty. This output performance can be measured either by customer satisfaction indices, or the willingness to recommend the product to other companies, or directly by the probability of continuing purchasing from the firm. Although customer loyalty is not easy to measure, Hauser et al. (1995) report that customer satisfaction is already often used as a basis for financial incentives to salespersons. Since such measures only represent subjective data and may not be reliable, and salespersons may manipulate the satisfaction ratings (Sharma, 1997), more research is needed to construct implementable long-term performance measures.

If output measures are not appropriate, salesforce control can only be exercised through input performance measures. This requires knowledge of the activities performed by salespeople. A comprehensive list is given by Marshall et al. (1999). However, effort is not only given by quantitative measures such as the number of calls, but also by qualitative assessments such as the quality of presentations and preparations for customer calls. Unfortunately, it is very difficult to obtain valid data for both types of input indicators. In general, salespeople work remote from the firm's headquarters in locations near to the customers. As a consequence, the efforts and skills of salespeople cannot be easily observed by management. Thus, management often must rely on self-reports by salespersons. However, very often it is not in the interest of a salesperson to provide correct and complete data. Therefore self-reports may not be accurate (Ramaswami et al., 1997). For example, salespeople might be reluctant to provide detailed calling report data that would enable the company to detect whether they are calling enough on the customers. Therefore, research has to be conducted on developing mechanisms to obtain correct self-report data. One naïve approach is to randomly contact customers to verify call reports. Unfortunately, these checks can have negative side-effects such as creating an atmosphere characterized by distrust rather than by trustful collaboration. Another approach is to create such incentives that motivate salespeople to provide correct data. If, for instance, the data of a call report enter into a recommendation system outlining which accounts are most profitable to call on in the next period, then it is in the interest of salespeople to provide accurate data (Siebel & Malone, 1996). While this is highly plausible, no system is reported so far that exhibits these features.

Instead of relying on data from salespeople, sales managers can also be asked to provide subjective judgments of inputs such as the level of preparation for calls, or the services provided for the customer. The accuracy of these reports depends on the closeness of the supervision. Problems with comparability arise when assessing salespeople across managers. If assessments are made using simple rating scales then the expectations of the sales managers may lead to errors in measuring absolute performance. Behaviorally anchored rating scales (BARS) have been developed to address this problem (Cocanougher & Ivancevich, 1978).

There is a stream of articles investigating in which situations companies use either output or input measures to control their salesforces. This is discussed under the heading of outcome-versus behavior-based control (Anderson & Oliver, 1987; Krafft, 1999). Empirical studies generally support the hypotheses that behavior-based control is preferred in cases of high environmental uncertainty, measurability of behavior and knowledge of the transformation process (Krafft, 1999). However, other studies show that high behavior-based performance also leads to high outcome performance. In addition, these empirical studies make clear that companies prefer hybrid types of control (Babakus et al., 1996; Cravens et al., 1993). The type of performance measure used can also affect the attitudes of salespeople toward their jobs and their companies. For example, Oliver & Anderson (1994) found that the use of input performance measures increases intrinsic motivation, job satisfaction, and commitment to the company; while the use of output performance measures increases extrinsic motivation.

Having obtained valid measures of output and input, the sales manager faces the problem of carrying out the final assessment of performance. To derive general conclusions on the factors influencing performance, researchers have applied models that range from simple regressions to very complex structural equation models. The results have been meta-analyzed by Churchill et al. (1985). While these results provide valuable knowledge to researchers, their managerial implications are limited. The conclusions are often highly plausible and therefore of little value to prove, because managers will intuitively assume such relationships. More information could be given to a manager if the magnitude of the influence of a certain factor could be quantified. Unfortunately, most studies only report the significance of influences rather than their magnitude. However, the magnitude of influence may depend on situational factors. Therefore, research is needed to develop methods that provide generalizable results, but also account for situational factors.

Various approaches can be used to quantify the impact of factors that are not under the control of a salesperson. For example, by regressing an output or input measure against external factors, estimation error represents the salesperson's individual performance (Albers, 1996). This method may also be applied for determining equitable sales quotas that control for the influence of external factors and thus can be achieved with equal effort. Alternatively, performance may be judged by the quotient of actual output to estimated output. While this method appears to be very favorable, it has the drawback of an omission bias resulting in biased estimators if substantial external factors have been left out. This causes major implementation problems when salespeople argue that important factors (affecting the value of their territories) are missing. Research is needed to find out whether such regression approaches are fair enough on an individual basis.

The method for controlling for external factors discussed above is based on estimating a single equation, relating input to output. When fitting this single response curve the sum of squared errors is minimized, resulting in estimates representing an average response such as in Ryans & Weinberg (1979, 1987) or Behrman & Perreault (1982). Instead of comparing performance with the average performance of salespeople that can be expected for the respective levels of external influence per territory, Horsky & Nelson (1996) compare salesperson performance to what can be expected from the best salespersons, based on efficient frontier analysis. If the possible output in a territory is calculated on the basis of a common combination of inputs across territories, it may discriminate against salespeople facing conditions in which they cannot combine the various input factors in the same way as suggested by the single efficient frontier equation. This limitation can be overcome by determining individual efficiency with the help of data envelopment analysis, by estimating weights for the different input factors so that the quotient of output divided by the weighted input is maximized relative to the same ratios of all other salespersons. If the output-input ratio is higher than or equal to all other ratios then the salesperson is efficiently combining his or her inputs. This method of data envelopment analysis has been applied, for example, by Mahajan (1991) and Boles, Donthu & Lohtia (1995). However, it is not known whether increasing the number of input factors creates so many degrees of freedom that nearly all salespeople are efficient.

In summary, we have seen that performance measurement is a complex problem. An individual performance assessment for the purpose of selection, training, and termination, as well as providing the basis for incentives, needs to be fair and requires equitable methods providing comparable assessments by correcting for external factors. While regression provides information about an average salesperson, a more helpful benchmark would involve comparing salespeople with what the best salesperson would do under those conditions.

3 Selection of Salespersons

Effective recruitment of salespeople involves determining the characteristics of high-performing salespeople. Some empirical studies provide information on companies' practices (Patton & King, 1992); however, it is not clear whether these practices are the best ones that could be used.

Numerous correlational studies have been conducted to identify characteristics elicited during the selection process related to sales success. A meta-analysis of these studies found only a low correlation between performance on the one hand, and background and experience variables, current status, lifestyle, attitude, personality, and skills on the other. The same weak results were reported with respect to the selection procedures (Churchill et al., 1985). Personal interviews, experiences of the applicant, biographical information from application forms, as well as reference checks, also show very low correlations with sales success. Composite tests and assessment centers appear to be far better selection approaches (Hunter & Hunter, 1984). In assessment centers, the working environment is simulated and then applicant behaviors are assessed in an environment similar to the one in which the salesperson will work. The problem here is to construct a selection procedure that is as close as possible to the eventual job setting, thereby providing the highest possible validity of assessment. Unfortunately, an assessment center is much more expensive than simply going through application forms (Randall & Randall, 1990). Rather than relying just on one assessment instrument, several instruments should be used. This recommendation is similar to the finding that the best forecast can be provided by combining different forecasting methods.

Another issue is evaluating the firm's selection procedures. One approach for conducting such an evaluation is examining the relationships between predictors of performance assessed at the time of hiring, to the eventual performance of the selected salespeople. Two problems arise in using this approach. First, the sample is censored – no performance data is available for salespeople rated below the selection criteria since they were not hired. Statistical methods can be used to correct for this bias. Second, there is an issue about the time at which performance is measured. There is little research on development of sales skills over time. In particular, the results of new salespeople may be unstable so that an assessment is only possible after months or even years of employment. When the length of time to make an accurate performance assessment is long, another bias may be introduced by the best performers in the sample through voluntary job change.

Finally, economic considerations need to be taken into account in selecting salespeople. The more effort required by the selection process, the higher the costs for the company. Thus, research is needed to find the best tradeoff between the cost of collecting suitable data and the gain of profit resulting from a better prediction. Another tradeoff is the effort placed in selection versus training.

4 Sales Training

El-Ansary (1993) found that top performing salesforces differ from low performing ones with respect to the content, source, length, and method of training. Specifically, the highest performing sales forces train their new salespeople longer and in greater depth in terms of methods and content. Research on the reasons for salespersons failure (Ingram et al., 1992; Morris et al., 1994) suggests the need for training in the following areas:

- *Knowledge* of technical characteristics of the company's products, all aspects of the company's policy, the offerings of relevant competitors, and benefits sought by customer segments.
- *Selling skills* – how to contact customers, approach them, listen to them, give presentations to decision makers at various levels and functional areas, overcome objections, and close the sale.
- *Time and territory management* – how to manage the sales territories with respect to the allocation of time across prospects and existing customers based on economic principles.
- *Motivation* to provide the highest possible effort to the task of selling. Achieving a high level of motivation is not a trivial task because salespeople are frequently exposed to demotivating conditions. For example, salespeople may be demotivated because they have experienced unsuccessful sales calls (Dixon et al., 2001), have not met quotas for several periods, or have been spending all of their time handling routine order processing tasks, or just achieve a satisfactory income and have no desire to increase it.

Given the necessity of sales training, sales management needs to make the following decisions:

Table 10.1 *Identification of Different Training Needs*

Actual sales compared to estimated sales based on potential	Number of calls relative to average			
		More effort than on average		Less effort than on average
Higher sales than estimated	1	Highly motivated and efficient salespersons	2	Poorly motivated but efficient salespersons
Lower sales than estimated	3	Highly motivated but inefficient salespersons	4	Poorly motivated and inefficient salespersons

- how much money to spend on training
- which salesperson should get what kind of training
- which training method should be applied.

In order to make these decisions, sales management ideally needs information on how different training methods and trainers affect profit contribution. Since there are no results from research available, sales executives indicate that the measurement of sales training effectiveness is an area with greatest need of additional research (Honeycutt et al., 1995). El-Ansary (1993) finds that there are no differences between high and low performing companies with respect to the level of spending, but differences arise with respect to the allocation of their budgets. This finding provides additional support of the flat-maximum principle, showing that profit does not vary much around a wide interval of budgets (Tull et al., 1986), but does vary significantly with small changes in the allocation of the budget. Thus potential profit improvements are higher for allocation decisions and, in this case, for decisions on the content of training.

Determining the right level of spending on sales training is rather difficult because, in general, it is not possible to separate the effects of sales training from the many other factors affecting sales. In such situations companies often base their decisions on what is practiced in the respective industry. Therefore, it is necessary to conduct surveys to find out numbers as in the study by El-Ansary (1993). Since operating with the average percentage of sales training spending with respect to sales volume is no guarantee for success, or even survival, it is preferable to conduct benchmarking studies with the goal of finding out what the successful companies are doing. However, Jacobson (1990) points out that success depends on so many factors, many of which are unobservable, that the derived statistical relationships may be artifacts. In addition, if all market players apply the same policy of increasing sales training, then at the very end, sales volume will remain unchanged while costs have increased.

Methods have to be developed that find out which salespeople need training and what specific training is needed. Of course, such decisions have to be based on an evaluation of each salesperson's performance with respect to knowledge, selling skills, managerial efficiency, and motivation. One proposal by the author of this review would be to quantify the effect of external factors such as potential and the number of calls as effort indicator. In this case one can estimate the sales in all territories that would result from the given values of potential and from an average number of calls. As a result, one can distinguish between a lack of motivation (as indicated by a lower number of calls than average) and a lack of efficiency (by comparing actual sales volume with the estimate, corrected for potential) (see Table 10.1).

Table 10.1 may be the basis for differentiated decisions on promotion, training and dismissal of salespersons. Cell 1 shows salespersons who are providing high effort with high efficiency, and therefore should be retained. On the other hand, salespeople in cell 4 are inferior with respect to both effort and efficiency, and may be subject to dismissal. In the two remaining cells the recommendations are quite differentiated. In cell 3 are salespeople with high effort and low efficiency that should be provided with sales training focusing on improving efficiency. On the other hand, salespeople in cell 2 with low effort and high efficiency have good sales skills but are no longer motivated, and thus need to be motivated. Unfortunately, no research has been carried out to determine the level of sophistication of analysis. Of course, it should be based on the economic principle that the company should not spend more money on finding out who needs training than can be gained from increased efficiency.

The final decisions concern the training content, as well as the method of training. Given the collinearity of many other variables influencing sales volume the best way of finding out about the effectiveness of sales training programs is to work with experiments. It is probably because of the high number of methods and contents offered in the market of sales training that such experimental studies have not been published so far. Companies, therefore, rely on surveys in practitioner magazines, on what other companies are doing, and on personal recommendations. From this discussion, it is clear that there is no single method for effective selling. Rather, salespeople need to be adaptive – to tailor their sales presentation and approach to sales situations and the needs of each individual customer (Weitz et al., 1986).

A big problem lies in the field of creating motivation through sales training. For example, there are about 6000 sales trainers offering their services in Germany alone. They are using more than 100 completely different training approaches and all of them claim success (Munkelt, 1992). In the face of these numbers, it is very hard to believe that only a few training approaches promise success. Rather, the success may be due to the 'Hawthorne effect,' namely that simply demonstrating concern for salespeople by exposing them to training motivates them, and thus improves their performance. Hence, it is no surprise that, like in soccer, new coaches can stimulate a sales team for a while irrespective of the method until the effect wears off and a new person (not so much a different approach) has to bring new motivation to the team. Longitudinal studies are required that investigate the impact of sales training and the pattern of change in trainers.

5 Dismissal of Salespersons

The employment of salespeople implies not only that a firm has to select appropriate salespersons and to train them in the best possible way, but also that the company has to determine the conditions under which they will be deemed unsatisfactory and dismissed. Unfortunately, the impact of dismissing under-performing salespeople is still unclear. Dismissing salespeople may improve the chances to attract good salespeople, as well as raise the motivation of employed salespersons, but can also distract salespeople who are interested in a stable relationship.

The effects of dismissal depend on the level of performance below which salespeople should be dismissed. Setting this level is not a trivial decision, because the dismissal of a salesperson and the recruitment of a new salesperson involve high costs which have to be covered by the higher efficiency of the new salesperson. However, it can never be clear beforehand whether a newly hired salesperson will perform better than the one fired. There remains a certain probability that the new salesperson performs even worse than the previous one. Such a complex decision can only be investigated with the help of dynamic models in which it is possible to tradeoff the costs of firing and recruitment against the higher profit contribution from sales generated by more efficient salespersons. Fernández-Gaucherand et al. (1995) formulated a Bayesian stochastic model for deriving optimal policies. The results of computational experiments show that an increase in the heterogeneity of the salesforce can lead to more stringent levels of minimal acceptable performance. However, such results depend on the recruitment policy, namely on hiring salespeople only at the entry level and promoting them, as compared to recruiting salespeople at all experience levels. This result arises because restricting the hiring to the entry-level increases salespersons' trust in the organization and reduces salesforce turnover as well as opportunistic behavior (Ganesan et al., 1993).

6 Motivation

Economic Foundation

Salesperson performance is clearly affected by their motivation and the subsequent effort they devote to selling. Thus, a major concern of salesforce management is choosing the right way of motivating its salespeople so that they act in the best interest of the company. Given the complexity of human beings and their needs and goals, it is not surprising to find a multitude of different approaches for motivating salespeople. Research distinguishes two different types of motivation – intrinsic and extrinsic (Churchill et al., 1997). If salespeople get reward from simply engaging in the task of selling, they are intrinsically motivated. If people, for example, love to interact with people and to sell, then they can be motivated by giving them a job which allows them to realize these rewards. If salespeople desire recognition from external sources such as their company or manager, they are more extrinsically motivated. Surveys (Churchill et al., 1979) suggest that salespeople typically are heavily motivated by financial incentives and thus are extrinsically motivated. However, the reason for this is still not clear. One may speculate that the extrinsic motivation arises because salespeople have to cope with more failures than successes when closing a sale only at every fifth or tenth attempt. In order to compensate for such a high failure rate, they might ask for strong financial incentives for the rare successes.

Psychologists are interested in finding out how motivation works (Teas & McElroy, 1986; Tyagi, 1985). This is closely linked with research on role perception. Salespeople have to play the role to serve the needs of the customers while at the same time playing the role to act in the best interest of their employer. It is generally assumed that motivation and role clarity improve job satisfaction, which in turn improves performance and the intention to stay with the company. There are numerous articles that have empirically investigated these relationships and found empirical support. A meta-analysis of the antecedents and consequences of salesperson job satisfaction is provided by Brown and Peterson (1993). How the intention to quit the job is formed and related to actual behavior is investigated, for example, by Chandrashekaran et al. (2000).

Given the managerial orientation of this book, this chapter takes more of an economic perspective.

Sales management has to find out which of the motivational devices or rewards are working and what mix of motivators should be applied. From this perspective, managers need to know the relationship between rewards and motivation and the costs incurred. Psychological theories mostly explain how motivation is affected by some factors, but do not give information about the most profitable device. Moreover, the results are not specific enough for salesforce management to really choose the right incentives from this research. Finally, empirical evidence suggests that valence for rewards differs across salespeople, for example, with respect to their career stage and personal characteristics like educational level and family background (Churchill et al., 1979). Thus, it is not only necessary to know about the heterogeneous effects of motivation, but also how to account for it. Consequently, research is concerned with ways to design incentives differently across salespeople without violating equitable treatment.

Strategic Evaluation of Motivational Devices

As we have discussed, theory distinguishes between intrinsic and extrinsic motivation. Many sales employees have an intrinsic motivation to do a good job because they love their work and get enough rewards from performing interesting activities. How this intrinsic motivation can be enhanced is obvious to sales managers: one can create good working conditions and delegate responsibility to enrich the job so that salespeople develop a sense of control and mastery. In addition, if salespeople are interested in communication and dislike reporting, then intrinsic motivation can be achieved by letting them do their selling job and finding other ways to get the necessary reports. Finally, the company may offer good career opportunities.

The critical question from an economic point of view is whether certain steps of creating motivation positively contribute to profit. If the cost for creating good working conditions and the respective return can be allocated precisely to this measure, then it is easy to decide on investing in such activities. However, very often the relationship between profit and working conditions is not a direct one, and it is hard to find a functional relationship in empirical data because so many other factors may have an impact on profit. Thus, how to determine how much money should be invested in intrinsic and how much in extrinsic motivation remains an open research question.

Extrinsic motivation is realized through external rewards. These may have the form of non-financial incentives such as external recognition, or of financial incentives such as bonuses for the achievement of quotas. If non-financial incentives can be given without substantial cost then it is trivial to work with them. For example, a very cheap activity with a good return could be to award a specific title like 'district manager,' which leads to recognition outside of the firm. If recognition can only be achieved by incentive programs, research is warranted on how to determine profitable non-financial incentives. For example, the return of such activities as spending a week in Monte Carlo, thereby making public that certain salespeople belong to the group of high-performers, has to be estimated and compared to its cost.

Financial incentives can be distinguished with respect to the form by which they depend on outputs or inputs. *Fixed salaries* are paid simply for doing the job of a salesperson. However, over time they may also depend on performance. *Commissions* reward the achievement of absolute levels of output such as sales volume and are paid regularly. *Bonuses* and *sales contest prizes* are paid from time to time for the achievement of certain goals (Albers, 1996). Bonuses on the achievement of sales quotas represent hybrid incentives: they are paid regularly but the goal may change over time. Prizes for winning sales contests also represent some kind of bonus. The difference between bonuses and prizes is that prizes are related to the achievement of relative goals (e.g., being the first among all salespeople), while bonuses are paid for the absolute achievement of a goal (like a quota).

The decision of which kind of financial incentives to choose and in which combination is a very complex one. While there is a good body of knowledge about the optimal combination of fixed salary and commissions (see Section 7) there are no research results with respect to the combination of the other forms of financial incentives. The literature, therefore, concentrates on a more strategic evaluation on the basis of advantages and disadvantages of financial incentives (Albers, 2000; Churchill et al., 1997), which are contrasted below.

Fixed salaries do not depend on performance and, thus, provide some financial stability for the salesperson. This can be advantageous in situations in which salespeople need patience to persist in closing difficult sales, perform tasks that do not immediately lead to sales (e.g., counseling) or are involved in sales with a long life cycle. However, there is no empirical support as to whether salespeople really perceive salaries in this way. Salaries are very simple to administer and do not require any adjustment if the company wants to change territories. Salaries also represent a fixed cost that leads to decreasing (increasing) selling costs per unit with increasing (decreasing) sales volume. This assessment is short-term oriented. Of course, salary can be adjusted over time and then may also depend on a performance measure. Research is needed to find out whether this variability over time is a stronger motivator than commissions.

Commissions depend on output such as sales volume or profit contribution in an absolute form. Because of the direct link between output and reward, commissions are considered a strong motivator. On the other hand, they imply that a firm transfers part of the selling risk to their salespeople. Commissions also allow for a differentiation of commission rates across products, thereby enabling the company to direct its salesforce towards certain activities. The problem is that commissions also involve some long-term side-effects. First, commissions may lead to myopic behavior in the sense that salespeople only sell when they are immediately rewarded with a commission, but neglect effort that may lead to future sales. Moreover, salespeople may overreact by ruining their health or engaging in unethical behavior in order to earn as much money as possible. Therefore, longitudinal studies are needed to investigate the motivational effects and side-effects of commissions.

Bonuses can be given for the achievement of outcome goals as well as for providing a certain input like a certain number of visits to customers. They are not paid regularly but only when the company wants to achieve a certain goal. This provides the company with a certain flexibility because it can change the goals for getting bonuses as the selling conditions change. With bonuses it is possible to motivate salespeople for a specific behavior, like the conversion of prospects into new accounts, or to emphasize sales of a specific product that is below target. Research has to be carried out to investigate whether bonuses can correct for a dysfunctional behavior caused by commissions.

Prizes for winning sales contests are awarded for relative output or input in a sense that achievement relative to other salespeople is rewarded. High prizes that can only be won by a few salespeople provide a strong incentive and increase motivation. In addition, through the payment of relative incentives, the company can filter out any external influence that affects all salespeople in the same way. However, contests create conditions comparable to a tournament, turning the salespeople into competitors. In this case, salespeople no longer cooperate with each other, which can worsen the working climate and, as a result, lead to lower motivation. Given these contradicting effects, research is needed to find out under which circumstances contests show overall positive or negative results.

Selection of Incentives

While the discussion of advantages and disadvantages provides strategic insights into the various forms of financial incentives, it does not help decision-makers sufficiently in selecting the appropriate ones. Decision-makers have to know how strong the motivational aspects and the side-effects of the different incentives are and which costs they involve. Therefore, research has been directed to conducting surveys assessing the valence of rewards for salespeople. Studies in which salespeople have been directly asked for the desirability of various rewards suggest that money is not the strongest motivator (Churchill et al., 1979; Ford et al., 1985), contradicting the attention that sales managers have devoted to the design of compensation systems. On the other hand, there are questions about the validity of such results. Salespeople may feel it is socially desirable to underrate the importance of money in the questionnaires. Therefore, it is better to employ motivational methods that force salespeople to tradeoff different rewards or utility components. Research on such a plan by Albers (1984) involves salespeople trading off income against leisure using nonlinear conjoint analysis. However, Churchill & Pecotich (1981) show that other methods produce similar conclusions compared to conjoint analysis.

Accounting for Heterogeneity

Sales managers have observed for decades that the motivation of salespeople varies across different career stages and characteristics (Churchill et al., 1979). In particular, researchers have found the phenomenon of a performance plateau that salespeople may reach after several years and continue to stay at without prospects for future growth (Cron et al., 1988). This performance plateauing suggests tailoring incentives to the specific needs of the various salespeople. Researchers have proposed to either set individual goals and reward the degree of its achievement, or to apply menus of incentives from which salespeople can select. Both alternatives are discussed in more detail below (page 258).

7 Compensation

Goals of Compensation

Companies that use financial incentives have to decide on the specific compensation plan they want to offer to their salespeople. Developing the compensation plan involves choosing from a fixed salary, commission rates, bonuses, or prizes for winning sales contests, or combinations of those. The design of the plan should be guided by economic reasoning since compensation represents a cost factor that should result in a higher profit contribution from sales. In order to achieve the maximum profit a company has to maximize the difference between profit contribution from sales and compensation cost. While, at first glance, this may appear to be a trivial objective it is very difficult in practice to get even close to the maximum because companies have incomplete knowledge about how compensation affects effort and on how effort affects sales. Before discussing the basic principles of the determination of optimal compensation plans in later subsections, note that such plans need to meet some further requirements to ensure successful implementation (Albers 2000; Churchill et al., 1997).

First, compensation plans should be simple enough for the company to administer the plan without high cost, and for salespeople to understand the plan and the goals of the company behind it. Second, compensation schemes should also be fair so that salespeople can be assured of the specific financial rewards if they perform in the desired way. Third, compensation plans should be equitable, which means that for equal performance salespeople should be rewarded with the same financial incentives. With these considerations serving as restrictions, the company has to find the profit-contribution-maximizing compensation plan. This involves the following decisions (Albers, 1996):

- How large should the expected income for the salespeople be?
- What is the optimal form of the financial incentives contract?
- How can the company determine the optimal parameter values of the compensation plan? This also answers the basic question, which percentage of total income should be fixed (salary) or variable (commissions, bonuses and sales contest prizes)?
- If the salesforce is heterogeneous, how can the company account for it?
- How can the company use compensation to direct its salespeople to favor specific activities such as selling the more profitable instead of high-volume products?
- If the company wants to achieve specific goals other than profit from sales, how does it select the appropriate goals, and does the plan involve achieving absolute levels or relative goals?

Level of Total Income

At first glance, the determination of the level of total income appears to be an optimization problem. The income level influences the motivation of salespeople to devote effort to selling, and thereby generates the sales volume at a cost justifying this income. Actually, the chosen income level mostly depends on the labor-market for salespeople. Incomes for salespeople vary with respect to their qualifications as well as to the regions in which different situations of supply and demand exist. Good data can be obtained from organizations like Dartnell Corporation in the USA and Kienbaum in Germany. There are also some empirical studies that examine the effects of various factors on compensation level (Coughlan & Narasimhan, 1992; Krafft, 1995).

Of course, companies may follow a more competitive policy of offering higher income opportunities such as IBM did during its golden years. However, offering high levels of compensation does not mean that IBM realized higher levels of motivation. It might have allowed IBM to hire more skilled salespeople who could achieve higher profit contributions than average salespeople. It is not clear whether such a policy is generally superior. If the market reflects the economic value of different qualifications, then it should make no difference which salespeople are hired. In reality, however, there are imperfect markets and companies may capitalize on that.

Optimal Form of Contract

Having determined the total income that salespeople should receive, the next question is the optimal form of the contract with the salespeople. This decision involves the choice of an optimal combination of financial incentives. More specifically, the company has to decide what percentage of income should be provided as a variable component depending on the performance of salespeople. By making part of the income variable, the company shifts part of the selling risk to the salespeople. Obviously, if the company wants its own risk taken over by someone else, it has to pay a risk premium to its salespeople. Thus, the question is how much risk should be shifted to the salespeople given the risk premium that has to be paid for it. All these problems are addressed by agency theory (Bergen et al., 1992; Eisenhardt, 1989).

Agency theory deals with the determination of an optimal contract between a principal – the company – and an agent – the salesperson – in situations where the agent has different objectives than the principal. This situation characterizes the salesperson–company relationship. A firm generally maximizes contribution from sales, while the salespeople maximize their utility from income minus disutility from working time. If there is no uncertainty, a firm can set up a so-called forced contract requiring the salespeople to do exactly what has been specified and paying an income only if the salespeople act as required. In the context of a salesforce such a forcing contract cannot be implemented for the following reasons. In general, sales management cannot observe the behavior of salespeople and, in addition, cannot infer behavior from sales success because there is no deterministic relationship between effort and sales (Albers, 1996). Many other factors influence sales, turning the relationship between sales and effort into a stochastic one.

A forcing contract involves on the one hand the risk for the company that the salespeople may not be able to sell the desired amount of products, and on the other hand, the risk for the salespeople that they may not obtain the desired rewards when they have devoted some level of effort to selling. With a variable income depending on sales volume the firm can shift part of its risk to the salespeople. This is not a trivial task since both parties may exhibit different risk attitudes. In general, the salespeople are considered to be more risk averse than the company because they cannot diversify the selling risk, whereas the company can do this across all of its salespeople. Now, agency theory provides an instrument to derive the optimal contract between the company and the salespeople, including the optimal split between a fixed salary and the variable components such as commissions.

Based on the work of Holmstrom (1979), Basu, Lal, Srinivasan, and Staelin (hereafter cited as BLSS) were the first to build a model for deriving the optimal form of a contract for salespeople (BLSS, 1985). They assume a risk neutral company that knows the response function of sales depending on effort by the salespeople. Of course, this relationship is stochastic. The company's objective is to maximize expected profit from sales minus cost from the compensation plan. Since a company can only hire salespeople if it pays according to market conditions, the compensation plan should guarantee a so-called minimum utility salespeople can achieve with alternative employments. More specifically, this means that the expected utility from income, which itself stochastically results from the effort decision by salespeople, minus the disutility from the required working time, should be greater than a minimum utility achievable on the market. Finally, a constraint is needed which postulates that the salespeople choose an effort level that maximizes their risk utility function. This can be incorporated as the constraint that the first derivative of this risk utility function has to be equal to 0.

Based on the assumption that the density function of the sales response is either gamma or binomial distributed, BLSS (1985) obtain a general solution that proposes to reward salespeople with a fixed and a variable component, thereby not fully shifting the risk to salespeople. The variable part may increase progressively in a linear form, or degressively, with sales depending on the risk aversion of salespeople. This result implies either a constant commission rate or an increasing or decreasing sliding commission rate function, which, in practical applications, is very often approximated by a piecewise linear function. In the case of constant risk aversion a decreasing commission rate function is optimal. All these plans have been empirically observed (Coughlan & Narasimhan, 1992; Krafft, 1995).

Even when nonlinear compensation turns out to be optimal, there are reasons for working with simpler plans. Plans with a fixed salary and a constant commission rate are simple to administer, easy to understand by salespeople, and very often not far from optimality (Basu & Kalyanaram, 1990). Even better are plans with a salary and a bonus for exceeding a certain sales quota, since they preserve the nonlinear nature of the BLSS solution and result in a sub-optimality of less than 1%, while the linear plan involves 8% on average (Raju & Srinivasan, 1996). However, nonlinear plans may motivate salespeople to vary effort over time in order to exploit the advantages of an intertemporal allocation (Lal & Srinivasan, 1993).

Finally, the BLSS model does not deal with the optimal compensation interval and with intertemporal interdependencies. Fudenberg et al. (1990) found that incentive pay should optimally be rewarded within the time horizon during which the actual outcomes are achieved. If there are intertemporal interdependencies in the sales response, the BLSS plan must be modified. For example, Dearden & Lilien (1990) demonstrate that, in a production learning-curve situation, commission rates should be set higher in the first period than would be optimal for a myopic firm.

The BLSS model, and the simplified one by Lal & Srinivasan (1993), have been used to derive general recommendations with respect to the form of the compensation plan and its adaptation to situational variables. How does the contract form change with higher uncertainty or more effective salespeople? These comparative static investigations suggest that the higher the uncertainty, the higher the fixed component should be, and that the more effective salespeople, the higher the variable component should be. Although this provides some basic insights into the structure of compensation plans it does not give quantitative results with respect to the exact levels of their components which are necessary for implementing compensation plans in practice.

Determining Exact Parameter Values of the Compensation Plan

In practical applications, one must determine the optimal parameter values that describe the shape of the compensation scheme. This specification can only be achieved if the company is able to specify the response function as well as the risk utility function of its salespeople. If the company has good subjective estimates from past experience, it may numerically solve the agency theoretic model, although such applications have not been reported so far. One reason may be that a closer investigation of the solutions by BLSS (1985), as well as Lal &

Table 10.2 *Optimal Form of Contracts for Salespeoples Derived from Agency Theory*

	Homogeneous salesforce	Heterogeneous salesforce
Information symmetry	(1) Fixed salary plus nonlinear commission rate function (BLSS, 1985)	(2) Fixed salary plus bonus for quota achievement level (Rao, 1990)
Information asymmetry	(3) Menu of contracts of form (1) (Gonik, 1978; Mantrala & Raman, 1990)	(4) Menu of contracts of form (2) (Lal & Staelin, 1986, Rao, 1990)

Srinivasan (1993), shows that in the case of high uncertainty, the optimal commission rate approaches the gross margin, which leaves a profit for the firm only if the fixed salary is negative (Albers, 1996). Although such a solution is sometimes observed in practice as a selling leasing contract, in which salespeople have to pay for the harvesting of a territory, this solution rarely occurs in practice. It therefore remains an open question why companies use plans with a positive fixed salary. In addition, the solution by BLSS implies that the optimal level of selling time approaches zero with increasing uncertainty. This result is also implausible, because salespeople with zero sales volume would be dismissed after the accounting period (Albers, 1996). Therefore, the basic model has been extended by introducing monitoring which, on the one hand, allows for lower incentive pay, but on the other, involves additional monitoring costs (Joseph & Thevaranjan, 1998). In a more recent paper the same authors offer a solution that simultaneously provides the optimal incentive level as well as the optimal monitoring level (Joseph & Thevaranjan, 1999). While these extensions solve some problems, it has not been empirically demonstrated that these models arrive at meaningful percentages of fixed to total income. Therefore one may suspect that there are issues still left unresearched by agency theory. In order to really get actionable results one needs an extension of these models such that the resulting levels of fixed salary as a percentage of total income are near to what industry is actually practicing (Albers, 1996).

Without an operational optimization model, the company has to rely on industry practice and may consult the same surveys already mentioned with respect to total income. Although professional surveys by Dartnell in the USA and Kienbaum in Germany break down percentages of variable income by sales position and industry, they do not investigate in detail which factors influence the choice of the percentage of the variable income. This is done in several empirical studies that test theoretical propositions. John and Weitz (1989) test transaction-cost theory in a cross-section of companies, and find that the percentage of fixed salary is higher when salespeople can be replaced and there is not a suitable output performance measure, while the size of the salesforce, contrary to the authors' hypothesis, is negatively related to fixed compensation.

Coughlan and Narasimhan (1992), Lal et al. (1994), Joseph and Kalwani (1995a) as well as Krafft et al. (1998) have tested agency theory empirically and found support for the propositions that the percentage of fixed to total income increases with education and tenure, but decreases with effectiveness of salespeople. It is interesting to note that the postulated positive influence of uncertainty and risk aversion on the percentage of fixed income is supported only in the studies by Lal et al. (1994) and Joseph and Kalwani (1995a), while the other studies are either inconclusive or show the opposite direction. In another study, the propositions of agency theory have been tested in controlled laboratory experiments creating the same conditions as in the BLSS model for a manager who wants to compensate his insurance agents (Umanath et al., 1993). The results confirm the finding that managers increase the percentage of variable income with increasing salesperson effectiveness, but disconfirm again that managers increase the percentage of fixed income with increasing environmental uncertainty. Ghosh & John (2000) found in other experiments that the prescriptions of agency theory are only supported in situations with risk-averse agents that undertake nonverifiable effort. The constant disconfirmation of the agency hypothesis with respect to uncertainty calls for research on the kind of uncertainty involved and other effects on the sign of the relationship.

Accounting for Heterogeneity and Information Asymmetry

The BLSS model (1985) assumes a relationship between the company and just one salesperson which implies homogeneity in the salesforce. In practice, however, salespeople differ in their abilities, selling skills, and motivation. Furthermore, salespeople may face different conditions in their sales territories which are due to external influences (Ryans & Weinberg, 1979, 1987). Finally, BLSS assume information symmetry, which means that the management knows, or can at least subjectively estimate, the response functions in each territory and the utility function of each salesperson. Of course, this is very often not the case. If these assumptions are relaxed and one distinguishes between the four combinations of homogeneity or heterogeneity with information symmetry or information asymmetry, one arrives at different forms for the incentive contract with salespeople, as shown in Table 10.2 (Albers, 1996).

When moving from a homogeneous to a heterogeneous salesforce, it would be ideal to work with idiosyncratic compensation plans that are individually optimized for each salespeople. Unfortunately, such a solution would violate equity considerations. Just because salespeople differ in their risk attitudes, utility functions with respect to income, and disutility with respect to working time, this cannot justify different compensation. In order not to destroy the morale of a salesforce, compensation must provide equal financial rewards for equal performance (Tyagi, 1990). This can be achieved by offering a fixed salary and a bonus which is no longer based on absolute sales volume (commission), but instead on relative quota achievement, where the quota reflects territorial differences beyond the control of individual salespeople (Rao, 1990). Raju and Srinivasan (1996) argue for a bonus function which only rewards quota overfulfillment to better capture the general BLSS solution.

If, in addition, management faces information asymmetry, then the company should apply menus of compensation plans from which the salespeople can select (Rao, 1990). A menu of compensation plans may be especially useful if the company employs salespeople with different levels of risk attitude. It may offer plans with high salary and low commissions as well as plans with a low salary and high commissions. The choice of a compensation plan also reveals each salesperson's sales response function and utility function. The logic of such menus is described by Lal & Staelin (1986). In the case of quotas, the company may be able to determine equitable quotas although it does not know the appropriate one for the individual salesperson. Therefore, it may offer a menu of quotas to be accepted by salespeople and bonuses for their achievement. Such a system is called the New Soviet Incentive system and will be described in more detail below.

Generally it is agreed that quotas should be high enough to represent real challenges but low enough so that they can really be reached. Otherwise, salespeople may become frustrated and perform even worse than without quotas. Motivational effects of quotas have been empirically investigated by Chowdhury (1993), who shows that salespeople increase effort with increasing quotas only up to a certain point, after which effort may even decrease with increasing quota levels. Quotas also influence the risk-taking behavior of salespeople in a way that salespeople who have already met the quota call on risky prospects, while salespeople who expect not to meet the quota tend to be risk averse (Ross, 1991). Gaba & Kalra (1999) find in five experiments that salespeople facing high (low) quotas engage in high-risk (low-risk) behavior. In order to develop effective quotas, the company must first ensure that quotas are equitable across territories and, second, to have quotas that are highly motivating but also as realistic as possible. Albers (1996) describes how such quotas can be determined.

The first step is to calibrate a response function of sales volume of an average salesperson depending on exogenous factors. Such a response function is best estimated by taking actual sales volume as the dependent variable and regressing it against the levels of relevant exogenous factors across all territories, such as in Ryans & Weinberg (1979, 1987). After having estimated the required parameter values of the response function, one can calculate the sales quotas by inserting the respective values for the exogenous factors as given in the various territories into the sales response function. This quota level represents the sales that can be expected from an average salesperson under the specific conditions in the various territories. These sales quotas are fair because they are equitable across territories. However, these quotas may not represent challenging targets. In particular, equitable quotas may even be below the currently achieved sales volumes. Thus, these quotas may be unrealistic and cannot be used for further planning purposes like adjusting the number of back-office personnel and determining the product capacity.

As a second step it is therefore necessary to offer a menu of quotas and bonuses from which salespeople can select the combination that they prefer. In order to be able to plan all other firm activities on the basis of accurate sales forecasts, the firm may also be interested in inducing salespeople to reveal their expected sales volume beforehand. There is one bonus system that fulfills all of these requirements. It starts with a prespecified quota q that the firm assumes to be fair and realistic (from step 1, above). It then allows the salespeople to agree to a quota Q that they think can be realistically achieved. In order to provide an incentive to choose a quota Q as high as their expected sales volume, the increase of the agreed quota Q over the prespecified one q is rewarded. However, if they do not meet the agreed quota later on, they will be penalized. If salespeople have underestimated sales, they should still get some reward for overfulfillment. This bonus system is identical to the New Soviet Incentive scheme (Weitzman, 1977) but gained popularity from the description of an application by IBM Brazil (Gonik, 1978). Mantrala & Raman (1990) show that it is in the best interest of salespeople to provide the highest sales quota they think they can realize. Unfortunately, the quotas accepted by salespeople heavily depend on their risk attitudes. If salespeople are highly risk averse, they will not accept a high sales quota. However, the relative difference of the bonuses and penalties can be used for influencing the risk attitude of salespeople.

This is a two-step procedure. Other researchers like Darmon (1987) and Mantrala et al. (1994) have proposed to implicitly infer the utility function of the salespeople by providing them with different combinations of quotas and bonuses and asking them for a preference order. Similarly, it is possible to learn about the unknown characteristics of a territory from the application of sales quota-bonus plans over a multi-period time horizon (Mantrala et al., 1997). Thus, it becomes possible simultaneously to derive the optimal quota levels and the optimal plan for compensating the different levels of quota achievement. While this approach provides a very operational method, Darmon does not deal with the equity of his bonus system. His optimization is restricted to a search for a common bonus function for overfulfillment of quotas that he assumes to be the current sales volume. This does not account for heterogeneity, but Darmon's framework is flexible enough to accommodate other bonus functions as well as utility functions of salespeople.

Optimal Differentiation of Compensation Plans for Directing the Allocation Decisions of Salespeople

If salespeople are responsible for selling multiple products to a set of customers, they have to allocate their selling time across both products and customers/prospects. If there are different gross margins across products, the firm must be interested in directing its salespeople to emphasize selling the most profitable products. The same situation arises if margins vary across customers. In addition, there is a conflict between the comfortable selling to established accounts and the more time-consuming and uncertain prospecting of new customers. The company may try to direct the allocation decision of salespeople by differentiating either commission rates or bonuses across products and/or customers.

In a pioneering article, Farley (1964) investigated what kinds of commissions are incentive compatible when there are differences in profitability across products. Based on the assumption of income maximizing salespeople, he demonstrates that the commission rates should be proportional to gross margins. This is a very attractive result because it is a simple rule that does not require knowledge of the true shape of the sales response functions. Later on, it has been shown that Farley's result holds even if one considers other plausible utility functions (Weinberg, 1978), or a dynamic problem with response depending on current as well as previous periods (Tapiero & Farley, 1975). If pricing authority is delegated to salespeople, Weinberg (1975) shows that commission rates based on realized profits (gross margin minus discounts) are still incentive compatible. However, it should be noted that an empirical investigation shows that full delegation of pricing authority is inferior to a restricted delegation, because salespeople tend to focus too much on price (Stephenson et al., 1979). Bhardwaj (2001) questions this result with the help of a theoretical investigation. In his model delegation is profitable under intense price competition because salespeople set higher prices.

The problem with Farley's solution is that it only provides the *relative* levels of the commission rates but not the absolute ones. Srinivasan (1981) was the first who tried to simultaneously determine the optimal level of the commission rates as well as the optimal differentiation across products. He proves that Farley's result no longer holds if the total time devoted to selling also depends on the commission rates. For a disutility function linear in selling time, Srinivasan shows that commission rates should be proportional to gross margins and sales elasticity with respect to selling time.

In the studies discussed so far, the authors have assumed deterministic relationships between sales and effort. Berger (1972) was the first to show that Farley's result is still valid for the stochastic case as long as utility is linear in income. If this assumption is relaxed it can only be shown that optimal commission rates depend on gross margin and the variance of the sales response. This is, however, not operational for implementations (Berger & Jaffe, 1991). Lal & Srinivasan (1993) extended their simplified BLSS model to the multiple-product case and find that commission rates expressed as percentages of gross margins for the various products should follow the same rank order as the selling effectiveness of effort per unit divided by standard deviation of sales. Finally, Zhang & Mahajan (1995) extend the work by Lal & Srinivasan (1993) to finding the optimal contract for multiple interdependent products in the original BLSS framework.

The above mentioned results refer to homogenous salesforces. If a company has a heterogeneous salesforce then heterogeneity can be captured through an optimal bonus function for quota achievement of multiple products. Mantrala et al. (1994) are the only ones to have proposed a solution for this problem so far. It is similar to QUOPLAN by Darmon (1987), in that it uses conjoint analysis for inferring the parameter values of the utility functions of the salespeople. Having obtained valid estimates for the parameter values, the authors apply the usual agency theoretic approach without the uncertainty issue. Since their model involves an allocation problem they first infer the selling time necessary to achieve a certain sales quota. In the next step, the utility function is estimated from preference judgments for different combinations of quotas per product and the corresponding quotas. Mantrala et al. claim to be able to optimize any bonus function on quota achievement. They describe applications in two pharmaceutical companies with two and four products, respectively. However, the individual quotas have been specified at a certain percentage of maximum sales, which is questionable with respect to equity. This model represents the most comprehensive and applicable approach for salesforce compensation at the moment. From the application it becomes clear that the optimal differentiation of incentives tends to produce extreme solutions which might be questionable in practice. In order to avoid this condition, Mantrala et al. (1994) present as the optimum a bonus function depending on joint quota achievement (multiplied by each other) for two products of significantly different size.

Achieving Specific Behaviors with Bonuses and Sales Contests

If the regular compensation system does not achieve an optimal level and allocation of effort by the salespeople on the various selling tasks, then the company may work with short-term incentives that reward specific behaviors (Good & Stone, 1991; Joseph & Kalwani, 1995b). If, for example, the acquisition of new accounts is not satisfactory because it involves a high risk and salespeople prefer to achieve more probable sales from existing accounts, and if salespeople are more myopic than the firm, then the company may be forced to provide specific rewards for the acquisition of new accounts. Otherwise it may lose the basis for future sales. Or if sales volume tends to fall behind expectations then it might be a good idea to provide special rewards for achieving short-term increases of sales volume. In such cases the company may work with rewards that are based on the achievement of a specific goal. The question is whether to base the rewards on the achievement of absolute or relative results.

In the case of absolute results, the company could specify, for example, a bonus of x if salespeople acquired new accounts. The advantage is that the company only has to pay the bonuses if salespeople really reach the specified quota. This approach is a very effective method of motivating salespeople to concentrate on specific tasks. The alternative is to reward the top x percent of salespeople depending on the achieved results. This approach creates a sales contest, and is very often applied in practice (Murphy & Dacin, 1998).

The popularity of sales contests stems from a twofold effect. Salespeople not only get financial incentives when performing very well, but they also gain recognition within the company and sometimes even outside. Good salespeople can be kept within the company even in situations of a poor industry climate for which individual salespeople are not responsible. Despite the popularity of sales contests, little is known about how to design them and about their effectiveness (Wildt et al., 1980/81). With the exception of a few empirical studies (Wildt et al., 1987; Wotruba & Schoel, 1983), all reported effects are theoretical. Sales contests are often used in order to achieve important short-term goals. With their double motivation and explicit focus on specific behavior, sales contests often have stronger effects than regular incentives. Thus, the question is not so much whether one achieves the goals of the contest but rather, which side-effects occur. Contests may lead salespeople to over-allocate effort to the tasks rewarded by the contest, thereby neglecting their regular selling tasks. This dysfunctional result may lead, for example, to a sales boom during the contest that borrows sales from the future. In addition, contests put all salespeople into rivalry. This competition may enhance motivation but also creates a more competitive climate with more reluctance to help each other. Gaba & Kalra (1999) show with the help of five experiments that salespeople may engage in high-risk (low-risk) behavior if only few (many) salespeople can become winners. Thus, it is still not clear what the best format for a sales contest is. What percentage of salespeople should win a prize? Should individuals, teams or both compete? How long should a contest last? These questions have been addressed by tournament theory (Lazear & Rosen, 1981; Nalebuff & Stiglitz, 1983). This theory shows that contests are attractive when there is the danger of collusion. Of course, participants should be as similar as possible, otherwise it is clear beforehand who is going to win the prizes. Tournaments are superior to incentives on absolute individual performance as long as there is a common changing environment. Otherwise contracts are better (Green & Stokey, 1983). Tournaments are also superior to the Multiple-Winners format because of motivating salespeople to fight for the best position possible outcome. If the participating salespeople are risk-averse it is favorable to increase the number of winners and to decrease the spread of prizes. Only in the case of risk-neutral salespeople is the winner-take-all format optimal

(Kalra & Shi, 2001). Empirical research is needed that tests these propositions. Because of the many complex behaviors involved, the best way of assessing the effectiveness of contests is to set up experiments with groups selling under different contest conditions.

Team Incentives

More and more, selling is not done by individual salespeople, but by selling teams (Jackson et al., 1999). For example, a salesperson is accompanied by an expert with specific product knowledge. A salesperson geographically responsible for a certain outlet of a customer is accompanied by the national account manager. Salespeople may form a team with back-end personnel responsible for working out engineering solutions and preparing offers. In all these cases, the output cannot be attributed to the effort of individuals. As a result, incentives have to be based on team rather than individual performance. Research is needed that proposes optimal compensation plans for teams (Moon & Armstrong, 1994). We only know from theory that we have to deal with the problem of free-riding behavior (Holmstrom, 1982). People with high disutility for working time may decide not to provide the appropriate effort because they rely on the effort of other persons, which results in a good income for a low level of effort. Such a behavior can only be avoided if the individual's contribution to the success of the team can be distinguished. Otherwise it is only possible to pay for team output, and have sales management monitor the team and dismiss any salespeople under suspicion of free-riding behavior.

8 Summary and Conclusions

Working with salespeople as a communication channel involves the task of managing the resource of human beings. This involves hiring the highest performing people, training them in effective selling, and motivating them to devote their best effort to selling. All these activities require a deep understanding of the problems of performance measurement. If one is only interested in general insights then it may be sufficient to operationalize output and input in a suitable way and to run structural equation models for explaining output by input measures. If the goal is, however, an individual performance assessment for the purpose of selection, training, and incentive determination, then one needs fair and equitable methods that attribute outputs only to controllable inputs and not to external factors. While regression analysis finds a relationship between sales and effort that is based on an average salesperson, it might be more helpful to estimate a common efficient frontier or individual degrees of efficiency by data envelopment analysis.

An important management task is to staff the salesforce with the highest performing salespeople. Unfortunately, there are only low correlations between characteristics of salespeople and performance. Therefore, the predictive validity of many traditional tools of selecting employees, such as application forms, biographical data, and interviews, is low. Only ability composite tests and assessment centers are promising. Companies are advised to constantly monitor the predictive validity of its selection methods by regressing actual performance of the existing salespeople against evaluations at the time of their selection. This can provide insights into possible improvements of the selection procedure. Salespeople need good training with respect to product, company, and market knowledge, as well as selling skills and time and territory management. It is not so much the *level* of the budget but the right choice of the content and methods, together with a good *allocation* of the budget that influences profitability. If salespeople turn out to be low performers, and training does not improve results, then a company has to decide whether to dismiss such salespeople. Given the high recruiting and dismissal costs, management should determine the critical level of performance below which the benefits of new and potentially better performing salespeople outweigh the costs of dismissal and recruitment.

Even well-trained salespeople have to be motivated to devote the highest possible effort to selling. While intrinsically motivated salespeople only require good working conditions and a rich job, extrinsically motivated people demand recognition mostly through financial incentives. In practice, many forms of financial incentives are offered, such as fixed salary, commissions, bonuses, and prizes for winning sales contests. When to use them can be explained by classifying them into fixed and variable incentives, and the latter into those based on absolute output measures such as sales volume versus those based on relative measures such as individual quota achievement or rank among colleagues. Optimal combinations of incentives require the estimation of a utility function of salespeople to know about their tradeoff with respect to the combined elements. If a salesforce is heterogeneous, then it is necessary to account for different external influences and preferences. This can be done by either basing compensation on relative output measures or by offering menus of compensation plans from which salespeople can choose.

The design of compensation plans also involves a decision on the level of total income which depends on the labor market as well as an assessment whether only high-performing people should be employed at high cost. In addition, the company has to decide on the percentage of income that should be provided as variable incentives depending on the output. This represents a shift of risk from the company to salespeople, which is only possible if a risk premium is paid. Agency theory suggests optimal contracts, trading off the risk premium against profit contribution from higher effort because of higher income opportunities. Unfortunately, agency theory does not yet provide plausible solutions that are implementable in practice, which calls for more research on the optimal design of suitable compensation plans. In the case of heterogeneity, a bonus payment on the achievement of quotas is the appropriate incentive. Fair and equitable quotas can only be calculated if one determines the functional relationship between output and external influences such as sales potential and dispersion of the territory. This allows for the calculation of the sales volume that an average salesperson should achieve in a certain territory with given external influences. In addition, salespeople should be motivated with the help of the Weitzman scheme to accept the highest quota that salespeople believe to be achievable. Moreover, bonuses can be used for rewarding specific behavior such as the acquisition of new accounts. Sales contests are an even stronger motivation tool. However, their effects are not quite clear, because they support competitive rather than collaborative behavior among salespeople and may lead to overreactions. The most difficult task is the design of compensation plans for selling teams. They can only be compensated on the basis of team output, which provokes free-riding behavior.

References

Albers, S. (1984) Fully nonmetric estimation of a continuous nonlinear conjoint utility function. *International Journal of Research in Marketing*, 1, 311–19.

——— (1996) Optimisation models for salesforce compensation. *European Journal of Operational Research*, 89, 1–17.

——— (2000) Sales-force management. In *The Oxford Textbook of Marketing*, edited by K. Blois. Oxford: Oxford University Press, pp. 292–317.

Anderson, E. & Oliver, R.L. (1987) Perspectives on behavior-based versus outcome-based salesforce control systems. *Journal of Marketing*, 51 (October), 76–88.

Anderson, R.E. (1996) Personal selling and sales management in the new millennium. *Journal of Personal Selling and Sales Management*, 6 (4), 17–32.

Babakus, E., Cravens, D.W., Grant, K., Ingram, T.N. & LaForge, R.W. (1996) Investigating the relationships among sales, management control, sales territory design, salesperson performance, and sales organization effectiveness. *International Journal of Research in Marketing*, 13, 345–63.

Basu, A.K. & Kalyanaram, G. (1990) On the relative performance of linear versus nonlinear compensation plans. *International Journal of Research in Marketing*, 7 (2–3), 171–8.

Basu, A.K., Lal, R., Srinivasan, V. & Staelin, R. (1985) Salesforce compensation plans: an agency theoretic perspective. *Marketing Science*, 4, 267–91.

Behrman, D.N. & Perreault, W.D. Jr. (1982) Measuring the performance of industrial salespersons. *Journal of Business Research*, 10, 355–70.

Bergen, M., Dutta, S. & Walker, O.C. (1992) Agency relationships in marketing: a review of the implications and applications of agency and related theories. *Journal of Marketing*, 56 (July), 1–24.

Berger, P.D. (1972) On setting optimal sales commissions. *Operations Research Quarterly*, 23, 213–15.

Berger, P.D. & Jaffe, L.J. (1991) The impact of risk attitude on the optimal compensation plan in a multi-product situation. *Journal of the Operational Research Society*, 42, 323–30.

Bhardwaj, P. (2001) Delegating pricing decisions. *Marketing Science*, 20, 143–69.

Boles, J.S., Donthu, N. & Lothia, R. (1995) Salesperson evaluation using relative performance efficiency: the application of data envelopment analysis. *Journal of Personal Selling and Sales Management*, 15 (Summer), 31–49.

Brown, S.P. & Peterson, R.A. (1993) Antecedents and consequences of salesperson job satisfaction: meta-analysis and assessment of causal effects. *Journal of Marketing Research*, 30, 63–77.

Chandrashekaran, M., McNeilly, K., Russ, F.A. & Marinova, D. (2000) From uncertain intentions to actual behavior: a threshold model of whether and when salespeople quit. *Journal of Marketing Research*, 37, 463–79.

Chowdhury, J. (1993) The motivational impact of sales quotas on effort. *Journal of Marketing Research*, 30, 28–41.

Churchill, G.A. & Pecotich, A. (1981) Determining the rewards salespeople value: a comparison of methods. *Decision Sciences*, 12, 456–70.

Churchill, G.A., Ford, N.M., Hartley, S.W. & Walker, O.C., Jr. (1985) The determinants of salesperson performance: a meta-analysis. *Journal of Marketing Research*, 22, 103–18.

Churchill, G.A., Ford, N.M. & Walker, O.C., Jr. (1979) Personal characteristics of salespeople and the attractiveness of alternative rewards. *Journal of Business Research*, 7, 25–50.

——— (1997) *Sales Force Management*, 5 edn. Homewood/Boston: Irwin.

Cocanougher, A.B. & Ivancevich, J.M. (1978) 'BARS' performance rating for sales force personnel. *Journal of Marketing*, 42 (July), 87–95.

Coughlan, A.T. (1993) Salesforce compensation: a review of MS/OR advances. In *Handbook in Operations Research and Management Science, Vol. 5: Marketing*, edited by J. Eliashberg & G.L. Lilien. Amsterdam: North-Holland, pp. 611–51.

Coughlan, A.T. & Narasimhan, C. (1992) An empirical analysis of sales-force compensation plans. *Journal of Business*, 65, 93–121.

Coughlan, A.T. & Sen, S.K. (1989) Salesforce compensation: theory and managerial implications. *Marketing Science*, 8, 324–42.

Cravens, D.W., Ingram, T.N., LaForge, R.W. & Young, C.E. (1993) Behavior-based and outcome-based salesforce control systems. *Journal of Marketing*, 57, 47–59.

Cron, W.L., Dubinsky, A.J. & Michaels, R.E. (1988) The influence of career stages on components of salesperson motivation. *Journal of Marketing*, 52 (January), 78–92.

Darmon, R.Y. (1987) QUOPLAN: a system for optimizing sales quota-bonus plans. *Journal of the Operational Research Society*, 38, 1121–32.

Dearden, J.A. & Lilien, G.L. (1990) On optimal salesforce compensation in the presence of production learning effects. *International Journal of Research in Marketing*, 7 (2–3), 179–88.

Dixon, A.L., Spiro, R.L. & Jamil, M. (2001) Successful and unsuccessful sales calls: measuring salesperson attributions and behavioral intentions. *Journal of Marketing*, 65 (July), 64–78.

Eisenhardt, K.M. (1989) Agency theory: an assessment and review. *Academy of Management Review*, 14 (1), 57–74.

El-Ansary, A.I. (1993) Sales force effectiveness research reveals new insights and reward-penalty patterns in sales force training. *Journal of Personal Selling and Sales Management*, 13 (2), 83–90.

Farley, J.U. (1964) An optimal plan for salesmen's compensation. *Journal of Marketing Research*, 1 (2), 39–43.

Fernández-Gaucherand, E., Jain, S., Lee, H.L., Rao, A.G. & Rao, M.R. (1995) Improving productivity by periodic performance evaluation: a Bayesian stochastic model. *Management Science*, 41, 1669–78.

Ford, N.M., Churchill, G.A. & Walker, O.C. Jr. (1985) Difference in the attractiveness of alternative rewards among industrial salespeople: additional evidence. *Journal of Business Research*, 13, 123–38.

Fudenberg, D., Holmstrom, B. & Milgrom, P. (1990) Short-term contracts and long-term agency relationships. *Journal of Economic Theory*, 51 (1), 1–31.

Gaba, A. & Kalra, A. (1999) Risk behavior in response to quotas and contests. *Marketing Science*, 18, 417–34.

Ganesan, S., Weitz, B.A. & John, G. (1993) Hiring and promotion policies in sales force management: some antecedents and consequences. *Journal of Personal Selling and Sales Management*, 13 (2), 15–26.

Ghosh, M. & John, G. (2000) Experimental evidence for agency models of salesforce compensation. *Marketing Science*, 19, 348–65.

Gonik, J. (1978) Tie salesmen's bonuses to their forecasts. *Harvard Business Review*, 56 (3), 116–23.

Good, D.J. & Stone, R.W. (1991) How sales quotas are developed. *Industrial Marketing Management*, 20, 51–5.

Green, J.R. & Stokey, N.L. (1983) A comparison of tournaments and contracts. *Journal of Political Economy*, 91, 349–64.

Hauser, J.R., Simester, D.I. & Wernerfelt, B. (1994) Customer satisfaction incentives. *Marketing Science*, 13, 327–50.

Holmstrom, B. (1982) Moral hazard in teams. *Bell Journal of Economics*, 13, 324–40.

Honeycutt, E.D. Jr., Ford, J.B. & Rao, C.P. (1995) Sales training: executives' research needs. *Journal of Personal Selling and Sales Management*, 15 (Fall), 67–71.

Horsky, D. & Nelson, P. (1996) Evaluation of salesforce size and productivity through efficient frontier benchmarking. *Marketing Science*, 15 (4), 301–20.

Hunter, J.E. & Hunter, R.F. (1984) Validity and utility of alternative predictors of job performance. *Psychological Bulletin*, 96, 73–96.

Ingram, T.N., Schwepker, C.H. Jr. & Hutson, D. (1992) Why salespeople fail. *Industrial Marketing Management*, 21, 225–30.

Ingram, T.N., LaForge, R.W., Schwepker, C.H., Avila, R.A. & Williams, M.R. (2000) *Sales Management – Analysis and Decision Making*, 4th edn. Chicago: The Dryden Press.

Jackson, D.W. Jr., Keith, J.E. & Schlacter, J.L. (1983) Evaluation of selling performance: a study of current practices. *Journal of Personal Selling and Sales Management*, 3 (November), 42–51.

Jackson, D.W. Jr., Schlacter, J.L. & Wolfe, W.G. (1995) Examining the bases utilized for evaluating salespeoples' performance. *Journal of Personal Selling and Sales Management*, 15 (Fall), 57–65.

Jackson, D.W. Jr., Widmier, S.M., Giacobbe, R. & Keith, J.E. (1999) Examining the use of team selling by manufacturers' representatives. *Industrial Marketing Management*, 28, 155–164.

Jacobson, R. (1990) Unobservable effects and business performance. *Marketing Science*, 9, 74–85.

John, G. & Weitz, B. (1989) Salesforce compensation: an empirical investigation of factors related to use of salary versus incentive compensation. *Journal of Marketing Research*, 26: 1–14.

Joseph, K. & Kalwani, M.U. (1995a) The impact of environmental uncertainty on the design of salesforce compensation plans. *Marketing Letters*, 6, 183–97.

——— (1995b) The role of bonus pay in salesforce compensation plans. *Industrial Marketing Management*, 27, 147–59.

Joseph, K. & Thevaranjan, A. (1998) Monitoring and incentives in sales organizations: an agency-theoretic perspective. *Marketing Science*, 17, 107–23.

——— (1999) Optimal monitoring in salesforce control systems. *Marketing Letters*, 10, 161–76.

Kalra, A. & Shi, M. (2001) Designing optimal sales contests: a theoretical perspective. *Marketing Science*, 20, 170–93.

Krafft, M. (1995). *Salesforce Compensation in the Light of the New Institutional Theories* (in German). Wiesbaden: Gabler Verlag.

——— (1999) An empirical investigation of the antecedents of sales force control systems. *Journal of Marketing*, 63 (3), 120–34.

Krafft, M., Lal, R. & Albers, S. (1998) Relative explanatory power of agency theory and transaction cost analysis in german salesforces. Working Paper, University of Kiel.

Lal, R. & Srinivasan, V. (1993) Compensation plans for single- and multi-product salesforces: an application of the Holmstrom-Milgrom model. *Management Science*, 39, 777–93.

Lal, R. & Staelin, R. (1986) Salesforce compensation plans in environments with asymmetric information. *Marketing Science*, 5, 179–98.

Lal, R., Outland, D. & Staelin, R. (1994) Salesforce compensation plans: an individual-level analysis. *Marketing Letters*, 5, 117–30.

Lazear, E.P. & Rosen, S. (1981) Rank-order tournaments as optimum labor contracts. *Journal of Political Economy*, 89, 841–64.

Mahajan, J. (1991) A data envelopment analytic model for assessing the relative efficiency of the selling function. *European Journal of Operational Research*, 53, 189–205.

Mantrala, M.K. & Raman, K. (1990) Analysis of a salesforce-incentive plan for accurate sales forecasting and performance. *International Journal of Research in Marketing*, 7, 189–202.

Mantrala, M.K., Raman, K. & Desiraju, R. (1997) Sales quota plans: mechanisms for adaptive learning. *Marketing Letters*, 8, 393–405.

Mantrala, M., Sinha, P. & Zoltners, A.A. (1994) Structuring a multiproduct sales quota-bonus plan for a heterogeneous salesforce: a practical approach. *Marketing Science*, 13, 121–44.

Marshall, G.W., Moncrief, W.C. & Lassk, F.G. (1999) The current state of sales force activities. *Industrial Marketing Management*, 28, 87–98.

Mason, J.L. (1965) The low prestige of personal selling. *Journal of Marketing*, 29 (4), 7–10.

Moncrief, W.C., Hart, S.H. & Robertson, D. (1988) Sales contests: a new look at an old management tool. *Journal of Personal Selling and Sales Management*, 8 (November), 55–61.

Moon, M.A. & Armstrong, G.M. (1994) Selling teams: a conceptual framework and research agenda. *Journal of Personal Selling and Sales Management*, 14 (1), 17–30.

Morris, M.H., LaForge, R.W. & Allen, J.A. (1994) Salesperson failure: definition, determinants, and outcomes. *Journal of Personal Selling and Sales Management*, 14 (1), 1–15.

Munkelt, I. (1992) Offers by sales trainers, (in German). *Absatzwirtschaft*, 7, 64–81.

Murphy, W.H. & Dacin, P.A. (1998) Sales contests: a research agenda. *Journal of Personal Selling and Sales Management*, 18 (Winter), 1–16.

Nalebuff, B. & Stiglitz, J. (1983) Prizes and incentives: towards a general theory of compensation and competition. *Bell Journal of Economics*, 14 (Spring), 21–43.

Oliver, R.L. & Anderson, E. (1994) An empirical test of the consequences of behavior-and outcome-based sales control systems. *Journal of Marketing*, 58 (4), 53–68.

Patton, W.E. III & King, R.H. (1992) The use of human judgement models in sales force selection decisions. *Journal of Personal Selling and Sales Management*, 12 (Spring), 1–14.

Raju, J.S. & Srinivasan, V. (1996) Quota-based compensation plans for multiterritory heterogeneous salesforces. *Management Science*, 42, 1454–62.

Ramaswami, S.N., Srinivasan, S.S. & Gorton, S.A. (1997) Information asymmetry between salesperson and supervisor: postulates from agency and social exchange theories. *Journal of Personal Selling and Sales Management*, 17 (3), 29–50.

Randall, E.J. & Randall, C.H. (1990) Review of salesperson selection techniques and criteria: a managerial approach. *International Journal of Research in Marketing*, 7, 81–95.

Rao, R.C. (1990) Compensating heterogeneous salesforces: some explicit solutions. *Marketing Science*, 10, 319–41.

Ross, W.T., Jr. (1991) Performance against quota and the call selection decision. *Journal of Marketing Research*, 28, 296–306.

Ryans, A.B. & Weinberg, C.B. (1979) Territory sales response. *Journal of Marketing Research*, 16, 453–65.

——— (1987) Territory sales response models: stability over time. *Journal of Marketing Research*, 24, 229–33.

Shapiro, C. & Varian, H.R. (1999) *Information Rules. A Strategic Guide to the Network Economy*. Boston, MA: Harvard Business School Press.

Sharma, A. (1997) Customer satisfaction-based incentive systems: some managerial and salesperson considerations. *Journal of Personal Selling and Sales Management*, 17 (2), 61–70.

Siebel, T.M. & Malone, M.S. (1996) *Virtual Selling – Going Beyond the Automated Sales Force to Achieve Total Sales Quality*. New York: The Free Press.

Skiera, B. & Albers, S. (1998) COSTA: contribution optimizing sales territory alignment. *Marketing Science*, 17, 196–213.

Srinivasan, V. (1981) An investigation of the equal commission rate policy for a multi-product salesforce. *Management Science*, 27, 731–56.

Stephenson, P.R., Cron, W.L. & Frazier, G.L. (1979) Delegating pricing authority to the sales force: the effects on sales and profit performance. *Journal of Marketing*, 43 (2), 21–28.

Tapiero, C.S. & Farley, J.U. (1975) Optimal control of salesforce effort in time. *Management Science*, 21, 976–85.

Teas, R.K. & McElroy, J.C. (1986) Causal attributions and expectancy estimates: a framework for understanding the dynamics of salesforce motivation. *Journal of Marketing*, 50 (1), 75–86.

Tull, D.S., Wood, V.R., Duhan, D., Gillpatrick, T., Robertson, K.R. & Helgeson, J.G. (1986) 'Leveraged' decision making in advertising: the flat maximum principle and its implications. *Journal of Marketing Research*, 23, 25–32.

Tyagi, P.K. (1985) Relative importance of key job dimensions and leadership behaviors in motivating salesperson work performance. *Journal of Marketing*, 49 (3), 76–86.

——— (1990) Inequities in organizations, salesperson motivation and job satisfaction. *International Journal of Research in Marketing*, 7, 135–48.

Umanath, N.S., Ray, M.R. & Campbell, T.L. (1993) The impact of perceived environmental uncertainty and perceived agent effectiveness on the composition of compensation contracts. *Management Science*, 39, 32–45.

Walker, O.C., Jr. Churchill, G.A., Jr. & Ford, N.M. (1977) Motivation and performance in industrial selling: present knowledge and needed research. *Journal of Marketing Research*, 14, 156–68.

Weinberg, C.B. (1975) An optimal commission plan for salesmen's control over price. *Management Science*, 21, 937–43.

——— (1978) Jointly optimal sales commissions for non-income maximizing salesforces. *Management Science*, 24, 1252–8.

Weitz, B.A., Sujan, H. & Sujan, M. (1986) Knowledge, motivation, and adaptive behavior: a framework for improving selling effectiveness. *Journal of Marketing*, 50 (4), 174–6.

Weitzman, M.L. (1977) The New Soviet Incentive model. *Bell Journal of Economics*, 7 (1), 251–7.

Wildt, A.R., Parker, J.D. & Harris, C.E., Jr. (1980/81) sales contest: what we know and what we need to know. *Journal of Personal Selling and Sales Management*, 1 (Fall/Winter), 57–64.

——— (1987) assessing the impact of sales-force contests: an application. *Journal of Business Research*, 15, 145–55.

Wotruba, T.R. & Schoel, D.J. (1983) Evaluation of salesforce contest performance. *Journal of Personal Selling and Sales Management*, 3 (1), 1–10.

Zhang, C. & Mahajan, V. (1995) Development of optimal salesforce compensation plans for independent, complementary and substitutable products. *International Journal of Research in Marketing*, 12, 355–62.

11

Pricing: Economic and Behavioral Models

CHEZY OFIR and RUSSELL S. WINER

Introduction

A major focus of academic research in marketing has been on what have traditionally been referred to as the marketing mix variables. Research on pricing, advertising, channels of distribution, sales promotion, and product policy (e.g., branding) are naturally important areas for research, as these are key decisions that marketing managers have to make. As an applied field, marketing has an obligation to perform not only basic research (e.g., how do buyers process information for new technological goods?) but also research that has the potential to help our practitioner counterparts do a better job.

The area of price, in particular, has been an extremely fertile ground for new concepts and methods. Not only is the number of papers published on the topic numerous, but a variety of edited volumes (see, for example, Devinney, 1988) and textbooks (Dolan & Simon, 1996; Monroe, 1990; Nagle & Holden, 2002) do an excellent job summarizing extant research and integrating it into marketing decision-making.

Pricing has received so much attention not only because of its key role in business but also because of its interdisciplinary nature. Academic researchers can and have attacked pricing issues from a traditional economics perspective, but also from a behavioral science perspective by incorporating psychological theories, constructs, and measurement tools into the research.

Given the many papers and books published on the topic of pricing, we decided to focus this chapter on the work that has been done within the last five years (the first section, on estimating price thresholds, is an exception). Even during this narrow time span, researchers have produced work that spans the set of topics covered in previous years, and have added some new perspectives. The areas covered in this chapter include:

- *Measurement and scaling issues:* An important basic question in pricing is how do we measure price response? Since the pioneering work of British researchers Gabor and Granger on price awareness and willingness-to-pay, researchers have developed more sophisticated approaches to price response measurement, such as price thresholds.
- *Behavioral models*: The classic approach to pricing is through the applications of microeconomic principles, as economists have been interested in the market clearing role of price for centuries. However, it is only relatively recently that academic researchers have looked to psychology to help understand that consumers are not simply price takers but actively process price information.
- *Empirical models*: Price and price-related promotions are routinely incorporated into brand choice models and other empirical research. This has been and continues to be the largest component of the academic body of work in marketing.
- *Competitive/normative models*: The last 10–15 years have witnessed the rapid diffusion of game theory into marketing. This set of work, although rather theoretical in nature, is a welcome addition to the literature because of

the importance of bringing competition into the models.

- *Pricing and the Internet*: The rapid growth of the Internet as a distribution and information channel has spawned interest in research on pricing issues in this context. With fixed prices rapidly disappearing in favor of a number of formats including auctions, the opportunities for price personalization, and the widespread availability of price comparison web services, a very interesting new avenue for research has opened up.

Measurement/Scaling Issues

Academic and applied researchers often measure consumer price knowledge and consumers' response to prices. This is essential for managers in the process of designing pricing and marketing strategies, and is an integral part of academic pricing research. Interestingly, although price response measurement is one of the oldest areas of pricing research, little has been done in this area for some time. Thus, this section relies more on past research and relatively little current research.

One may argue that given 50 years of applied and academic research in the pricing area, reviewing and examining measurement issues may be unnecessary. However, recent findings in behavioral pricing convincingly suggest that measurement task characteristics may bias the results and distort research conclusions.

An example of this potential for measurement bias can be drawn from research that focuses on consumer price knowledge. Marketing researchers have attempted to assess the degree to which consumers remember prices of recently purchased products (Dickson & Sawyer, 1990). The overall conclusion stemming from a substantial body of empirical research is that a relatively low percentage of consumers can recall prices accurately. This finding is opposed to neoclassical economic thinking, according to which consumers have complete knowledge of product prices (Marshall, 1890), and may suggest that consumers do not pay attention to prices they pay. Recently, Estalami et al. (2001) investigated the effects of macroeconomic factors on consumer price knowledge. They found that a simple task characteristic might have significantly biased the results. Using meta-analysis, they examined more than 200 studies and found that not forcing respondents to provide an exact price estimate accounted for a significant reduction in the percent of average deviations from actual prices. Removing these consumers' responses reduces the relative deviation from actual prices by more than 50 percent. Monroe (1976) found similar biases regarding price comparison tasks among brands. Thus, attention to a seemingly trivial measurement format may bias the results and change the scope of the conclusions.

The objective of this subsection is to review and examine measurement procedures and models designed to assess consumers' perceptions of prices, highlight limitations, and suggest new directions. Topics covered include:

- historical perspective
- current research on estimating price thresholds.

Past Research on Price Thresholds

Early research in behavioral pricing highlighted the difference between objective and subjective reactions to prices, and the comparative nature of processes underlying consumer judgments (e.g., Scitovsky, 1944–1945). Other early attempts at assessing consumer reactions to price, e.g., Stoetzel et al. (1954), Adam (1958), Fouilhé (1960), and Gabor and Granger (1961, 1966), reported that low prices tend to be less acceptable because they are perceived as reflecting low quality, and that high prices tend to be less acceptable simply because they are increasingly judged as too expensive. These results led to the postulation of an inverted U-shaped price acceptability function linking subjective price acceptability and actual prices. The findings ran counter to the implications of economic theory that consumers will, in general, prefer lower to higher prices, leading to a price acceptability function decreasing from left (lower prices) to right (higher prices).

An idea emerging from this early work is that consumers have a lower and upper threshold: a lower threshold below which prices may signal suspect product quality, and therefore unacceptable, and an upper price threshold above which prices of a product are too expensive and not worth the product. It should be noted that economists only refer to an upper price threshold (referred to as reservation price), since it is assumed that 'cheaper is better' and, therefore, no lower price limit is assumed.

Stoetzel et al. (1954) criticized economic theory for its assumptions regarding prices, and highlighted psychological aspects of price. In their research, exploring consumer perceptions of prices, they introduced a simple and easily implemented procedure in which consumers were asked to indicate minimum and maximum prices for a product, as follows: 'Below what price would you suspect that [a product] was of poor quality?' 'Above what price would you judge [a product] to be too dear?' (Stoetzel, 1970: 72). The results led them to conclude that consumers possess two thresholds and an acceptable range of prices between the thresholds.

Adam (1958) investigated price perception and the effects of historical pricing on consumer perceptions and demand. He explicitly assumed the existence of lower and upper thresholds. In several studies he used the same direct questions of Stoetzel (1970) to measure upper and lower thresholds, suggesting to consumers the existence of a price acceptability range with a lower threshold. Following Stoetzel and Adam, Fouilhé (1960) further investigated the methodology of direct questions regarding price thresholds and some distributional assumptions. His results, based on using this methodology, led him to conclude and reconfirm the existence of minimum and maximum thresholds, but also indicated some empirical problems with the lower price thresholds and the distributional assumptions suggested by Adam (1958).

Stimulated by the early work of the French researchers, Gabor and Granger (1961, 1966) further advanced the ideas of lower and upper price thresholds and the resultant price acceptability range. They assumed three basic types of consumer responses to prices: too expensive, too cheap, and acceptable. The thrust of their work was to develop the distributional assumptions initially suggested by Adam (1958) and test them empirically. Gabor and Granger (1966) also compared various measures of direct questions and obtained similar results, leading Marbeau (1987) to conclude that the two direct questions suggested by Stoetzel are superior and simple to implement. An extension of these measurement procedures is provided by the Price Sensitivity Meter method (Van Westendorp, 1976; for discussion see Monroe, 1990). This procedure required consumers to respond to four questions presenting different positions along a price acceptability continuum ranging from unacceptable–cheap ('At what price would you consider this [product/brand] to be so inexpensive that you would have doubts about its quality?') to unacceptable–too expensive ('... that the product is so expensive that regardless of its quality it is not worth buying?'). Monroe added a fifth question to complete this scale (Monroe, 1990: 114).

Some Current Work

The above-mentioned measurement methods and procedures are based on the assumption that consumer response to price is represented by an inverted U-shape function; hence the direct questions force respondents to associate low prices with low quality and high prices as being too expensive. A potential problem with these methods is that they direct the consumer to perceive low prices as unacceptable due to potential quality problems and, therefore, it precludes the possibility that this assumption may not apply to all products and consumers. Low prices may be quite acceptable and highly attractive in some contexts. If this is the case, these methods and measurement procedures are inherently biased. Different methods are needed to avoid this problem (Ofir, 2001).

In order to empirically assess the existence of a potential bias, a recent study (Ofir et al., 2000) administered two measurement procedures to relatively low and below-average income consumers. The first procedure entails presenting a list of 10 prices for each product. Consumers were asked to indicate their price acceptability for each price on a seven-point scale (1 = very unacceptable price, and 7 = very acceptable price). Separated by several unrelated tasks, consumers then were asked to respond to Price Sensitivity Meter questions, which directly assess thresholds. The data revealed by the price acceptability rating for each product provide a clear indication whether a consumer for each product is concerned with low prices. As expected, a substantial proportion of low-income consumers were not concerned with low prices; rather they found them more acceptable. That is, their reaction to price is represented by a decreasing price acceptability function. Out of those economically price-oriented consumers, a substantial portion were biased by the direct questions regarding thresholds and responded to the Price Sensitivity Meter as if they possessed a lower price threshold. Specifically, the majority of low-income consumers had no problem with very low prices of rice, jam, flour and body lotion, exhibiting an economic price acceptability function. Out of those consumers, the majority were biased by direct questions, regarding low prices as being too cheap and directly to indicate a lower threshold. These results provide clear evidence supporting the criticism that direct questions regarding thresholds bias the results. Specifically, there are consumers who prefer cheaper products. The implications for these consumers is that they only have an upper threshold (the reservation price) and not a lower threshold as well.

Given the need for unbiased methods to research consumer reactions to price, an additional method is suggested: paired-comparisons. As researchers have observed throughout the last five decades, price judgments are inherently comparative (e.g., Emery, 1970; Monroe, 1990; Scitovsky, 1944–1945). Price paired-comparison task is assumed to be a natural task for consumers. Graded paired-comparisons were used. Overall, the results among hundreds of consumers are very consistent (transitive) and reliable. Moreover, in this research two functional forms were observed: one exhibiting the 'cheaper is better' reaction as implied by economic theory, and the second function, an inverted U-shape function, suggested by the marketing literature.

In another study, the effects of income and its involvement on the shape of the price acceptability function were examined. Each of the two functions reflected different price perception and acceptability judgments. It is reasonable to assume that low income consumers are more price-conscious than high income consumers. This line of reasoning implies the hypothesis that higher income consumers, being less sensitive to price, less price-conscious, and more engaged in price-quality inference, will tend to perceive low prices as being an indication of low quality and, therefore, will be more likely to react to price acceptability in a manner represented by an inverted U-shaped function. Hence, compared to low-income consumers, it is postulated that a significantly higher proportion of high income consumers will have an inverted U-shaped acceptability function. It was also postulated that involved customers are more concerned with the benefits of the product than with its price. It is hypothesized, therefore, that an increase in product involvement will be accompanied by an increase in the proportion of inverted U-shape acceptability functions among both low and high-income consumers.

The results, based on about 280 consumers who responded to a paired-comparison task regarding 12 products, suggest highly consistent and reliable responses. Moreover for each product, a significantly higher proportion of higher income consumers, exhibited an inverted U-shape price acceptability function than low-income consumers. The results also suggest that the proportion of inverted U-shaped functions significantly vary as a positive function of the level of involvement. It is evident that both reactions to price (i.e., the 'cheaper is better' and an inverted U-shaped function) exist. Moreover, the cumulative results suggest that the price paired-comparisons method produces reliable and valid price scales.

Researchers have used direct questions to confirm the existence of price threshold and to obtain the acceptable price range. Attempts were also made to aggregate these results to determine the proportion of consumers accepting the resultant price range. Gabor and Granger (1961, 1966), building on the work of Adam (1958) and Fouilhé (1960), assumed a lognormal distribution. This work was developed further by Monroe (1971b). Unfortunately, all these studies (and most of the follow-up ones since used) potentially biased direct questions to obtain consumer responses. These approaches are potentially biased since direct questioning assumes *ex ante* that people actually form price thresholds and can retrieve them from memory.

An interesting approach to measure thresholds and obtain the relevant consumers' scales was suggested by Monroe (1971a). Consumers were provided with a list of prices which they classified into categories. These consumers were asked to use labels for each category (i.e., acceptable prices, etc.). The labels did not direct consumers in any way and thus were likely to be unbiased. In his recent discussion of this method, Monroe (1990) presented a mail survey version used in industry, which is potentially biased by directing consumers to labels such as 'Unacceptable – too expensive' (Monroe, 1990: 120). Thus, the use of category labels associated with various acceptability levels (without directing the consumer in any way) provides a viable method to obtain consumer reactions to price. Ofir et al. (2000) adopted a scaling model integrating a version of Monroe's (1971a) classification method. The basic assumption, in line with the pricing literature, is that consumers compare prices with latent thresholds. This assumption is explicit in Thurstone's method of successive intervals. Similar to Winer (1986), it assumes heterogeneous price acceptability across consumers. Two functional relationships are obtained from the model. The first is the proportion of price acceptors at different price levels. The second is the relation between subjective price acceptability and actual prices.

Finally, a recent study by Wertenbroch and Skiera (2002) develops an interesting lottery-based approach for estimating willingness-to-pay (WTP), or the upper price threshold, at point-of-purchase. A sample of consumers is drawn and are told that they can buy a target product without spending more money than they want to. They then learn that the buying price is p and will be determined randomly. They are then asked to offer a price s for the product which should equal their WTP. Next, the consumers each draw a p from a pre-specified random distribution (unknown to the consumers). If p is less than or equal to s, they are required to buy the product at price p. If p is greater than s, they are not permitted to buy the product. The consumer thus has an incentive to state his or her true WTP, since a too low s reduces the probability of buying with a surplus, and overstating s increases the probability of buying at a loss. The method is tested successfully on two inexpensive grocery items and an inexpensive durable good.

Behavioral Models

Many customers actively process price information; that is, they are not just price 'takers' (to use the conventional term from microeconomics). Customers continually assess the prices charged for products based on prior purchasing experience, formal communications (e.g., advertising) and informal communications (e.g., friends and neighbors), and point-of-purchase or web-derived listings of prices, and use those assessments in the ultimate purchase decision.

Some key concepts relating to the psychological aspects of pricing that have been the subject of recent research in marketing are the following:

- price judgments
- reference price
- 'odd' pricing
- the communication aspects of price.

Price Judgments

The previous section of this paper focused on measuring price thresholds, or judgments about whether prices are too high or too low. However, additionally, when confronted with a price or a set of prices, consumers process the price information and form preferences about the product or service in question. The prices could be in the same store, from multiple stores, from several types of channels (e.g., retail, Internet, catalog), and take a variety of forms (even price endings, endings with nines). In addition, consumers often have to make judgments about prices occurring over a period of time. For example, when asked to sign up for a fitness club, people are given the option of paying all at once or on a monthly basis. All of these different scenarios in which price processing occurs shows the importance of context in understanding how consumers form judgments of price.

The question of how consumers react to alternative pricing strategies has been studied by Alba et al. (1994, 1999). In the former study, the investigation concerned how consumers form judgments of how expensive one store is to another based on a market basket of goods and alternative pricing strategies utilized: everyday low pricing (EDLP) vs. high-low (regular retail prices using frequent temporary discounts). Although the two stores had equivalent market-basket prices, consumers judged the prices in the high-low stores to be lower. In the 1999 study, the authors add a longitudinal dimension to see how discounting patterns over time affect the results from the first study. In fact, the findings reverse: deep discounts (EDLP) lead to lower perceived prices than frequent, shallow discounts (high-low). Thus, it is clear that the competitive environment has an impact on how consumers form price judgments, both at a point in time and longitudinally.

Other research has examined alternative pricing strategies. One common marketing strategy is to make a large expense look small by advertising it in terms of the smaller amounts. For example, a \$1,000 fitness club membership can be promoted as being only \$3 each day. Gourville (1998) examined this phenomenon and called it the 'pennies-a-day' or PAD strategy. In the terminology of the field of judgment and decision making, this is an issue of 'framing.' Gourville found that a PAD framing strategy can be effective. Other research in this area could use reverse PAD strategies for undesirable products (e.g., showing how much cigarette users spend annually vs. a per-pack mentality). A similar strategy is to partition prices into two parts such as one part for the product and the other for shipping and handling. Interestingly, Morwitz et al. (1998) show that partitioned prices decrease customers' recalled total costs and increase their demand.

An interesting area of research involving price judgments is how consumers process the digits of a price. A large number of studies have documented that certain price endings (0, 5, 9) occur much more often than others. In particular, interest has centered around 9 endings, often called 'odd' prices. In an effort to explain the frequent use of odd prices, academics often propose that consumers round prices down, essentially ignoring the right-hand digits. Other potential explanations are that consumers discern meaning from prices that end in 9 (e.g., good value) and that consumers compare prices from left to right. The main point of this work is that consumers do not necessarily process prices holistically but, instead, use some heuristic to process the digits separately. Almost all work in price assumes holistic processing.

This research area has been attacked from two perspectives. Work by Schindler and his co-authors (see, for example, Schindler & Kirby, 1997) have used field experimental methods to infer why certain digits occur more often than others. They have found support for the argument that the reason the numbers 0 and 5 occur more frequently is due to the high cognitive accessibility of those numbers, as the use of these round-number endings makes price information easier for consumers to perceive, compare, and remember. Endings with 9 occur most frequently with high potential underestimation prices, that is, those where the 9s represent a large psychological drop in price from the price with one penny added (e.g., \$49.99 vs. \$50.00).

The alternative perspective estimates empirical choice models with alternative formulations to capture different price processing heuristics (Stiving & Winer, 1997). Using two different frequently purchased product categories, the authors found consistent support for left-to-right price processing rather than holistic processing or rounding. These empirical results are consistent with those of Schindler and Kirby's (1997) findings with respect to the 9 endings, since a large psychological drop in price using a 9 would occur if left-to-right processing was being used.

Not only does price represent revenues to the firm, it is also a communications device. High prices can be interpreted by customers as high quality, for example. There is a vast literature in this particular area of research (see Monroe, 1990). More currently, researchers have investigated the interpretation of promotions by consumers. Grewal et al. (1996) analyze the different wording or semantic cues of discounts such as 'was \$50, now \$34.99.' They consider different contexts (e.g., in-home or in the store) and discount sizes. Among a set of results, they find that consumers find a within-store price comparison more useful when they are situated in a retail store. Conversely, semantic cues that compare prices between stores are more effective on perceptions of value when consumers are at home. Raghubir (1998) hypothesizes that consumers use the values of coupons to infer the retail prices of products. Her main finding is that higher percentage discounts are associated with higher prices, which can undermine the effectiveness of the promotion. Practitioners feel that prices endings with 9s are interpreted by consumers as 'good deals.' However, some recent work by Schindler (2001) on 99 price endings shows that they are not always the lowest priced in a shopping area. A comparative price survey involving a wide array of product categories provides evidence that 99-ending prices are actually likely to be higher prices than those prices ending in the digits 00–98.

Reference Prices

A particular form of a price judgment is a reference price. A reference price is any standard of comparison against which an observed price is compared. There are two kinds of reference prices: internal and external, sometimes referred to as *temporal* and *contextual* respectively (Briesch et al., 1997; Rajendran & Tellis, 1994). External reference prices are usually observed prices that, in a retailing setting, are typically posted at the point of purchase as the 'regular retail price.' Internal reference prices are mental prices used to assess an observed price. Some empirical work has found that different market segments use the internal and external reference prices (Mazumdar & Papatla, 2000). Since the product manager cannot easily manipulate internal reference prices, yet they have a strong effect on buying behavior, we discuss them in more detail.

A large number of internal reference prices have been proposed (Winer, 1988), including:

- the 'fair' price, or what the product ought to cost the customer
- the price frequently charged
- the last price paid
- the upper amount someone would pay (reservation price)
- the lower threshold or lowest amount a customer would pay
- the price of the brand usually bought
- the average price charged for similar products
- the expected future price
- the typical discounted price

Many of these considerations contribute to the concept we call the *perceived* price, the price the customer thinks is the current actual price of the product.

The research literature has generally found that reference price has a significant impact on brand choice of both durable and nondurable goods (see Kalyanaram & Winer, 1995, for a review), and that it can have important normative implications (Greenleaf, 1995). In particular, when the observed price is higher than the reference price (a 'loss'), it can negatively affect purchasing because the consumer perceives this situation as an unpleasant surprise or a bad deal. For example, the large price increases for cars in the 1970s created what became known as a 'sticker shock' effect when consumer reference or perceived prices for cars were significantly lower than the prices they saw in the showroom. A happier situation occurs when the observed price is either at or below the reference price (a 'gain'). This happens when a brand a consumer might buy anyway is being promoted at a lower price. Interestingly, following Kahneman and Tversky's Prospect Theory, most empirical studies on reference price have found that the unpleasant surprises have a greater impact on purchasing probabilities than the pleasant surprises (see, for example, Mayhew & Winer, 1992).

Some research has followed up on the reference price asymmetry. Kopalle, Rao and Assunção (1996) and Kopalle and Winer (1996) show the normative impact of reference price asymmetry. Erdem, Mayhew, and Sun (2001) find that loss-sensitive households show stronger reactions to price, display, and newspaper feature advertisements than the average household, while gain-sensitive households show no striking characteristics. Two studies have questioned this finding of reference price asymmetry. Chang et al. (1999) and Bell and Lattin (2000) both find that heterogeneity in price responsiveness can potentially confound asymmetric reference price effects.

A second important concept of reference price is expected future price. This is a particularly important concept for any product category that experiences significant price changes over time. For example, new consumer durables are subject to this phenomenon. The prices of personal computers, camcorders, DVD players, etc. are falling so rapidly that customers are worried they will overpay. Discretionary purchasers can simply wait until the prices decrease further as they are willing to forego the utility from owning the product sooner. This reference price concept has been studied much less in the literature, an exception being Winer (1985).

Janiszewski and Lichtenstein (1999) propose a new reference point generated from range theory. Reference price models generally use Adaptation-Level theory (Helson, 1964) to make the assertion that consumers compare observed prices to some internal reference point. However, Janiszewski and Lichtenstein propose that the range of values of price can determine the value of any one price in the range. In other words, consumers may use a range of recalled price experiences to set a lower and upper boundry of price expectations; in this case, the attractiveness of a particular observed price is a function of its location in the range.

Empirical Price Response

As long as marketing academics have been interested in estimating market response functions, price response in the form of elasticities or other measures have been obtained. The famous Guadagni and Little (1983) paper sparked new interest in price response because of its focus on brand choice. The amount of work is sufficiently large that it has produced a meta-analysis over 10 years ago (Tellis, 1988) showing that the average price elasticity is about eight times larger (in absolute value) than the effects of advertising produced from a similar meta-analysis (Assmus et al., 1984).

Empirical research on price at the brand or store level has continued at a brisk pace. Some of the more recent topics examined include:

- short- and long-term effects of promotions
- the interaction of advertising and price
- retailing issues
- price search by consumers
- improvements in methodology.

Short- and Long-term Effects of Sales Promotion

Conventional wisdom from practitioners is that sales promotions (coupons, in-store price reductions, etc.) can have significant impact on sales in the short-term but rarely, if ever, have long-term effects. This is because consumers (and retailers) use the promotions to stock up, which creates a 'peak' in purchasing, but as the inventory is used, a 'trough' follows. Thus, long-term effects on a brand's sales are negligible as the promotion tends to affect timing but not loyalty. In addition, many categories create deal loyal rather than brand loyal customers due to the frequent use of promotions.

Recent research has examined this assertion using improved modeling approaches and longer time-series of purchasing data. Using a dynamic brand choice model, Papatla and Krishnamurthi (1996) find both traditional, negative aspects of promotions on brand loyalty but some positive results for the long-run. In particular, they find (for one product category) that the promoted brand does exhibit a decrease in brand loyalty and increased price sensitivity. However, they also find that prior purchases made on display and feature promotions, as well as purchases made when price decreases are paired with displays or features, improve subsequent response to such promotions. Mela, Gupta, and Lehmann (1997) use over eight years of scanner panel data to examine this issue. They find that promotions do indeed make both loyal and non-loyal consumers more price sensitive, and that these effects are more than four times greater for the latter group. Jedidi, Mela & Gupta (1999) incorporate competitive effects, but confirm the results of the Mela, Gupta & Lehmann (1997) study. In addition, based on their model and some cost and margin assumptions, they show that regular price decreases should have a generally negative impact on long-term profitability and increases in price promotions to be uniformly unprofitable. Nijs et al. (2001) examined the effects of brand promotions on product category demand using Dutch data for 560 product categories over a four-year period. They found that the average effects lasted about 10 weeks, but that there was no persistent, long-term positive impact on category sales.

Another area of promotion research is on what is called the asymmetric price effect. Earlier research by Blattberg and Wisniewski (1989) showed that when a high-priced, higher-quality brand is promoted, consumers of a lower-priced/quality brand will switch. However, the reverse is not true. Several papers have continued to work in this area. Sethuraman (1996) questions if this asymmetric effect still holds depending upon whether the higher-price brand's discounted price is still higher, equal, or lower than the lower-quality brand's price. Assuming three tiers of brands, high quality, medium quality national brands, and a discount brand, he finds that the highest-priced brand needs to discount to only just above the medium-quality brand's price for the promotion to be effective, that is, the highest-tier brand does not have to lower its price to the discount brand. Sivakumar and Raj (1997) extend this work to the category decision and find that the basic results hold. That is, high-priced/quality brands not only do better than low-priced/quality brands when they cut prices, but they also are less hurt from category defections when they raise prices. The basic asymmetry results are supported in a meta-analysis conducted by Sethuraman et al. (1999). The authors analyzed 1,060 cross-price effects on 280 brands from 19 different grocery product categories. Their results not only support the basic asymmetric effects, but they also find a strong 'neighborhood' effect whereby brands that are closer to each other in price have larger cross-price effects than brands priced farther apart.

A more general issue in the area of promotional effects is what category characteristics are associated with different levels of promotional elasticities. A study by Narasimhan et al. (1996) across 108 product categories showed that promotional elasticities are higher for product categories with fewer numbers of brands, higher category penetration, shorter interpurchase times, and higher consumer propensity to stockpile.

The Interaction of Advertising and Price

There are two competing hypotheses for the interaction between advertising and price. The first, termed the market power hypothesis, is that advertising creates brand loyalty and product differentiation and, therefore, lower price elasticities. The competing hypothesis is that advertising is information; it increases consideration sets and thus competition, and therefore leads to greater price sensitivity. These theories have led to a considerable amount of empirical research, with mixed results (Kaul & Wittink, 1995). Some of these results have been rationalized by examining the kind of advertising used. Price-oriented advertising, not unexpectedly, does lead to greater price sensitivity, while non-price-oriented advertising has the reverse effect. There are also consumer behavior implications that come into play (Mitra & Lynch, 1995).

Some recent research has continued to examine the advertising – price interaction. Besides the promotion results noted previously, Mela, Gupta, and Lehmann (1997) also found that advertising decreased price sensitivity in their data. Kalra and Goodstein (1998) examine different advertising positioning strategies and find that only a value-oriented positioning decreased willingness-to-pay.

Naik et al. (2000) study the advertising–promotion interaction. Conventional wisdom is that sales promotion, being price-focused, should have a negative interaction with brand-focused advertising in that it draws attention away from brand equity and creates more price competition. In a dynamic, competitive framework, the authors do find empirical support for this notion, which has significant normative implications. More work is needed in this area of research.

Retailing

The increased availability of electronic scanner data and interest in 'micro' marketing (product assortments customized to the local clientele) have generated research focusing on the retailer's pricing problem. Hoch et al. (1995) estimate store-level price elasticities for 18 product categories from a chain of 83 supermarkets. The authors then relate 11 demographic and competitive variables to these elasticities and find that they explain two-thirds of the variation in the elasticities. This provides empirical support for the micro-marketing concept. Montgomery (1997) improves the estimation procedure for store price elasticities using hierarchical Bayes estimation, and using a normative model, shows that micro-marketing strategies can increase gross profits anywhere from 3.9–10% over a uniform chain pricing strategy.

Some work has examined the impact of retailers' promotions policies on product, category, and store sales. Anderson and Simester (2001) study the impact of sales signs and in-store promotions. They find that the impact of a sales sign on the demand for an item is decreased when more products are on sale at the same time, and that sales of a product category are maximized when some but not all of the brands in the category are on sale. Lam et al. (2001) break down sales into four components: front traffic, store-entry ratio, closing ratio, and average spending. Using store data and infrared counters to measure front and store traffic by the hour, they found that price promotions have little impact on front traffic, but that they have a positive impact on store entry and the likelihood that a consumer will make a purchase.

Other retailing issues that can be studied relate to the types of promotions run in stores. Two types are off-the-shelf price discounts automatically deducted at the check-out, and in-store coupons available right by the product. After running a series of field experiments, Dhar and Hoch (1996) show that, on average, coupons lead to a 35% greater increase in sales and a 108% greater increase in retailer profits. Little other work of this type has been done.

Price Search

An interesting area of pricing research at the consumer level is price search. Prior work in this area has relied on Stigler's search theory: people will search for price information to the point where the marginal benefits from search equal the marginal costs. Urbany et al. (1996) propose a model of price search incorporating three broad sets of factors: habit, non-economic returns to search (e.g., shopping enjoyment), and economic returns. They find that the first two additional categories help to explain price search behavior better than in previous studies. Bronnenberg and Vanhonacker (1996) incorporate search into a logit model of brand choice. They specify and estimate a two-stage model, where the first stage is how price affects the consideration set, that is, for how many brands the household actually searches for price. The second stage of the model is brand choice. They find that response to variations in shelf price is limited to the brands in the choice or consideration set.

Methodological Advances

Like other areas of academic marketing research, a considerable amount of effort in the pricing area has been devoted to improving our methods for estimating price elasticities. Kalyanam and Shively (1998) take a stochastic spline approach to estimating market response to price. The authors use the new method to better estimate price response functions that are often far from smooth due to promotions, small price variations around category price points, etc. Montgomery and Rossi (1999) use Bayesian methods to improve the estimation of store-based price elasticities by combining store-level and 'pooled' or aggregate information across stores and brands.

Competitive/Normative Models

The last 10 years or so have witnessed an increased interest in the application of game-theoretic methods into marketing. Game theory allows modelers to add an important dimension to research: competition. Using these methods permits the researcher to characterize equilibria under a variety of assumptions about competitive actions and reactions which are not possible using more static, empirically based models. In many cases, the 'competition' is between channel members competing for profit margin, that is, not necessarily between firms. The price of incorporating competitive interactions is that institutional richness is often forsaken for model solvability.

A number of areas relevant to pricing have been examined using competitive strategy tools. These include:

- sales promotion
- channels of distribution
- product policy issues.

While some of this work does have an empirical component, what separates it from the research described in the previous section is that the theoretical model is based on competitive interactions described above.

Sales Promotion Research

Promotions are offered by both manufacturers (consumer-oriented and trade) and retailers. One of the purposes of trade promotions is to induce retailers to pass some of promotion incentive on to consumers and to therefore stimulate sales. This is called the 'pass-through.' This can range from 0%, where the retailer basically pockets the money, to 100% where it is all given to the consumer. Tyagi (1999) analyzes this situation with a number of alternative demand functions, and finds, surprisingly, that the optimal amount of pass-through depends heavily on the specification of the demand function and that in some cases (convex demand functions), the optimal amount is greater than 100%.

A more complicated situation is where there are multiple competing manufacturers and retailers and a number of different market segments (e.g., price sensitive vs. insensitive) (Lal & Villas-Boas, 1998). The setup of the model assumes two manufacturers each selling two products through two competing retailers. The manufacturers set wholesale prices to the retailers. The retailers carry all products and set retail prices. Of particular importance are the four types of consumer loyalty: no loyalty, loyalty to a manufacturer, loyalty to a retailer, and loyalty to a particular brand at a particular retail outlet. The key finding is that the results are a function of the segment structure – in particular, the ratio of switchers to loyal consumers for the highest priced brand relative to the ratio of switchers to loyals for the lowest priced brand.

A common practice in many supermarkets is double and sometimes triple couponing, where the retailer offers to multiply the value of a manufacturer coupon. Krishnan and Rao (1995) study whether such a policy is profitable and how it affects retail pricing in a product category. They produce three main findings: (1) manufacturers may increase coupon values in retail trade areas using double coupons; (2) double-coupon retailers try to prevent consumers from using them by discounting non-couponed brands; and (3) non-double-couponing retailers reduce their prices on the brands for which the double coupons are offered.

Channels of Distribution Research

One channel issue is how supermarkets compete against each other using different pricing formats: everyday low pricing (EDLP) vs. high-low or regular prices with in-store promotions. Lal and Rao (1997) examine the conditions under which EDLP can be successful. They assume two segments of consumers: time constrained, and 'cherry pickers' who go from store to store seeking the lowest prices. The show that EDLP and high-low strategies are more than simply pricing strategies, in that EDLP stores use lower basket prices to attract both segments, and high-low stores use service to compete in the time-constrained segment and price specials for the cherry-picking segment. Their study has implications for communications strategies as well.

One of the manifestations for a firm of having a channel system other than direct sales is that the power in the channel may be controlled by either the firm or the channel, depending upon a number of factors. At the same time, there has been considerable interest among marketers in what has become known as the New Empirical Industrial Organization literature in economics, which specifies a model with strategic interactions common to game theory. Kadiyali et al. (2000) examine the channel power issue in this context and develop a method to measure the power that channel members have and the underlying reasons for that power. They find that for two grocery items, the retailer's market power is very significant.

Another characteristic of channel relationships is that often a substantial amount of bargaining is conducted among the members. For example, retailers may try to extract better promotional allowances, while manufacturers attempt to get more shelf space. Srivastava et al. (2000) analyze a situation where a manufacturer and an exclusive, independent distributor are negotiating the transfer or wholesale price of a new product. They adapt a game-theoretic model (sequential equilibrium) to predict bargaining behavior and outcomes for this scenario. They derive predictions from the model about how the participants should behave. However, after conducting experiments, they find that the players bargained suboptimally, took longer to agree, and differed in a number of other respects. This experimental economics approach to understanding bargaining situations is a fruitful avenue for future research.

Product Policy

A variety of pricing issues relating to product policy have also been studied by marketing academics, each of which opens up a potential area for research. Vandenbosch and Weinberg (1995) extend prior game theory work looking at product differentiation from a single-dimension to two dimensions, product positioning and price. They find that unlike the one-dimensional differentiation model, firms do not tend toward maximum differentiation, but rather maximum differentiation on one dimension and minimum differentiation on the other. An interesting product policy question is how to price products that have branded components, such as Intel inside Compaq personal computers (Venkatesh & Mahajan, 1997). Desiraju & Shugan (1999) examine the pricing problems facing service companies such as airlines where, since the product is perishable, revenue is lost forever when a plane takes off with empty seats. This is referred to as 'yield management.' Krishnan et al. (1999) take the Generalized Bass Model (Bass et al., 1994) and develop optimal pricing policies for new product introductions that do not follow observed sales-growth patterns (which is commonly assumed) and are more consistent with observed pricing patterns, which either decline monotonically or increase and then decrease.

Pricing and the Internet

The increased penetration of the Internet and its emphasis on personalization has created a new pricing environment for marketing managers. The notion of a fixed price charged to all customers has virtually disappeared in the e-commerce world in favor of 'personalized' pricing. In addition, the Internet is characterized by shopping agents checking for the lowest price, customers specifying the prices they are willing to pay, and the lower search costs creating an environment where it is very easy to comparison shop even without shopping agents. Some industries such as music distribution are investigating the use of 'micro' or small payments for unbundled products, such as individual songs that can be downloaded to create customized CDs. Despite the recent drop in interest in the Internet as a way to make money, it is an exciting area for future research and the relative newness of the area means that there is little extant research.

One way to conceptualize the pricing structure afforded by the Internet is the following (Dolan & Moon, 2000):

Type I: The Set Price Mechanism

Many retail websites, such as BarnesandNoble.com, offer fixed prices for their products. As in the off-line or catalog contexts, customers can choose to buy or not buy at the posted prices. These are the kinds of sites that are heavily affected by price search tools such as MySimon.com, as it is simple for the customer to type in the name of a brand or book title and find the lowest price available. Except for the segment of customers that is uninformed about the price comparison mechanisms available, in this situation the marketing manager has only two choices: match the lowest price available or add value through branding or other mechanisms. Amazon.com does not have the lowest prices for books or CDs. However, the company has been able to develop loyal customers by adding value through brand-building and convenient shopping through its one-click purchasing process.

A useful framework for thinking about how e-tailers and other web participants can differentiate themselves and subdue price competition was offered by Alba et al. (1997). The authors suggested the following five possible approaches to seeking competitive advantage in electronic retailing:

- distribution efficiency
- assortments of complementary merchandise
- collection and utilization of customer information
- presentation of information through electronic formats
- unique merchandise.

Some sites can change prices at the time a parti-cular shopper is at the site depending upon his or her past history, the prices of the products being examined, and the sites from which they came. This is an excellent application of first-degree price discrimination and has the potential to optimize profits. For example, if you are visiting a site and do a price comparison, some sites will automatically adjust their prices to the lowest price as they 'sense' that you are price elastic.

Other than research on how to implement dynamic pricing in this context, interesting issues are the brand equity and ethical dimensions of price discrimination. Although it is not illegal to price discriminate to end customers, recent discoveries by Amazon customers that they were receiving different prices did not create favorable public relations for the firm. More importantly, a company can get into serious trouble if the pricing mechanism is tied to demographics such as race, resulting in a kind of electronic redlining.

Type II: Buyer/Seller Negotiation

On-line price negotiation is an alternative to face-to-face interactions, which many people dislike. While popular in B-to-B applications (e.g., energy, metals), of the three types of pricing mechanisms, this kind of real-time negotiation is the least common.

Type III: Auctions and Exchanges

One of the most popular innovations of the Internet, on-line auctions are forecasted to generate over $20 billion in sales by 2003 (*Industry Standard*, April 24, 2000). There are three types of pricing mechanisms in this category where competition across buyers and/or sellers results in prices that can vary widely across transactions.

(a) In this case, competition across buyers leads to a price. This is the classic auction model, also called the English auction. Yahoo! and eBay offer this kind of system for consumers to interact with each other. The classic auction has been around for hundreds if not thousands of years.
(b) A reverse auction is where sellers compete for a buyer's business. The most noteworthy example of this is Priceline.com that started with auctions for airline seats and has moved to hotel rooms and groceries. Some sites, such as Mercata.com, permit groups to get together and offer a larger sale to potential bidders.
(c) Exchanges are electronic marketplaces where a group of buyers and sellers interact to trade and set prices for transactions. Most of the Internet sites in this category are designed around a particular industry such as metals, steel, and automobile parts. Some companies such as VerticalNet, Ariba, and Commerce One have been very successful in this segment. Other companies focus on small businesses.

Research on Auctions

The research literature on auctions is vast as it has been an active area of research for economists since Vickrey's 1961 paper describing basic auction mechanisms. Some recent papers in the marketing and economics literatures shed some light on possible research areas related to Internet auctions.

One stream of literature relates to the basic auction format (Lucking-Reiley, 1999). Other than the English auction described above or its variants (reverse English auctions), three other basic auction mechanisms are Dutch, first-price sealed-bid, and second-price sealed-bid. A Dutch auction involves decreasing prices: a public price clock starts out at a very high level and the price falls until a participant bids. Both the Dutch and English auctions are 'real time' auctions, in contrast to sealed-bid auctions where bidders submit a bid by a deadline. In the first-price auction, the highest bidder wins. In the second-price auction, the winning bidder pays the second-highest bid. Vickrey (1961) showed that under some standard bidding assumptions, the expected revenue to be collected by the auctioneer is the same in all four formats. Using a real Internet context (magic game cards), Lucking-Reiley (1999) showed that the Dutch auction format produced significantly higher revenues than the others, violating the theoretical predictions.

Even within a format, there are often characteristics of particular auctions that can be tested. In English auctions, for example, sellers can set what is called a reserve, the minimum acceptable price that is unobservable to buyers. Greenleaf (2000) argues that behavioral phenomena such as anticipated regret and rejoicing can affect the seller's reserve level. In a related paper, Greenleaf and Sinha (1996) examine buy-in penalties – the amount a seller must pay if the item does not sell. These and other auction format issues can be studied in Internet contexts.

An interesting question is how to attract customers to an auction (Sinha & Greenleaf, 2000). While more customers are almost always incrementally profitable to a firm using 'posted' prices, more bidders does not necessary increase actual profits from an auction. Are there types of people who are attracted to auctions? Do they have different risk profiles than non-auction customers? How does an auction site optimally allocate resources between bidders and sellers?

The Internet and Information

A key characteristic of the Internet is the low cost of information search. While the Internet has the potential to permit firms to differentiate along a number of dimensions and thus extract a high price from that value, economic theory would dictate that low search costs ultimately create price competition. Interestingly, some studies show that prices on the Internet are actually higher than they are in the offline world (Smith et al., 1999) and that consumers are often willing to pay more for the same good from a brand name retailer (Smith & Brynjolfsson, 2001). An important research area, therefore, is how the information environment on the web affect customer and firm behavior.

One area of potential research is on the efficiency aspects of the web, that is, is the web more efficient than its offline counterpart? Smith et al. (1999) describe four dimensions of web efficiency that can be investigated:

- Price levels: are the prices charged on the Internet lower?
- Price elasticity: are consumers more sensitive to small price changes on the Internet?
- Menu costs: do retailers adjust their prices more finely or frequently on the Internet?
- Price dispersion: is there a smaller spread between the highest and lowest prices on the Internet?

While lower search costs should make it possible for customers to easily collect price information, it could also lower the cost of collecting information about product quality. Some research has found that lowering the search costs for quality for differentiated products (e.g., wine) decreases price sensitivity (Lynch & Ariely, 2000). An interesting question is whether there is learning in this kind of environment. Theoretical work has examined the impact of search costs on market structure and firm incentives with differentiated products (Bakos, 1997).

Some work has focused about the implications of the Internet for price competition among firms, both online and offline. Lal and Sarvary (1999) look at the conditions under which the Internet could actually decrease price competition and show that two factors – the attribute types of the products in question and the channels being used – can lead to higher prices and less search. Zettelmeyer (2000) relates the 'size' of the Internet in terms of its reach to competitive pricing and communications policies.

Conclusion

Of the five areas covered, we believe that three in particular deserve more attention from marketing academics.

As we noted earlier, except for the several studies described in this paper, issues related to measurement and scaling have not been extensively studied since the 1970s. This is a very important, practical area in which marketing academics can have a large impact. In today's price-sensitive market, understanding price thresholds and willingness-to-pay is critical to marketing managers' being able to price appropriately and not succumb to extreme pressure to drop prices. Yet, both authors have seen numerous instances of poor marketing research methods used to help set price.

More work is also needed to better understand customers' reactions and processing of price information. Measurement research can help set prices, but we also need to study how customers are utilizing the price information they see and make decisions.

Finally, given the rapid growth of the Internet and e-commerce, we need to better understand appropriate pricing policies and mechanisms for this new distribution channel and communications medium. It is clear that the Internet is attracting both price-sensitive and price-insensitive customers. In addition, pricing policy is inextricably tied into product policy: mass customization or individually tailored products and services should imply pricing flexibility. Price experimentation should be easy and inexpensive to do. However, at this stage in the development of the Internet, we do not know very much about optimal pricing policies or behavioral aspects.

References

Adam, Daniel (1958) Consumer reactions to price. *Observation Economics*, 15, 15–21.

Alba, Joseph W., Broniarczyk, Susan M., Shimp, Terence A. & Urbany, Joel E. (1994) The influence of prior beliefs, frequency cues, and magnitude cues on consumers' perceptions of comparative price data. *Journal of Consumer Research*, September, 219–35.

Alba, Joseph, Lynch, John, Weitz, Barton, Janiszewski, Chris, Lutz, Richard, Sawyer, Alan & Wood, Stacy (1997) Interactive home shopping: consumer, retailer, and manufacturer incentives to participate in electronic marketplaces. *Journal of Marketing*, July, 38–53.

Alba, Joseph W., Mela, Carl F., Shimp, Terence A. & Urbany, Joel E. (1999) The effect of discount frequency and depth on consumer price judgments. *Journal of Consumer Research*, September, 99–114.

Anderson, Eric T. & Simester, Duncan I. (2001) Are sales signs less effective when more products have them? *Marketing Science*, Spring, 121–42.

Assmus, Gert, Farley, John U. & Lehmann, Donald R. (1984) How advertising affects sales: meta analysis of econometric results. *Journal of Marketing Research*, 21 (May), 153–8.

Bakos, J. Yannis (1997) Reducing buyer search costs: implications for electronic marketplaces. *Management Science*, December, 1676–92.

Bass, Frank M., Krishnan, Trichy V. & Jain, Dipak C. (1994) Why the Bass Model fits without decision variables. *Marketing Science*, 13, 203–23.

Bell, David R. & Lattin, James M. (2000) Looking for loss aversion in scanner panel data: the confounding effect of price response heterogeneity. *Marketing Science*, Spring, 185–200.

Blattberg, Robert C. & Wisniewski, Kenneth J. (1989) Price-induced patterns of competition. *Marketing Science*, 8 (Fall), 291–309.

Briesch, Richard A., Krishnamurthi, Lakshman, Mazumdar, Tridib & Raj, S.P. (1997) A comparative analysis of reference price models. *Journal of Consumer Research*, September, 202–14.

Bronnenberg, Bart J. & Vanhonacker, Wilfried R. (1996) Limited choice sets, local price response, and implied measures of price competition. *Journal of Marketing Research*, May, 163–74.

Chang, Kwangpil, Siddarth, S. & Weinberg, Charles B. (1999) The impact of heterogeneity in purchase timing and price responsiveness on estimates of sticker shock effects. *Marketing Science*, 18, 178–92.

Desiraju, Ramarao & Shugan, Steven M. (1999) Strategic service pricing and yield management. *Journal of Marketing*, January, 44–56.

Devinney, Timothy M. (1988) *Issues in Pricing: Theory and Research*. Lexington, MA: Lexington Books.

Dhar, Sanjay K. & Hoch, Stephen J. (1996) Price discrimination using in-store merchandising. *Journal of Marketing*, January, 17–30.

Dickson, Peter R. & Sawyer, Alan G. (1990) The price knowledge and search of supermarket shoppers. *Journal of Marketing*, 54, July, 42–53.

Dolan, Robert J. & Moon, Youngme (2000) Pricing and market making on the internet. Harvard Business School case #9-500-065.

Dolan, Robert J. & Simon, Hermann (1996) *Power Pricing*. New York: The Free Press.

Emery, Fred (1970) Some psychological aspects of price. In *Pricing Research*, edited by B. Taylor & G. Wills. Princeton, NJ: Brandon/Systems, pp. 98–111.

Erdem, Tulin, Mayhew, Glenn & Sun, Baohong (2001) Understanding reference-price shoppers: a within- and cross-category analysis. *Journal of Marketing Research*, 38, (November), 445–57

Estalami, Hooman, Holden, Alfred & Lehmann, Donald R. (2001) Macro-economic determinants of consumer price knowledge: a meta-analysis of four decades of research. *International Journal of Research in Marketing*, 18, December, 341–55.

Fouilhé, Pierre (1960) Evaluation subjective des prix. *Revue Française de Sociologie*, 1, 163–72.

Gabor, Andre & Granger, C.W.J. (1961) On the price consciousness of consumers. *Applied Statistics*, 10, 170–88.

——— (1966) Price as an indicator of quality: report on an inquiry. *Economica*, 33, 43–70.

Gourville, John T. (1998) Pennies-a-Day: the effect of temporal reframing on transaction evaluation. *Journal of Consumer Research*, March, 395–408.

Greenleaf, Eric A. (1995) The impact of reference price effects on the profitability of price promotions. *Marketing Science*, 14, Winter, 82–104.

Greenleaf, Eric A. (2000) Reserves, regret, and rejoicing in open English auctions: an experimental study. Unpublished working paper, Stern School of Business, New York University.

Greenleaf, Eric A. & Sinha, Atanu R. (1996) Combining buy-in penalties with commissions at auction houses. *Management Science*, April, 529–40.

Grewal, Dhruv, Marmorstein, Howard & Sharma, Arun (1996) Communicating price information through semantic cues: the moderating effects of situation and discount size. *Journal of Consumer Research*, September, 148–56.

Guadagni, Peter M. & Little, John D.C. (1983) A logit model of brand choice calibrated on scanner data. *Marketing Science*, Summer, 203–38.

Helson, Harry (1964) *Adaptation-Level Theory*. New York: Harper and Row.

Hoch, Stephen J., Kim, Byung-Do, Montgomery, Alan L. & Rossi, Peter E. (1995) Determinants of store-level price elasticity. *Journal of Marketing Research*, February, 17–29.

Janiszewski, Chris & Lichtenstein, Donald R. (1999) A range theory account of price perception. *Journal of Consumer Research*, March, 353–68.

Jedidi, Kamel, Mela, Carl F. & Gupta, Sunil (1999) Managing advertising and promotion for long-run profitability. *Marketing Science*, 18, 1–22.

Kadiyali, Vrinda, Chintagunta, Pradeep & Vilcassim, Naufel (2000) Manufacturer-retailer channel interactions and implications for channel power: an empirical investigation of pricing in a local market. *Marketing Science*, 2, 127–48.

Kalra, Ajay & Goodstein, Ronald C. (1998) The impact of advertising positioning strategies on consumer price sensitivity. *Journal of Marketing Research*, May, 210–24.

Kalyanam, Kirthi & Shively, Thomas S. (1998) Estimating irregular pricing effects: a stochastic spline regression approach. *Journal of Marketing Research*, February, 16–29.

Kalyanaram, Gurumurthy & Winer, Russell S. (1995) Empirical generalizations from reference price and asymmetric price response research. *Marketing Science*, 14, part 2 of 2, G161–69.

Kaul, Anil & Wittink, Dick R. (1995) Empirical generalizations about the impact of advertising on price sensitivity and price. *Marketing Science*, 14, part 2 of 2, G151–60.

Kopalle, Praveen & Winer, Russell S. (1996) A dynamic model of reference price and reference quality. *Marketing Letters*, 7, 41–52.

Kopalle, Praveen K., Rao, Ambar G. & Assunção, Joao L. (1996) Asymmetric reference price effects and dynamic pricing policies. *Marketing Science*, 15, 60–85.

Krishnan, Trichy V. & Rao, Ram C. (1995) Double couponing and retail pricing in a couponed product category. *Journal of Marketing Research*, November, 419–32.

Krishnan, Trichy V., Bass, Frank M. & Jain, Dipak C. (1999) Optimal pricing strategy for new products. *Management Science*, December, 1650–63.

Lal, Rajiv & Rao, Ram (1997) Supermarket competition: the case of everyday low pricing. *Marketing Science*, 16, 60–80.

Lal, Rajiv & Sarvary, Miklos (1999) When and how is the Internet likely to decrease price competition? *Marketing Science*, 18, 4, 485–503.

Lal, Rajiv & Villas-Boas J. Miguel (1998) Price promotions and trade deals with multiproduct retailers. *Management Science*, 44, July, 935–49.

Lam, Shun Yin, Vandenbosch, Mark, Hulland, John & Pearce, Michael (2001) Evaluating promotions in shopping environments: decomposing sales response into attraction, conversion, and spending effects. *Marketing Science,* Spring, 194–215.

Lucking-Reiley, David (1999) Using field experiments to test equivalence between auction formats: magic on the internet. *American Economic Review*, December, 1063–80.

Lynch, John G. & Ariely, Dan (2000) Wine Online: search costs affect competition on price, quality, and distribution. *Marketing Science*, Winter, 83–103.

Marbeau, Yves (1987) What value pricing research today? *Journal of the Market Research Society*, 29, 153–82.

Marshall, Alfred (1890) *Principles of Economics*. London: Macmillan.

Mayhew, Glenn E. & Winer, Russell S. (1992) An empirical analysis of internal and external reference price effects using scanner data. *Journal of Consumer Research*, June, 62–70.

Mazumdar, Tridib & Papatla, Purushottam (2000) An investigation of reference price segments. *Journal of Marketing Research*, May, 246–58.

Mela, Carl F., Gupta, Sunil & Lehmann, Donald R. (1997) The long-term impact of promotion and advertising on consumer brand choice. *Journal of Marketing Research*, May, 248–61.

Mitra, Anusree & Lynch, John G. Jr. (1995) Toward a reconciliation of market power and information theories of advertising effects on price elasticity. *Journal of Consumer Research*, 21 (March), 644–59.

Monroe, Kent B. (1971a) Measuring price thresholds by psychophysics and latitudes of acceptance. *Journal of Marketing Research*, 8, November, 460–4.

——— (1971b) The information content of price: a preliminary model for estimating buyer response. *Management Science*, 17, B519–32.

——— (1976) The influence of price differences and brand familiarity on brand preferences. *Journal of Consumer Research*, 3, 42–9.

——— (1990) *Pricing: Making Profitable Decisions*, 2nd edn. New York: McGraw-Hill.

Montgomery, Alan L. (1997) Creating micro-marketing pricing strategies using supermarket scanner data. *Marketing Science*, 4, 315–37.

Montgomery, Alan L. & Rossi, Peter E. (1999) Estimating price elasticities with theory-based priors. *Journal of Marketing Research*, November, 413–23.

Morwitz, Vicki G., Greenleaf, Eric A. & Johnson, Eric J. (1998) Divide and prosper: consumers' reactions to partitioned prices. *Journal of Marketing Research*, November, 453–63.

Nagle, Thomas T. & Holden, Reed K. (2002) *The Strategy and Tactics of Pricing*, 3rd edn. Upper Saddle River, NJ: Prentice-Hall.

Naik, Prasad A., Raman, Kalyan & Winer, Russell S. (2000) The long-term impact of promotions: a double-edged sword in the battle for market share. Unpublished working paper, UC-Davis.

Narasimhan, Chakravarthi, Neslin, Scott A. & Sen, Subrata K. (1996) Promotional elasticities and category characteristics. *Journal of Marketing*, April, 17–30.

Nijs, Vincent R., Dekimpe, Marnik G., Steenkamp, Jan-Benedict E.M. & Hanssens, Dominique M. (2001) The category-demand effects of price promotions. *Marketing Science*, Winter, 1–23.

Ofir, Chezy (2001) Reexamining latitude of price acceptability. Unpublished working paper, Hebrew University.

Ofir, Chezy, Bechtel, Gordon G. & Winer, Russell S. (2000) Price acceptability thresholds: a thurstonian approach. Unpublished working paper, The Hebrew University.

Papatla, Purushottam & Krishnamurthi, Lakshman (1996) Measuring the dynamic effects of promotions on brand choice. *Journal of Marketing Research*, February, 20–35.

Raghubir, Priya (1998) Coupon value: a signal for price? *Journal of Marketing Research*, August, 316–24.

Rajendran, K.N. & Tellis, Gerard J. (1994) Contextual and temporal components of reference price. *Journal of Marketing*, January, 22–34.

Schindler, Robert M. (2001) Relative price level of 99-ending prices: image versus reality. *Marketing Letters*, August, 239–48.

Schindler, Robert M. & Kirby, Patrick N. (1997) Patterns of rightmost digits used in advertised prices: implications for nine-ending effects. *Journal of Consumer Research*, September, 192–201.

Scitovsky, Tibor (1944–45) Some consequences of the habit of judging quality by price. *Review of Economic Studies*, 12, 100.

Sethuraman, Raj (1996) A model of how discounting high-priced brands affects the sales of low-priced brands. *Journal of Marketing Research*, November, 399–409.

Sethuraman, Raj, Srinivasan, V. & Kim, Doyle (1999) Asymmetric and neighborhood cross-price effects: some empirical generalizations. *Marketing Science*, 18, 23–41.

Sinha, Atanu R. & Greenleaf, Eric A. (2000) Valuing and attracting bidders and sellers: traditional auctions and the Internet. Unpublished working paper, Stern School of Business, New York University.

Sivakumar, K. & Raj, S.P. (1997) Quality tier competition: how price change influences brand choice and category choice. *Journal of Marketing*, July, 71–84.

Smith, Michael D. & Erik Brynjolfsson (2001) Consumer decision-making at an Internet shopbot. Unpublished working paper.

Smith, Michael D., Bailey, Joseph & Brynjolfsson, Erik (1999) Understanding digital markets: review and assessment. In *Understanding the Digital Economy*, edited by E. Brynjolfsson & B. Kahin. Cambridge, MA: MIT Press, pp. 99–136.

Srivastava, Joydeep, Chakravarti, Dipankar & Rapoport, Amnon (2000) Price and margin negotiations in marketing channels: an experimental study of sequential bargaining under one-sided uncertainty and opportunity cost of delay. *Marketing Science*, 2, 163–85.

Stiving, Mark & Winer, Russell S. (1997) An empirical analysis of price endings with scanner data. *Journal of Consumer Research*, June, 57–68.

Stoetzel, Jean (1970) Psychological/sociological aspects of price. In *Pricing Strategy*, edited by B. Taylor & G. Wills. Princeton, NJ: Brandon/Systems, pp. 70–4.

Stoetzel, Jean, Sauerwein, Jacque & de Vulipan, Alain (1954) Reflections: French research: consumer studies. In *La psychologies economique*, edited by P.L. Reynaud. Libraire Marcel Riviere et Cie, pp. 183–8.

Tellis, Gerard J. (1988) The price elasticity of selective demand: a meta-analysis of econometric models of sales. *Journal of Marketing Research*, November, 331–41.

Tyagi, Rajeev K. (1999) A characterization of retailer response to manufacturer trade deals. *Journal of Marketing Research*, 36, November, 510–16.

Urbany, Joel E., Dickson, Peter R. & Kalapurakal, Rosemary (1996) Price search in the retail grocery market. *Journal of Marketing*, April, 91–104.

Van Westendorp, P. (1976) NSS-Price Sensitivity Meter: a new approach to the study of consumer perception of prices. *ESOMAR Congress*, 139–67.

Vandenbosch, Mark B. & Weinberg, Charles B. (1995) Product and price competition in a two-dimensional vertical differentiation market. *Marketing Science*, 2, 224–49.

Venkatesh, R. & Mahajan, Vijay (1997) Products and branded components: an approach for premium pricing and partner selection. *Marketing Science*, 2, 146–65.

Vickrey, William (1961) Counterspeculation, auctions, and competitive sealed tenders. *Journal of Finance*, May, 302–14.

Wertenbroch, Klaus & Skiera, Bernd (2002) Measuring consumer willingness to pay at the point of purchase. *Journal of Marketing Research*, 39, May, 228–241.

Winer, Russell S. (1985) A price vector model of demand for consumer durables: preliminary evidence. *Marketing Science*, Winter, 74–90.

——— (1986) A reference price model of brand choice for frequently purchased consumer products. *Journal of Consumer Research*, 13, September, 250–6.

——— (1988) Behavioral perspectives on pricing: buyers' subjective perceptions of price revisited. In *Issues in Pricing: Theory and Research*, edited by T. Devinney, Lexington, MA: Lexington Books, pp. 35–57.

Zettelmeyer, Florian (2000) Expanding to the Internet: pricing and communications strategies when firms compete on multiple channels. *Journal of Marketing Research*, August, 292–308.

12

Marketing Communications

DAVID W. STEWART and MICHAEL A. KAMINS

Introduction

Effective marketing and business strategies require obtaining the attention, informing and influencing relevant constituencies of the firm. Potential customers do not buy products or services that they are unaware of. Communication of the reasons a particular product should be purchased, e.g., the benefits associated with the product, and the ways in which a given brand within a product category is different or superior to competitive products, e.g., how the brand is differentiated, are fundamental to marketing success. Kotler (2000: 550) observes, 'the question is not whether to communicate, but rather what to say, to whom and how often.'

Research on marketing communications has a long and rich history. It has roots in early research on verbal learning in psychology (Ebbinghaus, 1885). The first systematic treatment of the role and influence of marketing communications was published by psychologist Walter Dill Scott (1908). Subsequently, the work of social psychologists such as McGuire (1969), Hovland et al. (1953), Lewin (1948), Merton (1946), Katz and Lazarsfeld (1955), and Klapper (1960), among others, played an important role in the development of both empirical research and theory focused on mass communications in general, and marketing communications more specifically. By the 1950s a rich tradition of research and theory development on marketing communications had begun to develop within the marketing discipline, but there continues to be a strong link between work on marketing communications and research in psychology on social influence, attitude change, and communications processes. Contemporary theories of marketing communications rest on such psychological foundations as the functional theory of attitudes (Fazio, 1990; Katz, 1960), the theory of reasoned action (Fishbein & Ajzen, 1975), the elaboration likelihood model (Petty & Cacioppo, 1981), social cognition (Bandura, 1994; Fiske & Taylor, 1992) and theories of goal-derived categorization (Barsalou, 1991). At the same time, research in communications (e.g., Bryant & Zillmann, 1994; Rogers, 1983) and other fields have offered insights into the influence of marketing communication. Finally, important work by practitioners and academics working with commercial data (e.g., Haley, 1985; Jones, 1995; Lodish et al., 1995; McDonald, 1996; Schwerin & Newell, 1981) have provided useful and important evidence regarding the effects of marketing communications.

The purpose of the present chapter is to review the generally accepted body of knowledge about the influence and effects of marketing communications. In addition, the chapter will examine factors that may mediate or moderate the influence of marketing communications. Page constraints prevent a detailed discussion of the rich theoretical foundations on which the body of knowledge rests. The focus of the chapter is the influence of marketing communications at the market or market segment level. Thus, the considerable literature on individual differences in response to marketing communication and on individual-level processes associated with marketing communication will not receive detailed treatment.

The advent of the Internet, other interactive media, and sophisticated customer relationship management systems, clearly create new opportunities for one-to-one targeting of consumers (Pavlou & Stewart, 2000). However, these opportunities are still largely untapped and the literature on such targeting is still in its infancy. To a large degree, the relatively recent origin of these technologies confounds the unique effects of this type of communication with the effects of the adoption of new technology by both consumers and marketers. For these reasons this chapter will not provide a comprehensive review of the role of interactive media and one-to-one marketing. A comprehensive review of interactive media can be found in Stewart et al. (2002), and Internet marketing is discussed elsewhere in this volume (see Chapter 21). While it is likely various new media will open new areas of research, it is also likely that much of the considerable theory and research related to more traditional forms of marketing communication will ultimately be found to be generalizable to various new media once the effects of technology adoption are sorted out. Thus, the goal of the present chapter is to provide a summary of a vast literature on marketing communication that can serve as an introduction to the rich empirical research and theory in the field.

The Role of Marketing Communication

The role of marketing communication is to convey an appropriate message to one or more of the firm's various constituencies. These constituencies include present and future customers, shareholders, competitors, employees, distributors, retailers, regulators, government officials, and the public at large. The messages, media, and objects of communication vary depending on the constituency involved. The reasons a firm may seek to convey a message also vary. It is not always the case that a firm uses marketing communications to sell its products or services. Firms may use marketing communications to create awareness of products, to provide specific information, or to establish or reinforce associations, attitudes, or preferences.

Lavidge and Steiner (1961) introduced a model termed the 'Hierarchy of Effects' to describe the steps or stages through which consumers typically pass when contemplating the purchase of a product. This model, which has its foundations in the earlier work on the social psychology of communication, posits that consumers move from being unaware to aware, to having knowledge, then to liking and preference, and finally to conviction and purchase. Although numerous variations of the hierarchy have subsequently been suggested (Moriarity, 1983) and there has been debate about the order in which various stages may occur (Ray, 1973), the general model has withstood the test of time as a means for conceptualizing the roles of marketing communication. The hierarchy of effects suggests that the goal of marketing communication is to move consumers through these various stages toward an ultimate purchase. Looked at more broadly, however, the model suggests that marketing communication may play a role in three processes: cognition (awareness and knowledge); affect (liking, preference, and conviction); conation or behavior (shopping, purchase). These underlying processes are linked to such marketing objectives as building product awareness and identity, brand building, and product choice, among others.

The relative importance of the various potential goals of marketing communication vary as a function of different moderating factors, including the product's stage in the life cycle, the competitive position of the firm, the intensity of competitive activity, and the degree of loyalty or brand switching in the product category. For example, creating awareness is much more important early in the life cycle of a product than it is for a mature product with a long and well-known history. Similarly, providing information about the positive dimensions of a product, to differentiate it from competitors' products, will be more important in the face of competition than in the absence of significant competition. These mediating factors will be considered in greater detail later in this chapter.

Types of Marketing Communication

Although there are many variations of marketing communication, there are five well-recognized types of communication over which marketers exercise some control: advertising, sales promotion, publicity and public relations, personal selling, and interactive or direct response marketing. To these five types of marketing communication under the control of the marketer must be added word-of-mouth communication – a powerful form of communication in markets, but one over which marketers have decidedly less control.

Advertising involves non-personal forms of communication offered through paid media under clear sponsorship. Major goals of advertising include building primary demand (product category sales) and selective demand (individual brand sales). Advertising may take a variety of forms, and different forms of advertising may produce different effects in the market and be differentially effective depending on various characteristics of the market, the advertised brand, and competitors' brands. Advertising has evolved over time as new media have been developed. Thus, advertising may be found in a variety of different media ranging from signs and outdoor billboards, to newspapers and magazines, to broadcast media. Each of these types of media impose different constraints on the kind of advertising message that can be effectively conveyed and the types of responses and outcomes that can be realistically expected in the market. Historically, much of advertising has tended to involve one-way interaction between the advertiser and the customer. The advent of the Internet and other interactive media has recently created the opportunity for interactive advertising, which has added to the types of response and outcomes that might be expected of advertising (Pavlou & Stewart, 2000).

Although advertising has frequently been depicted in the popular press as a powerful force (cf. Galbraith, 1967; Packard, 1957), it has generally been shown to have relatively modest effects on customers (Lodish et al., 1995; Stewart, 1992). Such modest effects do not mean that advertising is unimportant, but they do suggest that not all advertising is effective. Even advertising that is effective, in the sense that it achieves its objectives, has less effect than other factors such as customers' underlying needs and preferences, the quality of the product or service offering, pricing, and availability.

Sales promotion represents an eclectic collection of various promotional incentives designed to stimulate volume or speed of purchase (Blattberg & Neslin, 1990). Such incentives include sampling, coupons, premiums or gifts, and price deals, among others. As a percentage of the total promotional budget, sales promotion expenditures exceed advertising (Kotler, 2000). Because of the frequency of sales promotion techniques it could be argued that consumers have become promotion elastic and that larger or more lucrative incentives will be required to encourage the goal of new trial or increased usage among current users. It is certainly the case that the primary message communicated by most sales promotions is related to the importance of price as a determinant of purchase. A study by Krishna, Currim and Shoemaker (1991) regarding the deal price component of sales promotions revealed that consumers are generally knowledgeable regarding when a particular brand has been on sale. In addition, the authors observed that the expected frequency of dealing is positively correlated with perceived past-deal frequency. Such knowledge may impact the consumer's image of the brand and result in the consumer only buying the brand when it is on sale. Sales promotion can play an important and complementary role in generating trial for new products and brands, however. Although sales promotion clearly plays a role in marketing communication, this chapter will not specifically deal with sales promotion (see Chapter 13 of the present book).

Publicity and public relations involves the use of non-paid media to reach relevant audiences. Firms use press releases, media events, press kits, product announcements and a variety of other tools that are directed at the media (journalists, reporters, etc.) rather than customers. The intent of public relations activities is to obtain coverage of the firm and its products in stories and editorials that appear in the media. Since such stories are not paid for (at least not directly) and are attributed to a neutral party, they tend to be much lower in cost and have greater credibility than advertising. On the other hand, the nature of the message and the size and character of the audience reached through publicity is not under the control of the marketer.

Personal selling involves direct interpersonal communication between a representative of the firm and the potential customer. Whereas advertising has traditionally carried on a monolog with the target market, personal selling is dyadic in nature and hence inherently offers many advantages as a communication device (Williams et al., 1990). These advantages are critical since a personal selling approach is often required to complete the sale. One especially important advantage of personal selling is that the marketer's message can be specifically tailored to the consumer. Weitz et al. (1986) note that salespeople may engage in adaptive selling based on their knowledge of customer types and sales strategies. A second advantage of personal selling is that salespeople can develop relationships with customers that may increase purchase probability and brand loyalty (Farber & Wycoff, 1992). Personal selling is generally more expensive than advertising, and the number of individuals with which a salesperson can have contact within a given period is severely constrained. Although many of the principles and concepts associated with communication in general apply in a personal selling context, the interpersonal and interactive nature of personal selling adds dimensions to the communication process that are beyond the scope of the present chapter. Chapter 10 of this volume focuses more specifically on communication in a personal selling context.

Direct response and interactive marketing involve the use of non-personal media to conduct a dialog with consumers. The role of such marketing communications is to facilitate reciprocal response between customers and marketers. It includes electronic shopping, voice mail, e-mail, facsimile, telemarketing, catalogs and TV shopping. The Direct Marketing Association defines an interactive marketing system as one that uses one or more advertising media to affect a measurable response and/or transaction at any location. Day and Montgomery (1999) observe that the adaptive company of the future will utilize *interactive* strategies to become more market driven. That is, the company will have 'the ability to address an individual and then remember the response of that individual. With each successive interaction, the firm learns more and uses this information from customers to personalize further communications in ways that take into account that unique response and the value proposition.'

Word-of-mouth communication (WOM) refers to communication among and between individual customers. Such communication is very common in many markets, and the role of customer-to-customer communication cannot be underestimated. Customer-initiated communication tends to have very high credibility and may have wide-ranging effects: it may influence where customers shop, what information customers seek, what customers buy, and how customers evaluate a purchase after the sale. Although marketers often attempt to facilitate word-of-mouth communication, it is not directly under the marketers' control. There is evidence that word-of-mouth communication may be growing in importance as interactive media, such as the Internet, make it easier for customers to communicate with one another (Pavlou & Stewart, 2000).

Integrated Marketing Communications. In the past decade there has been an increasing recognition by both marketing scholars and practitioners of marketing communications that the various forms of marketing communication can and should work together to reinforce the goals and objectives of the marketer. This recognition has produced a focus on what has come to be called Integrated Marketing Communications (IMC) (Thorson & Moore, 1996). IMC explicitly recognizes the fact that consumers are exposed to information from many different sources. This exposure, in turn, results in the need for marketers to coordinate communications across media and consider how various forms of communication will reinforce and complement one another. In addition, various new media, such as the Internet, tend to blur the elements of the marketing mix (Stewart et al., 1996). Thus, the same medium may be a communications channel, a distribution channel, and, in some cases, even the product itself. This blurring of the boundaries of communication channels and of the larger marketing mix suggest a need to understand the context in which an individual medium or message may be embedded. It is certainly the case that marketers need to understand how all the elements of the communication and marketing mix will work together to produce a particular outcome.

Effects of Marketing Communication

The questions as to whether marketing communication is effective and what its effects are, are, on their face, simple questions. Yet, they are not so simple. For example, the question of effectiveness leads to issues regarding how success or failure is measured, and what is the time frame to be considered? A particular communication may be readily recalled but only because it is so irritating and obnoxious that it persuades consumers *not* to buy the product. By one measure, awareness, the communication 'worked'; by another, the number of persons persuaded to buy the product, it is a dismal failure. One cannot make a determination of whether communication has had an effect or has been successful without first specifying the purpose of the communication. Specification of purpose, in turn, requires an understanding of how communication influences the customer. Recognition of this fact led marketers to develop various approaches for identifying communications objectives and for conceptualizing the relationships among these objectives and their in-market measurement. The ubiquitous hierarchy-of-effects model, in its many forms (Moriarity, 1983; Vaughn, 1980), is one example of such an approach. Much of the research and theory related to the effects of marketing communications, at least communications involving impersonal media, has focused on advertising. For this reason, much of the discussion of the effects of marketing communication in the remainder of this chapter will focus on advertising effects.

Advertising and Primary Demand

A reading of marketing textbooks suggests that it is almost axiomatic that advertising increases product category sales. A frequent criticism of marketing communication – that it creates demand for products that have little utility – is also predicated on the assumption that one effect of communication is the creation of generic demand (Galbraith, 1967). This assumption rests on what appear to be reasonable premises. There is little doubt that various types of marketing communication are very efficient means for creating awareness of new products. Communication may also be a very useful and efficient means for stimulating the trial of a new product when the product itself is a new-to-the-world product. Thus, it is not difficult to identify a link between advertising, or marketing communication more generally, and product purchase early in the life cycle of a product. This link does not establish that communication is the primary determinant of demand, however, even for new-to-the-world categories. More importantly, there is little evidence that advertising, or other types of marketing communication, can increase the consumption of products within a mature product category (Ehrenberg, 1983; Lambin, 1976). The evidence that does exist suggests that such effects are small and short-lived.

One of the most comprehensive studies of the effects of advertising on sales was carried out by Lambin (1976). He investigated the effects of advertising for 16 different product categories in as many as 9 different countries over a 10-year period. With respect to the question of advertising's effects on aggregate category demand, Lambin concluded (1976: 136): 'Limited empirical support is given to the view that advertising increases primary demand.' In the four product categories where advertising did have a significant effect on primary demand, all four product classes were early in the product life cycle, and

> The economic power of advertising '*per se*' has been overstated by advertising critics and apologists. Socioeconomic forces are more important, and advertising has a limited capacity to stimulate total market growth. (Lambin, 1976: 136)

It is useful to note that some advertising campaigns that appear directed at increasing sales for a product category as a whole are, in fact, competitive advertisements in a broader context of competition. Examples of such campaigns include the California Raisins campaign (the dancing raisins) and the V-8 Vegetable Juice campaign ('Wow! I could have had a V-8.'). This type of marketing communication tends to be rare, however, since many products do not have close indirect substitutes. Other exceptions to these general findings are cases where marketing communication suggests new uses for an established product (the well-known Arm and Hammer Baking Soda campaign is an example), and where a product with a low level of top-of-mind awareness is made more salient to consumers (advertising campaigns for dot.com companies such as EBAY and IVILLAGE are recent examples). In all of these instances the product on which communications focuses is more similar to a new product than an established product. The suggestion of new uses for a product is essentially the same as developing a new market. In the case of a product or brand with low awareness and usage, the influence of marketing communication is closely akin to the development of a new market.

Several of the empirical studies that suggest communication has an effect on a primary demand have, in fact, been carried out in markets for various agricultural products, where low levels of awareness or indirect substitutes exist (Henderson & Brown, 1961; Henderson et al., 1961; Hoofnagle, 1963). Thus, these studies are consistent with the proposition that marketing communication has an effect on aggregate demand only under a narrow set of circumstances.

Empirical support for the proposition that marketing communication creates generic demand largely rests on studies that have shown correlations between growth of aggregate sales in a market and increases in total advertising expenditures (see, for example, the study by Taylor and Weiserbs, 1972). These studies seldom consider the influence of market conditions in interpreting results, however. For example, in markets that are growing, it is likely that advertising expenditures will increase in response to the growing market. The growing market, in turn, will result in increases in sales. When advertising budgets are based on a percent-of-sales rule, which remains the most common budgeting practice, it will always be the case that rising demand will be associated with rising expenditures on advertising. It would be incorrect to conclude that the increase in expenditures was the cause of the increase in sales in this instance. Rather, market growth drives the increase in both sales and advertising.[1]

Market growth may be attributable to factors other than a product being early in its life cycle. Demographic changes in a population often increase demand for whole product classes. As this demand is recognized by marketing organizations, expenditures on marketing communications are also likely to grow. This will produce a correlation between expenditures on advertising and growth in market demand. Such expenditures did not create the demand, however. The increase in expenditures is a *response* to the growth in demand.[2]

Among the most frequently cited studies of the purported effect of marketing communications on aggregate demand is that of Taylor and Weiserbs (1972). This study, which concluded that advertising does influence the aggregate consumption function, has been criticized for its methodological and conceptual flaws (see Lambin, 1976: 137–8). Among these flaws is a failure to consider marketplace factors other than advertising that may influence demand: the Taylor and Weiserbs study (1972) did not account for new product introductions during the period of the study.

Another frequently cited study (Roberts & Samuelson, 1988) examined data on the United States' cigarette market during 1971–1982. This study concluded that cigarette advertising expenditures had a significant positive impact on total demand in the category, while individual market shares of competing firms depended more on the number of brands offered. This study failed to consider an important determinant of demand during the period of study, however. The period 1971–1982 was a period in which large numbers of consumers attained an age when smoking often begins. The baby-boom generation entered adolescence and young adulthood during this period. In fact, the final wave of the baby-boom generation, those born in 1964, would have been 18 years of age in 1982. Indeed, a subsequent study of the cigarette market (Pollay et al., 1996) concluded that the primary effect of advertising in this market was to influence brand choice.

The influence of demographic trends can be observed in a variety of markets and the effects of marketing communications on primary demand can only be estimated correctly when such trends are also considered. For example, during the same period of the Roberts and Samuelson study, 1971–1982, there was an explosion of demand in the soft drink category. This huge increase in demand was also accompanied by large increases in expenditures on marketing communications by soft drink marketers. Such increases in marketing communications expenditures was a response to the increased demand that was created as a large segment of the population moved into the years of high soft drink consumption.[3]

There are, of course, determinants of demand other than demographics. There are cultural, social, and familial influences. People often want things that society suggests are important; they often want what others have. Most products have utility of one type or another; they make life easier, they move us from place to place, they cover our bodies, they provide excitement or relaxation, they make us feel better about ourselves, they provide nourishment, or they just taste or feel good. Some of this utility is inherent in the product itself; some of it may be a kind of learned utility. Such learned utility is a function of the culture, social relationships, and personal and observed experiences. Insofar as marketing communication reflects the values of a culture, it may serve to reinforce these values.

Increases and decreases in the demand for products are generally the result of broad changes in a society. These changes may be demographic; they may be economic; they may be technological; or they may be related to the fabric of values that define a society. Sometimes, these changes may be the result of new information. For example, more consumers are concerned about the amount of cholesterol in their diets today than 20 years ago. This concern has changed the eating habits of many consumers. It has also resulted in changes both in food products and in what is communicated about food products. That is, attributes of the product linked to cholesterol and, more broadly, to health concerns, become more salient to the consumer (e.g., fat and vitamin content) and hence are emphasized more frequently and prominently in marketing communications.

Both the empirical evidence and logical deduction offer compelling evidence that marketing communication does not create demand; it is a response to demand. People buy things because they want them, not because advertising somehow compels them to purchase. When the influence of primary drivers of demand, like demographic changes, broad societal changes, and the effects of other marketing actions, such as lower price, are controlled, there are no studies that demonstrate that marketing communication creates demand for established products.

In light of the evidence to the contrary, why does the belief that marketing communication creates demand persist? History and the human tendency to confound correlation with causation are the likely culprits. Much of the history of advertising was written during a period of very rapid growth in markets. As Blair et al. (1987) note, the period of history that began with the end of World War II and ended in the late 1970s was a time of enormous growth in the domestic market of the United States. This growth was driven by both a growth in population and a growth in the affluence of the population. This growth offered opportunities for business firms who responded by introducing a plethora of new products. At the same time, there was rapid growth in the media available for communicating with consumers about goods and services. One result of these broad societal changes was increased demand for a wide array of products and a concomitant increase in expenditures on marketing communication. Marketing communication during this period did speed the rapidity of the product adoption process by facilitating consumer awareness. It is not too difficult a leap to conclude that marketing communication was at least partially responsible for the growth in aggregate demand. Galbraith (1967) popularized this view of advertising in his book, *The Affluent Society*. Yet, this view was fundamentally incorrect.

Advertising and Selective Demand

If advertising or other types of marketing communications do not create aggregate product demand, at least in relatively mature product categories, it may, nonetheless, increase demand for the advertised brand. A common assumption about advertising is that its effect should always be manifest in an increase in demand. This increase in demand may be the result of one or both of two events: 1) communication may induce users of competing brands to switch brands; or 2) communication may induce users of a particular brand to buy more of the brand. In order to examine the influence of advertising on these two events, it is necessary to distinguish between two classes of consumers.

It has long been recognized that product categories differ appreciably in terms of the amount of switching among brands that takes place over time (Adtel, 1974; Carpenter & Lehmann, 1985; Colombo & Morrison, 1987; Ehrenberg, 1972; Frank & Massy, 1967; Jeuland, 1979; Raj, 1982; Schwerin & Newell, 1981; Stewart & Furse, 1986; Tellis, 1988). Some product categories are characterized by very high rates of brand switching among consumers, while others are characterized by relatively high brand loyalty and very low rates of brand switching among product users. These differences in switching rates are the result of a multitude of factors that will not be reviewed here. It is sufficient to note that these differences tend to be very stable over time (Ehrenberg, 1972). Further, there is evidence that within certain product categories, individual brands may also have unique switching rates.

The differences in brand switching rates across product categories are related to the mix of consumers who are loyal to a given brand or brands and those consumers who are not brand loyal. Certain product categories, for example cigarettes and laundry detergent, tend to exhibit very low rates of brand switching and high loyalty (as measured by repeat purchase rates) to individual brands. These types of product categories may have many or few product alternatives, but there is little switching from one product to another, i.e., the rate of switching does not appear to be related to the number of alternatives available. On the other hand, some product categories, e.g., paper towels and ready-to-eat cereals, tend to exhibit very high levels of brand switching. Thus, product categories differ with respect to the relative mix of brand loyal consumers and brand switchers.

Empirical research has consistently shown the existence of these two classes of consumers and has clearly demonstrated that marketing communication has differential effects on these two classes (Belch, 1981, 1982; Cacioppo & Petty, 1985; Carpenter & Lehmann, 1985; Eskin & Baron, 1977; Information Resources, Inc., 1989; Jeuland, 1979; Naples, 1979; Pechmann & Stewart, 1990; Raj, 1982; Schwerin & Newell, 1981; Simon & Arndt, 1980; Stephens & Warren, 1984; Tellis, 1988). Unfortunately, much of the empirical research on marketing communication has examined the effects of communication at the aggregate market level, rather than examine the effects within these two classes of consumers (Columbo & Morrison, 1987). This has frequently resulted in contradictory findings and misleading conclusions about the effects of marketing communication.

Advertising Effects on Loyals

The effect of advertising on loyals is obviously not to persuade them to buy the advertised brand, since they already do so. Rather, if there is an effect at all it must be to reinforce loyalty to the brand or persuade the consumer to buy more of the brand. Thus, in markets with very large numbers of loyal consumers relative to switchers, it would be unreasonable to expect that marketing communication should produce incremental sales unless the loyal users could be induced to buy more product.

There is some empirical evidence that suggests that advertising may induce loyal consumers to purchase larger quantities of their preferred brand, at least in the short run (Raj, 1982; Tellis, 1988). Such volume effects may be explained, at least in part, by a lessened tendency on the part of the consumer to purchase competitive brands (Carpenter & Lehmann, 1985; Raj, 1982), however. It is not at all clear that these effects are the result of an increase in the long-term demand for either the specific brand or the generic product. In other words, the effect of marketing communication on loyals appears to be to discourage switching (reinforce loyalty). Such reinforcement effects may or may not manifest themselves in increases in purchase volume, depending on the propensity of consumers to switch among brands and the frequency of purchase. Among the most loyal of consumers, those who purchase a single preferred brand, there would be no manifest effect of advertising even when the communication serves to reinforce loyalty.

An important question, with both theoretical and empirical implications, is the process by which marketing communication has its effect on loyal consumers. A substantial body of research speaks directly to this issue. Empirical studies that have examined the influence of advertising on loyals have consistently found that these consumers are more likely to pay attention to and remember information about products (brands) that they use, and are less likely to pay attention or remember information about products (brands) they do not use (Belch, 1981; Craig et al., 1976; Pechmann & Stewart, 1990; Politz Media Studies, 1960; Tolley, 1994). Such findings are quite consistent with theories of attention (Broadbent, 1977; Greenwald & Leavitt, 1984; Krugman, 1988) and selective exposure (Atkin, 1985; Axsom & Cooper, 1981; Baugh, 1982; Condry, 1989; Fenigstein & Heyduk, 1985; Gunter, 1985; Ratneshwar et al., 1989; Zillmann & Bryant, 1985), and with theories of cognitive dissonance (Akerlof & Dickens, 1982; Calder, 1981; Cotton, 1985). The former theories simply assert that people are more likely to attend to things that are more relevant to their needs and consistent with their own beliefs. The latter theory asserts that consumers often seek justification for making a decision or behaving in a particular way. Thus, Ehrlich et al. (1957) found new car buyers more attentive to automobile advertising *after* the purchase than before.

Studies in contexts other than marketing also support the view that people selectively attend to information (Axsom & Cooper, 1981; Brehm, 1956; Davis & Jones, 1960; Glass, 1964; Knox & Inkster, 1968). Thus, it is not surprising to find studies that reveal a high correlation between advertising recognition and product use (Chapman & Fitzgerald, 1982; Goldstein et al., 1987; McCarthy, 1986). Such findings suggest that attention to advertising is a natural consequence of using a particular product or brand.

The phenomena of selective exposure and cognitive dissonance explain why it is so hard to change brand loyal behavior once it is established. Consumers are simply less likely to attend to marketing communications for a brand they do not currently purchase. These phenomena also explain why repetition and creativity are such important elements in advertising. Attracting the attention of the non-user of a brand or product with a short message that is surrounded by enormous clutter is very difficult. Creative content or frequent repetitions of a product message represent the only avenues for attracting attention from an otherwise disinterested consumer. Attention and memory are not the only factors that are influenced by loyalty, however.

Modern attitude theory holds that individuals are not mere passive recipients of messages (Petty & Cacioppo, 1986). Rather, they actively screen and operate on information as it becomes available (assuming they choose to attend to it at all). They tend to seek information that reinforces existing beliefs, a phenomenon referred to as perceptual vigilance (Runyon & Stewart, 1987), and selectively ignore information that is counter to existing beliefs, a phenomenon known as perceptual defense (Runyon & Stewart, 1987). Individuals also elaborate on messages. They add arguments of their own, they counter-argue, and they have thoughts about the veracity of the source (Belch, 1981; Wright, 1973). These thoughts, not the message that gave rise to them, are what form or change attitudes. The numbers of these thoughts and the strength of resultant attitudes are a function of how involved the consumer is in the processing of a message (Petty & Cacioppo, 1986). When there is the potential for serious consequences associated with a decision (the decision is one of high involvement), individuals tend to do more thinking and form attitudes that are more resistant to change. When the potential for consequences is small (the decision is one of low involvement), the number of thoughts tends to be small and the attitudes that are formed tend to be weak (Kamins & Assael, 1989; Wright, 1974). There is little incentive in these types of low involvement situations for consumers to revisit decisions and attitudes once they are formed, however.

Most decisions about *brands* of frequently purchased consumer goods are low involvement decisions. Among loyal consumers of these products there are few incentives for switching brands. As a consequence, marketing communication related to competitive brands is unlikely to attract the attention of the loyal consumer, and this consumer is likely to have few thoughts in response to any given communication that does happen to obtain his or her attention. This is not a scenario in which marketing communication is likely to have a strong effect.

For loyal consumers, marketing communication simply serves to reinforce decisions of little consequence. Recognition of this role of advertising led Andrew Ehrenberg (1983, 1988) to propose the Awareness-Trial-Reinforcement (ATR) model of advertising. The ATR model suggests that advertising is a weak force rather than a strong, persuasive influence. It asserts that advertising may influence the consumer in one of several ways; advertising may create awareness, induce trial, or reinforce product purchase. It is the last stage, where the role of advertising is to reinforce feelings of satisfaction after purchase or to re-awaken awareness, that Ehrenberg emphasizes. He argues that the role of repetitive communication for mature products is predominantly defensive – to reinforce already developed repeat buying habits – since most buying behavior involves the repeat purchase of familiar products. Since the consumer is more likely to attend to communications for the brands he or she is already buying, repetition enables the purchase habit for a particular brand to continue to operate in the face of competitive advertising and other marketing programs.

Ehrenberg mounts a strong argument in defense of his position. He notes that there is little direct evidence that advertising for established brands operates by any other means, and such evidence as does exist is negative (Achenbaum, 1972) or only partially supportive (Barnes, 1971; McDonald, 1971; Palda, 1966). He argues that other models of advertising response do not explain how small- to medium-brands retain share in the face of vast amounts of advertising by brand leaders or why cuts in advertising seldom result in large losses of sales over the short run. Ehrenberg also notes that advertisements frequently provide little product information, a fact that would be more consistent with advertising being suggestive or reinforcing rather than strongly persuasive. Because the buyers of frequently purchased goods are not ignorant of them, Ehrenberg reasons that the aim of marketing communications is to inform the experienced customer that brand 'X' is as good as other brands.

Thus, ATR suggests that advertising is a price that firms pay to stay in the market by defending or maintaining their share of a market that is well established. Advertising might also create new sales for a given brand (but not for the category as a whole) by reawakening consumers' awareness and interest in it and by stimulating trial, but ultimately these consumers will be lost if they do not like the product and their new purchase behavior is not reinforced. Indeed, this is a particularly likely occurrence among brand switchers, whose response to marketing communication will be discussed below. The ATR model suggests that reinforcement reduces cognitive dissonance, increases brand satisfaction, and rekindles brand awareness. Communication has such a reinforcing effect because it predisposes the consumer to notice certain aspects of the brand, while ignoring others.

The marketing literature has for some time acknowledged that one effect of advertising is to provide a rationale for purchasing a specific brand within a category by calling attention to significant product differences or minor differences among products that are otherwise commodity products. This view of how marketing communication works is consistent with an impressive array of empirical studies and theory development in marketing, psychology, and economics, which suggests that providing a way to think about a decision, 'framing the problem,' has a significant effect on behavior (Hauser, 1986; Kahneman & Tversky, 1979, 1982; Plott & Levine, 1978; Stewart & Furse, 1986; Thaler, 1985; Tversky & Kahneman, 1974). One mechanism by which communication may reinforce habitual purchase behavior is through reminding consumers of a specific decision rule. The conceptualization of marketing communication as a reinforcer of the purchase behavior of loyal consumers is also consistent with the empirical observation that the more time that elapses between purchase events, the less likely that consumer loyalty will persist over time. This is one reason for findings that advertising has differential effects on heavy users and light users of a product (Ackoff & Emshoff, 1975a, 1975b, 1975c).

The preceding discussion suggests that most advertising is defensive; it is designed to hold current share of marketing. Marketing communications is part of the price of doing business in a mature market. This view is also consistent with empirical findings that market share is frequently closely related to share of voice (the percentage of a brand's advertising relative to all advertising for the product category (Horsky, 1977; Little, 1975; Stewart, 1989)).

This is not to suggest that advertising cannot ever be used for building market share in a product category. A particular competitor within a given category may choose to spend well above the equilibrium level of expenditures (that is, this competitor might raise its relative spending or share of voice above its market share). Research suggests that such competitive tactics are most likely to succeed when accompanied by a significant product improvement, a particularly compelling message, or when at least a subset of competitors is unable or unwilling to respond to the competitive threat. Short of the presence of these situational factors in the market, market response to increases in advertising in mature markets appears to be very short-lived (Little, 1979; also see below).

Several empirical studies offer evidence that is consistent with this view of marketing communication as a reinforcer of brand loyalty. In a carefully controlled study of print advertising carried out by Time, Inc. and Seagram (Time, Inc./Seagram, 1981), the largest changes in awareness, brand attitude, and purchase behavior were associated with brands that were low in awareness among consumers. While there were gains associated with advertising for high awareness brands as well, it is important to note that none of the products used in the study had been recently advertised in the test markets in which the study was carried out. Among high awareness brands, the greatest increase in awareness occurred following the first insertions of the print advertising. Changes in brand ratings (attitudes toward the brand) were very modest for high awareness brands. Although the advertising did increase consumers' willingness to buy the high awareness brands, willingness to buy was unrelated to the number of opportunities consumers had to see the advertising. These findings are consistent with the view that for established brands, the role of advertising is largely that of reinforcing existing attitudes and behavioral patterns. When such brands have not been advertised for some time, advertising may serve to raise the general awareness of the brand, and thereby remind consumers of the availability of the brand and their previously formed attitudes toward the brand. For new brands, or brands with low levels of awareness, regardless of the length of time on the market, advertising may not only increase awareness, it may also serve as one means, along with product trial, for creating attitudes toward the brand among consumers who have not previously formed such attitudes.

The role of marketing communication as a reinforcer of behavior may also be the reason that one of the more comprehensive studies of advertising (Information Resources, Inc., 1989; see also Lodish et al., 1995) found that about half of all of the advertising for more than 360 frequently purchased consumer goods produced no increase in sales. Among new products, almost 60% of the commercials examined in the study produced immediate increases in sales, but only 46% of the advertising executions for established products manifested any immediate increase in sales.

The results reported by Information Resources, Inc. are consistent with a study conducted by Raj (1982), who found that advertising had its only effect on brand loyal consumers in the product category he studied. Likewise, Tellis (1988) found that consumers who are loyal to a brand responded more strongly to advertising for that brand than those who were not loyal. He concludes, 'advertising has a small effect in winning new buyers (from competitors' offerings) but a relatively strong effect in reinforcing intensity of preference.' Several other studies also suggest that taking share away from competitive products is difficult, expensive, and often of only short-term benefit (Adams & Blair, 1989; Appel, 1984; Axelrod, 1980; Haley, 1978; Simon, 1982; Tellis, 1988).

Advertising Effects on Switchers

Advertising appears to have different effects on switchers than loyals. Much of the research in both industry and academe has focused on this capricious group. Switchers have little or no brand loyalty. They most certainly make purchase decisions on the basis of something other than brand. Switching may be associated with price, availability, top-of-mind awareness, or any number of other factors that may enter into decision making (Tellis, 1988). In the case where price is the determinant characteristic, price promotions are likely to be the most effective vehicle for inducing brand switching. Where the determinant factor in decision making is familiarity, top-of-mind awareness, image, or some other communications-driven element, marketing communications may play an important role. It is useful to note, however, that the effect of advertising on switchers is likely to be short-lived.

There is a significant body of literature that suggests brand familiarity, or top-of-mind awareness, plays an important role in consumer choice (Aaker & Day, 1974; Axelrod, 1968; Burke & Schoeffler, 1980; Grubar, 1969; Holman & Hecker, 1983; Sutherland & Galloway, 1983; Taylor et al., 1979; Wilson, 1981). The role of awareness also appears to be far greater for low involvement types of decisions, where the consumer is looking for a simple rule for decision making (Batra & Ray, 1985). Further, there is evidence that the repetition of brand advertising and the intensity of competitive advertising play key roles in producing these effects. Several studies have demonstrated that repetition has a far greater effect on awareness than on attitude (Ray, 1982; Ray & Sawyer, 1971; Ray et al., 1971; Sawyer, 1974; Strang et al., 1975). There is also evidence that competitive marketing communications can reduce the salience or top-of-mind awareness of a brand (Alba & Chattopadhyay, 1985; Burke & Srull, 1988; Geiger, 1971; Stewart, 1989). Thus, in product categories where consumers use a simple familiarity rule, switching may simply be a manifestation of changes in the most salient brand. In the most extreme case, this may be the brand to which the consumer was most recently exposed.

Familiarity is but one type of decision rule that consumers faced with low involvement choices may use for deciding among purchase alternatives. Virtually any differentiating characteristic of a product or its advertising will do. The use of a likable spokesperson, a credible sales person, a strong image with which consumers identify, a catchy tune, or any of dozens of other creative devices might serve to predispose the consumer to purchase one brand over another. Such predispositions in low involvement situations have been shown to be highly transient and easily changed (Chaiken, 1980; Petty & Cacioppo, 1986; Petty et al., 1983). These predispositions must be constantly reinforced or they will fade rapidly, often within a week (Petty & Cacioppo, 1986). This is one reason that research on advertising execution has found that more effective commercials, both in terms of memorability and in terms of eliciting brand switching behavior, contain brand differentiating messages, that is, statements, demonstrations, images, or other devices that distinguish the advertised brand from competitors (Stewart, 1986; Stewart & Furse, 1986; Stewart & Koslow, 1989). This research has also shown that differentiating messages are even more important for established products than for new products, where being new may, in itself, be a basis for differentiation.

Unlike firmly established attitudes, these transient predispositions are likely to change in the face of marketing communications by competitors that offer different cues that the consumer might use to make a brand selection. As in the case where familiarity is the critical factor in determining switching behavior, predispositions based on other factors must be constantly reinforced. This is a different kind of reinforcement than is required for loyal consumers, and it is more expensive to execute. This is one reason why product categories characterized by a high number of switchers typically require substantially greater expenditures on advertising.

In any given product category there exists some mixture of both loyals and switchers. Thus, marketing communication must reinforce loyal consumers and reinforce the decision rules of consumers with a predisposition to switch brands. If the objective of marketing communication is to attract loyal users of competing products, the communication must also cut through the selective attention of these consumers and offer a compelling reason for switching. These are not easy tasks. This is one reason good creative directors are well paid. Indeed, research suggests that the quality of advertising, i.e., the creative execution, the strength of the selling message, plays a very substantial role in determining the effectiveness of communication in the marketplace (Adams & Blair, 1992; Arnold et al., 1987; Blair, 1987/88; Drane, 1988; Stewart & Furse, 1986; Stewart & Koslow, 1989). Even if such effective advertising can be created, there is still the question of how long it will have an effect. The evidence suggests that the effects tend to be short-lived (Appel, 1984; Axelrod, 1980; Blair, 1987/88; Krishnamurthi et al., 1986; Tele-Research, Inc., 1968).

Temporal Characteristics of Advertising

There is a pervasive view that advertising has very long-term effects. This view received some early support from studies by Palda (1964) and Ackoff and Emshoff (1975a, 1975b). These studies suggested that the effects of advertising might persist for a year or more. There are numerous other studies that indicate that communication effects may persist beyond the initial or last exposure (Bass & Clarke, 1972; Clarke, 1976, 1977c, 1977d; Clarke & McCann, 1973; Dean, 1966; Houston & Weiss, 1974, 1975; Kuehn et al., 1964; Lambin, 1972; Lavidge & Steiner, 1961; Sawyer & Ward, 1977, 1979). Thus, there is no question that advertising, and other marketing communication effects, can be long lasting: a consumer who learns about a product via advertising does not immediately forget the product. Having learned about a product via advertising, tried the product, and had a satisfactory experience, a consumer may continue to buy the product into the future. These are certainly examples of the long-term effects of marketing communication. The mechanism by which these effects occur is a different matter, however. There are two competing views as to how these long-term effects arise. The differences in these two views are subtle, but they have important implications.

Cumuluative Effects Versus Current Effects

One perspective, the *cumulative effects* view, suggests that marketing communications do not have their full impact on sales in the period in which the communications occur. Rather, this view holds that the effect of marketing communication builds over time; the full effect of communication in a given period can only be identified by looking across multiple periods after exposure to the communication. A competing perspective, the *current effects* hypothesis, suggests that sales are a function of current expenditures on marketing communication and a carryover effect that cannot be completely attributable to past expenditures. These carryover effects are posited to be the result of an interaction of marketing communication and product use. For example, marketing communication in the form of advertising may create awareness of the product and induce trial (Marks & Kamins, 1988). Product trial may, in turn, result in a positive product experience. If the product experience is positive, a loyal user may be created. This loyalty may persist over time. It would be incorrect to attribute this effect exclusively or even directly to advertising, however. Product satisfaction is the primary determinant of loyalty (Churchill & Surprenant, 1982).

In this view, advertising contributes to loyalty only insofar as it generates product awareness and trial. The generation of awareness and trial are not unique functions of advertising; there are other means by which consumers become aware of products and are encouraged to try a product. Thus, the current effects model suggests that advertising has its primary effect in the period in which it occurs. It manifests longer-term effects only because there is a long-term consequence associated with a positive product experience.

The cumulative effects model suggests that the effects of marketing communications build over time. Thus, a single exposure to a communication may be insufficient to have a detectable effect on consumers, but it does have an effect that is added to subsequent exposures until a detectable effect occurs. This view is at least implicit in any research that looks at the relationship of aggregate spending on marketing communications and market demand over multiple time periods. Indeed, the notion that multiple exposures may be necessary for communication to manifest a measurable and/or optimal effect has a long history, and is frequently referred to as 'wear-in.' For example, Zielske (Zielske, 1959; Zielske & Henry, 1980) observed that recall increased for a message with repeated exposures. However, the pattern was different as a function of whether the messages were viewed monthly or weekly. A review of advertising repetition by Pechmann and Stewart (1991) led them to the general conclusion that both cognitive and affective responses to an advertisement (e.g., attention, recall, attitude) initially increase with increasing repetition over the first few months of an ad campaign.

The current effects model, on the other hand, suggests that the only appropriate analysis of the relationship between demand and marketing communications is one that examines the immediate effect of communication, that is, an analysis of the influence of the communications in a given period on sales in the same period. The most appropriate definition for a given period will vary by product category, but it is probable that the interval would correspond closely to the inter-purchase time, that is, the length of time that elapses between purchases of a brand (Krishnamurthi et al., 1986). For frequently purchased consumer goods this inter-purchase time interval is likely to vary from a few days to a few weeks.

A study of 22 frequently purchased brands (Harvey et al., 1989) concluded that advertising had a very immediate effect, but that gains began to fall back after eight to twelve weeks. Similarly, Krishnamurthi et al. (1986) found that the effect of advertising was immediate and had a duration of roughly the same interval as the purchase cycle for the brand (one-and-a-half weeks in this particular case). A collaborative study carried out by Time, Inc. and Seagram (1981) found that response to advertising was immediate for eight low usage products. Finally, the results of a large-scale study of 360 brands of consumer-packaged goods over a 10-year span (Information Resources, Inc., 1989), while finding that advertising effects may be long lasting, concluded:

> For new products, advertising can provide significant help when it is fulfilling its role of communicating product news. The data show that increasing weight behind new product advertising is a very productive strategy. Deferring spending may not work. Because new product advertising is primarily affecting trial, its effectiveness is likely to be long term because of the repeat purchases of these new triers generated by advertising …
>
> Once the new product advertising has performed its role of generating trial and positioning the new product in the market, the same large advertising budgets may not always be needed. Without new, compelling copy, the evidence shows that some established brand advertising might not be causing incremental sales. New, fresh copy for established products can be very effective even if run for a relatively short period. The data show that the incremental sales effects of new copy are found within six months.

Various researchers (e.g., Gibson, 1996; Jones, 1995; McDonald, 1996; Schroeder et al., 1997) have argued and offered empirical demonstrations that only one exposure is enough to trigger a maximum response to advertising. All of these findings are consistent with a current effects model of advertising response. If communication is effective, it works quickly upon exposure to the individual consumer. To the extent that different types of communication, media schedules and expenditures result in more or less rapid exposure of all consumers in the market, there may appear to be some lagged effects of advertising. These effects are artifacts of aggregating data, however; they are not real effects.

There is an impressive array of studies that can be brought to bear on the question of the length of communication effects, though almost all of this work has focused only on advertising. Econometric studies carried out using historical data, behavioral studies carried out in the laboratory, and field experiments involving controlled market testing and split cable testing, agree that the impact of advertising occurs quickly (Assmus et al., 1984; Bagozzi & Silk, 1983; Batra & Ray, 1984; Clarke, 1976, 1977b; Frank & Massy, 1967; Haley, 1978; Massy et al., 1970; Nakanishi, 1973; Sawyer & Ward, 1979; Schwerin & Newell, 1981; Sethi, 1971; Sexton, 1970; Zielske, 1959; Zielske & Henry, 1980). These studies also suggest that the effects of advertising erode over time and that this erosion is most rapid in the face of competitive advertising and other marketing programs. Generally, the more intense the competitive pressure, the more rapid the loss of advertising effects. This dissipation of effect holds for top-of-mind awareness, attitude, and purchase behavior.

These studies do not resolve the question of whether the cumulative effects model or the current effects model is the more appropriate, however. They do suggest that the direct effects of marketing communication tend to be immediate and short-lived. Indeed, even though Lavidge and Steiner (1961) took the position that 'the effects of much advertising are long term,' they also acknowledged, 'if something is to happen in the long run, something must be happening in the short run, something that will ultimately lead to eventual sales results.' Similarly, Tellis and Weiss (1995) raise the question of how communication can have a long-term impact if it has little impact in the period in which exposure occurs.

The Role of Message Frequency

There are a variety of potential explanations for the appearance of cumulative effects of communication. As noted above, the effects of communication may persist through an influence on product awareness, satisfaction and loyalty. In addition, many studies that appear to provide support for the cumulative effects model have examined aggregate market data. Such data provide insight into how communication effects influence the market as a whole, but do not indicate anything about what is happening at the level of the individual consumer. Any apparent cumulative effect in such studies may simply reflect the differential rates of exposure within the target audience. Ephron (1997) argues that advertising works most directly with the few consumers who are in the market at the time of exposure to the communication. Since consumers are continually entering the market, it may appear that advertising has a long-term, albeit weak impact on sales.

Differential exposure to a message among consumers is a function of both the consumers in the market at any one point in time and the marketer's selection of schedule and budget for advertising. Effective communication will have an impact in the marketplace only to the extent that it reaches consumers. The level and timing of media expenditures influence the rapidity with which consumers are exposed to an advertising message. Heavy expenditures result in reaching consumers most quickly. Lesser expenditures result in a more gradual reach of consumers. Blair (1987/88) demonstrated that advertising loses its effectiveness once all consumers have been exposed to the message. Adams and Blair (1992) also found that market share gains were immediate in response to a new commercial, but the gains peaked within a few weeks and brand share started to slip back, partially as a result of a new commercial launched by a competitor. Use of a new commercial resulted in sales again increasing. Similar results have been reported by Drane (1988).

Tellis (1997) also argues that frequency in and of itself is not the key driver of communication effectiveness. He maintains that the effect of the frequency of exposure to a communication is more complex than the question of the number of exposures alone. Rather, he suggests that three factors influence the effectiveness of any given exposure. The first factor is brand familiarity. A consumer's familiarity with a brand (measured by knowledge or purchase behavior) tends to produce communication effects with fewer exposures as a result of increased attention to communications for a familiar brand, desire for consistency between beliefs and behavior and the habituation-tedium theory of ad response (Sawyer, 1981). Second, message complexity requires more exposures for the ad to be effective since more complex concepts are being conveyed (Pechmann & Stewart, 1988; Sawyer, 1981). Finally, the need for message novelty results in either the need for new executions to refresh the message or the need for more spacing between executions to delay wearout of the message (Zielske, 1959; Zielske & Henry, 1980). The issue of wearout is considered later in this chapter.

A key factor in reconciling research on the relationship between frequency of exposure to a message and the effect of the message is recognition of the difference between opportunities for exposure to a message and actual exposure. Research that focuses on such measures of advertising intensity such as expenditures, rating points, appearances or mentions, or similar measures of the frequency of message occurrence are, in fact, measuring only opportunities for exposure to a message by individual consumers. An opportunity for exposure is not the same as an actual exposure. In addition, not every exposure that occurs will necessarily represent an undistracted, high quality exposure to the message. Thus, it may be necessary for a marketer to repeat a message several times before an individual consumer actually attends to and processes the message. This need for repetition, and the differential impact of such repetition across the target market, may produce what appear to be cumulative effects of communication. In reality, it is the cumulative effect of *opportunities* for message exposure that is at work rather than the cumulative effect of actual exposure to the message.

Also confounding research on the cumulative effect of advertising is that research that focuses on expenditures, or opportunities for exposure, tends to ignore the important role played by message quality and changes in messages over time. As discussed below, message quality is an especially critical factor in determining whether communication has any effect at all. In addition, studies that focus on expenditures or opportunities for exposure frequently ignore the fact that messages change over time (Stewart, 1999). There may well be a cumulative effect of multiple messages over time as consumers learn more about a product or service.

Communication Wearout

Wearout has been defined by Corkindale and Newall (1978) as: 'That level of advertising which corresponds to the point at which an individual, or group of individuals, fails to respond to the advertising stimulus. Beyond this point, the likelihood that the individual or group of individuals will fail to respond increases despite continued repetition of the stimulus.' The presence of advertising wearout has important implications for the debate regarding the cumulative effects model of communication and the current effects model. If communication does 'wear out' it is unlikely that it would have a cumulative effect. However, as Stewart (1999) observes, wearout is an ill-defined term; it means many different things, and whether it even exists is a function of how it is defined and how it is measured. Because communication has many potential goals, various studies have examined wearout with respect to very different goals: attention (Grass & Wallace, 1969), attitude (Greenberg & Suttoni, 1973), recall (Appel, 1984; Craig et al., 1976), sales (Alexrod, 1980), and brand choice (Adams & Blair, 1992; Blair, 1987/88; Drane, 1988). In addition, wearout has been defined as the absence of further incremental effects (Blair & Rabuck, 1998) and as a diminution in or negative effect in response to additional exposures to the message (Pechmann & Stewart, 1988; Scott & Solomon, 1998). Finally, there has been confusion in the literature between wearout of an individual message and wearout of entire advertising campaigns consisting of many different messages. Thus, it should not be a surprise that the literature on advertising wearout is filled with seeming contradictions.

Quite apart from issues of definition and measurement, empirical determination that wearout has occurred is difficult for two other reasons. First, marketing communication does not occur in a vacuum, there are exogenous factors and components of the communication strategy itself that may influence various measures of interest. Competitors' actions (including competitors' own responses to a successful communications program), changes in communication strategy, and general economic conditions, may produce changes in various in-market measures of communication effectiveness. Second, it may not be easy to verify the presence of wearout, particularly if results for one important dependent measure (e.g., attention) are stable or increasing, whereas those for another (e.g., recall) are declining. Indeed, it is probably not appropriate to discuss wearout in a general sense. Rather, it may be more useful to define wearout with respect to a specific measure of communications effect.

Given the differences in definitions and measures of wearout, it is not surprising that different reasons have been offered for its occurrence. Some researchers (e.g., Grass & Wallace, 1969; Greenberg & Suttoni, 1973; Jacobovitz, 1965) suggest that ceiling effects are in part responsible for wearout. It is certainly the case that no incremental effect of communication can be observed with respect to such measures as recognition and recall once 100% of the message recipients have processed the message. In addition, repeated exposure to a given message may result in a lack of attention to the message with additional repetition. This lack of attention may reduce recall of the message over time through a process of forgetting or through the interference of competing messages (Stewart, 1989).

On the other hand, Calder and Sternthal (1980) hypothesize that wearout is a function of changes in information processing in response to a given message over time. These researchers focus more on changes in attitude rather than memory. They posit that thoughts in response to initial exposures to a message are likely to be closely linked to the message. As message repetition continues, however, thoughts of message recipients turn from 'message-related thoughts' to 'own thoughts.' Since message-related thoughts are likely to be more positive toward the product than one's own thoughts, wearout in this begins to occur. Wearout this context is defined as a more negative attitude toward the product after multiple exposures to a given message. Interestingly, this view predicts that wearout can occur despite the implementation of strategies designed to increase attention.

The most common definition of wearout has focused on the absence of incremental effects associated with the repetition of a message (Stewart, 1999). Pechmann and Stewart (1988) observe that negative effects associated with repetition of a message are most likely to be observed in laboratory settings where the message is repeated frequently within a very short period of time. They suggest that such negative effects are far less likely to occur in the marketplace since marketing communications tend to be spread over time and are frequently varied. On the other hand, an absence of incremental effects is far more likely. A communication that is fully learned across all consumers cannot exhibit higher awareness, recall or comprehension. Similarly, a communication that has already produced a strong change in attitude or behavioral intention is unlikely to produce further change. It is important to recognize, however, that failure to observe further incremental change is not the same as the communication having no effect. A communication may very well reinforce memory or an existing attitude, and failure to repeat the communication (in the absence of other communications) may well result in decay in memory or positive attitude over time. Thus, wearout need not mean that a communication is not producing an effect; rather it means only that the communication is not producing any observable *incremental* effect.

Various strategies have been suggested for dealing with communication wearout. For example, Rossiter and Percy (1997), as well as Grass and Wallace (1969), suggest that strategies designed to increase attention to the message may be effective in countering wearout. This can be accomplished by using multiple executional variations on a similar theme so that the rate of wearout at any given exposure frequency could be slowed (cf. Gorn et al., 1997). Similarly, new messages that contain additional information may provide a means for obtaining incremental effects in attitude, intention, and purchase behavior (Blair & Rabuck, 1998; Lodish et al., 1995).

Evidence regarding communications wearout further weakens the case for the cumulative effects model of advertising. If repetition of a message produces no incremental effect, and, on occasion, can produce negative effects, there is little basis for concluding that communication effects build over time. Such building of effects over time and with repetition appears likely to occur only when the communications involved are themselves incremental in terms of the information provided to the consumer. Repetition alone does not appear to increase the effect of a message.

Long-term Effects of Advertising

Although the optimal frequency of communication is arguably a function of other identifiable factors, the question remains as to how long exposure to a communication remains effective over time. There are numerous studies focusing on sales that indicate that advertising effects may persist beyond the initial or last exposure (Bass & Clarke, 1972; Clarke, 1976, 1977a, 1977b; Clarke & McCann, 1973; Dean, 1966; Houston & Weiss, 1974, 1975; Kuehn et al., 1964; Lambin, 1972; Lavidge & Steiner, 1961; Sawyer & Ward, 1977, 1979). Thus, there is no question that communication effects appear to be long lasting. However, as noted above, these effects appear to be the result of an indirect effect that communication has on sales. This indirect effect is mediated through product awareness and trial and product satisfaction. Marketing communication precipitates and reinforces a process that produces a tendency to respond in a particular way toward a product. Communication is an important part of this process, but it is not the entire process.

Factors Moderating the Effects of Advertising

In the course of the preceding discussion of communication effects, several important characteristics of the marketplace in which communication takes place, and of communications strategy, have been identified. These characteristics have been shown to influence the effect of marketing communication. They include:

1. the stage in the life cycle of the *product category*, that is, whether the category is new or established;
2. the competitive position of the advertised product and the intensity of competitive activity within the market;
3. the familiarity of the product within the target audience;
4. whether the decision to purchase a specific brand is highly involving or one that is 'low involvement';
5. the nature and execution of the communication message.

All of these factors interact with marketing communication in ways that change the nature of consumer response to the communication. While there are, no doubt, numerous other mediating factors, these five are among the most frequently studied, and are among the most general of factors that may influence the effects of communication in the marketplace.

The Role of the Product Life Cycle

As noted earlier, the objectives of marketing communication are frequently different for a new product and an established product. There is sound empirical evidence that different types of messages, executional factors, and exposure schedules have differential effects for new versus established products (Belch, 1981; Calder & Sternthal, 1980; Politz Media Studies, 1960; Ray & Sawyer, 1971; Stewart & Furse, 1986; Stewart & Koslow, 1989; Stephens & Warren, 1984; Time, Inc./Seagram, 1981). Thus, any discussion of how marketing communication works must consider the life cycle of the product category, as well as the life cycle of the individual brand.

In *product categories* that are new (in contrast to new brands in established categories), the market itself is growing. Thus, expenditures on marketing communications and sales will tend to grow together as the market expands, but both are driven by market growth. Communication may stimulate sales in the sense that it increases awareness of the product among individuals who are not yet aware of it, but this effect will not influence sales unless the product itself provides a benefit or relative advantage.

Marketing communication for *new brands* within an established product category clearly must have as its objective the creation of awareness and the stimulation of trial. In established categories, however, awareness and trial are more likely to be generated among current users of competitive products. For established products, awareness and trial are less important objectives since high levels of awareness and trial are likely to be present among consumers. In an established product category, emphasis shifts from building awareness and trial to the reinforcement of brand loyalty. In this latter case, the effect of marketing communication will not be revealed in incremental sales. Rather, the effect of marketing communication will only become apparent when it is eliminated.

The Role of Competition

In most markets the purchase of a specific brand is but one of a number of possible responses available to consumers. There are frequently directly competitive products, that is, different brands of essentially similar products, and indirect competitors, that is, products that are perceived and used by the consumer as substitutes for the same purpose even though the products themselves are not necessarily comparable. Examples of these latter types of substitutes would be candy vs. raisins, vegetable juice vs. soft drinks, and an in-theater movie vs. a rented videotape.

Within any given market the availability of competitive products, of whatever type, is an important determinant of the extent to which advertising has longer or shorter-term effects. Further, the intensity of the marketing efforts for these competitive products mediates the effect of advertising. Thus, a firm that advertises a brand that holds a virtual monopoly, or that operates in a market composed of relatively weak competitors, may find that its advertising has effects that last over some time. Some of the early empirical studies of the duration of advertising effects, for example, Palda's (1964) classic work on the advertising of Linda Pinkham's Vegetable Compound, and the work of Ackoff and Emshoff (1975a, 1975b, 1975c) with Anheuser-Busch, suggested that the effects of advertising might persist for a year or more after its elimination. In both of these cases the brands were the dominant product in the category and faced relatively weak competition. However, in competitive markets, the communications and other marketing activities of competitors tend to mitigate the effects of marketing communications. Thus, the intensity of competition is one important factor that must be examined when examining the effects of marketing communication.

Stewart (1989) has offered a theoretical model to explain the effects of communication within a competitive market. This model is based on a well-known model of learning within the field of psychology, the accumulation model (Herrnstein, 1970, 1974; Mazur & Hastie, 1978). The model simply states that, at any one point in time, there exist numerous competing response tendencies within an individual consumer, some of which are stronger than others. Marketing communications for a particular brand, even if effective, does not displace dispositions to purchase competitive products: it merely strengthens the tendency to buy the brand for which the new communication has been received. Likewise, communications about competitive products, if effective, simply increases the tendency to purchase those products. Ultimately, the brand purchased will be the one with the strongest response tendency at the time of purchase.

Numerous studies have offered empirical evidence of the important role that competitive actions have in mediating the influence of marketing communication (Alba & Chattopadhyay, 1985; Burke & Srull, 1988; D'Souza & Rao, 1995; Geiger, 1971; Keller, 1991; Lambin, 1976; Moran, 1988; Pechmann & Stewart, 1988, 1990; Roediger & Schmidt, 1980; Schwerin & Newell, 1981; Unnava & Sirdeshmukh, 1994). This evidence suggests that competitive communications have an effect on memory as well as purchase behavior (Burke & Srull, 1988; Geiger, 1971). In addition, Lambin (1976: 109) concluded, 'the order of magnitude and the opposite sign of own and competitive advertising coefficients indicate a tendency toward reciprocal cancellation in the market as a whole.' This conclusion is consistent with the view offered earlier that much of the marketing communication for mature products serves to defend the firm's share of market from loss to competitors, rather than taking share from competitors.

The Role of Product Familiarity

Product familiarity has been shown to have a pronounced influence on the effects of advertising in the marketplace (Adtel, 1974; Alba & Chattopadhyay, 1985; Belch, 1981, 1982; Cacioppo & Petty, 1985; Calder, 1981; Calder & Sternthal, 1980; Craig et al., 1976; Dedeo, n.d.; Krugman, 1972; Naples, 1979; Petty & Cacioppo, 1986; Petty et al., 1983; Politz Media Studies, 1960; Raj, 1982; Ray & Sawyer, 1971; Sawyer, 1973, 1981; Simon & Arndt, 1980; Stephens & Warren, 1984; Tellis, 1997). As noted above, there is a significant body of literature that suggests brand familiarity, or top-of-mind awareness, plays an important role in consumer choice (Aaker & Day, 1974; Axelrod, 1968; Burke & Schoeffler, 1980; Grubar, 1969; Holman & Hecker, 1983; Sutherland & Galloway, 1983; Taylor et al., 1979; Wilson, 1981).

The role of familiarity also appears to be far greater for low involvement types of decisions, where the consumer is looking for a simple rule for decision making (Batra & Ray, 1985). Further there is evidence that the repetition of brand advertising and the intensity of competitive advertising play key roles in producing these effects. Several studies have demonstrated that advertising repetition has a far greater effect on awareness than on attitude (Ray, 1982; Ray & Sawyer, 1971; Ray et al., 1971; Sawyer, 1974; Strang et al., 1975). There is also evidence that competitive advertising can reduce the salience or top-of-mind awareness of a brand (Alba & Chattopadhyay, 1985; Burke & Srull, 1988; Geiger, 1971; Stewart, 1989). Thus, in product categories where consumers use a simple familiarity rule, it is important for advertisers to be constantly in the marketplace with communications, in order to maintain consumer awareness and combat competitive efforts to build even higher levels of awareness.

The Role of Consumer Involvement

Another factor that appears to mediate the influence of advertising is the level of involvement of the consumer in the purchase decision. Certain decisions, those that involve high risk for the consumer, appear to predispose consumers to greater information search and more effortful decision-making strategies.

It is useful to recognize that in most purchase situations, two different types of decisions are involved: 1) the decision to use (purchase) the generic product (product category), and 2) the decision about which specific brand within a product category to select. Most *brand* decisions involve rather little risk, and for most consumers are relatively trivial. Choices among brands of a frequently purchased consumer good are relatively trivial, inasmuch as there are usually relatively small differences among competing products. When making such decisions consumers frequently look for very simple rules of choice, or heuristics, that serve to reduce the effort involved in the decision. Marketing communication may be a particularly useful means for suggesting such heuristics.

The Role of the Message and Execution Factors

A very significant literature on message factors that influence the effectiveness of marketing communications now exists. This literature suggests that a focus of the message on the product or service is especially important, as is the offering of a brand differentiating message: a statement of how the product differs from competitive products, or a reason to buy the product instead of a competitive product (Stewart & Furse, 1986; Stewart & Koslow, 1989). In a carefully controlled study of 20 different commercials in several product categories, Blair (1987/88) found that the effects of advertising were highly dependent on the 'quality' of the advertising message. When the message was not persuasive, as measured by a laboratory measure of pre-post exposure brand switching, no amount of spending on advertising media produced any effects on sales. When the message was persuasive, increased spending on advertising resulted in an increase in market share. This sales increase was immediate and the duration of the effect was directly related to media expenditures. The findings of this study are consistent with the findings of several other empirical studies that have found that the content and execution of advertising is an important determinant of consumer response to such advertising (Adams & Blair, 1992; Arnold et al., 1987; Drane, 1988; Jones, 1995; Stewart & Furse, 1986; Stewart & Koslow, 1989).

Research on advertising effects has demonstrated positive effects for changes in either the advertising execution or the advertising campaign itself on sales (Batra et al., 1995; Eastlack & Rao, 1989; Lodish et al., 1995). But an important question still remains: what message factors should be considered in the creation of a 'effective/quality' communication?

One such message factor involves message content in the form of the order of presentation of persuasive arguments. That is, should the strongest arguments be placed at the beginning, middle or end of the communication? Research generally shows that people best remember the first item in a series of similar items they are exposed to, remember second best the last item, and remember the items in between less well (Ebbinghaus, 1885). Therefore, it is common knowledge that strong arguments should be either placed first or last in a promotional communication. However, if the goal is attitude change, and the target market is opposed to the content of the communication, the communicator may be better off by presenting strong arguments first in an attempt to diffuse ensuing counter-arguments.

Such strong arguments may also serve to attract attention to the communication and to cut through advertising clutter. In fact, the use of a two-sided refutational argument early on in the communication may be extremely effective in diffusing counter-arguments specifically, if the targeted consumers entertain negative thoughts toward the product or service advertised. Using a biological analogy that McGuire (McGuire & Papageorgis, 1961) termed 'inoculation theory,' Kamins and Assael (1987) found that the use of a communication that presented both product benefits and refuted weaknesses led to less counter argumentation on the part of the customer, than did a communication that only presented the product in a positive light. Thus, by presenting diluted product negatives in advance, the consumer is inoculated against the effectiveness of a competitor's use of these negatives in an attempt to derail the purchase of the firm's brand. Consistent with Inoculation Theory, overall counter argumentation may be reduced as refuted arguments generalize (McGuire & Papageorgis, 1961). However, this counter argumentation reduction comes at a cost of reducing the credibility of the advertiser (Kamins & Assael, 1987). That is, two-sided appeals that do not refute a negative claim are viewed by the recipient as significantly more credible than those that do refute the claim. This finding has a basis in attribution theory in that it is expected that the communicator would refute a negative claim.

Another message-related consideration deals with whether the communicator should draw a conclusion for the audience (closed-ended ads) or let the audience freely draw their own conclusion (open-ended ads). Although one could argue that consumers may resent being told what to infer from a given advertisement, there is a danger in not summarizing the main advertising claims for the reader. Jacoby and his colleagues (Jacoby & Hoyer, 1987; Jacoby et al., 1980) demonstrated that for advertising communications appearing in mass media magazines, the median miscomprehension rate for individual meanings is 11.8%. That is, the probability is greater than one in ten that a given consumer will miscomprehend a specific meaning conveyed in an advertisement (e.g., such as who is sponsoring the advertisement). Typically, since a given advertisement contains multiple meanings, Jacoby's finding suggests that the probability is probably close to certainty that a given consumer will miscomprehend some component of an advertisement that has just been read. This finding suggests there is an obvious need to summarize advertising messages for consumers.

Interestingly, research has shown that the open-ended ad is particularly effective in enhancing consumer attitudes and purchase intentions for those who are highly involved in the product class (Sawyer & Howard, 1991). This is because those consumers with high involvement tend to be motivated to draw their own conclusion from an advertisement. According to Sawyer and Howard (1991),

> Attitudes resulting from effortful self-generated conclusions should be more positive than attitudes resulting from less effortful processing of conclusions explicitly provided in a message (Linder & Worchel, 1970).

The goal(s) and objective(s) of advertising play, or should play, a significant role in influencing the need for and impact of various message and execution factors. For example, if an advertisement is designed to create an affectively based desire for the product, then a fear appeal as an executional approach may be appropriate (Ray & Wilkie, 1970; Sternthal & Craig, 1974). These appeals are typically operationalized by showing the consumer the unfavorable consequence of not using a particular brand of product (e.g., the consequences of losing your traveler checks if they are not American Express; the risk of a poor connection if you are not using AT&T). The effectiveness of fear appeals in advertising has been linked theoretically to the learning process (McGuire, 1969) through both drive and cue functions. That is, as a drive, fear has the impact of increasing message acceptance (facilitating effect). However, as a cue, fear has the potential to arouse message avoidance, which decreases message processing and ultimately attitude change (inhibiting effect). Therefore the impact of a fear appeal is hypothesized to be a function of two opposite forces and the empirical question that remains, related to the 'optimal' level of fear that should be induced by the advertiser. The research of Keller and Block (1996) answered this latter question by showing that moderate levels of fear led to the greatest degree of message persuasion consistent with the perspective that the decrease in message reception accelerates faster than an increase.

If an advertising goal is cognitively based, then the use of humor may be appropriate (Sternthal & Craig, 1973). Humor works at three levels. First, it helps to cut through the clutter by attracting the receiver's attention to the advertisement. Secondly, it serves to weaken counter-arguments to the message through distraction, by directing the receiver to focus on the message form as opposed to the message content. Finally, it works on an affective level by enhancing the receiver's mood. There are some concerns regarding the use of humorous ads, however. First, it can be argued that if the receiver's attention is focused on the joke then the processing of the advertisement content is compromised. Therefore humor may be more appropriate for those with low as opposed to high involvement with the product, since such an ad may cut through the clutter with its entertaining characteristics (Weinberger & Campbell, 1990/91). However, the longer term impact of the humorous commercial may be compromised for all consumers because the humor in the advertisement may lose its impact with repetition. One could easily construct an argument that humorous ads may wear out at a faster rate than if the humor were absent.

Some 30 years ago the FTC decided to allow the use of comparative advertisements as an executional device, so that consumers would have more complete information as they moved closer to the purchase decision. However, research has shown that direct comparative claims are differentially effective as a function of the relative market share of the sponsoring brand. That is, for low share brands direct comparative ads enhance attention, resulting in increased purchase intentions. However, for high share brands the use of comparative advertising may be detrimental, due to exposure of the competition and confusion about the sponsor (Pechmann & Stewart, 1990, 1991). This finding suggests a continued need for specific research on how marketers can increase top-of-mind awareness of their brands relative to competing brands in any context, as well as for a more compete understanding of those mediating factors which impact advertising structure.

Finally, there is a stream of research that examines the combined impact of visual and verbal components of advertising through what is known as the Dual Component Model (Mitchell & Olson, 1981). This research shows that both verbal and visual cues affect brand attitudes in two ways. First, brand attitude may be impacted through the effect of the visual/written stimuli on product attribute beliefs. Secondly, attitude might be changed as a function of the impact of the visual/written stimuli upon one's attitude toward the advertisement.

In general, research has shown that pictures that elicit a favorable mood (i.e., a tropical sunset, a canoe gently drifting on a lake at dusk) have an impact on attitude toward the advertisement and brand that extends beyond the effect they have on product beliefs (Miniard et al., 1991, 1992). This can be explained by the fact that a visual image has many different interpretations, and therefore while a favorable image may be reflected in terms of a generally more favorable attitude toward the advertiser or product, it would be difficult to expect such an image to impact specific product characteristics that make up brand belief.

For advertisements in which the visual image conveyed in the advertisement is designed to be congruent with the advertising copy, findings vary as a function of the degree to which the verbal copy is laden with imagery value. For copy with low imagery value, inclusion of visuals in the ad increased both immediate and delayed recall of product attributes. When the copy was high in imagery value, inclusion of visuals in the advertisement had little impact (Unnava & Burnkrant, 1991). Some research has been undertaken to examine the impact of advertising content that is inconsistent with respect to copy and visual imagery. Here it has been found that inconsistency results in generally greater recall and processing of the information presented (Houston et al., 1987). Such an approach offers a possible solution for those consumers who normally would not attend to the advertisement. However, although recall may be enhanced, the link to more favorable attitude and purchase intention may still be lacking.

Clearly the advertiser has many different message and execution factors at his/her fingertips. The use of a specific factor should be considered in light of the intention or goal of the advertisement, with the knowledge that sometimes increases in cognition, for example, may come at a cost of a decrease in affect or purchase intention. Changes in ad content or message structure should come incrementally so that the effect of each change can be studied and examined independently of the interaction of other factors that may be introduced.

Whereas marketers have control over the content of advertising and other forms of marketing communications, they do not have control over an especially powerful form of communications in the marketplace. This form of communication is communication between and among consumers, generally called word-of-mouth (WOM) communication. While marketers do not have the type of control over WOM communication that they have over advertising, considerable time and expenditures go into efforts to influence and induce WOM among consumers. Thus, marketers often attempt to create advertising that will be talked about at the water cooler. Event marketing, in which products or marketing communications play a prominent role, may also facilitate WOM among consumers. Thus, it is appropriate to consider the role and influence of WOM communication within a marketing communications context.

Word-of-Mouth Communication

WOM is a form of media and is probably the oldest, the most extensive and one of the most effective. In a marketing context it is a form of communication that conveys information about products and services in a verbal format mainly through conversations and group discussions (Brown & Reingen, 1987; Herr et al., 1991; Katz & Lazarsfeld, 1955; Reingen & Kernan, 1986). WOM communication about products has been shown to influence product evaluation to an even greater extent than information from a well-known objective source such as

Consumer Reports (Herr et al., 1991). In fact, estimates have maintained that as much as 80% of all buying decisions are influenced by an individual's direct recommendation (Voss, 1984).

The question remains as to why WOM exerts such a strong influence on consumer choice and judgment? To answer this question Herr et al. (1991) manipulated information vividness as a function of the manner in which information was presented to respondents. That is, half of their subjects were presented with anecdotal information presented in a face-to-face manner (the vivid WOM condition), and the other half were exposed to the same information in a printed mode (the pallid condition). The authors concluded that the effectiveness of WOM information could be explained by the fact that information that is received in a face-to-face manner is more accessible from memory than information presented in a less vivid format. Others seem to suggest that the effectiveness of WOM can be directly attributed to the confidence and perceived credibility the receiver has in the information. That is, oftentimes it is sought out from people in whose opinions the receiver has extreme confidence (Kapferer, 1990). Although some advertisements may achieve vividness through the use of imagery (Kisielius & Sternthal, 1986), advertising is not as credible or influential a source of information as that gleaned from family and friends.

WOM has been found to be more pervasive under certain market conditions inclusive of the evaluation of high involvement products and services (Feldman & Spencer, 1965). Kapferer (1990) explains this phenomenon in that high involvement products are important to the consumer and services can be characterized as credence goods (i.e., goods that the buyer normally finds hard to evaluate even after consumption (Ostrom & Iacobucci, 1995)). Moreover service quality is not necessarily standardized (as is production quality) and hence can vary considerably. Therefore, under these conditions, the consumer must rely on information that represents both the experiences of others and is perceived as credible. Similar to what has been observed in a personal selling context, under high involvement purchase conditions, the information supplied *verbally* by the salesperson was found to be important, not necessarily, however, for its credibility, but rather for its flexibility in responding to purchase concerns.

The importance of WOM as an informational source also seems to become prominent during the final stages of the consumer's decision-making process when a choice must be made. Here consumers seek out credible sources of information, and speaking with opinion leaders, market mavens and experts (Feick & Price, 1987) and/or friends and family is often a strategy of choice. It is clear that advertising and WOM information can effectively interact with each other. As Kapferer (1990) notes, advertising can be used to inform the consumer that a product or service has entered the market (e.g., advertising for a new movie). WOM informs the viewer whether it is worth going to see it.

One of the limitations of WOM is that the company has little control over its valence or degree to which it is spread. Therefore it is important to consider strategies designed to minimize the potential for negativity. One such strategy involves the obvious – producing quality products and services under strict, quality control standards. Responding to consumer complaints in a timely manner can also go far to diffusing potential negative WOM (File et al., 1992; Folkes, 1984).

As noted earlier, unlike advertising and other forms of marketing communication, neither the timing nor the content of WOM is under the control of the manufacturer. Compounding this is the fact that WOM communication often includes negative accounts of products or services because consumers often use WOM to express dissatisfaction (Folkes et al., 1987; Richins, 1983; Swan & Oliver, 1989). Hence, firms are often particularly concerned about negative WOM, especially when there is no evidence of it being true – that is, when it is a rumor.

Kamins, Folkes and Perner (1997) reported that, on average, consumers are exposed to approximately one rumor about companies or brands in a given year. Although this may not appear to be extensive, it should be noted that 92.6% of these rumors were classified as negative. Consistent with prior research, the authors observed that consumers typically attach lower credibility and importance to rumor relative to other sources of marketing communication (e.g., advertising, published sources and product trial). Although, rumor's low credibility and importance might be suggestive of a minimal impact on purchase decisions, Tybout et al. (1981) suggest that this is not the case. According to these authors, 'even when an association is disbelieved, it may be stored in memory and may influence evaluation.' Hence rumor is impactful simply because it is processed. This led these authors to propose three potential strategies based on information processing theory, in order to forestall the impact of rumor.

The first strategy, called 'refutation,' involved an attempt to discredit the rumor by presenting facts that supposedly proved it false. This approach was found to be ineffective since by refuting the rumor, it served to increase the rehearsal of it in the consumer's mind, thereby strengthening the association of the product or brand with the rumor itself. A second strategy involved what was termed a 'storage' strategy. Here at the point at which the rumor is spread, an attempt is made to associate the focus of the rumor with a second, more favorable object rather than with the object originally specified in the rumor. So, for example in the context of the rumor that a McDonald's hamburger had worms in it, one could mention that worms are a delicacy and that they are often used in fancy sauces at expensive French restaurants (Tybout et al., 1981). Finally, a third strategy used to counteract rumor is known as 'retrieval,' since it impacts information retrieval. Here subjects' attention is directed to a new stimulus that is designed to redirect thoughts about the rumor object away from the rumor. Again, in terms of McDonald's, consumers could be asked about the cleanliness of the nearest location, whether it has a children's playground, and the price of the Big Mac. Even if the new stimulus does not completely inhibit the retrieval of associations between the object and the rumor, it does have the potential to dilute these associations with other thoughts in active memory. It seems that the most effective strategy to forestall rumor is that of 'retrieval,' since 'storage' only works at the point at which the rumor is being spread. Clearly, it is impossible to be everywhere a rumor is disseminated. These strategies, designed to forestall the impact of rumor, are extremely important in light of the findings of Kamins, Folkes and Perner (1997), who reported that the majority of consumers made no attempt to verify the truthfulness of rumors they confronted and that consumers are more likely to spread rumors with negative as opposed to positive outcomes.

According to Shibutani (1966), rumors develop as a function of the importance and ambiguity of the issue in question. This of course is suggestive of future research in the area designed to forestall rumor. For example, would an approach designed to clarify as opposed to refute be more effective in forestalling rumor? Can the spread of rumor be slowed by de-emphasizing the importance of the rumor situation or the rumor attribute? Given the increasing prevalence of rumor in relation to global companies, answers to these research questions are imperative.

The Future of Research on Marketing Communications

Marketing communications is one of the most highly investigated areas within marketing. As this review has demonstrated, there is an impressive body of research and theory related to how marketing communications works, what factors influence its effectiveness, and how its effects should be measured. Few areas within marketing have received as much attention from academic and industry researchers. Given the impressive body of research on marketing communications it might seem that the area is largely understood. In fact, important questions remain to be examined.

Within the past decade, a new form of communication has emerged. This new form of communication is electronic, but it is similar to other forms of communication: 1) it shares many of the characteristics of print and/or broadcast advertising, at least with respect to the more traditional advertising that appears on it (banner ads, e-announcements); 2) it can be interactive, but without the interpersonal dimensions of personal selling; and 3) it provides the opportunity for direct response from and to the customer. The fact that electronic interactive marketing communication shares many of the characteristics of other forms of communication implies that much of what is known about communication applies in this new medium.

On the other hand, there are unique dimensions of electronic interactive media. There is interaction but this interaction is without the personal, face-to-face dimensions of such interpersonal communication modes as personal selling and WOM. Electronic interactive communication also provides a wider and more immediate scope of communication among customers (Pavlou & Stewart, 2000). Such communication remains a source of new ideas for empirical research and development of theory. Although the Internet is widely heralded as a new medium for interactive communications (Alba et al., 1997; Hoffman & Novak, 1996; Stewart & Zhao, 2000), consumers have already begun to provide evidence that they have integrated the Internet experience into their broader media use. Almost half of all personal computers are in the same room as the television set, and simultaneous viewing of television and access to the Internet are common (Cox, 1998). Such consumer-directed integration of television and the Internet is but one example of interactivity involving the integration of media by consumers. Combinations of older media, such as traditional print and broadcast advertising with the telephone (especially, but not exclusively, 800 telephone numbers), have long provided a degree of interactivity. At the most general level, feedback via sales reflects interactivity. Interactivity is, therefore, a characteristic of the consumer, not a characteristic of the medium; consumers can choose to respond or not. Thus, in this sense interactivity is not really new. What is new are the speed, scope, and scale of interactivity that is provided by new information and communication technologies.

Investigation of the role of interactivity is still in its infancy. Much remains to be learned about how consumers will use the new interactive media. In addition, much remains to be learned about how the various elements of the marketing mix interact to produce outcomes in the marketplace. A great deal of the extant research on marketing communication has tended to focus on one or a few isolated elements of the marketing mix. Rather little systematic work has been done on how various forms of marketing communication and of the larger marketing mix interact. Much of this integration is self-directed by consumers, at least in part. Research that integrates the behavior of consumers and their goals into an understanding of the effects of marketing communications would be especially useful for developing theory and guiding practice.

The rise of new interactive media and the growing ability of marketers (and others) to capture and manage data at the level of the individual consumer using information technology also raises new questions about the economics of marketing activity. Interactivity and data capture are not costless. In addition, individual consumers have preferences related to how they wish to interact (or whether they wish to interact at all), and concerns about the use of personal data. Thus, for the marketer there are questions of how to determine the optimal level of interaction with an individual consumer. This question has given rise to questions about the lifetime value of consumers under different scenarios of interaction (Niraj et al., 2001; Reinartz & Kumar, 2000). From the perspective of the consumer, a variety of issues related to privacy and intrusiveness beg investigation (Milne, 2000). Finally, the ease with which consumers can communicate with one another about common interests, about experiences with products, services and companies, and otherwise share information raises interesting questions regarding the relative balance of power between buyers and sellers. Thus, despite the substantial body of literature that already exists on the effects of marketing communications there remain important and largely unexplored areas of research for the future.

Notes

1. Critiques of empirical studies of the relationship between aggregate advertising expenditures and market growth consistently note the failure of these studies to account for the stage in the product life cycle of the product, as well as other factors that may contribute to market growth during the period of study (Clarke, 1977; Ehrenberg, 1983; Lambin, 1976; Schmalensee, 1972; Telser, 1962).

2. Another common response to increased demand is the creation of new brands designed to attract specific segments of the larger market. These new brands do not stimulate demand; they simply cause consumers to switch from one brand to another.

3. It is useful to note that soft drink producers also created numerous new products in response to the growth in demand, an action similar to that in the cigarette industry.

References

Aaker, David A. & Day, George S. (1974) A dynamic model of relationships among advertising, consumer awareness, attitudes, and behavior. *Journal of Applied Psychology*, 59 (3), 281–6.

Achenbaum, A.A. (1972) Advertising doesn't manipulate consumers. *Journal of Advertising Research*, 12 (2), 3–13.

Ackoff, Russell L. & Emshoff, James R. (1975a) Advertising research at Anheuser-Busch, Inc. (1963–68). *Sloan Management Review*, Winter, 1–15.

——— (1975b) Advertising research at Anheuser-Busch, Inc. (1968–74). *Sloan Management Review*, Spring, 1–15.

——— (1975c) A reply to the comments of Yvan Allaire. *Sloan Management Review*, Spring, 95–8.

Adams, Anthony J. & Blair, Margaret Henderson (1992) Persuasive advertising and sales accountability: past experience and forward validation. *Journal of Advertising Reseach*, 32 (March/April), 20–5.

Adtel (1974) Reported in Michael J. Naples, *Effective Frequency*. New York: Advertising Research Foundation, pp. 44–56.

Akerlof, George A. & Dickens, William T. (1982) The economic consequences of cognitive dissonance. *The American Economic Review*, 72 (June), 307–19.

Alba, Joseph W. & Chattopadhyay, Amitava (1985) Effects of context and part-category cues on recall of competing brands. *Journal of Marketing Research*, 22 (August), 340–9.

Alba, Joseph, Lynch, John, Weitz, Barton, Janiszewski, Chris, Lutz, Richard, Sawyer, Alan & Wood, Stacy (1997) Interactive home shopping: consumer, retailer, and manufacturer incentives to participate in electronic marketplaces. *Journal of Marketing*, 61 (July), 38–53.

Appel, Valentine (1984) On advertising wear out. *Journal of Advertising Research*, 24 (September), 42–4.

Arnold, Stephen J., Oum, Tae H., Pazderka, Bohumir & Snetsinger, Douglas W. (1987) Advertising quality in sales response models. *Journal of Marketing Research*, 24 (February), 106–13.

Assmus, Gert, Farley, John U. & Lehmann, Donald R. (1984) How advertising affects sales: meta-analysis of econometric results. *Journal of Marketing Research*, 21 (February), 65–74.

Atkin, Charles K. (1985) Informational utility and selective exposure to entertainment media. In *Selective Exposure to Communication*, edited by Dorf Zillmann & Jennings Bryant. Hillsdale, NJ: Lawrence Erlbaum Associates, pp. 63–92.

Axelrod, Joel N. (1968) Attitude measures that predict purchase. *Journal of Advertising Research*, 8 (March), 3–17.

——— (1980) Advertising wearout. *Journal of Advertising Research*, 20 (October), 13–18.

Axsom, Danny & Cooper, Joel (1981) Reducing weight by reducing dissonance: the role of effort justification in inducing weight loss. In *Readings for the Social Animal*, 3rd edn, edited by Elliot Aronson. San Francisco: W.H. Freeman.

Bagozzi, Richard P. & Silk, Alvin J. (1983) Recall, recognition, and the measurement of memory for print advertisements. *Marketing Science*, 2 (Spring), 95–134.

Bandura, Albert (1994) Social cognitive theory of mass communications. In *Media Effects: Advances in Theory and Research*, edited by Jennings Bryant & Dorf Zillmann. Hillsdale, NJ: Lawrence Erlbaum Associates, pp. 61–90.

Barnes, M. (1971) *The Relationship Between Purchasing Patterns and Advertising Exposure*. London: J. Walter Thompson Co.

Barsalou, Lawrence W. (1991) Deriving categories to achieve goals. In *The Psychology of Learning and Motivation: Advances in Research and Theory*, Vol. 27. New York: Academic Press, pp. 1–64.

Bass, Frank M. & Clarke, Darral G. (1972) Testing distributed lag models of advertising effect. *Journal of Marketing Research*, 9 (August), 298.

Batra, Rajeev & Ray, Michael L. (1984) Identifying opportunities for repetition minimization. *Marketing Science Institute Working Paper No. 84–108*. Cambridge, MA: Marketing Science Institute.

——— (1985) How advertising works at contact. In *Psychological Processes and Advertising Effects: Theory, Research, and Application*, edited by L. Alwitt & A.A. Mitchell. Hillsdale, NJ: Erlbaum, pp. 13–43.

Batra, Rajeev, Lehman, Donald R., Burke, Joanne & Pae, Jae (1995) When does advertising have an impact? A study of tracking data. *Journal of Advertising Research*, 35 (Sept./Oct.), 19–32.

Baugh, John A. (1982) Attention and automaticity in the processing of self-relevant information. *Journal of Personality and Social Psychology*, 43 (2), 425–36.

Belch, George E. (1981) An examination of comparative and non-comparative television commercials: the effects of claim variation and repetition on cognitive response and message acceptance. *Journal of Marketing Research*, 18 (August), 333–49.

——— (1982) The effects of television commercial repetition on cognitive response and message acceptance. *Journal of Consumer Research*, 9 (June), 56–65.

Blair, Margaret Henderson (1987/88) An empirical investigation of advertising wearin and wearout. *Journal of Advertising Research*, 27 (Dec./Jan.), 45–50.

——— & Rabuck, Michael J. (1998) Advertising wearin and wearout: ten years later – more empirical evidence and successful practice. *Journal of Advertising Research*, 38 (October), 7–18.

——— Kuse, Allan R., Furse, David H. & Stewart, David W. (1987) Advertising in a new competitive environment: persuading customers to buy. *Business Horizons*, 30 (November/December), 20–6.

Blattberg, Robert C. & Neslin, Scott A. (1990) *Sales Promotion: Concepts, Methods and Strategies*. Upper Saddle River, NJ: Prentice-Hall.

Brehm, Jack (1956) Postdecision changes in interpersonal perception as a means of reducing cognitive dissonance. *Journal of Abnormal and Social Psychology*, 52 (May), 384–389.

Broadbent, Donald (1977) The hidden pre-attentive processes. *American Psychologist*, 32 (2), 109–18.

Brown, Jacqueline J. & Reingen, Peter H. (1987) Social ties and word-of-mouth referral behavior. *Journal of Consumer Research*, 14 (3), 350–62.

Bryant, Jennings & Zillman, Dorf (1994) *Media Effects: Advances in Theory and Research*. Hillsdale, NJ: Lawrence Erlbaum Associates.

Burke, Raymond R. & Srull, Thomas K. (1988) Competitive interference and consumer memory for advertising. *Journal of Consumer Research*, 15 (6), 55–68.

Burke, William L. & Schoeffler, Sidney (1980) *Brand Awareness as a Tool for Profitability*. Boston: The Strategic Planning Institute and Cahners Publishing Co.

Cacioppo, John T. & Petty, Richard E. (1985) Central and peripheral routes to persuasion: the role of message repetition. In *Psychological Processes and Advertising Effects*, edited by L. Alwitt & A.A. Mitchell. Hillsdale, NJ: Erlbaum.

Calder, Bobby J. (1981) Cognitive consistency and consumer behavior. In *Perspectives in Consumer Behavior*, edited by Harold H. Kassarjian & Thomas S. Robertson. Glenview, IL: Scott, Foresman, and Co., pp. 258–69.

——— & Sternthal, Brian (1980) Television commercial wearout: an information processing view. *Journal of Marketing Research*, 17 (May), 173–86.

Carpenter, Gregory S. & Lehmann, Donald R. (1985) A model of marketing mix, brand switching and competition. *Journal of Marketing Research*, 22 (August), 318–29.

Chaiken, Shelley (1980) Heuristic versus systematic information processing and the use of source versus message cues in persuasion. *Journal of Personality and Social Psychology*, 39 (November), 752–66.

Chapman, S. & Fitzgerald, B. (1982) Brand preference and advertising recall in adolescent smokers: some implications for health promotion. *American Journal of Public Health*, 72 (May), 491–4.

Churchill, Gilbert A. Jr. & Surprenant, Carol (1982) An investigation into the determinants of customer satisfaction. *Journal of Marketing Research*, 19 (November), 491–504.

Clarke, Darral G. (1976) Econometric measurement of the duration of advertising effect on sales. *Journal of Marketing Research*, 13 (November), 345–57.

——— (1977a) *Cumulative Advertising Effects: Sources and Implications*. Cambridge, MA: Marketing Science Institute.

——— (1977b) Editor's Note. In *Cumulative Advertising Effects: Sources and Implications*. Cambridge, MA: Marketing Science Institute, pp. 190–2.

——— (1977c) Cumulative advertising effects: a synthesis. In *Cumulative Advertising Effects: Sources and Implications*, edited by Darral G. Clarke. Cambridge, MA: Marketing Science Institute, pp. 1–28.

——— (1977d) Econometric measurement of the duration of the advertising effect on sales. In *Cumulative Advertising Effects: Sources and Implications*, edited by Darral G. Clarke. Cambridge, MA: Marketing Science Institute, pp. 29–70.

——— & McCann, John M. (1973) Measuring the cumulative effects of advertising: a reappraisal. *Proceedings*, American Marketing Association. Chicago: American Marketing Association.

Colombo, Richard & Morrison, Donald G. (1987) A brand-switching model with implications for marketing strategies. *Working Paper No. 87–110, Marketing Science Institute*. Cambridge, MA: Marketing Science Institute.

Condry, John (1989) *The Psychology of Television*. Hillsdale, NJ: Lawrence Erlbaum Associates.

Corkindale, D. & Newall, J. (1978) Advertising thresholds and wearout. *European Journal of Marketing*, 12 (3), 327–78.

Cotton, John L. (1985) Cognitive dissonance in selective exposure. In *Selective Exposure to Communication*, edited by Dorf Zillmann & Jennings Bryant. Hillsdale, NJ: Lawrence Erlbaum Associates, pp. 11–34.

Cox, Beth (1998) Report: TV, PC get equal time. Advertising Report Archives, *InternetNews.com*, November 17.

Craig, C. Samuel, Sternthal, Brian & Leavitt, Clark (1976) Advertising wearout: an experimental analysis. *Journal of Marketing Research*, 13 (November), 365–72.

Davis, Keith & Jones, Edward E. (1960) Changes in interpersonal perception as a means of reducing cognitive dissonance. *Journal of Abnormal and Social Psychology*, 61 (November), 402–10.

Day, George S. & Montgomery, David B. (1999) Charting new directions for marketing. *Journal of Marketing*, 63 (Special Issue), 3–13.

Dean, Joel (1966) Does advertising belong to the capital budget? *Journal of Marketing*, 30 (October), 15–21.

DeBeo, Joseph E. (n.d.) Why over $109,800,000,000 was spent on advertising in America last year. New York: Young and Rubicom, Inc.

Drane, Robert (1988) Boosting the odds of advertising success. Paper presented to Marketing Science Institute Conference on Evaluating the Effects of Consumer Advertising on Market Position Over Time, June 8–10, Babson College Campus, Wellesley, MA.

D'Souza, Giles & Rao, Ram C. (1995) Can repeating an advertisement more frequently than the competition affect brand preference in a mature market? *Journal of Marketing*, 59 (4), 32–42.

Eastlack, Joseph O., Jr. & Rao, Ambar G. (1989) Advertising experiments at the Campbell Soup Company. *Marketing Science*, 8 (Winter), 57–71.

Ebbinghaus, Hermann (1885) *Memory: A Contribution to Experimental Psychology*, translated by Ruger and Bussenius. New York: Teachers College, Columbia University, 1913.

Ehrenberg, Andrew S.C. (1972) *Repeat Buying: Theory and Applications*. New York: American Elsevier.

——— (1983) Repetitive advertising and the consumer. *Journal of Advertising Research*, 23 (September), 29–38.

——— (1988) Advertising: reinforcing not persuading. Paper presented to Marketing Science Institute Conference on Evaluating the Effects of Consumer Advertising on Market Position Over Time, June 8–10, Babson College Campus, Wellesley, MA.

Ehrlich, D., Guttman, I., Schonbach, P. & Mills, J. (1957) Postdecision exposure to relevant information. *Journal of Abnormal and Social Psychology*, 54, 98–102.

Ephron, Erwin (1997) Recency planning. *Journal of Advertising Research*, 37 (4), 61–5.

Eskin, Gerald J. & Baron, Penny H. (1977) Effects of price and advertising in test market experiments. *Journal of Marketing Research*, 14 (November), 499–508.

Farber, Barry J. & Wycoff, Joyce (1992) Relationships: six steps to success. *Sales and Marketing Management*, (April), 50–8.

Fazio, Russell H. (1990) Multiple processes by which attitudes guide behavior: the MODE model as an integrative framework. *Advances in Experimental Social Psychology*, 23, 75–109.

Feick, Lawrence F. & Price, Linda L. (1987) The market maven: a diffuser of marketplace information. *Journal of Marketing*, 51 (1), 83–97.

Feldman, Sidney & Spencer, Merlin C. (1965) The effect of personal influence in the selection of consumer services. In *Proceedings of the Fall Conference of the American Marketing Association*, edited by Peter D. Bennett. Chicago, IL: American Marketing Association, pp. 440–52.

Fenigstein, Allan & Heyduk, Ronald G. (1985) Thought and action as determinants of media exposure. In *Selective Exposure to Communication*, edited by Dorf Zillmann & Jennings Bryant. Hillsdale, NJ: Lawrence Erlbaum Associates, pp. 113–40.

File, Karen M., Judd, Ben B. & Prince, Russ A. (1992) Interactive marketing: the influence of participation on positive word-of-mouth referrals. *Journal of Services Marketing*, 6 (Fall), 5–14.

Fishbein, Martin & Ajzen, Icek (1975) *Belief, Attitude Intention and Behavior: An Introduction to Theory and Research*. Reading, MA: Addison-Wesley.

Fiske, Susan T. & Taylor, Shelley E. (1992) *Social Cognition*, 2nd edn. New York: McGraw-Hill.

Folkes, Valerie S. (1984) Consumer reactions to product failure: an attributional approach. *Journal of Consumer Research*, 10 (4), 398–409.

——— Koletsky, Susan & Graham, John L. (1987) A field study of causal inferences and consumer reaction: the view from the airport. *Journal of Consumer Research*, 13 (4), 534–9.

Frank, Ronald F. & Massy, William F. (1967) Effects of short-term promotional strategy in selected market segments. In *Promotional Decisions Using Mathematical Models*, edited by Patrick J. Robinson. Cambridge, MA: Marketing Science Institute with Allyn and Bacon.

Galbraith, John K. (1967) *Affluent Society*. Boston: Houghton Mifflin.

Geiger, Joan A. (1971) Seven brands in seven days. *Journal of Advertising Research*, 11, 15–22.

Gibson, Larry D. (1996) What can one TV exposure do? *Journal of Advertising Research*, 36 (2), 9–18.

Glass, David (1964) Changes in liking as a means of reducing cognitive discrepancies between self-esteem and aggression. *Journal of Personality*, 32 (December), 531–49.

Goldstein, A.O., Fischer, P.M., Richards, J.W. & Creten, D. (1987) Relationship between high school student smoking and recognition of cigarette advertisements. *Journal of Pediatrics*, 110 (3), 488–91.

Gorn, Gerald J., Chattopadhyay, Amitava, Yi, Tracey & Dahl, Darren W. (1997) Effects of color as an executional cue in advertising: they're in the shade. *Management Science*, 43 (10), 1387–400.

Grass, Robert C. & Wallace, Wallace H. (1969) Satiation effects of TV commercials. *Journal of Advertising Research*, 9 (September), 3–8.

Greenberg, Allan & Suttoni, Charles (1973) Television commercial wearout. *Journal of Advertising Research*, 13 (October), 47–54.

Greenwald, Anthony G. & Leavitt, Clark (1984) Audience involvement in advertising: four levels. *Journal of Consumer Research*, 11 (June), 581–92.

Grubar, Alin (1969) Top-of-mind awareness and share of families: an observation. *Journal of Marketing Research*, 6 (May), 227–31.

Gunter, Barrie (1985) Determinants of television viewing preferences. In *Selective Exposure to Communication*, edited by Dorf Zillmann & Jennings Bryant. Hillsdale, NJ: Lawrence Erlbaum Associates, pp. 93–112.

Haley, Russell I. (1978) Sales effects of media weight. *Journal of Advertising Research*, 18 (June), 9–18.

——— (1985) *Developing Effective Communications Strategy: A Benefit Segmentation Approach*. New York: Wiley.

Harvey, Bill, Norman, Russ & Losey, Bill (1989) Advertising needs more frequent new releases. *The Marketing Pulse*, 9 (11), 1–4.

Hauser, John R. (1986) Agendas and consumer choice. *Journal of Marketing Research*, 23 (August), 199–212.

Henderson, P.L. & Brown, S.E. (1961) Effectiveness of a special promotional campaign for frozen concentrated orange juice. Report No. 356. Washington, DC: USDA Economic Research Service.

Henderson, P.L., Hind, J.F. & Brown, S.E. (1961) Sales effects of two campaign themes. *Journal of Advertising Research*, 6 (December), 2–11.

Herr, Paul M., Kardes, Frank R. & Kim, John (1991) Effects of word-of-mouth and product attribute information on persuasion: an accessibility-diagnosticity perspective. *Journal of Consumer Research*, 17 (4), 454–62.

Herrnstein, R.J. (1970) On the law of effect. *Journal of the Experimental Analysis of Behavior*, 13, 243–66.

——— (1974) Formal properties of the matching law. *Journal of the Experimental Analysis of Behavior*, 21, 159–64.

Hoffman, Donna L. & Novak, Thomas P. (1996) Marketing in computer-mediated environments: conceptual foundations. *Journal of Marketing*, 60 (July), 50–68.

Holman, Rebecca H. & Hecker, Sid (1983) Advertising impact: creative elements affecting brand saliency. *Current Issues and Research in Advertising*. Ann Arbor: The University of Michigan, pp. 157–72.

Hoofnagle, W.S. (1963) The effectiveness of advertising for farm products. *Journal of Advertising Research*, 3 (4), 2–6.

Horsky, Daniel (1977) An empirical analysis of the optimal advertising policy. *Management Science*, 23, 1037–49.

Houston, Franklin S. & Weiss, Doyle L. (1974) An analysis of competitive market behavior. *Journal of Market Research*, 11 (May), 151.

Houston, Franklin S. & Weiss, Doyle L. (1975) Cumulative advertising effects: the role of serial correlation. *Decision Sciences*, 6 (July), 471–81.

Houston, Michael, Childers, Terry & Heckler, Susan (1987) Picture-word consistency and the elaborative processing of print advertisements. *Journal of Marketing Research*, 24, 359–69.

Hovland, Carl I., Janis, I.L. & Kelley, Harold H. (1953) *Communication and Persuasion*. New Haven, CT: Yale University Press.

Information Resources, Inc. (1989) *Advertising Works*. Chicago: Information Resources, Inc.

Jacobovitz, L.A. (1965) Semantic satiation in concept formation. *Psychological Reports*, (17), 113–14.

Jacoby, Jacob & Hoyer, Wayne D. (1987) *The Comprehension/Miscomprehension of Print Communication*. Hillsdale, NJ: Lawrence Erlbaum.

——— & Sheluga, David A. (1980) *The Miscomprehension of Televised Communication*. New York: American Association of Advertising Agencies.

Jeuland, Abel P. (1979) Brand choice inertia as one aspect of the notion of brand loyalty. *Management Science*, 25 (July), 671–82.

Jones, John Philip (1995) *When Ads Work: New Proof That Advertising Triggers Sales*. New York: Lexington Books.

Kahneman, Daniel & Tversky, Amos (1979) Prospect theory: an analysis of decision under risk. *Econometrika*, 47, 263–91.

——— (1982) The psychology of preferences. *Scientific American*, 246, 160–73.

Kamins, Michael A. & Assael, Henry (1987) Two-sided versus one-sided appeals: a cognitive perspective on argumentation, source derogation, and the effect of disconfirming trial upon belief change. *Journal of Marketing Research*, 24 (February), 29–39.

——— (1989) Effects of appeal type and involvement on product disconfirmation: a cognitive response approach through product trial. *Journal of the Academy of Marketing Science*, 17 (Summer), 197–207.

Kamins, Michael A., Folkes, Valerie S. & Perner, Lars (1997) Consumer responses to rumors: good news, bad news. *Journal of Consumer Psychology*, 6 (2), 165–87.

Kapferer, Jean-Noel (1990) *Rumors*. New Brunswick, NJ: Transaction Publishers.

Katz, Daniel (1960) The functional approach to the study of attitudes. *Public Opinion Quarterly*, 24 (Summer), 163–204.

Katz, Elihu & Lazarsfeld, Paul F. (1955) *Personal Influence: The Part Played by People in the Flow of Mass Communications*. New York: Free Press.

Keller, Kevin Lane (1991) Memory and evaluation effects in competitive advertising environments. *Journal of Consumer Research*, 17 (3), 463–76.

Keller, Punam Anand & Block, Lauren Goldberg (1996) Increasing the persuasiveness of fear appeals: the effect of arousal and elaboration. *Journal of Consumer Research*, 22 (March), 448–59.

Kisielius, Jolita & Sternthal, Brian (1986) Examining the vividness controversy: an availability-valence interpretation. *Journal of Consumer Research*, 12 (4), 418–31.

Klapper, Joseph T. (1960) *The Effects of Mass Communication*. New York: Free Press.

Knox, Robert E. & Inkster, James A. (1968) Postdecision dissonance at post time. *Journal of Personality and Social Psychology*, 8 (April, Part I), 319–23.

Kotler, Phillip (2000) *Marketing Management*, 10th edn. Upper Saddle River, NJ: Prentice-Hall.

Krishna, Aradna, Currim, Imran S. & Shoemaker, Robert W. (1991) Consumer perceptions of promotional activity. *Journal of Marketing*, 55 (April), 4–16.

Krishnamurthi, Lakshman, Narayan, Jack & Raj, S.P. (1986) Intervention analysis of a field experiment to assess the buildup effect of advertising. *Journal of Marketing Research*, 23 (November), 337–45.

Krugman, Herbert E. (1972) Why three exposures may be enough. *Journal of Advertising Research*, 12 (December), 11–14.

——— (1988) Point of view: limits of attention to advertising. *Journal of Advertising Research*, 28 (October/November), 47–50.

Kuehn, Alfred A., McGuire, Timothy W. & Weiss, Doyle L. (1964) Measuring the effectiveness of advertising. In *Science Technology and Marketing*, edited by R.M. Hass. Chicago: American Marketing Association.

Lambin, Jean J. (1972) Is gasoline advertising justified? *Journal of Business*, 45 (October), 505.

——— (1976), *Advertising, Competition, and Market Oligopoly Over Time, An Investigation in Western European Countries*. New York: Elsevier Publishing Co.

Lavidge, Robert J. & Steiner, Gary A. (1961) A model for predictive measurement of advertising effectiveness. *Journal of Marketing*, 25, 59–62.

Lewin, Kurt (1948) *Resolving Social Conflicts*. New York: Harper and Row.

Linder, Darwyn E. & Worchel, Stephen (1970) Opinion change as a result of effortfully drawing a counterattitudinal conclusion. *Journal of Experimental Social Psychology*, 6 (October), 432–8.

Little, John D.C. (1975) Brandaid: a marketing mix model, parts I and 2. *Operations Research*, 23, 628–73.

——— (1979) Aggregate advertising models: the state of the art. *Operations Research*, 27 (July–August), 629–65.

Lodish, Leonard M., Abraham, Magid, Kalmenson, Stuart, Livelsberger, Jeanne, Lubetkin, Beth, Richardson, Bruce & Stevens, Mary Ellen (1995) How T.V. advertising works: a meta-analysis of 389 real world split cable T.V. advertising experiments. *Journal of Marketing Research*, 32 (May), 125–39.

Marks, Lawrence J. & Kamins, Michael A. (1988) The use of product sampling and advertising: effects of sequence of exposure and degree of advertising claim exaggeration on consumers' belief strength, belief confidence, and attitudes. *Journal of Marketing Research*, 25 (August), 266–81.

Massy, William F., Montgomery, David B. & Morrison, Donald G. (1970) *Stochastic Models of Buying Behavior*. Cambridge, MA: MIT Press.

Mazur, J.E. & Hastie, R. (1978) Learning as accumulation: a reexamination of the learning curve. *Psychological Bulletin*, 65 (6), 1256–74.

McCarthy, W.J. (1986) Testimony at the Hearings on Advertising of Tobacco Products before the Subcommittee on Health and the Environment of the Committee on Energy and Commerce, House of Representatives, 99th Congress, July 18, August 1.

McDonald, Colin (1971) What is the short-term effect of advertising? *Marketing Science Institute Report No. 71–142*. Cambridge, MA: Marketing Science Institute.

——— (1996) *Advertising Reach and Frequency: Maximizing Advertising Results Through Effective Frequency*. Lincolnwood, IL: NTC Business Books.

McGuire, William J. (1969) The nature of attitude change. In *The Handbook of Social Psychology*, edited by G. Lindzey & E. Aronson. Vol. 3. New York: Random House, pp. 177–257.

——— & Papageorgis, D. (1961) The relative efficacy of various types of prior belief-defense in producing immunity against persuasion. *Journal of Abnormal & Social Psychology* 62, 327–37.

Merton, Robert K. (1946) *Mass Persuasion*. New York: Harper and Row.

Milne, George R. (2000) Privacy and ethical issues in database/interactive marketing and public policy: a research framework and overview of the Special Issue. Special Issue on Privacy and Ethical Issues in Database/Interactive Marketing and Public Policy, *Journal of Public Policy and Marketing*, 19 (1), 1–6.

Miniard, Paul W., Sirdeshmukh, Deepak & Innis, Daniel E. (1992) Peripheral persuasion and brand choice. *Journal of Consumer Research*, 19 (2), 226–39.

Miniard, Paul W., Bhatla, Sunil, Lord, Kenneth R., Dickson, Peter R. & Unnava, H. Rao (1991) Picture-based persuasion processes and the moderating role of involvement. *Journal of Consumer Research*, 18 (1), 92–107.

Mitchell, Andrew A. & Olson, J.C. (1981) Are product attitude beliefs the only mediator of advertising effects on brand attitudes? *Journal of Marketing Research*, 18 (August), 318–21.

Moran, William T. (1988) A personal perspective on advertising principles and issues. Paper presented to Marketing Science Institute Conference on Evaluating the Effects of Consumer Advertising on Market Position Over Time, June 8–10, Babson College Campus, Wellesley, MA.

Moriarity, Sandra Ernest (1983) Beyond the Hierarchy of Effects: a conceptual framework. *Current Issues and Research in Advertising*, 6 (1), 45–55.

Nakanishi, Masao (1973) Advertising and promotion effects on consumer response to new products. *Journal of Marketing Research*, 10 (August), 242–52.

Naples, Michael J. (1979) *Effective Frequency*. New York: Association of National Advertisers.

Niraj, Rakesh, Gupta, Mahendra & Narasimhan, Chakravarthi (2001) Customer profitability in a supply chain. *Journal of Marketing*, 65 (3), 1–16.

Ostrom, Amy & Iacobucci, Dawn (1995) Consumer trade-offs and the evaluation of services. *Journal of Marketing*, 59 (1), 17–28.

Packard, Vance (1957) *The Hidden Persuaders*. New York: Pocket Books.

Palda, Kristian (1964) *The Measurement of Cumulative Advertising Effects*. Englewood Cliffs, NJ: Prentice-Hall.

——— (1966) The hypothesis of a Hierarchy of Effects: a partial evaluation. *Journal of Marketing Research*, 3, 13–24.

Pavlou, Paul A. & Stewart, David W. (2000) Measuring the effects and effectiveness of interactive advertising: a research agenda. *Journal of Interactive Advertising*, 1 (1). URL: http://www.jiad.org/vol1/no1/pavlou/.

Pechmann, Connie & Stewart, David W. (1988) Advertising repetition: a critical review of wearin and wearout. *Current Issues and Research in Advertising*, 11 (2), 285–330.

——— (1990) The role of comparative advertising: documenting its effects on attention, recall, and purchase intentions. *Journal of Consumer Research*, 17 (Sept.), 180–91.

——— (1991) The effect of comparative advertising on sales of low, moderate, and high share brands. *Journal of Advertising Research*, 31 (Dec./Jan.), 47–55.

Petty, Richard & Cacioppo, John T. (1981) *Attitudes and Persuasion: Classic and Contemporary Approaches*. Dubuque, IA: William C. Brown Company.

——— (1986), *Communication and Persuasion: Central and Peripheral Routes to Attitude Change*. New York: Springer-Verlag.

——— & Schumann, David (1983) Central and peripheral routes to advertising effectiveness: the moderating role of involvement. *Journal of Consumer Research*, 10, 135–46.

Plott, Charles R. & Levine, Michael E. (1978) A model of agenda influence on committee decisions. *The American Economic Review*, 68 (March), 146–60.

Politz Media Studies (1960) *The Rochester Study*. New York: Saturday Evening Post.

Pollay, Richard W., Siddarth, S., Siegel, Michael, Haddix, Anne, Merritt, Robert K., Giovino, Gary A. & Eriksen, Michael P. (1996) The last straw? Cigarette advertising and realized market shares among youths and adults, 1979–1993. *Journal of Marketing*, 60 (April), 1–16.

Raj, S.P. (1982) The effects of advertising on high and low loyalty consumer segments. *Journal of Consumer Research*, 9 (June), 77–89.

Ratneshwar, S., Mick, David G. & Reitinger, Gail (1989) Selective attention in consumer information processing: the role of chronically accessible attributes. In *Advances in Consumer Research*, edited by M. Goldberg, G. Gorn & R. Pollay. Provo, UT: Association for Consumer Research, Vol. 18, pp. 547–53.

Ray, Michael L. (1973) *Marketing Communication and the Hierarchy of Effects*. Cambridge, MA: Marketing Science Institute.

——— (1982) *Advertising and Communication Management*. Englewood Cliffs, NJ: Prentice-Hall.

——— & Sawyer, Alan G. (1971) Repetition in media models: a laboratory technique. *Journal of Marketing Research*, 8 (Feb.), 20–9.

——— Wilkie, William L. (1970) Fear: the potential of an appeal neglected by marketing. *Journal of Marketing*, 34 (Jan.), 54–62.

——— Sawyer, Alan G. & Strong, Edward C. (1971) Frequency effects revisited. *Journal of Advertising Research*, 11, 14–20.

Reinartz, W. & Kumar, V. (2000) On the profitability of long lifetime customers: an empirical investigation and implications for marketing. *Journal of Marketing*, 64 (4), 17–35.

Reingen, Peter H. & Kernan, Jerome B. (1986) Analysis of referral networks in marketing: methods and illustration. *Journal of Marketing Research*, 23 (November), 370–8.

Richins, Marsha L. (1983) Negative word-of-mouth by dissatisfied customers: a pilot study. *Journal of Marketing*, 47 (1), 68–78.

Roberts, Mark J. & Samuelson, Larry (1988) An empirical analysis of dynamic, nonprice competition in an oligopolistic industry. *Rand Journal of Economics*, 19 (Summer), 200–20.

Roediger, Henry L. & Schmidt, Stephen R. (1980) Output interference in the recall of categorized and paired-associate lists. *Journal of Experimental Psychology: Human Learning and Memory*, 6, 91–105.

Rogers, Everett M. (1983) *Diffusion of Innovations*, 3rd edn. New York: Free Press.

Rossiter, John R. & Percy, Larry (1997) *Advertising Communications and Promotion Management*. New York: McGraw-Hill Companies, Inc.

Runyon, Kenneth & Stewart, David W. (1987) *Consumer Behavior and the Practice of Marketing*, 4th edn. Columbus, OH: Merrill Publishing.

Sawyer, Alan G. (1973) The effects of repetition of refutational and supportive advertising appeals. *Journal of Marketing Research*, 10 (February), 23–33.

——— (1974) The effects of repetition: conclusions and suggestions about experimental laboratory research. In *Buyer/Consumer Information Processing*, edited by G.D. Hughes & M.L. Ray. Chapel Hill, NC: University of North Carolina Press, pp. 190–219.

——— (1981) Repetition, cognitive responses and persuasion. In *Cognitive Responses in Persuasion*, edited by Thomas M. Ostrom, Richard E. Petty & Timothy C. Brock. Hillsdale, NJ: Lawrence Erlbaum Associates, pp. 237–61.

——— & Howard, Daniel J. (1991) Effects of omitting conclusions in advertisement to involved and uninvolved audiences. *Journal of Marketing Research*, 28 (November), 467–74.

——— & Ward, Scott (1977) Carry-over effects in advertising communication: evidence and hypotheses from behavioral science. In *Cumulative Advertising Effects: Sources and Implications*, edited by Darral G. Clarke. Cambridge, MA: Marketing Science Institute, pp. 71–170.

——— (1979) Carry-over effects in advertising communication. In *Research in Marketing*, Vol. 2, edited by J. Sheth. Greenwich, CT: JAI Press, pp. 259–314.

Schmalensee, Richard (1972) *The Economics of Advertising*. Amsterdam: North Holland Publishing.

Schroeder, Gary, Richardson, Bruce & Sankaralingham, Avu (1997) Validating STAS using BehaviorScan. *Journal of Advertising Research*, 37 (4), 33–42.

Schwerin, Horace S. & Newell, Henry H. (1981) *Persuasion in Marketing*. New York: John Wiley.

Scott, Douglas R. & Solomon, Debbie (1998) What is wearout anyway? *Journal of Advertising Research*, 38 (October), 19–28.

Scott, Walter Dill (1908) *Psychology of Advertising*. Boston: Small, Maynard.

Sethi, S. Prakook (1971) A comparison between the effect of pulse versus continuous TV advertising on buyer behavior. *Proceedings of the American Marketing Association*. Chicago: American Marketing Association.

Sexton, Donald E. (1970) Estimating marketing policy effects on sales of a frequently purchased product. *Journal of Marketing Research*, 7 (August), 338–47.

Shibutani, T. (1966) *Improvised News: A Sociological Study of Rumor*. Indianapolis: Bobbs Merrill.

Simon, Hermann (1982) ADPLUS: an advertising model with wearout and pulsation. *Journal of Marketing Research*, 19 (August), 352–63.

Simon, Julian L. & Arndt, Johan (1980) The shape of the advertising response function. *Journal of Advertising Research*, 20 (August), 11–30.

Stephens, Nancy & Warren, Robert A. (1984) Advertising frequency requirements for older adults. *Journal of Advertising Research*, 23 (December), 23–32.

Sternthal, Brian & Craig, C. Samuel C. (1973) Humor in advertising. *Journal of Marketing*, 37 (Oct.), 12–18.

——— (1974) Fear appeals: revisited and revised. *Journal of Consumer Research*, 1 (3), 22–34.

Stewart, David W. (1986) The moderating role of recall, comprehension, and brand differentiation on the persuasiveness of television advertising. *Journal of Advertising Research*, 26 (April/May), 43–7.

——— (1989) Measures, methods, and models of advertising response over time. *Journal of Advertising Research*, 29 (June/July), 54–60.

——— (1992) Speculations on the future of advertising research. *Journal of Advertising*, 21 (Sept.), 1–18.

——— (1999) Advertising wearout: what and how you measure matters. *Journal of Advertising Research*, 39 (Sept./Oct.), 39–42.

——— Furse, David H. (1986) *Effective Television Advertising: A Study of 1000 Commercials*. Lexington, MA: Lexington Books.

——— Koslow, Scott (1989) Executional factors and advertising effectiveness: a replication. *Journal of Advertising*, 18 (3), 21–32.

——— Zhao, Qin (2000) Internet marketing, business models, and public policy. *Journal of Public Policy and Marketing*, 19 (2), 287–96.

——— Frazier, Gary & Martin, Ingrid (1996) Integrated channel management: merging the communication and distribution functions of the firm. In *Integrated Communication: Synergy of Persuasive Voices*, edited by Esther Thorson & Jeri Moore. Hillsdale, NJ: Erlbaum, pp. 185–216.

——— Pavlou, Paul & Ward, Scott (2002) Media influences on marketing communications. In *Media Effects: Advances in Theory and Research*, edited by Jennings Bryant & Dorf Zillmann. Hillsdale, NJ: Erlbaum, pp. 353–96.

Strang, Roger A., Prentice, Robert M. & Clayton, Alden (1975) The relationship between advertising and promotion in brand strategy. *Marketing Science Institute Report No. 75–119*. Cambridge, MA: Marketing Science Institute.

Sutherland, Max & Galloway, John (1983) Role of advertising: persuasion or agenda setting. *Journal of Advertising Research*, 23 (Sept.), 52–6.

Swan, John E. & Oliver, Richard L. (1989) Postpurchase communication by consumers. *Journal of Retailing*, 65, 516–33.

Taylor, L.D. & Weiserbs, D. (1972) Advertising and the aggregate consumption function. *The American Economic Review*, 62 (4), 642–55.

Taylor, S.E., Crocker, J., Fiske, S.T., Sprinzen, M. & Winkler, J.D. (1979) The generalizability of salience effects. *Journal of Social Psychology*, 37, 357–68.

Tele-Research, Inc. (1968) Do TV commercials wear out? *Tele/Scope Bulletin*, February.

Tellis, Gerard J. (1988) Advertising exposure, loyalty and brand purchase: a two-stage model of choice. *Journal of Marketing Research*, 25 (May), 134–44.

——— (1997) Effective frequency: one exposure or three factors? *Journal of Advertising Research*, 37 (4), 75–80.

——— & Weiss, Doyle L. (1995) Does TV advertising really affect sales? The role of measures, models and data aggregation. *Journal of Advertising*, 24 (3), 1–12.

Telser, Lester G. (1962) Advertising and cigarettes. *Journal of Political Economy*, 70, 471–99.

Thaler, Richard (1985) Mental accounting and consumer choice. *Marketing Science*, 4 (Summer), 199–214.

Thorson, Esther & Moore, Jeri (1996) *Integrated Communication: Synergy of Persuasive Voices*. Mahwah, NJ: Lawrence Erlbaum Associates.

Time, Inc./Seagram (1981) *A Study of the Effectiveness of Advertising Frequency in Magazines*. New York: Time, Inc.

Tolley, R. Stuart (1994) The search: patterns of newspaper readership. In *Attention, Attitude, and Affect in Response to Advertising*, edited by E. Clark, T. Brock & D.W. Stewart. Hillsdale, NJ: Erlbaum Publishing.

Tversky, Amos & Kahneman, Daniel (1974) Judgment under uncertainty: heuristics and biases. *Science*, 185, 1124–31.

Tybout, Alice M., Calder, Bobby J. & Sternthal, Brian (1981) Using information processing theory to design marketing strategies. *Journal of Marketing Research*, 18, 73–9.

Unnava, H. Rao & Burnkrant, Robert E. (1991) An imagery processing view of the role of pictures in print advertisements. *Journal of Marketing Research*, 28, 226–31.

Unnava, H. Rao & Sirdeshmukh, Deepak (1994) Reducing competitive ad interference. *Journal of Marketing Research*, 31 (8), 403–11.

Vaughn, Richard (1980) How advertising works: a planning model. *Journal of Advertising Research*, 20 (October), 30–2.

Voss, P., Jr. (1984) Status shifts to peer influence. *Advertising Age*, May 17, M-10.

Weinberger, Marc G. & Leland, Campbell (1990/91) The use and impact of humor in radio advertising. *Journal of Advertising Research*, 30 (Dec./Jan.), 44–51.

Weitz, Barton A., Sujan, Harish & Sujan, Mita (1986) Knowledge, motivation and adaptive behavior: a framework for improving selling effectiveness. *Journal of Marketing*, 50 (October), 174–91.

Williams, Kaylene C., Spiro, Rosann & Fine, Leslie M. (1990) The customer-salesperson dyad: an interaction/communication model and review. *Journal of Personal Selling and Sales Management*, 10 (Summer), 29–43.

Wilson, C.E. (1981) A procedure for analysis of consumer decision making. *Journal of Advertising Research*, 21 (2), 31–38.

Wright, Peter L. (1973) The cognitive processes mediating acceptance of advertising. *Journal of Marketing Research*, 10 (February), 53–62.

——— (1974) Analyzing media effects on advertising responses. *Public Opinion Quarterly*, 38 (Summer), 192–205.

Zielske, Henry A. (1959) The remembering and forgetting of advertising. *Journal of Marketing*, 23 (January), 239–43.

——— & Henry, Walter A. (1980) Remembering and forgetting television advertising. *Journal of Advertising Research*, 20 (April), 7–16.

Zillmann, Dorf & Bryant, Jennings (1985) *Selective Exposure to Communication*. Hillsdale, NJ: Lawrence Erlbaum Associates, Inc.

13

Sales Promotion

SCOTT A. NESLIN

Introduction

Sales promotion is a ubiquitous, and in some cases dominant, component of the firm's marketing mix. It can be defined as an 'action-oriented marketing event whose purpose is to have a direct impact on the behavior of the firm's customers' (Blattberg & Neslin, 1990: 3). Sales promotions include price discounts, feature advertising, special displays, trade deals, reward programs, coupons, rebates, contests, and sweepstakes. As implied by their definition, promotions have a noticeable impact on the behavior of customers. However, they tap into and induce important psychological processes in the consumer, as well as significant competitive response. As a result, all three foundations of the marketing field: behavioral science, economics, and management science (particularly econometrics), have contributed significantly to our knowledge base on sales promotion. In fact, there has been a veritable explosion of research over the past decade, and although we have learned a lot, there is still much more to understand.

The purpose of this chapter is to synthesize what we know and don't know about sales promotion. The focus is on substantive knowledge rather than methodology *per se*. However, we discuss methodological issues as they pertain to our ability to pinpoint substantive knowledge. We have organized the chapter into three domains: 'Why Sales Promotion' briefly reviews the behavioral and economic bases for the existence of sales promotion. 'How Promotion Works' discusses the various customer behaviors that are influenced by sales promotion. 'Promotion Types' discusses what we know about specific forms of promotion. We conclude with a brief discussion of future research opportunities.

Why Sales Promotion?

Managers often justify their use of promotions simply as the most reliable way to increase sales. The sales impact is tangible, immediate, and therefore attractive to results-oriented managers. However, academics try to answer the questions: Why promotion? What makes promotion so powerful? Why not simply decrease the everyday price? Is there a profit motive for promotion? Both economic and behavioral literatures provide insights on these questions.

Economic Viewpoint

Price Discrimination

Price discrimination means selling 'the same physical good … at different prices, either to the same consumer or different consumers' (Tirole, 1988: 133). The strategy behind price discrimination is to increase profits by selling the product at a higher price to consumers who are willing to pay more, and a lower price to consumers who are willing to pay less (Farris & Quelch, 1987). In marketing terms, price discrimination is market segmentation based on price sensitivities. Researchers have identified several ways that promotion can segment the market:

- *Informed vs. Uninformed Consumers* (Varian, 1980): Informed consumers are aware of prices and are willing to shop at different stores to get those prices. Uninformed consumers simply shop at the most convenient stores. Stores use price promotions so that informed consumers pay less than uninformed consumers (see also Shilony, 1977).

- *Loyals vs. Switchers* (Lal, 1990; Narasimhan, 1988; Raju et al., 1990): Manufacturers use promotions so that their loyal users pay more and switchers pay less. Loyals will buy the product even if the price is high, while switchers will only buy if the price is low. Narasimhan & Lal both formally model loyal segments and switcher segments. Raju et al. model all consumers as loyal to one brand, but their loyalty is not absolute, so they are willing to switch for the right price.
- *Stockpilers vs. Non-Stockpilers* (Blattberg et al., 1981): Retailers use promotions so that households with low inventory carrying costs can stockpile the product. The stockpilers pay lower prices than non-stockpilers. The retailer saves money by shifting its inventory costs to the stockpilers.
- *Heavy vs. Light Users* (Jeuland & Narasimhan, 1985): Light users are willing to stockpile and consume more of the product when price is low, whereas heavy users do not stockpile and are willing to pay the regular price when they have to. The firm makes money by increasing primary demand among light users, and by heavy users paying higher prices.
- *High vs. Low Cost of Time* (Narasimhan, 1984): Consumers with high opportunity costs of time (because of high wage rates or time demands) will not make the effort to buy on promotion. Low time-cost consumers are willing to make the effort and pay lower prices.

In the informed/uninformed and loyal/switcher segmentations, promotions arise as mixed strategy equilibria to a multi-firm game. Neither a single high price nor a single low price is stable (there is always a temptation to undercut prices, but firms have some monopoly power so do not have to charge constant low prices), so randomized prices become the mixed strategy equilibrium. Obviously firms do not promote randomly, but the key element is that consumers and firms do not know exactly when a particular product will go on sale.

Lal (1990) provides an exception to the mixed strategy approach. Firms cooperate by alternating weeks when they promote (e.g., Coke and Pepsi in US supermarkets). Two national brands, each with loyal customers, compete for the switching segment against a lower tier brand (e.g., a private/ own label) that has no loyal customers. The nationals want to offer price discounts to attract switchers, but when they do so, their loyals also pay the low price. In order to compensate for this cost, the nationals alternate weeks when they are on promotion. This enables the nationals to gain most of the switchers when they promote, and not cannibalize each other's efforts. What enforces this arrangement is a punishment strategy – if a national brand deviates from the alternate week schedule, there will be a ruinous price war. As long as both firms have ample marketing funds and care about future profits, the strategy is an equilibrium.

Non-Price Discrimination

Forecast Error (Pashigian & Bowen, 1991): Firms use promotions as 'clearance sales,' to sell off extra inventory accumulated because they cannot acc rately predict demand. This might occur in industries such as perishable food products, automobiles, and clothing.

Trial: No researchers have developed a formal theory of this. However, Blattberg et al. (1981) argue that the role of promotions may be to induce trial by lowering the costs of perceived risk.

Post-promotion Effects: Researchers have posited that the long-term impact of promotion encourages its use. These long-term effects include reference prices (Kopalle, Rao, and Assunção, 1996), baseline sales (Kopalle, Mela & Marsh, 1999), purchase event feedback (Freimer & Hersky, 2001) and consumption (Bell, Iyer, and Padmanabhan, 2002).

The Behavioral Perspective

Transaction Utility

Transaction utility (Thaler, 1985) is most readily understood by contrasting it with its companion concept, acquisition utility. Acquisition utility is the value derived from the intrinsic utility provided by an item, relative to its purchase price. Transaction utility is the purchase price of an item relative to a subjective benchmark known as a reference price. Acquisition utility represents utility generated by the economic value of the purchase. Transaction utility represents the value of the deal. The purpose of promotion, therefore, is to provide transaction utility to a 'deal prone' consumer segment that values transaction utility.

Researchers have demonstrated that transaction utility can be measured, distinguished from acquisition utility, and that it contributes to utility (Lichtenstein et al., 1990; see Grewal et al., 1998 and Urbany et al., 1997 for further elaboration). Perhaps the strongest evidence of transaction utility comes from the reference price literature. Winer (1986) was the first to show that the term (actual price – reference price) contributed significantly to a choice model, over and above price itself (see section 'Post-Promotion Brand Effects, p. 314 for further discussion of reference prices). Chandon et al. (2000) expand the concept of transaction utility beyond its price orientation, and enumerate the utilitarian vs. hedonic benefits of promotion. Utilitarian benefits include price savings, but also convenience and quality upgrade. Hedonic benefits include exploration, entertainment, and self-expression.

There is a well-developed literature that shows demographic and psychographic characteristics can identify the deal-prone segment (Bawa and Shoemaker, 1987a; Blattberg & Neslin, 1990). An emerging view is that psychographics play the direct role in determining deal proneness; demographics

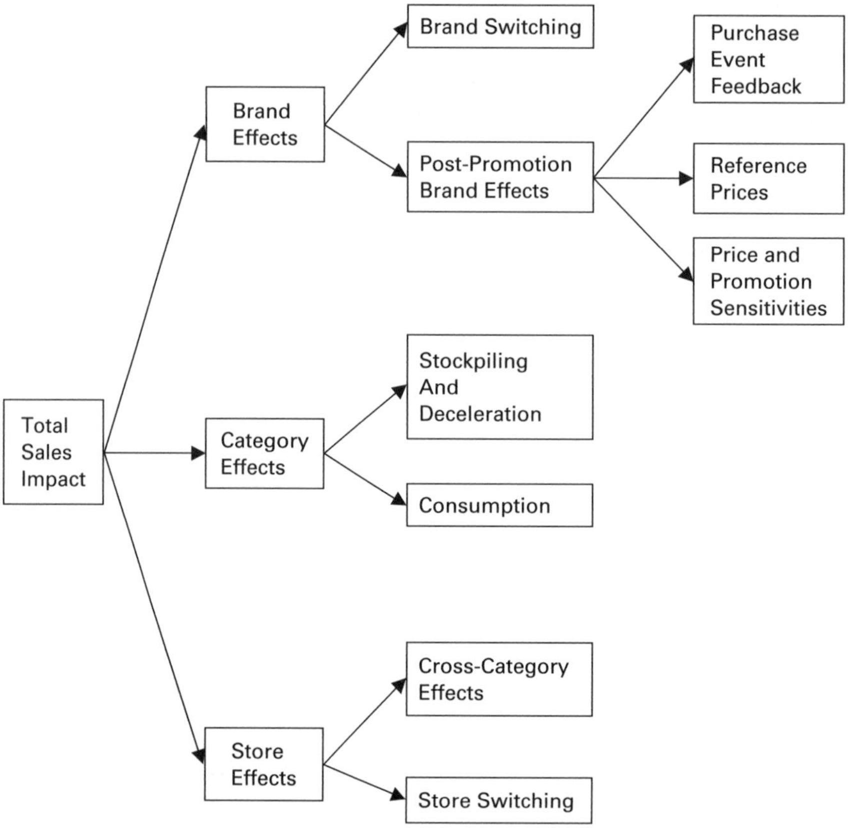

Figure 13.1 *How Promotion Affects Sales*

act to help determine the psychographics (Ailawadi, Neslin & Gedenk, 2001).

The Behaviorist Perspective

The behaviorist perspective is based on Skinner's theory of behavioral learning (Skinner, 1938). The concept is that rewarded behavior is more likely to persist. Sales promotions may act as rewards that encourage repeated purchase of the brand (Rothschild & Gaidis, 1981). An important quarrel with this argument is that rather than training customers to buy the brand, promotions may train customers to buy on promotion, i.e., become deal prone (Rothschild, 1987).

How Promotion Affects Sales and Profits

Promotions induce a pronounced and immediate increase in sales. Doubling, tripling, or even higher multiple sales increases are commonly observed while a promotion is in effect (Blattberg & Neslin, 1990; Doyle & Saunders, 1985; Guadagni & Little, 1983; Narasimhan et al., 1996). A rich literature has developed regarding the various ways in which promotions affect sales (see Blattberg et al., 1995). We organize these into brand, category, and store-level effects (see Figure 13.1).

Brand Effects

Brand Switching

From an economic perspective, (price) promotions induce a brand switch by increasing the utility of a brand that otherwise would not have been purchased. From a behavioral perspective, transaction utility provides an added impetus for buying a brand that otherwise would not have been purchased. The earliest evidence on promotion effectiveness suggested a strong brand switching effect (Dodson et al., 1978). Blattberg & Neslin (1990: 117) found that while 32% of coffee purchase occasions without promotions involved brand switches, the range was 40–66% when the purchase involved various types of promotion. Gupta (1988) attributed 85% of the effect of promotion in the coffee category to brand switching, with the remaining 15% attributable to stockpiling.

A key aspect of the switching impact of promotions is that it can be *asymmetric* between brands (Blattberg & Wisniewski, 1989). Blattberg and Wisniewski's concept was twofold: First,

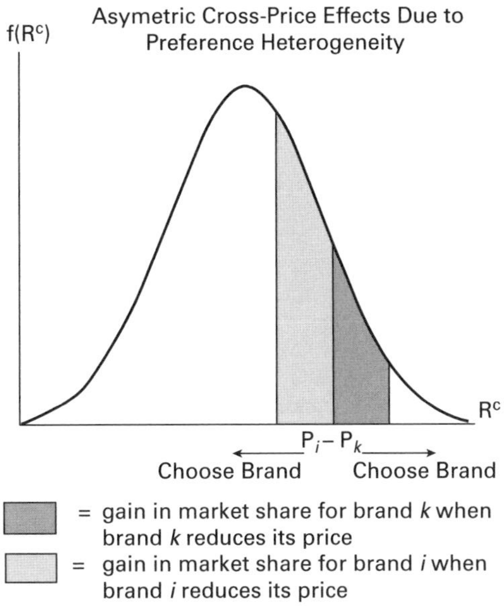

Figure 13.2 *Source: Blattberg & Wisniewski (1989)*

promotion-induced switching is asymmetric; what Brand A takes from Brand B is not necessarily the same as what Brand B takes from Brand A. Second, the asymmetry favors the high 'tier' brand. High tier brands – defined as higher quality and higher price – draw more from low tier brands than the reverse.

Evidence of tier-based asymmetry is stated in absolute numbers of sales, or in terms of elasticities. Evidence of asymmetric absolute effects includes Blattberg & Wisniewski (1989), Kumar & Leone (1988), Mulhern & Leone (1991), Walters (1991), Allenby & Rossi (1991), Sivakumar & Raj (1997), and Heath et al. (2000).[1] Evidence of asymmetric elasticities includes Kamakura & Russell (1989), and Bemmaor & Mouchoux (1991). Researchers have advanced several explanations for tier-related asymmetries:

Preference Heterogeneity (Blattberg & Wisniewski, 1989): Blattberg & Wisniewski show how asymmetries can arise due to consumer heterogeneity. They represent consumer *c*'s utility for Brand *i* (U_i^c) as:

$$U_i^c = \theta^c q_i^c - p_i \qquad [1]$$

where θ^c is how strongly the consumer cares about quality relative to price, q_i^C is consumer *c*'s perception of the quality of Brand *i*, and p_i is the price of Brand *i*. Without loss of generality, assume Brand *i* is in a higher tier than Brand *k*. Equation (1) implies that consumer *c* will choose Brand *i* over brand *k* if:

$$R^c \equiv \theta^c (q_i^c - q_k^c) > p_i - p_k \qquad [2]$$

where R^c is the quality advantage of Brand *i* over Brand *k*, weighted by consumer *c*'s valuation of quality. Note that R^c is distributed across consumers. The market shares of Brands *i* and *k* are determined by the location of $p_i - p_k$ relative to this distribution. As shown in Figure 13.2, Brand *i*'s market share will be the area to the right of $p_i - p_k$, because this area represents consumers for whom Equation [2] holds. Conversely, Brand *k*'s market share will equal the area to the left of $p_i - p_k$.

If Brand *i* decreases its price, it moves $p_i - p_k$ to the left and captures the shaded area to the left of the original $p_i - p_k$. If Brand *k* cuts its price, it moves $p_i - p_k$ to the right and captures the shaded area to the right of the original $p_i - p_k$. Depending on the distribution of R^c ($f(R^c)$) and the original value of $p_i - p_k$, we get asymmetric switching. In the example in Figure 13.2, Brand *i* price cuts draw more from Brand *k* than Brand *k* price cuts draw from Brand *i*.

This theory explains why there can be asymmetries between brands, but does not explain why the direction need be in favor of the higher tier brand. In Figure 13.2, the asymmetry comes out that way, but if $p_i - p_k$ were originally located to the left of the mode of the R^c distribution, the asymmetry would favor Brand *k*, the lower tier brand. Blattberg & Wisniewski (1989) conjecture that the distribution of R^c is such that asymmetries favor the high tier brand. Their evidence in favor of tier-based asymmetry implicitly supports this.

Income Effect (Allenby & Rossi, 1991): Allenby & Rossi draw on the economic theory of substitution and income effects to explain tier-based asymmetry (e.g., Ferguson, 1972: 70). A price decrease for Brand A increases sales of Brand A because consumers now find it more attractive than Brand B (the substitution effect), and because the consumer can now spend more on the product category (income effect). Allenby & Rossi posit that while both high tier and low tier brands will benefit from a substitution effect, the high tier brand benefits from the income effect, while the low tier brand loses. The model starts with the observation that the total utility a consumer can attain in a category increases if a brand drops its price. The key assumption is that the marginal utility for a high tier brand increases as the attainable utility in the category increases, while the marginal utility for a low tier brand decreases. Allenby & Rossi estimate their model and find evidence for their assumptions. They then calculate elasticities and show graphically the cross-price effects.

Loss Aversion (Hardie et al., 1993): This theory is based on the following empirically supported findings: (1) consumers evaluate brands by comparing them to a reference brand; (2) the last brand purchased serves as the reference brand; and (3) a disadvantage on an attribute results in a larger loss in utility than the gain in utility from having an advantage on an attribute. These three factors result in tier-based asymmetries because the higher tier brand decreases a loss relative to the lower tier brand (it decreases its price disadvantage), while a lower tier brand increases its gain relative to the higher tier brand (it increases its price advantage). Hardie et al. find support for this theory by showing that the last brand purchased serves as a reference point for future evaluations, and that losses decrease utility more than gains increase utility.

Dominance Effects (Heath et al., 2000): Heath et al. draw on the dominance effect (e.g., Huber et al., 1982). The dominance effect is that if Brand A supercedes Brand B on all attributes, Brand A gets an extra boost in utility. There are 'near dominance effects' as well. For example, assume that Brand A has superior quality to Brand B, then as the price of Brand A comes close to Brand B, it is 'assimilated' or perceived to be equal, thus providing an extra advantage to Brand A (Heath et al., 2000). Dominance results in tier-based asymmetry because the high tier brand can dominate the low tier brand by decreasing its price. But the low tier brand cannot dominate the high tier brand no matter how low it cuts its price – it will still have a quality disadvantage.

Heath et al. found support for dominance effects in a laboratory setting because large price decreases induced asymmetry, but small price decreases (where the high tier brand would not establish dominance) did not. They also found that consumers changed their valuation of product attributes in response to large price decreases, consistent with the notion of a synergistic gain in utility when one product dominates another.

Assessments of Alternative Theories of Asymmetry: Abe (1998) used nonparametric statistics to estimate the distribution of R^c and found unimodal distributions that he interprets to mean that the smaller share brand will draw more from a larger share brand than *vice versa*, so there is a market share effect rather than a price tier effect.[2] Abe also estimates a discretized version of Allenby & Rossi's model and finds that he cannot support the income effect theory either.

Heath et al. (2000) find strong support for dominance theory. They also find support for heterogeneity in that attribute weights (representing quality valuation) were correlated with switching. They also find support for loss aversion, in that consumers appear to use the last purchased brand as the reference brand. Interestingly, Heath et al. find not only asymmetries in price but quality as well. A lower tier brand gains more from the high tier brand when it increases its quality than the high tier brand gains from the low tier brand when it increases its quality. This illustrates the potential of private labels to gain market share by improving their quality (Hoch & Banerji, 1993).

Bronnenberg & Wathieu (1996) show mathematically that loss aversion in price does not necessarily guarantee tier-based asymmetry. In fact, they conclude that strong loss aversion in price tilts the asymmetry in favor of the low tier brand, not the high tier brand. Bronnenberg & Wathieu predict and show that asymmetries favor the lower tier brand in the orange juice category. They also show that the key variables predicting asymmetries are 'positioning,' the difference in quality between two brands relative to the difference in price, and 'distance,' the absolute difference in quality. The ability of Brand A to draw consumers from Brand B is a positive function of its positioning advantage and a negative function of its distance.

Sethuraman et al. (1999) conduct a meta-analysis of 1060 cross-price effects across 280 brands in 19 categories. They find that tier-based asymmetries exist with regard to elasticities, but not with regard to absolute price effects. They show that the elasticity result is potentially a numerical artifact due to the association between price tier and market share. In a recent paper, Sethuraman and Srinivasan (2002) find empirical support for their theory of absolute asymmetric effects favoring the lower share brand.

The above two studies question whether high tier brands enjoy a consistent cross-price asymmetry versus low tier brands. However, Sethuraman et al.'s paper, despite its extensive analysis, is not definitive. While it draws on several databases, it does not include the Allenby & Rossi (1991), Walters (1991), Mulhern & Leone (1991), Kumar & Leone (1988), and Sivakumar & Raj (1997) studies that showed an absolute tier-based asymmetry in favor of the high tier brand.

In summary, we have a strong theoretical and empirical thesis that high tier brands take more from low tier brands than the reverse. We have a smaller but convincing set of papers that provides a credible antithesis and there is emerging evidence that market share is the key factor. Researchers need to sort this out, determine what types of asymmetries exist, and what causes them.

Post-Promotion Brand Effects

Purchase Event Feedback: The fundamental question here is what the effect of promotion on brand preference is. Two relevant theories are self-perception and behavioral learning. Self-perception posits that consumers question their actions, and their answers direct future behavior (Dodson et al., 1978). If the consumer concludes that he or she bought the brand because of the promotion rather than brand preference, the consumer's underlying attitude toward the brand is 'discounted,' or weakened (Dodson et al., 1978). Over time, the consumer's preference for the brand is reduced. Promotion has undermined brand loyalty.

As discussed earlier, behavioral learning theory proposes that if promotions are working well, they reinforce purchase behavior and enhance repeat purchasing (Rothschild & Gaidis, 1981). This should happen if the brand is the 'primary reinforcer.' However, Rothschild (1987) points out that if the brand is not the primary reinforcer – because it is not high quality or serves needs no differently than other brands – promotion can simply reinforce the behavior of buying on promotion.

Self-perception and behavioral learning theories are far apart in their theoretical underpinnings, but they are saying similar things. If promotions are easily available and of high monentary value – the

Table 13.1 *Current and Post-Promotion Effects of a Price Promotion (Keane, 1997)*

Purchase Occasion	Baseline Sales	Promotion Sales*	Incremental Sales	Percent of Total Incremental Sales
1	168	168	0	0
2	143	448	305	84.5
3	113	131	18	5.0
4	85	95	10	2.8
5	58	67	9	2.5
6	62	69	7	1.9
7	44	46	2	.6
8	35	38	3	.8
9	29	32	3	.8
10	23	27	4	1.1
Total	760	1121	361	100%

* Promotion available at Purchase Occasion 2.

causes of preference discounting according to Dodson et al. (1978) – they become primary reinforcers and undermine brand preference. It is useful to have these polar theories identify the same risk – that promotions undermine brand preference.

Initial evidence on purchase event feedback found a negative association between promotion purchasing and repeat rates (Dodson et al., 1978; Shoemaker & Shoaf, 1977). The evidence was gathered by separating household purchase panel data into promotion purchases versus non-promotion purchases, and observing the purchase rate on the next purchase.

Neslin and Shoemaker (1989) noted that this type of analysis could result in aggregation bias, in that the promotion purchases represented a disproportional number of brand switchers, whereas the non-promotion purchases represented a disproportional number of brand loyals. It was no wonder, then, that promotion purchases were associated with lower repeat rates than non-promotion purchases. The crucial issue was to control for brand preference. Around this time, additional evidence appeared (Davis et al., 1992; Ehrenberg et al., 1994) that in fact promotion might not have any effect on repeat rates. This set the stage for more formal modeling of the phenomenon.

The basic notion behind purchase event feedback is that purchasing a brand in period t affects preference for the brand in period $t+1$. This is also known as 'state dependence' (Heckman, 1981; Keane, 1997; McAlister & Srivastava, 1991). We use the term 'purchase event feedback' rather than state dependence, because the former is more descriptive. The simplest way to model purchase event feedback is through a lagged purchase term in the utility function, i.e.:

$$U_t = (\alpha + \beta_1 PROMO_t + \beta_2 f(I_{t-1}) + \varepsilon_t \quad [3]$$

U_t is the consumer's utility for the brand at purchase occasion or time t, $PROMO_t$ measures the presence or absence of a promotion at time t, I_{t-1} is an indicator variable equaling 1 if the brand were purchased on the previous purchase occasion, and 0 if not, and ε represents other causes of utility at purchase occasion t. α, β_1, and β_2 are parameters to be estimated – β_1 measures the switching effect of promotions, β_2 measures the purchase event feedback effect. There are two common forms of $f(I_{t-1})$:

$$f(I_{t-1}) = LAST_{t-1} = I_{t-1} \quad [4]$$

$$f(I_{t-1}) = BLOY_t = \lambda BLOY_{t-1} + (1-\lambda)I_{t-1} \quad [5]$$

LAST has been used by a number of researchers (e.g., Seetharaman et al., 1999). BLOY was pioneered by Guadagni & Little (1983). It represents an exponentially smoothed measure of previous purchasing. The value of λ measures the degree to which previous learning persists over time. A large value of λ means that habits are difficult to change, and that a new purchase does not change preferences very much. LAST is a special case of BLOY, with $\lambda = 0$.[3]

The key question is whether purchase event feedback exists. There are arguments against it, for example that purchasing of frequently purchased products is low involvement and 'zero order,' with little learning or post-purchase evaluation (Neslin & Shoemaker, 1989). Econometrically, feedback can become confounded with cross-sectional effects such as brand preference (Allenby & Rossi, 1991; Keane, 1997). In addition, purchase event feedback can be confounded with serial correlation in the error term of the utility function (ε_t in Equation [3]). Serial correlation could be due to persistence in factors such as the weather or an advertising campaign.

Several papers have measured purchase event feedback (see Ailawadi et al., 1999 for an extensive list). In addition, two papers (Abramson et al., 2000; Ailawadi et al., 1999) have investigated methodological and bias issues associated with purchase event feedback. Perhaps the most convincing empirical demonstration is found in Keane (1997). Keane controlled for several different forms of preference and price sensitivity heterogeneity, plus serial correlation, and consistently found a statistically significant feedback effect.

Seetharaman et al. (1999) find significant feedback effects in four of five product categories (the exception was tuna). They find that consumer-level values of β_2 are correlated across categories. They also find that the percentage of consumers with statistically significant feedback effects ranged from 0% (tuna) to 21% (stick margarine). There may be a lack of statistical power since there are not many observations per consumer. However, the results remind us that it is possible that a minority of individuals actually manifest the behavior represented by an average parameter.

The overall finding, then, is that purchase event feedback does exist. This opens the door for a repeat purchase effect of promotion. Keane simulated the effect of a price promotion on sales of a particular brand-size of ketchup over a 60-week period. The results are shown in Table 13.1. The numbers generally decrease from top to bottom because fewer and fewer consumers had that many purchase occasions over the six-week period; however, there are consistently more purchases in the promotion case. The results show that the repeat purchase effect of buying persists over several purchase occasions (the estimate of λ in this case was .91[4]), that the promotion resulted roughly in a net 50% increase in sales, and that incremental post-promotion purchases represented 15% of that increase.

Gedenk & Neslin (1999) develop a feedback model where the degree of feedback in BLOY depends on whether the purchase is made on promotion.[5] They find that an in-store sampling program is associated with enhanced feedback, while price promotions detract from feedback. The net feedback effect of promotion, calculated by combining the 'promotion usage effect' and the 'purchase effect' (see Blattberg & Neslin, 1990, pp. 118–19) was still positive, even for price promotions. In short, purchasing on price promotion provides positive feedback, but not as positive as when the consumer buys not on promotion.

Papatla & Krishnamurthi (1996) find that repeated purchase on promotion decreases β_2. That is, the importance of the BLOY variable decreases over time if consumers purchase on promotion. Papatla & Krishnamurthi do not calculate the effects on purchase probability; in fact, it could be that purchase probabilities might be enhanced for the promoted brand even if the effect of promotion on β_2 is negative. This is because all brands experience a decrease in the impact of BLOY. In any event, this study provides important collaborative evidence of feedback.

In summary, there is strong evidence that purchase event feedback exists. The effect holds on average, although not all consumers may be subject to feedback, and is relatively consistent across consumers from category to category. Feedback means that promotions have a post-purchase effect on purchase probabilities, since promotions induce more purchase events in the first place. There is still the concern of whether current methods completely control for cross-sectional heterogeneity, so further work is needed similar to Keane's (1997), to cement the generalization that feedback exists and to quantify its magnitude.

Price and Promotion Sensitivity: In behavioral learning theory, the counterpoint of not reinforcing brand attitudes is that consumers learn to be price and promotion sensitive. Papatla & Krishnamurthi (1996) investigated this possibility by developing a choice model where the coefficients of price and promotion were functions of previous purchases on promotion. They found that price promotions increase price, display, and feature sensitivity; coupons increase price sensitivity; displays increase display sensitivity; and features increase feature sensitivity.

Mela et al. (1997) investigated these issues utilizing a six-year natural experiment, in which promotions increased and advertising decreased. They found that price promotions increased consumer sensitivity to price, while non-price promotions (features, displays) decreased sensitivity to price among loyal consumers, and increased it among non-loyals.

Boulding et al. (1994) examined quarterly data for 826 business units. They hypothesized that promotions would increase sensitivity to price for above average price firms because the promotions would draw attention to an aspect (price) that was not their distinct competence. They hypothesized that promotions would decrease sensitivity to price for below average price firms because the promotions would draw attention to an aspect (price) that was their distinct competence. The researchers found that promotions were associated with higher price sensitivity for higher priced firms, and lower price sensitivity for lower priced firms. The price sensitivity of average or slightly below average price firms were not apparently affected by promotions.

Overall, there is fairly strong evidence that promotions increase price or promotion sensitivity. It should be noted, however, that this evidence is subject to the same methodological concerns as the feedback studies (inferring causality and separating dynamic from cross-sectional effects).

Reference Prices: The reference price effect, rooted in Helson's adaptation-level theory (Blattberg & Neslin, 1990: 41–7; Helson, 1964), is that consumers judge the attractiveness of a currently available price by comparing it to a benchmark, or reference price. Reference prices also fit Kahneman & Tversky's (1979) prospect theory and form the basis for the transaction utility provided by promotions.

The simplest formulation of the reference price effect is:

$$U_{jt} = \beta_o + \beta_1 PRICE_{jt} + \beta_2(RPRICE_{jt} - PRICE_{jt}) \quad [6]$$

where U_{jt} equals the utility of Brand *j* at time *t*, $PRICE_{jt}$ is the available price of Brand *j* at time *t*, and $RPRICE_{jt}$ is the reference price for Brand *j* at time *t*. The term β_2 represents the absolute price effect, acquisition utility. The term β_2 represents the reference price effect, transaction utility, and should be positively signed. The presence of β_2 makes a price promotion more effective – not only do we get a gain in utility from a lower absolute price, but we gain additional utility because of the positive gap between price and reference price.

An important extension of equation [6] differentiates between 'gains' and 'losses' (Hardie et al., 1993). If the currently available price is below the reference price, we have a 'gain,' or a 'good deal.' If the currently available price is above the reference price, we have a 'loss,' or 'sticker shock.' There are then two reference price parameters, one for gains and one for losses.

The existence of reference prices is supported by several studies. Much of this research has utilized scanner data (Breisch et al., 1997; Winer, 1986; see Kalyanaram & Winer, 1995 for a summary). One study (Kalwani & Yim, 1992) explicitly measured reference prices in a lab setting. This may have accentuated their importance, but this study provides important convergent validity with the scanner data work.

Much research has investigated how consumers form reference prices. Two major mechanisms have emerged: temporal and contextual (Rajendran & Tellis, 1994). The temporal mechanism is that reference prices are formed based on previously observed prices. It is common to model this with an exponential smoothing model:

$$RPRICE_{jt} = \alpha\ (RPRICE_{jt} + (1-\alpha)\ PRICE_{jt-1} \quad [7]$$

There are several variations on this, including just last price ($\alpha = 0$) or a weighted geometric mean of recent price, and various 'rational expectations' models that use all information available such as price and market share trends, along with inflation (Briesch et al., 1997; Winer, 1986).

The contextual mechanism is that consumers utilize a currently available price as the reference price. That may be the price of the previously purchased brand (Hardie et al., 1993), the lowest currently available price (Rajendran & Tellis, 1994), or a weighted average of currently available prices (Mazumdar & Papatla, 1995).

Briesch et al. (1997) conducted an extensive comparison of temporal versus contextual reference prices. The authors found the exponential model was best in all four product categories, with the reference brand mechanism performing almost as well in one product category. Overall, this study supported temporal, brand-specific reference price formation. One aspect the study did not consider was whether temporal and contextual reference prices exist in the same model. Rajendran & Tellis (1994) found this to be the case (see also Mazumdar & Papatla, 2000). They found the best temporal formation model was equation [7], while the best contextual reference price was the lowest available price in the category.

Whether reference price gains are weighted differently than reference price losses is important for both theoretical and managerial reasons. From a theoretical standpoint, prospect theory predicts that losses should loom larger than gains. This says that the market share gains from buying a brand on promotion are significantly offset by the sticker shock that comes when the consumer then finds the brand at regular price in the next period. However, if the gain is greater than the loss effect, promotions become attractive. This is demonstrated by Kopalle et al. (1996), who show that if gains outweigh losses, and reference prices are formed via equation [7], price promotions are an optimal firm pricing strategy.

The evidence leans toward losses outweighing gains, but the results are not clear-cut. Kalyanaraman & Winer (1995) cite several studies that find losses outweigh gains. However, Briesch et al. (1997) consistently find, across four product categories, that gains outweigh losses. Greenleaf (1995) & Krishnamurthi et al. (1992) also find evidence that gains outweigh losses.

The most notable challenge to the estimation of reference prices is by Chang et al. (1999) (see also Bell & Lattin, 2000). Their argument is that estimated reference price effects arise because price sensitive consumers time their purchases to promotions. As a result, observations with lower prices are more likely to represent price sensitive consumers, so the model derives misleadingly strong reference price effects. Chiang et al. show that after controlling for heterogeneity in purchase timing for price sensitive consumers, the reference price effect is no longer statistically significant. This is a striking finding. It needs further investigation using various reference price formation models and additional product categories.

Another argument against reference prices is that the consumer should learn that price promotions exist and should not be surprised by sticker shock or a good deal. Lattin & Bucklin (1989), indeed, find that consumers form reference promotions apart from reference prices, and Krishna et al. (1991) find that a segment learns promotion frequency and depth.

A final argument against reference prices is that consumers barely remember the price of an item they have just purchased (Dickson & Sawyer, 1990), so how can they remember the prices of all the brands in the market! Kalyanaram & Little (1994) provide a rejoinder to this through the concept of lattitude of acceptance – consumers do not necessarily remember prices, but remember enough to know if an available price is exceptional. Krishna et al. (1991) also would suggest it is a market segment, not all consumers, who form reference prices.

Category Effects

Stockpiling and Deceleration

Promotions can induce consumers to purchase earlier than usual ('purchase acceleration'), defer purchase until a promotion is available ('purchase deceleration'), or purchase extra quantity of the product. We refer to acceleration and quantity effects as consumer stockpiling.[6]

The theoretical motivation for stockpiling is that consumers trade-off inventory carrying cost versus price (Blattberg et al., 1981; Krishna, 1992). Deceleration is motivated by consumer expectations (Gonul & Srinivasan, 1996; Krishna, 1994; Mela et al., 1998).

The empirical support for stockpiling is very strong, and one of the few promotion effects that have been documented for durables as well as packaged goods. The earliest evidence on stockpiling is due to Shoemaker (1979) & Wilson et al. (1979). They found that promotions were associated with shorter interpurchase times (from the previous purchase to the current promotion purchase) and larger purchase quantities. Blattberg, Eppen & Lieberman (1981) followed with similar evidence. Neslin, Henderson & Quelch (1985) synthesized these findings in a structural model:

Purchase Quantity = f(Promotion, Inventory, Interpurchase Time) [8a]

Interpurchase Time = f(Promotion, Inventory) [8b]

Purchase quantity was hypothesized to be a positive function of promotion and interpurchase time, and a negative function of inventory. Interpurchase time was hypothesized to be a negative function of promotion and a positive function of inventory. This shows that one has to control for household inventory levels to measure stockpiling. Researchers virtually always do this. The difficulty is that measures of inventory are not available directly, and must be estimated using observed purchase quantities and estimated average consumption rates. Neslin et al. (1985) found that featured price cuts increased purchase quantities and decreased interpurchase times. They found that loyal users were at least as likely to stock-up as were non-loyal consumers, and that heavy users were more likely to stock-up. There was no relationship between income and stockpiling behavior.

Several researchers have developed more formal purchase incidence and quantity models (Bucklin & Gupta, 1992; Bucklin et al., 1998; Chingtagunta, 1993; Gupta, 1988; Jain & Vilcassim, 1991; Mela et al., 1998). The overwhelming evidence supports the existence of stockpiling. Note however that instead of studying interpurchase times, this research typically studies whether a category purchase occurs in a given time period ('purchase incidence'). A positive promotion effect obviously is necessary evidence of acceleration (a category purchase is occurring now that otherwise would not have), but not sufficient. This is because a significant incidence effect could represent an increase in category consumption (Neslin & Schneider Stone, 1996).

In addition to the above evidence, Doyle & Saunders (1985) found that promotions accelerate purchases of furniture. Thompson & Noordewier (1992) found that rebates induced purchase acceleration of automobile sales. Bucklin & Gupta (1992) and Bucklin et al. (1998) showed that there are different market segments in terms of purchase incidence and quantity. Chintagunta & Haldar (1998) found that purchase acceleration of one category (e.g., spaghetti sauce) can induce accelerated purchasing of another category (e.g., pasta).[7]

One mystery was that while panel data analyses invariably found stockpiling of packaged goods, these effects did not show up in weekly sales data in the form of post-promotion 'dips.' Logic dictated that if consumers are stockpiling, there should be a dip in weekly category or brand sales in the weeks following a promotion, as consumers work through their inflated inventory. Interestingly, however, analyses of weekly supermarket scanner data did not find such dips (Abraham & Lodish, 1993; Moriarty, 1985; Neslin & Schneider Stone, 1996; Wittink et al., 1987).

Neslin & Schneider Stone (1996) posited several potential explanations for the lack of a post-promotion dip. These included: deal-to-deal buying (consumers who respond to promotions buy only on promotion), increases in consumption, competitive promotions, positive repeat purchase effects canceling the post-promotion dip, retailers extending promotions beyond the period officially indicated in the data; mixing acceleration and quantity effects, lack of consumer inventory sensitivity, and deceleration masking acceleration. Undoubtedly all these phenomena are present in weekly data and make it difficult to measure post-promotion dips.

Recent work by Van Heerde et al. (2000) shows that careful time series regressions with large sample sizes can uncover post as well as pre-promotion dips. The authors investigated three time series regression models. The simplest was a 'unrestricted' model of the form:

$$S_t = \alpha_o + \alpha_1 PI_t + \sum_{u=1}^{S} \beta_u PI_{t-u} + \sum_{v=1}^{S'} \gamma_v PI_{t+v} + \varepsilon_t \quad [9]$$

S_t represents (natural log of) sales in week t, whereas PI_t represents (natural log) of price index (the ratio of current to regular price) in week t. The β's represent lagged effects of promotion, and should be positive, corresponding to post-promotion dips (stockpiling). The γ's represent lead effects of promotion, and should also be positive, corresponding to pre-promotion dips (deceleration).

Van Heerde et al. investigated nine brands in two product categories – tuna fish and toilet tissue. They estimated their models by pooling data across stores (after appropriate tests). This resulted in 1456 observations for tuna and 1248 observations for tissue. Van Heerde et al. found evidence for both stockpiling and deceleration. They found that the dynamic sales effect (stockpiling plus deceleration) ranged from 3.6% to 25.1% of the average brand's current promotion effect. See Macé and Neslin (2001) for how these effects correlate with brand, category, store, and household characteristics.

In addition to Van Heerde et al., Doyle & Saunders (1985) found deceleration (which they attributed to salespeople telling their clients of an upcoming promotion). Mela et al. (1998) found that consumers decreased their baseline purchase incidence rates and purchased greater quantities as promotion levels increased over time. This is consistent with deceleration.

Consumption

Promotion could increase consumption through three inter-related mechanisms: more purchase occasions, fewer stock outs, and higher consumption rate. The purchase occasion mechanism is that consumers purchase the category more often over a finite period of time. Examples include services such as dining, airlines, and entertainment. The fewer stockout mechanism is appropriate for products that can be inventoried. It ensures that the product is on hand more often, and is therefore consumed more often. For example, a household may use one roll of paper towels per week, when paper towels are in the house. Promotions can ensure that paper towels are in the house more often by inducing consumers to stockpile paper towels.

The usage rate mechanism is that promotions encourage consumers to use a product at a faster rate. For example, if the household has one roll of paper towels in the house, it uses paper towels at a rate of one roll per week. However, if there are two rolls in the house, the household might use paper towels at a rate of one-and-a-half rolls per week. This mechanism is supported by both economic and behavioral theory. Assunacão & Meyer (1993) show that higher inventory levels provide the consumer with flexibility to consume at any desired rate, without having to worry about going back into the market and possibly paying a high replacement price. Folkes et al. (1993) provide evidence for 'scarcity theory.' The view is that smaller quantities are perceived as more valuable and therefore consumed more slowly (see also Wansink, 1996). Wansink & Deshpandé (1994) provide evidence that higher inventory levels create higher in-home awareness of the product, and therefore it is consumed more often.

All three mechanisms are related to each other and to consumer stockpiling. Stockpiling leads to higher inventories, which increase consumption either through fewer stockouts or higher usage rates. Purchase acceleration can also increase consumption. Consider the case of automobiles. A household may normally purchase a car every four years. A promotion may induce the household to buy a car now, even though it's only been three years since the last purchase. The question of whether this one-year acceleration results in higher consumption depends on the time until the next purchase. Here are the possibilities:

Year:	1	2	3	4	5	6	7	8	9	10
I. Purchase	x				x				x	
II. Purchase	x			x					x	
III. Purchase	x			x				x		
IV. Purchase	x			x			x			x

Case I is normal purchasing – the consumer buys a car every four years. In Case II, the promotion causes the consumer to buy a year earlier, but the consumer then waits five years to purchase again, getting back on the regular schedule. There is no increased consumption. In Case III, however, the consumer waits his or her normal time, four years, before buying again. This means that consumption has been increased, because over an eight-year time horizon, there are three purchases rather than two. In Case IV, the consumer adopts the new interpurchase time, three years, and thus clearly increases consumption of automobiles. Over ten years, there are four purchases instead of three in Case I.

The interplay between stockpiling and consumption makes it very difficult to disentangle the two. Dillon & Gupta (1996), in their study of 'category volume' versus brand choice, note that they are unable to tell whether their category volume elasticities may be due to either stockpiling or higher consumption. It is for this reason that Neslin & Schneider Stone (1996) run simulations for an extended time to measure the degree to which higher purchase incidence results in stockpiling versus increased consumption.

One of the few studies aimed directly at measuring the impact of promotion on consumption is by Ailawadi & Neslin (1998). The authors attempt to investigate the usage rate mechanism. Similar to other researchers, they calculate current consumer inventory as previous inventory, plus new purchases, minus consumption. However, previous researchers assumed the consumption rate was constant. Ailawadi and Neslin allowed consumption rate to be a function of inventory, reflecting the usage rate mechanism.

Ailawadi & Neslin (1998) find that yogurt consumption changes flexibly as a function of inventory, whereas ketchup consumption is less flexible. The authors conduct simulations that reveal for the yogurt category, 35% of the total effect of a promotion on brand sales represents increased consumption. The corresponding figure for ketchup was 12%. Silva-Risso et al. (1999) estimate Ailawadi & Neslin's model for spaghetti sauce and find consumption is not very flexible, similar to ketchup. Bell et al. (1999) provide additional evidence for the usage rate mechanism in the bacon, potato chips, soft drinks, and yogurt categories.

While the above research shows encouraging evidence for the faster usage rate mechanism, there is much more work needed to generalize these results, as well as investigate the stockpiling and increased purchase incidence mechanisms. See Nijs et al. (2001) for important recent evidence of the impact of promotion on consumption.

Store Effects

Cross-Category

Cross-category effects can either be complementary or substitution. A collection of empirical studies has shown that promotions increase sales of items in complementary categories (Manchanda et al., 1999;

Mulhern & Leone, 1991; Walters, 1991). All three studies conclude that cross-category effects are asymmetric. Typically there is a 'primary' category that increases sales in the 'secondary' category more strongly than the secondary category increases sales in the primary category. For example, cake mix is the primary category in all three studies, while frosting is the secondary category. In other examples, detergent was primary while softener was secondary; spaghetti was primary and sauce was secondary. The pattern seems to be that the secondary product is the one that augments or enhances the other, primary, product. However, this conjecture needs to be generalized and understood better.

It is true that cake mix promotions enhance frosting sales, but what do they do to in-store bakery sales or sales of other desserts? The best evidence for these substitution effects is from Walters & MacKenzie (1988). Walters & MacKenzie studied total store sales divided into four components: sales of loss leaders, sales of products bought with a coupon, sales of in-store promoted products, and sales of non-promoted products. The authors found that loss leader and coupon sales had no effect on non-promoted products – either there were no complementary effects or complementary and substitution effects balanced out. However, they found that in-store promotion sales decreased non-promotion sales, so the balance of complementarity and substitution resulted in a net loss in regular non-promoted sales. Walters & MacKenzie is just one study and we obviously cannot generalize from it. But the results strongly point out the need to study substitution as well as complementarity.

Store Switching

For retailers, store switching plays out the game theoretic competition analyzed by Varian (1980). This is not profitable for the manufacturer, however, if the only effect of a retailer promotion were to transfer sales of its brand from Store B to Store A.

Kumar and Leone (1988) analyze both store switching and brand switching and find that both effects exist. They found that store switching was strongly related to geographic proximity. Kumar & Leone's results were reinforced by Walters (1991). Walters studied brand switching, store switching, and complementarity effects, and found them all to be statistically significant.

Bucklin & Lattin (1992) proposed two store-switching effects – 'direct' and 'indirect.' The direct effect is what we would more commonly think of as a store switch, namely the consumer shops at Store A rather than Store B as a result of the promotion. The indirect effect acknowledges that consumers shop at several stores and promotions don't change that. However, a promotion in Store A causes the consumer to buy the category in Store A rather than Store B. This is a pre-emption or acceleration effect. Bucklin & Lattin show theoretically that the indirect effect will be larger if there is a lot of cross-shopping and if the consumer highly prefers the brand being promoted. They find, in fact, that the direct effect of promotions on store switching is insignificant, but that the indirect effect is significant. They also show that the pattern of competition between stores is defined not only by proximity but also by the preferences of customers that cross-shop particular store pairs.

Walters & MacKenzie (1988) study the effect of 'loss-leader' promotions on store traffic, and find that promotions have only a limited impact. However, there may be some methodological issues with Walters & MacKenzie's study. It appears that stores in their sample ran loss-leader promotions virtually every week. In this situation, the loss-leader variable measured not so much the presence versus absence of a loss-leader promotion, but which category was the loss leader in that particular week. Their variable therefore represents which categories are better than others at generating store traffic, not whether loss leaders *per se* increase store traffic.

In summary, there is some evidence for store switching effects. These can either be based on an indirect switch (promotions cause the cross-shopper to purchase in Store A versus Store B) or a direct switch (an increase in store traffic).

Decomposing the Total Effect of Promotions

Gupta (1988) decomposed promotion effects into brand switching, acceleration, and quantity by showing that the total elasticity of sales with respect to promotion can be represented as the sum of brand choice, purchase incidence, and quantity elasticities. Based on these calculations, Gupta found that the decomposition was 84% due to brand choice (switching), 14% due to purchase incidence (acceleration), and 2% due to quantity increases. This 84/14/2 finding reinforced the notion that promotion is primarily a switching device. The finding was upheld by Chiang (1991), who suggests approximately 80% of promotion's effect is due to switching, although Bucklin et al. (1998) found that the split in the yogurt category is 58% switching versus 42% incidence and quantity.

Bell et al. (1999) generalize these results by studying 13 categories. They find that on average the decomposition is 75/11/14. The switching percentage ranges from 49% (butter) to 94% (margarine). The incidence percentage ranges from .7% (liquid detergent) to 42.3% (butter). The quantity percentage ranges from .4% (margarine) to 45% (coffee).

Bell et al. find that higher switching effects are associated with high storability, low share of budget, necessity goods, low perceived differentiation, low brand loyalty, low price, and low price variability.

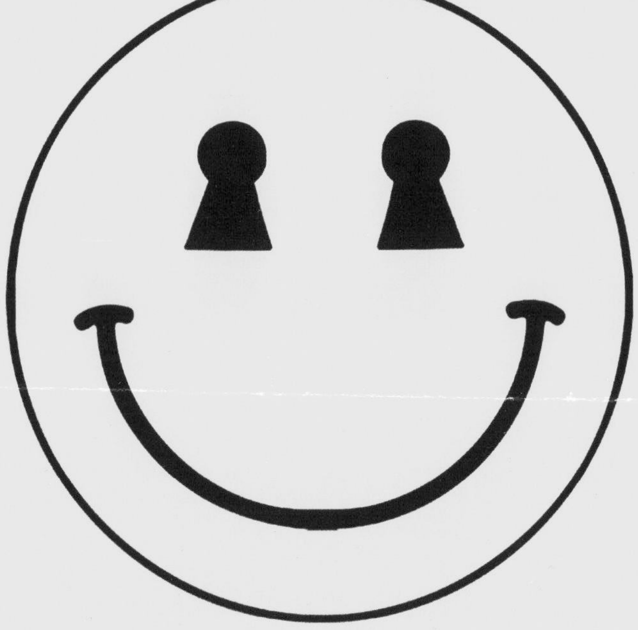

RAVER?

Stronger incidence effects are associated with high differentiation, low size assortment, low price variability, and high brand experience. Stronger quantity effects are associated with high brand and size assortment, high storability, high share of budget, high differentiation, low purchase frequency, low price variability, high deal depths, and high brand loyalty. This would suggest that for strong brands (with high loyalty), promotions induce loyal users to stock up.

Van Heerde (1999) decomposes the promotion effect into brand switching, stockpiling and deceleration, and 'category expansion' (store switching, increased consumption, and category switching). Depending on the type of promotion, he finds ample support for all three effects, but acknowledges that he cannot distinguish between store switching, consumption, and category switching. Dillon & Gupta (1996) model brand switching and category volume, but acknowledge they cannot disentangle stockpiling versus consumption impacts on category volume. Pauwels et al. (2002) use vector autoregression (VAR) and find an 11/89 breakdown for canned soup and a 39/61 breakdown for yogurt, where the first number is percent brand switching and the second number is percent category expansion.

There are significant methodological challenges in estimating the decomposition. One is that timing effects can become confounded with switching effects. For example, the effect of promotions on timing might bias logit models in favor of a strong switching effect (Sun et al., 2001). This is because the logit model can only attribute a strong correlation between promotions and brand purchases as a switching effect, so it does so.

Perhaps the best way to decompose the effects of promotion is through simulation of panel data (e.g., Ailawadi & Neslin, 1998; Silva-Risso et al., 1999). This is especially true to dissociate stockpiling and consumption effects. The reason is that, as pointed out earlier, a positive promotion coefficient in an incidence or quantity equation is ambiguous – it could signify stockpiling, or increased inventories, leading to higher consumption through either fewer stockouts or higher usage rates.

PROMOTION TYPES

Figure 13.3 depicts the three major forms of promotion: trade deals, retailer promotions, and consumer promotions. Consumer promotions are promotions targeted by manufacturers directly at consumers. Retailer promotions are promotions targeted by retailers directly to consumers. Trade deals are promotions targeted by manufacturers directly to retailers. Often the motivation for a trade deal is to induce retailers to undertake retailer promotions.

Trade Deals

Scope and Importance

Trade promotions currently command 50–60% of the marketing budget for many packaged goods firms (Cannondale Associates, 1999; Cox Direct, 1998), more than either consumer promotions or advertising. In a recent survey, 93% of executives at packaged goods companies indicated that trade deal inefficiency was either a very or extremely important concern to them (Cannondale Associates, 1999).

Although there are many types of trade deals (e.g., Blattberg & Neslin, 1990), three basic forms have emerged: off-invoice, discretionary funds, and bill-backs (Cannondale Associates). With off-invoice, the manufacturer offers a certain dollar discount for each case it sells to the retailer during a specified period of time. Discretionary funds often involve lump sum payments made by the manufacturer to the retailer in return for the retailer promoting the brand to consumers. Discretionary funds can be accrued based on previous retailer performance. Bill-backs are similar to off-invoice in that a discount is offered on a per-case basis. However, the difference is that the discount is per case the retailer *sells* during the trade promotion period, not per case the retailer *buys* during the trade promotion period. The amount the retailer needs to 'bill-back' the manufacturer may be based on internal retailer records, or on scanner data tabulated by a third party.

Passthrough

Passthrough is the degree to which trade deal dollars translate into retailer promotional efforts. One measure of passthrough, relevant for off-invoice and bill-back trade deals, is the percentage of the discount that is passed on to the consumer in the form of a price reduction. Published numbers on passthrough range from 0% to 200% (Tyagi, 1999; Walters, 1989). Passthrough is often less than 100% – often it is literally 0%, meaning the retailer accepts a discount from the manufacturer but does not change its retail price at all.

There have been a few empirical studies on the determinants of retailer passthrough. Curhan & Kopp (1986) measured passthrough for 570 trade deals in five retail chains. Walters (1988) studied 202 trade deals in two chains. We summarize their findings as follows:

- *Economics of the deal*: This involves the trade deal discount and regular item profitability. The economics of the deal emerge as a very important determinant of passthrough in both studies.
- *Promotion elasticity*: Both studies find higher passthrough for items that command stronger promotion response from consumers.
- *Brand sales level*: Walters finds no support for the notion that larger brands obtain more

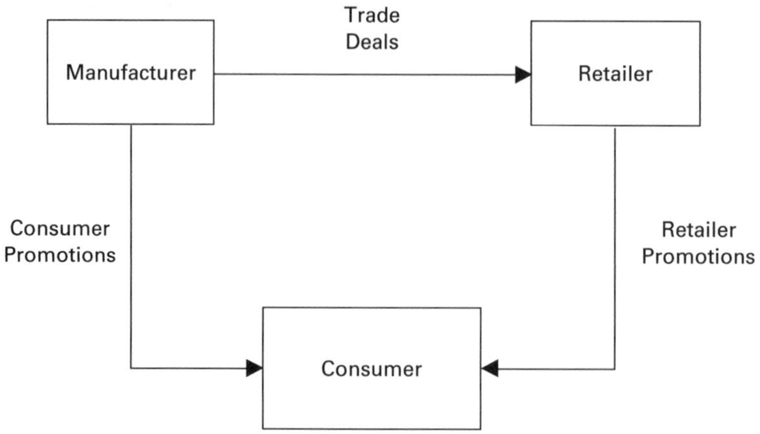

Figure 13.3 *Types of Promotion*

passthrough. Curhan & Kopp find mixed to no support.

- *Category volume*: Both studies find evidence that items in larger, more important categories to the retailer are likely to gain more passthrough.
- *Manufacturer accommodation*: This issue involves the manufacturer's willingness to accommodate special retailer needs. This factor achieves fairly strong support from both Curhan & Kopp and Walters.
- *Promotion wearout*: This is the notion that recently promoted items are less likely to receive passthrough. Walters finds this to be a very important factor, but Curhan & Kopp find it not to be significant.
- *Manufacturer merchandizing support*: This is the degree to which manufacturers undertake additional efforts to create demand for the product, via activities such as coupon drops, advertising, etc. Both studies found absolutely no support for this factor, contrary to commonly held industry beliefs.

Amplifying the above discussion, Murry & Heide (1998) conducted a conjoint analysis study of incentive, pay-for-performance requirements, monitoring efforts, and personal attachments, as factors influencing passthrough. Consistent with the above research, they found that incentives and pay-for-performance were the most important factors governing passthrough. Kumar et al. (2001) examine the role of consumer knowledge in determining passthrough.

Tyagi (1999) found the degree of passthrough depends on the following function:

$$\varphi = \frac{q(p^*)q''\,q(p^*)}{q'(p^*)} \qquad [10]$$

where, q is the demand function at the retail level, p* is the optimal retail price, and the primes stand for first or second derivatives of the demand function. Tyagi finds that passthrough increases as φ gets larger. In fact, if φ is greater than 1, we will have more than 100% passthrough; if φ is less than 1, we will have less than 100% passthrough. Equation [10] shows why passthrough may not be affected by brand sales level or market share. Large brands certainly will have a higher $q(p^*)$, however, to balance this, q' might be large, while q'' might be relatively small, resulting in a small value of φ.

In recent working papers, Moorthy (2001) and Besanko et al. (2001) deepen this line of work by considering the impact of passthrough for Brand A on the retail price of Brand B.

Kim & Staelin (1999) consider retailer competition and category profit, not just brand profit as in Tyagi. They show that passthrough should be a negative function of the degree of brand switching, because all else being equal, promotions that just cause consumers to switch brands are not attractive to retailers. Passthrough should be positively related to the degree of store switching, because promotions then represent incremental sales to the retailer.[8] Passthrough is negatively related to the extent to which promotions increase primary demand. This is because manufacturer allowances increase, allowing retailers to provide a good deal to consumers even though they pass through less.

Forward Buying

Forward buying is associated with off-invoice trade deals. The retailer purchases product during the promotion period to satisfy demand in future periods. The retailer trades off the price-per-case discount versus the cost of carrying extra cases of inventory in determining whether and how much to forward buy. Blattberg & Neslin (1990: 459–61) show how these considerations can be quantified to determine the optimal forward buy. Both Abraham & Lodish (1987) and Blattberg and Levin (1987) find evidence of forward buying.[9]

Discretionary fund and bill-back trade promotions eliminate the motivation to forward buy. The lump-sum payment does not compensate the retailer on a per case basis. The bill-back approach rewards retailers on a case-by-case basis, but only for product sold, not bought, during the promotion period. It is for this reason that manufacturers have put increased emphasis on discretionary and bill-back trade deals, rather than off-invoice promotions (Cannondale Associates, 1999). Perhaps the impetus for this movement was provided by Procter and Gamble's value pricing strategy, which attempted to eliminate off-invoice trade deals.

Neslin et al. (1995) show that forward buying decreases manufacturer profits because product is sold at discount to satisfy future demand, when retailers would otherwise have paid full price. However, Lal et al. (1996) argue that forward buying cushions price competition among manufacturers. Their arguments are indirectly consistent with the growth of manufacturer profits during the years most associated with the growth of off-invoice trade deals (Ailawadi et al., 1995).

Incremental Sales and Profits

Abraham & Lodish (1987) and Blattberg & Levin (1987) find that trade deals generate incremental sales, but are often unprofitable when evaluated on a per-event basis (see Blattberg & Neslin, 1993 for how to calculate profits for a trade deal). These calculations are for off-invoice trade deals. Research needs to be undertaken for discretionary fund and bill-back trade deals.

Incremental sales are typically calculated by subtracting baseline sales (the sales level that would occur without the promotion) from actual sales. However, forward buying makes it difficult to estimate baseline sales. Abraham & Lodish (1987) argue that most retailers do not buy on a 100% deal-to-deal basis, and they can infer the baseline by examining periods not affected by promotions. Blattberg & Levin (1987) argue that this is very difficult to do, especially when one is also aggregating across retailers or across stores. Blattberg & Levin (1987) believe that the best way to measure incremental sales is by considering both manufacturer shipments (what the manufacturer sells to the retailer) and retail sales (what the retailer sells to the consumer).

Kruger (1987) finds the Abraham & Lodish approach based on shipments data to be attractive because it is implementable and generates results of 'managerial accuracy given tolerable resource commitments.' He does, however, believe that deal-to-deal buying can produce inaccuracies using shipments data, so recommends the use of retail sales data to infer accurate baselines.

Normative Models

Neslin et al. (1995) devise an optimization model for the manufacturer to determine a joint trade deal/advertising calendar. Their conclusions include: (1) forward buying decreases optimal promotion expenditures and the depth of trade discounts; (2) promotion wearout at the retail level decreases manufacturer profits and causes manufacturers to promote less often; and (3) consumer stockpiling decreases manufacturer profits and decreases trade promotion expenditures. One implication of the forward-buy result is that trade deal discounts should be steeper for bill-back trade promotions, since these eliminate forward buying. The wearout effect warns manufacturers not to promote more frequently in response to poor passthrough. Note that only off-invoice trade deals induce forward buying, while all trade deals can induce consumer stockpiling, because the cause of the stockpiling is the passed-through retailer promotion.

Silva-Risso et al. (1999) combine a mathematical program for optimizing trade deals and a model to estimate the consumer demand function. They use household panel data for the demand function, which provides precise estimates of repeat purchase and acceleration effects. They find that acceleration is important – not including it results in a trade dealing policy that generates about 25% less profits than optimal. In their application, the authors find that the manufacturer is promoting too steeply, and recommend more promotions with lower depth.

Turning now to equilibrium models, Zenor (1994) shows that industry profits increase if manufacturers adopt a category-management perspective, because price competition is lessened. In addition, Zenor shows that the benefits of manufacturer category management are higher when (1) the manufacturers' own brands are more readily substitutable for each other, (2) the manufacturers' market share is higher, and (3) the retailer is also a category manager. Zenor's paper concerns pricing rather than trade dealing, but the results seem applicable to trade promotions. Lal & Villas-Boas (1998) show that the extent of trade dealing depends, importantly, on the extent of brand loyalty and store loyalty.

Kim & Staelin (1999) find that brand switching, store switching, and primary demand effects all result in higher trade deal allowances. However, while brand switching and store switching decrease profits, primary demand increases profits. Kim & Staelin also provide an interesting explanation for the concurrent growth in both trade dealing and decrease in retailer profits (Ailawadi et al., 1995). The key is store switching. As stores lose loyalty and there is more store switching, retailers are more likely to pass through trade deals, and this encourages more trade dealing (Neslin et al., 1995; Silva-Risso et al., 1999). However, retailer profits are generally lower because there is less store loyalty.

Two recent papers portray trade deals as a mechanism for increasing channel efficiency. Drèze and Bell (2000) show how scan-back deals can save inventory costs. Ailawada, Farris, and Shames (1994) argue that quantity discounts can improve efficiency.

Retailer Promotions

Effectiveness

There are three major types of retailer promotions: in-store price cuts, feature advertising, and in-store displays. Price cuts are also called 'temporary price reductions' or TPRs. They typically last 1–5 weeks. Feature advertising emphasizes the store's price for selected items and is often distributed through newspaper inserts. Displays include end-of-aisle, in-aisle, and other special efforts to make the product more prominent in the store.

Information Resources, Inc. (P-O-P Times, 1991) calculated 'lift' for the average brand in 164 categories:

Promotion Type	Mean Percent Increase in Sales
15% TPR	35%
Feature + 15% TPR	173%
Display + 15% TPR	279%
Feature + Display + 15% TPR	545%

Features and displays add significantly to the effectiveness of a 15% price reduction. One possibility is that they encourage the consumer to process the deal in depth to decide whether it is a good one. Another is that consumers use features and displays as convenient mechanisms for deciding what product to buy. This is consistent with the strong sales increases brought about by features and displays even if there is no accompanying price discount (Inman et al., 1990; Wittink et al., 1987). Note, however, that Anderson and Simester (1998, 2001) caution that overuse of sales signs can erode their credibility and effectiveness. In addition, the particular way in which the price discount is communicated can influence response (Krishna et al., 2000).

Also of interest is the consistent superiority of displays over feature advertising. The reasons for this are potentially twofold. First, more shoppers notice displays than read feature advertising. Second, displays may be more conducive to consumer stockpiling. (The statistics in the table above are not net of stockpiling.)

The different forms of retailer promotion may interact, i.e., the effect when two or more types are combined is not equal to the sum of the separate effects of these promotions. Wittink et al. (1987) find both positive and negative interactions between features and displays. The results above from the IRI study suggest that features and displays (when accompanying a 15% price reduction) interact positively on average. The nature and reasons for these interactions are not known in general. See Lemon and Nowlis (2002) for recent insights.

Researchers have investigated why retailer promotion elasticities vary across brands, categories, and stores. Bolton (1989) found that elasticity first decreases and then increases as a function of market share. Interestingly, category promotion activity had a stronger effect on elasticities than brand promotion activity, suggesting that consumers learn habits from category promotion activity that carry over to their purchasing of all brands. Bolton found that category display activity dampens price elasticities, while feature activity tends to accentuate it. In addition, Bolton found that manufacturer advertising and relative price level had no effects on promotional price elasticities.

Narasimhan et al. (1996) found that elasticities were generally larger in categories with high penetration, short interpurchase times, and small numbers of brands, that were easily stockpiled. The number of brands result is interesting. Narasimhan et al.'s logic was that categories with large numbers of brands suggest that there are many niches in the market, and hence less brand switching and lower elasticities. Equally interesting were that private label market share and impulse buying were not related to elasticities. For example, the authors found that other variables such as penetration, interpurchase time, and the number of brands in the category, predicted elasticities rather well irrespective of the level of impulse buying.

Hoch et al. (1995) found that demographics and competitive activity played important roles in determining price elasticities. Higher education and housing values tended to depress elasticities. High concentrations of ethnic groups, higher family size, and the presence in the family of a working woman tended to increase elasticities. Income and age had mixed results. The researchers found that the presence of a large volume warehouse operation near the store increased the store's price elasticity, but supermarket competitors had no relationship with elasticity. These results imply that pricing should be store-specific. Indeed, Montgomery (1997) shows that profits can be increased significantly by adjusting prices for individual stores. His results emphasize everyday regular prices rather than promotions, but it is apparent that promotion policies should vary for individual stores as well.

Strategic Issues

Everyday Low Pricing (EDLP): Everyday low pricing is a strategy emphasizing prices that stay constant over time. EDLP is the antithesis of promotional pricing, often referred to as HI/LO. EDLP can take place at either the retail (also called 'front-door' EDLP (Hoch et al., 1994)), or wholesale (also called 'back-door' EDLP) levels. Retail EDLP in its pure form arguably does not exist. An IRI study cited by Hoch et al. (Information Resources, Inc., 1993) concluded that self-proclaimed EDLP stores have lower everyday prices, price promote less steeply, but sell equal amounts on promotion, compared to HI/LO stores. Thus EDLP in practice is consistent with the notion of relatively constant low prices, but EDLP stores do not appear to eliminate price promotions.

Lattin & Ortmeyer (1991) showed theoretically that EDLP and HI/LO retailing can co-exist by segmenting the consumer market. The EDLP store appeals to 'expected price shoppers' who are time-constrained and thus interested in obtaining a low price on average, while realizing that they may not get the lowest available price in any given week. The HI/LO store appeals to 'cherry-pickers' who are willing to search out the lowest prices in each week. Coupled with this market segmentation are important differences in costs for the two stores. EDLP benefits from lower fixed costs associated with advertising and price management. HI/LO benefits from manufacturer trade deals by selling more low-priced cases, thus reducing its overall product cost. Surprisingly, the EDLP store is found to invest less in store service and more in forward buying.

Lal & Rao (1997) reach several similar conclusions as Lattin and Ortmeyer. Lal and Rao find, for example, that EDLP and HI/LO are segmentation strategies, and that HI/LO invests more in store service. However, Lal & Rao find the co-existence equilibrium exists even when costs are identical, and emphasize the need for effective communication of the expected price benefits of EDLP. Contrary to Lattin & Ortmeyer, Lal & Rao find that after taking into account the additional service provided by the HI/LO store, HI/LO winds up serving proportionately more time-constrained shoppers, and EDLP serves more cherry-pickers. Reconciling Lattin & Ortmeyer and Lal & Rao, they both agree that EDLP and HI/LO can co-exist, that they serve different market segments, and that HI/LO puts more emphasis on service. However, they disagree on the role of costs and exactly what segment is served by each format.

Hoch et al. (1994) conducted a field experiment where they compared EDLP to HI/LO pricing for specific categories. EDLP categories were assigned lower everyday prices, lower percentage price reductions, but equal promotion frequency to HI/LO categories. They found that EDLP did not increase sales enough to justify the loss in margin from lowering everyday prices. Hoch et al.'s results show that EDLP, on a category level, does not have instant drawing power for consumers. However, as the researchers note, the pricing policy was not advertised. These results suggest that if EDLP is to succeed as a retail strategy, it needs to be adopted on a store-wide basis and communicated effectively (cf. Lal & Rao). In short, it is better to think of EDLP as a segmentation and positioning strategy rather than as a pricing strategy.

Procter and Gamble's value pricing strategy (Shapiro, 1992) provides a 'natural experiment' for examining the potential for EDLP. P&G's strategy was to adopt wholesale EDLP by lowering its everyday wholesale prices but eliminating off-invoice trade promotions. P&G reportedly hoped that retailers would in turn adopt EDLP pricing at the retail level. Ailawadi, Lehmann & Neslin (2001) charted the changes that occurred at retail, and the consumer and competitive reactions to this response. They found that there was a significant reduction in the amount of retail promotion of P&G brands, but that net price to the consumer increased, and, coupled with the reduction in promotion, this resulted in lower market share for P&G brands.

Private Labels: Private labels, or store brands, are an important component of retailer strategy. Raju et al. (1995) found that it makes sense for the retailer to introduce store brands when cross-price elasticities between national brands are low, and cross-price elasticities between national brands and private labels are high. The low cross-price elasticities between the national brands make the category attractive because there isn't as much price competition. The high elasticity between the private label and the national brands means that the store brand can capture market share if it is introduced.

In a cross-category empirical analysis, Hoch & Banerji (1993) found that promotion intensity was not associated with the market share of private labels, whereas advertising was associated with lower private label share. This would suggest that national brand promotions do not reduce the shares of private labels. However, there could be two forces at work. First is that national brand promotions might decrease market share of private labels, but that manufacturers use promotions to combat private labels with high market shares. This would result in a net mixed relationship between promotion and private label shares.

Dhar & Hoch (1997) studied the variation in private label market share across retail chains. Their overall finding is that national brand promotion indeed decreases private label market share. Also noteworthy is that private label promotions can increase market share of the private labels as well.

Ailawadi, Neslin & Gedenk (2001) show that national brand deal proneness and store brand purchasing are fundamentally different consumer behaviors, driven by different consumer psychographics. Store brand purchasers are highly price conscious, less quality conscious, and not stockpilers. Deal buyers enjoy shopping, are planners and stockpilers, but are also willing to buy on impulse. The authors show that this yields two segments – deal purchasers and store brand purchasers. There is also a segment that will buy both store brands and purchase on deal. These results show why national brand promotions can reduce private label share, but will not be completely effective. There is a store brand prone segment that simply is not interested in national brand promotions.

Competitive Effects: A relatively recent but important literature investigated competitive reactions. The questions include: how do competitors react to promotions initiated by a given firm? How does retail competition differ from manufacturer competition? What determines competitive interactions? We have just begun to scratch the surface on these issues.

Leeflang & Wittink (1996) examined how firms should react to a promotion in order to preserve market shares. Their theory suggested that firm j's response to firm i's actions was positively related to cross-brand market share elasticity (if firm j is hurt more, it should respond more), and inversely related to firm *j*'s own elasticity (firm *j* does not have to respond as strongly if its own promotions are highly effective). They find empirical support for these hypotheses. Leeflang & Wittink also identified situations of apparent over- and under-reaction. For example, if the cross market share and own market share elasicities are non-zero, yet the firm does not react, that is under-reaction. Leeflang & Wittink uncovered more instances of over-reaction than under-reaction, and attributed this to firm-specific compensation and performance incentives.

A key assumption in Leeflang & Wittink's analysis is that firms react to preserve a given market share equilibrium. However, it is not clear that this would be the profit-maximizing reaction. The 'New Empirical Industrial Organization' (NEIO) paradigm analyzes competition from a profit-maximizing perspective (Breshnahan, 1989; Cotterill et al., 2000; Gasmi et al., 1992; Kadiyali et al., 2000; Vilcassim et al., 1999). The basic approach of these models is to derive a game-theoretic solution to a competitive market, and then use the equilibrium conditions implied by this solution as equations to be estimated empirically. The estimates to these equations provide insight on competitive behavior.

An interesting quantity often incorporated in these models is the 'conduct parameter,' or 'conjectural variation.' It measures how firm *j* will change its price in response to a change by firm *h*. Firm *h* is assumed to know firm *j*'s conduct parameter, and *vice versa*, and the conduct parameters figure directly into the equilibrium solution. Vilcassim et al. (1999) find that the conduct parameters for two firms were both positive, meaning that if firm 1 raises its price, so will firm 2, even though there are significant price cross-elasticities between the firms. The authors interpret this as cooperative behavior (see also Kadiyali et al., 2000).

The NEIO approach is very promising for providing a description of competitive interaction. There are a few technical concerns with the method; for example, the results may depend on the functional form of the demand function, and there are many simplifying assumptions needed to identify the estimation. In addition, Leeflang & Wittink (1996) showed that reactions should be an explicit function of demand parameters. However, in the conjectural variations approach, the conduct parameters exist as separate entities. This begs the question of why the conduct parameters are a certain value. Perhaps they are accounting for firm-specific factors such as compensation, company capabilities, or strategic interactions between the two firms beyond the market being studied.

This issue was investigated by Ailawadi, Lehmann & Neslin (2001) as part of their study of market response to Procter and Gamble's value pricing strategy. The researchers estimated manufacturer reaction functions similar to Leeflang & Wittink. They found these functions depended on own and cross-elasticities (as in Leeflang & Wittink) but also on market share position, potential for multi-market interaction, as well as unobservable firm-specific factors (such as compensation or capabilities). It would be very beneficial to integrate the rigor of the NEIO studies with the breadth of this study.

Decision Models

Tellis & Zufryden (1995) embed a scanner panel data demand model within a retailer profit optimization that includes ordering, inventory, and product costs. For a given set of trade promotions, the model prescribes a schedule of retailer promotions to optimize category profits. Tellis & Zufryden find that retailers should promote less steeply if consumers are brand loyal and their decision to purchase the category is highly influenced by their inventories. The reason for the inventory result is that if consumers are highly influenced by their inventories, promotion is not needed to induce them to buy the category. Tellis & Zufryden find it is best for the retailer to avoid promoting brands at the same time. The reason is that for any promotion, the retailer trades off the gains from consumers who switch to the promoted brand versus the losses from consumers (the loyals) who would have bought the brand anyway. When two brands are promoted at once, the retailer doubles the loyalty losses (since loyals can just stay with their brands) but incur no additional switching benefits (a similar argument is used by Lal, 1990).

Inman & McAlister (1993) develop a similar model to help the retailer decide whether to implement a pure feature promotion or a feature with a price cut. The decision depends on the relative sizes of the segments that respond to pure features (theoretically, low need-for-cognition consumers, Inman et al., 1989), versus features plus price cuts promotions (both the low and high NFCs). They field test their model and consistently recommend pure feature promotions. This is because the pure feature segment is sizeable and the retailer does not have to grant a price discount in order to capture this segment. The authors compare their model on a hold-out sample to the decisions made by real managers. They find that their model exceeds the profit performance of the real managers.

An entirely different approach to studying optimal promotion behavior is provided by Midgley et al. (1997). They use genetic algorithms to generate pricing and promotion decisions for a given set of competitive demand functions. They find that genetic algorithms promote more frequently and generate higher profits than actually occur in the marketplace. The authors conjecture that the ability of the genetic algorithm to promote more frequently yet produce higher profits may be due to institutional constraints facing real managers.

Some progress on incorporating cross-category effects in retail promotion planning is provided by Mulhern & Leone (1991), Dreze & Hoch (1998), and Chen et al. (1999). Mulhern & Leone show that these effects influence retailer passthrough and profits. Dreze & Hoch distinguish between categories for which consumers develop loyalties to a particular retailer, and those that do not. The authors show that a destination category program – essentially a frequency reward program for consumers who shop at a given store for a given category – increases sales in the destination category as well as other categories.

Chen et al. (1999) build on this idea formally by distinguishing between accounting and marketing profits. Accounting profits are the profits for a given product category. Marketing profits are the profits from the market segment that decides on its store choice based on the attractiveness of a certain category. Chen et al. argue that feature allocation decisions should be made on the basis of marketing profits, not accounting profits. The reason is that by targeting the categories that have the highest marketing profits, the retailer is creating significant cross-category externalities by attracting more customers to the store. The authors find that retailers in fact have learned to do this.

Practical promotion planning requires the retailer to be able to forecast sales if it runs a promotion. A retail chain may have to make tens of thousands of promotion decisions per year, and needs a robust and general method for forecasting promotion sales. Cooper et al. (1999) estimate a large regression model based on 20,000,000 promotion events and 150,000 UPCs. The dependent variable is the sales level achieved in a particular promotion. The authors use 67 independent variables, related to type of promotion event (feature, display, etc.), item promotion history, store promotion history, and seasonality. In one test, they are able to forecast promotion sales to within one case 69% of the time, and within two cases 83% of the time. Cooper & Giuffrida (2000) show how forecast accuracy can be improved by using rules-based data mining techniques.

Consumer Promotions

Coupons

Coupons are distributed directly to consumers by either the manufacturer or retailer. 'Vehicles' for distributing coupons include: free-standing inserts (color newspaper inserts), in or on package, magazines, newspapers, and direct mail. Recent vehicles gaining in popularity include in-store shelf distributed, in-store checkout distributed, and Internet distributed. In the packaged goods arena, however, the most common vehicle is free-standing inserts (FSIs), accounting for 81% of coupons in 1999 (NCH, 2000).

Coupon distribution rose rapidly in the US during the 1970s and 1980s, from around 35 billion in 1975 to a peak of 310 billion coupons in 1992. Since then, distribution has declined to 256 billion in 1999. Face value has increased over time and now averages 65.5 cents for grocery products and 89.4 cents for health and beauty aids (NCH, 2000). The reasons for these trends have not been thoroughly researched, but one view is that while coupons are effective at gaining market share, they were overused and were not paying out. Bucklin and Gupta (1999) report that industry use of logit models documented instances where couponing was ineffective and therefore played a role in decreasing coupon usage.

Redemption Rates: The factors that have been found to influence redemption rates are coupon vehicle, brand market share, face value, expiration date, and size of the coupon drop (Blattberg & Neslin, 1990; Inman & McAlister, 1994; NCH, 1999; Neslin & Clarke, 1987; Reibstein & Traver, 1982). Redemption rates are highest for in and on-package coupons (7–9%), moderate for direct mail (4%), low for FSIs (1.5%), and lowest for magazine and newspaper coupons (less than 1%) (NCH, 1999). Redemption rates increase as a function of market share and face value, and decrease as a function of expiration date (how long the coupon is valid) and size of the coupon drop. The reason why redemption rates decrease as a function of the size of the coupon drop is not readily apparent. It may be that the deal prone segment simply is of limited size, so larger coupon drops become wasteful. Redemption rates can be expected to decline for shorter expiration dates. However, Inman & McAlister (1994) demonstrate a regret effect, resulting in a spike in coupon redemptions around the time of the redemption date.

Redemption rates have been steadily declining. The average redemption rate for grocery product FSIs was 4.2% in 1985, 2.4% in 1992, and 1.5% in 1998. The question is why redemption rates have declined. There is no sign that retailer promotions or other forms of promotion are less effective, so why the problem with couponing? There are several possible reasons. First, coupons require effort and consumers, while still deal-prone, no longer want to make the effort. Second, redemption declines as distribution increases, and distribution levels have become too high. Third, use of coupons may have shifted from high market share to low market share brands. Fourth, manufacturers have recently shifted toward shorter expiration dates.

Regression models provide reasonable although not perfect predictions of redemption rates for a given brand as a function of market share, face value, vehicle, etc. (Blattberg & Neslin, 1990; Neslin & Clarke, 1987; Reibstein & Traver, 1982). Bawa et al. (1997) recently proposed an item response model for predicting redemption intentions at the household level. The model considers the attractiveness of the coupon, the deal-proneness of the household, and the ability of the coupon to separate deal prone from non-deal prone consumers.

Incremental Sales: Initial evidence on coupon-generated incremental sales was provided by field experiments conducted by Information Resources, Inc. (Irons et al., 1983), and by Neslin & Clarke (1987), Bawa & Shoemaker (1987b), and Shoemaker & Tibrewala (1985). These studies showed that loyal users of a brand were disproportionately likely to redeem that brand's coupons. This would hamper the ability of coupons to generate incremental sales.[10]

Neslin (1990) formulated a simultaneous model with equations for market share and coupon redemptions. The market share equation translated redemptions into share, providing a direct measure of the degree to which coupons are redeemed by loyal users. The redemptions equation modeled the dynamics of redemption (high in the first week of availability, then declining exponentially). Neslin found that for the median brand, 44% of coupon redemptions represent short-term incremental sales. While this is a significant number, it is probably not high enough to make many coupon promotions profitable (Neslin, 1990). Further insight on incremental sales per coupon redemption is provided by field experiments conducted by Information Resources, Inc., as reported in Leclerc and Little (1997). They show that incremental sales decreases as a function of market share for the brand (since there are more loyal users who use the coupon without it influencing their choice), and increases as a function of face value (since deeper price cuts are required to induce consumers to switch brands).

Household-level choice models that include couponing are hampered because we only know if a particular household has redeemed a coupon, not what coupons were available. Erdem et al. (1999) argue that since the coupon redemption lowers the price for the purchased brand, and the brand was purchased, there is a simultaneity bias in modeling either coupon effects or price effects that include prices net of coupon redemptions. They devise a method for addressing this bias and demonstrate that it results in lower estimated price elasticities.

Gonul & Srinivasan (1996) formulated a model whereby consumers choose products in a couponing environment according to a stochastic dynamic program. The need for a dynamic program arises because coupons arrive at a known but probabalistic distribution over time. Methodologically this was pioneering work, because it showed how to formulate and estimate a dynamically rational consumer choice model. Substantively, it showed that consumers – at least a segment of consumers – follow such a model, form expectations of upcoming coupon availability, and trade off current versus future costs of purchasing.

Dhar & Hoch (1996) found in a field experiment that a shelf-distributed coupon was more profitable than an in-store price cut of the same amount. Partially this was because not every person who purchased the couponed product used the coupon, as opposed to the TPR. What was very surprising, however, was that incremental sales generated by the coupon often exceeded that of the TPR. One reason could be that coupons communicate a much more convincing reference price for the brand. The consumer sees that the price is say $2.50 for the brand without the coupon, and this is unarguably true. The TPR communicates that the regular price is $2.50, but this is not as believable (Blair & Landon, 1981).

Coupon Design: FSIs typically include an advertisement along with the coupon. The question is whether the advertisement has any value. Leclerc & Little (1997) found that incremental sales are higher for high involvement categories when information-oriented advertising is part of the coupon. They also found that FSI coupons were more effective for attracting brand switchers when they included informational advertising, and more effective for attracting consumers loyal to competitive brands when they included image-oriented advertising.

Another issue receiving attention is expiration dates. Manufacturers have shortened expiration dates ('fuse lengths') from an average of 4.9 months in 1990 to 3.1 months in 1998 (NCH, 1993, 1999). NCH (1998) argues that this has decreased redemption rates because more coupons get lost or are not available when the consumer wants to buy the category. Also relevant is that Neslin (1990) found that earlier redeemed coupons were more likely to be associated with incremental sales, suggesting that those who delay redeeming are loyal users saving coupons for the brands they prefer. Krishna & Zhang (1999) show analytically that high share brands should offer shorter fuse dates to maximize profits. The reason is that high share brands have more loyal users, and the longer fuse dates give these loyal users time to save the coupon. The small share brand should have a longer fuse date to ensure it is available to the consumer when the consumer runs out of coupons for their preferred brand. Krishna & Zhang show empirically that higher market share is associated with shorter expiration dates.

Raju et al. (1994) show why on-pack coupons can generate more sales than either instantly redeemable or in-pack coupons. The reason is that on packs are effective at attracting brand switchers and retaining loyals. Instantly redeemable coupons focus on brand switchers, and in-packs focus on retaining loyals. The authors verified their hypotheses in a series of field experiments. Zhang et al. (2000) compared the profitability of 'front-loaded' versus 'rear-loaded' incentives, which in this context would correspond to regular FSI coupons versus in-pack coupons. They show that rear-loaded incentives are more profitable in environments where consumers seek variety – in-packs counteract this tendency by retaining consumers. Front-loaded incentives such as regular FSIs are more effective, however, in environments where consumers are inertially loyal to the last brand purchased.

A final design issue is the use of cross-ruff coupons – coupons distributed in the package of Brand A (the carrier) that are good for Brand B (the target). Dhar and Raju (1998) show that cross-ruff coupons are most effective when the carrier and target brands have unequal market shares. If the target brand has a low share, it is good to use a high share carrier brand to effectively increase coupon distribution for the low share brand. If the target brand has a high share, the cross-ruff serves mostly to make the carrier brand more attractive, a benefit that is greatest for a low share brand. The researchers also show that when categories are complementary, it is better to use the high share brand as the carrier, whereas if the categories are substitutes, it is better to use the low share brand as the carrier.

Rebates

Rebates have become ubiquitous for products such as software, automobiles, and durables. However, there is very little research on rebates. Thompson & Noordeweir (1992) provide the best demonstration that automobile rebates can be effective, if they are not overused. They analyze three successive years of major rebate programs offered by US automobile manufacturers. In the first year, the rebate programs generated many incremental sales. In the second year, the rebates generated some incremental sales, but consumers also began to accelerate their automobile purchases – there were significant post-promotion 'dips' after the rebate expired. In the third year, the rebates generated still fewer incremental sales, and most of these were wiped out by consumer acceleration. The study provides a significant example of the dangers of overusing promotions in a predictable way. The decreasing effectiveness of the rebates could have been due to exhausting the deal-prone segment, the rebates losing their transaction utility appeal, competitive response, or retailer behavior.

Perhaps the most fascinating aspect of rebates, 'slippage,' has received virtually no research attention. Slippage is the phenomenon that the consumer purchases a product that has a rebate available, but does not turn in the rebate. Slippage rates have been reported to be as high as 90% for software products (*Wall Street Journal*, 1998). Slippage is potentially a source of profit for manufacturers if the presence of the rebate can attract customers, yet those customers do not bother to mail in the rebate. We need studies that compare incremental sales generated by rebates to the number of rebates turned in. This would show whether rebates generate purchases without being subsequently redeemed.

Tat, Cunningham, & Babakus (1988) offered some explanations as to why consumers use rebates. Using a survey, they identified three factors underlying rebate usage: 'Effort,' 'Faith,' and 'Motives.' Effort involved the effort required to use rebates. Faith involved beliefs that manufacturers are well-meaning and that the rebate offers can be trusted. Motives involved beliefs that rebates induce consumers to buy brands or products that they don't need. The greatest differences between users and non-users of rebates involved the efforts and motives dimensions. While these results are interesting, they only scratch the surface on the consumer decision-making process behind rebate usage.

Reward Programs

Reward programs differ from most promotions in that their intended use is for retaining, not attracting customers. Reward programs have been used in a wide variety of industries, including airlines, telecommunications, hotels, car rentals, retailing, and financial services. The theme of a reward program is that it provides the customer with a reward for repeat purchasing the brand. The reward can be free product, cash reward, special services, or even frequency reward 'points' on another reward program.

Kopalle, Neslin & Singh (1999) report several potential benefits of reward programs. These include: softening price competition (Beggs & Klemperer, 1992; Klemperer, 1987); increasing profits, because it is purportedly cheaper to retain a customer than to acquire one (Orr, 1995); and building a database for direct marketing (Butscher, 1997; Reynolds, 1995). However, others have cited the high costs of reward programs (Dowling & Uncles, 1997), whether in fact they actually increase loyalty (Dowling & Uncles, 1997; Sharp & Sharp, 1997), and the impact of competitive response (Dowling & Uncles, 1997).

The most common argument for reward programs is that they increase consumer switching costs or 'loyalty,' thereby imbuing firms with monopoly power they can use to increase profits (Beggs & Klemperer, 1992). Kopalle, Neslin & Singh (1999) assume the customer maximizes long term utility and that firms play a two-stage game, deciding first whether to use the reward program or traditional pricing, and second, what should be their actual prices. Consumers vary in their preferences for the brands and are uncertain about future preferences. For example, they know in the current period their preferences for various flights, but are not sure of their preferences for flights in subsequent periods. Therefore it is possible, even if they have built up frequent flier miles on airline A, that they may want to take airline B if the flight and price are attractive. This feature makes Kopalle et al.'s scenario more competitive than Beggs & Klemperer's.

Kopalle et al. find that reward programs are more desirable when consumers highly value future rewards. This is not surprising. They also find that reward programs are more desirable when they can expand the market. In fact, they result in ruinous price competition in zero-sum market share battles. A possible reason is that reward programs accentuate competition in both attracting and retaining customers. Competition to attract customers is fierce because then the firm can increase switching costs through rewards. Competition to retain customers is also fierce, because customers vary in their preferences and may switch to another firm even if they have points accumulated for one firm.

Kopalle et al. therefore view reward programs as an excellent way for firms within an industry to compete against an outside industry, i.e., one that will not respond with reward programs. They argue and provide some empirical evidence that frequent flyer programs were adopted by the major airlines in the early 1980s as a means to compete against the new, low cost airlines that were entering the airline business after deregulation. The reward program allowed the majors to grow their market *vis-à-vis* the new entrants.

Kim et al. (2001) investigate the relative merits of rewards paid in hard cash versus paid in free product. They find that hard cash, while costing more to the firm than free product, can be the best type of reward. This is contingent on there being a heavy user group that is price sensitive. In this case, the cash reward commits the firms to charging high prices, which are paid by light users, while heavy users earn the reward and pay lower prices. The result is a subsidization of heavy users by light users, or price discrimination.

Sharp & Sharp (1997) investigate empirically the effects of a loyalty program in Australia whereby shoppers at participating retailers earned points that could be redeemed for air travel. The researchers found that this program had very little, if any, effect on consumer loyalty to participating retailers. The problem was that because so many retailers participated in the program, consumers could earn rewards without changing their purchase habits. While this research is just a first step, it does put the onus on those who purport that reward programs increase loyalty. In fact, one has to be careful here to distinguish between attitudinal and behavioral loyalty. It seems that reward programs should increase behavioral loyalty because there will be more repeat purchasing of the brand. However, it is not at all clear that reward programs enhance the attitudinal component of brand loyalty. Roehm et al. (2002) provide evidence that the type of reward used in the program can either enhance or undermine brand attitudes.

Klemperer, Kopalle et al., and Kim et al. assume consumers rationally solve stochastic dynamic programs. The extent to which consumers do so needs to be investigated. Soman (1997) shows through laboratory experiments that customers under-estimate the effort required to earn a long-term reward. (See Kivetz and Simonson (2002) for insights on the relationship between effect and type of reward consumers prefer). This would make reward programs more effective.

Targeted Promotions

One aspect of promotions that make them less profitable is that consumers make use of the promotion even though it does not influence their choice. Database marketing offers a way out of this dilemma, by using a customer data file to target promotions to the consumers who are more likely to respond in the desired fashion. The basic idea is to develop a consumer 'response model' that predicts how individual consumers will respond to an 'offer,' and then target the promotion to the high responders (David Sheppard Associates, Inc., 1995; Roberts & Berger, 1999; see also Ansari & Mela, 2000, and Knott et al., 2002).

Rossi et al. (1996) estimate a choice model and then predict at the household level the difference in choice probability with and without a targeted incentive. This yields incremental choice probability at the household level. The authors use a probit model where heterogeneity in response parameters is modeled using a Bayesian approach. Rossi et al. examine a coupon whose face value can be customized to each household. They investigate the usefulness of using demographics versus prior choices to estimate household-specific response coefficients. Their results suggest that the customized coupon can increase profits over a blanket-mailed coupon, and that previous choice information is more valuable than demographics only, although the two combine synergistically.

Rossi et al.'s results suggest strong potential for database marketing and customized promotions. While at first blush this appears to be a sure way to increase firm profits, one must also consider the competitive effects. What happens if all firms pursue targeting? Shaffer & Zhang (1995) show that if firms can target promotions at brand switchers, the result is a prisoner's dilemma where the net impact is a decrease in firm profits. Chen et al. (2001), however, show that if firms cannot perfectly identify customers, this can mitigate the prisoner's dilemma and increase profits.

Advertising and Promotion

Data from the packaged goods industry (Cox Direct, 1998) indicate that promotion spending has come to dominate advertising spending, currently comprising 75% of the marketing budget (roughly 50% is trade promotion and 25% is consumer promotion). Statistics are not available for non-packaged goods companies, but there is certainly a belief that promotions are crowding out advertising programs.

Agrawal (1996) conducts a game-theoretic analysis to show that the allocation between advertising and promotion depends on brand loyalty, e.g., brands with large loyal segments require more advertising to maintain that segment. Neslin et al. (1995) find, not surprisingly, that money should be allocated toward advertising and promotion proportional to their effectiveness (consistent with Dorfman & Steiner, 1954). More interestingly, they find that advertising and trade promotion are natural substitutes, in that an increase in advertising expenditure drives down promotion expenditures, and *vice versa*. For example, an increase in advertising increases the brand's non-promoted baseline.

However, one of the costs of promotion is sacrificing margin on baseline sales. So increased advertising results in higher promotion costs and hence less promotion. Consider the case that promotion expenditures increase. Since the promotion decreases the profit margin (assuming an off invoice or bill-back trade deal), this devalues the marginal benefit of advertising and advertising should be cut.

Neslin et al. note that if advertising and promotion reinforce each other, this could negate the above arguments. Unfortunately, there is little direct evidence on synergies between advertising and promotion. Leclerc & Little (1997) found that FSI advertising copy can enhance the effectiveness of FSIs. Buchanan et al. (1999) found that retailer displays that mix high equity with other brands can erode equity, depending on which brand is given precedence and consumer familiarity with other brands. They extol the value of separate displays because then consumers rely on previous beliefs on brand equity. This points out a potential benefit of price promotional displays (although the research did not examine price promotions *per se*). Lodish et al. (1995), in their study of over 300 advertising field experiments, find that incremental sales generated by advertising tends to decrease for brands that are displayed heavily. This could be a saturation effect – there are just a limited number of potential new triers.

Boulding et al. (1994) and Mela et al. (1997) find that advertising decreases price sensitivity, although Mela et al. examined price and non-price promotion separately and found that advertising had no effect on price promotion sensitivity (similar to Bolton, 1989) and actually enhanced the impact of non-price promotions. Mela et al. also found that promotion decreased advertising sensitivity over time.

The overall findings therefore are mixed on advertising/promotion synergy. There is some evidence that advertising can enhance the effectiveness of coupons and displays, and some evidence that displays can enhance advertising-induced brand equity. However, promotion can decrease advertising sensitivity in the long run and the two can cannibalize each other in the short run.

Two recent papers compare the long-term effects of advertising versus promotion, and find different results. Jedidi et al. (1999) analyze household-level scanner data in one product category and find that promotion increases choice probabilities in the short term but decreases them in the long term, whereas advertising has a positive long-term effect. Promotion also increases promotion and price sensitivity in the long term, while advertising has no effect on price or promotion sensitivity. Perhaps the one surprising result is that increased promotion actually decreases subsequent sales levels. This happens in their model because promotion decreases the brand choice constants in subsequent periods. However, it is not clear whether the researchers combined this with positive purchase event feedback. As we saw earlier, a promotion purchase is not as reinforcing of future purchases as a regular purchase, but is better than no purchase at all. This is why Keane (1997) and Gedenk & Neslin (1999) find that promotion increases long-term sales.

Ailawadi, Lehmann & Neslin (2001) analyze Procter and Gamble's value pricing strategy of 1992, using seven years of data across 24 product categories. P&G's strategy resulted in a reduction in promotion and an increase in advertising. The researchers found that the net effect was a decrease in market share. They decomposed market share into penetration (how many customers buy the brand), share of requirements (the brand's market share among customers who buy the brand at least once), and category usage (category usage of the brand's customers relative to the category norm). Higher loyalty would presumably be manifested in higher SOR. According to Ailawadi et al., the net decrease in share was because advertising was relatively ineffective and that the reduction in promotion resulted in much lower penetration without a concomitant increase in SOR. Competition on the whole was cooperative in that their combination of responses cushioned the market share decrease, i.e., P&G would have lost more market share if the competition had acted differently.

The Ailawadi et al. and Jedidi et al. studies need to be reconciled. While both agree that promotion is not necessarily profitable at the margin, Ailawadi et al. find that it does increase sales in the long run (so reducing promotion reduces sales), while Jedidi et al. seem to indicate that promotion reduces sales in the long run.

Assessment and Future Research Opportunities

Figure 13.4 provides a summary of progress to date in learning how promotion affects sales. There are some areas (the effect of promotion on response sensitivities, consumption, cross-category purchasing, and store switching) where there is a critical mass of research but major inroads are needed to fully understand the phenomenon. There is one area (stockpiling) that has seen a significant research that has generated a fairly clear understanding of the issue. There are three areas where there has been a lot of work but there are conflicts that need to be resolved. For brand switching, the issue is the existence and nature of asymmetric switching. For feedback, the issue is the existence and magnitude of the effect. For reference prices, the issues are the existence and magnitudes of loss aversion and of the reference price phenomenon itself. There is one final area, decomposition, where there is a critical mass of research on switching versus category effects. But there are questions as to the relative magnitudes of these effects, and much more work is needed to

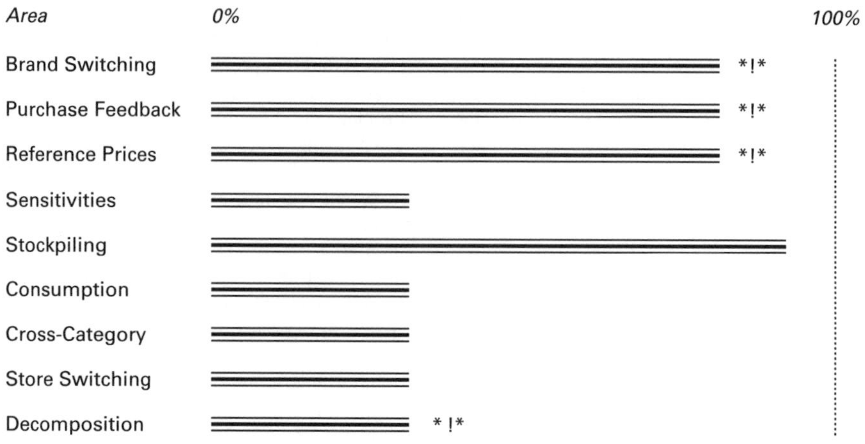

Figure 13.4 *Summary of Progress: How Promotion Affects Sales*

Note: The width of each line represents a combination of how much research has been done in the area and how completely we understand the issue. A *!* signifies a need to reconcile conflicting findings.

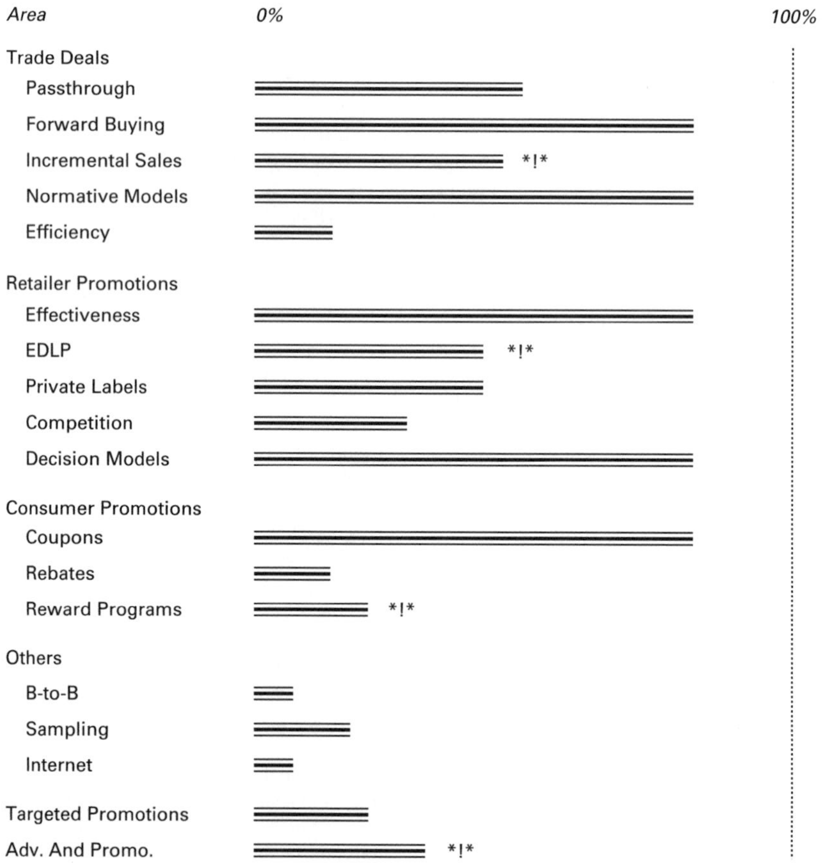

Figure 13.5 *Summary of Progress: Promotion Types*

Note: The width of each line represents a combination of how much research has been done in the area and how completely we understand the issue. A *!* signifies a need to reconcile conflicting findings.

incorporate other effects such as store switching and decoupling stockpiling from consumption.

Figure 13.5 summarizes progress about various promotion types. There are areas (forward buying, normative models of trade deals and retailer promotions, retailer promotion effectiveness, and coupons) that have seen much research and we have a firm understanding of the issue. Other areas have a critical mass of research work but we need much more. These include passthrough, private labels, and competitive effects of retailer promotions. There are some areas with a critical mass of work but conflicts that need to be reconciled. These include the appropriate way to measure incremental sales from trade deals, the long-term viability of EDLP, the value and effectiveness of reward programs, and the relative roles and effectiveness of advertising and promotion. There are other areas (trade promotion as a tool for channel efficiency, rebates, B-to-B promotions such as trade shows (Gopalakrishna & Lilien, 1995), sampling and other promotions such as contests, sweepstakes, and quantity promotions, Internet promotions, and database marketing, where we have barely scratched the surface.

In conclusion, the sales promotion area is one where academic researchers have been able to make a valuable contribution to theory and practice. Given that track record, plus the clear need for further research, the future looks promising for continued progress.

Acknowledgements

The author expresses appreciation to the participants in the Marketing Workshop at the Tuck School, the Marketing Doctoral Seminar at University of Michigan, and to Timothy Heath, Carl Mela, and Koen Pauwels for important comments and ideas. Special thanks go to reviewers Randy Bucklin, Aradhna Krishna, and Robert Shoemaker for detailed and invaluable suggestions.

Notes

1. The Heath et al. findings are based on a laboratory experiment. The other findings are based on supermarket scanner data.

2. Sethuraman (1995) also investigates the role of market share in elasticities and finds that it is the *large share* national brands that enjoy an asymmetric advantage with respect to private labels.

3. Note both LAST and BLOY must be initialized to begin any estimation process. LAST is easy to initialize, since we just drop the first purchase and use it for initialization. BLOY however is non-trivial to initialize. See Guadagni & Little (1983), Ailawadi et al. (1999), and Hsiao (1986).

4. Please note that Keane uses 'α' as the symbol for λ, and 'λ' as the symbol for β_2.

5. This was done by adjusting BLOY for whether purchase was made on or off promotion.

6. The stockpiling term fits inventoryable products well, since both acceleration and quantity increases result in higher than usual inventory. The term applies less readily to durables and services, but the general sense of the term is applicable.

7. Interestingly, the reverse effect (pasta => sauce) was much weaker, due to much lower incidence elasticity for pasta. This resulted in an asymmetric cross-incidence elasticity effect.

8. Although overall retailer profits decrease because the competing retailer responds with its own promotions, i.e., we have a prisoner's dilemma in promotions between competing retailers.

9. A related practice is 'diversion,' which is when the retailer buys extra inventory and ships the inventory to another part of the country where the trade deal is not available. The economic trade-off in this case for the retailer is the additional profit they can generate by selling the merchandise below local prices yet above their deal-reduced costs, versus transportation and inventory costs of buying the extra inventory.

10. The same problem exists with all promotions (Neslin & Shoemaker, 1989), but the issue has received particular attention for couponing.

References and Bibliography

Abe, Makoto (1998) Behavioral explanations for asymmetric price competition. *Marketing Science Institute Working Paper Report No. 98–123*. Cambridge, MA: Marketing Science Institute.

Abraham, Magid M. & Lodish, Leonard M. (1987) PROMOTER: an automated promotion evaluation system. *Marketing Science*, 6 (2): 101–23.

——— (1993) An implemented system for improving promotion productivity using store scanner data. *Marketing Science*, 12 (3): 248–69.

Abraham, Magid M., Lodish, Leonard & Blattberg, Robert C. (1987) Replies. *Marketing Science*, 6 (2): 152–5.

Abramson, Charles, Andrews, Rick L., Corrim, Imran & Jones, Morgan (2000) Parameter bias from unobserved effects in the multinomial logit model of consumer choice. *Journal of Marketing Research*, 37 (4): 410–26.

Agrawal, Deepak (1996) Effect of brand loyalty on advertising and trade promotions: a game theoretic analysis with empirical evidence. *Marketing Science*, 15 (1): 86–108.

Ailawadi, Kusum L. & Neslin, Scott A. (1998) The effect of promotion on consumption: buying more and consuming it faster. *Journal of Marketing Research*, 35 (August): 390–8.

Ailawadi, Kusum L., Borin, Norm & Farris, Paul (1995) Market power and performance: a cross-industry analysis of manufacturers and retailers. *Journal of Retailing*, 71 (3): 211–48.

Ailawadi, Kusum L., Farris, Paul & Shames, Ervin (1999) Trade promotion: essential to selling through resellers. *Sloan Management Review*, 41 (1): 83–92.

Ailawadi, Kusum L., Gedenk, Karen & Neslin, Scott A. (1999) Heterogeneity and purchase event feedback in choice models: an empirical analysis with implications for model building. *International Journal of Research in Marketing*, 16: 177–98.

Ailawadi, Kusum L., Lehmann, Donald R. & Neslin, Scott A. (2001) Market response to a long-term change in marketing mix: learning from P&G's value pricing strategy. *Journal of Marketing*, 65 (1): 44–61.

Ailawadi, Kusum L., Neslin, Scott A. & Gedenk, Karen (2001) Pursuing the value conscious consumer: store brands versus national brand promotions. *Journal of Marketing*, 65 (1): 71–89.

Ainslie, Andrew & Rossi, Peter E. (1998) Similarities in choice behavior across product categories. *Marketing Science*, 17 (2): 91–106.

Allenby, Greg M. & Rossi, Peter E. (1991) Quality perceptions and asymmetric switching between brands. *Marketing Science*, 10 (3): 185–204.

Anderson, Eric & Simester, Duncan I. (1998) The role of sales signs. *Marketing Science*, 17 (2): 91–106.

Anderson, Eric & Simester, Duncan I. (2001) Are sales signs less effective when more products have them? *Marketing Science*, 20 (2): 121–42.

Ansari, Asim & Mela, Carl (2000) 'E-Customization'. Working Paper, Columbia Business School, Columbia University, New York, NY.

Assuncão, Joao L. & Meyer, Robert, J. (1993) The rational effect of price promotions on sales and consumption. *Management Science*, 39 (5): 517–35.

Bawa, Kapil & Shoemaker, Robert W. (1987a) The coupon-prone consumer: some findings based on purchase behavior across product classes. *Journal of Marketing*, 51 (4): 99–110.

——— (1987b) The effects of a direct mail coupon on brand choice behavior. *Journal of Marketing Research*, 21 (February): 65–74.

Bawa, Kapil, Srinivasan, Srini S. & Srivastava, Rajendra K. (1997) Coupon attractiveness and coupon proneness: a framework for modeling coupon redemption. *Journal of Marketing Research*, 34 (November): 499–516.

Beggs, Alan & Klemperer, Paul (1992) Multi-period competition with switching costs. *Econometrica*, 60 (3): 641–66.

Bell, David R. & Lattin, James M. (1998) Looking for loss aversion in scanner panel data: the confounding effect of price-response heterogeneity. *Wharton Marketing Department Working Paper No. 98-032.*

Bell, David R. & Lattin, James M. (2000) Looking for loss aversion in scanner panel data: the confounding effect of price-response heterogeneity. *Marketing Science*, 19 (2): 185–200.

Bell, David R., Chiang, Jeongwen & Padmanabhan, V. (1999) The decomposition of promotional response: an empirical generalization. *Marketing Science*, 18 (4): 504–26.

Bell, David R., Iyer, Ganesh & Padmanabhan, V. (2002) Price competition under stockpiling and flexible consumption. *Journal of Marketing Research* (forthcoming).

Bemmaor, Albert C. & Mouchoux, Dominique (1991) Measuring the short-term effect of in-store promotion and retail advertising on brand sales: a factorial experiment. *Journal of Marketing Research*, 28 (May): 202–14.

Besanko, David, Dubé, Jean-Pierre & Gupta, Sachin (2001) Retail pass-through on competing brands. Working Paper, Johnson School of Management, Cornell University, Ithaca, NY.

Blair, Edward A. & Landon, E. Laird Jr. (1981) The effects of reference prices in retail advertisements. *Journal of Marketing*, 45 (2): 61–9.

Blattberg, Robert C. & Levin, Alan (1987) Modeling the effectiveness and profitability of trade promotions. *Marketing Science*, 6 (2): 124–46.

Blattberg, Robert C. & Neslin, Scott A. (1990) *Sales Promotion: Concepts, Methods, and Strategies*. Englewood Cliffs, NJ: Prentice-Hall, Inc.

——— (1993) Sales promotion models. In *Handbooks in Operations Research and Management Science: Marketing*, edited by J. Eliashberg & G.L. Lilien. Amsterdam: North-Holland, pp. 553–609.

Blattberg, Robert C. & Wisniewski, Kenneth J. (1989) Price induced patterns of competition. *Marketing Science*, 8 (4): 281–309.

Blattberg, Robert C., Briesch, Richard & Fox, Edward J. (1995) How promotions work. *Marketing Science*, 14 (3; Part 2 of 2): G122–32.

Blattberg, Robert C., Eppen, Gary & Lieberman, Joshua (1981) A theoretical and empirical evaluation of price deals for consumer nondurables. *Journal of Marketing*, 45 (1): 116–29.

Bolton, Ruth N. (1989) The relationship between market characteristics and promotional price elasticities. *Marketing Science*, 8 (2): 153–69.

Boulding, William, Lee, Eunkyu & Staelin, Richard (1994) Mastering the mix: do advertising, promotion, and sales force activities lead to differentiation? *Journal of Marketing Research*, 31 (May): 159–72.

Breisch, Richard A., Krishnamurthi, Lakshman, Mazumdar, Tridib & Raj, S.P. (1997) A comparative analysis of reference price models. *Journal of Consumer Research*, 24 (September): 202–24.

Breshnahan, Timothy F. (1989) Empirical studies of industries with market power. In *Handbook of Industrial Organization*, Vol. 2, edited by Richard Schmalensee & Robert Willig. New York: North-Holland, Chapter 17.

Bronnenberg, Bart J. & Wathieu, Luc (1996) Asymmetric promotion effects and brand positioning. *Marketing Science*, 15 (4): 379–94.

Buchanan, Lauranne, Simmons, Carolyn J. & Bickart, Barbara A. (1999) Brand equity dilution: retailer display and context brand effects. *Journal of Marketing Research*, 36 (August): 345–55.

Bucklin, Randolph E. & Gupta, Sunil (1992) Brand choice, purchase incidence, and segmentation: an integrated approach. *Journal of Marketing Research*, 29 (May): 201–15.

——— (1999) Commercial use of UPC scanner data: industry and academic perspectives. *Marketing Science*, 18 (3): 247–73.

Bucklin, Randolph E. & Lattin, James M. (1992) A model of product category competition among grocery retailers. *Journal of Retailing*, 68 (Fall): 271–93.

Bucklin, Randolph E., Gupta, Sunil & Siddarth, S. (1998) Determining segmentation in sales response across consumer purchase behaviors. *Journal of Marketing Research*, 35 (May): 189–97.

Butscher, Stephan A. (1997) Limited loyalty programs create strategic databases. *Marketing News*, 31 (October 27): 13.

Cannondale Associates (1999) *Trade Promotion Spending and Merchandising: 1999 Industry Study*. Wilton, CT: Cannondale Associates, Inc.

Chandon, Pierre, Wansink, Brian & Laurent, Gilles (2000) A benefit congruence framework for sales promotion effectiveness. *Journal of Marketing*, 64 (October): 65–81.

Chang, Kwangpil, Siddarth, S. & Weinberg, Charles B. (1999) The impact of heterogeneity in purchase timing and price responsiveness on estimates of sticker shock effects. *Marketing Science*, 18 (2): 178–92.

Chen, Yuxin, Hess, James D., Wilcox, Ronald T. & Zhang, Z. John (1999) Accounting profits versus marketing profits: a relevant metric for category management. *Marketing Science*, 18 (3): 208–29.

Chen, Yuxin, Narasimhan, Chakravarthi & Zhang, Z. John (2001) Individual marketing with imperfect targetability. *Marketing Science*, 20 (1): 23–41.

Chiang, Jeongwen (1991) A simultaneous approach to the whether, what, and how much to buy questions. *Marketing Science*, 10 (4): 297–315.

——— (1995) Competing coupon promotions and category sales. *Marketing Science*, 14 (1): 105–22.

Chintagunta, Pradeep (1993) Investigating purchase incidence, brand choice, and purchase quantity decisions of households. *Marketing Science*, 12 (2): 184–208.

Chintagunta, Pradeep K. & Haldar, Sudeep (1998) Investigating purchase timing behavior in two related product categories. *Journal of Marketing Research*, 35 (February): 43–53.

Cooper, Lee G. & Giuffrida, Giovanni (2000) Turning datamining into a management science tool: new algorithms and empirical results. *Management Science*, 46 (2): 249–64.

Cooper, Lee G., Baron, Penny, Levy, Wayne, Swisher, Michael & Gogos, Paris (1999) PromoCast™: a new forecasting method for promotion planning. *Marketing Science*, 18 (3): 301–16.

Cotterill, Ronald W., Putsis, William P. Jr. & Dhar, Ravi (2000) Assessing the competitive interaction between private labels and national brands. *Journal of Business*, 73 (1): 108–37.

Cox Direct (1998) *20th Annual Survey of Promotional Practices*. Largo, FL: Cox Direct.

Curhan, Ronald C. & Kopp, Robert J. (1986) Factors influencing grocery retailers' support of trade promotions. *MSI Report No. 86–104* (July). Cambridge, MA: Marketing Science Institute.

David Shepard Associates, Inc. (1995) *The New Direct Marketing*, 2nd edn. New York: Irwin.

Davis, Scott, Inman, J. Jeffrey & McAlister, Leigh (1992) Promotion has a negative effect on brand evaluations – or does it? Additional disconfirming evidence. *Journal of Marketing Research*, 29 (February): 143–8.

Dhar, Sanjay K. & Hoch, Stephen J. (1996) Price discrimination using in-store merchandising. *Journal of Marketing*, 60 (1): 17–30.

——— (1997) Why store brand penetration varies by retailer. *Marketing Science*, 16 (3): 208–27.

Dhar, Sanjay K. & Raju, Jagmohan S. (1998) The effects of cross-ruff coupons on sales and profits. *Management Science*, 44 (11, Part 1): 1501–16.

Dickson, Peter R. & Sawyer, Alan G. (1990) The price knowledge and search of supermarket shoppers. *Journal of Marketing*, 54 (3): 42–53.

Dillon, William R. & Gupta, Sunil (1996) A segment-level model of category volume and brand choice. *Marketing Science*, 15 (1): 38–59.

Dodson, Joe A., Tybout, Alice M. & Sternthal, Brian (1978) Impact of deals and deal retraction on brand switching. *Journal of Marketing Research*, 15 (February): 72–81.

Dorfman, R. & Steiner, P.O. (1954) Optimal advertising and optimal quality. *The American Economic Review*, 44: 826–36.

Dowling, Grahame R. & Uncles, Mark (1997) Do customer loyalty programs really work? *Sloan Management Review*, 38 (Summer): 71–82.

Doyle, Peter & Saunders, John (1985) The lead effect of marketing decisions. *Journal of Marketing Research*, 22 (February): 54–65.

Drèze, Xavier & Bell, David R. (2000) Creating win-win trade promotions: theory and empirical analysis of scan-back trade deals. Working Paper, Marshall School of Business, University of Southern California, Los Angeles, CA.

Dreze, Xavier & Hoch, Stephen J. (1998) Exploiting the installed base using cross-merchandising and category destination programs. *International Journal of Research in Marketing*, 15: 459–71.

Ehrenberg, Andrew S.C., Hammond, Kathy & Goodhardt, G.J. (1994) The after-effects of price-related consumer promotions. *Journal of Advertising Research*, 34 (July/August): 11–21.

Erdem, Tulin, Keane, Michael P. & Sun, Baohong (1999) Missing price and coupon availability data in scanner panels: correcting for the self-selection bias in choice model parameters. *Journal of Econometrics*, 89 (1–2): 177–96.

Farris, Paul W. & Quelch, John A. (1987) In defense of price promotion. *Sloan Management Review*, 28 (Fall): 63–9.

Ferguson, C.E. (1972) *Microeconomic Theory*, 3rd edn. Homewood, IL: Richard D. Irwin, Inc.

Folkes, Valerie S., Martin, Ingrid M. & Gupta, Kamal (1993) When to say when: effects of supply on usage. *Journal of Consumer Research*, 20 (December): 467–77.

Freimer, Marshall & Horsky, Dan (2001) Try it you will like it – does consumer learning lead to competitive price promotions? Working Paper, Simon School of Business, University of Rochester, Rochester, NY.

Gasmi, Farid, Laffont, J.J. & Vuong, Quang H. (1992) Econometric analysis of collusive behavior in a soft-drink market. *Journal of Economics and Management Strategy*, 1 (2): 277–312.

Gedenk, Karen & Neslin, Scott A. (1999) The role of retail promotion in determining future brand loyalty: its effect on purchase event feedback. *Journal of Retailing*, 75 (4): 433–59.

Gonul, Fusun & Srinivasan, Kannan (1996) Estimating the impact of consumer expectations of coupons on purchase behavior: a dynamic structural model. *Marketing Science*, 15 (3): 262–79.

Gopalakrishna, Srinath & Lilien, Gary L. (1995) A three-stage model of industrial trade show performance. *Marketing Science*, 14 (1): 22–42.

Greenleaf, Eric (1995) The impact of reference prices on the profitability of promotions. *Marketing Science*, 14 (1): 82–104.

Grewal, Dhruv, Monroe, Kent B. & Krishnan, R. (1998) The effects of price-comparison advertising on buyers' perceptions of acquisition value, transaction value, and behavioral intentions. *Journal of Marketing*, 62 (2): 46–59.

Guadagni, Peter M. & Little, John D.C. (1983) A logit model of brand choice calibrated on scanner data. *Marketing Science*, 2 (3): 203–38.

Gupta, Sunil (1988) Impact of sales promotions on when, what, and how much to buy. *Journal of Marketing Research*, 25 (November): 342–55.

Hardie, Bruce G.S., Johnson, Eric J. & Fader, Peter S. (1993) Modeling loss aversion and reference dependence effects on brand choice. *Marketing Science*, 12 (4): 378–94.

Heath, Timothy B., Ryu, Gangseog, Chatterjee, Subimal, McCarthy, Michael S., Mothersbaugh, David L., Milberg, Sandra & Gaeth, Gary J. (2000) Asymmetric competition and the leveraging of competitive disadvantages. *Journal of Consumer Research*, 27 (3): 291–308.

Heckman, James J. (1981) Heterogeneity and state dependence. In *Studies in Labor Markets*, edited by S. Rosen. Chicago: University of Chicago Press, pp. 91–139.

Helson, Harry (1964) *Adaptation-Level Theory*. New York: Harper and Row.

Hoch, Stephen J. & Banerji, Shumeet (1993) When do private labels succeed? *Sloan Management Review*, 34 (Summer): 57–67.

Hoch, Stephen J., Dreze, Xavier & Purk, Mary E. (1994) EDLP, Hi-Lo, and Margin Arithmetic. *Journal of Marketing*, 58 (October): 16–27.

Hoch, Stephen J., Kim, Byung-Do, Montgomery, Alan L. & Rossi, Peter E. (1995) Determinants of store-level price elasticity. *Journal of Marketing Research*, 32 (February): 17–29.

Hsiao, Cheng (1986) *Analysis of Panel Data*. Cambridge: Cambridge University Press.

Huber, Joel, Payne, John W. & Puto, Christopher (1982) Adding asymmetrically dominated alternatives: violations of regularity and the similarity hypothesis. *Journal of Consumer Research*, 9 (June): 90–8.

Information Resources, Inc. (1989) *InfoScan Topical Marketing Report*. Chicago: Information Resources, Inc.

——— (1993) *Managing Your Business in an EDLP Environment*. Chicago: Information Resources, Inc.

Inman, J. Jeffrey & McAlister, Leigh (1993) A retailer promotion policy model considering promotion signal sensitivity. *Marketing Science*, 12 (4): 339–56.

——— (1994) Do coupon expiration dates affect consumer behavior? *Journal of Marketing Research*, 31 (August): 423–8.

Inman, J. Jeffrey, McAlister, Leigh & Hoyer, Wayne D. (1990) Promotion signal: proxy for a price cut? *Journal of Consumer Research*, 17 (June): 74–81.

Irons, Karl W., Little, John D.C. & Klein, Robert L. (1983) Determinants of coupon effectiveness. In *Proceedings of the 1983 ORSA/TIMS Marketing Science Conference*, edited by Fred Zufryden. Los Angeles, CA: University of Southern California, pp. 157–64.

Jain, Dipak C. & Vilcassim, Naufel J. (1991) Investigating household purchase timing decisions: a conditional hazard function approach. *Marketing Science*, 10 (1): 1–23.

Jedidi, Kamel, Mela, Carl F. & Gupta, Sunil (1999) Managing advertising and promotion for long-run profitability. *Marketing Science*, 18 (1): 1–22.

Jeuland, Abel P. & Narasimhan, Chakravarthi (1985) Dealing – temporary price cuts – by seller as a buyer discrimination mechanism. *Journal of Business*, 58 (3): 295–308.

Kadiyali, Vrinda, Chintagunta, Pradeep & Vilcassim, Naufel (2000) Manufacturer–retailer channel interactions and implications for channel power: an empirical investigation of pricing in a local market. *Marketing Science*, 19 (2): 127–48.

Kahneman, Daniel & Tversky, Amos (1979) Prospect theory: an analysis of decision under risk. *Econometrica*, 47: 263–91.

Kalwani, Manohar U. & Yim, Chi Kin (1992) Consumer price and promotion expectations: an experimental study. *Journal of Marketing Research*, 29 (February): 90–100.

Kalwani, Manohar U., Yim, Chi Kin, Rinne, Heikki J. & Sugita, Yoshi (1990) A price expectations model of customer brand choice. *Journal of Marketing Research*, 27 (August): 251–62.

Kalyanaram, G. & Little, John D.C. (1994) An empirical analysis of latitude of price acceptance in consumer package goods. *Journal of Consumer Research*, 21 (December): 408–18.

Kalyanaram, Gurumurthy & Winer, Russell S. (1995) Empirical generalizations from reference price research. *Marketing Science*, 14 (3, Part 2): G161–G169.

Kamakura, Wagner A. & Russell, Gary J. (1989) A probabilistic choice model for market segmentation and elasticity structure. *Journal of Marketing Research*, 26 (November): 379–90.

Keane, Michael P. (1997) Modeling heterogeneity and state dependence in consumer choice behavior. *Journal of Business and Economic Statistics*, 15 (3): 310–27.

Kim, Byungdo, Shi, Mengze & Srinivasan, Kannan (2001) Reward programs and tacit price collusion. *Marketing Science*, 20 (2): 99–120.

Kim, Sang Yong & Staelin, Richard (1999) Manufacturer allowances and retailer pass-through rates in a competitive environment. *Marketing Science*, 18 (1): 59–76.

Kivetz, Ran & Simonson, Itomar (2002) Earning the right to indulge: effort as a determinant of customer preferences toward frequency reward programs. *Journal of Marketing Research*, 99 (2): 155–70.

Klemperer, Paul D. (1987) Markets with cosumer switching cost. *Quarterly Journal of Economics*, 102 (May): 375–94.

Knott, Aaron, Hayes, Andrew & Neslin, Scott A. (2002) Next-product-to-buy models for cross-selling applications. *Journal of Interactive Marketing*, 16 (3): 59–75.

Kopalle, Praveen K., Mela, Carl F. & Marsh, Lawrence (1999) The dynamic effect of discounting on sales: empirical analysis and normative pricing implications. *Marketing Science*, 18 (3): 317–32.

Kopalle, Praveen K., Neslin, Scott A. & Singh, Medini (1999) The economic viability of frequency reward programs in a strategic competitive environment. Working Paper, Amos Tuck School of Business, Dartmouth College, Hanover, NH.

Kopalle, Praveen K., Rao, Ambar G. & Assuncão, Joao L. (1996) Asymmetric reference price effects and dynamic pricing policies. *Marketing Science*, 15 (1): 60–8.

Krishna, Aradhna (1991) Effect of dealing patterns on consumer perceptions of deal frequency and willingness to pay. *Journal of Marketing Research*, 28 (November): 441–51.

——— (1992) The normative impact of consumer price expectations for multiple brands on consumer purchase behavior. *Marketing Science*, 11: 266–86.

——— (1994) The effect of deal knowledge on consumer purchase behavior. *Journal of Marketing Research*, 31 (February): 76–91.

Krishna, Aradhna & Zhang, Z. John (1999) Short- or long-duration coupons: the effect of the expiration date on the profitability of coupon promotions. *Management Science*, 45 (8): 1041–56.

Krishna, Aradhna, Briesch, Richard, Lehmann, Donald R. & Yuan, Hong (2000) A meta-analysis of the impact of price presentation on deal evaluation. Working Paper, University of Michigan Business School, Ann Arbor, MI.

Krishna, Aradhna, Currim, Imran S. & Shoemaker, Robert W. (1991) Consumer perceptions of promotional activity, *Journal of Marketing*, 55 (2): 4–16.

Krishnamurthi, Lakshman, Mazumdar, Tridib & Raj, S.P. (1992) Asymmetric response to price in consumer choice and purchase quantity decisions. *Journal of Consumer Research*, 19 (3): 1041–56.

Kruger, Michael W. (1987) Commentary: steps toward mastering trade promotions. *Marketing Science*, 6 (2): 147–9.

Kumar, Nanda, Rajiv, Surendra & Jeuland, Abel (2001) Effectiveness of trade promotions: analyzing the determinants of retail pass through. *Marketing Science*, 20 (4): 382–404.

Kumar, V. & Leone, Robert P. (1988) Measuring the effect of retail store promotions on brand and store substitution. *Journal of Marketing Research*, 25 (May): 178–85.

Lal, Rajiv (1990) Price promotions: limiting competitive encroachment. *Marketing Science*, 9 (3): 247–62.

Lal, Rajiv & Rao, Ram (1997) Supermarket competition: the case of Every Day Low Pricing. *Marketing Science*, 16 (1): 60–80.

Lal, Rajiv & Villas-Boas, J. Miguel (1998) Price promotions and trade deals with multiproduct retailers. *Management Science*, 44 (July): 935–49.

Lal, Rajiv, Little, John D.C. & Villas-Boas, J. Miguel (1996) A theory of forward buying, merchandising, and trade deals. *Marketing Science*, 15 (1): 21–37.

Lattin, James M. & Bucklin, Randolph E. (1989) Reference effects of price and promotion on brand choice behavior. *Journal of Marketing Research*, 26 (August): 299–310.

Lattin, James M. & Ortmeyer, Gwen (1991) A theoretical rationale for everyday low pricing by grocery retailers. *Research Paper No. 1144*. Graduate School of Business, Stanford University, Stanford, CA.

Leclerc, France & Little, John D.C. (1997) Can advertising copy make FSI coupons more effective? *Journal of Marketing Research*, 34 (November): 473–84.

Leeflang, Peter S.H. & Wittink, Dick R. (1996) Competitive reaction versus consumer response: do managers overreact? *International Journal of Research in Marketing*, 13: 103–19.

Lemon, Katherine W. & Nowlis, Stephen M. (2002) Developing synergies between promotions and brands in different price-quality tiers. *Journal of Marketing Research*, 39 (2): 171–85.

Lichtenstein, Donald R., Netemeyer, Richard G. & Burton, Scot (1990) Distinguishing coupon proneness from value consciousness: an acquisition-transaction utility theory perspective. *Journal of Marketing*, 54 (3): 54–67.

Lodish, Leonard M., Abraham, Magid, Kalmenson, Stuart, Livelsberger, Jeanne, Lubertkin, Beth, Richardson, Bruce & Stevens, Mary Ellen (1995) How T.V. advertising works: a meta-analysis of 389 real world split cable T.V. advertising experiments. *Journal of Marketing Research*, 32 (May): 125–39.

Macé, Sandrine & Neslin, Scott A. (2001) The determinants of promotion-induced stockpiling and deceleration. Working Paper, Tuck School of Business, Dartmouth College, Hanover, NH.

Manchanda, Puneet, Ansari, Asim & Gupta, Sunil (1999) The 'Shopping Basket': a model for multicategory purchase incidence decisions. *Marketing Science*, 18 (2): 95–114.

Mazumdar, Tridib & Papatla, Purushottam (1995) Loyalty differences in the use of internal and external reference prices. *Marketing Letters*, 6 (March): 111–22.

——— (2000) An investigation of reference price segments. *Journal of Marketing Research*, 37 (2): 246–58.

McAlister, Leigh & Srivastava, Rajendra (1991) Incorporating choice dynamics in models of consumer behavior. *Marketing Letters*, 2 (3): 241–52.

Mela, Carl F., Gupta, Sunil & Lehmann, Donald R. (1997) The long-term impact of promotion and advertising on consumer brand choice. *Journal of Marketing Research*, 34 (May): 248–61.

Mela, Carl F., Jedidi, Kamel & Bowman, Douglas (1998) The long-term impact of promotions on consumer stockpiling behavior. *Journal of Marketing Research*, 35 (May): 250–62.

Midgley, David F., Marks, Robert E. & Cooper, Lee G. (1997) Breeding competitive strategies. *Management Science*, 43 (3): 257–75.

Montgomery, Alan L. (1997) Creating micro-marketing pricing strategies using supermarket scanner data. *Marketing Science*, 16 (4): 315–37.

Moorthy, Sridhar (2001) On retail pass-through: intrabrand and interbrand competition effects. Working Paper, Rotman School of Management, University of Toronto, Toronto, Canada.

Moriarty, Mark (1985) Retail promotional effects on intra- and interbrand sales performance. *Journal of Retailing*, 6: 27–48.

Mulhern, Francis J. & Leone, Robert P. (1991) Implicit price bundling of retail products: a multiproduct approach to maximizing store profitability. *Journal of Marketing*, 55 (4): 63–76.

Murry, John P. & Heide, Jan B. (1998) Managing promotion program participation within manufacturer-retailer relationships. *Journal of Marketing*, 62 (1): 58–68.

Narasimhan, Chakravarthi (1984) A price discrimination theory of coupons. *Marketing Science*, 3 (2): 128–47.

——— (1988) Competitive promotional strategies. *Journal of Business*, 61 (4): 427–49.

Narasimhan, Chakravarthi, Neslin, Scott A. & Sen, Subrata K. (1996) Promotion elasticities and category characteristics. *Journal of Marketing*, 60 (2): 17–30.

NCH (1993) *Worldwide Coupon Distribution and Redemption Trends*. Chicago, IL: NCH Promotional Services.

——— (1998) *Worldwide Coupon Distribution and Redemption Trends*. Lincolnshire, IL: NCH NuWorld Marketing Limited.

——— (1999) *Worldwide Coupon Distribution and Redemption Trends*. Lincolnshire, IL: NCH NuWorld Marketing Limited.

——— (2000) *Worldwide Coupon Distribution and Redemption Trends*. Lincolnshire, IL, NCH NuWorld Marketing Limited.

Neslin, Scott A. (1990) A model for evaluating the profitability of coupon promotions. *Marketing Science*, 2 (4): 361–88.

Neslin, Scott A. & Clarke, Darral G. (1987) Relating the brand use profile of coupon redeemers to brand and coupon characteristics. *Journal of Advertising Research*, 27 (1): 23–32.

Neslin, Scott A. & Schneider Stone, Linda (1996) Consumer inventory sensitivity and the post-promotion dip. *Marketing Letters*, 7 (1): 77–94.

Neslin, Scott A. & Shoemaker, Robert W. (1983) A model for evaluating the profitability of coupon promotions. *Marketing Science*, 2 (4): 361–88.

——— (1989) An alternative explanation for lower repeat rates after promotion purchases. *Journal of Marketing Research*, 26 (2): 205–13.

Neslin, Scott A., Henderson, Caroline & Quelch, John (1985) Consumer promotions and the acceleration of product purchases. *Marketing Science*, 4 (2): 147–65.

Neslin, Scott A., Powell, Stephen G. & Schneider Stone, Linda (1995) The effects of retailer and consumer response on optimal manufacturer advertising and trade promotion strategies. *Management Science*, 41 (May): 749–66.

Nijs, Vincent R., Dekimpe, Marnik G., Steenkamp, Jan-Benedict E.M. & Hanssens, Dominique M. (2001) The category-demand effects of price promotions. *Marketing Science*, 20 (1): 1–22.

Orr, Alicia (1995) Customers for life! *Target Marketing*, 18 (March): 20.

Papatla, Purushottam & Krishnamurthi, Lakshman (1996) Measuring the dynamic effects of promotions on brand choice. *Journal of Marketing Research*, 33 (February): 20–35.

Pashigian, B. Peter & Bowen, Brian (1991) Why are products sold on sale? Explanations of pricing regularities. *Quarterly Journal of Economics* (November): 1015–38.

Pauwels, Koen, Hanssens, Dominique M. & Siddarth, S. (2002) The long-term effects of price promotions on category incidence, band choice, and purchase quantity. *Journal of Marketing Research* (forthcoming).

P-O-P Times (1991) Latest IRI data confirm the effectiveness of P-O-P. July/August: 37–42.

Raghubir, Priya (1998) Coupon value: a signal for price? *Journal of Marketing Research*, 35 (August): 316–24.

Raghubir, Priya & Corfman, Kim (1999) When do price promotions affect pretrial brand evaluations? *Journal of Marketing Research*, 36 (May): 211–22.

Rajendran, K.N. & Tellis, Gerard J. (1994) Contextual and temporal components of reference price. *Journal of Marketing*, 58 (January): 22–34.

Raju, Jagmohan S., Dhar, Sanjay K. & Morrison, Donald G. (1994) The effect of package coupons on brand choice. *Marketing Science*, 13 (2): 145–64.

Raju, Jagmohan S., Sethuraman, Raj & Dhar, Sanjay K. (1995) The introduction and performance of store brands. *Management Science*, 41 (6): 957–78.

Raju, Jagmohan S., Srinivasan, V. & Lal, Rajiv (1990) The effects of brand loyalty on competitive price promotional strategies. *Management Science*, 36 (3): 276–304.

Reibstein, David J. & Traver, Phillis A. (1982) Factors affecting coupon redemption rates. *Journal of Marketing*, 46 (Fall): 102–13.

Reynolds, Jonathan (1995) Database marketing and customer loyalty: examining the evidence. *European Retail Digest*, 7 (July). Oxford: Oxford Institute of Retail Management, pp. 31–8.

Roberts, Mary Lou & Berger, Paul D. (1999) *Direct Marketing Management*, 2nd edn. Upper Saddle River, NJ: Prentice-Hall, Inc.

Roehm, Michelle L., Pullins, Ellen Bulman & Roehm, Harper A. Jr. (2002) Designing loyalty programs for packaged goods brands. *Journal of Marketing Research*, 39 (2): 202–13.

Rossi, Peter E., McCulloch, Robert E. & Allenby, Greg M. (1996) The value of purchase history data in target marketing. *Marketing Science*, 15 (4): 321–40.

Rothschild, Michael L. (1987) A behavioral view of promotions effects on brand loyalty. In *Advances in Consumer Research*, Vol. XIV, edited by Melanie Wallendorf & Paul Anderson. Provo, UT: Association for Consumer Research, pp. 119–20.

Rothschild, Michael L. & Gaidis, William C. (1981) Behavioral learning theory: its relevance to marketing and promotions. *Journal of Marketing*, 45 (2): 70–8.

Seetharaman, P.B., Ainslie, Andrew & Chintagunta, Pradeep K. (1999) Investigating household state dependence effects across categories. *Journal of Marketing Research*, 36 (November): 488–500.

Sethuraman, Raj (1995) A meta-analysis of national brand and store brand cross-promotional price elasticities. *Marketing Letters*, 6 (4): 275–86.

Sethuraman, Raj & Srinivasan, V. (2002) The asymmetric share effect: an empirical generalization on cross-price effects. *Journal of Marketing Research* (forthcoming).

Sethuraman, Raj, Srinivasan, V. and Kim, Doyle (1999) Asymmetric and neighborhood cross-price effects: some empirical generalizations. *Marketing Science*, 18 (1): 23–41.

Shaffer, Greg & Zhang, Z. John (1995) Competitive coupon targeting. *Marketing Science*, 14 (4): 395–416.

Shapiro, Eben (1992) P&G takes on the supermarkets with uniform pricing. *The New York Times*, April 26.

Sharp, Byron & Sharp, Anne (1997) Loyalty programs and their impact on repeat-purchase loyalty patterns. *International Journal of Research in Marketing*, 14: 473–86.

Shilony, Y. (1977) Mixed pricing in oligopoly. *Journal of Economic Theory*, 14 (April): 373–88.

Shoemaker, Robert W. (1979) An analysis of consumer reactions to product promotions. In *Educators' Conference Proceedings*, edited by Neil Beckwith, Michael Houston, Robert Mittelstaedt, Kent B. Monroe & Scott Ward. Chicago: American Marketing Association, pp. 244–8.

Shoemaker, Robert W. & Shoaf, F. Robert (1977) Repeat rates of deal purchases. *Journal of Advertising Research*, 17 (2): 47–53.

Shoemaker, Robert W. & Tibrewala, Vikas (1985) Relating coupon redemption rates to past purchasing of the brand. *Journal of Advertising Research*, 25 (5): 40–7.

Silva-Risso, Jorge M., Bucklin, Randolph E. & Morrison, Donald G. (1999) A decision support system for planning manufacturers' sales promotion calendars. *Marketing Science*, 18 (3): 274–300.

Sivakumar, K. & Raj, S.P. (1997) Quality tier competition: how price change influences brand choice and category choice. *Journal of Marketing*, 61 (3): 71–84.

Skinner, B.F. (1938) *The Behavior of Organisms: An Experimental Analysis*. New York: Appleton-Century-Crofts.

Soman, Dilip (1997) The illusion of delayed incentives: evaluating future effort-money transactions. *Journal of Marketing Research*, 35 (November): 427–37.

Sun, Baohong, Neslin, Scott A. & Srinivasan, Kannan (2001) Measuring the impact of promotions on brand switching under rational consumer behavior. Working Paper, Kenan-Flagler Business School, University of North Carolina, Chapel Hill, NC.

Tat, Peter, Cunningham, William A. III & Babakus, Emin (1988) Consumer perceptions of rebates. *Journal of Advertising Research*, 28 (August/September): 45–50.

Tellis, Gerald J. & Zufryden, Fred F. (1995) Tackling the retailer decision maze: which brands to discount, how much, when, and why? *Marketing Science*, 14 (3): 271–99.

Thaler, Richard (1985) Mental accounting and consumer choice. *Marketing Science*, 4 (3): 199–214.

Thompson, Patrick A. & Noordewier, Thomas (1992) Estimating the effects of consumer incentive programs on domestic automobile sales. *Journal of Business and Economic Statistics*, 10 (4): 409–17.

Tirole, Jean (1988) *The Theory of Industrial Organization*. Cambridge, MA: MIT Press.

Tyagi, Rajeev K. (1999) A characterization of retailer response to manufacturer trade deals. *Journal of Marketing Research*, 36 (November): 510–16.

Urbany, Joel E., Bearden, William O., Kaicker, Ajit & Borrero, Melinda (1997) Transaction utility effects when quality is uncertain. *Journal of the Academy of Marketing Science*, 25 (1): 45–55.

Van Heerde, Harald J. (1999) *Models for Sales Promotion Effects Based on Store-Level Scanner Data*. Capelle a/d IJssel, The Netherlands: Labyrint Publication.

Van Heerde, Harald J., Leeflang, Peter S.H. & Wittink, Dick R. (2000) The estimation of pre- and postpromotion dips with store-level scanner data. *Journal of Marketing Research*, 37 (3): 383–95.

Varian, Hal R. (1980) A model of sales. *American Economic Review*, 70 (4): 651–60.

Vilcassim, Nafel J., Kadiyali, Vrinda & Chintagunta, Pradeep K. (1999) Investigating dynamic multifirm market interactions in price and advertising. *Management Science*, 45 (4): 486–98.

Wall Street Journal (1998) Rebates' secret appeal to manufacturers: few consumers actually redeem them. February 10, page B1.

Walters, Rockney G. (1989) An empirical investigation into retailer response to manufacturer trade promotions. *Journal of Retailing*, 65 (2): 253–72.

——— (1991) Assessing the impact of retail price promotions on product substitution, complementary purchase, and interstore sales displacement. *Journal of Marketing*, 55 (2): 17–28.

Walters, Rockney G. & MacKenzie, Scott B. (1988) A structural equations analysis of the impact of price promotions on store performance. *Journal of Marketing Research*, 25 (February): 51–63.

Wansink, Brian (1996) Does package size accelerate usage volume? *Journal of Marketing*, 60 (3): 1–14.

Wansink, Brian & Deshpandé, Rohit (1994) Out of sight, out of mind: pantry stockpiling and brand-usage frequency. *Marketing Letters*, 5 (1): 166–82.

Wilson, R. Dale, Newman, Larry M. & Hastak, Manoj (1979) On the validity of research methods in consumer dealing activity: an analysis of timing issues. In *Educators' Conference Proceedings*, edited by Neil Beckwith, Michael Houston, Robert Mittelstaedt, Kent B. Monroe & Scott Ward. Chicago: American Marketing Association, pp. 41–6.

Winer, Russell S. (1986) A reference price model of brand choice in frequently purchased consumer products. *Journal of Consumer Research*, 13 (September): 250–6.

Wittink, Dick R., Addona, Michael J., Hawkes, William J. & Porter, John C. (1987) SCAN*PRO®: a model to measure short-term effects of promotional activities on brand sales, based on store-level scanner data. Working Paper, Johnson School of Management, Cornell University, Ithaca, NY.

Zenor, Michael (1994) The profit benefits of category management. *Journal of Marketing Research*, 31 (May): 202–13.

Zhang, Z. John, Krisha, Aradhna & Dhar, Sanjay K. (2000) The optimal choice of promotional vehicles: front-loaded or rear-loaded incentives? *Management Science*, 46 (3): 348–62.

14

Understanding and Improving Service Quality: A Literature Review and Research Agenda

A. PARASURAMAN and VALARIE A. ZEITHAML

INTRODUCTION

The proliferation of look-alike products in many sectors, coupled with escalating competition and more demanding customers, have made service excellence one of the key marketing tools for achieving competitive differentiation and fostering customer loyalty. Service quality continues to occupy center stage in the marketing arena even as a growing number of company–customer exchanges through traditional channels are being replaced by Internet-based transactions and e-commerce. For instance, a survey of Internet shoppers revealed customer service to be the top-most determinant of repeat visits to websites (Hanrahan, 1999). Jeff Bezos, founder and CEO of Amazon.com, a company that is arguably the pioneer in the field of e-commerce, had this to say about the role of service:

> In the offline world … 30% of a company's resources are spent providing a good customer experience and 70% goes to marketing. But online … 70% should be devoted to creating a great customer experience and 30% should be spent on 'shouting' about it. (*Business Week*, March 22, 1999: EB 30)

Scholarly research on service quality has paralleled practitioner interest in understanding and leveraging superior service delivery. Much of this research has occurred within the past two decades. As of the early 1980s only a handful of writings had discussed the nature of service quality (Gronroos, 1982; Lehtinen & Lehtinen, 1982; Lewis & Booms, 1983; Sasser et al., 1978). However, since the mid-1980s, service quality and its measurement have occupied an increasingly prominent position in the published literature. Service quality has been one of the most researched topics in the services field, particularly in the early years of the evolution of services marketing as a significant subdiscipline of marketing (Fisk et al., 1993).

The goals of this chapter are:

(a) to summarize the literature pertaining to the conceptualization and definition of service quality;
(b) to examine the role of service quality in customer loyalty and profitability;
(c) to examine the relationship of service quality to the related construct of perceived value;
(d) to review conceptual frameworks for improving service quality;
(e) to discuss the development and applications of SERVQUAL, a multiple-item scale to measure service quality, and compare it with alternative measurement approaches;
(f) to examine the role and measurement of customer service in technology mediated customer–company interactions; and
(g) to propose a research agenda for addressing unresolved and emerging issues pertaining to service quality.

Conceptualization of Service Quality

Definition of Service Quality

Early writing on the topic of service quality (Gronroos, 1982; Lehtinen & Lehtinen, 1982; Lewis & Booms, 1983; Sasser et al., 1978) suggested that service quality results from a comparison of what customers feel a service provider should offer (i.e., their expectations), with how the provider actually performs. For instance, according to Lewis & Booms (1983), 'service quality is a measure of how well the service level delivered matches customer expectations. Delivering quality service means conforming to customer expectations on a consistent basis.'

The notion that service quality is a function of the expectations-performance gap was reinforced by an extensive multi-sector study conducted by Parasuraman, Zeithaml, and Berry – hereafter referred to as PZB – (1985). This study involved 12 customer focus-group interviews – three in each of four different service sectors (retail banking, credit card, stock brokerage, and appliance repair and maintenance) – to explore how customers assessed service quality. Based on common insights from the focus groups, PZB formally defined service quality, as perceived by customers, as *the degree and direction of discrepancy between customers' service perceptions and expectations.*

Dimensions of Service Quality

Early conceptualizations suggested several general service facets that customers might use to assess service quality. Sasser et al. (1978) proposed three different dimensions of service performance, all dealing with the *process* of service delivery: *levels of material*, *facilities*, and *personnel*. Gronroos (1982) proposed two types of service quality: *technical quality*, which involves what customers actually receive from the service provider (i.e., the *outcome* of the service), and *functional quality*, which involves the manner in which customers receive the service (i.e., the *process* of service delivery). Lehtinen & Lehtinen (1982) discussed three kinds of quality: *physical quality*, involving physical aspects associated with the service such as equipment or building; *corporate quality*, involving a service firm's image or reputation; and *interactive quality*, involving interactions between service personnel and customers, as well as among customers.

A consistent theme emerging from these dimensions is that customers use more than just the service outcome or 'core' in assessing service quality. Customer assessments are also influenced by the service process and the peripherals associated with the service. The customer focus-group research conducted by PZB (1985) confirmed that both outcome and process dimensions influence customers' evaluation of service quality. In addition, common patterns of responses from the focus group interviews revealed 10 general evaluative criteria that customers might use, regardless of the type of service sector. These criteria, while consistent with the service constructs mentioned earlier, are more specific and, as a group, constitute a more comprehensive set of service quality dimensions. Listed below are the 10 dimensions, their definitions, and illustrative questions pertaining to them based on responses from the focus group participants.

- **Tangibles:** Appearance of physical facilities, equipment, personnel, and communication materials. Do the tools used by the repairperson look modern? Does the equipment seem modern and effective? Are personnel dressed neatly and appropriately?
- **Reliability:** Ability to perform the promised service dependably and accurately. Does my stockbroker follow my exact instructions to buy or to sell? Is the service performed right the first time? At the right time?
- **Responsiveness:** Willingness to help customers and provide prompt service. Is my banker willing to answer my questions? When there is a problem with my bank statement, does the bank resolve the problem quickly? How quickly are my calls returned and my questions answered?
- **Competence:** Possession of the required skills and knowledge to perform the service. When I call my credit card company, is the person at the other end able to answer my questions? Does the repairperson appear to know what he or she is doing?
- **Courtesy:** Politeness, respect, consideration, and friendliness of contact personnel. Does the bank teller have a pleasant demeanor? Does my broker refrain from acting busy or being rude when I ask questions?
- **Credibility:** Trustworthiness, believability, and honesty. Does my bank have a good reputation? Does the repair firm guarantee its services?
- **Security:** Freedom from danger, risk, or doubt. Is it safe for me to use the bank's automatic teller machines? How confidential are my financial transactions with the company?
- **Access:** Approachability and ease of contact. How easy is it for me to get through to my broker over the telephone? Does the credit card company have a 24-hour, toll-free telephone number?
- **Communication:** Keeping customers informed in language they can understand and listening to them. Does my broker avoid using technical jargon? Does the repair firm call when they are unable to keep a scheduled repair appointment?

- **Understading the customer:** Making the effort to know customers and their needs. Does someone in my bank recognize me as a regular customer? Is the credit limit set by my credit card company consistent with what I can afford (i.e., neither too high nor too low)?

The definitions and illustrations of the 10 dimensions suggested that some of them may be interrelated. PZB (1985) acknowledged the possibility of overlapping dimensions and noted that measurement of overlap across the 10 criteria, as well as determination of whether some can be combined, would be examined empirically.

After the empirical analysis – which produced SERVQUAL, a five-dimensional service quality instrument described in a later section – three of the original ten dimensions remained intact in the final set of five dimensions. These three dimensions were tangibles, reliability, and responsiveness. The remaining seven original dimensions clustered into two broader dimensions. Based on the content of the items falling under these two dimensions, PZB labeled them *assurance* and *empathy*. Definitions of the final set of five dimensions, including the two new dimensions, are as follows:

- **Assurance:** Knowledge and courtesy of employees and their ability to inspire trust and confidence.
- **Empathy:** Caring, individualized attention the firm provides its customers.
- **Reliability:** Ability to perform the promised service dependably and accurately.
- **Responsiveness:** Willingness to help customers and provide prompt service.
- **Tangibles:** Appearance of physical facilities, equipment, personnel, and communication materials.

Assurance is basically a combination of the original dimensions of competence, courtesy, credibility, and security. Empathy represents the remaining dimensions of access, communication, and understanding the customer. Thus, although the final set contains only five dimensions, they capture the essence of all the original ten.

Comparison with Product Quality

The concept of perceived quality (covering both services and products) has been broadly defined as 'superiority or excellence' (Zeithaml, 1988). Consistent with what has been described about service quality, perceived quality is different from objective or actual quality, a higher-level abstraction rather than a specific attribute of a product, a global assessment that in some cases resembles attitude, and a judgment made within a consumer's evoked set (Zeithaml, 1988: 3). The literature on product quality, while wide-ranging and prolific, has not produced a consensus on the dimensions although some work has attempted to do so. Bonner and Nelson (1985), for example, found that sensory signals such as rich/full flavor, natural taste, fresh taste, good aroma, and appetizing looks were relevant across 33 food product categories. Brucks, Zeithaml and Naylor (2000) contend, on the basis of both exploratory and empirical work, that six abstract dimensions (ease of use, functionality, performance, durability, serviceability, and prestige) can be generalized across categories of durable goods. Garvin (1983) proposed, but did not empirically validate, eight dimensions of quality: performance, features, reliability, conformance, durability, serviceability, aesthetics, and image.

Besides the lack of consensus in the dimensions in product quality, researchers have also tended not to emphasize the comparison between expectations and perceptions when conceptualizing and operationalizing product quality. While customers are likely to have expectations for products just as they do for services, this point is not explicitly made or tested in existing research.

Contribution of Service Quality to Customer Loyalty and Profitability

Behavioral Consequences of Service Quality

Published research offers evidence that positive service-quality perceptions affect customer intentions to behave in positive ways – praising the firm, preferring the company over others, increasing the volume of purchases, or agreeing to pay a price premium. Most of the early research operationalized behavioral intentions in a uni-dimensional way, rather than delineating specific types of behavioral intentions. Woodside, Frey & Daly (1989), for example, found a significant association between overall patient satisfaction and intent to choose a hospital again. Cronin & Taylor (1992), using a single-item purchase-intention scale, found a positive correlation with service quality and customer satisfaction.

Several academic studies have examined the association between service quality and more specific behavioral intentions. In a series of studies (see Parasuraman, Berry & Zeithaml (PBZ), 1991b; PZB, 1988, 1994b) researchers found a positive and significant relationship between customers' perceptions of service quality and their willingness to recommend the company. Boulding and colleagues (1993) found a positive correlation between service quality and a two-item measure of repurchase intentions and willingness to recommend. In a second study involving university students, they found strong links between service quality and other behavioral intentions that are of strategic importance to a university, including saying positive things about the school, planning to contribute money to the class pledge upon graduation, and planning to recommend the school to employers as a place from which to recruit (Boulding et al., 1992).

Zeithaml, Berry, & Parasuraman (ZBP) (1996) empirically examined the quality–intentions link using a behavioral intentions battery with four dimensions – loyalty, propensity to switch, willingness to pay more, and external response to service problems – comprised of 14 specific behavioral intentions likely to result from perceived service quality. The dimensions and the battery were significantly correlated with customer perceptions of service quality.

Individual companies have also monitored the impact of service quality on selected behavioral intentions. Toyota found that intent to repurchase a Toyota automobile increased from a base of 37% to 45% with a positive sales experience, from 37% to 79% with a positive service experience, and from 37% to 91% with both positive sales and service experiences (McLaughlin, 1993). A similar study by Gale (1992) quantitatively assessed the relationship between the level of service quality and willingness to purchase at AT&T. Of AT&T's customers who rated the company's overall quality as excellent, over 90% expressed willingness to purchase from AT&T again. For customers rating the service as good, fair, or poor, the percentages decreased to 60%, 17% and 0% respectively. According to these data, willingness to repurchase increased at a steeper rate (i.e., by 43%) as the service-quality rating improved from fair to good, than when it went from poor to fair (17%) or from good to excellent (30%). These results suggest that the impact of service quality on willingness to repurchase is most pronounced in some intermediate level of service quality.

Service Quality and Profitability

For the first decade of quality improvement, expenditures on quality were not explicitly linked to profit implications (Aaker & Jacobson, 1994), largely because the evidence was not readily available. Because cost and cost savings due to quality were more accessible, they were the main financial variables considered. The relationship between service and profits took time to verify, part of the delay due to the unfounded expectation that the connection was simple and direct. Investments in service quality, however, do not track directly to profits for a variety of reasons. First, in much the same way as advertising, service-quality benefits are rarely experienced in the short term and, instead, accumulate over time, making them less amenable to detection using traditional research approaches. Second, many variables other than service improvements (such as pricing, distribution, competition, and advertising) influence company profits, leading the individual contribution of service to be difficult to isolate. Third, mere expenditures on service are not what lead to profits; instead spending on the right variables and proper execution are responsible.

The Direct Relationship between Service Quality and Profitability

At the aggregate level, a growing body of evidence is emerging about the relationship between service quality and profitability. Managerially, this research stream began when firms sought documentation that their investments in service quality, and in total quality management (TQM) in general, were paying off. Because individual firms found it difficult to substantiate the impact of their investments, they turned for insight to a group of early studies conducted by management consulting firms that explored effects across a broad sample of firms. The news was not encouraging. McKinsey and Co. found that nearly two-thirds of quality programs examined had either stalled or fallen short of delivering real improvements (Matthews & Katel, 1992). In two other studies, A.T. Kearney found that 80% of British firms reported no significant impact as a result of TQM, and Arthur D. Little claimed that almost two-thirds of 500 US companies saw 'zero competitive gain' from TQM (*The Economist*, 1992).

Partially in response to early versions of these studies, in 1991 the US General Accounting Office sought grounds for belief of the financial impact of quality in companies that had been finalists or winners of the Malcolm Baldrige National Quality Award. While an anecdotal rather than a rigorous study, the GAO found that these elite quality firms had benefited in terms of market share, sales per employee, return on sales and return on assets. Based on responses from 22 companies who won or were finalists in 1988 and 1989, the GAO found that 34 of 40 financial variables measured in the years the companies won or were finalists for the award showed positive performance improvements, while only 6 measurements were negative or neutral (US General Accounting Office, 1991).

More rigorous academic studies soon followed in the early 1990s, documenting both negative and positive relationships. Studies showing negative or no effects were typically not focused solely on service quality, but examined TQM in general. Easton (1993), for example, showed that departmental self interest and turf battles led to lack of effectiveness in TQM programs in both product and service companies. Bounds et al. (1994) and Reger et al. (1994) identified implementation problems that interfered with quality's impact on business performance. Sterman et al. (1997) found that a variety of quality strategies failed to deliver anticipated business performance improvements in many companies. Ittner & Larcker (1996) found that only 29% of executive respondents could link quality to accounting returns such as return on assets, and only 12% could link their TQM initiatives to stock price returns or the creation of economic value for shareholders.

Evidence from research also uncovered positive associations. Rust et al. (1992) documented the favorable financial impact of complaint recovery systems. Nelson et al. (1992) found a significant and positive relationship between patient satisfaction and hospital profitability. In their study, specific dimensions of hospital service quality, such as billing and discharge processes, explained 17–27% of the variance in financial measures such as hospital earnings, net revenues, and return on assets. Extending the definition of financial performance to include stock returns, Aaker & Jacobsen (1994) found a significant positive relationship between stock return and changes in quality perceptions, while controlling for the effects of advertising expenditures, salience, and ROI. In their study, the explanatory power of the quality measure was comparable to that of ROI, which was viewed as strong corroboration of the connection between perceived quality and business performance.

Indications from companies large enough to have multiple outlets also suggested a positive quality–profitability relationship. For example, the Hospital Corporation of America found a strong link between perceived quality of patient care and profitability across its many hospitals (Koska, 1990). The Ford Motor Company also demonstrated that dealers with high service-quality scores have higher-than-normal profit, return on investment, and profit per new vehicle sold (Ford Motor Company, 1990).

Ittner & Larcker (1996) correlated the 1994 American Customer Satisfaction Index results of 130 publicly traded firms with available accounting and stock price data, and documented a positive correlation between customer variables (satisfaction, repurchase intention, perceived quality, perceived value, and loyalty) with financial measures (return on assets, market-to-book ratio, and price-earnings ratio). Quality improvement has also been linked in other studies to stock price shifts (Aaker & Jacobson, 1994), the market value of the firm (Hendricks & Singhal, 1997), and overall corporate performance (Easton & Jarrell, 1998).

One stream of research, based largely in the operations and management literatures, has investigated the impact of service programs and managerial approaches within an organization on dependent measures, some of them profitability measures. For example, Fitzerald & Erdman (1992) estimated the impact of continuous improvement on profits in 280 automotive suppliers, and found a 17% increase in profits over a two- to three-year period. Mann & Kehoe (1994) revealed that delegated teams were particularly effective at improving people aspects of quality (e.g., employee motivation, satisfaction, and performance) and that statistical process control was most effective in improving processes in TQM programs. Ittner & Larcker (1997) explored the cross-sectional association between process management techniques and profit measures (return on sales and return on assets), and found that long-term partnerships with suppliers and customers are associated with higher performance. Furthermore, they found that other techniques (e.g., statistical process control, process capability studies, and cycle time analysis) vary by industry and are not universally related to the performance measures. A marketing study in this stream was conducted by Hauser et al. (1994), who demonstrated analytically the financial implications of using customer satisfaction in employee incentive systems.

Rust, Zahorik & Keiningham (1995) provided the most comprehensive framework for examining the impact of service quality improvements on profits. Called the return on quality (ROQ) approach, their framework is based on the following assumptions: (1) quality is an investment; (2) quality efforts must be financially accountable; (3) it is possible to spend too much on quality; and (4) not all quality expenditures are equally valid.

The framework is unique in that it begins with the key drivers of service and extends all the way to profits, showing that the behavioral impact stemming from service quality leads to improved profitability and other financial outcomes. The approach begins by gauging a service improvement effort that produces an increased level of customer satisfaction at the process or attribute level (e.g., Bolton & Drew, 1991a, 1991b; Rust et al., 1998; Simester et al., 1998). Increased customer satisfaction at the process or attribute level then leads to increased overall customer satisfaction or perceived service quality (Kordupleski et al., 1993; Rust et al., 1994, 1995). Overall satisfaction leads to behavioral impact, including repurchase or customer retention, positive word-of-mouth and increased usage. Behavioral impact then leads to improved profitability and other financial outcomes. The methodology allows for the tracking of these impacts throughout the entire chain, providing a measure of the effect of individual changes in service quality investments in overall profitability.

The ROQ approach is informative because it can help distinguish among all the company strategies, processes, approaches, and tactics that can be altered. In this way, it can be applied in companies to direct their individual strategies. Huge progress can be made in this area using the ROQ framework because it provides a solid structure for guiding practice and research.

Offensive Effects of Service Quality on Profits

Fornell & Wernerfelt (1987, 1988) have defined 'offensive effects' as the impact of service on obtaining new customers. Only a small set of studies exists on offensive effects, usually involving the relationship between service quality and the antecedents of profitability such as market share, firm reputation, and the ability to command a price premium. Virtually all of these studies are at the aggregate level, examining a cross-section of firms. Seminal studies using the PIMS (Profit Impact of Market Strategy) database uncovered significant associations among service quality, marketing variables, and profitability. Findings from these studies showed that companies offering superior service achieve higher-than-normal market share growth (Buzzell & Gale, 1987) and that the mechanisms by which service quality increased profits included higher market share and premium prices (Phillips et al., 1983). In one study, Gale (1992) found that businesses in the top quintile of relative service quality on average realize an 8% higher price than their competitors. One of the major criticisms leveled at PIMS research, and one with high relevance to linking service quality and profits, is that in PIMS perceived service quality is reported from the firm's perspective rather than the customer's. While we can therefore connect the firm's perception of the customer's perception of service quality and profits, this is not the relationship between customer perceived quality and profits. Difficulties in data collection, specifically connecting customer data with firm data, impede these research efforts.

Kordupleski, Rust & Zahorik (1993) conceptually delineated the path between quality and market share, claiming that satisfied customers spread positive word-of-mouth messages, which lead to the attraction of new customers and then to higher market share. They claim that advertising without sufficient quality to back up the communications will not increase market share. Further, they contend that there are time lags in market share effects, making the relationship between quality and market share difficult to discern in the short term.

Defensive Effects of Service Quality and the Service Profit Chain

Anecdotes about the superior financial value of existing customers over new customers are ubiquitous. Two of the most frequently espoused are that it costs five times as much to obtain a new customer as to keep an existing one, and that selling costs for existing customers are much lower (on average 20% lower) than selling to new ones (Peters, 1988). When it comes to keeping the customers a firm already has, an approach called 'defensive marketing' (Fornell & Wernerfelt, 1987, 1988), researchers and consulting firms have in the past 10 years documented and quantified the financial impact of existing customers. Among their findings are that numerous intervening variables can be isolated, calibrated, and measured within companies. In this section, we discuss the evidence published to date on the aspects of defensive marketing that have been studied.

Research shows linkages between customer retention and profits through the identified intervening factors of cost, increased purchases, price premium, and word-of-mouth communication. These four intermediate factors were identified by Reichheld and Sasser (1990) and others (Rose, 1990; Dawkins & Reichheld, 1990) who focused their attention on the association between customer retention and profits. Heskett et al. (1997) have conceptualized their research as the 'service–profit chain.' They argue that the longer customers stay with companies, the lower the costs to serve them, the higher the volume of purchases they make, the higher the price premium they tolerate, and the greater the positive word-of-mouth communication they engage in. They have provided evidence from multiple companies such as Sears, Intuit, and Taco Bell to document these relationships (Heskett et al., 1997). Customer loyalty can produce profit increases from 25% to 85% (Reichheld & Sasser, 1990).

Perhaps the strongest demonstration of the service–profit chain has been in Sears. The year 1992 was the worst in the history of Sears, with a net loss of $3.9 billion on sales of $52.3 billion. Between 1993 and 1998, however, Sears transformed itself into a company built around its customers by developing a model called the 3Cs and 3Ps. The 3Cs were known as the three 'compellings': make Sears into a 'compelling place to work, shop and invest.' The 3Ps were the company's three shared values – 'passion for the customer, our people add value, and performance leadership.' Using an ongoing process of data collection and analysis, the company created a set of Total Performance Indicators, or TPI – measures that showed how well it was doing with customers, employees, and investors. The company developed sets of specific objectives and measures to capture the 3Cs so that the company could be managed according to them. These objectives included customer loyalty and excellent service. Believing that these objectives could be obtained only if employees were committed and involved, parallel goals and measures were established for that group of internal customers. Sears' management spent a great deal of time and effort in communication and education for store-level personnel about their value and the worth of the customer. In 1998, the company declared the model successful:

> [I]n the course of the last 12 months, employee satisfaction on the Sears TPI has risen by almost 4% and customer satisfaction by 4% ... if our model is correct – and its predictive record is extremely good – that 4% improvement in customer satisfaction translates into more than $200 million in additional revenues in the past 12 months. (Ricci et al., 1998: 97)

The Impact of Selecting Profitable Customers

Most published research on the connection between service quality and profitability has reported relationships in the aggregate rather than by segments or individual customers. This is understandable, for most service quality efforts in the past treated all customers alike, usually attempting to deliver high quality to all customers. Lately, however, both managers and scholars have come to believe that all customers are not alike. Viewing and serving all customers the same is a key reason why the tie between service quality and profitability has been elusive.

In recent years, both scholars and managers have discussed the need to distinguish among levels or tiers of customers in providing service (Zeithaml et al., 2001). Companies have successfully tiered customers by usage (often undertaking frequent-flyer or buyer programs) in industries such as airlines, hotels, and rental car companies. Where heavy usage runs parallel to profitability, these programs are effective. However, many companies and industries are challenging that notion, discovering that heavy users require both high servicing and deep discounting, leading them to be less profitable than other categories of customers.

Reichheld (1993) showed that building a high-loyalty customer base of the right customers increased profits. At MBNA, a 5% increase in retention of the right customers grew the company profits 60% by the fifth year. In a later work, Reichheld (1996b) stated that companies must concentrate their efforts on that subset of customers to whom they can deliver consistently superior value. He suggests that companies isolate their 'core customers' by asking (1) which customers are the most profitable and loyal, require less service and seem to prefer stable, long-term relationships, (2) which customers place the greatest value on what you offer, and (3) which customers are worth more to you than to your competitors?

Heskett et al. (1997) call this 'potential-based marketing,' combining measures of loyalty with data describing potential levels of usage. Companies then attempt to increase shares of purchases by customers who either have the greatest need for the services or show the greatest loyalty to a single provider. By lengthening relationships with the loyal customers, increasing sales with existing customers, and increasing the profitability on each sale opportunity, they thereby increase the potential of each customer. Few rigorous academic studies have yet been published documenting the moderating effect of tiers of customers on profits. While both Reichheld (1996a) and Blattberg & Deighton (1996) have offered arguments, heuristics, and methodologies for determining segment profitability, these methods need to be applied and their results disseminated to affirm these concepts. In one of the few academic studies conducted to demonstrate the importance of focusing on profitability with individual customers, Grant & Schlesinger (1995) estimated the full profit potential across tiers of customers. Using a Canadian grocery store context, they calculated the impact of expanding the customer base by 2% with primary shoppers: a profitability increase of more than 45%. Converting only 200 of the company's existing secondary customers into primary customers would increase profits by 20%.

Improving Service Quality

The evidence presented in the preceding sections demonstrates that delivering superior service to the right customer segments offers a wide variety of benefits that ultimately add to the bottom line. However, enhancing service quality from inferior or mediocre to superior is a major challenge for many organizations. One conceptual framework that offers a starting point for tackling this challenge is the 'gaps model' of service quality, discussed below.

The Gaps Model of Service Quality

As discussed earlier, service quality, from the perspective of customers, can be formally defined as the gap between customers' service expectations and perceptions (PZB, 1985). Closing this customer gap – delivering quality service – is a complex undertaking involving many different organizational and employee skills and tasks (ZBP, 1988). Executives of services organizations have long been confused about how to approach this complicated topic in an organized manner. PZB (1985) developed one approach to viewing the delivery of service quality in a structured and integrated way, and called it the 'gaps model' of service quality.

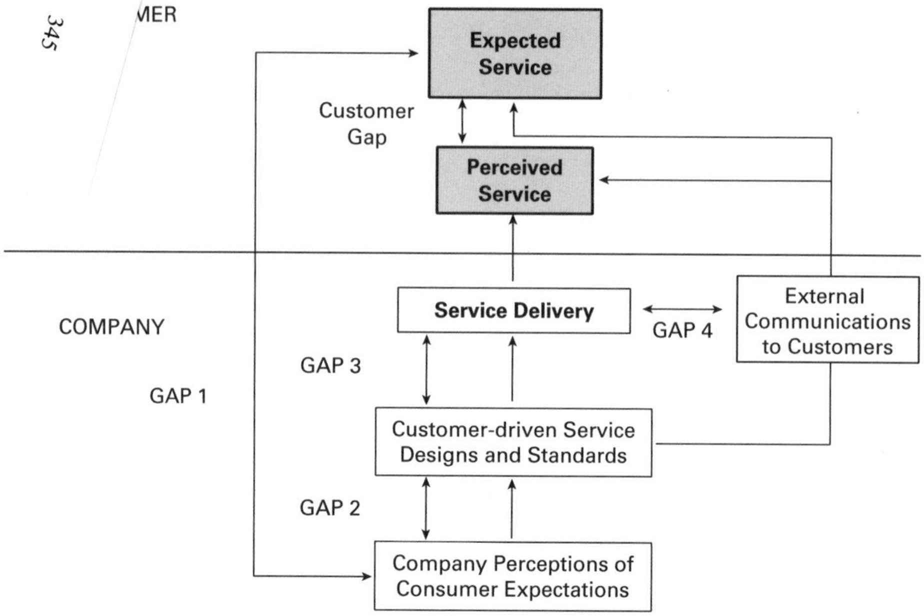

Figure 14.1 *Gaps Model of Service Quality*

The gaps model positions the key concepts, strategies, and decisions in delivering quality service in a manner that begins with the customer, and builds the organization's tasks around what is needed to close the gap between customer expectations and perceptions. The integrated gaps model of service quality is shown in Figure 14.1.

The figure shows that the central focus (top half) of the gaps model is the customer gap. To close this all-important customer gap, the model suggests that four other gaps – the provider gaps – need to be closed. The following four provider gaps, shown under the horizontal line in Figure 14.1, are the underlying causes behind the customer gap:

Gap 1: Not knowing what customers expect
Gap 2: Not selecting the right service designs and standards
Gap 3: Not delivering to service standards
Gap 4: Not matching performance to promises

Provider Gap 1: Not Knowing What Customers Expect

Provider Gap 1 is the difference between customer expectations of service and company, particularly management, understanding of those expectations. Many reasons exist for managers not being aware of what customers expect: they may not interact directly with customers, be unwilling to ask about expectations, or be unprepared to address them. Further, because there are few clearly defined and tangible cues for services, the gap between what consumers expect and what managers think they expect may be considerably larger than it is in firms that produce tangible goods (Gronroos, 1982; Webster, 1992). When people with the authority and responsibility for setting priorities do not fully understand customers' service expectations, they may trigger a chain of bad decisions and sub-optimal resource allocations that result in perceptions of poor service quality.

A number of factors have been shown to be responsible for Provider Gap 1, key among them an inadequate marketing research orientation. Evidence indicates that service firms lag behind goods firms in their use of marketing research and in other facets of customer orientation. Because marketing research is a key vehicle for understanding consumer expectations and perceptions of services, the size of Gap 1 depends greatly on the amount of marketing research conducted (ZBP, 1988). A second key factor is lack of upward communication. Front-line employees often know a great deal about customers (Schneider & Bowen, 1985), but if management is not in contact with front-line employees and does not understand what they know, the gap widens. A third factor involves the lack of company strategies to retain customers and strengthen relationships with them (Berry, 1983; Gwinner et al., 1998). A fourth factor is service recovery – understanding why people complain, what they expect when they complain, and how to develop effective strategies for dealing with inevitable service failures (Tax & Brown, 1998).

Provider Gap 2: Not Having the Right Service Quality Designs and Standards

A recurring theme in service companies is the difficulty experienced in translating customers' expectations into service-quality specifications. These problems are reflected in Provider Gap 2, the difference between company understanding of customer expectations and the development of customer-driven service designs and standards. Customer-driven standards differ from the conventional performance standards that most service companies establish, in that they are based on pivotal customer requirements that are visible to and measured by customers (Zeithaml & Bitner, 2000). They are operations standards set to correspond to customer expectations and priorities rather than to company concerns such as productivity or efficiency. Standards signal to contact personnel what management priorities are and which types of performance really count. When service standards are absent or when the standards in place do not reflect customers' expectations, quality of service as perceived by customers is likely to suffer (Levitt, 1976).

Because services are intangible, they are difficult to describe and communicate: a particular problem when new services are being developed. When all the people involved (managers, front-line employees, and behind-the-scenes support staff) are not working with the same concepts of the new service, based on customer needs and expectations, service design will likely be poor (Shostack, 1992). For a service that already exists, any attempt to improve it will also suffer unless everyone has the same vision of the service, else the result will be oversimplification, incompleteness, subjectivity, and bias (Shostack, 1992).

Provider Gap 3: Not Delivering to Service Standards

Provider Gap 3 is the discrepancy between the development of customer-driven service standards and actual service performance by company employees. Even when guidelines exist for performing services well and treating customers correctly, high quality service performance is not a certainty. Standards must be backed by appropriate resources (people, systems, and technology) and also must be enforced to be effective – that is, employees must be measured and compensated on the basis of performance along those standards (ZBP, 1988). Thus, even when standards accurately reflect customers' expectations, if the company fails to provide support for them – if it does not facilitate, encourage, and require their achievement – standards do no good. When the level of service-delivery performance falls short of the standards, it misses what customers expect as well. Narrowing Gap 3, by ensuring that all the resources needed to achieve the standards are in place, reduces the customer gap.

Research and company experience has identified many of the critical inhibitors to closing Gap 3 (Schneider & Bowen, 1993). These include employees who not clearly understand the role they are to play in the company (Katz & Kahn, 1978; Walker et al., 1977), employees who feel in conflict between customers and company management (Rizzo et al., 1970), the wrong employees (Bettencourt & Gwinner, 1996; Schneider & Schechter, 1991), inadequate technology, inappropriate compensation and recognition (Ouchi & McGuire, 1975), and lack of empowerment and teamwork (Bowen & Lawler, 1992). These factors all relate to the company's human resource function, involving internal practices such as recruitment, training, feedback, job design, motivation, and organizational structure.

Other issues creating problems involve the challenge in delivering service through such intermediaries as retailers, franchisees, agents, and brokers (Bongiorno, 1993). Most service (and many manufacturing) companies face formidable problems in attaining service excellence and consistency in the presence of intermediaries who represent them, interact with their customers, and yet who are not under their direct control (Serwer, 1995). Even if contact employees and intermediaries are 100% consistent in their service delivery, the customer can introduce heterogeneity into service delivery (Grove & Fisk, 1997). If customers do not perform their roles appropriately – if, for example, they fail to provide all the information necessary to the provider, or neglect to read and follow instructions – service quality is jeopardized (Kelley et al., 1992).

A final issue in Gap 3 is the need in service firms to synchronize demand and capacity; because services are perishable and cannot be inventoried, service companies frequently face situations of overdemand or underdemand.

Provider Gap 4: When Promises Do Not Match Performance

Provider Gap 4 is the difference between service delivery and the service provider's external communications. Promises made by a service company through its media advertising, sales force, and other communications may potentially raise customer expectations that serve as the standard against which customers assess service quality (ZBP, 1988). The discrepancy between actual and promised service therefore has an adverse effect on the customer gap. Broken promises can occur for many reasons: overpromising in advertising or personal selling, inadequate coordination between operations and marketing, and differences in policies and procedures across service outlets (George & Berry, 1981). In addition to unduly elevating expectations through exaggerated claims, there are other, less obvious ways in which external communications influence customers' service-quality assessments. Service companies frequently fail to capitalize on opportunities to educate customers to use services appropriately (Legg & Baker, 1991). They also frequently fail to manage customer expectations of what they will receive in service transactions and relationships.

Strategies for Closing the Gaps

Closing Gap 1: Determining What Customers Expect

To close Gap l, companies must use multiple research approaches among different customer groups to ensure that they are hearing what customers expect. Berry & Parasuraman (1997) argue that companies need to establish ongoing listening systems to capture, organize, and disseminate service-quality information to support decision making. Among the necessary research approaches that extend beyond those used with goods are transactional surveys, service reviews, and mystery shopping, which deal with the performance of service employees and effectiveness of service encounters. One research technique that has been found particularly useful in identifying service performance issues is the critical incident technique (Bitner, 1990), which asks customers to recall their positive and negative service experiences and then elaborate on what made them effective or ineffective. Traditional techniques such as focus-group interviews; new, declining and lost-customer surveys; and surveys are also part of an effective ongoing listening system.

A good listening system should incorporate approaches to address all the reasons for Gap 1 cited above. It could, for example, continuously solicit employee input through employee satisfaction surveys that would allow for upward communication, use traditional approaches to identify market segments, encourage management–customer interaction to allow managers to understand what front-line employees know, focus on understanding customer relationships, and identify the failures that require service recovery.

Customer relationship management, commonly called CRM, has become an increasingly common and pivotal strategy for closing Gap l. This approach, previously termed relationship management or relationship marketing, has long been used in industrial, commercial and professional settings where individual clients were significant contributors to company revenues and profitability. However, database marketing and Internet technologies now allow companies to interact with individual customers in a customized manner. The more a company can understand the individual needs of a customer, the more the first gap will be closed.

Closing Gap 2: Developing Customer-driven Standards and Designs

To close Gap 2, service providers must match customer expectations to new-service innovations and actual service process designs. Research shows that adaptations of the new-product design process can make service offerings more explicit and avoid failures (Zeithaml & Bitner, 2000). Service blueprinting is a particularly useful technique in the new-service development process (Kingman-Brundage, 1991; Shostack, 1992). The purpose of a blueprint is to make a complex and intangible service concrete through its visual depiction of all of the steps, actors, processes, and physical evidence of the service (Bitner, 1993). The key feature of service blueprints is their focus on the customer – the customer's experience is documented before any of the internal processes are determined. Quality function deployment (QFD) is another tool for linking customer requirements to internal elements of service design (Fitzsimmons & Fitzsimmons, 1997).

The other key strategy essential for closing Gap 2 is establishing customer-driven service standards, which can either take the form of operational (hard) or perceptual (soft) standards. Zeithaml & Bitner (2000) recommend a nine-step process for developing these standards: (1) identify the existing or desired service encounter sequence; (2) translate customer expectations into behaviors and actions for each service encounter; (3) select behaviors and actions for standards; (4) decide whether hard or soft standards are appropriate; (5) develop feedback mechanisms for measurement to standards; (6) establish measures and target levels; (7) track measures against standards; (8) provide feedback about performance to employees; and (9) periodically update target levels and measures. Successful development of customer-driven standards is discussed in Levitt (1976), Camp (1989), Ehrenfeld (1991), and Carroll (1992).

Closing Gap 3: Improving Service Performance

Because most services are delivered by people to people in real time, closing the service performance gap is heavily dependent on human resource strategies. Research shows that employee and customer satisfaction are positively correlated (Schlesinger & Heskett, 1991), as are climate for service, climate for employee well-being and customer perceptions of service quality (Schneider & Bowen, 1993). Considerable research has been conducted on strategies for integrating appropriate human resource practices into service firms. Among these strategies are: addressing role ambiguity and role conflict (Hartline & Ferrell, 1996; Singh et al., 1994), optimizing employee-technology-job fit (Berry & Parasuraman, 1991; Fisher, 1998; Schneider & Schechter, 1991), training (Normann, 1984), developing appropriate evaluation and compensation systems (Chung & Schneider, 1999), empowerment (Bowen & Lawler, 1992), teamwork (Dickson, 1994), and developing a service culture (Schneider & Bowen, 1995). These strategies are aimed at allowing employees to be effective in satisfying customers as well as efficient and productive in their jobs. Strategies designed to manage the customer in Gap 3 have also been proposed and studied. Zeithaml & Bitner (2000) organized these into three approaches: defining customer jobs (Winslow, 1992), managing the customer mix (Martin & Pranter, 1989), and recruiting, educating and rewarding customers (e.g., Bowen, 1986; Goodwin, 1988).

Service intermediaries perform many important functions for the service principal – co-producing the service, making services locally available, and functioning as the bond between the principal and the customer. In contrast to channels for products, channels for services are almost always direct, if not to the customer then to the intermediary that sells to the customer. In the process of service distribution, considerable conflict occurs – conflict over objectives and performance, costs and rewards, controlling quality and consistency across outlets, tension between empowerment and control and channel ambiguity. To solve these problems, the following strategies have been successfully pursued: control strategies, including measurement and review; empowerment strategies, including helping the intermediary develop customer-oriented service processes; providing needed support systems, including developing intermediaries to deliver service quality and changing to a cooperative management structure; and partnering strategies, including alignment of goals and consultation and cooperation.

Strategies to manage demand and capacity depend upon which of four scenarios – excess demand, demand exceeds optimum capacity, demand and supply are balanced, and excess capacity – exist (Lovelock, 1994). To shift demand to match capacity, approaches include varying the service offering, communicating with customers, modifying timing and location of service delivery, and differentiating on price (Clemmer & Schneider, 1989). To flex capacity to meet demand, approaches include stretching existing capacity (time, labor, facilities or equipment), aligning capacity with demand fluctuations (using part-time employees, rental or sharing of facilities or equipment, scheduling downtime during periods of low demand, and cross-training employees) (Lovelock, 1992). Yield management is another approach that balances capacity utilization, pricing, market segmentation and financial return (Desiraji & Shugan, 1999). Finally, when demand and capacity cannot be aligned, waiting line strategies can be effective, and involve employing operational logic (Fitzsimmons & Fitzsimmons, 1997), establishing a reservation process, differentiating waiting customers (Fitzsimmons & Fitzsimmons, 1997), and making waiting tolerable (Hui & Tse, 1996; Taylor, 1995).

Closing Gap 4: Managing Service Promises

One of the most important strategies in managing service promises involves aligning all of the company's individual external and internal messages so that integrated marketing communication (IMC) is achieved. This is more difficult to attain in services than in goods because many of the most important communication exchanges are between employees, customers, and management. Therefore, companies have more to manage in service communication than in goods communication. External marketing communication – messages from the company direct to customers – must be managed in both goods and services, but two other types of communication must be aligned with services. First, interactive marketing communication – messages employees give to customers – must be managed and must be consistent with the messages the company sends through advertising, public relations, the Internet and other channels (Bell & Leavitt, 1998). Second, internal marketing communication – messages from the company to employees – must be carefully coordinated so that employees know what is being promised in external communications.

Among the issues associated with achieving IMC are managing service promises (George & Berry, 1981; Legg & Baker, 1991), managing internal marketing communications, improving customer education, and managing customer expectations (Clemmer & Schneider, 1993; PBZ, 1991a).

Measuring Service Quality

A sound measure of service quality is necessary for identifying the attributes needing performance improvement, ascertaining how much improvement is needed on each attribute, and assessing the impact of improvement efforts. Unlike goods quality, which can be measured objectively by such indicators as durability and number of defects (Crosby, 1979; Garvin, 1983), service quality is an abstract and elusive construct because of three features unique to services: intangibility, heterogeneity, and inseparability of production and consumption (PZB, 1985). In the absence of objective measures, one has to rely on survey-based measures. One of the first such measures is the five-dimensional SERVQUAL scale mentioned before, developed by PZB (1988).

The original SERVQUAL scale involves a two-part survey containing 22 service attributes, grouped into the five general service quality dimensions of reliability, responsiveness, assurance, empathy and tangibles. The survey asks customers to provide two different ratings on each attribute – one reflecting the level of service they would expect from excellent companies in a sector, and the other reflecting their perception of the service delivered by a specific company within that sector. The difference between the expectation and perception ratings constitutes a quantified measure of service quality. The first part of Appendix 1 describes the development, testing and refinement of the original SERVQUAL instrument. This instrument, in addition to spawning many commercial and academic studies focusing on service quality assessment, triggered a lively debate in the literature pertaining to questions about SERVQUAL's psychometric soundness and usefulness. The second part of Appendix 1 summarizes the key concerns and the debate surrounding them.

Potential Uses of SERVQUAL

The refined SERVQUAL scale (including instructions to respondents) is shown in Appendix 2. In addition to the expectations and perceptions sections, this appendix contains a 'point-allocation question' that was used to ascertain the relative importance of the five dimensions by asking respondents to allocate a total of 100 points among the dimensions. In one major study involving customers of five different companies (PBZ, 1991b), results from the point-allocation question were consistent across the five company samples: reliability always emerged as the most critical dimension (its average allocation was 32 points) and tangibles as the least critical dimension (its average allocation was 11 points). The average allocations for responsiveness, assurance, and empathy were 23, 19, and 17 points, respectively.

Data gathered through a questionnaire incorporating the three sections in Appendix 2 (after appropriate adaptations, if necessary) can be used for a variety of purposes, as outlined below (analytical and other details concerning these potential applications are available in ZPB, 1990: 175–80).

1. To determine the average gap score (between customers' perceptions and expectations) for each service attribute.
2. To assess a company's service quality along each of the five SERVQUAL dimensions.
3. To compute a company's overall *weighted* SERVQUAL score that takes into account not only the service quality gap on each dimension but also the relative importance of the dimension (as reflected by the number of points allocated to it).
4. To track customers' expectations and perceptions (on individual service attributes and/or on the SERVQUAL dimensions) over time.
5. To compare a company's SERVQUAL scores against those of competitors.
6. To identify and examine customer segments that differ significantly in their assessments of a company's service performance.
7. To assess *internal* service quality (i.e., the quality of service rendered by one department or division of a company to others within the same company).

Illustrative Applications of SERVQUAL

A series of published studies have used SERVQUAL and adaptations of it in a variety of contexts, e.g., real estate brokers (Johnson et al., 1988); physicians in private practice (Brown & Swartz, 1989); public recreation programs (Crompton & Mackay, 1989); a dental school patient clinic, a business school placement center, and a tire store (Carman, 1990); motor carrier companies (Brensinger & Lambert, 1990); an accounting firm (Bojanic, 1991); discount and department stores (Finn & Lamb, 1991; Teas, 1993); a gas and electric utility company (Babakus & Boller, 1992); hospitals (Babakus & Mangold, 1992; Carman, 1990); banking, pest control, dry cleaning, and fast food (Cronin & Taylor, 1992); higher education (Boulding et al., 1993; Ford et al., 1993). Some of these studies have been critical of the instrument and have raised concerns about its psychometric properties (details are in Part 2 of Appendix 1). On the other hand, commercial applications of SERVQUAL have demonstrated the instrument's utility.

SERVQUAL has been productively used in multiple contexts, cultures and countries for measuring service quality in commercial as well as public-sector organizations. The nature of and findings from virtually all of these applications are unpublished and/or proprietary. However, based on the authors' knowledge of some of these applications, and with appropriate disguise to protect their confidentiality, two are briefly described below to provide readers with a flavor for the use of SERVQUAL in real life contexts.

Consumer-Service Context

A large Australian bank used SERVQUAL to measure its quality of service as evaluated by several segments of individual customers. The three sections in Appendix 1 were incorporated virtually unchanged into the bank's mail-survey questionnaire. The bank analyzed the data to assess service quality deficiencies on individual attributes and on the five SERVQUAL dimensions, as well as to compute weighted gap scores. The bank also benchmarked its SERVQUAL scores against those of two similar banks in the US that had participated in studies conducted by PZB. While some differences between the results for the Australian and US banks were found on specific service attributes, there were striking similarities in the overall pattern of results. For instance, the relative importance of the five dimensions (as measured by the point-allocation question) were as follows:

	Points Allocated		
	Australian Bank	US Bank 1	US Bank 2
Tangibles	13	10	11
Reliability	28	31	32
Responsiveness	22	22	22
Assurance	19	20	19
Empathy	18	17	16

The Australian bank set up a measurement system to track service quality at regular intervals and to assess the impact of service improvement efforts.

Industrial-Product Context

The Ceramic Products Division of Corning, Inc., a large manufacturing company in the US, developed a systematic process for monitoring and improving its service quality as perceived by customer organizations to which it supplied its manufactured products. The SERVQUAL approach was an integral component of this process. Details about the development and implementation of the process are documented in Farley et al. (1990). Only an overview of the adaptation and application of SERVQUAL in the process is provided here.

Corning's Ceramic Products Division began its service-improvement process by focusing on its largest client, a multinational company. This division modified the SERVQUAL instrument for assessing its service quality as perceived by multiple levels within this company. Corning's survey was adapted from the one shown in Appendix 1 as follows: (1) the wording of some of the items was changed to be more customized to the Corning context; (2) the separate expectation and perception questions were combined into a single-scale question in which the upper end of the 7-point scale was anchored as 'world class,' thereby 'fixing' customers' expectations at a level of 7; and (3) customers' assessment of not only Corning but also its primary competitor relative to world class were obtained. Thus, although the adapted instrument assumed that the expectation level was the same for all service attributes and customers (i.e., a level of 7 representing world class) – perhaps a debatable assumption – it is more parsimonious by not repeating the battery of statements.

Individuals at various functional levels completed the survey. Analysis of the responses revealed seven service attributes on which Corning's performance was weak relative to world class. Corning further condensed this short-list of attributes to four 'vital few' attributes on which its performance was worse than that of its major competitor, then formed a corrective action team to identify and implement action plans to improve its service quality on the vital attributes.

The SERVQUAL survey was readministered a year later to assess the impact of the corrective actions. Results indicated significant improvements in most of the targeted attributes, and also identified additional areas for further corrective action. The success of using SERVQUAL in this pilot application prompted Corning to make this process an ongoing activity in the Ceramics Product Division, and to expand its implementation to other divisions and customer groups.

Corning's use of SERVQUAL touches on virtually all of the potential applications of the instrument listed earlier. It also illustrates the fact that SERVQUAL is a generic, skeletal instrument that can be adapted for use in a variety of contexts, including industrial-product and internal-service contexts.

Recent Enhancements to SERVQUAL

The core of the conceptual model of expectations developed by ZBP (1993) is that customers use two different comparison standards in assessing service quality:

Desired Service – the level of service representing a blend of what customers believe 'can be' and 'should be' provided

Adequate Service – the minimum level of service customers are willing to accept.

Separating these two levels is a **Zone of Tolerance** that represents the range of service performance a customer would consider satisfactory.

Because SERVQUAL's expectations component measures *normative* expectations, the construct represented by it reflects the *desired service* construct defined above. However, the existing SERVQUAL's structure did not capture the *adequate service* construct. Therefore, in a multi-sector study (PZB, 1994b), SERVQUAL was augmented and refined to capture not only the discrepancy between perceived service and desired service, labeled as *measure of service superiority* (or MSS), but also the discrepancy between perceived service and adequate service, labeled as *measure of service adequacy* (or MSA). This multi-sector study tested two alternative measurement approaches (involving difference-score and direct measures of MSS and MSA) and, at the same time, also addressed the various concerns raised about the SERVQUAL scale. The results suggested that the difference-score measure had acceptable psychometric properties and offered richer diagnostics than did the direct measure. Part 3 of Appendix 1 describes this study and discusses findings from it.

Electronic Service Quality

Considerable business evidence shows a widespread lack of adequate service quality delivered through the Internet. A study conducted by International Customer Service Association (ICSA) and e-Satisfy.com (2000) found that only 36% of e-customers are satisfied with their Internet purchasing experiences. Boston Consulting Group (2000) research shows that four out of five online purchasers have experienced one failed purchase, and 28% of all online purchases fail. These failures disappoint consumers and have a detrimental impact on the future of electronic retailers: 28% of customers frustrated by their e-commerce experience report that they will not shop online again, and 23% will not buy from the offending site again.

Measuring Electronic Service Quality

While commercial surveys of customer satisfaction with websites (e.g., BizRate.com surveys) have been in existence for several years, the published scholarly literature is limited. However, working papers have now begun to appear (Wolfinbarger & Gilly, 2001).

One example of these studies (Zeithaml, Parasuraman & Malhotra, 2000) deals specifically with how customers assess electronic service quality (e-SQ) and what the antecedents and consequences of e-SQ are. In that research, e-SQ is defined as the extent to which a website facilitates efficient and effective shopping, purchasing and delivery. In exploratory research involving focus groups of experienced and inexperienced users, consumers reported that they used 11 dimensions to evaluate e-SQ. These included access, ease of navigation, efficiency, flexibility, reliability, personalization, security/privacy, responsiveness, assurance/trust, site aesthetics, and price knowledge. The empirical phase of the research involved the development of a scale to measure e-SQ, administration of the scale, then scale-reduction/refinement analyses (Parasuraman, Zeithaml & Malhotra, 2002). The analysis resulted in a core e-service quality scale with 22 items on four dimensions:

- **Efficiency:** the ease and speed of accessing and using the site
- **Fulfillment:** the extent to which the site's promises about order delivery and item availability are fulfilled
- **Reliability:** the correct technical functioning of the site
- **Privacy:** the degree to which the site is safe and protects customer information

The analysis also resulted in an e-recovery service quality scale consisting of 11 items on three dimensions.

- **Responsiveness:** handling of problems and returns through the site
- **Compensation:** the degree to which customers are compensated for problems
- **Contact:** the degree to which help can be accessed by telephone or online representatives

Equivalence of Dimensions and Perceptual Attributes for Service Quality and e-SQ

In comparing the dimensions of traditional service quality and e-SQ, we can make several observations. First, the dimensions of SERVQUAL and e-SERVQUAL are similar in some ways but different in others. Reliability and responsiveness are shared dimensions, but new Internet-specific dimensions appear to be critical in that context. Efficiency and fulfillment are core dimensions in e-SQ. Even though the attributes for fulfillment are similar to the attributes of reliability for the SERVQUAL scale, the dimensionality differs.

Second, as reported in Parasuraman, Zeithaml & Malhotra (2002), customers cannot report on the recovery dimensions unless they have experienced a problem or needed information beyond that presented on the site. The personal (i.e., friendly, empathetic, understanding) flavor of perceived service quality's empathy dimension is not required on the Internet, except to the extent it makes transactions more efficient or in non-routine situations.

Third, perceptual attributes related to the dimensions of perceived e-SQ and service quality differ, as might be expected, because the contexts differ. Compared to service quality, e-SQ seems to be a more cognitive evaluation than an emotional one. While emotions such as anger and frustration were expressed when reporting on problems arising from e-SQ, these appeared to be less intense than those associated with service quality experiences. Moreover, positive feelings of warmth or attachment that are engendered in service quality situations did not surface in the focus groups as being characteristics of e-SQ experiences.

Directions for Future Research

Consequences of Service Quality

The link between service quality and purchase intentions has been frequently researched and confirmed. However, the more compelling relationship between purchase intentions and *actual* purchase behavior lacks equal confirmation. It has long been known that customers do not always behave in ways they say they will; they tend in general to over-report their intentions to buy products and services. They are also not particularly good predictors of their own behavior. Therefore, an important relationship to contemplate and capture is between purchase intentions and purchase behavior. The relationship between customer purchase intentions and *initial* purchase behavior will be one of the most difficult to document, because to do so would mean matching data from customers before purchase (usually obtained anonymously) with post-purchase data.

Post-purchase data can be collected through warranty cards or other means, but to try to connect these data to pre-purchase intentions means having both customer identification and a mechanism to relate the two forms. One context where this connection might be observed is with electronic services for which surveys are disseminated before purchases are made. Using e-mail or other electronic coding, a company could query survey participants about the desirability of a given service, and then follow up to see if they purchase the services.

Other issues pertaining to the impact of service quality and worthy of further research include:

- *How does service compare in effectiveness to other retention strategies such as price?* Statistical analysis that allows us to examine the relative contribution of different marketing variables in retention needs to be conducted. To date no studies have incorporated all or most potential explanatory variables to examine their relative importance in keeping customers. A number of different methodologies could be appropriate for studying this question, including consumer questionnaires that examine the explained variance of customers' remaining with companies as a function of their assessments of companies' marketing mix. Many companies actually have survey data containing these variables but have either not analyzed the data for this purpose or have not reported their findings.
- *What aspects of service are most important for customer retention?* The only studies that have examined specific aspects of service and their impact on customer retention have been early studies looking at customer complaint management (Fornell & Wernerfelt, 1987, 1988). A decade ago this was appropriate as service was often equated with customer service, the after-sale function that dealt with dissatisfied customers. However, service is multi-faceted, consisting of a wide variety of customer-perceived dimensions including reliability, responsiveness, and empathy and resulting from innumerable company strategies such as technology and process improvement. In research exploring the relative importance of service dimensions on overall service quality or customer satisfaction, the bulk of the support confirms that reliability is most critical (Boulding et al., 1993; PZB, 1988; ZBP, 1996), but others have demonstrated the importance of customization (Fornell et al., 1996) and other factors. Because in many cases the dimensions and attributes are delivered with totally different internal strategies, resources must be allocated where they are most needed, and study on this topic could provide direction.
- *What are the relative impacts of traditional and electronic service quality on customers touched by both?* While research to date suggests similarities between traditional and electronic service quality, it also suggests some important differences. As such, a fruitful area for further research is to understand the process through which customers assess the overall service image of companies that interact with customers through both conventional and electronic channels. One key aspect would involve the creation of an instrument that could measure service quality appropriately across online and traditional channels.

Service Quality Measurement Issues

Part 3 of Appendix 1 describes a multi-sector study that incorporated the most recent refinements to SERVQUAL and tested the three-column and two-column format surveys (Appendix 3 presents the two survey formats) for quantifying the measure of service superiority (MSS) and measure of service adequacy (MSA). The empirical results from this study raise a number of issues for further investigation. First, although the three-column format is superior to the two-column format, especially in terms of diagnostic value, administering it in its entirety may pose practical difficulties, particularly in telephone surveys or when the list of generic items is supplemented with more context-specific items, as suggested by PBZ (1991b). Therefore, it would be useful to explore the soundness of administering logical subsections of the questionnaire (e.g., sections pertaining to the five dimensions) to comparable subsamples of customers so as to still achieve its full diagnostic value.

Second, research is needed to explore why the actual results from this study, and earlier studies (cf. Brown et al., 1993; PBZ, 1993), apparently do not fully support the alleged psychometric deficiencies of difference-score measures of service quality. Such research might provide a more enlightened understanding of the pros and cons of using difference scores in service-quality measurement.

Third, based on the findings reported in Appendix 1, and consistent with recent calls issued by PZB (1994b) and Perreault (1992), there is a need for explicitly incorporating practical criteria such as diagnostic value into the traditional scale-assessment paradigm that is dominated by psychometric criteria.

Fourth, as suggested by results from the study discussed in Part 3 of Appendix 1, direct measures of service quality may tend to produce upwardly biased ratings. This possibility warrants further exploration. Insights from research aimed at understanding the causes of this tendency, and estimating the extent of upward bias it produces, would be helpful in reducing the bias, or at least correcting for it in interpreting direct-measure ratings.

Fifth, additional research on the dimensionality of the SERVQUAL items is warranted. Although support for SERVQUAL's five-dimensional configuration exists, considerable interdimensional overlap has been found, especially among responsiveness, assurance, and empathy. PBZ (1991b) have speculated about possible reasons for this overlap, and have proffered directions for future research on this issue. Research is also needed to uncover the underlying causes and managerial implications of the empirical correlations among the dimensions.

Finally, further empirical work is needed to evaluate and revise as necessary the preliminary scales developed thus far to measure customers' assessments of the core and recovery service quality of websites.

Summary

Service quality has been one of the most researched topics in the services field, particularly in the early years of the evolution of services marketing as a significant subdiscipline of marketing (Fisk et al., 1993). This chapter began with a synthesis of the literature pertaining to the conceptualization of service quality and its contribution to profitability and customer loyalty. It then discussed studies offering conceptual frameworks and approaches for improving service quality. The chapter also discussed the measurement of service quality, which is a prerequisite for identifying service facets requiring improvement and for assessing the impact of improvement efforts. The chapter concluded with an agenda for further research to address unresolved and emerging issues, and to add to extant knowledge about assessing and improving service quality.

APPENDIX 1

Part 1: Development and Refinement of Original SERVQUAL

Operationalization of the Service Quality Gap

Consistent with the definition of service quality, PZB (1988) operationalized the construct as the difference between two 7-point rating scales – one to measure customers' expectations about companies in general within the service sector or category being investigated, and the other to measure customers' perceptions about a particular company whose service quality was to be assessed. Both rating scales were anchored by 'Strongly Agree' (7) at one end, and 'Strongly Disagree' (1) at the other. The expectations scale measured the extent to which customers felt companies in the sector in question *should* possess a specified service attribute. The corresponding perceptions scale measured the extent to which customers felt a given company (say XYZ Company) *did* possess the attribute. The attributes were cast in the form of statements with which customers were asked to express their degree of agreement or disagreement on the 7-point scale. The following statements illustrate:

Expectations Statements:

- The behavior of employees of banks should instill confidence in customers.
- Banks should give customers individual attention.

Corresponding Perceptions Statements:

- The behavior of employees of XYZ Bank instills confidence in customers.
- XYZ Bank gives customers individual attention.

Construction of SERVQUAL

PZB, drawing upon insights and examples from their extensive focus group interviews, developed a comprehensive set of statements (such as the ones listed in the preceding section) to represent various specific facets of the 10 service-quality dimensions. This process yielded 97 statements, which formed the basis for constructing an initial two-part instrument. The first part consisted of 97 expectations statements. The corresponding set of 97 perceptions statements formed the second part. In accordance with recommended procedures for scale development (Churchill, 1979), roughly half of the expectations statements and the corresponding perceptions statements were worded negatively.

To refine the initial instrument, PZB administered it to a sample of 200 customers representing five different service categories – appliance repair and maintenance, retail banking, long-distance telephone, securities brokerage, and credit cards. Analyses of the perception-minus-expectation gap scores on the 97 items resulted in a more parsimonious, 34-item instrument, with statements grouped into seven dimensions (the analyses included item-to-total correlation analysis, factor analysis, and assessment of internal consistency of items in each dimension).

To further assess the reliability, validity, and dimensionality of the 34-item instrument, PZB used it to collect data pertaining to the service quality of four nationally known, US-based companies (a bank, a company offering appliance repair and maintenance services, a credit-card company, and a long-distance telephone company). Four independent samples, consisting of 200 customers from each of the four companies, participated in this research phase. Results of analyses (similar to those mentioned above) of the perception-expectation gap scores were consistent across the four independent samples. The common pattern of findings resulted in two changes to the instrument: (1) further elimination of items to create a 22-item instrument, and (2) grouping of the 22 items into five general dimensions. Strong evidence supporting the reliability, validity, and dimensionality of this condensed instrument – labeled SERVQUAL – is documented in PZB (1988). A complete listing of statements in the two parts of SERVQUAL, as well as instructions for the two parts, are also provided in PZB (1988).

It is important to note that SERVQUAL is not a panacea for all service-quality measurement problems, nor should it be treated by companies as the sole basis for assessing service quality. As PZB (1988) have observed:

> The instrument has been designed to be applicable across a broad spectrum of services. As such, it provides a basic skeleton through its expectations/perceptions format encompassing statements for each of the five service-quality dimensions. The skeleton, when necessary, can be adapted or supplemented to fit the characteristics or specific research needs of a particular organization. SERVQUAL is most valuable when it is used periodically to track service quality trends, *and when it is used in conjunction with other forms of service quality measurement.* (PZB, 1988: 30–1; emphasis added)

Refinement of SERVQUAL

In another multi-sector study, discussed in PBZ (1991b), SERVQUAL was further refined by measuring customer assessments of service quality for telephone repair, retail banking, and insurance services. Five nationally known companies – one telephone company, two insurance companies, and two banks – participated in the study. The refinements to SERVQUAL were suggested by results from a pretest of the original version through a mail survey of a sample of 300 customers of the telephone company that participated in the study. The refined SERVQUAL was then further tested in the main study, wherein data were collected through mail surveys of independent samples of customers of each of the five companies. Refinements involved changes to the instructions and to some statements in the original SERVQUAL, but not to its five-dimensional structure or to the 7-point rating scale. The refinements and brief rationales for them are outlined below (a more detailed discussion is available in PBZ, 1991b).

The distribution of expectations ratings obtained in the pretest was highly skewed toward the upper end of the 7-point scale (mean expectation score was 6.22). Suspecting that the 'should' terminology in the expectations statements might be responsible for the high ratings, the statements were revised to capture what customers *will* expect from companies delivering *excellent* service. For example, the original expectations statement 'Banks *should* give customers individual attention' was revised to read '*Excellent* banks *will* give customers individual attention.' The instructions for the expectations section were also appropriately altered.

The negatively worded statements in the original SERVQUAL instrument were problematic for several reasons: (1) they were awkward; (2) they were confusing respondents (the pretest data showed substantially higher standard deviations for the negatively worded statements than for those worded positively); and (3) they seemed to lower the reliabilities (coefficient alpha values) for the dimensions containing them. Therefore, all negatively worded statements were changed to a positive format.

Finally, two original items – one each under tangibles and assurance – were replaced with two new items to reduce redundancy and to more fully capture the dimensions. These changes also reflected suggestions from company managers who reviewed the pretest questionnaire.

The psychometric properties of the refined SERVQUAL instrument were reassessed with data from the five companies. The results indicated strong reliability for the five multiple-item components of the instrument: across the five companies, the coefficient alpha values ranged from .80 to .86 for tangibles, .88 to .92 for reliability, .88 to .93 for responsiveness, .87 to .91 for assurance, and .85 to .89 for empathy. The five components also possessed high predictive and convergent validity, as indicated by their ability to explain the variance in customers' perceptions of the companies' overall service quality. Regression analyses, in which overall service quality (measured on a 10-point scale) was the dependent variable and the mean perception-expectation gap scores on the five SERVQUAL dimensions were the independent variables, yielded adjusted R-squared values ranging from .57 to .71 across the five companies.

The evidence of reliability and validity reported above was stronger than the corresponding results obtained for the original SERVQUAL instrument (PZB, 1988), indicating improved cohesiveness of the items under each dimension and demonstrating the ability of gap scores on the dimensions to predict overall service quality. However, results of factor analyses of the gap scores obtained from the refined instrument revealed somewhat greater overlap among the five dimensions, especially responsiveness and assurance, than in the case of the original SERVQUAL. Thus, the discriminant validity or uniqueness of the five components of the refined SERVQUAL instrument is in question, and is one of the key concerns discussed next.

Part 2: Concerns and Debate Surrounding SERVQUAL

Many published SERVQUAL-based studies have critically examined the instrument and raised questions about its psychometric soundness and its usefulness. These questions relate to the need for SERVQUAL's expectations component (e.g., Babakus & Mangold, 1992; Cronin & Taylor, 1992), the interpretation and operationalization of expectations (Teas, 1993), the reliability and validity of SERVQUAL's difference-score formulation (e.g., Babakus & Boller, 1992; Brown et al., 1993), and SERVQUAL's dimensionality (e.g., Carman, 1990; Finn & Lamb, 1991). In response to these questions, PZB have presented counterarguments, clarifications, and additional evidence to reaffirm the instrument's psychometric soundness and practical value (PBZ, 1991b, 1993; PZB, 1994a). As details of this debate are well documented in the sources cited, they are not repeated here. However, the major unresolved questions are outlined below.

Is It Necessary to Measure Expectations?

Studies have shown consistently that scores on the perceptions-only component of SERVQUAL are able to explain significantly more variance in customers' overall evaluations of an organization's service quality (measured on a single-item, overall-perceptions rating scale) than are the perception-expectation difference scores. Thus, from a strictly *predictive validity* standpoint, measuring expectations is not warranted. Moreover, measuring expectations increases survey length. However, SERVQUAL's developers have argued that measuring expectations has *diagnostic value* (i.e., it generates information that would pinpoint *shortfalls* in service quality), and that basing service-improvement decisions solely on perceptions data might lead to sub-optimal or erroneous resource allocations (PZB, 1994a). Thus, an important unresolved issue is the tradeoff between the empirical and diagnostic value of expectations in service quality measurement.

How Should the Expectations Construct Be Operationalized?

Although the definition of service quality as the gap between customers' expectations and perceptions is conceptually simple, the operationalization of this definition has been controversial because of the multiple ways the term 'expectation' can be and has been interpreted. While service quality researchers have generally viewed expectations as *normative* standards (i.e., customers' beliefs about what a service provider *should* offer), researchers working in the area of customer satisfaction/dissatisfaction have typically considered expectations to be *predictive* standards (i.e., what customers feel a service provider *will* offer). However, both 'should' and 'will' expectations have been used in measuring service quality (Boulding et al., 1993). Furthermore, other types of expectations (e.g., 'ideal,' 'deserved') have also been proposed and defended as appropriate comparison standards (for a comprehensive review, see Woodruff et al., 1991).

The multiplicity of comparison standards and the absence of a comprehensive theoretical framework delineating their interrelationships are implicit in a call issued by Woodruff et al. for developing 'a classification scheme ... to reduce the many possible standards to a relatively few categories' (1991: 108). In an attempt to address unresolved issues in the area of customer expectations, ZBP (1993) developed a conceptual model of expectations by combining insights from past research with findings from a multi-sector study aimed at understanding the nature and determinants of customers' service expectations. The core of this model served as the foundation for the latest enhancements to the SERVQUAL instrument and will be discussed in a later section.

Is It Appropriate to Operationalize Service Quality as a Difference Score?

Operationalizing any construct as a difference between two other constructs has been questioned for psychometric reasons, especially if the difference scores are to be used in multivariate analyses (for a recent review of the concerns raised, see Peter et al., 1993). SERVQUAL's difference-score formulation has also been questioned for the same psychometric reasons (Babakus & Boller, 1992; Brown et al., 1993). Critics of difference scores have suggested that direct (i.e., non-difference score) measures of the perception-expectation gap will be psychometrically superior (e.g., Carman, 1990; Peter et al., 1993). However, the available empirical evidence comparing SERVQUAL and direct measures of service quality has not established conclusively that the direct measures are superior (PBZ, 1993). Thus, the relative superiority of the direct versus difference-score operationalization of service quality is another unresolved issue.

Does SERVQUAL Have Five Distinct Dimensions That Transcend Different Contexts?

Replication studies incorporating SERVQUAL have not been able to reproduce as 'clean' a five-dimensional factor structure as was obtained in the original study (PZB, 1988). For instance, in an article comparing and synthesizing results from several replication studies, PBZ (1991b) point out that the number of final SERVQUAL dimensions vary from two (Babakus & Boller, 1992) to five (Brensinger & Lambert, 1990) to eight (Carman, 1990). PZB (1991b) also offer alternative explanations for these differences:

> Respondents may indeed consider the SERVQUAL dimensions to be conceptually distinct; however, if their evaluations of a specific company on individual scale items are similar *across* dimensions, fewer than five dimensions will result as in the Babakus & Boller (1992) study. Alternatively, if their evaluations of a company on scale items *within* a dimension are sufficiently distinct, more than five dimensions will result as in Carman's (1990) study. In other words, differences in the number of empirically derived factors across replications may be primarily due to across-dimension similarities and/or within-dimension differences in customers' evaluations of a *specific* company involved in each setting. At a *general* level, the five-dimensional structure of SERVQUAL may still serve as a meaningful framework for summarizing the criteria customers use in assessing service quality. (1991: 440)

Nevertheless, the dimensionality of SERVQUAL continues to be debated (e.g., Cronin & Taylor, 1992; PZB, 1994a) and, as such, is an issue warranting further research.

Part 3: A Multi-Sector Study to Expand and Further Test SERVQUAL

PZB (1994b) conducted a multi-sector study to (1) augment SERVQUAL to incorporate the measure of service superiority (MSS) and the measure of service adequacy (MSA) corresponding to the desired and adequate expectation levels in an expanded conceptual model of service expectations (ZBP, 1993), and (2) assess the relative merits and demerits of the difference-score and direct operationalizations of the service quality gap measures (i.e., MSS and MSA). This study tested two alternative measurement formats:

- Three-column Format – This format involves obtaining separate ratings of desired, adequate, and perceived service with three identical, side-by-side scales, requiring the computation of differences between ratings to quantify MSS and MSA. Its operationalization of service quality is similar to that of SERVQUAL except that it does not repeat the battery of items.
- Two-column Format – Unlike SERVQUAL, this format involves obtaining *direct* ratings of MSS and MSA with two identical, side-by-side scales.

Appendix 3 illustrates the two questionnaire formats. Only one sample SERVQUAL item is shown in Appendix 3. The questionnaires used in the study contained the full battery of items in Appendix 2 (but after each item was abbreviated to a form similar to the sample item in Appendix 3). The term *minimum service* rather than *adequate service* was used in the questionnaires, based on the recommendation of customers in focus groups that pretested earlier questionnaire drafts.

The two questionnaire formats were used in mail surveys of independent samples of customers from four large companies in the US – a computer manufacturer, a retail chain, an auto insurance company, and a life insurance company. Relevant results from the mail surveys are discussed next to address the previously expressed concerns about SERVQUAL.

Is It Necessary to Measure Expectations?

Consistent with findings from earlier studies, the perceptions-only ratings (obtained from the third column of the three-column format) had the most predictive power. Specifically, regressing customer ratings on a 9-point, overall service quality scale on the perceptions scores on the five SERVQUAL dimensions yielded R-squared values ranging from .72 to .86 across the four companies. In contrast, when difference-score ratings of MSS (i.e., perception-minus-desired service ratings) on the five dimensions were used as independent variables, in the regression analyses, the R-squared values ranged from .51 to .60 across companies. When direct ratings of MSS (from the two-column format questionnaire) were used as independent variables, the R-squared values ranged from .45 to .74 across companies. Thus, measuring perceptions alone should suffice if the sole purpose of service quality measurement on individual attributes is to try to maximize the explained variance in overall service ratings. However, from a practitioner's standpoint, an equally important purpose is to pinpoint service quality shortfalls and take appropriate corrective action. From this *diagnostic-value* perspective, it is prudent to measure perceptions against expectations, as discussed below.

The importance of assessing perceptions relative to expectations was evident from several patterns of results for the four companies. For instance, consider the following mean ratings (on a 9-point scale) obtained for the computer company on the reliability and tangibles dimensions:

	Desired Service	Adequate Service	Perceptions
Reliability	8.5	7.2	7.5
Tangibles	7.5	6.0	7.5

On the basis of perceptions ratings alone, the company's performance is identical on both dimensions and, as such, the company may place the same level of service-improvement emphasis on each. That such a strategy will be sub-optimal becomes evident when the perceptions ratings are interpreted in conjunction with the desired- and adequate-service expectations. Performance on tangibles far exceeds the adequate service level (the MSA rating is 1.5) and actually meets the desired service level (the MSS rating is 0). In contrast, performance on reliability barely exceeds the adequate service level (the MSA rating is .3) and is substantially short of the desired service level (the MSS rating is −1). Clearly, devoting equal attention to both dimensions would be wasteful; instead, the company should give far higher priority to improving performance on reliability.

Thus, measuring expectations is warranted from the standpoint of being able to pinpoint the most serious service shortfalls and make wise resource-allocation decisions. Before expending effort to make improvements on any service attribute, a company should ascertain, at a minimum, whether perceived performance on the attribute falls below, within, or above the customers' zone of tolerance. Such a comparative assessment is not possible if perceptions alone are measured. For instance, in PZB's (1994b) multi-sector study, the retail-chain customers' mean perceptions ratings on the 9-point scale for reliability, responsiveness, assurance, empathy and tangibles were 6.6, 6.2, 6.7, 6.2 and 7.2, respectively. Although these ratings suggest room for improvement, the chain might still consider them to be 'decent' ratings, especially since even the lowest rating of 6.2 is more than a full point above the scale's mid-point of 5. However, the adequate service ratings for reliability, responsiveness, assurance, empathy and tangibles were 7.1, 6.6, 6.9, 6.6 and 6.6, respectively. Thus, except on the dimension of tangibles, the retail chain's perceived performance does not even meet customers' minimum expectations. The retail chain's service quality is much worse than what one might infer from the perceptions ratings alone.

The results from the study also shed light on whether increased questionnaire length due to measuring expectations adversely affects response rate. Both the two-column and three-column format questionnaires (illustrated in Appendix 3) are physically shorter than the current two-part SERVQUAL (shown in Appendix 2) because they do not repeat the battery of items. However, the two-column format is 'shorter' than the three-column format in that the former requires one less set of ratings. Thus, if questionnaire length (reflected by the number of sets of ratings respondents are requested to provide) has a detrimental effect on response rate, one would predict a higher response rate for the two-column format than for the three-column format. The actual response rates obtained run counter to this prediction – in all four companies the response rate for the three-column format was equal to or higher than the response rate for the two-column format (the mean response rates across companies for the two-column and three-column formats were 22% and 24%, respectively). These results suggest that measuring expectations separately is not likely to lower response rates.

How Should the Expectations Construct Be Operationalized?

Although the results of the study do not directly address this issue, they provide support for the meaningfulness of using the zone of tolerance (bounded by the desired and adequate service expectations) as a yardstick against which to compare perceived service performance. As implied by the illustrative findings discussed above, operationalizing customer expectations as a zone or range of service levels is not only feasible empirically, but also valuable from a diagnostic standpoint. Using the zone of tolerance as a comparison standard in evaluating service performance can help companies in understanding how well they are meeting at least customers' minimum requirements, and how much improvement is needed before they achieve the status of service superiority.

Is It Appropriate to Operationalize Service Quality as a Difference Score?

As already discussed, while the two-column format measures the gap between perceptions and expectations *directly*, the three-column format involves operationalizing the gap as a difference score. Therefore, relevant results from the comparative study can be used to assess the reliability, validity, and diagnostic value of the direct and difference-score measures.

Based on values of coefficient alpha – the conventional criterion for assessing the reliability (or internal consistency) of items making up a scale – both the direct and difference-score measures of service quality fared well.

For instance, the range of coefficient alpha values across companies for the five SERVQUAL dimensions (based on the MSS scores representing the measure of service superiority or the gap between perceptions and desired-service expectations) were as follows:

	Direct Measure	Difference-Score Measure
Reliability	.90 to .96	.87 to .95
Responsiveness	.83 to .95	.84 to .91
Assurance	.88 to .94	.81 to .90
Empathy	.91 to .97	.85 to .93
Tangibles	.88 to .97	.75 to .88

As the above results indicate, although the reliability coefficients are somewhat higher for the direct measure, all the values for the difference-score measure exceed the lower threshold value of .7 suggested by Nunnally (1978). However, some concern has been raised in the psychometric literature about the appropriateness of computing coefficient alphas for difference scores, and an alternative formula has been recommended specifically for assessing the reliability of a difference-score measure (Peter et al., 1993). The reliability coefficients obtained through this formula for the difference-score operationalization of MSS were somewhat lower than the coefficient alpha values reported above, but were still quite high. In fact, the coefficient values for the SERVQUAL dimensions across all companies exceeded .8 with just two exceptions in one company (the coefficients for assurance and tangibles in the computer company were .71 and .65, respectively). Thus, the reliability of the difference-score operationalization of service quality, although lower than that of the direct measure, seems acceptable.

Both the direct and the difference-score measures of service quality have *face validity* in that both are consistent with the conceptual definition of service quality as the discrepancy between perceptions and expectations. And, as implied by the regression results reported earlier, both measures have good *predictive validity* – the R-squared values for the regressions with overall quality as the dependent variable range from .45 to .74 for the direct measure and .51 to .60 for the difference-score measure.

Because service quality is proposed in the literature to be an antecedent of *perceived value* (e.g., Zeithaml, 1988), one can assess the *nomological validity* of the service quality measures by the degree to which they are related to perceived value. In the present study, customers rated the 'overall value for money' offered by their respective companies on a 9-point scale. As in the case of the overall quality ratings, the overall value ratings for each company were regressed on the MSS scores for the five SERVQUAL dimensions. The range of R-squared values from these regression analyses was .34 to .57 for the direct measure, and .31 to .58 for the difference-score measure. These results support the nomological validity of both measures. Moreover, comparing these ranges of R-squared values for the value regressions, with the corresponding ranges reported above for the quality regressions, reveals that the variance explained is higher for quality, the construct the direct and difference-score formats purport to measure, than for value, a different construct. This pattern of results offers some support for the *discriminant validity* of both measures as well.

The two measures did differ in terms of possible *response error*, a potential threat to their validity. Response error was assessed by examining the logical consistency of the MSA and MSS ratings from the two-column format, and of the adequate-service and desired-service ratings from the three-column format. An instance of response error occurs when the MSS rating on an item exceeds the MSA rating, or when the adequate-service rating exceeds the desired-service rating. The percentages of respondents who committed one or more such errors ranged from 8.6% to 18.2% for the two-column format, and from 0.6% to 2.7% for the three-column format. Thus, the validity threat due to possible response error is far greater for the direct measure than for the difference-score measure.

The study's results also suggested a need for caution in interpreting the direct-measure ratings because of possible upward bias in them. To illustrate, with just two exceptions, the mean values for the direct measures of service superiority (i.e., MSS) along the five SERVQUAL dimensions were *greater than* 5, the scale point at which the desired and perceived service levels are equal (the exceptions were mean ratings of 4.9 and 5.0 for the retail chain's responsiveness and empathy, respectively). This consistent pattern implied that perceived service performance was *above* the desired service level for virtually all dimensions in each company. In contrast, except for tangibles in the computer company, the difference-score values of MSS were negative, implying that perceived service performance was *below* the desired service level. Given that the desired level represents a form of *ideal* standard, perceived performance falling below that level (on at least several dimensions) seems a more plausible and face valid finding than a consistent pattern of perceptions exceeding the desired service level. As such, the direct measures may be producing upwardly biased ratings that can mislead executives into believing that their companies' service performance is better than it actually is.

From a practical or diagnostic-value standpoint, the three-column format questionnaire (from which the difference-score measures are derived) has yet another advantage – by virtue of its generating separate ratings of the adequate-service, desired-service, and perception levels, this format is capable of *pinpointing* the position of the zone of tolerance and the perceived service level relative to the zone. The direct measures obtained from the two-column format questionnaire can indicate whether the perceived service level is above the tolerance zone (MSS score greater than 5), below the tolerance zone (MSA score less than 5), or within the tolerance zone (MSS score less than or equal to 5 and MSA score greater than or equal to 5). However, ratings from the two-column format cannot identify the tolerance zone's position on a continuum of expectation levels; nor can they pinpoint the perceived service level relative to the zone.

In summary, the difference-score operationalization of service quality appears to have psychometric properties that are as sound as that of the direct-measure operationalization. Moreover, the three-column format questionnaire yields richer diagnostics than the two-column format questionnaire. Thus, operationalizing service quality as difference scores seems appropriate.

Does SERVQUAL Have Five Distinct Dimensions That Transcend Different Contexts?

To verify the dimensionality of the direct-measure and difference-score versions of SERVQUAL, the MSA and MSS scores on the individual items were factor analyzed to extract five factors. The results showed that for both questionnaire versions the reliability items formed a distinct factor. The responsiveness, assurance and empathy items primarily loaded on the same factor. The tangibles items, though distinct from the other dimensions, were split among the three remaining factors. The splitting of tangibles into several factors has occurred in past studies as well (PBZ, 1991b), and might be an artifact of extracting five factors (i.e., because the items for the other four dimensions were captured by just two factors, the tangibles items may have split up to represent the remaining factors).

To further evaluate the distinctiveness of the SERVQUAL dimensions, confirmatory factor analyses were conducted using LISREL to assess the tenability of two alternative measurement models. One was a five-construct model in which the items loaded on the five SERVQUAL dimensions according to the *a priori* groupings of the items. The second model was a three-construct model in which the reliability and tangibles items loaded on two distinct constructs, while the remaining items loaded on the third construct (acknowledging the possible uni-dimensionality of responsiveness, assurance and empathy). The analyses showed both models to be defensible on the basis of the traditional criteria of GFI (goodness-of-fit index), AGFI (adjusted GFI), and RMSR (root-mean-squared residual). Additional analyses, conducted to assess the *relative* fit of the two models and to explore further the distinctiveness of the five dimensions, provided stronger support for the five-dimensional structure than for the three-dimensional structure (details of these analyses are available in PZB, 1994b). In summary, although the results showed evidence of discriminant validity among SERVQUAL's five dimensions, they also support the possibility of a three-dimensional structure where responsiveness, assurance and empathy meld into a single factor.

APPENDIX 2

Refined SERVQUAL Instrument

Note: In what follows, telephone repair services are used as an illustrative context.

Directions: Based on your experiences as a customer of telephone repair services, please think about the kind of telephone company that would deliver excellent quality of repair service. Think about the kind of telephone company with which you would be pleased to do business. Please show the extent to which you think such a telephone company would possess the feature described by each statement. If you feel a feature is *not at all essential* for excellent telephone companies such as the one you have in mind, circle the number '1.' If you feel a feature is *absolutely essential* for excellent telephone companies, circle '7.' If your feelings are less strong, circle one of the numbers in the middle. There are no right or wrong answers – all we are interested in is a number that truly reflects your feelings regarding telephone companies that would deliver excellent quality of service.

Note: Each of the statements was accompanied by a 7-point scale anchored at the ends by the labels 'Strongly Disagree' (= 1) and 'Strongly Agree' (= 7). Intermediate scale points were not labeled. Also, the headings (Tangibles, Reliability, etc.), shown here to indicate which statements fall under each dimension, were not included in the actual questionnaire.

Tangibles

1. Excellent telephone companies will have modern-looking equipment.
2. The physical facilities at excellent telephone companies will be visually appealing.
3. Employees of excellent telephone companies will be neat-appearing.
4. Materials associated with the service (such as pamphlets or statements) will be visually appealing in excellent telephone companies.

Reliability

5. When excellent telephone companies promise to do something by a certain time, they will do so.
6. When customers have a problem, excellent telephone companies will show a sincere interest in solving it.
7. Excellent telephone companies will perform the service right the first time.
8. Excellent telephone companies will provide their services at the time they promise to do so.
9. Excellent telephone companies will insist on error-free records.

Responsiveness

10. Employees of excellent telephone companies will tell customers exactly when services will be performed.
11. Employees of excellent telephone companies will give prompt service to customers.
12. Employees of excellent telephone companies will always be willing to help customers.
13. Employees of excellent telephone companies will never be too busy to respond to customer requests.

Assurance

14. The behavior of employees of excellent telephone companies will instill confidence in customers.
15. Customers of excellent telephone companies will feel safe in their transactions.
16. Employees of excellent telephone companies will be consistently courteous with customers.
17. Employees of excellent telephone companies will have the knowledge to answer customer questions.

Empathy

18. Excellent telephone companies will give customers individual attention.
19. Excellent telephone companies will have operating hours convenient to all their customers.
20. Excellent telephone companies will have employees who give customers personal attention.
21. Excellent telephone companies will have the customers' best interests at heart.
22. The employees of excellent telephone companies will understand the specific needs of their customers.

Perceptions Section

Directions: The following set of statements relates to your feelings about XYZ Telephone Company's repair service. For each statement, please show the extent to which you believe XYZ has the feature described by the statement. Once again, circling a '1' means that you strongly disagree that XYZ has that feature, and circling a '7' means that you strongly agree. You may circle any of the numbers in the middle that show how strong your feelings are. There are no right or wrong answers – all that we are interested in is a number that best shows your perceptions about XYZ's repair service.

Tangibles

1. XYZ has modern-looking equipment.
2. XYZ's physical facilities are visually appealing.
3. XYZ's employees are neat-appearing.
4. Materials associated with the service (such as pamphlets or statements) are visually appealing at XYZ.

Reliability

5. When XYZ promises to do something by a certain time, it does so.
6. When you have a problem, XYZ shows a sincere interest in solving it.
7. XYZ performs the service right the first time.
8. XYZ provides its services at the time it promises to do so.
9. XYZ insists on error-free records.

Responsiveness

10. Employees of XYZ tell you exactly when services will be performed.
11. Employees of XYZ give you prompt service.
12. Employees of XYZ are always willing to help you.
13. Employees of XYZ are never too busy to respond to your requests.

Assurance

14. The behavior of employees of XYZ instills confidence in customers.
15. You feel safe in your transactions with XYZ.
16. Employees of XYZ are consistently courteous with you.
17. Employees of XYZ have the knowledge to answer your questions.

Empathy

18. XYZ gives you individual attention.
19. XYZ has operating hours convenient to all its customers.
20. XYZ has employees who give you personal attention.
21. XYZ has your best interests at heart.
22. Employees of XYZ understand your specific needs.

Point-Allocation Question

Directions: Listed below are five features pertaining to telephone companies and the repair services they offer. We would like to know how important each of these features is to *you* when you evaluate a telephone company's quality of repair service. Please allocate a total of 100 points among the five features *according to how important each feature is to you* – the more important a feature is to you, the more points you should allocate to it. Please ensure that the points you allocate to the five features add up to 100.

The appearance of the telephone company's physical facilities, equipment, personnel, and communications materials. _____points

The ability of the telephone company to perform the promised service dependably and accurately. _____points

The willingness of the telephone company to help customers and provide prompt service. _____points

The knowledge and courtesy of the telephone company's employees and their ability to convey trust and confidence. _____points

The caring, individualized attention the telephone company provides its customers. _____points

Total points allocated 100 points

APPENDIX 3

Enhanced Version of SERQUAL

Note: Both formats are for the auto insurer (one of four companies that participated in the study) and only one illustrative item is shown in each.

Three-column Format

We would like your impressions about _________'s service performance relative to your expectations. Please think about the two different levels of expectations defined below:

> *MINIMUM SERVICE LEVEL* – the *minimum* level of service performance you consider adequate.
>
> *DESIRED SERVICE LEVEL* – the level of service performance you desire.

For each of the following statements, please indicate: (a) your *minimum service level* by circling one of the numbers in the *first* column; and (b) your *desired service level* by circling one of the numbers in the *second* column; and (c) your *perception of _____________'s service* by circling one of the numbers in the *third* column.

When it comes to …	My *Minimum* Services Level is:	My *Desired* Services Level is:	My Perception of ________'s Service Performance is:
1. Prompt service to policyholders	Low High	Low High	Low High No Opinion
	1 2 3 4 5 6 7 8 9	1 2 3 4 5 6 7 8 9	1 2 3 4 5 6 7 8 9 N

Two-column Format

Please think about the quality of service _________ offers compared to the two different levels of service defined below:

> *MINIMUM SERVICE LEVEL* – the *minimum* level of service performance you consider adequate.
>
> *DESIRED SERVICE LEVEL* – the level of service performance you desire.

For each of the following statements, please indicate: (a) how ________'s performance compares with your *minimum service level* by circling one of the numbers in the *first* column; and (b) how ________'s performance compares with your *desired service level* by circling one of the numbers in the *second* column.

When is comes to …	Compared to My *Minimum* Service Level ____'s Service Performance is:										Compared to My *Desired* Service Level ____'s Service Performance is:									
	Lower		The Same			Higher				No Opinion	Lower		The Same			Higher				No Opinion
1. Prompt service to policyholders	1	2	3	4	5	6	7	8	9	N	1	2	3	4	5	6	7	8	9	N

References

Aaker, David A. & Jacobson, Robert (1994) The financial information content of perceived quality. *Journal of Marketing*, 58 (May): 191–201.

Babakus, Emin & Boller, Gregory W. (1992) An empirical assessment of the SERVQUAL scale. *Journal of Business Research*, 24, 253–68.

Babakus, Emin & Mangold, W. Glynn (1992) Adapting the SERVQUAL scale to hospital services: an empirical investigation. *Health Services Research*, 26 (6), 767–86.

Bell, David E. & Leavitt, Donald M. (1998) Bronner Slosberg Humphrey. *Harvard Business School Case* 9-598-136. 5.

Berry, Leonard L. (1983) Relationship marketing. In *Emerging Perspectives on Services Marketing*, edited by Leonard L. Berry, G. Lynn Shostack & Gregory D. Upah. Chicago: American Marketing Association, pp. 25–8.

Berry, Leonard L. & Parasuraman, A. (1991). Marketing to employees. *Marketing Services*. New York: Free Press, Chapter 9.

——— (1997) Listening to the customer: the concept of a service-quality information system. *Sloan Management Review*, 38, Spring, 65–76.

Bettencourt, Lance A. & Gwinner, Kevin (1996) Customization of the service experience: the role of the frontline employee. *International Journal of Service Industry Management*, 7, 2, 3–20.

Bitner, Mary Jo (1990) Evaluating service encounters: the effects of physical surrounding and employee responses. *Journal of Marketing*, 54 (April), 69–82.

——— (1993) Managing the evidence of service. In *The Service Quality Handbook*, edited by Eberhard E. Scheuing & William F. Christopher. New York: American Management Association, pp. 358–70.

Blattberg, Robert C. & Deighton, John (1996) Manage marketing by the customer equity test. *Harvard Business Review*, July–August, 136–44.

Bojanic, David C. (1991) Quality measurement in professional services firms. *Journal of Professional Services Marketing*, 7 (2), 27–36.

Bolton, Ruth N. & Drew, James H. (1991a) A longitudinal analysis of the impact of service changes on customer attitudes. *Journal of Marketing*, 55 (January), 1–9.

——— (1991b) A multistage model of customer's assessments of service quality and value. *Journal of Consumer Research*, 17 (March), 375–84.

Bongiorno, Lori (1993) Franchise fracas. *Business Week*, March 22, 68.

Bonner, P. Greg & Nelson, Richard (1985) Product attributes and perceived quality: foods. In *Perceived Quality*, edited by J. Jacoby & J. Olson. Lexington, MA: Lexington Books, pp. 64–79.

Boston Consulting Group (2000) http://www.nua.ie/surveys/index.cgi?f=VS&art_id=905355643&rel=true

Boulding, William, Kalra, Ajay, Staelin, Richard & Zeithaml, Valarie (1993) A dynamic process model of service quality: from expectations to behavioral intentions. *Journal of Marketing Research*, 30 (February), 7–27.

Boulding, William, Staelin, Richard, Kalra, Ajay & Zeithaml, Valarie A. (1992) Conceptualizing and testing a dynamic process model of service quality. *Report Number 92–121*, Marketing Science Institute.

Bounds, Greg, York, Lyle, Adams, Mel & Ranney, Gipsie (1994) *Beyond Total Quality Management Toward the Emerging Paradigm*. New York: McGraw-Hill.

Bowen, David E. (1986) Managing customer as human resources. *Human Resource Management*, 25, 3, 371–83.

Bowen, David E. & Lawler, Edward E. (1992) The empowerment of service workers: what, why, how, and when. *Sloan Management Review*, 33 (Spring), 31–9.

Brensinger, Ronald P. & Lambert, Douglas M. (1990) Can the SERVQUAL scale be generalized to business-to-business services? In *Knowledge Development in Marketing*, 1990 AMA's Summer Educators' Conference Proceedings, p. 289.

Brown, Stephen W. & Swartz, Teresa A. (1989) A gap analysis of professional service quality. *Journal of Marketing*, 53 (April), 92–98.

Brown, Tom J., Churchill, Gilbert A. Jr. & Peter, J. Paul (1993) Improving the measurement of service quality. *Journal of Retailing*, 69 (Spring), 127–39.

Brucks, Merrie, Zeithaml, Valarie A. & Naylor, Gillian (2000) Price and brand name as indicators of quality dimensions for consumer durables. *Journal of the Academy of Marketing Science*, 28 (Summer), 359–374.

Buzzell, Richard & Gale, Bradley (1987) *The PIMS Principles: Linking Strategy to Performance*. New York: The Free Press.

Camp, Robert (1989) *Benchmarking: The Search for Industry Best Practices that Lead to Superior Performance*. Milwaukee: American Society for Quality Control.

Carman, James M. (1990) Consumer perceptions of service quality: an assessment of the SERVQUAL dimensions. *Journal of Retailing*, 66 (Spring), 33–55.

Carroll, Doug (1992) Expert: being on time isn't everything for airlines. *USA Today*, March 5, 6B.

Chung, Beth G. & Schneider, Benjamin (1999) Correlates of service employees' role conflict. Working Paper, School of Hotel Administration, Cornell University.

Churchill, Gilbert R., Jr. (1979) A Paradigm for Developing better measures of marketing constructs. *Journal of Marketing Research*, 16 (February), 64–73.

Clemmer, Elizabeth C. & Schneider, Benjamin (1989) Toward understanding and controlling customer dissatisfaction with waiting during peak demand times. In *Designing a Winning Service Strategy*, edited by Mary Jo Bitner & Lawrence A. Crosby. Chicago, IL: American Marketing Association, pp. 87–91.

——— (1993) Toward understanding and controlling customer dissatisfaction. In Pruyn, A. Th. H. & Smidts, A. Customer Evaluation of Queues: Three Exploratory Studies. *European Advances in Consumer Research*, 1, 371–82.

Crompton, John L. & Mackay, Kelly J. (1989) Users' perceptions of the relative importance of service quality dimensions in selected public recreation programs. *Leisure Sciences*, 11, 367–75.

Cronin, J. Joseph, Jr. & Taylor, Stephen A. (1992) Measuring service quality: a reexamination and extension. *Journal of Marketing*, 56 (July), 55–68.

Crosby, Philip B. (1979) *Quality Is Free: The Art of Making Quality Certain*. New York: New American Library.

Dawkins, Peter & Reichheld, Frederick F. (1990) Customer retention as a strategic weapon. *Directors and Boards*, 14 (Summer), 41–7.

Desiraji, Ramarao & Shugan, Steven M. (1999) Strategic service pricing and yield management. *Journal of Marketing*, 63, 1, 44–56.

Dickson, Peter (1994) *Marketing Management*. Fort Worth, TX: Dryden Press.

Easton, George S. (1993) The 1993 state of US Total Quality Management: a Baldrige examiner's perspective. *California Management Review*, 35 (3), 32–54.

Easton, George S. & Jarrell, Sherry L. (1998) The effects of Total Quality Management on corporate performance. *Journal of Business*, 71 (April), 253–308.

Ehrenfeld, Tom (1991) Merit evaluation and the family of measures. *Harvard Business Review*, September–October, 54–7.

Farley, John M., Daniels, Carson F. & Pearl, Daniel H. (1990) Service quality in a multinational environment. *Proceedings of the ASQC Quality Congress Transactions*. San Francisco, CA: ASQC, pp. 25–9.

Finn, David W. & Lamb, Charles W. Jr. (1991) An evaluation of the SERVQUAL scales in a retail setting. In *Advances in Consumer Research*, 18, edited by Rebecca H. Holman & Michael R. Solomon. Provo, UT: Association for Consumer Research, p. 18.

Fisher, Lawrence M. (1998) Here comes front-office automation. *Strategy and Business*, 13 (Fourth Quarter), 53–65.

Fisk, Raymond P., Brown, Stephen W. & Bitner, Mary Jo (1993) Tracking the evolution of the services marketing literature. *Journal of Retailing*, 69 (Spring), 61–103.

Fitzerald, C. & Erdman, T. (1992) *Actionline*. American Automotive Industry Action Group (October).

Fitzsimmons, James A. & Fitzsimmons, Mona J. (1997) *Service Management*, 2nd edn. New York: Irwin/McGraw-Hill.

Ford, John B., Joseph, Mathew & Joseph, Beatriz (1993) Service quality in higher education: a comparison of universities in the United States and New Zealand using SERVQUAL. In *Enhancing Knowledge Development in Marketing*, 1993 AMA Educators' Proceedings, pp. 75–81.

Ford Motor Company (1990) *Memorandum to Dealers*, October 3.

Fornell, Claes & Wernerfelt, Birger (1987) Defensive marketing strategy by customer complaint management: a theoretical analysis. *Journal of Marketing Research*, 24 (November), 337–46.

——— (1988) A model for customer complaint management. *Marketing Science*, 7 (Summer), 271–86.

Fornell, Claes, Johnson, Michael D., Anderson, Eugene W., Cha, Jaesung & Bryant, Barbara Eviritt (1996) The American customer satisfaction index: nature, purpose, and findings. *Journal of Marketing*, 60 (October), 7–18.

Gale, Bradley (1992) Monitoring customer satisfaction and market-perceived quality. *Worth Repeating Series*, Number 922CSO1. Chicago: American Marketing Association.

Garvin, David A. (1983) Quality on the line. *Harvard Business Review*, 61, September–October, 65–73.

George, William R. & Berry, Leonard L. (1981) Guidelines for the advertising of services. *Business Horizons*, May–June, 52–6.

Goodwin, Cathy (1988) 'I Can Do It Myself': Training the service consumer to contribute to service productivity. *Journal of Services Marketing*, 2 (Fall), 71–8.

Grant, Alan W. & Schlesinger, Leonard A. (1995) Realize your customers' full profit potential. *Harvard Business Review*, 73, September–October, 59–72.

Gronroos, Christian (1982) *Strategic Management and Marketing in the Service Sector*. Helsingfors: Swedish School of Economics and Business Administration.

Grove, Steven & Fisk, Raymond (1997) The impact of other customers on service experiences: a critical incident examination of 'getting along.' *Journal of Retailing*, 73, 1, 63–85.

Gwinner, Kevin P., Gremler, Dwayne D. & Bitner, Mary Jo (1998) Relational benefits in service industries: the customer's perspective. *Journal of the Academy of Marketing Science*, 26, 2 (Spring), 101–14.

Hanrahan, Timothy (1999) Price isn't everything: companies scramble to make sure customer service doesn't get lost in cyberspace. *The Wall Street Journal*, July 12, R20.

Hartline, Michael D. & Ferrell, O.C. (1996) The management of customer-contact service employees: an empirical investigation. *Journal of Marketing*, 60 (October), 52–70.

Hauser, John R., Simester, Duncan I. & Wernerfelt, Birger (1994) Customer satisfaction based incentive systems. *Marketing Science*, 16 (Spring), 129–45.

Hendricks, Kevin B. & Singhal, Vinod R. (1997) Does implementing an effective TQM program actually improve operating performance? Empirical evidence from firms that have won quality awards. *Management Science*, 43 (9), 1258–74.

Heskett, James L, Sasser, W. Earl Jr. & Schlesinger, Leonard A. (1997) *The Service Profit Chain*. New York: The Free Press.

Hui, Michael K. & Tse, David K. (1996) What to tell consumers in waits of different lengths: an integrative model of service evaluation. *Journal of Marketing*, 60 (April), 81–90.

International Customer Service Association (ICSA) and e-Satisfy.com (2000) http://sellitontheWeb.com/ezine/news0382.shtml

Ittner, Christopher & Larcker, David F. (1996) Measuring the impact of quality initiatives on firm financial performance. In *Advances in the Management of Organizational Quality*, edited by Soumeh Ghosh & Donald Fedor. Vol 1. Greenwich, CT: JAI Press, pp. 1–37.

——— (1997) The performance effects of process management techniques. *Management Science*, 43 (4), 523–34.

Johnson, Linda L., Dotson, Michael J. & Dunlop, B.J. (1988) Service quality determinants and effectiveness in the real estate brokerage industry. *The Journal of Real Estate Research*, 3, 21–36.

Katz, B. & Kahn, R. (1978) *The Social Psychology of Organizations*. New York: John Wiley and Sons, Inc.

Kelley, Scott W., Skinner, Steven J. & Donnelly, James H. Jr. (1992) Organizational socialization of service customers. *Journal of Business Research*, 25, 197–214.

Kingman-Brundage, Jane (1991) Technology, design and service quality. *International Journal of Service Industry Management*, 2 (3), 47–59.

Kordupleski, Raymond E., Rust, Roland T. & Zahorik, Anthony J. (1993) Why improving quality doesn't improve quality (or whatever happened to marketing?). *California Management Review*, 35 (3), 82–95.

Koska, Mart T. (1990) High quality care and hospital profits: is there a link? *Hospitals*, March 5, 62–3.

Legg, Donna & Baker, Julie (1991) Advertising strategies for service firms. In *Services Marketing*, edited by Christopher Lovelock. Englewood Cliffs, NJ: Prentice-Hall, pp. 282–91.

Lehtinen, Uolevi & Lehtinen, Jarmo R. (1982) Service quality: a study of quality dimensions. Unpublished working paper, Helsinki: Service Management Institute, Finland.

Levitt, Ted (1976) The industrialization of service. *Harvard Business Review*, September–October, 63–74.

Lewis, Robert C. & Booms, Bernard H. (1983) The marketing aspects of service quality. In *Emerging Perspectives on Services Marketing*, edited by Leonard L. Berry, G. Lynn Shostack & Gregory Upah. Chicago, IL: American Marketing Association, pp. 99–107.

Lovelock, Christopher (1992) Strategies for managing capacity-constrained service organizations. In *Managing Services: Marketing, Operations, and Human Resources*, 2nd edn., edited by Christopher Lovelock. Englewood Cliffs, NJ: Prentice Hall, pp. 154–68.

——— (1994) Getting the most out of your productive capacity. In *Product Plus*. Boston, MA: The McGraw-Hill Companies, Inc., pp. 239–61.

Mann, Robin and Kehoe, Dennis (1994) An evaluation of the effects of quality improvement activities on business performance. *The International Journal of Quality and Reliability Management*, 11 (4), 29–45.

Martin, Charles I. & Pranter, Charles A. (1989) Compatiblity management: customer-to-customer relationships in service environments. *Journal of Services Marketing*, 3, 3, 5–15.

Matthews, J. & Katel, P. (1992) The cost of quality: faced with hard times, business sours on Total Quality Management. *Newsweek*, September 7, 48–9.

McLaughlin, John P. (1993) Ensuring customer satisfaction is a strategic issue, not just an operational one. Presentation at the AIC Customer Satisfaction Measurement Conference, Chicago (December 6–7).

Nelson, Eugene, Rust, Roland T., Zahorik, Anthony, Rose, Robin L., Batalden, Paul & Siemanski, Beth (1992) Do patient perceptions of quality relate to hospital financial performance? *Journal of Healthcare Marketing*, December, 1–13.

Normann, Richard (1984) Getting people to grow. *Service Management: Strategy and Leadership in Service Business*. New York: John Wiley and Sons, pp. 44–50.

Nunnally, Jum C. (1978) *Psychometric Theory*, 2nd edn. New York: McGraw-Hill.

Ouchi, William G. & McGuire, Mary Ann (1975) A conceptual framework for the design of organizational control mechanisms. *Management Science*, 25 (September), 833–48.

Parasuraman, A., Berry, Leonard L. & Zeithaml, Valarie A. (1991a) Understanding customer expectations of service. *Sloan Management Review*, 3 (Spring), 39–48.

——— (1991b) Refinement and reassessment of the SERVQUAL scale. *Journal of Retailing*, 67 (Winter), 420–50.

——— (1993) More on improving service quality measurement. *Journal of Retailing*, 69 (Spring), 40–147.

Parasuraman, A., Zeithaml, Valarie A. & Berry, Leonard L. (1985) A conceptual model of service quality and its implications for future research. *Journal of Marketing*, 49 (Fall), 41–50.

Parasuraman, A., Zeithaml, Valarie A. & Berry, Leonard L. (1988) SERVQUAL: a multiple-item scale for measuring consumer perceptions of service quality. *Journal of Retailing*, 64 (Spring), 12–40.

——— (1994a) Reassessment of expectations as a comparison standard in measuring service quality: implications for further research. *Journal of Marketing*, 58 (January), 111–124.

——— (1994b) Moving forward in service quality research: measuring different customer-expectation levels, comparing alternative scales, and examining the performance-behavioral intentions link. Marketing Science Institute monograph, Report Number 94–114.

Parasuraman, A., Zeithaml, Valarie A. & Malhotra, Arvind (2002) An empirical examination of the service quality-value-behavioral chain in an electronic context. Working paper.

Perreault, William D., Jr. (1992) The shifting paradigm in marketing research. *Journal of the Academy of Marketing Science*, 20 (Fall), 367–75.

Peter, J. Paul, Churchill, Gilbert A. Jr. & Brown, Tom J. (1993) Caution in the use of difference scores in consumer research. *Journal of Consumer Research*, 19 (March), 655–62.

Peters, Thomas J. (1988) *Thriving on Chaos*. New York: Alfred A. Knopf.

Phillips, Lynn, Chang, Dae R. & Buzzell, Robert (1983) Product quality, cost, and business performance: a test of some key hypotheses. *Journal of Marketing*, Spring, 26–43.

Reger, Rhonda K., Gustafson, L.T., Demarie, S.M. & Mulland, J.V. (1994) Reframing the organization: why implementing total quality is easier said than done. *Academy of Management Review*, 19 (3), 565–84.

Reichheld, Frederick (1993) Loyalty-based management. *Harvard Business Review*, March–April, 64–74.

——— (1996a) Learning from customer defections. *Harvard Business Review*, March–April, 56–69.

——— (1996b) *The Loyalty Effect: The Hidden Force Behind Growth, Profits, and Lasting Value*. Boston: Harvard Business School Press.

Reichheld, Frederick & Sasser, W. Earl Jr. (1990) Zero defections: quality comes to services. *Harvard Business Review*, 68, September–October, 105–11.

Ricci, Anthony J., Kirn, Steven P. & Quinn, Richard T. (1998) The employee-customer profit chain at Sears. *Harvard Business Review*, January–February, 83–97.

Rizzo, John, House, R.J. & Lirtzman, S.I. (1970) Role conflict and ambiguity in complex organizations. *Administrative Science Quarterly*, 15, 150–63.

Rose, S. (1990) The coming revolution in credit cards. *The Journal of Retail Banking*, Summer, 17–19.

Rust, Roland, Subramanian, Bala & Wells, Mark (1992) Making complaints a management tool. *Marketing Management*, 3, 40–5.

Rust, Roland T., Zahorik, Anthony J. & Keiningham, Timothy L. (1994) *Return on Quality*. Chicago: Probus Publishing Company.

——— (1995) Return on Quality (ROQ): making service quality financially accountable. *Journal of Marketing*, 59 (April), 58–70.

Rust, Roland T., Keiningham, Timothy, Clemens, Stephen & Zahorik, Anthony (1998) Return on Quality at Chase Manhattan Bank. Working Paper, Center for Service Marketing, Vanderbilt University, Nashville, TN.

Sasser, W. Earl, Jr., Olsen, R. Paul & Wyckoff, D. Daryl (1978) *Management of Service Operations: Text and Cases*. Boston: Allyn & Bacon.

Schlesinger, Leonard A. & Heskett, James L. (1991) The service-driven service company. *Harvard Business Review*, September–October, 71–81.

Schneider, Benjamin & Bowen, David E. (1985) Employee and customer perceptions of service in banks: replication and extension. *Journal of Applied Psychology*, 70 (3), 423–33.

——— (1993) The service organization: human resources management is crucial. *Organizational Dynamics*, Spring, 39–52.

——— (1995) *Winning the Service Game*. Boston: Harvard Business School Press.

Schneider, Benjamin & Schechter, Daniel (1991) Development of a personnel selection system for service jobs. In *Service Quality, Multidisciplinary and Multinational Perspectives*, edited by Stephen W. Brown, Evert Gummesson, Bo Evardsson & BengtOve Gustavsson. Lexington, MA: Lexington Books, pp. 217–36.

Serwer, Andrew E. (1995) Trouble in franchise nation. *Fortune*, March 6, 115–18.

Shostack, G. Lynn (1992) Understanding services through blueprinting. In *Advances in Services Marketing, and Management: Research and Practice*, Vol. 1, edited by Teresa A. Swartz, David E. Bowen & Stephen W. Brown. Greenwich, CT: JAI Press Inc., pp. 75–90.

Simester, Duncan I., Hauser, John R., Wernerfelt, Birger & Rust, Roland T. (1998) Implementing quality improvement programs designed to enhance customer satisfaction: quasi-experiments in the US and Spain. Working Paper, Sloan School of Management, MIT.

Singh, Jagdip, Goolsby, Jerry R. & Rhoads, Gary K. (1994) Burnout and customer service representatives. *Journal of Marketing Research*, 31 (November), 558–69.

Sterman, John D., Repenning, Nelson P. & Kofman, Fred (1997) Unanticipated side effects of successful quality programs: exploring a paradox of organizational improvement. *Management Science,* 43 (4), 503–21.

Tax, Stephen S. & Brown, Stephen W. (1998) Recovering and learning from service failure. *Sloan Management Review*, Fall, 75–88.

Taylor, Shirley (1995) The effects of filled waiting time and service provider control over the delay on evaluations of service. *Journal of the Academy of Marketing Science*, 23, 1, 34–48.

Teas, R. Kenneth (1993) Expectations, performance evaluation and consumer's perceptions of quality. *Journal of Marketing*, 57 (October), 18–34.

The Economist (1992) The cracks in quality. April 18, 67–8.

US General Accounting Office (1991) *Management Practice, US Companies Improve Performance Through Quality Efforts,* Report No. GAO/NSIAD-91-190. Washington, DC: US General Accounting Office.

Walker, Orville, Churchill, Gilbert & Ford, Neil (1977) Motivation and performance in industrial selling: present knowledge and needed research. *Journal of Marketing Research*, 14 (May), 156–68.

Webster, Frederick E., Jr. (1992) The changing role of marketing in the corporation. *Journal of Marketing*, October, 1–17.

Winslow, Ron (1992) Videos, questionnaires aim to expand role of patients in treatment decisions. *The Wall Street Journal*, February 25, B1.

Wolfinbarger, Mary & Gilly, Mary (2001) Shopping online for freedom, control and fun. Working Paper, University of California, Irvine.

Woodruff, Robert B., Clemons, D. Scott, Schumann, David W., Gardial, Sarah F. & Burns, Mary Jane (1991) The standards issue in CS/D research: a historical perspective. *Journal of Consumer Satisfaction, Dissatisfaction and Complaining Behavior*, 4, 103–9.

Woodside, Arch G., Frey, Lisa L. & Daly, Robert Timothy (1989) Linking service quality, customer satisfaction, and behavioral intention. *Journal of Health Care Marketing*, 9 (December), 5–17.

Zeithaml, Valarie A. (1988) Consumer perceptions of price, quality, and value: a conceptual model and synthesis of research. *Journal of Marketing*, 52 (July), 2–22.

Zeithaml, Valarie & Bitner, Mary J. (2000) *Services Marketing: Integrating Customer Focus Across the Firm*. Burr Ridge, IL: Irwin/McGraw-Hill.

Zeithaml, Valarie A., Berry, Leonard L. & Parasuraman, A. (1988) Communication and control processes in the delivery of service quality. *Journal of Marketing*, 52 (April), 35–48.

——— (1993) The nature and determinants of customer expectations of service. *Journal of the Academy of Marketing Science*, 21 (1), 1–12.

——— (1996) The behavioral consequences of service quality. *Journal of Marketing*, 60 (April), 31–46.

Zeithaml, Valarie A., Parasuraman, A. & Berry, Leonard L. (1990) *Delivering Quality Service: Balancing Customer Perceptions and Expectations*. New York, The Free Press.

Zeithaml, Valarie A, Parasuraman, A. & Malhotra, Arvind (2000) A conceptual framework for understanding e-service quality: implications for future research and managerial practice. Cambridge, MA: Marketing Science Institute, Report #00-115.

Zeithaml, Valarie A., Rust, Roland T. and Lemon, Katherine N. (2001) Making profitability the basis for service. *California Management Review*, Summer, 118–42.

PART FOUR

Marketing Management

15

Individual Decision-making

J. EDWARD RUSSO and KURT A. CARLSON

What is a Decision?

A decision is the identification of and commitment to a course of action. It may be as simple as choosing one from a fixed set of available options, such as picking a secretary from the three applicants sent by personnel. However, a decision may also be much more complex. Choosing a Director of Market Research may include, *inter alia*, crafting a job description, assembling a set of candidates, a sequence of decisions that reduce that set, and accountability to others for the chosen individual's performance.

How are the identification and commitment made? We view the commitment as the termination of a process whose overarching goal is the distinguishing of one option as superior in overall value. Thus, first and foremost, decision-making is a process, which means a series of cognitive (and emotional) activities that occur over time. This is not to deny that some decisions result from sudden insight. However, most of the important decisions that people make require a sequence of efforts to understand the situation, identify options, gather information, and draw the needed inferences. Further, that process is aimed at distinguishing one alternative from all others (Svenson, 1992, 1996, 2002).[1] That is, the inferences that are drawn from the information acquired are aimed at identifying the one option that is superior in overall value.

What should be the basis of overall value? We dismiss economics' strong assumption that, for all options, decision-makers have known stable tastes or preferences that correspond to numerical 'utilities.' Even if such preferences existed, humans are not capable of recalling them fully and consistently. Alternatively, it has been argued that decision-makers have core values (Keeney, 1996) or principles (Beach, 1998) that underlie the overall worth of the available alternatives. In this view, consistent preferences require knowing oneself fully and fundamentally. Though more reasonable than the economists' fixed exogenous preferences, basing overall value on a set of primitive principles or values also entails cognitive ability and effort that seem to overtax human resources.

What then can be used as the primitive antecedent of overall value? This is a deep question that we do not claim to answer satisfactorily. However, as a working complement to our view of the decision process, we propose that the driver of overall value is the achievement of goals. We do not mean the simple maximizing of utility, with its attendant tautology of utility as what is being maximized and a choice revealing the alternative with the maximum utility. Instead, we base value on a psychologically deeper use of goals.

Plan of the Chapter

The body of the chapter is organized by two distinctions. First, decision-making is a process whose time progression we partition into discrete phases. Although the decision process has occasionally been viewed as a continuum (e.g., Busemeyer & Townsend, 1993), the great majority of the literature considering the entire process is organized into a sequence of distinct phases or stages. Second, within each phase the documented decision behaviors are partitioned into two groups. The first, called errors of untutored performance, can be corrected or improved. The second, challenges to skilled performance, capture the factors that make decisions difficult even for skilled decision-makers. These two categories, errors and challenges, correspond roughly to the controllable (or internal) and uncontrollable (or external) obstacles to a satisfactory decision. The distinction between them is not unlike that between what coaching can and cannot do for an athlete's performance. A coach can detect, communicate, and correct the common errors of naïve performance in sports like swimming and basketball (e.g., making contact with the opponent while boxing out for a rebound). However, even after all the physical and strategic inefficiencies have been 'coached out' of individuals, their performance is still limited by personal and environmental factors (e.g., the relative height and strength of the player and opponent). In summary, novice decision-makers must deal with both errors and challenges. Skilled decision-makers, no matter how great their expertise (we avoid calling them 'experts'), must still confront the uncontrollable obstacles to a successful decision.

We also make one disclaimer. The content of this chapter is individual decision-making. It is not the decision-making of organizations, or even of individual decision-making in the organizational context. For an entry to the literature on organizational decision-making, as well as to the debate over whether organizational and individual decision-making are fundamentally different, see the edited volume by Shapira (1997). Within the domain of individual decision-making, our primary focus is managers and the decisions that confront them. However, both the theories and the empirical findings of the field typically extend to consumers and other individual decision-makers.

The Process of Making a Decision

This chapter is based on the view of decision-making as a process that is driven by goals. We first discuss goals as fundamental to the process, then overview the phases of the process itself.

Goals

Goals in Psychology

Dating back to James (1890) and Ach (1905), goals have been seen as directing human behavior. Reviewing 'goal-like constructs' in the last half century, Austin & Vancouver (1996: 339) list more than 25 social and cognitive goal-based theories. Unfortunately, there is less agreement on what goals are than on their importance. To Lewin (1935, 1943) goals were cognitions over desirable end states. This definition, or one very similar to it, remains popular (e.g., Huffman et al., 2001; Karniol & Ross, 1996; Kleindorfer et al., 1993; Slade 1994). To others, goals serve as a bridge between motivation and cognition. Though some use the terms 'motivation' and 'goal' interchangeably (e.g., Kunda, 1990), others contend that goals should be viewed as a transaction point between motivation and cognition. For example, Schutz (1994: 137) contends that 'thoughts [cognitions] are about something and are directed [motivated] toward some purpose or end.' We adopt this latter view and apply it to decision-making. Thus, goals represent the end states the decision-maker attempts to attain, while cognitions and motivations capture, respectively, what the decision-maker is thinking and where that thought is being directed during the decision process.

Sources of Goals. Goals can be activated from within the decision-maker or from the environment (see Showers & Cantor, 1985 for a review). Numerous sources of goal activation have been proffered, including emotional states (Raghunathan & Pham, 1999), personal values (Beach, 1998), personality traits (Saunders & Stanton, 1976), the presence of others (Ariely & Levav, 2000; Earley & Kanfer, 1985), subtle environmental cues (Bargh, 1990), task requirements (Tubbs & Dahl, 1991) and so-called 'chronic pursuits' or those goals that tend to be generally active (Moskowitz et al., 2000).

Conflict Among Goals. Multiple goals may be activated and pursued simultaneously, and their activation levels may change over time. The acceptance of multiple active goals requires the resolution of the competition among those goals. How this resolution occurs is an open question, with several distinct answers. Each may be valid depending on the situation. Thus, goal conflicts may be reconciled in a deliberate and sensitive tradeoff, through a priority based on their relative levels of activation, or by such arbitrary means as letting certain goals always override others. Alternatively, like Simon's (1991: 367) 'committee of goals,' they may not be resolved with any finality, but may coexist (Medin & Bazerman, 1999).

Goals in Decision-Making

The achievement of goals as the driving force of a decision process is a familiar assumption in theories of decision-making (Bagozzi, 1993; Bagozzi & Dholakia, 1999; Beach, 1998; Beach & Mitchell, 1987; Bettman, 1979; Bettman et al., 1998; Huffman et al., 2001; Payne et al., 1992; Slade, 1994). Further, the empirical evidence of the role

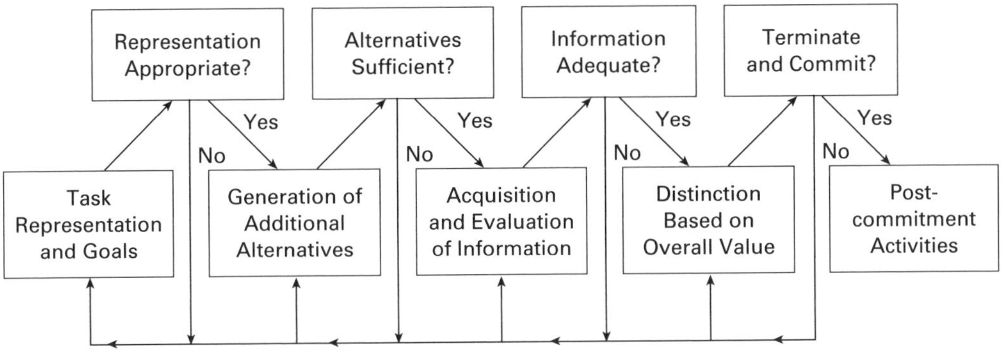

Figure 15.1 *Framework for Decision-making*

of goals in decision-making is substantial. Decision-makers faced with different goals exhibit different decision processes (Tubbs & Ekeberg, 1991) – and even post-decisional processes (Svenson, 1996; Vroom, 1966; Vroom & Deci, 1971). Goals have also been used to explain such anomalous decision behaviors as the asymmetric dominance effect (Ariely & Wallsten, 1995; Simonson, 1989), exaggerated preference for variety (Ariely & Levav, 2000), maladaptive use of strategies (Payne et al., 1996), resistance to disconfirming information (Meloy, 2000), and risk preference reversals (Raghunathan & Pham, 1999). There are many decision-relevant goals that can be activated, and they may be active at various intensities or levels. Goals like effort conservation are so general that they are likely to be active under almost all representations. Others may be elicited more selectively, like seeking a dominating alternative (Montgomery, 1983) or avoiding the choice of a poor alternative.

Goals in Managerial Decision-making

Decision-makers are assumed to be free to choose their own goals. Thus, the rationality of a decision does not depend on decision-makers' personal goals. Instead, rationality is confined to the method or 'means' for achieving the chosen goals or 'ends.' 'Reason … signifies the choice of the right means to an end that you wish to achieve. It has nothing whatever to do with the choice of ends' (Russell, 1954: 8). This assumption is broadly accepted by economists and psychologists, e.g., 'rational … denote[s] that the behavior is appropriate to the goal' (Newell & Simon, 1972: 53).

The decision-maker's full autonomy in the choice of goals does not apply to many managerial decisions. Managers must often strive to achieve not only their own internally activated goals, but also goals suggested or imposed by others (sometimes called objectives). A marketing manager responsible for a series of decisions regarding a new product launch is likely to be held accountable for objectives like market share and revenue. Thus, the freedom to choose goals on a purely subjective basis is, for managers, constrained to include their also achieving externally imposed objectives.

Phases of the Decision Process

The phases of the decision process have been extended both forward and back to complete a framework for decision-making. This framework is composed of the five sequential phases shown in Figure 15.1. It is only one in a long line of phase-based structures for decision-making (e.g., Bagozzi & Dholakia, 1999; Bettman, 1979; Payne et al., 1999). These range in detail from only two stages (e.g., Lussier & Olshavsky, 1974; Sheridan et al., 1975) to three stages (e.g., Pennington & Hastie, 1993; Russo & Leclerc, 1994) to as many as 19 distinct operations (Edwards & Fasolo, 2001).

Phase 1. Mental Representation of the Decision Task

The decision-maker's mental representation of the decision task is a stable, coherent, cognitive structure that resides in memory, can be invoked automatically, and focuses the decision-maker's attention on certain aspects of the problem while occluding others (McNamara, 1994; Ranyard, 1997). By helping decision-makers organize and simplify the task, the representation enables them to perceive, interpret, judge, choose, and act (Schoemaker & Russo, 2001).

The decision task is recognized and accepted in Phase 1. The created mental representation of the task (and context) combines with individual tendencies to activate multiple goals. These, in turn, lead to an anticipated process and drive all further action. Note, however, that as the decision process unfolds, the activation levels of the goals may change and entirely new ones be elicited.

Returning to the decision about whom to hire as the Director of Market Research, when the Vice-President of Marketing learns that the existing position will be vacated, she recognizes the need to fill it. Various aspects of the task are acknowledged, such as time and budget constraints, and some desired characteristics of a new research director. The representation may be elaborated to include such contextual elements as corporate policy (maybe giving preference to internal candidates or to minorities and women), political considerations (acceptance by other groups may be greater if the new director has an information technology background or a doctoral degree), and interpersonal fit with the department's employees (especially the new department leader's four direct reports). The result is a plan for the remainder of the process, maybe starting by announcing the position internally, recruiting colleagues outside Market Research to interview applicants, organizing a timetable, and considering a contingency plan if no internal candidate proves satisfactory. Finally, and as important as anything else, certain goals are activated. Foremost among these is the overarching goal of distinguishing one candidate as superior, but others may include respecting the constraints, re-evaluating the job requirements, or even something as personal as hosting interview dinners at favored restaurants.

Metadecisions. Sometimes the first action that follows recognition and acceptance of a decision is deciding how to decide. This activity, sometimes called a metadecision, is an initial structuring of the approach to be taken to the current decision by considering how decisions like this one should be made. From the particulars, it abstracts the fundamental elements of the decision and uses an appreciation of them to guide the specific process to be followed. If the position of Director of Market Research must be filled, the Vice-President of Marketing might consider the best way to identify, recruit, evaluate, and attract highly qualified candidates for a generic upper management position. Such consideration may include a review of lessons learned from past senior hiring decisions, a recognition of the constraints of time and money, and an analysis of which part of the process is likely to cause the most difficulty (e.g., finding applicants versus determining which one can best do the job).

Based on our unsystematic observations, the metadecision is rarely performed. One can move through all the other phases, and do so successfully, without making a metadecision. Little has been written on the metadecision (for an exception, see Russo & Schoemaker, 2002, Chapter 1). However, there is a small literature on 'deciding how to decide' (e.g., Johnson & Payne, 1985) that is more tightly focused than our meaning as an initial strategic structuring of the entire decision process. Because making a metadecision is optional and little treated either theoretically or empirically, we do not discuss it further.

Phase 2. Generation of Alternatives

The quality of the alternative finally chosen depends directly on having a sufficiently rich pool of options. Sometimes the possible alternatives are obvious – as when a consumer buys one brand of toothpaste on a supermarket shelf. At other times, however, creativity, effort, time, and money are needed to generate better options. With luck, the internal candidates for Director of Market Research are fully satisfactory. If not, however, an executive search firm may be hired, personal networks explored, and the vacant position advertised externally. If no adequate candidates can be found, the Vice-President may have to return to Phase 1 and restructure the position.

Phase 3. Acquisition and Evaluation of Information

Productive decision processes require pertinent information. The search for information is guided by a combination of the mental representation from Phase 1, the possible courses of action from Phase 2, and general guidelines of information gathering. Also, to the extent that the needed information is stored in memory, effective retrieval strategies are needed. Finally, whether the information is acquired or retrieved, it automatically receives an initial evaluation that cannot be suppressed. Evaluation, 'defined as the assessment of the positive and/or negative qualities of an object, is assumed to be among the most pervasive and dominant human responses' (Jarvis & Petty, 1996: 172). Note, however, that Phase 3 contains only the evaluation of the individual units of information, not the combined evaluation of multiple units, which is reserved to Phase 4.

Phase 4. Resolution of Multiple Units of Information to Distinguish One Alternative as Superior

Much of the hard thinking occurs in Phase 4, where the evaluated units of information must be reconciled. Because it is rare that all the information points to one alternative as best, the decision-maker is confronted with opposing evaluations. One candidate for Directorship may have more experience, while another has the desired technology skills, while a third seems like the superior manager of people. The tradeoff among opposing units of information is the work of Phase 4.

Phase 5. Post-commitment Distinction, Implementation, and Learning

Even after a commitment has been made to one course of action, decision-makers tend to reflect on the chosen option, on the rejected ones, and on the information that supported or opposed them. This process is often oriented toward justification, even if only to oneself. The commitment is also followed by a process of implementing the selected course of action, during which parts of it may be fine-tuned or, if necessary, substantially altered. The new Director of Market Research may need coaching or, as one executive said to us about a new hire, 'a kick in the pants.' Finally, there is learning. Increasingly, important decisions are followed by a formal 'lessons learned' analysis that captures and preserves the conclusions to be usefully carried forward to similar future decisions.

Flow of the Decision Process

Transitions

The sequence of phases in Figure 15.1 is augmented by the four transitions between them. Note that each of these involves its own decision about the progress of the process: are the representation and goals appropriate to the task? Has a sufficient number of options been generated? Is the current information adequate? Has one alternative been sufficiently distinguished from the others so that the process can be terminated?

The value of explicitly recognizing these transitions may be clearest for the last one. Whenever Phase 4 is terminated, how could any alternative other than the one leading in overall value be chosen (with the exception of no option being good enough, in which case postponement is considered the best course of action). In other words, is a decision, in the commonly accepted sense of choosing the best option, any more than the obvious action at the time of termination? Thus, although the observable act of decision-making is selecting one alternative, the real decision may be when to terminate the distinction process and commit to the leading alternative.

Flexibility

The left-to-right linearity of this multi-phase process should not create the impression of a unidirectional path. The decision process is more adaptively flexible. For instance, if the previous Director of Market Research identified and groomed a nearly ideal replacement, the generation of alternatives (Phase 2) is unnecessary. More generally, there should be an efficient flow back and forth through the phases that is guided by the four transition decisions. The capacity for any of these transition decisions to send the process back to an earlier stage is indicated by the downward arrows to the backward directed line at the bottom of Figure 15.1. Continuing our example, if none of the internal candidates meets the job requirements (as determined in the termination decision), Phase 2 needs to be re-entered, possibly by hiring an executive search firm. What is not done, however, is to scour the universe of candidates so that Phase 2 is completed with finality before Phases 3 and 4 are begun. Alternatively, if no internal candidate proves acceptable but organization policies (or politics) require that the Directorship be filled internally, the job may have to be restructured and the process returned to Phase 1. Whatever the particulars, the essential point is that the transition decisions enable a flexible process that is not constrained to a one-pass sequence through each phase (see also Mintzberg & Westley, 2001).

Phase 1: Representation and Goals

Phase 1 begins the main overview of research in decision-making. Each phase is covered in sequence, and the content of each is partitioned into the errors of untutored behavior and the challenges to skilled performance. Most of the published literature falls into the category of errors, and does so uniformly across all five phases. Although we proceed through the phases in sequence, it is worth remembering that the actual process of decision-making usually exhibits a back-and-forth efficient flexibility.

Representation and Goals: Errors of Untutored Behavior

The representation adopted for a particular decision task is influenced by task requirements (Best & Ladd, 1985), situational context, and individual tendencies. Task requirements obligate the decision-maker to engage in particular procedures during the decision process, such as instructions to choose one alternative versus rank order all of them. They also activate certain goals, such as to select a restaurant as part of a romantic evening versus one suitable for a business dinner. They can be thought of as directives that require the decision-maker to focus on particular aspects of the problem and, in some cases, to implement specific decision routines.

Context

The representation will also be guided by the situational context, which includes both the options themselves and peripheral factors from the decision's environment (Goldstein & Weber, 1995; Markman & Gentner, 2001). The impact of the decision domain on the task representation, while holding the logical structure of the alternatives constant, was shown by Rettinger & Hastie (2001). The same choice between a sure loss and a two-stage gamble was represented differently in the context of a casino gamble (a straightforward numerical calculation) versus a traffic ticket (where moral principles were elicited).

In the task of selecting a new Director of Market Research, salient characteristics of the internal candidates, such as relevant experience and technical knowledge, will almost certainly find their way into the representation of 'an acceptable candidate.' However, what might be overlooked in the construction of the representation are characteristics possessed by none of these candidates, such as the ability to recruit from outside the company. Similarly, how might the attitudes or anxieties of the market research department's personnel affect the representation of 'an acceptable candidate'? Note that situational context, and possibly the individual tendencies discussed below, may guide the formation of the representation so subtly that decision-makers are unaware of their effect.

Individual Tendencies

Individual tendencies are personal characteristics of the decision-maker, such as her needs, style, experience, etc., that influence the representation. These tendencies include, *inter alia*, expertise (Hollenbeck & Brief, 1987), mood (Meloy, 2000), need for uniqueness (Simonson & Nowlis, 2000), processing capacity (Bettman et al., 1990), and regulatory focus orientation (Higgins, 1997). The representation of the decision can also be influenced by subtle prior experience, such as priming (Chartrand & Bargh, 1996).[2] Finally, it is also affected by such conscious experiences as having been endowed with an option (Thaler & Johnson, 1990), having chosen an option once before (Muthukrishnan & Kardes, 2001), or having incurred sunk costs (Arkes & Blumer, 1985; Zeelenberg & van Dijk, 1997). Note that these last factors may also influence later phases of the decision process.

Framing

The bulk of the published research on decision representations alters the description of the alternatives in order to generate different representations or frames (e.g., Kahneman & Tversky, 1979; Meyerowitz & Chaiken, 1987; Roney et al., 1995; Tversky & Kahneman, 1981, 1988). As visible as these demonstrations have been, it is important to appreciate the range of factors, beyond the specific alternatives, that have been shown to influence framing. These include accountability (Huber & Seiser, 2001; Lerner & Tetlock, 1999), analogies (Klein, 1998), boundaries and constraints, both stated and presumed (Bazerman et al., 2001; Knoblich et al., 1999), decision importance (Billings & Scherer, 1988; Tyszka, 1998), points of comparison (Hinsz et al., 1997), a requisite sequence of subordinate choices (Dawes, 1998), and whether the decision requires that one option be selected or multiple options be rejected (Chernev, 2001; Dhar & Wertenbroch, 2000).

Framing effects have been demonstrated to arise from broad paradigms or worldviews (e.g., Beach, 1998; Johnson & Russo, 1994; Maddi, 1998; Nisbett et al., 2001; Slovic, 1997; Tetlock, 1991). Tetlock (2000) shows that managers with a conservative political ideology are more likely to prefer simple philosophies of corporate governance (the shareholder view over the broader notion of stakeholders), and simple structures of accountability. These same effects on task representation may derive from still broad, but more specific knowledge structures, like those of job or functional area within a company (see Dearborn & Simon, 1958 for an early illustration). Included in this work is an extensive literature on mental accounting (Thaler, 1980, 1999). Maybe the two specific phenomena most deeply studied are sunk costs (e.g., Bazerman & Neale, 1992; Boulding et al., 1997; Camerer & Weber, 1999; Heath, 1995; Soman & Gourville, 2001; Staw & Hoang, 1995; Staw & Ross, 1989) and the endowment effect (Thaler & Johnson, 1990; see also the review and analysis by Camerer, 1995).

The most detailed or 'micro' framing effects may be the impact of different yardsticks (or metrics) and reference points of a single attribute. Consider shifting a reference point to frame the same outcomes as losses versus gains (Bazerman, 1984; Kahneman & Tversky, 1979, 1984; and see reviews in Dawes, 1998, and Camerer, 1995). In their well-known 'Asian disease' problem, Kahneman & Tversky (1979) presented individuals with a choice between two treatment options. When the alternative treatments highlighted the number of deaths, decision-makers were more likely to select the risky (all or nothing) treatment. In contrast, when the alternatives highlighted the number of lives to be saved, decision-makers were more likely to select the safe option (see also Highhouse & Yuece, 1996, and McNeil et al., 1982). Thus, a point of reference, as a detail of the framing of the options, can elicit valuations that are based not only on merit but also on whether the options are perceived as gains or losses relative to that reference point.

The framing of decisions has been one of the most active areas of decision research in the last two decades (Levin et al., 1998, 2002). As a natural consequence, its results have been challenged rigorously. Unsurprisingly, some of the reported results are narrower, or generalize less well, than originally claimed (Frisch, 1993; Schneider, 1992; van Schie & van der Pligt, 1995; see especially the critique in Mellers et al., 1998: 456). Nonetheless, the research on the framing of decisions has produced findings that are generally robust and have expanded the traditional focus of the field (i.e., Phases 3 and 4) to include the mental representation of the task. The topic of framing is likely to remain central to decision research.

Almost all of the above errors of untutored behavior deal with the representation of the decision rather than its goals. The latter both guide the construction of the representation and, in turn, are activated by it so that they then guide the processes that occur in subsequent phases. However, because there is so little empirical literature that measures and reports the activation of goals, there is little written above about them. As will become clear, this situation characterizes all five phases of the decision process. Indeed, the paucity of empirical studies of goals is explicitly addressed in the conclusion.

Summary of Errors of Untutored Behavior

Errors occur in all of the above categories of phenomena. With respect to framing, most of the published work demonstrates the susceptibility of the representation to superficial or irrelevant aspects of the task. With regard to the decision context, many contextual elements improperly influence the task representation. Individual tendencies should also, for the most part, not be allowed to influence the task representation, yet they do. This is true, notably, for mood, regulatory focus orientation, and various 'needs' like those for cognition and for uniqueness. The exception to individual tendencies as a source of errors is the decision-maker's expertise, which should legitimately affect the fullness or complexity of the representation. Although there has been nothing approaching an ecologically valid evaluation of the quality of decision-makers' mental representations, there is ample evidence of the intrusive influence of irrelevant elements of the task, and irrelevant characteristics of the individual.

Representation and Goals: Challenges to Skilled Performance

The mental representation of a decision task should, first of all, be ecologically valid. This is the locus of the errors described above: namely, an invalid representation of the task (and its context). Yet even with no errors of untutored behavior, a valid representation of the logical essence of a decision is often difficult, especially for new or complex decisions. Furthermore, should ecological validity be achieved, the mental representation must also trade off fullness and simplicity. This means capturing the important elements of the decision while discarding, or at least de-emphasizing, the unimportant ones so that the decision-maker's cognitive (and emotional) resources are focused where they can produce the most value.

The empirical work on the construction of decision representations is still very sparse, as are techniques for aiding such construction. At the same time, a valid and usable mental representation is crucial to most important managerial (and other) decisions. It would seem to be a challenge that deserves more scholarly attention.

Transition: Are the Representation and Goals of the Decision Task Appropriate?

Decision-makers typically do not recognize the need for a deliberate, careful construction of a mental representation of the decision task. This implies, in turn, that the related transition decision is largely non-strategic. Certainly, decision-makers' cessation of representation-building and movement to a new phase is unstudied. We know little or nothing about how decision-makers decide that a representation is adequate or that appropriate goals have been activated. Maybe in the future more will be known, but at present there is little to report.

Phase 2. Generation of Alternatives

Most frameworks for decision-making do not include a phase devoted solely to option generation. Rather, the options are presumed to be known and the task is only to select the best one. In most complex decisions, however, generating good options can play as great a role in success as recognizing when one is superior (Kleindorfer et al., 1993).

Generation of Alternatives: Errors of Untutored Behavior

The uncoached errors of option generation are few but general. The mental representation from Phase 1 can limit the options considered. Companies that frame themselves as a family of employees may insist that they develop and promote only from within. We know of one such internally focused firm that, when it was absolutely forced to go outside for its Director of Market Research, hired the individual from one of its main research suppliers who had been for many years that supplier's chief contact with the hiring firm. It was as if, when they couldn't put a family member in the job, they accepted a neighbor of long and close standing. What is needed to avoid such errors is an awareness of the boundaries or blindspots of the task representation or, better yet, the consideration of alternative representations to expand those boundaries or expose those blindspots. Related to, but distinct from, the above, Fiedler (1988) showed that negative mood can narrow the focus of attention and cause a failure to search for new alternatives. Similarly, a feeling of ownership of the current set of alternatives can inhibit the expansion to incorporate new ones, especially if that ownership resulted from a process of elimination.

Another representation-driven error derives from a sense of completeness that obviates the need to search for more alternatives. If the Director's position is represented today just as it was when the last Director was hired (rather than re-evaluated to reflect changed conditions or to prepare for future ones), the set of candidates may be inappropriately limited. Some of the excluded candidates, if asked to describe how they 'see the job,' might well have stimulated the needed updating of Phase 1's representation.

The generation of alternatives is often considered to be in the domain of problem-solving or creativity, rather than decision-making. The research literature on problem-solving has been dominated by insight problems where the challenge is to generate the single correct option (e.g., Dunker, 1945; Wason, 1960). Implicit is the ease of recognizing the solution once it has been generated. Thus, there is a natural complementarity between the field of decision-making's dominant focus on evaluating options and that of problem-solving's on generating them. For reviews of the latter, see Klahr & Simon (1999) and Nickerson (1996). For an entrée to the diverse literature on creativity, see Sternberg (1988); and for the link between creativity and option generation, see MacCrimmon & Wagner (1994).

Generation of Alternatives: Challenges to Skilled Performance

The challenges of option generation are substantial. We have already noted that the decision representation can limit the generation of new options. To these can be added time pressure and mood. Shanteau and Dino (1993) show that greater time pressure undermines the creative process of option generation.

Finally, we note that the options themselves can sometimes be modified, especially if they are designed to be flexible in the first place (Russo & Schoemaker, 2002, Interlude A). The so-called 'real options' approach argues for flexible options in the face of uncertainty (Hamilton, 2000). We know one CEO who, when faced with no acceptable candidates for COO, considered hiring two applicants in a job-sharing arrangement. This would have postponed an all-or-none commitment to one of them, and bought time both to observe them on the job and determine whether one of them could develop into a COO.

Transition: Is the Set of Alternatives Sufficient?

Because we know of no empirical work on this transition decision, we can offer no deeper comment than a cost-benefit analysis that translates the work in information search into the task of option generation. One empirical result, however, suggests caution in the presumption that it is always better to have more alternatives than fewer. Several studies have found that, at the store level, the reduction of low-selling stockkeeping units (SKUs) can lead to an increase in total category sales when the perceived assortment of important category attributes is not reduced (e.g., Boatwright & Nunes, 2001). At the individual level, Iyengar & Lepper (2000) found that consumers were more satisfied with their choices from six than when there were 24 alternatives (e.g., flavors of jam). They experienced choosing one from the larger set as more difficult and frustrating, producing what the authors termed choice overload. Thus, estimating the benefits of generating (or searching for) additional alternatives may need to be modified by the additional costs of processing them.

Phase 3. Acquisition and Evaluation of Relevant Information

Phase 3 is entered, or re-entered, because more information is required. It consists of two activities. The first is determining the kind of information that is needed, along with its source, either in memory or the external environment. The second is the interpretation and evaluation of the acquired information.

Information Acquisition: Errors of Untutored Performance

When more information is needed, the first step is to determine what that information should be. The prescriptive answer to this question is whatever information permits the decision-maker to distinguish the options most effectively and efficiently. Unfortunately, this is guidance more easily stated than implemented.

The errors of an untutored search for information fall into three categories. The first is an all-too-natural tendency to create rather than discover separation among the alternatives. This tendency can lead decision-makers to be overly confident in their decisions: specifically, to believe that their decision is strongly supported when, in reality, it is not. Second, there is a variety of memory-based errors. Finally, we discuss mood and user control. All three classes of factors play an important role in the determination of what information to acquire.

The Problem of Manufactured Distinctions

The desire to distinguish one alternative as superior can lead to the creation, as opposed to the recognition, of a distinction (Svenson, 1996; Tyszka, 1998). Distinction-creation often leads decision-makers to seek information that supports (rather than informs) the currently observed distinctions or currently favored hypotheses (Einhorn & Hogarth, 1978; Lord et al., 1979). This biased testing of current hypotheses, preferences, or other beliefs can lead to a confirmation bias (for general conditions, see Klayman, 1995; Klayman & Ha, 1987; Rabin & Schrag, 1999). The tendency to seek more confirming than disconfirming evidence is particularly broad, though by no means universal (Klayman & Ha, 1987). This bias may be driven by the motivation to bolster one's feeling of competence by finding information that supports the decision-maker's leading option, currently preferred hypothesis, or other 'owned' belief. Alternatively, seeking confirming evidence may be driven by the goal of effort conservation, because such information increases the separation of the leading alternative and thereby brings the process closer to termination. Finally, a bias toward more confirmatory searches may follow from unintended attentional factors, such as a biased focus on the reasons for supporting the leading alternative (versus supporting the trailing alternatives).

Illusion of Control. A comforting presumption that highly uncertain, even random, events can be controlled by the decision-maker's skill is known as the illusion of control (Langer, 1975; Permuter & Monty, 1977). Two mundane examples are the numerous heuristics for gambling like throwing the dice harder to produce a higher number, and the robust demand for commercial advice on picking lottery numbers (Thompson et al., 1998). In management, senior executives tend to overestimate the amount of control they have over their organization's performance. They underappreciate the impact of global, national, and industry-wide factors in favor of the intra-company actions that they control. When dealing with risky alternatives, the illusion of control enables decision-makers to distinguish as superior the alternative over which they can exercise the most control.

Memory-based Errors

A second class of errors in information search derives from memory retrieval. Among the seven sins of memory identified by Schacter (1999, 2001), four may influence what information individuals believe should be acquired. Two of these – bias and suggestibility – lead to errors of untutored performance. The remaining two, transience and misattribution, are challenges to skilled performance.

Bias is the tendency for one's current beliefs, knowledge, or feelings to influence memory for prior experience. It has been repeatedly demonstrated that in order to cohere with currently held beliefs and feelings, people distort their memories of past ones (Levine, 1997; Marcus, 1986). Ego enhancement may also bias memory. College students recalled correctly about nine of ten high school grades that were an A, but only three of ten that were a D (Bahrick et al., 1996).

Suggestibility refers to the recall of experiences that did not occur (see Loftus et al., 1995 for a review). Representative examples are the leading question (Loftus et al., 1978) and eyewitnesses' identification of a transgressor. For instance, Wells & Bradfield (1998) showed to eyewitnesses a photospread that did not include the picture of the actual bank robber. However, confirmation of an incorrect identification caused eyewitnesses to express greater confidence in and provide more detailed descriptions of the identified robber (compared to those who were given no feedback).

Mood

Although atmospheric and often irrelevant, in some situations mood can impact the information acquisition phase of the choice process. Each of the three most common explanations of this generalized positive affect account for some of its effects. According to the mood maintenance view, people wish to avoid information that would disrupt a positive mood (Isen, 1987; Wegener et al., 1995). In a two-alternative choice, Meloy (2000) showed that individuals in a good mood were more likely to ignore disconfirming information, presumably to preserve their progress in the distinction process and, thereby, maintain their good mood. In the second view, the decision-maker's affective state primes mood-consonant information in memory (Isen, 1987; Mackie & Worth, 1989). As a result, decision-makers exhibit a tendency to acquire information that is consistent with their mood, whether good or bad (Adaval, 2001). The final view suggests that the overall affective state signals how well things are going and, as such, provides useful information to the decision process (Bless et al., 1996; Loewenstein et al., 2001). For the present purpose, it is unnecessary to resolve the competing explanations for mood's effects. We note only that all three agree on the potential role of mood in determining what information decision-makers seek.

User Control

We address one last topic under information seeking: the ability of the decision-maker to actively control how, when, and what information is acquired (as opposed to having to use a presented body of evidence). Unsurprisingly, allowing decision-makers to fit the information to their needs or goals increases efficiency (Alba & Hutchinson, 1987; Payne et al., 1993). Moreover, control has also been found to positively impact learning (Klayman, 1988), creativity (Kuhn & Ho, 1980), and the enjoyment of the decision task (Klein, 1999). However, along with its positive impact on the decision process, control can entail processing costs. Ariely (2000) showed that any expected benefits of user control are constrained to situations where managing that control did not place too heavy a burden on the decision-maker's cognitive resources.

Information Acquisition: Challenges to Skilled Performance

Estimating Likelihoods

A constant challenge for decision-makers is the estimation of likelihoods. These may be for repeated events, like achieving monthly sales quotas, or unique ones, like the success of any specific candidate for Director of Market Research. Likelihoods also occur for internal events, such as whether a decision-maker's recollection of an event is correct.

Missing Information

The challenge of missing information offers three options: inferring what is missing, discounting information when only part of it is missing (e.g., Slovic & MacPhillamy, 1974) or ignoring what is simply unavailable. Which action is chosen depends upon the particular task and context (Kivetz & Simonson, 2000). A frequent situation is the presence of some attributes or elements of an object while others are unknown and must be inferred. The estimates of the missing values are conditioned on the interdependencies among the attributes. For instance, in the determination of a superior brand, the inference about the relative value of the competing products on a missing attribute depends on whether the attributes are positively or negatively correlated (Chernev & Carpenter, 2001).

Memory Challenges

Transience refers to the tendency to forget over time. For example, past situations may be temporarily inaccessible to recall because of interference from related situations (Postman & Underwood, 1973). Such a failure can impede the decision-maker's ability to acquire the best information for the problem by undermining the ability to match the current problem to relevant situations from the past.

Misattribution refers to decision-makers' failure to recall the source of some information. They may mistakenly attribute the information to their own insight or imagination, which may grant this information an undue status (Schacter, 1999). Consider how such a tendency might cause problems in the task of finding a new Director of Market Research. To the extent that members of the search committee forget where valuable information about potential prospects was obtained, they may be inclined to believe they simply 'knew it all along' or that their intuition is better than it actually is. This could lead the committee to rely too heavily on internal sources.

Summary

The natural challenges of uncertainty, missing information, and imperfect memory illustrate a general problem. Even if all the correctable error of unskilled information acquisition could be removed, there remain substantial difficulties to executing this part of the decision process.

Interpreting and Evaluating Acquired Information: Errors of Untutored Performance

The errors of untutored approaches are partitioned into those of focus and of generation. We then consider the task of dealing equitably with different formats of information.

Errors of Focus

One cause of errors might be broadly characterized as an overfocus on one part of the information so that its overall value is mis-estimated. Consider the underadjustment from an anchor (Slovic & Lichtenstein, 1971; Tversky & Kahneman, 1974). An estimate of next year's sales is commonly reached by starting with this year's sales and adjusting appropriately. This year's sales offer a conveniently precise and known starting point, called the anchor. Adjusting appropriately means moving up or down from the anchor, depending on what is known about the differences between this year and next, and doing so to the correct degree. Unfortunately, the anchor offers a clearer focus than does the adjustment. The result is a tendency to underadjust or to fail to move far enough from the anchor. Anchoring with insufficient adjustment has been invoked to explain a broad class of behaviors, including egocentric biases (Gilovich et al., 2000), overconfidence (Griffin & Tversky, 1992), effects of product promotion (Wansink et al., 1998), and the influence of others' opinions on product evaluation (Wooten & Reed, 1998). For recent discussions of anchoring and adjustment, see Chapman & Johnson (1999, 2001), Epley & Gilovich (2001), Hastie & Dawes (2001), and Mussweiler & Strack (2001).

Another focusing phenomenon is the relative attention paid to positive versus negative aspects of a product or service experience. Ofir & Simonson (2001) show that informing people in advance that they will be asked to evaluate a product or service leads to lower evaluations and purchase intentions. They trace the cause of this 'negativity effect' to a focus during consumption on the negative elements of the product or service.

False Consensus. A very different focus is one's own beliefs or circumstances. The false consensus effect is a biased belief that others behave or believe more like us than they really do (Marks & Miller, 1987; Mullen, 1983; Ross & Sicoly, 1979; Ross et al., 1977; Srull & Gaelick, 1983). In estimating a national sample's agreement with various statements such as 'Our family is too heavily in debt today,' people tend to bias those estimates toward their own position (Hoch, 1987). Here the information about oneself, acting somewhat like the anchor discussed above, is better known than the information about others. The result is too great an influence of one's own beliefs on the estimate of others'. It must be noted that the false consensus effect is not universally observed (Hoch, 1987), and that the reverse presumption of dissimilarity between oneself and others may occur. Nonetheless, the effect is robust and, as Nickerson (1999, 2001) has argued, is part of the more general phenomenon of projecting what we know onto others, or 'over-imputation of our own knowledge' (2001: 170).

Confirming Beliefs. An entire subcategory of focus errors are those where the evaluation of the information is biased to confirm a currently held or otherwise preferred belief. The desirability bias, known variously as optimism (e.g., Darvill & Johnson, 1991; Messick & Bazerman, 1996), outcome bias (e.g., Cohen & Wallsten, 1992), value bias (e.g., Slovic, 1966; Yates, 1990), and wishful thinking (e.g., McGuire & McGuire, 1991; Slovic, 1966), is the distortion of information to make preferred outcomes seem more likely. For instance, voters tend to believe that their preferred candidate is likely to win an election (Fischer & Budescu, 1995). This phenomenon is quite robust (but see Bar-Hillel & Budescu, 1995, for one limitation), and has been found with professionals in finance (Olsen, 1997) and in medicine (Poses & Anthony, 1991).

Lord et al. (1979) showed that, after reviewing the same information, people who are opposed to capital punishment become more opposed, while those in favor of capital punishment become more favorable. They contend that such polarization occurs because people 'accept confirming evidence at face value while subjecting disconfirming evidence to critical evaluation and as a result ... draw undue support for their initial positions from mixed or random empirical findings' (1979: 2098; also see Kuhn & Lao, 1996 for a critique). Another demonstration of the impact of a prior belief on the evaluation of new information is the 'agreement effect' of Koehler (1993). Using practicing scientists, he showed that judgments of the quality of scientific evidence are biased to favor prior beliefs. There is a large empirical literature on the prior belief effect (e.g., Edwards & Smith, 1996), and accessible reviews are provided in the books by Gilovich (1991, see especially Chapter 5) and by Nisbett & Ross (1980, especially Chapters 4 and 8).

Temporal Perspective. A focus on the past versus the future can alter the evaluation of information. Maybe the most well-known exhibition of the effect of temporal perspective is the hindsight bias, which we postpone discussion of until the post-decisional phase. The differences in temporal perspective have been explained in several ways, each probably valid in particular situations (Jungermann & Thuring, 1987; Weick, 1979). Einhorn and Hogarth categorized retrospective analysis as diagnostic and 'largely intuitive and suggestive,' while for the more predictive prospective thinking 'the decision-maker must assemble and weigh a number of variables' (1987: 66). Jung (2001) claims that retrospective searches for causal explanations of outcomes focus mainly on the actor or agent, while prospective ones include a balance between the agent and situational factors. Mitchell, Russo & Pennington (1989) showed that a retrospective view of a future event, so-called prospective hindsight, generated more detailed causal explanations. They further showed that the advantage of moving forward in time and looking back was not due to temporal perspective *per se*, but to the increased certainty associated with hindsight.

Explanation Bias. A biasing focus can be caused by the very process of information evaluation itself. One example is the explanation bias. For instance, individuals who explained how one particular outcome of a hypothetical football game might occur increased their estimated likelihood of that outcome (Hirt & Sherman, 1985). Similarly, individuals who explained why two variables might be related were more likely to judge the variables as related (Anderson & Sechler, 1986). Sengupta & Fitzsimons (2000) found that analyzing the reasons for preferring a brand increased the likelihood of choosing that brand. However, the reverse happened when a delay of several days was inserted between the reasons analysis and product choice. This result echoes the finding of the disruptive effect of reason generation on attitude-behavior consistency (Wilson et al., 1989, 1993).

Similar to the explanation bias is the effect of elaboration. The evaluation of a positive option, like an ideal vacation, increases under more extensive elaboration (e.g., Shiv & Huber, 2000). Several studies have demonstrated that a judgment task, in comparison to a choice task, leads to the increased elaboration that can drive the above effect (e.g., Schkade & Johnson, 1989).

Relation to a Standard. Information is often evaluated relative to some standard or reference point. A high reference point versus a low one can lead to negative versus positive evaluations of the same information. When these standards of comparison emerge during Phase 3 (in contrast to their being embedded in the representation of the task from Phase 1), the error in evaluation is assigned to this later phase. For instance, if the previous Director of Market Research was a Ph.D., the educational credentials of all candidates may be compared to this standard.

Another source of standards is past experience, especially recent experience that tends to shift standards of evaluation. Wedell (1998) used two initial decisions, such as two choices between pairs of airline tickets, to widen the range of values on one dimension, either layover time or price. He then observed in a third choice that the values on the widened dimension shifted in accord with the range principle of Parducci's range-frequency theory (Parducci, 1974; see also Mellers & Cooke, 1994).

Errors of Generation

The previous errors of focus encompass problems that occur after enough information has been acquired but needs to be explained, to be viewed in a temporal perspective, or to be judged relative to a standard. In contrast, the second category of evaluation errors results from decision-makers' failure to generate a complete set of instances, evidence or obstacles. Errors of insufficient generation include the biases resulting from the use of the availability heuristic and planning fallacy.

Availability. Due to the resource constraints of time, money, and cognitive capacity, decision-makers are usually forced to assemble only a subset of instances from all those available and to base their decisions on this incomplete information. If the sampling procedure is flawed, then a biased set of instances may result and the quality of the decision may be compromised. When decision-makers draw instances from memory, those instances recalled are often the most vivid or self-relevant. Basing judgments on such a biased sampling of salient instances from memory is called the availability heuristic (see Dawes, 1998 for a thorough discussion). Use of this heuristic typically results in biases of incompleteness due to inadequate retrieval of nonevents or self-irrelevant events. For example, when asked whether strokes or motor vehicle accidents cause more deaths in the US each year, more people respond accidents. In fact, strokes, though less well-publicized, cause more deaths each year in the US (Fischhoff et al., 1981; see also Koepsell et al., 1983).

In another illustration of memory-based availability, Dube-Rioux & Russo (1988) asked professionals from the hospitality industry to estimate the likelihood that a restaurant failure was primarily due to each of several possible categories of causes, including a category for 'all other' events. If these professionals were generating a complete set of possible causes for the outcome, then pruning one cause from the fault tree of all possible causes would lead to a compensatory increase in the likelihood of the 'all other' category. However, if the availability of causes from memory was incomplete, then this pruned cause might not be generated and the likelihood of the 'all other' category would not be augmented sufficiently. Consistent with imperfect availability, the likelihood of the pruned cause was mostly assigned to the remaining named categories rather than to the 'all other' category as it should have been (see also Fischhoff et al., 1978; Hirt & Castellan, 1988; Russo & Kolzow, 1994).

Planning Fallacy. Individuals repeatedly underestimate how long it will take to complete a task (Buehler et al., 1994). One explanation for this error is the failure to predict the obstacles that will thwart the plan's progress. This planning fallacy is sometimes exacerbated by the dismissal of obstacles to implementation that have occurred in the past because they are considered unique, non-repeating events. Because it is difficult to generate the specific future events that will disrupt execution of the plan (Atance & O'Neill, 2001), there is a tendency to adopt a 'no fault' scenario that systematically underestimates the completion time (Merrow et al., 1979, 1981).

Information Format

A general set of evaluation biases derives from the task of dealing equally with different information formats, such as pictorial, verbal, or numerical. Decision analysts argue for the superior clarity of numerical information. Their case is bolstered by the sometimes alarming variance in the perceived numerical equivalent of a verbal description. In their summary of this literature, Budescu, Weinberg & Wallsten note that '[t]he overwhelming result is great variability in the values assigned to words and large overlap among the ranges assigned to the various [verbal] expressions' of likelihood (1988: 281). Outside the laboratory, this kind of variance has been observed in audit managers of a Big Five public accounting firm (Amer et al., 1994) and physicians (Bryant & Norman, 1980; Kenney, 1981). In early 1961, the general responsible for the military evaluation of the CIA's plan to invade Cuba at the Bay of Pigs gave it a 'fair' chance of success. He meant 30%. The invasion's planners thought higher. The result was a military failure (Behn & Vaupel, 1982).

Sometimes verbal descriptions are not only variable, and therefore subject to preferred slants, they are also indiscriminate. Jurors in a mock civil trial were asked to find for the plaintiff or defendant based on three increasingly strict criteria of strength of evidence: 'preponderance,' 'clear and convincing,' or 'beyond a doubt' (Kagehiro, 1990). The proportions of guilty verdicts (i.e., favorable to the plaintiff) were .44, .41, and .45, respectively. Thus, these verbal characterizations of the different requirements for culpability had no differential impact on people's verdicts. A second group judged the same cases under the same three criteria, but with numerical specifics added: 'preponderance' meant at least a 50% likelihood of culpability; 'clear and convincing' meant at least a 70% likelihood; and 'beyond a doubt' meant at least a 90% likelihood. The respective verdict proportions changed, in order, to .62, .45, and .30 – a very systematic difference across the three criteria for culpability. Thus, the numbers and not the words conveyed the differences in the required strength of evidence.

Yet, a downside to precise numerical communication of information can occur when the numbers are only estimates but are taken as precise fact (Wallsten, 1990). That is, when the uncertainty of numerical estimates is conveniently ignored because it is unpleasant or complicating, those numbers may command an unjustified impact on decisions (Singer, 1971). More than a few senior managers have railed at their marketing groups' sales estimates as too fuzzy, as if intelligence or effort could yield perfect predictions of the future.[3] In spite of numerical descriptions' susceptibility to overly precise interpretations, and verbal descriptions' defense as more flexibly suited to imprecise beliefs like likelihoods, on balance the evidence supports numbers when making decisions. In a typical finding, Budescu et al. (1988) contrasted numbers versus words (and graphical displays) in a bidding task. They found performance worst with verbal expressions of probability. Possibly reflecting this, decision-makers tend to prefer numeric information to verbal information, particularly when they are receiving as opposed to providing the information (Olson & Budescu, 1997).

Interpreting and Evaluating Acquired Information: Challenges to Skilled Performance

Evaluating information properly faces a standard range of potential challenges. How credible is the information? For instance, suppose that the Vice-President of Marketing speaks with a former boss of one of the candidates for the Directorship. How truthful will that person be, given the risk of a lawsuit if something negative is said? Unfortunately, the credibility of information seems not to be as well estimated as its strength, as demonstrated by Griffin & Tversky (1992) who use this imbalance to illuminate the overconfidence phenomenon (discussed shortly). Credibility is only one source of uncertainty, which typically complicates the evaluation of information. Closely related to uncertainty is ambiguity. Unsurprisingly, ambiguity aversion has been consistently found, from Ellsberg's (1961) ambiguity-driven paradox (Becker & Brownson, 1964) to the series of papers by Curley & Yates (1985, 1989; Curley, Yates & Abrams, 1986).

Excluding uncertainty, there remains what might be called the general challenge of evaluation. Briefly, all the information must be interpreted and compiled to provide the appropriate value on one attribute or aspect of an alternative. Thus, the observations of all the people who interviewed a candidate for Director of Market Research must be combined, possibly with other information (e.g., the opinions of a prior boss or someone else listed as a reference), to yield a value on, say, oral communication skills. Fischhoff et al. (1980: 399) contend that valuation is clearest when the attribute is 'familiar, simple, and directly experienced.' Thus, this challenge is so specific to each decision, that we can do little more than acknowledge it.

Finally, we note a few empirical regularities of how information that is time-dependent is evaluated. The two main findings are that values that are delayed are discounted, and that a time trend matters. The discounting of the value of a delayed outcome is a long-recognized phenomenon (e.g., Loewenstein & Elster, 1992). As consistent as time-based discounting is, there are wide differences in the slope of discounting depending on the nature of those outcomes, for instance a gain versus a loss (Shelley, 1994), risky versus riskless (Stevenson, 1993), and health versus money (Chapman, 1996). One of the most intriguing applications of the negative evaluation of a downward time trend is Hsee et al.'s (1991) demonstration of a preference for Job A paying, in consecutive years, $12,000, $13,000, $14,000, and $15,000, over Job B, paying in those same years $18,000, $17,000, $16,000 and $15,000. Note that Job B dominates Job A, yet was less preferred by Hsee et al.'s subjects solely because of its downward trend in salary.

Similarly, research by Kahneman and colleagues (Fredrickson & Kahneman, 1993; Redelmeier & Kahneman, 1996; Varey & Kahneman, 1992) has examined remembered pain experienced during a prior procedure. One astounding result of this work is that duration of the experience fails to predict remembered discomfort during the procedure. However, Ariely & Loewenstein (2000) present evidence that duration does matter, when conversational norms and scale effects are accounted for. In related work, Kahneman et al. (1993) demonstrated that overall evaluations of a painful experience were reduced by adding a sequence of diminishing pain to the very end of the procedure. This finding, that the latter portion of the sequence plays a major role in the evaluation of the whole sequence, has found support elsewhere (Ariely, 1998; Baumgartner et al., 1997).

Transition: Is the Information Adequate?

The acquisition and evaluation of information (Phase 3) and the reconciliation of opposing information to distinguish one option as superior (Phase 4) are proximal activities that often cycle back and forth. A respect for efficiency means that the conclusion of enough information to usefully move to Phase 4 only means enough for the moment, not enough forever. It is simply expected that, at the present time, more progress toward the ultimate goal can be achieved by carrying the currently available information forward into the reconciliation and distinction process.

The one error of untutored decision-making that seems to recur and affect the judgment of information sufficiency is overconfidence (Ayton & McClelland, 1997; Klayman et al., 1999). If decision-makers believe that they are, say, 95% certain that next quarter's sales will fall in a specified interval, they may well conclude that no more market research can justify its cost, and enter Phase 4 with this range as a key fact. If, however, they are overconfident, the true probability might be only 80%. Thus, in reality they should collect more evidence (i.e., remain in Phase 3) before basing any decision on the current estimated range of sales.

Although overconfidence is pervasive (Russo & Schoemaker, 1992), much can be done about it. For repetitive judgments, feedback is effective when combined with accountability (see, for example, Murphy & Winkler, 1984 on weather forecasters). For unique decisions, listing pro and con reasons can reduce this error (Koriat et al., 1980), with the con reasons doing most of the work. This last result points to the inadequate generation of negative or disconfirming evidence (discussed above) as one cause of overconfidence.

Once the tendency toward too much confidence in our own estimates and judgments is overcome, decision-makers still face the general challenge of judging when they have sufficient information. A precise computation of information sufficiency is exceedingly difficult. Indeed, as with much of decision-making, such guidelines exist only for situations so constrained by simplifying assumptions as to be nearly useless to managerial decisions. The best approach may be one of successive refinement in which decision-makers use the current information in Phase 4, see where the remaining important gaps in information lie, and cycle back to Phase 3 to acquire as much of that needed evidence as can be done at reasonable cost. A repeated cycle of this nature means that decision-makers' best judgments of information sufficiency need only be approximate – which may be all that can be realistically achieved.

Phase 4. Distinguishing One Alternative as Superior

The core task of what has traditionally been thought of as decision-making occurs in Phase 4. It is reconciling the multiple units of information that support the competing alternatives in order to identify the superior option. Initially, this task was accomplished with formal models like expected utility (see Schoemaker, 1982 for a review) and the weighted additive rule (e.g., Anderson, 1982; Dawes, 1979; Hammond & Adelman, 1976; Meehl, 1954). Although some psychologists participated in model building and testing, others directly addressed the phenomenon of the conflict among opposing units of information (e.g., Shepard, 1964; for a review, see Payne et al., 1992, and for recent work, see Weber et al., 2001).

The present discussion of conflict reconciliation is organized around three approaches – intuition, rule-following, and compensatory processes. Intuition means that a substantial portion of the reconciliation process is automatic, unable to be described, and based on 'gut feel.' Rules are effort-conserving rules of thumb, often termed heuristics, that are approximations to accurate tradeoffs. Compensatory processes attempt to use all the information by trading off sensitively the evidence for one alternative against that for the other alternative(s). From intuition to rule-following to compensatory processes, these three approaches tend to increase in the accuracy with which they identify the superior alternative, in the effort required, and in the clarity or transparency of the process itself (Schoemaker & Russo, 1993). The best approach depends on the parameters of the decision, such as the costs of errors and effort, time pressure, and the demand for a justification of the reasoning process. Yet whichever approach is selected, each has its errors of untutored performance, and each its unavoidable challenges.

Intuition

We all rely on intuition to some degree. Indeed, some people see themselves as very good intuitive decision-makers. They acquire evidence, often including the overall recommendations of others, then let it all nonconsciously percolate in their minds until, somehow, the best option emerges. How or why is never clear. It just happens. Of course, thoughtful managers are sometimes troubled by the absence of any reasoning process that can be examined for weaknesses. However, there is no conscious process available to inspection. Then, because nothing can be done, many comfortingly assume that their intuition is sound. Excellent reviews of intuition are provided by Hayashi (2001) and Hogarth (2001), and Lieberman (2000) takes the analysis of intuition down to the neural level.

Although the process of intuitive reasoning is opaque to the decision-maker, scholars have made progress in understanding it. To a large degree, intuition is nonconscious pattern matching. Salient characteristics of the current decision, like the alternatives, information, and constraints, are automatically connected to related past decisions. If there is a good match, 'intuition' dictates choosing the identified alternative (Massaro, 1994). Sometimes the process is extended over time, but is still based on matched connections that remain opaque to the decision-maker. Finally, the match is sometimes transparent to others or, rarely, even to decision-makers themselves (e.g., when the VP of Marketing realizes that she favors one candidate because he most closely resembles the successful Director of Market Research who just resigned).

When is intuition useful, even necessary, as opposed to when does it lead decision-makers in the wrong direction? Sometimes intuition is based on 'automated expertise' (Simon & Prietula, 1989). This means that the match is (a) accurate, because it is based on valid knowledge in the decision domain, and (b) automatic or opaque, because all that knowledge has become, over time, inaccessible to conscious awareness. Though novice automobile drivers must, at first, think about the operation of the machine, the rules of the road, and the surrounding traffic, over years of experience they learn to drive with most of those thoughts automated. Similarly, great experience can leave sound reasoning automatic and unavailable to inspection.

The problem comes when the automatic matching of the new situation to an old one is based on apparent characteristics of the new situation that do not accurately reflect the underlying causal drivers of a good choice. Maybe the intuitively indicated candidate for Director of Market Research resembles the former one in physical appearance, educational credentials, or social style, but not in some crucial areas of competence. The real problem is that because intuitive reasoning is opaque, there is no way for decision-makers to tell whether an intuitive choice is valid (i.e., based on genuine, if automated, expertise) or when the match is a false one in terms of the true drivers of overall value. For an illustration of the danger of intuition in medicine, see Redelmeier et al. (1993a, 1993b).

Any implication that revealing the (associative) process underlying an intuitive choice would enable better decision-making needs to be qualified. The attempt to introspect rapid or automated processes can backfire, either by inhibiting insight or yielding a biased evaluation (Schooler et al., 1993, 2002). This problem is very closely related to the explanation bias discussed in Phase 3's errors of focus. As one illustration of this danger, Wilson et al. (1993) let people observe, rate, choose, and keep art posters. Those who rated the posters (compared to a control group that did not) reported two weeks later both lower satisfaction with the poster they had chosen and a lower likelihood of having hung the poster in their homes. Wilson et al. argue that the act of evaluation distorted the true attractiveness of the posters.

When should decision-makers use their intuition? The most obvious situation is when time is very short. Gary Klein and his associates have studied emergency decisions in several natural environments, like fire-fighting, military combat, neonatal nursing, and nuclear power plant operation (Klein, 1998; Klein & Weick, 2000). Klein's recognition-primed view of 'naturalistic decision-making' describes the matching of the current situation to those familiar ones stored in the memory of experienced professionals.

Intuition's Errors and Challenges

Because intuition is an automated approach to Phase 4's task of combining all the available information to distinguish one option as superior, decision-makers' challenge is always to recognize when to trust that the current situation is one where they have 'automated expertise.' To the extent that this matching task is performed poorly, possibly because of time pressure, decision-makers risk a superficial match that is fundamentally flawed, with all the context-specific costs that such an error entails.

Rule-following

A decision rule is a mental shortcut that is usually a good guide to the right course of action and which saves time and effort. Marketing managers adopt shortcut rules, or heuristics, like the following.

- If our main competitor lowers prices, follow.
- Avoid being the first client of a start-up service provider. Wait until the company has established a record of success.
- Never publicly acknowledge anything negative about our products.
- Set the price by adding X% to the cost of the labor and materials.

In the search for a new Director of Market Research, the VP of Marketing might simplify her reconciliation of opposing information by adopting the *dictionary rule*. 'Pick the candidate on the final list that is rated highest by my colleagues. If two or more candidates are tied (or nearly so) on the interviewers' ratings, pick the one with the most relevant experience. If there's still a tie (or nearly so), go with the direct reports' preference.' Note how this heuristic (like ordering words in a dictionary by the first letter, second letter, etc.) avoids making the hard tradeoffs on differences in ratings, experience, and staff preferences.[4] The main danger is not matching the current case to those where the rule is a good fit. If decision-makers are unaware that they are using a heuristic, or unaware of what it requires to fit a situation, they are exposing themselves to the risk of choosing an inferior alternative.

Consider the following true story (Russo & Schoemaker, 2002: 139–40). A food manufacturer used the dictionary rule to guide product reformulation. The most important criterion was consumers' rating of different products in standard taste tests. The second consideration, used only to break ties on taste, was production cost. The company's rule was 'Substitute a new product formulation (e.g., use a cheaper cooking oil) only when cost is lower but taste is not.' The rule was backed by valid consumer taste tests and standard statistical criteria. The result: steadily declining market share in several unrelated product categories that defied all attempts at explanation. The reason: small annual decrements in taste were not statistically significant, but over several annual product reformulations those decrements accumulated to yield a noticeably inferior product (for an experimental example of this same accumulation, see Tversky, 1969). When the brand manager was told of the flawed use of the dictionary rule, he rejected the explanation – as did his boss. They had insufficient understanding of the dictionary rule in particular, and of heuristics in general.

Heuristics for Likelihood

Combining observations or other information to estimate likelihoods relies on its own set of simplifying rules that substitute for the more complex probability calculus. Consider the representativeness heuristic and the following clever demonstration devised by Tversky & Kahneman (1983). If a regular six-sided die with four Red (R) faces and two Green (G) faces is tossed 20 times, which of the following subsequences is most likely?

1. RGRRR
2. GRGRRR
3. GRRRRR

Many of the experimental subjects who received this problem chose Sequence 2, though the correct answer is Sequence 1. Indeed, the latter is exactly Sequence 2 with the first Green deleted. Because this Green occurs only in Sequence 2, it *must* be less likely than Sequence 1. Tversky & Kahneman explain the majority choice of Sequence 2 as the use of the representativeness heuristic. The combination of four Reds and two Greens is more representative of the die than is the four to one sample of Sequence 1.

We list below several of the more prominent violations of the laws of probability. At the same time, we caution that their applicability to decision-making is sometimes narrow. Their generalizability is limited because highly structured situations are needed for the demonstrations of error, whereas most managerial tasks are far less structured.

- *Conjunction Fallacy.* The example of the red-green die illustrates a larger problem. The conjunction of two events, in this case the subsequences G and RGRRR, must always have a lower probability than either component event. Tversky & Kahneman (1983) have shown several systematic violations, including the well-known Linda problem. For a review, see Payne et al. (1992) and the arguments about probabilistic reasoning by Beach et al. (1986) and by Ginossar & Trope (1987).
- *Gambler's Fallacy.* An event, say five Tails in successive tosses of a fair coin, lowers the estimated likelihood of its recurrence, though it should not. This is another illustration of the representativeness heuristic, in which five Tails followed by a Head is more representative of a fair coin than the same five Tails followed by yet another Tail. For an illustration of the gambler's fallacy in the choice of numbers that are chosen in a state lottery, see Clotfelter & Cook (1993).
- *Hot Hand Fallacy.* This is the opposite of the gambler's fallacy, because it is based on skill rather than pure chance. People tend to believe too much in streaks, like players making numerous

successive shots in a basketball game because they have a 'hot hand' (Gilovich et al., 1985). Indeed, Gilovich et al. analyze NBA statistics to show that, contrary to popular belief and frequent anecdotes, the hot hand phenomenon does not exist in professional basketball.

- *Baserate Neglect.* Dull baserates are sometimes underweighted compared with more vivid case-specific information (Kahneman & Tversky, 1972). Contrary to the laws of (Bayesian) probability (Dawes, 1998), a single highly vivid event – like one person's story of the mechanical problems of their Ford Windstar – may outweigh the frequency-of-repair data from years of J.D. Power surveys.
- *Law of Small Numbers.* People sometimes overestimate the resemblance of a small sample of events to the population from which it was drawn (Rabin, 2002; Tversky & Kahneman, 1974).

For other violations of the laws of probability, see Camerer (1995) and Dawes (1998). We also acknowledge problems with likelihood that are not strictly violations of laws. For instance, the illusion of control presumes too small a role for randomness or for factors outside the decision-maker's control (e.g., Thompson et al., 1998).

In contrast to the numerous published examples of violations of the laws of probability is the assertion of Gigerenzer and his associates that (many of) these errors of reasoning about likelihoods disappear when relative frequencies are used instead of probabilities (Gigerenzer & Hoffrage, 1995; Sedlmeier & Gigerenzer, 2001). The debate over probabilities versus relative frequencies remains active (Gigerenzer & Hoffrage, 1999; Kahneman & Tversky, 1996; Lewis & Keren, 1999; Mellers & McGraw, 1999). In spite of Gigerenzer's argument, it does seem fair to conclude that people's untutored treatment of likelihood deviates from the probability calculus or from other desirable criteria sufficiently often to be worrisome.

There are many general decision rules for simplifying the reconciliation process. Other examples are the *threshold rule*, in which the winning option must exceed a threshold value (or hurdle) on every criterion, and the *majority of confirming* dimensions, in which alternatives are compared in pairs and the winner is the one with the most criteria favoring it (Russo & Dosher, 1983). Some heuristics are quite complex, like the policy making process described by Janis (1989). However, all such decision rules, even Janis' policy process, are substantially simpler than a full analysis.

Rule-Following: Errors and Challenges

The errors of rule-following all derive from using a heuristic when it is not a good approximation to a full and sensitive use of the available information. This type of error may occur because decision-makers are unaware of the heuristic they are actually employing (e.g., Dhami & Ayton, 2001), are unaware of its dangers, use it mainly as a way of coping with emotion (Luce et al., 2000, 2001), or miscalculate the tradeoff among accuracy, effort, and transparency. Assuming that the first three are mastered, the continuing challenge lies in the final error, namely to make that tradeoff well. That is, the challenge is always knowing when to use a particular decision rule and when its expected costs exceed its benefits. A review of heuristics and rule-following can be found in Mellers et al. (1998).

Trading Off Multiple Pieces of Information: Errors of Untutored Behavior

There are many phenomena that result from decision-makers' inequitable treatment of pieces of information when they are combined with the ultimate goal of identifying the single best course of action. In what follows, we organize these phenomena into three groups according to their origin: contrasting whole alternatives, contrasting their components (i.e., attributes or features), or the nature of the information being traded off.

Contrasting of the Alternatives

Fundamental to the contrast among alternatives is their position relative to each other, the status they attain during the choice process, and how they have been represented or framed at the outset of that process. We consider each, in turn.

Effects Due to Positioning of the Alternatives. In the direction-of-comparison effect, assessing the difference between two attractive alternatives enhances the preference for the 'focal' option, or the one to which the other was compared (Dhar et al., 1999). In contrast, when the two options are unattractive, the focal option is relatively less preferred. Thus, the positioning of an alternative as the benchmark or standard of comparison can significantly affect its perceived value. Mantel & Kardes (1999) qualify this finding to situations where the comparison is based on the individual attributes (rather than holistic judgments of the competing alternatives), and where low involvement leads to attribute processing that is less thorough or systematic.

A second kind of positioning effect derives from the alternatives' relative status that emerges during the decision process. This is the pre-decisional distortion of information, or the tendency to see new information about a pair of alternatives as overly supportive of whichever one is currently leading

(Russo et al., 1996, 1998). Russo, Meloy, & Wilks (2000) showed that when sales representatives of a major pharmaceutical firm decided which of two physicians to call on, the evaluation of new information was distorted to favor whichever physician they were already leaning toward visiting. This error of evaluation is quite robust (for auditors, see Russo et al., 2000; for prospective jurors in a mock trial, see Carlson & Russo, 2001; and for a Bayesian interpretation see Boulding et al., 1999). It is also substantial – about twice the magnitude of post-decisional distortion due to cognitive dissonance reduction (Russo et al., 1996, 1998). Finally, because people are largely unaware that they are distorting new information to conform to old information, their choices can be manipulated. In consumer choice, Russo, Carlson & Meloy (2002) targeted one alternative by putting a single attribute that slightly but clearly favored the targeted alternative in the first position (and equivalent information favoring the nontargeted alternative later). The targeted alternative was selected 69% of the time, regardless of which alternative was targeted. The effect was traced to the first attribute's being made the leading alternative, combined with decision-makers' tendency to distort all subsequent information to favor that alternative/brand.

The pre-decisional distortion of information is closely related to the halo effect, in which an overall opinion biases the evaluation of a new piece of information (Bagozzi, 1996). The halo effect is usually confined to information that reflects a component of the alternative (as opposed to a cue; see Connolly & Srivastava, 1995). An example would be how an overall judgment of how much a person is liked then influences the separate evaluations of that person's intelligence, social skills, physical attractiveness, and so on. There is no consensus on the causal nature of the halo effect (Balzer & Sulsky, 1992; Murphy et al., 1993).

Effects Due to an Alternative's Inherited Character. Inequitable treatment of pieces of information can follow from an inherited character of one or more of the options. For example, assuming the absence of political incentives for project completion, unrecoverable costs that have already been incurred on a project should play no role in the current decision-making process. Instead, the decision-maker should value alternatives in terms of their benefits and costs from this point forward. If the expected future benefits outweigh the expected future costs, then support for the project should continue; otherwise, the project should be killed. However, as discussed earlier, decision-makers frequently take sunk costs into account and remain committed to projects that continue to lose money, largely because of the commitment built by sunk costs (Heath, 1995; Moon, 2001; Simonson & Nye, 1992; Thaler, 1991). That is, the alternative to continue the project for which resources have already been spent has a special status over the alternatives of killing the project or launching a new one.

Endowment also confers a special status. If one of the alternatives is the default or endowed option, decision-makers tend to over-value it (Chapman, 1998; Thaler, 1991; Van Boven et al., 2000; van Dijk & van Knippenberg, 1998). For example, Madrian and Shea (2001) showed that automatic enrollment in a 401(k) plan led to significantly increased participation in the plan, suggesting that decision-makers often find the default option sufficiently superior to the alternative options, regardless of what alternative is made the default option. Another naturally occurring example is Johnson et al.'s (1993) finding that 20% of New Jersey drivers purchased the right to sue when their default insurance plan omitted this provision, whereas 75% of Pennsylvania drivers purchased the right to sue (by not opting to drop it for a savings) when it was included as a default in their insurance plan.

Contrasting the Attributes

Errors in the valuation stage of the distinction process can also derive from how the individual attributes or other units of information are contrasted. We focus on errors associated with inequitable attention to certain aspects of the alternatives.

Attribute Comparability. By comparability we mean the degree to which the attributes are measured on the same units (i.e., metrics or yardsticks). When alternatives have common (versus unique) features, Gentner & Gunn (2001) showed that the act of comparing two alternatives (as opposed to merely coprocessing them) leads to greater noticing of both commonalities and differences between the alternatives. This recognition of differences is critical to the distinction process of Phase 4. Dhar & Sherman (1996) showed that the likelihood that decision-makers select an alternative (versus postponing the choice) increases when the alternatives share bad attributes and possess unique good attributes (relative to when the two alternatives share good attributes and have unique bad ones). Chernev (1997, 2001) extended this work on the impact of common versus unique features to include the role of attribute importance. In related work on comparable (or 'alignable') attribute differences, Zhang & Markman (2001) show that differences on alignable attributes have a larger impact on the decision for low-motivation (relative to high-motivaton) participants. This suggests that under conditions of high motivation, decision-makers exert the effort necessary to process nonalignable attribute differences.

Ritov (2000) has proposed an expectation-based explanation for both the relatively greater impact of unique or distinctive features and of alignable attribute differences. A distinctive feature may receive greater weight because it is unexpected, where expectation derives either from the cohesiveness of the attributes that comprise the alternatives or from the environmental frequencies of these same components. Ritov discusses the general importance of expected structure, both for individual alternatives (the cohesiveness among the attributes) and for comparisons between alternatives (the likelihood that a feature is included in both alternatives).

Joint versus Separate Evaluation. There are several phenomena that arise from the contrast between evaluating alternatives in isolation versus choosing between those same alternatives. Maybe the most well known is Lichtenstein & Slovic's (1971, 1973) observation that individuals who choose between a low probability of winning a large amount and a high probability of winning a small amount tend to select the latter, but when asked to price each of the same gambles, they often set a lower price on the gamble they selected. There is some controversy over what is the exact source of this effect (Dawes, 1998; Fischer & Hawkins, 1993; Mellers et al., 1998; Tversky et al., 1988). However, most explanations contend that the decision-maker gives different weight to the attributes (payoff and probability) in choice versus pricing because of compatibility between the attribute's units and those of the required response (e.g., Slovic et al., 1990). Hsee (1996) suggests that joint evaluation provides information that makes certain attributes easier to value. These attributes gain impact under choice because they are inherently easier to evaluate in choice than they are in a single-alternative judgment. Though Hsee's explanation fits well for the choice settings he explores (e.g., choices between dishes of ice cream), it seems less capable of accounting for the gambling scenarios above.

Nowlis & Simonson (1997) found that participants who chose between alternatives gave more weight to comparable attributes than participants who provided purchase likelihood ratings (single-alternative valuations). This is consistent with the above, if we assume that comparable attributes are easier to process and, thus, have more impact. An implication of this conjecture, based on Zhang & Markman's (2001) evidence, is that we might anticipate Nowlis & Simonson's pattern of data to be less pronounced when decision-makers are highly motivated.

Attribute Character

In addition to inequitable treatment of information arising from how decision-makers contrast alternatives and attributes, errors can arise from the character of the attributes. Attribute character captures a broad class of factors, such as whether the attribute is numeric or verbal, ambiguous or unambiguous, dull or vivid, relevant or irrelevant, etc.

Numeric versus Verbal Information. The discussion of Phase 3 considered the impact of different formats for representing individual units of information, especially numeric (e.g., 28 mpg) versus verbal (e.g., above-average fuel efficiency). Now, in Phase 4, we take up the errors made when the individual units of information are combined to distinguish the alternatives on overall value. Briefly, numeric information is associated with more compensatory processing (Stone & Schkade, 1991), more accurate preference predictions (Lindberg et al., 1991), and less variable probability forecasts that an event will occur (Budescu & Wallsten, 1990). Finally, numeric information tends to carry more weight in preferential prediction tasks (Lindberg et al., 1991; Svenson & Karlsson, 1986). Thus, and without surprise, the numeric format facilitates the ease and accuracy of combining individual information units.

Ambiguous Information. A characteristic of the numerical–verbal difference is information ambiguity. Indeed, researchers often study the impact of ambiguity on the decision process by contrasting verbal and numerical information (Teigen & Wibecke, 2000; Wallsten, 1990). As with the preference for numeric information, research on ambiguity has found that decision-makers prefer information that is less ambiguous (Keren & Gerritsen, 1999) and tend to overweight certain (relative to uncertain) outcomes (Kahneman & Tversky, 1979). However, this finding is not universal. Smithson (1999) found that individuals were willing to embrace ambiguous information when the alternative – unambiguous information – led to conflict. In fact, individuals preferred ambiguous information to unambiguous, conflicting information when the outcome was positive. In related work, Hsee (1995, 1996) showed that decision-makers relied more on appealing dimensions (e.g., enjoying one's self) that were not pertinent to the primary task when uncertainty in the justifiable dimension existed. This finding, which Hsee refers to as 'elastic justification,' can be treated as a variant of ambiguity aversion, where the ambiguity in a particular dimension motivates the individual to use factors that are attractive but not justifiable under normal circumstances.

Dull versus Vivid Information. The character of information includes its vividness. How vivid or striking the available information is has been shown to influence mock jurors' judgments (Wilson, Northcraft & Neale, 1989), consumer preferences (Keller & Block, 1997), and estimates of probabilities (Shedler & Manis, 1986). The general result is that vivid information has more impact than non-vivid information. As an example of vividness, consider the case of shark attacks during the summer of 2001. Even though the number of shark attacks and consequent fatalities from them were not extreme by historical standards, there existed a perception that shark attacks were becoming more common. One possible reason is a particularly vivid shark attack in early July that drew the world's attention to the topic. Part of a CNN report from Pensacola, Florida, read as follows.

> The boy was wading in knee-deep water at the Gulf Islands National Seashore on July 6 when he was mauled by a 7-foot bull shark, which tore off his arm and bit a large portion of his thigh. Jessie's uncle, Vance Flosenzier, wrestled the shark to shore and pulled the arm from its mouth. The boy's arm was reattached in an 11-hour operation later that night at Baptist Hospital in Pensacola.

The vividness here comes from several remarkable events, including that a seven-foot bull shark bit off a boy's arm in knee-deep water, the uncle wrestled the shark to the shore, and the arm was recovered from the shark's mouth and reattached.

Irrelevant Information. Decision-makers sometimes rely on irrelevant information when making predictions and choices. The dilution effect is the tendency for irrelevant information to reduce the use or impact of relevant information in prediction tasks (Nisbett et al., 1981; Tetlock et al., 1996). Tetlock & Boettger (1989) found that accountability caused individuals to use a wider range of information, but it did not universally eliminate the dilution effect.

In addition to irrelevant information, decision-makers are sometimes influenced by irrelevant alternatives. Huber, Payne & Puto (1982) showed that consideration of an alternative that was dominated by one of two other alternatives in the choice set led decision-makers to select the dominating option more often than when the dominated option was not present. This violation of the normative principle of regularity is striking because it means that adding irrelevant options to the consideration set can change the choice proportions of the viable options. This phenomenon, known as asymmetric dominance, has been extensively replicated and discussed (Ariely & Wallsten, 1995; Simonson & Tversky, 1992; Wedell, 1991).

Order of Information and Illusory Correlation

The order in which information appears can greatly influence its impact on the decision process. *Primacy* refers to greater weight given to information that appears early in the information sequence. Similarly, information that appears late in the information sequence tends to have greater impact, termed a *recency* effect. The literature on order effects is large and varied. It includes effects not only of the order of information (Asare, 1992; Pennington & Hastie, 1988), but the order in which the alternatives are considered (Dean, 1980), and of a sequence of tasks (Davis et al., 1984).

Illusory correlation refers to the tendency for decision-makers to perceive a positive correlation among units of information when little or no correlation exists. This false perception of correlation among the different attributes of the options or units of information has several possible sources. It may arise from the goal to achieve coherence among the multiple pieces of information (Holyoak & Simon, 1999) or consistency between the expected and observed amounts of separation (or distinction) in the overall value of the alternatives (Carlson, 2000). The goal of separating the alternatives may yield an illusory correlation when new information is perceived as overly consistent with prior information in order to increase separation (Russo et al., 1998; Svenson, 1996, 1998). Even a desire to minimize effort may drive illusory correlation. If the evaluation of new information is distorted toward that of prior information, decision-makers can achieve more rapidly the distinction between alternatives that is deemed sufficient to terminate the process of Phase 4.

Trading Off Multiple Units of Information: Challenges to Skilled Performance

The task of combining the individual pieces of information always poses the challenge of comparing different attributes or features. The difficulty of this challenge is influenced by the expertise of the decision-maker and by the comparability of the attributes themselves (Fischer et al., 2000; Johnson, 1984, 1988). Further, the task is easier when the separation between the best and all other alternatives is large.

In addition, it must be acknowledged that some attributes are very difficult to trade off because the decision-maker has granted them protected status (Baron & Spranca, 1997; Luce et al., 2000; Ritov & Baron, 1999). For many people, human life is one of these dimensions. For example, every automobile manufacturer faces the difficult determination of how safe to make a car, knowing that extra safety means higher cost. The idea that engineers would determine how safe the car should be, and thus how many lives will be lost in car crashes involving the car, is unpalatable because human lives are a protected attribute or 'value' (Lukes, 1996).[5] Nevertheless, the determination must be made because the extremes (the car is either a deathtrap, or is entirely safe and probably useless as a vehicle) are unacceptable. Indeed, there is evidence that people can make tradeoffs between opposing protected values when they must (Baron & Leshner, 2000).

Finally, we also want to acknowledge the complicating effect of time pressure (which is a challenge to every part of the decision process) and of cognitive limitations. The cognitive computational burden is often heaviest in the tradeoffs of Phase 4. Decision analysts might say that this occurs because most decision-makers choose not to quantify value and, therefore, deny to themselves the arithmetic concatenation operations. Managers might respond that the effort to generate valid numerical estimates, whether the momentary demand on cognitive resources or the total work over time, is not worth the benefit. Thus, most decision-makers face the challenge of 'keeping it all straight in their heads' as they deal with the inevitable tradeoffs among different attributes.

Transition: Is Distinction Sufficient for Termination and Commitment to the Leading Option?

This important transition decision is little studied. Only a few errors of untutored performance are known to affect the termination decision. As with most of these phase transitions, there is little theory and less empirical work. Some errors derive from mistakes made earlier in the process, such as false confidence in the completeness of the set of options (Phase 2), or of the information used to evaluate them (Phase 3).

Tversky & Shafir (1992) show that postponement, which is neither terminating nor returning to an earlier phase, is sensitive to the conflict felt among the competing alternatives. When this conflict was increased by adding more options, an act that should only make the best available option at least as attractive, postponement increased as well.

Even if these errors are eliminated, the decision to terminate may be complicated by time pressure or the kind of perceived overload that underlies the postponement result of Tversky & Shafir. An important question is whether termination is based on a sensitive cost-benefit analysis or on rule-following. Several studies have shown an increased use of heuristics or other rule-like strategies under time pressure (e.g., Mano, 1988; Payne et al., 1988; Wright & Weitz, 1977).

Whether the termination analysis is sensitive or approximate, how does it incorporate external factors like incentives, as they influence effort? And how does it incorporate individual preferences, like risk-seeking (Weber, 1999; Weber & Milliman, 1997), that might lead to an earlier termination based on a less resolved conflict among opposing units of information? Some evidence is provided by Mano (1990), who found that time pressure and error penalties shifted the goal of completely processing the information. A related issue is the assessment of the decision-maker's perceived value of accuracy or of effort. For instance, Mellers et al. (1998) have argued that experimenters may fail to take into account the other uses that subjects have for the time they are spending in an experiment. This omission can lead to a discrepancy between what the observer (experimenter) and the decision-maker (subject) believe is rational behavior.

Phase 5. Post-commitment Distinction, Implementation, and Learning

Post-commitment Errors of Untutored Behavior

Decision-makers are prone to error even after they have made a decision and begun to implement it. In this section, we consider two post-decisional errors, bolstering and hindsight, that can exact substantial costs on subsequent decision processes.

Post-decisional Bolstering

Decision-makers tend to bolster their judgment of the selected alternative (Geller & Pitz, 1968; Peterson & DuCharme, 1967). The conventional explanation for the bias toward bolstering is that the act of deciding requires knowledge that one must forgo the positive features of the rejected alternatives and accept the negative features of the chosen one. This knowledge can lead to dissonance (Festinger, 1964) or regret (Loomes & Sugden, 1982), which the decision-maker attempts to quell by avoiding disconfirming information and/or distorting encountered information to bolster the chosen alternative. Evidence that decision-makers are, in fact, more critical of disconfirming information than of supporting information is provided by Ditto & Lopez (1992) and by Edwards & Smith (1996).

There are at least three mechanisms for this differential criticality of opposing (versus supportive) information. First, decision-makers can prefer and seek out information that is supporting of their choice (Frey, 1986; Janis & Mann, 1977; Jonas et al., 2001). Second, decision-makers can distort the evaluation of new information to support the selected alternative (Russo et al., 1998; Svenson, 1996). Third, decision-makers can mistakenly remember the original information as more supportive of the selected alternative than it actually was (Mather et al., 2000).

The cost of post-decisional bolstering is undervaluing the new information. That is, decision-makers who bolster the chosen alternative may remain too committed to it when new information suggests they should abandon it (and the environment allows them to do so freely). Note that this is closely related to the sunk cost phenomenon that we have addressed above.

Hindsight Bias

The second post-decisional error commonly exhibited by decision-makers is hindsight bias – when decision-makers believe that they always knew what they currently know (Fischhoff, 1975; Hawkins & Hastie, 1990). Hindsight bias presents a challenge to the conventional notion of learning from experience because decision-makers exhibiting it fail to appreciate that they have learned something (Bukszar & Connolly, 1988).

Research has shown that hindsight bias is larger for negative and unexpected outcomes than it is for positive and expected ones (Schkade & Kilbourne, 1991). Some of the settings in which this bias has been observed include auditors' going concern judgments (Anderson et al., 1993), business decisions (Connolly & Bukszar, 1990), eyewitness identification of suspects (Wells & Bradfield, 1999), and general retrospective likelihood judgments (Tversky et al., 1992).

In general, hindsight bias is attributed to the reconstructive nature of memory (Carli, 1999; Hoffrage et al., 2000; Stalhberg & Maass, 1998). Individuals are most likely to exhibit hindsight bias when they are motivated and able to claim they always knew what history has demonstrated to be true (Louie, 1999). This bias can be mitigated by increased effort during the choice process (Creyer & Ross, 1993) and by timely feedback (Hoch & Loewenstein, 1989). However, prior instruction to avoid the bias seems to be fruitless (Kamin & Rachlinsky, 1995).

Post-commitment Challenges to Skilled Performance

Regret

Even if decision-makers avoid post-decisional bolstering and hindsight bias, they still must cope with the emotional burden of having made mistakes, at least some of the time. These mistakes include both failing to select the best course of action and selecting an inferior one.

Assuming that decision-makers recognize, learn from, and account for their mistakes, the issue of getting beyond the regret associated with these mistakes still remains. Coping with mistakes is not merely a matter of emotional maintenance, because regret can affect current and future choices (Mellers, 2000; Tsiros & Mittal, 2000). Recall the result reported earlier that people were more satisfied with their choice from six items than from a much larger set of 24 or 30 items (Iyengar & Lepper, 2000). One claimed driver of this effect was the greater regret associated with the choice from the larger set. More generally, decision-makers who feel regret over a particular action (or inaction) may be more likely to be hesitant (impulsive) in a new, related choice. Thus, decision-makers should recognize how regret is manifest and under what conditions it is likely to be greatest.

Gilovich & Medvec (1995) show that people feel more regret in the short run for actions, and more regret in the long run for inactions. Though there is some debate over exactly why this difference exists (Gilovich & Medvec, 1995; Kahneman, 1995), there is consensus that regret requires consequences and that the consequences of action take less time to be realized than the consequences of inaction (Gilovich et al., 1998). The implication is that decision-makers should be wary of regret-induced hesitance in time-constrained decisions, and of regret-induced impulsivity in decisions without a time constraint.

Closely related to regret is disappointment. Regret derives mainly from realizing that a rejected alternative would have been superior to the actual choice. Disappointment follows from learning that the chosen option is worse than was expected. For a comparative discussion of both regret and disappointment, see Zeelenberg et al. (2000).

Other Emotional Responses

Regret is not the only emotion-based response to decision outcomes that has been explored. After a choice between gambles, individuals learned the outcome of the selected gamble and described their emotional response to the outcome (Mellers et al., 1997). The emotional responses revealed that unexpected wins are more pleasurable than expected wins, and any outcome is less pleasant if that which might have been was better.

Implementation

To complete Phase 5, we acknowledge two last activities, implementation and feedback. The former's connection to decision-making is mainly in cases where the original decision may be successively refined as more details are specified (each of which may entail its own subsidiary decision) or revised as unexpected events dictate 'midcourse corrections.' For a brief introduction to the challenges of implementation, see Interlude C of Russo & Schoemaker (2002).

There is little empirical work that touches on the implementation of decisions. In one such study, decision-makers expressed a choice for each of two gambles that were played sequentially (Barkan & Busemeyer, 1999). After the outcome of the first gamble was known, those decision-makers were allowed to revise their choice for the second gamble. The experience of a gain (loss) on the first gamble, even when it was fully expected, led to a shift toward risk aversion (seeking) in the second gamble – in accord with Prospect Theory (Kahneman & Tversky, 1979).

Learning from Experience

Although learning from feedback has never been a large part of decision research, it has received some attention for over two decades (Einhorn & Hogarth, 1978). There are two broad perspectives on the task of learning: causal explanation and noncausal prediction. The latter is exemplified by forecasting, on which there is an extensive literature (e.g., Armstrong & Collopy, 2001). A common error of untutored performance is not using all the feedback or outcomes that are available. A tragic example is the decision to launch the Challenger space shuttle in January 1986 based on an analysis of all past failures but omitting past successes (Dalal et al., 1989). Remarkably, a clear relation between launch success and launch temperature only emerged when the data from all past launches were plotted, including the normally less pertinent cases of successful launches. Feedback is often not available to a learning analysis for the simple reason that decision-makers do not take the trouble to keep track of it (e.g., Goldberg, 1959). Even when decision-makers do all they can to gather and use past outcomes for the prediction of future cases, difficulties remain. Sometimes the feedback is inherently incomplete, as when the VP of Marketing never learns how the rejected applicants for Director of Market Research would have performed (Einhorn & Hogarth, 1978). At other times, the quality of the feedback is degraded by noise in the environment, especially when there is a long delay between the decision and its outcome (e.g., Jennings et al., 1982). Finally, even with complete and precise feedback, delay alone can inhibit learning (Gibson, 2000).

The task of learning as causal explanation (to be distinguished from prediction-oriented learning that is noncausal or statistical) is fraught with obstacles to success. It is much easier to know what happened than to know why it happened. Errors of untutored performance include an array of ego-supporting actions. Self-serving attributions of cause overweigh the decision-maker's skill when performance is good, and overweigh the role of chance when the outcome is bad (e.g., Bettman & Weitz, 1983; Curren et al., 1992; Salancik & Meindl, 1984). Decision-makers resist attributing the cause of a negative result to themselves, thereby accepting blame. They may distort their memory of earlier statements (e.g., predictions), claim that those statements were misunderstood (i.e., reinterpret them), or even change their preferences to make the outcome feel less noxious (the sour grapes effect). Finally, sometimes decision-makers confuse their decision with its implementation. That is, a causal analysis of the outcome must distinguish between the quality of the decision (which, in this chapter, means the quality of the decision process) and of the implementation. Failure to appreciate the role of implementation is a kind of 'treatment effect,' with the most extreme case (known as self-fulfilling prophecy) occurring when a treatment (or implementation) is totally ignored as a cause of the decision's outcome (Jussim, 1986; Kierein & Gold, 2000). In summary, the challenges to effective learning of multiple partial causes are aggravated by several self-imposed obstacles.

CONCLUSION

This chapter adopted a process view of decision-making with goals as the drivers of the decision process. A five-phase structure and a distinction between the correctable and unavoidable obstacles facing decision-makers was used to organize the task of effective decision-making, as well as some of the known findings of the field. This concluding section addresses two questions. First, how far can this process view be taken or, more specifically, what would be required to raise its status from framework to theory to model? Second, what intellectual paths have decision researchers traveled and which way do these paths point as we look toward the future?

Completing the Framework

What's Missing?

Even a casual inspection through the lens of our framework reveals many gaps in our knowledge of decision processes. For instance, we know relatively little about the formation of a problem representation, as crucial as it is. Furthermore, systematic experimentation has been focused on such specifics as the reference points of components of the alternatives, with much less exploration of full mental models. Similarly understudied, at least in the domain of decision-making, is the generation of options (Phase 2). The bulk of research has focused on the information collection and resolution activities of Phases 3 and 4.

Goals. We argued for the central role of goals as the guiding force of the entire decision process. Yet goals played only a minor role in our discussion of Phases 2 through 5. And this role was limited largely to theorizing, because there is so little direct empirical evidence on the activation of specific goals during the decision process. Before decision research can be reliably linked to goals, we need direct evidence of goal activation during the decision process. Unfortunately, as mentioned above, attempts to recover goals directly during the decision process have largely failed. For instance, Chartrand & Bargh (1996) showed that even though participants assigned to different goal-prime conditions assessed information consistently with their condition, they were unable to retrospectively report goals as differentially active across those same conditions. Similarly, Markman & Brendl (2000) report little success recovering the goals that drive consumers' choice processes, whether participants were queried during or after the choice process. Only when consumers were asked to report why attributes were important did they begin to reveal goal-relevant information.

Using a newly developed method, Carlson (2001) has successfully recovered decision-making goals. He tracked the activation levels of 15 general decision process goals (viz., achieve certainty, avoid the worst, be consistent, choose the best, conserve effort, consider all information, develop an impression, enjoy the process, justify, learn about the options, learn my preferences, narrow the set, pick at random, remember the information, separate the options). His method conjoins training for goal recognition with retrospective memory prompts to aid goal recall. These substantial prompts include the original choice alternatives, the responses to progress questions answered during the choice process, and playback of a videotaped verbal (and visual) protocol. Results revealed that decision-makers can report the activation levels of multiple goals at several points during the choice process and that these reports varied with individual expertise, composition of the choice set, and phase of the decision process. Perhaps methods that enable the measurement of the goals active during the decision process will encourage development of the goal component of the framework.

Theory and Model

Can a theory be based on an organized collection of validated cognitive processes or must it be fully computer-implemented as Simon (1992) has urged? If the latter is to be achieved, what must be added to the framework to create a complete theory? Maybe the most glaring inadequacy of the current framework is the lack of specification of the transitions. Given how little is known empirically about the transition decisions, this is understandable. A complete theory will require something like rules that specify the computations on which the transitions are based.

Two other elements that are almost entirely missing are memory and emotion. A model for the former is provided by Dougherty et al. (1999); see also Hastie & Park (1986). As illustrations of the potential value of integrating a memory mechanism into decision-making, see Dougherty's (2001) application of his memory model to account for aspects of overconfidence, and Seifert & Patalano's (2001) predictive encoding model to explain goal activation. The topic of emotion is more complex and pervasive than memory. Fortunately, more is known about the role of emotion in decisions. See the extensive work of Luce et al. (2001) and, more generally, the special issue of *Cognition and Emotion* (Schwarz, 2000) and the volume edited by Martin & Clore (2001).

The final aspect of behavior, and maybe the most difficult, is nonconscious processes (Alba et al., 2002). Like goals, they have been difficult to study empirically, but their importance is becoming clear. One such phenomenon is the mere-measurement effect, in which merely responding to a question about the intent to perform a behavior increases the likelihood of that behavior (Sherman, 1980). For example, Morwitz et al. (1993) found that when over 40,000 consumers were asked, 'When will the next new car be purchased by someone in your household?,' the proportion of automobiles purchased over the next six months rose from 2.4% to 3.3%. The mere-measurement effect is primarily due to nonconscious processes (Fitzsimons & Williams, 2000), which suggests that reducing it by warnings or other conscious interventions is unlikely to succeed (see also Wilson & Brekke, 1994, and Fitzsimons & Shiv, 2001). Because other nonconscious phenomena will undoubtedly be found to affect decisions, this should remain an active area of work.

Model

A fully articulated model might take one of two forms. The first is a computational model like those described in Newell & Simon's (1972) *Human Problem Solving*. Carpenter & Just (1999) make the case for such models applied to higher-order cognition, though their several applications do not include decision-making. The alternative model form is the associative network. These models represent concepts as nodes in a network and contain some form of diffusion of activation along the connecting links between nodes (e.g., Holyoak & Simon, 1999; Janiszeuski & van Osselaer, 2000; Leven & Levine, 1996; Roe et al., 2001; Simon et al., 2001; Thagard & Millgram, 1995; West et al., 1997). Any interest in speculating which of these two directions might be more productive must be dampened by how much detailed empirical evidence is still lacking. It may well be that more specifics of the process of making decisions need to be revealed not only before one direction can be chosen over the other, but before the superior model can be adequately specified.

PAST AND FUTURE

In the beginning, there was only the guidance of the Ancients. Plato urged decision-makers to 'choose that course of action in which the painful is exceeded by the pleasant' (Jowett, 1953: 184). Two millennia later the economists who addressed value and the mathematicians who addressed likelihood began to formalize that ancient advice into numerically precise measurements and rigorous theories of rational decision-making. Their efforts culminated in von Neumann & Morgenstern's axiomatization of Expected Utility (1944, 1947). This theory was extended to subjective probabilities (Edwards, 1954), augmented by Bayesian updating and, to a lesser extent, combined with a general additive utility structure. Taken together, this conceptual corpus formed the theoretical content of the optimality paradigm (Schoemaker, 1982) that dominated decision research in the 1950s and 1960s.

The descriptive failures of the various manifestations of this source of models were also beginning to be exposed in these decades. Joining these empirical shortcomings were the obvious invalidities of the behavioral assumptions made or implied by the economists. In terms of the decision process, the economists presumed that every course of action could be valued accurately (and precisely) and, of course, that the one with the greatest overall value would be chosen. Even when this valuation process was composed of a fully specified sequence of mathematical operations, there was no serious claim that the operations described a cognitive process. As Simon (1991: 366) noted, 'Economics dodged the problem [of a theory of the mind] for two centuries with its *a priori* assumptions of human rationality. But those assumptions are no longer fruitful; they must be replaced by a more veridical theory of the human mind.'

After behavioral researchers began exposing the descriptive failures of the economic/statistical models, they naturally speculated on the actual cognitive reasoning or processes. They proposed conservatism (Edwards, 1968; Phillips & Edwards, 1966), anchoring (Slovic & Lichtenstein, 1971), overconfidence (Adams & Adams, 1961; Lichtenstein et al., 1977; Oskamp, 1965), and so on. Most of this work demonstrated some violation of a rational standard (Arkes, 1991). They became known first as biases and later as anomalies (Thaler, 1994). While some went no further than confirming a violation (e.g., Grether & Plott, 1979), others led to 'behavioral regularities' like those that emerged from Prospect Theory (Kahneman & Tversky, 1979) and asymmetric dominance (Huber et al., 1982). In general, this work yields 'cognitive processes described at an intermediate level of generality' (Kahneman, 1991: 142), a description that echoes Robert Merton's famous 'theories of the middle range' (namely, as general as possible while constrained to the formulation of specific hypotheses vulnerable to empirical refutation). The anomalies stream has grown to dominate decision research in the last two decades (e.g., Shafir & LeBoeuf, 2002).

Other behavioral researchers have drawn less from the economics/statistics tradition of rigorous rationality, and more from the cognitive revolution of the 1970s. Their focus is primarily on increasingly detailed description. Thus, whereas the economists' decision process is straightforward – and 'positivist' (Thaler, 1980) or 'paramorphic' (Doherty & Brehmer, 1997) – and the anomalies-focused behaviorists infer more than trace the decision process, the process-oriented behavioralists seek process-based explanations of increasing detail.

The present chapter reflects this last perspective and reveals how far this enterprise is from success. After dividing the decision process into phases and into errors and challenges within phases, many of the preceding sections are characterized by a noncoherent list of phenomena. Where will the explanations be found that unify these many phenomena into a detailed, coherent description of the decision process?

Should the trend continue of increasingly detailed analyses of the decision process? Will a unifying explanation be found there, or must our theorizing shift to associative neurocognition (e.g., Holyoak & Simon, 1999) or even neurophysiology itself (Platt & Glimcher, 1999)? This question lies at the level of paradigms (Simon, 1983). History teaches that, at some point, the fruitfulness of paradigms declines. That appears to be what has happened to the optimality view. We do not attempt to predict the future of the anomalies or process paradigms – or the emergence of any new competitors (Johnson & Russo, 1994). Instead, it may be best to recognize that the choice of a productive paradigm and the difficult shift from one to another may be at least as important to the field's progress as the normal, if formidable, challenges of theory construction, experimentation, and insightful inference.

Acknowledgements

The authors thank Joe Alba, Jim Bettman, Lyle Brenner, Joel Huber & Meg Meloy for their comments on earlier drafts of this chapter. Its preparation was supported by NSF Grant SES-0112039 to the first author.

Notes

1. The distinction of one alternative as superior to all others is variously labeled separation or differentiation. The latter term is used to convey the dual processes of detecting differences among alternatives (in overall value) and of enlarging those differences (e.g., Svenson, 1996) until they are sufficient to justify a clear choice. The term distinction indicates only the first of those processes, namely perceiving or discovering the differences that are genuinely present. Thus, while differentiation (or separation) may more inclusively describe the processes that actually occur, distinction seems like the better description of the decision-maker's goal.

2. Chartrand & Bargh (1996) show that participants who are nonconsciously primed with a goal-relevant

concept engage in goal-consistent information processing. One interpretation of this result is that the nonconscious prime changed the decision-maker's representation of the task, as well as altering the goals that were active in the decision-maker's mind.

3. This has been called the Sherlock Holmes phenomenon, meaning that 'if we are only clever enough, we should be able to make some elementary yet invariably accurate deductions from very meager evidence' (Behn & Vaupel, 1982: 90).

4. When ties on one attribute are not exact, the dictionary or lexicographic rule is actually a lexicographic semi-order (Luce, 1956; Tversky, 1969).

5. Addressing societal choices, LeGrand (1990) distinguishes between production tradeoffs and value tradeoffs. The former involve the mundane attributes of most managerial decisions such as competing new products' expected sales, launch costs, fit with the product portfolio, etc. Value tradeoffs deal with 'principles' (i.e., protected values) whose potential status makes compromising them more difficult and painful.

References

Ach, Narziss K. (1905) *Über die Willenstaetigkeit und dad Denken (Willing and Thinking)*. Gottingen, Germany: Vandenhoek and Ruprecht.

Adams, J.K & Adams, P.A. (1961) Realism of confidence judgments. *Psychological Review*, 68, 33–45.

Adaval, Rashmi (2001) Sometimes it just feels right: the differential weighting of affect-consistent and affect-inconsistent product information. *Journal of Consumer Research*, 28 (June), 1–17.

Alba, Joseph W. & Hutchinson, Wesley J. (1987) Dimensions of consumer expertise. *Journal of Consumer Research*, 13 (4), 411–54.

Alba, Joseph W., Chartrand, Tanya L., Fitzsimons, Gavan J., Huber, Joel, Hutchinson, J. Wesley, Kardes, Frank R., Menon, Geeta, Raghubir, Priya, Russo, J. Edward, Shiv, Baba, Tavassoli, Nader T. & Williams, Patti (2002) Non-conscious influences on consumer choice. *Marketing Letters*, forthcoming.

Amer, Tarek, Hackenbrack, Karl & Nelson, Mark (1994) Between-auditor differences in the interpretation of probability phrases. *Auditing: A Journal of Practice and Theory*, 13 (1), 126–36.

Anderson, Craig A. & Sechler, Elizabeth S. (1986) Effects of explanation and counterexplanation on the development and use of social theories. *Journal of Personality and Social Psychology*, 50 (1), 24–34.

Anderson, John C., Lowe, Jordan D. & Reckers, Philip M.J. (1993) Evaluation of auditor decisions: hindsight bias effects and the expectation gap. *Journal of Economic Psychology*, 14 (4), 711–37.

Anderson, Norman H. (1982) *Methods of Information Integration Theory*. New York: Academic Press.

Ariely, Dan (1998) Combining experience over time: the effects of duration, intensity changes and on-line measurements on retrospective pain evaluations. *Journal of Behavioral Decision-making*, 11 (1), 19–45.

——— (2000) Controlling the information flow: effects on consumers' decision-making and preferences. *Journal of Consumer Research*, 27 (2), 233–48.

Ariely, Dan & Levav, Jonathan (2000) Sequential choice in group settings: taking the road less traveled and less enjoyed. *Journal of Consumer Research*, 27 (3), 279–90.

Ariely, Dan & Loewenstein, George (2000) When does duration matter in judgment and decision-making? *Journal of Experimental Psychology: General*, 129 (4), 508–23.

Ariely, Dan & Wallsten, Thomas S. (1995) Seeking subjective dominance in multidimensional space: an explanation of the asymmetric dominance effect. *Organizational Behavior and Human Decision Processes*, 63 (3), 223–32.

Arkes, Hal R. (1991) Costs and benefits of judgment errors: implications for debiasing. *Psychological Bulletin*, 110 (3), 486–98.

Arkes, Hal R. & Blumer, Catherine (1985) The psychology of sunk cost. *Organizational Behavior and Human Decision Processes,* 35, 124–40.

Armstrong, J. Scott & Collopy, Fred (eds) (2001) *Principles of Forecasting: A Handbook for Researchers and Practitioners*. Boston, MA: Kluwer Academic Publishers.

Asare, Stephen K. (1992) The auditor's going-concern decision: interaction of task variables and the sequential processing of evidence. *The Accounting Review*, 67 (2), 379–93.

Atance, Cristina M. & O'Neill, Daniela K. (2001) Episodic future thinking. *Trends in Cognitive Sciences*, 5 (12), 533–8.

Austin, James T. & Vancouver, Jeffrey B. (1996) Goal constructs in psychology: structure, process, and content. *Psychological Bulletin*, 120 (3), 338–75.

Ayton, Peter & McClelland, Alastair G.R. (1997) How real is overconfidence? *Journal of Behavioral Decision-Making*, 10 (3), 279–86.

Bagozzi, Richard P. (1993) On the neglect of volition in consumer research: a critique and proposal. *Psychology and Marketing*, 10 (3), 215–37.

——— (1996) The role of arousal in the creation and control of the halo effect in attitude models. *Psychology and Marketing*, 13 (3), 235–64.

Bagozzi, Richard P. & Dholakia, Utpal (1999) Goal setting and goal striving in consumer behavior. *Journal of Marketing*, 63 (Special Issue), 19–32.

Bahrick, Harry P., Hall, Lynda K. & Berger, Stephanie A. (1996) Accuracy and distortion in memory for High School grades. *Psychological Science*, 7 (5), 265–71.

Balzer, William K. & Sulsky, Lorne M. (1992) Halo and performance appraisal research: a critical examination. *Journal of Applied Psychology*, 77 (6), 975–85.

Bargh, John A. (1990) Auto-motives: preconscious determinants of social interaction. In *Handbook of Motivation and Cognition*, Vol. 2, edited by E.T. Higgins & R.M. Sorrentino. New York: Guilford Press, pp. 93–130.

Bar-Hillel, Maya & Budescu, David (1995) The elusive wishful thinking effect. *Thinking and Reasoning*, 1 (1), 71–103.

Barkan, Rachel & Busemeyer, Jerome R. (1999) Changing plans: dynamic inconsistency and the effect of experience on the reference point. *Psychonomic Bulletin and Review*, 6 (4), 547–54.

Baron, Jonathan & Leshner, Sarah (2000) How serious are expressions of protected values? *Journal of Experimental Psychology: Applied*, 6 (3), 183–94.

Baron, Jonathan & Spranca, Mark (1997) Protected values. *Organizational Behavior and Human Decision Processes*, 70 (1): 1–16.

Baumgartner, Hans, Sujan, Mita & Padgett, Dan (1997) Patterns of affective reactions to advertisements: the integration of moment-to-moment responses into overall judgments. *Journal of Marketing Research*, 34 (May), 219–32.

Bazerman, Max H. (1984) The relevance of Kahneman and Tversky's concept of framing to organizational behavior. *Journal of Management*, 10 (3), 333–43.

Bazerman, Max H. & Neale, Margaret (1992) Negotiator cognition and rationality: a behavioral decision theory perspective. *Organizational Behavior and Human Decision Processes*, 51 (2), 157–75.

Bazerman, Max H., Baron, Jonathan & Stronk, Katherine (2001) *You Can't Enlarge the Pie: The Psychology of Ineffective Government*. New York, Basic Books.

Beach, Lee Roy (1998) *Image Theory: Theoretical and Empirical Foundations*. Mahwah, NJ: Erlbaum.

Beach, Lee Roy & Mitchell, Terence R. (1987) Image theory: principles, goals, and plans in decision-making. *Acta Psychologica,* 66 (3), 201–20.

Beach, Lee Roy, Barnes, V.E. & Christensen-Szalanski, J.J.J. (1986) Beyond heuristics and biases: a contingency model of judgmental forecasting. *Journal of Forecasting*, 5, 143–57.

Becker, S.W. & Brownson, F.O. (1964) What price ambiguity? Or the role of ambiguity in decision-making. *Journal of Political Economy*, 72, 62–73.

Behn, Robert D. & Vaupel, James W. (1982) *Quick Analysis for Business Decision-makers*. New York: Basic Books, Inc.

Best, J.B. & Ladd, B. (1985) Generation and development of strategy on a logical-deduction task. *Psychological Reports*, 57 (3), 939–46.

Bettman, James R. (1979) *An Information Processing Theory of Consumer Choice*. Reading, MA: Addison-Wesley.

Bettman, James R. & Weitz, Bart (1983) Attributes in the board room: causal reasoning in corporate annual reports. *Administrative Science Quarterly*, 28, 165–83.

Bettman, James R., Johnson, Eric J. & Payne, John W. (1990) A componential analysis of cognitive effort in choice. *Organizational Behavior and Human Decision Processes*, 45 (1), 111–39.

Bettman, James R., Luce, Mary Frances & Payne, John W. (1998) Constructive consumer choice processes. *Journal of Consumer Research*, 25, 187–217.

Billings, Robert S. & Scherer, Lisa L. (1988) The effects of response mode and importance on decision-making strategies. *Organizational Behavior and Human Decision Processes*, 41 (1), 1–19.

Bless, Herbert, Clore, Gerald, Schwarz, Norbert, Golisano, Verena, Rabe, Christina & Wolk, Marcus (1996) Mood and the use of scripts: does a happy mood really lead to mindlessness? *Journal of Personality and Social Psychology*, 71 (4), 665–79.

Boatwright, Peter & Nunes, Joseph C. (2001) Reducing assortment: an attribute-based approach. *Journal of Marketing*, 65 (July), 50–63.

Boulding, William, Kalra, Ajay & Staelin, Richard (1999) The quality double whammy. *Management Science*, 18, 4, 463–84.

Boulding, William, Morgan, Ruskin & Staelin, Richard (1997) Pulling the plug to stop the new product drain. *Journal of Marketing Research*, 34 (February), 164–76.

Bryant, G.D. & Norman, G.R. (1980) Expressions of probability: words and numbers. *New England Journal of Medicine*, 302, 411.

Budescu, David V. & Wallsten, Thomas S. (1990) Dyadic decisions with numerical and verbal probabilities. *Organizational Behavior and Human Decision Processes*, 46 (2), 240–63.

Budescu, David V., Weinberg, S. & Wallsten, Thomas S. (1988) Decisions based on numerically and verbally expressed uncertainties. *Journal of Experimental Psychology: Human Perception and Performance*, 14, 281–94.

Buehler, Roger, Griffin, Dale & Ross, Michael (1994) Exploring the 'planning fallacy': why people underestimate their task completion times. *Journal of Personality and Social Psychology*, 67 (3), 366–81.

Bukszar, Ed & Connolly, Terry (1988) Hindsight bias and strategic choice: some problems in learning from experience. *Academy of Management Journal*, 31 (3), 628–41.

Busemeyer, Jerome R. & Townsend, James T. (1993) Decision field theory: a dynamic cognition approach to decision-making. *Psychological Review*, 100, 432–59.

Camerer, Colin (1995) Individual decision-making. In *Handbook of Experimental Economics*, edited by J. Kagel & A. Roth. Princeton, NJ: Princeton University Press, pp. 587–703.

Camerer, Colin F. & Weber, Roberto A. (1999) The econometrics and behavioral economics of escalation of commitment: a re-examination of Staw and Hoang's NBA data. *Journal of Economic Behavior and Organization*, 39 (1), 59–82.

Carli, L.L. (1999) Cognitive reconstruction, hindsight, and reactions to victims and perpetrators. *Personality and Social Psychology Bulletin*, 25 (8), 966–79.

Carlson, Kurt A. (2000) Disparity pursuit theory: the role of expectation in product choice. *Advances in Consumer Research*, 27, 301–6.

——— (2001) In search of consumer goals. Doctoral dissertation, Cornell University, August.

Carlson, Kurt A. & Russo, J. Edward (2001) Distorted evaluation of evidence in legal trials. *Journal of Experimental Psychology: Applied*, 7 (2), 91–103.

Carpenter, Patricia A. & Just, Marcel Adam (1999) Computational modeling of high-level cognition versus hypothesis testing. In *The Nature of Cognition*, edited by Robert J. Sternberg. Cambridge, MA: The MIT Press, pp. 245–93.

Chapman, Gretchen B. (1996) Expectations and preferences for sequences of health and money. *Organizational Behavior and Human Decision Processes*, 67, 59–75.

——— (1998) Similarity and reluctance to trade. *Journal of Behavioral Decision-making*, 11 (1), 47–58.

Chapman, Gretchen B. & Johnson, Eric J. (1999) Anchoring, activation, and construction of values, *Organizational Behavior and Human Decision Processes*, 79 (2), 115–53.

——— (2001) Incorporating the irrelevant: anchors in judgments of belief and value. In *The Psychology of Judgment: Heuristics and Biases*, edited by T. Gilovich, D.W. Griffin & D. Kahneman. New York: Cambridge University Press.

Chartrand, Tanya L. & Bargh, John A. (1996) Automatic activation of impression formation and memorization goals: nonconscious goal priming reproduces effects of explicit task instructions. *Journal of Personality and Social Psychology*, 71 (3), 464–78.

Chernev, Alexander (1997) The effect of common features on brand choice: moderating effect of attribute importance. *Journal of Consumer Research*, 23 (March), 304–11.

——— (2001) The impact of common features on consumer preferences: a case of confirmatory reasoning, *Journal of Consumer Research*, 27 (4), 475–88.

Chernev, Alexander & Carpenter, Gregory S. (2001) The role of market efficiency intuitions in consumer choice: a case of compensatory inferences. *Journal of Marketing Research*, 38 (August), 349–61.

Clotfelter, Charles T. & Cook, Philip J. (1993) Notes: The 'Gambler's Fallacy' in lottery play. *Management Science*, 39 (12), 1521–5.

Cohen, Brent L. & Wallsten, Thomas S. (1992) The effect of consistent outcome value and judgments and decision-making given linguistic probabilities. *Journal of Behavioral Decision-making*, 5, 53–72.

Connolly, Terry & Bukszar, Edward W. (1990) Hindsight bias: self-flattery or cognitive error? *Journal of Behavioral Decision-making*, 3 (3), 205–11.

Connolly, Terry & Srivastava, Joydeep (1995) Cues and components in multiattribute evaluation. *Organizational Behavior and Human Decision Processes*, 64 (2), 219–28.

Creyer, Elizabeth & Ross, William T. (1993) Hindsight bias and inferences in choice: the mediating effect of cognitive effort. *Organizational Behavior and Human Decision Processes*, 55 (1), 61–77.

Curley, Shawn P. & Yates, J. Frank (1985) The center and range of the probability interval as factors affecting ambiguity preferences. *Organizational Behavior and Human Decision Processes*, 36, 272–87.

——— (1989) An empirical evaluation of descriptive models of ambiguity reactions in choice situations. *Journal of Mathematical Psychology*, 33, 397–427.

Curley, Shawn P., Yates, J. Frank & Abrams, Richard A. (1986) Psychological sources of ambiguity avoidance. *Organizational Behavior and Human Decision Processes*, 38, 230–56.

Curren, Mary T., Folkes, Valerie S. & Steckel, Joel H. (1992) Explanations for successful and unsuccessful marketing decision: the decision-maker's perspective. *Journal of Marketing*, 56, 18–31.

Dalal, Siddhartha R., Fowlkes, Edward B. & Hoadley, Bruce (1989) Risk analysis of the space shuttle: pre-Challenger prediction of failure. *Journal of the American Statistical Association*, 84 (408), 945–57.

Darvill, Thomas J. & Johnson, Ronald C. (1991) Optimism and perceived control of life events as related to personality. *Personality and Individual Differences*, 12 (9), 951–4.

Davis, James H., Tindale, R. Scott, Nagao, Dennis H., Hinsz, Verlin B. & Robertson, Bret (1984) Order effects in multiple decisions by groups: a demonstration with mock juries and trial procedures. *Journal of Personality and Social Psychology*, 47 (5), 1003–12.

Dawes, Robyn M. (1979) The robust beauty of improper linear models in decision making. *American Psychologist*, 34, 571–82.

——— (1998) Behavioral decision-making and judgment. In *The Handbook of Social Psychology*, 4th edn., edited by Daniel T. Gilbert, Susan T. Fiske & Gardner Lindzey. New York: Oxford University Press, pp. 497–548.

Dean, Michael L. (1980) Presentation order effects in product taste tests. *Journal of Psychology*, 105 (1), 107–10.

Dearborn, DeWitt C. & Simon, Herbert A. (1958) Selective perception: a note on the departmental identification of executives. *Sociometry*, 21, 140–4.

Dhami, Mandeep K. & Ayton, Peter (2001) Bailing and jailing the fast and frugal way. *Journal of Behavioral Decision Making*, 14 (2), 141–68.

Dhar, Ravi & Sherman, Steven (1996) Comparison effects on preference construction. *Journal of Consumer Research*, 26 (3), 293–306.

Dhar, Ravi & Wertenbroch, Klaus (2000) Consumer choice between hedonic and utilitarian goods. *Journal of Marketing Research*, 37 (1), 60–71.

Dhar, Ravi, Nowlis, Stephen M. & Sherman, Steven J. (1999) Comparison effects on preference construction. *Journal of Consumer Research*, 26 (3), 293–306.

Ditto, Peter H. & Lopez, David F. (1992) Motivated skepticism: use of differential decision criteria for preferred and nonpreferred conclusions. *Journal of Personality and Social Psychology*, 63 (4), 568–84.

Doherty, Michael E. & Brehmer, Berndt (1997) The paramorphic representation of clinical judgment: a thirty-year retrospective. In *Research on Judgment and Decision-Making*, edited by William M. Goldstein & Robin M. Hogarth. Cambridge: Cambridge University Press, pp. 537–52.

Dougherty, Michael R.P. (2001) Integration of the ecological and error models of overconfidence using a multiple-trace memory model. *Journal of Experimental Psychology: General*, 130 (4), 579–99.

Dougherty, Michael R.P., Gettys, Charles F. & Ogden, Eve E. (1999) MINERVA-DM: a memory processes model for judgments of likelihood. *Psychological Review*, 106 (1), 180–209.

Dube-Rioux, Laurette & Russo, J. Edward (1988) An availability bias in professional judgment. *Journal of Behavioral Decision Making*, 1 (4), 223–37.
Dunker, Karl (1945) On problem solving (translated by L.S. Lees). *Psychological Monographs*, 58 (270).
Earley, Christopher P. & Kanfer, Ruth (1985) The influence of component participation and role models on goal acceptance, goal satisfaction, and performance. *Organizational Behavior and Human Decision Processes*, 36 (3), 378–90.
Edwards, Kari & Smith, Edward E. (1996) A disconfirmation bias in the evaluation of arguments. *Journal of Personality and Social Psychology*, 71(1), 5–24.
Edwards, Ward (1954) The theory of decision making. *Psychological Bulletin*, 51, 380–417.
——— (1968) Conservatism in human information processing. In *Formal Representation of Human Judgment*, edited by B. Kleinmuntz. New York: John Wiley & Sons, pp. 17–52.
Edwards, Ward & Fasolo, Barbara (2001) Decision technology. *Annual Psychology Review*, 52, 581–606.
Einhorn, Hillel J. & Hogarth, Robin M. (1978) Confidence in judgment: persistence of the illusion of validity. *Psychological Review*, 85 (5), 395–416.
——— (1987) Decision-making: going forward in reverse. *Harvard Business Review*, 65 (1), 66–70.
Ellsberg, Daniel (1961) Risk, ambiguity, and the savage axioms. *Quarterly Journal of Economics*, 75, 643–69.
Epley, Nicholas & Gilovich, Thomas (2001) Putting adjustment back in the anchoring and adjustment heuristic: differential processing of self-generated and experimenter-provided anchors. *Psychological Science*, 12 (5), 391–6.
Felcher, Marla E., Malaviya, Prashant & McGill, Ann L. (2001) The role of taxonomic and goal-derived product categorization in, within, and across category judgments. *Psychology and Marketing*, 18 (8), 865–87.
Festinger, Leon (1964) *Conflict, Decision, and Dissonance*. Stanford, CA: Stanford University Press.
Fiedler, Klaus (1988) Emotional mood, cognitive style, and behavioral regulation. In *Affect, Cognition, and Social Behavior*, edited by K. Fiedler & J. Forgas. Toronto: Hogrefe Int., pp. 100–19.
Fischer, Gregory W. & Hawkins, Scott A. (1993) Strategy compatibility, scale compatibility, and the prominence effect. *Journal of Experimental Psychology: Human Perception Performance*, 19, 580–97.
Fischer, Gregory W., Luce, Mary Frances & Jia, Jianmin (2000) Attribute conflict and preference uncertainty: effects on judgment time and error. *Management Science*, 46 (1), 88–103.
Fischer, Ilan & Budescu, David V. (1995) Desirability and hindsight bias in predicting results of a multi-party election. In *Contributions to Decision Making I*, edited by Jean-Paul Caverni, M. Bar-Hillel, F.H. Barron & H. Jungermann. Amsterdam, NY: Elsevier Science, pp. 193–211.
Fischhoff, Baruch (1975) Hindsight is not equal to foresight: the effect of outcome knowledge on judgment under uncertainty. *Journal of Experimental Psychology: Human Perception and Performance*, 1 (3), 288–99.
Fischhoff, Baruch, Lichtenstein, Sarah, Slovic, Paul, Derby, S.L. & Keeney, Ralph L. (1981) *Acceptable Risk*. Cambridge: Cambridge University Press.
Fischhoff, Baruch, Slovic, Paul & Lichtenstein, Sarah (1978) Fault trees: sensitivity of estimated failure probabilities to problem representations. *Journal of Experimental Psychology: Human Perception and Performance*, 4, 330–44.
——— (1980) Knowing what you want: measuring labile values. In *Cognitive Processes in Choice and Decision Behavior*, edited by Thomas Wallsten. Hillsdale, NJ: Erlbaum, pp. 117–41.
Fitzsimons, Gavan J. & Shiv, Baba (2001) Nonconscious and contaminative effects of hypothetical questions on subsequent decision making. *Journal of Consumer Research*, 28 (2), 224–38.
Fitzsimons, Gavan J. & Williams, Patti (2000) Asking questions can change choice behavior: does it do so automatically or effortfully? *Journal of Experimental Psychology: Applied*, 6 (3), 195–206.
Fredrickson, Barbara L. & Kahneman, Daniel (1993) Duration neglect in retrospective evaluations of affective episodes. *Journal of Personality and Social Psychology*, 65 (1), 45–55.
Frey, Dieter (1986) Recent research on selective exposure to information. In *Advances in Experimental Social Psychology*, Vol. 19, edited by L. Berkowitz. New York: Academic Press, pp. 41–80.
Frisch, D. (1993) Reasons for framing effects. *Organizational Behavior and Human Decision Processes*, 54, 399–429.
Geller, E. Scott & Pitz, Gordon F. (1968) Confidence and decision speed in the revision of opinion. *Organizational Behavior and Human Decision Processes*, 3 (2), 190–201.
Gentner, Dedre & Gunn, Virginia (2001) Structural alignment facilitates the noticing of differences. *Memory and Cognition*, 25 (4), 565–77.
Gibson, Faison P. (2000) Feedback delays: how can decision makers learn not to buy a new car every time the garage is empty? *Organizational Behavior and Human Decision Processes*, 83 (1), 141–66.
Gigerenzer, Gerd & Hoffrage, Ulrich (1995) How to improve Bayesian reasoning without instruction: frequency formats. *Psychological Review*, 102, 684–704.
——— (1999) Overcoming difficulties in Bayesian reasoning: a reply to Lewis and Keren (1999) and Mellers and McGraw (1999). *Psychological Review*, 106, 425–30.
Gilovich, Thomas (1991) Seeing what we want to see: motivational determinants of belief. *How We Know What Isn't So: The Fallibility of Human Reason in Everyday Life*. New York: The Free Press, pp. 75–87.
Gilovich, Thomas & Medvec, Victoria Husted (1995) The experience of regret: what, when, and why. *Psychological Review*, 102 (2), 379–95.
Gilovich, Thomas, Medver, Victoria Husted & Savitsky, Kenneth (2000). The spotlight effect in social judgment: an egocentric bias in estimates of the salience of one's own actions and appearance. *Journal of Personality and Social Psychology*, 78 (2), 211–22.

Gilovich, Thomas, Medvec, Victoria Husted & Kahneman, Daniel (1998) Varieties of regret: a debate and partial resolution. *Psychological Review*, 105 (3), 602–5.

Gilovich, Thomas, Vallone, R. & Tversky, Amos (1985) The hot hand in basketball: on the misperception of random sequences. *Journal of Personality and Social Psychology*, 17, 295–314.

Ginossar, Zvi & Trope, Yaacov (1987) Problem solving in judgment under uncertainty. *Journal of Personality and Social Psychology*, 17, 464–74.

Goldberg, Lewis R. (1959) The effectiveness of clinicians' judgments: the diagnosis of organic brain damage from the Bender Gestalt Test. *Journal of Consulting Psychology*, 23, 25–33.

Goldstein, William M. & Weber, Elke U. (1995) Content and discontent: indications and implications of domain specificity in preferential decision-making. In *Decision-making from a Cognitive Perspective*, 32, edited by J. Busmeyer, D.L. Medin & R. Hastie. San Diego: Academic Press, pp. 83–126.

Grether, David M. & Plott, Charles R. (1979) Economic theory of choice and the preference reversal phenomenon. *American Economic Review*, 69, 623–38.

Griffin, Dale & Tversky, Amos (1992) The weighing of evidence and the determinants of confidence. *Cognitive Psychology*, 24 (3), 411–35.

Hamilton, William F. (2000) Managing real options. In *Wharton on Emerging Technologies*, edited by George S. Day & Paul J.H. Schoemaker. New York: John Wiley & Sons, pp. 271–88.

Hammond, Kenneth R. & Adelman, Leonard (1976) Science, values, and human judgment. *Science*, 194, 389–96.

Hastie, Reid & Dawes, Robyn M. (2001). *Rational Choice in an Uncertain World: The Psychology of Judgment and Decision-Making*. Thousand Oaks, CA: Sage.

Hastie, Reid & Park, Bernadette (1986) The relationship between memory and judgment depends on whether the judgment task is memory-based or on-line. *Psychological Review*, 93 (3), 258–68.

Hawkins, Scott A. & Hastie, Reid (1990) Hindsight: biased judgments of past events after the outcomes are known. *Psychological Bulletin*, 107, 311–27.

Hayashi, Alden M. (2001) When to trust your gut. *Harvard Business Review*, 79, 59–66.

Heath, Chip (1995) Escalation and de-escalation of commitment in response to sunk costs: the role of budgeting in mental accounting. *Organizational Behavior and Human Decision Processes*, 62 (1), 38–54.

Higgins, E. Tory (1997) Beyond pleasure and pain. *American Psychologist*, 52 (12), 1280–1300.

Highhouse, Scott & Yuece, Pavam (1996) Perspectives, perceptions, and risk-taking behavior. *Organizational Behavior and Human Decision Processes*, 65 (2), 159–67.

Hinsz, Verlin B, Kalnbach, Lynn R. & Lorentz, Nicole R. (1997) Using judgmental anchors to establish challenging self-set goals without jeopardizing commitment. *Organizational Behavior and Human Decision Processes*, 71 (3), 287–308.

Hirt, Edward R. & Castellan, John N. Jr. (1988) Probability and category identification in the fault tree paradigm. *Journal of Experimental Psychology: Human Perception and Performance*, 14, 112–31.

Hirt, Edward R. & Sherman, Steven J. (1985) The role of prior knowledge in explaining hypothetical events. *Journal of Experimental Social Psychology*, 21 (6), 519–43.

Hoch, Stephen J. (1987) Perceived consensus and predictive accuracy: the pros and cons of projection. *Journal of Personality and Social Psychology*, 53, 221–34.

Hoch, Stephen J. & Loewenstein, George F. (1989) Outcome feedback: hindsight and information. *Journal of Experimental Psychology: Learning, Memory, and Cognition*, 15 (4), 605–19.

Hoffrage, Ulrich, Hertwig, Ralph & Gigerenzer, Gerd (2000) Hindsight bias: a by-product of knowledge updating? *Journal of Experimental Psychology: Learning, Memory, and Cognition*, 26 (3), 566–81.

Hogarth, Robin (2001) *Educating Intuition*. Chicago: University of Chicago Press.

Hollenbeck, John R. & Brief, Arthur P. (1987) The effects of individual differences and goal origin on goal setting and performance. *Organizational Behavior and Human Decision Processes*, 40 (3), 392–414.

Holyoak, Keith J. & Simon, Dan (1999) Bidirectional reasoning in decision-making by constraint satisfaction. *Journal of Experimental Psychology: General*, 123 (1), 3–31.

Hsee, Christopher K. (1995) Elastic justification: how tempting but task-irrelevant factors influence decisions. *Organizational Behavior and Human Decision Processes*, 62 (3), June, 330–7.

——— (1996) Less is better: when low-value options are valued more highly than high-value options. *Journal of Behavioral Decision-making*, 11 (2), 107–21.

Hsee, Christopher K., Abelson, Robert P. & Salovey, P. (1991) The relative weighting of position and velocity in satisfaction. *Psychological Science*, 2, 263–6.

Huber, Joel, Payne, John & Puto, Christopher (1982) Adding asymmetrically dominated alternatives: violations of regularity and the similarity hypothesis. *Journal of Consumer Research*, 9 (1), 90–8.

Huber, Oswald & Seiser, Gabriele (2001) Accounting and convincing: the effect of two types of justification on the decision process. *Journal of Behavioral Decision-making*, 14, 69–85.

Huffman, Cynthia, Ratneshwar, Srinivas & Mick, David Glen (2001) Consumer goal structures and goal determination processes: an integrative framework. In *The Why of Consumption: Contemporary Perspectives on Consumer Motives, Goals and Desires*, edited by S. Ratneshwar, D.G. Mick & C. Huffman. London and New York: Routledge, pp. 9–35.

Isen, Alice M. (1987) Positive affect, cognitive processes, and social behavior. In *Advances in Experimental Social Psychology*, Vol. 20, edited by Leonard Berkowitz. San Diego: Academic Press, Inc., pp. 203–53.

Iyengar, Sheena S. & Lepper, Mark R. (2000) When choice is demotivating: can one desire too much of a good thing? *Journal of Personality and Social Psychology*, 79 (December), 995–1006.

James, William (1890) *Principles of Psychology*. New York: Holt.

Janis, Irving L. (1989) *Crucial Decisions: Leadership in Policymaking and Crisis Management*. New York: The Free Press.

Janis, Irving L. & Mann, Leon (1977) *Decision-Making: A Psychological Analysis of Conflict, Choice, and Commitment*. New York: The Free Press.

Janiszewski, Chris & van Osselaer, Stijn M.J. (2000) A connectionist model of brand-quality associations. *Journal of Marketing Research*, 37 (3), 331–50.

Jarvis, W., Blair, G. & Petty, Richard E. (1996) The need to evaluate. *Journal of Personality and Social Psychology*, 70 (1), 172–94.

Jennings, Dennis L., Amabile, Teresa M. & Ross, Lee (1982) Informal covariation assessment: data-based versus theory-based judgments. In *Judgment Under Uncertainty: Heuristics and Biases*, edited by Daniel Kahneman, Paul Slovic & Amos Tversky. Cambridge: Cambridge University Press.

Johnson, Eric J. & Payne, John W. (1985) Effort and accuracy in choice. *Management Science*, 31 (4), 395–414.

Johnson, Eric J. & Russo, J. Edward (1994) Competitive decision-making: two and a half frames. *Marketing Letters*, 5 (3), S289–S302.

Johnson, Eric J., Hershey, John C., Meszaros, Jacqueline & Kunreuther, Howard C. (1993) Framing, probability distortions, and insurance decisions. *Journal of Risk and Uncertainty*, 7 (1), 35–51.

Johnson, Michael D. (1984) Consumer choice strategies for comparing noncomparable alternatives. *Journal of Consumer Research*, 11 (3), 741–53.

——— (1988) Comparability and hierarchical processing in multialternative choice. *Journal of Consumer Research*, 15 (December), 303–14.

Jonas, Eva, Schulz-Hardt, Stefan, Frey, Dieter & Thelen, Norman (2001) Confirmation bias in sequential information search after preliminary decisions: an expansion of dissonance theoretical research on selective exposure to information. *Journal of Personality and Social Psychology*, 80 (4), 557–71.

Jowett, Benjamin (1953) Translation of Plato's *Protagoras* in *The Dialogues of Plato*, 4th edn, Vol. 1. Oxford: Clarendon Press, pp. 183–4.

Jung, Susan H. (2001) The effects of temporal perspective on new product evolution. Working Paper, Kellogg School of Management, Northwestern University, November.

Jungermann, Helmut & Thuring, Manfred (1987) The use of mental models for generating scenarios. In *Judgmental Forecasting*, edited by G. Wright & P. Ayton. New York: John Wiley and Sons, Ltd., pp. 245–66.

Jussim, Lee (1986) Self-fulfilling prophecies: a theoretical and integrative review. *Psychological Review*, 93 (4), 429–45.

Kagehiro, Dorothy K. (1990) Defining the standard of proof in jury instructions. *Psychological Science*, 1 (May), 194–200.

Kahneman, Daniel (1991) Judgment and decision making: a personal view. *Psychological Science*, 2 (3), 142–5.

——— (1995) Varieties of counterfactual thinking. In *What Might Have Been: The Social Psychology of Counterfactual Thinking*, edited by N.J. Roese & J.M. Olson. Mahwah, NJ: Erlbaum, pp. 375–96.

Kahneman, Daniel & Tversky, Amos (1972) Subjective probability: a judgment of representativeness. *Cognitive Psychology*, 3, 430–54.

——— (1979) Prospect theory: an analysis of decision under risk. *Econometrica*, 47 (2), 263–91.

——— (1984) Choices, values, and frames. *American Psychologist*, 39 (4), 341–50.

——— (1996) On the reality of cognitive illusions. *Psychological Review*, 103, 582–91.

Kahneman, Daniel, Fredrickson, Barbara L., Schreiber, Charles A. & Redelmeier, Donald A. (1993) When more pain is preferred to less: adding a better end. *Psychological Science*, 4 (6), 401–5.

Kamin, Kim A. & Rachlinski, Jeffrey J. (1995) Ex post not equal ex ante – determining liability in hindsight. *Law and Human Behavior*, 19 (1): 89–104.

Karniol, Rachel & Ross, Michael (1996) The motivational impact of temporal focus: thinking about the future and the past. *Annual Review of Psychology*, 47, 593–620.

Keeney, Ralph (1996) *Value-Focused Thinking: A Path to Creative Decisionmaking*. Cambridge, MA: Harvard University Press.

Keller, Punam & Block, Lauren G. (1997) Vividness effects: a resource-matching perspective. *Journal of Consumer Research*, 24 (3), 295–304.

Kenney, R.M. (1981) Between never and always. *New England Journal of Medicine*, 305, 1098–9.

Keren, Gideon & Gerritsen, Leonie E.M. (1999) On the robustness and possible accounts of ambiguity aversion. *Acta Psychologica*, 103 (1–2), 149–72.

Kierein, Nicole M. & Gold, Michael A. (2000) Pygmalion in work organizations: a meta-analysis. *Journal of Organizational Behavior*, 21, 913–28.

Kivetz, Ran & Simonson, Itamar (2000) The effects of incomplete information on consumer choice. *Journal of Marketing Research*, 37, 427–448.

Klahr, David & Simon, Herbert A. (1999) Studies of scientific discovery: complementary approaches and convergent findings. *Psychological Bulletin*, 125 (5), 524–543.

Klayman, Joshua (1988) Cue discovery in probabilistic environments: uncertainty and experimentation. *Journal of Experimental Psychology: Learning, Memory, and Cognition*, 14 (2), 317–30.

——— (1995) Varieties of confirmation bias. *The Psychology of Learning and Motivation*, 32, 385–418.

Klayman, Joshua & Ha, Young won (1987) Confirmation, disconfirmation, and information in hypothesis testing. *Psychological Review*, 94 (2), 211–28.

Klayman, Joshua, Soll, Jack-B, Gonzalez-Vallejo, Claudia & Barlas, Sema (1999) Overconfidence: it depends on how, what, and whom you ask. *Organizational Behavior and Human Decision Processes*, 79 (3), 216–47.

Klein, Gary (1998) *Sources of Power: How People Make Decisions*, Cambridge, MA: MIT Press.

Klein, Gary & Weick, Karl E. (2000) Decisions: making the right ones, learning from the wrong ones. *Across the Board*, 37 (6), 16–22.

Klein, Lisa R. (1999) Creating virtual experiences in the new media. Unpublished doctoral dissertation, Marketing Department, Harvard Graduate School of Business Administration, November.
Kleindorfer, Paul R., Kunreuther, Howard C. & Schoemaker, Paul J.H. (1993) *Decision Sciences: An Integrative Perspective*. Cambridge: Cambridge University Press.
Knoblich, Gunther, Ohlsson, Stellan, Haider, Hilde & Rhenius, Detlef (1999) Constraint relaxation and chunk decomposition in insight problem solving. *Journal of Experimental Psychology: Learning, Memory, and Cognition*, 25 (6), 1534–56.
Koehler, Jonathan J. (1993) The influence of prior beliefs on scientific judgments of evidence quality. *Organizational Behavior and Human Decision Processes*, 56 (1), 28–55.
Koepsell, T.D., Christensen-Szalanski, J.J.J., Beck, D.E. & Christensen-Szalanski, C.M. (1983) Effects of expertise and experience on risk judgments. *Journal of Applied Psychology*, 68, 278–84.
Koriat, Asher, Lichtenstein, Sarah & Fischhoff, Baruch (1980) Reasons for confidence. *Journal of Experimental Psychology: Human Learning and Memory*, 6, 107–18.
Kuhn, Deanna & Ho, Victoria (1980) Self-directed activity and cognitive development. *Journal of Applied Developmental Psychology*, 1 (2), 119–33.
Kuhn, Deanna & Lao, Joseph (1996) Effects of evidence on attitudes: is polarization the norm? *Psychological Science*, 7 (2), 115–20.
Kunda, Ziva (1990) The case for motivated reasoning. *Psychological Bulletin*, 108 (3), 480–98.
Langer, Ellen (1975) The illusion of control. *Journal of Personality and Social Psychology*, 32, 311–28.
LeGrand, Julian (1990) Equity versus efficiency: the elusive trade-off. *Ethics*, 100, 554–68.
Lerner, Jennifer S. & Tetlock, Philip E. (1999) Accounting for the effects of accountability. *Psychological Bulletin*, 125 (2), 255–75.
Leven, Samuel J. & Levine, Daniel S. (1996) Multiattribute decision-making in context: a dynamic neural network methodology. *Cognitive Science*, 20 (2), 271–99.
Levin, Irwin P., Gaeth, Gary J., Schreiber, Judy & Lauriola, Marco (2002) A new look at framing effects: distribution of effect sizes, individual differences, and independence of types of effects. *Organizational Behavior and Human Decision Processes*, 88 (1), 411–29.
Levin, Irwin P., Schneider, Sandra L. & Gaeth, Gary J. (1998) All frames are not created equal: a typology and critical analysis of framing effects. *Organizational Behavior and Human Decision Processes*, 76, 149–88.
Levine, Linda J. (1997) Reconstructing memory for emotions. *Journal of Experimental Psychology: General*, 126 (2), 165–77.
Lewin, Kurt (1935) *A Dynamic Theory of Personality*. New York: McGraw-Hill.
——— (1943) Defining the field at a given time. *Psychological Review*, 50, 292–310.
Lewis, Charles & Keren, Gideon (1999) On the difficulties underlying Bayesian reasoning: a comment on Gigerenzer and Hoffrage. *Psychological Bulletin*, 106 (2), 411–16.
Lichtenstein, Sarah & Slovic, Paul (1971) Reversal of preferences between bids and choices in gambling decisions. *Journal of Experimental Psychology*, 89, 46–55.
——— (1973) Response-induced reversals of preference in gambling: an extended replication in Las Vegas. *Journal of Experimental Psychology*, 101, 16–20.
Lichtenstein, Sarah, Fischhoff, Baruch & Phillips, Lawrence D. (1977) Calibration of probabilities: the state of the art to 1980. In *Decision Making and Change in Human Affairs*, edited by H. Jungermann & G. deZeeuw. Dordrecht, Holland: D. Reidel Publishing Company, pp. 275–324.
Lieberman, Matthew D. (2000) Intuition: a social cognitive neuroscience approach. *Psychological Bulletin*, 126 (1), 109–37.
Lindberg, Erik, Gaerling, Tommy & Montgomery, Henry (1991) Prediction of preferences for and choices between verbally and numerically described alternatives. *Acta Psychologica*, 76 (2), 165–76.
Loewenstein, George F. & Elster, Jon (eds) (1992) *Choice Over Time*. New York: Russell Sage Foundation.
Loewenstein, George F., Weber, Elke U., Hsee, Christopher K. & Welch, Ned (2001) Risk as feelings. *Psychological Bulletin*, 127 (2), 267–86.
Loftus, Elizabeth F., Feldman, Julie & Dashiell, Richard (1995) The reality of illusory memories. In *Memory Distortions: How Minds, Brains, and Societies Reconstruct the Past*, edited by Daniel L. Schacter. Cambridge, MA: Harvard University Press, pp. 47–68.
Loftus, Elizabeth F., Miller, David G. & Burns, Helen J. (1978) Semantic integration of verbal information into a visual memory. *Journal of Experimental Psychology: Human Learning and Memory*, 4 (1), 19–31.
Loomes, G. & Sugden, Robert (1982) Regret theory – an alternative theory of rational choice under uncertainty. *Economic Journal*, 92 (368), 805–24.
Lord, Charles G., Ross, Lee & Lepper, Mark R. (1979) Biased assimilation and attitude polarization: The effects of prior theories on subsequently considered evidence. *Journal of Personality and Social Psychology*, 37 (11), 2098–109.
Louie, Therese A. (1999) Decision-makers' hindsight bias after receiving favorable and unfavorable feedback. *Journal of Applied Psychology*, 84 (1), 29–41.
Luce, Mary Frances, Payne, John W. & Bettman, James R. (2000) Attribute identities matter: subjective perceptions of attribute characteristics. *Marketing Letters*, 11 (2), 103–16.
——— (2001) *Emotional Decisions: Tradeoff Difficulty and Coping in Consumer Choice*. Chicago: University of Chicago Press.
——— (2000) Coping with unfavorable attribute values in choice. *Organizational Behavior and Human Decision Processes*, 81 (2), 274–99.
Luce, R. Duncan (1956) Semi-orders and a theory of utility discrimination. *Econometrica*, 24, 178–91.
Lukes, Steven (1996) On trade-offs between values. In *Ethics, Rationality, and Economic Behaviour*, edited by

Francesco Farina, Frank Hahn & Stefano Vannucci. Oxford: Clarendon Press, pp. 36–49.

Lussier, Denis A. & Olshavsky, Richard W. (1974) An information processing approach to individual brand choice behavior. Paper presented at the ORSA/TIMS Joint National Meeting, San Juan, Puerto Rico.

Maddi, Salvatore R. (1998) *The Human Quest for Meaning: A Handbook of Psychological Research and Clinical Applications*. Mahwah, NJ: Erlbaum.

Madrian, Brigitte C. & Shea, Dennis F. (2001) The power of suggestion: inertia in 401(K) participation and savings behavior. *Quarterly Journal of Economics*, 116 (4), 1149–87.

Mano, Haim (1988) Deadlines and cognitive effort: a cost-benefit approach. Washington University, St. Louis, John M. Olin School of Business, Typescript.

——— (1990) Anticipated deadline penalties: effects on goal levels and task performance. In *Insights in Decision-making*, edited by Robin M. Hogarth. Chicago: University of Chicago Press, pp. 154–172.

Mantel, Susan Powell & Kardes, Frank R. (1999) The role of direction of comparison, attribute-based processing, and attitude-based processing in consumer preference. *Journal of Consumer Research*, 25 (March), 335–52.

Marcus, George B. (1986) Stability and change in political attitudes: observe, recall and explain. *Political Behavior*, 8, 21–44.

Markman, Arthur B. & Brendl, C. Miguel (2000) The influence of goals on value and choice. *The Psychology of Learning and Motivation*, 3, 97–128.

Markman, Arthur B. & Gentner, Dedre (2001) Thinking. *Annual Review of Psychology*, 52, 223–47.

Marks, G. & Miller, N. (1987) Ten years of research on the false-consensus effect: an empirical and theoretical review. *Psychological Review*, 102, 72–90.

Martin, Leonard L. & Clore, Gerald L. (eds) (2001) *Theories of Mood and Cognition: A User's Guidebook*. Mahwah, NJ: Lawrence Erlbaum Associates.

Massaro, Dominic W. (1994) A pattern recognition account of decision-making. *Memory and Cognition*, 22 (5), 616–27.

Mather, Mara, Shafir, Eldar & Johnson, Marcia K. (2000) Misremembrance of options past: source monitoring and choice. *Psychological Science*, 11 (2), 132–8.

MacCrimmon, Kenneth R. & Wagner, Christian (1994) Stimulating ideas through creativity software. *Management Science*, 40 (11), 1514–32.

McGuire, William J. & McGuire, Claire V. (1991) The content, structure, and operation of thought systems. In *Advances in Social Cognition*, Vol. 4, edited by Robert S. Wyer, Jr. & Thomas K. Srull. Hillsdale, NJ: Lawrence Erlbaum Associates.

Mackie, Diane M. & Worth, Leila T. (1989) Processing deficits and the mediation of positive affect in persuasion. *Journal of Personality and Social Psychology*, 57 (1), 27–40.

McNamara, Timothy P. (1994) Knowledge representation. In *Thinking and Problem Solving*, edited by Robert J. Sternberg. New York: Academic Press, pp. 81–117.

McNeil, Barbara J., Pauker, Steven G., Sox, Harriet C. Jr. & Tversky, Amos (1982) On the elicitation of preferences for alternative therapies. *New England Journal of Medicine*, 306, 1259–62.

Medin, Douglas L. & Bazerman, Max H. (1999) Broadening behavioral decision research: multiple levels of cognitive processing. *Psychonomic Bulletin and Review*, 6 (4), 533–46.

Meehl, Paul E. (1954) *Clinical versus Statistical Prediction: A Theoretical Analysis and a Review of the Evidence*. Minneapolis: University of Minnesota Press.

Mellers, Barbara A. (2000) Choice and the relative pleasure of consequences. *Psychological Bulletin*, 126 (6), 910–24.

Mellers, Barbara A. & Cooke, Alan D.J. (1994) Tradeoffs depend on attribute range. *Journal of Experimental Psychology: Human Perception and Performance*, 20, 1055–67.

Mellers, Barbara A. & McGraw, A. Peter (1999) How to improve Bayesian reasoning: comment on Gigerenzer and Hoffrage (1995). *Psychological Bulletin*, 106 (2), 417–24.

Mellers, Barbara A., Schwartz, Alan & Cooke, Alan D.J. (1998) Judgment and decision-making. *Annual Review of Psychology*, 49, 447–77.

Mellers, Barbara A., Schwartz, Alan, Ho, Katty & Ritov, Ilana (1997) Decision affect theory: emotional reactions to the outcomes of risky options. *Psychological Science*, 8 (6), 423–9.

Meloy, Margaret G. (2000) Mood-driven distortion of product information. *Journal of Consumer Research*, 27 (3), 345–59.

Merrow, Edward W., Chapel, Stephen W. & Worthy, Christopher (1979) A review of cost estimation in new technologies: implications for energy process plants. *Rand Corporation Report* R-2481-DOE.

Merrow, Edward W., Phillips, Kenneth E. & Myers, Christopher W. (1981) Understanding cost growth and performance shortfalls in pioneer process plants. *Rand Corporation Report* R-2569-DOE.

Messick, David M. & Bazerman, Max H. (1996) Ethical leadership and the psychology of decision-making. *Sloan Management Review*, 37 (2), 9–22.

Meyerowitz, Beth E. & Chaiken, Shelley (1987) The effect of message framing on breast self-examination attitudes, intentions, and behavior. *Journal of Personality and Social Psychology*, 52, 500–10.

Mintzberg, Henry & Westley, Frances (2001) Decision making: it's not what you think. *MIT Sloan Management Review*, Spring, 89–93.

Mitchell, Deborah J., Russo, J. Edward & Pennington, Nancy (1989) Back to the future: temporal perspective in the explanation of events. *Journal of Behavioral Decision-making*, 2, 25–38.

Montgomery, Henry (1983) Decision rules and the search for dominance structure: towards a process model of decision-making. In *Analyzing and Aiding Decision Processes*, edited by P. Humphreys, O. Svenson & A. Vari. Amsterdam: North-Holland, pp. 343–69.

Moon, Henry (2001) Looking forward and looking back: integrating completion and sunk-cost effects within an escalation-of-commitment progress decision. *Journal of Applied Psychology*, 86 (1), 104–13.

Morwitz, Vicki G., Johnson, Eric & Schmittlein, David (1993) Does measuring intent change behavior? *Journal of Consumer Research*, 20, 46–61.

Moskowitz, Gordon B., Salomon, Amanda R. & Taylor, Constance M. (2000) Preconsciously controlling stereotyping: implicitly activated egalitarian goals prevent the activation of stereotypes. *Social Cognition*, 18 (2), 151–77.

Mullen, B. (1983) Egocentric bias in estimates of consensus. *Journal of Social Psychology*, 121, 31–8.

Murphy, Alan H. & Winkler, Robert L. (1984) Probability forecasting in meteorology. *Journal of the American Statistical Association*, 79, 489–500.

Murphy, Kevin R., Jako, Robert A. & Anhalt, Rebecca L. (1993) Nature and consequences of halo error: a critical analysis. *Journal of Applied Psychology*, 78 (2), 218–25.

Mussweiler, Thomas & Strack, Fritz (2001) The semantics of anchoring. *Organizational Behavior and Human Decision Processes*, 86 (2), 234–55.

Muthukrishnan, A.V. & Kardes, Frank R. (2001) Persistent preferences for product attributes: the effects of the initial choice context and uninformative experience. *Journal of Consumer Research*, 28 (June), 89–104.

Newell, Allen & Simon, Herbert A. (1972) *Human Problem Solving*. Englewood Cliffs, NJ: Prentice-Hall.

Nickerson, Raymond S. (1996) Ambiguities and unstated assumptions in probabilistic reasoning, *Psychological Bulletin*, 120 (3), 410–33.

——— (1999) How we know – and sometimes misjudge – what others know: imputing one's own knowledge to others. *Psychological Bulletin*, 125, 737–59.

——— (2001) The projective way of knowing: a useful heuristic that sometimes misleads. *Current Directions in Psychological Science*, 10 (5), 168–72.

Nisbett, Richard E. & Ross, Lee (1980) Theory maintenance and theory change. In *Human Inference: Strategies and Shortcomings of Social Judgment*. Englewood Cliffs, NJ: Prentice Hall, pp. 167–92.

Nisbett, Richard E., Zukier, H. & Lemley, R.E. (1981) The dilution effect: non-diagnostic information weakens the implications of diagnostic information. *Cognitive Psychology*, 13 (2), 248–77.

Nisbett, Richard E., Peng, Kaiping, Choi, Incheol & Norenzayan, Ara (2001) Culture and systems of thought: holistic versus analytic cognition. *Psychological Review*, 108 (2), 291–310.

Nowlis, Stephen M. & Simonson, Itamar (1997) Attribute-task compatibility as a determinant of consumer preference reversals. *Journal of Marketing Research*, 34, 205–18.

Ofir, Chezy & Simonson, Itamar (2001) In search of negative customer feedback: the effect of expecting to evaluate on satisfaction evaluations. *Journal of Marketing Research*, 38 (May), 170–82.

Olsen, Robert A. (1997) Desirability bias among professional investment managers: some evidence from experts. *Journal of Behavioral Decision-making*, 10 (1), 65–72.

Olson, Michael J. & Budescu, David V. (1997) Patterns of preference for numerical and verbal probabilities. *Journal of Behavioral Decision-making*, 10 (2), 117–31.

Oskamp, Stuart (1965) Overconfidence in case-study judgments. *Journal of Consulting Psychology*, 29, 261–5.

Parducci, Allen (1974) Contextual effects: a range-frequency analysis. In *Handbook of Perception*, Vol. 2, edited by E.C. Carterette & M.P. Friedman. New York: Academic Press, pp. 127–41.

Payne, John W., Bettman, James R. & Johnson, Eric J. (1988) Adaptive strategy selection in decision-making. *Journal of Experimental Psychology: Learning, Memory, and Cognition*, 14, 534–52.

——— (1992) Behavioral decision research: a constructive processing perspective. *Annual Psychology Review*, 43, 87–131.

——— (1993) *The Adaptive Decision-maker*. Cambridge: Cambridge University Press.

Payne, John W., Bettman, James R. & Luce, Mary Frances (1996) When time is money: decision behavior under opportunity-cost time pressure. *Organizational Behavior and Human Decision Processes*, 66 (2), 131–52.

Payne, John W., Bettman, James R. & Schkade, David A. (1999) Measuring constructed preferences: toward a building code. *Journal of Risk and Uncertainty*, 19 (1–3), 243–70.

Pennington, Nancy & Hastie, Reid (1988) Explanation-based decision-making: effects of memory structure on judgment. *Journal of Experimental Psychology: Learning, Memory, and Cognition*, 14 (3), 521–33.

——— (1993) Reasoning in explanation-based decision-making. *Cognition*, 49 (1–2), 123–63.

Permuter, Lawrence C. & Monty, Richard A. (1977) The importance of perceived control: fact or fantasy? *American Scientist*, 65, 759–65.

Peterson, Cameron R. & DuCharme, Wesley M. (1967) A primacy effect in subjective probability revision. *Journal of Experimental Psychology*, 73 (1), 61–5.

Phillips, Lawrence & Edwards, Ward (1966) Conservatism in a simple probability inference task. *Journal of Experimental Psychology*, 72 (3), 346–54.

Platt, Michael L. & Glimcher, Paul W. (1999) Neural correlates of decision variables in parietal cortex. *Nature*, 400, 233–8.

Poses, Roy M. & Anthony, Michele (1991) Availability, wishful thinking, and physicians' diagnostic judgments for patients with suspected bacterium. *Medical Decision-making*, 11 (3), 159–68.

Postman, Leo & Underwood, Benton J. (1973) Critical issues in interference theory. *Memory and Cognition*, 1 (1), 19–40.

Rabin, Matthew (2002) Inference by believers in the law of small numbers. *Quarterly Journal of Economics*, August, forthcoming.

Rabin, Matthew & Schrag, Joel L. (1999) First impressions matter: a model of confirmatory bias. *Quarterly Journal of Economics*, 114 (1), 37–82.

Raghunathan, Rajagopal & Pham, Michel Tuan (1999) All negative moods are not equal: motivational influences of anxiety and sadness on decision-making. *Organizational Behavior and Human Decision Processes*, 79 (1), 56–77.

Ranyard, Rob (1997) *Decision-making: Cognitive Models and Explanations*. London and New York: Routledge.

Redelmeier, Donald A. & Kahneman, Daniel (1996) Patients' memories of painful medical treatments: real-time and retrospective evaluations of two minimally invasive procedures. *Pain*, 66 (1), 3–8.

Redelmeier, Donald A., Rozin, Paul & Kahneman, Daniel (1993a) Patient decision-making – Reply. *Journal of the American Medical Association*, 270 (20), 2432.

——— (1993b) Understanding patients' decisions: cognitive and emotional perspectives. *Journal of the American Medical Association*, 270 (1), 72–6.

Rettinger, David A. & Hastie, Reid (2001) Content effects on decision making. *Organizational Behavior and Human Decision Processes*, 85 (2), 336–59.

Rettinger, David A. & Hastie, Reid (forthcoming) Comprehension and decision-making. In *Emerging Perspectives in Judgment and Decision-making*, edited by S. Schneider & J. Shanteau. New York: Cambridge University Press.

Ritov, Ilana (2000) The role of expectations in comparisons. *Psychological Review*, 107 (2), 345–57.

Ritov, Ilana & Baron, Jonathan (1999) Protected values and omission bias. *Organizational Behavior and Human Decision Processes*, 79 (2), 79–94.

Roe, Robert M., Busemeyer, Jerome R. & Townsend, James T. (2001) Multialternative decision field theory: a dynamic connectionist model of decision-making. *Psychological Review*, 108 (2), 370–92.

Roney, C.J.R., Higgins, E. Tory & Shah, J. (1995) Goals and framing: how outcome focus influences motivation and emotion. *Personality and Social Psychology Bulletin*, 21 (11), 1151–60.

Ross, Lee & Sicoly, Fiore (1979) Egocentric biases in availability and attribution. *Journal of Personality and Social Psychology*, 37, 322–36.

Ross, Lee, Greene, David & House, P. (1977) The 'false consensus effect': an egocentric bias in social perception and attribution process. *Journal of Experimental Social Psychology*, 13, 279–301.

Russell, Bertrand (1954) *Human Society in Ethics and Politics*. New York: Simon & Schuster.

Russo, J. Edward & Dosher, Barbara A. (1983) Strategies for multiattribute binary choice. *Journal of Experimental Psychology: Learning, Memory, and Cognition*, 9 (4), 676–96.

Russo, J. Edward & Kolzow, Karen J. (1994) Where is the fault in fault trees? *Journal of Experimental Psychology: Human Perception and Performance*, 20 (1), 17–32.

Russo, J. Edward & Leclerc, France (1994) An eye fixation analysis of choice processes for consumer non-durables. *Journal of Consumer Research*, 21, 274–90.

Russo, J. Edward & Schoemaker, Paul J.H. (1992) Managing overconfidence. *Sloan Management Review*, 33 (2), 7–17.

——— (2002) *Winning Decisions: Getting It Right the First Time*. New York: Doubleday.

Russo, J. Edward, Carlson, Kurt A. & Meloy, Margaret G. (2002) The impact of information distortion on choice. Working Paper, Cornell University.

Russo, J. Edward, Medvec, Victoria H. & Meloy, Margaret G. (1996) The distortion of information during decisions. *Organizational Behavior and Human Decision Processes*, 66 (April), 102–10.

Russo, J. Edward, Meloy, Margaret G. & Medvec, Victoria Husted (1998) Predecisional distortion of product information. *Journal of Marketing Research*, 35 (4), 438–52.

Russo, J. Edward, Meloy, Margaret G. & Wilks, T. Jeffrey (2000) Predecisional distortion of information by auditors and salepersons. *Management Science*, 46, 13–27.

Salancik, Gerald & Meindl, James (1984) Corporate attributions as strategic illusions of management control. *Administrative Science Quarterly*, 29, 238–54.

Saunders, George B. & Stanton, John L. (1976) Personality as influencing factor in decision-making. *Organizational Behavior and Human Decision Processes*, 15 (2), 241–57.

Schacter, Daniel L. (1999) The seven sins of memory: insights from psychology and cognitive neuroscience. *American Psychologist*, 54 (3), 182–203.

——— (2001) *The Seven Sins of Memory: How the Mind Forgets and Remembers*. Boston, MA: Houghton Mifflin Co.

Schkade, David A. & Johnson, Eric J. (1989) Cognitive processes in preference reversals. *Organizational Behavior and Human Decision Processes*, 44 (October), 203–31.

Schkade, David A. & Kilbourne, Lynda M. (1991) Expectation-outcome consistency and hindsight bias. *Organizational Behavior and Human Decision Processes*, 49 (1), 105–23.

Schneider, Sandra L. (1992) Framing and conflict: aspiration level, contingency, the status quo, and current theories of risky choice. *Journal of Environmental Economics*, 26, 88–109.

Schoemaker, Paul J.H. (1982) The expected utility model: its variants, purposes, evidence and limitations. *Journal of Economic Literature*, 20, 529–63.

Schoemaker, Paul J.H. & Russo, J. Edward (1993) A pyramid of decision approaches. *California Management Review*, 36, 9–31.

——— (2001) Managing frames to make better decisions. In *Wharton on Making Decisions*, edited by Steven J. Hoch, Howard C. Kunreuther & Robert E. Gunther. New York: John Wiley and Sons, Inc, pp. 131–55.

Schooler, Jonathan W., Ariely, Dan & Loewenstein, George (2002) The pursuit and monitoring of happiness can be self-defeating. Chapter in preparation for *Psychology and Economics*, edited by Brocas, Isabelle & Carrillo, Juan D. Oxford: Oxford University Press.

Schooler, Jonathan W., Ohlsson, Stellan & Brooks, Kevin (1993) Thoughts beyond words: when language overshadows insight. *Journal of Experimental Psychology: General*, 122, 166–83.

Schwarz, Norbert (2000) Special Issue. *Cognition and Emotion*.

Schutz, Paul A. (1994) Goals as the transactive point between motivation and cognition. In *Student Motivation, Cognition, and Learning: Essays in Honor of Wilbert J. McKeachie,* edited by Paul R. Pintrich,

Donald R. Brown, et al. Hillsdale, NJ: Erlbaum, pp. 135–56.

Sedlmeier, Peter & Gigerenzer, Gerd (2001) Teaching Bayesian reasoning in less than two hours. *Journal of Experimental Psychology: General*, 130 (3), 380–400.

Seifert, Colleen M. & Patalano, Andrea L. (2001) Opportunism in memory: preparing for chance encounters. *Current Directions in Psychological Science*, 10 (6), 198–201.

Sengupta, Jaideep & Fitzsimons, Gavan J. (2000) The effects of analyzing reasons for brand preferences: disruption or reinforcement? *Journal of Marketing Research*, 37 (August), 318–30.

Shafir, Eldar & LeBoeuf, Robyn A. (2002) Rationality. *Annual Review of Psychology*, 53, 491–517.

Shanteau, James & Dino, Geri Anne (1993) Environmental stressor effects on creativity and decision-making. In *Time Pressure and Stress in Human Judgment and Decision-Making*, edited by Ola Svenson & A. John Maule. New York: Plenum Press, pp. 293–308.

Shapira, Zur (ed.) (1997) *Organizational Decision Making*. New York: Cambridge University Press.

Shelley, Marjorie K. (1994) Gain/loss asymmetry in risky intertemporal choice. *Organizational Behavior and Human Decision Processes*, 59, 124–59.

Shedler, Jonathan & Manis, Melvin (1986) Can the availability heuristic explain vividness effects? *Journal of Personality and Social Psychology*, 51, 26–36.

Shepard, Roger N. (1964) On subjectively optimum selections among multi-attribute alternatives. In *Human Judgments and Optimality*, edited by M.W. Shelby & G.L. Bryan. New York: John Wiley and Sons, pp. 257–81.

Sheridan, John E., Richards, Max D. & Slocum, John W. (1975) Comparative analysis of expectancy and heuristic models of decision behavior. *Journal of Applied Psychology*, 60, 361–8.

Sherman, Steven J. (1980) On the self-erasing nature of errors of prediction. *Journal of Personality and Social Psychology*, 39 (August), 211–21.

Shiv, Baba & Huber, Joel (2000) The impact of anticipating satisfaction on consumer choice. *Journal of Consumer Research*, 27 (September), 202–16.

Showers, Carolin & Cantor, Nancy (1985) Social cognition: a look at motivated strategies. *Annual Review of Psychology*, 36, 275–305.

Simon, Dan, Pham, Lien B., Le, Quang A. & Holyoak, Keith J. (2001) The emergence of coherence over the course of decision-making. *Journal of Experimental Psychology: Learning, Memory, and Cognition*, 27 (5), 1250–60.

Simon, Herbert A. (1983) *Reason in Human Affairs*. Stanford, CA: Stanford University Press.

——— (1991) *Models of My Life*. Cambridge, MA: MIT Press.

——— (1992) What is an 'explanation' of behavior? *Psychological Science*, 3 (3), 150–61.

Simon, Herbert A. & Prietula, Michael J. (1989) The experts in your midst. *Harvard Business Review* 67 (1), 120–4.

Simonson, Itamar (1989) Choice based on reasons: The case of attraction and compromise effects. *Journal of Consumer Research*, 16 (2), 158–74.

Simonson, Itamar & Nowlis, Stephen M. (2000) The role of explanations and need for uniqueness in consumer decision-making: unconventional choices based on reasons. *Journal of Consumer Research*, 27 (1), 49–68.

Simonson, Itamar & Nye, Peter (1992) The effect of accountability on susceptibility to decision errors. *Organizational Behavior and Human Decision Processes*, 51 (3), 416–46.

Simonson, Itamar & Tversky, Amos (1992) Choice in context: tradeoff contrast and extremeness aversion. *Journal of Marketing Research,* 29 (3), 281–95.

Singer, Max (1971) The vitality of mythical numbers. *The Public Interest*, 23, 3–9.

Slade, David (1994) *Goal-Based Decision-Making: An Interpersonal Model*. Hillsdale, NJ: Erlbaum.

Slovic, Paul (1966) Value as a determiner of subjective probability. *IEEE Transactions on Human Factors in Electronics,* HFE-7 (1), 22–8.

——— (1997) Trust, emotion, sex, politics, and science: surveying the risk-assessment battlefield. In *Environment, Ethics, and Behavior: The Psychology of Environmental Valuation and Degradation*, edited by Max H. Bazerman & David M. Messick. San Francisco, CA: The New Lexington Press/Jossey-Bass Inc., pp. 277–313.

Slovic, Paul & Lichtenstein, Sarah (1971) Comparison of Bayesian and regression approaches to the study of information processing in judgment. *Organizational Behavior and Human Performance*, 6, 649–744.

Slovic, Paul & MacPhillamy, Douglas (1974) Dimensional commensurability and cue utilization in comparative judgment. *Organizational Behavior and Human Decision Processes*, 11 (2), 172–94.

Slovic, Paul, Griffin, Dale & Tversky, Amos (1990) Compatibility effects in judgment and choice. In *Insights in Decision-making*, edited by Robin M. Hogarth. Chicago: University of Chicago Press, pp. 5–27.

Smithson, Michael (1999) Conflict aversion: preference for ambiguity vs. conflict in sources and evidence. *Organizational Behavior and Human Decision Processes*, 79 (3), 179–98.

Soman, Dilip & Gourville, John T. (2001) Transaction decoupling: how price bundling affects the decision to consume. *Journal of Marketing Research*, 38 (February), 30–44.

Srull, Thomas & Gaelick, Lisa (1983) General principles and individual differences in the self as a habitual reference point: an examination of self-other judgments of similarity. *Social Cognition*, 2, 108–21.

Stalhberg, Dagmar & Maass, Anne (1998) Hindsight bias: impaired memory or biased reconstruction? In *European Review of Social Psychology*, Vol. 8, edited by Wolfgang Stroebe & Miles Hewston. New York: John Wiley & Sons, Inc., pp. 105–32.

Staw, Barry M. & Hoang, Ha T. (1995) Sunk costs in the NBA: why draft order affects playing time and survival in professional basketball. *Administrative Science Quarterly*, 40, 474–94.

Staw, Barry M. & Ross, Jerry (1989) Understanding behavior in escalation situations. *Science*, 246, 216–20.
Sternberg, Robert J. (ed.) (1988) *The Nature of Creativity*. New York: Cambridge University Press.
Stevenson, Mary K. (1993) Decision-making with long-term consequences: temporal discounting for single and multiple outcomes in the future. *Journal of Experimental Psychology: General*, 122, 3–22.
Stone, Dan N. & Schkade, David A. (1991) Numeric and linguistic information representation in multiattribute choice. *Organizational Behavior and Human Decision Processes*, 49 (1), 42–59.
Svenson, Ola (1992) Differentiation and consolidation theory of human decision-making: a frame of reference for the study of pre- and post-decision processes. *Acta Psychologica*, 80 (1–3), 143–68.
——— (1996) Decision-making and the search for fundamental psychological regularities: what can be learned from a process perspective? *Organizational Behavior and Human Decision Processes*, 65 (3), 252–67.
——— (2002) Values and affect in human decision-making: a differentiation and consolidation theory perspective. In *Emerging Perspectives on Judgment and Decision Research*, edited by Sandra L. Schneider & James Shanteau. Cambridge: Cambridge University Press, pp. 357–404.
Svenson, Ola & Karlsson, Gunnar (1986) Attractiveness of decision alternatives characterized by numerical and non-numerical information. *Scandinavian Journal of Psychology*, 27 (1), 74–84.
Teigen, Karl H. & Wibecke, Brun (2000) Ambiguous probabilities: when does P = 0.3 reflect a possibility, and when does it express a doubt? *Journal of Behavioral Decision-making*, 13 (3), 345–62.
Tetlock, Philip E. (1991) An alternative metaphor in the study of judgment and choice: people as politicians. *Theory and Psychology*, 1 (4), 451–75.
——— (2000) Cognitive biases and organizational correctives: do both disease and cure depend on the politics of the beholder? *Administrative Science Quarterly*, 45, 293–326.
Tetlock, Philip E. & Boettger, R. (1989) Accountability: a social magnifier of the dilution effect. *Journal of Personality and Social Psychology*, 57, 388–98.
Tetlock, Philip E., Lerner, Josh & Boettger, R. (1996) The dilution effect: judgmental bias, conversational convention, or a bit of both? *European Journal of Social Psychology*, 26, 915–35.
Thagard, Paul & Millgram, Elijah (1995) Inference to the best plan: a coherence theory of decision. In *Goal-directed Learning*, edited by A. Ram & D.B. Leake. Cambridge, MA: MIT Press, pp. 439–54.
Thaler, Richard H. (1980) Toward a positive theory of consumer choice. *Journal of Economic Behavior and Organization*, 1, 39–60.
——— (1991) *Quasi-Rational Economics*. New York: Russell Sage.
——— (1994) *Winner's Curse: Paradoxes and Anomalies of Economic Life*. Princeton, NJ: Princeton University Press.
——— (1999) Mental accounting matters. *Journal of Behavioral Decision-making*, 12, 183–206.
Thaler, Richard H. & Johnson, Eric J. (1990) Gambling with the house money and trying to break even: the effects of prior outcomes on risky choice. *Management Science*, 36, 643–60.
Thompson, Suzanne C., Armstrong, Wade & Thomas, Craig (1998) Illusions of control, underestimations, and accuracy: a control heuristic explanation. *Psychological Bulletin*, 123 (2), 143–61.
Tsiros, Michael & Mittal, Vikas (2000) Regret: a model of its antecedents and consequences in consumer decision-making. *Journal of Consumer Research*, 26, 401–22.
Tubbs, Mark E. & Dahl, James G. (1991) A within-persons examination of the effects of goal assignment on choice of personal goal. *Psychological Reports*, 69 (1), 263–70.
Tubbs, Mark E. & Ekeberg, Steven E. (1991) The role of intentions in work motivation: implications for goal-setting theory and research. *Academy of Management Review*, 16 (1), 180–99.
Tversky, Amos (1969) The intransitivity of preferences. *Psychological Review*, 76, 31–48.
Tversky, Amos & Kahneman, Daniel (1974) Judgment under uncertainty: heuristics and biases. *Science*, 185, 1124–31.
——— (1981) The framing of decisions and the psychology of choice. *Science*, 211 (30), 453–8.
——— (1983) Extensional versus intuitive reasoning: the conjunction fallacy in probability judgment. *Psychological Review*, 90 (4), 293–315.
——— (1988) Rational choice and the framing of decisions. In *Decision-making: Descriptive, Normative, and Prescriptive Interactions*, edited by David E. Bell, Howard Raiffa & Amos Tversky. Cambridge: Cambridge University Press, pp. 167–92.
Tversky, Amos & Shafir, Eldar (1992) Choice under conflict: the dynamics of deferred decision. *Psychological Science*, 3 (6), 358–61.
Tversky, Amos, Sattath, Shmuel & Slovic, Paul (1988) Contingent weighting in judgment and choice. *Psychological Review*, 95 (3), 371–84.
Tversky, Amos, Kahneman, Daniel, Gentner, Dedre, Collins, Allan, Fischhoff, Baruch, Hoch, Stephen J. & Loewenstein, George F. (1992) Inferential aspects and judgment under uncertainty. In *Metacognition: Core Readings*, edited by Thomas O. Nelson. Needham Heights, MA: Allyn & Bacon, Inc., pp. 377–436.
Tyszka, Tadeusz (1998) Two pairs of conflicting motives in decision-making. *Organizational Behavior and Human Decision Processes*, 74 (3), 189–211.
Van Boven, Leaf, Dunning, David & Loewenstein, George (2000) Egocentric empathy gaps between owners and buyers: misperceptions of the endowment effect. *Journal of Personality and Social Psychology*, 79 (1), 66–76.
van Dijk, Eric & van Knippenberg, Daan (1998) Trading wine: on the endowment effect, loss aversion, and the comparability of consumer goods. *Journal of Economic Psychology*, 19 (4), 485–95.

van Schie, Els C.M. & van der Pligt, Joop (1995) The effects of framing and salience. *Organizational Behavior and Human Decision Processes*, 63 (3), 264–75.

Varey, Carol A. & Kahneman, Daniel (1992) Experiences extended across time: evaluation of moments and episodes, *Journal of Behavioral Decision-making*, 5 (3), 169–85.

von Neumann, John & Morgenstern, Oskar (1944, 1947) *Theory of Games and Economic Behavior*, 1st edn, 2nd edn. Princeton, NJ: Princeton University Press.

Vroom, Victor H. (1966) Organizational choice: a study of pre- and postdecisional processes. *Organizational Behavior and Human Decision Processes*, 1 (2), 212–25.

Vroom, Victor H. & Deci, Edward L. (1971) The stability of post-decision dissonance: a follow-up study of the job attitudes of business school graduates. *Organizational Behavior and Human Decision Processes*, 6 (1), 36–49.

Wallsten, Thomas S. (1990) The costs and benefits of vague information. In *Insights in Decision-making: A Tribute to Hillel J. Einhorn*, edited by Robin Hogarth. Chicago: The University of Chicago Press, pp. 28–43.

Wansink, Brian, Kent, Robert H. & Hoch, Stephen J. (1998) An anchoring and adjustment model of purchase quantity decisions. *Journal of Marketing Research*, 35 (1), 71–81.

Wason, P.C. (1960) On the failure to eliminate hypotheses in a conceptual task. *Quarterly Journal of Experimental Psychology*, 12, 129–40.

Weber, Elke U. (1999) Who's afraid of a little risk? New evidence for general risk aversion. In *Decision Science and Technology: Reflections on the Contributions of Ward Edwards,* edited by James Shanteau, Barbara A. Mellers & David A. Schum. Boston, MA: Kluwer Academic Publishers, pp. 53–63.

Weber, Elke U. & Milliman, Richard A. (1997) Perceived risk attitudes: relating risk perception to risky choice. *Management Science*, 43 (2), 123–44.

Weber, Elke U., Baron, Jonathan & Loomes, Graham (eds) (2001) *Conflict and Tradeoffs in Decision-making*. Cambridge: Cambridge University Press.

Wedell, Douglas H. (1991) Distinguishing among models of contextually induced preference reversals. *Journal of Experimental Psychology: Learning, Memory, and Cognition*, 17 (4), 767–78.

——— (1998) Testing models of trade-off contrast in pairwise choice. *Journal of Experimental Psychology: Human Perception and Performance*, 24 (1), 49–65.

Wegener, Duane T, Petty, Richard E. & Smith, Stephen M. (1995) Positive mood can increase or decrease message scrutiny: the hedonic contingency view of mood and message processing. *Journal of Personality and Social Psychology*, 69 (1), 5–15.

Weick, Karl E. (1979) *The Social Psychology of Organizations*. Reading, MA: Addison-Wesley.

Wells, Gary L. & Bradfield, Amy L. (1998) Good, you identified the suspect: feedback to eyewitnesses distorts their reports of the witnessing experience. *Journal of Applied Psychology*, 83 (3), 360–76.

——— (1999) Distortions in eyewitnesses' recollections: can the postidentification-feedback effect be moderated? *Psychological Science*, 10 (2), 138–44.

West, Patricia M., Brockett, Patrick L. & Golden, Linda L. (1997) A comparative analysis of neural networks and statistical models for predicting consumer choice. *Marketing Science*, 16 (4), 370–91.

Wilson, Marie G., Northcraft, Gregory B. & Neale, Margaret A. (1989) Information competition and vividness effects in on-line judgments. *Organizational Behavior and Human Decision Processes*, 44 (1), 132–9.

Wilson, Timothy D. & Brekke, Nancy. (1994) Mental contamination and mental correction: unwanted influences on judgments and evaluations. *Psychological Bulletin*, 116, 117–42.

Wilson, Timothy D., Dunn, Dana S., Kraft, Dolores & Lisle, Douglas J. (1989) Introspection, attitude change, and attitude-behavior consistency: the disruptive effects of explaining why we feel the way we do. *Advances in Experimental Social Psychology*, 22, 289–343.

Wilson, Timothy D., Lisle, Douglas J., Schooler, Jonathan W., Hodges, Sara D., Klaaren, Kristen J. & LaFleur, Suzanne J. (1993) Introspecting about reasons can reduce post-choice satisfaction. *Personality and Social Psychology Bulletin*, 19 (3), 331–9.

Wooten, David B. & Reed II, Americus (1998) Informational influence and the ambiguity of product experience: order effects on the weighting of evidence. *Journal of Consumer Psychology*, 7 (1), 79–99.

Wright, Peter & Weitz, Bart (1977) Time horizon effects on product evaluation strategies. *Journal of Marketing Research*, 14, 429–43.

Yates, J. Frank (1990) *Judgment and Decision-making*, Englewood Cliffs, NJ: Prentice-Hall.

Zeelenberg, Marcel & van Dijk, Eric (1997) A reverse sunk cost effect in risky decision making: sometimes we have too much invested to gamble. *Journal of Economic Psychology*, 18, 677–91.

Zeelenberg, Marcel, van Dijk, Wilco W., Manstead, Anthony S.R. & van der Pligt, Joop (2000) On bad decisions and disconfirmed expectancies: the psychology of regret and disappointment. *Cognition and Emotion*, 14 (4), 531–41.

Zhang, Shi & Markman, Arthur B. (2001) Processing product unique features: alignability and involvement in preference construction. *Journal of Consumer Psychology*, 11 (July), 13–27.

16

Allocating Marketing Resources

MURALI K. MANTRALA

1. Introduction

A key responsibility of marketing managers is to decide the allocation of scarce marketing resources, e.g., advertising dollars, selling hours, retail shelf-space or merchandise inventories. Organizationally, these decisions begin with the basic 'marketing mix' issues of setting the size and allocation of the total marketing investment across advertising, personal selling, promotions and retailing efforts. Then, managers must decide how should the budget for a specific marketing instrument or activity, e.g., advertising or personal selling, be allocated across organizational planning units (*market entities*) such as products, geographic areas, media, accounts, and *time periods*, so as to optimize an objective function (short- or long-term contributions, profits).

Marketing resource allocation decisions are complicated, and managers tend to address them with fairly arbitrary and simplifying heuristics and decision rules. For example, the pervasive and persistent uses of 'percentage-of-sales' and 'proportionate' rules for advertising, sales promotion and personal selling budgeting and allocation decisions are well documented (e.g., Lilien et al., 1992; Ingram & LaForge, 1992). Such rules usually result in sub-optimal decisions and significant waste of resources. Improving these decisions is important because they have a significant impact on aggregate sales and profits realized by a firm. For example, based on salesforce size and resource-allocation studies at 50 companies, Sinha & Zoltners (2001) report that a size and resource-allocation strategy was available that would produce, on average, a 4.5% contribution improvement over the company's current or base case strategy. Such improvements are possible with normative models.

Following Zoltners (1981), normative models may be classified into *theoretical models*, which are designed to develop normative theory, and *decision models*, which are designed to provide optimal solutions to specific decision problems. A normative-theoretical model is built around a mathematical expression for the *market response function*, i.e., the representation of how a market responds to the marketing effort(s), whereas a decision model is built around a concrete empirical expression for the sales response function. The solution of a theoretical model provides conditions, generalizable across market settings, under which a single- or multi-variable objective function is optimized. However, these optimality conditions do not by themselves tell a firm what specific adjustments it needs to make in a particular marketing effort or the mix of these efforts if it is not currently operating optimally. Such specific insights and guidance for a specific market setting can only come from empirically evaluating the theoretical conditions within the context of the appropriate decision model.

This chapter surveys selected normative-theoretical and decision models and related insights for allocating marketing resources, *directly* controlled by the decision-maker, that have appeared in the marketing literature over the last 50 years, with the emphasis on contributions within the last decade. Research into incentive mechanisms for indirectly controlling marketing effort allocation decisions by autonomous agents such as independent distributors or salespeople (e.g., Anderson et al., 1987) is not covered in this paper. In particular, the area of salesforce compensation and incentive mechanisms (e.g., Lal & Srinivasan, 1993; Mantrala et al., 1994) is the subject of a separate chapter in this Handbook (Chapter 10). The present chapter has three broad objectives:

- to provide an overview of selected academic research in each problem area to help scholars understand issues in the problem area and how specific articles and approaches address these issues
- to offer a bibliography of important research in each problem area
- to identify productive areas for future research.

Important advances in knowledge about the optimal allocation of marketing resources have typically occurred as a result of advances in response measurement and/or optimization models and methods. However, an entire book rather than a single book chapter such as this for the general marketing student would be needed to provide an adequate treatment of the variety of data, estimation models and/or optimization procedures that have been applied in normative research on marketing resource allocation problems. Therefore, we concentrate on summarizing the substantive issues and normative insights contributed by selected works in the literature, encouraging the interested reader to go to the original papers for more details.

The chapter surveys research bearing on the optimal allocation of the following marketing resources: advertising spending (Section 2); salesforce effort (Section 3); manufacturer trade promotions (Section 4); retailer merchandising and promotions (Section 5); and marketing mix expenditures (Section 6). Therefore, this chapter largely focuses on marketing *communication* and *retailing* efforts on behalf of existing products. That is, we do not deal with resource allocation issues related to new product development or line extensions (e.g., Cohen et al., 1997; Srinivasan et al., 1997), marketing research (e.g., Chatterjee et al., 1988) or marketing channel design (e.g., Rangan, 1987). Further, while recognizing that price is a key element of the marketing mix that needs to be jointly optimized with communication efforts, we do not treat optimal pricing strategies in this chapter. Unless otherwise stated, the discussion assumes that the (regular) price of a good and its marginal cost of production are fixed parameters of the problem under consideration.

Within each of the categories of marketing resource allocation problem areas that we do cover in this chapter, we summarize normative-theoretical guidelines, common decision rules, decision models and insights from applications. Outstanding areas for future research are summarized in the closing Section 7.

We begin with advertising budgeting and allocation decisions and, in fact, devote considerably more space to these advertising management problems than to the other problem areas. This is because, first, advertising decisions have attracted the greatest amount of research attention over the last few decades, and second, advertising can be viewed as a surrogate for other forms of marketing communication efforts. That is, a number of issues and principles we discuss in relation to advertising allocation decisions apply to these other efforts as well.

2. Advertising Budgeting and Allocation Models

Companies spend billions of dollars annually on advertising. Such advertising spending decisions are usually made in two stages. First, in the budgeting stage, the firm's management decides *how much* to spend on advertising and then, in the planning stage, the firm decides *how to spend* the given budget during the upcoming year. These decisions may include questions of how to allocate the advertising budget over multiple brands or product categories, over geographic areas or regions, across available media and across time periods of the planning horizon, i.e., scheduling decisions.

The next section reviews selected normative models and decision rules for determining annual advertising budgets, i.e., the advertising investment (monetary expenditures or *adspend*) decision with respect to a single market. Subsequently, we focus on decision problems concerning the distribution or allocation of advertising monies across multiple market entities.

Advertising Budgeting

The 'State-of-the-Art' in Practice

For many companies, especially in the consumer packaged goods sector, determining how much should be spent to advertise their products and services is perhaps the single most important marketing decision they make every year. Given this importance and the amount of normative research it has attracted since the time of Dean (1951), and the very great profit potential of formal response measurement and analysis described by Bass (1979), one might assume that the science of advertising budgeting would now be firmly grasped and implemented in most businesses. However, as recently as 1998, preliminary findings of the 'MAX' study sponsored by the American Association of Advertising Agencies ('4 As') indicate that advertising budgeting continues to be viewed as a complex, poorly structured, and risk-laden process by many business executives (Farris et al., 1998). Further, the study observes that normative models are used by many companies, but not really to generate optimal budgets. Instead, models seem to be used more for 'reality checks' on 'ballpark' target budgets set using simpler percentage-of-sales type heuristics (e.g., Bigne, 1995; Broadbent, 1988; Mitchell, 1993). Eventually, of course, norms, negotiations, politics, exogenous budget constraints, fairness, and financial considerations all may enter into the organizational review and finalization of the advertising budget, making advertising budget-setting a much more complex process than the rote application of a rule of thumb, e.g., Piercy (1987a, 1987b), Jones (1992), Low & Mohr (1997, 1999). Still, however, the higher the budget review level in the corporation, the more likely it is that financial ratios will dominate the review process (Farris et al., 1998).

The 4 As' MAX study indicates that there are still a number of significant common problems and issues that need to be resolved in advertising budgeting that represent opportunities for research with potential near-term payoff. A number of these are perceived to be related to the gaps between normative budgeting theory and practice, but it is not clear whether these gaps exist because practice lags theory, or *vice versa*. The following review of extant normative ad budgeting models, decision rules, and related insights in the academic literature should serve to develop this research agenda.

Normative Ad Budgeting Models

Response Function The notion of a market response function relating advertising spending rate (e.g., dollars/period) to a brand's sales rate (units per period) in a target market lies at the heart of all normative models for advertising budgeting. The generally accepted criteria for the form of the steady-state (static) sales response function of an established product are: (1) sales are non-negative at zero units of advertising effort with positive sales at zero advertising implying a *sales carryover effect*; (2) sales increase as effort is increased but at a decreasing rate; (3) sales approach a ceiling or saturation sales level (e.g., Hanssens et al., 2001; Little, 1979). Little (1979) allows that steady-state advertising-sales response can be concave or S-shaped. However, the empirical support available for S-shaped ad-sales response functions, e.g., Zentler & Ryde (1956), Ackoff & Emshoff (1975), Rao & Miller (1975), Eastlack & Rao (1986), is limited and far outweighed by the evidence favoring concave functions, e.g., Simon and Arndt (1980), Hanssens et al. (2001). Common theoretical specifications for a firm's concave advertising-sales response function include the *modified exponential*, *power*, and 'ADBUDG' (Little, 1970) forms, while Gompertz or logit functions are utilized to capture S-shaped response. Comprehensive reviews of response functional forms are provided by Leeflang et al. (2000), Lilien et al. (1992), and Saunders (1987).

Next, it is generally recognized that advertising has dynamic effects, i.e., advertising in one period can impact sales beyond that period by way of either a *delayed response effect* or *customer holdover effect* (Kotler, 1971). Such carryover effects should be taken into account by firms interested in maximization of long-term rather than short-term profits when setting advertising budgets. Normative-theoretical dynamic advertising-sales response models in the literature have tended to be formulated as continuous-time models using differential equations. On the other hand, discrete-time models employing difference equations have been popular in empirical and applied research, mainly because most econometric techniques have been developed for estimating such models (Bass, 1979; Rao, 1986). One well-known example of a dynamic, discrete-time advertising-sales response function is that proposed in Little's (1975) Brandaid model for marketing mix optimization. A special case of this model equation is:

$$S_t = \lambda S_{t-1} + (1 - \lambda)\, g(A_t) \qquad [1]$$

where S_t = sales in period t, λ is a sales carryover constant and $g(A_t)$ is the long-run (steady-state) sales (dollars/period) response to advertising spending A_t in period t assuming the product's price, other marketing efforts, and market conditions including competing firms' actions do not change. Structurally, as Little (1979) has shown, discrete-time approximations of the Vidale & Wolfe (1957) and Nerlove & Arrow (1962) differential equation models are special cases of the Brandaid model.

In Equation [1], one plausible specification of $g(A_t)$ is the ADBUDG form proposed by Little (1970). Dropping the subscript t for convenience, this is given by:

$$g(A) = M[A^{\gamma}/ (A^{\gamma}+\rho)];\ A \geq 0,\ \rho > 0,\ \gamma \geq 0 \qquad [2]$$

In Equation [2], the parameter $M > 0$, denotes the saturation sales (market potential) level; γ and ρ are *shape* parameters such that with ρ fixed, the function is S-shaped when $\gamma > 1$ and concave when $\gamma \leq 1$. Equation [2] is actually a special case of a 'us/(us+them)' advertising share attraction model and the fixed parameter ρ can be interpreted to be an index of 'average competitive effects' (Leeflang et al., 2000: 120).

Optimality Condition for a Profit-Maximizing Monopolist With the product gross margin as a fraction of the price, m, held fixed, let us now consider the advertising budgeting problem of a profit-maximizing monopolist in a deterministic world where advertising is the only instrument. In theory, the advertising budget that maximizes profits $\pi = mg(A) - A$, can be found by applying marginal analysis (e.g., Naert, 1972, 1973). For example, given a concave sales response function, advertising should be employed to the point where the marginal revenue product of advertising equals its marginal cost, i.e., $mg'(.) - 1 = 0$, where $g'(.)$ is the derivative with respect to advertising. Equivalently, the optimality condition for the profit-maximizing budget is given by:

$$\alpha^* = A^*/g(A^*) = m\eta(A^*) \quad [3]$$

where A^* = the profit-maximizing ad budget, $g(A^*)$ = sales realized at the optimal budget, $\eta(A^*)$ = the advertising-sales elasticity $(A^*/g(A^*))g'(A^*)$ at the optimum and α^* = optimal ad-sales ratio. If we allow for the long-term effect of advertising as in the Brandaid model [1] then the optimal ad-sales ratio is:

$$\alpha^* = A^*/g(A^*) = m[(1 - \lambda)/[(1-r\lambda)]\ \eta(A^*) \quad [4]$$

where r is the discount factor related to the firm's cost of capital.

'Percentage-of-Sales' Decision Rule Versus Normative Solution

That the dynamic optimality condition [4] for the profit-maximizing ad budget can be expressed as an advertising-sales ratio is interesting in that it seems to support the popular use of percentage-of current or expected sales decision rules to set at least ballpark target budgets (Farris et al., 1998). There are actually a number of variants of these rules (e.g., Broadbent, 1988) but most take the generic form of the monetary advertising budget in period t+1 being linearly related to the sales revenues in period t (see, e.g., Mantrala, 1996). Many managers' underlying belief appears to be that this type of decision rule can determine ad budgets that are close to the optimum values found with more sophisticated but complicated normative models (Aaker & Myers, 1987). Is this belief justified? The answer is a qualified 'yes' according to research by Welam (1982) that assumes a constant ad-sales elasticity power response function of the form $g(.) = A^{\eta}$. More specifically, Welam notes that the value of the factor $[(1 - r\lambda)/(1 - \lambda)]$ in [4] is approximately one for realistic combinations of values of r and λ. He then shows that with an advertising-sales ratio α set approximately equal to $m\eta(A^*)$, repeated application of the percentage-of-sales rule over time will, in fact, drive advertising investment to a stable equilibrium level equal to A^*. Welam concludes that, given a reasonably stable environment, if management knows the gross margin and can produce a reasonable estimate of the advertising-sales elasticity, then optimal results may be obtained at equilibrium 'without completing a full-blown marginal analysis and estimation of the sales response function.' Raman (1990) also demonstrates the dynamic optimality of the advertising-sales ratio rule in a stochastic environment assuming a constant-elasticity response function.

The key to the optimality or near-optimality of percentage-of-sales rule for advertising budgeting is, of course, the choice of the specific ad-sales ratio employed by the user of the decision rule, and this can be fairly arbitrary (e.g., Broadbent, 1988). Basing the ratio on a simple estimate of the ad-sales elasticity, as suggested by Welam (1982), may work reasonably well in the case of a constant elasticity response function. But, how well does the percentage-of-sales rule perform – in terms of both budgets and profits – when the market is characterized by *a varying elasticity* response function? Clearly, in this scenario, it would be more difficult for a manager to pin down the optimal ad-sales ratio. Therefore, the question is how do errors in the choice of the ad-sales ratio affect budgets and resulting profits? Mantrala (1996) utilizes a nonlinear difference equation framework to investigate this issue, and finds results that are not so encouraging as those of Welam (1982), as shown in the following illustration using the Brandaid model [1] with the ADBUDG specification [2].

Illustration: Setting $\gamma = 1$ in [2], note that the ad-sales elasticity at some advertising level A is given by $\eta(A) = \rho/(A + \rho)$. That is, the ad-sales response elasticity declines with the advertising level. Further, it can be shown that corresponding to any selected ad-sales ratio $\alpha > 0$, repeated application of the decision rule converges to the equilibrium advertising level or fixed point A_E given by $A_E = \alpha M - \rho$.

Thus, to achieve a positive advertising-sales equilibrium, the chosen percentage-of-sales should be greater than $\alpha_0 = M/\rho$, a number that could be treated as the 'minimum efficient level of spending.' A lower value of the selected ad-sales ratio is 'suicidal' because it would drive sales down to zero. Peckham (1976) describes several actual cases of firms' own advertising policies leading to the extinction of own established brands. Interestingly, an important finding of the MAX study was that no companies were able to justify exactly how minimum efficient levels of advertising were set, but most companies believe that there is such a lower limit to the advertising budget (Farris et al., 1998). Next, application of marginal analysis yields the following set of results:

Optimal advertising

$$A^* = (mM\rho)^{1/2} - \rho,\ M > \rho/m \quad [5]$$

*Sales at A**

$$g(A^*) = [M\{(mM\rho)^{1/2} - \rho\}]/(mM\rho)^{1/2} \quad [6]$$

Maximized profits

$$\pi(A^*) = mM - 2(mM\rho)^{1/2} + \rho \quad [7]$$

*Advertising-sales elasticity at A**

$$\eta(A^*) = (\rho/Mm)^{1/2} \quad [8]$$

Table 16.1

Sales response Function no.	Parameters			Optimal values				
	M	ρ	*m*	A*	η(A*)	g(A*)	π(A*)	α*
(1)	1000	8	.8	72	.10	900	648	.08
(2)	1000	32	.8	128	.20	800	512	.16
(3)	1000	128	.8	192	.40	600	288	.32

Optimal ad-sales ratio

$$\alpha^* = (m\rho/M)^{1/2} \quad [9]$$

Now, let us denote any arbitrary selected percentage-of-sales decision rule ratio as $\alpha = (w + 1)\alpha^*$ where w is a fractional deviation from α^*. Similarly let $A_E = (v + 1)A^*$ where $v \geq -1$ is the fractional deviation of A_E from A^* corresponding to w deviation of α from α^*. Then, the relationship between v and w can be derived to be as follows:

$$v = (mM\rho)^{1/2}\, w/[(mM\rho)^{1/2} - \rho] \quad [10]$$

Next, let $\pi(A_E) = (D + 1)\, \pi(A^*)$ where $-1 \leq D \leq 0$ is the fractional deviation of $\pi(A_E)$ from $\pi(A^*)$ corresponding to w deviation of α from α^*. Then, we can derive the following relationship between D and w:

$$D = -\,[(mM\rho)^{1/2}\, w^2] \,/\, [(w + 1)\pi(A^*)] \quad [11]$$

Table 16.1 displays three sets of assumed values of the sales response parameters M and ρ with m set equal to .8. The corresponding elasticity values in Table 16.1 (right-hand side) are in the range commonly seen in empirical advertising-sales response studies (Assmus et al., 1984; McNiven, 1980).

For each of these three numerically specified sales response functions, let us consider four values of w in a range ± 0.5, namely, −.50, −.25, +.25 and +.50. Figure 16.1 displays corresponding plots of the resulting ad budgets and profit deviations from optimal values, v_i, and D_i at different values of w, for $i = 1, 2, 3$ respectively. We see that $v > w$ for any value of w, and for any specific sales response function, the difference $(v–w)$ increases as w increases. We also see that for any fixed w, the value of v dramatically increases as the value of the response parameter ρ, increases. Thus, a ± 25% error in the choice of α results in a ± 28% investment error when ρ = 8 but nearly a ± 42% investment error when ρ = 128. Higher values of ρ imply higher values of the ad-sales elasticity η(A*). However, for any level of w, the corresponding level of D is of much lower magnitude than v. For example, in the case of sales response function No.1, a ± 42% investment error due to a ± 25% error in the choice of α results in less than ± 1% reduction from maximum profits. The result with respect to *the insensitivity of profits to significant investment errors* is an example of what has been coined the *flat maximum principle* by Tull et al. (1986). We shall return to this important principle in a later section.

The results displayed in Figure 16.1 clearly indicate that there is no guarantee that percentage-of-sales rules will *determine budgets close to the optimum* budget as presumed by some practitioners. That would occur only if the optimal ad-sales ratio is chosen, and even small errors in this choice can lead to significant investment errors in both percentage and absolute terms. However, the corresponding percentage drops from the maximum profits can be quite small, especially if the advertising-sales elasticity is in the typical range for established products. Therefore, a stronger defense of this decision rule can be made on the basis of *near-optimal profits rather than budgets*. However, even this defense is of little consolation if the response function were S-shaped, i.e., $\gamma > 1$ in [2] as might be the case with relatively new products. Mantrala (1996) shows that in such scenarios, even small underestimates of the optimal ad-sales ratio can rapidly drive advertising and sales to extinction, were the rule to be repeatedly applied without correction.

Advertising Budgeting in the Presence of Competition

So far, we have considered advertising budgeting by a monopoly firm, assuming competitive advertising is fixed. Normative models for budgeting in the presence of active competition involve the use of game theory, as illustrated by Moorthy (1993) in a static, deterministic and symmetric duopoly model framework. His analysis is based on the competitive generalization of the steady-state response model [2] of the following form:

$$g_i(A_i) = M(A_i/(A_i + A_{3-i})) \text{ for } i = 1, 2 \quad [12]$$

Then firm i's objective is to maximize its profits accounting for the other firm's best response function. The *Nash equilibrium* solution to this game is found by simultaneously solving the firms' first-order conditions, and is given by:

$$A_i^* = mM/4,\ i = 1, 2 \quad [13]$$

It follows from [13] that each firm's market share in equilibrium is a half, the same as it would have been if they had spent nothing on advertising. In

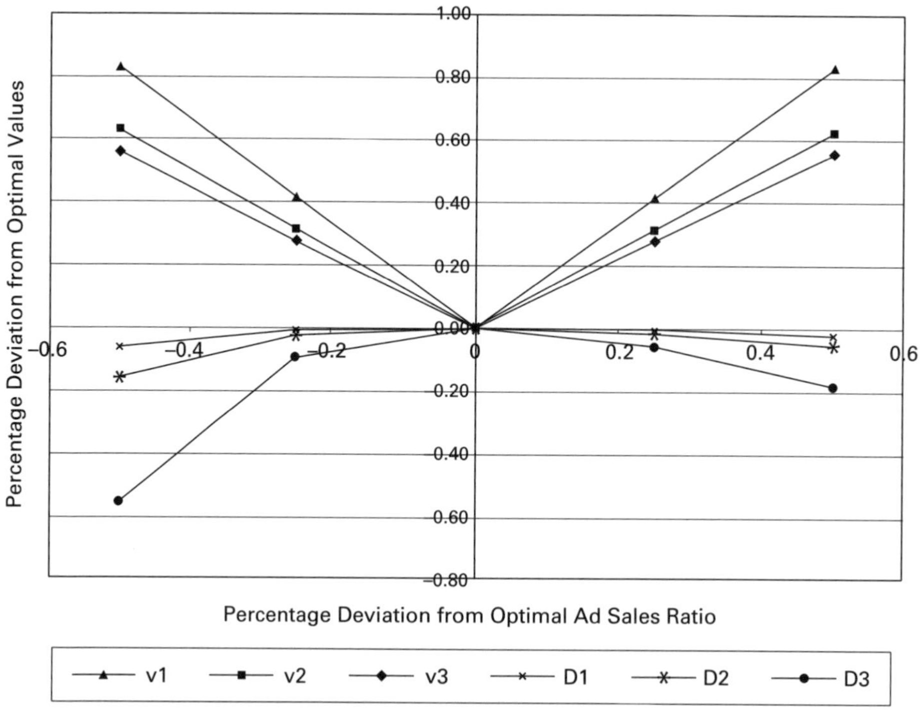

Figure 16.1 *Effects of Deviations from Optimal Ad-Sales Ratio on Advertising and Profit Levels*

other words, the firms are bound in a prisoner's dilemma situation. Unable to trust the other firm to hold its spending level down, each firm ends up spending more than is collectively optimal. If the firms have symmetric response functions, but differing gross margins, then it can be shown that the ratio of each competitor's budget is proportional to the ratio of the competitor's profit margins. That is, the ratio of the competitors' efforts expended per unit profit margin is constant across firms (Mills, 1961). Interestingly, this result is consistent with the 'percentage of current gross profits (or contribution)' ad budgeting rule where the percentage in question is usually the average 'A/P' ratio of the industry (e.g., Schonfeld, 1979). Recall, however, that this consistency depends on the assumptions of competitors with symmetric ad-sales response and objective functions that are unlikely to hold in reality. Thus, we can expect that without any more information about competitors other than their A/P ratios, advertising budgeting using the average A/P rule will lead a firm to set a sub-optimal budget. However, again, profit sensitivity to such errors is likely to be limited due to the flat maximum phenomenon. Indeed, a numerical analysis of a response model of form [12] by Weinberg (1975) led him to propose that a firm should set its advertising budget at about 23% of the maximum gross profits available to it. His analysis showed that this is close to the firm's optimum over a wide range of competitive advertising levels. However, Weinberg cautions that a firm's advertising budget should not exceed 25% of the maximum gross profits available to it, because the profit losses from spending above this 25% level are quite significant. Interestingly, Weinberg's rule is consistent with the symmetric static duopoly solution [13] noted above. (Chintagunta & Vilcassim, 1992, 1994, and Erickson, 1991 provide treatments of optimal advertising strategies in dynamic duopolies.)

Uncertainty and Advertising Budgeting

The normative models we have discussed so far have ignored uncertainty and assume risk-neutral decision-makers. The 4 As-sponsored MAX project work makes special mention of the need to gain a better understanding of how advertising budgets are and should be set in the face of sales response uncertainty, taking into account decision-makers' risk preferences (Farris et al.,1999). Two sources of uncertainty of particular interest are *generalized (environmental) uncertainty* and *estimation uncertainty*, i.e., the uncertainty associated with estimated relationships utilized in a decision model. The research questions of interest are how and when is the optimal advertising budget under uncertainty different from the deterministic solution?

Jagpal and Brick (1982) examined the impact of estimation uncertainty on the optimal advertising budget, in a Capital Asset Pricing Model (CAPM) 'value maximization' rather than individual expected utility maximization framework. They show that at equilibrium, the ratio of the 'risk-adjusted' value marginal product of advertising (i.e., the value product of advertising measured with respect to the *certainty equivalent* of sales) equals the unit cost of advertising. The result generalizes the optimality condition under certainty given by [3] and establishes that the deterministic and stochastic budget solutions can be different. Little (1966), Pekelman & Tse (1980) and Nguyen (1985) also consider both types of uncertainty in a multi-period adaptive control system framework in which the uncertain sales response parameters are subject to periodic Bayesian updating based on observed sales response. In Little's formulation, the budgeting problem is intertemporally separable, i.e., 'the decisions of one period do not affect the decisions of the next.' This is not the case in Pekelman and Tse's analysis and they find the optimal advertising rule involves a tradeoff between the short-term profits dictated by basing decisions on the response parameters' expected values, or exchanging lower short-term profits for future reductions in parameter variance and enhanced later-period profits. Nguyen's (1985) analysis of a similar 'learning-by-doing' model shows that whether or not it is optimal for the firm to experiment at an advertising rate higher or lower than the myopic (one-period) level depends on the very specification of the response function. The result follows regardless of the firm's attitude towards risk.

The research by Aykac et al. (1989) is noteworthy as they analytically derive the conditions for optimal advertising budgeting considering both estimation and environmental uncertainty within an expected utility-maximizing framework that allows for decision-makers to be risk-averse or risk-neutral. In their model, the advertising management's utility is a function of uncertain profits that are, in turn, a nonlinear function of advertising. Aykac et al. then approximate the advertisers' utility function by a second-order Taylor expansion, and solve for the expected utility maximizing budget. They find that if the decision-maker is risk-neutral, he/she would maximize expected profits and the optimality condition is similar to the deterministic result. On the other hand, a risk-averse manager would trade off some expected profits in order to reduce the profit variance. More specifically, Aykac et al. show that risk-averse managers will spend more (less) than risk-neutral mangers if the minimum profit variance occurs at higher (lower) outlays than are required for maximizing expected profits.

Flat Maximum Principle and Over-advertising

The phenomenon of the 'flat maximum principle' deserves closer attention because of its significant managerial implications. Specifically, following their single-period, monopoly firm analyses, Tull et al. (1986) suggest that advertising managers can afford to over-spend to gain share without much loss in terms of foregone profits. Motivated by these observations, Chintagunta (1993) investigates the robustness of the flat maximum principle in myopic and dynamic duopoly competition contexts, and reaches conclusions that are basically consistent with those of Tull et al. (1986). More specifically, within the context of his response function assumptions, Chintagunta found that the flat maximum principle continues to apply in static and dynamic competitive settings. As he points out, technically, a flat maximum occurs because a percentage change in profits is of 'second order,' whereas a percentage change in ad expenditures is of the first order. This mitigates the effects on profits of changes in ad levels and could justify both over-spending in good times and under-spending in bad times.

The observations by Tull et al. (1986) and Chintagunta (1993) are interesting because the bulk of empirical studies of firms' advertising budgets suggest that most firms *over-advertise* (Aaker & Carman, 1982; Abraham & Lodish, 1990; Prasad & Sen, 1999). The question is why does this happen? Our discussion so far suggests three possible answers: first, excess budgets may be simply due to the rote application of percentage-of-sales rules-of-thumb, with the driving ad-sales ratio set too high, perhaps because the minimum efficient level is unknown (Farris et al. 1998; Tellis & Weiss, 1995). Second, managers may be aware of the flat maximum principle, and Tull et al.'s (1986) suggested strategy of over-spending to gain share at little cost in terms of foregone profits is already common practice. Third, as pointed out by Aykac et al. (1989), what appears to be over-spending relative to the optimum budget in a deterministic analysis may, in fact, be a risk-averse management's optimal response to estimation uncertainty.

In the next section, we turn our attention to advertising allocation decision problems.

Advertising Effort Distribution Problems

In this section, we will deal with problems of distribution of advertising effort subject to an exogenous budget constraint, as well as where the budget can be endogenously determined. In such problems, the objective is to *maximize the sum* of all entities' contributions to profits.

Static and Deterministic Resource Allocation Problems

As in the case of the budgeting problem, the sales response functions characterizing the market entities (e.g., geographic areas, products, and media) competing for the resource lie at the heart of allocation models. Frequently these disaggregate response functions are heterogeneous in their parameters if not shapes. The basic rule for optimal (profit-maximizing) distribution of a fixed budget over concave sales response functions is well-known: the allocation should be such that the marginal contribution responses at the assigned allocations of all entities should be equal and the advertising budget be exhausted. A number of papers in the operations research literature have presented algorithms and procedures for solving the distribution of effort problems when the sales response functions are concave or S-shaped (see, e.g., Charnes & Cooper, 1958; Freeland & Weinberg, 1980; Koopman, 1953; Lodish, 1971; Luss & Gupta, 1975; Mjelde, 1975; Rao & Rao, 1983; Shih, 1974; Sinha & Zoltners, 1979).

These optimization model solutions can sometimes be dramatically different from the intuition of managers (Mantrala et al., 1992). In practice, allocation decisions are often done applying *constant proportion of investment* (CPI) allocation rules. Examples include allocation of budgets according to the ratio of entities' sales potentials, consumer population sizes, etc. The basic problem with such allocation rules is that they ignore the responsiveness of each entity to allocated effort. Consequently, the optimal allocation ratios considering responsiveness are often quite different from those of CPI allocations. Further, under CPI rules all entities receive positive allocations regardless of the size of the budget and, also, all entities' allocations alter proportionately as the budget is increased or decreased. However, given sales response heterogeneity, optimization prescribes that for budgets below a certain critical size, only some entities should receive positive allocations, while others should get nothing. Moreover, even when the given budget is greater than the critical budget size, optimal allocations to entities often increase disproportionately as the budget size is increased. This means there can be reversals in the ratios of divisions of incremental budgets among the entities. Indeed, if the response functions are S-shaped, there may even be reversals in not just allocation ratios but *allocation levels* as well. That is, an entity that received a higher allocation than another at one level of the budget is allocated a lower amount than the other upon increasing the budget. In many organizations, such reversals in the context of increasing overall budgets would come as a rude shock to the manager concerned! Mantrala et al. (1992) present illustrations of all these phenomena and their impact on the total profitability of the investment decision. A major conclusion that emerges from their analyses is that improvements in the distribution of effort decision often have a much more significant impact on profitability than changes in the size of the total budget without correcting proportionate rule-based allocations occurring at the disaggregate level.

The analyses summarized above assume that competitors' actions are held fixed. What are the rules for optimal advertising allocations when a firm is in active competition with another in multiple markets? Monahan (1987) addresses this question and examines profit-maximizing competitive resource allocations in a duopoly where payoffs to each firm have a market share attraction form, of which [2] is a special case. Allowing that each firm wishes to allocate a fixed, but perhaps different sized budget so as to maximize total firm profits, Monahan derives the Nash equilibrium solution and obtains several interesting analytical results. First, he establishes that at equilibrium, the ratio of each competitor's effort allocated to the *i*th market is proportional to the ratio of the competitors' profit margins. Second, Monahan shows that as the attraction elasticity of effort in a market increases, it can become optimal for the firm with the larger budget to shift resources *away* from that market and use them more profitably elsewhere. In equilibrium, the second firm's allocation to any market is proportional to that of the first firm. Thus it is possible that as the responsiveness of a market increases, the overall effort allocated to it should decrease rather than increase – as might be first assumed.

A number of factors that complicate advertising resource allocation problems in practice have yet to be considered, such as multiple product demand interdependencies, spillover effects, dynamic effects, interacting media and demand uncertainty. Clearly, the value of applying normative allocation models and analyses becomes even more pronounced when some or all of these complications are present. Below, we briefly review some selected examples of models that highlight the allocation implications of each of these complexities.

Multi-product Allocation with Demand Interdependencies

Most manufacturers and retailers market multiple brands or products that compete for advertising funds. Such problems are challenging because they must cope with the issue of demand interdependencies such as when advertising of one product has a positive (*complementary*) effect, or negative (*substitution*) effect, on the demand of another product. Gijsbrechts & Naert (1984) present a general model of a multi-product marketing resource allocation problem that takes into account demand complementarity and substitutability. In practice, however, advertising decisions often ignore possible demand interdependencies, particularly when a *bottom-up approach* is used in decision-making. Doyle & Saunders (1990) discuss this issue within the context of a retailing environment. Under the bottom-up approach, individual merchandise group managers propose the products they want to advertise and how much they want to spend. Such budgets often reflect manufacturer's allowances and the rules of thumb which typify advertising decisions generally, e.g., 'how much can we afford to allocate as a percentage of sales?' The latter approach often leads to advertising being spread thinly across a wide range of products, rather than being targeted on those most likely to generate the best results.

Doyle & Saunders propose a multi-product advertising budgeting model that was used by a leading European variety store retailer to allocate expenditures to different product categories and media, accounting for both own- and cross-item advertising effects. Specifically, they assume sales in a given product category are a semilog response function of advertising for that category, advertising for other categories, lagged advertising terms, and a general store campaign. Doyle and Saunders estimated these category-level advertising response functions using three years of weekly electronic point-of-sales data, and found ample evidence of cross-effects between campaigns. Compared to the results of actual bottom-up allocations that ignored cross-effects, Doyle and Saunders projected that the optimal allocations based on the estimated response functions could improve projected profits by 37% and sales by 31%, and justify a budget four times as large as the existing budget.

Advertising Allocation Across National/Local Regions with Spillovers

Advertising is particularly amenable to regional variation (e.g., Ingene & Parry, 1990). Some firms allocate the total budget in proportion to last year's sales in an area or on a per capita basis. These decision rules reflect only some of the inter-area differences and may lead to significant over- or under-allocation to areas. Better solutions are offered by several allocation decision models that allow for heterogeneous ad-sales response functions, e.g., Rao & Miller (1975), and Urban (1975a, 1975b). An interesting twist in these problems is that advertising in a local area is usually a combination of national and local media advertising. Urban (1975a) therefore uses a 'weighted advertising' measure as the independent variable in the local area advertising-sales response function. This measure combines the pressure of national advertising expenditure that falls in an area with that due to its own local advertising. Urban's model algorithm is then able to determine the optimal 'split' of the total budget between national and local advertising, as well as allocations across local areas.

Another complication in allocating advertising geographically is the possibility of *spillovers*, i.e., advertising in one area or market segment affecting the demand in another. An early paper by Gensch & Welam (1973) formulates a model for optimum budget allocation for dynamic, interacting market segments. More recently, Brody & Finkelberg (1997) describe an implementable model for addressing a similar, multinational (pan-European) advertising allocation problem. They describe an example application wherein Belgian and Dutch consumer markets receive considerable spillover from advertising in neighboring nations, e.g., Germany. The optimal solution they determined was that local spending in both Belgium and Holland could be reduced to the minimum level, with Germany getting the bulk of the allocation. Because the model was able to reallocate resources to where they have greater impact, the expected overall revenue was $7.5 million higher (+3.5%) than following the traditional rule of allocating solely on the basis of the population size of the market, without any increase in advertising budget. Further, although revenues from France, Belgium and Holland were reduced, these reductions were outweighed by increased revenue from Germany, resulting in a total European gain. Of course, the reward structure for local managers must equitably reflect this.

Advertising Allocation Across Synergistic Media Vehicles

The allocation of an advertising budget across media vehicles, or media planning, is a classic problem that has been the subject of considerable research and the focus of many well-known decision models, e.g., Little & Lodish (1969), and Aaker (1975). Detailed treatments of media models are provided by Rust (1986), and Danaher & Rust (1994) among others. Here, we concentrate on the specific issue of allocation across interacting media. Interaction effects are different from interdependencies (Longman & Pauwels, 1998) and occur when two marketing elements combine to have a joint effect on sales of a single product. *Synergy* occurs when the combined effect of multiple activities exceeds the sum of their individual effects (e.g., Belch & Belch, 1998). The issue of synergy frequently arises in the context of advertising media models and is a key driver of the *Integrated Marketing Communications* (IMC) perspective (Schultz, 1993: 17).

Naik & Raman (2001) investigate the theoretical and empirical effects of synergy between TV and print media by employing a linear, additive dynamic model with interactions. Using market data on Dockers® brand advertising and sales, they apply Kalman filtering methodology to establish that there exists synergy between TV and print ads. Given this empirical support for the response model, they derive the following propositions:

1. As the effectiveness of a medium increases, the advertiser should increase spending on that medium, thus increasing the media budget.
2. As the carryover effect increases, the advertiser should increase the media budget. This rate of increase in the media budget increases as synergy increases.
3. As synergy increases, advertisers should not only *increase the total media budget*, but also *allocate a higher proportion of funds to the less effective medium*.
4. If the various activities are equally effective, then the advertiser should allocate the media budget equally amongst them, regardless of the magnitude of synergy.
5. Advertisers should *not* eliminate the budget for activities that have a negligible direct impact (main effect) on sales, if they show synergy with another medium that does have a main effect.

Advertising Media Scheduling with Dynamic Advertising Quality

An important managerial question that has been the focus of much academic research is whether ad expenditures should be evenly distributed over periods of a given time horizon or concentrated in limited bursts (e.g., Little, 1979). The latter policy is known as pulsing or flighting. The necessary condition for pulsing is that advertising has a dynamic carryover effect. The rationale is intuitive. If a current-effects model is correct, there are no temporal interdependencies. Consequently, the optimal advertising policy can be chosen period-by-period (i.e., pulsing is inappropriate).

Normative models have shown that a continuous spending strategy is optimal when brand awareness or sales is a concave function of advertising spending, while a very rapid switching between 'on' and 'off' advertising ('chattering') is optimal when the function has an S-shape (e.g., Mahajan & Muller, 1986; Sasieni, 1971). However, a chattering policy is not implementable in practice and is perceptually indistinguishable from the continuous one (e.g., Feinberg, 1992). Given the limited empirical support for S-shaped advertising response functions (Simon & Arndt, 1980), this body of research suggests that continuous advertising should be optimal in most practical circumstances. However, managers do pulse. This prompted Little (1986) to ask what form of response model could support a pulsing strategy?

Simon (1982) offers a model that allows a pulsing strategy to dominate the continuous strategy when sales response to advertising is not S-shaped. In this model, the superiority of pulsing is driven by an asymmetry of sales response. Specifically, the gain in sales volume when ad spending is increased by a certain amount is greater than the loss in sales when the spending is reduced by the same amount. In such situations, alternating between high and low spending levels makes sense. However, as noted by Sasieni (1989), there is only limited empirical support for this model specification (Haley, 1978). Also, Simon's model, and its extension by Mesak (1992), does not resolve the issues of optimal duration and spacing between advertising bursts. Further, the preceding normative models have ignored the question of how the impact of advertising spending is mediated by *advertising quality*, and how this may vary as a function of message or copy repetition, style, 'freshness,' etc. over time (e.g., Arnold et al., 1987; Little, 1975a; Parsons & Schultz, 1976). This appears to be an important omission given the mounting evidence that the creative component of advertising ad message quality is often more important than the level of expenditure (Eastlack & Rao, 1986; Lodish et al., 1995).

Motivated by these questions, Naik, Mantrala and Sawyer (1998) develop a model that shows that pulsing can generate greater total awareness than continuous advertising when the effectiveness (quality) of the advertising varies over time. Specifically, they postulate that ad quality declines because of repetition and copy *wearout* during periods of continuous advertising, and it restores, due to forgetting effects, during periods of no advertising. Such dynamics make it worthwhile for advertisers to stop advertising when ad quality becomes very low and wait for ad quality to restore before starting the next burst again, as is common in practice. Naik et al. (1998) embed these ad quality dynamics within the classic Nerlove & Arrow (1962) dynamic response model framework and provide empirical support for the model. They then present an implementable approach based on a genetic algorithm-Kalman filter procedure for evaluating large numbers of alternative media schedules and determining the best set for consideration in media planning. Applying this approach in case studies of cereal and milk chocolate brand advertising in the UK, Naik et al. show that the form of the best advertising spending strategies in each case was a pulsing strategy while continuous spending was in fact the worst policy. Further, they found many schedules that were an improvement over the media schedule actually used in each campaign.

Advertising Budget Allocations Under Uncertainty

As we already saw in the case of budgeting, optimal allocations across market entities characterized by sales response uncertainty are likely to vary with the decision-makers' risk preferences. Further, as shown by Mantrala et al. (1992) for a two-entity example, the optimum total budgets will vary with these differences in allocations and risk-preferences. In another example, Holthausen & Assmus (1982) address the problem of allocation of an advertising budget across geographic market areas with uncertain and heterogeneous response functions. Assuming a risk-return framework, they show that basing allocations on the mean sales response to advertising in each segment leads to a solution that maximizes expected return but is also associated with a relatively high risk. This may render it non-optimal to a risk-averse management. Holthausen and Assmus's model derives an efficient frontier in terms of the expected profit and its variance resulting from alternative budget allocations. The manager then chooses the optimal allocation based on his/her preference function. In their applications, Holthausen and Assmus assume modified exponential-form sales response functions whose variance increases with advertising. The parameters of these functions cannot be estimated independently since covariances between sales of different segments in the model must be dealt with explicitly. Therefore, the authors used a nonlinear, seemingly unrelated regressions algorithm based on three-stage, least squares method to estimate the system of equations. The allocations between territories significantly shift at different risk-return combinations.

3. Salesforce Strategy and Effort Deployment Decisions

The salesforce is the Number 1 marketing investment for firms in many industries, e.g., pharmaceuticals. As a result, several *salesforce strategy* issues arise repeatedly in these industries. What is the optimal size (number of salespeople)? What is the best way to organize or structure the salesforce? How should salesforce effort (number of sales calls or selling hours) be allocated across products sold and the markets served? Once these higher-level salesforce strategy questions are settled, there are still more micro-level allocation decisions to be addressed. How should salespeople be deployed across sales territories? What is the best allocation of a salesperson's effort or call time across his/her assigned target customers or accounts?

In reality, answers to these questions of sales force strategy and deployment are all intimately related and have to be considered simultaneously for best results. Still, we find it useful to organize our discussion of research in this area into two parts: Salesforce Strategy and Salesforce Deployment. Further, we move from separate to more integrated salesforce strategy and deployment models as our discussion proceeds.

Salesforce Strategy

Salesforce Sizing

The determination of the total salesforce size has been traditionally approached using either a top-down 'breakdown' approach or a bottom-up workload build-up approach. Under the breakdown approach, the total salesforce budget (or 'costs') may be set as a 'cost-of-sales' percentage of a sales forecast. The sizing decision may be as simple as dividing this dollar budget by the average salesperson salary to come up with a salesforce size. Effectively, therefore, this amounts to a *cost containment* approach. Sinha & Zoltners (2001) report that many companies in their consulting experience like to constrain the ratio of salesforce costs as a percentage of total sales to be smaller than a preset value. Apparently, the US average is 6.8%. This heuristic ignores the principle that salesforce effort drives sales, and the fact that greater attention to salesforce productivity may actually support an increase in the salesforce size. For example, Sinha and Zoltners provide an illustration that shows that salesforce cost ratios and profits are *negatively correlated* for salesforce sizes less than the profit-maximizing size. Companies that favor small salesforce sizes tend to under-size their salesforces.

The 'bottom-up' workload build-up approach to salesforce sizing is more detailed but continues to be problematic. For example, in the pharmaceutical industry, the workload build-up approach usually divides the total physician population into segments according to specialty and prescribing level (or 'deciles'). A subset of targeted physicians to be called on, the *reach*, is chosen for each physician segment. An annual call norm, the *frequency*, is established for each targeted segment. Multiplying the physician counts by the call norms, i.e., reach times frequency, produces the estimate of required total salesforce calls. Under this formula, field force size then equals the total number of calls required divided by the average number of calls sales representatives make in a year. The problem with this approach is that it prevents effective evaluation of resource allocation decisions. Many combinations of reach and frequency of detailing yield the same field force size, but can result in dramatically different sales and profits when companies allocate effort in various combinations of products and markets.

To summarize, the cost-of-sales approach is driven by a predetermined output forecast, while the workload build-up approach is driven by a predetermined total effort per person. Both approaches ignore the full relationship between output and effort, i.e., the sales response function, and market entities' differing responsiveness to selling effort. Recognizing these limitations, a number of normative models for salesforce sizing incorporating market response functions have been proposed. Early models focused on utilizing either historical or experimental data to relate sales levels to territorial potential and workload, e.g., Lucas et al. (1975), and Waid et al. (1956), and then derived normative implications for sizing decisions. Meidan (1982) provides an overview and evaluation of these and other methods for salesforce sizing. However, these approaches derive aggregate relationships that assume the firm's current salesforce effort-allocation program will remain unchanged. Thus, they ignore the fact that sales revenues are also a function of how the salesforce effort is allocated across products, markets, districts, sales regions and so forth (see, e.g., Mantrala et al., 1992).

Salesforce Allocation Across Products and Markets

As already discussed within the context of advertising, optimization theory tells us that the resource is optimally allocated if the incremental returns are equal across all marketing entities that want the resource. How close do companies actually come to allocating their salesforce effort optimally? Usually not very much, according to Sinha & Zoltners (2001). They provide an assessment based on estimated sales response functions for over 400 products promoted by 50 companies and find that if these companies were to implement their planned strategies, the ratio of the largest incremental return to the smallest incremental return averaged more than eight! As already noted, the nature of sales effort allocations across products and markets is more critical than the size of the salesforce. This is again because of the flat maximum principle that has been observed to operate in numerous salesforce studies. That is, profits remain unresponsive to salesforce size over fairly broad ranges. On the other hand, it has been observed that a better or worse allocation of effort across products and markets can make a difference in profits between 5 and 20% (Sinha & Zoltners, 2001).

The simultaneous or integrated consideration of both salesforce sizing and allocation of effort decisions can be developed using 'bottom-up' (more disaggregated) or 'top-down' (more aggregated) approaches. Classic examples of the disaggregated approach are the models of Lodish (1971, 1980) and Montgomery et al. (1971) (see also Vandenbosch & Weinberg, 1993; Zoltners & Sinha, 1980). One of the most well-known applications of such models is the salesforce sizing and allocation across products and customer types (physician specialties) using a decision calculus model at Syntex Laboratories described by Lodish et al. (1988). Lodish (2001) revisits this application and reports that Syntex credited the model with increasing profits by over 20%.

Horsky and Nelson (1996) propose a different approach that takes a 'top-down' perspective in the sense that it is based on aggregated data, which allows top management an independent assessment of the salesforce size, i.e., with little or no input from the salesforce. Horsky and Nelson follow a geographic area time-allocation approach where the national salesforce size decision is based on estimated district sales response functions. The innovation in Horsky and Nelson's approach is that their methodology estimates a district sales response function that reflects the '*efficient frontier*' sales response to salesforce size, effort and other variables. This efficient frontier sales response function reflects the productivity of only the firm's top performing districts. Using this response function, the profit-maximizing size can be determined, inefficient districts can be identified and the extent of these inefficiencies can be revealed. Several possible reasons for these inefficiencies can be uncovered by comparing with more traditional regression-based estimates of the average sales response functions. Efficient frontiers can be estimated using econometric techniques or linear programming methods such as Data Envelopment Analysis (DEA); see, e.g., Mahajan (1991).

Salesforce Structure

Many existing salesforce decision models for sizing and resource allocation assume that the structure of the salesforce is fixed. However, as pointed out by Rangaswamy et al. (1990), by altering the structure of the salesforce, management can influence the level and direction of effort deployment on a long-term basis. The salesforce structure problem is concerned with two key questions. How many salesforces should the firm use? And which products should be assigned to each salesforce? The optimal salesforce structure is closely related to the issues of salesforce size and sales effort deployment. One cannot evaluate a particular salesforce structure without simultaneously examining the total amount of salesforce effort (size) and the manner in which the effort is allocated across products and markets (deployment). For example, a salesforce utilizing two specialty field forces comprised of 100 people, each deploying their resources optimally, can outperform a single field force of 300 that is deploying the resources inappropriately. At the same time, a single field force of 175 that is optimally deployed may outperform two 100-salesperson field forces that are also optimally deployed. In order to choose between two alternate structures, one has to be assured that both structures will be efficiently sized and deploy their effort optimally.

Considering a repetitive buying environment, e.g., prescription drug markets, Rangaswamy et al.

present a mathematical programming model for integrated salesforce structure, sizing and effort allocation that incorporates a product sales response function-based methodology. At the outset, the set of partitions of the firm's product line that correspond to the feasible set of salesforce structures is defined. The product sales response functions represent the sales from a particular product *j* in a market segment *k* under salesforce structure *s* and allow for product-line interdependencies. The approach to calibrate these functions combines analysis of historical data with a judgmental data estimation procedure. The decision model derives recommendations for the optimal number of salesforces, optimal product assignments to salesforces, optimal size of each salesforce and optimal effort allocation for the plan period for each product-market-structure combination.

Salesforce Deployment

Salesforce deployment involves the simultaneous resolution of four interrelated subproblems: salesforce sizing, salesman location, sales territory alignment, and sales resource allocation. The first subproblem deals with selecting the appropriate number of salesmen. The salesman location aspect of the problem involves determining the location of each salesman in one sales coverage unit (SCU). SCUs are usually defined in terms of a geographic planning unit for which the required data can be obtained. Counties, zip codes, and company trading areas are some examples. Sales territory alignment may be viewed as the problem of grouping SCUs into larger geographic clusters called sales territories. Sales resource allocation refers to the problem of allocating scarce salesman time to the aligned sales coverage units. All four subproblems have to be resolved in order to maximize profit of the selling organization (Drexl & Haase, 1999).

A number of models for sales territory alignment have been proposed and implemented (Zoltners & Sinha, 1983). From their meta-analysis of actual applications, Sinha & Zoltners (2001) report that most sales territories (55%) are either too large or too small. Further, good sales-territory alignment enhances customer coverage and increases sales. Sales will increase between two and seven percent when sales territories optimize coverage. But, what is a good alignment? Some authors suggest that a good alignment is profit-maximizing (Lodish, 1975; Skiera & Albers, 1998; Zoltners, 1976). Most managers feel it should be (customer relationship) disruption minimizing. In practice, good alignments balance territory workload. The best workload measures are calibrated to account for territory market potential.

Glaze & Weinberg (1979) address the three subproblems of locating the salesmen, aligning accounts, and allocating calling time. More specifically, they present the procedure territory alignment model and account planning system (TAPS), which seeks to maximize sales for a given salesforce size while also attempting to achieve equal workload between salespersons and, in addition, minimize total travel time. Recently, Skiera & Albers (1998) proposed a new approach, COSTA, an acronym for 'contribution optimizing sales territory alignment,' that operates with aggregated concave sales response functions at the level of SCUs that require less data than previous profit maximization approaches. COSTA models sales as a function of calling time and travel time, assuming a constant ratio of travel to calling time. Using a simulated annealing heuristic (Kirkpatrick et al., 1983) the decision model simultaneously solves the optimal allocation of a salesperson's selling time across the SCUs of his/her territory, and the assignment of SCUs to territories. Motivated by the COSTA approach, Drexl and Haase (1999) propose a novel nonlinear, mixed-integer programming model to solve all four subproblems of salesforce sizing, location, alignment and allocation of effort simultaneously. Drexl & Haase present fast approximation methods capable of solving large-scale, real-world instances of their model formulation.

4. Manufacturer Sales Promotion Allocation Decisions

Sales promotion is an area that has attracted a vast amount of study (see, e.g., Blattberg & Neslin, 1990). The bulk of this research has been with respect to sales promotions by consumer packaged goods (CPG) manufacturers and retailers that spend heavily on this type of marketing effort. Research on promotions and their effects is the subject of a separate chapter in this handbook (Chapter 13). Therefore, in this section, we confine our attention to selected normative models for guiding CPG manufacturer trade promotion. Retailer merchandising and promotion resource allocation decisions are the subject of the next section of this chapter.

Manufacturer trade promotions include case allowances, advertising allowances, display allowances, and contests. Major CPG manufacturers budget at least one-half of their total marketing expense to trade promotions. These trade promotions frequently fund retailers' temporary price reductions (TPRs), displays, and feature advertising. Blattberg & Neslin (1990) review and suggest a number of models and approaches that have been proposed or should be considered in dealing with promotional issues and decisions. Two prominent contributions among these are the models for evaluating the effectiveness of trade promotions proposed by Blattberg & Levin (1987) and

Abraham & Lodish (1987). The Abraham-Lodish PROMOTER methodology provides a better baseline for evaluating promotion effectiveness than the typical approach of simply comparing the average weekly shipments during the promotional period with the average weekly sales over the previous two or three years. Both the Blattberg-Levin and Abraham-Lodish approaches were designed to use the store audit and warehouse withdrawal data typically purchased by CPG manufacturers at that time, but held out the possibility of capitalizing on the emerging UPC scanner-based data services. Consequently, we concentrate on a few more recent models that utilize these newer databases (store-level and household panel scanner data). More specifically, we focus on two types of manufacturer trade promotion resource allocation decisions: (1) allocation of trade promotional support across local geographic markets or key accounts; and (2) planning the *sales promotion calendar* (or the sequence of weekly price discounts, features and displays).

Trade Promotion Allocation across Markets and Accounts

Abraham & Lodish (1993) describe the traditional way many CPG brand managers allocate promotional resources. Typically, markets are grouped by their category development indices (CDI) and brand development indices (BDI). These indices respectively portray whether category sales per household, or brand sales per household, in a market are above or below average. Then, it is common to apply allocation decision rules such as allocating more to markets with high CDI and low BDI (viewed as high potential markets), or allocating more to markets with high BDI ('follow your strengths'). To improve these decisions, Abraham and Lodish advocate a market response approach that directly relates promotional activity with the incremental response that has occurred and permits allocation of resources to areas where they will get more marginal revenue per promotional dollar. They note that incremental sales volume can be either short-term or long-term.

Short-term incremental volume is volume generated in the promotion week, in the promoting store, that is incremental to 'normal' sales in that store during that week that would have occurred if the promotion had not been run. The short-term incremental volume, adjusted downward for any purchase acceleration by loyal consumers, provides the long-term incremental volume. Abraham & Lodish's (1993) PROMOTIONSCAN system uses store-level scanner data to measure short-term promotion effects and relate them to retailer merchandising activity. Subsequently, the PROMOTIONSCAN data is integrated with corporate promotion costs and profit margins to calculate the short-term incremental profitability of specific promotion events and the cost per incremental case sold on promotion. Abraham and Lodish describe applications that demonstrate that this information is very useful for senior-level total budget and brand allocation decisions.

The production version of PROMOTIONSCAN employs simple cross-tabulations to summarize incremental sales associated with various retail promotion activities – features, displays, and price cuts. There have also been efforts to develop multivariable sales response models at the 'key account' level, i.e., for a specified retailer in a given geographic market, e.g., Kroger in Columbus. This type of measurement is important because most consumer goods manufacturers actually do allocate trade promotion budgets separately by various key accounts that can number more than 100. The typical approach is to allocate dollars according to the relative sales volume of key accounts for either the category of interest or the entire ACV (all commodity volume) of the key accounts. Such an approach to allocation ignores heterogeneity in consumer responses to promotion in different markets. As already mentioned, a market that displays greater promotional response than average at the consumer level deserves a greater allocation of promotional dollars. The need is to estimate consumer sales response models at the account level. However, attempts to fit account-level sales response models using standard statistical methods such as least squares regression are usually frustrated by the propagation of a large number of coefficients with the wrong sign or unreasonable magnitude. Therefore, Boatwright et al. (1999) propose a more advanced, hierarchical Bayesian modeling approach to estimating account-specific response coefficients that overcomes the common difficulties in response model estimation, yet yields results that facilitate trade promotion allocation decisions. Their approach to the trade promotion allocation process is demonstrated with an analysis of weekly scanner data for Kraft sliced cheese sold in 77 key accounts. The sales response model calibrates the effect of prices, display, and feature activity on brand sales units. The authors present an optimal allocation scheme whereby key accounts are ranked in descending order of predicted promotional impact. Results show that such an allocation approach outperforms the typical proportional allocation method that relies solely on key account volume.

Planning Sales Promotion Calendars

How should a manufacturer structure the trade promotion offer to a retailer so as to get the right promotion calendar in front of consumers? The sales promotion calendar summarizes tactical decisions regarding levels of TPRs, feature ads, and in-store displays, each executed at the level of individual retail accounts and brand stock-keeping units (SKUs) over several months or a year. Silva-Risso et al. (1999) combine scanner modeling technology and optimization methods to develop a Decision Support System (DSS) that addresses this question. Silva-Russo et al. note that two limitations of the Abraham-Lodish (1993) approach are, first, it uses store-level data and therefore does not decompose the promotional lift (i.e., the volume of sales above baseline) into sales that are truly incremental versus those that are borrowed. Second, Abraham and Lodish do not incorporate dynamics in consumer response or the effects of previous marketing activity on future promotional events. In contrast, Silva-Russo et al. use household scanner panel ('wand') data to capture the dynamics and heterogeneity of consumer response, and estimate the purchase acceleration and/or stockpiling induced by a promotion and decompose total sales into incremental and non-incremental (baseline plus borrowed). The response model forms the basis of a market simulator that permits a search for the manufacturer's optimal promotion calendar (subject to a set of constraints, some of them imposed by the retailer) via the simulated annealing algorithm. Calendar profits are the net result of the contribution from incremental sales, minus the opportunity cost from giving away discounts to non-incremental sales, and the fixed costs associated with implementing promotional events (e.g., retagging, features, displays).

Incremental sales result from promotion-induced switching, the acceleration and quantity promotion, effects on those switchers, increased consumption, and the carryover effect from purchase event feedback. In an application, Silva-Russo et al. found that the manufacturer could substantially improve the profitability of its sales promotion activity, and that there would be a concurrent positive effect on retailer profit and volume levels. Sensitivity analyses revealed that changes in retailer passthrough have a significant effect on the optimal depth and number of weeks of trade promotion that a manufacturer should offer. This emphasizes the importance to manufacturers of having accurate estimates of passthrough for purposes of promotion budgeting and planning.

5. Allocating Retailer Merchandising and Promotion Resources

Retailer merchandising variables include shelf-space, floor-space, quantities and assortment of goods offered across categories, and promotions. Retailer promotions to consumers include temporary price cuts, displays, feature advertising, free goods, retailer coupons, premiums, and contests. In this section, we review selected resource allocation problems involving these variables.

Space Allocation Problems

Display Space Allocation Problems

Determining the amount of scarce self-service display space (e.g., linear feet, facings or square inches) to allocate to different categories and stocked brands so as to maximize the store's profit is a classic and critical retail management decision. Self-service display areas constitute a purchase setting where the products and brands must stimulate their own demand without the direction or encouragement of sales personnel. There have been a number of studies with respect to the effects of display space (e.g., Curhan, 1973), and an empirical generalization emerging from these studies is that increasing store shelf (display) space has a positive impact on sales of nonstaple grocery items (Hanssens et al., 2001). An early review of 20 studies found a mean shelf-space elasticity of 0.15 (1977 study by Heinsbroek reported by Bultez & Naert, 1988). However, there are ultimately decreasing returns to increasing shelf-space for a brand. Recently, Dreze et al. (1994) employed the S-shaped Gompertz growth function to model the effect of shelf-space on store sales. These researchers found that the Gompertz function was statistically significant in seven out of eight product categories that were studied.

The shelf-space decision is essentially a multi-product marketing resource allocation problem. However, a number of the early normative models for shelf-space allocation (e.g., Hansen & Heinsbroek, 1979; Lynch, 1974) assume decreasing returns shelf-space response functions, but ignore product demand interdependencies. The apparent interdependencies between one product's sales and another product's resource allocation in their models occur only because of the existence of a total space constraint. Other models that do explicitly include interdependencies in the demand model specification are those of Anderson (1979), Corstjens and Doyle (1981 – and its dynamic extension, Corstjens & Doyle, 1985). Anderson is concerned with the allocation of shelf-space between two brands and models the market share of one brand as a logistic function of its share of display space. In contrast, Corstjens and Doyle's aim is to optimize space allocation across product classes or categories, and they model the demand for each product group as a multiplicative power function of the display areas allocated to all of the product groups. Thus, cross-elasticities explicitly enter into the picture. Corstjens and Doyle incorporate these response functions within a geometric programming framework, to derive the space allocation across product classes or categories that maximizes store profit, taking into account the interactions between product classes.

Bultez & Naert's (1988) SH.A.R.P. model (SHelf Allocation for Retailer's Profit) expands and extends the Corstjens and Doyle model by considering not only interactions between product classes but also interactions between items within a product class. To estimate shelf-space elasticities at both levels, Bultez and Naert use an attraction model specification of the sales response function that corresponds to a flexible multivariate logistic relationship. They incorporate the interdependent product response functions in a nonlinear programming model formulation of the profit-maximizing retailer's constrained shelf-space allocation problem. Solving this problem using the Lagrangean approach, Bultez and Naert derive the optimal allocation formula, or 'SH.A.R.P. rule,' which implies that priority should be given to products whose display contributes most to boosting the sales of the most profitable ones and reducing handling costs. They report an empirical application to multiple assortments in Belgian supermarket chains. The SH.A.R.P. optimal allocation formula or rule is nontrivial to apply since all of its terms depend themselves on space allocation. Bultez and Naert use a computer heuristic to solve the system of nonlinear equations defined by the SH.A.R.P. rule. Reallocations of shelf-space according to their model resulted in increases in profit varying from 7 to 34%.

An interesting feature of the Bultez-Naert paper is that it provides an analysis of how the SH.A.R.P rule compares with the commonly used rules-of-thumb for shelf-space allocation actually used by supermarkets. As we have observed in the case of advertising and personal selling efforts, several of the well-known space allocation heuristics are, in fact, variants of rules of proportionality to sales, revenue or profit. These include 'PROGALI,' which suggests allocation based on either sales volume or on sales revenue; 'OBM,' which sets allocations proportional to gross margin revenues; and 'CIFRINO,' which recommends allocations proportional to relative profit contributions of the product groups. The SH.A.R.P rule, however, looks quite different from these common rules of thumb. Rather restrictive conditions have to be imposed to derive the rules as special cases. In fact, the SH.A.R.P rule can be interpreted as defining each item's space-share as a weighted mean of its relative contribution to the assortment profitability and its share of the assortment total sales volume. In other words, optimality lies somewhere between the two extreme benchmarks used by retailers: the CIFRINO/OBM and the PROGALI rules.

The classic problem of optimal retailer shelf-space allocation in combination with retail category assortment decisions (e.g., Borin et al., 1994) have become particularly relevant issues today as an increasing number of CPG retailers shift from traditional brand-centered management to category management (CM) (see e.g., Basuroy et al., 2001). Below, we review some recent work that considers the implications for the allocation of other merchandising resources such as feature advertising space.

'Marketing' vs 'Accounting' Profits

One key aspect of the category management philosophy is that profits of one product category may be affected by merchandising decisions in another category. Chen et al. (1999) argue that the traditional accounting measure of category profits offers imperfect help in making merchandising decisions, since it does not take into account cross-category effects of merchandising on store profitability. They propose that a profit measure that takes into account these important cross-effects is the most relevant performance metric for CM and they call this new construct *marketing profits*. Chen et al.'s aim is to draw out the relationship between accounting and marketing profits and implications for decisions such as feature advertising space allocation. Interestingly, central to their theoretical structure is the assumption that in the face of a deluge of new products and the substantial profit opportunities available through slotting allowances, retailers' shelf-space allocation decisions are reasonably *close-to-optimal*. This, they argue, could be achieved by using either an automated planogram such as Apollo or SPACEMAN (Levy & Weitz, 1998) or simply by trial-and-error (Borin et al., 1994; Dreze et al., 1994).

Chen et al. clearly believe that shelf-space management practice has improved since the time of Bultez and Naert's (1988) work. They argue that this is so because the conditions under which the retailer makes the shelf-space decision are considerably more stable than those impinging on other merchandising decisions such as feature advertising, point-of-purchase displays, stocking, and price discounts. For example, the different co-op advertising allowances available to the retailer often shift dramatically from week-to-week, while the total amount of shelf-space available or the basic composition of the different categories remain the same over time. Given the assumption of optimal shelf-space allocation, Chen et al. derive the implied relationship between accounting and marketing profits and show how the latter can be measured. They then demonstrate how the marketing profits approach can be applied to decide the allocation of promotional resources such as feature advertising space. In an illustration, Chen et al. show that allocation based on compartmentalized accounting profits always leads to an overall lower profit for the store than the allocation based on marketing profits, which considers all indirect effects. They also show that the marketing profits approach offers estimation benefits to the analyst.

Planning Optimal Timing and Depth of Price Promotions and Order Quantities

Tellis & Zufryden (1995) propose a nonlinear, integer programming model to help retailers determine the optimal timing and depth of retail price discounts (possibly accompanied by in-store displays and feature newspaper inserts) in conjunction with the optimal timing and quantity of the retailer's promotion-related order over multiple brands and time periods. This decision model incorporates an integrated model of a consumer's purchase incidence, brand choice, and purchase quantity in response to retailer promotion. The consumer response model is parameterized using IRI household scanner panel data. The decision model also includes a retailer model that captures the dynamics of retail inventory in response to retail orders and consumer purchases. Tellis and Zufryden report an application that shows how the optimum depth and timing of retail discounts over a planning horizon vary with the parameters of the problem. In particular, they show that retailers should give higher discounts to consumers as retail margins, consumer responsiveness, and category attractiveness increase, and lower discounts as consumer loyalty increases.

Allocating Promotion Merchandise Inventories across Stores

A key problem faced by retailers in the domain of retail promotion planning is deciding the chain-wide order quantity of a product on promotion and allocation of this stock across stores in the chain. Cooper et al. (1999) focus on the need for accurate sales forecasts based on *promotion-event data* to guide allocation of a chain-wide order to stores in the trading area. The most common practice involves classifying stores into three or four store-size groups and allocating stock proportional to these sizes. Some chains group stores according to the size of the category involved in the promotion, rather than by overall store size. Cooper et al. provide examples that show that such decision rules not supported by accurate response forecasting can result in significant misallocation of the merchandise inventory (as much as 25–35% errors in allocation). Therefore, they propose a promotion-event data-based methodology that captures store-specific information for an item to develop chain-level and store-by-store forecasts. In one field test, they forecast the results of 20,710 upcoming events. Subsequently, after the results came in, Cooper et al. report that 69% of the forecasts using their methodology were within one case of the actual level, and 83% of the forecasts were within two cases. The corresponding historical averages matched on ad and display conditions predicted only 39% within one case and 62% of the events within two cases.

6. Marketing Mix Allocation Models

In previous sections we have dealt with single-variable, e.g., advertising, personal selling, promotions, and retail merchandising resource allocation problems. In this section we review research and planning models that consider two or more of these marketing instruments in combination. We begin with the seminal normative analysis of Dorfman and Steiner (1954).

The Dorfman-Steiner Theorem

Dorfman and Steiner consider the single-period marketing mix optimization problem of a myopic profit-maximizing monopolist, and derive marketing mix optimality conditions assuming that the selection of the levels of various marketing instruments are independent decisions. The Dorfman-Steiner results can be summarized as follows. If the selection of the levels of various marketing resources are independent decisions, the conditions for the optimal mix of price, advertising expenditures, and distribution (personal selling) expenditures are that the negative of the price elasticity equals the marginal revenue product of advertising, equals the marginal product revenue of distribution, equals the reciprocal of the gross margin fraction. Note that [3] is simply a special case of this result. (It is assumed that the second-order conditions for profit-maximization are satisfied. They would be if the multi-variable sales response function is a concave function of advertising or personal selling expenditures, price is greater than marginal cost of production at all production levels, and the marginal cost is constant or an increasing function of quantity produced.)

If we recast the Dorfman-Steiner result entirely in terms of elasticities of different policy instruments (modified by other terms), then the theorem states that at optimality, the ratio of marketing resource elasticities will be equal to the ratio of the respective expenditure levels. In the case of a fixed budget, it can be shown that the optimal fraction that expenditure on one resource should constitute of the total budget is given by the ratio of its elasticity to the sum of all instrument elasticities. If the equality is not satisfied at the present levels of the policy instruments, then the instruments should be adjusted in the appropriate direction. If the appropriate direction is not obvious, some trial and error may be necessary. The Dorfman-Steiner theorem does not directly give the optimal values of the marketing policy variables, but rather the conditions that will be satisfied when the optimal values are found.

Dorfman and Steiner's static, monopoly and deterministic problem assumptions about sales response have been extended to incorporate dynamics, competition and uncertainty, e.g., Nerlove & Arrow (1962), Lambin et al. (1975), Jagpal & Brick (1982), and Morey & McCann (1983). Raman (2001) investigates the joint effect of both dynamics and uncertainty on the optimal marketing mix using the methodology of stochastic optimal control. He shows that uncertainty has important consequences in a dynamic optimization context even when it may have no effect in the corresponding static optimization problem. Raman (2001) finds that the strategies offering greatest value to managers in uncertain and risky environments are feedback policies because they optimally adapt to changing market conditions. Feedback policies facilitate optimal utilization of uncertainty to improve expected profit.

Returning to the case of a monopoly firm in a static and deterministic setting, Ingene and Parry (1995) reexamine the original Dorfman-Steiner optimality conditions in a multi-regional marketing context, i.e., where a vertically integrated firm operates in multiple geographically distinct regions. In such settings, Ingene and Parry draw a distinction between national or global, and regional or local marketing efforts. They demonstrate that when a multi-regional firm sets each marketing mix variable on a region-by-region basis, the standard Dorfman-Steiner optimality conditions obtain. However, if the firm finds it economical to manipulate one of the marketing variables 'globally,' say, national umbrella advertising, while the other variables are set regionally, say, local 'service-provision' variables, then Ingene and Parry find that the Dorfman-Steiner conditions do not yield profit-maximizing results. Interestingly, they determine there are conditions when the 'Global-Regional' scenario yields an optimal solution in which the global marketing variable may have a *negative marginal impact* on sales in some regions.

A number of normative marketing mix decision models have been proposed in the literature, including those of Balachandran and Gensch (1974), Little (1975a, 1975b), and Lambin (1972). A comprehensive review of these decision models is provided in Lilien and Kotler (1983). Below, we focus on normative analyses of some special marketing mix problems that have attracted research attention in recent years.

Marketing Communications Mix Problems

Advertising and Personal Selling Mix

Many organizations' marketing programs rely on both advertising and personal selling and naturally interactions between these marketing instruments and their implications for budget allocation have been the focus of a fair amount of research. Intuitively, advertising and personal selling should be synergistic. Gatignon & Hanssens (1987) in fact did find that personal selling effectiveness in Navy recruiting increased with local advertising support (see, e.g., Gatignon, 1993 for a comprehensive review of the literature on marketing interactions, and methods for calibrating models with interaction terms).

In another study in an industrial marketing context, Gopalakrishna & Chatterjee (1992) modeled, estimated and assessed the joint impact of advertising and personal selling on sales of a mature industrial product of low complexity. Their customer account-level sales response model allows for a synergistic effect and fit the data well in the illustrative application, and all parameter estimates were found to be highly significant with low standard errors. Gopalakrishna and Chatterjee employed the model to derive analytically some results pertaining to the impact of key market factors on the optimal level and allocation of the total communications budget. Their findings indicate that:

1. The optimal total communications budget and the optimal advertising budget increase as the number of accounts increases.
2. Optimal spending on both advertising and personal selling is higher if the account potential is larger with the advertising to personal selling ratio tending to 1 (an equal split of the budget) as account potential increases.
3. Greater personal selling effort per account must be directed to the segment that has a greater average potential if the segments are equally responsive to communications effort.
4. As competitive activity (spending) increases, it is optimal to gradually increase communications expenditures to fight the competition. However, beyond a certain level of competitive activity, it is optimal to cut back on expenditure to minimize dissipation of effort.

Competition in Gopalakrishna and Chatterjee's illustrative application was assumed to be passive and constant over time. A worthwhile direction for future research would be to allow for active competitive response to marketing actions.

Advertising and Promotions Mix

Several researchers have examined the tradeoffs between advertising and trade discounts. Sethuraman & Tellis (1991) analyze whether price discounts are more profitable than increases in advertising. Their analysis incorporates two new factors affecting the profitability of price discounts into the classic Dorfman-Steiner (1954) problem: (1) the opportunity loss from buyers who would have bought the brand at a regular price; and (2) the opportunity loss from retailers who 'pass through' only a fraction of the manufacturer's discounts to the consumers. Key results of Sethuraman and Tellis's theoretical analysis are that the elasticity of price and advertising are major factors determining the profitability of a price discount and an advertising increase. Further, when both advertising and a price-cut are profitable, the ratio of the elasticities plays a key role in the price-advertising tradeoff. Specifically, the amount of advertising necessary to match the profits from a 1% price cut increases with the ratio of the elasticities, advertising-to-sales ratio, and passthrough ratio, and decreases with the fraction of original demand bought at the discounted price. Sethuraman and Tellis also performed a meta-analysis of the ratios of the estimated price and advertising elasticities reported in previous empirical studies. They conclude that the price elasticity is 'on average' 20 times the advertising elasticity in the case of nondurable goods, and only about five times in the case of durable goods. Also, the elasticity ratio is higher for mature products than for products in the early stage of the life cycle, suggesting that price discounts may be much more profitable than advertising in the case of mature, nondurable products.

Neslin, Powell & Schneider Stone (1995) also investigate optimal advertising and trade promotion strategies but go further than Sethuraman & Tellis (1991) by building a dynamic model that incorporates retailer forward buying. More specifically, Neslin et al. develop a dynamic optimization model to examine how the manufacturer's optimal advertising and trade promotion plans are influenced by retailer and consumer response influences. The manufacturer's problem is to maximize its profits by advertising directly to consumers and offering periodic trade deal discounts to the retailer in the hope that the retailer will in turn pass through a retailer promotion to the consumer. Neslin et al. formulate and solve a discrete-time nonlinear program and show that the manufacturer's optimal allocation depends on the consumer response to advertising, consumer response to retailer promotions, retailer inventory carrying cost, and retailer passthrough behavior. Interestingly, they find a natural tendency for advertising and trade dealing to substitute for each other in an optimal plan. This follows from the costs and benefits of these activities, and occurs even if advertising has a positive carryover effect. The explanation is that at optimality, the marginal benefit of advertising must equal its marginal cost. An increase in trade discount then lowers the marginal benefit of advertising because the net profit margin has been lowered. Advertising expenditures must then decrease to bring the marginal benefits and costs of advertising back into equilibrium. These findings establish the robustness of the basic Dorfman-Steiner result even in a dynamic context that incorporates retailer behavior.

The increasing disposition of CPG manufacturers toward the use of sales promotions, often at the cost of advertising, has been a cause for concern among both academics and practitioners (e.g., Low & Mohr, 2000). As discussed in Section 4, sales promotions are inherently short-term oriented. Interest, therefore, has shifted to assessing the long-term effects of promotions versus advertising. Jedidi et al. (1999) point out that companies must be able to assess both the short-term and long-term effects of advertising and promotion to arrive at an appropriate budget allocation. They used scanner panel data for a mature, nonfood product to estimate the effects on brand choice and sales levels of advertising, regular price, price promotion depth and frequency over an eight-year period. The results of this analysis show that advertising has a positive long-term effect on brand equity (as represented by consumer loyalty over time), while price discounting has a negative effect. The results are brand-specific. Jedidi et al. perform simulations to assess the profit impact of long-term changes in price, advertising, and promotions and find that increases in advertising would have mixed effects on profitability; increasing price would generally not be profitable; and increased promotions would have a deleterious impact on profits.

Advertising, Personal Selling and Promotions Mix

Research that examines the optimal mix of advertising, personal selling and promotions within one study is limited in the marketing literature. This may be because of the concentration of research attention on CPG companies' dominant promotions and advertising programs that could be studied with readily available store-level and household panel scanner data during the last decade. Today in the pharmaceuticals industry, however, there is growing interest in the rigorous measurement of the joint effectiveness of detailing (personal selling) to physicians, 'direct-to-the-consumer' (DTC) advertising, medical journal advertising, and 'meetings and events' (promotions) (e.g., Kumble et al., 2000). Combined spending on these marketing efforts was in the region of $12 billion in year 2000, according to Scott-Levin Audit reports. Such measurements and optimizing expenditures based on them have become increasingly feasible with the availability of disaggregated prescription sales data from sources such as IMS Health, NDC and Scott-Levin (e.g., Liebman, 1998). For example, a recent study by Neslin (2001) focused on measuring the ROI for detailing (DET), DTC ads, medical journal ads (JAD) and physician meetings and events (M&E) using data provided by Scott-Levin and PERQ/HCI for 391 pharmaceutical brands over 60 months. Using a pooled cross-section/time series regression approach (e.g., Leeflang et al., 2000), Neslin found detailing to be very effective, DTC ads to be hardly effective, 'impressive' returns for journal advertising, and a high overall ROI for M&E. Based on this research, Neslin provides budget allocation recommendations for a 'median brand' in several scenarios that indicate that funds should be shifted from DTC toward DET and JAD.

7. Future Research Opportunities and Conclusions

Most of the papers surveyed in this chapter discuss their limitations and offer interesting directions for further work in their lines of research. Therefore, in this section, we adopt a broader perspective, to identify five general areas that we believe offer significant and substantial opportunities for future research bearing on the allocation of marketing resources.

Customer Equity Management

Virtually all of the models we have reviewed in this chapter have been brand- or product-oriented. That is, the driving objective was to allocate resources so as to maximize profits derived from sales of a brand or product category. Recently, however, there has been rapidly growing interest in directing marketing resources to maximize 'customer equity,' rather than brand equity and sales (e.g., Blattberg et al., 2001; Rust et al., 2000). Blattberg et al. argue that the fundamental goal of businesses should be keeping customers, not selling products. Setting a marketing budget, then, becomes the task of balancing what is spent on customer acquisition and what is spent on customer retention so as to maximize customer equity. In their seminal paper, Blattberg and Deighton (1996) define customer equity as the sum of the discounted net present values of each customer's lifetime expected contributions to offsetting the company's fixed costs.

Assessing customer 'lifetime values' (LTVs) and viewing each customer as a revenue-producing asset over time has been a central tenet of the direct marketing industry for many years (e.g., Shepard, 1990). However, the LTV concept is now becoming more commonplace in general marketing due to advances in firms' databases of customers, related customer relationship management (CRM) software and Internet communications technologies. The convergence of these technologies has made finer information-based target marketing feasible in many industries (e.g., Blattberg et al., 2001; Rust et al., 2000). Blattberg and Deighton show how the relationships between customer acquisition spending-acquisition rate, and retention spending-retention rate, can be modeled and assessed via a decision calculus approach and utilized to decide the levels of acquisition and retention expenditures. However, theirs is only a first step and there is great scope for more research into both normative-theoretical and decision modeling and measurement of customer profitability and analyses of related marketing expenditure allocation decisions (e.g., Berger & Nasr, 1998; Mulhern 1999).

Perishable-asset Yield Management

Capacity-constrained service and retailing firms seek to maximize revenue or yield of the firm. The operations research field has made significant contributions to the development of yield (or revenue) management systems (YMS). It is only recently that the marketing literature has begun to focus on such YMS problems even though YMS depends on the fundamental concepts of market segmentation (Desiraju & Shugan, 1999; Harris & Peacock, 1995). YMS can be approached from two perspectives. They can be viewed as tools for implementing an optimal multiperiod pricing strategy, in which each price is a function of forecasted excess capacity (Desiraju & Shugan, 1999). Alternatively, YMS can be viewed from a marketing resource allocation perspective where the resource in question is the limited capacity or inventory of a finite marketable resource, e.g., airline seats (Belobaba, 1987) or seasonal style-goods of a retailer (Gallego & van Ryzin, 1994). Managers must decide how much of each type of capacity (inventory) to allocate to different potential stochastic demand segments. Mantrala and Rao (2001) take this perspective in assessing the results of an application of a decision model for jointly optimizing order quantity and retail markdown pricing policy for a fashion good that has a limited selling season and uncertain demand. Their results suggest that like other marketing resources, expected profits are relatively insensitive to changes in inventory around the optimum order quantity, but much more sensitive to improvements of the allocation of the inventory to different demand segments or price tiers.

A related problem that faces a central planner or allocator of a retail chain is deciding the optimal order quantity and allocation of a style-good across different stores in the chain that are operating in heterogeneous and uncertain demand environments (see, e.g., Levy & Weitz, 1998; Mantrala & Raman, 1999). This and related problems of optimal assortment, pricing, advertising and promotion are challenging resource allocation problems faced by fashion retailers and service firms offering important opportunities for more research by marketing scientists.

Category Management

The growing practice of category management (CM) is an important development among both CPG manufacturers and retailers (e.g., Basuroy et al., 2001; Zenor, 1994). However, there has not been as much rigorous normative research on CM as one might expect considering the great amount of importance, attention and space that has been given to this practice by industry consultants, executives and the trade press over the last decade. In particular, other than pricing and shelf-space allocations, few normative analyses of optimal marketing resource allocation decisions under CM have appeared in the academic literature. For example, questions such as how to decide the optimal product and marketing mix for a product category taking into account product interdependencies, competitive effects and category managers' risk-preferences have yet to be systematically addressed. More analytical research such as that of Chen et al. (1999), as well as behavioral research, is needed in this area.

Micromodeling and Micromarketing

Most of the marketing resource allocation models we have reviewed in this chapter utilize macro- or aggregate response models, based on either historical national or market level time series data, field experimental data, or managers' judgmental data, rather than models of individual customer response behavior. This is partly because much of the research reviewed occurred when there was little or no 'convincing' individual-level data on sales and/or marketing control variables readily available (e.g., Little, 1979).

Moreover, most of the decisions we have treated are about budgeting and allocation of marketing resources to markets rather than individual consumers, and common sense does suggest that a model should be specified at the same level of aggregation at which decisions are made. For example, if the problem is one of allocating advertising resources across all stores and households of a market, then the model should be estimated with market-level data. Conversely, if one is concerned about, say, better allocation of salespeople's calls to individual doctors who are likely to be heterogeneous in their preferences and responsiveness, then physician-level data analyses would be more relevant, provided such data were available (e.g., Manchanda et al., 2000; Winer, 1979). Recent research, however, indicates that this conventional argument is flawed as it ignores *aggregation bias* problems that arise due to heterogeneity in consumer-level demand parameters and nonlinear responses to marketing actions to which consumers are exposed (e.g., Christen et al., 1997; Gupta et al., 1996). The emerging conclusion of this research is that even if individual-level heterogeneity is of no immediate interest to the manager, it is helpful to use data (if available) that contain such differences in order to obtain valid market-level estimates of marketing activities' effects, e.g., Leeflang et al. (2000).

Disaggegate-level analyses are, of course, also necessary when the manager's interest is in fact micromarketing, i.e., tailoring a firm's marketing mix to individual households. Marketing practices that are designed to exploit consumer differences require flexible models of heterogeneity, coupled with an inference procedure that adequately describes uncertainty in consumer-level estimates. However, the amount of data obtained through surveys or household purchase histories available for drawing inferences about any specific consumer is usually sparse, although there may exist many consumers in a particular study (Allenby & Rossi, 1999; Rossi et al., 1996). Therefore, Allenby and Rossi advocate the use of hierarchical Bayes models of heterogeneity that pool data across individuals while allowing for the analysis of individual model parameters. Models that do so successfully will permit more refined target marketing and profitable allocation of marketing resources at the individual-level. Building such models appears to be a major research opportunity today.

Marketing Resource Allocation Strategies in Evolving Markets

Many models covered in this chapter can be characterized as being short-run focused while assuming an essentially stable environment. A number of recent studies, however, have examined the strategic or long-term effects of marketing efforts such as advertising or promotion, e.g., Dekimpe and Hanssens (1995), and Mela et al. (1997). Examples of issues of interest are the long-term impact of marketing spending strategies on brand equity, competitors' reactions and positions, and profits. However, as argued by Dekimpe and Hanssens (1999), what constitutes the long-term and how it should be measured is often not very clear. To rigorously define the 'long-term,' Dekimpe and Hanssens propose that both marketing effort and market response be classified as either short-lived (temporary or stationary) or persistent (evolving), and derive four strategic scenarios for marketing resource allocation decisions.

1. *Business as usual* – where marketing expenditure and sales patterns are stable except for short promotion-based swings.
2. *Escalation* – where marketing expenditures increase over time with little or no improvements in performance.
3. *Hysteresis* – where temporary marketing actions lead to sustained changes in purchase behavior.
4. *Evolving business practice* – where sustained marketing efforts lead to persistent results.

Dekimpe and Hanssens argue that in allocating promotion expenditures, managers should consider which of the four strategic scenarios prevails, and that this issue can be investigated by applying new empirical methods, e.g., vector-autoregressive (VAR) models, to high-quality time-series (tracking) data. The dynamically optimal marketing resource allocation strategy depends on the prevailing scenario. For example, if the condition of hysteresis (see, e.g., Simon, 1997) prevails partially or fully, then the marketer can replace costly maintenance spending with one 'triggering' or upfront, temporary marketing investment (Hanssens & Ouyang, 2001). Using dynamic programming, Hanssens and Ouyang obtain exact expressions for the allocation of a marketing budget between trigger and maintenance spending. The long-term resource allocation strategy issues raised by the above research are provocative and need to be pursued in future research.

In conclusion, this chapter has surveyed many topics in the domain of allocating marketing resources. The issues are of great practical and immediate importance to managers. While many normative models have been proposed and successfully applied, it is clear that new management systems, data sources, estimation, and optimization methods all represent opportunities for further research, leading to more productive and profitable expenditure of marketing resources. We hope that this chapter will facilitate the development of this research.

References

Aaker, David A. (1975) ADMOD: an advertising decision model. *Journal of Marketing Research*, 8 (February), 37–45.

Aaker, David A. & Carman, James M. (1982) Are you overadvertising? *Journal of Advertising Research*, 22 (August–September), 57–70.

Aaker, David A. & Myers, John G. (1987) *Advertising Management*. Englewood Cliffs, NJ: Prentice-Hall Inc.

Abraham, Magid M. & Lodish, Leonard M. (1987) Promoter: an automated promotion evaluation system. *Marketing Science*, 6 (Spring), 101–23.

Abraham, Magid M. & Lodish, Leonard M. (1990) Getting the most out of advertising and promotion. *Harvard Business Review*, May–June, 50–8.

——— (1993) An implemented system for improving promotion productivity using store scanner data. *Marketing Science*, 12 (Summer), 248–69.

Ackoff, Russell L. & Emshoff, James R. (1975) Advertising research at Anheuser-Busch (1963–68). *Sloan Management Review*, 16, 1–16.

Allenby, Greg M. & Rossi, Peter E. (1999) Marketing models of consumer heterogeneity. *Journal of Econometrics*, 89, 57–78.

Anderson, Erin, Lodish, Leonard M. & Weitz, Barton A. (1987) Resource allocation behavior in conventional channels. *Journal of Marketing Research*, 24, 1 (February), 85–97.

Anderson, Evans E. (1979) An analysis of retail display space: theory and methods. *Journal of Business*, 52, 1, 103–18.

Arnold, Stephen J., Oum, Tae H., Pazderka, Bohumir & Snetsinger, Douglas W. (1987) Advertising quality in sales response models. *Journal of Marketing Research*, 24, 1 (February), 106–13.

Assmus, Gert, Farley, John U. & Lehmann, Donald R. (1984) How advertising affects sales: meta-analysis of econometric results. *Journal of Marketing Research*, 21, 1 (February), 65–74.

Aykac, A., Corstjens, Marcel, Gautschi, David & Horowitz, Ira (1989) Estimation uncertainty and optimal advertising decisions. *Management Science*, 35, January, 42–50.

Balachandran, V. & Gensch, Dennis H. (1974) Solving the marketing mix problem using geometric programming. *Management Science*, 21, October, 160–71.

Bass, Frank M. (1979) Advertising spending levels and promotion policies: profit potential for the applications of management science. The Eleventh Annual Albert Wesley Frey Lecture, April, Graduate School of Business, University of Pittsburgh.

Basuroy, Suman, Mantrala, Murali K. & Walters, Rockney G. (2001) The impact of category management on retail prices; theory and evidence. *Journal of Marketing*, 65 (October), 16–32.

Belch, George E. & Belch, Michael A. (1998) *Advertising and Promotion: An Integrated Marketing Communications Perspective*, 4th Edn. Boston, MA: Irwin-McGraw Hill Inc.

Belobaba, Peter P. (1987) Airline yield management: an overview of seat inventory control. *Transportation Science*, 21, 2 (May), 63–73.

Berger, Paul D. & Nasr, Nada I. (1998) Customer lifetime value: marketing models and applications. *Journal of Interactive Marketing*, 12, 1 (Winter), 17–30.

Bigne, E. (1995) Advertising budget practices: a review. *Journal of Current Issues and Research in Advertising*, 17, 2, 17–33.

Blattberg, Robert C. & Deighton, John (1996) Manage marketing by the customer equity test. *Harvard Business Review* (July–August), 136–44.

Blattberg, Robert C. & Levin, Alan (1987) Modeling the effectiveness and profitability of trade promotions. *Marketing Science*, 6 (Spring), 124–46.

Blattberg, Robert C. & Neslin, Scott A. (1990) *Sales Promotion: Concepts, Methods and Strategies*. Englewood Cliffs, NJ: Prentice-Hall.

Blattberg, Robert C., Getz, Gary & Thomas, Jacquelyn S. (2001) *Customer Equity: Building and Managing Relationships as Valuable Assets*. Boston, MA: Harvard Business School Press.

Boatwright, Peter, McCulloch, Robert & Rossi, Peter (1999) Account-level modeling of trade promotion: an application of a constrained parameter hierarchical model. *Journal of the American Statistical Association*, 94, 448 (December), 1063–73.

Borin, Norm, Farris, Paul & Freeland, James R. (1994) A model for determining retail product category assortment and shelf-space allocation. *Decision Sciences*, 25, 359–84.

Broadbent, Simon (1988) *The Advertiser's Handbook for Budget Determination*. Lexington, MA: Lexington Books.

Brody, Edward J. & Finkelberg, H. (1997) Allocating marketing resource. In *Brand Valuation*, edited by R. Perrier. London: Premier Books.

Bultez, Alain & Naert, Philippe (1988) S.H.A.R.P.: Shelf Allocation for Retailers' Profit. *Marketing Science*, 7, 3, 211–31.

Charnes, A. & Cooper, W.W. (1958) The theory of search: optimal distribution of search effort. *Management Science*, 5, 44–9.

Chatterjee, Rabikar, Eliashberg, Jehoshua, Gatignon, Hubert & Lodish, Leonard M. (1988) A practical Bayesian approach to selection of optimal market testing strategies. *Journal of Marketing Research*, 25, November, 363–75.

Chen, Yuxin, Hess, James D., Wilcox, Ronald T. & Zhang, Z. John (1999) Accounting profits versus marketing profits: a relevant metric for category management. *Marketing Science*, 18, 3, 208–29.

Chintagunta, Pradeep K. (1993) Investigating the sensitivity of equilibrium profits to advertising dynamics and competitive effects. *Management Science*, 39, 9 (September), 1146–62.

Chintagunta, Pradeep K. & Vilcassim, Naufel J. (1992) An empirical investigation of advertising strategies in a dynamic duopoly. *Management Science*, 38, 9 (September), 1230–44.

——— (1994) Marketing investment decisions in a dynamic duopoly: a model and empirical analysis. *International Journal of Research in Marketing*, 11, 3, 287–306.

Christen, Marcus, Gupta, Sachin, Porter, John C., Staelin, Richard & Wittink, Dick R. (1997) Using market-level data to understand promotion effects in a nonlinear model. *Journal of Marketing Research*, 34, 3 (August), 322–34.

Cohen, Morris A., Eliashberg, Jehoshua & Ho, Teck H. (1997) An anatomy of a decision-support system for developing and launching line extensions. *Journal of Marketing Research*, 34, 1 (February), 117–29.

Cooper, Lee G., Baron, Penny, Levy, Wayne, Swisher, Michael & Gogos, Paris (1999) PromoCast: a new forecasting method for promotion planning. *Marketing Science*, 18, 3, 301–16.

Corstjens, Marcel & Doyle, Peter (1981) A model for optimizing retail space allocations. *Management Science*, 27, 7 (July), 822–33.

——— (1985) An application of geometric programming to marketing problems. *Journal of Marketing*, 49, Winter, 137–44.

Curhan, Ronald C. (1973) Shelf space allocation and profit maximization in mass retailing. *Journal of Marketing*, 37, July, 54–60.

Danaher, Peter J. & Rust, Roland T. (1994) Determining the optimal level of media spending. *Journal of Advertising Research,* 34, 1, 28–34.

Dean, Joel (1951) *Managerial Economics*. Englewood Cliffs, NJ: Prentice-Hall Inc.

Dekimpe, Marnik & Hanssens, Dominique M. (1995) Empirical generalizations about market evolution and stationarity. *Marketing Science*, 14, Part 2 of 2, G109–G121.

——— (1999) Sustained spending and persistent response: a new look at long-term marketing profitability. *Journal of Marketing Research*, 36, 4 (November), 1–31.

Desiraju, Ramarao & Shugan, Steven M. (1999) Strategic service pricing and yield management. *Journal of Marketing*, 63, 1 (January), 44–56.

Dorfman, R. & Steiner, P.O. (1954) Optimal advertising and optimal quality. *American Economic Review*, 44, 826–36.

Doyle, Peter & Saunders, John (1990) Multiproduct advertising budgeting. *Marketing Science*, 9, Spring, 97–113.

Drexl, Andreas & Haase, Knut (1999) Fast approximation methods for sales force deployment. *Management Science*, 45, 10 (October), 1307–23.

Dreze, Xavier, Hoch, Stephen J. & Purk, Mary E (1994) Shelf management and space elasticity. *Journal of Retailing*, 70, 4 (Winter), 301–26.

Eastlack, Joseph O. & Rao, Ambar G. (1986) Modeling response to advertising and pricing changes for 'V-8' cocktail vegetable juice. *Marketing Science*, 5, 6, 245–59.

Erickson, Gary M. (1991) *Dynamic Models of Advertising Competition: Open- and Closed-Loop Extensions*. Boston, MA: Kluwer Academic Publishers.

Farris, Paul W., Reibstein, David J. & Shames, Ervin R. (1999) Insights and lessons from the MAX budgeting field study. Presentation at 1999 INFORMS Marketing Science Conference, Syracuse University, May.

Farris, Paul W., Shames, Ervin R. & Reibstein, David J. (1998) *Advertising Budgeting: A Report from the Field*. New York: American Association of Advertising Agencies.

Feinberg, Fred (1992) Pulsing policies for aggregate advertising models. *Marketing Science*, 1, 1, 221–34.

Freeland, James R. & Weinberg, Charles B. (1980) S-shaped response functions: implications for decision models. *Journal of the Operational Research Society*, 31, 11, 1001–7.

Gallego, Guillermo & van Ryzin, Garrett (1994) Optimal dynamic pricing of inventories with stochastic demand over finite horizons. *Management Science*, 40, 8 (August), 999–1020.

Gatignon, Hubert (1993) Marketing mix models. In *Marketing, Handbooks in Operations Research and Management Science 5*, edited by Jehoshua Eliashberg & Gary L. Lilien. Amsterdam: North-Holland, pp. 697–732.

Gatignon, Hubert & Hanssens, Dominique M. (1987) Modeling marketing interactions with application to salesforce effectiveness. *Journal of Marketing Research*, 24, 3 (August), 247–57.

Gensch, Dennis H. & Welam, Ulf (1973) Optimal advertising budget allocation for interacting market segments. *Management Science*, 20, 10 (October), 200–9.

Gijsbrechts, E. & Naert, Philippe, A. (1984) Toward hierarchical linking of marketing resource allocation to market areas and product groups. *International Journal of Research in Marketing*, 1, 2, 97–116.

Glaze, T.A. & Weinberg, C.B. (1979) A sales territory alignment program and account planning system (TAPS). In *Sales Management: New Developments from Behavioral and Decision Model Research*, edited by R.P. Bagozzi. Cambridge, MA: Marketing Science Institute, pp. 325–43.

Gopalakrishna, Srinath & Chatterjee, Rabikar (1992) A communications response model for a mature industrial product: application and implications. *Journal of Marketing Research*, 29, 2 (May), 189–200.

Gupta, Sachin, Chintagunta, Pradeep, Kaul, Anil & Wittink, Dick R. (1996) Do household scanner data provide representative inferences from brand choices: a comparison with store data. *Journal of Marketing Research*, 33, 4 (November), 342–55.

Haley, Russell L. (1978) Sales effects of media weight. *Journal of Advertising Research*, 18 (June), 9–18.

Hansen, Pierre & Heinsbroek, Hans (1979) Product selection and space allocation in supermarkets. *European Journal of Operational Research*, 3, 474–84.

Hanssens, Dominique M. & Ouyang, Ming (2001) Hysteresis in market response: when is marketing spending an investment? *Review of Marketing Science* Working Paper, University of Texas at Dallas.

Hanssens, Dominique M., Parsons, Leonard J. & Schultz, Randall L. (2001) *Market Response Models: Econometric and Time Series Analysis.* Boston, MA, Dordrecht, London: Kluwer Academic Press.

Harris, Frederick H. & Peacock, Peter (1995) Hold my place please. *Marketing Management*, 4, Fall, 34–46.

Holthausen, Duncan M. & Assmus, Gert (1982) Advertising budget allocation under uncertainty. *Management Science*, 28, May, 487–99.

Horsky, Dan & Nelson, Paul (1996) Evaluation of salesforce size and productivity through efficient frontier benchmarking. *Marketing Science*, 15, 4, 301–20.

Ingene, Charles A. & Parry, Mark E. (1990) A model of multi-regional advertising. Working Paper, University of Washington.

——— (1995) A note on multi-regional marketing. *Management Science*, 41, 7 (July), 1194–201.

Ingram, Thomas N. & LaForge, Raymond W. (1992) *Sales Management: Analysis and Decision Making.* Orlando, FL: The Dryden Press.

Jagpal, Harsharanjeet & Brick, Ivan (1982) The marketing-mix decision under uncertainty. *Marketing Science*, 1, Winter, 79–92.

Jedidi, Kamel, Mela, Carl F. & Gupta, Sunil (1999) Managing advertising and promotion for long-run profitability. *Marketing Science*, 18, 1, 1–22.

Jones, John Philip (1992) *How Much Is Enough? Getting the Most from Your Advertising Dollar.* New York: Lexington Books.

Kirkpatrick, S., Gellat, C.D Jr. & Vecchi, M.P. (1983) Optimization by simulated annealing. *Science*, 220 (May), 671–80.

Kumble, Ranjit, Mantrala, Murali K. & Mulhern, Francis (2000) Improving pharmaceutical sales and promotional resource allocation using physician prescription databases. Presentation to Marketing Research SIG, American Marketing Association Summer Marketing Educators' Conference (August).

Koopman, B.O. (1953) The optimal distribution of effort. *Operations Research*, 1, 2, 52–63.

Kotler, Philip (1971) *Marketing Decision Making: A Model Building Approach.* New York: Holt, Rinehart and Winston.

Lal, Rajiv & Srinivasan, V. (1993) Compensation plans for single- and multi-product salesforces: an application of the Holmstrom-Milgrom model. *Management Science*, 39, 7 (July), 777–93.

Lambin, Jean-Jacques (1972) A computer on-line marketing mix model. *Journal of Marketing Research*, 9, 2 (May), 119–26.

Lambin, Jean-Jacques, Naert, Philippe & Bultez, Alain (1975) Optimal marketing behavior in oligopoly. *European Economic Review*, 6, 105–28.

Leeflang, Peter, Wittink, Dick R., Wedel, Michel & Naert, Philippe A. (2000) *Building Models for Marketing Decisions*. Boston, MA: Kluwer Academic Publishers.

Levy, Michael & Weitz, Barton A. (1998) *Retailing Management.* Homewood, IL: Irwin.

Liebman, Milton (1998) Finally, predictable returns on promotional investments. *Medical Marketing & Media*, 33, 6, 64–74.

Lilien, Gary L. & Kotler, Philip (1983) *Marketing Decision Making: A Model-Building Approach.* New York: Harper & Row.

Lilien, Gary L., Kotler, Philip & Moorthy, K. Sridhar (1992) *Marketing Models.* Englewood Cliffs, NJ: Prentice-Hall.

Little, John D.C. (1966) A model of adaptive control of promotional spending. *Operations Research*, 14, November, 1075–97.

——— (1970) Models and managers: the concept of a decision calculus. *Management Science*, 16, 8 (April), B466–B484.

——— (1975a) BRANDAID: a marketing mix model, Part I: structure. *Operations Research*, 23, 628–55.

——— (1975b) BRANDAID: A marketing mix model, Part II: Implementation, calibration, and case study. *Operations Research*, 23, 656–73.

——— (1979) Aggregate advertising models: the state of the art. *Operations Research*, 27, 4 (July–August), 629–67.

——— (1986) Comments on advertising pulsing policies for generating awareness for new products. *Marketing Science*, 5, Spring, 107–8.

Little, John D.C. & Lodish, Leonard M. (1969) A media planning calculus. *Operations Research*, 17, January–February, 1–35.

Lodish, Leonard M. (1971) CALLPLAN: an interactive salesman's call planning system. *Management Science*, 18 (December), 25–40.

——— (1975) Sales territory alignment to maximize profit. *Journal of Marketing Research*, 12, 1 (February), 30–6.

——— (1980) A user oriented model for sales force size, product and market allocation decisions. *Journal of Marketing*, 44, Summer, 70–8.

——— (2001) Building marketing models that make money. *Interfaces*, 31, 3, Part 2 (May–June), S45–S55.

Lodish, Leonard M., Curtis, Ellen, Ness, Michael & Simpson, M. Kerry (1988) Sales force sizing and deployment using a decision calculus model at Syntex Laboratories. *Interfaces*, 18, January–February, 5–20.

Lodish, Leonard M., Abraham, Magid, Kalmenson, Stuart, Livelsberger, Jeanne, Lubetkin, Beth, Richardson, Bruce & Stevens, Mary E. (1995) How T.V. advertising works: a meta analysis of 389 real world split cable T.V. advertising experiments. *Journal of Marketing Research*, 32, 2 (May), 125–39.

Longman, Marc & Pauwels, Wilfried (1998) Analysis of marketing mix interaction effects and interdependencies: a normative approach. *Managerial and Decision Economics*, 19, 6 (September), 343–53.

Low, George S. & Mohr, Jakki J. (1997) *Marketing Communications Budget Allocations: Antecedents and Outcomes*. Cambridge, MA: Marketing Science Institute.

——— (1999) Setting advertising and promotion budgets in multi-brand companies. *Journal of Advertising Research*, 39, 1 (January–February), 67–78.

——— (2000) Advertising vs sales promotion: a brand management perspective. *Journal of Product and Brand Management*, 9, 6, 389–414.

Lucas, H.C., Weinberg, C.B. & Clowes, K. (1975) Sales response as a function of territorial potential and sales representative workload. *Journal of Marketing Research*, 12, August, 298–305.

Luss, Hanan & Gupta, Shiv K. (1975) Allocation of effort resources among competing activities. *Operations Research*, 23, March–April, 360–5.

Lynch, M. (1974) A comment on Curhan's 'The relationship between shelf space and unit sales in supermarkets'. *Journal of Marketing Research*, 11, May, 218–20.

Mahajan, Jayashree (1991) A data envelopment analytic model for assessing the relative efficiency of the selling function. *European Journal of Operational Research*, 53, 189–205.

Mahajan, Vijay & Muller, Eitan (1986) Advertising pulsing policies for generating awareness for new products. *Marketing Science*, 5, 2 (Spring), 86–106.

Manchanda, Puneet, Chintagunta, Pradeep & Gertzis, Susan (2000) Responsiveness of physician prescription behavior to salesforce effort: an individual-level analysis. Working Paper, University of Chicago.

Mantrala, Murali K. (1996) Taking a closer look at the workings of advertising budgeting rules. Working Paper, University of Florida.

Mantrala, Murali K. & Raman, Kalyan (1999) Demand uncertainty and supplier's returns policies for a multi-store style-good retailer. *European Journal of Operational Research*, 115, 270–84.

Mantrala, Murali K. & Rao, Surya (2001) A decision-support system that helps retailers decide order quantities and markdowns for fashion goods. *Interfaces*, 31, 2 (May–June Part 2), S146–S165.

Mantrala, Murali K., Sinha, Prabhakant & Zoltners, Andris A. (1992) Impact of resource allocation rules on marketing investment-level decisions and profitability, *Journal of Marketing Research*, 29, 2 (May), 162–75.

——— (1994) Structuring a multiproduct sales quota-bonus plan for a heterogeneous sales force: a practical model based approach. *Marketing Science* 13 (2), 121–44.

McNiven, Malcolm A. (1980) Plan for more productive advertising. *Harvard Business Review*, 58, March–April, 130–6.

Meidan, A. (1982) Optimizing the number of industrial salespersons. *Industrial Marketing Management*, 11, 63–74.

Mela, Carl F., Gupta, Sunil & Lehmann, Donald R. (1997) The long-term impact of promotions and advertising on consumer brand choice. *Journal of Marketing Research*, 34, 2 (May), 248–61.

Mesak, Hani (1992) An aggregate advertising pulsing model with wearout effects. *Marketing Science*, 11, 3, 310–26.

Mills, Harland D. (1961) A study in promotional competition. In *Mathematical Models and Methods in Marketing*, edited by F.M. Bass & R.D. Buswell. Homewood, IL: Richard D. Irwin, pp. 271–88.

Mitchell, Lionel A. (1993) An examination of methods of setting advertising budgets: practice and literature. *European Journal of Marketing*, 27, 5, 5–22.

Mjelde, K.M. (1975) The optimality of an incremental solution of a problem related to distribution of effort. *Operations Research Quarterly*, 26, 4, 867–70.

Monahan, George E. (1987) The structure of equilibria in market share attraction models. *Management Science*, 33, 2 (February), 228–43.

Montgomery, David B., Silk, Alvin J. & Zarazoga, C.E. (1971) A multiple-product sales force allocation model. *Management Science*, 18, 4, Part 2 (December), 3–24.

Moorthy, K. Sridhar (1993) Competitive marketing strategies. In *Marketing, Handbooks in Operations Research and Management Science 5*, edited by Jehoshua Eliashberg & Gary L. Lilien. Amsterdam: North-Holland, pp. 697–732.

Morey, Richard C. & McCann, John M. (1983) Estimating the confidence interval for the optimal marketing mix: an application of lead generation. *Marketing Science*, 2, Spring, 193–202.

Mulhern, Francis J. (1999) Customer profitability analysis: measurement, concentration, and research directions. *Journal of Interactive Marketing*, 13, 1 (Winter), 25–40.

Naert, Philippe A. (1972) Observations on applying marginal analysis in marketing: Part I. *Journal of Business Administration*, 4, Fall, 49–65.

——— (1973) Observations on applying marginal analysis in marketing: Part II. *Journal of Business Administration*, 4, Spring, 3–14.

Naik, Prasad A. & Raman, Kalyan (2001) Understanding the impact of synergy in multimedia communications. Working Paper, University of California, Davis.

Naik, Prasad A., Mantrala, Murali K. & Sawyer, Alan G. (1998) Planning media schedules in the presence of dynamic advertising quality. *Marketing Science*, 17, 3, 214–35.

Nerlove, M. & Arrow, Kenneth J. (1962) Optimal advertising policy under dynamic conditions. *Economica*, 29, May, 129–42.

Neslin, Scott A. (2001) Measuring 'ROI' for pharmaceutical detailing, DTC, journal advertising, and meetings and events. Presentation at the Chicago-Kellogg-ZS Associates Conference on Measuring and Managing Promotional Effectiveness in the Pharmaceutical Industry, Evanston, June 7–8.

Neslin, Scott A., Powell, Stephen G. & Schneider Stone, Linda (1995) The effects of retailer and consumer response on optimal manufacturer advertising and trade promotion strategies. *Management Science*, 41, 5 (May), 749–66.

Nguyen, Dung (1985) An analysis of optimal advertising under uncertainty. *Management Science*, 31, 5 (May), 622–33.

Parsons, Leonard & Schultz, Randall (1976) *Marketing Models and Econometric Research*. New York: North-Holland.

Peckham, J.O. (1976) Why advertise established brands. *Nielsen Researcher*, 3, 1–12.

Pekelman, D. & Tse, E. (1980) Experimentation and budgeting in advertising: an adaptive control approach. *Operations Research*, 28, March–April, 321–47.

Piercy, Nigel F. (1987a) Advertising budgeting: process and structure as explanatory variables. *Journal of Advertising*, 16, 2, 34–40.

——— (1987b) The marketing budgeting process: marketing management implications. *Journal of Marketing*, 52, October, 45–59.

Prasad, Arbind & Sen, Subrata (1999) Are firms advertising too much? Presentation at the INFORMS 1999 Marketing Science Conference, Syracuse University, May.

Raman, Kalyan (1990) Stochastically optimal advertising policies under dynamic conditions: the ratio rule. *Optimal Control Applications and Methods*, 11, 283–8.

——— (2001) Optimizing the marketing program dynamically under uncertainty. Working Paper, University of Michigan-Flint.

Rangan, V. Kasturi (1987) The channel design decision: a model and an application. *Marketing Science*, 6, 2 (Spring), 156–74.

Rangaswamy, Arvind, Sinha, Prabhakant & Zoltners, Andris (1990) An integrated model-based approach for sales force structuring. *Marketing Science*, 9, 4 (Fall), 279–98.

Rao, Ambar G. & Miller, Peter B. (1975) Advertising/sales response functions. *Journal of Advertising Research*, 15, April, 7–15.

Rao, Ambar G. & Rao, Mendu R. (1983) Optimal budget allocation when response is S-shaped. *Operations Research Letters*, December, 225–30.

Rao, Ram C. (1986) Estimating continuous time advertising-sales models. *Marketing Science*, 5, Spring, 125–42.

Rossi, Peter, McCulloch, R. & Allenby, Greg (1996) On the value of household purchase history information in target marketing. *Marketing Science*, 15, 321–40.

Rust, Roland T. (1986) *Advertising Media Models*. Lexington, MA: Lexington Books.

Rust, Roland T., Zeithaml, Valarie & Lemon, Katherine N. (2000) *Driving Customer Equity*. New York: The Free Press.

Sasieni, Maurice W. (1971) Optimal advertising expenditure. *Management Science*, 18, December, 64–72.

——— (1989) Optimal advertising strategies. *Marketing Science*, 8, 4 (Fall), 358–70.

Saunders, John (1987) The specification of aggregate market models. *European Journal of Marketing*, 21, 2, 5–47.

Schonfeld, Eugene (1979) Common sense rules in setting ad budgets. *Industrial Marketing*, (December), 53–8.

Schultz, Don E. (1993) Integrated marketing communications: maybe definition is in the point of view. *Marketing News*, 27, 2 (January 18), 17.

Sethuraman, Raj & Tellis, Gerald J. (1991) An analysis of the tradeoff between advertising and price discounting. *Journal of Marketing Research*, 27, 2 (May), 160–74.

Shepard, D. (1990) *The New Direct Marketing*. Homewood, IL: Business One Irwin.

Shih, W. (1974) A new application of incremental analysis of resource allocations. *Operational Research Quarterly*, 25, 4, 587–97.

Silva-Risso, Jorge M., Bucklin, Randolph E. & Morrison, Donald G. (1999) A decision-support system for planning manufacturers' sales promotion calendars. *Marketing Science*, 18, 3, 274–300.

Simon, Hermann (1982) ADPULS: an advertising model with wearout and pulsation. *Journal of Marketing Research*, 19, August, 352–63.

——— (1997) Hysteresis in marketing – a new phenomenon? *Sloan Management Review*, 38, 3 (Spring), 39–49.

Simon, Julian L. & Arndt, Johan (1980) The shape of the advertising response function. *Journal of Advertising Research*, 20, August, 11–28.

Sinha, Prabhakant & Zoltners, Andris A. (1979) The multiple-choice knapsack problem. *Operations Research*, 27, May–June, 503–15.

——— (2001) Sales-force decision models: insights from 25 years of implementation. *Interfaces*, 31, 3 (Part 2 of 2: May–June), S8–S44.

Skiera, Bernd & Albers, Sonke (1998) COSTA: contribution optimizing sales territory alignment. *Marketing Science*, 17, 196–213.

Srinivasan, V., Lovejoy, William S. & Beach, David (1997) Integrated product design for marketability and manufacturing. *Journal of Marketing Research*, 34, 1 (February), 154–63.

Tellis, Gerald J. & Weiss, Doyle L. (1995) Does TV advertising really affect sales? The role of measures, models and data aggregation. *Journal of Advertising Research*, 24, 3 (Fall), 1–12.

Tellis, Gerald J. & Zufryden, Fred S. (1995) Tackling the retailer decision maze: which brands to discount, how much, when and why? *Marketing Science*, 14, 3, 271–89.

Tull, Donald S., Wood, Van R., Duhan, Dale, Gillpatrick, Tom, Robertson, Kim R. & Helgeson, James G. (1986) Leveraged decision making in advertising: the flat maximum principle and its implications. *Journal of Marketing Research*, 23, February, 25–32.

Urban, Glen L. (1975a) Allocating ad budgets geographically. *Journal of Advertising Research*, 15 (December), 7–16.

——— (1975b) National and local allocation of advertising dollars. *Journal of Marketing Research*, 15, 6, 7–16.

Vandenbosch, Mark B. & Weinberg, Charles B. (1993) Salesforce operations. In *Marketing, Handbooks in Operations Research and Management Science 5*, edited by Jehoshua Eliashberg & Gary L. Lilien. Amsterdam: North-Holland, pp. 653–94.

Vidale, H.L. & Wolfe, H.B. (1957) An operations research study of sales response to advertising. *Operational Research Quarterly*, 5, June, 370–81.

Waid, C., Clark, D.F. & Ackoff, R.L. (1956) Allocation of sales effort in the Lamp Divisions of the General Electric Company. *Operations Research Quarterly*, 4, December, 629–47.

Weinberg, Charles (1975) Advertising decision rules for market share models. *Decision Sciences,* 6, 25–36.

Welam, Ulf Peter (1982) Optimal and near optimal price and advertising strategies. *Management Science*, 28, November, 1313–27.

Winer, Russell S. (1979) On consumer- versus firm-level analysis of advertising effectiveness: implications for model-building. *Decision Sciences*, 10, 547–61.

Zenor, Michael J. (1994) The profits benefits of category management. *Journal of Marketing Research*, 31, 2 (May), 202–13.

Zentler, A.P. & Ryde, Dorothy (1956) An optimal geographic distribution of publicity expenditures in a private organization. *Management Science*, 4, July, 337–52.

Zoltners, Andris A. (1976) Integer programming models for sales territory alignment to maximize profit. *Journal of Marketing Research*, 13 (November), 426–30.

——— (1981) Normative marketing models. In *Marketing Decision Models*, edited by R.L. Schultz & A.A. Zoltners. New York: North Holland, pp. 55–76.

Zoltners, Andris A. & Sinha, Prabhakant (1980) Integer programming models for sales resource allocation. *Management Science*, 26, March, 242–60.

——— (1983) Sales territory alignment: a review and model. *Management Science*, 29, 11 (November), 1237–56.

17

Marketing Decision Support and Intelligent Systems: Precisely Worthwhile or Vaguely Worthless?

ERIC M. EISENSTEIN and LEONARD M. LODISH

Our goal in this chapter is to review the marketing decision support system (MDSS) literature so as to provide maximal guidance to researchers and practitioners on how best to improve marketing decision-making using decision support systems. In order to achieve this goal, we lay out a taxonomy of decision support systems, create an integrative framework showing the drivers that maximally aid successful implementation, and propose future research that will help to resolve the inconclusive results in the literature. Throughout the chapter, we also attempt to reunite the divided decision support system literature by examining the assumptions underlying different research traditions in a broad, integrative context.

The chapter is structured as follows. We first place decision support system research in context by characterizing the major assumptions used in the two research traditions that form the backbone of the DSS field. We also make the case that decision support can be helpful even to expert decision-makers. Second, we define the basic constructs that are antecedent to decision support system design. Third, in light of these basic constructs, we construct a taxonomy of the types of decision support systems that we will be discussing. Fourth, we propose a metric for evaluating DSS success and we present an integrative framework that reflects the factors that appear most directly to affect the success of marketing decision support systems. We also relate existing systems to the taxonomy and framework. Fifth, we review the factors in our framework to identify the most important and to provide guidance about best practices. Sixth, we answer the question: does an MDSS work? Seventh, we examine the research on knowledge-based systems in marketing, assess whether they work, and discuss the relationship between these systems and other types of decision support systems. Eighth, we briefly review recent developments in machine learning and data mining. Finally, we provide general comments and our thoughts on future directions for research. Readers who are interested in another recent review should see Wierenga et al. (1999).

Decision Support Systems – Overview

There are two conceptually distinct traditions of decision support system research, which have origins in the disciplines of computer science and decision theory. Computer science gave rise to knowledge-based system design (also called expert systems, or artificial intelligence). Decision theory developed across multiple fields, including psychology, operations research, engineering, and a variety of business disciplines. Because of the wide differences in training of researchers, decision-theory research has been broader in scope than computer science. However, the most typical decision-theoretic approaches have concentrated on providing statistical or optimization-based models to improve decision-making. In this section, we examine the different assumptions that researchers trained in these traditions have brought to the design of decision support systems. We also justify an assumption common to both decision support traditions, that decision support is necessary even for experienced experts.

Who Needs Decision Support?

Success in business is based on making better decisions than one's competitors. The volume and complexity of information that is available as an input to decisions has been increasing, particularly in marketing and other fields where computerized data collection is the norm (Huber, 1983; King, 1993; Little, 1970). The overall greater complexity of decision environments has brought about increased reliance on specialists and experts in many disciplines (Wright & Bolger, 1992), including marketing, and this increased reliance on experts-motivated researchers to examine the decision-making process more rigorously.

These research efforts have been motivated by two (often opposing) goals. The first is to understand how people *actually* make decisions – a descriptive goal. The second is to understand how people should *ideally* make decisions – a normative goal. A smaller group of researchers have been motivated by a desire to improve decisions – a prescriptive goal. Prescriptive research takes as given that there is a discrepancy between normative and descriptive decision-making that leaves room for improvement.

It is intuitively clear why a novice needs a decision support system. It is less obvious why an experienced, senior decision-maker would need one. Both the computer science and the decision theory traditions assume that decisions by seasoned decision-makers can be improved (a prescriptive stand). Furthermore, both traditions agree that some experienced decision-makers (experts) are better than others. Where the groups disagree is on the normative theory, the 'gold standard,' that represents best performance in a field.

Assumptions in the Tradition of Computer Science

The computer-science tradition starts with two plausible assumptions. First, it is assumed that experienced, senior decision-makers (such as experienced marketing managers) are able to achieve excellent decision-making performance and that these decision-makers outperform novices (such as recent graduates) in their field of expertise. Second, it is assumed that the most experienced and expert individuals in a field represent the normative standard against which both other practitioners and computerized systems should be judged (Hayes-Roth et al., 1983; Turban & Aronson, 1998). These assumptions lead to the conclusion that to improve decisions, we should capture the knowledge and process of reasoning of the best experts, codifying it in computer code. Systems that attempt to accomplish this task are termed knowledge-based (or expert) systems. Once developed, these systems can be used by less seasoned decision-makers or novices to improve their decision-making, or as replacements for the original expert(s). The assumption of outstanding expert judgment is rarely challenged in the computer-science tradition.

Assumptions in the Decision Theory Tradition

By contrast, researchers in decision theory have concluded that even the top experts in a field rarely represent the appropriate gold standard. Decision theorists base this conclusion on the substantial evidence of a 'process-performance paradox' (Camerer & Johnson, 1991). The paradox is that although seasoned experts display considerable advantages in memory, cue use, richness of problem structure, and other cognitive aspects of expert decision-making, they frequently demonstrate little or no performance advantage in decision quality. In some studies, experts are found to perform no better than novices (Oskamp, 1962). In other studies, it is found that experts are out-performed by simple linear models (Dawes & Corrigan, 1974; Dawes et al., 1989; Einhorn & Hogarth, 1975; Meehl, 1954). Experts can fall prey to the same array of cognitive biases that affect novices, resulting in sub-optimal performance and unreliability (Carroll & Payne, 1976; Christensen-Szalanski & Bushyhead, 1981; Einhorn, 1974; Northcroft & Neale, 1987; Oskamp, 1962). More controversial research implies that experts should be completely replaced by statistical models, where possible, since the models have been shown to be more accurate under certain circumstances (Dawes & Corrigan, 1974; Dawes et al., 1989).

The decision-theory literature is not monolithic with respect to the opinion of experts. The expert-disparaging results are challenged by a smaller number of studies that indicate that expert judgment can have utility. Experts appear to be especially good when they can take advantage of rare but highly predictive information in the environment – so-called 'broken-leg cues' (Blattberg & Hoch, 1990; Johnson, 1988; Meehl, 1954; Phelps & Shanteau, 1978). Shanteau (1987, 1988, 1992a) shows that in domains such as weather forecasting, auditing, chess, physics, etc., experts can be quite good. These domains are characterized by greater opportunities for feedback, greater problem structure, and less noise. Shanteau (1987) also finds that lack of feedback, low structure, or noisy environments, tend to predict poor performance. Examples of the latter groups of decision-makers include clinical psychologists, stockbrokers, physicians, and court judges.

The process-performance paradox sets the stage for the assumptions in the decision-theory tradition. Decision theorists assume that even seasoned experts are sub-optimal, and that data-based statistical models should be provided to aid or replace human decision-makers. An implicit assumption that guides the types of systems that are developed, and are developable, in this tradition is that problems are sufficiently structured that we can build models, collect data, and have an appropriate idea of the functional form of the underlying relationship.

The Need for Decision Support

Researchers are in agreement that some experts are better than others, and therefore that the decision-making performance of many seasoned decision-makers can be improved (theoretically, decisions can at least be improved to the level of the best experts). Hence, formal decision support can have utility. Researchers disagree on the form that formal decision support should take. The computer-science tradition holds the top experts in a field to be the normative standard, leading to a knowledge-based approach. The decision-theoretic tradition holds experts to be fallible and places greater stock in statistical models – a data-based view that leads to an emphasis on statistics, models, and optimization.

Scope of Consideration

Nothing described thus far requires a computer. Early techniques for decision support predated the widespread availability of computers, and included decision trees, structured decision aids, and diagnostic flowcharts, many of which had their origins in operations research, economics, or in engineering. With the advent of the computer, both more complex and more integrative systems could be created. Only these interactive, computer-based models are usually considered to be DSS. Hence, we will not review marketing management support systems that are non-computer-based (e.g., marketing models).

Although we concentrate our review of decision support systems on those developed for marketing, it is clear that marketing scientists owe a debt to researchers in other fields who have investigated similar problems. Throughout this chapter, we follow the terminology of Little (1979) and use the phrase *marketing decision support systems* (MDSS) as an umbrella category that includes simple, robust, judgmentally calibrated decision calculus models (Little & Lodish, 1969), such as CALLPLAN (Lodish, 1971) and ADBUDG (Little, 1970); marketing decision support systems such as ASSESSOR (Silk & Urban, 1978); expert systems for marketing such as ADCAD (Burke et al., 1990) and NEGOTEX (Rangaswamy et al., 1989); and other computer-based, interactive systems whose purpose is to improve decision-making.

Antecedents to MDSS

In this section we define the necessary antecedents to thinking about MDSS success. First, we define what we mean by a decision, and then what we mean by an MDSS. Third, we create a taxonomy of decision support systems. The disparate traditions in computer science and decision theory have been largely preserved in the marketing domain. Hence, the taxonomy delineates the boundaries of DSS from other types of management science models and decision aids. It also differentiates knowledge-based systems that stem from the computer-science tradition from the marketing decision support systems that are based on decision theory.

What is a Decision?

Because decision-making has been investigated in many disciplines and across a broad span of time, there is no standardized definition of a decision. What is a decision? For our purposes, we will adopt a consequentialist definition, noting: 'all the knowledge we have learned and the information we have acquired only add value when the decision is made and the chosen action is executed ... a decision is the identification of and commitment to a course of action' (Russo and Carlson, this volume). This definition fits nicely into the spirit of MDSS research, in that it is focused on actions that managers need to take. It also emphasizes the economic nature of marketing by making it clear that decisions are bound to economic actions that the manager and the firm then take.

What is a Marketing Decision Support System (MDSS)?

Little (1979) defines an MDSS with direct reference to an action-based definition of a decision. He defines an MDSS as: 'a coordinated collection of data, systems, tools and techniques with supporting software and hardware by which an organization gathers and interprets relevant information from business and environment and *turns it into a basis for marketing action*' [emphasis added]. Little also notes that decision support systems should possess other characteristics, such as interactivity, robustness, and completeness on important issues. There is widespread agreement that decision support systems are meant to support and not to replace the decision-maker, and that the systems should improve decisions (cf. Alter, 1980; Keen & Scott-Morton, 1978). Numerous other definitions of MDSS exist in the literature, but since Little's definition seems to incorporate the most commonly mentioned characteristics, we will use it. In keeping with these definitions, we will not discuss systems that do not support decisions as we have defined the term (e.g., marketing creativity-enhancement programs, and pure forecasting methodologies). One other common part of the definition of MDSS is that the decision is repeated. Thousands of computerized analyses are developed every year in support of one-time decisions. Although these analyses are a form of decision support, they are not considered decision support *systems*, and we will not discuss them.

Taxonomy of Decision Support Systems

Researchers in marketing have paralleled the broader decision-support literature. Some researchers have adopted the assumption set of computer science, and others the assumptions of decision theory. Within marketing, there are prominent examples of the two major types of decision support system: knowledge-based systems (also called expert systems, intelligent management systems, and artificial intelligence), and 'plain vanilla' DSS. Not every system can be neatly characterized as either vanilla or knowledge-based, because the systems form a continuum and hybrid systems have been created (Rangaswamy et al., 1987). The taxonomy that follows differentiates the various types of DSS that marketers have created.

Vanilla MDSS play a passive role in the human–machine interaction. They may execute computations, present data, and respond to queries. But they cannot explain their logic, deal with incomplete information, or make logical inferences. Vanilla systems may have a great deal of knowledge built into them, but they are incapable of even simple reasoning. Hence they do not serve as intelligent assistants to a decision-maker.

Some decision environments benefit from having an intelligent computerized assistant. This is the realm of knowledge-based systems. These systems are designed to substitute, in whole or in part, for human expertise. They are sophisticated, specialized computer programs whose goal is to capture and reproduce experts' decision-making processes and to achieve expert-level performance (Naylor, 1983; Turban & Aronson, 1998). Typically, they are restricted to a narrow domain, in which they follow the type of heuristic reasoning used by experts. Another useful taxonomy can be found in Wierenga and van Bruggen (1997).

Contrasting Vanilla and Knowledge-based MDSS

Three essential features differentiate vanilla MDSS and knowledge-based systems: the use of symbolic processing, the use of heuristics rather than algorithms, and the use of inference techniques which are usually based on logical relationships. This allows the two types of systems to be used under different circumstances. Rangaswamy et al. (1987) recommend that knowledge-based systems should be used when: (1) the key relationships are logical rather than arithmetical; (2) the problem is structured, but not to a level that would allow algorithmic solution; (3) knowledge in the domain is incomplete; and (4) problem solving in the domain requires a direct interface between the manager and the computer system. Knowledge-based systems also differ from vanilla DSS in their ability to offer an explanation of how they arrived at their output, and to explain the logic behind their advice (Awad, 1996).

Vanilla MDSS are based on the tradition of decision theory, management science, and statistics. The emphasis of their development has been on the statistical quality of their predictions. Knowledge-based systems originate from the computer-science tradition. The emphasis of their development has been less on improving decision-making and more on mimicking the process of reasoning and the performance of a recognized expert (or experts) in the domain area. This means that another characterization of knowledge-based systems is to consider them to be descriptive models of the current state of knowledge in a domain. Knowledge-based systems will improve decision-making to the extent that (a) the expert(s) upon whom the system is based are better than the user (and are better than a statistical baseline prediction), and (b) the extent to which the system replicates the experts' knowledge and reasoning processes. Vanilla MDSS can improve decision-making to the extent that the output from the model is superior to that of the decision-maker. Obviously neither type of system will improve decisions if their recommendations are not accepted and implemented by decision-makers.

It should be clear that there is a continuum of MDSS architectures that range from simple facilitation of what-if questions (the simplest vanilla systems) to built-in intelligence, structured knowledge, and intelligent enabling (the most advanced knowledge-based systems). This range includes advanced hybrid systems that combine elements of both traditional DSS as well as knowledge-based reasoning, and it is this continuum of systems that is the focus of the remainder of this chapter.

Integrative Framework for Marketing Decision Support System Success

In this section, we review previous frameworks, contrast different metrics of success, propose a metric of success that we believe is the proper metric, and create an integrative framework that identifies the factors that are most likely to contribute to the success of an MDSS. In this we are indebted to Wierenga et al. (1999), who have also created an excellent overarching framework. Finally, we review the factors that most directly contribute to the success of MDSS.

Review of Existing Frameworks

The classic framework for decision support systems was proposed by Gorry and Scott-Morton (1971), later updated by Keen and Scott-Morton (1978), who combined the work of Simon (1977) and Anthony (1965). Simon argued that decision-making processes fall along a continuum that ranges from highly structured (programmed) to unstructured decisions. Structured processes are routine, repetitive problems for which standard solutions exist. Unstructured processes are fuzzy, complex problems for which there are no known algorithmic solutions. Structure also incorporates the noisiness (predictability) of the system, since adding noise frequently results in a breakdown of standardized solutions. Anthony (1965) defined three broad categories that encompass all managerial activities: strategic planning – the long-range goals and policies for resource allocation; management control – the acquisition and efficient use of resources in the accomplishment of organizational goals; and operational control – the efficient and effective execution of specific tasks. Keen and Scott-Morton (1978) divide the structure dimension into three categories – structured, semi-structured, and unstructured – and then create a nine cell matrix with the three Anthony categories, which can be used to classify problems and to select appropriate decision support alternatives. This framework is used with minor modifications by many other authors (e.g., Turban & Aronson, 1998; Wierenga & Ophuis, 1997; Wierenga et al., 1999).

Wierenga and coworkers (Wierenga & Ophuis, 1997; Wierenga et al., 1999) position their integrative framework for MDSS success as a generalization of the Keen and Scott-Morton framework. Their framework consists of five factors: decision situation characteristics, characteristics of the MDSS, the match between demand and supply of decision support, design characteristics, and implementation process. These factors contribute to the success of an MDSS. The framework also properly recognizes that there are important factors that contribute to the success of an MDSS that are not captured by the Keen and Scott-Morton framework. These omitted factors include characteristics of the implementation process, problem characteristics other than structure, and decision-maker characteristics.

We agree with Wierenga et al. that the classic framework does not fully characterize the factors contributing to the success of an MDSS, but we feel that it is possible to create an even simpler framework. Our framework has only three major stages. Problem characteristics includes the problem definition and the constraints on our knowledge. Adoption and use includes those factors that change the likelihood that an MDSS will be implemented and used, including characteristics of the system itself. These factors lead to success, which we argue should be measured by increased profit to the firm. A further review of the controversy surrounding the choice of a measure of success is discussed in more detail later. We believe that this framework is more general than either the Keen and Scott-Morton or the Wierenga et al. frameworks. Our integrative framework appears below.

Integrative Framework of the Factors that Determine MDSS Success

1. *Problem characteristics*
   (a) Structuredness includes amount of noise, knowledge of causal drivers and relationships among the drivers
   (b) Availability of data
   (c) Stationarity of the process
   (d) Type of answer required recognizes that choosing a discrete option (such as acquiring or not acquiring a competitor) is fundamentally different from predicting a continuous measure (such as how much money to allocate to advertising).
2. *System design*
   (a) Technical validity is the quintessential component of the system. Systems cannot add value without giving good answers for the right reasons.
   (b) Other system characteristics include ease of use, validity, accuracy, and the quality of alternative systems.
3. *Adoption and use*
   (a) Decision-maker characteristics relate to the experiences and abilities that the users possess, which change the likelihood of using the system.
   (b) Organizational factor characteristics relate to the way that the organization

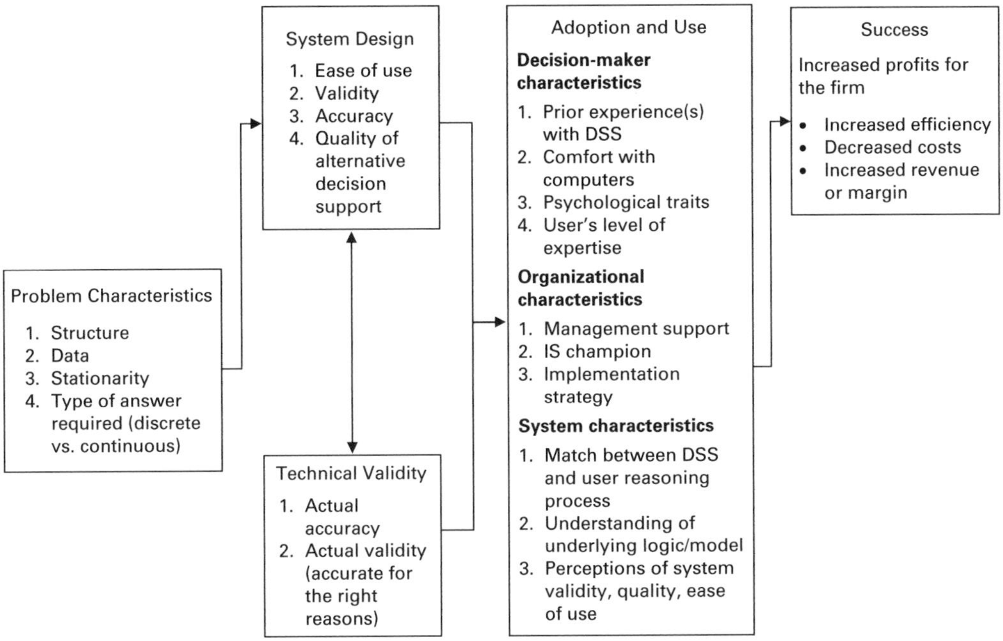

Figure 17.1 *Framework for MDSS Success*

chooses to implement the system, and how the system is developed.

(c) System characteristics reflect user perceptions of the validity, accuracy, ease of use, and quality of alternative systems, as well as user understanding of how the system generates its output.

4. *Success* is defined as increased profit for the corporation, or perhaps a subsidiary goal such as increased market share or sales.

What is Success?

Success in the Plain Vanilla Tradition

The question of the dependent variable in DSS research has been a matter of considerable debate. As Wierenga et al. (1999) point out, 'DeLone and McLean (1992), who examined dependent variables in 100 empirical DSS/IS studies, find that "there are nearly as many measures as there are studies."' In marketing, the main discussion of measures of success is due to Wierenga and his colleagues (Wierenga & van Bruggen, 1997; Wierenga et al., 1999). They distinguish four different measures of MDSS success: (a) technical validity, which is the extent to which the underlying MDSS model is valid and makes statistically accurate predictions; (b) the adoption and use of the MDSS; (c) impact for the user, usually measured by user satisfaction; and (d) impact for the organization, which are variables such as profit, sales, or market share. These output measures are frequently used by researchers who are studying MDSS success.

Comparison of Metrics

We feel that the criterion for MDSS success must be increased profits for the corporation. This is not to say that the other measures posited by Wierenga et al. (and other researchers) are not relevant. Technical validity is the *sine qua non* of success. Decisions cannot reliably be improved by a model that does not make accurate predictions for the right reasons, which is what is meant by technical validity. Another advantage of technical validity is that it can be tested in the absence of being implemented. Since implementation is costly, technical validity serves as a useful screen – we do not need to implement models that are not technically valid. Technical validity is not viewed as a metric of success in our framework. Instead, it is a necessary system characteristic, and a consequence of system design. This positioning highlights that technical validity is not an end, but a means to achieve the end of better decisions and greater profits.

The two frameworks agree that adoption and use by individual decision-makers must occur if the system is to affect decision performance. Much of the research in the DSS literature on adoption concentrates on users' satisfaction or perceptions of usefulness of a system. These perceptions are called user impact variables. Our framework subsumes user impact into adoption and use. We do this because it seems logical to assume that systems that are perceived to perform well by users are more likely to be adopted and implemented. On the other hand, there is no logical reason to believe that systems do in fact perform well just because users think they do, or because users perceive them as useful. Therefore, the use of user impact as a measure of success is problematic (Ives & Olson, 1984), and we look at user impact as part of adoption.

Success in the Knowledge-based System Tradition

The vanilla DSS tradition acknowledges that success ideally ought to be measured by better performance on objective, economically relevant measures. By contrast, the literature on knowledge-based systems and expert systems tends to de-emphasize many of the measures of success that are used in vanilla DSS research. In some cases, this lack of emphasis stems from the fact that external validation is difficult to obtain. Such situations arise because even *post hoc* it may not be clear what the proper answer should have been (e.g., what negotiation strategy should be adopted, what clause should be inserted into a contract).

The most apparent example of differences in success metrics is that knowledge-based systems research tends virtually to ignore technical validity (Carroll, 1987; Turban & Aronson, 1998). This is a consequence of the assumption that human experts are the normative standard and that the experts are able to achieve an outstanding level of decision-making performance (Hayes-Roth et al., 1983), and also reflects the difficulty of validating output in knowledge-based environments. In addition, researchers in knowledge-based systems use other criteria that are not used by vanilla DSS researchers. For example, a major goal of knowledge-based systems is to mimic the reasoning process that an expert would have used (Carroll, 1987; Davis & Lenat, 1980; Rangaswamy et al., 1987, 1989; Turban & Aronson, 1998).

Our framework incorporates these additional measures for both vanilla and knowledge-based systems. However, we incorporate them as process measures rather than measures of success. The reason is that a good match to the reasoning process of experts is not a substitute for technical validity, increased profit, or for improving decisions. But the match between reasoning processes is relevant if it can be shown that a better match results in greater likelihood of use or implementation. The potential for increased adoption through matched reasoning holds for both vanilla and knowledge-based systems. Thus we place this factor into the system characteristics dimension of the framework, rather than as a success factor.

Success in the Real World

Carroll (1987) points out that success depends critically on who the users will be. This is because 'improving' decisions requires a baseline for comparison. If the system users are themselves seasoned experts (such as experienced managers or salespeople) then the hurdle is raised. The system must do sufficiently better than those experts to justify the investment and ongoing costs of the MDSS. If the users are novices, then even a substantially non-optimal system might improve performance and generate greater profits for the firm. This is especially true if users are more likely to use a less complex, non-optimal, but easier to understand MDSS. Little (1970) made a similar point, noting that models should be 'simple, robust, easy to communicate with, adaptive, and complete on important issues.' If the definitions of 'simple,' 'complete,' etc. are understood to be defined relatively rather than absolutely, then we arrive at a vision of MDSS success that is quite similar to Urban and Karash's (1971) view of evolutionary model building (Lilien et al., 1992).

In summary, success in MDSS research requires: (1) technical validity; (2) adoption and use; and (3) generation of positive profit for the organization. Technical validity is necessary but not sufficient. Adoption and use is also necessary but not sufficient, because users may adopt and use invalid systems and believe that they are beneficial. A more granular metric could differentiate the impact on individuals' decisions from impact at the firm level. This distinction recognizes that implementation failures due to organizational factors beyond the control of an individual manager (e.g., lack of capital or constraints on production) may reduce the impact of an MDSS for the corporation, even though decisions would be improved by following the recommendations of the MDSS.

Increasing the Likelihood of MDSS Success

In this section we examine the factors of our framework that contribute to the success of MDSS. We review the literatures that have been written about the factors and attempt to provide guidance to researchers and practitioners on how to make MDSS development successful. We follow our integrative framework, first focusing on problem characteristics, then on the dimensions of adoption and use – decision-maker characteristics, organizational characteristics, and system characteristics.

Problem Characteristics

The integrative framework characterizes decision problems along four dimensions: structure, availability of data, the stationarity of the system, and the type of decision to be made.

Structure, Data, and Stationarity

The most important characteristic of the decision problem in terms of the impact on the development of MDSS is the structuredness of the problem (Keen & Scott-Morton, 1978; Russell & Norvig, 1995; Simon, 1977; Turban & Aronson, 1998; Wierenga & Ophuis, 1997; Wierenga et al., 1999). Structure incorporates both the predictability (amount of noise) of the system as well as our knowledge of the underlying causal factors and the relationship among these causal elements. A closely related concept is depth of knowledge, which includes the degree to which our understanding of the structure has been codified by scientific research. The precision with which we know the functional form of the response is an example of depth of knowledge. High structure problems are those with standardized solutions; low structure problems lack standard solutions (Simon, 1977). Availability of data is obviously necessary for developing statistically based MDSS, such as regression or other probability models. Data may not be as helpful if the environment is non-stationary. At a minimum, the underlying analytic models in the MDSS must model the nature of the nonstationarity. Nonstationarity may also impugn the validity of many types of data-based models, and the technical modeling requirements increase. Nonstationarity is less well defined for knowledge-based systems, since these systems are not fundamentally based on data. However, maintaining the knowledge base of the system and keeping the rules and reasoning processes up-to-date is costly and time consuming (Gill, 1995), and is the analogue of nonstationarity in a data-based system.

Type of Output

The type of output that the decision support system is expected to produce is closely related to the type of decision that a manager is required to make. Decisions are differentiated from non-decisions in that an action accompanies a decision. These actions vary on many dimensions, but one central difference among them is whether the action to be taken is discrete or continuous. Conceptually, the spectrum of actions is a continuum that ranges from binary actions, through choose *k* of *n*, to continuous or near continuous allocations. This dimension is frequently ignored in the literature – an oversight in our view. The requirements for decision support depend critically on this dimension, because in the case of a binary action we may need only directional information from the MDSS. Requiring only directional advice may allow for the construction of helpful models even in low structure, low depth of knowledge, low data arenas. Conversely, continuous outputs, such as exact dollar allocations across many marketing projects, will require greater predictability, structure, and depth of knowledge. It is obviously a contradiction to create exact models under conditions of very low structure. As Wierenga et al. (1999: 198) state '... we find no papers addressing issues where there is low structure and the environment is turbulent'. One reason for the lack of papers may be the focus on continuous rather than categorical decisions. Hence, an area for additional research in low structure environments is to search for directional (categorical), 'vaguely right,' models, rather than having no models or 'precisely wrong' specifications (Lodish, 1974; Lodish & Reibstein, 1986).

After examining the literature, it appears to us that the most important problem characteristics that contribute to the eventual success of an MDSS are the structuredness of a problem and the type of output that is required. Marketing problems exhibit enormous variation along both dimensions (Wierenga et al., 1999).

Factors Relating to Adoption and Use of MDSS

MDSS adoption and use is primarily affected by decision-maker characteristics, organizational characteristics, and characteristics of the system. We discuss these factors below.

Decision-maker Characteristics

Individual-specific factors influence both the use of MDSS as well as the benefits derived from such use. These factors can be divided into psychological characteristics of users (e.g., cognitive style, problem solving or decision style, personality, etc.), and user-situational characteristics (e.g., user involvement in design and implementation, prior experience with DSS or computers, expertise in the decision domain). There is only a small amount of research within marketing on the interactions between decision-maker characteristics and MDSS success. Where the effects have been studied in a marketing-specific setting, the results have been similar to those in the general DSS literature (Wierenga et al., 1999; Zinkhan et al., 1987). We thus review both marketing-specific results as well as results from the general literature.

Psychological Characteristics of Decision-makers The most commonly mentioned decision-maker characteristics in the general DSS literature are psychological traits. However, most articles focus on one trait, called cognitive style (Alavi & Joachimsthaler, 1992; Turban, 1995; Turban & Aronson, 1998; Wierenga & Ophuis, 1997; Wierenga et al., 1999). As a construct, cognitive style is not as well-defined as it might be. A consensus definition is that cognitive style is a multidimensional construct that describes the characteristic ways that individuals process and use information in the course of solving problems and making decisions (Huysmans, 1970; van Bruggen et al., 1998). It seems reasonable to believe that such a trait would influence MDSS use, but there are numerous problems with using it to predict MDSS success. First, most research in the DSS field focuses on only one subdimension of cognitive style, the analytic/heuristic subdimension (Huber, 1983; Wierenga & Ophuis, 1997; Wierenga et al., 1999; Zinkhan et al., 1987; Zmud, 1979). This subdimension is usually further simplified to a binary classification with opposite types of decision-makers at the extremes. At one end of the spectrum are presumed to be high analytical decision-makers, who prefer reductionist reasoning to a core set of underlying relationships; at the other end are low analytical decision-makers, who tend to look for heuristic solutions or to solve problems by analogy, frequently in a more holistic manner (Huysmans, 1970; van Bruggen et al., 1998).

The problem with this approach is pointed out by Huber (1983), who notes that the dichotomization is an oversimplification, since cognitive style is actually a continuous variable, and most people are neither completely analytic nor completely non-analytic. Furthermore, no research appears to exist that quantifies the relationship between a given score on a personality test and the degree to which heuristic (low analytical) reasoning will be used (a result also found by van Bruggen et al., 1998: 647). Worse, much of the research on cognitive style has used personality measures that were not developed to accurately measure the type of specific analytic or analogical reasoning that might interact with decision support system use (Alavi & Joachimsthaler, 1992). Finally, substantial evidence from the literature on expertise suggests that expertise is domain specific (Chi et al., 1988; Ericsson, 1996; Ericsson & Smith, 1991). This means that decision-making within the area of expertise can use a different cognitive style than ordinary day-to-day thinking (Shanteau, 1992a, 1992b). It is day-to-day thinking (general patterns of thought) that are measured by the personality test. However, it is usually decision-making within the area of expertise that we measure in MDSS research.

The most damning evidence against the use of cognitive style as a basis for recommendations in MDSS design is that the psychological factors that have been measured, including cognitive style, appear to be poor predictors of DSS success. Alavi and Joachimsthaler (1992) note in their meta-analysis of DSS implementation research:

> overall, these results suggest that the relationship between cognitive style and DSS performance is small ... [it] translates to a correlation of .122, which implies that, on average, less than 2 percent of DSS performance can be explained by this dimension ... [the] meta-analytic results indicate that [general] psychological factors have only a small to moderate effect on DSS performance and user attitudes. (1992: 103, 109)

Huber (1983) reaches similar conclusions about the use of cognitive style in DSS research.

Despite the small effect sizes associated with cognitive style, researchers seem to agree that high analytical decision-makers outperform heuristic decision-makers, and that they also have more positive attitudes towards DSS (Alavi & Joachimsthaler, 1992; Larreche, 1979; Leonard et al., 1999; Ramaprasad, 1987; van Bruggen et al., 1998; Zinkhan et al., 1987). Lusk and Kersnick (1979) and Cole and Gaeth (1990) have both shown that high analytical decision-makers structure and solve problems in a manner that positively affects decision performance. Whether structuring problems in a manner which increases performance interacts with better use of decision support systems remains a contentious topic. Research on the interaction of psychological characteristics with preference for the use of decision support systems (De Waele, 1978; Hunt et al., 1989) as well as performance improvements/declines (Benbasat & Dexter, 1982, 1985) is inconclusive.

We believe that these inconclusive results are likely to have been caused by heterogeneity in the user population. For example, some studies have found that decision-makers prefer a DSS that will complement their weaker cognitive style, but other studies have found that decision-makers prefer to match their stronger style. Similar ambiguities exist when looking at the interaction of cognitive style DSS use and performance improvements. These reversals and small effect sizes could easily be due to unobserved heterogeneity of preferences (Hutchinson et al., 2000): some high analytical decision-makers prefer to complement their weaker style, others their stronger style, and the same is true for low-analyticals. This is a critical area for further research, and an example of an area where greater experimental rigor would yield valuable theoretical and practical results.

Other User Characteristics Another frequently studied user characteristic is the expertise of the MDSS user. The use of decision support systems and decision aids is generally believed to help novices more than experts, and low-analyticals more than high (Benbasat & Dexter, 1982, 1985; van Bruggen et al., 1998). Spence and Brucks (1997) demonstrate the expert–novice comparison using a (non-computerized) decision aid. They found that novices especially benefited from the use of a decision aid in a structured housing valuation task. Experts performed equally well with and without the aid. This result underscores the need to specify the user pool for the MDSS. Depending on whether the primary users will be experts or novices, the design of the MDSS may change, and the system must also work better than the alternative option of non-use if decisions are to improve.

A final user characteristic is prior experience with a decision support system. Not surprisingly, prior positive experience increases likelihood of adoption and use (Alavi & Joachimsthaler, 1992). We believe that prior experience with computer technology in general might also be predictive. This is not a user characteristic that is often studied. But it is not difficult to believe that a manager who does not know how to read his email is unlikely to use a decision support system, or that a technological wizard is more likely to do so. Over the last several years the authors of this chapter have seen enormous increases in the computer sophistication of salesforce managers in executive education. This type of increased familiarity with computers, spreadsheets, and financial models can only increase the likelihood of MDSS use. One troubling aspect of increasing familiarity is that the nonstationary nature of the 'familiarity base' limits our ability to draw inferences from research that may be 20 to 30 years old, as much of it is.

Organizational Characteristics

Organizational characteristics include the support of top management, implementation strategy, and user involvement in design and implementation.

Management Support 'The evidence for the need for management support is so strong that any attempt to implement a system without it or without the related conditions of commitment and authority to implement will probably result in failure' (Hanssens et al., 1990: 324). The need for top management support appears to be especially important for knowledge-based or expert systems (Tyran & George, 1993). It seems equally intuitive that the existence of an IS champion increases implementation success, though the literature is unclear how important this characteristic is.

Implementation Strategy Implementation strategy encompasses a wide variety of activities that help users learn and use a new MDSS. Training and user involvement in the design process are two of the most frequently mentioned aspects of implementation strategy.

Many decision-makers must justify their decisions to more senior management, or to outside parties such as analysts, courts, or clients. Adoption and use become much less likely when managers do not understand the workings of the MDSS, or the logic behind the output. We strongly feel that MDSS cannot be mere black-boxes. In their meta-analysis, Alavi and Joachimsthaler (1992) find that training in the use of the DSS aids implementation. They also point out that most studies interpret training very narrowly. These studies tend to train very specific aspects of use (the specific hardware and software skills needed to interact with the DSS). They point out that adoption and use might increase more with training in how the model works. Although the authors note wide variance in the reported effect sizes of the component studies, the larger (better) effect sizes are related to the training variable in field studies rather than laboratory studies, which lends support to the importance of training in real-world environments.

User involvement is generally defined as the participation in the system development process by the users. It is stridently advocated throughout the process of DSS development, and is viewed as essential for success (Lilien et al., 1992; Sprague & Watson, 1993; Turban & Aronson, 1998). In their meta-analysis, Alavi and Joachimsthaler (1992) find support for user involvement increasing the success of implementation, but they also find large measurement error. They attribute this error to the construct being poorly defined. A more critical view is espoused by Ives and Olson (1984), who also examined the relationship between user involvement and MDSS success. Their review of the role of involvement in MIS success concludes that 'much of the existing research is poorly grounded in theory and methodologically flawed; as a result the benefits of user involvement have not been convincingly demonstrated' (Ives & Olson, 1984: 586). They note that involvement in the design process increases user satisfaction and perceived usefulness of the system (and may therefore help implementation). But since these constructs are not logically related to technical validity or to the appropriate use of the system (e.g., users might like the system because its recommendations are easy to override), the link between involvement and better decisions is weak.

Decision Support System in Marketing – Do They Work?

As we remarked in the introduction, Wierenga et al. (1999) is also an excellent review of decision support system research in marketing.

Field Studies

Many authors have lamented the lack of studies that investigate the effects of MDSS in the field rather than in the lab (Sharda et al., 1988; Wierenga et al., 1999). Field studies with control groups are the gold-standard, since the magnitudes and directions of the performance changes are most likely to mirror what practitioners would achieve. Perhaps the best-known field study is Fudge and Lodish (1977), who implemented the CALLPLAN model (Lodish, 1971) in a field test with matched pairs of sales representatives. The result was that the average salesperson with access to the model had 8.1% greater sales than those without model support (though not every model-user performed better than every non-user). The authors achieved this result in spite of the fact that the control group judgmentally estimated the parameters of the model; they just did not receive the model's recommendations. The carefulness of this study, combined with its matched pair comparison, make it the gold-standard against which other research can be judged. Furthermore, this study fits directly into our integrative framework. The users were trained on the use of CALLPLAN, adopted and used it, and the output measure was profit. There were no claims that CALLPLAN generated completely optimal allocations. CALLPLAN is a decision-calculus model – its parameters are judgmentally calibrated, users have the flexibility to arrive at nearly any answer they desire, and the model is not 100% complete. Nevertheless, the model works better than the average salesperson's intuition, is simple enough to be understood, and was therefore more likely to be adopted by the test users.

Other field studies include Lodish et al. (1988) and Gensch et al. (1990). The Gensch study compared two districts that used the MDSS against control districts. The MDSS-using districts had large increases in sales at a time when the market as a whole was going down; the control districts showed declines in sales. In this case, the model was rolled out company-wide on the basis of its success, making it difficult to quantify exactly what the gains due to the model were, but they were very likely positive. Lodish et al. implemented a salesforce size and deployment model, with parameters calibrated by a modified Delphi technique. Although the full recommendations of the model were not implemented, substantial gains in sales were documented even with the more limited implementation. These successes in the field support our claim that for many problem types it is only necessary to get directionally correct, order of magnitude information, rather than 'precisely wrong' optimized output from a technically deficient model. Directional output was sufficient to increase profits and sales in these studies, and made the model and recommendations more likely to be accepted by the users.

Laboratory Studies

Most other studies of MDSS success have been performed in the laboratory. Chakravarti et al. (1979) conducted a laboratory study using a simplified version of ADBUDG (Little, 1970), the original decision calculus model, in the context of a game simulation. Participants in an executive education program played the game, making advertising allocation decisions over several rounds. After participants received some experience (training), a portion of the participants were given access to ADBUDG. If the model were properly calibrated, it would have generated the optimal solution, but the executives did not know this. Oddly, those who used the model earned *less* profit than those in the control group, implying that the MDSS had actually led to worse accuracy in predicting share.

In a very similar experiment, however, McIntyre (1982) used CALLPLAN with a group of MBA students in a game setting. He found that access to the MDSS enhanced decisions along multiple dimensions, including better average profit earned, fewer large errors, and faster learning. The number of allocation units and the noise level in the environment had little interaction with the benefits – the model helped across problem sizes and noise levels.

Several different commentators (Little & Lodish, 1981; McIntyre, 1982; Wierenga et al., 1999) attempt to reconcile the results of these two studies by looking at the study characteristics. These reconciliations generally point out that Chakravarti et al. use a more complicated functional form for the advertising response that incorporated lagged effects from the previous period. These carryover effects induce a nonstationarity in the response that is then confounded with previous treatments. This explanation squares with the research of Sterman (1987, 1989), who found that people have a very difficult time dealing with lagged effects, even within the setting of a simple game. Little and Lodish point out that using ADBUDG rather than BRANDAID was unfortunate, since BRANDAID removes the confound between carryover and current advertising changes. Similar changes to the parameter input structure are found in Lodish (1980), who modified DETAILER (Montgomery et al., 1971) to simplify the dynamics, with corresponding success on implementation.

Van Bruggen et al. (1998) found positive effects of MDSS use on market share and profit in the context of the MARKSTRAT game. They believe that their MDSS is effective because it assists users in identifying the important variables and by aiding decisions that are based on those variables. They also found that decision-makers using an MDSS are less susceptible to applying the anchoring and adjustment heuristic, which often results in poor outcomes.

Blattberg and Hoch (1990) demonstrated that a combination of managerial judgment and MDSS output resulted in superior performance compared with using either by itself. They attribute the result to the fact that managers and models have complementary skills. Models are more consistent and better at integrating information; humans are better at identifying 'broken-leg cues' (Meehl, 1954) – diagnostic variables that have not yet been incorporated into the model. They recommend placing 50% weight on manager and model judgment as an heuristic.

Hoch and Schkade (1996) performed a laboratory experiment that attempted to determine whether it is better to design a MDSS that will capitalize on managerial strengths or compensate for weaknesses. There is a tradeoff because designing to capitalize on human strengths may exacerbate the weaknesses. They varied both the predictability of the environment and the type of decision aid. One decision aid was a pure database lookup, which capitalizes on humans' strength in pattern matching. The other MDSS was a statistical model, which compensates for human inconsistency. A third group had access to both models. The authors conclude that in a highly predictive environment, the various MDSS improve decision performance about equally. In low predictive environments, database lookup was the worst possible support strategy. Supporting decision-makers' strengths will not necessarily improve decisions.

Hybrid and Problem-oriented MDSS

A whole class of marketing decision support systems fall in between the more classic DSS, expert systems, and test marketing. Systems such as ASSESSOR (Silk & Urban, 1978), Promotionscan (Abraham & Lodish, 1987), the segment selection methodology developed by Montoya-Weiss and Calantone (Montoya-Weiss & Calantone, 1999), and various product design and positioning optimizers (e.g., Green & Krieger, 1985, 1992) are hybrid systems (also called 'problem-oriented systems,' Rangaswamy et al., 1987). These systems do not make explicit the reasons for their recommendations, operate in a higher structure world where algorithmic solutions exist, and require all data inputs to be present, making them superficially similar to vanilla DSS. But these systems also have logical structures that are easy to follow, robust and complex models of the world, and 'what if' capabilities for sensitivity analysis. These characteristics make them more similar to knowledge-based systems because: (1) the easily understandable logical structure makes it possible to make explicit the reason for the recommendation; (2) the complex and more complete underlying models incorporate a great deal of accumulated knowledge; and (3) 'what-if' and sensitivity analysis reduces the need for every input to be filled in precisely, and also allows recommendations to be accompanied by a measure of confidence.

ASSESSOR is a pre-test evaluation system for new packaged goods. Using it, a sample of consumers are surveyed about current category usage. They are then shown advertising for a new product and its major competitors, and participate in a simulated shopping experience. At a later time, subjects report their repeat purchase intentions. Measures taken during the process are used to forecast the product's expected market share and to diagnose product problems. The MDSS has been implemented for hundreds of product evaluations across many companies, and has helped lower the failure rate of new products in test market by almost half, and thus significantly increases corporate profits (Urban & Katz, 1983). Within our framework, it is technically valid, easy to use and understand, and implementable with the support of top management. This makes it very successful.

Promotionscan (Abraham & Lodish, 1993) is an automated system for measuring short-term incremental volume due to promotions by automatically computing an appropriate baseline sales volume and by adjusting for other variables that might be confounded with the promotional effect. The output of the system is used by managers to determine which retail promotional options should be chosen or negotiated. The system (or a similar system based on it) is in use in firms that sell over 50% of the frequently purchased packaged goods revenue in the US (Lodish, pers. comm.). The initial sample application showed a 15% increase in incremental sales with the use of Promotionscan. Anecdotally, one manager says:

> The system provides answers to questions such as what the competition is doing, which distribution outlet is most effective, what merchandising strategy would prove productive and other questions plaguing our sales force. To get the same information from the paper reports would take three to four times longer. (Progressive Grocer, 1994)

A recent advance on Promotionscan is due to Silva-Risso et al. (1999), who disaggregate the store level estimates used in Promotionscan so that a more precise measure of incremental vs. borrowed sales can be estimated. A constrained model's recommendations were implemented by a firm, who reported positive results from the implementation.

Montoya-Weiss & Calantone (1999) used a company-wide implementation of a 'problem-oriented' MDSS for the selection of industrial product markets. The DSS is actually a complete system of methodologies that includes problem structuring, segment formation, segment evaluation and selection, and segment strategy description. These steps are accomplished by a conjoint analysis, cluster analysis, product design optimization, and a multi-objective integer programming model. They implemented the entire MDSS at an automotive supply company, and the company adopted most of the model recommendations, blended with managerial judgment. In the two years after implementation, the company realized a 5% savings in operating expenses, a 4.5% increase in sales revenue, a 3% decrease in cost of goods sold, and a 15.8% increase in net profit. The authors also simulated the company's performance without the system as a comparison metric, and compared the model's estimates to actual performance. Compared with their simulation, actual performance represented a 36% increase in net profit, and a 41% reduction in communication costs. A controlled implementation would have made a stronger test, but these results are impressive nonetheless.

Product line optimizers such as SIMOPT (Green & Krieger, 1992) use a combination of conjoint and optimization techniques to aid in the optimal design and positioning of products. They have not been extensively validated in the field, but it is possible to look to the success of conjoint in general for the likely performance of these MDSS (Wind et al., 1989).

Knowledge-based Systems in Marketing – Do They Work?

Knowledge-based systems enjoyed their heyday in marketing from the mid-1980s to the early 1990s, paralleling the golden age of expert systems in computer science. Two of the most significant attempts at system design are NEGOTEX (Rangaswamy et al., 1989) and ADCAD (Burke et al., 1990), which help to prepare strategies for international negotiations and advertising strategies respectively. Other systems include INNOVATOR (Ram & Ram, 1988; Ram & Ram, 1989), which helps to screen new product ideas in the financial services. Business Strategy Advisor (Schumann et al., 1989; see also Wierenga, 1990) uses a BCG-like matrix to make strategic recommendations. These systems share a number of characteristics. First, they all operate in domains for which there is no easily agreed upon algorithmic solution, making the expert systems methodology appropriate (Rangaswamy et al., 1987, 1989). Second, the knowledge base underlying each of these systems is derived from industry experts, published material, the authors' experiences, or a combination of the three. Third, in keeping with the computer-science tradition, which tends to de-emphasize technical validity measures, these systems were not tested against established experts or other systems in either field tests or laboratory settings at the time of publication.

The lack of strong tests of validity makes it difficult to determine whether the systems 'work,' especially in the context of our framework for implementation and the previous discussion. ADCAD was informally validated by expert comments. INNOVATOR's authors used an *ad hoc* comparison with an expert in their initial article, and then tested the completeness of the knowledge base, the consistency and accuracy of the decisions made by the system, and the reasoning process by which the system made decisions several years after initial publication (Ram & Ram, 1996). The most in-depth validation was performed for NEGOTEX. It included full reviews using formal questionnaires by seven leading academics who specialized in negotiations, and by MBA students taking a marketing strategy class, as well as informal feedback from several practitioners. These validations do not comprise field trials, nor do they use laboratory experiments (for example, by having a group of experts rate the recommendations of subjects with and without access to the systems). We should stress that the approach to validation employed by these authors is in keeping with the normal validation methods in the expert systems literature. Rangaswamy et al. (1989) point out that the validation of expert systems has been a topic of controversy, and quote Sheil (1987), saying: 'there is no way to check that all knowledge is "correct" and no way to prove that the system has no significant gaps in its coverage' (1989: 32). Sheil is correct, but his point fails to address the larger issue.

Knowledge-based systems should be validated better. One reason that the expert system golden age faded is that lack of validation made it difficult to justify the substantial costs of development and system maintenance. Yet, it is possible to validate a knowledge-based system. Its recommendations can be compared to recommendations of experts in the field. Alternatively, a split-pool of likely users can be constructed, and the responses of the pool with access to the system can be compared against those without access. To be careful, the procedure followed in the test of CALLPLAN should be followed, where the control group still answers all the questions that the system-enabled group answer, just without the model output.

Carroll (1987) examines expert system performance across numerous application areas. She examines the two major standards of validation: comparison of the recommendations to those of experts, and comparison of the logical process. Recall that one of the main selling points of knowledge-based systems is the similarity in the reasoning process between model and user. In outcome performance, she finds that expert systems do about as well on average as the humans on whom they are trained under ideal circumstances. But the quality of knowledge-based systems' recommendations deteriorates much faster than human experts' at the boundary of the problem domain, or if the underlying logical relationships change slightly (Carroll, 1987; Davis, 1984; Davis & Lenat, 1980; Davis et al., 1987). Carroll also finds that 'expert systems are generally not superb [descriptive] models of human expertise' (Carroll, 1987: 285), meaning that the logic patterns followed by the system are not fully consistent with those of the human expert. This is because most knowledge-based systems are limited to rule-based inference, but rules make up only a subset of human inferential techniques, and because the rule elicitation process is necessarily inaccurate (see Nisbett & Wilson, 1977 for more discussion on this).

There is no definitive answer to the question 'do knowledge-based systems in marketing work?' By the success metrics that we have defined, we have almost no data. Evaluated against subordinate necessary conditions such as technical validity, the systems appear to perform well under ideal circumstances, but are likely to be non-robust. In general, systems only partially match the reasoning processes used by experts in the domain. Knowledge-based systems are more expensive to build (Turban, 1995; Turban & Aronson, 1998). They are also abandoned more frequently than vanilla DSS once implemented, primarily due to lack of acceptance by users, and the costs of transitioning from a development to an ongoing maintenance outlook (Gill, 1995; Turban, 1992, 1995).

Amidst these apparent disadvantages, Rangaswamy et al. (1989) provide a completely different rationale for the continued importance of knowledge-based systems. They note that 'the mere process of building an expert system can contribute to the marketing discipline independent of whether the final system is used by decision makers' (Rangaswamy et al., 1989: 33). The meta-analytic synthesis performed while developing knowledge-based systems may help to point out gaps and inconsistencies in current knowledge and may help the developers to develop empirical generalizations. Although these are both worthy goals, it then remains to be shown that expert system design is a better way to accomplish this goal than other approaches to research synthesis.

Cutting Edge Systems

Cutting edge systems that have been developed by computer scientists are just beginning to hit marketing. Firms are increasingly attempting to resurrect AI under the new names of 'machine learning' and 'rule discovery.' Machine learning encompasses various ways to allow the coefficients of a model to automatically update over time. Rule discovery is the process of generating symbolic rules of the form 'if <pattern> then <action>' using discrete variables as the inputs (Cooper & Giuffrida, 2000).

The most common technique used for machine learning is neural networks (Turban & Aronson, 1998). Neural networks process information in a similar manner to biological neural systems. They accept multiple inputs into a processing element, integrate the inputs according to a weighting function, and then the processing element either produces an output or does not (binary activation). The output from the first layer of processing elements is typically fed into another layer of elements, and then to an output node or nodes (which recommends an action). When used to recommend an action, a neural network is mathematically equivalent to a nonlinear discriminant function whose parameters are determined by the pattern of weights among the processing units.

Neural networks have been found to be particularly good in pattern recognition, generalization and abstraction of prototypical patterns, and interpretation of noisy inputs. All of these uses are of course 'trained' into the network, rather than having a modeler input and test a structural equation. Their primary successes thus far have been in speech and handwriting recognition, and in prediction of credit default and business failure (Tam & Kiang, 1992; Wilson & Sharda, 1994). Their advantages include the ability to learn from past data, to model highly complex relationships among the data, to be easily maintained and updated (just train them on new data), and to process data quickly. The major disadvantage of neural networks is the nearly complete lack of explanation or reasoning behind the output. This black-box nature is because the function is nonlinear and the connection weights between processing elements have no obvious interpretation (Turban & Aronson, 1998).

Rule discovery refers to procedures that automatically create 'if-then' types of rules from existing data. Cooper & Giuffrida (2000) provide an excellent taxonomy and summary of rule discovery methods as they apply rule discovery techniques to the residuals of a promotion forecasting system (PromoCast™). Because they apply the rule discovery techniques to the residuals of a forecasting model, the discovered rules represent local variations that would not have been captured by a standard market response model. Furthermore, the rules include a measure of confidence so that managers can know how 'certain' they should be in applying the rule. Their extensive validation on a holdout sample demonstrates a significant improvement in forecast accuracy.

Conclusions and Future Research

We have placed MDSS in context, offered a taxonomy of decision support systems, clearly defined a measure of success, created an integrative framework of factors contributing to MDSS success, and have examined the assumptions that underlie the relationship between our framework and existing MDSS. In summary, both the computer science and decision theory research traditions have reached the conclusion that it is possible to improve even expert decision-making. Computer science assumes that the top expert(s) in a field are the gold standard of performance. This assumption has given rise to knowledge-based decision support, which attempts to capture the knowledge and reasoning process of an expert in the form of a computer system. By contrast, decision theorists have argued that the normative standard should be an objective outcome measure, either a statistical model or an expert, depending on which is better. The decision theory and psychology literatures conclude that statistical models are frequently better than human experts. This conclusion has led to a focus on data-based, statistically grounded systems. These two types of system anchor the ends of a continuum. On one end are plain vanilla systems that almost never mimic the reasoning process of human experts, and may be just simple 'what-if' simulators. At the other end of the continuum are knowledge-based systems, which are 'sophisticated and highly specialized computer programs that try to capture and reproduce experts' decision-making processes (Naylor 1983)' (Carroll, 1987: 280). In the middle are hybrid systems that include automatic diagnostic tools such as Promotionscan, and test-forecast models such as ASSESSOR.

Regardless of what type of system is contemplated, we argue that increased profit is the proper metric to use to measure DSS success. Our insistence on profit as the proper metric of success is a departure from most previous literature. In most prior literature, system validity and implementation have been treated separately, with user opinions of system efficacy or measures of adoption and use frequently substituting for profit as the metric of success. By proposing that increased profits for the firm is the proper metric, we propose that the standard for success must include both accuracy *and* implementation. This reconceptualization of success implies that there is a valid tradeoff between factors that affect adoption and use and the accuracy of the system, if increasing accuracy has the potential to decrease probability of implementation. Such a situation may arise under a variety of conditions, notably when the increase in accuracy comes along with increased system complexity or when the increase in accuracy comes only with the use of a model that the users do not understand (a black-box model). It should be clear that optimizing accuracy of the system is not necessary, and in fact would be viewed negatively under our metric if adoption and use is negatively related to the factors that increase accuracy. Similarly, characteristics of the system, such as the similarity of the system to human reasoning or the ability to explain why certain output has been generated, are relevant only if they increase accuracy or increase the likelihood of adoption and use. The existence of the tradeoffs outlined here should not be taken to be an abandonment of theory. Technical validity is still the *sine qua non* of DSS construction – the system must be accurate for the right reasons. But, although models should be 'simple, robust, easy to communicate with, adaptive, and complete on important issues' (Little, 1970), the definitions of 'simple,' 'robust,' etc. should be viewed relatively. Accuracy should also be viewed relatively – better to have a vaguely right and implemented solution that is better than what previously existed, than to have a precise, misspecified model that is wrong, or an ideal model that is not used.

MDSS Success

With the exception of Chakravarti et al., studies of vanilla DSS effectiveness in marketing generally find a positive main effect of the MDSS on performance. These results are somewhat anomalous within the broader field of DSS research. Sharda et al. (1988) review this general literature (including many of the marketing results) and conclude: 'field and laboratory tests investigating superiority of DSS over non-DSS decisions show inconclusive results' (Sharda et al., 1988: 144). As Sharda et al. point out, part of the reason that many DSS may not appear to improve decision-making is that most of the non-significant studies are based on a one-time measurement of performance. Furthermore, in most of the inconclusive studies the DSS was a 'black-box' – subjects did not know or understand the workings of the model. They go on to note that MDSS are likely to be used more than once, users are likely to be trained, and some understanding of how the DSS works is likely to be transmitted. These criticisms imply that the inconclusive studies confound lack of training with measures of the ability of the DSS to improve decision-making. In marketing, the MDSS used are rarely black-boxes, and most subjects receive some training on how the MDSS works. This may explain the positive effects of MDSS in marketing. However, Sharda et al. raise a critical point about the rigor of MDSS (and more broadly, DSS research). Many inconclusive results are likely to have been caused by heterogeneity in the user or test populations. We raised this point in the context of examining the evidence of the effect of individual differences on successful DSS adoption and use, but the argument applies to almost every aspect of DSS measurement. Users of DSS may be heterogeneous on a variety of dimensions, including familiarity with computers, expertise in the decision-making task, psychological traits, and prior use of DSS. These differences will affect the success of DSS, and must be controlled for and modeled in the research. Hutchinson et al. (2000) provide extensive recommendations and procedures for diagnosing unobserved heterogeneity.

Future Research

In this section we summarize some emerging technologies and trends in DSS and knowledge-based systems. We also make recommendations to researchers. Wierenga et al. (1999) make a number of excellent recommendations as well.

One important area for future research is to engage in more validation along the continuum of validation approaches. The most important priority is to generate more controlled field studies with both existing and new models. This is critical if we are to get information about the entire process of MDSS development, implementation, and measures of success in complex environments. Secondly, we should encourage systems to be evaluated in the laboratory as thoroughly as possible if they are not going to be implemented in the field. One way to do this is to use subjects who are representative of the user pool in as realistic a decision-making environment as possible. Assuming a representative user pool, researchers should collect measures of likelihood of adoption and use, in addition to assessing improvement in decision quality (or efficiency). Where possible, simpler models should be compared to more complex models on both the accuracy and likelihood of adoption measures so that the tradeoff between complexity and adoption can be found (if it exists). Prior to extensive laboratory testing, every system (including knowledge-based systems) should be assessed for technical validity – against an appropriate array of possible other decision-making systems and human experts at a minimum.

Although field studies are the gold standard in MDSS research, simpler non-DSS solutions could also prove very helpful. One simple and informative area of research would be to just keep track of the decisions that are made within a company. Then one could at least compare the before, during, and after DSS-use performance, controlling for other variables. Many firms keep detailed records of their plans, but virtually no information about what they actually did. With the help of researchers, these firms could then at least directionally determine the effect of the MDSS on decision performance.

We also recommend an increased emphasis on solving more complex problems. In order to do this, three separate research streams must be united. The psychological literature on managerial decision-making should be employed to determine whether and under what circumstances DSS should reinforce managerial strengths versus compensating for weaknesses (along the lines of Hoch & Schkade, 1996). Second, more hybrid systems should be constructed, with data-gathering methodologies, intuitive processing models, and a combination of logical and data-processing capabilities built into them. Third, we need to renew the emphasis on directionally correct solutions and the validation of such solutions. This is a reasonable initial goal in highly complex environments. We need more research into the process of how managers go about making directional decisions, and the level of expertise that they can achieve in complex environments.

Finally, it is the dream of most marketing managers to have automated systems that can extract relevant information from customer and transaction databases. With the explosion of transactions in the online world, data-mining, machine learning, and rule discovery will become more important. Marketers should be leading this wave of research with colleagues in computer science.

Acknowledgements

The authors would like to thank Arvind Rangaswamy, Robin Wensley, and Christopher Van den Bulte for comments on earlier drafts of this paper.

References

Abraham, Magid M. & Lodish, Leonard M. (1987) Promoter: an automated promotion evaluation system. *Marketing Science*, 6 (2), 101–23.

——— (1993) An implemented system for improving promotion productivity using store scanner data. *Marketing Science*, 12, 3 (Summer), 248–269.

Alavi, Maryam & Joachimsthaler, Erich A. (1992) Revisiting DSS implementation research: a meta-analysis of the literature and suggestions for researchers. *MIS Quarterly*, 16 (1), 95–116.

Alter, Steven (1980) *Decision Support Systems: Current Practice and Continuing Challenges*. Reading, MA: Addison-Wesley Publishers.

Anthony, R.N. (1965) Planning and control systems, a framework for analysis. Boston, MA: Division of Research, Graduate School of Business Administration, Harvard University.

Awad, Elias M. (1996) *Building Expert Systems*. Minneapolis, St. Paul: West Publishing Company.

Benbasat, Izak & Dexter, Albert S. (1982) Individual differences in the use of decision support aids. *Journal of Accounting Research*, 20 (1), 1–12.

——— (1985) An experimental evaluation of graphical and color-enhanced information. *Management Science*, 31 (11), 1348–65.

Blattberg, Robert C. & Hoch, Stephen J. (1990) Database models and managerial intuition: 50% model + 50% manager. *Management Science*, 36 (8), 887–99.

Burke, Raymond R., Rangaswamy, Arvind, Wind, Jerry & Eliashberg, Jehoshua (1990) A knowledge-based system for advertising design. *Marketing Science*, 9 (3), 212–29.

Camerer, Colin F. & Johnson, Eric J. (1991) The process-performance paradox in expert judgment: how can experts know so much and predict so badly? In *Toward a General Theory of Expertise: Prospects and Limits*, edited by K. Anders Ericsson & Jacqui Smith. New York: Cambridge University Press, pp. 195–217.

Carroll, Barbara (1987) Expert systems for clinical diagnosis: are they worth the effort? *Behavioral Science*, 32 (4), 274–92.

Carroll, John S. & Payne, John W. (1976) The psychology of parole decision process: a joint application of attribution theory and information-processing psychology. In *Cognition and Social Behavior*, edited by John S. Carroll & John W. Payne. Hillsdale, NJ: Lawrence Erlbaum Associates.

Chakravarti, Dipankar, Mitchell, Andrew et al. (1979) Judgment based marketing decision models: an experimental investigation of the decision calculus approach. *Management Science*, 25 (3), 251–63.

Chi, Michelene T.H., Glaser, Robert & Farr, Marshall J. (eds) (1988) *The Nature of Expertise*. Hillsdale, NJ: Lawrence Erlbaum Associates.

Christensen-Szalanski, Jay J. & Bushyhead, James B. (1981) Physicians' use of probabilistic information in a real clinical setting. *Journal of Experimental Psychology: Human Perception & Performance*, 7 (4), 928–35.

Cole, Catherine A. & Gaeth, Gary J. (1990) Cognitive and age-related differences in the ability to use nutritional information in a complex environment. *Journal of Marketing Research*, 27 (2), 175–84.

Cooper, Lee G. & Giuffrida, Giovanni (2000) Turning datamining into a management science tool: new algorithms and empirical results. *Management Science*, 46 (2), 249–64.

Davis, Donald L., Davis, R. Dean & Shrode, William S. (1987) Decision support systems (DSS) design for operations managers: an empirical study of the impact of report design and decision style on effective choice. *Journal of Operations Management*, 7 (1–2), 47–62.

Davis, R. (1984) Amplifying expertise with expert systems. In *The AI Business: The Commercial Uses of Artificial Intelligence*, edited by Karen A. Prendergast & Patrick Henry Winston. Cambridge, MA: MIT Press, pp. 17–40.

Davis, Randall & Lenat, Douglas B. (1980) *Knowledge Based Systems in Artificial Intelligence*. New York: McGraw-Hill International Book Co.

Dawes, Robyn M. & Corrigan, Bernard (1974) Linear models in decision making. *Psychological Bulletin*, 81 (2), 95–106.

Dawes, Robyn M., Faust, David & Meehl, Paul E. (1989) Clinical versus actuarial judgment. *Science*, 243 (4899), 1668–74.

DeLone, W.H. & McLean, E.R. (1992) Information systems success: the quest for the dependent variable. *Information Systems Research*, 3 (1), 60–95.

De Waele, M. (1978) Managerial style and the design of decision aids. *OMEGA*, 6 (1), 5–13.

Einhorn, Hillel J. (1974) Expert judgment: some necessary conditions and an example. *Journal of Applied Psychology*, 59 (5), 562–71.

Einhorn, Hillel J. & Hogarth, Robin M. (1975) Unit weighting schemes for decision making. *Organizational Behavior & Human Decision Processes*, 13 (2), 171–92.

Ericsson, K. Anders (ed.) (1996) *The Road to Excellence: The Acquisition of Expert Performance in the Arts and Sciences, Sports, and Games*. Mahwah, NJ: Lawrence Erlbaum Associates.

Ericsson, K. Anders & Smith, Jacqui (eds) (1991) *Toward a General Theory of Expertise: Prospects and Limits*. New York: Cambridge University Press.

Fudge, W.K. & Lodish, L.M. (1977) Evaluation of the effectiveness of a model based salesman's planning system by field experimentation. *Interfaces*, 8 (1, part 2), 97–106.

Gensch, D.H., Aversa, N. et al. (1990) A choice modeling market information system that enabled ABB Electric to expand its market share. *Interfaces*, 20 (1), 6–25.

Gill, T. Grandon (1995) Early expert systems: where are they now? *MIS Quarterly*, 19 (1), 51–84.

Gorry, G.A. & Scott-Morton, M.S. (1971) A framework for management information systems. *Sloan Management Review*, 13 (1), 55–70.

Green, Paul E. & Krieger, Abba M. (1985) Models and heuristics for product line selection. *Marketing Science*, 4 (1), 1–19.

——— (1992) An application of a product positioning model to pharmaceutical products. *Marketing Science*, 11 (2), 117–32.

Hanssens, Dominique M., Parsons, Leonard J. & Schultz, Randall L. (1990) *Market Response Models: Econometric and Time Series Analyses*. Boston: Kluwer.

Hayes-Roth, Frederick, Waterman, Donald A. & Lenat, Douglas B. (1983) An overview of expert systems. In *Building Expert Systems*, edited by Frederick Hayes-Roth, Donald A. Waterman & Douglas B. Lenat. Vol. 1. Reading, MA: Addison-Wesley Publishing Co., pp. 3–29.

Hoch, S.J. & Schkade, D.A. (1996) A psychological approach to decision support systems. *Management Science*, 42 (1), 51–64.

Huber, George P. (1983) Cognitive style as a basis for MIS and DSS designs: much ado about nothing? *Management Science*, 29 (5), 567–79.

Hunt, Raymond G., Krzystofiak, Frank J., Meindl, James R. & Yousry, Abdalla M. (1989) Cognitive style and decision making. *Organizational Behavior & Human Decision Processes*, 44 (3), 436–54.

Hutchinson, J. Wesley, Kamakura, Wagner A. & Lynch, John G. Jr. (2000) Unobserved heterogeneity as an alternative explanation for 'reversal' effects in behavioral research. *Journal of Consumer Research*, 27 (3), 324–44.

Huysmans, J.H.B.M. (1970) The effectiveness of the cognitive constraint in implementing operations research proposals. *Management Science*, 17 (1), 92–104.

Ives, Blake & Olson, Margrethe H. (1984) User involvement and MIS success: a review of research. *Management Science*, 30 (5), 586–604.

Johnson, Eric J. (1988) Expertise and decision under uncertainty: performance and process. In *The Nature of Expertise*, edited by Michelene T.H. Chi & Robert Glaser. Hillsdale, NJ: Lawrence Erlbaum Associates, Inc.

Keen, Peter G.W. & Scott-Morton, Michael S. (1978) *Decision Support Systems: An Organizational Perspective*. Reading, MA: Addison-Wesley.

King, David (1993) Intelligent support systems: art, augmentation, and agents. In *Decision Support Systems: Putting Theory into Practice*, edited by Ralph H. Sprague Jr. & Hugh J. Watson. 3rd edn. Englewood Cliffs, NJ: Prentice-Hall, pp. 137–59.

Larreche, Jean C. (1979) Integrative complexity and the use of marketing models. In *The Implementation of Management Science*, edited by Robert L. Doktor, R.L. Schultz & D.P. Slevin. New York: North-Holland Pub. Co.

Leonard, Nancy H., Scholl, Richard W. & Kowalski, Kellyann Berube (1999) Information processing style and decision making. *Journal of Organizational Behavior*, 20 (3), 407–20.

Lilien, Gary L., Kotler, Philip & Moorthy, K. Sridhar (1992) *Marketing Models*. Englewood Cliffs, NJ: Prentice-Hall.

Little, John D.C. (1970) Models and managers: the concept of a decision calculus. *Management Science*, 16 (8), 466–85.

——— (1979) Decision support systems for marketing managers. *Journal of Marketing*, 43 (3), 9–26.

Little, John D.C. & Lodish, Leonard M. (1969) A media planning calculus. *Operations Research*, 17 (1), 1–33.

——— (1981) Commentary on 'Judgment based marketing decision models'. *Journal of Marketing*, 45 (Fall), 24–9.

Lodish, Leonard M. (1971) CALLPLAN: an interactive salesman's call planning system. *Management Science*, 18 (December), 25–40.

——— (1974) A vaguely right approach to sales force allocation decisions. *Harvard Business Review*, 52 (January–February), 119–24.

——— (1980) A user-oriented model for sales force size, product, and market allocations. *Journal of Marketing*, 44 (Summer), 70–8.

Lodish, Leonard M. & Reibstein, David J. (1986) New gold mines and minefields in market research. *Harvard Business Review*, 64 (1), 168–82.

Lodish, L.M., Curtis, E. et al. (1988) Sales force sizing and deployment using a decision calculus model at Syntex Laboratories. *Interfaces*, 18 (1), 5–20.

Lusk, Edward J. & Kersnick, Michael (1979) The effect of cognitive style and report format on task performance: the MIS design consequences. *Management Science*, 25 (8), 787–98.

McIntyre, Shelby H. (1982) An experimental study of the impact of judgment-based marketing models. *Management Science*, 28 (1), 17–33.

Meehl, Paul E. (1954) *Clinical vs. Statistical Prediction: A Theoretical Analysis and a Review of the Evidence*. Minneapolis: University of Minnesota Press.

Montgomery, D., Silk, Alvin J. & Zaragoza, C. (1971) A multiple product sales force allocation model. *Management Science*, 18 (December), 3–24.

Montoya-Weiss, Mitzi & Calantone, Roger J. (1999) Development and implementation of a segment selection procedure for industrial product markets. *Marketing Science*, 18 (3), 373–95.

Naylor, Chris (1983) *Build Your Own Expert System*. Wilmslow, Cheshire: Sigma Technical Press.

Nisbett, Richard E. & Wilson, Timothy D. (1977) Telling more than we can know: verbal reports on mental processes. *Psychological Review*, 84 (3), 231–59.

Northcroft, M.A. & Neale, G.B. (1987) Experts, amateurs and real-estate: an anchoring and adjust perspective in property pricing decisions. *Organizational Behavior & Human Decision Processes*, 39, 84–97.

Oskamp, Stuart (1962) The relation of clinical experience and training methods to several criteria of clinical prediction. *Psychological Monographs*, 76 (28, Whole No. 547), 27.

Phelps, Ruth H. & Shanteau, James (1978) Livestock judges: how much information can an expert use? *Organizational Behavior & Human Decision Processes*, 21 (2), 209–19.

Progressive Grocer (1994) Case studies: Hormel Foods Corp. turning data into useful information. *PROMO: Progressive Grocer Special Report*: S14.

Ram, Sudha & Ram, Sundaresan (1988) INNOVATOR: an expert system for new product launch decisions. *Applied Artificial Intelligence*, 2, 129–48.

——— (1996) Validation of expert systems for innovation management: issues, methodolgy, and empirical assessment. *Journal of Product Innovation Management*, 13 (1), 54–68.

Ram, Sundaresan & Ram, Sudha (1989) Expert systems: an emerging technology for selecting new product winners. *The Journal of Product Innovation Management*, 6 (2), 89–99.

Ramaprasad, Arkalgud (1987) Cognitive process as a basis for MIS and DSS design. *Management Science*, 33 (2), 139–48.

Rangaswamy, Arvind, Burke, Raymond R., Wind, Jerry & Eliashberg, Jehoshua (1987) Expert systems for marketing. Working Paper, Marketing Science Institute, Report No. 87–107 (November).

Rangaswamy, Arvind, Eliashberg, Jehoshua, Burke, Raymond R. & Wind, Jerry (1989) Developing marketing expert systems: an application to international negotiations. *Journal of Marketing*, 53 (4), 24–39.

Russell, Stuart J. & Norvig, Peter (1995) *Artificial Intelligence: A Modern Approach*. Upper Saddle River, NJ: Prentice-Hall, Inc.

Schumann, M., Gongla, Patricia, Lee, Kyoung-Sang & Sakamoto, J. Gene (1989) Business Strategy Advisor: an expert systems implementation. *Journal of Information Sciences Management*, 6 (2), 16–24.

Shanteau, James (1987) Psychological characteristics of expert decision makers. In *Expert Judgment and Expert Systems*, edited by Jeryl L. Mumpower, Ortwin Renn, Lawrence D. Phillips & V.R.R. Uppuluri. Berlin: Springer-Verlag.

——— (1988) Psychological characteristics and strategies of expert decision makers. *Acta Psychologica*, 68 (1–3), 203–15.

——— (1992a) Competence in experts: the role of task characteristics. *Organizational Behavior & Human Decision Processes*, 53 (2), 252–66.

——— (1992b) The psychology of experts: an alternative view. In *Expertise and Decision Support*, edited by George Wright & Fergus Bolger. New York: Plenum Press.

Sharda, Ramesh, Barr, Steve H. & McDonnell, James C. (1988) Decision support system effectiveness: a review and an empirical test. *Management Science*, 34 (2), 139–59.

Shiel, B. (1987) Thinking about artificial intelligence. *Harvard Business Review*, 65 (July–August), 91–7.

Silk, Alvin J. & Urban, Glen L. (1978) Pre-test-market evaluation of new packaged goods: a model and measurement methodology. *Journal of Marketing Research*, 15 (2), 171–91.

Silva-Risso, J.M., Bucklin, R.E. et al. (1999) A decision support system for planning manufacturers' sales promotion calendars. *Marketing Science*, 18 (3), 274–300.

Simon, Herbert A. (1977) *The New Science of Management Decision*, rev. edn. Englewood Cliffs, NJ: Prentice-Hall.

Spence, M.T. & Brucks, M. (1997) The moderating effects of problem characteristics on experts' and novices' judgements. *Journal of Marketing Research*, 34 (2), 233–47.

Sprague, Ralph H. Jr. & Watson, Hugh J. (1993) *Decision Support Systems: Putting Theory into Practice*, 3rd edn. Englewood Cliffs, NJ: Prentice-Hall.

Sterman, John D. (1987) Testing behavioral simulation models by direct experiment. *Management Science*, 33 (12), 1572–92.

——— (1989) Modeling managerial behavior: misperceptions of feedback in a dynamic decision making experiment. *Management Science*, 35 (3), 321–39.

Tam, Kar Yan & Kiang, Melody Y. (1992) Managerial applications of neural networks: the case of bank failure predictions. *Management Science*, 38 (7), 926–47.

Turban, Efraim (1992) *Expert Systems and Applied Artificial Intelligence*. New York: Macmillian Publishing.

——— (1995) *Decision Support and Expert Systems: Management Support Systems*, 4th edn. Englewood Cliffs, NJ: Prentice-Hall.

Turban, Efraim & Aronson, Jay E. (1998) *Decision Support Systems and Intelligent Systems*. Upper Saddle River, NJ: Prentice-Hall.

Tyran, Craig K. & George, Joey F. (1993) The implementation of expert systems: a survey of successful implementations. *Data Base*, 24 (1), 5–15.

Urban, G.L. & Karash, R. (1971) Evolutionary model building in the analysis of new products. *Journal of Marketing Research* 8 (February): 62–6.

Urban, Glen L. & Katz, Gerald M. (1983) Pre-test-market models: validation and managerial implications. *Journal of Marketing Research*, 20 (3), 221–35.

van Bruggen, Gerrit H., Smidts, Ale & Wierenga, Berend (1998) Improving decision making by means of a marketing decision support system. *Management Science*, 44 (5), 645–58.

Wierenga, Berend (1990) *The First Generation of Marketing Expert Systems*. Philadelphia, PA: Wharton School, University of Pennsylvania.

Wierenga, Berend & Ophuis, Peter A.M. Oude (1997) Marketing decision support systems: adoption, use, and satisfaction. *International Journal of Research in Marketing*, 14 (3), 275–90.

Wierenga, Berend & van Bruggen, Gerrit H. (1997) The integration of marketing problem-solving modes and marketing management support systems. *Journal of Marketing*, 61 (3), 21–37.

Wierenga, Berend, van Bruggen, Gerrit H. & Staelin, Richard (1999) The success of marketing management support systems. *Marketing Science*, 18 (3), 196–207.

Wilson, Rick L. & Sharda, Ramesh (1994) Bankruptcy prediction using neural networks. *Decision Support Systems*, 11 (5), 545–58.

Wind, Jerry, Green, Paul E., Shifflet, Douglas & Scarbrough, Marsha (1989) Courtyard by Marriott: designing a hotel facility with consumer-based marketing models. *Interfaces*, 19 (1), 25–48.

Wright, George & Bolger, Fergus (1992) *Expertise and Decision Support*. New York: Plenum Press.

Zinkhan, George M., Joachimsthaler, Erich A. & Kinnear, Thomas C. (1987) Individual differences and marketing decision support system usage and satisfaction. *Journal of Marketing Research*, 24 (2), 208–14.

Zmud, Robert W. (1979) Individual differences and MIS success: a review of the empirical literature. *Management Science*, 25 (10), 966.

PART FIVE

Special Topics

18

Global Marketing: Research on Foreign Entry, Local Marketing, Global Management

JOHNY K. JOHANSSON

INTRODUCTION

As we all know, markets are opening up around the world and companies are increasingly 'going global,' at least in their managers' mindsets. Not to be left behind, academic research in marketing has also an increasingly strong international component, whether explicitly introduced or not. Among practitioners international experience and a posting abroad are becoming the *sine qua non* of the organizational career path. In business schools deans prescribe an 'internationalized' curriculum to characteristically ambivalent faculty. These developments are not surprising. Global marketing as an area of academic inquiry and practical management provides fascinating challenges, is hugely stimulating, and is in tune with the 'victory' of the free market system. Unfortunately, however, global marketing is also theoretically paradoxical, complex in practice, and always subject to the vagaries of larger political and economic forces. These contrasts have created problems as well as opportunities for practitioners, business schools, and academic researchers alike. This chapter will assess the state of the art, and also suggest areas for future inquiry.

Terminology. In a narrow sense, 'global marketing' refers to the coordination of marketing activities across the world's markets (as in, for example, Backhaus et al., 1998). Characteristic topics include global branding, standardization of products and services, global advertising, and the use of information technology and organizational innovations to implement coordinated marketing strategies.

The present survey, however, adopts a broader definition of global marketing – one that includes most marketing activities across borders. It distinguishes the typical *global* marketing management problems from *foreign entry* questions and *local marketing* in a foreign country. Foreign entry and local marketing together constitute what was traditionally 'international marketing.'

One reason for such an inclusion is simply that a number of marketing researchers have contributed to knowledge development in these areas. Still, foreign entry questions involve issues such as exporting, trade barriers, and mode of entry – not your typical marketing topics. Thus they pose different problems than global coordination, where the company typically is already present in most major markets.

A separate focus on 'local marketing' helps identify the domain where standard marketing know-how is often directly applicable. That is, topics such as 'marketing in China,' even though they typically emphasize adaptation to local conditions, and at the same time often underscore the robustness of the basic marketing principles.

In global marketing coordination, standardization of the marketing mix is common. Uniform marketing might be useful for global control and synergy, but it means the mix is not adapted to the local market. Thus, paradoxically, global marketing tends to go counter to a true market orientation.

Outline. The present chapter will deal with these three research areas in order. It starts with *foreign entry*, followed by *local marketing* abroad, and then *global management*. The emphasis will be on the global part, the three areas accounting for approximately 25%, 25%, and 50% of the chapter respectively. The chapter will first identify the managerial problems faced in an area, then discuss published research in the area, and then examine unexplored topics in need of further investigation. The chapter ends with an overall assessment of publication opportunities and problems in global marketing.

Foreign Entry

General Overview

The area of foreign entry raises issues that are rarely, if ever, covered in the standard marketing literature. Nevertheless, the researcher in global marketing, as well as the practitioner of global marketing, has to face foreign entry issues in order to understand the possibilities and constraints of entering foreign markets. It is not simply a matter of assessing the promise of markets abroad, but also the way one goes about entering those markets and whether the company has the capability of operating there. In strategic terms, successful entry depends as much on available resources as on market potential.

In the area of foreign entry, four different marketing research directions can be distinguished.

- Mode of Entry. The most developed sub-area in terms of theory involves *mode of entry* studies, the management choice between exporting, licensing, or some other form of entering a foreign market. Here, in addition to marketers, economists have been active.
- Internationalization. A second area is that of *internationalization*, the process by which firms grow from intermittent exporters to full-fledged global companies.
- Exporting. A third area is that of special *exporting* studies, largely empirically based research into what factors can predict how actively a firm will pursue export markets.
- Negotiations. *Negotiations* undertaken with potential partners and middlemen for entry into a foreign market constitute a very fruitful and important research area in global marketing.

Mode of Entry

Firms traditionally choose between three basic modes of entry, viz. *exporting*, *licensing*, and *foreign direct investment* (FDI) in production. The exporting mode involves choices between independent channels (importers, distributors, and agents) or establishing a sales subsidiary in the market country. Licensing includes, for example, choosing between franchising or contracting with a foreign manufacturer to produce and market the product. FDI might involve 100% ownership, or a joint venture. Recently popular, non-equity *alliances* with other firms have been added as another mode of entry. The latest mode, not yet analyzed much in the academic literature, is *direct marketing*, with or without Internet involvement.

This is an area where economists have traditionally been active. There is not so much marketing know-how involved in analyzing these options, and academic marketers have, in a sense, been latecomers to the area.

Research on mode of entry into foreign markets drew its early inspiration from the economic theory of international trade. Comparative advantages were identified as a driver of a country's exports and imports, and the choice of entry mode depended on barriers to trade, including transportation costs, companies' levels of market knowledge, and tariffs. In the last couple of decades, the theory has been extended to account for endogeneous changes in a country's underlying resource endowments (Porter, 1990), the fact that intra-industry trade takes place because of product differentiation (Krugman, 1988), and the role of firm-specific advantages in determining trade patterns (Dunning, 1988). Such firm-specific advantages (FSAs) might include, for example, patents, market know-how, and a strong brand name.

This 'new' theory of the multinational (Buckley, 1987) stresses the need for companies to use FDI to 'internalize' their FSAs to protect against dissipation. According to the internalization school, when trade barriers are high, companies avoid licensing in favor of FDI in wholly-owned subsidiaries, because licensees cannot be controlled. As transportation costs and tariffs come down, exporting becomes an increasingly efficient mode of entry for these companies, which can now avoid not only the dangers of licensing but also the financial exposure of FDI. This theory can be seen as a extension of Vernon's product cycle theory (Wells, 1968), which tracks the gradual diffusion of production technology across countries. Vernon's theory predicts a shift of production to lower wage countries – the internalization theory suggests that the new plant will be a wholly-owned subsidiary of the innovating company.

Among marketers, couching entry mode in terms of choice of distribution channels abroad, researchers have successfully used transaction cost theory to predict entry mode (Anderson & Coughlan, 1987; Anderson & Gatignon, 1986). Conceptualizing the costs of establishing representation abroad as transaction specific investments, and introducing depth of commitment and level of trust into the model, choosing channels to minimize transaction costs becomes a very attractive managerial and research recipe. An added benefit is that the framework closely parallels recent distribution channel studies in the home market, making the reviewers at top marketing journals more comfortable in assessing the value of the research.

Internationalization

Marketing research into foreign entry mode has typically been more empirically based than economists' research. To some extent, the marketing research has even contradicted the theoretical propositions of economics. This is particularly true in the analysis of the path of global expansion followed by firms.

The 'Cultural Distance' Effect

When companies first expand abroad, they find it natural to look for countries abroad where their experiences in the home market would be most useful. This 'reasoning by analogy' leads to selecting countries with conditions similar to the home market's. Most of the export expansion paths followed by firms begin in countries 'psychologically' or 'culturally' similar to their own or to countries they already export to. Geographical proximity plays a role, but is only one part of the broader notion of 'cultural distance' at the heart of expansion by gradually internationalizing (Johanson & Vahlne, 1977).

The cultural distance effect works so as to create very natural 'biases,' which are not necessarily misplaced. Factors that make for cultural proximity also make previous experience relevant, and if the company is successful in one country, it is more likely to be successful doing the same thing in a similar country. In general, however, the blind acceptance of the easy cultural distance path leads to a superficial analysis of possibly very real differences among the countries, and also to a predictability of company action that can be a disadvantage from a competitive standpoint. And, what's more, potentially better markets might be ignored.

The International Learning Curve

The cultural distance path can be justified not only on the basis that it seems to achieve a maximal capitalization on previous experience. It also allows the gradual accumulation of know-how about how to do business abroad, like following a learning curve which gradually increases the productivity of the managers involved. At least in the initial stages of expansion, this learning effect is a common rationale for choosing countries to enter.

After building up experience and confidence, internationalizing companies start considering a more orderly and strategic export expansion. According to some researchers, when companies find that over 15% of their revenues comes from overseas markets, management starts paying more systematic attention to overseas potential (Czinkota & Ronkainen, 1999: 257). Then an export expansion strategy seems needed to manage the increasing dependence on overseas markets.

Internationalization Stages

As several researchers have found, this gradual internationalization sequence is reflected in the mode of entry chosen (see, for example, Cavusgil, 1980; Nordstrom, 1991). Although companies differ, the general pattern is for gradually increased commitment to foreign markets. The stages may differ somewhat between companies, but follow this general pattern:

Stage 1: Indirect exporting, licensing
Stage 2: Direct exporter, via independent distributor
Stage 3: Establishing foreign sales subsidiary
Stage 4: Local assembly
Stage 5: Foreign production

Several variations of these internationalization stages have been proposed. For example, as we saw above, the early use of licensing has been questioned by proponents of the 'internalization' school. Also, in recent years, as strategic alliances have become common, companies utilize joint ventures and alliances at almost any stage in the process. The process of sequential moves from one stage to the next has been challenged in studies which demonstrate how some firms exit markets and then re-launch entry with a lower commitment mode (Pauwels & Matthyssens, 2001).

Entry Strategies Internationalization studies naturally touch on the strategy followed when entering new markets abroad.

The entry strategy of companies typically follows one of two alternative patterns. Under the 'waterfall' scenario, the product or service is gradually moved into overseas markets, while in the 'sprinkler' mode the product is introduced into several countries' markets simultaneously or within a limited period of time (Riesenbeck & Freeling, 1991).

Traditionally, the *waterfall* strategy was the preferred choice. It goes well with the cultural distance and learning patterns already discussed. After success in the home market, the product is gradually moved out to culturally close country markets, then to other mature and high growth markets, and finally to less-developed country markets. This is the pattern followed by many well-known companies, including Matsushita, BMW, and General Electric.

The advantage of the waterfall strategy is that the expansion can take place in an orderly manner, and the same managers can be used for different countries, which helps to capitalize on skills developed (Kalish et al., 1995). For the same reasons it is also a relatively less-demanding strategy in terms of resource requirements. This is why it still is the most common approach for newer companies such as Dell, Benetton, and The Body Shop. But in fast moving markets the waterfall strategy may be too slow.

Compared with the waterfall, the *sprinkler* strategy has the opposite strengths and disadvantages. It is a much quicker way to product introduction across the globe, it generates first-mover advantage, and it pre-empts competitive countermoves by sheer speed. The sprinkler strategy is a good strategy in hypercompetition and time-based competition. The drawback is the amount of managerial, financial, and other resources required, and the risk potential of major commitments without proper country knowledge or research.

Examples of the sprinkler approach are becoming more frequent as the competitive climate heats up and as global communications such as the Internet make access to country markets easier. The typical cases involve new product launches by companies with an established global presence such as Sony (the handheld camcorder, for example, and the Walkman), Microsoft (Windows 95, 98 and Me), and Gillette (the Sensor, for example).

Today the sprinkler strategy is also used by domestic companies to establish a global presence. Even though not 'Born Globals' (see below), these firms first solidify their home market success and then expand across the globe quickly. For example, catalog-based retailers such as Land's End, Eddie Bauer, and L.L. Bean have entered a large number of foreign countries within a limited time period. Telecommunications companies have also followed the sprinkler strategy, although partly by necessity: not many country markets were open to foreign competitors before deregulation and privatization. With the great advances in global communications in the last decade, the sprinkler approach has become much less resource demanding, and companies can reach almost anywhere on the globe to sell their wares (Hanson, 2000: 60–1).

Born Global Recently, the gradual increase in commitment to overseas markets has been challenged by some researchers. As studies in Australia, the US and elsewhere shows, in the new free trade economy where global communication is easy, technology is King, and entrepreneurship is beautiful, there are numerous smaller firms whose markets at the inception are globally conceived. These 'born global' firms are the subject of new and interesting work by academics (Knight & Cavusgil, 1997).

Based on research among newly formed high technology start-ups, the term *born global* was apparently first coined by a consulting report (McKinsey & Co., 1993). Born global firms are firms which, from the outset, view the world as one market. They are typically small, technology based businesses, and their FSAs lie in new innovations and technological breakthroughs. The entrepreneurial spirit of the founder, coupled with the threat of competitive imitation and alternative technologies, means that rapid internationalization is necessary to capture the first-mover advantages in world markets.

Born global firms rely on networking for most of their expansion abroad. They may start as exporters, selling to customers identified and reached through alliances and network relationships. Their FSAs involve technical eminence, with substantial added-value, and differentiated designs. Because of limited organizational and managerial resources, the born globals tend to rely on advanced communications technologies to reach their customers in different countries – facsimile, electronic mail, the Internet, and electronic data interchange, EDI. The advanced communications allow the company low-cost exchange with partners and customers. In addition, substantial market data availability on the Internet, previously unavailable to smaller firms, facilitates their overseas penetration. In a pioneering Swedish study of smaller firms' internationalization paths, the importance of creating a strong network of communications and logistics is similarly stressed (Hertz & Mattsson, 1998).

At the present, it looks like the advances in global communication have made traditional internationalization patterns simply history. Although high technology markets differ from mainstream markets, there are reasons to suspect that in the future many small companies will see the world as their market from the beginning, using the Internet to research foreign markets, identify distributors and potential partners on the world-wide web, and create alliances and relationships through e-mail and voice-mail (for a number of case studies see Westland & Clark, 1999).

Exporting Studies

Marketing researchers in the exporting area have tended to focus on what determines whether companies decide to fully exploit the market opportunities abroad. This is not surprising among US researchers, considering that the size of the American home market easily dwarfs most foreign markets. Thus, the effectiveness of various export promotion programs has been studied (Czinkota, 1982), as has the export consciousness on the part of company managers (Dichtl et al., 1990), and the industry structure and company characteristics which lead to high share of export revenues (for an excellent review, see Leonidou et al., 1998). Also continuing to grow is a body of studies focused on relating export entry to performance, identifying the strategic factors which explain superior export earnings (Aaby & Slater, 1989; Aulakh et al., 2000; Cavusgil & Zou, 1994).

Performance-oriented export research is also a trend in Europe, where researchers seem not so worried about stimulating exports. The smaller size of their home countries and the proximity to foreign lands have made exporting a necessary and logical step for companies to achieve higher volumes and reap returns to scale. Thus, European researchers find that firms have long-established channel and customer contacts abroad, and the questions research revolve more naturally around questions of managing networks and leveraging relationships (Homburg et al., 1997; Madsen, 1989). The Swedish 'cultural distance' concept has been extended into a network paradigm of relationships and linkages which can be leveraged for expansion abroad (Forsgren & Johanson, 1992).

A share of the exporting research is focused on how international institutions constrain or facilitate trade between countries. Still very much in evidence in the typical textbook, the research is basically institutional and comparative, dealing with differences across countries in market access and export-import regulations. Also common are analyses of the role of international institutions such as the WTO, the World Bank, and the United Nations. Although hardly involving typical marketing problems, these issues need careful analysis by marketers expanding abroad.

When it comes to evaluating country attractiveness as a market and forecasting sales, standard market estimation tools can be used, with some adaptation. Moyer's (1968) article is an early example, further refined by Kumar et al. (1994), who suggest an interactive multi-criteria procedure. The classic Armstrong (1970) study shows Kodak's approach to forecasting film sales in different countries. Lindberg (1982) shows how to estimate penetration rates in different countries, and the applicability of forecasting by using lead countries for lagging markets. Root (1987) provides a good overview of the techniques available.

Negotiations Research

A strong area of research relating to foreign entry involves cross-cultural negotiations. International expansion, including entry into new markets, of course often involves face-to-face negotiations with potential distributors, importers, business customers, and alliance partners. But the negotiations encompass more than straight marketing issues, and although marketing journals will publish such research, much of the negotiation literature fits better with general management and organizational behavior journals.

Unavoidably, international negotiation research has to deal with cultural issues. In fact, much of the research published suggests that the negotiation strategies and tactics employed in successful negotiations are based firmly on a thorough understanding of the other party's particular culture (see, for example, Hall & Hall, 1990). Thus, the research is primarily normative, explaining why certain behaviors are preferable – learn something about the host country's history and language – while others should be avoided – don't prop your feet on the table, don't show impatience. The advice is often very specific, down to the number of people that accompany the main negotiator (a status symbol), the dress (formal to show respect and seriousness of purpose, or informal to feel at ease), and the level of voice (if not loud at least very clear in the United States, more intimate in other countries).

Traditional negotiation research suggests that the straightforward, no-nonsense approach favored by some Americans is less likely to be successful than a more indirect and subtle approach favored by countries in Europe and Asia (see, for example, Tung, 1988). But in fast-growing high-technology products and services, the negotiations often involve younger people whose exposure to global TV programs, fellow students, and the Internet have made them less sensitive about behavior that to some of their older compatriots may seem outrageous (Francis, 1991).

Foreign entry negotiations represent a fruitful area for academic research, partly because mock negotiations can be staged in a controlled setting, and strong hypotheses can be scientifically tested. A good example is the excellent article by Graham et al. (1994), demonstrating the limits of the typical American negotiation approach (in particular, the tendency to 'get down to business quickly,' and to focus on 'what's in it for me?') in other countries.

Local Marketing Abroad

General Overview

In contrast to foreign entry studies, local marketing studies fall squarely in the domain of marketing. In fact, many academic researchers who view 'international' marketing simply as marketing under different constraints have primarily local marketing issues in mind.

Local marketing studies generally deal with the applicability of marketing principles in different countries and markets. It is fundamentally comparative, trying to assess whether consumers and competitors generally behave 'differently' in different countries. Not only are these studies empirical, they tend to be ethnocentric in the sense that they assume a home country (typically the American market) to serve as the baseline for the comparisons.

Academic research in local marketing can be broken down into three categories.

- Local Consumer Behavior. Studies dealing with consumer behavior in a country. These studies usually focus on cultural factors and local marketing research problems.
- Business-to-Business Marketing. Although of practical importance, relatively little academic research has been undertaken to track the effect of cultural influences on personal selling and relationship marketing.
- Local Marketing Environment. Studies dealing with marketing management in various environments, including institutional differences, different regulations, and 'area studies' into different ways of doing business.

Local Consumer Behavior

Culture

By necessity and logic, research into consumer behavior in a foreign country usually starts with culture. Culture focuses the discussion on the basics of the marketing effort, that of satisfying customers' wants. Those wants, if not needs, are inextricably linked to culture in the broadest sense.

The standard source for cultural analysis tends to be Hofstede's (1980) classic survey of the employees from various countries in a large multinational firm (IBM). From his large-scale factor analysis, Hofstede developed his four cultural dimensions:

1. *Individualism vs. collectivism*. In a collective society, the identity and worth of the individual is rooted in the social system, less in individual achievement (affecting decision-making speed).
2. High vs. low *power distance*. High power distance societies tend to be less egalitarian, while democratic countries exhibit low power distance (determining who makes the buying decision).
3. *Masculine vs. feminine*. Captures the degree to which a culture is dominated by assertive males rather than nurturing females (impacting innovativeness).
4. Weak vs. strong *uncertainty avoidance*. Rates nations according to the level of risk tolerance or risk aversion among the people (influencing the speed of new product acceptance).

In a later study Hofstede (1988) added a fifth dimension, *Confucianist dynamics*, to distinguish the long-term orientation among Asian people, influenced by Confucius, the Chinese philosopher, from the more short-term outlook of Western people.

Another cultural source commonly used in marketing research is the work by Hall (1976), who proposed the distinction between *high* and *low context* societies. In a high context society (such as Japan), the choice and meaning of words differ depending on the context. In a low context society (like the USA) words will be interpreted literally.

In global marketing writings, the importance attributed to culture for buyer behavior actually varies greatly. There are those who, like Usunier (1996) in his intriguing textbook, treat culture as the dominating factor in international marketing, guiding not only customer behavior but also that of managers and competitors. Nakata and Sivakumar (1996) offer an intriguing review of cultural factors in new product development. Other researchers have studied the cultural problems with local marketing research. The book by Douglas and Craig (2000) represents an excellent survey of the many complications involved in doing marketing research in different cultures.

Most textbook approaches see culture as only one of the environmental forces which underlies buyer behavior in every country, and basically view culture as another fixed and given constraint on the global marketer's options (Kotabe & Helsen, 1998). In his book, Johansson (2000) attempts to meld two traditions by treating culture partly as a fundamental factor which affects people's values and attitudes, but also one which is manifested directly in behaviors and is changing over time.

Representative studies in local consumer behavior include the Ford et al. (1997) cross-cultural analysis of women's reactions to sex roles in advertising, and the study of information seekers in different cultures by Thorelli (1990). There are also articles testing the applicability of various theories in different countries, such as the perceived risk study across three countries by Hoover et al. (1978), and Lee and Green (1991) testing Fishbein's attitude model on Asian data. Belk (1995) gives a postmodern and humorous view of the degree to which certain cultures are likely to take to the American popular culture sweeping the world.

Among the more common studies in consumer behavior have been assessments of country-of-origin effects. The typical focus in these studies has been the perceptions, biases, and stereotypes that are associated with the product's or service's home country (as indicated by the 'made-in' label). Already by the early 1980s, Bilkey and Nes (1982) were able to do a large survey of a number of contributions in the country-of-origin area. One common replicated finding is that people seem to favor their own country's products, unless they come from a less-developed country. In one study, for example, Shimp and Sharma (1987) developed a culturally based scale measuring the degree of an individual's ethnocentricity, and used it successfully to show how consumers are inclined to downgrade foreign products.

There is also an *emotional* aspect of country-of-origin effects. A 'halo' feedback effect from the liking of a brand to over-rating it on salient perceptual attributes is not uncommon. People may feel pressured to buy (or not buy) products from a certain country. This can happen, for example, because of a media campaign ('Buy American') or because of social norms operating on the buyer. These and similar effects are reported in Papadopoulos and Heslop (1993).

With the possibility of markets becoming more homogeneous, and with many product components produced and assembled in a variety of countries (so-called 'hybrid' products), some of the country-of-origin effect diminishes (Han & Terpstra, 1988). Overall, however, the effect has proven quite resistant and robust, partly because people's identities are still strongly tied to nationality (see, for example, Keillor et al., 1996).

Business-to-Business Marketing

Global business-to-business marketing is, in a practical sense, further advanced than global consumer marketing. The reason has to do with the age-old tradition of shipping industrial goods and raw materials from exporters to importers, which naturally engenders international industrial marketing. It has to do also with what is now called relationship marketing. As foreign entry is undertaken, the middlemen in the market country become the entering firm's natural customers. The linkage between the parties, which initially may be arms-length and market-based, gradually grows from simple exchange into a stronger business-to-business relationship. This development is also natural when entry into new sourcing countries occurs. Supply chains are often international from the outset. In fact, industrial marketing is one area where the qualifiers 'international' and 'global' are arguably unnecessary.

In the past, the major contributions in business-to-business global marketing centered on *logistics*, *sales force management*, and the organization of *after-sales service* and support. Apart from the question of transfer pricing to subsidiaries, there were few articles discussing pricing issues, and promotional questions were also rarely researched. Recently, however, there are articles on customer satisfaction and purchasing managers' attitudes, including their country-of-origin perceptions (Dzever, 1999). A new research area concerns the role of the world-wide web in providing unparalleled communication between countries (Evans & King, 1999), and how the Internet's opportunities for creative marketing efforts in business-to-business relationships can be captured (Honeycutt et al., 1998).

Networks

One major research thrust in the business-to-business area is the emphasis on network linkages among buyers and sellers. As business customers become more assemblers, with outsourcing abroad replacing domestic suppliers, many multinationals become simply one central node in a larger network, even a 'virtual' corporation. The conceptualization used by researchers and the research questions asked typically involve the sociology of a network – how linkages are created, the role of personal contact, the development of trust – rather than the marketing capabilities as such (see, for example, Hakansson, 1989).

These networks of linkages between independent firms in different countries are a source of competitive advantage in local markets. Creating a strong relationship with a foreign buyer takes on a greater strategic role than a narrow focus on the particular transaction would suggest. Over time, the seller gains further understanding of the new market, expansion into related products, and access to other potential customers. In Sweden, for example, companies use these networks to compensate for their strategic weakness of a limited home market. To be strategically useful, the relationship has to involve a long-term commitment and tasks that can grow and change.

The Local Marketing Environment

Even though the same marketing principles may be applicable to any country market, special local conditions usually mandate some changes, if not in the overall strategy then at least in its implementation.

Each country presents its own particular obstacles, and the environments can be roughly subdivided by market maturity, from emerging to growth to mature markets. The demand situation is likely to differ among these three types of markets, including the relative preference for domestic over foreign products, the degree of brand loyalty, and the intensity of competition. It is in the mature markets (Western Europe, North America, Japan) that the assertion that 'international marketing' is simply 'marketing' has most validity.

One early research approach in local environment studies involved a comparative assessment of appropriate marketing strategies in different countries. An early classic was the MSI comparative study of foreign markets by Liander et al. (1967).

More country-specific, the laws and regulations governing price maintenance and in-store promotions, the lack of available advertising media and weak infrastructure, or language and religious differences are just a few of the factors which might place constraints on the local marketing effort. In implementation, even a standardized strategy has to be 'localized.'

Multidomestic markets

Across local markets where customer preferences are different, the so-called 'multidomestic' markets (Kashani, 1992), the localization effort needs to be extended to true adaptation. The difference between localization and adaptation is a matter of degree, but localization can be defined as changes which are necessary for a product or service to function in the local environment, while adaptations are changes which aim to re-position the offering closer to market preferences.

Market Life Cycle

The relationship between emerging market evolution and the growth path of mature markets is not very well researched or understood yet. Entering an emerging market with an existing product, the emphasis is necessarily on basics (usage infrastructure, channels of distribution, income and demographics, payment options). However, as the product moves up the life cycle curve and the market gradually matures, a similar maturing process is likely to happen in the local marketing environment. This is one example of the positive spillover from international marketing efforts. Partly because it is a relatively recent phenomenon, the way emerging markets evolve is still an underrepresented topic in the literature, providing a potentially rewarding area for future research.

Area Studies

A good part of the research in local marketing involves what in academe is usually called 'area studies.' This type of research focuses on a country or region, and presents an in-depth description of some salient features of the area. Although this kind of research is mainly published in trade journals and books, rarely in academic journals, there are contributions which legitimately claim a place in academic publications.

Many of these publications deal with new developments, such as the European integrated market, the opening of markets in communist countries, and the surge in Asia. Pan-European examples include Dalgic (1992) and Halliburton and Jones (1994). Ambler et al. (1999) deal with the role of guanxi (roughly 'personal obligations') in managing channels in China. A number of writers have analyzed the complex Japanese distribution structure, and how it has slowly been transformed under political pressure and new competition (Czinkota & Kotabe, 1993 present a good collection of articles).

The trade publications in area studies do offer a good introduction for prospective academic researchers. For example, anyone contemplating doing research on marketing in Asia would do well to consult the books by Lasserre and Schütte (1995) and Yip (1998).

Global Management

General Overview

In terms of truly *global* marketing management, the volume of published academic research is surprisingly thin. The managerial problems facing the typical global marketing manager revolve around coordination and control of marketing programs and campaigns across countries, and the associated allocation of resources between regions and countries. The administrative problems are obviously complex, and one would expect that academic researchers would have interesting tools to apply. But the effort is stymied at the inception for two reasons. One, there is internal dissension in many multinationals about the legitimacy of global coordination, since it almost invariably involves a certain degree of reduced autonomy for country subsidiaries. The resistance slows the implementation of a global strategy, and the critical research problems involve organizational behavior as much as pure marketing.

Two, there are difficult data problems with global marketing research. Reaching across countries to collect comparable data is a time-consuming and expensive effort, even when possible. The most common solution is to use academic colleagues at foreign institutions as co-workers and co-authors, but the organization and coordination of this network is itself a difficult managerial task. Another solution is to use one company's national subsidiaries and alliance partners, but this limits the kind of hypotheses a researcher can test. Using secondary data is easier now that databases and Internet sites are making the data increasingly accessible, but the reliability and validity are low except for very aggregate figures.

Added to these woes is also the fact that there are differences of opinion between many academics concerning the viability of globalized marketing. Consequently, academic researchers in global marketing have, from the start, one strike against them among many reviewers.

These obstacles have made some researchers into global strategies focus on the *feasibility* of global marketing. These studies emphasize the need for open two-way communication between headquarters and the country subsidiaries, and the flexibility needed to avoid making simple mistakes in odd-sounding brand names, rigid pricing policies, or promotional tools which are prohibited in some countries.

Another area of research concerns the comparative performance of global strategies versus locally adapted programs. Here the findings reflect mostly anecdotal evidence that standardization can have some cost benefits, but that the cost of coordination can become quite high, canceling the scale returns in production. This research represents an emerging area as companies begin to master the coordination problems through intranets, extranets, and the Internet. One would expect future research efforts here to show how successful implementation can be accomplished, and then proceed to more theoretical issues of how the various dimensions of global strategies play out against local competitors and culturally distinct markets.

The functional areas (pricing, product, promotion, distribution) have not been covered very much by academic research. Pricing coordination across countries and regions, a constant managerial headache in times of fluctuating exchange rates and gray trade, has been analyzed in a few articles, mainly concerned with the effects of European integration. Global advertising is, next to product standardization, the most often covered area in global marketing research. Other promotions have been given limited coverage, presumably because differing regulations make sales promotions largely a local matter. Global events and sponsorships, increasingly powerful, have drawn attention, but very little in terms of serious academic research. Distribution is similar, with a lot going on in terms of express mail, the Internet, and global logistics, but not much covered in terms of theoretical perspectives. In products and services, global branding has received a lot of scholarly attention, and here the research has managed to combine theory and empiricism well. Finally, although not strictly marketing, the important area of global sourcing has been analyzed in depth, not only by marketing scholars but also in the supply chain literature.

For ease of presentation, the global marketing research discussed will be grouped into typical marketing management categories.

- Strategy formulation. The seminal sources for globalized marketing.
- Market segmentation. The way companies can group country markets into macro-segments, and the role of micro-segments within each country.
- Product positioning. The factors that are uniquely associated with global positioning of standardized products and service.
- Product policy. The dominant question in product policy is the question of standardization versus adaptation of globally marketed products and services.
- Global services. Because of the intangibility and other aspects of services, there are unique complications when globalizing services.
- Global branding. An area that has attracted a lot of attention recently from researchers and practitioners, global branding research involves identifying the reasons and factors that make global brands 'power brands.'
- Global promotion. An area where the old meets the new: global advertising and the Internet.
- Global distribution. The 'death of distance' is not yet here, but global logistics is getting increasingly sophisticated.
- Global organization. Globalizing marketing usually involves a number of organizational changes which can make or break the program.

Strategy Formulation

Keegan's Global Strategies

In an early seminal article, Keegan (1969) suggested that there are typically four marketing alternatives to be considered when global strategies are contemplated.

The most common strategy is *product-communications extension*, simply extending the existing product line, pricing policies, advertising appeals, and promotional themes to the new countries entered. This approach naturally involves lower expenditures and is convenient, but does not always work. It fits a company such as Coca-Cola, since consumer preferences and competitive conditions for colas tend to be similar across countries (although even Coke has found it beneficial to tinker with its secret formula in different countries, such as reducing its sweetness). On the whole, though, it works best where cultural distances are small, and is a natural for a company adopting a focus (as opposed to diversification) strategy to expansion.

A second marketing alternative is *product extension – communications adaptation*. When use conditions are the same or similar as those in the domestic market but the need to be fulfilled is different, the product line can be extended but the communications must adapt. This involves repositioning a global product. The Minolta Maxxum, a leading automatic single lens reflex (SLR) camera, is a good example. The global product is identical in terms of technology and design, but the positioning varies across countries. In Japan and Europe it is a camera for serious amateurs, young adults who are interested in the technology. In the US, on the other hand, the camera's appeal is to a broader group of people, including families and older adults.

A third strategy, *product adaptation – communications extension*, can work well when use conditions change, but positioning is the same. The well-known Exxon slogan, 'Put a Tiger in Your Tank,' has worked well across the globe for many years. The gasoline itself, however, has been adapted by the use of additives to account for differences in climate, season, and performance requirements in various countries.

The fourth strategy alternative is *dual adaptation*, involving both product and communications adaptation. This case is most likely to be necessary when a diversification strategy is attempted, entering countries where use conditions and positioning requirements differ. This alternative involves higher costs and often more uncertainty as well, since cultural distance is likely to be larger and market know-how less. Benetton, the Italian apparel maker, has faced this problem in Southeast Asian markets. Because people's body proportions are not the same the world over, and because the preferred range and intensity of colors also differ, the designs have to be altered. Also, attempts to extend Benetton's politically charged European advertising has met with resistance from local retailers, whose customers are willing to buy the Italian design image but not the societal concern.

Keegan suggests a fifth strategy alternative, *product invention*, which he recommends for truly global companies. It involves developing entirely new products for the market abroad, less common as an entry strategy since it presupposes thorough knowledge of market conditions. Global companies with presence in many countries do this often. The Nissan Primera was developed for the European market, the Volkswagen Rabbit was developed for the American market (on the European Golf platform), and Procter and Gamble's Vizir detergent was developed for Europe.

Levitt's Homogeneous Markets

In 1983, over 10 years after Keegan's article, a strong argument for companies to globalize marketing without much adaptation was made by Ted Levitt. Earlier, Buzzell (1968) had suggested that marketing standardization might be profitable globally without targeting segments, because the potential losses due to mis-targeting could be recouped by scale economies. This theme was taken up again by Levitt (1983) who argued that, in addition to scale economies from fully exploiting technological advances, standardization was preferable because markets were growing more homogeneous.

Levitt argued that markets were being globalized because of two factors: *global communications* and rapid *technology diffusion*. With satellite TV broadcasts beaming the same programs all over the world and with instantaneous global telecommunications, the world will supposedly move inexorably toward greater homogeneity of markets. At the same time, the increasing speed of technological innovation and diffusion makes today's products soon outdated by the onslaught from global competitors able to incorporate the latest product inventions. The joint effect of these two forces makes a global product or brand not only a potent competitor but the preferred alternative.

Against Globalization Levitt's point of view generated a controversy and induced rebuttals from a few marketing academics as well as practitioners (e.g., Douglas & Wind, 1987). The basic counterargument was that granted that these forces are at work, the world's markets were as yet far from homogeneous. Many domestic producers were still marketing competitive products that could only be dislodged by even more attractive offerings tailored to local conditions and tastes. Further, the advantages of scale have become diminished with the emergence of computerized flexible manufacturing systems that can produce many different product models and versions without incurring extra costs.

One research study (Baden-Fuller & Stopford, 1991) showed how globalization failed in white goods appliances, precisely the example used by Levitt (1983) to argue for globalization. The study analyzed the performance of regional and national competitors in the domestic appliance industry in Europe. The reasons were several. First, the predicted convergence of tastes failed to materialize. Tastes did change in the various countries but not toward the same standard. For example, in the 1960s the British preferred top-loading washing machines, while the French demanded front-loaders. By the 1980s the preferences had changed in both countries but, curiously enough, in opposite directions. The researchers are at a loss to explain this development, except to blame it on the traditional rivalry between the two countries!

In another test of Levitt's globalization argument, Boddewyn et al. (1986) demonstrated empirically that there was at least some truth to the assertion that markets were becoming more homogeneous. The early failures of marketing globalization – the Parker Pen fiasco, the ill-fated global Ford Fiesta, the Polaroid SX-70 camera – were seen as due to heavy-handed implementation rather than failure of policy.

One might hypothesize that the spillover from the events at the end of the 1990s – the global financial crisis, the setbacks of large multinationals such as Coca Cola in soft-drinks, Whirlpool in appliances, and Nissan in automobiles – would lead to increased power for local and domestic products and services. So far this has not been borne out in published studies. Globally recognized brands, for example, have continued as 'power brands,' although as Yavas et al. (1992) suggest, they have to be 'locally responsive.'

Perhaps fittingly, at the start of the new millennium, the watchword seems to be 'global localization.' Most writers seem to favor this 'middle-of-the-road' solution, a contingency theory of globalization. Yip (1992) discusses the industrial preconditions favoring a global strategy. In an award winning article, Solberg (1997) integrated several global strategy propositions into a general framework for choosing marketing strategies, contingent on the level of industry globality and the firm's preparedness for standardization.

Global Market Segmentation

One of the first contributions to global market segmentation was by Wind and Douglas (1972) who introduced the concepts of macro- and micro-segmentation. The macro-segmentation process involves the identification and selection of groups of similar countries into 'macro' segments. The basis for the grouping consists of basic demographic, cultural and economic variables. The similarity among the countries in a macro-segment ensures that the fundamentals for product and service standardization are met. The global marketer can then choose between macro-segments, picking those where the firm's specific advantages can be put to best use (for a good discussion of the robustness of this process, see Shocker's treatment of market segmentation, this Handbook).

The micro-segments resemble those customarily identified in domestic-only marketing. Within each of the countries in a macro-segment there are likely to be micro-segments with a high degree of similarity, and these can be targeted using a homogeneous marketing strategy (see, for example, Hofstede et al., 1999). The two-step procedure ensures that both the underlying drivers of behavior and the specific buying criteria for the product or service are accounted for.

Country Clusters

To identify macro-segments of countries, it is possible to use computerized techniques such as cluster analysis. Clustering maps show a picture of which countries are similar and which are far apart. To incorporate more than two criteria at a time, it is common to do an initial factor analysis before clustering the countries. The factor analysis helps combine all the criteria into a manageable few dimensions, although at the price of making interpretation of the dimensions less clear. Cavusgil (1990) provides a good illustration of the approach.

The use of broad economic indicators in macro-segmentation has been challenged by marketers who argue that these indicators are too general to be really predictive of buyer behavior and market response. In an effort to test the predictive ability of the country groupings based on broad economic, social, and political criteria, one study examined the new product diffusion pattern for three products (color TVs, VCRs, and CD-players) in different country clusters (Helsen et al., 1993). If the clusters are useful, one would expect the new product rate of penetration to be similar for the countries in a cluster, and different across clusters. The study found little evidence of this. The new product diffusion patterns varied within clusters, and some countries from different clusters showed similar patterns. The study concluded with a caution, however. The clusters can still be useful in other ways. In particular, echoing other studies, the authors suggest that clusters of countries can be useful to gain scale economies in the execution of marketing research, uniformity of packaging, simplifying logistics, and similar promotions. Overall, managerial judgment is necessary to fully evaluate the benefits of these broadly defined clusters.

Diversification vs. Focus

The clustering approach to macro-segmentation leads generally to the identification of similar markets. However, in developing a global strategy, some companies make a conscious effort to be a player in different markets. This is done in order to balance market countries so that the international 'portfolio' of countries provides diversification protection against the risk of large losses. This has become increasingly important with the global financial turmoil spreading quickly through tightly integrated markets.

Examples of diversification strategies are common. Volvo, the Swedish car maker, limited its US market involvement to 25% of total output for many years. In personal interviews with top management, Toyota executives have been reported as feeling uneasy when their exports take more than 50% of their home market demand. However, even though there may be strong diversification benefits from entering several markets or regions, a case can be made for focusing on a few similar markets in the same cluster. These markets can be given more attention and market positions fortified. Since the countries are relatively similar, spillover effects can be shared more easily. Product lines can be the same. Good advertising copy is more likely to play well in a similar country. How should a company strike a balance between diversifying and possibly overextending itself, versus being too dependent on a few single markets?

In a classic article, Ayal and Zif (1979) attempted to answer that question. Using theoretical arguments, they argued that high-growth markets require more marketing support for a brand, and a focused strategy tends to be desirable. On the other hand, instability and competitive rivalry in the market increase the benefits of diversification. When decisions have to be custom-tailored to the local market, there is greater need for focus. If the markets respond strongly to an increase in expenditures (the sales response curve shows a region of increasing returns), it will pay to focus and spend more, since every dollar spent brings in increasingly more sales.

Empirical research has shown that, generally, diversified strategies tend to lead to greater sales abroad, while concentrated or focused strategies tend to result in somewhat higher profitability (Lee, 1987; Piercy, 1982). One prime determinant of profitability is whether the firm can identify and track cost effectiveness, something which is easier in focused strategies. In firms aiming for diversification, sales objectives and market orientation tend to be more important than costs, leading to greater sales.

Micro-segmentation

One implication of Buzzell's and Levitt's standardization propositions is that there is little if any need for macro-segmentation. Global segmentation becomes virtually synonymous with domestic-only segmentation. Nationality and borders can be ignored. The usual criteria – demographics, benefits sought, or lifestyle – are dominant. Teenagers all over the world are similar.

This line of reasoning was refined by Takeuchi and Porter (1986), who suggested that perceived benefits may vary across countries, so that the same offering may be purchased for different reasons in different countries. This led to the notion that a standardized product or service may end up targeting different segments in different countries. This proposition has been empirically tested and confirmed. For example, Du Preez et al. (1994) demonstrated this effect for the case of automobiles in Korea, Spain, and France.

To explain the success of standardized products and brands, one argument is that the segments will crystallize only after the product is made available. In other words, the target segment has not formed (in fact does not exist) before the product is introduced, and thus one should not try to adapt to the market. The success of new technology products where pre-launch customer reaction was negative (H-P's hand-held calculator, Sony's Walkman, Toshiba's lap-top computer) has helped reinforce the notion that preferences and thus segments are created by the marketplace, making it of no use to attempt to actually identify segments *a priori*. This line of reasoning was taken to new heights by Hamel and Prahalad (1991), with the advice that rather than trying to hit a bull's-eye it was better to try to shoot many arrows at a target hoping that at least one will hit the mark. Use a shotgun, not a rifle! Needless to say, given these disagreements, global segmentation is an area waiting for more research to be done.

Global Product Positioning

The amount of academic research on global product or service positioning is very limited. In practice, of course, positioning always 'happens,' whether by deliberate policy or by default. For example, standardized offerings become positioned somehow everywhere, although, as Takeuchi and Porter (1986) point out, perhaps differently in different countries. But there is little research on global positioning as such.

The research questions in global positioning involve, for example, analyses of how consumers perceive domestic versus foreign brands, how new entrants from abroad affect an existing product space, and the extent to which global power brands stretch the space, add new dimensions, and/or shift preferences. In one example, Nebenzahl and Jaffe (1993) discuss how country-of-origin effects can shift preferences and thus demand.

These are mainly empirical questions, of course, but have clearly more fundamental counterparts. For example, what is the role of 'familiarity' with products or brands in the perceptions? One would expect less familiarity to lead to a downward bias in perceptions. Is there a NIH (not invented here) bias? If so, past favorites, including domestic brands, might be awarded an upward bias when foreign makes enter. How do people reconfigure the perceptual space from the 'shock' of new entries in a previously closed market? Does 'pent-up demand' mean that the established product space maps have already incorporated the previously unavailable products? And so on. Educated conjectures about these and similar phenomena can be made on the basis of existing studies of product positioning and perceptual processes, but these conjectures need more testing.

One international positioning article by Johansson and Thorelli (1985) focuses on how perceptions of car makes are influenced by country-of-origin cues. Not surprisingly, the authors discover a perceptual bias in the direction of the stereotypes of a country's products. For example, Japanese cars may not be quite as fuel efficient as people think, German cars not quite as outstanding technologically as many expect, and American cars not quite as bad as some would say. The authors emphasize that these findings are product and country specific. It is possible, for example, that perceptual country-of-origin biases decrease as manufacturing technology gets diffused globally (so that high quality can be produced in many places), and also decrease if a country displays variable quality (so that the country-of-origin signal is 'noisy').

Over time, as global competition intensifies and objectively the products become more comparable, many of these misperceptions are likely to be corrected. Still they may linger on for some time, rewarding or penalizing a country's companies accordingly.

Global Product Policies

Research on the global product policies of multinationals tends to focus on the standardization issue. Several important contributions have appeared since the early Buzzell (1968) and Levitt (1983) articles discussed above.

Performance Effects

Tying level of product or service standardization to performance has been the subject of recent studies. In a carefully executed large-scale study, Samiee and Roth (1992) examined the financial performance differences among standardizing and not standardizing firms in 12 global industries. One would expect that in a global industry, firms that standardize product and services would perform better than those that do not standardize, but the authors found this not to be the case. Standardizing firms showed significant differences in strategy components and perceptions, but not a superior financial performance. The authors attribute the lack of significant differences to implementation problems and industry-specific omitted variables, including competitive intensity in the industry.

These results were confirmed in another broad industry study by Carpano and Chrisman (1995). Using a contingency framework, this article employs the match between the international product strategy and the international market served as the driver of performance. A good match for a standardized product is one where demand is homogeneous across markets. The authors find no evidence of higher financial performance for firms with a superior match. On the other hand, when performance is measured in terms of sales growth, the matching level does affect performance positively.

Most studies so far suggest that standardization of products or services can have positive benefits on the top line items of revenues and market share, but that the impact on the bottom line (return on investments, return on assets, profits) is still uncertain. This is quite paradoxical, since the general argument is that standardized products may miss local targets, but be counterbalanced by lower costs. Thus, one would expect revenues to slow down, while the bottom line would rise as costs are lowered. More research is clearly needed here.

Product Line

It is well known that, in practice, most companies offer slightly different product lines in different markets, a tactic that helps target local tastes and also makes gray trade more difficult. For example, camera companies tend to have slightly different feature combinations in different regional markets, making it easier to spot models sold through unauthorized outlets. Little or no theory-oriented research has been done in the area of parallel distribution, but the phenomenon has been extensively documented in newspaper accounts and special reports (for a good normative discussion, see Cavusgil & Sikora, 1988).

New Products

In the area of new product development, there are several contributions which touch on global products. Graber (1996) comes closest, describing the approach used by Black & Decker to develop global products, including the use of a Worldwide Household Board. Although not specifically focused on global products, Song & Parry (1997) present an in-depth analysis of how new product development practices differ between the US and Japan. Lynn & Gelb (1996) spell out a method for the identification of innovative country market segments which can be targets for a new technical product. Johansson and Nonaka (1996: 118–20) explain how Nissan developed the Primera car for the EU market.

The general thrust of these descriptions is the need for adaptation of the new product to market preferences. The issue of the extent to which preferences can be ignored in favor of a standardized version is typically not faced head-on. Rather, as in the Black & Decker case cited above, the standardized global product is one which serves a global need and where the benefits are similar across markets, making the standardized product in fact well adapted to the markets. There is obviously room for the study of the tradeoffs made by consumers when facing a standardized brand and having the option of picking a local (well-targeted) product instead. Kotabe & Helsen (1998: Chapter 11) show a hypothetical use of conjoint analysis for this evaluation.

Research on the global diffusion of innovative new products is another area which has received considerable attention. Typically adapting the Bass model to diffusion across borders, the research has been successful at tracking and predicting the penetration of durable goods in foreign markets. An early contribution is Lindberg (1982), followed by Gatignon et al. (1989) and Takada & Jain (1991).

Global Services

Global services might seem a relatively recent phenomenon, but that is mainly because international trade in services is not a very tangible activity (in personal services, for example, 'exports' might involve sending a representative abroad). Also, many services do not fall under the aegis of the WTO, despite vigorous US efforts during the last negotiation round. But the franchising of hotels, fast food chains, and apparel retailers has been common for quite a long time, as has the global reach of banks, advertising agencies, and engineering firms. More recently, lawyers, accountants, management consultants, and other professional groups have also developed global ambitions.

To some extent, academic researchers in the past tended to treat services as similar to products (by, for example, defining products as 'embodied' services). This approach might still make sense in the case where the issue is after-sales service – the service offered after a product has been sold. But in recent years free-standing services have come to be seen as quite distinct from products, something which has also affected global service expansion (Erramilli & Rao, 1993). Intangibility, reliance on functioning infrastructure, the personal content making replication difficult, differences in national regulations, even culturally contingent expectations of what constitutes good service, are some of the factors that have made services unlikely global candidates.

The key to the recent expansion is the recognition that in services standardization of key features is a pre-requisite for global expansion. Franchising has shown how it can be done. And deregulation has opened up foreign markets to a much greater degree than before.

The feasibility of globalizing a service business depends on three conditions unique to services: life cycle, infrastructure, and localization.

Life Cycle

As with the product life cycle, the development over time of a business service follows a cycle from birth, through growth and maturity, to decline. In the typical marketing illustration, the product life cycle follows an S-curve, with the growth period corresponding to the point where the S has its steepest ascent. This is when a new product is often introduced in foreign markets to capture first-mover advantages. However, for services, it is in the maturity stage that the potential for global expansion of the service concept is the highest.

In the early and growth stages of the cycle, the 'production process' employed by the service company is often still under development. The concept is still being created. In maturity, the soft- and hardware ingredients in the service have been fully developed, and the standardization of key components and features takes place. It is this standardization – whether it be in advertising, medical care, fast-food restaurants, accounting, or hotels – which is the basis for global expansion of the service (Normann, 1984). Firm-specific advantages in services are often in innovative standardization – from McDonald's strict procedures for cleanliness and friendliness, to the Hilton Hotels' training of how to greet guests, to Amazon.com's one-click payment procedure.

Infrastructure

The global applicability of a service depends on whether the infrastructure through which the service is offered exists in foreign markets. In brokerage firms, for example, a very sophisticated service concept, that works very well under a certain type of regulatory and economic environment, might lose all relevance when the financial regulations and/or the institutional members change character. The buying and selling of call and put options or other derivatives, for example, is not feasible where there is no futures market.

Localization

Another important inhibitor of services exporting is that many service systems exist as ingenious solutions to very special problems faced in the home country. The typical supermarket in the US developed partly as a response to the growing availability of automobiles and parking lot space in many suburban areas of the nation. Similar idiosyncratic factors determine the specific shape of the service organizations found in many countries. This helps explain, for example, why Japanese service firms have been very slow in globalizing.

Since the 'production' of the service is typically inseparable from the distribution of the service, foreign direct investment is usually needed to transfer the complete service delivery system. In particular, if the competitive advantages are lodged in augmented personal service, to globalize without the loss of these advantages one needs to train the personnel delivering the service as well. Globalizing this type of service becomes tantamount to establishing a whole separate 'production' unit in the market country – a stark contrast to exporting a physical good.

Fast-Food Franchising

To show the research potential in global services it is useful to examine two in more depth: global fast food, for its amazing success; and professional services, for their unlikely globalization.

The franchising of fast-food restaurants has witnessed an unprecedented growth in the last two decades. The brand names McDonald's, Kentucky Fried Chicken, Dunkin' Donuts, Wendy's, and others are well known the world over. How and why have these 'exports' proven so viable?

The basic and necessary first step in franchising abroad is analogous to that of developing any geographically dispersed franchise organization (McIntyre & Huszagh, 1995). The core service features of the service system and the firm's specific advantages have to be identified and then formulations developed that travel well. These features will form the basic building blocks for the system as exported. In the case of a company like McDonald's it consists not only of the cooking method and serving procedure, but also of the training of the workers, their attire and attitude, and the management and bookkeeping system.

Successful fast-food franchising firms provide a lot of preplanning tools to help the prospective local investor. These include analyses of key factors in choice of location (traffic patterns, competition and synergy from similar outlets, offices versus residential), checklists of positive and negative attraction factors in the market area (population mix, income levels, age and family size), and building advice (size, layout, construction materials).

Professional Services

Despite the presence of domestic regulations that typically require local certification (and thus effectively block foreign entry), professional services have recently expanded in step with the expansion of global firms. A gradual move toward making regulations more homogeneous has also played a role. In the EU region, for example, certification of lawyers and doctors in one member country is recognized in other EU countries as well. As accounting standards converge, large Western firms, such as Arthur Andersen and Price Waterhouse, are also going global. Their main customers are still multinationals from their own countries, but even this is changing. Large European firms such as Siemens and BMW retain American accountants, and Japanese firms such as Canon and Sony are now clients of the Tokyo offices of American accounting firms.

The global expansion of professional services has been facilitated by the increased sophistication in creating strategic alliances. Traditionally, professional services went global through the establishment of local branch offices managed by expatriates, who would come and spend a few years as the country head. The system worked, but always made the branch office subservient to headquarters – not a useful arrangement to attract the best local professionals. Today, firms often expand through the use of looser affiliations such as strategic alliances with local firms, allowing the local firm to keep much of its identity – and the fees. Even though sometimes this makes the service offered to global customers uneven in quality, the client is served in name by the same firm everywhere. The result is a lower-cost global reach for the main office, and a motivated local force in the field.

For the many industry-specific regulations affecting international trade in many service sectors, there are a number of articles analyzing the regulatory constraints in different countries. For example, Sambharay and Phatak (1990) offer a comprehensive review of restrictions on international data transfers and their impact on multinational operations. The more strategic requirements for successful service expansion abroad began to be outlined by Normann (1984). Later, Erramili and Rao (1993) presented an empirically based transaction-cost analysis of service firms' entry modes into foreign markets. Lovelock and Yip (1996) further developed the strategic options available to global service firms. The role of after-sales services in international marketing was analyzed by Asugman et al. (1997). Measuring firm-level export performance in services, and how the measures should differ from performance measures for products, was discussed by White et al. (1998). Most recently, Song et al. (1999) studied the first-mover advantages of global service firms from Japan and the US, finding pioneering advantages of service firms smaller than those of manufacturing firms.

Research into global services is clearly only at the starting point. The next step will be to extend the current conceptual models in service marketing to the global arena, for example by identifying Bitner's (1992) 'service-scapes' as experienced by customers in different countries. The Aubert-Gamet and Cova (1999) contribution is a very promising first step in this direction.

Global Branding

One of the most fertile but still largely unexplored developments in global marketing is global branding. It is, of course, a natural outgrowth of the voluminous 1990s research on brand equity. A unique brand name and logo are for most global companies a major standardized feature of their marketing strategy. Still, much of traditional branding research typically acknowledges the global character of powerful brands only implicitly. Truly global brand research takes the global dimensions of well-known brands explicitly into account.

International branding research has actually a rather long and, to some extent, illustrious history. The list of mistakes made by marketers attempting to standardize brand names whose meaning in a different language is misleading, comical, or otherwise an affront to local sensibilities is long (Ricks, 1993). Rosen et al. (1989) show that while of American consumer brands more than half (66%) are used identically abroad, the majority of sales (80%) come from the home market. More recent research, however, suggests that there are important scale returns associated with a unified brand identity across the globe.

Two large brand research firms, US-based Landor and Interbrand in London, have developed brand equity ratings for many of the world's brands. The global reach of the brands figure prominently in the ratings. Interbrand's criteria are illuminating in this respect. Four dimensions are used to score each brand. First, its 'Dominance,' mainly in terms of market share; second the brand 'Stretch,' suggesting a capability of brand extensions into new products and markets. A third dimension is 'Franchise,' which indicates the degree to which a brand can cross social, cultural, and national boundaries. Fourth is 'Commitment,' the degree to which the brand has managed to develop a followership among its customers, usually on the basis of shared values. The globality of the brand logically enters into all four of these dimensions, and it is hardly surprising to find that the top 'power' brands are those with global presence. The empirical validity of these measures, in particular the extent to which these dimensions are universally applicable, is still an unresolved issue, and a fruitful area for further investigation.

The shift toward brand equity has led to a conception of brands as one of the major assets of large multinationals. Growing that asset has become a major preoccupation of marketing managers (Douglas et al., 2001). Consequently, recent research into global brands has come to focus on the implementation and management of global branding strategies, rather than the value of those strategies as such. This research is still in its emerging stages, although promising efforts have been made. Kapferer's updated publication (1997) is focused more on how to globalize a brand portfolio, and Brandt & Johnson (1997) discuss global branding strategies in high technology firms.

Articles and books on international branding include a significant number from European-based authors, possibly because of the new pan-European branding possibilities (Gad, 2001; Macrae, 1996). By contrast, a striking majority of US contributions are focused on the domestic market. For example, while Keller's (1998) textbook does discuss the international dimension, and Aaker and Joachimsthaler's 2000 book, *Brand Leadership*, covers global branding strategies, in both cases the content is fitted into one single chapter.

The basic thrust of these managerially oriented efforts is the advice to balance global uniformity against local sensitivity – the classic Doz and Prahalad paradigm. That is, the more-or-less implicit assumption is that there has to be local sensitivity coupled with global power. How this balance is to be struck is not easy to discern, depending as it is on the specific product and country involved. Nevertheless, it seems the global branding is easier for technology-based products. Strikingly, with the exception of Kapferer (1997), very little attention and systematic research have so far been given to the local customer reaction to a global brand entry. Kapferer is strong on identifying possible negative or positive reactions, but his work is still mainly concerned with solutions to managerial problems, not underlying behavioral mechanisms.

Research on country-of-origin cues by Tse and Gorn (1993) has shown how a brand can have a definite national identity despite being produced elsewhere. In particular, this is the case for brands whose country-of-origin is well established – planned or not, their positioning always involves a nationality cue. For example, a Sony television set made in the US is apparently still 'Japanese' to many consumers. Coca-Cola soft-drinks and Levi jeans are typically 'American' wherever produced and sold, eliciting either favor or rejection depending upon time and place.

There is still a lot of fruitful research to be done on global branding. One question revolves around the way customer perceptions are affected by the globality of a brand. The opinions here differ among observers. Some argue that the customer will not care about the globality itself, always seeing the purchase as a local phenomenon. The typical anecdotal evidence includes the youngster from Hong Kong who, when on a US vacation with his family, exclaims 'They got McDonald's here too!' On the other side of the argument is the notion that in many markets the global brand possesses a cachet that local brands lack. This does not only happen in previously closed, emerging markets with their pent-up demand, but even in a market such as the US, where previously ethnocentric customers now allow themselves the luxury of finally enjoying world-leading cellular phone makes, foreign beers, and soccer. As Alden et al. (1999) find in a path-breaking article, it is possible to target an emerging global consumer culture with a global advertising message, where the globality of the brand does enter into the buyer's evaluative criteria. Of course, with the recent rise of a very visible anti-globalization movement, the fact that a brand is global might actually deter consumers (see Klein, 2000).

Global Pricing

Global pricing, whether it be the same price everywhere, perhaps adjusted for differences in costs, or pricing according to different demand elasticities in different countries, is conceptually simple. However, in practice most firms find it an unsolvable puzzle, and even academics have trouble developing transparent and justifiable procedures. Typically, a pricing text such as Nagle and Holden (1995) does not cover global pricing problems, and Royal and Lucas (1995) refer to global pricing as a 'hazard.'

One problem is that different countries have different regulations concerning the extent to which manufacturers and/or middlemen can control the prices facing the customer. This is true also for what rebates and discounts are legally permitted. Another complication is that with fluctuating exchange rates the typical multinational cannot easily coordinate prices across national subsidiaries for which costs and demand can vary greatly. Transfer pricing, used to charge subsidiaries for components and finished products, also needs to take into account differences in tax structures between countries and also potential dumping charges. Then there is the very real threat of gray trade: customers (and middlemen) shopping across countries for lower prices and arbitraging on exchange rate shifts. Universal credit cards and the Internet have made it possible for almost anyone to 'buy elsewhere.'

Before the lowering of trade barriers, and when exchange rates were fixed (before the 1970s), it was possible to use a polycentric pricing approach, essentially pricing products based on costs and demand characteristics for each country separately. The global problem was limited to optimizing transfer pricing, and academic researchers studying the problem involved mostly operations researchers (see, for example, the excellent discussion in Rutenberg, 1982: Chapter 5).

As markets opened up and foreign competitors could enter freely from abroad, scale advantages of large plants could be leveraged and prices abroad could be cut. With the discovery of the experience curve effect, prices in new markets could even be cut below home country prices, despite transportation costs. A good reference to this phase is Dolan and Jeuland (1981). Not surprisingly, the result for many entrants was accusations of dumping, and a number of legal proceedings took place as wounded firms claimed injury from dumping foreigners (Nagle & Holden, 1995: Chapter 14, offer a good overview of the legal briefs emerging from these skirmishes).

The central problem in global pricing – that of coordinating prices across countries and regions – has been tackled directly mainly in a few contributions emanating out of Germany. This is perhaps not surprising considering the increased harmonization of EU regulations and Germany's preeminence in potential gray trade categories such as autos, chemicals, and pharmaceuticals. Simon (1995) developed the concept of pricing 'corridors,' limited ranges within which national subsidiaries could vary prices with impunity. The limits allow both for adjustments to local demand conditions and to fluctuating exchange rates. The autonomy of the local subsidiary is not threatened directly, and gray trade opportunities can be held down. The exact width of the corridors depends on a number of contingent factors, and can vary between countries depending upon geographical distances and transportation costs, as well as each country's internal market.

Two other German contributions come from Assmus and Wiese (1995) and Bacher et al. (1997). The latter discuss the problem of identifying the actual level of the common price across the EU countries. They point out the adjustments that need to be made in order to make the common price attractive in each local market, such as selecting psychological price points. Assmus and Wiese deal with the implementation of a coordinated price pattern across a company's national subsidiaries, and use empirical case evidence to develop alternative implementation procedures. They show how the choice between various global pricing approaches is affected by many factors, and two in particular: level of marketing standardization, and strength of local resources.

When marketing standardization is high, target segments and the elements of the marketing mix are known well-enough for headquarters to help set local prices.

If local resources are strong, economic controls tend to be preferable, since raising and lowering transfer prices or rationing will send clear signals to local representatives without imposing final prices. But if local resources are weak, centralization of the pricing decisions may be necessary, creating limits beyond which prices may not deviate.

In the low standardization case, when marketing is multidomestic in orientation, with locally adapted mix elements, headquarters' role will be less directive. Local managers are likely to be better informed about local conditions than headquarters.

When local representatives are less resourceful, formalization of procedures can be helpful in ensuring that the appropriate factors are taken into account when local prices are set. However, with strong local resources, informal coordination is likely to be preferable, preserving local autonomy, but still using a stick if the carrot is not enough.

There are many global pricing questions left to explore. In terms of normative research, a hedging model against currency fluctuations might be used to identify the currency in which the common price should be quoted. But the models have to be extended to incorporate the use of credit cards by consumers, as the introduction of the Euro currency has demonstrated. Also, the optimal level for a common price is not easy to calculate. As Bacher et al. (1997) indicate, the price will have to come closer to the competitive level in the leading countries, in all probability lowering the average prices. This normative suggestion can be inferred from formal models, but the prediction of lower prices to consumers should be tested against actual data.

In terms of explanatory research, the interesting issues include at least two types of questions. One concerns consumers' inclination to engage in arbitrage practices versus staying loyal to local vendors. The ease of transactions on the Internet, and the raw sales data so far, point toward a shift towards arbitrage and buying on-line, but it is not clear how long this trend will hold, or in what product and service categories it will dominate. The harvest reaped by on-line retailers seems mostly bought through loss-leading price-cuts and discounts.

Another promising area of global pricing marketing research is the extent to which the loss of local market adaptation implicit in a common price level encourages domestic and foreign entrants. *A priori* this is simply a case of evaluating the price elasticity of demand, and assessing whether the contemplated price gap might entice consumers to shift. But the counterargument is that with a completely integrated market, the price elasticities will converge into a single demand curve, and a common price will be optimal. This is one possible theoretical conjecture which could be tested against empirical evidence.

Global Promotion

In some ways, global promotion is the most developed sub-area of international marketing, not only in practice but also in terms of academic research. Even before the world's nationalized broadcast networks were opened up to competition from commercial stations and channels, and networks with global reach such as CNN appeared, advertising agencies had gone global – helping multinational manufacturers to generate brand recognition across continents. Marlboro's cowboy, Coca-Cola's red-and-white logo, and Exxon's 'Tiger in the Tank' were recognized the world over. As global communications technology developed and national control over airwaves and print media loosened, the agency networks were already in place for truly global promotions.

Media Advertising

With communication satellites, global telecommunications, and, more recently, the Internet, any one source can communicate with people all over the world (in the case of the Internet, even interactively). It quickly became clear that not only was a unique brand name and positioning desirable (a type of large-scale benefit), but so would be the cost-reductions of world campaigns. This idea received strong support from the initial success of Saatchi & Saatchi, the leading British ad agency, with its global 'Manhattan Landing' commercial for British Airways (Quelch, 1984). Others followed suit, including Maidenform with its 'Wonderbra,' Nike with Michael Jordan, and, more recently, Apple's 'Collect all five' slogan for its iMac computer. An informative description of what is involved in developing such a global ad campaign is given by Hanni et al. (1995), analyzing Goodyear's steps to develop a pan-regional Latin-American ad campaign.

To be sure, a completely standardized campaign is still not the typical strategy. Rather, companies use 'pattern standardization,' where the basic visual idea and storyboard are used, usually with unchanged slogan and brand name (Hite & Fraser, 1988). The national ads may be re-shot with local actors and settings. In this way scale advantages can be retained, while still adapting to local preferences.

The extent to which advertising can be the same across countries and regions is still a hotly contested issue. As highly touted as the successes are, failures are perhaps equally well known. Parker Pen's ill-fated excursion into uniform ads and standardized product line in the 1980s has been well-documented by Keegan (1995: 780–95). British Airways' decision to let artists from different countries paint its planes encountered a storm of British protests, led by an indignant Margaret Thatcher. The large number of blunders in translating slogans and brand names makes for enjoyable, albeit sometimes painful, reading (Ricks, 1993).

There has been a fair amount of research into the degree to which global advertising is actually practiced. The answer found by Hill and Shao (1994) for 347 branches of US ad agencies is that although two-thirds of the branches' work covered more than one country, only 10% was completely global. Similarly, Harris (1994) finds that among 38 European and US multinationals, only three practice complete standardization of advertising.

What is really needed in terms of global advertising research now is perhaps not so much what companies and agencies *are* doing, but rather what they *should* do. In particular, it would be very useful to identify factors in the marketplace and in the product or service category which favor standardization, and factors which hinder it. Different languages and perhaps cultures are obvious drawbacks, but it is not clear whether they rule out standardization entirely. What is needed is a careful analysis of the conditions under which such obvious obstacles can be overcome, and when they cannot.

E-commerce

Media advertising is, of course, only one promotional activity, and with the arrival of the Internet and one-to-one marketing perhaps it is not the most important for many products. Direct marketing, whether through on-line communications, direct mail catalogs, or telemarketing, has gone global as communication channels open up. Chat-box names on the Internet, e-mail addresses, and credit records with phone numbers have been added to the various address lists which are compiled from sales records, subscriptions, and warranties, making it increasingly possible to customize offers to individual buyers in different countries. It is not surprising if some people, inside and outside the US, find the 'American-style' one-to-one marketing efforts intrusive and a threat to privacy (Culnan, 1994). Still, with the advent of e-commerce, the upward trend is even steeper than before (Parke, 1994; Siwolop, 1998).

Academic research on global direct marketing is still relatively scant. Most of the coverage comes in industry and trade publications, with the occasional newspaper report. There are several issues that could profitably be investigated. One is the customer reaction to buying direct as compared to going to a store, for example. What considerations go into this choice, and how and when is it made – case-by-case, or as individual style? Do cultural factors play a role? Another question is the degree to which loyalty can be engendered in direct marketing, compared to what store and face-to-face relationships offer.

With the advent of e-commerce, there has been more action among marketing researchers. Still, the global aspects have not been covered extensively. Quelch and Klein (1996) were among the first to explore some of the new issues affecting international marketers, paying special attention to the cost-efficiency of on-line contacts for customer service and supplier contacts. Peterson (1997) edited a volume with contributions focused on the consumer reactions to the new electronic marketing channel. At the end of 1999 MSI sponsored a conference which focused on marketing contributions in e-commerce, but most speakers were practitioners, not academic researchers (the presentations are available on www.msi.org).

Even though publications on e-commerce marketing are now appearing at an accelerated pace, so far relatively little attention is paid to the global aspects (see, for example, Allen et al., 1998). The reason is partly that many countries do not yet have the infrastructure to support global e-commerce. But things are rapidly changing, especially in Japan and Europe (see Merrill Lynch, 1999; Strassel, 1998). The greater reason seems to be the lack of attention given to national borders once global networks can be used to send data and 'digitalized' products. Seybold and Marshak's (1998) treatment of the successes of Dell's computers, Cisco's software, and American Airlines' reservation system is symptomatic. All three companies have international reach, but the analysis ignores the global dimension.

Of course, to some extent the global dimension can be ignored in these cases. The 'products' sold are basically information, and words and numbers can be easily sent abroad in digital format. High technology, either in terms of communications or in the products themselves, tends to be less culture-specific than other products or services. And most customers could be expected to know at least some English, especially the technical terms used.

But if these criteria are key, e-commerce will be limited to a relatively small percentage of the global market. For most products nationality still matters. Orders have to be executed by people who may or may not know English, shipments have to be made using other countries' middlemen, logistics costs are incurred in foreign currencies, and customs and tariff assessments have to be paid.

Since there is no limit to human ingenuity, one might expect that e-commerce will increasingly create its own solutions to some of these problems. In the meantime, however, even successful endeavors such as Amazon.com carry the burden of high inventory and shipping costs, with profitable operations still out of sight.

As seen in some of the contributions referenced above, some of the current academic research attempts to define a working business model for e-commerce. This is clearly a very worthwhile effort, especially if the global aspects are integrated into the models. For Internet businesses, global marketing is not simply a necessity but an unavoidable opportunity, presently masquerading as a problem.

Other Promotions

Sales promotion, including in-store p-o-p activities, is an area which has trouble globalizing. The problem is mainly the differences in what is permitted by law in different countries. Boddewyn's (1988) classic account might be out of date, but presents vividly the problems involved – and despite the attempts at harmonization, even in the EU, retail regulations differ considerably still. Once full deregulation comes, if ever, the focus (including academic research) can turn to the more interesting marketing questions such as the reaction of different promotional tools in different cultures. If history is any guide, protectors of people's welfare in different countries will lament the new methods, while consumers will be quick to pick up on offers that increase choices and lower prices.

A promotional area which is shaping up as an important global marketing tool is publicity, whether generated by event sponsorship or public relations. Sponsorship of sports events such as of Formula 1 racing events, championship soccer matches, and World Cup downhill racing have long been used by firms to create positive brand associations globally. But recently the list has been extended by companies that create their own events, including glamorous parties to introduce new Swatch designs, Microsoft's launch of Windows 95, and Disney's cross-marketing of a new movie. Product placement and the Internet are also used to advantage in cases such as the release of the James Bond *Golden Eye* movie featuring the new BMW Roadster. There is plenty of room for academic effect research here, evaluating the global impact, cost effectiveness, and long-term results of these tactics.

Global Distribution

The logistical aspects of distribution have been globalized to a great extent in recent years. In transportation, shipping companies have merged or developed alliances to create seamless global networks. Warehousing is now outsourced to carriers such as Federal Express and UPS. Processing at customs borders is simplified and customized for recurring items.

As Yip & Johansson (1993) show, the rest of distribution is one of the least globalized marketing functions for some multinationals. To be sure, there are some aspects of distribution that have been globalized, and one would expect more in the future. Wholesalers like SuperValu in Washington state have branched out into Russia. A few retailers are also going global. Walmart, the large drug store chain, for example, has entered Latin-America, where French Carrefour has a strong presence. The largest chain in South East Asia is Makro, a Dutch-based operation. Arrow Electronics, the largest electronic component distributor, does business around the world.

Most of the material on global distribution comes from the trade press, and documents how some firms have expanded (see, for example, Rapoport, 1995; Simmons, 1990). However, academic researchers have been very active in analyzing the interesting question of how culture affects retail structure and channel relationships and makes globalization difficult. An early example is Goldman's (1974) analysis of retailing in developing markets. Kale and McIntyre (1991) show how culture affects the degree to which personal relationships influence the channel member choices in different cultures. Alexander (1990) analyzes the degree to which the various national cultures translate into country-specific channel characteristics.

Global channel relationships present a challenging area of academic research. The different way conflicts are resolved in different countries, the global threats to established roles of various middlemen, and the potential for blocking access to channels are all topics worth investigating. From various news reports and trade press surveys one can get a sense of the extent of the problems, but it would seem important for academics to analyze the 'whys' of the difficulties, and suggest solutions based on the findings and the theories confirmed. Frazier (1999) provides a comprehensive theoretical framework which could serve as a first step in such a research effort.

Marketing Organization

Since implementation of a global marketing strategy is so crucial and so difficult, marketing organization is a key global marketing area. In the early days, the multinational company relied on the national subsidiaries to direct the local marketing effort, typically giving autonomy to the local managers. Coordinating global strategies threatens this autonomy and the local head's status.

Research has shown that if the global strategy is formulated with inputs from the local subsidiaries, the chances of locals accepting a global marketing strategy are much improved (Kim & Mauborgne, 1993). Still, as the overview of global marketing organization by Gates (1995) shows, there is still a lot of friction. Implementing global strategies is not smooth sailing, but requires a lot of personal intervention and stroking of egos (Taylor, 1992).

Some of the coordinating mechanisms have been analyzed by academic researchers. The important role of cross-national teams has been stressed by Bartlett (1983), and Yip and Madsen (1996) showed the increased significance of global accounts for serving multinational customers. Forsgren and Johanson (1992) show what management of the international network linkages between headquarters and subsidiaries involves. Homburg et al. (1997) show how the governance mechanism tends to move away from trust and toward more formal contracts as the network expands beyond the headquarter country's borders.

There are many unresolved issues which could be further analyzed by empirical research. For example, it is still not clear whether the top-down centralization implicit in globalized strategies is superior to the more dispersed transnationalism proposed by Bartlett and Ghoshal (1989) or Hedlund's (1986) decentralized 'heterarchy.' But the overriding question in the near-term future will be the effect of global communication technology. With the growth of the Internet, company 'intranets,' and the 'extranets' which tie in also suppliers, the organizational coordination parameters and problems across the globe will be completely changed – and will probably still be very acute.

Future Directions

Because of the relative newness of global marketing as a field of inquiry, most of the topics discussed here still warrant further examination. Nevertheless, there are some areas where the immediate needs are clear and future research would be particularly welcome.

Foreign Entry

Mode of entry is still a vital research area, partly because of the rise of non-equity alliance tie-ups which challenge existing theories and past assumptions. For example, the dissipation potential of licensing technology seems in practice to be less important as firms agree to share R&D efforts. Another issue is the degree of marketing control that can be exercised with various forms of entry modes.

In the internationalization research as well, past theories are coming under close scrutiny as empirical studies continue to uncover unorthodox and unsettling irregularities. The 'born globals' paradigm and the leapfrogging of intermediate steps in the degree of commitment to a foreign market contradict theories inferred from past behaviors. The learning hypothesis underlying much of the theorizing in the past would seem well-suited for extension into the new strategic emphasis on knowledge as a key asset, and one would expect this area to produce a new and richer paradigm soon.

As we have seen, exporting research continues apace, as does cross-cultural negotiation research. Both areas offer opportunities for strong academic research, and are aided by the practical importance of identifying factors relating to successful performance.

Local Marketing

In the area of local marketing, the opportunities for strong academic research are much fewer. The most promising issues revolve around culture and the effect of culture on buyer behavior. Culture has recently, in fact, become a major focus of marketing research and analysis. Here the paradoxical result of increasing ethnocentricity among peoples as globalization proceeds has played a crucial role. Apparently not everybody wants to be a citizen of the world or adopt the American way of life. Research on trust in different cultures, on the applicability of Hofstede's cultural categories, on what distinguishes national versus ethnic culture, and how these things relate to various marketing phenomena represent a growing area of inquiry, of interest to top academic journals, some outside of marketing (e.g., Blankenburg-Holm et al., 1999).

On the other hand, area studies, including the analysis of institutional differences in various markets, although important for doing marketing, tend to be less suitable for top quality academic journals. Research that uncovers differences in import tariffs, explains counter-trade options, describes what is involved in shipping abroad or finding an alliance partner is too mundane, too narrow, and too descriptive for leading academic journals. More theory development and generalizable results are required. The degree to which French consumers of packaged goods are different from American consumers is only an empirical question – why they are different requires some theorizing. With such theory, the research is publishable in top academic journals (as we have seen), especially if the countries' citizens can be conceptualized as representatives of a certain cultural or economic group.

Global Management

Somewhat surprisingly, given its relatively long history, the viability of global marketing standardization remains a vital area for further research. Proponents for global strategies point to successes, while opponents list the failures. It seems futile to attempt to settle the argument by simple empirical numbers on either side. Rather, the research has to become more fine-tuned, work with 'more or less' standardization instead of yes-no, and attempt to develop the contingencies where 'more' is better than 'less,' and conversely. The start has already been made, by, for example, Samiee and Roth (1992), but much more is needed. The key is to approach the topic from both the managerial angle, including implementation questions, and the customer angle, focusing on the malleability of attitudes engrained by traditional and less global home markets.

In the new product area, strong quantitative research on the diffusion of new products and on cross-country product development processes has helped spawn new interest for global marketing among traditional marketing researchers. These areas are likely to continue strongly well into the future, with a good record in top quality publication outlets.

In other functional areas, global pricing research is an area acutely in need of more investigation. The research involves not only the feasibility of coordinated pricing to avoid gray trade. Various policies such as skimming versus penetration, loss-leadership, and every-day low pricing need to be re-evaluated against competitive conditions and customer expectations in other markets. The whole area of so-called psychological pricing also needs to be validated against cultures in other countries.

Much research in functional areas has already helped our understanding of how theories and practices successful in one country might have to be adapted in foreign contexts. The pros and cons of global advertising, for example, have been widely debated, but, as one would expect, its success depends in a complex way on product, audience, and timing. By contrast, although the basic psychological mechanisms and social linkages through which country-of-origin effects work are fairly well established, we still know little about when and how the mechanisms and linkages are activated.

At the behavioral level, we really know very little about consumer reactions to global brands. Even though such research can be done inside any one domestic market, there has been a reluctance by mainstream researchers to face up to the global versus local dimensions. The country-of-origin literature has touched on the issue tangentially, by treating the national origin of a brand similarly to the 'made-in' label. But there is clearly more work to do in terms of identifying the meaning of a 'global' brand and measuring its impact on consumer behavior. For example, one would expect a global brand to exhibit differences from local-only brands in the meaning of its relationship to the consumer.

A firm-level area for further research is on the question of implementing global marketing strategies. The managerial difficulties of coordination have long been a drawback of globalization, relatively well documented through case studies and several systematic investigations. But with the advent of the Internet as a truly global channel of internal and external communication, as well as distribution of services and some products, implementation is likely to be much more feasible. The way companies adapt to the new medium and the diffusion of innovative new practices is clearly a promising area for firm-level studies.

Journal Publication

Global marketing outlets span a wide range of academic journals, both in terms of topics and in terms of scientific rigor (and consequently academic ranking). Compared to the more fine-tuned approaches in, say, *Journal of Marketing Research*, academic research that focuses on the broader issues facing global marketers is generally less rigorous. The driving conceptualization is typically less precise, approached at a more empirical level and with more diffuse concepts. This means the data are necessarily noisy, and construct validity is more difficult to achieve. The number of relevant variables is larger, creating a need for larger data sets to preserve degrees of freedom. At a more practical level, because data collection often involves different foreign markets, comparable data is difficult to assemble. These factors help explain why there are relatively so few articles in the leading marketing journals. But these things are fast changing, and likely to continue improving.

Apart from the top-tier marketing journals, the major journals in global marketing include *Journal of International Business Studies*, *Journal of International Marketing*, *International Marketing Review*, and *The European Journal of Marketing*. In these journals one can find articles on mode of entry, export expansion, local receptiveness to global brands, and global strategies. None is yet in a league with the top-tier marketing journals, but they are all on the upswing, especially the *Journal of International Business Studies*, which is closing in on the leaders.

In addition to marketing journals, studies of globalized marketing strategies have a natural home in the *Strategic Management Journal*. Checking the Table of Contents in *SMJ* during the last few years, however, relatively few articles on global marketing can be found. The reason is mainly, again, problems with noisy data, spanning several industries and product categories (as is natural since the unit of analysis is typically the firm). These studies are consequently often case-based, making positive reviews less likely. But again, things are changing as marketing researchers become increasingly sophisticated. The award for the most seminal *SMJ* article in a decade to Lieberman and Montgomery (1988), although not strictly in the global marketing area, undoubtedly helps global marketing studies as well.

For a specific area such as services, there are specialized journals (*The Services Industries Journal*, *The International Journal of Service Industries*), with a majority of articles covering international aspects. This is a logical development, just as production journals today are inherently international, and given that services happen to fall most naturally in the marketing functional area. By the same token, business-to-business marketing journals (such as *Journal of Industrial Marketing* and *Industrial Marketing Management*) also provide outlets for many articles with an international flavor.

Overall, the future for academic research in global marketing looks very bright. The reason is that as more research is done, the conceptualizations are getting more carefully articulated, the methodology used is becoming more rigorous, and the data quality is improving. Consequently, articles do stand a good chance of publication in the best marketing and economics journals. For example, the more theoretical articles in foreign entry – mode of entry models, transaction cost analysis of the distribution channel – are already appearing in top journals, as we have seen. Marketing research that analyzes local customers as representatives of general cultural groupings, rather than countries as such, offer more general and valid findings than studies which simply report national differences. Already country-of-origin studies, one of the more popular sub-areas of culture-based marketing, do appear in top journals. So do the more rigorous studies in the new product diffusion and innovation areas. Global branding studies are likely to follow. And so on.

Of course, more rigor comes at a price: the subject matter tends to be more narrowly defined, limiting the external impact of the results. Not surprisingly, the studies have been criticized by other global marketers as being of limited relevance and value in the bigger picture of global marketing strategy. The critique is not only understandable, it is also healthy. When it comes to global marketing research it is necessary to strike a balance between internal rigor and external impact. It is sometimes better to be 'vaguely right' than 'precisely wrong' – even in academic research.

References

Aaby, Nils-Erik & Slater, Stan F. (1989) Management influences on export performance: a review of the empirical literature 1978–88. *International Marketing Review*, 6, Fall, 7–26.

Aaker, David A. & Joachimsthaler, Erich (2000) *Brand Leadership*. New York: The Free Press.

Alden, Dana L., Steenkamp, Jan-Benedict E.M. & Batra, Rajeev (1999) Brand positioning through advertising in

Asia, North America and Europe: the role of global consumer culture. *Journal of Marketing*, 63, Jan, 75–87.

Alexander, Nicholas (1990) Retailers and international markets. *International Marketing Review*, 7, 4, 75–85.

Allen, Cliff, Kania, Deborah & Yaeckel, Beth (1998) *Internet World: Guide to One-to-One Web Marketing*. New York: John Wiley and Sons.

Ambler, T., Styles, C. & Wang, X. (1999) The effect of channel relationships and guanxi on the performance of inter-province export ventures in the People's Republic of China. *International Journal of Research in Marketing*, 16, 1 (Feb), 75–88.

Anderson, Erin & Coughlan, Anne T. (1987) International market entry and expansion via independent or integrated channels of distribution. *Journal of Marketing*, 51, Jan, 71–82.

Anderson, Erin & Gatignon, Hubert (1986) Modes of foreign entry: a transaction cost analysis and propositions. *Journal of International Business Studies*, 3, 1–26.

Armstrong, J. Scott (1970) An application of econometric models to international marketing. *Journal of Marketing Research*, 7 (May), 190–8.

Assmus, Gert & Wiese, Carsten (1995) How to address the gray market threat using price coordination. *Sloan Management Review*, 36, 3, 31–42.

Asugman, Gulden, Johnson, Jean L. & McCullough, James (1997) The role of after-sales service in international marketing. *Journal of International Marketing*, 5, 4, 11–28.

Aubert-Gamet, Veronique & Cova, Bernard (1999) Servicescapes: from modern non-places to postmodern common places. *Journal of Business Research*, 44, 1 (Jan), 37–45.

Aulukah, Preet S., Kotabe, Masaaki & Teegen, Hildy (2000) Export strategies and performance of firms from emerging economies: evidence from Brazil, Chile, and Mexico. *Academy of Management Journal*, 43, 3, 342–61.

Ayal, Igal & Zif, Jehiel (1979) Market expansion strategies in multinational marketing. *Journal of Marketing*, 43, Spring, 84–94.

Bacher, Matthias R., Heger, Thomas & Köhler, Richard (1997) Euro pricing by consumer goods manufacturers. Institut für Markt- und Distributionsforschung, Universität zu Köln.

Backhaus, Klaus, Büsschken, Joachim & Voeth, Markus (1998) *Internationales Marketing*. 2. Auflage. Stuttgart: Schäffer-Poeschel.

Baden-Fuller, Charles W.F. & Stopford, John M. (1991) Globalization frustrated: the case of white goods. *Strategic Management Journal*, 12, 493–507.

Bartlett, Christopher A. (1983) Procter & Gamble Europe: Vizir launch. Harvard Business School case no. 384-139.

Bartlett, Christopher A. & Ghoshal, Sumantra (1989) *Managing Across Borders: The Transnational Solution*. Boston: Harvard Business School Press.

Belk, Russell W. (1995) Hyperreality and globalization: culture in the age of Ronald McDonald. *Journal of International Consumer Marketing*, 8, 3/4, 23–37.

Bilkey, Warren J. & Nes, Eric (1982) Country-of-origin effects on product evaluations. *Journal of International Business Studies*, 8, 1 (Spring–Summer), 89–99.

Bitner, Mary-Jo (1992) Servicescapes: the impact of physical surroundings on customers and employees. *Journal of Marketing*, April, 57–71.

Blankenburg-Holm, Desiree, Eriksson, Kent & Johanson, Jan (1999) Creating value through mutual commitment to business network relationships. *Strategic Management Journal*, 20, 5 (May), 467–86.

Boddewyn, Jean J. (1988) *Premiums, Gifts, and Competitions*. New York: International Advertising Association.

Boddewyn, Jean J., Soehl, Robin & Picard, Jacques (1986) Standardization in international marketing: is Ted Levitt in fact right? *Business Horizons*, November–December, 69–75.

Buckley, Peter J. (1987) *The Theory of the Multinational Enterprise*. Studia Oeconomiae Negotiorum 26. Uppsala, Sweden: Acta Universitatis Upsaliensis.

Brandt, Marty & Johnson, Grant (1997) *Power Branding*. San Francisco: International Data Group.

Buzzell, Robert (1968) Can you standardize multinational marketing? *Harvard Business Review*, 46 (November–December), 98–104.

Carpano, Claudio & Chrisman, James J. (1995) Performance implications of international product strategies and the integration of marketing activities. *Journal of International Marketing*, 3, 1, 9–28.

Cavusgil, S. Tamer (1980) On the internationalization process of firms. *European Research*, 8, 6, 273–81.

——— (1990) A market-oriented clustering of countries. In *International Marketing Strategy*, 3rd edn, edited by Hans B. Thorelli & S. Tamer Cavusgil. New York: Pergamon, pp. 201–12.

Cavusgil, S. Tamer & Sikora, Ed (1988) How multinational can counter gray market imports. *Columbia Journal of World Business*, Winter, 75–85.

Cavusgil, S. Tamer & Zou, Shaomin (1994) Marketing strategy-performance relationship: an investigation of the empirical link in export market ventures. *Journal of Marketing*, 58, January, 1–21.

Culnan, Mary (1994) Privacy guidelines for the 'new' direct marketer. *Privacy and American Business*, 1, 4, 5.

Czinkota, Michael R. (1982) *Export Development Strategies: U.S. Promotion Policy*. New York: Praeger.

Czinkota, Michael R. & Kotabe, Masaaki (1993) *The Japanese Distribution System*. Chicago: Probus.

Czinkota, Michael R. & Ronkainen, Ilkka A. (1999) *International Marketing*, 5th edn. Fort Worth, TX: Harcourt Brace Jovanovich.

Dalgic, Tevfik (1992) Euromarketing: charting the map for globalization. *International Marketing Review*, 9, 5, 31–42.

Dichtl, Erwin, Köglmayr, Hans-Georg & Müller, Stefan (1990) International orientation as a precondition for export success. *Journal of International Business Studies*, 21, 1, 23–40.

Doland, Robert & Jeuland, Abel (1981) Experience curves and dynamic demand models: implications for optimal pricing strategies. *Journal of Marketing*, 45 (Winter), 52–73.

Douglas, Susan & Craig, Samuel R. (2000) *International Marketing Research*, 2nd edn. Upper Saddle River, NJ: Prentice-Hall.

Douglas, Susan & Wind, Yoram (1987) The myth of globalization. *Columbia Journal of World Business*, Winter, 1–9.

Douglas, Susan, Craig, Samuel R. & Nijssen, Edwin J. (2001) Integrating branding strategy across markets: building international brand architecture. *Journal of International Marketing*, 9, 2, 97–114.

Du Preez, Johann P., Diamantopoulos, Adamantios & Schlegelmilch, Bodo B. (1994) Product standardization and attribute saliency: a three-country empirical comparison. *Journal of International Marketing*, 2, 1, 7–28.

Dunning, John H. (1988) The eclectic paradigm of international production. *Journal of International Business Studies*, Spring, 1–31.

Dzever, S. (1999) Country-of-origin effects on purchasing agents' product perceptions: an Australian perspective. *Industrial Marketing Management*, 28, 2, 165–75.

Erramilli, M.K. & Rao, C.P. (1993) Service firms' international entry-mode choice: a modified transaction cost approach. *Journal of Marketing*, 57, 3, 19–38.

Evans, J.R. & King, V.E. (1999) Business-to-business marketing and the world wide web: planning, managing, and assessing web sites. *Industrial Marketing Management*, 28, 4, 343–58.

Ford, John B., LaTour, Michael S. & Honeycutt, Earl D. (1997) An examination of the cross-cultural female response to offensive sex role portrayals in advertising. *International Marketing Review,* 14, 6, 409–23.

Forsgren, Mats & Johanson, Jan (eds) (1992) *Managing Networks in International Business*. Philadelphia: Gordon and Breach.

Francis, June N.P. (1991) When in Rome? The effects of cultural adaptation on intercultural business negotiations. *Journal of International Business Studies*, Third Quarter, 403–28.

Frazier, Gary L. (1999) Organizing and managing channels of distribution. *Journal of The Academy of Marketing Science*, 28, Spring, 226–40.

Gad, Thomas (2001) *4-D Branding*. London: Financial Times/Prentice-Hall.

Gates, Stephen (1995) The changing global role of the marketing function: a research report. The Conference Board, report no. 1105-95-RR.

Gatignon, Hubert, Eliashberg, Jehoshua & Robertson, Thomas S. (1989) Modeling multinational diffusion patterns: an efficient methodology. *Marketing Science*, 8, Summer, 231–47.

Goldman, Arieh (1974) Outreach of consumers and the modernization of urban food retailing in developing countries. *Journal of Marketing*, 38, October, 8–16.

Graber, D.R. (1996) How to manage a global product development process. *Industrial Marketing Management*, 25, 6, 483–9.

Graham, John L., Mintu, Alma T. & Rodgers, Waymond (1994) Explorations of negotiations behaviors in ten foreign cultures using a model developed in the United States. *Management Science*, 40, 1 (January), 72–95.

Hakansson, Hakan (1989) *Corporate Technological Behaviour: Cooperation and Networks*. London: Routledge.

Hall, Edward T. (1976) *Beyond Culture*. Garden City, NY: Anchor.

Hall, Edward T. & Hall, Mildred Reed (1990) *Understanding Cultural Differences*. Yarmouth, ME: Intercultural Press.

Halliburton, Chris & Huenerberg, Reinhard (1993) Pan-European marketing – myth or reality? *Journal of International Marketing*, 1, 3, 77–92.

Halliburton, Chris & Jones, Ian (1994) Global individualism – reconciling global marketing and global manufacturing. *Journal of International Marketing*, 2, 4, 79–88.

Hamel, Gary & Prahalad, C.K. (1991) Corporate imagination and expeditionary marketing. *Harvard Business Review*, July–August, 81–92.

Han, C. Min & Terpstra, Vern (1988) Country-of-origin effects for uni-national and bi-national products. *Journal of International Business Studies*, 19, 2, 235–55.

Hanni, David A., Ryans, John K. & Vernon, Ivan R. (1995) Coordinating international advertising – the Goodyear case revisited for Latin America. *Journal of International Marketing*, 3, 2, 83–98.

Hanson, Ward (2000) *Principles of Internet Marketing*. Cincinnati, OH: South-Western College Publishing.

Harris, Greg (1994) International advertising standardization: what do the multinationals actually standardize? *Journal of International Marketing*, 2, 4, 13–30.

Hedlund, Gunnar (1986) The hypermodern MNC: a heterarchy? *Human Resource Management*, 25, 9–36.

Helsen, Kristian, Jedidi, Kamel & de Sarbo, Wayne (1993) A new approach to country segmentation utilizing multinational diffusion patterns. *Journal of Marketing*, 57, 4 (October), 60–71.

Hertz, Susanne & Mattsson, Lars-Gunnar (1998) *Mindre foretag blir internationella: Marknadsforing i natverk* (Smaller firms Go International: Marketing in a Network). Lund, Sweden: Liber Ekonomi (in Swedish).

Hill, John S. & Shao, Alan T. (1994) Agency participants in multicountry advertising: a preliminary examination of affiliate characteristics and environments. *Journal of International Marketing*, 2, 2, 29–48.

Hite, Robert E. & Fraser, Cynthia L. (1988) International advertising strategies of multinational companies. *Journal of Advertising Research*, Aug/Sept, 9–17.

Hofstede, Frenkel ter, Steenkamp, Jan-Benedict E.M. & Wedel, Michel (1999) International market segmentation based on consumer-product relations. *Journal of Marketing Research*, 36, 1 (February), 30–45.

Hofstede, Geert (1980) *Culture's Consequences*. Beverly Hills, CA: Sage.

——— (1988) The Confucius connection: from cultural roots to economic growth. *Organizational Dynamics*, 16, 4 (Spring), 5–21.

Homburg, Christian, Kiedaisch, Ingo & Cannon, Joseph P. (1997) Governance mechanisms in transnational business relationships. ZMU Working Paper No. 6, WHU-Otto Beisheim Graduate School, Koblenz, Germany.

Honeycutt, E.D. Jr., Flaherty, T.B. & Benassy, K. (1998) Marketing industrial products on the Internet. *Industrial Marketing Management*, 27, 1, 63–72.

Hoover, Robert J., Green, Robert T. & Saegert, Joel (1978) A cross national study of perceived risk. *Journal of Marketing*, 42, July, 102–8.

Johanson, Jan & Vahlne, J.E. (1977) The internationalization process of the firm – a model of knowledge development and increasing foreign market commitments. *Journal of International Business Studies*, Spring–Summer, 23–32.

Johansson, Johny K. (2000) *Global Marketing*, 2nd edn. Boston: Irwin/McGraw-Hill.

Johansson, Johny K. & Nonaka, Ikujiro (1996) *Relentless: The Japanese Way of Marketing*. New York: HarperBusiness.

Johansson, Johny K. & Thorelli, Hans B. (1985) International product positioning. *Journal of International Business Studies*, 16, 3 (Fall), 57–76.

Kale, Sudhir H. & McIntyre, Roger P. (1991) Distribution channel relationships in diverse cultures. *International Marketing Review*, 8, 31–45.

Kalish, Schlomo, Mahajan, Vijay & Muller, Eitan (1995) Waterfall and sprinkler new product strategies in competitive global markets. *International Journal of Research in Marketing*, 12, July, 105–19.

Kapferer, Jean-Noel (1997) *Strategic Brand Management*, 2nd edn. London: Kogan-Page.

——— (1992) *Managing Global Marketing*. Boston: PWS-Kent.

Keegan, Warren J. (1969) Multinational product planning: strategic alternatives. *Journal of Marketing*, January, 58–62.

——— (1995) *Global Marketing Management*, 5th edn. Englewood Cliffs, NJ: Prentice-Hall.

Keillor, Bruce, Hult, Tomas M., Erffmeyer, Robert C. & Babakus, Emin (1996) NATID: the development and application of a national identity measure for use in international marketing. *Journal of International Marketing*, 4, 2, 57–73.

Keller, Kevin Lane (1998) *Strategic Brand Management*. Upper Saddle River, NJ: Prentice-Hall.

Kim, W. Chan & Mauborgne, Renee A. (1993) Making global strategies work. *Sloan Management Review*, Spring, 11–27.

Klein, Naomi (2000) *No Logo*. London: Flamingo.

Knight, Gary A. & Cavusgil, S. Tamer (1997) Early internationalization and the born-global firm: an emergent paradigm for international marketing. Center for International Business Education and Research, Michigan State University, East Lansing, MI, Working Paper.

Kotabe, Masaaki & Helsen, Kristian (1998) *Global Marketing Management*. New York: John Wiley and Sons.

Krugman, Paul R. (1988) *Geography and Trade*. Cambridge, MA: MIT Press.

Kumar, V., Stam, Antonie & Joachimsthaler, Erich A. (1994) An interactive multicriteria approach to identifying potential foreign markets. *Journal of International Marketing*, 2, 1, 29–52.

Lasserre, Philippe & Schütte, Hellmut (1995) *Strategies for Asia Pacific*. London: Macmillan.

Lee, Chol & Green, Robert T. (1991) Cross-cultural examination of the Fishbein behavioral intentions model. *Journal of International Business Studies*, 22, 2, 289–305.

Lee, Chong Suk (1987) Export market expansion strategies and export performance: a study of high technology manufacturing firms. Doctoral Dissertation, University of Washington.

Leonidou, Leonidas C., Katsikeas, Constantine S. & Piercy, Nigel F. (1998) Identifying managerial influences on exporting: past research and future directions. *Journal of International Marketing*, 6, 2, 74–102.

Levitt, Ted (1983) The globalization of markets. *Harvard Business Review*, May–June, 92–102.

Liander, Bertil, Terpstra, Vern, Yoshino, M.Y. & Sherbini, Aziz A. (1967) *Comparative Analysis for International Marketing*. Boston: Allyn & Bacon.

Lieberman, Marvin & Montgomery, David (1988) First-mover advantages. *Strategic Management Journal*, 9, Summer, 41–58.

Lindberg, Bertil (1982) International comparison of growth in demand for a new durable consumer product. *Journal of Marketing Research*, August, 364–71.

Lovelock, Christopher H. & Yip, George S. (1996) Developing global strategies for service businesses. *California Management Review*, 38, 2 (Winter), 64–86.

Lynn, Michael & Gelb, Betsy D. (1996) Identifying innovative national markets for technical consumer goods. *International Marketing Review*, 13, 6, 43–57.

McIntyre, Faye S. & Huszagh, Sandra M. (1995) Internationalization of franchise systems. *Journal of International Marketing*, 3, 4, 39–56.

McKinsey & Co. (1993) *Emerging Exporters: Australia's High Value-Added Manufacturing Exporters*. Melbourne: Australian Manufacturing Council.

Macrae, Chris (1996) *The Brand Chartering Handbook*. Harlow, England: Addison-Wesley.

Madsen, Tage K. (1989) Successful export marketing management: some empirical evidence. *International Marketing Review*, 6, 4, 41–57.

Merrill Lynch (1999) *The Internet Tsunami*. Merrill Lynch Bulletin, Sept 21.

Moyer, Reed (1968) International market analysis. *Journal of Marketing Research*, 5, Nov, 353–60.

Nagle, Thomas T. & Holden, Reed K. (1995) *The Strategy and Tactics of Pricing*, 2nd edn. Englewood Cliffs, NJ: Prentice-Hall.

Nakata, Cheryl & Sivakumar, K. (1996) National culture and new product development: an integrative review. *Journal of Marketing*, 60, January, 61–72.

Nebenzahl, Israel & Jaffe, Eugene (1993) Estimating demand functions from the country-of-origin effect. In *Product-Country Images: Impact and Role in International Marketing*, edited by Nicolas

Papadopoulos & Louise A. Heslop. New York: International Business Press, pp. 159–78.

Nordstrom, Kjell A. (1991) *The Internationalization Process of the Firm: Searching for New Patterns and Explanations*. Stockholm: Institute of International Business.

Normann, Richard (1984) *Service Management*. New York: John Wiley and Sons.

Papadopoulos, Nicolas & Heslop, Louise A. (eds) (1993) *Product-Country Images: Impact and Role in International Marketing*. New York: International Business Press.

Parke, Jo Anne (1994) The case for going global: globalization in direct marketing. *Target Marketing*, 17, 11 (November), 8.

Pauwels, Pieter & Matthyssens, Paul (2001) Strategic flexibility and the internationalization process model: an exploratory study. Paper presented at the AIB Conference, Sydney.

Peterson, Robert A. (ed.) (1997) *Electronic Marketing and the Consumer.* Beverly Hills, CA: Sage.

Piercy, Nigel (1982) Export strategy: concentration on key markets vs. market spreading. *Journal of International Marketing*, 1, 1, 56–67.

Porter, Michael (1990) *The Competitive Advantage of Nations*. New York: The Free Press.

Quelch, John (1984) British Airways. Harvard Business School case 585-014.

Quelch, John & Klein, Lisa R. (1996) The Internet and international marketing. *Sloan Management Review*, Spring, 60–74.

Rapoport, Carla with Martin, Justin (1995) Retailers go global. *Fortune*, February 20, 102–8.

Ricks, D.A. (1993) *Blunders in International Business*. Cambridge, MA: Blackwell.

Riesenbeck, Hajo & Freeling, Anthony (1991) How global are global brands? *McKinsey Quarterly*, 4, 3–18.

Root, Franklin R. (1987) *Entry Strategies for International Markets*, rev. edn. New York: D. C. Heath.

Rosen, Barry Nathan, Boddewyn, Jean J. & Louis, Ernst A. (1989) US brands abroad: an empirical study of global branding. *International Marketing Review*, 6, 1, 7–19.

Royal, Weld & Lucas, Allison (1995) Global pricing and other hazards. *Sales & Marketing Management,* 147, 8 (August), 80–3.

Rutenberg, D.P. (1982) *Multinational Management*. Boston: Little, Brown.

Sambharay, Rakesh B. & Phatak, Arvind (1990) The effect of transborder data flow restrictions on American multinational corporations. *Management International Review*, 30, 1, 267–81.

Samiee, Saeed & Roth, Kendall (1992) The influence of global marketing standardization on performance. *Journal of Marketing*, 56, 2 (April), 1–17.

Seybold, Patricia B. with Marshak, Ronni T. (1998) *Customers.com: How to Create a Profitable Business Strategy for the Internet and Beyond*. New York: Times Business.

Shimp, Terence A. & Sharma, Subhash (1987) Consumer ethnocentrism: construction and validation of the CETSCALE. *Journal of Marketing Research,* 24, August, 280–9.

Simmons, Tim (1990) A global brand of dialog; food products manufacturers moving to market products globally. *Supermarket News*, 40, 28 (July 9), 2.

Simon, Hermann (1995) Pricing problems in a global setting. *Marketing News*, October 9, 4.

Siwolop, Sana (1998) Books did it for Amazon, but what's next? *New York Times*, August 23, D1, D5.

Song, X. Michael & Parry, Mark E. (1997) The determinants of Japanese new product successes. *Journal of Marketing Research*, 34, February, 64–76.

Song, X. Michael, Di Benedetto, C.A. & Zhao, Y.L. (1999) Pioneering advantages in manufacturing and service industries: empirical evidence from nine countries. *Strategic Management Journal*, 20, 9 (Sept), 811–36.

Strassel, Kimberley A. (1998) E-commerce finally blooms as Europe takes to the Net. *Wall Street Journal*, Interactive edition, December 7.

Solberg, Carl Arthur (1997) A framework for analysis of strategy development in globalizing markets. *Journal of International Marketing*, 5, 1, 10–22.

Takada, Hirokazu & Jain, Dipak (1991) Cross-national analysis of diffusion of consumer durable goods in Pacific Rim countries. *Journal of Marketing*, 55, April, 48–54.

Takeuchi, Hirotaka & Porter, Michael E. (1986) Three roles of international marketing in global strategy. In *Competition in Global Industries*, edited by Michael E. Porter. Boston, MA: Harvard Business School Press, pp. 111–46.

Taylor, William (1992) The logic of global business: an interview with ABB's Percy Barnevik. In *Transnational Management*, edited by Christopher A. Bartlett & Sumantra Ghoshal. Homewood, IL: Irwin, pp. 892–908.

Thorelli, Hans B. (1990) The information seekers: multinational strategy targets. Reading no. 25. In *International Marketing Strategy*, 3rd edn, edited by Hans B. Thorelli & S. Tamer Cavusgil. New York: Pergamon, pp. 341–351.

Tse, David K. & Gorn, Gerald J. (1993) An experiment on the salience of country-of-origin in the era of global brands. *Journal of International Marketing*, 1, 1, 57–76.

Tung, Rosalie (1988) Toward a concept of international business negotiations. In *Advances in International Comparative Management*, edited by Richard Farmer. Greenwich, CT: JAI Press, pp. 203–19.

Usunier, Jean-Claude (1996) *Marketing Across Cultures*, 2nd edn. London: Prentice-Hall.

Vernon, Raymond (1966) International investment and international trade in the product cycle. *Quarterly Journal of Economics*, 80 (May), 190–207.

Wells, Louis T. (1968) A product life cycle for international trade? *Journal of Marketing*, July, 1–6.

Westland, J. Christopher & Clark, Theodore H.K. (1999) *Global Electronic Commerce*. Cambridge, MA: MIT Press.

White, D. Steven, Griffith, David A. & Ryans, John K. Jr. (1998) Measuring export performance in service industries. *International Marketing Review*, 15, 3, 188–204.

Wind, Jerry & Douglas, Susan (1972) International market segmentation. *European Journal of Marketing,* 6, 1, 12–23.

Yavas, Ugur, Verhage, Bronislaw J. & Green, Robert T. (1992) Global consumer segmentation versus local market orientation: empirical findings. *Management International Review,* 32, 3, 265–72.

Yip, George S. (1992) *Total Global Strategy*. Englewood Cliffs, NJ: Prentice-Hall.

——— (1998) *Asian Advantage: Key Strategies for Winning in the Asia-Pacific Region.* Reading, MA: Addison-Wesley.

Yip, George S. & Johansson, Johny K. (1993) Global market strategies of U.S. and Japanese business. Working Paper, Marketing Science Institute, Cambridge, MA.

Yip, George S. & Madsen, Tammy L. (1996) Global account management: the new frontier in relationship marketing. *International Marketing Review*, 13, 3, 24–42.

19

Service Marketing and Management: Capacity as a Strategic Marketing Variable

STEVEN M. SHUGAN

Overview of this Chapter: Marketing with Capacity Constraints

We start this chapter with the classical discussion of whether service marketing is different from the marketing of manufactured and extractive (e.g., agriculture, fishing, mining) goods. We conclude that although philosophical debates are inconclusive, certain problems are prevalent for service providers. One of those problems, faced by many but not all service providers, is the problem of coordinating marketing and operations. This problem is often made difficult by the presence of capacity constraints. We devote this chapter to the topic of marketing with capacity constraints.

After that general discussion, we argue that both service quality and service strategy are integrally related to capacity decisions. For it is capacity (i.e., available employee hours, available physical facilities, lengths of queues, etc.) that ultimately determines whether the service provider can satisfy and retain buyers. Capacity decisions also impact costs and profitability. There are basic compromises between creating additional capacity to better serve customers and increasing costs.

After discussing the relationship between capacity strategy and service strategy, we discuss capacity-constrained strategies in two settings. In the first, we examine the case when demand is predictable. This arises when factors such as predictable seasonality allow us to accurately forecast peak and off-peak demand. Seasonality may be related to the time of day, the day of week, the month of the year, or particular holidays.

The section on capacity-constrained strategies considers strategies such as demand shifting. Demand shifting occurs when service providers attempt to shift demand from peak to off-peak periods. We discuss both the social welfare as well as the profitability implications associated with these strategies. Beyond demand shifting, we also consider other strategies, including non-price rationing, offering different levels of service at times of peak demand, and the bundling of services.

One interesting part of peak pricing strategies occurs when the opportunity cost of a resource changes over time. For example, consider a restaurant where table space is severely limited but only during peak hours. In this situation, the price of foods (e.g., coffee) that take more time to consume should have much higher prices during peak hours because these foods consume more capacity. Off-peak, however, excess capacity lowers the opportunity cost of consuming capacity to zero.

The last section of this chapter considers the case of capacity-constrained strategies with unpredictable demand. This case often occurs when exogenous and unpredictable events impact the arrival of buyers. A change in interest rates, a change in weather conditions, a special event, or just randomness could all cause a sudden increase or decrease in demand.

This section discusses how unpredictable demand usually decreases service quality and causes longer waiting times. The section also discusses the impact of unpredictable demand on the capacity decision and whether to build excess capacity into the system. We discuss marketing strategies with unpredictable demand when prices are flexible, and when they are not. We also discuss rationing and different methods for allocating capacity when service providers are unable to satisfy all customers.

The chapter ends with conclusions and directions for future research.

Is Service Marketing Different?

Most discussions of service marketing start with a justification for service marketing (Zeithaml & Bitner, 2000). Some authors argue that service marketing is vastly different from the marketing of manufactured goods (Berry, 1980; Onkvisit & Shaw, 1991; Shostack, 1977). However, it is obvious that when services include such diverse activities as banking, retailing, wholesaling, consulting, litigation, and surgery, then there are very few characteristics shared by all services (Lovelock et al., 1998; Rust et al., 1995). Therefore, it is counterproductive to argue that manufactured goods and services each have unique characteristics not shared by each other.

Instead, we should merely state the obvious. Service providers find some problems more prevalent than manufacturers (Folland et al., 1988; Sirdeshmukh et al., 2002). Service providers face problems not frequently encountered in other sectors, i.e., manufacturing and agriculture (Spicer & Bernhardt, 1997). Consider, for example, the product-line manager for soup. This manager is responsible for developing and implementing a marketing-plan for soup. The plan probably includes specific marketing instruments such as trade promotions that offer discounts to retailers. The plan also includes coupons, package design and shelf facings. The plan could also include some ideas for a new eight-ounce size. This manager needs to understand marketing instruments such as trade promotions, coupons, package design, shelf facings, and package size.

Now consider the marketing manager for a major hospital. The manager of the major hospital has different concerns about the implementation and dissimilar marketing instruments. Legal constraints force the hospital to offer some services and not offer others. More business comes from physician and other referrals than customer choices. Marketing plans must consider the reaction of patients, physicians, insurance companies, government regulators, hospital staff, and private agencies. Prices are only flexible for elective procedures. Promotional efforts must consider capacity and location constraints. Hours of operation and allocation of employee time are primary considerations (Hirschberg, 2000).

Although this argument suggests service providers face different problems than manufacturing firms, this argument also applies within the service sector. Given the broad definition of the service sector (Shugan, 1994), the sector embraces very different service providers. In fact, the service section is the miscellaneous sector of the economy for businesses not classified elsewhere. It is expected, therefore, that many service organizations are not only different from organizations in manufacturing and agriculture, but also different from each other. Services such as museums and railroads appear to have less in common than agricultural organizations such as cattle ranches and cash-crop farms. Similarly, banks and electric utilities appear to have far less in common than automobile manufacturers and electronics manufacturers. Hence, although it is important to understand problems that are prevalent among service providers, not all service providers will face all these problems.

We might wonder whether service businesses are unique in any way. At one level, everything is unique. Industry terminology, for example, is often specific. Different industries may have different terms for the same concept. Bridge-buying, forward-buying, stockpiling, stacking, cross-purchasing, inventorying are different terms used in different industries for exactly the same concept. At this level of analysis, only experience in the specific industry applies.

However, it is wrong to conclude that service providers are entirely different and require completely new and unique approaches. Many marketing principles and marketing research tools apply equally well to both service providers and manufacturers. We should never conclude a business is unique. That conclusion is very dangerous and encourages each manager to ignore knowledge accumulated in other industries. It also encourages an inward focus so that managers ignore valuable innovations just because they do not occur in the same industry.

We should only conclude that most service providers face many common problems, such as capacity constraints (Desiraju & Shugan, 1999) and intensive use of human resources (Szymanski & Henard, 2001). Given these common problems, there is a set of common principles and methods useful to these service providers. All service providers should be aware of existing tools for capacity management and development of human resources. Most marketing principles apply to every context, including the marketing of agricultural products, durable goods, industrial products, services, and even ideas. Let us not use superficial differences between service sector firms and other firms as an excuse to forget basic principles. We should not claim every industry is unique merely to avoid the work associated with learning advanced methods developed elsewhere. Many service firms do exactly that. They waste time reinventing the wheel and, in many cases, inventing an inferior wheel.

There are several good marketing textbooks (Hoffman & Bateson, 1997; Kurtz & Clow, 1997; Zeithaml & Bitner, 2000) dealing with the important consumer behavior issues in services marketing (Zeithaml, 2000). There are also several good service operations textbooks (Hart et al., 1990) dealing with the critical issues in service delivery. However, very few articles or textbooks deal with the integration of managing demand with operational considerations. This chapter focuses on that topic.

This chapter argues one key problem faced by many services is the management of demand, given capacity constraints. We argue that capacity constraints are a primary motivator of marketing activities in a wide variety of services. We also argue the capacity decision is linked to the service quality decision. In fact, in many industries, capacity decisions may be the most important aspect of service quality.

Service Capacity as a Competitive Advantage

Service Capacity and Service Quality

Service Capacity as Service Quality

We can think of capacity as a very general term. In many ways, service capacity is an important measure of our ability to deliver service quality. Capacity represents our capabilities. Greater capacity implies a greater capability to supply service quality. Considering all the aspects of service quality (Parasuraman et al., 1985), we realize that it is capacity that allows us to deliver them.

Our capacity strategy, therefore, directly impacts service strategy. For example, we can increase capacity by expanding the number of servers. As we increase the number of servers, our customers may enjoy shorter waiting times in the service queue or benefit from a higher probability of service. With greater capacity, we also have the capability of providing each customer with more service. Increasing capacity, therefore, actually improves the quality of the service output. We expect that capacity should be directly related to customer satisfaction (Anderson, 1995; Anderson & Fornell, 1999, 2000; Hauser et al., 1994).

In many service industries, we can equate superior service to higher capacity. In retailing, for example, increasing the number of trained floor employees helps customers find assistance more quickly. In medical services, increasing the number of employees can decrease waiting times and allow health-care workers to spend more time with each patient. In the airline industry, increasing the number of flights might allow passengers to choose more convenient flight times. For many home repair services, having more employees increases the probability the home repair provider can make a repair on the same day that the customer calls. We see that customer satisfaction (Anderson et al., 1994, 1997) is directly related to available capacity.

We also see that selecting capacity often indirectly determines the level of service that we provide. Stated differently, a superior service strategy requires a greater investment in capacity. More capacity in the form of more employees, larger facilities, or just a faster processing speed, all translate into higher service levels. The result is more ability to provide customer service and a greater reliability when demand is uncertain (Herk, 1993).

Finally, setting capacity can sometimes deter or prevent competitive entry (Perrakism & Warskett, 1983; Spence, 1977) and, at other times, can encourage collusive behavior by competitors (Brock & Scheinkman, 1985; Compte et al., 2002). Similar to increasing quality, increasing capacity and allowing advance sales can also create a dominant position in the market (Lee and Ng, 2001). Of course, advance selling alone can increase profits whether capacity constraints are binding or not (Shugan & Xie, 2000, 2002; Xie & Shugan, 2001).

Capacity as Strategic Advantage

In this section, we will explore the ability of a firm to either compete on service capacity or use service capacity as a competitive advantage. Capacity may be the seller's most important resource (Wernerfelt, 1995). It can lead to customer satisfaction on a multitude of dimensions (Hauser, 2001).

Here, capacity means differentiation (Bergen et al., 1996). We ask whether we can be different on capacity and, in doing so, insulate ourselves to some degree from competition. As we have seen, choosing capacity is similar to choosing the level of service because, when we choose a lower capacity, we also choose a lower level of service quality. Less capacity often implies longer waiting times in service queues and, in industries such as airlines, the probability of any service may decrease. Here, the ability to compete on capacity is similar to the ability to compete on service. Hence, we are exploring whether firms can compete on service itself.

In more service industries than previously believed (Allen & Liu, 1995), scale economies are critical to achieving profitability. The need for these scale economies may limit a service provider's ability to choose capacity and compete on capacity. Large benefits from scale economies, for example, may require all service producers to invest in relatively large capacity. Without these economies, small service providers may face an overwhelming cost disadvantage. Consequently, competition may create a market with only a very small number of very large capacity providers. For these few producers, capacity is seldom the key differentiating factor. In office-products retailing, for example, nearly all retailers are relatively large and often of similar size. Similarly, many wholesale distributors in various device industries are small, but of similar size because of a lack of economies-of-scale. Here, capacity fails to provide higher quality service or a benefit for the customer.

There is another situation when capacity may provide very little advantage. In some industries, all users may want very similar levels of service. For example, when developing film, most users may want 1 hour processing and are not willing to pay much more for 1/2 hour processing. If the cost of providing 1/2 hour processing is much greater than the cost of providing 1 hour processing, all service providers would be forced into charging for providing the same level of service, i.e., 1 hour processing.

We see that in some industries, cost considerations, such as economies-of-scale, may require all service providers to make specific investments in capacity. We also see that a lack of heterogeneity in user wants also limits our ability to increase capacity as a source of competitive advantage. Later in this section, we discuss other factors influencing capacity decisions. At this point, however, we further explore the topic of when capacity can be a source of competitive advantage or, at least, differentiation.

To differentiate on capacity, both low-capacity and high-capacity strategies must be viable. In other words, if some service providers are already profitable at some level of capacity, we want to know whether we can enter the market with a different level of capacity and still be profitable. We want to know whether a corporate strategy using a different level of capacity is viable. For simplicity, we refer to this different strategy as a high-capacity strategy. In the following section, we examine the viability of a high-capacity strategy when profitable low-capacity providers are already in the market. The concepts in this section are equally applicable to adopting a low-capacity strategy in a market already containing profitable high-capacity service providers. Our interest here is in whether service providers can compete by adopting different levels of capacity, thereby offering different levels of service quality.

The Impact of Service Capacity Constraints

Interpreting Capacity Constraints

The meaning of capacity varies from industry to industry. We will refer to capacity constraints as being either hard or soft. A hard capacity constraint strictly constrains or limits the service provider's ability to serve customers. As the service provider reaches capacity, the service provider becomes unable to serve additional customers.

When a hard capacity constraint becomes binding, the service provider can no longer serve additional customers. A restaurant, for example, may have insufficient seating capacity to serve additional customers during the peak dinner hour. When all tables at a restaurant become occupied, the capacity constraint is binding and the restaurant can no longer seat additional customers. At capacity, an accounting firm may have an insufficient number of accountants to complete additional tax returns during the tax season. Its capacity constraint becomes binding.

Note that when hard capacity constraints are binding, unused demand may be lost forever. Although granting refunds may provide customer benefits, these refunds must be coupled with the opportunity cost associated with unused capacity. These opportunity costs are irrelevant when surplus capacity exists (Chu et al., 1999).

In addition to hard capacity constraints, there are also soft capacity constraints. These constraints are not strictly binding, and it may be possible to serve additional customers. Serving these customers, however, may be very costly. For example, consider an electric utility. During the peak summer season, the utility may be unable to generate sufficient power to feed the many hungry air conditioners. Despite that constraint, the electric utility can purchase power from other utilities and use that power to meet the increased demand from its customers. Buying electric power on the open market, however, may be much more costly for the electric utility than generating the electric power itself.

Another feature of soft capacity constraints is the ability to expand capacity by decreasing service levels. Here, the firm may decrease service times or service rates as it approaches capacity. A health-care provider, for example, may spend less time helping each patient as the medical facility approaches capacity. An airline may give passengers less seating choices as a plane approaches capacity. An amusement park may close particular attractions as the park approaches capacity or as demand for those attractions exceeds available seating. In each case, the service provider temporarily expands capacity to serve more users, but each user receives some qualitatively lower level of service.

Note that in some industries, such as entertainment (Sawhney & Eliashberg, 1996), service providers often offer a line of services. In that event, insufficient capacity in one service may encourage buyers to switch to another service that may be as profitable as the unavailable service. The consequence of this switching is a much lower opportunity cost associated with capacity constraints than for service providers with only one service.

We see that capacity constraints are sometimes not constraints but rather abrupt changes in the cost of serving customers. Hence, we can view capacity constraints as high costs. As the service provider approaches capacity, the cost of serving additional customers dramatically increases. As an aircraft reaches capacity, the airline must substitute a larger plane or put passengers on a competitor's plane. As a professional service approaches capacity, the service must employ workers over-time at higher wages or employ temporary workers at still higher wages. As a telephone network approaches capacity, it becomes necessary to purchase additional capacity on the spot market.

Another factor influencing capacity constraints is the length of the planning horizon. A binding capacity constraint, in the short-term, can be relaxed in the long-term. Consider an airline. In the very short-term, airlines are unable to add an additional seat to a full airplane. Given more time, however, the airline could use a larger plane on a particular route to accommodate additional passengers. Given a still longer planning horizon, the airline could purchase additional landing slots and fly additional flights. Given the very long-term, the airline could buy additional airplanes. Hence, short-term capacity constraints could become less binding as the planning horizon increases.

To some extent, all capacity constraints can be soft given a sufficiently long planning horizon. Restaurants, for example, can build additional rooms. Telephone companies can lay additional lines. Accounting firms can hire additional accountants. It is, therefore, necessary to consider both the degree to which the capacity constraint is binding and the length of the planning horizon.

Long-term versus Short-term Constraints

In the short-term, a capacity constraint is not a managerial decision. It is a binding constraint faced by management. Rather than deciding on capacity, the short-term decision is how to ration capacity in times of high demand and how to forecast when rationing will be necessary.

At this point, we focus our attention on long-term capacity constraints. This distinction is important because we will view the capacity decision as an integral part of the overall corporate strategy. For example, when designing the Washington–New York shuttle, Eastern Airlines decided to commit to full capacity by allocating sufficient planes to meet maximum demand. Subsequent airlines that entered the same market often took other strategies. New York Air, for example, allocated only sufficient capacity for average demand. When the number of potential passengers exceeded the number of available seats, New York Air turned those additional potential passengers away.

We see that, in the long-term, a firm can always decide to purchase sufficient capacity to accommodate maximum or peak demand. Purchasing that additional capacity, however, can be expensive and increase the costs of the service provider. An airline, for example, that has many empty unused planes has higher costs than an airline with fewer planes.

In a competitive market, service providers who choose to have more capacity than other service providers will have higher expenses than service providers who choose a lower level of capacity. An airline that desires more capacity, for example, would have the additional cost of purchasing more planes. Additional revenues caused by servicing additional customers will offset some of these expenses. The airline with additional capacity, for example, has more planes to fly additional flights. The airline, however, will only achieve additional revenues during periods when peak demand exceeded available seating. Moreover, the additional revenues are limited to the number of passengers who wanted to fly but were unable to fly because of limited capacity.

We see that having additional capacity alone may not generate sufficient revenue to justify the additional capacity. In many cases, additional revenues will fail to offset all the costs associated with additional capacity. There are at least three reasons for this situation. First, additional revenue made possible by more capacity is limited to times of peak demand. Second, additional revenue from added capacity is limited to the amount of excess demand during times of peak demand. Third, a better pricing strategy may be able to decrease demand during peak periods and generate additional revenue without the cost of additional capacity. Finally, having additional capacity may fail to attract more customers when that capacity provides no tangible benefit for customers.

Now consider two service providers who are very similar, but one provider chooses to have more capacity than the other provider. The low-capacity provider acquires sufficient capacity to serve all customers in times of off-peak demand, but far less capacity than necessary to serve customers during times of peak demand. The high-capacity provider acquires sufficient capacity to serve most, if not all, customers during peak demand.

We see that the high-capacity provider will have the ability to serve more customers during times of peak demand than the low-capacity provider. The high-capacity service provider will also have a disadvantage. During times of low demand, the high-capacity provider will suffer from more excess capacity. The high-capacity provider will more often be in a position of excess capacity than the low-capacity service provider. Those situations will cause the high-capacity service provider to have a lower capacity utilization rate than the low-capacity provider. In other words, the high-capacity provider will have less revenue per unit of capacity. In strategic terms, the high-capacity provider becomes the high-cost provider.

Note that the excess capacity is not what makes the high-capacity provider into a high-cost provider. It is the absolute amount of capacity owned by the high-capacity provider that inflicts the higher costs. The high-capacity provider would be the higher cost provider regardless of whether the capacity is fully exploited or goes idle. This distinction is important because a better understanding of the problem provides us with the proper focus. Our focus should not be on capacity utilization but, instead, on maximizing long-term profits. When we become a high-capacity provider, we expect additional revenue during periods of peak-demand. During those periods, we expect greater profits than our low-capacity competitors. During off-peak periods, the excess capacity is irrelevant to our decisions.

With higher costs, the high-capacity service provider must either be able to charge a higher rate (that is, price) than the low-capacity service provider, or to save costs elsewhere. At this point, let us consider only the case where the high-capacity producer gets a higher price. This higher price compensates the high-capacity service provider for times of excess capacity. The additional revenue from the high price enables the service provider to support the excess capacity during off-peak periods and satisfy additional customers during the peak periods. In the next section, we explore situations when a high-capacity, high-price strategy is viable.

Capacity-Constrained Strategies with Predictable Demand

Peak and Off-peak Marketing Objectives

The last section discussed marketing strategies when the capacity constraint was non-binding or there was a threat of it becoming non-binding. This section discusses marketing strategies when the capacity constraint becomes binding. The constraint may be binding for only a short, and sometimes predictable, time each year. That predictability often comes from predictable seasonality. For services such as retailing, a peak season may correspond to only 16 to 33 days a year. During these days, the retailer encounters peak customer traffic. Moreover, these days may generate the critical sales volume that determines whether the retailer is profitable or not. The rest of the year may only generate sufficient profit to cover overhead expenses. Every dollar during the season, however, may represent the retailer's profit for the year (Greenidge, 1983).

When the capacity constraint is binding, the service provider may be unable to serve all available customers. The capacity constraint becomes binding when the service provider decides to have less capacity than needed to meet peak-demand. As a service provider with insufficient capacity to meet peak-demand, we must consider implementing two strategies. These strategies are not mutually exclusive. Most service providers attempt to employ both.

The first strategy is to reduce demand during the peak period by extracting greater user-surplus during the peak period. Either charging a higher price during the peak period or offering a less costly service during the time of peak-demand often accomplishes this strategy. A hotel, for example, may raise rates while a retailer may offer fewer specials or promotions. The result is less demand during the peak-period. A very large price increase during peak-demand may reduce demand to the actual level of capacity. There are also non-pricing strategies, which we discuss later.

The second strategy is to shift demand from the peak season to the off-peak season. Here, the service provider gives users incentives to use the service during the off-peak season rather than during the peak season. A restaurant, for example, may offer an 'early-dinner special,' which offers a lower price for dinner if the patron arrives at the restaurant before the peak-time. The restaurant hopes that some patrons will choose to eat earlier. If some patrons do, the restaurant will get better utilization of capacity before the peak-dining period, and still fill all tables during the peak-dining period.

Note that more strategies are viable during the peak-period because potential competitors are already at capacity. At capacity, they pose less of a threat. For example, Haskel and Martin (1994), using survey data on capacity constraints merged into a panel industry data set, show a positive relationship between profits and binding capacity constraints.

Marketing Strategies at the Peak

Pricing Strategies with One Capacity Constraint

Different Objectives for Private and Public Sectors When managing public services, reducing peak demand may itself be an objective (Crew et al., 1995). Within a larger context, it may be socially desirable to encourage citizens to consume less during times of peak demand. The benefits may be associated with the conservation of scarce resources. Public services may attempt to avoid, for example, socially undesirable consequences of peak demand including congestion, undue burden of scarce public resources, destruction of public goods and regressive taxation. These events occur in public services including the national parks, electrical utilities, the public highway system, and the environment.

In private services, however, the objective is seldom as simple as merely decreasing peak demand. In private services, the reduction of peak demand is only important when it leads to additional revenues. These revenues can occur during the peak period, during the off-peak period, or both. For example, increasing the rate charged for accounting services during the peak season may, first, increase the revenue from billed hours during the peak period, and, second, shift some demand to the off-peak period, generating more revenue during the off-peak period.

In this section we discuss how to increase revenues during the peak season. We refer to this type of revenue generation as price discrimination because users pay different prices during different time periods. A telephone caller, for example, who makes a call during a weekday at noon, pays more per minute than when making a call during a weekend at noon. Prices explicitly depend on demand.

New competition, unfortunately, sometimes limits our ability to fully exploit the peak by raising prices. During times of peak demand, temporary entry of competitors may occur. For example, when the Christmas season nears and toy retailers approach capacity, other retailers, who usually fail to carry toys, do carry toys for the short peak period of Christmas. Hence, as a toy retailer, we may be unable to significantly raise prices during the Christmas season. Moreover, having more capacity does not necessarily make one the dominant firm in the market (Van Cayseele & Furth, 2001).

Pricing to Maximize Profits

The Theory

In the last section, we discussed the optimal off-peak price when capacity is non-binding. We said that the capacity constraint is irrelevant and that it should not distract us from setting the best price. We should not attempt to decrease our price to fill any excess capacity. The excess capacity is irrelevant to our pricing decision.

To set prices, we should start by determining the best price assuming we face no capacity constraints. We call this price the best-unconstrained price. It is the price we would set were there no capacity constraints.

If the best-unconstrained price results in excess capacity, we are finished. We should use that optimal price and ignore the capacity. This situation should occur in situations of off-peak demand because we should set off-peak capacity to be non-binding. Hence, setting the off-peak price can be equivalent to setting a price without capacity constraints. The size of capacity has no effect on the off-peak price.

If, however, the best-unconstrained price results in a binding capacity constraint, then capacity does have an impact on the optimal price. The best-unconstrained price is not optimal and we need to take another step. We need to increase the price to diminish demand to the point when the capacity is just sufficient to meet demand. Let us explore the reason for this action.

Once we fill capacity, we have little opportunity to extract any revenue from customers who are denied service. Increasing the price accomplishes this goal. Conceptually, we want to continue to increase our price until the peak-demand exactly equals our available capacity. At that point, we obtain the maximum revenues allowable given our current capacity. If our price is any lower, we fail to extract revenues from customers denied service. If our price is any higher, we no longer have a binding capacity constraint. At the optimal price, peak-demand exactly equals current capacity.

For example, consider electric utility industry. In this industry, peak price could be many times off-peak prices. Surveys of customers suggest that, on average, customers would be willing to pay at least 100 times the off-peak price rather than forego peak service for any period of time (Rose & Mann, 1995). However, peak prices fail to reach those levels for three reasons. First, given that customers' willingness-to-pay is very high, electrical utilities maintain large amounts of excess capacity to insure against blackouts during peak periods. Some plants may only operate at the time of peak demand. Second, because electricity can easily move long distances, competition provides some downward pressure on peak prices. Finally, public sentiment combined with extensive regulation provides some pressure for peak and off-peak prices to equate. Of course, the consequence may be higher off-peak prices.

Implementing the Theory

In concept, the theory is clear. We should increase our price to diminish demand to the point that we have exactly sufficient capacity to meet demand. In practice, however, service providers may be reluctant to increase prices beyond a certain level. There are several reasons for this reluctance.

The primary reason is our inability to predict demand. With uncertainty, it may be inadvisable to raise prices to diminish demand. We discuss this issue in the next section, which further discusses unpredictable demand. Another reason is the difficulty of continuous changing prices over time. Many service providers must announce prices and these providers become committed to their announced prices. They cannot renege on those prices and insist on higher prices just because it is temporarily profitable to do so. Of course, whenever an overbooked airplane fills, the airline probably wishes it could increase the fare to everyone on the plane.

Finally, it is administratively difficult to set complex pricing schemes. A restaurant might prefer to charge a different price for every item for different hours of the day and different days of the week. Complexity prevents it from doing so. Restaurants, instead, have different menus for lunch and dinner, have early-bird specials, have happy hours and adopt other simpler mechanisms for approximating optimal prices.

Despite the fact that pricing schemes must be simpler than theoretically desirable, it is still important to understand the optimal price. We must know the optimal price before we choose among, possibly, simpler schemes. Knowing the optimal price helps us better choose among available options when we are unable to increase the price to the point of maximizing profits.

We know, for example, we want to raise the prices of all capacity consuming services that provide little contribution to profits. In the restaurant example, after-dinner coffee may cause patrons to occupy the table longer and cause the restaurant to forego profits from another patron occupying the table. The other patron might order a complete dinner, and the coffee price should reflect that fact. When possible, the restaurant should charge a very high price for coffee.

Framing Peak Prices Psychological theory tells us that presentation or framing is important. Customers may like a concept when presented in one-way but not another. Considerable research suggests that price is no exception. How we present prices influence how customers respond to them.

It is often useful to present peak prices as regular prices rather than premium prices. In that way, off-peak prices become discounts from the regular price. Hence, the matinee price for a movie is considered to be a discount off the regular price. Weekend and night telephone rates are discounts from the daytime rate. In each case, the consumer who uses the service during the peak pays a regular price, but the regular price is higher than the off-peak price. Other examples include family nights at sporting events, two-for-one drink specials, free off-peak upgrades on car rentals or hotel rooms, coupons valid only during off-peak hours, early-bird dinner specials, special resident off-peak admission to amusement parks, and so on.

Whether to Announce Peak Prices In most cases, the off-peak price is lower than the peak price. Moreover, in most cases, the service provider announces both the off-peak and peak prices. Telephone companies, resort hotels, car rentals, and accounting services, for example, announce higher rates during their peak periods of demand. Here, the user knows the price during the peak period. This knowledge gives many users a greater ability to shift demand to off-peak periods.

The primary reason for announcing peak-prices is to shift some demand to off-peak periods. As a service provider, we hope to shift the demand that we are unable to satisfy, because of capacity constraints, to a time when capacity is non-binding. That leaves only the most price-insensitive users who will pay the highest price for our limited capacity.

When demand is unpredictable, there is another reason for announcing peak-prices. With unpredictable demand, more capacity implies a higher probability of service or a shorter waiting time. When we announce a high price, we signal users that our capacity is sufficient to meet demand. The high price only works with a competitive market because, as a high-priced provider, we could not survive unless we offered some service associated with our higher price. This reason for announcing price is only valid when demand uncertainty exists.

We see there are several reasons to announce peak-prices. There are also reasons not to announce them. Rather than announcing prices, we can vary prices as capacity fills. We can link rates directly to demand conditions. Rates begin to change as capacity fills. Here, neither the service provider nor the user knows tomorrow's rate. Consider, for example, a hotel booking space for a date in the future. On that date, the hotel plans to offer the first 20% of its rooms at a discount rate, the next 50% of its rooms at a regular rate, the next 20% at a high rate and the last 10% at a very high premium rate. As the date approaches, the hotel implements the plan and the rate rises as the hotel fills. When the date is about to arrive, however, the hotel risks that any remaining rooms may remain empty. At that point, the hotel may no longer have a binding capacity constraint and we face the conditions described in the previous section. Without binding capacity, in some cases, there may be a sudden decrease in rates.

Another reason for not announcing peak-prices is the opportunity to auction limited capacity. As capacity fills, we would like to sell the remaining capacity at the highest price. Remember, demand that exceeds our capacity generates no revenue. Auctioning the last available capacity does extract the maximum revenue.

Despite the theoretical attractiveness of auctions, they are rare. Airlines do auction overbooked seats by offering greater and greater payments to flyers willing to surrender their current seats for seats on the next flight. Ushers may extract higher and higher tips for the best of the remaining seats. Tickets for sporting events may increase as the stadium fills. However, social pressures and transaction costs usually make auctions infeasible.

Shadow Prices and Multiple Constraints

Defining a Shadow Price To understand how to construct pricing strategies for meeting peak demand with multiple prices, we need to understand the concept of a shadow price. Shadow prices represent the additional profit that we would make if we could expand the underlying resource. The shadow price is higher when the capacity or resource constraint is more important. Capacity constraints with larger shadow prices are usually hard, i.e., difficult to relax, and are more likely to be binding when demand increases. Constraints with small shadow prices are less likely to be binding and, when binding, are relatively soft. When a constraint is non-binding, it has a shadow price of zero.

For example, suppose we own a restaurant. We face a capacity constraint on our ability to seat dinner parties. The constraint is based on the underlying resource consisting of the number of tables. During the off-peak Monday-night period, there are sufficient tables to meet demand and the shadow price for a table is zero. During the peak Friday-night period, there are insufficient tables to meet demand. It may be impossible to seat additional patrons when all tables become filled and so the resource, consisting of tables, is binding. In that case, the shadow price on the resource consisting of the number of tables is strictly positive, i.e., it is greater than zero.

Suppose that during Friday night, when all tables are filled, we can earn $40 from a one-hour dinner at a table for two people. Here, the shadow price of the table resource would be approximately $40. A $40 shadow price implies that we would be willing to pay up to $40 to add an additional table during Friday night. It also implies that anything that consumes a two-person table for one hour, on Friday night, should be priced at $40 more than during off-peak Monday night.

Finally, note that we have failed to discuss how to set optimal capacity. Although that decision is important, it may be possible to use price to adjust for mistakes in setting capacity. Hence, pricing decisions can compensate for sub-optimal capacity (Skiera & Spann, 1999) and reduce the loss in customer welfare (Berg & Tschirhart, 1988). This later finding is important when uncertainty and long lag times can cause many firms to operate at sub-optimal capacity (Bar-Ilan Sulem & Zanello, 2001).

Using Shadow Prices to Set Peak-Prices We see that a shadow price represents the opportunity cost of a resource. As a service consumes more of a limited resource, i.e., one with a binding capacity constraint, the service requires a higher price. The price should reflect the off-peak profit plus the shadow price of the limited resource. The optimal peak-price is the off-peak price plus the shadow price of the resource being consumed.

Consider our restaurant example. Suppose a dessert causes a table to be occupied for another six minutes; we should charge $40 × 6 minutes/60 minutes or $4 more for the two desserts during Friday night than during the off-peak period. Alternatively, we could offer a $4 discount from the peak-price during off-peak periods.

Hence, the true cost of a service during the peak-period includes the shadow price of the capacity it consumes. While an after-dinner coffee may consume no resources during the off-peak period, that coffee consumes a valuable table during the peak-period. A restaurant should charge more for the coffee during the peak period, or offer a large discount during the off-peak period. When charging different prices is not possible, the restaurant should discourage after-dinner coffee during the peak-period.

Note that the concept of a shadow price implies a different strategy for managing a restaurant's offerings. It suggests that we could offer a new appetizer rather than a new dessert. The appetizer would need to be ready-made, so that we could serve it quickly. Unlike desserts, we can serve appetizers while patrons already would be seated at a table waiting for their main courses. In that way, the appetizer consumes no capacity and provides additional revenue during peak demand. Moreover, a filling appetizer may become a substitute for dessert. That would free additional capacity because the average patron who eats an appetizer rather than a dessert may spend less time at the table.

Finally, remember that, during times of off-peak demand and non-binding capacity constraints, the shadow price for desserts becomes zero, because they do not consume a table. Consequently, we should have different prices for desserts during the peak and off-peak period. We should, in contrast, offer approximately the same price for appetizers during the peak and off-peak periods, or possibly, charge less for appetizers during times of peak demand. Any service that does not consume a constrained resource should have the same price during the peak and off-peak period.

Shadow Prices with Multiple Services When we offer several services, the shadow price may become more complex. The sum of the resources consumed by the separate services may be less than the required resources for all of the services. This situation often occurs when customers simultaneously use several services.

Consider again our restaurant example. Suppose we have two desserts, an ice cream and a fruit dessert, that are equally expensive to prepare. The ice cream dessert requires three minutes of preparation by the server, while the fruit dessert requires no preparation. Assume that, because of this preparation, dinner at a table that orders the ice-cream dessert is three minutes longer than a table that orders the fruit dessert. According to our prior analysis, the ice-cream dessert should cost more. The shadow price of the ice cream dessert is

$40 × 3 minutes/60 minutes or $2. Hence, the ice cream dessert should cost $2 more than the fruit dessert during Friday night.

These computations assume that the table would be available three minutes sooner were it not for the ice cream dessert. This assumption holds if one person orders the ice cream dessert while the other orders the fruit dessert. Were both people at the table to order the ice cream dessert, the second dessert consumes no capacity because the table would not be free three minutes sooner. When the table orders two ice cream desserts, we should charge each person only $2/2 or $1.00 more for the ice cream dessert than the fruit dessert. Of course, in practice, we may be unable to implement this optimal pricing strategy.

Now suppose that one person at the table orders still another dessert that takes five minutes to prepare. In that case, the ice cream dessert consumes none of the table resource constraint. The table would be occupied anyway and the ice cream dessert has no effect on the time the table is occupied. Hence, the peak-price of the ice cream dessert may depend on the dessert ordered by the other person at the table. The shadow price for the ice cream dessert can be $2.00, $1.00, or $0 more than the off-peak price. It depends on what other dessert is ordered.

In practice, we may not know which desserts a table will order, nor can we charge a different price for different pairs of desserts. We can, however, determine the peak-price for the ice cream dessert based on our expectations about the likelihood of different orders. Suppose, for example, ice cream desserts have a 20% share of all of our desserts, while fruit desserts have a 40% share, we might expect a shadow price of 20% × $2.00 plus 40% × $1.00 or $0.80. Hence, we give diners a $1.20 discount for the ice cream dessert during off-peak periods.

Multiple Constraints So far, we have considered a single capacity constraint on a single resource. With one resource, each service consumes some of that resource. A shadow price is a price that represents the value of the resource. When the capacity constraint is non-binding, the shadow price is zero. When the constraint becomes binding, it has a positive shadow price. The shadow price represents the importance of the resource in generating profits. Hence, we need to increase the prices of services by the amount of the resource consumed, times the shadow price.

In this section, we consider the situation when the service provider faces multiple constraints and more than one may be binding at times of peak-demand. For every binding constraint, there is a shadow price associated with that underlying resource. During times of peak-demand, we have several shadow prices for each underlying resource. The price of a service needs to increase during times of peak-demand by the quantity of each resource consumed, times the respective price of each resource.

Conceptually, we start by identifying all capacity constraints on limited resources. We should then determine which constraints are most likely to be binding during times of peak-demand. We should determine which of those binding constraints, when relaxed, would generate the most incremental profits. These are our primary constraints. These are the constraints that have the highest shadow prices. Constraints whose relaxation leads to less incremental profits are secondary constraints. These constraints have smaller shadow prices. Finally, constraints whose relaxation leads to no incremental profits are not binding, and have no shadow prices.

Let us return to our restaurant example. In that example, the constraint on the number of tables is our primary constraint. It is the primary constraint because one additional table could generate a profit of $40 per hour, a relatively high shadow price.

In addition to tables, we face constraints on other resources, such as the number of servers and the amount of food in the kitchen. The number of servers is a secondary constraint. We might stretch current servers across more tables and allow servers to devote less time to each table. That action would generate less than $40. Slower service would result. It might also suggest somewhat neglected patrons might decrease tips and, consequently, require us to pay servers larger salaries to compensate for the lower tips. Moreover, fewer servers may suggest less revenue from appetizers, alcoholic drinks, and other revenue encouraged by servers. At this point, let us only consider the service time implications.

Suppose, for example, having one less server reduces available service time per table. Although we may have some surplus of server time, having one less server may still slow service time. Suppose, for example, the average service time per table decreases, on average, 1 minute per table per hour for our 30 tables. Hence, losing one server costs us 30 minutes of service time. In that case, the shadow price for a server is $40 × 30 minutes/60 minutes or $20 per hour. In sum, we would be willing to spend up to $20 to add an additional server during this hour. Adding an additional server would provide 30 minutes of empty table space capable of generating $20 in revenue.

Of course, this calculation is only approximate. We might want to do a more detailed calculation considering other effects of slow service time, including failure to obtain customer orders for drink refills and the consequence of giving customers less attention. For illustrative and conceptual purposes, however, our $20 computation illustrates the general approach. Moreover, our attempt here is not to advocate complex mathematical computations, but to suggest a conceptual framework on how to think about capacity constraints.

Returning to our example, we also have a constraint on the amount of food in the kitchen. This tertiary constraint may be non-binding because the amount of food may be sufficient. At worst, we may have an insufficient quantity of a popular item and may need to substitute a less popular item. We could assign a small shadow price to reflect the cost of goodwill and, perhaps, the smaller profit margin associated with the surrogate item.

We can now use these shadow prices to determine the prices of different services. When we price off-peak, no capacity constraints are binding so we set prices without consideration of capacity. We call these prices the non-binding prices. When we approach capacity, the best or optimal prices for each service should equal the non-binding price plus the sum of the shadow prices of the resources consumed at capacity.

A dish that takes longer to prepare causes a longer occupation of a table. For example, a dish that takes three minutes more than average to prepare causes a table to be occupied three minutes longer. The cost of that dish, during peak-times, should increase by $40 × 3 minutes/60 minutes or $2. That same dish might also require two minutes more of server time to either prepare the dish or present the dish to the customer. During times of off-peak demand, this server time is non-binding and should not influence the price. During times of peak-demand, the server time is binding and the peak-price should increase to include the cost of the additional server time as well as the table space. At a rate of $20 per hour, for example, the two minutes of server time costs us $20 × 2 minutes/60 minutes or 67¢. Hence, a dish, that takes three minutes longer to prepare and occupies a server for two minutes of presentation time, should have a price $2.67 higher during the peak period than during the off-peak period.

Conceptually, therefore, we should think of peak-prices as off-peak prices plus the sum of the shadow prices of resources with binding constraints. This conceptualization of an optimal peak-price with multiple resource constraints provides numerous pricing and non-pricing implications.

For example, this reasoning suggests a focus on services that consume the most important resource. Consider, for example, a large party. In a large party, it is more likely that some member of the party will order something that requires maximum preparation or server time than in a small party. Hence, large parties are more likely to occupy more table space, and more of other resources. The implication is that we should charge more for meals at larger tables. Alternatively, we should offer larger off-peak discounts to tables with larger parties. Although practicality may limit our ability to do so, we should recognize the strategic implications. We should recognize the objectives of pricing strategy given binding capacity constraints.

There are also many non-pricing strategic implications. For example, we might want to develop special services to offer during times of peak-demand. These services would either be complementary or substitutable. In either case, we should develop services that do not consume valuable capacity. For example, serving drinks to waiting customers does not consume table capacity. Selling magazines to passengers on a train does not consume seating capacity on the train. We discuss these non-pricing strategies in the next section.

Non-pricing Strategies for Peak Demand

Problems Raising Prices Despite the obvious advantages of raising prices when facing peak-demand, there are also many reasons that service providers are reluctant to do so. Most of these reasons are long-term in nature and relate to the long-term consequences of price increases. For example, non-profit service providers may fear public outcry and political repercussions. Private-sector service providers may fear that price increases may encourage competitors to enter the market. Price increases may encourage our customers to try competitive service providers and, if they like the competitive services, we may lose those customers off-peak. We may also permanently lose those customers. Price increases may also generate ill will among customers, leading to alienated customers and diminished off-peak demand. This reason is frequently cited for the failure to raise prices for popular sporting events and music concerts. Another reason is that price increases may encourage industrial customers to make long-term adjustments, such as changing procedures or finding alternative suppliers that might diminish long-term demand. Finally, price increases might conflict with a long-term growth strategy. They may be counterproductive for building customer loyalty, lowering costs (Bailey & White, 1974) or getting customer referrals (Biyalogorsky et al., 2001).

There may also be short-term factors discouraging a temporary price increase during times of peak demand. These factors include transaction costs involved in changing the price. For example, retailers might have problems continuously changing prices. Direct marketers may have problems continuously changing catalog prices or other announced prices.

Non-pricing Objectives When discussing non-pricing strategies, we should remember that the objective of public sector services is different from private sector services. Public sector services tend to look for creative ways of decreasing demand such as brown-outs[1] for electricity conservation, express lanes for car-pooling during peak rush-hours, and ordinances that outlaw the watering of lawns during specific hours.

Private sector services, in contrast, usually have the objective of extracting additional profit from the peak-demand period. It is usually insufficient to merely decrease peak demand. Therefore, non-pricing mechanisms for decreasing demand must have the property that they also increase profits, and there are only two ways to do that. To increase profits without changing price, we can do one of the following. The first is to cut the cost of service delivery. The second is to shift revenue to future periods, increasing the profitability of future periods. At this point, we discuss non-pricing strategies for reducing costs.

As we said earlier, an off-peak discount is often equivalent to a peak price increase. This is also the case for non-pricing strategies. A decrease in service during the peak cuts costs, and it can be framed as an increase in service during the off-peak. No matter how we present the strategy to customers, the idea is increase peak profitability by decreasing peak costs. Examples of profitable non-pricing strategies for decreasing costs during peak periods include providing less service, forgoing investments to off-peak periods, increasing customer waiting times, giving less manufactured product, and increasing customer participation in the service delivery process. Let us discuss each of these strategies.

More Service Off-peak The most obvious way to cut costs during peak periods is lowering the level of service. A retail floor employee may spend less time helping customers during peak periods and spend a greater percentage of total time handling transactions. A bus service may make fewer stops during times of peak demand and only stop at designated locations. A bakery may only offer stock items during times of peak demand but offer more customization (Anderson & Shugan, 1991) during times of off-peak demand. An accountant may also offer only standard services during times of peak demand and much more customized services during off-peak periods. Off-peak seating at entertainment events may be more spacious.

To accomplish this strategy, it is necessary to be somewhat ambiguous about the nature of the service. The added services during the off-peak period are somewhat special and unexpected by the customer. Off-peak services may be more creative and go the extra mile. The best or optimal level of service during peak demand is usually lower than the optimal level of off-peak service.

The higher optimal level for off-peak service does have a disadvantage. Optimal off-peak activities often involve more service for every provider. For that reason, service providers often consider off-peak periods as more competitive. They attribute some of that competition to having reduced primary demand (i.e., industry demand for all providers), but having the same number of competitors. The additional reason for that increased competition is the surplus of capacity and the fact that optimal service levels are higher for all service providers.

It is, therefore, very intuitive that off-peak periods bring different problems. In the peak-demand period, we need to work at capacity and stretch our resources to the limit. In off-peak demand periods, we face decreased demand, increased competition and the need to deliver more service. Off-peak periods present the opportunity to provide better service and get customer loyalty to carry us through the peak-demand periods.

Forgoing Investments to Off-peak Periods There are many activities done by service providers that represent important investments in the future. These activities include the training of employees, improvement of service facilities, developing relationships with key customers, giving employees vacation time, and experimenting with new procedures and new delivery systems. All of these activities are important for the future of the service. Off-peak demand periods provide an excellent opportunity for these activities.

Longer Customer Waiting Times One of the most frequent consequences of peak demand is an increase in the waiting time for customers. At supermarkets, amusement parks, medical facilities, banks, copying services, and many other services, customers can face very long waits during the peak period. In each case, there is a greater chance that a larger number of customers will arrive at the same time. Anytime the number of recent arrivals outnumbers the number of available servers, a waiting line or queue develops.

Service providers can shorten the queue by adding more servers. Banks can add tellers. Supermarkets can add checkout people. Accounting firms can add accountants. Unfortunately, the cost of adding people is very high because the peak demand for one service provider usually coincides with the peak demand for competitive service providers. Consequently, every service provider is trying to hire temporary, but already trained, help at the same time. The result is an inability to systematically add servers.

Another problem with adding servers occurs when the service provider experiences daily or hourly peaks. It is very difficult to hire an additional employee for just a few scattered hours during the day. A restaurant, for example, might find it difficult to get waiters and waitresses who would only work during the lunch and dinner hours. An accounting firm would have great difficulty finding accountants to work just a few months out of the year.

As we noted earlier, it is often best to build insufficient capacity to meet peak demand. The result is, unfortunately, longer waiting times. We should plan for these waiting times and try to manage them. Some firms provide entertainment during the wait, they provide seating for waiting customers, they provide comfortable waiting areas, and many firms try to carefully control their queues. Some restaurants, for example, encourage waiting customers to visit the lounge and enjoy a cocktail until their table is ready. Some large buildings install mirrors in waiting areas so that customers can preen themselves while waiting for the elevators, restaurants, and other services in the building.

Less Manufactured Products The easiest way to cut costs is to provide less manufactured products during peak periods and more off-peak. Examples include two-for-one drinks, early-dinner specials that include a free dessert, an accounting firm that provides a free service during the off-season, and a season pass to several sporting events might include free team merchandise.

Bundling is a useful way to implement this strategy (Oren et al., 1985). Here, the service provider offers a bundle of items during the off-peak period that includes items consuming capacity-constrained resources. Of course, during the off-peak period, these resource constraints are non-binding and, therefore, have a shadow price of zero. The early-dinner special at a restaurant, for example, includes a free dessert. The free dessert causes the party to stay at the table longer, consuming the table resource. During peak-hours the shadow price would be high and the corresponding cost to the service provider would be high. During off-peak hours, however, the shadow price is low and there is no capacity cost to the service provider. The cost of the dessert is only the direct cost of the dessert; there are no indirect costs associated with using the table resource.

Increasing Customer Participation During times of peak-demand, the server resource is binding because all servers are busy. This creates a high shadow price for the server resource. As we discussed earlier, the service provider could hire additional servers, but when all competitors share the same times for peak-demand, there may be an insufficient number of temporary servers. This situation creates the opportunity to allow the customer to take a greater role in the production of the service.

For example, during times of peak-demand, a retailer may either charge more for gift-wrapping services or require consumers to do their own gift-wrapping. During times of peak-demand, an airline may require passengers to check some carry-on baggage that, during off-peak times, the airline would allow on the plane. Banks encourage the use of automated equipment such as ATMs during times of peak-demand. Restaurants have self-service buffet.

For most services, users already participate in the production of the service. The user's time is an important resource. During peak-periods when all servers are busy, the user's time carries a much smaller shadow price than the servers' time.

Substitute Peak Services One of the best non-pricing strategies for peak-demand management is the development of new services that have low shadow prices. After developing these services, we attempt to switch customers to these new services from existing services with very high shadow prices during times of peak-demand.

Consider the example of an amusement park where afternoons bring peak daytime demand. During that peak time, the park can add substitute amusements such as parades, fireworks, outdoor shows, outdoor concerts, and pageantry. These substitute amusements siphon people from amusements with high shadow prices such as popular rides with limited system capacity (e.g., a limited number of people per vehicle or a small number of vehicles), indoor shows with limited seating and 'stop-and-go rides' that shut down for loading and unloading.

We see that the key to developing new substitute services is to go beyond user benefits. In addition to user benefits, we must focus on the resources the new services consume. These services may provide slightly less benefits to users during off-peak periods than existing services, but during peak-periods, these services provide a good value. Once we consider shadow prices, these substitute services have the same customer benefit at a much lower cost and, probably, price to the user. Hence, they provide the user with greater value.

Off-peak Marketing Strategies

The Objective

For non-profit services, shifting demand from peak to off-peak periods may be socially desirable (Burness & Patrick, 1991; Radas & Shugan, 1998a). It may lessen congestion, pollution, conserve societal resources and provide other socially desirable outcomes. For profit-making services, the situation is different.

As we recall, decreasing peak demand was not itself an objective. Similarly, shifting peak-demand to off-peak periods is itself not an objective. It is only important when the shifted demand produces additional profits. That usually occurs when the demand lost from the peak-period does not significantly decrease revenues during the peak-period. For example, consider the postal service's campaign to get people to mail early for Christmas

(Shostack, 1984). In this example, the same package would have been mailed later at the same postage. It is profitable to shift demand because the shifted demand has no impact on total demand but decreases peak-period costs. It is also profitable to shift demand to off-peak when the peak demand would have been otherwise lost.

We must remember, however, that merely shifting demand often generates no additional profits (Radas & Shugan, 1998a, 1998b). If we follow a good off-peak strategy, we need not necessarily concern ourselves about whether the demand comes from peak periods or from increasing the overall off-peak demand. We could very well decrease profits by shifting customers to the off-peak. We must worry about which customers we shift. We want to keep price-insensitive customers buying at the peak because these customers allow us to charge higher prices during the peak period. So we want to shift only price-sensitive customers to the off-peak period. Accomplishing this objective requires a specific separating strategy.

We either need to identify price-sensitive customers, or make an offer that causes price-sensitive customers to reveal themselves. For this reason, many firms keep extensive databases on customers. For example, the US's largest hotel chain, Marriott Hotels & Resorts, uses a four million-person database of Honored Guest Awards members to plan off-peak promotions.

Competitive Factors Influencing Our Strategy

During periods of peak demand, we lose some customers because of our inability to meet all demand. With insufficient capacity, we must ration customers and deny service to some users. These users may be lost either temporarily or permanently. If losing customers during the peak were inevitable, it would be better to lose them temporarily than permanently by shifting lost customers to the off-peak period. However, we must remember that demand shifting is not necessarily a good strategy. It depends on the cost of demand shifting relative to other ways of increasing off-peak demand.

Consider a situation when a service provider believes that demand may exceed supply. The service provider may attempt to switch customers to an off-peak period by signaling customers, that is, telling customers that the service provider is near capacity. For example, consider reservations as a technique for signaling customers. Users may call an airline, a restaurant, or another service provider. The service provider may then tell some users that no reservations are available. That information may cause some users to shift their purchases to off-peak periods. Some airline passengers may make reservations on another flight. Some diners may make dinner reservations at a different time. Patients at a health maintenance organization may make reservations on a less busy day. Unlike an HMO, however, in other industries some customers may switch to competitive services. Some airline passengers may call competitive airlines. Some diners may visit competitive restaurants. In these cases, the service provider permanently loses these users by trying to shift demand.

It might be a better strategy to over-book or raise prices as demand nears capacity. Unable to forecast demand exactly, a restaurant must choose between possible long customer waits and possible lost customers from charging too much (with excess capacity). If the restaurant fails to take reservations, for example, customers may risk a very long wait for service. If the restaurant takes reservations and some customers fail to arrive, the restaurant may have empty tables while their reservation systems shifts customers to competitors. Strategies such as reservations are complex and we discuss those strategies later.

Remember here, our goal is to extract the maximum profits during the peak period. We never want to shift customers merely to increase off-peak demand. It is only profitable to shift customers when that is the most profitable way to increase off-peak demand. In other words, we must compare the profitability of demand shifting to the profitability of merely creating new demand during the off-peak period. Remember, demand shifting may be only one of many methods of generating off-peak demand.

The most important factor influencing the profitability of a demand shifting strategy is the nature of the competition and competitive demand. In some cases, our peak demand coincides with our competitors' peak demand. In other cases, our peak demand is independent of our competitors' demand. The precise timing of competitive peaks is very important. Let us consider why.

With more competitors, it becomes more difficult to shift demand because our competitors may capture our lost customers during the peak-period. Competitors, of course, may be unable to accept our lost customers when these competitors share the same peak-demand periods as us. Consider, for example, Florida resort hotels during Christmas. All of these hotels face the same peak, that is, Christmas. When our hotel fills, our competitors' also fill. Consequently, some demand must shift to off-peak, and some people will postpone their Florida trip to an off-peak month.

We see that when all competitors share the same peak, demand shifting becomes easier. It is also easier to extract maximum profits from the peak period. It is easier to either raise prices or execute an alternative non-pricing strategy when competitors are also at capacity. When competitors have a different peak period, we would have less ability to increase prices or extract additional profits because users could easily get service from a competitor. Moreover, when competitors are not at capacity, they are most attractive to our users because our competitors will likely have lower off-peak prices and higher off-peak levels of service.

The timing of competitive peak periods also influences our capacity and service strategy. When we face long periods of peak demand, and we face the same periods of peak demand as competitors, we have a relatively easy task managing demand. We can invest in larger capacity because we can more easily extract profits during periods of peak demand. In contrast, suppose that we face short periods of peak demand and that we face different periods of peak demand than competitors. Here, we have a far more difficult task. We cannot invest as much in capacity because we are unable to extract sufficient profits during the peak period for two reasons. First, the brevity of the peak period shortens the duration of peak profits and, thereby, decreases our total peak profits. Second, competitors offer credible alternatives for customers during times of our peak demand. So we are less able to extract profits during the peak because we would quickly lose customers to our competitors.

Pricing Strategies

To some extent, all price increases during times of peak-demand indirectly shift demand to off-peak periods. A higher rate for telephone calls during peak hours often causes some callers to shift their calls to lower-rate off-peak periods. Hence, we may not need an explicit strategy for shifting demand.

When demand is perfectly predictable, we need not consider shifting when setting the peak price. We should increase the peak price until the capacity constraint is just binding. In other words, we increase the peak price until peak demand exactly equals our capacity. We should have no excess capacity and no excess demand.

We do, however, need to consider shifting when we set the peak price when demand is somewhat unpredictable. Shifting may further increase the optimal price during the peak-period. Suppose, for example, that we overestimate peak demand and our price is higher than optimal. With that price, our peak demand falls below our maximum capacity and we unnecessarily lose some sales.

Shifting demand lessens this loss because some of those unnecessarily lost sales are merely shifted to the off-peak period. We still enjoy many of those sales, albeit at the lower off-peak price. So shifting decreases the loss from incorrectly forecasting demand and accidentally pricing too high during the peak period.

Faced with uncertain demand, the presence of shifting makes us willing to risk a higher price during the peak period than otherwise. Suppose, for example, we manage an airline that flies two flights. One flight is during the peak late afternoon. The other flight is in the off-peak evening period. Assume that without capacity constraints, we would maximize profits with a price of $400. At a price of $400, there would be 200 travelers wanting to board the late-afternoon flight.

Now assume the plane's capacity is 150 passengers. We should continue to increase the fare until only 150 of the original travelers still want to board the plane. Suppose that happens at $450. At $450, exactly 150 passengers want to board the plane.

Finally, assume we are wrong and only 149 passengers want to board the late-afternoon plane. The plane has one empty seat on the fight. We lose the opportunity to enjoy revenue from that empty seat. The loss, however, might be small when demand shifting is present because the lost passenger flies the evening flight. Although that passenger pays a lower fare, we enjoy the revenue from that fare. Without demand shifting, the total fare is lost and we would adopt a lower peak price.

Non-pricing Strategies

Multiple Services with Different Peaks We said that excess capacity should not affect our off-peak decisions. We should not develop off-peak services to fill excess capacity. However, the optimal capacity decision depends on the extent of demand and duration of the peak and off-peak period. We should purchase less capacity with a short peak period and a long off-peak period. We should purchase more capacity with a longer peak period. In other words, it is hard to justify a very large capacity to satisfy demand for only a short time period.

With several services, each generating peak demand during a different time period, we can extend the period of peak demand. With a longer period of peak demand, the optimal capacity increases. In other words, we can justify a larger capacity given more demand. Consequently, with counter-cyclic services that generate peak demand during different time periods, we invest more in capacity. With a larger capacity, we can serve more customers during the longer periods of peak demand and we receive a higher corresponding profit for those periods. The result may be better service during every peak period.

Suppose, for example, we are a manufacturer's representative for several winter-sports equipment manufacturers. The representative may offer numerous services from order taking to constructing in-store displays. To provide our services, we employ a number of sales representatives and own a small warehouse. All of our services are highly seasonal, with demand growing strongly at the end of summer, peaking at the beginning of the winter and minimal during the spring.

Were we to begin distributing summer sports equipment, we could maintain a larger number of full-time employees and a larger warehouse, because we could now generate more profit from having additional capacity. In other words, by carrying summer sports equipment, we would have more employees and a larger warehouse throughout the year. With those additional resources, we could provide more service to our original winter sports equipment manufacturers.

We see that by smoothing demand with new off-peak services, we can deliver better service during peak periods. That creates a strong incentive to smooth demand because it increases our ability to compete in all time periods. The problem is being sufficiently creative to find services that have different peaks and that we can profitably deliver with the same resources.

Children's software writers, who face peak demand near Christmas, would find it profitable to develop financial software, peaking in the winter, if their programmers could write for both markets. Mortgage companies, who face peak demand during the construction season, would find it profitable to develop other services, such as automobile loans, that peak during the autumn.

Smoothing Demand with Bundling across Time As we discussed earlier, we would like to substantially increase price during times of peak demand. Sometimes, unfortunately, there are upper limits on the extent to which we can increase prices. Huge price increases may convey the perception of price gauging. Moreover, when facing uncertain demand, constantly changing prices may create transaction costs. This is true in many industries where service providers announce prices in advance. A ski resort, for example, that books rooms months in advance, would find it difficult to suddenly increase prices after a heavy snowfall.

Here, bundling services across time provides a possible solution. Consider, for example, a season pass for a series of ten football games. Suppose we would like to charge \$20 for the five less popular games and \$50 for the more popular games. Public relations, unfortunately, prevents us from charging more than \$35 for a game. Here, we charge \$35 for all the games, but we limit the number of single tickets to a very small number. We offer season passes to all ten games for $\$35 \times 10$ or \$350. Note that the season pass price is equivalent to charging \$20 for the five less popular games plus \$50 for the five popular games, because $\$20 \times 5$ plus $\$50 \times 5$ equals \$350.

We see that bundling across time provides a way of hiding the individual prices. In that way, we effectively charge more during the peak periods than our single period price suggests. We transfer profits from the peak period to the off-peak period by bundling purchase in each period.

Note that bundling may have an additional advantage when time-sensitive people are also price-insensitive. In those cases, the price-insensitive customers may not attend events during the off-peak. They may buy a bundled ticket and only use tickets for popular events. As a result, we incur lower costs during the off-peak because we incur no costs for those users, who have a ticket, but fail to attend off-peak events.

Advertising and Offering Coupons at the Peak The peak demand period provides an excellent opportunity to contact customers who may be interested in off-peak service. Unlike customers reached through less directed tools, such as television advertising, the peak identifies high potential customers. These users have already revealed a propensity to like our service because they have already used the service. It is now only necessary to interest them in additional off-peak services. This strategy is viable for all services that could be used again during the off-peak such as lodging services, transportation services, restaurant services, insurance services, and many others.

When customers use the service during the peak, we can expose them to advertising concerning our off-peak service. These advertisements depend on the type of services. Restaurants place clear plastic displays, often called tents, on the table to advertise off-peak specials and attempt to enhance repeat usage.

There are many other creative ways of using peak periods to reach potential off-peak customers. We can target customers during the peak with coupons for off-peak services. During the peak, we can offer discounted tickets or passes for off-peak periods. We can also inform customers about price reductions and special promotions associated with off-peak usage of our service.

We must, however, be careful not to overdo our selling effort during the peak-period and subject customers to unrelenting advertising. Customers, unhappily waiting in line, may find advertising unattractive. In one case, a supermarket installed 13-inch color television monitors mounted at each checkout counter. The television monitors exposed customers, waiting in its queues, to paid advertising. They went beyond advertising items at the supermarket and included general commercials. Customer response was overwhelmingly negative. Customers complained that the commercials were annoying, distracting, and noisy.

Giving Priority to Loyal Customers Another non-pricing strategy for using peak demand to increase off-peak demand is the establishment of priority queues. With priority queues, loyal customers get special priority during peak periods. Here, we define a loyal customer as a user who uses the service off-peak. Therefore, priority queues during the peak period encourage loyalty and enhance demand during the off-peak period. Customer loyalty leads to increased retention (Bolton, 1998) and higher future profits.

There are examples of priority queues in many industries. Airlines gives priority seating to frequent flyers that show demand during both peak and off-peak periods. Restaurants give priority seating to regular customers. Loyal industrial customers may get faster delivery during times of peak demand. Banks sometimes have special lines for regular commercial customers. Any services that schedule appointments can give priority to loyal customers and encourage off-peak demand.

We see that giving priority during the peak to loyal customers can help create off-peak demand. This strategy works best when loyal customers are also price-insensitive customers such as business travelers or high-income individuals. This strategy may not work as well when our loyal customers are also price-sensitive customers. Let us consider the case when our most loyal customers are also more sensitive to price than our average customers at the peak.

Consider, for example, Disney World resort customers in Florida. Here, Disney enjoys regular visits by Florida residents throughout the year. Florida residents are quick to take advantage of off-peak specials and unexpected lulls in peak-demand. These loyal residents, however, are far more flexible with their travel plans than customers who fly to Disney from the north or corporations who must schedule conferences on particular dates. Florida residents, consequently, are both more loyal, while being far more price sensitive.

When loyal customers are more price sensitive, it becomes more costly to give loyal customers higher priority. By giving priority to price-sensitive customers, we may need to lower the optimal peak price to account for the high price sensitivity during the peak. As a consequence, we increase off-peak profitability at the cost of peak profitability. In general, demand shifting is not a good strategy. It is better to focus merely on generating off-peak demand, than shifting peak demand.

Requiring Reservations There are many ways reservations can help service providers stimulate off-peak demand. The most obvious way is to shift customers who would otherwise be lost at the peak, to the off-peak. With reservations, we are able to fill to capacity and then transfer all excess demand to the off-peak. When a user calls, we try to match that user with a time period when capacity is available. We may also be able to extract the highest price by shifting the user to the most desirable time slot whose price does not exceed the user's reservation price.

Reservation systems work best when either little competition exists or our competitors face the same peak demand that we do. When users lack alternatives, we have maximum flexibility in assigning reservations. During the peak, we can completely book our capacity at very high prices. When either a user is unable to reserve our service at the peak, because of insufficient capacity, or when the user desires a lower price, we can provide the user with an off-peak reservation. The lack of user alternatives encourages the user to accept our off-peak reservation in lieu of switching to a competitor.

With many competitors that face different peak demand, the situation changes. We would have less flexibility. When we deny a user a peak-reservation and offer an off-peak reservation, the user may prefer a competitive peak-reservation. We, consequently, observe reservations in industries where few alternatives exist, such as physician or other professional services, or when all competitors face the same peak demand, such as hotels and restaurants.

Beyond competition, user preferences may also affect the profitability of reservation systems. Remember that a reservation is an insurance against either being denied service or a long wait for service. Some reservations provide more complete coverage than others. The greater the coverage, the greater the benefit to users. Greater coverage also produces a greater cost for the service provider. Reservation systems are costly to the service provider because of both administration costs and the opportunity costs associated with customers who fail to use their reservation. Customers who fail to honor their reservations often cause less than ideal idle capacity during peak-periods and considerable opportunity costs. An airline, for example, may fly with an empty seat that would have otherwise earned a premium fare.

Promoting to New Customers The cost of giving free service, on a trial basis, is cheaper during the off-peak periods. Here, we only incur the incremental cost associated with the additional service. We offer trial services at a lower price. The intent, here, is to overcome the initial hesitation that a customer might have with our service. Our goal is to get that customer to continue using our service after the trial period. Therefore, it is important that we only offer trial prices to clients who have the potential to become permanent customers. We should also avoid offering trial prices to existing customers who may only seek to obtain our service at lower prices.

Trial prices are common in many service industries. In promoting cellular phones, for example, one company offers free time during off-peak hours to potential new clients.

Capacity-Constrained Strategies with Unpredictable Demand

The Impact of Unpredictable Demand

How Unpredictable Demand Decreases Service Quality

The previous section discussed service strategy when demand for our service had predictable peaks.

This section discusses service strategy when demand is relatively constant, but is characterized by sudden and unpredictable peaks. This type of demand is found in many service industries when several customers, by chance, arrive at the same moment.

Consider, for example, a bank in the middle of the afternoon. Suppose there is one teller on duty. About 30 customers arrive each hour and it takes approximately one minute to serve a customer. Customers, in our example, arrive independently. In other words, the arrival of one customer neither increases nor decreases the probability that another customer will arrive sooner or later. Moreover, in this example, the bank has sufficient capacity to serve all customers and, therefore, should not deny service to any customers. In fact, we would expect the teller would be idle 30 minutes of every hour because the teller would be with customers only 30 minutes of every hour. In other words, the bank has twice the capacity needed to meet the demand of 30 minutes of teller-time per hour.

From a quick look at the situation, we might conclude that our system is inefficient because the teller is idle 50% of the time. We might also conclude that this excess capacity will provide a very high level of service because customers need not wait in line. Despite the presence of excess capacity, however, long lines may still develop at the bank. Suppose, for example, that rather than arriving in two-minute intervals, by chance, the 30 customers all arrive at the same time. In that event, the one teller starts to serve the first customer, and the other 29 customers begin to wait in a line or queue. The queue starts with a length of 29. With a one-minute per customer service time, and assuming that no new customers arrive, it takes 29 minutes before the teller serves the last person in line. We see that the average customer in the queue waits 435/29 or 15 minutes for service to be completed.[2] Moreover, the last customer in the queue waits 29 minutes for service.

It is unlikely that many customers will wait 29 minutes or more, but it is very likely that some customers will wait. In fact, we can compute the average time we would expect customers to wait. Computing the average wait time requires a mathematical formula from queuing theory. That formula reveals that with an average two-minute arrival rate for customers, and an average service time of one minute, we predict that the average customer will wait one minute. Stated another way, the average customer spends two minutes in the bank and half of that time is spent waiting in line. Hence, customers spend 50% of their time waiting in line while tellers spend 50% of their time idle.

In our example, the arrival of customers was independent and evenly distributed throughout the hour. This situation implies that we do not expect customers to arrive together, except by chance. Chance arrival by customers, of course, suggests a high probability that customers will sometimes arrive together. In addition, when customers arrive in groups, because they are traveling together as friends or co-workers, the situation is worse. Expected queues will be longer and the average customer will spend more time in the bank.

In general, we can think of capacity as a measure of our ability to provide service quality, and queue length as a measure of actual service quality. Our previous example suggests that as demand becomes unpredictable, we require more capacity to provide the same level of service quality. We can have many idle servers, yet, with some positive probability, many of our customers may still suffer long waits in queues. In the next section, we discuss how different types of demand uncertainty affect service quality.

Factors Influencing Service Quality and Waiting Times

Time for Service Delivery Two key components of uncertainty are service times and customer arrival rates. Service time is the time it takes for a customer to receive complete service. Customers often prefer faster service to slower service, keeping constant the benefits from the service. Despite customer preferences for faster service, service time is important for another reason. Service time has a dramatic impact on the total time that the average customer spends in the system.

The time the average customer spends in the system is the sum of the time being served and the time waiting for service. For example, at a healthcare facility, patients must first wait for care and, subsequently, obtain care. Their total time in the system is the sum of the time waiting for care plus the time actually receiving care from, say, a physician. Were one patient to spend more time with the physician, it would increase that patient's time in the system. In addition, the longer service time for the one patient would delay all patients currently waiting in line as well as any new patients who arrive during the delay. Hence, delays in service time can quickly increase the total time spent by all customers in the service system.

We often measure service time as the rate at which service occurs. The rate is the number of customers served per unit time. For example, if it takes two minutes to serve one customer, we say the service has a rate of 1/2 or .5 customers per minute. The service rate is a function of several factors including organization of the service, server training, and customer preparation. A well-organized service sequences tasks to maximize efficiency. A retail check-out clerk, for example, may follow an efficient script of first asking for all merchandise, asking the type of payment, removing price tags for the merchandise, entering prices from tags into the computer, bagging the merchandise while printing the receipt, and so on. Server training assists servers in maintaining efficiencies by developing contingent procedures for handling special problems. Finally, work progress analysis and other special methods can reduce server time.

The service rate varies from industry to industry. In some industries, the average service rate is relatively short. In other industries, the average service rate is relatively long. In the next section, we explore the effect of service rate on service strategy and customer waiting.

How Often Customers Arrive For some services, customers arrive frequently but service time is relatively fast. By frequent arrivals, we mean that we expect many customers to arrive in each time interval. By relatively fast service, we mean that a server can serve many customers within a short time. Examples of frequent arrival/fast service situations include express lines in grocery stores, tollbooths on interstate highways, collection of tickets at entrances to theaters, and directory assistance by telephone companies. For these services, one server usually serves many customers each hour. The server spends little time with a customer and queues move quickly. As a consequence, these services can provide higher levels of service with less capacity.

To see why, consider the unlikely, but possible, event of multiple arrivals. Suppose that 30 customers usually arrive per hour and all 30 customers arrive at the same time. If the service is fast, the line moves quickly and, despite the unfortunate timing, the last customer in the queue still has a relatively short wait. This reasoning suggests a less disastrous impact associated with simultaneous arrivals. Fast service allows us to quickly overcome the problems associated with simultaneous arrival.

Now let us consider the situation of infrequent customer arrival with relatively slow service times. For example, consider an interstate automobile towing and on-site repair service. The facility may expect very few calls in any day, but a single call may take several hours of time. With situations of infrequent arrival but slow service rates, we expect one server to spend more time with customers. We also expect shorter lines because we expect fewer customers. Despite these expectations, infrequent arrival but slow service situations require more capacity to provide the same level of service. In other words, when lines do develop, our customers wait much longer than in the frequent arrival/fast service case.

To see way, let us consider our previous example where, on average, 30 customers arrive per hour and it takes, on average, one minute to serve a customer. That situation is a frequent arrival/fast service case. For the infrequent arrival/slow service case, consider a situation where only six customers arrive per hour but it takes five minutes to serve each of them. In each case, we expect one server to spend 30 minutes of every hour serving customers. In the first case, on average, in each hour the server would spend one minute with each of 30 customers and 30 minutes idle. In the second case, on average, each hour the server would spend five minutes with each of six customers and 30 minutes idle. The two cases appear somewhat similar.

When it comes to average waits, however, the two cases are very different. Queuing theory formulas tell us that the average wait for the frequent arrival/fast service case is one minute while the average wait for the infrequent arrival/slow service case is five times longer, or five minutes. The average time spent in the service system for the frequent arrival/fast service case is one minute waiting and one minute being serviced, a total of two minutes. The average time spent in the service system for the infrequent arrival/slow service case is five minutes waiting and five minutes being serviced, a total of 10 minutes.

We see that in both cases we have similar capacities, because in each case our server is idle, on average, 50% of the time. In every hour, our server spends about 30 minutes with customers. However, when customer arrivals are infrequent and service is slow, our customers wait five times longer. To keep average waiting times constant, for the two cases, we would need more servers in the second case. We conclude that infrequent arrival/slow service providers require more capacity to provide the same waiting times as frequent arrival/fast service. Both cases may have the same amount of idle capacity, but the expected wait times are very different. It therefore costs us more to provide the same waiting times, and customers must pay more for the benefit of the same waiting time when service is slow. The consequence is an inherent efficiency problem in infrequent arrival/slow service situations.

Strategic Implications

Technological Constraints on Service Quality

Uncontrollable Service Rates

In many cases, the nature of the business dictates the quality of the service in terms of service rates. For example, a travel agency that books vacations will have slower service than a tollbooth on an expressway. The technology of a travel agency service requires more time spent with customers to evaluate options and assess customer preferences. The technology of a tollbooth, in contrast, allows very fast interactions with customers and minimum contact.

Services such as unemployment agencies, traffic court, eye-glass examinations, and hospital emergency rooms will require more lengthy service times than services such as dry cleaning drop-offs, car washes and toll booths. These differences in service time are a function of the service technology and are somewhat beyond the control of the service provider.

Services that have technologically slow service rates will face a technological disadvantage. Not only must they provide more servers to compensate for slower service rates, but they must add still more servers to keep waits short. Here, a service that has twice the service time must have more than twice as many servers to remain even with the faster service.

Consequently, the payoff from improving service rates is much higher for services with slower service rates than services with faster service rates. Services with low service rates gain on both time with the server as well as shorter waits when they improve service. Unfortunately, services with slower rates often require more customization of their service, which limits their ability to improve service rates.

With slower service rates, we require more capacity because each server will be busy longer. For example, when a server takes six minutes to serve a customer, we will need more servers than when each server takes only one minute. When a server takes six minutes, that server is busy for six minutes and will be unable to serve another customer for six minutes. Consequently, we need more servers to accommodate multiple arrivals. Otherwise, when multiple customers arrive in close proximity, we will either lose some customers or decrease the quality of service by increasing average waiting times.

Controllable Customer Arrival Rates

Similar to service rates, the arrival rates of customers are somewhat of a function of the service technology. Travel agencies will have few arrivals per hour, while tollbooths will have many arrivals per hour. Museums will have a continuous flow of customers, while new car dealers may encounter more sporadic arrivals. As a service provider, we should seek to influence arrival rates. Service technology, however, may place limits on our influence.

Consider a situation when the rate of service is relatively slow. As we discussed earlier, the average wait time will be higher. It may take, for example, an hour to fully serve one customer. In that case, the unfortunate event of multiple arrivals has a more adverse effect on waiting time. With one server and the arrival of three customers, we will be able to serve only one of the customers. The second customer must wait one hour while the third customer must wait two hours. Our average wait times will be one hour.

As a service provider, we can insure against multiple arrivals by having more servers. Of course, having more servers suggests more idle capacity. More idle capacity, in turn, suggests a higher fixed cost and a higher rate to the consumer. In other words, customers must pay for insurance against long waits by subsidizing excess capacity.

The compromise between excess capacity and insufficient capacity depends on both the arrival rate and the incremental fixed cost associated with additional capacity. When the arrival rate increases, we are better able to justify more capacity. More frequent arrivals suggest a high probability that many customers will be in the service delivery system. As the number of customers increase, we expect more even demand and better utilization of capacity. We also expect to be better able to manage average customer waiting time because demand is more evenly distributed over time.

Combining Arrival Rates and Service Rates

To get the same average wait time, we said that arrivals that are more frequent and slower service require more capacity than less frequent arrivals and faster service. In general, industries with slow service and frequent arrivals require the highest capacity. Industries with slow service and infrequent arrivals require the second highest capacity. Industries with fast service and frequent arrivals require the next highest level of capacity. Industries with fast service and infrequent arrivals require the least capacity.

Table 19.1 provides examples from different industries of the four cases. Table 19.2 illustrates the expected wait times for these different cases, holding constant capacity (i.e., the number of servers).

To determine whether the appropriate strategy involves higher levels of service and shorter waiting times, we must determine whether our customers are willing to pay for decreased waiting times. In industries such as medical services, where insurance companies and government agencies sometimes limit pricing strategies, there may be little incentive to decrease waiting times. In other industries, such as business travel, users may place great value on their time and be very willing to pay for shorter waits.

In many cases, some customers will prefer a higher price for insurance against a long wait while other customers would prefer a lower price and a risk of a long wait. It is, therefore, necessary to segment the market into customers who are willing to risk a wait and customers who are willing to pay more to avoid the risk of a wait. Remember that it is always best to provide sufficient service so that some servers are idle some of the time.

This segmentation can be either explicit or by self-selection. With explicit segmentation, we attempt to identify and classify each customer by his or her willingness-to-wait. Having identified the customer, we then offer that customer the appropriate service. With self-selection, we might announce two services – a premium service and an economy service. The economy service provides a basic

Table 19.1 *Arrival and Service Rate Examples*

	Many Customers	Few Customers
Slow Service	Unemployment Agency	Travel Agency
	Traffic Court	Eye Glass Service
	Hospital Emergency Room	Clothes Alteration
	Dental Service	New Car Dealer
	Tax Preparation	Many Repair Services
Fast Service	Dry Cleaning Drop-off	Off-peak ATM
	Convenience Store	Self-serve Gas Station
	Car Wash	Vending Machine
	Parking Garage	Expensive Boutique Check-out
	Toll Booth	Museum Admission

Table 19.2 *Expected Waiting Times*

	Many Customers	Few Customers
Slow Service	Very Long Waits	Long Waits
Fast Service	Medium Waits	Short Waits

service at a minimum price. The premium service consists of an additional bundle of benefits including insurance against long waits.

Strategic Implications of Larger Scale Suppose we have two service providers. The first provider has one server, the service rate is .5 minutes and customers arrive, on average, every two minutes. The second service provider has twice the capacity and twice the arrival rate. The second provider has two servers, a service rate of .5 and customers arrive, on average, every minute. In this situation, the first service provider will have 60% more customers in line and customers will spend 80% more time in line.

Hence, when the service rate is slow, the penalty imposed on customers is greater than when service rates are higher. This penalty is greater even when the slow service rate provider has additional services to compensate for the slower service rate. An unlucky customer, who arrives shortly after another customer, will need to wait a long time. The customer would need to wait the entire time required for service. The longer the service time, the longer the wait unless there were two servers. With two servers the second customer would not need to wait. As we will see, however, a service with twice the service time and twice the servers still has a greater risk of a long wait than a server with both half the number of servers and half the service time.

Now suppose there are two servers but customer arrivals occur at twice the rate. Of course, in this case, lines will be longer than with a more infrequent arrival rate. Nevertheless, as we mentioned, average waits will be less than the situation with only one server but half the arrival rate.

Although it is possible to demonstrate this conclusion with some complex mathematical calculations, we will, instead, examine the intuition underlying the conclusions. Suppose that we have two service providers, A and B. Provider A has one server and gets one customer every two hours, i.e., an arrival rate of .5 customers per hour. Provider B has two servers and gets ten customers every two hours, i.e., an arrival rate of one customer per hour.

Provider B is similar to provider A. For simplicity, suppose that Provider B has two lines, one for each server. Each line would behave similarly to Provider A's line. People arrive in each line and wait. The wait in each line at Provider B is, on average, identical to the wait at Provider A. In short, Provider B looks completely identical to Provider A except there are two lines rather than one.

However, Provider B offers an important advantage over Provider A. When one line at Provider B is busy, a customer can switch to the other line. When one line at Provider B gets longer than the other line, customers can switch to the shorter line. In fact, Provider B can make the whole process extremely efficient by having one line and, as customers move to the front of that line, assigning them to the first available server.

In other words, as we scale-up the operation, the average wait decreases. Double the arrival rate and add twice as many servers and the wait goes down. Triple the arrival rate and add three times as many servers and the wait goes down further. Increasing the scale decreases the probability of a long wait.

There are, therefore, important economies-of-scale associated with services. These economies will be most important when increasing the size of the operation proportionally increases arrivals. In short, when doubling the size of the operation doubles the market, we should double the size of the operation. The operation should continue to increase in size until further increases in the size of the operation fail to generate sufficiently large increases in arrivals.

The advantage of larger size or scale is particularly important in industries that have both large markets of customers and exhibit very slow service rates. When an industry's service technology requires long service times, service providers in that industry gain an important competitive advantage by growing larger. Larger service providers gain the capacity to provide better service by merely doubling their size. This advantage continues as long as the market is sufficiently large.

New entry, in contrast, is easier in smaller markets with more rapid service. In these markets, a small service provider can serve the entire market or a segment of that market at approximately the same cost as a larger service provider. Holding other factors constant, there is little advantage to scale from the perspective of waiting times.

Profiting from Imbalances in Service Capacity and Demand

Profiting from Excess Capacity

Is Excess Capacity Needed? As we increase the number of servers, we provide our customers with benefits. We decrease the expected wait times and insure our customers against a long wait. We also incur a higher fixed cost for the capacity that enables us to deliver these benefits. These benefits are desirable for us provided that we are able to increase our price to cover that capacity.

With a constant marketing strategy, it is seldom profitable to have sufficient capacity to cover the maximum possible demand. It depends on the distribution of customer arrivals. Suppose, for example, we must decide on the service capacity of a retailer. Here, we must decide the size of the floor service staff.

We would certainly have additional staff on weekends, holidays and other periods when we anticipate above-average demand. During weekdays, we would have a smaller staff. However, it is possible to have unexpected busy periods each weekday.

Suppose, on average, there are two customers in the store that require service. There is a 5% chance that five customers will arrive together and all require service. There is a 1% chance that 10 customers will require service and a .1% chance that 50 customers will require service.

Were we to maintain 50 service employees, 48 employees would usually be idle. The prices for our products must include the salaries of the 50 service employees. Few of our customers would pay the higher prices to insure against not receiving service with a probability of .1%. Hence, we would not employ 50 service employees.

Were we to maintain five staff people, three would usually be idle. Again, our retail prices must include the salaries of the three idle employees as well as the two busy employees. Our decision about the number of staff depends on our service strategy. We must decide whether to be a high service/high price or lower service/lower price provider.

Whatever our strategic decision, we will have excess capacity because we would never hire sufficient service employees to meet the maximum possible, but improbable, demand. It is always possible, with some small probability, that demand will exceed the optimal capacity. Stated another way, optimal capacity is always less than the maximum possible demand.

The consequence, therefore, of our capacity decision is to have periods when demand apparently exceeds capacity. This conclusion, however, may be false when we allow the marketing strategy to vary. We might implement a marketing strategy that reduces demand during periods of insufficient capacity. In general, these marketing strategies involve some type of rationing.

Finally, we should end this section by remembering that we can always eliminate excess capacity by lowering the price of our service. At a sufficiently low price, we would generate sufficient demand to fill capacity. A hotel, for example, at a sufficiently low room rate would fill the rooms with permanent guests. This point illustrates that filling capacity is not a goal and is merely a deceptive distraction for the service provider.

Selling Excess Capacity As authors such as Lovelock (1992) note, off-peak periods with excess capacity provide an opportunity to rest, plan for the peak, train new employees, accomplish required maintenance, and develop new services consistent with the overall service strategy. All of these activities provide indirect help that contributes to the efficiency and profitability of the service provider at the peak. They are real benefits that are often difficult to measure.

Beyond these indirect benefits, service providers often seek direct revenue gains from excess capacity. We should again remember that filling excess capacity is not a goal in itself. Just as a manufacturer should not produce products which the manufacturer is unable to sell, a service provider should not lose money merely to fill capacity.

It would be foolish to switch high-paying peak customers to off-peak by offering deep discounts. We would only be forgoing possible profits. Off-peak periods should not cannibalize peak-period profits. We should only try to maximize revenues given the possible resource of excess capacity.

Having said that, let us consider how we can use excess capacity. With excess capacity, we can often produce additional service at very little additional cost. That is, of course, the key to using excess capacity. We must try to accomplish this task by not shifting specific buyers from higher priced purchases at the peak. A restaurant, for example, should not have early-bird dinner specials that merely take customers from the peak. These specials, rather, should target customers who would be unwilling to pay the higher prices at the peak. They may also target customers whom they are unable to serve at the peak because of insufficient capacity.

Another approach to profiting from excess capacity is to sell that capacity. A public utility, for example, could sell excess electricity or telephone line capacity. This strategy is feasible when demand is unpredictable and uncorrelated across the industry. Here, when one electric utility has reached capacity, another may be well-below capacity and can sell the first utility some of its excess.

To sell excess capacity, it is necessary to establish a spot market. On this market, buyers and sellers can negotiate short-term agreements for excess capacity. In many cases, these spot markets take the form of subcontracting. An advertising agency, for example, faced with demand that exceeds capacity might subcontract work to an agency operating at under capacity. A hotel, whose demand exceeds capacity, may send guests to another hotel that is operating below capacity.

Remember that when demand is unpredictable, the timing of excess capacity is also unpredictable. Hence, we must develop procedures long before the excess capacity develops. The hotel, for example, that absorbs the overflow from another hotel must develop a long-term relationship with the second hotel. The same is true for rental car companies, airlines and other services that either strategically overbook or just find themselves with unexpected demand.

Profiting from Insufficient Capacity

Peak Strategies with Price Flexibility Previously, we discussed the pricing decision when demand varied by season but varied in a predictable way. In this case, when demand for the service was certain, the pricing decision was straightforward. As noted earlier, the optimal price is independent of capacity, provided we have sufficient capacity at the optimal price. When we have insufficient capacity at the optimal price, we should set a sufficiently high price so that demand exactly equals available capacity. Hence, we must first determine the optimal price without a capacity constraint. Only then can we determine whether capacity is sufficient. Moreover, we should make no attempt to fill excess capacity, but instead, ignore it by merely setting price to maximize profits.

In this section, we turn our attention to the case of uncertain demand. When demand is uncertain, the situation can become more complex. When demand is uncertain, the capacity constraint is probabilistic or uncertain. In short, we do not know whether we have sufficient capacity. Only after setting our price do we observe actual demand. At that point, demand may or may not exceed available capacity. The outcome is uncertain.

When demand is uncertain, the old rules for certain demand may or may not hold. The best pricing rule depends on whether we have the ability to change prices when unexpected peaks in demand develop. That ability is usually specific to the service industry. In industries such as consulting, accounting, law, architecture, air travel, and so on, a service provider can change prices when unexpected demand develops. A consultant who gets unexpectedly busy, for example, can raise prices for new projects. As the consultant reaches capacity, the price can approach infinity and the consultant declines new business regardless of the client's willingness to pay.

When the pricing decision is flexible and we can change our price as unexpected demand conditions develop, the old pricing rules for certain demand apply. We should again ignore capacity and price at that price that maximizes profits. We should only consider capacity constraints when we have insufficient capacity to meet demand at the optimal price. In that case, we should raise the price until demand exactly equals capacity.

Peak Strategies with Price Inflexibility When price is inflexible, the situation is far more complex. This situation occurs in many industries, such as restaurants, retailing, and most personal services. For these industries, we post prices before we know demand conditions. It becomes very difficult, after demand becomes known, to change prices. Retailers can mark down merchandise with disappointing demand; however, they cannot suddenly raise prices on an unexpectedly busy day.

Here, the pricing decision is much more complex because the optimal price always depends on the probability that demand will exceed available capacity. Hence, the optimal price depends on capacity regardless of whether the capacity constraint is binding. The mere possibility of a binding capacity constraint changes the optimal price.

Suppose, for example, that a car wash finds that the best price for a car wash, without considering capacity constraints, is $10. Lowering the price below $10 would generate additional customers, but the number of additional customers fails to compensate for the loss in profit per wash. Raising the price above $10 would increase the profit per wash, but that increase in profits does not compensate for the decrease in the total number of car washes caused by the higher price.

Now suppose that, at $10, the car wash attracts sufficient demand that long waits can develop. To be precise, 20% of the time, the car wash permanently loses customers who are unwilling to wait in line. So, 20% of the time, the car wash can raise prices and do the same number of washes. Hence, the car wash should raise prices, continue to operate at capacity and earn greater profits.

The car wash, however, is unable to predict when a busy period will develop. Moreover, it is unable to temporarily raise prices when a busy period develops. Hence, the car wash must raise prices during all periods with the anticipation that during busy times, the higher price will generate greater profits. During slack periods, unfortunately, the higher price generates less profit. After balancing price and demand, the best price with a capacity constraint will be higher than the best price without the capacity constraint, regardless of whether the capacity constraint is binding.

Remember that this conclusion is only valid when the service provider is unable to change prices when a peak develops. As we have said, the usual cause for this situation is that the peak was unexpected. Other causes for this might include problems with image. Many service providers may feel that their image with the public would suffer if they were to raise prices at times of peak demand (e.g., consider increasing the price of fresh water after a hurricane). The loss in image would suggest a loss in goodwill and an eventual loss in sales. Given these conditions, the service provider would not have a different price during the peak and non-peak times. Note, however, that the best price is now greater than the off-peak price and less than the peak price. In short, customers pay more during off-peak periods so that the service provider does not need to raise prices at the peak.

Rationing: Balancing Service Capacity and Demand

Price Rationing

For a variety of reasons, many economists argue that rationing capacity on price is the most efficient means of allocating capacity. In short, most economists argue that when demand exceeds available capacity, the capacity should go to the highest bidder. If the demand for a theater exceeds seating capacity, for example, the available seats should go to the highest bidders. Alternatively, the theater could raise the price of each seat until the number of buyers exactly equals the number of seats.

One of the primary justifications for price rationing is supply-side efficiency. As the price of a scarce resource increases, the service provider enjoys more revenue from the available capacity. As that revenue increases, the service provider finds it profitable to expand available capacity. Without the additional revenue, there would be less incentive to expand capacity.

This fact is true for both the service provider and competitive service providers. Were a theater, for example, to consistently find that demand exceeded capacity, the theater might raise its price. With a higher price, the theater would find that additional capacity is more profitable. Competitive theaters would also find that additional capacity is more profitable. As a consequence, the entire industry would build additional capacity. The industry would enjoy increased profits from higher prices. Those profits would encourage existing service providers to increase capacity and increased profits would attract new service providers into the market.

The combined service capacity of all competitors continues to increase until the price drops. This drop in price suggests a balance between the demand for the service and its supply. Were we to allocate capacity on a basis other than price, there would be no incentive to increase capacity to meet demand. The result would be less than optimum levels of capacity.

A second argument for price rationing is that customers reveal their true preferences for the service. For example, consider a theater that is hosting two events, a musical production and a drama. For both events, demand for tickets exceeds the number of available seats. Suppose, rather than raising price, the theater allocates scarce theater tickets for the two events using a random lottery. Here, chance determines which customers receive which ticket. In this case, customers who are more interested in the drama may receive a ticket for the musical. Moreover, some customers, who have only a moderate interest in either event, may receive, by chance, tickets to both events.

We see that price rationing is often a desirable means of balancing capacity and demand. It is an efficient way of reducing demand while increasing revenue. It is also an efficient way of allocating capacity in the event that demand still exceeds capacity. Here, a waiting line or queue develops. We use price rationing to prioritize customers in the queue and determine who receives service first. Those customers willing to pay a higher price move to the front of the queue. More price-sensitive customers risk waiting in line longer for the reward of a lower price. This type of queue is known as a priority queue.

A perfect priority queue would prioritize customers exactly according to their willingness to wait as expressed by their willingness to pay. The customer willing to pay the highest price would take the first position in the queue and be the first to receive service. The customer willing to pay the second highest price would take the second position in the queue. The customers would queue so that the last customer in line bids the lowest price for immediate service.

In reality, we seldom see pure priority queues except in highly technical markets such as queues for computing resources allocations, natural gas delivery services, or financial markets. The complexity of the priority queue makes it difficult to implement in its pure form. Far more often, we see random queues with priority rules such as first-come first-served. Nevertheless, the priority queue remains an important concept.

A simple means of simulating a priority queue is a useful goal. Commonly practiced methods such as yield management (Desiraju & Shugan, 1999; Smith et al., 1992) create weaker forms of priority queues. These methods fail to perfectly align customers with their willingness to pay. Although they are not perfect, these methods do achieve some degree of success toward that goal.

Yield management, for example, creates a partial priority queue by segmenting customers by their willingness to pay and, then, allocating capacity by segment (Dana, 1998, 1999a, 1999b, 2001). The better the yield management system, the more the system resembles a priority queue. An airline, for example, tries to allocate limited seating first by full-priced first class, full-priced business class, full-priced economy class, followed by discounted fares. In this way, the airline creates an imperfect, but effective, priority queue.

Yield management also allows overselling of capacity (Biyalogorsky et al., 1999). Overselling is useful when demand is uncertain and advance purchases are not completely binding. Overselling also gives the seller the potential to make very profitable buyback transactions during the spot period. When capacity is insufficient, sellers can buy back capacity at lower prices than the expected spot price.

However, recent research suggests that non-price rationing, although inefficient for society, may be more profitable than price rationing (Gilbert & Klemperer, 2000). This situation occurs when customers must make large sunk investments to enter the market.

Why Non-price Rationing

The discussion of rationing is important both in this section, which discusses unpredictable demand peaks, and the last section, which discussed predictable demand peaks. Rationing capacity is important whenever demand for the service exceeds the capacity needed to supply the service. It is less important whenever the service provider has the ability to forecast when capacity will be insufficient to satisfy demand.

There is, however, at least one important difference between rationing when demand is predictable and when it is unpredictable. The difference comes in the ability to react to changes in demand. In the last section, the service provider knew well in advance when demand would exceed capacity. The service provider had sufficient time to plan for the event and take necessary actions. A tour operator, for example, could announce higher prices during periods of peak demand and lower prices during off-peak periods. An accounting firm could similarly announce higher prices for tax services during the peak season. When demand is unpredictable, the service provider knows that demand will sometimes exceed capacity. The service provider, however, does not know when that will occur. In this case, the service provider is unable to announce higher prices during periods of peak demand. That inability often leads to forms of non-price rationing.

Consider a taxi service, for example, which may suddenly find itself faced with higher demand because of inclement weather. The service would like to increase fares during these unexpected peak-periods. Unfortunately, the service seldom has the ability to take that action. The taxi service, therefore, resorts to other forms of non-price rationing.

The taxi service may, for example, focus on more profitable routes. Drivers may focus on airports, hotels, and locations where long hauls are more likely. The service may also attempt temporarily to expand capacity by postponing breaks for drivers, calling in additional drivers, and deploying all available cars.

We see that uncertainty in forecasting peak demand may prevent price rationing. In addition, there are other arguments against price rationing such as perceived equity, simplicity in implementation and legal constraints. Perceived equity, which occurs in services such as health-care and public utilities, suggests that customers who are unable to pay a very high price should still be allowed access to the service. Simplicity in implementation, which occurs in industries such as amusement parks and toll roads, suggests that it would be operationally costly to implement complex rationing systems because of difficulties in explaining and maintaining those systems. Finally, legal constraints often prevent many forms of price rationing because of either regulatory rules or laws against price discrimination.

Before discussing forms of non-price rationing, we should again note that higher prices do solve the capacity constraint problem. We can reduce demand to the level of capacity with higher prices. Moreover, higher prices provide the long-term incentive to increase capacity to serve more customers. However, there are equity arguments against price rationing.

Consider the National Development Bank (i.e., the Banco Naçional de Fomento, BNF), in Ecuador. This bank had the responsibility for granting credit services to the agricultural sector. The bank, on an equity basis, decided to reject price rationing in favor of non-pricing methods for allocating available credit. Given non-price rationing, the demand for credit exceeded available funds. Therefore, the bank used methods such as higher requirements for collateral, a more involved application process and increased delays in granting loans (Morrison, 1994). The consequence was a bias in favor of larger loans to customers who could endure both the more onerous application process and the long wait for the loan. This outcome left small farms at a distinct disadvantage, leaving many of them strapped for funds.

Now consider the health-care system. Here, policy makers rejected price rationing for donor hearts as inequitable. A system of first-come first-served became the policy. Unfortunately, this method of rationing scarce donor hearts has another drawback. The first-come first-served method rejects hearts for sicker patients who often find waiting more costly, and sometimes die waiting for a heart (Frank, 1992).

Obviously, equity concerns are important when choosing a rationing system. However, service providers must face a difficult compromise between equity and gaining additional profits that could help expand future capacity. Higher levels of profit justify both additional investments in capacity as well as maintaining higher capacity off-peak. Service providers who are unable to generate sufficient funds during times of peak demand should choose lower levels of overall capacity.

Finally, non-price rationing might be directed at gaining customer loyalty or rewarding better customers. This concept is consistent with the Zeithaml, Rust & Lemon (2001) concept of a customer pyramid.

Public Attitudes Toward Rationing

When determining a rationing plan, we should consider both the profitability of the rationing plans as well as customer opinion. This is a difficult compromise because customers often prefer less profitable rationing methods. Moreover, many customers are somewhat unhappy about priority queues when they view the service as essential. Fortunately, they do recognize the need for rationing when faced with limited capacity.

One survey, for example, found that many people would support some form of rationing for public health-care services. Forty-four percent of those surveyed would prefer the same rationing rules regardless of the patient's ability to pay; 40% of the respondents said they preferred rationing of treatments based on the likelihood of success rather than rationing based on first-come first-served; 29% of the respondents said that we should deny smokers heath-care services for diseases caused by smoking; 26% of the respondents said that children should have priority over the elderly. Finally, only 16% of the respondents thought that rationing should not be used for privately funded health-care services.[3]

Advance Selling with Capacity Constraints

Advance selling of capacity can be extremely profitable. Shugan & Xie (2000) show that giving buyers the ability to advance purchase capacity provides many potential advantages. If the advance price is discounted, it allows a much larger increase in demand than the same price discount in the spot period (Shugan & Xie, 2000; Xie & Shugan, 2001). Lee & Ng (2001) also find this result. Shugan & Xie (2002) show that this result survives the introduction of competition.

Advance selling can also allow price-discrimination where more price-sensitive buyers advance purchase, allowing high spot prices (Dana, 1999a; Desiraju & Shugan, 1999). It does, however, often require the sequential servicing of buyers (Rosen & Rosenfield, 1997). Advance selling can also help to efficiently adjust uncertain demand to fill more capacity across services (Dana, 1999b).

When buyers want to insure future capacity (Png, 1989), the advance price can be at a premium to the spot price (Shugan & Xie, 2002). Sellers profit from selling at a higher advance price than selling at the lower spot price.

Advance selling can also decrease the pressure to attract new buyers with lower prices (Serel et al., 2001). Advance selling impacts the compromise between selling only to current customers in the spot period at high prices and trying to increase demand by attracting new customers. The reason is that by advance selling, spot capacity is reduced and, with less spot capacity, there is less incentive to attract more buyers (Shugan & Xie, 2002).

Finally, recent research examines the connection between bundling, rationing, and advance selling. DeGraba and Mohammed (1999) suggest that by advance selling in bundles and subsequently selling individually, a multi-service seller can earn more profit than individually selling each service. Given limited capacity, and possibly insufficient capacity, less price-sensitive (i.e., high-valuation) customers will advance buy. The reason is that they expect rationing when units are individually sold. It is these bundled purchases that cause the shortages that result in rationing. In this case, the bundle's price exceeds the sum of the individual prices. Future research might further integrate capacity constraints with product line strategy (Hess & Gerstner, 1998; Noble & Gruca, 1999; Shugan & Desiraju, 2001).

Conclusions and Future Research

This chapter discussed many ways in which capacity constraints impact the marketing strategies for service providers. Although not all service providers face capacity constraints, many do. This section reviews 11 of the more significant conclusions in this area.

First, capacity often dictates service strategy. Second, service providers can only compete on capacity when different buyers want different levels of service. Third, operational adjustments to changing capacity become a marketing strategy because they have a direct impact on customer satisfaction and demand. Fourth, marketing strategies must change during times of peak demand to emphasize services or aspects of services requiring less capacity. Fifth, it is important how we communicate with buyers about changes in price and quality during peak demand. Sixth, an important marketing decision is whether to announce peak prices or retain flexibility about them. Seventh, non-pricing rationing of capacity during times of peak demand creates the opportunity to reward loyal customers and sell new services. Eighth, there is an essential conflict between providing more service per customer and creating waiting times that diminish total service quality. Ninth, price rationing is often the most profitable form of rationing but it does create problems and is often difficult to implement. Tenth, advance selling of services provides enormous potential to increase profits. Eleventh, we can create sophisticated marketing strategies by combining dynamic pricing strategies, non-price rationing, bundling, advance selling and changing service quality over time.

We expect that future research on marketing strategies in the presence of capacity constraints will continue. We expect future research will focus on new strategies made possible by advancing technology. These strategies include strategies involving more complex pricing, strategies involving advance selling, and strategies that continuously adjust over time to adapt to changing conditions (possibly, instantaneously). We need a deeper understanding of how to market bundles of services, each facing different capacity constraints. We need a deeper understanding of how to implement multi-service strategies where different services face different competitive and demand conditions. We need a deeper understanding of what the best ways are to implement the rationing of capacity. Finally, we need a deeper understanding of how to build capacity consistent with our service strategy.

Notes

1 A "brown-out" is a significant drop in line-voltage below the regular voltage setting. A voltage decrease greater than 20% could be considered a brown-out and is also called a power "sag."

2 $1 + 2 + 3 + \cdots + 29 = 435$.

3 Northwestern National Life Insurance Company, *Americans Speak out on Health Care Rationing*. Minneapolis: The Company, November 1990.

References

Allen, W. Bruce & Liu, Dong (1995) Service quality and motor carrier costs: an empirical analysis. *The Review of Economics and Statistics*, 77 (3), 499–510.

Anderson, Eugene W. (1995) An economic approach to understanding how customer satisfaction affects buyer perceptions of value. *Marketing Theory and Applications*, Vol. 6, edited by David W. Stewart & Naufel Vilcassim.

Anderson, Eugene W. & Fornell, Claes (1999) The customer satisfaction index as a leading indicator. *Handbook of Services Marketing and Management*, edited by Teresa A. Swartz & Dawn Iacobucci. New York: Sage.

——— (2000) Foundations of the American customer satisfaction index. *Journal of Total Quality Measurement*, 11 (7), S869–S882.

Anderson, Eugene W. & Shugan, Steven M. (1991) Repositioning for changing preferences: the case of beef versus poultry. *Journal of Consumer Research*, 18, 2 (September), 219–32.

Anderson, Eugene W., Fornell, Claes & Lehmann, Donald R. (1994) Customer satisfaction, market share, and profitability. *Journal of Marketing*, 58, 3 (July), 53–66.

Anderson, Eugene W., Fornell, Claes & Rust, Roland (1997) Customer satisfaction, productivity, and profitability: differences between goods and services. *Marketing Science*, 16, 2, 129–45.

Bailey, Elizabeth E. & White, Lawrence J. (1974) Reversals in peak and off-peak prices. *Bell Journal of Economics and Management Science*, 5, 75–92.

Bar-Ilan Sulem, A.S. & Zanello, A. (2001) Time-to-build and capacity choice. *Journal of Economic Dynamics and Control*, 26 (1), 69–98.

Berg, Sanford V. & Tschirhart, John (1988) *Natural Monopoly Regulation*. Cambridge: Cambridge University Press.

Bergen, Mark, Dutta, Shantanu & Shugan, Steven M. (1996) Branded variants: a retail perspective. *Journal of Marketing Research*, 33 (1), 9–19.

Berry, Leonard L. (1980) Services marketing is different. *Business Horizons*, May/June, 24–29.

Biyalogorsky, E., Gerstner, E. & Libai, B. (2001) Customer referral management: optimal reward programs. *Marketing Science*, 20 (1), 82–95.

Biyalogorsky, E., Carmon, Z., Fruchter, G. & Gerstner, E. (1999) Overselling with opportunistic cancellations. *Marketing Science*, 18 (4), 605–10.

Bolton, R.N. (1998) A dynamic model of the duration of the customer's relationship with a continuous service provider: the role of satisfaction. *Marketing Science*, 17 (1), 45–65.

Brock, William A. & Scheinkman, Jose A. (1985) Price setting supergames with capacity constraints. *The Review of Economic Studies*, 52 (3), 371–82.

Burness, H. Stuart & Patrick, Robert H. (1991) Peak-load pricing with continuous and interdependent demand. *Journal of Regulatory Economics*, 3 (1), 69–88.

Chu, W., Gerstner, E. & Hess, J.D. (1995) Cost and benefits of hard sell. *Journal of Marketing Research*, 32 (February), 97–102.

——— (1999) Managing dissatisfaction, how to decrease customer opportunism by partial refunds. *Journal of Service Research*, 1 (2), November, 140–54.

Compte, O., Jenny, F. & Rey, P. (2002) Capacity constraints, mergers and collusion. *European Economic Review*, 46 (1), 1–29.

Crew, M.A., Fernando, C.S. & Kleindorfer, P.R. (1995) The theory of peak-load pricing – a survey. *Journal of Regulatory Economics*, 8, 3 (November), 215–48.

Dana, James D. Jr. (1998) Advance-purchase discounts and price discrimination in competitive markets. *The Journal of Political Economy*, 106 (2), 395–422.

——— (1999a) Equilibrium price dispersion under demand uncertainty: the roles of costly capacity and market structure. *Rand Journal of Economics*, 30 (3), 632–60.

——— (1999b) Using yield management to shift demand when the peak time is unknown. *Rand Journal of Economics*, 30 (3), 456–74.

——— (2001) Competition in price and availability when availability is unobservable. *Rand Journal of Economics*, 32 (3), 497–513.

DeGraba, P. & Mohammed, R. (1999) Intertemporal mixed bundling and buying frenzies. *Rand Journal of Economics*, 30 (4), 694–718.

Desiraju, Ramarao & Shugan, Steven M. (1999) Strategic service pricing and yield management. *Journal of Marketing*, 63 (January), 44–56.

Folland, Sherman, Ziegenfuss, James T. Jr. & Chao, Paul (1988) Implications of prospective payment under DRGs for hospital marketing. *Journal of Health Care Marketing*, 8 (December), 29–36.

Frank, Jacqueline (1992) Many on heart waiting list may not need transplants study. *Reuters News Service*, November 19.

Gilbert, R.J. & Klemperer, P. (2000) An equilibrium theory of rationing. *Rand Journal of Economics*, 31 (1), 1–21.

Greenidge, C.D. (1983) Let customers go with the flow: analyzing store layout. *Skiing Trade Monthly News*, 7 (January), 10.

Hart, C., Heskett, J. & Sasser, W.E. Jr. (1990) *The Service Management Course*. New York: Free Press.

Haskel, Jonathan & Martin, Christopher (1994) Capacity and competition: empirical evidence on UK panel data. *Journal of Industrial Economics*, 42 (1), 23–44.

Hauser, J.R. (2001) Metrics thermostat. *Journal of Product Innovation Management*, 18 (May, 3), 134–53.

Hauser, J.R., Simester, D.I. & Wernerfelt, B. (1994) Customer satisfaction incentives. *Marketing Science*, 13 (4), 327–50.

Herk, Leonard F. (1993) Consumer choice and cournot behavior in capacity-constrained duopoly competition. *Rand Journal of Economics*, 24 (3), 399–417.

Hess, J.D. & Gerstner, E. (1998) Yes, bait and switch really benefits consumers. *Marketing Science*, 17 (3), 273–82.

Hirschberg, J.G. (2000) Modelling time of day substitution using the second moments of demand. *Applied Economics*, 32 (June, 8), 979–86.

Hoffman, K.D. & Bateson, J.E.G. (1997) *Essentials of Services Marketing*. Orlando, FL: The Dryden Press.

Kurtz, David L. & Clow, Kenneth E. (1997) *Services Marketing*. New York: John Wiley and Sons.

Lee, K.S. & Ng, I.C.L. (2001) Advanced sale of service capacities: a theoretical analysis of the impact of price sensitivity on pricing and capacity allocations. *Journal of Business Research*, 54 (3), 219–25.

Lovelock, C. (1992) Seeking synergy in service operations: seven things marketers need to know about service operations. *European Management Journal*, 10 (March, 1), 22–9.

Lovelock, C., Patterson, P.G. & Walker, R. (1998) *Services Marketing*. Sydney: Prentice-Hall.

Morrison, Andrew R. (1994) Capital market imperfections, labor market disequilibrium and migration: a theoretical and empirical analysis. *Economic Inquiry*, 32, 2 (April), 290.

Noble, P.M. & Gruca, T.S. (1999) Industrial pricing: theory and managerial practice. *Marketing Science*, 18 (3), 435–54.

Onkvisit, S. & Shaw, J.J. (1991) Is services marketing 'really' different? *Journal of Professional Services Marketing*, 7 (2), 3–17.

Oren, Shmuel, Smith, Stephen & Wilson, Robert (1985) Capacity pricing. *Econometrica*, 53 (3), 545–66.

Parasuraman, A., Zeithaml, V.A. & Berry, L. (1985) A conceptual model of service quality and its implications for future research. *Journal of Marketing*, 49 (Fall), 41–50.

Perrakism, Stylianos & Warskett, George (1983) Capacity and entry under demand uncertainty. *The Review of Economic Studies*, 50 (3), 495–511.

Png, I.P.L. (1989) Reservations – customer insurance in the marketing of capacity. *Marketing Science*, 8 (3), 248–64.

Radas, Sonja & Shugan, Steven M. (1998a) Managing service demand: shifting and bundling. *Journal of Service Research*, 1, 1 (August), 47–64.

Radas, Sonja & Shugan, Steven M. (1998b) Seasonal marketing and timing new product introductions. *Journal of Marketing Research*, 35, 3 (August), 296–315.

Rose, Judah & Mann, Charles (1995) Unbundling the electric capacity price in a deregulated commodity. *Public Utilities Fortnightly*, 133, 22 (December), 20–6.

Rosen, S. & Rosenfield, A.M. (1997) Ticket pricing. *Journal of Law & Economics*, 40 (2), 351–76.

Rust, Roland T., Zahorik, A.J. & Keiningham, T.L. (1995) Return on quality (ROQ) – making service quality financially accountable. *Journal of Marketing*, 59, 2 (April), 58–70.

Rust, R., Zahorik, A. & Keiningham, T. (1996) *Service Marketing*, New York: HarperCollins.

Sawhney, M.S. & Eliashberg, J. (1996) A parsimonious model for forecasting gross box-office revenues of motion pictures. *Marketing Science*, 15 (2), 113–31.

Serel, Dogan A., Dada, Maqbool & Moskowitz, Herbert (2001) Sourcing decisions with capacity reservation contracts. *European Journal of Operational Research*, 131 (3), 635–48.

Shostack, G. Lynn (1977) Breaking free from product marketing. *Journal of Marketing*, 41 (April), 73–80.

——— (1984) Designing services that deliver. *Harvard Business Review*, 62 (January–February), 133–9.

Shugan, Steven M. (1994) Explanations for service growth. In *Service Quality*, edited by Richard Oliver & Roland Rust. Thousand Oaks, CA: Sage Publications, pp. 223–40.

Shugan, Steven M. & Desiraju, Ramarao (2001) Retail product-line pricing strategy when costs and products change. *Journal of Retailing*, Spring, 77 (1), 17–38.

Shugan, Steven M. & Radas, Sonja (1999) Services and seasonal demand. In *Handbook of Services Marketing and Management*, edited by Teresa A. Swartz & Dawn Iacobucci. New York: Sage Publications, pp. 147–70.

Shugan, Steven M. & Xie, Jinhong (2000) Advance pricing of services and other implications of separating purchase and consumption. *Journal of Service Research*, 2 (February), 227–39.

——— (2002) Advance-selling strategies with competition. University of Florida, Working Paper.

Sirdeshmukh, Deepak, Singh, Jagdip & Sabol, Barry (2002) Consumer trust, value, and loyalty in relational exchanges. *Journal of Marketing*, 66, 1 (Winter), 15.

Skiera, Bernd & Spann, Martin (1999) The ability to compensate for suboptimal capacity decisions by optimal pricing decisions. *European Journal of Operational Research*, 118, 450–63.

Smith, B.C., Leimkuhler, J.F. & Darrow, R.M. (1992) Yield management at American-Airlines. *Interfaces*, 22 (1), 8–31.

Spence, A. Michael Entry (1977) Capacity, investment and oligopolistic pricing. *Bell Journal of Economics*, 8 (2), 534–44.

Spicer, John & Bernhardt, Dan (1997) Durable services monopolists do better than durable goods monopolists. *The Canadian Journal of Economics*, 30 (4a), 975–90.

Szymanski, David M. & Henard, David H. (2001) Customer satisfaction: a meta-analysis of the empirical evidence. *Journal of the Academy of Marketing Science*, 29 (Winter), 16–35.

Van Cayseele, P. & Furth, D. (2001) Two is not too many for monopoly. *Journal of Economics*, 74 (3), 231–58.

Wernerfelt, B. (1995) The resource-based view of the firm – 10 years after. *Strategic Management Journal*, 16 (3), 171–74.

Xie, Jinhong & Shugan, Steven M. (2001) Electronic tickets, smart cards, and online prepayments: when and how to advance sell. *Marketing Science*, 20 (3), 219–43.

Zeithaml, Valarie A. (2000) Service quality, profitability and the economic worth of customers: what we know and what we need to learn. *Journal of the Academy of Marketing Science*, 28, 1 (Winter), 67–85.

Zeithaml, Valarie A. & Bitner, Mary Jo (2000) *Services Marketing: Integrating Customer Focus Across the Firm*, 2nd edn. New York: McGraw-Hill.

Zeithaml, V.A., Rust, R.T. & Lemon, K.N. (2001) The customer pyramid: creating and serving profitable customers. *California Management Review*, 43, 4 (Summer), 118.

20

Marketing in Business Markets

HÅKAN HÅKANSSON and IVAN SNEHOTA

Business markets are generally defined as markets where both sellers and buyers are businesses or other organizations. Markets where not only sellers but also customers are businesses and other organizations are of great significance in all developed economies. It is estimated that the value of transactions that are carried out between businesses in an economy such as Sweden's is about 3–4 times more than the value of transactions between businesses and households. That is only a crude indicator of the importance of these markets. Apart from the volume of exchange, business markets are important arenas for economic and technological development that affect economies of regions and countries. The telecom and biotech markets are but two recent examples of markets that have had important effects both on regional developments and our way of living.

Over the last few decades there has been considerable research into the nature of business markets and on the marketing practices in companies that operate in these markets. Research findings show that business markets display several peculiar features that impact on marketing practices. The peculiarity of business markets has its origin in the symmetry of market relationships. We have the same type of actor on both sides – both the selling and buying side are companies or other professional organizations. The symmetry of actors has far-reaching consequences for the market processes.

The aim of this chapter is to review the picture of business markets as it comes out in contemporary research, to outline their peculiarities and to explore their consequences for marketing management and future directions of marketing research.

The chapter is organized around five sections. The first section deals with the distinctive traits of business markets recurrently reported in empirical studies. We will focus in particular on three features evidenced in numerous studies: (1) the existence of continuous interactive buyer–seller relationships; (2) interdependencies that confer on these markets what might be called network form; and (3) interactive dynamics of business markets. Since the empirical evidence of these phenomena is extensive and mounting, the question has to be raised whether they affect the marketing practices in business and, in particular, how do they fare with the more normative body of knowledge in the discipline of marketing.

In the second section we will explore how the existence of buyer–seller relationships in business markets has been interpreted from different theoretical perspectives. We will develop the concept of relational exchange, as opposed to transactional exchange, and contrast it with other perspectives on business relationships. In particular we will contrast the market-as-network perspective with how relationships are looked upon in transaction cost approaches and with how they are studied and interpreted from sociological perspectives. Our argument will be that the perspective of the market-as-network research tradition points to the formation of relationships being an opportunity driven process, where technical, social, and economic dimensions interact. Our point will be that the contemporary research on business relationships suggests that the formation of relationships follow an economic logic and play an important role both in the achievement of economic efficiency and in fuelling innovation.

The scope of the third section is to assess and explain the variety of business relationships found in business markets. We will therefore examine the processes of business relationships' development, focus on the processes that generate change and stability in relationships, and outline an analytical framework to assess and categorize business relationships in two dimensions: their content and function. Both content and function of business relationships will be related to the economic consequences at relationship level, both for a single company and at network level.

The fourth section takes up the task of marketing management in business markets. Given the prominence of relationships in business markets and their impact on the economic performance of business organizations, the task of marketing management in business markets can be framed, in the market-as-network perspective, as acting in relationships. The claim will be that developing business relationships, the core of marketing in business markets, entails developing new patterns of connections and interactions. Such a perspective will be contrasted with the assumption of autonomous decision taking that underlies the mainstream conception of marketing management.

In the fifth and last section we will deal with the theme of strategy development in business markets, as well as with the need for future research. In markets where relationships matter, the main issue of market strategy appears to be not only the status of the company in the market network but also how the changes in it can be exploited and achieved. Adopting the market-as-network perspective, market strategy development entails managing the relationship set (customer portfolio) and leveraging business relationships in order to build up and maintain the technical problem solving and organizational capability of the company. We will argue that the strategy dimension is likely to be the most important one in future research. There are at least two important strategic issues where there is an urgent need for better understanding. One is how relationships affect the way companies reach a certain position, and the other is how relationships need to be combined more systematically so as to exploit a certain position.

The Distinctive Features of Business Markets

Hundreds of research studies conducted all over the world have documented at least three recurrent features of the economic landscape of business markets. (For a review of these findings see, for example, Axelsson & Easton, 1992; Easton & Håkansson, 1997; Ford, 1997; Gemunden et al., 1997; Håkansson & Snehota, 2000; Iacobucci, 1996; Möller & Wilson, 1995; Naude & Turnbull, 1998; Reid & Plank, 2000; Sharma, 1993.)

The first feature evidenced by the research is that companies, as a rule, keep buying from and selling to each other with a certain continuity. It is, as a rule, a flow of exchanges rather than single order transactions that arises between companies, and single buyers and sellers with whom business is contracted continuously tend to play an important role for companies (Håkansson & Snehota, 1995; Hallen et al., 1991; Wynstra, 1998). In most industries there is a relatively high degree of market concentration in the sense that the absolute number of potential suppliers or customers is relatively limited. The concentration becomes even more evident if examined for the single companies. The 10 largest customers and/or the 10 largest suppliers of a company often account for 60–80% of the total sold and bought volumes respectively (Håkansson, 1989), and single business counterparts become thus important. At single company level the supplier and the customer base appears to be relatively stable over time. Business with new customers and suppliers accounts, as a rule, for only a minor portion of the total volume bought and sold (Gadde & Mattsson, 1987; Håkansson, 1989; Hallen, 1986). Few percentage points of sales or purchases are done with new customers or suppliers in a year. The turnover in the customer/supplier base over time tends to be gradual. Furthermore there is the complexity of exchange; large volumes of several different items are bought and sold between a seller and buyer. There is the involvement of numerous individuals (actors) who intervene in the flow of products and services and interact with each other. Both parties tend to intervene actively, which reflects the symmetry in resources and competencies among buyers and sellers.

The first distinctive feature of business markets is thus the *existence of continuous business relationships* in which behaviours of buyers and sellers are interlocking. These relationships evolve as buyer and seller companies interact. The complex flow of products and services in relationships between companies is subject to continuous interventions and adaptations as the need arises.

The second distinctive feature of business markets evidenced by the research is the interdependencies between the relationships. Because of the concentration, both the cost and revenue sides of a company depend as a rule on a limited number of business relationships. The main relationships to customers and suppliers are important because through these the necessary resources are acquired both on the input side and on the output side. They are important for the economic performance directly because of the costs and revenues they generate, but also for other less evident reasons that appear only upon closer examination. Numerous studies demonstrate how technical development in companies originates in and depends on customer and supplier relationships (Ford & Saren, 2001; Håkansson, 1989; Håkansson & Waluszewski, 2002; Laage-Hellman, 1997; Lorenzoni & Bader-Fuller, 1995; von Hippel, 1988; von Hippel et al., 1999;

Helper & Sako, 1995). A company's performance depends to large extent on the performance of suppliers and customers with which it maintains relationships. Furthermore, what happens in one of these relationships (e.g., to a certain customer) affects what happens in others.

Companies can take advantage of a relationship (e.g., a lead-user customer) and leverage it in other relationships (e.g., to some other customers or suppliers). At the same time the very same relationships may be severely limiting the degrees of freedom of companies (Håkansson & Snehota, 1998).

Numerous interdependencies thus exist between different business relationships. The interdependencies exist in several steps (e.g., from different tiers of suppliers to customers' customers). Because of the interdependencies the roles of actors in business markets tend to become differentiated (so, for example, suppliers can be at the same time customers and competitors). The interdependencies between relationships and actors make business markets appear tightly knit, organized and structured. Business markets thus display a typical *network form*, which is the second distinctive feature of business markets evidenced by the research (Håkansson & Johanson, 1993; Araujo & Easton, 1996).

The third feature documented in research regards the dynamics of business relationships and market networks. Whatever dimension of the content of business relationships is observed (products, services, prices, contact patterns) it appears to be continuously changing (Dwyer et al., 1987; Ford, 1980; Gadde & Mattsson, 1987; Håkansson, 1989; Halinen, 1997; Halinen & Törnros, 1995; Halinen et al., 1999; Lundgren, 1995). Products do not last long, adaptations are frequently made, the service packages likewise, not to mention the logistics and administrative routines.

Individuals in companies on both sides interact. Different competing perceptions of problems and solutions are confronted and bring about the new solutions, and changed technical and organizational arrangements in and between the companies. This process is relentless. Because of the interaction the content and strength of the single buyer–seller relationships change. As single business relationships change, the structure of the market network is, as a consequence, changing. Changes in one relationship flow over to other relationships because of the existing interdependencies, and changes made elsewhere in the network impact on a relationship in which no apparent changes have been made. What the research has evidenced is the *continuous change* in the content of relationships and in the form of the market network; continuous change to which companies adapt but that they themselves generate.

The empirical evidence of these three phenomena – interactive exchange relationships, network forms, and continuous change in business markets – raises questions regarding their explanation. None of the three features of business markets can be easily explained relying on traditional interpretations of the market processes that focus on single discrete exchange transactions and their conditions. The presence of continuous relationships in business markets, substantiated in the empirical research, suggests a somewhat peculiar market process. That in turn raises the question about effective marketing management in such a context. It appears that the normative body of knowledge of the marketing discipline needs to be developed if it has to offer guidance to management in such a context.

Relationship Rationale – The Existence of Relational Exchange

Research documenting the existence and role of business relationships provides evidence of the variety of relationships that exists in business markets (Håkansson, 1989; Håkansson & Snehota, 1995; Keep et al., 1998). It has shown that a relationship cannot be simply described as on/off and that there is no such thing as a standard relationship. Buyer–seller relationships in business markets vary in strength, scope, content, duration, and other dimensions. This variety can be captured and explained in varying ways, dependent on the perspective that is taken. There is thus a large variety both in the phenomenon 'business relationships' itself, but also in how the relationships are looked upon in different theoretical approaches. There seems to be a consensus in the larger research community that relationships are important (e.g., Alter & Hage, 1993; Anderson et al., 1994; Håkansson, 1982, 1989; Kalwani & Narayandas, 1995; Sheth & Parvatiyar, 1995, 2000; Webster, 1992), but much less agreement about why they arise and what consequences their existence has for business behaviour.

The existence of interactive, continuous relationships between buyers and sellers in business markets can be explained in different ways. Different scholars offer different answers to why they develop and what functions they serve. In the traditional economics' perspective the relationships appear an obstacle to effective functioning of the market – a market imperfection. The argument is that they are binding the sellers and buyers to circumstances that exist outside the exchange transaction and thus can be claimed to introduce economically improper and ineffective behaviours. A relationship is some kind of monopolistic/monopsonistic situation. Building on this basis the transaction-cost approach explains the existence of relationships as a hybrid mode of governance – parallel to markets and hierarchies (Rindfleisch & Heide, 1997; Williamson, 1975, 1985). The transaction cost perspective thus offers the explanation that relational arrangement, in some specific situations (small numbers, high asset specificity), can reduce the transaction costs more effectively than market or hierarchy (Heide, 1994; Heide & John, 1992). The relationship will function as a governance mechanism and facilitate economic exchange and resource allocation. The key mechanism of interest within relationships is trust and can be compared with price mechanism within markets, and authority within hierarchies (Bradach & Eccles, 1989; Haugland & Reve, 1993; Wathne & Heide, 2000; Rindfleish & Moorman, 2001). To see a relationship as a co-ordination mechanism that can be useful in certain situations instead of price or authority is the way to relate systematically the phenomenon of relationships to traditional economics.

There is yet another stream of thought and research in economics that can be linked to the existence of relationships, the so-called Austrian school in economics. The emphasis on market process (Kirzner, 1973, 1979) and on the time and knowledge dimensions of it (Hayek, 1945) in the Austrian school provides some bases to explain the formation and role of relationships. It stresses the importance of uncertainty and therefore of the impact of market interaction on the relative knowledge about scope and effective use of resources of market actors. It has been used occasionally in business studies to explain the role of innovation in the development of exchange relationships in markets and consequently in market strategy (Foss, 1999; Hunt, 2000; Jacobson, 1992; Reekie & Savitt, 1982; Snehota, 1990). This stream of research, however, has little interest in explaining the variety in the relationship phenomenon.

Relationships in general have also been a central phenomenon in sociology and, in particular, in economic sociology. The social exchange is seen, in contrast with economic exchange, as an important ingredient in social structures (Blau, 1964; Burt, 1992; Cook & Emerson, 1984; Granovetter, 1973, 1985; Swedberg, 1994; Uzzi, 1997). Also in the sociological perspective trust is a central dimension of relationships, but it is argued that exchange relationships can also have other effects, which might include normative values (Mitchell, 1973), and impact on information processing which, in turn, offers an explanation to the variety of relationships (Powell, 1987). The sociological tradition, compared with economics, emphasizes explanations of relationships not only as the coordinating mechanism but also as a force influencing and changing the actors.

Early studies of industrial markets, antecedent of the market-as-network research tradition, pointed to social exchange as an important ingredient in business relationships, but also to the dimension of technical adaptations and their economic consequences (Håkansson, 1982; Håkansson & Östberg, 1975; Cunningham & Homse, 1986; Turnbull & Valla, 1986). Buyer–seller relationships have been approached and analysed as an economic entity connecting to each other a set of organizational units as well as resource elements. This stream of research has focused on behavioural rather than attitudinal dimensions of business relationships. It has approached relationships as interlocking behaviours with economic consequences and emphasized in the concept of relationships the coordination and mutual influence of behaviours of the interacting parties.

The starting point of the subsequent research in the market-as-network tradition has been to explore more closely how businesses operate with respect to their customers and suppliers. It has focused on the economic rationale of relationships in business markets – and introduced the notion of *relational exchange*. It can be related to some early studies of market system and processes in marketing perspective (Alderson, 1957; Arndt, 1979; Bagozzi, 1975). As we observed earlier, companies in business markets produce and use large volumes repeatedly in a environment where typically only a limited number of counterparts exist and both buying and selling is professional, i.e., subject to economic criteria. The values in exchange, that is the economic consequences to the two companies involved, under such circumstances are not limited to the transfer of products/services that are objects of market transactions. Rather, the behaviours of buyers and sellers reflects a broader set of variables.

This point can be illustrated starting from the buyer/user perspective. (While we will here take the buyer/user perspective the same applies to the economic consequences for the seller/provider.) What do companies value in supply relationships, and what motivates their behaviours such as the choice of suppliers? The more we explore their motivations the more the claim is 'economy' (Gadde & Håkansson, 2001; Lamming, 1993; Torvatn, 1996; van Weele, 2000; Wynstra, 1998). However, the economic consequences of a supplier relationship for the buyer/user do not originate only in the features of the product supplied and its price. Other elements of relationship interaction such as, for example, learning, coordination and adaptations have economic consequences for the customer company. Flexibility in supplier logistics and administrative routines may affect the costs of the buying company or its revenues. Willingness to adapt the product or production process may result in product development that can be used in other supplier relationships or in customer relationships to provide economically superior solutions. In other words, the interaction itself among the buyer's own and the supplier's personnel can be of value if it brings about new technical or organizational solutions.

Different elements of the relationship can thus originate economic consequences for a party. So the values in exchange originate in the relationship and not only in the transaction content of it. It has to be observed, however, that the consequences will depend on the features of the parties and of the context and not simply on the relationship behaviours as such. The same behaviours (i.e., interaction content) in a relationship will produce different consequences dependent on the context of those involved. What emerges from such micro-processes is a picture of 'relational' rather than 'transactional' exchange. We use this notion of *relational exchange* to describe circumstances when values in exchange that motivate behaviours of the parties depend on consequences of the relationships (of the mutually directed behaviours), rather than simply on features of the products/services that are the object of transfer between the parties.

The relational nature of exchange in business markets is related to the symmetry of the actors' buying and selling, their interdependence, and the uncertainty they are both facing. It is our understanding that much of the peculiarities of business markets can be explained by the 'relational nature of exchange'. The point is that under such circumstances the relationships that exist in business markets become an economically sensible and rational arrangement, rather than an impediment to economic efficiency.

The other two features – the network form and interactive dynamics – appear also to make sense if their economic consequences for businesses are examined. The relative stability and continuity in the network form is cost-effective in order to generate resource combinations and provide a stable platform for development. Likewise the interaction dynamics within relationships provide continuous opportunities and impulses to improvement (Håkansson & Johanson, 2001). Relationships with consequent interdependencies (networks) and peculiar change dynamics are thus functional to both the producer and the user in search of joint solutions. It is important, however, to notice that a network can be very dysfunctional for those who are not part of it. Networks do not allocate resources in an efficient way in some general sense. Networks are good for those highly involved in them and who want to continue to develop together.

Evolution of Business Relationships

Assuming and postulating relational exchange in business markets implies that the behaviours of the involved are driven by factors exogenous to the transaction. How a relationship will develop is not given by the characteristics of the situation but by the enactment by the involved actors, who are motivated by expected economic outcomes of interaction (Ebers, 1997; Grabher, 1993; Thibault & Kelly, 1959; Kelly & Thibault, 1978). Relationships' development and their economic consequences are enactment driven. That can also explain the content of exchange

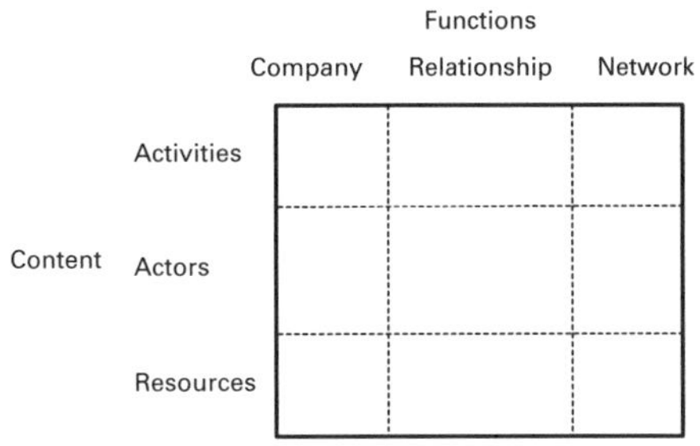

Figure 20.1 *Content and Function of Business Relationships*

in continuous evolution. Issues connected to this development are probably one of the most central for future research on business relationships.

If we are to explain the processes of enactment and thus development in business relationships we need a framework to capture the variety of business relationships and their complexity. Håkansson and Snehota (1995) suggest a model of business relationships consisting of two basic dimensions: the content and the function of relationships. The model is illustrated in Figure 20.1.

Relationship Content

Three dimensions of a business relationship can be used to characterize its content and its economic consequences: actor dimension, activity dimension, and resource dimension.

The *actor dimension* of content of a business relationship regards the interpersonal interaction of the individuals involved. This has very much to do with the social content – the degree to which the actors feel close to each other; how they trust, appreciate and influence each other and become mutually committed (Huemer, 1998; Smith & Barday, 1997; Wilkinson & Young, 1996; Wilson, 1995). The notion of actor bonds can be introduced to describe this content dimension of the business relationship. Bonds that arise between actors can be more or less strong and will influence to varying extents what the individuals involved perceive as possible and feasible directions of enactment. They are important for the 'learning' of parties about opportunities and solutions, as pointed out in some of the studies of learning in relationships (Dahlqvist, 1998; Håkansson & Johanson, 2001). The strength of the actor bond is thus an important dimension of the relationship content, with economic consequences.

The *activity dimension* is the mutual coordination of the activities of the parties involved. The coordination can be more or less extensive. So, for example, the production activities of the two companies can be more or less integrated and linked together, and the same with regards to deliveries, information handling, and other activities. In this way the two companies' activity structures can become more or less tightly linked (Dubois, 1998; Richardson, 1972; Torvatn, 1996). The systematic relating and co-ordination of activities between firms has attracted a great deal of interest in management, as can be witnessed by the popularity of concepts like Just-in-Time, Total Quality Control or Time-Based Management that can easily be related to the activity dimension of relationship content. The relative strength of activity links that arise in a business relationship has been shown to have great economic consequences.

Finally, the relationship content has a *resource dimension*. In the development of the relationship the two actors' resources can be more or less adapted and developed in relation to each other. The resources of the two parties become thus more or less closely mutually tied. Resource ties arise as the two parties in a relationship confront and mutually adapt their resources over time (Hallen et al., 1991). The specific mutual adaptation can involve tangible resources such as physical items, but also intangible resources such as knowledge. Adaptations will make the resources of the two companies more complementary, but the systematic conjoining of resources also, more importantly, leads to development of new joint resource combinations – innovation that in turn has economic consequences (Biemans, 1992; Håkansson, 1987, 1989; Holmen, 2001; Laage-Helman, 1997; Lundgren, 1995).

The three layers of content of buyer–seller relationships are interrelated. Firstly, there is a time-related connection: the first phase in most relationships is characterized by social interaction. There is a need for the parties to get to know each other and to build up trust and confidence in the counterpart. There is an apparent need for a social platform before any more substantial adaptation or change can be done. Secondly, there is the functional connection between activities and resources. When activities are linked it will often also affect resources on both sides. Thirdly, there is for all three dimensions a cumulative aspect as they are successively embedded into each other as the two sides interact. The fact that they are interrelated will both stimulate and hinder the future development. Activity links might limit the interaction in resource terms; resource ties may limit the possibilities of activity coordination; the actor bond the perceived possibilities of adaptations and coordination.

It is the interplay of the three dimensions of relationship content that creates and re-creates tension in buyer–seller relationships that necessitates finding/uncovering new patterns of connections of resources, activities and actors between the two companies. Exploring and enacting new patterns entails economic consequences and thus represents a powerful motive in both parties' behaviours. In order to assess the economic consequences, however, we need to look at the functions of relationships.

Function

Actor bonds, resource ties and activity links do have consequences that go beyond the specific relationship in which they arise. This is what leads to the need to explore the functions of relationships. The function of the relationship (cf. Figure 20.1) can be conceived to fall in three categories: for the relationship itself, the single company, and the network. This division has to do with how the relationship is activated and related by the two sides, to what they are doing outside the relationship and also to how other actors view and behave in relation to it.

The starting point in an attempt to explore the consequences of a relationship is the relationship itself. In order to have a function in the two other respects a relationship must have a function in itself; that is, to have some content meaningful to those that take part in it. It requires that there are some persons on each side who have the view that there is at least the potential for meaningful connections between the two – that the other side has something that can be of use in a joint process. The more function a relationship has in itself, the more it can have a function in the two other aspects (Blois, 1998).

A relationship that has some content can be used: activated in different ways by the two sides. Each of the two companies involved can, to different degrees, relate the relationship to internal processes and to other relationships it is involved in. The more a company is leveraging a relationship the greater will be the impact on other activities of the company. The function of a relationship can in this respect vary from being the relationship that is forming the company to a marginal relationship that has to live its life separated from what the company does in general. Again it is obvious that in this way relationships offer opportunities, but it is the two companies and their way of acting that determines to what degree such opportunities offered are captured and enacted in the relationship itself (Johanson & Mattsson, 1985; Loasby, 1998; Ghosh & John, 1999).

Similarly there are third parties to the relationship that can take advantage of the development within the relationship and in this way add to its function. The most important category of third parties is other companies that have relationships with the two principal companies. These can enhance or work against the relationship in a number of ways (Blankenburg-Holm et al., 1996; Easton & Lundgren, 1992; Holmen & Pedersen, 2000). The network of related relationships is thus functionally related to the content of the relationship itself.

We concluded earlier that the three types of content were interrelated, and the same is the case for the three types of function. It is not just the two actors that have different environments, but their activities as well as resources are also parts of larger activity patterns and resource constellations (Håkansson & Snehota, 1995). Every relationship in its content and functions is thus embedded into different specific contexts. Every relationship is a heterogeneous practice of interaction in which a number of aspects and issues is brought together and confronted. The economic consequences that motivate the interactive behaviour of actors will depend on the enacted solutions to this multiplicity of dimensions. There are different changes or suggestions for changes in all these dimensions. The relationship is both a means of handling those changes as well as protection against them. Relationship interaction is a way of creating a specific interface between a set of resources and pattern of activities and web of issues. That may explain the variety of business relationships evidenced in the empirical studies of business markets.

The Task of Marketing – Managing Economy in Interaction

Up to this point we have been concerned with the distinctive features of business markets and the main theme can be summarized as follows: in business markets relationships matter. Business markets are characterized by relational exchange. It is the content of buyer–seller relationships that can be described in at least three dimensions of resource ties, activity links and actor bonds that has the economic consequences that motivate behaviours of actors. It is through relationships that customers can access suppliers' resources, connect into their various activities and make use of suppliers' know-how and capabilities. With whom customers will develop relationships depends on perceived expected economic consequences for their own business. Development of business relationships is a function of the interaction of those involved. Relationships evolve through enactment of opportunities perceived in the relationship, but also of the impact on the two companies and on a broader network of relationships in which the two companies are embedded. The multiple connections that relationships contain are both a consequence and a base of enactment. Buyer–seller relationships are the loci of these complex and changing interdependencies and account for the peculiar dynamics of business markets – their apparent continuity and continuous change.

Highlighting these features of the market context leads to the question of how does it affect the tasks of marketing in companies, that is, the nature of marketing management in business markets? Under these circumstances the task of marketing becomes somewhat peculiar and the normative body of the mainstream marketing management discipline becomes problematic. That is because it is based on the transaction exchange logic and focused on discrete decisions regarding parameters of market transactions (such as product, price, place, and promotion) that are, as we argued, even difficult to identify. When relational exchange matters the main determinants of market performance of the company are different from the single transaction parameters. The problem with applying the transaction exchange logic strictly has been hinted at before by some scholars of industrial marketing (e.g., Ames, 1970; Corey, 1976; Hutt & Speh, 1984) even though voices to the contrary have not been absent (Fern & Brown, 1984).

What are the determinants of market performance of a company in business markets when relationships matter? In the broadest sense the sales development and profitability will depend on how a company performs in two areas. The first is coping with situations as they arise in single customer relationships. Facing the relational exchange the core task of marketing is developing the offering and managing the economic consequences of customer relationships. The second is maintaining and developing the existing customer base and the portfolio of relationships that define the market position of the company. The first area can be related to the general issues of marketing management, the second to market strategy development. The latter will be dealt with in the subsequent section.

As we have explored the role of supplier relationships from the user/customer perspective, we argued that the perceived expected economic consequences of relationships are customers' main concern and motivate their behaviours. Coping successfully with developing relationships is therefore about providing economic value for the customer's business (Anderson & Narus, 1999) and for their own. In business markets it becomes evident that the heart of marketing is managing the economy of customer relationships, which depends on the various dimensions of their content and function.

It has been argued (Håkansson & Snehota, 1995) that the economic consequences originate in connecting the operations of one's own company with those of the customer's and other connected actors in the market. Using the scheme outlined in Figure 20.1 the economic values can be traced to co-ordination, adaptation and interaction of activities, resources and individuals involved in both companies; that is, they reflect the activity links, resource ties and actor bonds enacted in a relationship. How these impact on the economy of business relationships is schematically illustrated in Figure 20.2. It points to three elements of economy of business relationships: perception of opportunities, productivity, and innovation, that all depend on how the two companies are connected in a relationship.

Basic dimension	*Relational effect*	*Economic outcome*
Communication	actor bonds	opportunity space
Co-ordination	activity links	productivity
Adaptations	resource ties	innovativeness

Figure 20.2 *Economy of Business Relationships*

What Figure 20.2 hints at is that economic consequences of a relationship stem from a combination of coordination, adaptations, and communication. As the combining can never be fully stabilized and accomplished it requires continuously finding solutions as to how to connect the two parties' operations. Managing the economy of a relationship thus entails a continuous connecting and re-connecting of the various dimensions in the relationship. That is one of the reasons why marketing management in business markets is primarily a problem of organizing. Marketing embraces managing all the three types of economies and entails not only the integration within a relationship but also integration of the relationship into one's own company and into other relationships to third parties. So the task of marketing in business markets is the one of organizing within the relationship, within the company, and within the network.

Under what conditions is the connecting in business relationships done and the economy managed? Firstly, it is done in interaction with others. The choices are interactive and both actions and reactions matter (Harrison, 1998). Secondly, it is done in conditions where, mainly because of the need to react, there are only limited possibilities to search for alternative solutions (Wedin, 2001). Thirdly, it is done locally by middle management that interacts and has the elements of feasible solutions (Boxer & Wensley, 1986). Finally, it is done over time. There is a time dimension, a process of trial and error that can be described as a continuous experimenting with different solutions (Eriksson et al., 1996).

Handling the three types of content requires quite different abilities as each of them activates different types of issues, which require different personnel be involved and different ways to organize the interaction. Formation of actor bonds requires regularity and time, and involves marketing and purchasing personnel as well as general management. The activity links and resource ties are much more event or project related; they are also much more technically oriented. Therefore technicians on both sides tend to play a more significant role.

The main issues in marketing management in business markets thus become *monitoring* and *sustaining the organizing process* on which the economic consequences depend. The process of enactment of this degree of complexity that we find in business relationships is difficult to monitor and to intervene into. Neither the monitoring nor sustaining the interactive organizing process is a simple task. A conscious and systematic approach can be beneficial for effective monitoring, but monitoring can never be exhaustive; nor should it be striven for to achieve full control. Under the circumstances that characterize business relationships, it appears more important to sustain a more-or-less continuous development than to try to control it. The reason is that each of the three types of content can always be developed further and there are always reasons to try to exploit these opportunities. As we concluded in the earlier section, relationships are about finding and exploiting opportunities. These opportunities do not just exist as potential opportunities inside the relationship – instead they have to be created, organized, structured, and implemented through the relationship. Given the involvement of various individual actors one important task is to try to provide the sense of taking part. Understanding is a key word, as knowledge of the circumstances can never be complete. The scope of management becomes to support the framing and reading of situations as individuals involved meet them, and to support the development of internal capabilities to deal with challenges appearing in the relationship (Dahlqvist, 1998).

Strategy Development in Business Markets

The concept of market strategy often used in research and practice is rich in connotations but is still not satisfactorily defined (e.g., Wensley, 1996). The central issue in market strategy has always been the fit between the resources and activities of a company and its environment. Much of the research has dealt with how such a fit can be achieved and maintained over time. Traditionally the emphasis in research and theory has been on how businesses identify and adapt to opportunities existing or emerging in the market environment (e.g., Abell, 1978). More recently, as in the resource-based or capability-based conception of strategy, it has shifted to how business can exploit and influence the environment (Conner & Prahalad, 1996; Grant, 1996).

The distinctive features of business markets suggest a need to reconsider the conception of market strategy and some of the key issues in market strategy development. The substantial symmetry of the actors, the textured nature of the context – presence of relationships and the network form – and the resulting dynamics, impact on the concept of strategy (Ford et al., 1998). Both in practice and in research we can see a shift in emphasis from some issues traditionally considered central to some that have been seen as less relevant. Three issues in particular acquire a prominent role: the boundaries of the business enterprise, the strategic choice, and strategy development process.

The interdependencies underlying buyer–seller relationships in business markets make the *boundaries* of the business enterprise much less clear-cut than is usually assumed. Activities, resources and actors of different organizations are more or less closely meshed and intertwined. It has been evidenced how the single specific relationships impact on the capabilities of the company, and how the need to adapt stems from these. In business markets it becomes evident that market relationships of a company – to customers, suppliers and others – become the main assets and liabilities of the company (Håkansson & Snehota, 1998) and the boundaries of the company somewhat arbitrary. On the one hand this makes the issue of adapting to and control of the market environment less central. Companies in business markets shape their market as much as they adapt to the market. The interactive business relationships contain simultaneously both processes (Dubois, 1998).

As the boundaries fade into the background two issues come to the forefront. The first is, somewhat paradoxically, the need to set and define boundaries of a business enterprise. Others, in particular customers, tend to pull the company to form a certain pattern of activities and to build up a certain collection of resources necessary to provide value to the counterparts. As the demands will inevitably diverge over time a company cannot follow all possible paths of development; some have to be sacrificed, others put in focus. The strategic intent of the company (Hamel & Prahalad, 1989) can only be defined by what falls beyond its boundaries, what it does not intend to exercise influence over. In practice the boundary setting takes the shape of a relationship portfolio problem (Fiocca, 1982; Turnbull, 1990; Bensaou, 1999). The key issue in customer portfolio management is not selecting the customers, but rather setting priorities in terms of concessions and initiative. The boundary setting, prioritizing of some and not other relationships, cannot be settled once and for all and not even for any extended time periods. The boundary setting has to be continuous, and requires monitoring and adaptations.

The second issue that stems from the fading of the boundaries is the need to mobilize the assets represented by relationships to others – mainly customers and suppliers. In business markets every single company's market strategy is to some extent collective (Astley, 1984), and entails both inducement and creating dependencies. The need to mobilize is mutual, which means a company has to mobilize others but also to accept being mobilized by others. In practice it takes the form of leveraging certain relationships to, say, a specific customer or supplier, for development of other relationships, to (for example) another customer or supplier. It also means the readiness to get involved. The problem with leveraging is that there are combination effects: it can never be conceived as one-to-one connection.

The issue of boundaries of business enterprise is linked to that of *strategic choice,* another issue traditionally central in both strategy research and practice. It regards the possibilities of a company to effectively control its performance. A common tenet in the very concept of market strategy is that a company's market performance depends on its capacity to create economic value for its customers. Once again the interdependencies underlying the formation of relationships in business markets make it less obvious how much autonomy a company has in producing value for customers, and what are the main variables it can play on.

The market performance in business markets is more difficult to separate from the overall business performance. Traditional measures of market performance, such as market share and competitiveness, become less relevant. Achieving economy both in the sense of static and dynamic efficiency for the firm is linked to achieving the economies for customers. Possibilities to develop customer relationships are related to the existing relationships – the macro-position of the company in the market network constitutes an asset in developing the micro-position of the company with respect to a single specific customer (Johanson & Mattsson, 1985).

Economies can only be created by change, by novel connecting of activities, resources and actors, which has two aspects: creating efficiency through incremental improvements within the on-going relationships, and developing new patterns in the market network (Ritter, 1999). The issue is not, however, to induce change – the change is always present both in the relationships of the company and in the relative network. Rather, the issue is how to stabilize a pattern in change so that activities, resources and actors within the strategic boundaries of the company, which embrace others, permit the creation of economic value. The 'economies' are the result of systematic connections and combinations. The economic values for customers do not exist *per se*, they are created through relating. The customer–supplier relationships are about division and sharing of resources, but primarily about value creation that stems from how these resources are combined. Resources are not given, but are very much a result of the interaction processes going on within the network. Their value depends on the existing structure and will disappear as soon as the structure is changed. The development of new patterns, in this way, affects the value of the company's resources as well as the value of each of the counterparts and their resources. Clearly, those losing in value will act against any such change, which points back to the importance of mobilizing some positive forces in order to get any change accepted.

The strategic choice the company has in business markets is thus limited by others, and given by synchronization with the processes of renewal in its relationship network. It can lead it or follow it, but can never fully control it (Håkansson & Ford, 2002).

Strategy development *processes* rather than strategy content comes to the forefront in business markets. It regards the processes underlying value proposition and delivery that, in turn, form the network position and capacity of the company to enact novel connections on which the economic consequences depend (Ford & Mcdowel, 1999). Strategy development requires that three issues need to be dealt with simultaneously. The first is the need to identify and read the changes taking place at the same time with several counterparts. It has very much to do with knowledge about what is taking place and how that is related to what has happened earlier and to what is happening at other places at the same time. The second is to find ways to combine single changes with each other. It has more to do with interpreting, experimenting and with entrepreneurial abilities. Finally, the third is to try to mobilize others in relation to the identified possibility. That has to do with the social dimension and requires both that the company is socially embedded into the network structure, and that it can find a way to persuade the actors around about it to make sense of relevant patterns.

The first issue regards getting and analysing information. Interaction processes in buyer–seller relationships are problematic in this respect because they tend to include a large number of people on both sides discussing and handling the ongoing exchange. Knowledge about these processes exists only locally and is highly embedded into the process. Furthermore, there is one level where the relationship and its content is discussed and another where the physical exchange takes place. The latter is important as it never can be fully controlled and can fail even if the communication works. The tension between the two layers, as well as between the two counterparts in each relationship, is of interest from a knowledge point of view. It accounts for the possibilities to develop the interface between single resource items, i.e., different development opportunities, that can only be seen by those directly involved. In order to gather information from several relationships some individuals must take part in several relationships or meeting places where individuals from several relationships have a chance to discuss and reflect. Knowledge must be built up (Håkansson & Johanson, 2001).

The second issue regards combining changes, relating the development in different relationships. Heterogeneous resources and practices are involved in renewal. As there always are some common resources (products or facilities) used in several relationships there are a number of natural knotting points. One problem can be that those responsible for these are not necessarily highly involved in the relationships and tend to follow a logic that puts a premium on stability and homogeneity. Every renewal entails a conflict which makes the renewal possible, but also potentially impossible.

This leads us to the third issue; the need to involve others. The change must be 'stabilized' by getting adaptations among related and influenced actors. One important dimension in all network structures is that the use of different resources is systematically related to each other. Mobilizing others requires actors to make sense of the pattern of change. The economic effects are a result of this systematic combining. Thus, if anyone wants to make a change there is a need to get others to adapt in order to increase the economic value.

Future Research Directions

Research over the past two decades reviewed in this chapter has undoubtedly contributed to further understanding of business markets and marketing. Major achievements have been to produce the evidence of relationships, to advance the notion of the network form of business markets, and to direct attention to interdependence and interaction processes underlying the development of business relationships.

It has produced sufficient empirical evidence to discard the assumption of autonomous actors in business markets. To dispense the assumption of autonomous actors in explanations of market behaviour is not simple. Such an assumption is a cornerstone of much of the normative body of marketing management. Conceptual frameworks, not to say theories that do not take into account interdependencies and interaction, not only fail to produce sustainable explanations of market behaviours; they also fail to provide reliable guidance for effective market conduct.

Ushering in the interdependence and interaction as explanatory constructs makes the task of conceptual development and theory building much more complex. Explaining the interactive behaviour, so central to business markets, represents a major challenge that is not likely to be easily solved. The complexity in modelling and theory construction becomes compounded, but cannot be avoided.

To this point the bulk of research on business marketing has been mostly descriptive and the resulting conceptual development inductive. That is, probably, typical of an initial phase of a paradigmatic change. The conceptual framework in course of elaboration does not lack weak spots. There has been only limited effort to make it systematic and fully consistent and, above all, to test some of the hypotheses it has produced. Yet, the conceptual platform it has produced appears fruitful. Future pathways of research in business marketing are difficult if not impossible to forecast; one can only identify a few areas where future research would be desirable.

The first is systematic testing and further development of the current conceptual framework. It requires formulating hypotheses that can be tested on larger scale, quantitatively measurable empirical observations. That would probably entail generating broader empirical databases relevant from the network perspective.

The second area for research is to explore other market contexts that might display features analogous to those of business markets. There are indications that marketing of services is one such area (Grönroos, 1996, 2000; Gwinner et al., 1998). Another area is that of distribution systems and channels (Bucklin & Sengupta, 1993). Such research might contribute to better insight into the issues of strategic interdependencies and autonomy of strategic choice.

Economy of business relationships is another broad area where future research is needed and possibly rewarding. The market-as-network perspective points to 'economy' as a primary explanatory factor in the formation of buyer–seller relationships in business markets. A central assumption is that relationships are economically rational arrangements under the circumstances that firms face in business markets. It deserves further elaboration and testing.

Finally, understanding better the economy of business relationships and their economic consequences for both buyers and sellers would constitute a base for formulating normative indications for marketing management, consistent with the findings of the market-as-network research. Elaborating such a normative body of knowledge is another desirable direction of research. It is likely to entail exploring collective best practices more systematically.

In hindsight, the past two decades have been an interesting time in research on business markets. It appears that it has in many ways anticipated some of the trends in the marketing discipline such as focusing on relationships and networking. It is likely to continue to remain an interesting arena because business markets appear to be such a good laboratory setting for the study of the market processes that are the focal point of marketing management.

References

Abell, D.F. (1978) Strategic windows. *Journal of Marketing*, 42 (July), 21–6.

Alderson, W. (1957) *Marketing Behavior and Executive Action*. Homewood, IL: Richard D. Irwin, Inc.

Alter, C. & Hage, J. (1993) *Organizations Working Together*. Newbury Park, CA: Sage.

Ames, B.C. (1970) Trappings versus substance in industrial marketing. *Harvard Business Review*, 48, 4, 93–102.

Anderson, J. & Narus, J. (1999) *Business Market Management: Understanding, Creating and Delivery Value*. Upper Saddle River, NJ: Prentice-Hall.

Anderson, J., Håkansson, H. & Johanson, J. (1994) Dyadic business relationships within a business network context. *Journal of Marketing*, 58 (October), 1–15.

Araujo, L. & Easton, G. (1996) Networks in socio-economic systems. In *Networks in Marketing*. edited by D. Iacobucci. Thousand Oaks, CA: Sage, pp. 63–107.

Arndt, J. (1979) Toward a concept of domesticated markets. *Journal of Marketing*, 43 (Fall), 69–75.

Astley, G.W. (1984) Toward an appreciation of collective strategy. *Academy of Management Review*, 9, 3, 526–35.

Axelsson, B. & Easton, G. (eds) (1992) *Industrial Networks: A New View of Reality*. London: Routledge.

Bagozzi, R.P. (1975) Marketing as exchange. *Journal of Marketing*, 39 (October), 32–9.

Bensaou, M. (1999) Portfolios of buyer-supplier relationships. *Sloan Management Review*, Vol. 40 (Summer), 35–44.

Biemans, W. (1992) *Managing Innovation within Networks*. London: Routledge.

Blankenburg-Holm, D., Eriksson, K. & Johanson, J. (1996) Business networks and cooperation in international business relationships. *Journal of International Business Studies*, 27 (5), 1033–53.

Blau, P. (1964) *Exchange and Power in Social Life*. New York: John Wiley and Sons.

Blois, K.J. (1998) Don't all firms have relationships? *Journal of Business & Industrial Marketing*, 13, 3, 256–70.

Boxer, P.J. & Wensley, J.R.C. (1986) The need for middle-out development of marketing strategy. *Journal of Management Studies*, 23, 2, 189–204.

Bradach, J.L. & Eccles, R.G. (1989) Price, authority and trust: from ideal types to plural forms. *Annual Review of Sociology*, 15, 97–118.

Bucklin, L.P. & Sengupta, S. (1993) Organizing successful co-marketing alliances. *Journal of Marketing*, 57, April, 32–46.

Burt, R.S. (1992) *Structural Holes*. Cambridge, MA: Harvard University Press.

Conner, K.R. & Prahalad, C.K. (1996) A resourse-based theory of the firm: knowledge versus opportunism. *Organisation Science*, 7, 5, 477–501.

Cook, K.S. & Emerson, R.M. (1984) Exchange networks and the analysis of complex organizations. *Research in the Sociology of Organizations*, 3, 1–30.

Corey, R.E. (1976) *Industrial Marketing: Cases and Concepts*. Englewood Cliffs, NJ: Prentice-Hall.

Cunningham, M. & Homse, E. (1986) Controling the marketing-purchasing interface: resource development and organizational implications. *Industrial Marketing and Purchasing*, 1, 2, 3–27.

Dahlqvist, J. (1998) Knowledge use in business exchange: Acting and thinking business actors. Ph.D. Thesis, Department of Business Studies, Uppsala University.

Dubois, A. (1998) *Coordinating Activities across Firm Boundaries*. London: Routledge.

Dwyer, F.R., Shurr, P.H. & Oh, S. (1987) Developing buyer-seller relationships. *Journal of Marketing*, 51 (April), 11–27.

Easton, G. & Håkansson, H. (1997) Market as networks. *International Journal of Research in Marketing*, 13, 5, 431–47.

Easton, G. & Lundgren, A. (1992) Changes in industrial networks as flow through nodes. In *Industrial Networks: A New View of Reality*, edited by B. Axelsson & G. Easton. London: Routledge, pp. 88–104.

Ebers, M. (ed.) (1997) *The Formation of Interorganizational Networks*. London: Oxford University Press.

Eriksson, K., Holm, D. & Johanson, J. (1996) Business networks and international business relationships. *Journal of International Business Studies*, 27, 5, 1033–53.

Fern, E.F. & Brown, J.R. (1984) The industrial/consumer dichotomy: a case of insufficient justification. *Journal of Marketing*, 48 (Spring), 68–77.

Fiocca, R. (1982) Account portfolio analysis for strategy development. *Industrial Marketing Management*, 11, 1, 53–62.

Ford, D. (1980) The development of buyer-seller relationships in industrial markets. *European Journal of Marketing*, 14, 5/6, 339–54.

——— (ed.) (1997) *Understanding Business Markets*. London: Dryden Press.

Ford, D. & Mcdowel, R. (1999) Managing business relationships by analysing the effects and value of different actions. *Industrial Marketing Management*, 28, 5, 429–42.

Ford, D. & Saren, M. (2001) *Technology Strategy for Business*, 2nd edn. London: International Thompson Press.

Ford, D., Gadde, L-E., Håkansson, H., Lundgren, A., Snehota, I., Turnbull, P. & Wilson, D. (1998) *Managing Business Relationships*. London: John Wiley and Sons.

Foss, N.J. (1999) The use of knowledge in firms. *Journal of Institutional and Theoretical Economics*, 155, 458–86.

Gadde, L-E. & Håkansson, H. (2001) *Supply Network Strategies*. London: John Wiley and Sons.

Gadde, L-E. & Mattsson, L-G. (1987) Stability and change in network relationships. *International Journal of Research in Marketing*, 4, 29–41.

Gemunden, H-G., Ritter, T. & Achim, W. (eds) (1997) *Relationships and Networks in International Markets*. Amsterdam: Pergamon Press.

Ghosh, M. & John, G. (1999) Governance value analysis and marketing strategy, *Journal of Marketing*, 63 (Special issue), 131–45.

Grabher, G. (ed.) (1993) *The Embedded Firm. On Socioeconomics of Industrial Networks*. London: Routledge.

Granovetter, M. (1973) The strength of weak ties. *American Journal of Sociology*, 78, 1360–80.

——— (1985) Economic action and social structure: the problem of embeddedness. *American Journal of Sociology*, 91, 3, 481–510.

Grant, R. (1996) Toward a knowledge-based theory of the firm. *Strategic Management Journal*, 17 (Winter), 109–22.

Grönroos, C. (1996) Relationship marketing logic. *Asia-Australia Marketing Journal*, 4, 1, 1–12.

——— (2000) Relationship marketing, the Nordic School Perspective. In *Handbook of Relationship Marketing*, edited by J.N. Sheth & A. Parvatiyar. Thousand Oaks, CA: Sage.

Gwinner, K.P., Gremler, D.D. & Bitner, M.J. (1998) Relational benefits in services industries: the consumer's perspective. *Journal of the Academy of Marketing Science*, 26, 2, 101–14.

Håkansson, H. (ed.) (1982) *International Marketing and Purchasing of Industrial Goods – An Interaction Approach*. New York: John Wiley and Sons.

——— (ed.) (1987) *Industrial Technological Development. A Network Approach*. London: Croom Helm.

——— (1989) *Corporate Technological Behaviour: Co-operation and Networks*. London: Routledge.

Håkansson, H. & Ford, D. (2002) How should companies interact. *Journal of Business Research*, 55, 133–9.

Håkansson, H. & Johanson, J. (1993) The network structure as a governance structure: interfirm co-operation beyond markets and hierarchies. In *The Embedded Firm: On the Socioeconomics of Industrial Networks*, edited by G. Grabher. London: Routledge, pp. 35–51.

——— (eds) (2001) *Business Network Learning*. Amsterdam: Pergamon.

Håkansson, H. & Östberg, C. (1975) Industrial marketing – an organizational problem? *Industrial Marketing Management*, 4, 113–23.

Håkansson, H. & Snehota, I. (eds) (1995) *Developing Relationships in Business Networks*. London and New York: Routledge.

——— (1998) The burden of relationships. In *Network Dynamics in International Marketing*, edited by P. Naude & P.W. Turnbull. Oxford: Pergamon Press, pp. 16–25.

——— (2000) The IMP perspective: asset and liabilities of business relationships. In *Handbook of Relationship Marketing*, edited by J. Sheth & A. Parvatiyar. Thousand Oaks, CA: Sage, pp. 69–93.

Håkansson, H. & Waluszewski, A. (2002) *Managing Technological Development. IKEA, the Environment and Technology*. London: Routledge.

Halinen, A. (1997) *Relationship Marketing in Professional Services. A Study of Agency-Client Dynamics in the Advertising Sector*. London: Routledge.

Halinen, A. & Törnros, J-Å. (1995) The meaning of time in the study of industrial buyer-seller relationship. In *Business Marketing: An Interaction and Network Perspective*, edited by K. Möller & D. Wilson. Boston: Kluwer, pp. 493–530.

Halinen, A., Salmi, A. & Havila, V. (1999) From dyadic change to changing business networks. An analytical framework. *Journal of Management Studies*, 36, 6, 779–94.

Hallen, L. (1986) A comparison of strategic marketing approaches. In *Strategies for International Industrial*

Marketing, edited by P. Turnbull & J-P. Valla. London: Croom Helm, pp. 235–49.
Hallen, L., Johanson, J. & Seyed-Mohammed, N. (1991) Interfirm adaptation in business relationships. *Journal of Marketing*, 55 (April), 29–37.
Hamel, G. & Prahalad, C.K. (1989) Strategic intent. *Harvard Business Review*, 67, 3, 63–76.
Harrison, D. (1998) Strategic responses to predicted events; the case of banning CFCs. Ph.D. Dissertation, Department of Marketing, University of Lancaster, UK.
Haugland, S. & Reve, T. (1993) Price, authority and trust in international distribution channel relationships. *Scandinavian Journal of Management*, 10, 3, 225–44.
Hayek, F.A. (1945) The use of knowledge in society. *American Economic Review*, 35 (September), 519–30.
Heide, J.B. (1994) Interorganizational governance in marketing channels. *Journal of Marketing*, 58, 71–85.
Heide, J.B. & John, G. (1992) Do norms matter in marketing relationships? *Journal of Marketing*, 56, 32–44.
Helper, S. & Sako, M. (1995) Supplier relationships in Japan and the United States: are they converging? *Sloan Management Review*, 36, 3, 77–84.
Holmen, E. (2001) Notes on a conceptualisation of resource-related embeddedness of interorganizational product development. Ph.D. Dissertation, Institute for Marketing, University of Southern Denmark.
Holmen, E. & Pedersen, A-C. (2000) Avoiding triadic reductionism: serial tetrads – a useful concept for studying connected relationships? In *Interaction, Relationships and Networks, Proceedings from the 16th IMP Conference, University of Bath*, edited by D. Ford, P. Naude, T. Ritter, P. Turnbull & S. Leek.
Huemer, L. (1998) *Trust in Business Relations: Economic Logic or Social Interaction?* Umeå: Boréa.
Hunt, S.D. (2000) *A General Theory of Competition*. Thousand Oaks, CA: Sage.
Hutt, M.D. & Speh, T.W. (1984) The marketing strategy center: diagnosing the industrial marketer's interdisciplinary role. *Journal of Marketing*, 48 (Fall), 53–61.
Iacobucci, D. (ed.) (1996) *Networks in Marketing*. Thousand Oaks, CA: Sage.
Jacobson, R. (1992) The Austrian school of strategy. *Academy of Management Review*, 17, 4, 782–807.
Johanson, J. & Mattsson, L-G. (1985) Marketing investments and market investments in industrial networks. *International Journal of Research in Marketing*, 2, 185–95.
Kalwani, M.U. & Narayandas, N. (1995) Long term manufacturer-supplier relationships: do they pay off for the supplier firms? *Journal of Marketing*, 59 (January), 1–16.
Kelly, H.H. & Thibaut, J.W. (1978) *Interpersonal Relations: A Theory of Interdependence*. New York: John Wiley and Sons.
Keep, W.W., Hollander, S.C. & Dickinson, R. (1998) Forces impinging on long-term business-to-business relationships in the United States: a historical perspective. *Journal of Marketing*, 62 (April), 31–45.
Kirzner, I. (1973) *Competition and Entrepreneurship*. Chicago: The University of Chicago Press.
——— (1979) *Perception, Opportunity and Profit; Studies in the Theory of Entrepreneurship*. Chicago: The University of Chicago Press.
Laage-Hellman, J. (1997) *Business Networks in Japan; Supplier-Customer Interaction in Product Development*. London: Routledge.
Lamming, R. (1993) *Beyond Partnership – Strategies for Innovation and Lean Supply*. London: Prentice-Hall.
Loasby, B.J. (1998) The organisation of capabilities. *Journal of Economic Behavior and Organisation*, 35, 139–60.
Lorenzoni, G. & Baden-Fuller, C. (1995) Creating a strategic center to manage a web of partners. *California Management Review*, 37, 3, 146–63.
Lundgren, A. (1995) *Technological Innovation and Network Evolution*. London: Routledge.
Mitchell, J.C. (1973) Networks, norms and institutions. In *Network Analysis*, edited by J. Boissevain & J.C. Mitchell. The Hague: Mouton.
Möller, K. & Wilson, D. (eds) (1995) *Business Marketing: An Interaction and Network Perspective*. Dordrecht: Kluwer Academic Press.
Naude, P. & Turnbull, P.W. (eds) (1998) *Network Dynamics in International Marketing*. Oxford: Pergamon Press.
Powell, W.W. (1987) Hybrid organizational arrangements: new form or transitional development? *California Management Review*, 30, 1, 67–87.
Reekie D.W. & Savitt, R. (1982) Marketing behaviour and entrepreneurship: a synthesis of Alderson and Austrian economics. *European Journal of Marketing*, 16, 7, 55–66.
Reid, D.A. & Plank, R.E. (2000) Business marketing comes of age: a comprehensive review of the literature. *Journal of Business-to-Business Marketing*, 7, 2/3, 9–185.
Richardson, G.B. (1972) The organisation of industry. *The Economic Journal*, September, 883–96.
Rindfleish, A. & Heide, J.B. (1997) Transaction cost analysis: past, present and future applications. *Journal of Marketing*, 61 (October), 30–54.
Rindfleish, A. & Moorman, C. (2001) The acquisition and utilisation of information in new product alliances. A strength of ties perspective. *Journal of Marketing*, 65 (April), 1–18.
Ritter, T. (1999) The networking firm. *Industrial Marketing Management*, 28, 5, 497–506.
Sharma, D. (ed.) (1993) *Advances in International Marketing*, Vol. 5. Cambridge, MA: JAI Press.
Sheth, J.N. & Parvatiyar, A. (1995) The evolution of relationship marketing. *International Business Review*, 4, 4, 397–418.
——— (eds) (2000) *Handbook of Relationship Marketing*. Thousand Oaks, CA: Sage.
Smith, J.B. & Barclay, D.B. (1997) The effects of organizational differences and trust on the effectiveness of selling partners' relationships. *Journal of Marketing*, 61 (January), 3–21.
Snehota, I. (1990) Notes on a theory of business enterprise. Ph.D. Thesis, Uppsala University: Department of Business Studies.

Swedberg, R. (1994) Markets as social structures. In *The Handbook of Economic Sociology*, edited by N.J. Smelser & R. Swedberg. Princeton, NJ: Princeton University Press, pp. 255–82.

Thibault, J.W. & Kelley, H.H. (1959) *The Social Psychology of Groups*. New York: Wiley.

Torvatn, T. (1996) Productivity in industrial networks. A case study of the purchasing function. Ph.D thesis, Trondheim: Norwegian University of Science and Technology.

Turnbull, P. (1990) A review of portfolio planning models for industrial marketing and purchasing manager. *European Journal of Marketing*, 24, 3, 7–22.

Turnbull, P. & Valla, J-P. (eds) (1986) *Strategies for International Industrial Marketing*. London: Croom Helm.

Uzzi, B. (1997) Social structure and competition in interfirm networks: the paradox of embeddedness. *Administrative Science Quarterly*, 42, 35–67.

van Weele, A. (2000) *Purchasing and Supply Chain Management: Analysis, Planning and Practice*. London: Thompson Learning.

von Hippel, E. (1988) *The Sources of Innovation*. New York: Oxford University Press.

von Hippel, E., Thomke, S. & Sonnak, M. (1999) Creating breakthroughs at 3M. *Harvard Business Review*, September–October, 47–57.

Wathne, H. & Heide, J.B. (2000) Opportunism in interfirm relationships: forms, outcomes and solutions. *Journal of Marketing*, 64 (October), 36–51.

Webster, F. (1992) The changing role of marketing in the corporation. *Journal of Marketing*, 56 (October), 132–6.

Wedin, T. (2001) Networks and demand: the use of electricity in industrial processes. Ph.D. Dissertation, Department of Business Studies, Uppsala University.

Wensley, R. (1996) Another oxymoron in marketing: marketing strategy. In *Marketing in Evolution*, edited by S. Shaw & N. Hood. London: MacMillan, pp. 36–54.

Wilkinson, I. & Young, L. (1996) Business dancing, the nature and role of interfirm relations in business strategy. *Asia-Australia Marketing Journal*, 1, 67–79.

Williamson, O.E. (1975) *Markets and Hierarchies: Analysis and Antitrust Implications*. New York: Free Press.

——— (1985) *The Economic Institutions of Capitalism*. New York: Free Press.

Wilson, D.T. (1995) Toward an integrated model of buyer-seller relationships. *Journal of the Academy of Marketing Science*, 23, 4, 335–45.

Wynstra, F. (1998) Purchasing involvement in product development. Ph.D. Thesis, Eindhoven University of Technology.

21

Marketing and the Internet

PATRICK BARWISE, ANITA ELBERSE and KATHY HAMMOND

1. Introduction: The Promise of Digital Marketing

How Important is the Internet in Marketing?

The Internet has become one of the most discussed topics in business and academia. The speed of development of electronic marketing has been fast by any standards, and especially compared with the slow process of academic research and publication in marketing and other social sciences.

At the time of writing, however, business and financial markets are recovering from earlier overexuberance about the Internet. It is now recognized that the fundamentals of business have not changed; that most pure-play dotcom business models were wildly over-optimistic, especially in business-to-consumer (B2C) markets; and that the future role of the Internet in marketing will be largely as part of an integrated combination of 'bricks and clicks.'

Despite this necessary reassessment, the Internet remains the most wide-ranging and significant area of current development in marketing:

- It allows *faster*, *cheaper*, *more personalized interactions* (and raises more privacy concerns) than any previous medium.
- It can dramatically reduce *customer search costs* and even support purchase decisions made on behalf of the customer by intelligent software agents.
- It allows seamless communication over *any distance*, local or global. Eventually, it will also support effective automatic language translation.
- It is becoming *ubiquitous*, allowing '24x7' communications with customers at home, at work, at the point of purchase, on the road, or anywhere else – including location-sensitive communications.
- Increasingly, it is evolving beyond a single, limited channel (a PC connected to a regular telephone line) to exploit a range of new, high-capacity fixed and mobile networks and '*convergent*' devices such as interactive digital television (iDTVs), online games computers, next generation cellphones and PDAs, in-car telematics, online vending machines, and utility meters.

These capabilities have the potential – in principle – to transform many aspects of marketing: segmentation and targeting, bundling, pricing, customer service and customer relationship management, marketing communication, promotion, channels and value chains, brand communities, global marketing, and the importance of brands.

Marketers are all still trying to discover the long-term implications for strategy and execution, but it is possible to draw some initial conclusions, including on many of the topics just listed. Our overall assessment is that, despite the earlier hype, the Internet remains the most important development in B2C markets since the growth of television and supermarkets 50 years ago, and the most important in business-to-business (B2B) markets since the railroad and telegraph 100–150 years ago.

Hoffman (2000: 1) described the Internet as 'the most important innovation since the development of the printing press,' with the potential to 'radically transform not just the way individuals go about conducting their business with each other, but also the very essence of what it means to be a human being in society.' Peppers and Rogers (1993, 1997) argued that digital marketing represents a complete transformation of the marketing paradigm, from a predominantly one-way broadcast model to a model of totally interactive, totally personalized one-to-one relationships. However, the extent to which digital media such as the Internet will revolutionize business, home life, and the relationship between marketer and consumer is still controversial. Earlier innovations such as the electric telegraph, the railroad, electricity, the telephone, the automobile, the airplane, radio, and television have all had widespread impact on both business and everyday life, although perhaps only electricity quite matches the combined speed and scale of the Internet's impact (Barwise & Hammond, 1998).

Many of the features associated with the Internet have appeared before in the context of technologies such as the electric telegraph (Standage, 1998) and radio (Hanson, 1998, 2000). Ethnographers such as Venkatesh (1985) have long studied people's everyday use of technology in the home. Mick and Fournier (1998) and Fournier, Dobscha and Mick (1998) found that much so-called technophobia among consumers is entirely rational and based on their previous experience of technology making life more complicated – not simpler, as claimed. Certainly many of the early claims about the likely speed of the Internet's impact, for example on the use of other media (Gilder, 1994; Negroponte, 1995), have turned out to be wide of the mark. Exaggerated visions of a wired society go back at least to E.M. Forster writing in 1909 (Baer, 1998).

What is clear is that the Internet combines many of the features of existing media with new capabilities of interactivity and addressability, as well as making it much easier for both companies and individuals to achieve a global reach with their ideas and products. By the start of the twenty-first century it had already been adopted on a massive scale, especially in North America, Australia and Northern Europe, and its effects will continue to be felt in almost every market and on almost every aspect of marketing. These impacts range from the most micro (such as ad agencies needing to experiment with the design of interactive advertisements) through to the most macro (such as whether corporate profitability will be lower in 'frictionless' markets).

A few researchers were quick to recognize the potential of new interactive media to affect all aspects of marketing. Blattberg and Deighton (1991: 8) noted that, by the early 1990s, technology was already allowing interactive marketing to take place to individually identifiable consumers: 'When a firm can go back to a customer to respond to what the customer has just said, it is holding a dialogue, not delivering a monologue.' They noted that good database design was key, that profiles of customer histories should be collected, and that privacy concerns would grow. Deighton built on this work by gathering together a collection of thoughts from marketing academics and industry experts on how interactivity might reshape the marketing paradigm (Deighton, 1996). He also foresaw the emergence of a new marketing paradigm that would bring about a convergence between consumer marketing and business-to-business marketing (Deighton, 1997). He suggested that

> the discipline of marketing, whose stock of knowledge amounts to a fund of insights on how to compensate for the imperfections of two kinds of tools – broadcast tools and sales agent tools – now has a new tool without some of those imperfections but with a whole new set of imperfections yet to be discovered. (Deighton, 1997: 348)

Hoffman and Novak (1996, 1997) identified the unique 'many-to-many' property of computer-mediated environments such as the web. They suggested that marketing activities will be difficult to implement in their traditional form, and predicted the evolution of a marketing paradigm compatible with the increased role of the consumer and of interactive technologies.

Other researchers have suggested similar far-reaching changes in business: Haeckel (1998: 69) proposed that the collaborative potential of information technology and the Internet might recast business as 'a game with customers, rather than … a game against competitors.' Taking a similar view, Achrol and Kotler (1999) suggested that, as the hierarchical organizations of the twentieth century disaggregate into a variety of network forms, customers will enjoy an increasing capacity to become organized, with marketers becoming agents of the buyer rather than the seller, and adopting the role of customer consultant rather than purveyor of goods and services. They cite examples such as Baxter Travenol in hospital supplies, McKesson in pharmaceuticals, Travelocity in flight booking, and Amazon (Achrol & Kotler, 1999: 157–8). Similarly, Nouwens and Bouwman (1995) explored the conditions likely to give rise to 'network organizations' such as the recorded music retail industry. They concluded that the role of a system integrator is crucial, but that a dominant actor (e.g., a copyright holder) could hinder the effective use of industry-wide communication networks.

In exploring the research agenda for marketers, Winer et al. (1997) examined the potential for marketing research associated with computer-mediated environments (CMEs). They suggested that the CME provides a new context in which to study existing theories as well as being an entirely new phenomenon meriting research in its own right. They identified five key areas of choice research likely to be impacted by the development of CME technology: decision processes, advertising and communication, brand choice, brand communities, and pricing. This review chapter covers research on all five, as well as on other topics.

Aims and Scope of this Chapter

Our aim is to review the research to-date on how the Internet is impacting marketing. The speed of development and the shortage of new theory to support hypothesis-testing necessarily mean that our review deals more with empirical research than with theory. There has, however, been a growing stream of theoretical development and discussion, from early essays on marketing in an information-intensive environment (Glazer, 1991), on the nature of interactivity in both marketing (Blattberg & Deighton, 1991; Rust & Oliver, 1994) and communication (Dutton, 1996; Morris & Ogan, 1996; Neuman, 1991; Pavlik, 1996), through ethnographic work which explores household–technology interactions (Venkatesh et al., 1996) to the work of Hoffman and Novak (1996) – the main pioneers of Internet research in marketing – who proposed one of the first models of consumer behavior in computer mediated environments – and to Bakos and Brynjolfsson (1999, 2000a, 2000b), and their work on online pricing strategies.

The Internet impacts marketing strategy, channel management, pricing, marketing communications, customer service, decision support systems, database marketing, global marketing, and business-to-business marketing. We here focus on research which looks at how the Internet is or can be used by both firms and consumers to support the marketing process. We concentrate on research in consumer behavior, advertising, pricing, channels, and marketing strategy, because empirical research is most advanced in these areas. We aim to provide an overview of the current state of research and briefly to identify opportunities for further work. We do not cover the extensive literature on supply chain management, information management, organizational behavior, or the broader impact of the Internet on productivity, profitability, employment, and international trade.

We searched for relevant literature in a number of ways. First, we used databases such as JSTOR, ABI Inform/ProQuest Direct and Web of Science, searching for key terms covering the topics under investigation. Second, we browsed volumes of relevant marketing journals (e.g., the *International Journal of Research in Marketing*, *Journal of Consumer Research*, *Journal of Electronic Commerce*, *Journal of Interactive Marketing*, *Journal of Marketing*, *Journal of Marketing Research*, *Management Science*, and *Marketing Science*) published after 1994 – roughly the time at which articles about the Internet started to appear. Third, we searched for articles on the Internet, usually starting at popular search engines, web pages published by academic institutions (e.g., the MIT E-commerce Forum, Wharton's Forum on Electronic Commerce, and references on UCLA's Anderson School website), as well as individual researchers' personal web pages. Fourth, we collected literature based on suggestions by colleagues who had read an earlier draft of our manuscript (which we had made publicly available on the web). In our search, we did not limit ourselves to published articles, book chapters and books; given the dynamic nature of the topic, we also sought to include working papers and manuscripts under review. In total, we collected nearly 400 publications.[1]

The rest of this chapter is organized as follows. Section 2 concerns Internet adoption, usage and the consumer's experience. Section 3 builds on this to discuss the evidence on consumers' online purchasing behavior. Section 4 covers Internet advertising. Section 5 then explores wider issues related to Internet economics and pricing, including the evidence on whether the Internet is, as is often claimed, leading to 'frictionless' markets characterized by fierce price competition. This leads into Section 6, on the impact on channels and intermediaries. Section 7 reviews the strategies and business models that firms are developing in response to the new threats and opportunities created by the Internet. Finally, Section 8 briefly summarizes the chapter and discusses future prospects and research opportunities.

2. Internet Adoption, Usage, and the Consumer Experience

In this section we start by reporting research on the factors that influence customers' adoption and usage of the Internet in general. We next discuss its adoption specifically for e-commerce, and factors such as site design, service quality and fulfillment, that can affect its continued use as an e-commerce channel. Finally we introduce the relevant literature on software agents.

Predictors of Internet Adoption and Usage

The use of the Internet as a marketing channel depends both on the growth in general Internet penetration and usage, and on how the Internet then influences the adoption and diffusion of other products and services. In both these contexts, there is the usual caveat that one must be careful not to assume that the predictors of early adoption will also hold for later adopters.

Rangaswamy and Gupta (1999) draw on the adoption and diffusion literature to propose how the

Internet will develop. They use the GVU database[2] and other surveys to explore early adopters' attitudes toward the Internet and perceptions of online versus offline vendors. They found that among very early adopters, especially those who were heavy users, the primary reason for using the web was for shopping.

Hammond et al. (2000) compared Internet users and non-users to determine if there were differences between these two groups in their attitudes toward technology, ownership of different technologies, and information versus entertainment needs. They found that, compared to non-users, Internet users were more interested in technology in general and the benefits it provided, especially if they thought it would save them effort or time. They were also more likely to think that technology was both important and fun. Internet users were primarily motivated by communication/information needs but this did not appear to be because they felt 'time-pressured' compared to non-users. A tentative implication of these findings is that the Internet may need to become more entertainment-oriented in order to attract a broader active user base.

Emmanouilides and Hammond (2000) used logistic regression to explore four successive waves of survey data on Internet users. They found that the main predictors of *active or continued use* of the Internet were: time since first use (very early adopters were the most likely to be active users, but this relationship was curvilinear, with middle adopters more likely than other groups not to have used the Internet in the previous month); location of use, particularly at home; and the use of specific applications, such as information services. However, the main predictors of *frequent or heavy* Internet use were: use of email for business purposes; time since first use of the Internet; and location of use (either at work or at home with two or more other people).

As the Internet matures as a consumer medium we begin to see studies which evaluate how it is used and what makes for a compelling experience. Novak et al. (2000) built on Hoffman and Novak's (1996) discussion of 'flow' to develop a model of the components of a compelling online experience. The model was validated using a web-based consumer survey. A compelling experience was found to be positively correlated with fun, recreational and experiential uses of the web, with expected use in the future, and with the amount of time consumers spend online, and negatively associated with work-related usage. Faster download and interaction were not, *per se*, associated with a compelling experience.

Other evidence supports the importance of the fun or hedonic aspect of Internet use. Hammond et al. (1998) explored the differences between novices and more experienced users and their appreciation of the web's informational and entertainment value. They found that, while prior experience was an important moderator of users' attitudes towards the web, its influence was nonlinear. The heaviest users were enthusiasts for the medium, while moderate and light users perceived it as a source of information, but not for entertainment or fun.

Exploring the different reasons people have for using the Internet, Hoffman et al. (2000) used the locus of control (LOC) construct to study differences in usage between those with an internal versus an external focus. They found that those who use the web as a substitute for other activities tend to have an external orientation, whereas those with an internal focus use it in a more goal-directed manner as a supplement to other information gathering activities.

Applying the uses and gratifications perspective to web users, Eighmey and McCord (1998) found similarities to the uses and gratifications reported for other media. However, there were additional factors related to personal involvement and continuing relationships that were associated with users' reactions to websites. As Venkatesh (1998) notes, consumers not only consume new technology and its products, but are also consumers of the market processes, which are themselves affected by new technology, and all these processes can affect the social order. Related to the experience of consumers in online environments, Gould and Lerman (1998) analyzed early consumer-to-consumer (C2C) exchanges on an online discussion forum, *NetGirl*, in a bid to describe and understand, in phenomenological terms, the consumer experience.

These adoption and usage studies treat the Internet as an additional medium in consumers' lives. We now turn to research which specifically evaluates its adoption and use as a channel for commerce.

Adoption of the Internet as an E-Commerce Channel

Hoffman et al. (1995) were the first researchers to propose a framework for examining the commercial development of the web. They explored its role both as a distribution channel and as a medium for marketing communication, evaluated the resulting benefits to consumers and firms, and discussed the barriers to its commercial growth from both supply- and demand-side perspectives. Their classification scheme categorized websites as either destination sites (online storefronts and other content sites), or as web traffic control sites (malls, incentive sites, and search agents). They proposed that the interactive nature of the web freed customers from their traditional passive role as receivers of marketing communications, giving them access to greater amounts of dynamic information to support decision-making.

In an early study comparing web shopping with buying through other channels, Palmer (1997) tested the buying of 120 different products across four retail formats: in store, catalog, cable television, and the web. Total product cost did not vary significantly between the four formats, but there were significant differences in product description, availability, delivery, and time taken to shop.

Consumer substitution between online, traditional retail, and direct mail has been explored by Ward and Davies (1999) using a transaction cost approach. Ward and Davies developed a model to investigate distribution channel choice and tested it using survey data, finding that consumers considered online shopping and direct marketing to be closer substitutes than either of them with traditional retail. Degeratu et al. (1999) hypothesized how online and traditional grocery stores differ in their influence on consumer choice. They found that brand names were more valuable online in categories where information on fewer product attributes was available; that 'non-sensory' attributes (e.g., the fat content of margarine) had more impact on online choice than 'sensory' ones (e.g., visual cues such as paper towel design); and that price sensitivity was higher online because online promotions were stronger signals of price discounts. The combined effect of price and promotion on consumer choice was found to be weaker online than offline.

Other research has covered the battle between bricks-and-mortar and Internet companies. Interesting in this regard is a study by Goolsbee (2000) on competition in the computer industry. Based on Forrester Research Survey data covering 90,000 households, he constructed a price index measuring the offline costs of a computer in different cities, and then calculated how likely a computer buyer would be to purchase online, taking into account prices of computers offered by offline retailers. He found that if local (offline) and online prices were initially equal, and local prices were to rise by 10%, bricks-and-mortar retailers would see their share of unit sales fall from 68% to 63%, assuming the total volume of purchases remained unchanged. Although the precise effect may vary among sectors and products, and the findings indicate that online and offline purchases are to some extent substitutes, these findings suggest that there is less rivalry between offline and online retailers than between retailers operating nearby stores.

Building on the channels literature, Morrison and Roberts (1998) explored the determinants of consumer consideration of new delivery channels for existing services in terms of preference for the service, preference for the delivery method, and the fit between the service and the delivery method. They suggested that adoption of new channels was being slowed by consumer doubts over the relative advantage of these new channels, and also the lack of fit between the service (their example was banking) and the new channel. They concluded that consumer e-commerce firms need to spend more effort explaining to consumers the fit and appropriateness of new delivery methods for their goods and services.

Using US survey data from the GVU Center, Bain (1999) examined factors related to the adoption of the Internet as a purchase medium. A strong (negative) relationship was found between consumer perceptions of the risk of web-shopping and purchase behavior, but not between perceptions concerning information privacy and purchase behavior. This suggests that consumers will not buy online if they are worried that there is a financial risk but they are less concerned about their personal details being kept, used, or traded by retailers.

The most likely candidates to be early adopters of retailer websites have been found to be consumers who were familiar with the Internet and already used to other modes of home shopping (Balabanis & Vassileiou, 1999). Consumers in higher income brackets were more enthusiastic about shopping on the Internet, but for this segment strong brands were key to shopping online. Li et al. (1999) found that education, experience, views on convenience, channel knowledge, perceived distribution utility, and perceived accessibility were robust predictors of the extent to which an Internet user was a frequent online buyer.

Bellman et al. (1999) surveyed over 9,000 online users and used logistic regression to identify factors that predicted whether an online user bought products online, and if so, how much they spent. The best predictors were 'time starvation' (how many hours a week the user worked) and the extent of their 'wired' lifestyle. Lohse et al. (2000) re-surveyed the same respondents to test whether and how their attitudes and behavior had changed over time. They found that the average annual spend per purchaser had increased over time; time starvation and a wired lifestyle were still major determinants of the amount of online spending; but time starvation no longer appeared to influence whether a person chose to buy from an online store. A further finding was that, while the percentage of respondents who made a purchase online increased over time, a significant minority (14%) who had previously bought online had ceased to do so. The authors suggest that this was mostly due to respondents having had bad experiences with online retailers.

Swaminathan et al. (1999), using an email survey of GVU Center respondents, found that concerns about privacy and security had minimal effect on consumers' online purchasing behavior, but that those who purchased frequently online were more likely to support new laws to protect privacy (perhaps because they knew more about what companies do with the data). The main determinant of online purchase frequency was perceived vendor characteristics, especially price competitiveness and the ease of canceling orders. Another factor was that consumers motivated by convenience (mostly men) were more likely to buy online than those who valued social interaction (mostly women).

Another key factor that has been found to determine whether consumers buy online is whether this fits into their lifestyle, and the extent to which they perceive it as easy and convenient (Becker-Olsen, 2000). She found that those not buying online felt that traditional shopping was easier, quicker, cheaper, and more convenient for their particular lifestyle. Even those who did buy online did not perceive it as quicker or less expensive, nor did they feel that they received better service. Neither group (online buyers and non-buyers) seemed strongly concerned with security risks, although the overall credibility of the company/site was seen as important, especially by those who had not purchased online. Other factors were the need to see/touch the product (in some categories) and consumers' need to have the product immediately.

Service Quality, Fulfillment, and Site Design

Building on Hoffman et al.'s (1995) framework for classifying Internet commerce sites, Spiller and Lohse (1998) surveyed 44 website features across 137 women's apparel retail sites. Using cluster and factor analysis they identified five distinct web catalog interface types: superstores, promotional stores, plain sales stores, one-page stores, and product listings. Differences between online stores centered on size, service offerings, and interface quality.

Again, building on the Hoffman and Novak framework, it has been proposed that there are three major components to a consumer's online shopping experience: interface quality, encounter quality, and fulfillment quality (Chang, 2000). We can think of these as: process, experience, and results, although in the online world these elements are often intertwined more than in traditional retail channels. To build brand equity, it is suggested that firms need to ensure excellence on all three dimensions. We now consider empirical research findings in these areas.

One of the key aspects of the online experience investigated by researchers is the time taken for consumers to access the information they require. Dellaert and Kahn (1999) investigated whether the waiting time experienced by consumers (e.g., while pages downloaded) affected subsequent evaluation of the web content. They found that the potential negative effects of waiting can be neutralized by improving the waiting experience. Consumers may feel negative effect as a result of waiting, but this did not necessarily impact on their evaluation of the web material itself, as long as the waiting time was signaled and expected.

This finding was amplified by Weinberg (2000), who showed that the perceived waiting time could be significantly influenced by providing a waiting time anchor *lower* than the actual waiting time. In an experiment where all subjects experienced an actual wait of 7.5 seconds, those given the message '*Please wait about 5 seconds*' on average estimated it was 5.6 seconds; those told '*Please wait about 10 seconds*' estimated 8.7 seconds. In a second experiment, subjects exposed to a 5-second wait anchor rated the quality of the homepage higher, and were more likely to continue searching the website, than those exposed to a 10-second wait anchor.

Related to consumer perceptions of the time they spend waiting for information to download is the time spent waiting for a response to an information request. Voss (2000) reported a survey of different sites' responsiveness to email inquiries. It was found that, in both the US and Britain, websites' response tended to be poor for web startups and even worse for established businesses. There was, however, wide variation, with some sites never responding and others having an excellent auto-acknowledge function followed by relatively fast full response. This paper proposed a set of key metrics in areas such as trust, response time, response quality, and navigability. Similarly, in the context of complaints, Strauss and Hill (2001) found that customer satisfaction was enhanced by quick responses to complaint emails. They, too, found a huge range in company response.

As many web startups discovered, service quality also includes fulfillment, which, for physical products, requires expensive bricks-and-mortar logistics. In many markets this can be subcontracted at low cost, but in some, notably groceries, home delivery is likely to be the limiting factor. Two articles in *McKinsey Quarterly* (Barsh et al., 2000; Bhise et al., 2000) and another in the Booz Allen *Strategy and Business* (Laseter et al., 2000) explored the issue of fulfillment. Barsh et al. describe how most e-tailers lose money on every transaction. The articles conclude that successful online retailing requires a scalable national sales and distribution channel, and that the main discriminator between those companies that succeed and those that fail will be large order volumes and deep reserves of capital.

The online experience has also been related to interface quality, specifically to website design. Ghose and Dou (1998) found that the more interactive the website, the more likely it is to be rated a 'top site.' Against this finding, however, are the crucial issues of simplicity, navigability, and especially the download and response times, as described above.

Bellman and Rossiter (2001) introduce and test the concept of a *web ad schema*, defined as the consumer's set of beliefs about information locations, and routes to those locations, for a web advertising site. They argue that consumers already have well-developed schemata for finding useful information in traditional media (e.g., they expect to find detailed product specifications towards the back of a brochure, and to see or hear the brand name in the final frames of a TV commercial). But on the web, some consumers are much better than others at finding information from an advertising website. Bellman and Rossiter contend that these adept consumers have web ad schemata which are both well developed and congruent with the structure of the site. Their paper reports a series of three studies which support the existence of web ad schemata and their influence on communications effectiveness (brand knowledge). The results also suggest that these schemata are motor-associative – acquired by exploring the site one click at a time – rather than map-like. The implications are first, that the site structure should be as simple as possible, and second, that (except for a very large site) in-site navigation should also be simple and motor-associative, providing 'local' information about the pages immediately accessible from the current page and *not* a 'menu' of the overall site structure, which is the usual approach (Hofacker, 2001). Although this research focuses only on advertising sites, the conclusions about navigability seem likely to generalize to other types of site.

Research by Mandel and Johnson (1999) showed that even minor peripheral cues such as background color and pictures could influence consumers' response to a site. For example, in one experiment, subjects who were shown a 'money' background gave more weight to price when asked to evaluate products than those who were shown a different background. Such priming effects were found to affect both search order and choice.

Another element of site design is the tools that are provided to help consumers choose between different products/brands. Building on the extensive literature on consumer information processing and consideration sets, Häubl and Trifts (2000) explored the impact that interactive decision aids have on consumers' decision-making. In a controlled experiment they introduced users to two decision aids. The first was a recommendation agent to allow consumers to screen a large set of alternatives and reduce these to a short list or consideration set. The second, a comparison matrix, helped users make in-depth comparisons among the selected alternatives. The study found that both these interactive decision aids had an impact on consumer decision-making, enabling consumers to make better decisions with less effort. The findings also suggest that the use of such tools can lead to an increase in the quality (but decrease in the size) of consumers' consideration sets.

Also on this topic, early work by Widing and Talarzyk (1993) on how consumers use decision aids suggested that not only did they like computer assistance and feel that it helped them to make better decisions, but that aids which enabled them to weight the importance of rated attributes (such as ease of use, or performance), and obtain a personalized rank order of brands, were more useful than other types of decision aid.

Ariely (2000) used a series of experiments to explore the characteristics and likely impact of information control on consumers' decision quality, memory, knowledge, and confidence. He found that controlling the flow of information can help consumers better match their preferences, have better memory and knowledge about the topics they are exploring, and be more confident in their judgments. However, he warns that controlling the information flow can create additional demands on the consumer's ability to process information, and so may not be suitable for situations where the task is difficult or novel.

Almost all the previous research focuses specifically on B2C interactions. Berthon et al. (1998) developed a conceptual framework for evaluating web communication activities (e.g., number of active users as a percentage of hits, number of purchases as a percentage of active users, etc.), and suggested how this might be applied to the B2B industrial purchasing decision-making process.

Software Agents

Devices such as the recommendation agents in Häubl and Trifts' (2000) study, discussed above, focus on improving the navigability and convenience of choosing a product or service supplied by the site owner. We now turn to the more advanced intelligent agents which act on behalf of individual consumers, knowing their preferences and searching the web for products that best meet their needs. Such an agent could significantly influence brand choice and/or which distribution channel is chosen to supply a particular brand. If requested, it can negotiate price and/or delivery, possibly by inviting suppliers to bid ('reverse auction') and/or by forming a cartel with other consumers (or their agents) to negotiate the best price (Dolan & Moon, 2000). Finally, the agent may be empowered in some contexts to make the actual purchase on behalf of the consumer. Initially, agents (or 'bots,' e.g., 'shopbots' in the case of those aimed at shopping applications) were controlled through the consumer's PC. Increasingly, they will also be controlled through mobile phones and interactive digital TVs, and eventually by voice rather than a keyboard or keypad (Barwise & Hammond, 1998).

The best known center for research on agent technology is the Media Laboratory at MIT. Patti Maes, who heads its software agent group, expects agent technology to have dramatic effects on the US economy (Maes, 1999). She predicts the disappearance of existing intermediaries and the emergence of some new types of intermediary, a reduction in the capital required to set up a business (and therefore more scope for small niche businesses), and efficiency gains for both buyers and sellers by dramatically reducing marketing and selling costs, but with a clear overall shift in the balance of power from sellers to buyers.

Guttman et al. (1998) summarize the Media Lab's research on e-commerce agents. These include: C2C 'smart' classified ads, merchant agents that provide interrogative negotiation, agents that facilitate expertise brokering and distributed reputation facilities, agents for point-of-sale comparison shopping, and agents for mobile devices. The Media Lab research has focused on the development, prototyping and evaluation of the agent technology itself, including the launch of an agent-based business, Firefly.com, which was bought by Microsoft in 1998 but shut down in 1999 in preparation for Microsoft's Passport service. Other researchers have sought to explore the potential and likely impact of agent technology from a marketing perspective (discussed below). Some of this research overlaps with work on buyer search costs and information economics, and on disintermediation, discussed in Sections 5 and 6.

Recommendation systems are assessed by Ansari et al. (2000) who investigate the two main methods of gathering recommendations: collaborative filtering (based on other users' weighted preferences) and content or attribute-based filtering (based on information provided by the user). Researchers at the Sloan School at MIT have investigated the use of recommendation agents as 'trust-based advisors' in both B2B and B2C contexts. Urban et al. (1999) described a prototype trusted agent system, and reported that consumers who are not very knowledgeable about the product, who visited more retailers, and who were younger and more frequent Internet users, had the highest preference for a virtual personal advisor.

Other researchers have proposed frameworks for thinking about the design of electronic agents. Gershoff and West (1998) and West et al. (1999) suggest a set of goals for agent design that include both outcome-based goals (e.g., improving decision quality) and process goals (e.g., increasing consumer satisfaction and trust). Kephart et al. (2000) describe an IBM research program into the potential impact of dynamic pricing agents on the economy. Iacobucci et al. (2000) focus on intelligent agents that compare a user's profile to data on other users to determine which users in the database are similar, in order to develop relevant recommendations of value to the focal user. Iacobucci and her colleagues characterize this as 'rediscovering the wheel' of cluster analysis and therefore draw from the cluster analysis literature to begin to address the questions being posed in this new application area.

All these decision-making aids and recommendation agents are provided with the aim of supporting purchase and repeat-purchase. The next section reviews the evidence on consumer purchase behavior online.

3. Online Purchasing Behavior

Retailer/Brand Choice and Loyalty on the Web

The impact that interactive shopping might have on consumer behavior, and therefore on retailer and manufacturer revenue, was addressed by Alba et al. (1997). They considered the relative attractiveness to consumers of alternative retail formats. They noted that technological advances offered consumers unmatched opportunities to locate and compare product offerings, but that price competition may be mitigated by the ability of consumers to search for more differentiated products better fitted to their needs. The authors examined the impact of the Internet as a function of both consumer goals and product/service categories, and explored consumer incentives and disincentives to purchase online versus offline. They also discussed implications for industry structure in terms of competition between retailers, competition between manufacturers, and retailer-manufacturer relationships. They concluded with a list of research questions raised by the advent of interactive home shopping.

Continuing the theme of the impact that interactive shopping might have on consumers, Peterson et al. (1997) suggested that many predictions regarding the growth of the Internet for consumer retail are overstated because they failed to consider the heterogeneity and complexity of consumer markets. Peterson et al. analyze channel intermediary functions that could be performed on the Internet, classify its potential impact by category type, and discuss how price competition might evolve. They propose a consumer decision-making process that takes account of the Internet as both an information channel and a purchase channel. They give a detailed list of questions to motivate and guide the development of research into the use of the Internet and its implications for marketing theory and strategy.

As Rubini et al. (1996: 70) argued, even with the arrival of new technology, 'the process of shopping remains unchanged. The underlying basis for all retail, whether physical or virtual, remains a problem-solving process with a value-for-value exchange at its heart.' They discuss consumer shopping behavior from a design perspective, stressing the role played by problem recognition, search and evaluation of alternatives, navigation, purchase, content, identity, infrastructure, and social space.

They propose further exploration of these issues using a test virtual world through which shoppers navigate. Such a world is explored by Burke (1996), who described early test virtual stores as used by a tire company, a snack-food maker, a frozen-food company, and a fast-food restaurant chain. Burke (1997) reviewed the ways in which conventional retailers can enhance the shopping experience for their customers using both in-store and virtual applications. He addresses the potential weaknesses of the Internet as a shopping medium and suggests how these might be overcome.

Moving on from the decision whether to shop online, to which retailer site to patronize, Ilfield and Winer (2001) explore the decision-making process behind consumers' website choices and the relative effects of the communication channels which aid this process. They compare the traditional 'persuasive' hierarchy of effects (think-feel-do) model with a 'low involvement' (think-do-feel) model and a 'no involvement' (do-think-feel) model. The models were tested across a wide range of Internet companies. The data include spending by each company on a variety of online and offline media, measures of website attractiveness, number of visits and page views, public relations mentions, website quality, links, and whether the firm had a non-Internet presence. The low involvement model gave the best fit. The authors concluded that high brand awareness is essential for an Internet firm's survival.

In line with this conclusion, Adamic and Huberman (2000) studied the distribution of website visitors by examining usage logs covering 120,000 sites. They found that, both for all sites and for sites in specific categories, the distribution of visitors per site follows a universal power law similar to that found by Pareto in income distributions. This implies that a small number of sites command the traffic of a large segment of the web population, which suggests that only a few winners will emerge in each market.

Once the prospective customer has visited a website, managers wish to maximize the breadth (time spent on a site) and depth (number of pages viewed) of site visits, plus the repeat-visit rate and, of course, where appropriate, the amount of money spent per customer. Evidence on the importance to consumers of the perceived value of time can be found in a study by Lohse and Spiller (1999) which assessed different features of website interface design that affect store traffic and amount spent. Product list navigation features that save consumers time online (i.e., reduce the time to purchase) accounted for 61% of the variance in monthly sales.

Several researchers have applied traditional repeat-buying models to the investigation of online brand loyalty in order to evaluate customer lifetime value and to test whether consumer loyalty operates in a similar manner online compared with offline. Fader and Hardie (2001) presented a non-stationary experiential gamma (NSEG) model, similar to a negative binomial distribution (NBD) model but with dynamic individual-level buying rates. The NSEG model outperformed the NBD in the context of repeat buying on the Internet, in terms of both forecast accuracy and parameter stability across calibration periods of different lengths. Fader and Hardie describe a modeling exercise applied to repeat sales at the online music retailer CDNOW. Their main finding is that most of CDNOW's sales growth was due to a constant stream of new customers rather than from earlier trialists increasing their loyalty (measured as share of category requirements) over time. The implication is that it will be hard for online stores to sustain their earlier rapid sales growth since most consumers who use them will continue to do so in combination with established channels, rather than gradually switching over to purchasing exclusively online.

Using similar techniques, Moe and Fader (2000) developed an individual-level model for online store visits based on Internet clickstream data. This model captured cross-sectional variation in store-visit behavior as well as changes over time as consumers gained experience with the store. The results confirmed that people who visit a store more often are, as is widely assumed, more likely to buy. However, changes in an individual's visit frequency over time can also provide additional information about which consumer segments are more likely to buy. The implication is that marketers should use a sophisticated segmentation approach that incorporates how much an individual's behavior is changing over time, rather than simply targeting all frequent shoppers.

Other modelers include Wu and Rangaswamy (1999), who used data from online grocer Peapod. Their model uses Fuzzy Set Theory to capture the two-stage process of (1) consideration set formation, and (2) evaluation of alternatives in the consideration set. They showed that previous models had failed to capture the richness of the choice processes that are increasingly feasible for consumers in online markets.

A key question for retailers and brand managers is whether consumers exhibit greater or lesser brand loyalty online compared with offline. Danaher et al. (2000) compared consumer brand loyalty (share of category requirements and average purchase frequency) for packaged goods purchased online versus at traditional grocery stores. They used a segmented-Dirichlet model with latent classes for brand choice to compensate for systematic deviations in the offline retail setting. This provided the benchmark against which loyalty was tested in the online setting. Brand loyalty for high market-share brands was significantly greater in the virtual environment (a 'winner-take-all' effect), with the reverse being the case for low-share brands. In an online purchase setting, 'niche' brands (those with a small but highly loyal following) did better than expected, while 'change-of-pace' brands (those bought infrequently but by a large segment of the relevant population) did worse than expected.

Brands, Trust and Customer Relationships

In the context of the Internet, 'the brand is the experience and the experience is the brand' (Dayal et al., 2000: 42). As in physical environments, the key goal of online marketing is to use the web, usually in combination with a range of other channels and activities, to build a positive and profitable long-term relationship with the customer.

Steinfield et al. (1995) argued that B2B electronic networks can be used either to support transactional marketplaces or to strengthen commercial relationships. Their review of the literature suggests that the latter relational ('electronic hierarchies') approach is more prevalent. They examined the theoretical rationales behind these competing approaches and presented evidence on the conditions under which electronic marketplaces or electronic hierarchies are likely to prevail. Their conclusions are supported by Bauer et al. (1999), who focused on the contribution the Internet can make to relationship marketing, and especially to commitment, satisfaction and trust. This paper provided empirical evidence that consumers' trust is reduced if their expectations are not met.

There is, however, also evidence that the Internet is used by consumers as 'merely' an alternative shopping channel rather than a means of strengthening their relationships with brands or other consumers. Becker-Olsen (2000) found that, among those who had bought online, the most important factors determining their purchase behavior were the ability of the site to load quickly, availability of familiar brand names, and a clear return policy. These findings throw some doubt on the conclusions of Steinfield et al. (1995), and Bauer et al. (1999), and on the claims of Armstrong and Hagel (1996) and Hagel (1999), who suggested that online brand communities can play a major role in creating loyal customers (discussed more fully below). Becker-Olsen's results imply that consumers are more interested in purchasing conveniently and quickly than in browsing and developing a relationship. This supports Peterson's (1997) view that marketing relationships are by nature mostly exchange-oriented rather than relational.

The need for online retailers to pay more attention than their offline counterparts to establishing trust in the minds of consumers is seen as key by many researchers. Reichheld and Schefter (2000) suggested that the outlays to acquire a customer are often considerably higher for online retailers than for traditional channels, but that encouraging repeat (i.e., loyal) customers is key to success as these customers not only increase their spend over time but contribute to further customer acquisition through positive recommendation (which is easier in an online environment, via email, etc.). In Reichheld and Schefter's words, 'Loyalty is not won with technology. It is won through the delivery of a consistently superior customer experience' (2000: 113). Part of their argument is that the Internet, like all database relationship-marketing channels, enables marketers to target resources on their most profitable customers and prospects. This argument is similar to that of Peppers and Rogers (1993), who proposed the ultimate segmentation approach: reducing the market to what is sometimes called 'segments of one'. (Peppers and Rogers themselves avoid this term, however, since they see one-to-one marketing as fundamentally different from even the most targeted 'push' marketing, being based on an ongoing dialogue between the supplier and customer.)

Hoffman et al. (1999) argued that part of consumers' low trust in online vendors arises from their perceived lack of control over web businesses' access to their personal information and the secondary use of this information. The solution they propose is a radical shift toward more cooperative interaction between a business and its customers. A reasonable hypothesis based on cooperation is that consumers are willing to disclose personal information and to have that information subsequently used to create customer profiles for business use, if they also perceive there to be fair processes in place to protect individual privacy. Support for this hypothesis was found by Culnan and Armstrong (1999). They concluded that privacy concerns need not hold back the development of consumer e-commerce, provided that firms observe procedural fairness.

Milne and Boza (1999), however, presented evidence that improving trust and reducing concerns are two distinct approaches to managing consumer information. Further, contrary to existing self-regulation efforts, they argued that, when managing consumer information, improving trust is more effective than efforts to reduce concern. Researching gender differences regarding privacy concerns, Sheehan (1999) found that women were generally more concerned about online privacy, but that those men who were concerned were more likely to adopt behaviors to protect their privacy.

The issue of when and how consumers use brands as a source of information when shopping online was addressed by Ward and Lee (2000). Applying theory from information economics, they hypothesized that recent adopters of the Internet would be less proficient at searching for product information and would rely more on brands; as users gained experience with the Internet they would become more proficient searchers, more likely to search for alternative sources of information, and so less reliant on brands. These hypotheses were tested and supported using claimed usage and opinion data collected in one of the GVU Center's regular surveys of web users (see note 2). Ward and Lee suggest that these findings are consistent with the substitutability of brand advertising for searches, especially for consumers with high search costs. Their results support the view that branding does not merely reinforce loyalty, but conveys useful product information that tends to make markets more efficient.

Returning to the theme that the Internet is better able to support buyer–seller relationships than offline media, Dellaert (1999) explored how it can facilitate increased consumer contributions to product/service design processes, branding (e.g., by discussing consumption experiences in online groups), service (helping other consumers in product searches and product usage), and the production process (by ordering electronically). In particular he examined the difference between the drivers of these consumer contributions and the drivers of online ordering. For instance, he found that consumer experience of the web was a driver of consumer contributions but not of online ordering. Similarly, online ordering increased linearly with consumer income, whereas consumer contributions had an inverted u-shaped relationship with income.

Also in support of the relationship approach, and in contrast to Becker-Olsen (2000) (see above), are two other studies. Mathwick (2000) reported a survey of online purchasers in the GVU database which found that not all respondents were 'exchange' orientated. For some users, a 'communal' orientation towards other users was claimed to be a defining characteristic of the online experience. Responses were categorized on a two-by-two matrix based on exchange orientation and communal orientation. Although a particular characteristic of the Internet is the ability to target consumers using behavioral data, Peltier et al. (1998) explored the use of relationship-oriented attitudinal data (trust, commitment, and relationship benefits) as the basis of market segmentation. This approach is also relevant to the use of online communities (see below) as a vehicle for increasing brand loyalty.

Taking a more strategic overview, Wind and Rangaswamy (2001), in a conceptual paper, propose that the next stage in the evolution of mass customization is customerization – 'a buyer-centric company strategy that combines mass customization with customized marketing' (Wind and Rangaswamy, 2001: 13). They state that customerization requires the effective integration of marketing, operations, R&D, finance, and information, plus a substantial change in the firm's orientation, processes and organizational architecture.

Turning to methodologies less often seen in marketing, network methods and analysis tools have been proposed by Iacobucci (1998) as useful for examining interactive marketing systems. She describes the content properties of interactive marketing: technology, intrinsic motivation, use of interactive marketing information, and the real-time aspect of interaction, together with the structural properties of interactive marketing: customization, responsiveness, interactions amongst relevant groups, and a structure of networked networks. Iacobucci suggests that interactive marketing is network-like, and can therefore be analyzed using the tools developed to help understand the meaning of intricate network structures.

Using Community to Reinforce Loyalty

Ever since the publication of Howard Rheingold's (1993) book *The Virtual Community: Homesteading on the Electronic Frontier*, commentators have been struck by the Internet's unprecedented capacity to support global communities of interest. In a business context, e-commerce models such as Hotmail's free email service and (to some extent) eBay's online auction system are centered on the firm's ability to use the web to facilitate consumer-to-consumer (C2C) communication. More controversial is the scope for building an online brand community based on a major established brand. The most prominent advocate of this strategy is John Hagel of McKinsey, who has argued that a virtual community can expand the market, increase the brand's visibility, and improve profitability (Hagel, 1999; Hagel and Armstrong, 1997; Hagel and Singer, 1999).

Research on online brand communities, like much Internet-related research, is still somewhat atheoretical. However, Wilde and Swatman (1999) explored a number of theories to support the concept of a telecommunications-enhanced community and attempted to develop an integrative model. McWilliam (2000) discussed the advantages, disadvantages and limitations of online brand communities, and the new and unfamiliar skills brand managers will need if they are to succeed in managing such communities. The problems identified include issues of scale (e.g., the number of active participants in discussion groups is tiny compared to the potential customer base) and especially control. She concluded that it is extremely hard for the firm, accustomed to controlling communications about its brand, to strike the right balance here.

Supporting the view that community, and especially C2C interactions, can help build loyalty, Dellaert (2000) explored how such contributions can be modeled and measured, and tested a model in the context of Dutch tourists' preferences for Internet travel websites with and without other tourists' contributions. The main finding was that consumers' evaluation of other consumers' contributions to a site was high relative to other website characteristics.

As part of a study aimed at developing theory and providing evidence on brand communities, Muniz and O'Guinn (2001) used both face-to-face ethnographic research and reported/observed computer-mediated communications to gauge the use and role of brand communities. They found evidence that involvement in brand communities (e.g., Saab, Apple Macintosh, Ford Bronco) was prevalent, and that the web provided much positive reinforcement; giving consumers a 'greater voice,' providing an important source of information (from the brand but more particularly from other members), and enabling social benefits (e.g., sharing rituals and traditions, promoting brand legitimacy). Membership of an online brand community was shown to positively affect the components of brand equity (e.g., perceived quality, brand loyalty, brand awareness and brand associations). However, the authors highlight that a strong brand community can also be a threat to marketers. For example, the community could collectively reject marketing efforts or product change, or it could be sabotaged by brand 'terrorists' or competitors.

4. Internet Advertising

The Role of Advertising Online

For most established businesses, the web's main role is either to reduce costs or to add value for existing customers, but it also has a potential role in customer acquisition, and in the case of a web startup, this role is crucial. Both large corporates and web startups see driving traffic to the site as one of the most important, as well as one of the most difficult, determinants of the site's success (Rosen and Barwise, 2000). A few startups such as Amazon have been extremely successful at generating free publicity. Others have been adept at so-called viral marketing (i.e., electronic word-of-mouth), the classic case being Hotmail: anyone with a free email account has a motive to encourage their friends to set one up too. More generally, however, Langford (2000) found that, although Free Traffic Builders (FTBs: search engines, directories, news groups, listservs, bulletin boards, and chat rooms) offer free online promotion, none of these had much impact in generating traffic. Indeed, the scale of their marketing expenditure relative to their revenue is one of the main causes of failure among web startups, especially B2C dotcoms (Higson and Briginshaw, 2000).

Several studies have looked at managers' perceptions of the Internet as an advertising medium (Ducoffe, 1996; Leong et al., 1998; Schlosser et al., 1999). Bush et al. (1999) found that, while advertisers were generally keen to use the web to communicate product information, they were concerned about security/privacy and uncertain how to measure the effectiveness of online advertising. Leong et al. (1998) reported that website managers perceived the web to be a cost effective advertising medium, well-suited for conveying information, precipitating action, creating brand or product image and awareness. However, it was seen as ineffective for stimulating emotions or getting attention.

Silk et al. (2001) explored the role of the Internet as an advertising medium in competition with other media. Their analysis built on an earlier econometric study of the substitutability and complementarity of traditional US national media, as revealed by cross-elasticities over the period 1960–94 (Silk et al., 1997). They reviewed the early evidence on four aspects of online advertising: household penetration, consumer demand for information, pricing and measurement, and fit with different product/service categories. They concluded that

> [the Internet's] longer-term impact on intermedia rivalry will be broad and substantial. [It] is emerging as an adaptive, hybrid medium with respect to audience addressability, audience control, and contractual flexibility ... [and] a potential substitute or complement for all the major categories of existing media. (Silk et al., 2001: 145)

Consumer Attitudes Toward Advertising on the Web

If we turn from firms' use of the web as an advertising medium to users' perceptions of web advertising, early researchers (Hoffman et al., 1995; Rust and Oliver, 1994) predicted that consumers might abandon their traditionally passive role and actively seek out advertisements of relevance to them. It has also been suggested that a decrease in consumers' search costs, coupled with technology to enable them to filter and block unwanted advertisements, and the ability of advertisers to offer targeted rewards for viewing ads, may lead to an 'unbundling' of advertising and content (Yuan et al., 1998).

Mehta and Sivadas (1995) found that, while early Internet users had a fairly negative attitude toward online advertising, they were more likely to respond to targeted than to non-targeted ads. Ducoffe (1996) reported that business users perceived web advertising as more informative than valuable or entertaining. Survey respondents were asked to rank seven media in terms of their value as a source of advertising. The web was placed near the bottom.

As Internet use became more widespread, however, Schlosser et al. (1999) found wide variation among users' attitudes toward Internet advertising – equal numbers of respondents liked, disliked, and felt neutral toward it. Enjoyment of looking at web adverts contributed more than the informativeness or utility of the ad toward developing positive consumer attitudes to web advertising. This finding was mirrored by the responses of a demographically matched sample who answered questions on advertising in general, showing that the reported perceptions of Internet advertising were not just a reflection of the demographics of early Internet users. Other research has looked at the relationship between the complexity of websites/ads and attitudes towards them (Bruner and Kumar, 2000). Positive attitudes were associated with greater web experience and with sites perceived as interesting but not complex.

Advertising Effectiveness Online

While it has been shown that the greater the degree of interactivity, the more popular the website (Ghose and Dou, 1998), interactivity does not always enhance advertising effectiveness as it can interrupt the process of persuasion, especially when ads are targeted (Bezjian-Avery et al., 1998). Related to this, Griffith and Krampf (2000) found that consumers viewing a retailer's product offering through a print ad were more involved with the offering, and recalled more about the product and the brand, than did consumers viewing the same offering online.

Most Internet users use search engines to find product or brand information. The ability of popular search engines to locate specific marketing/management phrases was modeled by Bradlow and Schmittlein (2000). They concluded that, in addition to the sheer size of the search engine (i.e., total number of pages indexed), its sophistication (depth of search, ability to follow frame links and image maps, and ability to monitor the frequency with which a page's content changes) also affected the probability that a given engine could locate a given web page.

Unsurprisingly, the nature of the ad copy also affects the clickthrough rate (Hofacker and Murphy, 1998). Building on this research the same authors modeled clickthrough probabilities and surprisingly found that the addition of an extra banner ad on a page did not reduce the clickthrough rate of the first banner ad (Hofacker and Murphy, 2000). Early work by the Millward Brown company (Briggs and Hollis, 1997) established that banner ads were not only a direct marketing vehicle but also worked much like offline advertising in that, even when no clickthrough occurred, they helped to build brand awareness and image for the advertised brand.

Flores (2000) reported results of extensive research on Internet advertising effectiveness at Ipson-ASI Interactive. He stressed that traditional banners accounted for only about half of online advertising expenditure in 1999 (versus 95% in 1997). Other forms included full-page ads ('interstitials'), 'rich media' ads, pop up ads, sponsorships, email ads (e.g., in electronic newsletters), and company or product websites. He argued that evaluation should depend on whether the main aim was direct response or brand-building. His findings include:

Larger ads (interstitials etc.) generated greater recall and clickthrough rates, but took longer to download, causing more annoyance.

Consumers found broadband ads almost as engaging as TV ads, and much more engaging than narrowband or print.

Copy quality was crucial (and generally low).

Experienced online consumers were less tolerant of online ads (and recall rates were generally declining over time).

Flores (2000: 17) also argued that the future challenge would be not only to understand how each medium (and format) works, but also how they work together, including in combination with new media such as advertising on wireless devices (Barwise and Strong, 2002) and iDTV (Brodin et al., 2002).

Drèze and Zufryden (1997) developed and evaluated a web-based methodology for evaluating the effectiveness of promotional websites. Using conjoint and efficient frontier analysis, the four site attributes tested were background, image size, sound file display, and celebrity endorsement. Their model aimed to provide a means of evaluating different trade-offs to achieve website configurations that result in the greatest time spent at the site plus the highest number of pages viewed.

Exploring the measurement of Internet advertising gross rating points (GRPs), reach and frequency, Drèze and Zufryden (1998) suggested that the two main measurement problems to be addressed were identification of an individual, and counting revisits of cached (i.e. stored) content. Leckenby and Hong (1998) continued the search for appropriate audience measures by developing and testing six reach and frequency models. They concluded that models developed for magazine or television data generally performed equally well with Internet data, with the simplest model, the Beta Binomial, providing the greatest accuracy. Wood (1998) also discussed how reach and frequency measures were evolving on the web. Other authors who conducted studies into the effects of web ads include Bellizzi (2000), who studied business-to-business advertising and found that mentioning or simulating the website in print ads significantly increased site traffic, Sen et al. (1998), who discuss the different variables available and appropriate for segmenting web users, and Yang (1997), who reported on an early study comparing the effect of interactive ads on students whose country of origin was Taiwan, China, and the US.

Advertising on the web has also been evaluated in terms of its comparative effectiveness compared with offline advertising. Hoffman and Novak (2000) discussed a range of customer acquisition methods used by CDNOW: traditional media (radio, television, and print), online advertising (e.g., banner ads), a revenue-sharing affiliate program, strategic partnerships with traffic generators such as AOL, plus PR, freelinks, and word-of-mouth. They concluded that revenue-sharing, a very different model from the impression-based advertising which still dominates broadcast media, was the most cost-effective means of acquiring customers online.

The Internet is more a 'pull' medium like classified advertising in print media (i.e., where interactions are initiated by the customer) than a 'push' medium like TV, but marketers are gradually learning how to use it in both modes (Braunstein and Levine, 2000; Hofacker, 2001). Overall, Internet advertising (including email) is still a growth area within marketing communications, despite the justifiable reaction against earlier over-optimistic expectations. Marketers are still learning how to use it in terms of brand strategy, creative execution, and evaluation.

5. Internet Economics and Pricing

Frictionless Markets?

Some commentators expect the Internet to lead to 'frictionless markets' in which empowered customers, increasingly supported by intelligent agents, trusted intermediaries and third parties, shop around with minimal effort, playing one supplier off against another and relentlessly driving down prices. In economic terms, the Internet can reduce buyer search costs, decreasing the ability of sellers to extract monopolistic profits and increasing the ability of markets to optimally allocate resources (Bakos, 1997). In this section we explore theoretical and empirical research to date on the impacts of the Internet on market prices and price dispersion. We start with theoretical notions on buyer search costs and the likelihood of 'frictionless' markets.

An early analysis of web-related information economics was given by Wigand and Benjamin (1995), who argued that the Internet holds great potential for efficiency gains along the whole industry value chain, primarily because of transaction cost savings (see also Rayport and Sviokla, 1995). The potential effects Wigand and Benjamin discussed include disintermediation, reduced profit margins, and consumer access to a broad selection of lower-priced goods, but also various opportunities to restrict consumers' access to the vast amount of available information and potential commerce opportunities. They developed an integrated model of electronic commerce and discussed implications for public policy 'to mitigate risks associated with market access and value chain reconfiguration.'

Bakos (1997) also addressed the impact of reducing search costs. He modeled the role of buyer search costs in markets with differentiated product offerings in the context of electronic marketplaces, and explored the implications for the incentives of buyers, sellers, and independent intermediaries to invest in such marketplaces. Among other things, his analysis provides formal support for the proposition that electronic marketplaces promote price competition and reduce the market power of sellers, as argued by Wigand and Benjamin (1995), Malone et al. (1987), and others who expected online markets to have less 'friction' than their offline counterparts.

More recently, Sinha (2000) argued that the ease of collecting and comparing information on the web, regarding prices, features and quality, means that costs are becoming increasingly transparent. This, according to Sinha, will impair sellers' ability to obtain high margins, turning most products and services into commodities. Sinha suggests that the Internet 'encourages highly rational shopping,' eroding the 'risk premium' that sellers have been able to extract from wary buyers. It also demands that companies with varying prices in different countries re-examine their price structure. One response for firms is 'smart' pricing through versioning and other mechanisms such as auctions. Sinha (2000: 50) argues that such 'smart' pricing may be extremely risky in the long term, as it may create perceptions of unfairness among consumers, now able to share price information easily. The solutions he recommends are a combination of product quality, innovation, and bundling.

Sinha's succinct but wide-ranging article touches on several topics that have been explored by researchers: price levels and price dispersion, bundling and versioning, and auctions. In the following sections, we look at studies in each of these areas.

Price Levels and Price Dispersion

Early empirical evidence on the Internet's impact on prices is reviewed by Smith et al. (2000), who found that Internet markets are more efficient than conventional markets with respect to price levels, menu costs, and price elasticity. However, despite the presence of conditions to foster efficiency, they also found substantial and persistent dispersion in prices. They suggested that this may be partly explained by heterogeneity in retailer-specific factors such as trust and awareness (i.e., brand equity). In addition, Internet markets are still at an early stage and may change dramatically in the coming years with the development of cross-channel sales strategies, intermediaries and shopbots, improved supply chain management, and new information markets.

Brynjolfsson and Smith (2000), one of the studies reviewed by Smith et al. (2000), analyzed the prices of books and CDs on 41 Internet and conventional retail outlets. They found that prices on the Internet averaged from 9% to 16% lower than in conventional outlets (depending on whether taxes, shipping and shopping costs are included in the price). They also found substantial price dispersion among Internet retailers, although weighting the prices by a proxy for market share reduced this dispersion. They concluded that, 'while there is lower friction in many dimensions of Internet competition, branding, awareness and trust remain important sources of heterogeneity among Internet retailers' (Brynjolfsson and Smith, 2000: 563).

Signs of less friction are present in several studies. For example, in a study on life insurance, Brown and Goolsbee (1999) found that prices for term life policies fell 8% to 15% between 1995 and 1997. Although other factors contributed to lower prices, the rising use of specialized websites for comparison shopping explained up to half of the total decline. Similarly, Scott-Morton et al. (1999) found that car buyers who used the Autobytel.com online referral service paid, on average, 2% less than customers who bought offline.

In another study of price and non-price competition in the online book industry, Clay et al. (1999) collected prices of 107 titles sold by 13 online and 2 physical bookstores. Controlling for book characteristics, prices in online and physical bookstores were found to be the same. In line with Brynjolfsson and Smith (2000), this study found significant price dispersion among online bookstores, providing indirect evidence of perceived product or brand differentiation, enabling Amazon in particular to charge a 'substantial premium, ... even relative to barnesandnoble.com and Borders.com' (Clay et al., 1999: 1).

Empirical research suggests that the Internet's impact on pricing has been limited. A theoretical study by Lal and Sarvary (1999) provides insight into possible explanations. Their model distinguishes between 'digital' product attributes (which can be communicated online at low cost), and 'non-digital' attributes (for which physical inspection of the product is needed). It assumes that consumers are faced with a choice of two brands but are familiar with the non-digital attributes of only the brand bought on the last purchase occasion. Based on this assumption, Lal and Sarvary showed that when (1) the proportion of Internet users is high enough, (2) non-digital attributes are relevant but not overwhelming, (3) consumers have a more favorable prior knowledge about the brand they currently own, and (4) the purchase situation can be characterized by 'destination shopping' (i.e., the fixed cost of a shopping trip is higher than the cost of visiting an additional store), the use of the Internet can lead not only to higher prices but also discourage consumers from engaging in search. Their explanation is that, under these conditions, an online consumer who wishes to do so can avoid visiting any stores at all and therefore also avoid comparing the non-digital attributes of competing brands. A further insight is that physical stores may have a growing role for product demonstration and online customer acquisition. The underlying theory is based on Nelson's (1970, 1974) distinction between search and experience goods.

In addition to Nelson's (1970) initial distinction between search goods (whose quality can be judged by inspection), and experience goods (whose quality can only be judged only through usage), a third category was added by Darby and Karni (1973), namely 'credence' goods, whose quality cannot be determined reliably even after usage. A classic example is wine. Online wine sales have been researched by Lynch and Ariely (2000) who found that first, lowering the cost of search for quality information reduced price sensitivity, and second, price sensitivity for goods common to two online stores increased when cross-store comparison was made easy. However, easy cross-store comparison had no effect on price sensitivity for unique goods. Third, making information environments more transparent by lowering all three search costs (for price information, for quality information within a given store, and for comparisons across the two stores) produced welfare gains for consumers. The implications are that retailers should aim to make information environments maximally transparent but try to avoid price competition by carrying more unique or differentiated merchandise.

Shankar et al. (1999), using data from the hospitality industry, also found that the Internet could dampen price sensitivity in some contexts. Specifically, the Internet increased consumers' price search, although it had no main effect on the importance they attached to price, and reduced price sensitivity by providing in-depth (price and non-price) information. The Internet also increased the range of products and prices offered and product/price bundling by an intermediary, thereby reducing price importance. Finally, it reduced the amount of price searching, thereby increasing the effects of brand loyalty – very much as Lal and Sarvary (1999) hypothesized, and in line with the empirical results of Brynjolfsson and Smith (2000) and Clay et al. (1999) for books and CDs.

Bundling and Versioning

In relation to the Internet, it is often said that 'information wants to be free.' Here, 'free' can mean both liberated and priced at zero. On the Internet, the marginal cost of providing information to a customer is usually zero, so any pricing model for an information product based on equating marginal cost to marginal revenue would eventually lead to the information being given away. This raises the question of how a firm can make money from content creation or packaging. Although this is not a new issue – it is one which has always been faced by broadcasting, publishing, and other media industries – the power and ubiquity of digital technology are increasing the scale of the problem.

Arthur (1996) argued that new knowledge-based industries are characterized by increasing returns to scale, i.e., that if a product gains a dominant market share its advantage is magnified by increasing returns. In this world, 'success accrues to the successful' and 'market share begets market share.' In contrast, traditional resource processing industries are characterized by diminishing returns. Arthur compared and contrasted these two interrelated worlds of business and offered advice to managers in knowledge-based markets. One important source of increasing returns in information and communication industries is network externalities, whereby the value of a product to one user depends on how many other users there are. Network externalities were first defined and discussed by Rohlfs (1974); Katz and Shapiro provided a comprehensive survey (Katz and Shapiro, 1994).

Turning our attention to *bundling*, optimal bundling strategies for a multi-product monopolist information supplier (i.e., with zero marginal cost) were modeled by Bakos and Brynjolfsson (1999). They suggested that bundling large numbers of unrelated information goods might be surprisingly profitable because the law of large numbers makes it easier to predict consumers' valuations for a bundle of goods than for the individual goods sold separately. They modeled the bundling of complements and substitutes, bundling in the presence of budget constraints, and the scope for offering a menu of different bundles if the market is highly segmented. They argued that the predictions from their analysis appear to be consistent with empirical observations of the markets for online content, cable TV programming, and music.

In Bakos and Brynjolfsson (2000a, 2000b) the authors extended their bundling model to a range of different settings. They argued that bundling can create 'economies of aggregation' for information goods, even in the absence of network externalities or economies of scale or scope. They draw four implications: (1) when competing for upstream content, larger bundlers are able to outbid smaller ones; (2) when competing for downstream consumers, bundling can discourage entry even when the prospective entrant has a superior cost structure or quality; (3) conversely, bundling by the new entrant can allow profitable entry; and (4) because a bundler can potentially capture a large share of profits in a new market, bundlers may have higher incentives to innovate than single-product firms.

Shapiro and Varian (1998a, 1998b) argued that 'the so-called new economy is still subject to the old laws of economics.' As they noted, the fixed costs of information products tend to be dominated by sunk costs – costs that are not recoverable if production is halted. They suggested that information providers therefore need strategies both to differentiate their products and to price them in such a way that the price varies between buyers, reflecting the sometimes markedly different value that the different segments place on the same, or almost the same, information product. The solution they proposed is *versioning*, i.e., offering the information in different versions targeted at different types of customer. This is similar to the series of release windows for movies and the way publishers often release a book first as a high-priced hardback and later in paperback. They described a wide range of dimensions of versioning: convenience, comprehensiveness, manipulation, community, annoyance, speed, and support. Some of these issues were also explored by Adar and Huberman (2000), who focused on the possibility of exploiting the different and regular patterns of surfing demonstrated by different Internet users, by implementing 'temporal discrimination' through dynamically configuring sites and versioning information services.

Auctions

Online auctions, with eBay as the best-known example, were a hot topic of the late 1990s. They offer a rich area of study for marketing researchers and economists. Lucking-Reiley (1999a) presented what he called 'an economist's guide' to online auctions, including a brief history, and the results of a survey of 142 auction sites that were online in the Fall of 1998. His paper summarized the various business models they used, what goods they offered for sale, and what kinds of auction mechanism they employed. Lucking-Reiley argued that established auction theory from economics could be used to improve Internet auctions. He also presented detailed data on the competition between the incumbent eBay and the two well-funded entrants into the B2C online auction arena, Yahoo! and Amazon, in 1999. Among other things, he showed that the different auctioneers' fee structures had measurable incentive effects on sellers' choices and transaction outcomes.

Building on this review, Lucking-Reiley (1999b) tested different auction formats using field experiments in which collectible trading cards were auctioned off. In addition, Lucking-Reiley et al. (2000) presented an exploratory analysis of the determinants of prices in online auctions for collectible coins at eBay. Three findings stand out. First, a seller's feedback ratings, reported by other eBay users, have a measurable effect on his auction prices. This is particularly true for negative feedback ratings. Second, minimum bids and reserve prices tend to have a positive effect on the final auction price. However, this finding does not take into account that these instruments also decrease the probability of the auction resulting in an actual sale. Third, when a seller chooses to have his auction last for a week or so, this significantly increases the average auction price.

A preliminary literature review and frameworks for analyzing auctions are also given by Klein and O'Keefe (1999) and Chui and Zwick (1999). Klein and O'Keefe described an example (Teletrade.com) of a telephone-based auction which now also uses the web; explored possible theoretical implications; and developed seven hypotheses for future empirical research. Chui and Zwick explored the scope and scale of online auctions and the range of business models, including B2C, B2B, and C2C auctions. DeKoning et al. (1999) explored consumer motivations in using C2C online auctions, focusing especially on the behavioral differences between global and local/regional online auctions.

Conclusion: Little Impact to Date and Brands are Not Dead

Overall, the dramatic early predictions that the Internet would lead to frictionless markets characterized by commoditization and the death of brands (e.g., Gates, 1995; Negroponte, 1995; Wigand and Benjamin, 1995) have so far proved wide of the mark. There is evidence that it has increased competition and reduced average prices slightly in some markets, but the impact on both price levels and price dispersion has been small. Brands are still here, and strong enough to attract critics (Klein, 2000).

The underlying reasons why brands exist have not gone away (Barwise, 1997). In fact, trusted brands may be even more important in a world of information overload, and money-rich, time-poor consumers, where product quality still cannot usually be reliably judged online (Barwise, 1997; Brynjolfsson and Smith, 2000; Dayal et al., 2000; Lal and Sarvary, 1999; Shankar et al., 1999). Also some firms can counter price competition by providing unique products that prevent direct comparisons (Lynch and Ariely, 2000). Finally, concerns about brand reputation should limit firms' enthusiasm for aggressive 'smart' pricing – a euphemism for charging more to less price-sensitive customers (Sinha, 2000).

The continuing importance of brands has been one lesson from the dotcom bubble. Another is that romanticized notions that the Internet would abolish economies of scale were largely mistaken. In addition to economies of scale in branding and fulfillment, and network externalities (e.g., in standards), even pure information businesses can gain from economies of bundling (Bakos and Brynjolfsson, 1999, 2000a, 2000b) and will likely also have more opportunities for versioning (Shapiro and Varian, 1998a, 1998b).

One area where the Internet is having more impact is auctions. In the B2C and C2C markets, eBay is a new type of business, but the number of viable firms seems likely to be small. In contrast, online markets and auctions are having a significant impact on B2B markets (Bloch and Catfolis, 2001).

It may be that the muted impact of the Internet on prices is still the quiet before the storm. As intelligent agent software becomes more powerful and more widely used, we may see more pressure on prices and on brand loyalty. Even this, however, may have more impact on channel choice (e.g., finding the cheapest place to buy the brand) than on the choice of brand itself.

We now turn from 'horizontal' competition within a market to 'vertical' competition along a value chain, i.e., channels and intermediaries. This is another area for which early predictions of dramatic change have proved overstated.

6. The Impact on Channels and Intermediaries

Disintermediation

The ability of easily accessible electronic information to increase the efficiency of markets was an early topic addressed by marketing academics. Bakos (1991) used economic theory to develop models which showed that, where product quality and price information are easily available (as in electronic markets), search costs are reduced and benefits for buyers increased, which, in turn, can reduce sellers' profits. Following on from Bakos's work, Benjamin and Wigand (1995) suggested that the so-called national information infrastructure (or NII, of which they believed the Internet was only a part) would cause a restructuring and redistribution of profits among stakeholders along the value chain, threatening all intermediaries between the manufacturer and consumer.

This issue of the role of intermediaries in buyer–seller relationships has been a recurring theme, with much of the earlier work suggesting *disintermediation* and later papers generally arguing for re- or cyber-intermediation. Rayport and Sviokla (1994) described how physical interactions in the marketplace were being replaced by virtual 'market*space*' transactions. They argued that the conventional value proposition was being disaggregated and that its three basic elements – content (the firm's offering), context (how the content is offered), and infrastructure – could now be managed in new and different ways. Building on these ideas,

Rayport and Sviokla (1995) suggested ways of managing and exploiting this new virtual value chain. Weiber and Kollman (1998) also evaluated the significance of virtual value chains and concluded that information, in its own right, will become a factor of competition in future markets.

Shaffer and Zettelmeyer (1999) and Wigand and Benjamin (1995) both sketched a pessimistic scenario for intermediaries. According to Shaffer and Zettelmeyer (1999), manufacturers traditionally have had to rely on retailers to provide product and category information that is either too technical or too idiosyncratic to be communicated effectively via mass media. The emergence of the Internet as a medium for marketing communications now makes it possible for manufacturers (and third parties) to also provide such information. Shaffer and Zettelmeyer show that this may lead to channel conflict. Specifically, manufacturers gain and retailers lose from information that makes a retailer's product offerings less substitutable. In an earlier paper, Wigand and Benjamin (1995), using a transaction cost perspective, suggested that intermediaries between the manufacturer and the consumer may be threatened as electronic commerce becomes ubiquitous and as information infrastructures reach out to the consumer. Profit margins, they posit, may be substantially reduced. The consumer is likely to gain access to a broad selection of lower-priced goods, but there will be many opportunities to restrict consumers' access to the potentially vast amount of commerce. An essential component of the evolution of the future world of electronic commerce, the authors suggest, is the 'market choice box' – the consumer's interface between the many electronic devices in the home and the information superhighway (Barwise, 2001; Wigand & Benjamin, 1995).

Reintermediation and 'Cybermediaries'

In contrast to these views, Sarkar et al. (1998) argued against the idea that intermediaries are likely to disappear. Drawing on channel evolution literature and transaction cost economics, they proposed instead that virtual channel systems and new '*cybermediaries*' would emerge. In a short *Harvard Business Review* perspectives article, Carr (2000) took this argument a step further, arguing that, far from the widely predicted disintermediation, the Internet is in fact leading to 'hypermediation,' in which transactions over the web, even very small ones, routinely involve many intermediaries – not only wholesalers and retailers, but also content providers, affiliate sites, search engines, portals, internet service providers, software makers, and many others. He suggested that it is these largely unnoticed intermediaries who stand to gain most of the profits from electronic commerce.

Jin and Robey (1999) focused on B2C cybermediaries such as Amazon, Virtual Vineyards, and 1-800-FLOWERS. They proposed six theoretical perspectives on cybermediation: transaction cost economics, consumer-choice theory, retailing as an institution, retailing as social exchange, retailers as bridges in social networks, and retailers as creators of knowledge. They conclude that a multitheoretical approach (in contrast to transaction cost theory alone) shows both that the disintermediation hypothesis was overstated and that cybermediaries can exist for many reasons. Bhargava et al. (2000) explored the aggregation benefits that consumers derive from having access to multiple providers through an intermediary. Their analysis is theoretical and economics-based. They concluded that when consumers are heterogeneous and differentiated in their willingness to pay for intermediation, the intermediary can offer two or more service levels at different price levels.

These theoretical propositions by Sarkar et al., Jin and Robey, and Bhargava et al. are consistent with empirical findings. Bailey and Bakos (1997) suggested that markets do not necessarily become disintermediated as they become facilitated by information technology. Thirteen case studies of firms participating in electronic commerce were explored, and evidence was found of new emerging roles for online intermediaries, including aggregating, matching sellers and buyers, providing trust, and supplying interorganizational market information. The authors discuss two specific examples to illustrate an unsuccessful strategy for electronic intermediation (BargainFinder) as well as a more successful one (Firefly).

Christensen and Tedlow (2000) categorized the Internet as a 'disruptive' technology, which enables innovative retailers to create new business models that significantly change the economics of the industry. They put this in an historical context by relating the Internet to three previous disruptive technologies in retailing: the department store, the mail order catalog, and the discount department store. They proposed that

> the essential mission of retailing has always had four elements: getting the right product in the right place at the right price at the right time and the Internet has great potential for improving performance on various combinations of the first three of these. For information products and services, the Internet can also perform outstandingly on the fourth, time, dimension, but for physical products it does not. When shoppers need products immediately, they will head for their cars, not their computers. (Christensen and Tedlow, 2000: 42)

They further argued that the Internet is unsuited for products which require 'touch and feel,' not to mention 'taste and smell.'

Based on their analysis of the three earlier disruptive technologies, Christensen and Tedlow noted that one pattern has been that generalist stores and catalogs dominate at the outset of the disruption but are then supplanted by specialists. A second pattern has been that the disruptive retailers initially sold easy-to-sell branded mass-market products and then moved up-scale with higher-margin, more complex products. They suggested that it is too soon to say whether the first of these two patterns will recur on the Internet – more likely, the pattern will vary between categories – but that there is some evidence that the second pattern is recurring, and probably much faster than with the previous disruptive technologies, since the Internet enables firms to swiftly achieve high market reach combined with high richness of content and range (also see Evans and Wurster, 1999). If this analysis is correct, we will see consumer e-commerce growth for complex, high-ticket items such as durables (but excluding those needing 'touch and feel') as well as for simple branded products such as books and music.

The corporate intranet represents another largely unresearched, new B2B channel (Barwise, 2001: 37). Increasingly, high-value corporate employees are using intranets for ordering office supplies, booking travel, etc. Some firms have extended this system to enable staff to make personal purchases (e.g., booking a leisure break at an attractive price that includes a corporate discount) through the intranet. This is seen as a tool for attracting and retaining key staff, as well as increasing their use of, and familiarity with, the intranet. For the supplier, it represents a low-cost, low-risk way of reaching money-rich, time-poor consumers.

Business-to-Business (B2B) Markets

Much of this previous research focuses on consumer services and it is these that have attracted the most media coverage. More important in business terms, at least initially, is the setting up of new B2B markets and exchanges or 'e-hubs.' Chircu and Kauffman (2000) describe a framework whereby a traditional intermediary is able to continue to compete by combining web technology with its existing specialist assets. The framework is based on literature from several disciplines and evidence from a study in the corporate travel industry. The results show that traditional travel firms have been able to avoid disintermediation and retain a highly profitable central role in this market.

Potentially more dramatic (in terms of changes in business processes) has been the emergence of entirely new B2B e-hubs. E-hubs can be defined as websites where industrial products and services can be bought from a wide range of suppliers. Ramsdell (2000) categorized B2B online markets into three kinds: 'vertical' markets, such as those for auto manufacturing or petroleum products; 'horizontal' markets, typically focusing on the supply of maintenance, repair and operations (MRO) products, such as safety supplies, hand tools, and janitorial services; and finally markets focusing on specific functions such as human resources. He concluded that these B2B markets would fundamentally change how firms and their suppliers interact, especially for MRO products and services. An alternative classification has been given by Kaplan and Sawhney (2000) based on *what* businesses buy (operating inputs versus manufacturing inputs) and *how* they buy (systematic sourcing versus spot sourcing). They give examples of each of the four types and also describe both forward and reverse aggregation models.

Since the dotcom meltdown, the number of pure-play B2B e-hubs has declined and many of those that survive are struggling. Currently, the growth is in less ambitious B2B online auctions, where individual firms use the web to support contract bids by their suppliers using technology provided by firms such as Freemarkets.com. There are, however, arguments that in the long term, the dominant e-market will be industry consortia delivering full supply chain integration (Bloch and Catfolis, 2001).

7. Online Marketing Strategy

Turning to implications for marketing strategy, below we first describe studies focused on general strategic implications of the Internet. We then turn to research on how firms should prepare themselves for the 'new economy,' and which business models they employ (or should employ) in online environments. We then briefly discuss research that has adopted an international perspective. Finally, we give some tentative conclusions. Even more than for the other sections, research described here is clearly 'marked' by the time at which it was conducted. Now that the Internet bubble has burst, we expect to see more research addressing issues related to the 'new economy slowdown' but, to date, such studies have not appeared in academic journals.

Strategy and the Internet

Many books and articles, and some research studies, have investigated the opportunities and challenges created by the Internet and the implications for marketing strategies. Baer (1998) is one of the few authors to take a long-term perspective. He described a century of failed visions and applications, drew some general lessons from past experience, documented why interactive services might now at last take off, and indicated some likely areas for growth. Also in 1998, the *Journal of Business*

Research devoted a special issue to business in the new electronic environment (see Dholakia, 1998 for the introduction to this issue).

Evans and Wurster (1999) argued that electronic commerce was no longer about 'grabbing land.' Instead, they suggested that the battle for competitive advantage in this arena will be waged along three dimensions: reach, affiliation, and richness. *Reach* is about access and connection – how many customers a business can connect with and how many products it can offer to those customers. *Richness* is the depth and detail of information that the business can give the customer, as well as the depth and detail of information it collects about the customer. *Affiliation* reflects whose interests the business represents. This logic poses a challenge for incumbent product suppliers and retailers: they have to recognize that their value chain is being deconstructed.

Zettelmeyer (2000) offered another perspective on the implications of Internet growth for firms. He showed how pricing and communication strategies may be affected by the size of the Internet. Firms have incentives to facilitate consumer search on the Internet, but only as long as its reach is limited. As the Internet is used by more consumers, firms' online pricing and communication strategies will mirror their offline strategies. According to Zettelmeyer, firms can increase their market power by strategically using information on multiple channels to achieve finer consumer segmentation.

Coltman et al. (2000) focused on the forces that determine the appropriateness of e-business to a firm. They sketched out the characteristics of organizations likely to survive in the new network economy. Three related questions guided their analysis: (1) Where is the revolution (or evolution) concentrated? (2) Why is the revolution (or evolution) occurring as it is? (3) Is it a revolution or natural evolution? They conclude that claims that e-business is driving revolutionary change are misleading and only partly correct. In contrast, Anderson (2000) proposed that e-business enables companies to transform not only their marketing operation, but also the entire way they do business, from procurement to communications to supply chain, massively improving their speed, global reach, efficiency, and cost structure. Cross (2000) also took into account the downside of these developments, which are forcing managers to rethink and reshape their business strategies, their use of technology, and their relations with suppliers and customers. In Cross's view, the convergence of new technologies, hypercompetitive markets, and 'heat-seeking' financial and human capital that quickly flow to new and untested business models threatens a number of traditional business models and processes.

In a recent article entitled 'Strategy and the Internet,' Porter (2001) argued that, contrary to what many observers think, the Internet is not disruptive to most existing industries and companies, because it does not nullify important sources of competitive advantage – in fact, it often makes them even more valuable. Rather than rendering strategy obsolete, because the Internet tends to weaken industry profitability without providing proprietary operational advantages, it is more important than ever for companies to distinguish themselves through strategy. For traditional companies, he suggests strategy should be based on the view that the Internet complements rather than cannibalizes existing ways of doing business.

How Firms Should Prepare for the New Economy

Not surprisingly, much research in the strategy area has centered on the question of how firms should adapt to their rapidly changing environment and 'get in shape' for the new economy. For example, Voss (2000) described how firms can develop a systematic strategy for delivering service on the web, while Weiber and Kollmann (1998) evaluated the significance of virtual value chains in opening up possibilities in the so-called 'marketplace' and 'marketspace' (Rayport and Sviokla, 1994).

Most authors see becoming an e-business as an evolutionary journey for firms. For example, Earl (2000) identified six stages, each determining the course of the next: external communications, internal communications, e-commerce, e-business, e-enterprise, and transformation (drop the "e"). These correspond to six lessons representing an agenda for evolving e-business: (1) perpetual content management, (2) architectural integrity, (3) electronic channel strategy, (4) high-performance processes, (5) information literacy, and (6) continuous learning and change. Similarly, Albrinck et al. (2000) argued that virtually all companies pursue e-business opportunities in a consistent way, passing through four stages: grassroots, focal point, structure and deployment, and endgame. Venkatraman (2000) described five steps to a 'dot-com strategy.' In his view, vision, governance, resources, infrastructure, and alignment are the stepping stones to a successful web strategy.

Chavez et al. (2000) outlined a multidimensional framework to help managers decide how to structure their Internet businesses: whether to keep them integrated into the parent company, establish them as wholly-owned subsidiaries, or spin them off (wholly or partially). They argued that firms must weigh the tradeoffs between what they called the 'three Cs': control, currency and culture. Above all, the decision must be made in the context of a company's total 'digital agenda': that is, as part of its overall strategy for creating and sustaining value in the new economy.

Dayal et al. (2000) specifically considered how firms can build digital brands. In their view, the '3 Ps' of a physical brand in the consumer's mind – its personality, presence, and performance – are also essential on the web. In addition, digital brand builders must manage the consumer's online experience of the product, from first encounter through purchase to delivery and beyond (see pages 532–533, Section 2). As discussed below, their paper also analyzes the range of business models underlying digital brands.

More recently, Moss Kanter (2001) described 'ten deadly mistakes of wanna-dots,' i.e., established firms seeking to incorporate the Internet into their businesses. Based on empirical research in North America, Europe, and Asia, she found evidence for several common barriers to change in emerging e-businesses, including lack of commitment and lack of knowledge about how to change. She argued that 'wanna-dots' should go beyond 'cosmetic changes' and be prepared to undergo a 'serious makeover.'

Business Models

How can firms use the web to achieve strategic and marketing benefits? This is clearly a key strategic marketing question but, to date, research on online business models is limited. Perhaps this is because a proper examination of the question necessitates a thorough understanding of the behavior of consumers, firms and other players in the Internet arena, while the first empirical generalizations in these areas are only just starting to emerge.

Nevertheless, some researchers have started to work in this area, mostly focusing on describing and classifying the various business models that are being used. Ward Hanson's *Principles of Internet Marketing* (2000) was the first advanced textbook on the topic. Hanson introduced a useful distinction between business models based on improvements in the product or service and those based directly on revenues. The first includes models focused on enhancement (e.g., brand building), efficiency (e.g., cost reduction), and/or effectiveness (e.g., information collection). The second includes models in which the provider pays (e.g., sponsorship or alliances) and those in which the user pays (e.g., product sales or subscriptions).

Ethiraj et al. (2000) examined the changes in opportunity space within firms' value chains arising from online technologies, and the implications for competitive advantage. They identified four key components of the business model – scalability, complementary resources and capabilities, relation-specific assets, and knowledge-sharing routines – and discussed how and why these may be important drivers of competitive advantage in Internet-based business models. Also looking to identify what makes Internet businesses successful, Dayal et al. (2000) argued that there are six basic business models: retail, media, advisory, made-to-order manufacturing, do-it-yourself, and information services. They posited that the success of an Internet brand rests on the skill with which its business model combines two or more of these.

Building on the entrepreneurship and strategic management literatures, Amit and Zott (2000) examined the value creation potential of a sample of American and European e-commerce companies. They developed a model that enables an evaluation of the value-creation potential of e-commerce business models along four dimensions: novelty, lock-in, complementarities, and efficiency. Dutta et al. (1998) sought to understand how the Internet has transformed business models across different types of business. Specifically, they investigated how the marketing mix and customer relationships are being transformed across different sectors and regions. They concluded that few firms are rethinking how their business models are being transformed and, consequently, that most firms' Internet presence is rather ineffective.

Focusing on business models specifically for online content services, Picard (2000) explored how such business models emerged, how new developments are affecting those models, and the implications for content producers. He divides the history of online content service providers into periods coinciding with four 'abandoned' business models (videotext, paid Internet, free web, and advertising push), one model in current use (portals and personal portals), and an emerging model (digital portals). The latter allows the combination of aspects of current content portals plus digitization of video and audio.

Werbach (2000) investigated another potential source of revenue for Internet firms that has received little attention: syndication. Syndication involves the sale of the same information good to many customers, who then integrate it with other offerings and redistribute it. It has its origins in the news and entertainment worlds but, Werbach argues, syndication is expanding to define the structure of e-business. As companies enter syndication networks, they will need to rethink their products, relationships, and core capabilities.

Most empirical research on revenue models has concerned one specific revenue source – Internet advertising (discussed mainly from an advertiser perspective, in Section 4).

For established businesses, Geyskens et al. (2001) studied the net impact of setting up an additional Internet channel on a firm's stockmarket return, reflecting the change in expected future cashflows. They found that, on average, Internet-channel investments had been profitable by this measure. They also identified firm strategies and market characteristics that influence the direction and size of the stockmarket reaction. For example, they found that early followers had a competitive advantage against both innovators and later followers (as also argued by Porter, 2001).

Geyskens et al.'s empirical analysis revolves around the newspaper industry – a widely-cited example of an industry struggling to respond to the digital revolution. According to Baer (1998), when videotext was first invented, newspapers such as the *LA Times* saw it as simply a new publishing medium. They were reluctant to accept that the 'content' of most interest to consumers was largely other consumers they knew well (colleagues, friends, family), i.e., via email or chat. Today, virtually all newspaper groups have implemented online versions, partly to protect their classified advertising revenue, partly to protect subscription/cover price revenue, and potentially to open up new revenue sources. In recent years, several other researchers have studied the (online) news industry, including Dans (2000), Dans and Pauwels (2001), Elberse (1998), and Pauwels (2001).

International Perspectives

To date, despite the fact that the Internet is likely to have far-reaching implications for international marketing, only a handful of studies have explored marketing and the Internet in an international context.

The question of how the Internet might revolutionize global marketing was raised by Quelch and Klein (1996). They discussed the opportunities and challenges that it offers to large and small companies worldwide. They examined the impact on global markets and new product development, the advantages of an intranet for large corporations, and the need for foreign government support and cooperation. More recently, Samiee (1998) studied two types of impediment to the Internet's adoption and growth in international marketing: structural (nations' differing infrastructures, languages, cultures, and legal frameworks) and functional (marketing program and process issues, including data management and customer discontent). His analysis suggested that the Internet will play a much greater role in B2B marketing across national boundaries than in international consumer marketing. For an exploratory study that examines how the Internet can help small and medium-sized firms (SMEs) reach a global market, see Lituchy and Rail (2000).

Developments in Europe versus those in the US have been studied by Cornet et al. (2000) and Hammond (2001). Cornet et al. (2000) discussed how Europe is 'playing catch-up' with the US in e-business. The European game, they argue, may well have a different outcome, as conditions specific to Europe give incumbents a better chance to win. Hammond (2001) surveyed a global panel of media experts after the bursting of the Internet bubble in 2000. She found that consumer usage of the web was expected to continue its growth much as previously predicted by the same panel. However, there were some regional differences. Experts from Europe, despite starting from a lower base in 2000, were more optimistic than those from North America for the five-year outlook for online purchasing (in their countries) of gambling, newspapers, and groceries. Eastern Europeans expected their countries to catch up with the West by 2005.

Within Europe, Rosen and Barwise (2000) compared business use of the web by corporates, and web startups in different countries. They confirmed the advanced development in the Nordic countries, but also found that French companies were in many respects as advanced as those in the UK, Germany, and Holland, despite the relatively low penetration of the web among consumers in France. Rosen and Barwise attribute this pattern to the earlier development of France Telecom's proprietary Minitel system, which retarded consumer adoption of the web but accelerated French businesses' development of online systems and data.

Using a series of exemplary cases, Berthon et al. (1999) illustrated how international firms can use the web to enhance the marketing of services across national boundaries. They argued that cyberspace 'gives the marketer undreamed control over the previously capricious characteristics of services,' and that innovative use of the web can address problems traditionally related to the marketing of international services (intangibility, simultaneity, heterogeneity, and perishability). In addition, they offered a 'diagnostic checklist' to evaluate the effectiveness of a firm's website in providing such services.

Online Marketing Strategy: Tentative Conclusions

As yet, there has been little systematic research on the implications of the Internet for marketing strategy. What has been done is still fragmented. Opinions vary between those, such as Evans and Wurster (1999) and Anderson (2000), who believe that the Internet will transform strategy, and those, such as Coltman et al. (2000), Porter (2001), and ourselves, who argue that the fundamental tenets of strategy and marketing still apply.

There is some consensus on how existing firms should prepare for the new economy, with most writers agreeing that the change process involves a series of recognizable stages, although different writers use somewhat different labels.

Business models still represent a big gap. Hanson (2000) provides a useful and balanced classification, but it remains the case that both dotcoms and established firms are generally still struggling to find business models which generate significant direct revenues online (with some notable, widely cited exceptions such as AOL, Yahoo!, and Dell). The emphasis today is mainly on what Hanson calls product/service improvement models rather than direct revenue models. For instance, there is evidence that among the main B2C beneficiaries of the web have been established retailers using a 'bricks-and-clicks' strategy, whereby consumers browse online but purchase at the physical store (Vishwanath and Mulvin, 2001).

Finally, although a striking feature of the Internet is its ability to transcend geography, there has been little research on its impact on international marketing. The most cited paper to-date is Quelch and Klein's (1996) early discussion of the opportuni-ties and threats it raises for firms operating internationally.

8. Conclusions and Research Opportunities

Overall Evaluation: The Impact of the Internet on Marketing

Until the bubble burst in Spring 2000, expectations of the Internet had been so overhyped that the reality was bound to disappoint. The danger now, especially in a much less confident financial and geopolitical climate, is that sentiment swings too far the other way and the Internet's significance is underestimated. We still believe that the Internet, and the digital revolution more generally, will have wide-ranging impacts on marketing as well as on many other aspects of society and business (Barwise and Hammond, 1998).

Contrary to some of the earlier hype, the Internet does not change the fundamental principles of marketing. Nor has its impact to-date (e.g., on consumer behavior, advertising, pricing, channels/intermediaries, strategy and globalization) been anything like as dramatic as predicted. However, we expect its impact to increase greatly over the next ten years for three reasons:

1. Even in the US, Northern Europe and Australasia, the Internet is only a recent part of most consumers' lives – and its penetration is still much lower than for traditional mass technologies (TV, radio, mail, telephone, automobile). In other countries, its penetration is even lower. Internet adoption and usage are still increasing among consumers and businesses, especially in countries with lower levels of penetration today. As it approaches universal adoption and usage, its role within marketing, especially international marketing, will continue to grow.
2. Marketers are still learning how to use the Internet as a medium in its own right and especially in combination with other media (Flores, 2000; Silk et al., 2001). Despite the rhetoric about integrated marketing communications, 'bricks-and-clicks' strategies, 'one-to-one marketing' (Peppers and Rogers, 1993, 1997), and 'permission marketing' (Godin, 1999), it will take years for most firms to turn these words into really cost-effective reality. Many of the issues relate to technology, database management, organization, and policy (e.g., addressing security and privacy concerns), as well as creative execution (Barwise and Strong, 2002). All of this is happening – for instance, the Internet is steadily increasing its share of advertising in most countries – but it will take time.
3. The technology is still developing fast. Current developments include broadband, mobile Internet, iDTV and virtual reality, wireless LANs (e.g., in the home and office), better intelligent agents, and more intuitive interfaces (Barwise, 2001; Barwise and Hammond, 1998; Maes, 1999). None of these technologies has significant penetration; none works very well yet; none has an agreed standard like the Internet Protocol; none is cheap enough yet to achieve mass market adoption. All of these developments seem likely to happen, but they will take several years. Over time, however, their combined effect on marketing practice will be great.

Online technology has the potential, depending on the context, to:

- Reduce customer search costs
- Allow low-cost customization of the marketing mix
- Support some market-related activities like auctions and brand communities in areas where they were not previously viable
- Give customers access to firms (and perhaps vice versa) any time, anywhere
- Abolish some types of intermediary and create other, new types
- Strongly reinforce globalization.

Which of these actually happens, and how much, will emerge over the next few years, but meanwhile, many specific insights have already emerged from the research to date.

Specific Insights from the Research to Date

- The Internet is already valued by a large minority of the population as an information-source, but it competes with other channels and has to offer clear benefits (Bellman et al., 1999; Morrison and Roberts, 1998). Convenience is a key benefit for such adopters; the development of recommendation systems and other agents will increase the Internet's perceived utility and use for such people (Ariely, 2000; Häubl and Trifts, 2000).

- As the Internet matures we can expect it to become somewhat more entertainment-orientated in order to attract a broader user base. This will increase its revenue potential (Hammond et al., 2000; Novak et al., 2000).
- Brand equity can, at least to some extent, be reinforced through online communities (Muniz and O'Guinn, 2001). Although brand loyalty may not be higher in online markets (Fader and Hardie, 2001), where brand loyalty is increased, high market share brands benefit most (Danaher et al., 2000). Brands are especially important for new adopters (Ward and Lee, 2000). This partially supports the view that online retailer choice is mostly a low involvement process (Ilfield and Winer, 2001).
- The Internet is emerging as a significant advertising medium, although more slowly than the enthusiasts predicted. Most of the advertising revenue is captured by the biggest sites (AOL, MSN, Yahoo!, etc.), leaving the business plans of most 'niche' advertising-funded dotcoms in tatters.
- As an advertising medium, the Internet can be used in many ways – e.g., mass/targeted, push/pull, local/national/global (Silk et al., 2001). It now includes a wide range of formats, with many alternatives to traditional banner ads (Bellman and Rossiter, 2001; Flores, 2000) and email, probably the fastest-growing part of Internet advertising. Clickthrough rates are low and falling, but underestimate the total consumer response (Flores, 2000). Relevance and permission are becoming increasingly important (Barwise and Strong, 2002).
- Early predictions that the Internet would lead to 'frictionless' markets (Gates, 1995; Wigand and Benjamin, 1995) have so far proved wide of the mark. There is evidence that it has somewhat increased competition and reduced prices in some markets, but the impact on both price levels and price dispersion has been small (Smith et al., 2000).
- By the same token, brands continue to be just as important in the post-Internet world (Barwise, 1997; Dayal et al., 2000; Lal and Sarvary, 1999; Shankar et al., 1999), as does product differentiation (Lynch and Ariely, 2000).
- Economies of scale will continue to be extremely important. In addition to physical (e.g., fulfillment) and network externality reasons, even for pure information products the larger players will have more scope for bundling (Bakos and Brynjolfsson, 2000a, 2000b) and versioning (Shapiro and Varian, 1998a, 1998b).
- Online markets and auctions have had limited impact on consumer (B2C, C2C) markets despite the success of a few businesses, notably eBay. But they are developing fast in B2B markets (Bloch and Catfolis, 2001; Kaplan and Sawhney, 2000).
- The expected 'disintermediation,' as existing intermediaries are replaced by direct communications between primary suppliers and consumers (Benjamin and Wigand, 1995; Rayport and Sviokla, 1995; Shaffer and Zettelmeyer, 1999), has not happened. Instead, the initial evidence is that, as predicted by Sarkar et al. (1995), when intermediaries disappear they are replaced by new web-based 'cybermediaries' (Bailey & Bakos, 1997; Sarkar et al., 1998).
- There is also evidence that bricks-and-mortar intermediaries who have successfully combined online technology with their existing assets (a 'bricks-and-clicks' strategy) have gained competitive advantage (Chircu and Kauffman, 2000; Vishwanath and Mulvin, 2001).
- At this stage, there is little empirical research on the impact of the Internet on marketing strategy. There is wide agreement that firms should prepare for the new economy in stages (Albrinck et al., 2000; Earl, 2000; Venkatraman, 2000) and that full preparation requires a transformation going well beyond marketing (Anderson, 2000; Moss Kanter, 2001).
- There is still no consensus on the long-term impact on strategy, nor on viable business models. At this stage, most successful business use of the Internet has been as a supplement to existing activities rather than as a way of generating significant direct revenue (see the classification in Hanson, 2000).
- An early article by Quelch and Klein (1996) on how the Internet may revolutionize global marketing has not been followed up by large-scale empirical research. Given the inherently global nature of the Internet, this represents an opportunity.

Future Research Opportunities

The discussion in this chapter has covered a wide range of topics, but several key areas have emerged where further research can add to the Marketing discipline. We list these under three headings: first, the application of existing approaches to measure the impact of online media on substantive topics in marketing strategy and consumer behavior; second, the development of new theory; third, the emergence of new (or the effects on existing) market research methodologies.

The Impact of the Internet on Marketing Strategy and Consumer Behavior

Under this broad heading we may expect to see the following types of questions addressed:

- Does consumer behavior change when the Internet is used as a channel for commerce?
- Are consumers more or less brand loyal when they buy online? What factors determine customer loyalty in an online environment?
- How does the role of brands differ in online versus offline environments?
- What are the short- and long-term effects of promotions in an online shopping environment?
- Is online advertising more or less effective than offline advertising? In what respects and contexts/roles?
- How should we measure marketing performance online?
- What CRM strategies are effective online?
- How should online and offline channels be combined? Do online channels 'cannibalize' offline channels?
- To what extent does the Internet affect international marketing and diffusion processes?
- How does the Internet fit into everyday life? How has it changed everyday life?
- How will Internet marketing evolve into marketing using a range of converging digital media (broadband, mobile, interactive television)?

We would expect to see explicit use of existing theory to address these questions – theory not only from marketing but also from economics, psychology, and anthropology.

The Development of New Theory

In addition to the use of existing theory, the rise of the Internet creates the need for new theory in a number of radically new areas, particularly:

- Consumer-to-consumer interaction
- Agent-consumer interaction
- Agent-to-agent (or machine-to-machine) interaction.

Emerging Marketing Research Methodologies

As Rangaswamy and Gupta (1999) indicate, the Internet will influence not only which research issues we pursue, but also how we will explore those issues, and how we disseminate research results, insights, and techniques to a broad audience. This review is a case in point. We used the web extensively to find relevant papers from a wide range of sources. We are also using it to disseminate the results (at www.marketingandtheinternet.com). As far as emerging market research methodologies are concerned, online real-time experiments promise to be an exciting area. The Internet generates huge quantities of unobtrusive data, which can be used to set up consumer behavior experiments that are more realistic and more complex than experiments in the offline world. Englis and Solomon (2000) review consumer research applications online, and describe one particular methodology for 'visually-oriented consumer research.' In addition, research into controversial, sensitive or ethical topics is challenging in a face-to-face (i.e., focus group) setting. Montoya-Weiss et al. (1998) suggest the advantages (and drawbacks) that electronic communication environments have for helping with communication apprehension (CA) problems in such research. Possible other applications include:

- Assessment of customer acquisition costs
- Measurement of responsiveness to advertising and promotions
- Investigation of price sensitivity
- Exploration of consumer-agent interaction.

We would like to thank everyone who contributed to this chapter, especially Tim Ambler, Kent Grayson, Bruce Hardie, Arvind Sahay, Craig Smith, and Naufel Vilcassim (all at London Business School), who provided detailed comments on an earlier draft, and many colleagues across the world who gave comments and suggestions about relevant literature.

Notes

1. Just over half these publications are referenced in this chapter.

2. The Graphics, Visualization and Usability (GVU) Center at Georgia Institute of Technology ran a series of WWW User Surveys from 1994 to 1998. The data from these surveys were made widely available for research and many studies mentioned in this chapter made use of one or more of these datasets. For more information see: http://www.gvu.gatech.edu/gvu/wwwinit/survey.html

References

Achrol, S.R. and Kotler, P. (1999) Marketing in the network economy. *Journal of Marketing*, 63 (Special Issue), 146–163.

Adamic, L.A. and Huberman, B.A. (2000) The nature of markets in the world wide web. *Quarterly Journal of Electronic Commerce*, 1 (2), 5–12.

Adar, E. and Huberman, B.A. (2000) The economics of surfing. *Quarterly Journal of Electronic Commerce*, 1 (3), 203–14.

Alba, J., Lynch, J.G.J., Weitz, B., Janiszewski, C., Lutz, R., Sawyer, A.G. & Wood, S. (1997) Interactive home shopping: consumer, retailer, and manufacturer incentives to participate in electronic marketplaces. *Journal of Marketing*, 61 (July), 38–53.

Albrinck, J., Irwin, G., Neilson, G. & Sasina, D. (2000) From bricks to clicks: the four stages of e-volution. *Strategy and Business*, 20, 63–72.

Amit, R. and Zott, C. (2000) Value drivers of e-commerce business models. Working Paper, The Wharton School, 1–14.

Anderson, D. (2000) Creating and nurturing a premier e-business. *Journal of Interactive Marketing*, 14 (3), 67–73.

Ansari, A., Essegaier, S. & Kohli, R. (2000) Internet recommendation systems. *Journal of Marketing Research*, 37 (3), 363–75.

Ariely, D. (2000) Controlling the information flow: effects on consumers' decision making and preferences. *Jounal of Consumer Research*, 27 (2, September), 233–48.

Armstrong, A. & Hagel, J. (1996) The real value of online communities. *Harvard Business Review*, May–June, 134–41.

Arthur, W.B. (1996) Increasing returns and the New World of business. *Harvard Business Review*, July–August, 100–9.

Baer, W.S. (1998) Will the Internet bring electronic services to the home? *Business Strategy Review*, 9, 1 (Spring), 29–36.

Bailey, J. & Bakos, J.Y. (1997) An exploratory study of the emerging role of electronic intermediaries. *International Journal of Electronic Commerce*, 1 (3), Spring, 7–20.

Bain, M.G. (1999) Business to Consumer eCommerce: an investigation of factors related to consumer adoption of the Internet as a purchase channel. *Centre for Marketing Working Paper*, 99-806.

Bakos, J.Y. (1991) A strategic analysis of electronic marketplaces. *MIS Quarterly*, September, 295–310.

——— (1997) Reducing buyer search costs: implications for electronic marketplaces. *Management Science*, 43 (12), 1676–92.

Bakos, J.Y. & Brynjolfsson, E. (1999) Bundling information goods: pricing, profits and efficiency. *Management Science*, 45 (12), 1613–30.

——— (2000a) Aggregation and disaggregation of information goods: implications for bundling, site licencing, and micropayment systems. In *Internet Publishing and Beyond: The Economics of Digital Information and Intellectual Property*, edited by D. Hurley, B. Kahin & H.R. Varian. Cambridge, MA: MIT Press, pp. 114–37.

——— (2000b) Bundling and competition on the Internet. *Marketing Science*, 19 (1), 63–82.

Balabanis, G. & Vassileiou, S. (1999) Some attitudinal predictors of home shopping through the Internet. *Journal of Marketing Management*, 15, 361–85.

Barsh, J., Crawford, B. & Grosso, C. (2000) How e-tailing can rise from the ashes. *McKinsey Quarterly*, 3, 100–9.

Barwise, P. (1997) Editorial: brands in a digital world. *Journal of Brand Management*, 4 (4), 220–3.

——— (2001) TV, PC or mobile? Future media for B2C e-commerce. *Business Strategy Review*, 12 (1), 35–42.

Barwise, P. & Hammond, K. (1998) *Predictions: Media*. London: Phoenix. www.predictionsmedia.com.

Barwise, P. & Strong, C. (2002) Permission-based mobile advertising. *Journal of Interactive Marketing*, 16 (1), 14–24.

Bauer, H., Gretcher, M. & Leach, M. (1999) Customer relations through the Internet. Working Paper, MIT Ecommerce Forum and University of Mannheim.

Becker-Olsen, K.L. (2000) Point, click and shop: an exploratory investigation of consumer perceptions of online shopping. Presented at the AMA Summer Conference.

Bellizzi, A.J. (2000) Drawing prospects to e-commerce websites. *Journal of Advertising Research*, January–April, 43–53.

Bellman, S. & Rossiter, J.R. (2001) The web ad schema. Working Paper, Graduate School of Management, University of Western Australia.

Bellman, S., Lohse, J. & Johnson, E.J. (1999) Predictors of online buying: findings from the Wharton Virtual Test Market. *Communications of the ACM*, December, 1–15.

Benjamin, R.I. & Wigand, R.T. (1995) Electronic markets and virtual value chains on the information superhighway. *Sloan Management Review*, Winter, 62–72.

Berthon, P., Lane, N., Pitt, L.F. & Watson, R.T. (1998) The world wide web as an industrial marketing communication tool: models for the identification and assessment of opportunities. *Journal of Marketing Management*, 14, 691–704.

Berthon, P., Pitt, L., Katsikeas, C.S. & Berthon, J.P. (1999) Virtual services go international: international services in the marketspace. *Journal of International Marketing*, 11 (3) (Sept–Oct), 84–105.

Bezjian-Avery, A., Calder, B. & Iacobucci, D. (1998) New media interactive advertising vs. traditional advertising. *Journal of Advertising Research*, July–August, 23–32.

Bhargava, H., Choudhary, V. & Krishnan, R. (2000) Pricing and product design: intermediary strategies in an electronic market. Working Paper, MIT Ecommerce Forum, 1–20.

Bhise, H., Faral, D., Miller, H., Vadnier, A. & Zainulbhai, A. (2000) The dual for the doorstep. *McKinsey Quarterly*, 2, 33–41.

Blattberg, C.R. & Deighton, J. (1991) Interactive marketing: exploring the age of addressability. *Sloan Management Review*, 33 (1), Fall, 5–14.

Bloch, N. & Catfolis, T. (2001) Business-to-business digital marketplaces: how to succeed? *Business Strategy Review*, 12 (3), 20–8.

Bradlow, E.T. & Schmittlein, D.C. (2000) The little engines that could: modelling the performance of world wide web search engines. *Marketing Science*, 19 (1), Winter, 43–62.

Braunstein, M. & Levine, E.H. (2000) *Deep Branding on the Internet: Applying Heat and Pressure Online to Ensure a Lasting Brand*. Roseville, CA: Prima.

Briggs, R. & Hollis, N. (1997) Advertising on the web: is there response before click-through? *Journal of Advertising Research*, March–April, 33–45.

Brodin, K., Barwise, P. & Canhoto, A.I. (2002) UK responses to iDTV. Future Media Report, London Business School, www.idtvconsumers.com.

Brown, J.R. & Goolsbee, A. (1999) Does the Internet make markets more competitive? Evidence from the life insurance industry. National Bureau of Economic Research, Working Paper.

Bruner, G. & Kumar, A. (2000) Web commercials and advertising hierarchy-of-effects. *Journal of Advertising Research*, January–April, 35–42.

Brynjolfsson, E. & Smith, M.D. (2000) Frictionless commerce? A comparison of Internet and conventional retailers. *Management Science*, 46 (4), 563–85.

Burke, R. (1996) Virtual shopping: breakthrough in marketing research. *Harvard Business Review*, 74 (2) (Mar–Apr), 120–9.

——— (1997) Do you see what I see? The future of virtual shopping. *Journal of the Academy of Marketing Science*, 25 (4), Fall, 352–60.

Bush, J.A., Bush, V. & Harris, S. (1999) Advertiser perceptions of the Internet as a marketing communications tool. *Journal of Advertising Research*, March–April, 17–27.

Carr, G.N. (2000) Hypermediation: commerce as clickstream. *Harvard Business Review*, January–February, 46–7.

Chang, T.Z. (2000) Online shoppers' perceptions of the quality of Internet shopping experience. *AMA Summer Educators Conference*, pp. 254–5.

Chavez, R., Leiter, M. & Kiely, T. (2000) Should you spin off your Internet business? *Business Strategy Review*, 11 (2), 19–31.

Chircu, A.M. & Kauffman, R.J. (2000) Reintermediation strategies in business-to-business electronic commerce. *International Journal of Electronic Commerce*, 4 (4), 7–42.

Christensen, C. & Tedlow, R.S. (2000) Patterns of disruption in retailing. *Harvard Business Review*, January–February, 42–5.

Chui, K. & Zwick, R. (1999) Auction on the Internet – a preliminary study. Working Paper, Department of Marketing, Hong Kong University of Science and Technology, 1–27.

Clay, K., Ramayya, K., Wolff, E. & Fernandes, D. (1999) Retail strategies on the web: price and non-price competition in the on line book industry. Working Paper, MIT Ecommerce Forum.

Coltman, T., Devinney, T.M., Latukefu, A. & Midgley, D.F. (2000) E-business: revolution, evolution or hype? Working Paper, MIT Ecommerce Forum, 2 January.

Cornet, P., Milcent, P. & Roussel, P.-Y. (2000) From e-commerce to €-commerce. *McKinsey Quarterly*, 2, 31–8.

Cross, G.J. (2000) How e-business is transforming supply chain management. *Journal of Business Strategy*, 21 (March/April) (2), 36–9.

Culnan, M.J. & Armstrong, P. (1999) Information privacy concerns, procedural fairness and impersonal trust: an empirical investigation. *Organization Science*, 10 (1), 104–15.

Danaher, J.P., Wilson, I.W. & Davis, R. (2000) Consumer brand loyalty in a virtual shopping environment. INFORMS Marketing Science Conference 2000.

Dans, E. (2000) Internet newspapers: are some more equal than others? *The International Journal of Media Management*, 2 (1), 4–13.

Dans, E. & Pauwels, K. (2001) Internet marketing the news: levering brand equity from marketplace to marketspace. *Journal of Brand Management*, 8 (4–5), 303–14.

Darby, M. & Karni, E. (1973) Free competition and the optimal amount of fraud. *Journal of Law and Economics*, 16, 67–88.

Dayal, S., Landesberg, H. & Zeisser, M. (2000) Building digital brands. *McKinsey Quarterly*, 2, 42–51.

Degeratu, A., Rangaswamy, A. & Wu, J. (1999) Consumer choice behavior in online and traditional supermarkets: the effects of brand name, price, and other search attributes. Working Paper, MIT Ecommerce Forum.

Deighton, J. (1996) The future of interactive marketing. *Harvard Business Review*, November–December, 151–62.

——— (1997) Commentary on 'Exploring the Implications of the Internet for Consumer Marketing'. *Journal of the Academy of Marketing Science*, 25 (4), 347–51.

DeKoning, V., Giles, T., Glufing, L. & Leigh, V. (1999) Online auctions: consumer behavior in local versus global formats. Working Paper, Owen Graduate School of Business, Vanderbilt University.

Dellaert, B. (1999) The consumer as value creator on the Internet. Working Paper, MIT Ecommerce Forum, 1–27.

——— (2000) Tourists' valuation of other tourists' contributions to travel websites. Working Paper, MIT Ecommerce Forum, 1–10.

Dellaert, B. & Khan, B.E. (1999) How tolerable is delay? Consumers' evaluations of Internet web sites after waiting. *Journal of Interactive Marketing*, 13 (1) (Winter), 41–54.

Dholakia, R.R. (1998) Special Issue: Conducting business in the new electronic environment: prospects and problems. *Journal of Business Research*, 41 (3), 175–7.

Dolan, R.J. & Moon, Y. (2000) Pricing and market making on the Internet. *Journal of Interactive Marketing*, 14 (2) (Spring), 56–73.

Drèze, X. & Zufryden, F. (1997) Testing web site design and promotional content. *Journal of Advertising Research*, 37 (2) (March–April), 77–91.

——— (1998) Is Internet advertising ready for primetime? *Journal of Advertising Research*, May–June, 7–18.

Ducoffe, R.H. (1996) Advertising value and advertising on the web. *Journal of Advertising Research*, 15 (1) (September–October), 21–35.

Dutta, S., Kwan, S. & Segev, A. (1998) Business transformation in electronic commerce: a study of sectoral and regional trends. *European Management Journal*, 16 (5) (October), 540–51.

Dutton, W.H. (1996) *Information and Communication Technologies: Visions and Realities*. New York: Oxford University Press.

Earl, M.J. (2000) Evolving the e-business. *Business Strategy Review*, 11 (2), 33–8.

Eighmey, J. & McCord, L. (1998) Adding value in the information age: uses and gratifications of sites on the world wide web. *Journal of Business Research*, 41, 187–94.

Elberse, A. (1998) Consumer acceptance of interactive news in the Netherlands. *Harvard International Journal of Press/Politics* (MIT Press), 3 (4), 62–83.

Emmanouilides, C. & Hammond, K. (2000) Internet usage: predictors of active users and frequency of use. *Journal of Interactive Marketing*, 14 (2) (Spring), 17–32.

Englis, B.G. & Solomon, M.R. (2000) Life/Style online, a web-based methodology for visually-oriented consumer research. *Journal of Interactive Marketing*, 14 (1) (Winter), 2–14.

Ethiraj, S., Guler, I. & Singh, H. (2000) The impact of Internet and electronic technologies on firms and its implications for competitive advantage. Working Paper, The Wharton School, 1–40.

Evans, P. & Wurster, T.S. (1999) Getting real about virtual commerce. *Harvard Business Review*, November–December, 85–94.

Fader, P.S. & Hardie, B.G.S. (2001) Forecasting repeat sales at CDNow: a case study. *Interfaces*, 31 (2), 94–107.

Flores, L. (2000) Internet advertising effectiveness: what did we learn and where are we going? Working Paper, Worldwide Advertising Conference, Rio de Janeiro, November, 1–18.

Fournier, S., Dobscha, S. & Mick, D.G. (1998) Preventing the premature death of relationship marketing. *Harvard Business Review*, 76 (Jan–Feb), 43–51.

Gates, B. (1995) *The Road Ahead*. New York: Viking.

Gershoff, A. & West, P.M. (1998) Using a community of knowledge to build intelligent agents. *Marketing Letters*, 9 (January), 79–91.

Geyskens, I., Gielens, K. & Dekimpe, M. (2001) The market valuation of Internet channel additions. Working Paper, Tilburg University & University of Leuven.

Ghose, S. & Dou, W. (1998) Interactive functions and their impacts on the appeal of Internet presence sites. *Journal of Advertising Research*, March–April, 29–43.

Gilder, G. (1994) *Life After Television*. New York: W.W. Norton & Company.

Glazer, R. (1991) Marketing in an information-intensive environment: strategic implications of knowledge as an asset. *Journal of Marketing*, 55, 1–19.

Godin, S. (1999) *Permission Marketing*. New York: Simon and Schuster.

Goolsbee, A. (2000) Competition in the computer industry: online versus retail. Working Paper, University of Chicago.

Gould, S.J. & Lerman, D.B. (1998) 'Postmodern' versus 'long-standing' cultural narratives in consumer behavior: an empirical study of NetGirl Online. *European Journal of Marketing*, 32 (7/8), 644–54.

Griffith, D.D. & Krampf, R.F. (2000) An empirical examination of consumer information processing: a print versus web-based retailing catalog context. AMA Summer Educators Conference, Chicago.

Guttman, R.H., Moukas, A.G. & Maes, P. (1998) Agent-mediated electronic commerce: a survey. *Knowledge Engineering Review*, 13 (2), 147–59.

Haeckel, S.H. (1998) About the nature and future of interactive marketing. *Journal of Interactive Marketing*, 12 (1) (Winter), 63–71.

Hagel, J. (1999) Net gain: expanding markets through virtual communities. *Journal of Interactive Marketing*, 13 (1) (Winter), 55–65.

Hagel, J. & Armstrong, A. (1997) Net gain: expanding markets through virtual communities. *McKinsey Quarterly*, 1, 140–53.

Hagel, J. & Singer, M. (1999) *Net Worth*. Boston, MA: Harvard Business School Press.

Hammond, K. (2001) B2C e-Commerce 2000–2010: what experts predict. *Business Strategy Review*, 12 (1), 43–50.

Hammond, K., McWilliam, G. & Diaz, A. (1998) Fun and work on the web: differences in attitudes between novices and experienced users. *Advances in Consumer Research*, 25, 372–8.

Hammond, K., Turner, P. & Bain, M. (2000) Internet users versus non-users: drivers of Internet uptake. *International Journal of Advertising*, 19, 665–81.

Hanson, W. (1998) The original www: web business model lessons from the early days of radio. *Journal of Interactive Marketing*, 12 (3) (Summer), 46–56.

——— (2000) *Principles of Internet Marketing*. Cincinnati, Ohio: South-Western College Publishing.

Häubl, G. & Trifts, V. (2000) Consumer decision making in online shopping environments: the effects of interactive decision aids. *Marketing Science*, 19 (1) (Winter), 4–21.

Higson, C. & Briginshaw, J. (2000) Valuing Internet businesses. *Business Strategy Review*, 11 (1), 10–20.

Hofacker, C.F. (2001) *Internet Marketing*. New York: John Wiley and Sons.

Hofacker, C.F. & Murphy, J. (1998) World Wide Web banner advertisement copy testing. *European Journal of Marketing*, 32 (7/8), 703–12.

——— (2000) Clickable world wide web banner ads and content sites. *Journal of Interactive Marketing*, 14 (1) (Winter), 49–59.

Hoffman, D.L. (2000) The revolution will not be televised: introduction to the Special Issue on Marketing Science and the Internet. *Marketing Science*, 19 (1), 1–3.

Hoffman, D.L. & Novak, T.P. (1996) Marketing in hypermedia computer-mediated environments: conceptual foundations. *Journal of Marketing*, 60 (3) (July), 50–68.

——— (1997) A new marketing paradigm for electronic commerce. *The Information Society*, 13 (Jan–March), 43–54.

——— (2000) How to acquire customers on the web. *Harvard Business Review*, May–June, 179–88.

Hoffman, D.L., Novak, T.P. & Chatterjee, P. (1995) Commercial scenarios for the web: opportunities and challenges. *Journal of Computer Mediated Communication*, Special Issue on Electronic Commerce (Online), 1 (3).

Hoffman, D.L., Novak, T.P. & Peralta, M.A. (1999) Building consumer trust in an online environment: the case for information privacy. *Communications of the ACM*, 42 (4), 80–5.

Hoffman, D.L., Novak, T.P. & Schlosser, A. (2000) Consumer control in online environments. Working Paper, ELab – Owen Graduate School of Management, Vanderbilt University.

Iacobucci, D. (1998) Interactive marketing and the meganet: network of networks. *Journal of Interactive Marketing*, 12 (1) (Winter), 5–16.

Iacobucci, D., Arabie, P. & Bodapati, A. (2000) Recommendation agents on the Internet. *Journal of Interactive Marketing*, 14 (3) (July), 2–11.

Ilfield, J.S. & Winer, R.S. (2001) Generating web site traffic: an empirical analysis of web site visitation behavior. Working Paper, Haas School of Business, University of California at Berkeley.

Jin, L. & Robey, D. (1999) Explaining cybermediation: an organisational analysis of electronic retailing. *International Journal of Electronic Commerce*, 3 (4) (Summer), 47–65.

Kaplan, S. & Sawhney, M. (2000) E-hubs: the new B2B marketplaces. *Harvard Business Review*, May–June, 97–103.

Katz, M. & Shapiro, C. (1994) Systems competition and network effects. *Journal of Economic Perspectives*, 8 (2), 93–115.

Kephart, J.O., Hanson, J.E. & Greenwald, A.R. (2000) Dynamic pricing by software agents. *Computer Networks*, 32 (6), 731–52.

Klein, N. (2000) *No Logo*. London: Flamingo.

Klein, S. & O'Keefe, R.M. (1999) The impact of the web on auctions: some empirical evidence and theoretical considerations. *International Journal of Electronic Commerce*, 3 (3) (Spring), 7–20.

Lal, R. & Sarvary, M. (1999) When and how is the Internet likely to decrease price competition? *Marketing Science*, 18 (4), 485–503.

Langford, B.E. (2000) The web marketer experiment: a rude awakening. *Journal of Interactive Marketing*, 14 (1) (Winter), 40–8.

Laseter, T., Houston, P., Chung, A., Byrne, S., Turner, M. & Devendran, A. (2000) The last mile to nowhere: floors and fallacies in Internet home-delivery schemes. *Strategy and Business*, 20, 40–8.

Leckenby, J.D. & Hong, J. (1998) Using reach/frequency for web media planning. *Journal of Advertising Research*, January–February, 7–20.

Leong, E.K.F., Huang, X. & Stanners, P.-J. (1998) Comparing the effectiveness of the web site with traditional media. *Journal of Advertising Research*, September–October, 44–9.

Li, H., Kuo, C. & Russell, G.M. (1999) The impact of perceived channel utilities, shopping orientations, and demographics on the consumer's online buying behavior. *Journal of Computer Mediated Communication*, 5 (2), 1–20.

Lituchy, T.R. & Rail, A. (2000) Bed and breakfasts, small inns, and the Internet: the impact of technology on the globalization of small businesses. *Journal of International Marketing*, 8 (2), 86–97.

Lohse, T. & Spiller, P. (1999) Internet retail store design: how the user interface influences traffic and sales. *Journal of Computer Mediated Communication* (Online), 5 (2).

Lohse, L.G., Bellman, S. & Johnson, E.J. (2000) Consumer buying behavior on the Internet: findings from panel data. *Journal of Interactive Marketing*, 14 (1) (Winter), 15–29.

Lucking-Reiley, D. (1999a) Auctions on the Internet: what's being auctioned and how? Working Paper, MIT Ecommerce Forum, 1–50.

——— (1999b) Using field experiments test equivalence between auction formats: magic on the Internet. *American Economic Review*, December, 1063–81.

Lucking-Reiley, D., Bryan, D., Prasad, D., Naghi, D. & Reeves, D. (2000) Pennies from eBay: the determinants of price in online auctions. Working Paper, Vanderbilt University.

Lynch, J.G.J. & Ariely, D. (2000) Wine online: search costs affect competition on price, quality, and distribution. *Marketing Science*, 19 (1) (Winter), 83–103.

Maes, P. (1999) Smart commerce: the future of intelligent agents in cyberspace. *Journal of Interactive Marketing*, 13 (3) (Summer), 66–76.

Malone, T., Yates, J. & Benjamin, R. (1987) Electronic markets and electronic hierarchies: effects of information technology on market structure and corporate strategies. *Communications of the ACM*, 30 (6), 484–97.

Mandel, N. & Johnson, E.J. (1999) Constructing preferences online: can web pages change what you want? Working Paper, MIT Ecommerce Forum, Wharton Ecommerce Forum.

Mathwick, C. (2000) Online relationship orientation. Presented at the AMA Summer Conference.

McWilliam, G. (2000) Building stronger brands through online communities. *Sloan Management Review*, 41 (3) (Spring), 43–54.

Mehta, R. & Sivadas, E. (1995) Direct marketing on the Internet: an empirical assessment of consumer attitudes. *Journal of Direct Marketing*, 9 (3) (Summer), 21–32.

Mick, D.G. & Fournier, S. (1998) Paradoxes of technology: consumer cognizance, emotions, and coping strategies. *Journal of Consumer Research*, 25 (September), 123–43.

Milne, G.R. & Boza, M.-E. (1999) Trust and concern in consumers' perceptions of marketing information management practices. *Journal of Interactive Marketing*, 13 (1) (Winter), 5–24.

Moe, W.W. & Fader, P.S. (2000) Which visits lead to purchases? Dynamic conversion behavior at e-commerce sites. Working Paper, Wharton Business School, University of Pennsylvania, 1–26.

Montoya-Weiss, M.M., Massey, A.P. & Clapper, D.L. (1998) On-line focus groups: conceptual issues and a research tool. *European Journal of Marketing*, 32 (7/8), 713–23.

Morris, M. & Ogan, C. (1996) The Internet as mass medium. *Journal of Communication*, Winter, 39–50.

Morrison, P.D. & Roberts, J.H. (1998) Matching electronic distribution channels to product characteristics:

the role of congruence in consideration set formation. *Journal of Business Research*, 41, 223–9.

Moss Kanter, R. (2001) The ten deadly mistakes of wanna-dots. *Harvard Business Review*, January, 91–100.

Muniz, A.M. & O'Guinn, T.C. (2001) Brand community. *Journal of Consumer Research*, 27, 412–32.

Negroponte, N. (1995) *Being Digital*. New York: Knopf.

Nelson, P. (1970) Information and consumer behavior. *Journal of Political Economy*, 78 (2), 311–29.

——— (1974) Advertising as information. *Journal of Political Economy*, 81 (July/August), 729–54.

Neuman, R.W. (1991) *The Future of the Mass Audience*. Cambridge, UK: Cambridge University Press.

Nouwens, J. & Bouwman, H. (1995) Living apart together in electronic commerce: the use of information and communication technology to create network organizations. *Journal of Computer-Mediated Communication* (Online), 1 (3).

Novak, T.P., Hoffman, D.L. & Yung, Y.-F. (2000) Measuring the customer experience in online environments: a structural modelling approach. *Marketing Science*, 19 (1) (Winter), 22–42.

Palmer, J.W. (1997) Electronic commerce in retailing: differences across retailing formats. *The Information Society*, 13 (1) (Winter), 97–108.

Pauwels, K. (2001) The drivers of online readership: a decomposition approach. Working Paper, Andersen School, UCLA.

Pavlik, J.V. (1996) *New Media and the Information Superhighway*. Boston: Allyn and Bacon.

Peltier, W.J., Schibrowsky, A.J. & Davis, J. (1998) Using attitudinal and descriptive database information to understand interactive buyer-seller relationships. *Journal of Interactive Marketing*, 12 (3), 32–45.

Peppers, D. & Rogers, M. (1993). *The One-To-One Future*. New York: Doubleday.

——— (1997) *Enterprise One-To-One: Tools for Building Unbreakable Customer Relationships in the Interactaive Age*. New York: Doubleday.

Peterson, R.A. (ed.) (1997) *Electronic Marketing and the Consumer*. Thousand Oaks, CA: Sage.

Peterson, R.A., Balasubramanian, S. & Bronnenberg, B.J. (1997) Exploring the implications of the Internet for consumer marketing. *Journal of the Academy of Marketing Science*, 25 (4), 329–46.

Picard, R.G. (2000) Changing business models of online content services and their implications for multimedia and other content producers. *The International Journal of Media Management*, 2 (2), 1–21.

Porter, M.E. (2001) Strategy and the Internet. *Harvard Business Review*, March, 62–78.

Quelch, J.A. & Klein, L.R. (1996) The Internet and international marketing. *Sloan Management Review*, Spring, 60–75.

Ramsdell, G. (2000) The real business of B2B. *McKinsey Quarterly*, 3, 174–83.

Rangaswamy, A. & Gupta, S. (1999) Innovation adoption and diffusion in the digital environment: some research opportunities. Working Paper, MIT Ecommerce Forum, 1–35.

Rayport, J.F. & Sviokla, J.J. (1994) Managing in the marketspace. *Harvard Business Review*, November–December, 141–50.

——— (1995) Exploiting the virtual value chain. *Harvard Business Review*, November–December, 75–85.

Reichheld, F. & Schefter, P. (2000) E-loyalty: your secret weapon on the web. *Harvard Business Review*, July–August, 105–13.

Rheingold, H. (1993) *The Virtual Community: Homesteading on the Electronic Frontier*. New York: Harper Perennial.

Rohlfs, J. (1974) A theory of interdependent demand for a communications service. *Bell Journal of Economics*, 5 (1), 16–37.

Rosen, N. & Barwise, P. (2000) Business.eu: corporates versus web start-ups. August: Online Research Agency, London Business School, Protégé.

Rubini, D., Tarlton, M. & White, D. (1996) Scenes from a virtual mall: the consumer experience in cyberspace. *Design Management Journal*, Fall, 62–71.

Rust, R.T. & Oliver, R.W. (1994) The death of advertising. *Journal of Advertising*, 23 (4), 71–7.

Samiee, S. (1998) The Internet and international marketing: is there a fit? *Journal of Interactive Marketing*, 12 (4), 5–21.

Sarkar, M., Butler, B. & Steinfield, C. (1995) Intermediaries and cybermediaries: a continuing role for mediating players in the electronic marketplace. *Journal of Computer Mediated Communication* (Online), 1 (3) (December).

——— (1998) Cybermediaries in electronic marketspace: toward theory building. *Journal of Business Research*, 41, 215–21.

Schlosser, A., Shavitt, S.K.A. & Kanfer, A. (1999) Survey of Internet users' attitudes towards Internet advertising. *Journal of Interactive Marketing*, 13 (3) (Summer), 34–54.

Scott-Morton, F., Zettelmeyer, F. & Silva-Risso, J. (1999) Internet car retailing. Working Paper, National Bureau of Economic Research.

Sen, S., Padmanabhan, B., Tuzhilin, A., White, N.H. & Stein, R. (1998) The identification and satisfaction of consumer analysis-driven information needs of marketers on the www. *European Journal of Marketing*, 32 (7/8), 668–702.

Shaffer, G. & Zettelmeyer, F. (1999) The Internet as a medium for marketing communications: channel conflict over the provision of information. Working Paper, MIT Ecommerce Forum.

Shankar, V., Rangaswamy, A. & Pusateri, M. (1999) The online medium and customer price sensitivity. Working Paper, MIT Ecommerce Forum, 1999.

Shapiro, C. & Varian, H.R. (1998a) *Information Rules: A Strategic Guide to the Network Economy*. Boston: Harvard Business School Press.

——— (1998b) Versioning: the smart way to sell information. *Harvard Business Review*, November–December, 106–14.

Sheehan, B.K. (1999) An investigation of gender differences in on-line privacy concerns and resultant behaviors. *Journal of Interactive Marketing*, 13 (4) (Autumn), 24–38.

Silk, A.J., Klein, L.R. & Berndt, E.R. (1997) Intermedia substitutability in the US national advertising market. Working Paper 98–005, Harvard Business School.

——— (2001) The emerging position of the Internet as an advertising medium. *Netnomics*, 3, 129–48.

Sinha, I. (2000) Cost transparency: the net's real threat to prices and brands. *Harvard Business Review*, March–April, 43–50.

Smith, M.D., Bailey, J. & Brynjolfsson, E. (2000) Understanding digital markets: review and assessment. In *Understanding the Digital Economy*, edited by E. Brynjolfsson & B. Kahin. Cambridge, MA: MIT Press, pp. 99–136.

Spiller, P. & Lohse, J. (1998) A classification of Internet retail stores. *International Journal of Electronic Commerce*, 2 (2), 29–56.

Standage, T. (1998) *The Victorian Internet: The Remarkable Story of the Telegraph and the Nineteenth Century's On-Line Pioneers.* New York: Walker & Co.

Steinfield, C., Kraut, R. & Plummer, A. (1995) The impact of interorganizational networks on buyer-seller relationships. *Journal of Computer Mediated Communication* (Online), 1 (3) (December).

Strauss, J. & Hill, D.J. (2001) Consumer complaints by e-mail: an exploratory investigation of corporate responses and customer reactions. *Journal of Interactive Marketing*, 15 (1), 63–73.

Swaminathan, V., Lepkowska-White, E. & Rao, P.B. (1999) Browsers or buyers in cyberspace? An investigation of factors influencing electronic exchange. *Journal of Computer Mediated Communication* (Online), 5 (2) (December).

Urban, G., Sultan, F. & Qualls, W. (1999) Design and evaluation of a trust based advisor on the Internet. Working Paper, MIT Ecommerce Forum, 1–41.

Venkatesh, A. (1985) A conceptualization of the household/technology interaction. *Advances in Consumer Research*, 12, 189–94.

——— (1998) Cybermarketscapes and consumer freedoms and identities. *European Journal of Marketing*, 32 (7/8), 664–76.

Venkatesh, A., Dholakia, R.R. & Dholakia, N. (1996) New visions of information technology and postmodernism: implications for advertising and marketing communications. In *The Information Superhighway and Private Households: Case Studies of Business Impacts*, edited by W. Brenner & L. Kolbe. Heidelberg, Germany: Physica, pp. 319–37.

Venkatraman, N. (2000) Five steps to dot-com strategy: how to find your footing on the web. *Sloan Management Review*, 41 (3) (Spring), 15–28.

Vishwanath, V. & Mulvin, G. (2001) Multi-channels: the real winners in the B2C Internet wars. *Business Strategy Review*, 12 (1), 25–33.

Voss, C. (2000) Developing an eService strategy. *Business Strategy Review*, 11 (1) (Spring), 21–33.

Ward, M.R. & Lee, M.J. (2000) Internet shopping, consumer search and product branding. *Journal of Product and Brand Management*, 9 (1), 6–18.

Ward, P. & Davies, B.J. (1999) The diffusion of interactive technology at the customer interface. *International Journal of Technology Management*, 17 (1/2), 84–108.

Weiber, R. & Kollmann, T. (1998) Competitive advantages in virtual markets – perspectives of 'information-based marketing' in cyberspace. *European Journal of Marketing*, 32 (7/8), 603–15.

Weinberg, B.D. (2000) Don't keep your Internet customers waiting too long at the (virtual) front door. *Journal of Interactive Marketing*, 14 (1) (Winter), 30–9.

Werbach, K. (2000) Syndication: the emerging model for business in the Internet era. *Harvard Business Review*, May–June, 85–93.

West, P.M., Ariely, D., Bellman, S., Bradlow, E.T., Huber, J., Johnson, E.J., Kahn, B., Little, J. & Schkade, D. (1999) Agents to the rescue? *Marketing Letters*, 10 (3), 285–300.

Widing, R.E. & Talarzyk, W.W. (1993) Electronic information systems for consumers: an evaluation of computer-assisted formats in multiple decision environments. *Journal of Marketing Research*, 30 (May), 125–41.

Wigand, R.T. & Benjamin, R.I. (1995) Electronic commerce: effects on electronic markets. *Journal of Computer Mediated Communication* (Online), 1 (3).

Wilde, W. & Swatman, P. (1999) A preliminary theory of telecommunications enhanced communities. *Telecommunications Journal of Australia*, 40 (2), 61–72.

Wind, J. & Rangaswamy, A. (2001) Customerization: the next revolution in mass customization. *Journal of Interactive Marketing*, 15 (1), 13–32.

Winer, R.S., Deighton, J., Gupta, S., Johnson, E.J., Mellers, B., Morwitz, V.G., O'Guinn, T., Rangaswamy, A. & Sawyer, A.G. (1997) Choice in computer-mediated environments. *Marketing Letters*, 8 (3), 287–96.

Wood, L. (1998) Internet ad buys – what reach and frequency do they deliver? *Journal of Advertising Research*, January–February, 21–8.

Wu, J. & Rangaswamy, A. (1999) A fuzzy set model of consideration set formation: calibrated on data from an online supermarket. Working Paper, MIT Ecommerce Forum, 1–46.

Yang, C.-C. (1997) An exploratory study of the effectiveness of interactive advertisements on the Internet. *Journal of Marketing Communications*, 3, 61–85.

Yuan, Y., Caulkins, J.P. & Roehrig, S. (1998) The relationship between advertising and content provision on the Internet. *European Journal of Marketing*, 32 (7/8), 677–87.

Zettelmeyer, F. (2000) Expanding to the Internet: pricing and communications strategies when firms compete on multiple channels. *Journal of Marketing Research*, August, 292–308.

PART SIX

Concluding Observations

ROBIN WENSLEY and BARTON WEITZ

Specific Future Research Challenges

We asked each of the contributors to identify and comment on the specific research issues for the future in their own chapters. Thus we will not repeat their very useful contributions here but refer readers to their relevant areas of interest. In this final set of observations we will consider some issues concerning the general direction of substantive marketing research. By understanding both the impact of dominant forces on the development of the overall field as well as the general context in which this development has taken place, we and others can appreciate more readily the options in terms of future development.

Domain of Marketing and Consumer Behavior

We start our final comments with the early decisions we made concerning the scope of this Handbook and its contents. As we explained in the Introduction, we chose not to include specific chapters on consumer behavior. While there is an excellent, although now somewhat dated, handbook in this area which covers this requirement, our primary reason for excluding this material is that consumer behavior research has become distinct from the practice of and academic rationale for marketing management. Consumer behavior research now often does not offer marketing management implications and even sometimes discourages the presentation of these implications in a particular article. Much of the research seems to be undertaken simply for the sake of understanding consumer behavior rather than providing insights for improving the benefits received by consumers. Indeed to some degree the key professional association – the Association of Consumer Research – conscientiously eschews such a managerial perspective.[1] This shift in the focus of consumer research, although understandable given the wish to privilege the consumer rather than the manager, has some unfortunate consequences. To define the domain of marketing overall without careful attention to the nature and behavior of the consumer limits our understanding of an essentially interactive process to the perspective of only one party. While the distinction serves us well in designing this research handbook, when, as in the majority of the book, we are considering research in areas of marketing management, it also prevents a wider analysis of the socio-economic context in which the overall marketing activity is located.

Much of the research in marketing that we have surveyed in this Handbook takes an unashamedly managerial perspective. It defines the nature of marketing activity implicitly or explicitly with the central caveat 'at a profit.' We do not wish to suggest that there is anything wrong in this, merely that in certain instances this tends to mean that the consumer gets framed as either the black box in this process or an entity to be managed. As Richard Scase (2002) recently commented, this is the Consumer Relationship Management view of the world, not the Consumer Managed Relationship view.

A more integrated and extensive focus on consumer behavior would allow us in principle to investigate alternative notions of the 'competent' or 'confident' consumer: to reframe the relationship with the suppliers so that instead of just responding to a specific set of product choices, the individual consumer is playing an active role in both reintegrating the individual choices into a meaningful pattern and, indeed, attributing meaning to the patterns themselves. As Richard Lutz noted, in his editorial for the *Journal of Consumer Research* (1991), to which we also referred in our introduction,

> By its very nature, the field of consumer research is defined by its focus on the set of substantive phenomena identified as consumer behaviors. Thus, the raison d'être for consumer research is to explain or understand consumer behavior phenomena of potential interest to scholars, managers, public policy officials, or even consumers themselves. More consumer research needs to emphasize substantive phenomena to a greater degree.

The longer-term question of whether we are likely to witness a more substantial reintegration of the field of consumer behavior into the overall marketing domain is probably outside the scope of this comment. At the moment, in these postmodern times, the inevitable trend seems to be toward fragmentation rather than integration. Even, however, to have some form of partial integration would require those whose principal perspective is managerial to adopt a more de-centered perspective on the nature of market choice, and the attendant issues of motivation and identity.

Research Resources: Databases and Analytical Tools

One general way of considering likely developments in any particular field of research is by looking at the nature of the key resources that may be available. In the context of research in marketing, we focus on two sets: one defined rather directly by the actual research process (the databases and analytical tools) and the other by the broader context (developments in the related disciplines).

It is undeniable that research in marketing has been strongly influenced by the nature of the databases that have been made available, as well as the emergence of new analytical tools in areas such as statistical modeling and structural equation analysis. Again we do not wish to go into specific areas which have been covered in detail by the individual chapters, but will note some of the broader implications of this almost inevitable process.

The first implication is most effectively communicated by the old joke about the drunk, his keys, and the lamp-post. A drunk is searching around at night underneath a street lamp-post. A passer-by asks him what he is doing:

> 'Looking for my keys,' says the drunk, to which the passer-by asks 'Where did you lose them?' 'Over there.' 'Then why are you looking under the lamp-post?' 'Because it is easier to see under the light,' explains the drunk.[2]

In the context of much research in marketing, the data and available tools have meant that we have tended to look for answers where it is convenient rather than collect the data where the answers might be more likely found. To take one example, much of our data have remained, in essence, transaction specific (and other notions such as 'relationships' tend therefore to be defined and measured in terms of a sequence of transactions).

The second implication is more subtle. Many of the analytical tools were actually developed primarily for a slightly different purpose from the way in which they are used for research within the marketing domain. For instance, much modeling work in econometrics, particularly relating to macro-economic variables, originated with systems of variables in which one could develop measures to explain well over 90% of the variance in the dependent variable. Yet we apply these measures to systems where getting over 10% is often quite an achievement (Wensley, 1997). Such substantial differences in empirical and practical contexts mean that we must be cautious both about the nature of truth claims derived from such econometric-based analysis (McCloskey, 1986, 1994; McCloskey & Ziliak, 1996) but also the nature of the understanding that we can expect from such forms of empirical quantitative analysis (Byrne, 2002).

In a rather similar manner, much structural equation modeling links to earlier notions of latent class analysis and its application in areas such as psychology. It is noteworthy that in such original areas, some of our criteria for significance, such as the infamous $p < 0.05$, have been subject to much greater scrutiny and indeed critique. (See, for instance, Wilkinson, 1999)[3]

Disciplinary Developments

It can be reasonably asserted that much of academic work in the marketing domain traces its disciplinary roots to one or more of economics, sociology, and psychology. Of course, there have been substantial developments in each of these areas themselves, and we may also be able to make some intelligent inferences about the future developments for research in marketing by looking more closely at some of these key developments. However, we should remember a similar caveat to the one we raised about resources and tools: in the marketing domain it is also important to retain a focus on the substantive research issue.

Game Theory in Economics

A number of commentators have described the development of game theory as the most significant single development in economics in the last 20 years. It does undoubtedly provide a systematic theoretical framework for the analysis of optimal behaviors, which have to anticipate to some significant degree the behavior of others – which is obviously a central concern in understanding competitive processes.

Game theory is covered in a range of economic texts such as Kreps (1990), and a recent review is to be found in Chatterjee & Samuelson (2001). However, game theory still seems rather bedeviled by experimental anomalies when it comes to asymmetric pay-offs (for instance see Goeree & Holt, 2001). Beyond this specific concern there is a much more fundamental methodological issue, as Shugan (2002) notes in a very useful paper on mathematical models and what he terms 'monopoly models,' that is ones in which we ignore competitive behavior:

> These remarks are not intended to suggest that the assumption of a competitive equilibrium has little value. It has monumental value. It is particularly valuable for answering many research questions including the impact of regulation or public policy on the players that adopt optimal behavior (of course, don't assume regulation is already optimal). It also has value for predicting how markets will develop and understanding how external shocks might impact markets. The only argument made here is that incorporating competition by assuming optimal behavior requires a set of approximating assumptions that often conflict with the objective of advising marketing decision-makers.
>
> The conclusion is that we should sometimes embrace monopoly models. The strong approximating assumption of no competitive response is sometimes better than the approximating assumption of optimal behavior. (Shugan, 2002: 5)

Following on from Shugan's comment about approximation, there is also a lot of difference between the strict, and sometimes complex, mathematics of academic game theory and the much more general approach often suggested of thinking through the potential strategies for other players. Green (2002) has recently tried to test the relative efficacy of these two approaches in a series of scenarios, and concludes that the more generic role-playing approach is more effective than analytical game theory. Armstrong (2002), commenting on the analysis, also suggests that, if anything, the experimental treatment is biased in favor of game theory.

Structuration and New Institutionalism in Sociology

'Structuration' is a concept in sociology particularly identified by Giddens (1984) as a way of understanding the nature of complex social processes. In this process agents and organizations are simultaneously both creators of structures and also have their actions constrained by those structures. It of course relates to other developments, such as actor-network theory and the dichotomy between agency and structure (see Latour et al., 1986). However, Ray Bhaskar notes:

> in opposition to the dichotomy of structure and agency, it argued for what I called the transformational model of social activity, which is not to identify structure or agency, but to trace their distinctive features and mutual interdependency, in a way that Margaret Archer and others have shown is distinct from, although related to, that position that Giddens has put forward under the theory of structuration. Basically, structure always tends to collapse into agency on his model, whereas on my model the agents themselves have natural and other perhaps transcendental components that can't be reduced to social structures. (http://www.philosophers.co.uk/current/bhaskar.htm)

This caveat is particularly important if in trying to understand the development of markets we need, as we discussed above, to recognize the central role of consumers and consumption. Hence, we all recognize the extent to which social and business structures and relationships both enable and influence choices that are made. However, we should also recognize that Cova (1999), for instance, has emphasized that the meaning or the links are to be seen as defined and interpreted by the individual themselves not by the producer, although use-value or functionality can also remain a central issue.

Meanwhile, under the broad term of the 'new institutionalism,' empirical research has been mostly interested with testing the sources of institutions and addressing the relationship of these sources to the organizational structures. The focus has, however, generally been on non-profit organizations and public agencies (schools, the mental health sector, and cultural institutions) to show similarities in the organizations across contexts (Powell, 1991: 183). Institutionalization is often approached from two timeframes: one is the essentialist view of the organization, where the cultural or social system is studied in the context of dependent and independent variables and causal relationships; the other conceives of institutionalization as a process where history has its own significant place and where 'path-dependent processes make it difficult for organizations to explore alternative options' (Powell, 1991: 193). However, there seem to be few process studies that have focused research on institutional mechanisms that are self-reinforcing (Scott, 1995: 80). In general, institutional theorists have paid greater attention to institutional forces than to the mechanisms engendering and sustaining those forces. Powell & DiMaggio (1991) argue for a more pro-active description of organizational choice of the actors involved in 'seeking legitimation for changes that enhance their prestige and power' (Powell, 1991: 194).

Selection Behaviors in Psychology

In understanding choice, or selection behavior in psychology, recent approaches have tended to focus either positively or negatively on the emerging area of evolutionary psychology. This provides us with potentially fruitful developments in our attempts to understand choice behaviors both among competitors as well as customers in a marketing context.

However, the current state of understanding of such choice behaviors seems to be one of contention. Broadly speaking, in a competitive context, because of the interactive nature of outcomes, optimal choice behavior involves some form of backward iteration. But there seems to be consistent evidence that cognitively we find difficulty in undertaking various relatively simple backward iteration reasoning tasks. This seems to be true even when we are presented with effectively full information. Sterman (1989) has used various versions of the classic 'beer game,' which is based on a simulation of the retail and wholesale supply chain for beer, to show that given stock and demand leads and lags, participants, even with effectively full information, have great difficulty avoiding decisions to 'reorder,' which themselves create further instabilities, much along the lines originally demonstrated by Forrester (1961) with his early system dynamics models.

More generally, over the past couple of decades, evidence has been building up that humans are amazingly bad at solving simple logical problems in terms of simple choice behavior. This is partly demonstrated by the original work of Tversky & Kahneman (1974) in experiments on decision-making in business-like contexts, but also goes much wider than this. In particular, Cosmides (1989) has argued that certain forms of representation in choice situations allow us to access well-established reasoning modules based on long-term evolutionary development, while Oaksford & Chater (1994) have argued that we need to distinguish between the nature of specific decision choice and the notion of underlying logic. Overall, Stenning & Van Lambalgen (2001), in reviewing a wide range of empirical work and interpretations, have suggested that a key issue should be much greater concern for semantics (the meaning and use of words) in understanding the ways in which the specific task is structured and understood by respondents.

Marketing as Management

We have emphasized at various stages in this Handbook that we cannot properly review the nature of research in marketing without recognizing the historical relationship between research in the marketing domain and the managerial role within the marketing function, or functions, of commercial organizations.

In many ways this remains an on-going debate, most recently to be found in a special edition of the *European Journal of Marketing* (Baker, 2002). However, one of its most common manifestations has been in the so-called twin hurdles of academic rigor and practical relevance.

Rigor and Relevance

The discussion about the relationship between academe and practice or, in its other form, the balance between rigor and relevance, in research has had a long history not only in marketing but both in management generally and also in allied domains. Most recently, outside marketing, it has provided the basis for special issues of *MIS Quarterly*, *Academy of Management Journal* and the *British Journal of Management*. Perhaps not surprisingly, the conclusions in each of these special issues are rather similar. For instance, Rynes et al. (2001) suggest that action is required in two domains. In the case of direct relationships between academics and practitioners they emphasize the need for more individual engagement and institutional interaction. In the case of publications they encourage greater editorial flexibility and the avoidance of specialist language. As they themselves note, these are hardly novel prescriptions and the relative failure to adopt them at earlier stages raises important questions about our understanding of the wider context in which the changes are supposed to take place.[4] This situation, as they recognize, itself requires an explanation. They suggest that a combination of lack of understanding and lack of interest remain the key reasons. In the case of the former, they view the 'new models of knowledge creation' – in which they refer, amongst others, to Argyris & Schon (1996) and Nonaka & Takeuchi (1995)[5] – as sources of a new understanding. In the case of the latter, they seem more evangelical than sanguine:

> If the goals of improved knowledge creation and enhanced use of knowledge are dominated by other goals, use of Nonaka's framework is unlikely to prove any more successful than previous efforts to narrow the science-practice gap. Previous research suggest that rigidity and complacency in the face of changed circumstances are two of the major causes of professional, organizational and institutional demise ... concerted efforts at all levels, but especially among gatekeepers at the institutional level will be needed. (Rynes et al., 2001: 351)

We would suggest a less pessimistic overall perspective, based on a rather broader systemic view about knowledge production and application in areas such as marketing.

Issues of this sort in marketing management are directly equivalent to those in the management field discussed by Pettigrew (2001). Pettigrew (1995, 1997) developed the notion of the 'double hurdle' for management research covering, roughly, academic rigor and practical relevance. More recently, Pettigrew (2001) has noted that his initial analysis has become oversimplified in that he was clear about the 'double hurdles' of engagement with the social science community and the world of practice, and he recognized that both of these were plural rather than singular. This plurality is very important: individuals, groups or institutions may claim the right to define their world exclusively but these claims are continually contested. Indeed, it can be argued that this continual process of contestation is a crucial policy component in the evolution and robust nature of any science domain.

This issue of contestation of knowledge claims links closely with an analogous point made by Lee (1999), in discussing issues of rigor and relevance in MIS research. He argues that in much of the critique of lack of relevance (such as Benbasat & Zmud, 1999, to which he is directly responding) itself lacks not only substantial empirical support but also a wider context:

> Research on the topic of relevance to practice would need to accomplish more than just provide empirically grounded statements on the state of relevance of IS research today. Such research could also explore all the different forms that relevance can take in addition to the forms presumed in the instrumental model and in critical social theory. Such research might also look for parallels between how relevant research has unfolded historically in professions such as medicine, law, engineering, and architecture and how it might therefore unfold in IS. Above all, it would not be enough for such research to offer speculative philosophical ponderings, such research would of course have to be relevant in its own way too. (Lee, 1999: 32)

Knowledge in the professions involves a process of contestation and challenge, with evidence submitted under various rules of procedure and subjected to rigorous scrutiny and interpretation: the model of the court provides a rather different perspective for notions of the 'evidence base' and its application.

Pettigrew (2001) specifically argues that there are challenging prospects for management research in what he and others have termed the 'after-modernism' era, but this must involve, where necessary, creating and interacting with the dense networks of social science disciplines and practice.

Endwords

Inevitably any listing of research topics over and above those already mentioned by our various esteemed contributors runs the risk of being rather idiosyncratic. However, we do think it is worth identifying three of these: two of which reflect very much the need for an interactive understanding of the relationship between suppliers and consumers, and the other which emphasizes the complex nature of market-focused organization and activity.

When it comes to the issue of the longer-term relationship with the customer, we would suggest that this particularly manifests itself in two general topics:[6]

1. The potential and implication for one-to-one marketing and the potential backlash. How are consumers going to react to differential treatment such as pricing and the potential invasion of privacy?
2. The increasing importance of customer retention and share of wallet.

In both of these areas, as we noted before, any robust research approach needs to incorporate a genuinely consumer-driven approach. As Fournier et al. (1998) noted, the term 'relationship' has often been misused in marketing management practice to define an interpretation which is exclusively one way, and frames the consumer as essentially passive.[7] Similar arguments could be applied to the often rather broad way in which 'loyalty' is used as a construct in these approaches. Indeed this is compounded by the fact that ever since Jacoby & Kyner (1973), we need to recognize that even measuring such items as 'loyalty' is fraught with problems. On top of this, in making sense of long-run consumer behavior and the balance between our developing notions of what has been termed routine and 'novelty seeking' behavior, we need to go back to some of the issues raised by Lattin & McAlister (1985) in their original approach.

Taken together such concerns mean that we need to be critical of our use of language, measurement, and underlying assumptions of the nature of the wider socio-economic context if we wish to research further in these areas.

Our other research priority concerns the issue of understanding the evolving nature of the marketing function within organizations, but also (more generally) the need to adopt a wider perspective in understanding the nature of market-focused activity and interfunctional coordination. The importance of multi-disciplinary perspectives was highlighted in the chapters on new product development and services management, while the coordination of multiple function in the firm lies at the center of any notion of market-focused organization. Yet here, as marketing academics, we face a further issue in our research: broadly speaking what is the specialist competence that we can bring to such analysis? If we are to move beyond the survey approaches that, ever since the pioneering work of Narver & Slater (1990) and Kohli & Jaworski (1990), have dominated empirical work on the nature of market orientation within the firm, we will need to be willing to delve deeper into the 'other' black box (compared with that of the consumer) – that of the organization – and perhaps also to study another Handbook – that of Organizational Studies (Clegg et al., 1996)!

Notes

1. 'In 1969, a group of interested researchers meeting informally at Ohio State University decided that an organization composed of those interested in consumer behavior research, regardless of discipline or affiliation, was necessary to advance and disseminate knowledge in this field. In 1970, the first conference was held in Amherst at the University of Massachusetts. Annual conferences have been held since that time. ACR is incorporated in the State of Georgia and presently has approximately 1700 members. In its early years, approximately 80 percent of ACR's members were employed in the academic world, especially in the fields of marketing, psychology, home economics and economics. About 15 percent of its membership were made up of employees and executives of commercial firms, especially from consumer goods marketing organizations, marketing research firms, and advertising agencies. Five percent were employed by government agencies and non-profit organizations. In recent years membership has shifted and now comes almost totally from the academic world with very few members from business firms and government.' (From the ACR website http://www.acrweb.org/aboutacr.htm, where ACR is also very clear about what it does not do as well.)

2. In terms of the history of this joke Donald Nilsen, an avid collector of sources of humor, particularly business humor, notes 'It's impossible to trace the history of such a joke because it goes back into oral (pre-written) history. I ran across this joke, for example, when I was in Afghanistan. It was one of a series of Mullah Nasrudin jokes that goes back hundreds of years.' (Donald Nilsen, pers. comm.)

3. Two further caveats and observations are worthwhile at this point, both relating to the question of increased analytical sophistication. The first is that, on the positive side, as Bob Jacobson has ably demonstrated in the case of the so-called 'market share effect' (Jacobson, 1995; Jacobson & Aaker, 1985), as our forms of analysis become more sophisticated we can find that an original strong effect becomes seen as more and more a result of biases in our earlier forms of measurement rather than substantive in its own right. On the other hand, to quote the article by Wilkinson (1999: 598):

> Although complex designs and state-of-the-art methods are sometimes necessary to address research questions effectively, simpler classical approaches often can provide elegant and sufficient answers to important questions.

A nice example of this is to be found in the experiment conducted by Jan Maganus & Mary Morgan (1999), which looked at various more sophisticated econometric approaches to the data originally interpreted by Tobin: it was very noteworthy that Tobin's 'less sophisticated' approach stood up very well to such a test.

4. Indeed, in marketing specifically, certain historical developments have clearly moved in the opposite direction, such as the gradual decrease in the number of practitioners on the editorial board of the *Journal of Marketing* (Wensley, 2000).

5. They see these new models as able to:

> provide powerful tools for understanding the great knowledge creation potential of increased academic-practitioner interaction, as well as crafting interactive, 'double-loop' ways of bringing about such interaction. (Rynes et al., 2001: 351)

6. Both of these topics form part of the Marketing Science Institute (MSI) Research priorities. Wensley (2000) has provided an analogous critique of the way in which these priorities are framed.

7. Wensley (1990) provides a rather earlier analysis of the ways in which marketing writing has used particular terms in the context of 'the user' to create a particular set of often implicit assumptions about their relationship with suppliers of products and services.

References

Argyris, C. & Schon, D.A. (1996) *Organizational Learning II: Theory, Method and Practice*. Reading, MA: Addison-Wesley.

Armstrong, S. (2002) Assessing game theory, role playing, and unaided judgement. *International Journal of Forecasting,* 18 (3), July–Sept, 345–52, also available at Armstrong's personal website: http://www.marketing.wharton.upenn.edu/people/faculty/armstrong.html).

Baker, M. (ed.) (2002) *European Journal of Marketing,* 3.

Benbasat, I. & Zmud, R.W. (1999) Empirical research in information systems: the practice of relevance. *MIS Quarterly*, 23 (1), May, 3–16.

Byrne, David (2002) *Interpreting Quantitative Data*. London: Sage.

Chatterjee, Kalyan & Samuelson, William F. (eds) (2001) *Game Theory and Business Applications*. Boston, MA: Kluwer Academic Publishing.

Clegg, S.R., Hardy, C. & Nord, W.R. (1996) *Handbook of Organization Studies*. London: Sage.

Cosmides, L. (1989) The logic of social exchange: has natural selection shaped how humans reason? Studies with the Wason selection task. *Cognition*, 31 (3), 187–276.

Cova, B. (1999) From marketing to societing: when the link is more important than the thing. In *Rethinking Marketing*, edited by D. Brownlie, M. Saren, R. Wensley & R. Whittington. London: Sage, pp. 64–83.

Forrester, Jay W. (1961) *Industrial Dynamics*. Cambridge, MA: MIT Press.

Fournier, S., Dobscha, S. & Mick, D.G. (1998) Preventing the premature death of relationship marketing. *Harvard Business Review*, Jan–Feb, 42–50.

Giddens, A. (1984) *The Constitution of Society: Outline of a Theory of Structuration*. Cambridge: Polity Press.

Goeree, J.K. & Holt, C.A. (2001) Ten little treasures of game theory and ten intuitive contradictions. *American Economic Review*, 91 (5), 1402–22.

Green, K. (2002) Forecasting decisions in conflict situations: a comparison of game theory, role-playing, and unaided judgement. *International Journal of Forecasting* 18 (3), July–Sept, 321–44.

Jacobson, R. (1995) The cost of the market share quest. Working Paper, University of Washington, Seattle, March.

Jacobson, R. & Aaker, D.A. (1985) Is market share all that it's cracked up to be? *Journal of Marketing*, 49, Fall, 11–22.

Jacoby, J. & Kyner, D.B. (1973) Brand loyalty vs repeat purchasing behavior. *Journal of Marketing Research*, 10 (1), 1–9.

Kohli, A.K. & Jaworski, B.J. (1990) Market orientation: the construct, research propositions and managerial implications. *Journal of Marketing*, April, 54 (2), 1–18.

Kreps, David M. (1990) *Game Theory and Economic Modelling*. Oxford: Clarendon Press.

Lattin, James M. & McAlister, Leigh (1985) Using a variety-seeking model to identify substitute and complementary relationships among competing products. *Journal of Marketing Research*, 22 (August), 330–9.

Latour, B., Woolgar, S. & Salk, J. (1986) *Laboratory Life*. Princeton, NJ: Princeton University Press.

Lee, A.S. (1999) Rigor and relevance in MIS research: beyond the approach of positivism alone. *MIS Quarterly*, 23, 1, March, 29–33.

Lutz, R. (1991) Editorial. *Journal of Consumer Research*, 17, March, 1–3.

Maganus, Jan R. & Morgan, Mary S. (eds) (1999) *Methodology and Tacit Knowledge*. Chichester, England: John Wiley and Sons.

McCloskey, D. (1986) *The Rhetoric of Economics*. Wisconsin, MD: University of Wisconsin Press.

——— (1994) *Knowledge and Persuasion in Economics*. Cambridge: Cambridge University Press.

McCloskey, D.N. & Ziliak, S.T. (1996) The standard error of regressions. *Journal of Economic Literature*, 34 (March), 97–114.

Narver, J.C. & Slater, S.F. (1990) The effect of market orientation on business profitability. *Journal of Marketing*, October, 54 (4), 20–35.

Nonaka, I. & Takeuchi, H. (1995) *The Knowledge-creating Company*. New York: Oxford University Press.

Oaksford, M.R. & Chater, N.C. (1994) A rational analysis of the selection task as optimal data selection. *Psychological Review*, 101, 608–31.

Pettigrew, A. (1995) The double hurdles for management research. Distinguished Scholar Address to the Organization and Management Theory Division of the US Academy of Management. Vancouver, Canada, August.

——— (1997) The double hurdles for management research. In *Advancement in Organizational Behaviour: Essays in Honour of D.S. Pugh*, edited by T. Clark. London: Dartmouth Press, pp. 277–96.

——— (2001) Management research after modernism. *British Journal of Management,* 12 (4), 561–70.

Powell, Walter W. (1991) Expanding the scope of institutional analysis. In *The New Institutionalism in Organizational Analysis*, edited by Walter W. Powell & Paul J. DiMaggio. Chicago: University of Chicago Press, pp. 183–203.

Powell, Walter W. & DiMaggio, Paul J. (eds) (1991) *The New Institutionalism in Organizational Analysis.* Chicago: University of Chicago Press.

Rynes S.L., Bartunek, J.M. & Daft, R.L. (2001) Across the great divide: knowledge creation and transfer between practitioners and academics. *Academy of Management Journal*, April, 44, 2, 340–55.

Scase, R. (2002) *Britian in 2010*. Oxford: Capstone Publishing.

Scott, R.W. (1995) *Institutions and Organizations.* Thousand Oaks, CA: Sage Publications, Inc.

Shugan, S. (2002) Marketing science, models, monopoly models and why we need them: an editorial. *Marketing Science* (forthcoming) (available at http://bear.cba.ufl.edu/centers/MKS/general/editorial0402.htm).

Stenning, K. & Van Lambalgen, M. (2001) Semantics as a foundation for psychology: a case study of Wason's selection task. *Journal of Logic, Language and Information*, 10 (3), 273–317.

Sterman, J. (1989) Misperceptions of feedback in dynamic decision making. *Organizational Behavior and Human Decision Processes*, 43 (3), 301–35.

Tversky, A. & Kahneman, D. (1974) Judgement under uncertainty heuristics and biases. *Science*, 185, September, 1124–31.

Wensley, R. (1990) 'The Voice of the Consumer?' Speculations on the limits to the marketing analogy. *European Journal of Marketing*, 24 (7), 49–60.

——— (1997) Explaining success: the rule of ten percent and the example of market share. *Business Strategy Review*, 8 (1), Spring, 63–70.

——— (2000) The MSI priorities: a critical view on researching firm performance, customer experience and marketing. *Journal of Marketing Management*, 16 (1–3) 11–27.

Wilkinson, Leland (1999) Statistical methods in psychology journals: guidelines and explanations. *American Psychologist*, August, 54, 8, 594–604 (also available at http://www.apa.org/journals/amp/amp548594.html).

Index

Page numbers in *italics* refer to figures.